					8A (18)
3A (13)	4A (14)	5A (15)	6A (16)	7A (17)	Helium 2 **He** 4.0026
Boron 5 **B** 10.811	Carbon 6 **C** 12.011	Nitrogen 7 **N** 14.0067	Oxygen 8 **O** 15.9994	Fluorine 9 **F** 18.9984	Neon 10 **Ne** 20.1797
Aluminum 13 **Al** 26.9815	Silicon 14 **Si** 28.0855	Phosphorus 15 **P** 30.9738	Sulfur 16 **S** 32.066	Chlorine 17 **Cl** 35.4527	Argon 18 **Ar** 39.948

2B (12)

Zinc 30 **Zn** 65.38	Gallium 31 **Ga** 69.723	Germanium 32 **Ge** 72.61	Arsenic 33 **As** 74.9216	Selenium 34 **Se** 78.96	Bromine 35 **Br** 79.904	Krypton 36 **Kr** 83.80
Cadmium 48 **Cd** 112.411	Indium 49 **In** 114.818	Tin 50 **Sn** 118.710	Antimony 51 **Sb** 121.760	Tellurium 52 **Te** 127.60	Iodine 53 **I** 126.9045	Xenon 54 **Xe** 131.29
Mercury 80 **Hg** 200.59	Thallium 81 **Tl** 204.3833	Lead 82 **Pb** 207.2	Bismuth 83 **Bi** 208.9804	Polonium 84 **Po** (208.98)	Astatine 85 **At** (209.99)	Radon 86 **Rn** (222.02)
— 112 — Discovered 1996	— 113 — Discovered 2004	— 114 — Discovered 1999	— 115 — Discovered 2004	— 116 — Discovered 1999		— 118 — Discovered 2002

Terbium 65 **Tb** 158.9254	Dysprosium 66 **Dy** 162.50	Holmium 67 **Ho** 164.9303	Erbium 68 **Er** 167.26	Thulium 69 **Tm** 168.9342	Ytterbium 70 **Yb** 173.054	Lutetium 71 **Lu** 174.9668
Berkelium 97 **Bk** (247.07)	Californium 98 **Cf** (251.08)	Einsteinium 99 **Es** (252.08)	Fermium 100 **Fm** (257.10)	Mendelevium 101 **Md** (258.10)	Nobelium 102 **No** (259.10)	Lawrencium 103 **Lr** (262.11)

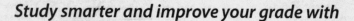
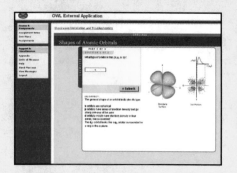

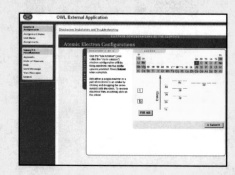

Student Guide

Contents

Revised June 2009

Technical Support

For **Technical Support for OWL,** including a full list of **Frequently Asked Questions**, please visit **www.cengage.com/owl.**

What You Need to Use OWL

1. An OWL Access Code, which you can obtain in these ways:

   a. You can purchase an access code from **www.cengage.com/owl**. Choose your subject, click **Buy an Access Code,** choose the correct course, book, and term length, and then you'll be taken to **www.ichapters.com** to complete your online purchase (which requires a credit card).

   b. Your professor may have arranged to package an access card like one of these with your textbook or your bookstore may sell the card separately:

2. An internet connection and browser. The browser version and plug-ins needed depend on which OWL course you take. Introductory assignments in OWL will specify browser requirements and provide tests to check if your browser is configured correctly for use with OWL.

Registration and Log In

To use OWL for the first time, go to **www.cengage.com/owl** to register your access code. If you need help, to go **www.cengage.com/owl/partners/brookscole/help** or to Technical Support at **www.cengage.com/owl**.

During the registration process, you'll be prompted to bookmark the log in page for future visits, but if you forget to bookmark it, you can always log in from **www.cengage.com/owl**.

OWL Left Menu Guide

After you have logged into OWL, familiarize yourself with the left menu bar, which helps you navigate through the system. Here is a brief explanation of the left menu options on most OWL screens.

ӘWL

Current Course Assignments

Course Home	View the home page for your OWL course.
My Courses	Click to view all available courses.
Assignments	View the list of current assignments due for your course.
Grades	View OWL grades or grades outside of OWL if your instructor has made them available.
Communication	Send and view messages from your OWL instructor.

Getting Started --------Help and guides for getting started with OWL.

Chemistry Tables ------Quick access to the periodic table and other resources.

e-Book------------------Link to the full version of the electronic textbook.

Go Chemistry™----------Download mini lectures on key concepts to your personal video player or desktop.

Thinkwell Videos ------Brief video lectures to review important concepts.

[instructor's link]---------Your instructor may add extra links to helpful websites here.

Answer Formatting in OWL

As with most computer-based homework systems, when you answer questions in OWL, your responses must be formatted in order to be graded correctly. For some answers, you must enter superscripts and subscripts in your answer. Proper answer formatting is especially important when entering chemical formulas, mathematical equations, and units of measurement. Improper formatting will lead to otherwise correct answers being marked wrong.

Be sure to complete the **Intro to OWL** assignments to learn the basics of answer formatting and setting up your browser correctly. Answer formatting basics are reviewed below.

To Write a Chemical Formula in OWL	
Enclose **subscripts** with *underscores* _.	Enclose **superscripts** with *carats* ^.
The *underscore* key is next to the number zero on the keyboard.	The *carat* key is the number six on the keyboard.
$H\_2\_O = H_2O$	$Cr\textasciicircum3+\textasciicircum = Cr^{3+}$
Combined: $SO\_4\_\textasciicircum2-\textasciicircum = SO_4^{2-}$	

Ions	Unit Charge Ions
Write the **number first** and then the charge.	Do **not** include the number one in unit charge ions.
$N\textasciicircum3-\textasciicircum = N^{3-}$ $Ca\textasciicircum2+\textasciicircum = Ca^{2+}$	$Na\textasciicircum+\textasciicircum = Na^{+}$ $Cl\textasciicircum-\textasciicircum = Cl^{-}$

Using the Chemical Formula Input

The chemical formula input box displays the superscripts and subscripts as you enter the formula. There are 3 ways to use the input box.

- **Keyboard:** Use the keyboard to enter underscores and carats on your own.
- **Buttons after:** Enter the formula without underscores or carats, then highlight each superscript and/or subscript, click the appropriate subscript or superscript button, and the underscores or carats will be filled in automatically.
- **Button during:** Use the subscript or superscript buttons to enter the underscores and carats while you type the formula.

Using the Chemical Formula Input Tool

Use the Chemical Formula Input Tool to help correctly format your answers with subscripts and superscripts.*

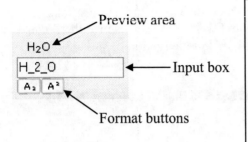

Preview area

Input box

Format buttons

Click [A₂] to subscript text and click [A²] to superscript text.

1. For example, to write the chemical formula for water, type a capital "H" in the input box.
2. Click [A₂] and then type "2."
3. Click [A₂] again to set the text format back to normal font. Note that you press the button before AND after you enter the character to be formatted.
4. Type a capital "O."

Check the Preview Area to see your entry before submitting it.

*If you are familiar with previous versions of OWL, you can still format your answers with underscores (Shift-minus) for subscripts and carats (Shift-6) for superscripts.

SCIENTIFIC NOTATION IN OWL

OWL uses a similar format to the "EE" or "EXP" format found on most calculators.

6.02×10^{23} should be entered as **6.02E23**

Where **"E23"** represents **"x 10^{23}"**

DO NOT confuse **SCIENTIFIC NOTATION** with entering **SUPERSCRIPTS!**

Use "E" notation for **NUMERICAL VALUES**. 6.02E23 **This is a numerical value.**

Use **"carat"** notation for **TEXT** input. Cu^2+^ **This is text.**

Examples:

Number to Enter	OWL Format	Calculator Format
6.02×10^{23}	6.02E23	6.02 EE 23 or 6.02 EXP 23
0.000000454	4.54E-7	4.54 EE -7 or 4.54 EXP -7

Note:
Also do not confuse this notation with the irrational number "e" = 2.718282 which forms the base for the natural log, ln. On calculators this is usually the e^x or **inv ln** key.

OWL Information Menu Bar

If you need a refresher on writing Chemical Formulas or Scientific Notation in OWL, you can click the **Chemical Formulas** or **Scientific Notation** links on the information menu bar at the top of each question page. The **Periodic Table** and **Tables** links on the left menu menu take you to appendix resources in OWL. You can also reach all these resources through the **Chemistry Tables** link in the left navigation menu.

And remember, for **Technical Support for OWL,** including **Frequently Asked Questions**, please visit **www.cengage.com/owl.**

Chemistry & Chemical Reactivity

Volume 2

Enhanced Seventh Edition

John C. Kotz | Paul M. Treichel | John Townsend

CENGAGE
Learning™

Australia • Brazil • Japan • Korea • Mexico • Singapore • Spain • United Kingdom • United States

Chemistry & Chemical Reactivity: Volume 2, Enhanced Seventh Edition

John C. Kotz | Paul M. Treichel | John Townsend

Executive Editors:
Maureen Staudt
Michael Stranz

Senior Project Development Manager:
Linda DeStefano

Marketing Specialist:
Sara Mercurio

Senior Production / Manufacturing Manager:
Donna M. Brown

PreMedia Supervisor:
Joel Brennecke

Rights & Permissions Specialist:
Kalina Hintz
Todd Osborne

Cover Image:
Getty Images*

* Unless otherwise noted, all cover images used by Custom Solutions, a part of Cengage Learning, have been supplied courtesy of Getty Images with the exception of the Earthview cover image, which has been supplied by the National Aeronautics and Space Administration (NASA).

For product information and technology assistance, contact us at
Cengage Learning Customer & Sales Support, 1-800-354-9706

For permission to use material from this text or product, submit all requests online at **cengage.com/permissions**
Further permissions questions can be emailed to
permissionrequest@cengage.com

ISBN-13: 978-1-4240-7066-4

ISBN-10: 1-4240-7066-X

Cengage Learning
5191 Natorp Boulevard
Mason, Ohio 45040
USA

Cengage Learning is a leading provider of customized learning solutions with office locations around the globe, including Singapore, the United Kingdom, Australia, Mexico, Brazil, and Japan. Locate your local office at:
international.cengage.com/region

Cengage Learning products are represented in Canada by Nelson Education, Ltd.

For your lifelong learning solutions, visit **www.cengage.com/custom**

Visit our corporate website at **www.cengage.com**

Printed in the United States of America

Custom Contents in Brief

Part 5
THE CHEMISTRY OF THE ELEMENTS

13 | The Chemistry of Solids

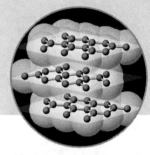

Graphite is composed of sheets of carbon atoms in six-member rings.

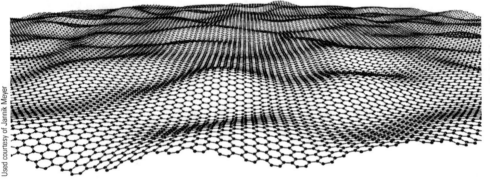

Used courtesy of Jannik Meyer

Graphene is a single sheet of six-member carbon rings. This latest material in the world of carbon chemistry has unusual electrical properties.

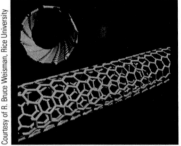

Courtesy of R. Bruce Weisman, Rice University

Carbon nanotubes are composed of six-member carbon rings.

Graphite to Graphene

One of the most interesting developments in chemistry in the last 20 years has been the discovery of new forms of carbon. First, there were buckyballs and then single-wall and multi-wall carbon nanotubes.

Common graphite, from which your pencil lead is made, consists of six-member rings of carbon atoms connected in sheets, and the sheets stack one on top of another like cards in a deck. But if carbon compounds are heated under the right conditions, the carbon atoms assemble into sheets, and the sheets close on themselves to form tubes. These are called **nanotubes** because the tubes are only a few nanometers in diameter. Sometimes they are single tubes, and other times there are tubes within tubes. Carbon nanotubes are at least 100 times stronger than steel but only one sixth as dense, and they conduct heat and electricity far better than copper. There has been enormous interest in their commercial applications, but there has also been difficulty in making them with consistent properties.

Now there is **graphene**, a single sheet of six-member carbon atoms. Researchers in England discovered them in a simple way: put a flake of graphite on Scotch tape, fold the tape over, and then pull it apart. The graphite layers come apart, and, if you do it enough times, only one layer—one C atom thick!—is left on the tape. This is clearly not the way to make graphene commercially, but methods have since been developed to make it in larger amounts. And now researchers are looking at ways to make graphene sheets in specific shapes, and to use them as transistors and other electronic devices.

Questions:

1. Based on a C—C distance of 139 pm, what is the side-to-side dimension of a planar, C_6 ring?
2. If a graphene sheet has a width of 1.0 micrometer, how many C_6 rings are joined across the sheet?
3. Estimate the thickness of a sheet of graphene (in pm). How did you determine this value?

Answers to these questions are in Appendix Q.

Chapter Goals

OWL *See Chapter Goals Revisited (page 610) for Study Questions keyed to these goals and assignable in OWL.*

- Understand cubic unit cells.
- Relate unit cells for ionic compounds to formulas.
- Describe the properties of solids.
- Understand the nature of phase diagrams.

Chapter Outline

13.1 Crystal Lattices and Unit Cells
13.2 Structures and Formulas of Ionic Solids
13.3 Bonding in Ionic Compounds: Lattice Energy
13.4 The Solid State: Other Kinds of Solid Materials
13.5 Phase Changes Involving Solids
13.6 Phase Diagrams

M any kinds of solids exist in the world around us (Figure 13.1 and Table 13.1). As the description of graphene shows, solid-state chemistry is one of the booming areas of science, especially because it relates to the development of interesting new materials. As we describe various kinds of solids, we hope to provide a glimpse of the reasons this area is exciting.

Chemistry.Now™

Throughout the text this icon introduces an opportunity for self-study or to explore interactive tutorials by signing in at **www.cengage.com/login**.

13.1 Crystal Lattices and Unit Cells

Module 18

In both gases and liquids, molecules move continually and randomly, and they rotate and vibrate as well. Because of this movement, an orderly arrangement of molecules in the gaseous or liquid state is not possible. In solids, however, the molecules, atoms, or ions cannot change their relative positions (although they vibrate and occasionally rotate). Thus, a regular, repeating pattern of atoms or molecules within the structure—a long-range order—is a characteristic of most solids. The beautiful, external (macroscopic) regularity of a crystal of salt (Figure 13.1) suggests it has an internal symmetry.

TABLE 13.1 Structures and Properties of Various Types of Solid Substances

Type	Examples	Structural Units	Forces Holding Units Together	Typical Properties
Ionic	NaCl, K_2SO_4, $CaCl_2$, $(NH_4)_3PO_4$	Positive and negative ions; no discrete molecules	Ionic; attractions among charges on positive and negative ions	Hard; brittle; high melting point; poor electric conductivity as solid, good as liquid; often water-soluble
Metallic	Iron, silver, copper, other metals and alloys	Metal atoms (positive metal ions with delocalized electrons)	Metallic; electrostatic attraction among metal ions and electrons	Malleable; ductile; good electric conductivity in solid and liquid; good heat conductivity; wide range of hardness and melting points
Molecular	H_2, O_2, I_2, H_2O, CO_2, CH_4, CH_3OH, CH_3CO_2H	Molecules	Dispersion forces, dipole–dipole forces, hydrogen bonds	Low to moderate melting points and boiling points; soft; poor electric conductivity in solid and liquid
Network	Graphite, diamond, quartz, feldspars, mica	Atoms held in an infinite two- or three-dimensional network	Covalent; directional electron-pair bonds	Wide range of hardness and melting points (three-dimensional bonding > two-dimensional bonding); poor electric conductivity, with some exceptions
Amorphous	Glass, polyethylene, nylon	Covalently bonded networks with no long-range regularity	Covalent; directional electron-pair bonds	Noncrystalline; wide temperature range for melting; poor electric conductivity, with some exceptions

FIGURE 13.1
Some common solids.

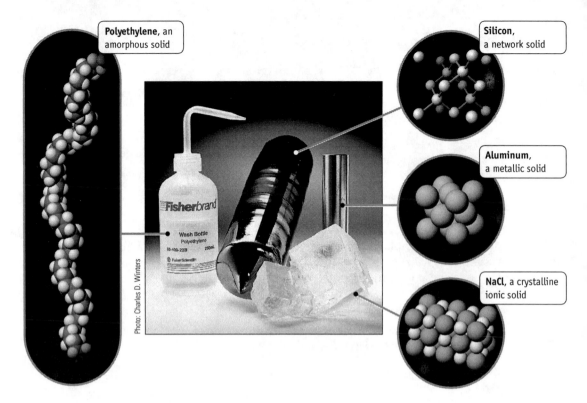

Polyethylene, an amorphous solid

Photo: Charles D. Winters

Silicon, a network solid

Aluminum, a metallic solid

NaCl, a crystalline ionic solid

Structures of solids can be described as three-dimensional lattices of atoms, ions, or molecules. For a crystalline solid, we can identify the **unit cell**, the smallest repeating unit that has all of the symmetry characteristic of the way the atoms, ions, or molecules are arranged in the solid.

To understand unit cells, consider first a two-dimensional lattice model, the repeating pattern of circles shown in Figure 13.2. The yellow square at the left is a unit cell because the overall pattern can be created from a group of these cells by joining them edge to edge. It is also a requirement that unit cells reflect the stoichiometry of the solid. Here, the square unit cell at the left contains one smaller sphere and one fourth of each of the four larger circles, giving a total of one small and one large circle per two-dimensional unit cell.

You may recognize that it is possible to draw other unit cells for this two-dimensional lattice. One option is the square in the middle of Figure 13.2 that fully encloses a single large circle and parts of small circles that add up to one net small circle. Yet another possible unit cell is the parallelogram at the right. Other unit

FIGURE 13.2 Unit cells for a flat, two-dimensional solid made from circular "atoms." A lattice can be represented as being built from repeating unit cells. This two-dimensional lattice can be built by translating the unit cells throughout the plane of the figure. Each cell must move by the length of one side of the unit cell. In this figure, all unit cells contain a net of one large circle and one small circle. Be sure to notice that several unit cells are possible, with two of the most obvious being squares.

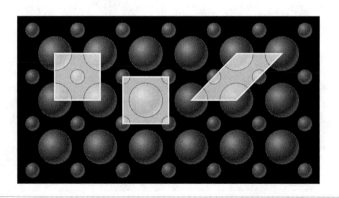

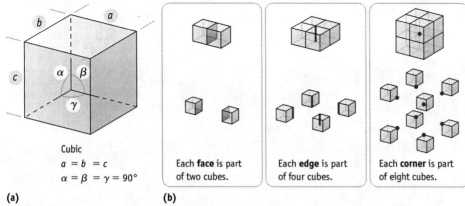

Cubic
$a = b = c$
$\alpha = \beta = \gamma = 90°$

(a)

Each **face** is part of two cubes.

Each **edge** is part of four cubes.

Each **corner** is part of eight cubes.

(b)

FIGURE 13.3 Cubic unit cells. (a) The cube is one of the seven basic unit cells that describe crystal systems. In a cube, all sides are of equal length, and all angles are 90°. In noncubic unit cells, the angles are not necessarily 90°, and the sides are not equal in length. (b) Stacking cubes to build a crystal lattice. Each crystal face is part of two cubes; each edge is part of four cubes; and each corner is part of eight cubes.

cells are possible, but it is conventional to draw unit cells in which atoms or ions are placed at the **lattice points;** that is, at the corners of the cube or other geometric object that constitutes the unit cell.

The three-dimensional lattices of solids can be built by assembling three-dimensional unit cells much like building blocks (Figure 13.3). The assemblage of these three-dimensional unit cells defines the **crystal lattice.**

To construct crystal lattices, nature uses seven three-dimensional unit cells. They differ from one another in that their sides have different relative lengths and their edges meet at different angles. The simplest of the seven crystal lattices is the **cubic unit cell,** a cell with edges of equal length that meet at 90° angles. We shall look in detail at just this structure, not only because cubic unit cells are easily visualized but also because they are commonly encountered.

Within the cubic class, three cell symmetries occur: **primitive cubic (pc), body-centered cubic (bcc),** and **face-centered cubic (fcc)** (Figure 13.4). All three have

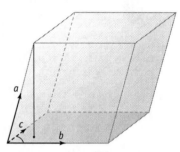

Unit cells. Of the possible unit cells, all are parallelepipeds (except for the hexagonal cell), figures in which opposite sides are parallel. In a cube, all angles (a-o-c, a-o-b, and c-o-b; where o is the origin) are 90°, and all sides are equal. In other cells, the angles and sides may be the same or different. For example, in a tetragonal cell, the angles are 90°, but $a = b \neq c$. In a triclinic cell, the sides have different lengths, the angles are different, and none equals 90°.

Primitive cubic

Body-centered cubic

Face-centered cubic

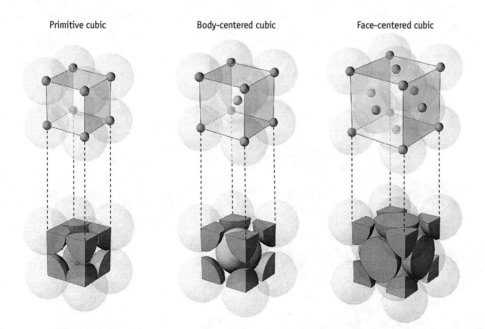

FIGURE 13.4 The three cubic unit cells. The top row shows the lattice points of the three cells, and the bottom row shows the same cells using space-filling spheres. The spheres in each figure represent identical atoms (or ions) centered on the lattice points. Because eight unit cells share a corner atom, only $\frac{1}{8}$ of each corner atom lies within a given unit cell; the remaining $\frac{7}{8}$ lies in seven other unit cells. Because each face of a fcc unit cell is shared with another unit cell, one half of each atom in the face of a face-centered cube lies in a given unit cell, and the other half lies in the adjoining cell.

FIGURE 13.5 Metals use four different unit cells. Three are based on the cube, and the fourth is the hexagonal unit cell (see page 595). (Many metals can crystallize in more than one structure.)

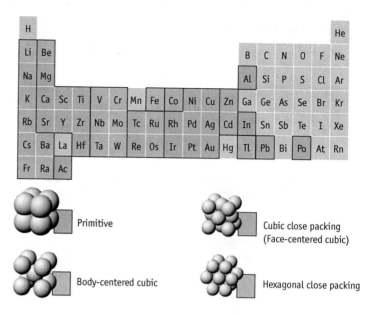

Primitive

Cubic close packing (Face-centered cubic)

Body-centered cubic

Hexagonal close packing

identical atoms, molecules, or ions at the corners of the cubic unit cell. The bcc and fcc arrangements, however, differ from the primitive cube in that they have additional particles at other locations. The bcc structure is called "body-centered" because it has an additional particle, of the same type as those at the corners, at the center of the cube. The fcc arrangement is called "face-centered" because it has a particle, of the same type as the corner atoms, in the center of each of the six faces of the cube. Examples of each structure are found among the crystal lattices of the metals (Figure 13.5). The alkali metals, for example, are body-centered cubic, whereas nickel, copper, and aluminum are face-centered cubic. Notice that only one metal, polonium, has a primitive cubic lattice.

When the cubes pack together to make a three-dimensional crystal of a metal, the atom at each corner is shared among eight cubes (Figures 13.3, 13.4, and 13.6a). Because of this, only one eighth of each corner atom is actually within a given unit cell. Furthermore, because a cube has eight corners, and because one eighth of the atom at each corner "belongs to" a particular unit cell, the corner atoms contribute a net of one atom to a given unit cell. Thus, *the primitive cubic arrangement has one net atom within the unit cell.*

(8 corners of a cube)(⅛ of each corner atom within a unit cell) =
1 net atom per unit cell for the primitive cubic unit cell

FIGURE 13.6 Atom sharing at cube corners and faces. (a) In any cubic lattice, each corner particle is shared equally among eight cubes, so one eighth of the particle is within a particular cubic unit cell. (b) In a face-centered lattice, each particle on a cube face is shared equally between two unit cells. One half of each particle of this type is within a given unit cell.

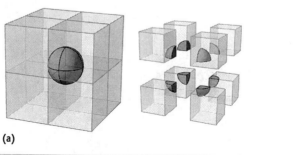

(a)

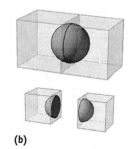

(b)

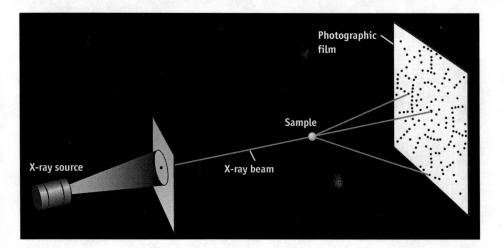

FIGURE 13.7 X-ray crystallography. In the x-ray diffraction experiment, a beam of x-rays is directed at a crystalline solid. The photons of the x-ray beam are scattered by the atoms of the solid. The scattered x-rays are detected by a photographic film or an electronic detector, and the pattern of scattered x-rays is related to the locations of the atoms or ions in the crystal.

In contrast to the primitive cubic lattice, a body-centered cube has an additional atom wholly within the unit cell at the cube's center. The center particle is present in addition to those at the cube corners, so *the body-centered cubic arrangement has a net of two atoms within the unit cell.*

In a face-centered cubic arrangement, there is an atom on each of the six faces of the cube in addition to those at the cube corners. One half of each atom on a face belongs to a given unit cell (Figure 13.6b). Three net particles are therefore contributed by the particles on the faces of the cube:

(6 faces of a cube)(½ of an atom within a unit cell) =
3 net face-centered atoms within a face-centered cubic unit cell

Thus, *the face-centered cubic arrangement has a net of four atoms within the unit cell,* one contributed by the corner atoms and another three contributed by the atoms centered in the six faces.

An experimental technique, x-ray crystallography, can be used to determine the structure of a crystalline substance (Figure 13.7). Once the structure is known, the information can be combined with other experimental information to calculate such useful parameters as the radius of an atom (Study Questions 13.7–13.10).

Chemistry Now™

Sign in at **www.cengage.com/login** and go to Chapter 13 Contents to see Screen 13.2 for a self-study module on **crystal lattices.**

■ **EXAMPLE 13.1 Determining an Atom Radius from Lattice Dimensions**

Problem Aluminum has a density of 2.699 g/cm³, and the atoms are packed in a face-centered cubic crystal lattice. What is the radius of an aluminum atom?

Strategy Our strategy for solving this problem is as follows:

1. Find the mass of a unit cell from the knowledge that it is face-centered cubic.

2. Combine the density of aluminum with the mass of the unit cell to find the cell volume.

3. Find the length of a side of the unit cell from its volume.

4. Calculate the atom radius from the edge dimension.

Aluminum metal. The metal has a face-centered cubic unit cell with a net of four Al atoms in each unit cell.

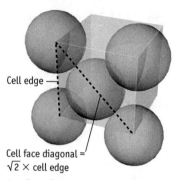

Cell edge ───

Cell face diagonal =
$\sqrt{2}$ × cell edge

One face of a face-centered cubic unit cell. This shows the cell face diagonal, $\sqrt{2}$ × edge, is equal to four times the radius of the atoms in the lattice.

Solution

1. *Calculate the mass of the unit cell.*

$$\text{Mass of 1 Al atom} = \left(\frac{26.98 \text{ g}}{1 \text{ mol}}\right)\left(\frac{1 \text{ mol}}{6.022 \times 10^{23} \text{ atoms}}\right) = 4.480 \times 10^{-23} \text{ g/atom}$$

$$\text{Mass of unit cell} = \left(\frac{4.480 \times 10^{-23} \text{ g}}{1 \text{ Al atom}}\right)\left(\frac{4 \text{ Al atoms}}{1 \text{ unit cell}}\right) = 1.792 \times 10^{-22} \text{ g/unit cell}$$

2. *Calculate the volume of the unit cell.*

$$\text{Volume of unit cell} = \left(\frac{1.792 \times 10^{-22} \text{ g}}{\text{unit cell}}\right)\left(\frac{1 \text{ cm}^3}{2.699 \text{ g}}\right) = 6.640 \times 10^{-23} \text{ cm}^3/\text{unit cell}$$

3. *Calculate the length of a unit cell edge.* The length of the unit cell edge is the cube root of the cell volume.

$$\text{Length of unit cell edge} = \sqrt[3]{6.640 \times 10^{-23} \text{ cm}^3} = 4.049 \times 10^{-8} \text{ cm}$$

4. *Calculate the atom radius.* Notice in the model of aluminum in the margin (and in Figure 13.4) that the Al atoms at the cell corners do not touch each other. Rather, the four corner atoms touch the face-centered atom. Thus, the diagonal distance across the face of the cell is equal to four times the Al atom radius.

$$\text{Cell face diagonal} = 4 \times (\text{Al atom radius})$$

The cell diagonal is the hypotenuse of a right isosceles triangle, so, using the Pythagorean theorem,

$$(\text{Diagonal distance})^2 = 2 \times (\text{edge})^2$$

Taking the square root of both sides, we have

$$\text{Diagonal distance} = \sqrt{2} \times (\text{cell edge})$$
$$= \sqrt{2} \times (4.049 \times 10^{-8} \text{ cm}) = 5.727 \times 10^{-8} \text{ cm}$$

We divide the diagonal distance by 4 to obtain the Al atom radius in cm.

$$\text{Al atom radius} = \frac{5.727 \times 10^{-8} \text{ cm}}{4} = 1.432 \times 10^{-8} \text{ cm}$$

Atomic dimensions are often expressed in picometers, so we convert the radius to that unit.

$$1.432 \times 10^{-8} \text{ cm}\left(\frac{1 \text{ m}}{100 \text{ cm}}\right)\left(\frac{1 \text{ pm}}{1 \times 10^{-12} \text{ m}}\right) = 143.2 \text{ pm}$$

This is in excellent agree with the radius in Figure 7.8.

EXERCISE 13.1 Determining an Atom Radius from Lattice Dimensions

Gold has a face-centered unit cell, and its density is 19.32 g/cm³. Calculate the radius of a gold atom.

EXERCISE 13.2 The Structure of Solid Iron

Iron has a density of 7.8740 g/cm³, and the radius of an iron atom is 126 pm. Verify that solid iron has a body-centered cubic unit cell. (Be sure to note that the atoms in a body-centered cubic unit cell touch along the diagonal across the cell. They do not touch along the edges of the cell.) (Hint: the diagonal distance across the unit cell is edge × $\sqrt{3}$.)

It is a "rule" that nature does things as efficiently as possible. You know this if you have ever tried to stack some oranges into a pile that doesn't fall over and that takes up as little space as possible. How did you do it? Clearly, the pyramid arrangement below on the right works, whereas the cubic one on the left does not.

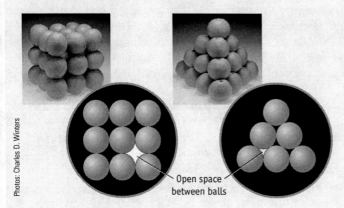

If you could look inside the pile, you would find that less open space is left in the pyramid stacking than in the cube stacking. Only 52% of the space is filled in the cubic packing arrangement. (If you could stack oranges as a body-centered cube, that would be slightly better; 68% of the space is used.) However, the best method is the pyramid stack, which is really a face-centered cubic arrangement. Oranges, atoms, or ions packed this way occupy 74% of the available space.

To fill three-dimensional space, the most efficient way to pack oranges or atoms is to begin with a hexagonal arrangement of spheres, as in this arrangement of marbles.

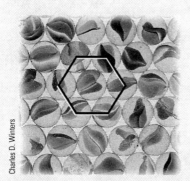

Succeeding layers of atoms or ions are then stacked one on top of the other in two different ways. Depending on the stacking pattern (Figure 1), you will get either a **cubic close-packed (ccp)** or **hexagonal close-packed (hcp)** arrangement.

In the hcp arrangement, additional layers of particles are placed above and below a given layer, fitting into the same depressions on either side of the middle layer. In a three-dimensional crystal, the lay-

ers repeat their pattern in the manner ABABAB. . . . Atoms in each A layer are directly above the ones in another A layer; the same holds true for the B layers.

In the ccp arrangement, the atoms of the "top" layer (A) rest in depressions in the middle layer (B), and those of the "bottom" layer (C) are oriented opposite to those in the top layer. In a crystal, the pattern is repeated ABCABCABC. . . . By turning the whole crystal, you can see that the ccp arrangement is the face-centered cubic structure (Figure 2).

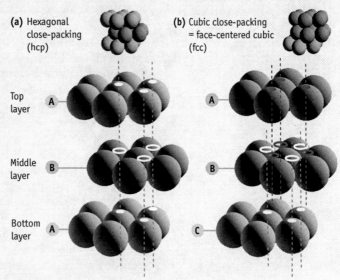

FIGURE 1 Efficient packing. The most efficient ways to pack atoms or ions in crystalline materials are hexagonal close-packing (hcp) and cubic close packing (ccp).

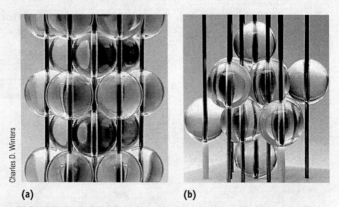

FIGURE 2 Models of close packing. (a) A model of hexagonal close-packing, where the layers repeat in the order ABABAB. . . . (b) A face-centered unit cell (cubic close-packing), where the layers repeat in the order ABCABC. . . . (A kit from which these models can be built is available from the Institute for Chemical Education at the University of Wisconsin at Madison.)

13.2 Structures and Formulas of Ionic Solids

The lattices of many ionic compounds are built by taking a primitive cubic or face-centered cubic lattice of ions of one type and placing ions of opposite charge in the holes within the lattice. This produces a three-dimensional lattice of regularly placed ions. The smallest repeating unit in these structures is, by definition, the unit cell for the ionic compound.

The choice of the lattice and the number and location of the holes that are filled are the keys to understanding the relationship between the lattice structure and the formula of a salt. Consider, for example, the ionic compound cesium chloride, CsCl (Figure 13.8). The structure of CsCl has a primitive cubic unit cell of chloride ions. The cesium ion fits into a hole in the center of the cube. (An equivalent unit cell has a primitive cubic unit cell of Cs^+ ions with a Cl^- ion in the center of the cube.)

Next, consider the structure for NaCl. An extended view of the lattice and one unit cell are illustrated in Figures 13.9a and 13.9b, respectively. The Cl^- ions are arranged in a face-centered cubic unit cell, and the Na^+ ions are arranged in a regular manner between these ions. Notice that each Na^+ ion is surrounded by six Cl^- ions. An octahedral geometry is assumed by the ions surrounding an Na^+ ion, so the Na^+ ions are said to be in **octahedral holes** (Figure 13.9c).

The formula of an ionic compound must always be reflected in the composition of its unit cell; therefore, the formula can always be derived from the unit cell structure. The formula for NaCl can be related to this structure by counting the number of cations and anions contained in one unit cell. A face-centered cubic lattice of Cl^- ions has a net of four Cl^- ions within the unit cell. There is one Na^+ ion in the center of the unit cell, contained totally within the unit cell. In addition, there are 12 Na^+ ions along the edges of the unit cell. Each of these Na^+ ions is shared among four unit cells, so each contributes one fourth of an Na^+ ion to the unit cell, giving three additional Na^+ ions within the unit cell.

(1 Na^+ ion in the center of the unit cell) + ($\frac{1}{4}$ of Na^+ ion in each edge × 12 edges)

= net of 4 Na^+ ions in NaCl unit cell

This accounts for all of the ions contained in the unit cell: four Cl^- and four Na^+ ions. Thus, a unit cell of NaCl has a 1:1 ratio of Na^+ and Cl^- ions, as the formula requires.

Another common unit cell again has ions of one type in a face-centered cubic unit cell. Ions of the other type are located in **tetrahedral holes**, wherein each ion is surrounded by four oppositely charged ions. As illustrated in Figure 13.10, there are eight tetrahedral holes in a face-centered unit cell. In ZnS (zinc blende), the sulfide

■ **Lattice Ions and Holes** Chemists usually think of ionic lattices as being built from the larger anions with the smaller cations located in the holes that remain. For NaCl, for example, an fcc lattice is built out of the Cl^- ions (radius = 181 pm), and the smaller Na^+ cations (radius = 98 pm) are placed in appropriate holes in the lattice.

FIGURE 13.8 Cesium chloride (CsCl) unit cell. The unit cell of CsCl may be viewed in two ways. The only requirement is that the unit cell must have a net of one Cs^+ ion and one Cl^- ion. Either way, it is a simple cubic unit cell of ions of one type (Cl^- on the left or Cs^+ on the right). Generally, ionic lattices are assembled by placing the larger ions (here Cl^-) at the lattice points and placing the smaller ions (here Cs^+) in the lattice holes.

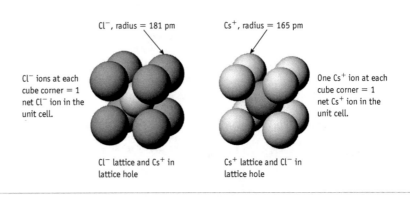

Cl⁻, radius = 181 pm

Cs⁺, radius = 165 pm

Cl^- ions at each cube corner = 1 net Cl^- ion in the unit cell.

One Cs^+ ion at each cube corner = 1 net Cs^+ ion in the unit cell.

Cl^- lattice and Cs^+ in lattice hole

Cs^+ lattice and Cl^- in lattice hole

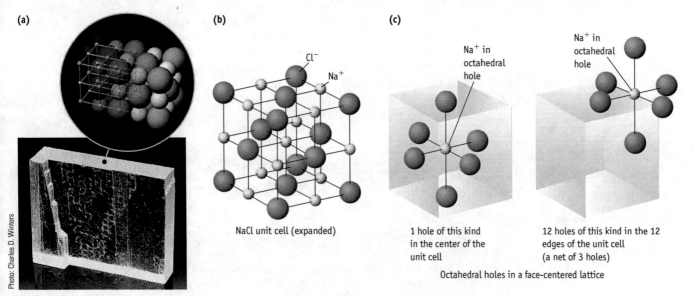

(a)

(b)

(c)

Cl⁻

Na⁺

NaCl unit cell (expanded)

Na⁺ in octahedral hole

1 hole of this kind in the center of the unit cell

Na⁺ in octahedral hole

12 holes of this kind in the 12 edges of the unit cell (a net of 3 holes)

Octahedral holes in a face-centered lattice

Photo: Charles D. Winters

FIGURE 13.9 Sodium chloride. (a) Cubic NaCl is based on a face-centered cubic unit cell of Na^+ and Cl^- ions. (b) An expanded view of a sodium chloride lattice. (The lines represent the connections between lattice points.) The smaller Na^+ ions (silver) are packed into a face-centered cubic lattice of larger Cl^- ions (yellow). (c) A close-up view of the octahedral holes in the lattice.

ions (S^{2-}) form a face-centered cubic unit cell. The zinc ions (Zn^{2+}) then occupy one half of the tetrahedral holes, and each Zn^{2+} ion is surrounded by four S^{2-} ions. The unit cell consists of a net of four S^{2-} ions and four Zn^{2+} ions, which are contained wholly within the unit cell. This 1 : 1 ratio of the ions is reflected in the formula.

In summary, compounds with the formula MX commonly form one of three possible crystal structures:

1. M^{n+} ions occupying all the cubic holes of a primitive cubic X^{n-} lattice. Example, CsCl
2. M^{n+} ions in all the octahedral holes in a face-centered cubic X^{n-} lattice. Example, NaCl
3. M^{n+} ions occupying half of the tetrahedral holes in a face-centered cube lattice of X^{n-} ions. Example, ZnS

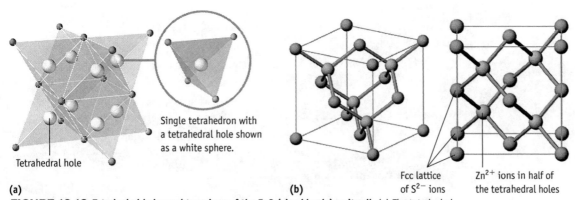

Single tetrahedron with a tetrahedral hole shown as a white sphere.

Tetrahedral hole

Fcc lattice of S^{2-} ions

Zn^{2+} ions in half of the tetrahedral holes

(a)

(b)

FIGURE 13.10 Tetrahedral holes and two views of the ZnS (zinc blende) unit cell. (a) The tetrahedral holes in a face-centered cubic lattice. (b) This unit cell is an example of a face-centered cubic lattice of ions of one type with ions of the opposite type in one half of the tetrahedral holes.

Chemists and geologists in particular have observed that the sodium chloride or "rock salt" structure is adopted by many ionic compounds, most especially by all the alkali metal halides (except CsCl, CsBr, and CsI), all the oxides and sulfides of the alkaline earth metals, and all the oxides of formula MO of the transition metals of the fourth period. Finally, the formulas of compounds must be reflected in the structures of their unit cells; therefore, the formula can always be derived from the unit cell structure.

Chemistry。ౢ.Now™

Sign in at **www.cengage.com/login** and go to Chapter 13 Contents to see Screen 13.3 to view an animation of **ionic unit cells.**

■ **EXAMPLE 13.2 Ionic Structure and Formula**

Problem One unit cell of the mineral perovskite is illustrated here. This compound is composed of calcium and titanium cations and oxide anions. Based on the unit cell, what is the formula of perovskite?

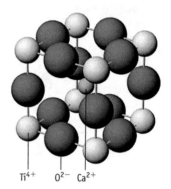

Ti^{4+} O^{2-} Ca^{2+}

Strategy Identify the ions present in the unit cell and their locations within the unit cell. Decide on the net number of ions of each kind in the cell.

Solution The unit cell has Ti^{4+} ions at the corners of the cubic unit cell, a calcium ion in the center of the cell, and oxide ions along the edges.

Number of Ti^{4+} ions:

(8 Ti^{4+} ions at cube corners) × (⅛ of each ion inside unit cell) = 1 net Ti^{4+} ion

Number of Ca^{2+} ions:

One ion is in the cube center = 1 net Ca^{2+} ion

Number of O^{2-} ions:

(12 O^{2-} ions in cube edges) × (¼ of each ion inside cell) = 3 net O^{2-} ions

Thus, the formula of perovskite is $CaTiO_3$.

Comment This is a reasonable formula. A Ca^{2+} ion and three O^{2-} ions would require a titanium ion with a 4+ charge, a reasonable value because titanium is in Group 4B of the periodic table.

■ **EXAMPLE 13.3 The Relation of the Density of an Ionic Compound and its Unit Cell Dimensions**

Problem Magnesium oxide has a face-centered cubic unit cell of oxide ions with magnesium ions in octahedral holes. If the radius of Mg^{2+} is 79 pm and the density of MgO is 3.56 g/cm³, what is the radius of the oxide ion?

Strategy The unit cell contains 4 MgO units, so we can calculate the mass of the unit cell. Combining the unit cell mass and the density of the solid gives us the unit cell volume, from which we can find the length of one edge of the unit cell. The edge of the unit cell is twice the radius of a Mg^{2+} ion (2 times 79 pm) plus twice the radius of an O^{2-} ion (the unknown).

Solution

1. *Calculate the mass of the unit cell.* An ionic compound of formula MX and based on a face-centered cubic lattice of X^- ions with M^+ ions in the octahedral holes has 4 MX unit per unit cell.

$$\text{Unit cell mass} = \left(\frac{40.31 \text{ g}}{1 \text{ mol MgO}}\right)\left(\frac{1 \text{ mol MgO}}{6.022 \times 10^{23} \text{ units of MgO}}\right)\left(\frac{4 \text{ MgO units}}{1 \text{ unit cell}}\right)$$
$$= 2.677 \times 10^{-22} \text{ g/unit cell}$$

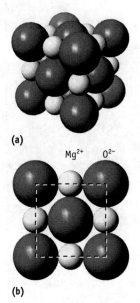

(a)

Mg^{2+} O^{2-}

2. *Calculate the volume of the unit cell from the mass and density.*

$$\text{Unit cell volume} = \left(\frac{2.667 \times 10^{-22} \text{ g}}{\text{unit cell}}\right)\left(\frac{1 \text{ cm}^3}{3.56 \text{ g}}\right) = 7.49 \times 10^{-23} \text{ cm}^3/\text{unit cell}$$

3. *Calculate the edge dimension of the unit cell in pm.*

$$\text{Unit cell edge} = (7.49 \times 10^{-23} \text{ cm}^3)^{\frac{1}{3}} = 4.22 \times 10^{-8} \text{ cm}$$

$$\text{Unit cell edge} = 4.22 \times 10^{-8} \text{ cm}\left(\frac{1 \text{ m}}{100 \text{ cm}}\right)\left(\frac{1 \times 10^{12} \text{ pm}}{1 \text{ m}}\right) = 422 \text{ pm}$$

(b)

Magnesium oxide. (a) A unit cell showing oxide ions in a face-centered cubic lattice with magnesium ions in the octahedral holes. (b) One face of the cell.

4. *Calculate the oxide ion radius.*

One face of the MgO unit cell is shown in the margin. The O^{2-} ions define the lattice, and the Mg^{2+} and O^{2-} ions along the cell edge just touch one another. This means that one edge of the cell is equal to one O^{2-} radius (x) plus twice the Mg^{2+} radius plus one more O^{2-} radius.

$$\text{MgO unit cell edge} = x \text{ pm} + 2(79 \text{ pm}) + x \text{ pm} = 422 \text{ pm}$$

$$x = \boxed{\text{oxide ion radius} = 132 \text{ pm}}$$

EXERCISE 13.3 Structure and Formula

If an ionic solid has an fcc lattice of anions (X) and all of the tetrahedral holes are occupied by metal cations (M), is the formula of the compound MX, MX_2, or M_2X?

EXERCISE 13.4 Density from Cell Dimensions

Potassium chloride has the same unit cell as NaCl. Using the ion sizes in Figure 7.12, calculate the density of KCl.

13.3 Bonding in Ionic Compounds: Lattice Energy

Ionic compounds typically have high melting points, an indication of the strength of the bonding in the ionic crystal lattice. A measure of that is the lattice energy, the main topic of this section.

Lattice Energy

Ionic compounds exist as solids under normal conditions. Their structures contain positive and negative ions arranged in a three-dimensional lattice (Figure 13.9). In an ionic crystal lattice, there are extensive attractions between ions of opposite charge and repulsions between ions of like charge. Each of these interactions is governed by an equation related to Coulomb's law (◀ page 78). For

TABLE 13.2 Lattice Energies of Some Ionic Compounds

Compound	$\Delta_{lattice}U$ (kJ/mol)
LiF	−1037
LiCl	−852
LiBr	−815
LiI	−761
NaF	−926
NaCl	−786
NaBr	−752
NaI	−702
KF	−821
KCl	−717
KBr	−689
KI	−649

Source: D. Cubicciotti: Lattice energies of the alkali halides and electron affinities of the halogens. *Journal of Chemical Physics*, Vol. 31, p. 1646, 1959.

example, $U_{ion\ pair}$, the energy of attractive interactions between 1 mol of ion pairs is given by

$$U_{ion\ pair} = C(N_A)\left(\frac{(n^+e)(n^-e)}{d}\right)$$

The symbol C represents a constant; d is the distance between the ion centers; n^+ is the number of positive charges on the cation; n^- is the number of negative charges on the anion; and e is the charge on an electron; n^+e is assigned a positive value, and n^-e is assigned a negative value due to the respective charges of the ions. Including Avogadro's number, N_A, allows us to calculate the energy change for 1 mol of ion pairs. Be sure to notice that the energy depends directly on the charges on the ions and inversely on the distance between them.

In an extended ionic lattice, there are multiple cation–anion interactions. Let us take NaCl as an example (Figure 13.9). If we focus on an Na^+ ion in the center of the unit cell, we see it is surrounded by, and attracted to, six Cl^- ions. Just a bit farther away from this Na^+ ion, however, there are 12 other Na^+ ions, and there is a force of repulsion between the center Na^+ and these ions. (These are 12 Na^+ ions in the edges of the cube.) And if we still focus on the "center" Na^+ ion, we see there are eight more Cl^- ions, and these are attracted to the "center" Na^+ ion. If we were to take into account *all* of the interactions between the ions in a lattice, it would be possible to calculate the **lattice energy, $\Delta_{lattice}U$**, the energy of formation of one mole of a solid crystalline ionic compound when ions in the gas phase combine (see Table 13.2). For sodium chloride, this reaction would correspond to

$$Na^+(g) + Cl^-(g) \rightarrow NaCl(s)$$

Lattice energy is a measure of the strength of ionic bonding. Often, however, chemists use **lattice enthalpy, $\Delta_{lattice}H$** rather than lattice energy because of the difficulty of estimating some energy quantities. The same trends are seen in both, though, and, because we are dealing with a condensed phase, the numerical values are nearly identical.

We shall focus here on the dependence of lattice enthalpy on ion charges and sizes. As given by Coulomb's law, the higher the ion charges, the greater the attraction between oppositely charged ions, and so $\Delta_{lattice}H$ has a larger negative value for more highly charged ions. This is illustrated by the lattice enthalpies of MgO and NaF. The value of $\Delta_{lattice}H$ for MgO (−4050 kJ/mol) is about four times more negative than the value for NaF (−926 kJ/mol) because the charges on the Mg^{2+} and O^{2-} ions [(2+) × (2−)] are twice as large as those on Na^+ and F^- ions.

Because the attraction between ions is inversely proportional to the distance between them, the effect of ion size on lattice enthalpy is also predictable: A lattice built from smaller ions generally leads to a more negative value for the lattice enthalpy (Table 13.2 and Figure 13.11). For alkali metal halides, for example, the lattice enthalpy for lithium compounds is generally more negative than that for potassium compounds because the Li^+ ion is much smaller than the K^+ cation. Similarly, fluorides are more strongly bonded than are iodides with the same cation.

■ **Born–Haber Cycles** Calculation of lattice energies by this procedure is named for Max Born (1882–1970) and Fritz Haber (1868–1934), German scientists who played prominent roles in thermodynamic research.

Calculating a Lattice Enthalpy from Thermodynamic Data

Lattice enthalpies can be calculated using a thermodynamic relationship known as a **Born–Haber cycle.** This calculation is an application of Hess's law (◄ page 233). Such a cycle is illustrated in Figure 13.12 for solid sodium chloride.

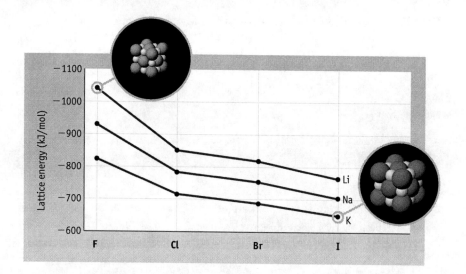

Steps 1 and 2 in Figure 13.12 involve formation of $Na^+(g)$ and $Cl^-(g)$ ions from the elements; the enthalpy change for each of these steps is known (Appendices F and L). Step 3 in Figure 13.12 gives the lattice enthalpy, $\Delta_{lattice}H$. $\Delta_f H°$ is the standard molar enthalpy of formation of NaCl(s) (Appendix L). The enthalpy values for each step are related by the following equation:

$$\Delta_f H° \; [NaCl(s)] = \Delta H_{Step\ 1a} + \Delta H_{Step\ 1b} + \Delta H_{Step\ 2a} + \Delta H_{Step\ 2b} + \Delta H_{Step\ 3}$$

Because the values for all of these quantities are known except for $\Delta H_{Step\ 3}$ ($\Delta_{lattice}H$), the value for this step can be calculated.

Step 1a. Enthalpy of formation of Cl(g)   = +121.3 kJ/mol (Appendix L)
Step 1b. ΔH for $Cl(g) + e^- \rightarrow Cl^-(g)$ = −349 kJ/mol (Appendix F)
Step 2a. Enthalpy of formation of Na(g)   = +107.3 kJ/mol (Appendix L)
Step 2b. ΔH for $Na(g) \rightarrow Na^+(g) + e^-$ = +496 kJ/mol (Appendix F)

The standard enthalpy of formation of NaCl(s), $\Delta_f H°$, is −411.12 kJ/mol. Combining this with the known values of Steps 1 and 2, we can calculate ΔH_{step3}, which is the lattice enthalpy, $\Delta_{lattice}H$.

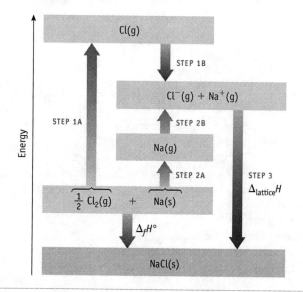

FIGURE 13.12 Born–Haber cycle for the formation of NaCl(s) from the elements. The calculation in the text uses enthalpy values, and the value obtained is the lattice enthalpy, $\Delta_{lattice}H$. The difference between $\Delta_{lattice}U$ and $\Delta_{lattice}H$ is generally not significant and can be corrected for, if desired. (Note that the energy diagram is not to scale.)

Step 3.   Formation of NaCl(s) from the ions in the gas phase = ΔH_{step3}

$\Delta H_{step3} = \Delta_f H° \, [NaCl(s)] - \Delta H_{Step\ 1a} - \Delta H_{Step\ 1b} - \Delta H_{Step\ 2a} - \Delta H_{Step\ 2b}$
$= -411.12 \text{ kJ/mol} - 121.3 \text{ kJ/mol} - (-349 \text{ kJ/mol})$
$- 107.3 \text{ kJ/mol} - 496 \text{ kJ/mol}$
$= -787 \text{ kJ/mol}$

Chemistry ⚛ Now™

Sign in at **www.cengage.com/login** and go to Chapter 13 Contents to see Screen 13.4 for an illustration of **lattice and lattice energy.**

EXERCISE 13.5 Using Lattice Enthalpies

Calculate the molar enthalpy of formation, $\Delta_f H°$, of solid sodium iodide using the approach outlined in Figure 13.12. The required data can be found in Appendices F and L and in Table 13.2.

13.4 The Solid State: Other Kinds of Solid Materials

So far, we have described the structures of metals and simple ionic solids. Now we will look briefly at the other categories of solids: molecular solids, network solids, and amorphous solids (Table 13.1).

Molecular Solids

Compounds such as H_2O and CO_2 exist as solids under appropriate conditions. In these cases, it is molecules, rather than atoms or ions, that pack in a regular fashion in a three-dimensional lattice. You have already seen one such structure, that of ice (Figure 12.8).

The way molecules are arranged in a crystalline lattice depends on the shape of the molecules and the types of intermolecular forces. Molecules tend to pack in the most efficient manner and to align in ways that maximize intermolecular forces of attraction. Thus, the water structure was established to gain the maximum intermolecular attraction through hydrogen bonding.

It is from structural studies on molecular solids that most of the information on molecular geometries, bond lengths, and bond angles discussed in Chapter 8 was assembled.

Network Solids

Network solids are composed entirely of a three-dimensional array of covalently bonded atoms. Common examples include two allotropes of carbon: graphite and diamond. Elemental silicon is also a network solid with a diamond-like structure.

Graphite consists of carbon atoms bonded together in flat sheets that cling only weakly to one another (Figure 2.7). Within the layers, each carbon atom is surrounded by three other carbon atoms in a trigonal planar arrangement. The layers can slip easily over another, which explains why graphite is soft, a good lubricant, and used in pencil lead. (Pencil "lead" is not the element lead, but rather a composite of clay and graphite.)

Diamonds have a low density ($d = 3.51 \text{ g/cm}^3$), but they are also the hardest material and the best conductor of heat known. They are transparent to visible light, as well as to infrared and ultraviolet radiation. Diamonds are electrically in-

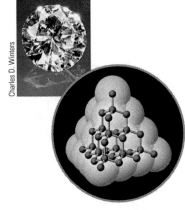

FIGURE 13.13 A diamond and the diamond lattice. The colors of diamonds may range from colorless to yellow, brown, or black. Poorer-quality diamonds are used extensively in industry, mainly for cutting or grinding tools. Industrial-quality diamonds are produced synthetically at present by heating graphite, along with a metal catalyst, to 1200–1500 °C and a pressure of 65–90 kilobars.

Charles D. Winters

sulating but behave as semiconductors with some advantages over silicon. In addition to their use in jewelry, many diamonds are used as abrasives and in diamond-coated cutting tools. In the structure of diamond (Figure 13.13), each carbon atom is bonded to four other carbon atoms at the corners of a tetrahedron, and this pattern extends throughout the solid.

Silicates, compounds composed of silicon and oxygen, represent an enormous class of chemical compounds. You know them in the form of sand, quartz, talc, and mica, or as a major constituent of rocks such as granite. The structure of quartz is illustrated in Figure 13.14. It consists of tetrahedral silicon atoms covalently bonded to oxygen atoms in a giant three-dimensional lattice.

Most network solids are hard and rigid and are characterized by high melting and boiling points. These characteristics reflect the fact that a great deal of energy must be provided to break the covalent bonds in the lattice. For example, silicon dioxide melts at temperatures higher than 1600 °C.

Amorphous Solids

A characteristic property of pure crystalline solids—whether metals, ionic solids, or molecular solids—is that they melt at a specific temperature. For example, water melts at 0 °C, aspirin at 135 °C, lead at 327.5 °C, and NaCl at 801 °C. Because they are specific and reproducible values, melting points are often used as a means of identifying chemical compounds.

Another property of crystalline solids is that they form well-defined crystals, with smooth, flat faces. When a sharp force is applied to a crystal, it will most often cleave to give smooth, flat faces. The resulting solid particles are smaller versions of the original crystal (Figure 13.15a).

Many common solids, including ones that we encounter every day, do not have these properties, however. Glass is a good example. When glass is heated, it softens over a wide temperature range, a property useful for artisans and craftsmen who can create beautiful and functional products for our enjoyment and use. Glass also possesses a property that we would rather it not have: When glass breaks, it leaves randomly shaped pieces. Other materials that behave similarly include common polymers such as polyethylene, nylon, and other plastics.

Photo: Charles D. Winters

FIGURE 13.14 Silicon dioxide. Common quartz, SiO_2, is a network solid consisting of silicon and oxygen atoms.

Charles D. Winters

(a) A salt crystal can be cleaved cleanly into smaller and smaller crystals that are duplicates of the larger crystal.

(b) Glass is an amorphous solid composed of silicon and oxygen atoms. It has, however, no long-range order as in crystalline quartz.

(c) Glass can be molded and shaped into beautiful forms and, by adding metal oxides, can take on wonderful colors.

FIGURE 13.15 Crystalline and amorphous solids.

The characteristics of these amorphous solids relate to their molecular structure. At the particulate level, amorphous solids do not have a regular structure. In fact, in many ways these substances look a lot like liquids. Unlike liquids, however, the forces of attraction are strong enough that movement of the molecules or ions is restricted.

Chemistry ⚛ Now™

Sign in at **www.cengage.com/login** and go to Chapter 13 Contents to see:
- Screen 13.5 for an exercise on **molecular solids**
- Screen 13.6 for a self-study module on **network solids**
- Screen 13.7 for a self-study module on **silicate minerals**

13.5 Phase Changes Involving Solids

The shape of a crystalline solid is a reflection of its internal structure. But what about physical properties of solids, such as the temperatures at which they melt? This and many other physical properties of solids are of interest to chemists, geologists, and engineers, among others.

Melting: Conversion of Solid into Liquid

The melting point of a solid is the temperature at which the lattice collapses and the solid is converted into a liquid. Like the liquid-to-vapor transformation, melting requires energy, called the enthalpy of fusion (given in kilojoules per mole) (◀ Chapter 5).

Energy absorbed as heat on melting = enthalpy of fusion = $\Delta_{fusion}H$ (kJ/mol)
Energy evolved as heat on freezing = enthalpy of crystallization = $-\Delta_{fusion}H$ (kJ/mol)

■ **Uncle Tungsten** *Uncle Tungsten* is the title of a book by Oliver Sacks (Alfred Knopf, New York, 2001). In it, he describes growing up with an uncle who had a light bulb factory and used tungsten. He also describes other "chemical adventures."

Enthalpies of fusion can range from just a few thousand joules per mole to many thousands of joules per mole (Table 13.3). A low melting temperature will certainly mean a low value for the enthalpy of fusion, whereas high melting points are associated with high enthalpies of fusion. Figure 13.16 shows the enthalpies of fusion for the metals of the fourth through the sixth periods. Based on this figure, we see that transition metals have high enthalpies of fusion, with many of those in the sixth period being extraordinarily high. This trend parallels the trend seen with the melting points for these elements. Tungsten, which has the highest melting point of all the known elements except for carbon, also has the highest enthalpy of fusion among the transition metals. For this reason, tungsten is used for the filaments in light bulbs; no other material has been found to work better since the invention of the light bulb in 1908.

Table 13.3 presents some data for several basic types of substances: metals, polar and nonpolar molecules, and ionic solids. In general, nonpolar substances that form molecular solids have low melting points. Melting points increase within a series of related molecules, however, as the size and molar mass increase. This happens because London dispersion forces are generally larger when the molar mass is larger. Thus, increasing amounts of energy are required to break down the intermolecular forces in the solid, a principle that is reflected in an increasing enthalpy of fusion.

The ionic compounds in Table 13.3 have higher melting points and higher enthalpies of fusion than the molecular solids. This trend is due to the strong ion–ion forces present in ionic solids, forces that are reflected in high lattice energies (page 599). Because ion–ion forces depend on ion size (as well as ion charge), there is a good correlation between lattice energy and the position of the metal or

TABLE 13.3 Melting Points and Enthalpies of Fusion of Some Elements and Compounds

Compound	Melting Point (°C)	Enthalpy of Fusion (kJ/mol)	Type of Interparticle Forces
Metals			
Hg	−39	2.29	Metal bonding; see pages 657–663.
Na	98	2.60	
Al	660	10.7	
Ti	1668	20.9	
W	3422	35.2	
Molecular Solids: Nonpolar Molecules			
O_2	−219	0.440	Dispersion forces only.
F_2	−220	0.510	
Cl_2	−102	6.41	
Br_2	−7.2	10.8	
Molecular Solids: Polar Molecules			
HCl	−114	1.99	All three HX molecules have dipole–dipole
HBr	−87	2.41	forces. Dispersion forces increase with size
HI	−51	2.87	and molar mass.
H_2O	0	6.01	Hydrogen bonding and dispersion forces
Ionic Solids			
NaF	996	33.4	All ionic solids have extended ion–ion inter-
NaCl	801	28.2	actions. Note the general trend is the same
NaBr	747	26.1	as for lattice energies (see Section 13.3 and
NaI	660	23.6	Figure 13.11).

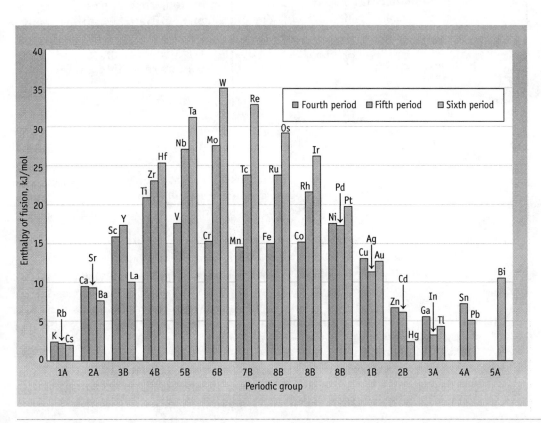

FIGURE 13.16 Enthalpy of fusion of fourth-, fifth-, and sixth-period metals. Enthalpies of fusion range from 2–5 kJ/mol for Group 1A elements to 35.2 kJ/mol for tungsten. Notice that enthalpies of fusion generally increase for group 4B–8B metals on descending the periodic table.

FIGURE 13.17 Sublimation.

Sublimation entails the conversion of a solid directly to its vapor. Here, iodine (I_2) sublimes when warmed. If an ice-filled test tube is inserted into the flask, the vapor deposits on the cold surface.

Iodine sublimes when heated.

Charles D. Winters

halogen in the periodic table. For example, the data in Table 13.3 show a decrease in melting point and enthalpy of fusion for sodium salts as the halide ion increases in size. This parallels the decrease in lattice energy seen with increasing ion size.

Sublimation: Conversion of Solid into Vapor

Molecules can escape directly from the solid to the gas phase by sublimation (Figure 13.17).

$$\text{Solid} \rightarrow \text{Gas} \qquad \text{Energy required as heat} = \Delta_{\text{sublimation}}H$$

Sublimation, like fusion and evaporation, is an endothermic process. The energy required as heat is called the **enthalpy of sublimation.** Water, which has a molar enthalpy of sublimation of 51 kJ/mol, can be converted from solid ice to water vapor quite readily. A good example of this phenomenon is the sublimation of frost from grass and trees as night turns to day on a cold morning in the winter.

13.6 Phase Diagrams

Depending on the conditions of temperature and pressure, a substance can exist as a gas, a liquid, or a solid. In addition, under certain specific conditions, two (or even three) states can coexist in equilibrium. It is possible to summarize this information in the form of a graph called a **phase diagram.** Phase diagrams are used to illustrate the relationship between phases of matter and the pressure and temperature.

Water

Figure 13.18 illustrates a phase diagram for water. The lines in a phase diagram identify the conditions under which two phases exist at equilibrium. Conversely, all points that do not fall on the lines in the figure represent conditions under which there is only one state that is stable. Line A–B represents conditions for solid–vapor equilibrium, and line A–C for liquid–solid equilibrium. The line from point A to point D, representing the temperature and pressure combination at which the liquid and vapor phases are in equilibrium, is the same curve plotted for water vapor pressure in Figure 12.17. Recall that the normal boiling point, 100 °C in the case of water, is the temperature at which the equilibrium vapor pressure is 760 mm Hg.

Point A, appropriately called the **triple point**, indicates the conditions under which all three phases coexist in equilibrium. For water, the triple point is at $P = 4.6$ mm Hg and $T = 0.01$ °C.

The line A–C shows the conditions of pressure and temperature at which solid–liquid equilibrium exists. (Because no vapor pressure is involved here, the pressure referred to is the external pressure on the liquid.) For water, this line has a negative slope; the change for water is approximately -0.01 °C for each one-atmosphere increase in pressure. That is, the higher the external pressure, the lower the melting point.

The negative slope of the water solid–liquid equilibrium line can be explained from our knowledge of the structure of water and ice. When the pressure on an object increases, common sense tells us that the volume of the object will become

Case Study   The World's Lightest Solid

The *Guinness Book of Records* calls it the "world's lightest solid" and the "best thermal insulator." Even though it is 99.8% air and has a density of only about 1 mg/cm^3, it is a light blue solid that, to the touch, feels much like Styrofoam chips that are used in packaging. It is also strong structurally, able to hold over 2000 times its weight (Figure A).

"It" is a silica aerogel, a low-density substance derived from a gel in which the liquid has been replaced by air (▶ page 666). There are aerogels based silicon and carbon as well as aluminum and other metals, but the silicon-based aerogel is the most thoroughly studied. This aerogel is made by polymerizing a compound like $Si(OC_2H_5)_4$ in alcohol. The resulting long-chain molecules form a gel that is

bathed in the alcohol. This substance is then placed in supercritical CO_2 (▶ page 609), which causes the alcohol in the nanopores in the gel to be replaced by CO_2. When the CO_2 is vented off as a gas, what remains is a highly porous aerogel with an incredibly low density.

Aerogels have been known for decades but have only recently received a lot of study. They do have amazing properties! Chief among them is their insulating ability, as illustrated in Figure B. Aerogels do not allow heat to be conducted through the lattice, and convective heat transfer is also poor because air cannot circulate throughout the lattice. One practical use for these aerogels is in insulating glass. However, before it can be truly useful for this purpose, researchers need to find a way to make completely transparent aerogel. (Silica aerogel is very light blue owing to Rayleigh scattering, the same process that makes the sky blue.) Aerogels are also biocompatible and have been studied as possible drug delivery systems.

Aerogel has been in the news in the past few years because it was used to catch comet dust in Project Stardust. A spacecraft was sent to intercept a comet in 2004 and returned to Earth in January 2006. On the spacecraft was an array holding blocks of aerogel. As the craft flew through the comet's tail, dust particles impacted the aerogel blocks and were "brought to a standstill as they tunneled through it without much heating or alteration, leaving carrot-shaped tracks." When the spacecraft was returned to Earth, scientists analyzed the particles and found that there were silicate minerals that seemed to have been formed in the inner regions of the solar

FIGURE B Aerogel as an insulator. http://stardust.jpl.nasa.gov/images/gallery/aerogelmatches.jpg

system. (See *Science*, Vol. 314, 15 December 2006.)

Questions:

1. *Assume the repeating unit in the aerogel polymer is $OSi(OC_2H_5)_2$. If the polymer is 99.8% air, how many silicon atoms are there in 1.0 cm^3 of aerogel?*

2. *Suppose you wish to make a superinsulating window and so fill the gap between two sheets of glass with aerogel. What mass of aerogel is needed for a 180 cm × 150 cm window with a gap of 2.0 mm between the glass sheets?*

Answers to these questions are in Appendix Q.

FIGURE A Silica aerogel. A 2.5-kg brick is supported by a piece of silica aerogel weighing about 2 g. (http://stardust.jpl.nasa.gov/photo/aerogel.html)

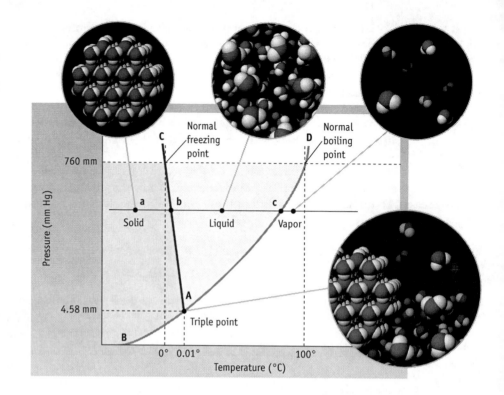

smaller, giving the substance a higher density. Because ice is less dense than liquid water (due to the open lattice structure of ice, Figure 12.8), ice and water in equilibrium respond to increased pressure (at constant T) by melting ice to form more water because the same mass of water requires less volume.

Phase Diagrams and Thermodynamics

Let us explore the water phase diagram further by correlating phase changes with thermodynamic data. Suppose we begin with ice at -10 °C and under a pressure of 500 mm Hg (point a on Figure 13.18). As ice is heated (at constant P), it absorbs about 2.1 J/g · K in warming from point a to point b at a temperature between 0 °C and 0.01 °C. At this point, the solid is in equilibrium with liquid water. Solid–liquid equilibrium is maintained until 333 J/g has been transferred to the sample and it has become liquid water at this temperature. If the liquid, still under a pressure of 500 mm Hg, now absorbs 4.184 J/g · K, it warms to point c. The temperature at point c is about 89 °C, and equilibrium is established between liquid water and water vapor. The equilibrium vapor pressure of the liquid water is 500 mm Hg. If 2260 J/g is transferred to the liquid–vapor sample, the equilibrium vapor pressure remains 500 mm Hg until the liquid is completely converted to vapor at 89 °C.

Carbon Dioxide

The features of the phase diagram for CO_2 (Figure 13.19) are generally the same as those for water but with some important differences.

In contrast to water, the CO_2 solid–liquid equilibrium line has a positive slope. Once again, increasing pressure on the solid in equilibrium with the liquid will shift the equilibrium to the more dense phase, but for CO_2 this will be the solid. Because solid CO_2 is denser than the liquid, the newly formed solid CO_2 sinks to the bottom in a container of liquid CO_2.

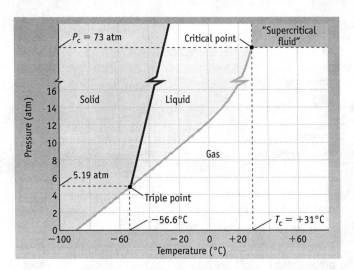

FIGURE 13.19 The phase diagram of CO₂. Notice in particular the positive slope of the solid–liquid equilibrium line. (For more on the critical point, see page 577.)

Another feature of the CO₂ phase diagram is the triple point that occurs at a pressure of 5.19 atm (3940 mm Hg) and 216.6 K (−56.6 °C). Carbon dioxide cannot be a liquid at pressures lower than this.

At pressures around normal atmospheric pressure, CO₂ will be either a solid or a gas, depending on the temperature. [At a pressure of 1 atm, solid CO₂ is in equilibrium with the gas at a temperature of 197.5 K (−78.7 °C).] As a result, as solid CO₂ warms above this temperature, it sublimes rather than melts. Carbon dioxide is called *dry ice* for this reason; it looks like water ice, but it does not melt.

From the CO₂ phase diagram, we can also learn that CO₂ gas can be converted to a liquid at room temperature (20–25 °C) by exerting a moderate pressure on the gas. In fact, CO₂ is regularly shipped in tanks as a liquid to laboratories and industrial companies.

Finally, the critical pressure and temperature for CO₂ are 73 atm and 31 °C, respectively. Because the critical temperature and pressure are easily attained in the laboratory, it is possible to observe the transformation to supercritical CO₂ (Figure 13.20).

Chemistry ☺ Now™

Sign in at **www.cengage.com/login** and go to Chapter 13 Contents to see Screen 13.8 to view animations of **phase changes** and to do an exercise on **phase diagrams**.

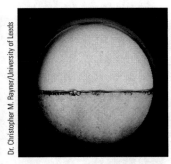

The separate phases of CO₂ are seen through the window in a high-pressure vessel.

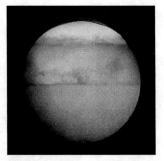

As the sample warms and the pressure increases, the meniscus becomes less distinct.

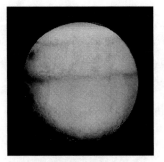

As the temperature continues to increase, it is more difficult to distinguish the liquid and vapor phases.

Once the critical *T* and *P* are reached, distinct liquid and vapor phases are no longer in evidence. This homogeneous phase is "supercritical CO₂."

FIGURE 13.20 Transformation to supercritical CO₂.

Chapter Goals Revisited

Now that you have studied this chapter, you should ask whether you have met the chapter goals. In particular, you should be able to:

Understand cubic unit cells

a. Describe the three types of cubic unit cells: primitive cubic (pc), body-centered cubic (bcc), and face-centered cubic (fcc) (Section 13.1).

b. Relate atom size and unit cell dimensions. Study Question(s) assignable in OWL: 7, 8, 10, 26, 29, 32, 34, 36, 43; Go Chemistry Module 18.

Relate unit cells for ionic compounds to formulas

a. Understand the relation of unit cell structure and formula for ionic compounds. (Section 13.2) Study Question(s) assignable in OWL: 4, 5, 6, 8; Go Chemistry Module 18.

Describe the properties of solids

a. Understand lattice energy and how it is calculated (Section 13.3). Study Question(s) assignable in OWL: 11, 13, 14, 16, 38.

b. Characterize different types of solids: metallic (e.g., copper), ionic (e.g., NaCl and CaF_2), molecular (e.g., water and I_2), network (e.g., diamond), and amorphous (e.g., glass and many synthetic polymers) (Table 13.1). Study Question(s) assignable in OWL: 17.

c. Define the processes of melting, freezing, and sublimation and their enthalpies (Sections 13.4 and 13.5). Study Question(s) assignable in OWL: 20.

Understand the nature of phase diagrams

a. Identify the different points (triple point, normal boiling point, freezing point) and regions (solid, liquid, vapor) of a phase diagram, and use the diagram to evaluate the vapor pressure of a liquid and the relative densities of a liquid and a solid (Section 13.5). Study Question(s) assignable in OWL: 21, 22, 23, 24.

STUDY QUESTIONS

⊌WL Online homework for this chapter may be assigned in OWL.

▲ denotes challenging questions.

■ denotes questions assignable in OWL.

Blue-numbered questions have answers in Appendix O and fully-worked solutions in the *Student Solutions Manual*.

Practicing Skills

Metallic and Ionic Solids

(See Examples 13.1–13.3 and ChemistryNow Screens 13.2 and 13.3.)

1. Outline a two-dimensional unit cell for the pattern shown here. If the black squares are labeled A and the white squares are B, what is the simplest formula for a "compound" based on this pattern?

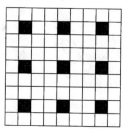

2. Outline a two-dimensional unit cell for the pattern shown here. If the black squares are labeled A and the white squares are B, what is the simplest formula for a "compound" based on this pattern?

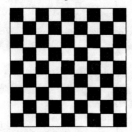

3. One way of viewing the unit cell of perovskite was illustrated in Example 13.2. Another way is shown here. Prove that this view also leads to a formula of $CaTiO_3$.

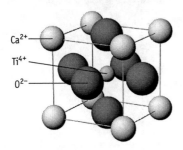

4. ■ Rutile, TiO_2, crystallizes in a structure characteristic of many other ionic compounds. How many formula units of TiO_2 are in the unit cell illustrated here? (The oxide ions marked by an x are wholly within the cell; the others are in the cell faces.)

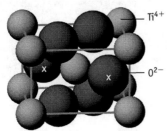

5. ■ Cuprite is a semiconductor. Oxide ions are at the cube corners and in the cube center. Copper ions are wholly within the unit cell.
   (a) What is the formula of cuprite?
   (b) What is the oxidation number of copper?

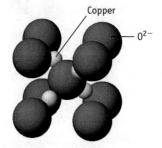

6. ■ The mineral fluorite, which is composed of calcium ions and fluoride ions, has the unit cell shown here.
   (a) What type of unit cell is described by the Ca^{2+} ions?
   (b) Where are the F^- ions located, in octahedral holes or tetrahedral holes?
   (c) Based on this unit cell, what is the formula of fluorite?

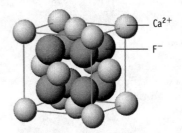

7. ■ Calcium metal crystallizes in a face-centered cubic unit cell. The density of the solid is 1.54 g/cm³. What is the radius of a calcium atom?

8. ■ The density of copper metal is 8.95 g/cm³. If the radius of a copper atom is 127.8 pm, is the copper unit cell primitive, body-centered cubic, or face-centered cubic?

9. Potassium iodide has a face-centered cubic unit cell of iodide ions with potassium ions in octahedral holes. The density of KI is 3.12 g/cm³. What is the length of one side of the unit cell? (Ion sizes are found in Table 7.12.)

10. ▲ ■ A unit cell of cesium chloride is shown on page 596. The density of the solid is 3.99 g/cm³, and the radius of the Cl^- ion is 181 pm. What is the radius of the Cs^+ ion in the center of the cell? (Assume that the Cs^+ ion touches all of the corner Cl^- ions.)

Ionic Bonding and Lattice Energy
(See ChemistryNow Screen 13.4.)

11. ■ List the following compounds in order of increasing lattice energy (from least negative to most negative): LiI, LiF, CaO, RbI.

12. Examine the trends in lattice energy in Table 13.2. The value of the lattice energy becomes somewhat more negative on going from NaI to NaBr to NaCl, and all are in the range of −700 to −800 kJ/mol. Suggest a reason for the observation that the lattice energy of NaF ($\Delta_{lattice}U = -926$ kJ/mol) is much more negative than those of the other sodium halides.

13. ■ To melt an ionic solid, energy must be supplied to disrupt the forces between ions so the regular array of ions collapses. If the distance between the anion and the cation in a crystalline solid decreases (but ion charges remain the same), should the melting point decrease or increase? Explain.

14. ■ Which compound in each of the following pairs should require the higher temperature to melt? (See Study Question 13.)
(a) NaCl or RbCl
(b) BaO or MgO
(c) NaCl or MgS

15. Calculate the molar enthalpy of formation, $\Delta_f H°$, of solid lithium fluoride using the approach outlined on pages 599-602. $\Delta_f H°$ [Li(g)] = 159.37 kJ/mol, and other required data can be found in Appendices F and L. (See also Exercise 13.5.)

16. ■ Calculate the lattice enthalpy for RbCl. In addition to data in Appendices F and L, you will need the following information:

$\Delta_f H°$ [Rb(g)] = 80.9 kJ/mol

$\Delta_f H°$ [RbCl(s)] = −435.4 kJ/mol

Other Types of Solids
(See ChemistryNow Screens 13.6 and 13.7.)

17. ■ A diamond unit cell is shown here.
(a) How many carbon atoms are in one unit cell?
(b) The unit cell can be considered as a cubic unit cell of C atoms with other C atoms in holes in the lattice. What type of unit cell is this (pc, bcc, fcc)? In what holes are other C atoms located, octahedral or tetrahedral holes?

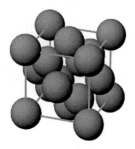

18. The structure of graphite is given in Figure 2.7.
(a) What type of intermolecular bonding forces exist between the layers of six-member carbon rings?
(b) Account for the lubricating ability of graphite. That is, why does graphite feel slippery? Why does pencil lead (which is really graphite in clay) leave black marks on paper?

Physical Properties of Solids

19. Benzene, C_6H_6, is an organic liquid that freezes at 5.5 °C (see Figure 12.1) to form beautiful, feather-like crystals. How much energy as heat is evolved when 15.5 g of benzene freezes at 5.5 °C? (The enthalpy of fusion of benzene is 9.95 kJ/mol.) If the 15.5-g sample is remelted, again at 5.5 °C, what quantity of energy as heat is required to convert it to a liquid?

20. ■ The specific heat capacity of silver is 0.235 J/g · K. Its melting point is 962 °C, and its enthalpy of fusion is 11.3 kJ/mol. What quantity of energy as heat, in joules, is required to change 5.00 g of silver from a solid at 25 °C to a liquid at 962 °C?

Phase Diagrams and Phase Changes
(See ChemistryNow Screen 13.8.)

21. ■ Consider the phase diagram of CO_2 in Figure 13.19.
(a) Is the density of liquid CO_2 greater or less than that of solid CO_2?
(b) In what phase do you find CO_2 at 5 atm and 0 °C?
(c) Can CO_2 be liquefied at 45 °C?

22. ■ Use the phase diagram given here to answer the following questions:

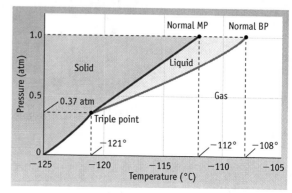

(a) In what phase is the substance found at room temperature and 1.0 atm pressure?
(b) If the pressure exerted on a sample is 0.75 atm and the temperature is −114 °C, in what phase does the substance exist?
(c) If you measure the vapor pressure of a liquid sample and find it to be 380 mm Hg, what is the temperature of the liquid phase?
(d) What is the vapor pressure of the solid at −122 °C?
(e) Which is the denser phase—solid or liquid? Explain briefly.

23. ■ Liquid ammonia, $NH_3(\ell)$, was once used in home refrigerators as the heat transfer fluid. The specific heat capacity of the liquid is 4.7 J/g · K and that of the vapor is 2.2 J/g · K. The enthalpy of vaporization is 23.33 kJ/mol at the boiling point. If you heat 12 kg of liquid ammonia from −50.0 °C to its boiling point of −33.3 °C, allow it to evaporate, and then continue warming to 0.0 °C, how much energy must you supply?

24. ■ If your air conditioner is more than several years old, it may use the chlorofluorocarbon CCl_2F_2 as the heat transfer fluid. The normal boiling point of CCl_2F_2 is −29.8 °C, and the enthalpy of vaporization is 20.11 kJ/mol. The gas and the liquid have specific heat capacities of 117.2 J/mol · K and 72.3 J/mol · K, respectively. How much energy as heat is evolved when 20.0 g of CCl_2F_2 is cooled from +40 °C to −40 °C?

General Questions

These questions are not designated as to type or location in the chapter. They may combine several concepts.

25. Construct a phase diagram for O_2 from the following information: normal boiling point, 90.18 K; normal melting point, 54.8 K; and triple point, 54.34 K at a pressure of 2 mm Hg. Very roughly estimate the vapor pressure of liquid O_2 at $-196\ °C$, the lowest temperature easily reached in the laboratory. Is the density of liquid O_2 greater or less than that of solid O_2?

26. ▲ ■ Tungsten crystallizes in the unit cell shown here.

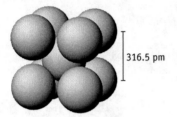

316.5 pm

    (a) What type of unit cell is this?
    (b) How many tungsten atoms occur per unit cell?
    (c) If the edge of the unit cell is 316.5 pm, what is the radius of a tungsten atom? (*Hint:* The W atoms touch each other along the diagonal line from one corner of the unit cell to the opposite corner of the unit cell.)

27. Silver crystallizes in a face-centered cubic unit cell. Each side of the unit cell has a length of 409 pm. What is the radius of a silver atom?

28. ▲ ■ The unit cell shown here is for calcium carbide. How many calcium atoms and how many carbon atoms are in each unit cell? What is the formula of calcium carbide? (Calcium ions are silver in color and carbon atoms are gray.)

29. ■ The very dense metal iridium has a face-centered cubic unit cell and a density of 22.56 g/cm³. Use this information to calculate the radius of an atom of the element.

30. Vanadium metal has a density of 6.11 g/cm³. Assuming the vanadium atomic radius is 132 pm, is the vanadium unit cell primitive cubic, body-centered cubic, or face-centered cubic?

31. ▲ Calcium fluoride is the well-known mineral fluorite. It is known that each unit cell contains four Ca^{2+} ions and eight F^- ions and that the Ca^{2+} ions are arranged in an fcc lattice. The F^- ions fill all the tetrahedral holes in a face-centered cubic lattice of Ca^{2+} ions. The edge of the CaF_2 unit cell is 5.46295×10^{-8} cm in length. The density of the solid is 3.1805 g/cm³. Use this information to calculate Avogadro's number.

32. ▲ ■ Iron has a body-centered cubic unit cell with a cell dimension of 286.65 pm. The density of iron is 7.874 g/cm³. Use this information to calculate Avogadro's number.

33. ▲ You can get some idea of how efficiently spherical atoms or ions are packed in a three-dimensional solid by seeing how well circular atoms pack in two dimensions. Using the drawings shown here, prove that B is a more efficient way to pack circular atoms than A. A unit cell of A contains portions of four circles and one hole. In B, packing coverage can be calculated by looking at a triangle that contains portions of three circles and one hole. Show that A fills about 80% of the available space, whereas B fills closer to 90% of the available space.

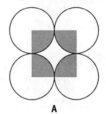 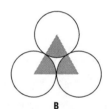

A   B

34. ▲ ■ Assuming that in a primitive cubic unit cell the spherical atoms or ions just touch along the cube's edges, calculate the percentage of empty space within the unit cell. (Recall that the volume of a sphere is $(4/3)\pi r^3$, where r is the radius of the sphere.)

35. ▲ The solid state structure of silicon is

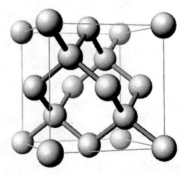

    (a) Describe this crystal as pc, bcc, or fcc. What type of holes are occupied in the lattice?
    (b) Calculate the density of silicon in g/cm³ (given that the cube edge has a length of 543.1 pm), and estimate the radius of the silicon atom. (Note: the Si atoms on the edges do not touch one another.)

36. ▲ ■ The solid state structure of silicon carbide, SiC, is shown below. Knowing that the Si—C bond length is 188.8 pm (and the Si—C—Si bond angle is 109.5°), calculate the density of SiC.

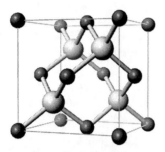

Unit cell of SiC.

Sample of silicon carbide.

37. Spinels are solids with the general formula AB_2O_4 (where A^{2+} and B^{3+} are metal cations of the same or different metals. The best-known example is common magnetite, Fe_3O_4 [which you can formulate as $(Fe^{2+})(Fe^{3+})_2O_4$]. Another example is the mineral often referred to as spinel, $MgAl_2O_4$.

A crystal of the spinel MgAl₂O₄ on a marble chip.

The oxide ions of spinels form a face-centered cubic lattice. In a *normal spinel,* cations occupy ⅛ of the tetrahedral sites and ½ of the octahedral sites.
(a) In $MgAl_2O_4$, in what type of holes are the magnesium and aluminum ions found?
(b) The mineral chromite has the formula $FeCr_2O_4$. What ions are involved, and in what type of holes are they found?

38. ■ Using the thermochemical data below, and an estimated value of -2481 kJ/mol for the lattice energy for Na_2O, calculate the value for the *second* electron affinity of oxygen $[O^-(g) + e^- \rightarrow O^{2-}(g)]$.

Quantity	Numerical Value (kJ/mol)
Enthalpy of atomization of Na	107.3
Ionization Energy of Na	495.9
Enthalpy of formation of solid Na₂0	−418.0
Enthalpy of formation of 0(g) from 0₂	249.1
First electron affinity of 0	−141.0

In the Laboratory

39. Lead sulfide, PbS (commonly called galena), has the same formula as ZnS.

Unit cell of PbS.

Sample of galena.

Does PbS have the same solid structure as ZnS? If different, how are they different? How is the unit cell of PbS related to its formula?

40. $CaTiO_3$, a perovskite, has the structure below.
   (a) If the density of the solid is 4.10 g/cm^3, what is the length of a side of the unit cell?
   (b) Calculate the radius of the Ti^{4+} ion in the center of the unit cell. How well does your calculation agree with a literature value of 75 pm?

Ca^{2+}
Ti^{4+}
O^{2-}

Unit cell of the perovskite CaTiO$_3$.

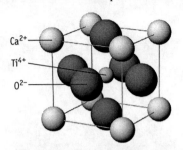

©DEA/C. Bevilacqua/Getty Images

A sample of perovskite CaTiO$_3$.

Summary and Conceptual Questions

The following questions may use concepts from this and previous chapters.

41.▲ Boron phosphide, BP, is a semiconductor and a hard, abrasion-resistant material. It is made by reacting boron tribromide and phosphorus tribromide in a hydrogen atmosphere at high temperature (> 750 °C).
   (a) Write a balanced chemical equation for the synthesis of BP. *(Hint: Hydrogen is a reducing agent.)*
   (b) Boron phosphide crystallizes in a zinc blende structure, formed from boron atoms in a face-centered cubic lattice and phosphorus atoms in tetrahedral holes. How many tetrahedral holes are filled with P atoms in each unit cell?
   (c) The length of a unit cell of BP is 478 pm. What is the density of the solid in g/cm^3.
   (d) Calculate the closest distance between a B and a P atom in the unit cell. (Assume the B atoms do not touch along the cell edge. The B atoms in the faces touch the B atoms at the corners of the unit cell. See page 594.)

42. ▲ Why is it not possible for a salt with the formula M_3X (Na_3PO_4, for example) to have a face-centered cubic lattice of X anions with M cations in octahedral holes?

43. ▲ ■ Two identical swimming pools are filled with uniform spheres of ice packed as closely as possible. The spheres in the first pool are the size of grains of sand; those in the second pool are the size of oranges. The ice in both pools melts. In which pool, if either, will the water level be higher? (Ignore any differences in filling space at the planes next to the walls and bottom.)

44. Spinels are described in Study Question 37. Consider two normal spinels, $CoAl_2O_4$ and $SnCo_2O_4$. What metal ions are involved in each? What are their electron configurations? Are the metal ions paramagnetic, and if so how many unpaired electrons are involved?

14 | Solutions and Their Behavior

© David Raboin, 2007

Safe Flying

You are sitting in an airport in the winter. Outside the weather is bad, with blowing snow and ice. You want to get on the plane home, but first the plane has to be de-iced. Ice and snow on the wings severely impairs the ability of wings to provide lift, so it is unsafe to try to take off unless the plane is de-iced. The fluid that is sprayed on the plane is a mixture of ethylene or propylene glycol and other substances. These are the same chemicals used in the antifreeze in your car's radiator.

Questions:
1. Why does ethylene glycol ($HOCH_2CH_2OH$) dissolve so well in water?
2. Why use a solution of ethylene glycol and water as an anti-freeze?
3. If you mix 100. g of ethylene glycol with 500. g of water, what is the freezing point of the mixture?

Answers to these questions are in Appendix Q.

Chapter Goals

OWL *See Chapter Goals Revisited (page 646) for Study Questions keyed to these goals and assignable in OWL.*

- Calculate and use the solution concentration units molality, mole fractions, and weight percent.
- Understand the solution process.
- Understand and use the colligative properties of solutions.

Chapter Outline

We come into contact with solutions every day: aqueous solutions of ionic salts, gasoline with additives to improve its properties, and household cleaners such as ammonia in water. We purposely make solutions. Adding sugar, flavoring, and sometimes CO_2 to water produces a palatable soft drink. Athletes drink commercial beverages with dissolved salts to match salt concentrations in body fluids precisely, thus allowing the fluid to be taken into the body more rapidly. In medicine, saline solutions (aqueous solutions containing NaCl and other soluble salts) are infused into the body to replace lost fluids.

A **solution** is a homogeneous mixture of two or more substances in a single phase. By convention, the component present in largest amount is identified as the solvent and the other component(s) as the solute(s) (Figure 14.1). Although other types of solutions exist (such as alloys, solid solution of metals), the objective in this chapter is to develop an understanding of gases, liquids, and solids dissolved in liquid solvents.

Experience tells you that adding a solute to a pure liquid will change the properties of the liquid. Indeed, that is the reason some solutions are made. For instance, adding antifreeze to the water in your car's radiator prevents the coolant from boiling in the summer and freezing in the winter. The changes that occur in the freezing and boiling points when a substance is dissolved in a pure liquid are two observations we shall examine in detail. These properties, as well as the osmotic pressure of a solution and changes in vapor pressure, are examples of colligative properties.

Chemistry ⚛ Now™

Throughout the text this icon introduces an opportunity for self-study or to explore interactive tutorials by signing in at **www.cengage.com/login**.

Photos: Charles D. Winters

(a) Copper(II) chloride, the solute, is added to water, the solvent.

(b) Interactions between water molecules and Cu^{2+} and Cl^- ions allow the solid to dissolve. The ions are now sheathed with water molecules.

FIGURE 14.1 Making a solution of copper(II) chloride (the solute) in water (the solvent). When ionic compounds dissolve in water, each ion is surrounded by water molecules. The number of water molecules is usually six, but fewer are possible.

Colligative properties are properties of solutions that depend only on the number of solute particles per solvent molecule and not on the identity of the solute.

14.1 Units of Concentration

To analyze the colligative properties of solutions, we need ways of measuring solute concentrations that reflect the number of molecules or ions of solute per molecule of solvent.

Molarity, a concentration unit useful in stoichiometry calculations, is not useful when dealing with most colligative properties. Recall that molarity (M) is defined as the number of moles of solute per liter of solution (◀ page 174), so using molarity does not allow us to identify the exact amount of solvent used to make the solution. This fact is illustrated in Figure 14.2. The flask on the right contains a 0.100 M aqueous solution of potassium chromate. It was made by adding enough water to 0.100 mol of K_2CrO_4 to make 1.000 L of solution. There is no way to identify the amount of solvent (water) that was actually added. If 1.000 L of water had been added to 0.100 mol of K_2CrO_4, as illustrated with the flask on the left in Figure 14.2, the volume of solution would be greater than 1.000 L.

Three concentration units are described here that reflect the number of molecules or ions of solute per solvent molecule: molality, mole fraction, and weight percent.

The **molality**, m, of a solution is defined as the amount of solute (mol) per kilogram of solvent.

$V_{soln} > 1.00$ L
V_{H_2O} added = 1.00 L
0.100 molal solution

$V_{soln} = 1.00$ L
V_{H_2O} added < 1.00 L
0.100 molar solution

FIGURE 14.2 Preparing 0.100 molal and 0.100 molar solutions. In the flask on the right, 0.100 mol (19.4 g) of K_2CrO_4 was mixed with enough water to make 1.000 L of solution. (The volumetric flask was filled to the mark on its neck, indicating that the volume is 1.000 L. Slightly less than 1.00 L of water was added.) If 1.00 kg of water was added to 0.100 mol of K_2CrO_4 in the flask on the left, the volume of solution is greater than 1.000 L. (The small pile of yellow solid in front of the flasks is 0.100 mol of K_2CrO_4.)

$$\text{Concentration } (c, \text{ mol/kg}) = \text{molality of solute} = \frac{\text{amount of solute (mol)}}{\text{mass of solvent (kg)}} \quad \textbf{(14.1)}$$

The molality of K_2CrO_4 in the flask on the left side of Figure 14.2 is 0.100 mol/kg. It was prepared from 0.100 mol (19.4 g) of K_2CrO_4 and 1.00 kg (1.000 L × 1.00 kg/L) of water.

Notice that different quantities of water were used to make the 0.100 M (0.100 molar) and 0.100 m (0.100 molal) solutions of K_2CrO_4. This means the *molarity and the molality of a given solution cannot be the same* (although the difference may be negligibly small when the solution is quite dilute).

The **mole fraction**, X, of a solution component is defined as the amount of that component (n_A) divided by the total amount of all of the components of the mixture ($n_A + n_B + n_C + ...$). Mathematically it is represented as

$$\text{Mole fraction of A } (X_A) = \frac{n_A}{n_A + n_B + n_C + ...} \quad \textbf{(14.2)}$$

Consider a solution that contains 1.00 mol (46.1 g) of ethanol, C_2H_5OH, in 9.00 mol (162 g) of water. The mole fraction of alcohol is 0.100, and that of water is 0.900.

■ **Molarity and Molality** The use of the terms "molar" (symbol M) and "molal" (symbol m) is common practice among chemists. Recently, however, NIST suggested that use of these terms and symbols to represent concentrations should be discontinued and replaced with the formal units of concentration (mol/L and mol/kg).

$$X_{ethanol} = \frac{1.00 \text{ mol ethanol}}{1.00 \text{ mol ethanol} + 9.00 \text{ mol water}} = 0.100$$

$$X_{water} = \frac{9.00 \text{ mol water}}{1.00 \text{ mol ethanol} + 9.00 \text{ mol water}} = 0.900$$

Notice that the sum of the mole fractions of the components in the solution equals 1.000, a relationship that is true for all solutions.

Weight percent is the mass of one component divided by the total mass of the mixture, multiplied by 100%:

$$\text{Weight \% A} = \frac{\text{mass of A}}{\text{mass of A} + \text{mass of B} + \text{mass of C} + \ldots} \times 100\% \qquad (14.3)$$

The alcohol–water mixture has 46.1 g of ethanol and 162 g of water, so the total mass of solution is 208 g, and the weight % of alcohol is

$$\text{Weight \% ethanol} = \frac{46.1 \text{ g ethanol}}{46.1 \text{ g ethanol} + 162 \text{ g water}} \times 100\% = 22.2\%$$

Weight percent is a common unit in consumer products (Figure 14.3). Vinegar, for example, is an aqueous solution containing approximately 5% acetic acid and 95% water. The label on a common household bleach lists its active ingredient as 6.00% sodium hypochlorite (NaOCl) and 94.00% inert ingredients.

Naturally occurring solutions are often very dilute. Environmental chemists, biologists, geologists, oceanographers, and others frequently use **parts per million (ppm)** to express their concentrations. The unit ppm refers to relative quantities by mass; 1.0 ppm represents 1.0 g of a substance in a sample with a total mass of 1.0 million g. Because water at 25 °C has a density of 1.0 g/mL, a concentration of 1.0 mg/L is equivalent to 1.0 mg of solute in 1000 g of water or to 1.0 g of solute in 1,000,000 g of water; that is, units of ppm and mg/L are approximately equivalent.

FIGURE 14.3 Weight percent. The composition of many common products is often given in terms of weight percent. Here, the label on the cat spray indicates it contains 1.15% active ingredients.

Chemistry⚛Now™

Sign in at **www.cengage.com/login** and go to Chapter 14 Contents to see Screen 14.2 for an exercise on **calculating solution concentrations in various units.**

■ **EXAMPLE 14.1 Calculating Mole Fractions, Molality, and Weight Percent**

Problem Assume you add 1.2 kg of ethylene glycol, $HOCH_2CH_2OH$, as an antifreeze to 4.0 kg of water in the radiator of your car. What are the mole fraction, molality, and weight percent of the ethylene glycol?

Strategy Calculate the amount of ethylene glycol and water, and then use Equations 14.1–14.3.

Solution The 1.2 kg of ethylene glycol (molar mass = 62.1 g/mol) is equivalent to 19 mol, and 4.0 kg of water represents 220 mol.

Mole fraction:

$$X_{\text{glycol}} = \frac{19 \text{ mol ethylene glycol}}{19 \text{ mol ethylene glycol} + 220 \text{ mol water}} = 0.080$$

Molality:

$$c_{\text{glycol}} = \frac{19 \text{ mol ethylene glycol}}{4.0 \text{ kg water}} = 4.8 \text{ mol/kg} = 4.8 \, m$$

Weight percent:

$$\text{Weight \%} = \frac{1.2 \times 10^3 \text{ g ethylene glycol}}{1.2 \times 10^3 \text{g ethylene glycol} + 4.0 \times 10^3 \text{ g water}} \times 100\% = 23\%$$

Commercial antifreeze. This solution contains ethylene glycol, $HOCH_2CH_2OH$, an organic alcohol that is readily soluble in water. Regulations specify that the weight percent of ethylene glycol in ethylene glycol–based antifreeze must be at least 75%. (The remainder of the solution can be other glycols and water.)

14.2 The Solution Process

■ **Unsaturated** The term unsaturated is used when referring to solutions with concentrations of solute that are less than that of a saturated solution.

If solid $CuCl_2$ is added to a beaker of water, the salt will begin to dissolve (see Figure 14.1). The amount of solid diminishes, and the concentrations of Cu^{2+}(aq) and Cl^-(aq) in the solution increase. If we continue to add $CuCl_2$, however, we will eventually reach a point when no additional $CuCl_2$ seems to dissolve. The concentrations of Cu^{2+}(aq) and Cl^-(aq) will not increase further, and any additional solid $CuCl_2$ added after this point will remain as a solid at the bottom of the beaker. We say that such a solution is **saturated**.

Although no change is observed on the macroscopic level, it is a different matter on the particulate level. The process of dissolving continues, with Cu^{2+} and Cl^- ions leaving the solid state and entering solution. Concurrently, a second process is occurring: the formation of solid $CuCl_2$(s) from Cu^{2+}(aq) and Cl^-(aq). The rates at which $CuCl_2$ is dissolving and reprecipitating are equal in a saturated solution, so that no net change is observed on the macroscopic level.

A Closer Look

Supersaturated Solutions

Although at first glance it may seem a contradiction, it is possible for a solution to hold more dissolved solute than the amount in a saturated solution. Such solutions are referred to as **supersaturated** solutions. Supersaturated solutions are unstable, and the excess solid eventually crystallizes from the solution until the equilibrium concentration of the solute is reached.

The solubility of substances often decreases if the temperature is lowered. Supersaturated solutions are usually made by preparing a saturated solution at a given temperature and then carefully cooling it. If the rate of crystallization is slow, the solid may not precipitate when the solubility is exceeded. Going to still lower temperatures results in a solution that has more solute than the amount defined by equilibrium conditions; it is supersaturated.

When disturbed in some manner, a supersaturated solution moves toward equilibrium by precipitating solute. This change can occur rapidly, often with the evolution of thermal energy. In fact, supersaturated solutions are used in "heat packs" to apply heat to injured

Charles D. Winters

Supersaturated solutions. When a supersaturated solution is disturbed, the dissolved salt (here sodium acetate, $NaCH_3CO_2$) rapidly crystallizes. (See ChemistryNow Screen 14.2 to watch a video of this process.)

Charles D. Winters

Heat of crystallization. A heat pack relies on the heat evolved by the crystallization of sodium acetate. (See ChemistryNow Screen 14.6 to watch a video of a heat pack.)

muscles. When crystallization of sodium acetate ($NaCH_3CO_2$) from a supersaturated solution in a heat pack is initiated, the tempera-

ture of the heat pack rises to about 50 °C, and crystals of solid sodium acetate are detectable inside the bag.

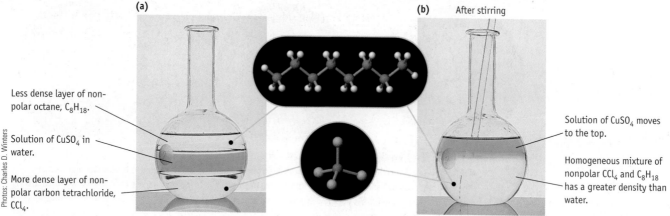

(a)

(b) After stirring

Less dense layer of non-polar octane, C_8H_{18}.

Solution of $CuSO_4$ in water.

More dense layer of non-polar carbon tetrachloride, CCl_4.

Photos: Charles D. Winters

Solution of $CuSO_4$ moves to the top.

Homogeneous mixture of nonpolar CCl_4 and C_8H_{18} has a greater density than water.

FIGURE 14.4 Miscibility. (a) The colorless, denser bottom layer is nonpolar carbon tetrachloride, CCl_4. The blue middle layer is a solution of $CuSO_4$ in water, and the colorless, less dense top layer is nonpolar octane, C_8H_{18}. This mixture was prepared by carefully layering one liquid on top of another, without mixing. (b) After stirring the mixture, the two nonpolar liquids form a homogeneous mixture. This layer of mixed liquids is under the water layer because the mixture of CCl_4 and C_8H_{18} has a greater density than water.

This process is another example of a dynamic equilibrium (◄ page 119), and we can describe the situation in terms of an equation with substances linked by a set of double arrows ($\rightleftharpoons$):

$$CuCl_2(s) \rightleftharpoons Cu^{2+}(aq) + 2\,Cl^-(aq)$$

A saturated solution gives us a way to define precisely the solubility of a solid in a liquid. **Solubility** is the concentration of solute in equilibrium with undissolved solute in a saturated solution. The solubility of $CuCl_2$, for example, is 70.6 g in 100 mL of water at 0 °C. If we add 100.0 g of $CuCl_2$ to 100 mL of water at 0 °C, we can expect 70.6 g to dissolve, and 29.4 g of solid to remain.

Liquids Dissolving in Liquids

If two liquids mix to an appreciable extent to form a solution, they are said to be **miscible**. In contrast, **immiscible** liquids do not mix to form a solution; they exist in contact with each other as separate layers (see Figures 12.5 and 14.4).

The polar compounds ethanol (C_2H_5OH) and water are miscible in all proportions as are the nonpolar liquids octane (C_8H_{18}) and carbon tetrachloride (CCl_4). On the other hand, neither C_8H_{18} nor CCl_4 is miscible with water. Observations like these have led to a familiar rule of thumb: *Like dissolves like.* That is, two or more nonpolar liquids frequently are miscible, just as are two or more polar liquids.

What is the molecular basis for the "like dissolves like" guideline? In pure water and pure ethanol, the major force between molecules is hydrogen bonding involving O—H groups. When the two liquids are mixed, hydrogen bonding between ethanol and water molecules also occurs and assists in the solution process. In contrast, molecules of pure octane or pure CCl_4, both of which are nonpolar, are held together in the liquid phase by dispersion forces (◄ Section 12.3). The energy associated with these forces of attraction is similar in value to the energy due to the forces of attraction between octane and CCl_4 molecules when these nonpolar liquids are mixed. Thus, little or no energy change occurs when octane–octane and CCl_4–CCl_4 attractive forces are replaced with octane–CCl_4 forces. The solution

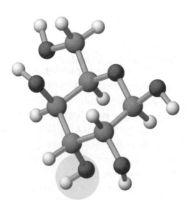

OH group

Like dissolves like. Glucose has five —OH groups on each molecule, groups that allow it to form hydrogen bonds with water molecules. As a result, glucose dissolves readily in water.

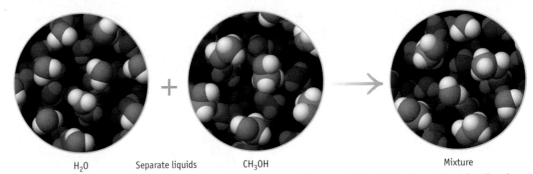

H₂O   Separate liquids   CH₃OH   Mixture

FIGURE 14.5 Driving the solution process—entropy. When two similar liquids—here water and methanol—are mixed, the molecules intermingle, and the energy of the system is more dispersed than in the two, separate pure liquids. A measure of this energy dispersal is entropy, a thermodynamic function described in more detail in Chapter 19.

process is expected to be nearly energy neutral. So, why do the liquids mix? The answer lies deeper in thermodynamics. As you shall see in Chapter 19, spontaneous changes, such as the mixing of liquids, are accompanied by an increase in entropy, a thermodynamic function that is a measure of the dispersal of the energy of the particles in the mixture relative to the pure liquids (Figure 14.5).

In contrast, polar and nonpolar liquids usually do not mix to an appreciable degree; when placed together in a container, they separate into two distinct layers (Figure 14.4). The explanation is complex and involves the interplay of the enthalpy of mixing and entropy. The enthalpy of mixing is zero or nearly so, but mixing dissimilar liquids leads to a decrease in entropy. As explained in Chapter 19, this means that mixing dissimilar liquids is not thermodynamically favorable.

Solids Dissolving in Water

The "like dissolves like" guideline also holds for molecular solids dissolving in liquids. Nonpolar solids such as naphthalene, $C_{10}H_8$, dissolve readily in nonpolar solvents such as benzene, C_6H_6, and hexane, C_6H_{14}. Iodine, I_2, a nonpolar inorganic solid, dissolves in water to some extent, but, given a choice, it dissolves to a larger extent in a nonpolar liquid such as CCl_4 (Figure 14.6). Sucrose (sugar), a polar molecular solid, is not very soluble in nonpolar solvents but is readily soluble in water, a fact that we know well because of its use to sweeten beverages. The presence of O—H groups in the structure of sugar and other substances such as glucose allows these molecules to interact with polar water molecules through hydrogen bonding.

"Like dissolves like" is a somewhat less effective but still useful guideline when considering the solubility of ionic solids. Thus, we can reasonably predict that ionic compounds, which can be considered extreme examples of polar compounds, will

■ **Entropy and the Solution Process** Although the energetics of solution formation are important, it is generally accepted that entropy is a more important contributor to the solution process. See Chapter 19 and T. P. Silverstein: "The real reason why oil and water don't mix." *Journal of Chemical Education*, Vol. 75, pp. 116–118, 1998.

Active Figure 14.6 **Solubility of nonpolar iodine in polar water and nonpolar carbon tetrachloride.** When a solution of nonpolar I_2 in water (the brown layer on top in the left test tube) is shaken with nonpolar CCl_4 (the color-less bottom layer in the left test tube), the I_2 transfers preferentially to the nonpolar solvent. Evidence for this is the purple color of the bottom CCl_4 layer in the test tube on the right.

Chemistry.Now™ Sign in at www. cengage.com/login and go to the Chapter Contents menu to explore an interactive version of this figure accompanied by an exercise.

Nonpolar I_2
Polar H_2O

Polar H_2O

Shake the test tube

Nonpolar CCl_4

Nonpolar CCl_4 and I_2

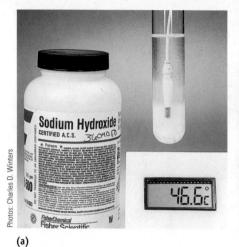

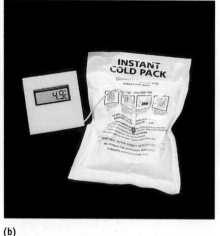

(a)　　　　　　　　　　　　　　　　　(b)

FIGURE 14.7 Dissolving ionic solids and enthalpy of solution.
(a) Dissolving NaOH in water is a strongly exothermic process. (b) A "cold pack" contains solid ammonium nitrate, NH_4NO_3, and a package of water. When the water and NH_4NO_3 are mixed and the salt dissolves, the temperature of the system drops, owing to the endothermic enthalpy of solution of ammonium nitrate ($\Delta_{soln}H° = +25.7$ kJ/mol).

not dissolve in nonpolar solvents. This fact is amply borne out by observation. Sodium chloride, for example, will not dissolve in liquids such as hexane or CCl_4, but the salt does have a significant solubility in water. Many ionic compounds are soluble in water, but, according to the solubility guidelines on page 126, there are many other ionic solids that are not.

Predicting the solubility of ionic compounds in water is complicated. As mentioned earlier, two factors—enthalpy and entropy—together determine the extent to which one substance dissolves in another. For ionic compounds dissolving in water, entropy usually (but not always) favors solution. A favorable enthalpy factor (negative ΔH) generally leads to a compound being soluble. For example, when sodium hydroxide dissolves in water, the solution warms up (Figure 14.7a), and sodium hydroxide dissolves readily in water. An unfavorable enthalpy factor, however, does not guarantee that an ionic compound will not be soluble. When ammonium nitrate dissolves in water, the solution becomes colder (Figure 14.7b), but ammonium nitrate is still very soluble in water.

Network solids, including graphite, diamond, and quartz sand (SiO_2), do not dissolve in water. Indeed, where would all the beaches be if sand dissolved in water? The covalent chemical bonding in network solids is simply too strong to be broken; the lattice remains intact when in contact with water.

Enthalpy of Solution

To understand the energetics of the solution process, let us view this process at the molecular level. We will use the process of dissolving potassium fluoride, KF, in water to illustrate what occurs, and the energy-level diagram in Figure 14.8 will assist us in following the changes.

Solid potassium fluoride has an ionic crystal lattice with alternating K^+ and F^- ions held in place by attractive forces due to their opposite charges. In water, these ions are separated from each other and *hydrated*; that is, they are surrounded by water molecules (Figure 14.1). Ion–dipole forces of attraction bind water molecules strongly to each ion. The energy change to go from the reactant, KF(s), to the products, K^+(aq) and F^-(aq), can be considered to take place in two stages:

1. Energy must be supplied to separate the ions in the lattice against their attractive forces. This is the reverse of the process defining the lattice enthalpy of an ionic compound with an enthalpy equal to $-\Delta_{lattice}H$ (◄ page 600).

FIGURE 14.8 Model for energy changes on dissolving KF. An estimate of the magnitude of the energy change on dissolving an ionic compound in water is achieved by imagining it as occurring in two steps at the particulate level. Here, KF is first separated into cations and anions in the gas phase with an expenditure of 821 kJ per mol of KF. These ions are then hydrated, with $\Delta_{hydration}H$ estimated to be −837 kJ. Thus, the net energy change is −16 kJ, a slightly exothermic enthalpy of solution.

(See ChemistryNow Screen 14.4 for exercises on the energetics of solution formation.)

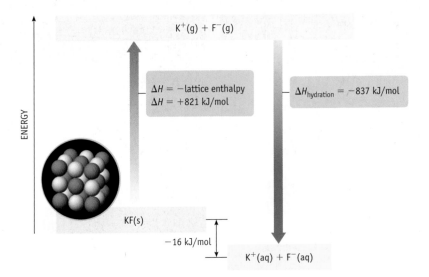

Separating the ions from one another is highly endothermic because the attractive forces between ions are strong.

2. Energy is evolved when the individual ions are transferred into water, where each ion becomes surrounded by water molecules. Again, strong forces of attraction (ion–dipole forces) are involved. This process, referred to as **hydration** when water is the solvent, is strongly exothermic.

We can therefore represent the process of dissolving KF in terms of these chemical equations:

Step 1 $KF(s) \longrightarrow K^+(g) + F^-(g)$ $\qquad\qquad -\Delta_{lattice}H$

Step 2 $K^+(g) + F^-(g) \longrightarrow K^+(aq) + F^-(aq)$ $\qquad \Delta_{hydration}H$

The overall reaction is the sum of these two steps. The enthalpy of the overall reaction, called the **enthalpy of solution** ($\Delta_{soln}H$), is the sum of the two enthalpies.

Overall $KF(s) \longrightarrow K^+(aq) + F^-(aq)$ $\qquad \Delta_{soln}H = -\Delta_{lattice}H + \Delta_{hydration}H$

We can use this to estimate the value of $\Delta_{hydration}H$. For example, we estimate the lattice energy for KF to be −821 kJ/mol using a Born-Haber cycle calculation (◀ page 600), and we measure the value of $\Delta_{soln}H$ in a calorimetry experiment to be −16.4 kJ/mol. From these two values, we can determine $\Delta_{hydration}H$ to be −837 kJ/mol.

As a general rule, to be soluble, a salt will have an enthalpy of solution that is exothermic or only slightly endothermic (Figure 14.9). In the latter instance, it is assumed that the enthalpy-disfavored solution process will be balanced by a favorable entropy of solution. If the enthalpy of solution is very endothermic—because of a low hydration energy, for example—then the compound is unlikely to be soluble. We can reasonably speculate that nonpolar solvents would not solvate ions strongly, and that solution formation would thus be energetically unfavorable. We therefore predict that an ionic compound, such as copper(II) sulfate, is not very soluble in nonpolar solvents such as carbon tetrachloride and octane (Figure 14.4).

It is also useful to recognize that the enthalpy of solution is the difference between two very large numbers. Small variations in either lattice energy or hydration enthalpies can determine whether a salt dissolves endothermically or exothermically.

Finally, notice that the two energy quantities, $\Delta_{lattice}H$ and $\Delta_{hydration}H$, are both affected by ion sizes and ion charges (◀ pages 557 and 600). A salt composed of smaller ions is expected to have a greater (more negative) lattice enthalpy because the ions can be closer together and experience higher attractive forces. However, the small

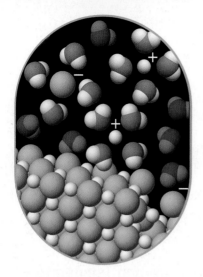

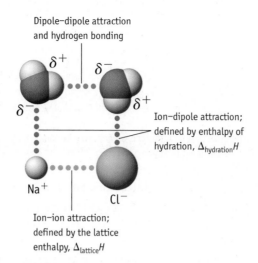

Dipole–dipole attraction and hydrogen bonding

δ^+ δ^-

δ^- δ^+

Ion–dipole attraction; defined by enthalpy of hydration, $\Delta_{hydration}H$

Na^+

Cl^-

Ion–ion attraction; defined by the lattice enthalpy, $\Delta_{lattice}H$

size will also allow a closer approach of solvent molecules and a greater solvation enthalpy. The net result is that simple correlations of solubility with structure (ionic radii) or thermodynamic parameters ($\Delta_{lattice}H$) are generally not successful.

Enthalpy of Solution: Thermodynamic Data

As mentioned earlier, the enthalpy of solution for a salt can be measured using a calorimeter. This is usually done in an open system such as the coffee-cup calorimeter described in Section 5.6. For an experiment run under standard conditions, the resulting measurement produces a value for the standard enthalpy of solution, $\Delta_{soln}H°$, where standard conditions refer to a concentration of 1 molal.

Tables of thermodynamic values often include values for the enthalpies of formation of aqueous solutions of salts. For example, a value of $\Delta_f H°$ for NaCl(aq) of −407.3 kJ/mol is listed in Table 14.1 and Appendix L. This value refers to the formation of a 1 m solution of NaCl from the elements. It may be considered to involve the enthalpies of two steps: (1) the formation of NaCl(s) from the elements Na(s) and Cl_2(g) in their standard states, and (2) the formation of a 1 m solution by dissolving solid NaCl in water:

Formation of NaCl(s):	$Na(s) + \frac{1}{2} Cl_2(g) \longrightarrow NaCl(s)$	$\Delta_f H° = -411.1$ kJ/mol
Dissolving NaCl:	$NaCl(s) \longrightarrow NaCl(aq, 1\ m)$	$\Delta_{soln}H° = +3.9$ kJ/mol
Net process:	$Na(s) + \frac{1}{2} Cl_2(g) \longrightarrow NaCl(aq, 1\ m)$	$\Delta_f H° = -407.3$ kJ/mol

TABLE 14.1   Data for Calculating Enthalpy of Solution

Compound	$\Delta_f H°$ (s) (kJ/mol)	$\Delta_f H°$ (aq, 1 m) (kJ/mol)
LiF	−616.9	−611.1
NaF	−573.6	−572.8
KF	−568.6	−585.0
RbF	−557.7	−583.8
LiCl	−408.7	−445.6
NaCl	−411.1	−407.3
KCl	−436.7	−419.5
RbCl	−435.4	−418.3
NaOH	−425.9	−469.2
NH_4NO_3	−365.6	−339.9

Chemistry‚Ọ‚Now™

Sign in at **www.cengage.com/login** and go to Chapter 14 Contents to see
• Screen 14.3 for a visualization of the process and for a problem on **the solution process**
• Screen 14.4 for an analysis of the dissolution of KF and an exercise on **solution energetics**

■ **EXAMPLE 14.2 Calculating an Enthalpy of Solution**

Problem Use the data given in Table 14.1 to determine the enthalpy of solution for NH_4NO_3, the compound used in cold packs.

Strategy Use Equation 5.6 and data from Table 14.1 for reactants and products.

TABLE 14.2 Henry's Law Constants (25 °C)*

Gas	k_H (mol/kg · bar)
N_2	6.0×10^{-4}
O_2	1.3×10^{-3}
CO_2	0.034

*From http://webbook.nist.gov/ chemistry/. Note: 1 bar = 0.9869 atm.

Solution The solution process for NH_4NO_3 is represented by the equation

$$NH_4NO_3(s) \longrightarrow NH_4NO_3(aq)$$

The enthalpy change for this process is calculated using enthalpies of formation given in Table 14.1:

$$\Delta_{soln}H° = \Sigma[\Delta_fH°(product)] - \Sigma[\Delta_fH°(reactant)]$$
$$= \Delta_fH°\left[NH_4NO_3(aq)\right] - \Delta_fH°\left[NH_4NO_3(s)\right]$$
$$= -339.9 \text{ kJ/mol} - (-365.6 \text{ kJ/mol}) = +25.7 \text{ kJ/mol}$$

The process is endothermic, as indicated by the fact that $\Delta_{soln}H°$ has a positive value and as verified by the experiment in Figure 14.7b.

EXERCISE 14.2 Calculating an Enthalpy of Solution

Use the data in Table 14.1 to calculate the enthalpy of solution for NaOH.

14.3 Factors Affecting Solubility: Pressure and Temperature

Pressure and temperature are two external factors that influence solubility. Both affect the solubility of gases in liquids, whereas only temperature is an important factor in the solubility of solids in liquids.

Dissolving Gases in Liquids: Henry's Law

The solubility of a gas in a liquid is directly proportional to the gas pressure. This is a statement of **Henry's law,**

$$S_g = k_H P_g \qquad\qquad (14.4)$$

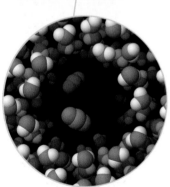

FIGURE 14.10 Gas solubility and pressure. Carbonated beverages are bottled under CO_2 pressure. When the bottle is opened, the pressure is released, and bubbles of CO_2 form within the liquid and rise to the surface. After some time, an equilibrium between dissolved CO_2 and atmospheric CO_2 is reached. Because CO_2 provides some of the taste in the beverage, the beverage tastes flat when most of its dissolved CO_2 is lost.

Photo: Charles D. Winters

where S_g is the gas solubility, P_g is the partial pressure of the gaseous solute, and k_H is Henry's law constant (Table 14.2), a constant characteristic of the solute and solvent.

Carbonated soft drinks illustrate how Henry's law works. These beverages are packed under pressure in a chamber filled with carbon dioxide gas, some of which dissolves in the beverage. When the can or bottle is opened, the partial pressure of CO_2 above the solution drops, which causes the solubility of CO_2 to drop. Gas bubbles out of the solution (Figure 14.10).

Henry's law has important consequences in SCUBA diving. When you dive, the pressure of the air you breathe must be balanced against the external pressure of the water. In deeper dives, the pressure of the gases in the SCUBA gear must be several atmospheres and, as a result, more gas dissolves in the blood. This can lead to a problem. If you ascend too rapidly, you can experience a painful and potentially lethal condition referred to as "the bends," in which nitrogen gas bubbles form in the blood as the solubility of nitrogen decreases with decreasing pressure. In an effort to prevent the bends, divers may use a helium–oxygen mixture (rather than nitrogen–oxygen) because helium is not as soluble in blood as nitrogen.

We can better understand the effect of pressure on solubility by examining the system at the particulate level. The solubility of a gas is defined as the concentration of the dissolved gas in equilibrium with the substance in the gaseous state. At equilibrium, the rate at which solute gas molecules escape the solution and enter the gaseous state equals the rate at which gas molecules reenter the solution. An increase in pressure results in more molecules of gas striking the surface of the liquid and entering solution in a given time. The solution eventually reaches a new equilibrium when the concentration of gas dissolved in the solvent is high enough that the rate of gas molecules escaping the solution again equals the rate of gas molecules entering the solution.

©Chris McGrath/ALLSPORT/Getty Images

Chemistry.⚛.Now™

Sign in at **www.cengage.com/login** and go to Chapter 14 Contents to see Screen 14.5 for an exercise and tutorial on **Henry's law.**

■ EXAMPLE 14.3 Using Henry's Law

Problem What is the concentration of O_2 in a fresh water stream in equilibrium with air at 25 °C and 1.0 bar? Express the answer in grams of O_2 per kg of solvent.

Strategy To use Henry's law to calculate the molar solubility of oxygen, the partial pressure of O_2 in air must first be calculated.

Solution The mole fraction of O_2 in air is 0.21, and, assuming the total pressure is 1.0 bar, the partial pressure of O_2 is 0.21 bar. Using this pressure for P_g in Henry's law, we have:

$$\text{Solubility of } O_2 = k_H P_g = \left(\frac{1.3 \times 10^{-3} \text{ mol}}{\text{kg} \cdot \text{bar}} \right)(0.21 \text{ bar}) = 2.7 \times 10^{-4} \text{ mol/l}$$

This concentration, in grams per liter, can then be calculated using the molar mass of O_2:

$$\text{Solubility of } O_2 = \left(\frac{2.7 \times 10^{-4} \text{ mol}}{\text{kg}} \right)\left(\frac{32.0 \text{ g}}{\text{mol}} \right) = \boxed{0.0087 \text{ g/kg}}$$

This concentration of O_2 (8.7 mg/kg) is quite low, but it is sufficient to provide the oxygen required by aquatic life.

EXERCISE 14.3 Using Henry's Law

What is the concentration of CO_2 in water at 25 °C when the partial pressure is 0.33 bar? (Although CO_2 reacts with water to give traces of H^+ and HCO_3^-, the reaction occurs to such a small extent that Henry's law is obeyed at low CO_2 partial pressures.)

Hyperbaric chamber, an illustration of Henry's law. A person is placed inside the chamber, and the partial pressure of oxygen is raised to several times the normal, atmospheric level. This raises the amount of oxygen dissolved in blood and tissues. This technique is used to treat, among other things, decompression sickness, carbon monoxide poisoning, severe anemia, and certain nonhealing wounds.

■ **Limitations of Henry's Law** Henry's law holds quantitatively only for gases that do not interact chemically with the solvent. It does not accurately predict the solubility of NH_3 in water, for example, because this compound gives small concentrations of NH_4^+ and OH^- in water.

Temperature Effects on Solubility: Le Chatelier's Principle

The solubility of all gases in water decreases with increasing temperature. You may realize this from everyday observations such as the appearance of bubbles of air as water is heated below the boiling point.

To understand the effect of temperature on the solubility of gases, let us reexamine the enthalpy of solution. Gases that dissolve to an appreciable extent in water usually do so in an exothermic process

$$\text{Gas + liquid solvent} \xrightleftharpoons{\Delta_{soln}H < 0} \text{saturated solution + energy}$$

The reverse process, loss of dissolved gas molecules from a solution, requires energy as heat. These two processes can reach equilibrium eventually.

To understand how temperature affects solubility, we turn to **Le Chatelier's principle**, which states that a change in any of the factors determining an equilibrium causes the system to adjust by shifting in the direction that reduces or counteracts the effect of the change. If a solution of a gas in a liquid is heated, for example, the equilibrium will shift to absorb some of the added energy. That is, the reaction

$$\underset{\xleftarrow{\hspace{2cm}}}{\text{Gas + liquid solvent} \xrightleftharpoons[\Delta_{soln}H \text{ is negative.}]{\text{Exothermic process}} \text{saturated solution + energy}}$$

Add energy. Equilibrium shifts left.

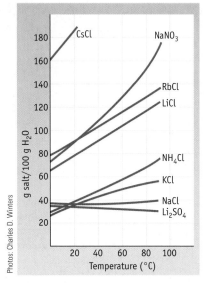

(a) Temperature dependence of the solubility of some ionic compounds.

(b) NH$_4$Cl dissolved in water.

(c) NH$_4$Cl precipitates when the solution is cooled in ice.

FIGURE 14.11 The temperature dependence of the solubility of some ionic compounds in water. Most compounds, such as NH$_4$Cl, increase in solubility with increasing temperature.

FIGURE 14.12 Giant crystals of potassium dihydrogen phosphate. The crystal being measured by this researcher at Lawrence Livermore Laboratory in California weighs 318 kg and measures 66 × 53 × 58 cm. The crystals were grown by suspending a thumbnail-sized seed crystal in a 6-foot tank of saturated KH$_2$PO$_4$. The temperature of the solution was gradually reduced from 65 °C over a period of about 50 days. The crystals are sliced into thin plates, which are used to convert light from a giant laser from infrared to ultraviolet.

shifts to the left if the temperature is raised because energy is absorbed in the process that produces free gas molecules and pure solvent. This shift corresponds to less gas dissolved and a lower solubility at higher temperature—the observed result.

The solubility of solids in water is also affected by temperature, but, unlike the situation involving solutions of gases, no general pattern of behavior is observed. In Figure 14.11, the solubilities of several salts are plotted versus temperature. The solubility of many salts increases with increasing temperature, but there are notable exceptions. Predictions based on whether the enthalpy of solution is positive or negative work most of the time, but exceptions do occur.

Chemists take advantage of the variation of solubility with temperature to purify compounds. If a compound is more soluble in a given solvent at higher temperatures, an impure sample of the compound is dissolved in the solvent at a high temperature. The solution is cooled to decrease the solubility (Figure 14.11c). When the limit of solubility is reached at the lower temperature, crystals of the pure compound form. If the process is done slowly and carefully, it is sometimes possible to obtain very large crystals (Figure 14.12).

Chemistry ⚛ Now™

Sign in at **www.cengage.com/login** and go to Chapter 14 Contents to see Screen 14.6 for a tutorial on **temperature and Le Chatelier's principle.**

 Module 19

14.4 Colligative Properties

If you dissolve some salt in water, the vapor pressure of the water over the solution will decrease, and the water will evaporate less rapidly under the same conditions. In addition, the solution will freeze below 0 °C and boil above 100 °C. These observations refer to the colligative properties of the solution, properties that depend

Sign in at **www.cengage.com/login** to download the Go Chemistry module for this section or go to **www.ichapters.com** to purchase modules.

on the relative numbers of solute and solvent particles in a solution and not on their identity.

Changes in Vapor Pressure: Raoult's Law

The equilibrium vapor pressure at a particular temperature is the pressure of the vapor when the liquid and the vapor are in equilibrium (◀ page 573). When the vapor pressure of the solvent over a solution is measured at a given temperature, it is experimentally observed that

- The vapor pressure of the solvent over the solution is lower than the vapor pressure of the pure solvent.
- The vapor pressure of the solvent, $P_{solvent}$, is proportional to the relative number of solvent molecules in the solution; that is, the solvent vapor pressure is proportional to the solvent mole fraction, $P_{solvent} \propto X_{solvent}$.

Because solvent vapor pressure is proportional to the relative number of solvent molecules, we can write the following equation for the equilibrium vapor pressure of the solvent over a solution:

$$P_{solvent} = X_{solvent}\, P^{\circ}_{solvent} \qquad\qquad (14.5)$$

This equation, called **Raoult's law**, tells us that the vapor pressure of solvent over a solution ($P_{solvent}$) is some fraction of the pure solvent equilibrium vapor pressure ($P^{\circ}_{solvent}$). For example, if 95% of the molecules in a solution are solvent molecules ($X_{solvent} = 0.95$), then the vapor pressure of the solvent ($P_{solvent}$) is 95% of $P^{\circ}_{solvent}$.

Like the ideal gas law, Raoult's law describes a simplified model of a solution. We say that *an ideal solution is one that obeys Raoult's law*. No solution is ideal, however, just as no gas is truly ideal. Nevertheless, Raoult's law is a good approximation of solution behavior in many instances, especially at low solute concentration.

For Raoult's law to hold, the forces of attraction between solute and solvent molecules must be the same as those between solvent molecules in the pure solvent. This is frequently the case when molecules with similar structures are involved. Solutions of one hydrocarbon in another (hexane, C_6H_{14}, dissolved in octane, C_8H_{18}, for example) follow Raoult's law quite closely. If solvent–solute interactions are stronger than solvent–solvent interactions, the actual vapor pressure will be lower than calculated by Raoult's law. If the solvent–solute interactions are weaker than solvent–solvent interactions, the vapor pressure will be higher.

■ **Raoult's Law** Raoult's law is named for Francois M. Raoult (1830–1901), a professor of chemistry at the University of Grenoble in France, who did the pioneering studies in this area.

Chemistry ⚛ Now™

Sign in at **www.cengage.com/login** and go to Chapter 14 Contents to see Screen 14.7 for an exercise and a tutorial on **Raoult's law**.

■ **EXAMPLE 14.4 Using Raoult's Law**

Problem Suppose 651 g of ethylene glycol, $HOCH_2CH_2OH$, is dissolved in 1.50 kg of water. What is the vapor pressure of the water over the solution at 90 °C? Assume ideal behavior for the solution.

Strategy To use Raoult's law (Equation 14.5), we first must calculate the mole fraction of the solvent (water). We also need the vapor pressure of pure water at 90 °C (= 525.8 mm Hg, Appendix G).

It was evening on Thursday, August 21, 1986. Suddenly, people and animals around Lake Nyos in Cameroon, a small nation on the west coast of Africa, collapsed and died. By the next morning, 1700 people and hundreds of animals were dead. The calamity had no apparent cause—no fire, no earthquake, no storm. What had brought on this disaster?

Some weeks later, the mystery was solved. Lake Nyos and nearby Lake Monoun are crater lakes, which formed when cooled volcanic craters filled with water. Lake Nyos is lethal because it contains an enormous amount of dissolved carbon dioxide. The CO_2 in the lake was generated as a result of volcanic activity deep in the earth. Under the high pressures found at the bottom of the lake, a very large amount of CO_2 dissolved in the water.

On that fateful evening in 1986, something happened to disturb the lake. The CO_2-saturated water at the bottom of the lake was carried to the surface, where, under lower pressure, the gas was much less soluble. Approximately one cubic kilometer of carbon dioxide was released into the atmosphere, much like the explosive release of CO_2 from a can of carbonated beverage that has been shaken. The CO_2 shot up about 260 feet; then, because this gas is more dense than air, it hugged the ground and began to move with the prevailing breeze at about 45 miles per hour. When it reached the villages 12 miles away, vital oxygen was displaced. The result was that both people and animals were asphyxiated.

In most lakes, this situation would not occur because lake water "turns over" as the seasons change. In the autumn, the top layer of water in a lake cools; its density increases; and the water sinks. This process continues, with warmer water coming to the surface and cooler water sinking. Dissolved CO_2 at the bottom of a lake would normally be expelled in this turnover process, but geologists found that the lakes in Cameroon are different. The chemocline, the boundary between deep water, rich in gas and minerals, and the upper

Thierry Orban/Corbis, Sygma

Lake Nyos in Cameroon (western Africa), the site of a natural disaster. In 1986, a huge bubble of CO_2 escaped from the lake and asphyxiated more than 1700 people.

layer, full of fresh water, stays intact. As carbon dioxide continues to enter the lake through vents in the bottom of the lake, the water becomes saturated with this gas. It is presumed that a minor disturbance—perhaps a small earthquake, a strong wind, or an underwater landslide—caused the lake water to turn over and led to the explosive and deadly release of CO_2.

Lake Nyos remains potentially deadly. Geologists estimate that the lake contains 10.6 to 14.1 billion cubic feet (300–400 million cubic meters) of carbon dioxide. This is

about 16,000 times the amount found in an average lake that size.

A team of geologists from France and the United States has been working to resolve this potential threat. In early 2001, scientists lowered a pipe, about 200 meters long, into the lake. Now the pressure of escaping carbon dioxide causes a jet of water to rise as high as 165 feet in the air. Over the course of a year, about 20 million cubic meters of gas will be released. While this has been a successful first step, more gas must be removed to make the lake entirely safe, so additional vents are planned.

Solution We first calculate the amounts of water and ethylene glycol and, from these, the mole fraction of water.

$$\text{Amount of water} = 1.50 \times 10^3 \text{ g} \left(\frac{1 \text{ mol}}{18.02 \text{ g}} \right) = 83.2 \text{ mol water}$$

$$\text{Amount of ethylene glycol} = 651 \text{ g} \left(\frac{1 \text{ mol}}{62.07 \text{ g}} \right) = 10.5 \text{ mol glycol}$$

$$X_{water} = \frac{83.2 \text{ mol water}}{83.2 \text{ mol water} + 10.5 \text{ mol glycol}} = 0.888$$

Next, we apply Raoult's law, calculating the vapor pressure from the mole fraction of water and the vapor pressure of pure water:

$$P_{water} = X_{water}P^\circ_{water} = (0.888)(525.8 \text{ mm Hg}) = \boxed{467 \text{ mm Hg}}$$

The dissolved solute decreases the vapor pressure by 59 mm Hg, or about 11%:

$$\Delta P_{water} = P_{water} - P^\circ_{water} = 467 \text{ mm Hg} - 525.8 \text{ mm Hg} = -59 \text{ mm Hg}$$

Comment Ethylene glycol dissolves easily in water, is noncorrosive, and is relatively inexpensive. Because of its high boiling point, it will not evaporate readily. These features make it ideal for use as antifreeze. It is, however, toxic to animals, so it is being replaced by less toxic propylene glycol for this application.

EXERCISE 14.4 Using Raoult's Law

Assume you dissolve 10.0 g of sucrose ($C_{12}H_{22}O_{11}$) in 225 mL (225 g) of water and warm the water to 60 °C. What is the vapor pressure of the water over this solution? (Appendix G lists P°(H_2O) at various temperatures.)

Adding a nonvolatile solute to a solvent lowers the vapor pressure of the solvent (Example 14.4). Raoult's law can be modified to calculate directly the lowering of the vapor pressure, $\Delta P_{solvent}$, as a function of the mole fraction of the solute.

$$\Delta P_{solvent} = P_{solvent} - P^\circ_{solvent}$$

Substituting Raoult's law for $P_{solvent}$, we have

$$\Delta P_{solvent} = (X_{solvent} P^\circ_{solvent}) - P^\circ_{solvent} = -(1 - X_{solvent})P^\circ_{solvent}$$

In a solution that has only the volatile solvent and one nonvolatile solute, the sum of the mole fraction of solvent and solute must be 1:

$$X_{solvent} + X_{solute} = 1$$

Therefore, $1 - X_{solvent} = X_{solute}$, and the equation for $\Delta P_{solvent}$ can be rewritten as

$$\Delta P_{solvent} = -X_{solute} P^\circ_{solvent} \qquad \text{(14.6)}$$

Thus, the change in the vapor pressure of the solvent is proportional to the mole fraction (the relative number of particles) of solute.

Boiling Point Elevation

Suppose you have a solution of a nonvolatile solute in the volatile solvent benzene. If the solute concentration is 0.200 mol in 100. g of benzene (C_6H_6) (= 2.00 mol/kg), this means that $X_{benzene}$ = 0.865. Using $X_{benzene}$ and applying Raoult's law, we can calculate that the vapor pressure of the solvent at 60 °C will drop from 400. mm Hg for the pure solvent to 346 mm Hg for the solution:

$$P_{benzene} = X_{benzene} \, P°_{benzene} = (0.865)(400. \text{ mm Hg}) = 346 \text{ mm Hg}$$

This point is marked on the vapor pressure graph in Figure 14.13. Now, what is the vapor pressure when the temperature of the solution is raised another 10 °C? The vapor pressure of pure benzene, $P°_{benzene}$, becomes larger with increasing temperature, so $P_{benzene}$ for the solution must also become larger. This new point, and additional ones calculated in the same way for other temperatures, define the vapor pressure curve for the solution (the lower curve in Figure 14.13).

An important observation we can make in Figure 14.13 is that the vapor pressure lowering caused by the nonvolatile solute leads to an increase in the boiling point. The normal boiling point of a liquid is the temperature at which its vapor pressure is equal to 1 atm or 760 mm Hg (◀ page 576). In Figure 14.13, we see that the normal boiling point of pure benzene (at 760 mm Hg) is about 80 °C. Tracing the vapor pressure curve for the solution, we also see that the vapor pressure reaches 760 mm Hg at a temperature about 5 °C higher than this value.

The vapor pressure curve and increase in the boiling point shown in Figure 14.13 refer specifically to a 2.00 *m* solution. We might wonder how the boiling point of the solution would vary with solute concentration. In fact, a simple relationship exists

FIGURE 14.13 Lowering the vapor pressure of benzene by addition of a nonvolatile solute. The curve drawn in red represents the vapor pressure of pure benzene, and the curve in blue represents the vapor pressure of a solution containing 0.200 mol of a solute dissolved in 0.100 kg of solvent (2.00 *m*). This graph was created using a series of calculations such as those shown in the text. As an alternative, the graph could be created by measuring various vapor pressures for the solution in a laboratory experiment.

(See ChemistryNow Screen 14.8 Colligative Properties, to view an animation of this vapor pressure lowering.)

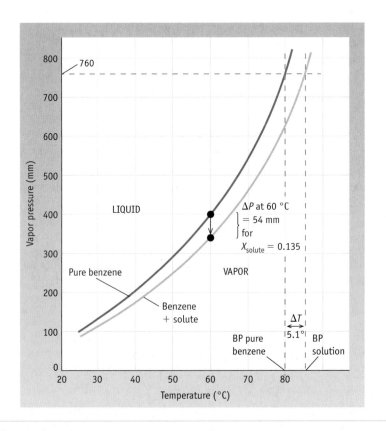

TABLE 14.3 Some Boiling Point Elevation and Freezing Point Depression Constants

Solvent	Normal Boiling Point (°C) Pure Solvent	K_{bp} (°C/m)	Normal Freezing Point (°C) Pure Solvent	K_{fp} (°C/m)
Water	100.00	+0.5121	0.0	−1.86
Benzene	80.10	+2.53	5.50	−5.12
Camphor	207.4	+5.611	179.75	−39.7
Chloroform ($CHCl_3$)	61.70	+3.63	—	—

between boiling point elevation and molal concentration: The boiling point elevation, ΔT_{bp}, is directly proportional to the molality of the solute.

$$\text{Elevation in boiling point} = \Delta T_{bp} = K_{bp}m_{solute} \qquad (14.6)$$

In this equation, K_{bp} is a proportionality constant called the **molal boiling point elevation constant**. It has the units of degrees/molal (°C/m). Values for K_{bp} are determined experimentally, and different solvents have different values (Table 14.3). Formally, the value corresponds to the elevation in boiling point for a 1 *m* solution.

Chemistry.$_{\odot}$.Now™

Sign in at **www.cengage.com/login** and go to Chapter 14 Contents to see Screen 14.8 for an exercise and a tutorial on the **effect of a solute on the solution freezing point.**

■ **EXAMPLE 14.5 Boiling Point Elevation**

Problem Eugenol, the active ingredient in cloves, has the formula $C_{10}H_{12}O_2$. What is the boiling point of a solution containing 0.144 g of this compound dissolved in 10.0 g of benzene?

Strategy We can use Equation 14.6 to calculate the change in boiling point. This value is then added to the boiling point of pure benzene to provide the answer. To use Equation 14.6, you need a value of K_{bp} and the molality of the solution. The K_{bp} value for benzene is given in Table 14.3, but you need to calculate the molality, *m*.

Solution

$$0.144 \text{ g eugenol} \left(\frac{1 \text{ mol eugenol}}{164.2 \text{ g}} \right) = 8.77 \times 10^{-4} \text{ mol eugenol}$$

$$c_{eugenol} = \frac{8.77 \times 10^{-4} \text{ mol eugenol}}{0.0100 \text{ kg benzene}} = 8.77 \times 10^{-2} \text{ m}$$

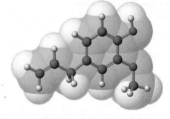

Eugenol, $C_{10}H_{12}O_2$, is an important component in oil of cloves.

Use the value for the molality to calculate the boiling point elevation and then the boiling point:

$$\Delta T_{bp} = (2.53 \text{ °C/m})(0.0877 \text{ m}) = 0.222 \text{ °C}$$

Because the boiling point rises relative to that of the pure solvent, the boiling point of the solution is

$$80.10 \text{ °C} + 0.222 \text{ °C} = \boxed{80.32 \text{ °C}}$$

EXERCISE 14.5 Boiling Point Elevation

What quantity of ethylene glycol, $HOCH_2CH_2OH$, must be added to 125 g of water to raise the boiling point by 1.0 °C? Express the answer in grams.

The elevation of the boiling point of a solvent on adding a solute has many practical consequences. One of them is the summer protection your car's engine receives from "all-season" antifreeze. The main ingredient of commercial antifreeze is ethylene glycol, HOCH₂CH₂OH. The car's radiator and cooling system are sealed to keep the coolant under pressure, ensuring that it will not vaporize at normal engine temperatures. When the air temperature is high in the summer, however, the radiator could "boil over" if it were not protected with "antifreeze." By adding this nonvolatile liquid, the solution in the radiator has a higher boiling point than that of pure water.

Freezing Point Depression

Another consequence of dissolving a solute in a solvent is that the freezing point of the solution is lower than that of the pure solvent (Figure 14.14). For an ideal solution, the depression of the freezing point is given by an equation similar to that for the elevation of the boiling point:

$$\text{Freezing point depression} = \Delta T_{\text{fp}} = K_{\text{fp}} m_{\text{solute}} \qquad (14.7)$$

where K_{fp} is the **freezing point depression constant** in degrees per molal $(°C/m)$. Values of K_{fp} for a few common solvents are given in Table 14.3. The values are negative quantities, so the result of the calculation is a negative value for ΔT_{fp}, signifying a decrease in temperature.

The practical aspects of freezing point changes from pure solvent to solution are similar to those for boiling point elevation. The very name of the liquid you add to the radiator in your car, antifreeze, indicates its purpose (see Figure 14.14a). The label on the container of antifreeze tells you, for example, to add 6 qt (5.7 L) of antifreeze to a 12-qt (11.4-L) cooling system to lower the freezing point to −34 °C and to raise the boiling point to +109 °C.

■ **EXAMPLE 14.6 Freezing Point Depression**

Problem What mass of ethylene glycol, HOCH₂CH₂OH, must be added to 5.50 kg of water to lower the freezing point of the water from 0.0 °C to −10.0 °C?

Strategy To use Equation 14.7, you need K_{fp} (Table 14.3). You can then calculate the molality of the solution and, from this value, the amount and quantity of ethylene glycol required.

FIGURE 14.14 Freezing a solution. (a) Adding antifreeze to water prevents the water from freezing. Here, a jar of pure water (left) and a jar of water to which automobile antifreeze had been added (right) were kept overnight in the freezing compartment of a home refrigerator. (b) When a solution freezes, it is pure solvent that solidifies. To take this photo, a purple dye was dissolved in water, and the solution was frozen slowly. Pure ice formed along the walls of the tube, and the dye stayed in solution. The concentration of the solute increased as more and more solvent was frozen out, and the resulting solution had a lower and lower freezing point. Eventually, the system contains pure, colorless ice that formed along the walls of the tube and a concentrated solution of dye in the center of the tube.

Photos: Charles D. Winters
(a)

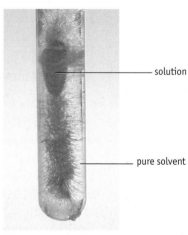
— solution

— pure solvent
(b)

Solution The solute concentration (molality) in a solution with a freezing point depression of $-10.0\ °C$ is

$$\text{Solute concentration } (m) = \frac{\Delta T_{fp}}{K_{fp}} = \frac{-10.0\ °C}{-1.86\ °C/m} = 5.38\ m$$

Because the solution contains 5.50 kg of water, we need 29.6 mol of ethylene glycol:

$$\left(\frac{5.38\ \text{mol glycol}}{1.00\ \text{kg water}}\right)(5.50\ \text{kg water}) = \boxed{29.6\ \text{mol glycol}}$$

The molar mass of ethylene glycol is 62.07 g/mol, so the mass required is 1840 g.

$$29.6\ \text{mol glycol}\left(\frac{62.07\ g}{1\ \text{mol}}\right) = \boxed{1840\ \text{g glycol}}$$

Comment The density of ethylene glycol is 1.11 kg/L, so the volume of glycol to be added is 1.84 kg (1 L/1.11 kg) = 1.66 L.

EXERCISE 14.6 Freezing Point Depression

In the northern United States, summer cottages are usually closed up for the winter. When doing so, the owners "winterize" the plumbing by putting antifreeze in the toilet tanks, for example. Will adding 525 g of $HOCH_2CH_2OH$ to 3.00 kg of water ensure that the water will not freeze at $-25\ °C$?

Osmotic Pressure

Osmosis is the movement of solvent molecules through a semipermeable membrane from a region of lower solute concentration to a region of higher solute concentration. This movement can be demonstrated with a simple experiment. The beaker in Figure 14.15 contains pure water, and the bag and tube hold a concentrated sugar solution. The liquids are separated by a semipermeable membrane, a thin sheet of material (such as a vegetable tissue or cellophane) through

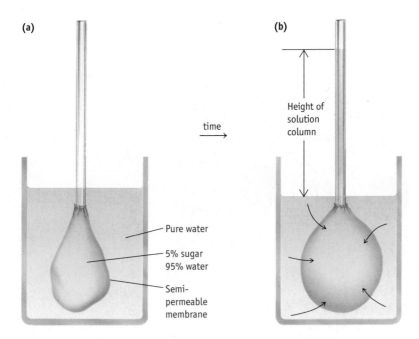

(a)

time

(b)

Height of solution column

Pure water

5% sugar
95% water

Semi-permeable membrane

FIGURE 14.15 The process of osmosis. (a) The bag attached to the tube contains a solution that is 5% sugar and 95% water. The beaker contains pure water. The bag is made of a material that is semipermeable, meaning that it allows water, but not sugar molecules, to pass through. (b) Over time, water flows from the region of low solute concentration (pure water) to the region of higher solute concentration (the sugar solution). Flow continues until the pressure exerted by the column of solution in the tube above the water level in the beaker is great enough to result in equal rates of passage of water molecules in both directions. The height of the column of solution (b) is a measure of the osmotic pressure.

(See ChemistryNow Screen 14.9 Colligative Properties, for an animation of **osmosis.**)

which only certain types of molecules can pass. Here, water molecules can pass through the membrane, but larger sugar molecules (or hydrated ions) cannot (Figure 14.16). When the experiment is begun, the liquid levels in the beaker and the tube are the same. Over time, however, the level of the sugar solution inside the tube rises, the level of pure water in the beaker falls, and the sugar solution becomes more dilute. Eventually, no further net change occurs; equilibrium is reached.

From a molecular point of view, the semipermeable membrane does not present a barrier to the movement of water molecules, so they move through the membrane in both directions. Over time, more water molecules pass through the membrane from the pure water side to the solution side than in the opposite direction. In effect, water molecules tend to move from regions of low solute concentration to regions of high solute concentration. The same is true for any solvent, as long as the membrane allows solvent molecules but not solute molecules or ions to pass through.

Why does the system eventually reach equilibrium? Clearly, the solution in the tube in Figure 14.15 can never reach zero sugar or salt concentration, which would be required to equalize the number of water molecules moving through the membrane in each direction in a given time. The answer lies in the fact that the solution moves higher and higher in the tube as osmosis continues and water moves into the sugar solution. Eventually, the pressure exerted by this column of solution counterbalances the pressure exerted by the water moving through the membrane from the pure water side, and no further net movement of water occurs. An equilibrium of forces is achieved. The pressure created by the column of solution for the system at equilibrium is called the **osmotic pressure**, Π. A measure of this pressure is the difference between the height of the solution in the tube and the level of pure water in the beaker.

FIGURE 14.16 Osmosis at the particulate level. Osmotic flow through a membrane that is selectively permeable (semipermeable) to water. Dissolved substances such as hydrated ions or large sugar molecules cannot diffuse.

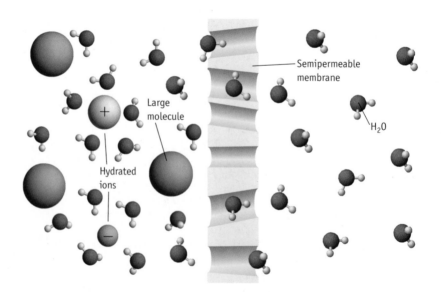

Semipermeable membrane

H_2O

Large molecule

Hydrated ions

Osmotic pressure is a colligative property. From experimental measurements on dilute solutions, it is known that osmotic pressure and concentration (c) are related by the equation

$$\Pi = cRT \qquad (14.8)$$

In this equation, c is the molar concentration (in moles per liter); R is the gas constant; and T is the absolute temperature (in kelvins). Using a value for the gas law constant of $0.082057 \; \text{L} \cdot \text{atm}/\text{K} \cdot \text{mol}$ allows calculation of the osmotic pressure Π in atmospheres. This equation is analogous to the ideal gas law ($PV = nRT$), with Π taking the place of P and c being equivalent to n/V.

Because pressures on the order of 10^{-3} atm are easily measured, concentrations of very dilute solutions (as low as about 10^{-4} M) can be determined through measurements of osmotic pressure.

Other examples of osmosis are shown in Figure 14.17. In this case, the egg's membrane serves as the semipermeable membrane. Osmosis occurs in one direction if the concentration of solute is greater inside the egg than in the exterior solution and occurs in the other direction if the concentration solution is less inside the egg than it is in the exterior solution. In both cases, solvent flows from the region of low solute concentration to the region of high solute concentration.

Colligative Properties and Molar Mass Determination

Early in this book, you learned how to calculate a molecular formula from an empirical formula when given the molar mass. But how do you know the molar mass of an unknown compound? An experiment must be carried out to find this crucial piece of information, and one way to do so is to use a colligative property of a

(a) A fresh egg is placed in dilute acetic acid. The acid reacts with the $CaCO_3$ of the shell but leaves the egg membrane intact.

(b) If the egg, with its shell removed, is placed in pure water, the egg swells.

(c) If the egg, with its shell removed, is placed in a concentrated sugar solution, the egg shrivels.

FIGURE 14.17 An experiment to observe osmosis. You can try this experiment in your kitchen. In the first step, use vinegar as a source of acetic acid.

(See ChemistryNow Screen 14.1, Puzzler, and Screen 14.9, Colligative Properties, for a video of this experiment.)

Photos: Charles D. Winters

solution of the compound. The same basic logic is used for each of the colligative properties studied:

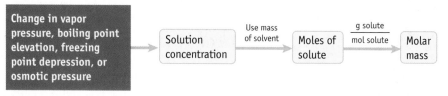

EXAMPLE 14.7 Determining Molar Mass from Boiling Point Elevation

Problem A solution prepared from 1.25 g of oil of wintergreen (methyl salicylate) in 99.0 g of benzene has a boiling point of 80.31 °C. Determine the molar mass of this compound.

Strategy Calculations using colligative properties to determine a molar mass always follow the pattern outlined in the text.

Solution We first use the boiling point elevation to calculate the solution concentration:

$$\text{Boiling point elevation } (\Delta T_{bp}) = 80.31 \text{ °C} - 80.10 \text{ °C} = 0.21 \text{ °C}$$

$$c_{solute} = \frac{\Delta T_{bp}}{K_{bp}} = \frac{0.21 \text{ °C}}{2.53 \text{ °C}/m} = 0.083 \ m$$

The amount of solute in the solution is calculated from the solution concentration:

$$\text{Amount of solute} = \left(\frac{0.083 \text{ mol}}{1.00 \text{ kg}}\right)(0.099 \text{ kg solvent}) = 0.0082 \text{ mol solute}$$

Now we can combine the amount of solute with its mass to obtain its molar mass:

$$\frac{1.25 \text{ g}}{0.0082 \text{ mol}} = \boxed{150 \text{ g/mol}}$$

Comment Methyl salicylate has the formula $C_8H_8O_3$ and a molar mass of 152.14 g/mol.

EXAMPLE 14.8 Osmotic Pressure and Molar Mass

Problem Beta-carotene is the most important of the A vitamins. Its molar mass can be determined by measuring the osmotic pressure generated by a given mass of β-carotene dissolved in the solvent chloroform. Calculate the molar mass of β-carotene if 10.0 mL of a solution containing 7.68 mg of β-carotene has an osmotic pressure of 26.57 mm Hg at 25.0 °C.

Strategy First, use Equation 14.8 to calculate the solution concentration from the osmotic pressure. Then, use the volume and concentration of the solution to calculate the amount of solute. Finally, find the molar mass of the solute from its mass and amount.

Solution The osmotic pressure can be used to calculate the concentration of β-carotene:

$$\text{Concentration (mol/L)} = \frac{\Pi}{RT} = \frac{(26.57 \text{ mm Hg})\left(\dfrac{1 \text{ atm}}{760 \text{ mm Hg}}\right)}{(0.082057 \text{ L} \cdot \text{atm/K} \cdot \text{mol})(298.2 \text{ K})}$$

$$= 1.429 \times 10^{-3} \text{ mol/L}$$

Now the amount of β-carotene dissolved in 10.0 mL of solvent can be calculated:

$$(1.429 \times 10^{-3} \text{ mol/L})(0.0100 \text{ L}) = 1.43 \times 10^{-5} \text{ mol}$$

We can combine the amount of solute with its mass to calculate its molar mass:

$$\frac{7.68 \times 10^{-3} \text{ g}}{1.43 \times 10^{-5} \text{ mol}} = \boxed{538 \text{ g/mol}}$$

Comment Beta-carotene is a hydrocarbon with the formula $C_{40}H_{56}$ (molar mass = 536.9 g/mol).

EXERCISE 14.7 Osmotic Pressure and Molar Mass

A 1.40-g sample of polyethylene, a common plastic, is dissolved in enough benzene to give exactly 100 mL of solution. The measured osmotic pressure of the solution is 1.86 mm Hg at 25 °C. Calculate the average molar mass of the polymer.

Colligative Properties of Solutions Containing Ions

In the northern United States, it is common practice to scatter salt on snowy or icy roads or sidewalks. When the sun shines on the snow or patch of ice, a small amount melts, and some salt dissolves in the water. As a result of the dissolved solute, the freezing point of the solution is lower than 0 °C. The solution "eats" its way through the ice, breaking it up, and the icy patch is no longer dangerous for drivers or for people walking.

Salt (NaCl) is the most common substance used on roads because it is inexpensive and dissolves readily in water. Its relatively low molar mass means that the effect

Putting salt on ice assists in melting the ice.

Osmosis and Medicine

Osmosis is of practical significance for people in the health professions. Patients who become dehydrated through illness often need to be given water and nutrients intravenously. Water cannot simply be dripped into a patient's vein, however. Rather, the intravenous solution must have the same overall solute concentration as the patient's blood: the solution must be isoosmotic or **isotonic** (Figures A and B, part a). If pure water was used, the inside of a blood cell would have a higher solute concentration

(lower water concentration), and water would flow into the cell. This hypotonic situation would cause the red blood cells to burst (lyse) (Figure B, part c). The opposite situation, hypertonicity, occurs if the intravenous solution is more concentrated than the contents of the

blood cell (Figure B, part b). In this case, the cell would lose water and shrivel up (crenate). To combat this, a dehydrated patient is rehydrated in the hospital with a sterile saline solution that is 0.16 M NaCl, a solution that is isotonic with the cells of the body.

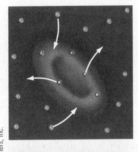
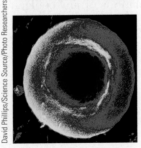
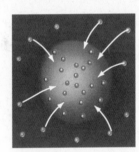

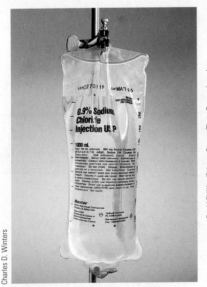

FIGURE A An isotonic saline solution. This solution has the same molality as body fluids.

(a) Isotonic solution **(b)** Hypertonic solution **(c)** Hypotonic solution

FIGURE B Osmosis and living cells. (a) A cell placed in an isotonic solution. The net movement of water into and out of the cell is zero because the concentration of solutes inside and outside the cell is the same. (b) In a hypertonic solution, the concentration of solutes outside the cell is greater than that inside. There is a net flow of water out of the cell, causing the cell to dehydrate, shrink, and perhaps die. (c) In a hypotonic solution, the concentration of solutes outside the cell is less than that inside. There is a net flow of water into the cell, causing the cell to swell and perhaps to burst (or lyse).

per gram is large. In addition, salt is especially effective because it is an electrolyte. That is, it dissolves to give ions in solution:

$$NaCl(s) \rightarrow Na^+(aq) + Cl^-(aq)$$

Recall that colligative properties depend not on what is dissolved but *only on the number of particles of solute per solvent particle*. When 1 mol of NaCl dissolves, 2 mol of ions form, which means that the effect on the freezing point of water should be twice as large as that expected for a mole of sugar. A 0.100 *m* solution of NaCl really contains two solutes, 0.100 *m* Na^+ and 0.100 *m* Cl^-. What we should use to estimate the freezing point depression is the *total* molality of solute particles:

$$m_{total} = m(Na^+) + m(Cl^-) = (0.100 + 0.100) \text{ mol/kg} = 0.200 \text{ mol/kg}$$

$$\Delta T_{fp} = (-1.86 \ ^\circ C/m)(0.200 \ m) = -0.372 \ ^\circ C$$

To estimate the freezing point depression for an ionic compound, first find the molality of solute from the mass and molar mass of the compound and the mass of the solvent. Then, multiply the molality by the number of ions in the formula: two for NaCl, three for Na_2SO_4, four for $LaCl_3$, five for $Al_2(SO_4)_3$, and so on.

Table 14.4 shows that as the concentration of NaCl decreases, ΔT_{fp} for NaCl approaches but does not quite reach a value that is two times larger than the value determined assuming no dissociation. Likewise, ΔT_{fp} for Na_2SO_4 approaches but does not reach a value that is three times larger. The ratio of the experimentally observed value of ΔT_{fp} to the value calculated, assuming no dissociation, is called the **van't Hoff factor** after Jacobus Henrikus van't Hoff (1852–1911), who was involved in studying this phenomenon. The van't Hoff factor is represented by *i*.

$$i = \frac{\Delta T_{fp}, \text{ measured}}{\Delta T_{fp}, \text{ calculated}} = \frac{\Delta T_{fp}, \text{ measured}}{K_{fp} \ m}$$

or

$$\Delta T_{fp} \text{ measured} = K_{fp} \times m \times i \qquad (14.9)$$

The numbers in the last column of Table 14.4 are van't Hoff factors. These values can be used in calculations of any colligative property. Vapor pressure lowering,

---

TABLE 14.4   Freezing Point Depressions of Some Ionic Solutions

Mass %	m (mol/kg)	ΔT_{fp} (measured, °C)	ΔT_{fp} (calculated, °C)	$\dfrac{\Delta T_{fp}, \text{ measured}}{\Delta T_{fp}, \text{ calculated}}$
NaCl				
0.00700	0.0120	−0.0433	−0.0223	1.94
0.500	0.0860	−0.299	−0.160	1.87
1.00	0.173	−0.593	−0.322	1.84
2.00	0.349	−1.186	−0.649	1.83
Na₂SO₄				
0.00700	0.00493	−0.0257	−0.00917	2.80
0.500	0.0354	−0.165	−0.0658	2.51
1.00	0.0711	−0.320	−0.132	2.42
2.00	0.144	−0.606	−0.268	2.26

boiling point elevation, freezing point depression, and osmotic pressure are all larger for electrolytes than for nonelectrolytes of the same molality.

The van't Hoff factor approaches a whole number (2, 3, and so on) only with very dilute solutions. In more concentrated solutions, the experimental freezing point depressions indicate that there are fewer ions in solution than expected. This behavior, which is typical of all ionic compounds, is a consequence of the strong attractions between ions. The result is as if some of the positive and negative ions are paired, decreasing the total molality of particles. Indeed, in more concentrated solutions, and especially in solvents less polar than water, ions are extensively associated in ion pairs and in even larger clusters.

EXAMPLE 14.9 Freezing Point and Ionic Solutions

Problem A 0.00200 *m* aqueous solution of an ionic compound, $Co(NH_3)_5(NO_2)Cl$, freezes at -0.00732 °C. How many moles of ions does 1.0 mol of the salt produce on being dissolved in water?

Strategy First, calculate ΔT_{fp} of the solution assuming no ions are produced. Compare this value with the actual value of ΔT_{fp}. The ratio will reflect the number of ions produced.

Solution The freezing-point depression expected for a 0.00200 *m* solution assuming that the salt does not dissociate into ions is

$$\Delta T_{fp} \text{ calculated} = K_{fp}m = (-1.86 \text{ °C})(0.0200 \text{ } m) = -3.72 \times 10^{-3} \text{ °C}$$

Now compare the calculated freezing point depression with the measured depression. This gives us the van't Hoff factor:

$$i = \frac{\Delta T_{fp}, \text{ measured}}{\Delta T_{fp}, \text{ calculated}} = \frac{-7.32 \times 10^{-3} \text{ °C}}{-3.72 \times 10^{-3} \text{ °C}} = 1.97 \approx 2$$

It appears that 1 mol of this compound gives 2 mol of ions. In this case, the ions are $[Co(NH_3)_5(NO_2)]^+$ and Cl^-.

EXERCISE 14.8 Freezing Point and Ionic Compounds

Calculate the freezing point of 525 g of water that contains 25.0 g of NaCl. Assume *i*, the van't Hoff factor, is 1.85 for NaCl.

14.5 Colloids

Earlier in this chapter, we defined a solution broadly as a homogeneous mixture of two or more substances in a single phase (page 617). To this definition we should add that, in a true solution, no settling of the solute should be observed and the solute particles should be in the form of ions or relatively small molecules. Thus, NaCl and sugar form true solutions in water. You are also familiar with suspensions, which result, for example, if a handful of fine sand is added to water and shaken vigorously. Sand particles are still visible and gradually settle to the bottom of the beaker or bottle. **Colloidal dispersions**, also called **colloids**, represent a state intermediate between a solution and a suspension. Colloids include many of the foods you eat and the materials around you; among them are JELL-O®, milk, fog, and porcelain (see Table 14.5).

Around 1860, the British chemist Thomas Graham (1805–1869) found that substances such as starch, gelatin, glue, and albumin from eggs diffused only very slowly when placed in water, compared with sugar or salt. In addition, the former substances differ significantly in their ability to diffuse through a thin membrane: Sugar molecules can diffuse through many membranes, but the very large molecules that make up starch, gelatin, glue, and albumin do not. Moreover, Graham found that

Gold colloid. A water-soluble salt of $[AuCl_4]^-$ is reduced to give colloidal gold metal. The colloidal gold gives the dispersion its red color. (Similarly, colloidal gold is used to give a beautiful red color to glass.) Since the days of alchemy, some have claimed that drinking a colloidal gold solution "cleared the mind, increased intelligence and will power, and balanced the emotions."

TABLE 14.5   Types of Colloids

Type	Dispersing Medium	Dispersed Phase	Examples
Aerosol	Gas	Liquid	Fog, clouds, aerosol sprays
Aerosol	Gas	Solid	Smoke, airborne viruses, automobile exhaust
Foam	Liquid	Gas	Shaving cream, whipped cream
Foam	Solid	Gas	Styrofoam, marshmallow
Emulsion	Liquid	Liquid	Mayonnaise, milk, face cream
Gel	Solid	Liquid	Jelly, JELL-O®, cheese, butter
Sol	Liquid	Solid	Gold in water, milk of magnesia, mud
Solid sol	Solid	Solid	Milkglass

(a) (b)

Photos: Charles D. Winters

FIGURE 14.18 The Tyndall effect.
Colloidal dispersions scatter light, a phenomenon known as the Tyndall effect. (a) Dust in the air scatters the light coming through the trees in a forest along the Oregon coast. (b) A narrow beam of light from a laser is passed through an NaCl solution (left) and then a colloidal mixture of gelatin and water (right).

he could not crystallize these substances, whereas he could crystallize sugar, salt, and other materials that form true solutions. Graham coined the word "colloid" (from the Greek, meaning "glue") to describe this class of substances that are distinctly different from true solutions and suspensions.

We now know that it is possible to crystallize some colloidal substances, albeit with difficulty, so there really is no sharp dividing line between these classes based on this property. Colloids do, however, have two distinguishing characteristics. First, colloids generally have high molar masses; this is true of proteins such as hemoglobin that have molar masses in the thousands. Second, the particles of a colloid are relatively large (say, 1000 nm in diameter). As a consequence, they exhibit the **Tyndall effect**; they scatter visible light when dispersed in a solvent, making the mixture appear cloudy (Figure 14.18). Third, even though colloidal particles are large, they are not so large that they settle out.

Graham also gave us the words **sol** for a colloidal dispersion of a solid substance in a fluid medium and **gel** for a colloidal dispersion that has a structure that prevents it from being mobile. JELL-O® is a sol when the solid is first mixed with boiling water, but it becomes a gel when cooled. Other examples of gels are the gelatinous precipitates of $Al(OH)_3$, $Fe(OH)_3$, and $Cu(OH)_2$ (Figure 14.19).

Colloidal dispersions consist of finely divided particles that, as a result, have a very high surface area. For example, if you have one millionth of a mole of colloidal particles, each assumed to be a sphere with a diameter of 200 nm, the total surface area of the particles would be on the order of 200 million cm^2, or the size of several football fields. It is not surprising, therefore, that many of the properties of colloids depend on the properties of surfaces.

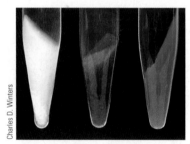

Charles D. Winters

FIGURE 14.19 Gelatinous precipitates. (left) $Al(OH)_3$, (center) $Fe(OH)_3$, and (right) $Cu(OH)_2$.

Types of Colloids

Colloids are classified according to the state of the dispersed phase and the dispersing medium. Table 14.5 lists several types of colloids and gives examples of each.

Colloids with water as the dispersing medium can be classified as **hydrophobic** (from the Greek, meaning "water-fearing") or **hydrophilic** ("water-loving"). A hydrophobic colloid is one in which only weak attractive forces exist between the water and the surfaces of the colloidal particles. Examples include dispersions of metals and of nearly insoluble salts in water. When compounds like AgCl precipitate, the result is often a colloidal dispersion. The precipitation reaction occurs too rapidly for ions to gather from long distances and make large crystals, so the ions aggregate to form small particles that remain suspended in the liquid.

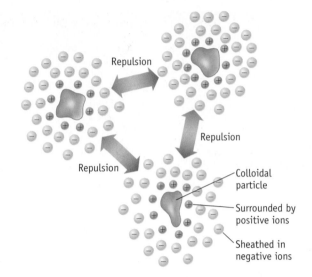

FIGURE 14.20 Hydrophobic colloids. A hydrophobic colloid is stabilized by positive ions absorbed onto each particle and a secondary layer of negative ions. Because the particles bear similar charges, they repel one another, and precipitation is prevented.

Repulsion

Repulsion

Repulsion

Colloidal particle

Surrounded by positive ions

Sheathed in negative ions

FIGURE 14.21 Formation of silt. Silt forms at a river delta as colloidal soil particles come in contact with salt water in the ocean. Here, the Ashley and Cooper Rivers empty into the Atlantic Ocean at Charleston, South Carolina. The high concentration of ions in sea water causes the colloidal soil particles to coagulate.

Why don't the particles come together (coagulate) and form larger particles? The answer is that the colloidal particles carry electric charges. An AgCl particle, for example, will absorb Ag^+ ions if the ions are present in substantial concentration; an attraction occurs between Ag^+ ions in solution and Cl^- ions on the surface of the particle. In this way, the colloidal particles become positively charged, allowing them to attract a secondary layer of anions. The particles, now surrounded by layers of ions, repel one another and are prevented from coming together to form a precipitate (Figure 14.20).

A stable hydrophobic colloid can be made to coagulate by introducing ions into the dispersing medium. Milk contains a colloidal suspension of protein-rich casein micelles with a hydrophobic core. When milk ferments, lactose (milk sugar) is converted to lactic acid, which forms lactate ions and hydrogen ions. The protective charges on the surfaces of the colloidal particles are overcome, and the milk coagulates; the milk solids come together in clumps called "curds."

Soil particles are often carried by water in rivers and streams as hydrophobic colloids. When river water carrying large amounts of colloidal particles meets sea water with its high concentration of salts, the particles coagulate to form the silt seen at the mouth of the river (Figure 14.21). Municipal water treatment plants often add salts such as $Al_2(SO_4)_3$ to clarify water. In aqueous solution, aluminum ions exist as $[Al(H_2O)_6]^{3+}$ cations, which neutralize the charge on the hydrophobic colloidal soil particles, causing these particles to aggregate and settle out.

Hydrophilic colloids are strongly attracted to water molecules. They often have groups such as —OH and —NH$_2$ on their surfaces. These groups form strong hydrogen bonds to water, thereby stabilizing the colloid. Proteins and starch are important examples of hydrophilic colloids, and homogenized milk is the most familiar example.

Emulsions are colloidal dispersions of one liquid in another, such as oil or fat in water. Familiar examples include salad dressing, mayonnaise, and milk. If vegetable oil and vinegar are mixed to make a salad dressing, the mixture quickly separates into two layers because the nonpolar oil molecules do not interact with the polar water and acetic acid (CH_3CO_2H) molecules. So why are milk and mayonnaise apparently homogeneous mixtures that do not separate into layers? The answer is that they contain an **emulsifying agent** such as soap or a protein. Lecithin is a phospholipid found in egg yolks, so mixing egg yolks with oil and vinegar stabilizes the colloidal dispersion known as mayonnaise. To understand this process

NASA/Peter Arnold, Inc.

further, let us look into the functioning of soaps and detergents, substances known as surfactants.

Surfactants

Soaps and detergents are emulsifying agents. Soap is made by heating a fat with sodium or potassium hydroxide (◄ page 476), which produces the anion of a fatty acid.

$$\underbrace{H_3C(CH_2)_{16}}_{\substack{\text{Hydrocarbon tail} \\ \text{Soluble in oil}}} - \underbrace{\overset{\displaystyle O}{\overset{\displaystyle \|}{C}} - O^- \ Na^+}_{\substack{\text{Polar head} \\ \text{Soluble in water}}}$$

sodium stearate, a soap

The fatty acid anion has a split personality: It has a nonpolar, hydrophobic hydrocarbon tail that is soluble in other similar hydrocarbons and a polar, hydrophilic head that is soluble in water.

Oil cannot be readily washed away from dishes or clothing with water because oil is nonpolar and thus insoluble in water. Instead, we add soap to the water to clean away the oil. The nonpolar molecules of the oil interact with the nonpolar hydrocarbon tails of the soap molecules, leaving the polar heads of the soap to interact with surrounding water molecules. The oil and water then mix (Figure 14.22). If the oily material on a piece of clothing or a dish also contains some dirt particles, that dirt can now be washed away.

Substances such as soaps that affect the properties of surfaces, and therefore affect the interaction between two phases, are called surface-active agents, or **surfactants**, for short. A surfactant used for cleaning is called a **detergent**. One function of a surfactant is to lower the surface tension of water, which enhances the cleansing action of the detergent (Figure 14.23).

Many detergents used in the home and industry are synthetic. One example is sodium laurylbenzenesulfonate, a biodegradable compound.

$$CH_3CH_2CH_2CH_2CH_2CH_2CH_2CH_2CH_2CH_2CH_2CH_2 - \text{⬡} - SO_3^- \ Na^+$$

sodium laurylbenzenesulfonate

■ **Soaps and Surfactants** A sodium soap is a solid at room temperature, whereas potassium soaps are usually liquids. About 30 million tons of household and toilet soap, and synthetic and soap-based laundry detergents, are produced annually worldwide.

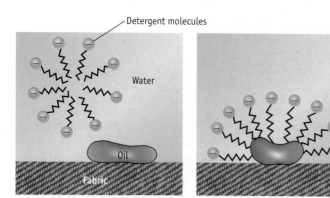
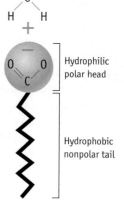

FIGURE 14.22 The cleaning action of soap. Soap molecules interact with water through the charged, hydrophilic end of the molecule. The long, hydrocarbon end of the molecule is hydrophobic, but it can bind through dispersion forces with hydrocarbons and other nonpolar substances.

FIGURE 14.23 Effect of a detergent on the surface tension of water. Sulfur (density = 2.1 g/cm³) is carefully placed on the surface of water (density, 1.0 g/cm³) (left). The surface tension of the water keeps the denser sulfur afloat. Several drops of detergent are then placed on the surface of the water (right). The surface tension of the water is reduced, and the sulfur sinks to the bottom of the beaker.

add surfactant →

Photos: Charles D. Winters

In general, synthetic detergents use the sulfonate group, $-SO_3^-$, as the polar head instead of the carboxylate group, $-CO_2^-$. The carboxylate anions form an insoluble precipitate with any Ca^{2+} or Mg^{2+} ions present in water. Because hard water is characterized by high concentrations of these ions, using soaps containing carboxylates produces bathtub rings and tell-tale gray clothing. The synthetic sulfonate detergents have the advantage that they do not form such precipitates because their calcium salts are more soluble in water.

Chapter Goals Revisited

Now that you have studied this chapter, you should ask whether you have met the chapter goals. In particular, you should be able to:

Calculate and use the solution concentration units molality, mole fraction, and weight percent

a. Define the terms solution, solvent, solute, and colligative properties (Section 14.1).

b. Use the following concentration units: molality, mole fraction, and weight percent. (Section 14.1). Study Question(s) assignable in OWL: 6, 9, 10, 12, 56.

c. Understand the distinctions between saturated, unsaturated, and supersaturated solutions (Section 14.2).

d. Define and illustrate the terms miscible and immiscible (Section 14.2).

Understand the solution process

a. Describe the process of dissolving a solute in a solvent, including the energy changes that may occur (Section 14.2). Study Question(s) assignable in OWL: 13, 16, 88, 93.

b. Understand the relationship of lattice enthalpy and enthalpy of hydration to the enthalpy of solution for an ionic solute (Section 14.2). Study Question(s) assignable in OWL: 77, 88.

c. Describe the effect of pressure and temperature on the solubility of a solute (Section 14.2).

d. Use Henry's law to calculate the solubility of a gas in a solvent (Section 14.2). Study Question(s) assignable in OWL: 21, 22, 67.

e. Apply Le Chatelier's principle to the change in solubility of gases with temperature changes (Section 14.2).

Understand and use the colligative properties of solutions

a. Calculate the mole fraction of a solvent ($X_{solvent}$) and the effect of a solute on solvent vapor pressure ($P_{solvent}$) using Raoult's law (Section 14.4). Study Question(s) assignable in OWL: 24, 74, 96.

b. Calculate the boiling point elevation or freezing point depression caused by a solute in a solvent (Section 14.4). Study Question(s) assignable in OWL: 28, 30, 32, 45, 53, 60; Go Chemistry Module 19.

c. Calculate the osmotic pressure (Π) for solutions (Section 14.4). Study Question(s) assignable in OWL: 47, 78, 84, 97.

d. Use colligative properties to determine the molar mass of a solute (Section 14.4). Study Question(s) assignable in OWL: 35, 39, 61, 64, 84, 85.

e. Characterize the effect of ionic solutes on colligative properties (Section 14.4). Study Question(s) assignable in OWL: 43.

f. Use the van't Hoff factor, i, in calculations involving colligative properties (Section 14.4). Study Question(s) assignable in OWL: 41, 79, 80.

KEY EQUATIONS

Equation 14.1 (page 618) Molality is defined as the amount of solute per kilogram of solvent.

$$\text{Concentration } (c, \text{ mol/kg}) = \text{molality of solute} = \frac{\text{amount of solute (mol)}}{\text{mass of solvent (kg)}}$$

Equation 14.2 (page 618) The mole fraction, X, of a solution component is defined as the number of moles of a given component of a mixture (n_A, mol) divided by the total number of moles of all of the components of the mixture.

$$\text{Mole fraction of A } (X_A) = \frac{n_A}{n_A + n_B + n_C + \ldots}$$

Equation 14.3 (page 619) Weight percent is the mass of one component divided by the total mass of the mixture (multiplied by 100%).

$$\text{Weight \% A} = \frac{\text{mass of A}}{\text{mass of A} + \text{mass of B} + \text{mass of C} + \ldots} \times 100\%$$

Equation 14.4 (page 626) Henry's law: the solubility of a gas, S_g, is equal to the product of the partial pressure of the gaseous solute (P_g) and a constant (k_H) characteristic of the solute and solvent.

$$S_g = k_H P_g$$

Equation 14.5 (page 629) Raoult's law: the equilibrium vapor pressure of a solvent over a solution at a given temperature, $P_{solvent}$, is the product of the mole fraction of the solvent ($X_{solvent}$) and the vapor pressure of the pure solvent ($P°_{solvent}$).

$$P_{solvent} = X_{solvent} P°_{solvent}$$

Equation 14.6 (page 631) The elevation in boiling point of the solvent in a solution, ΔT_{bp}, is the product of the molality of the solute, m_{solute}, and a constant characteristic of the solvent, K_{bp}.

$$\text{Elevation in boiling point} = \Delta T_{bp} = K_{bp}m_{solute}$$

Equation 14.7 (page 634) The depression of the freezing point of the solvent in a solution, ΔT_{fp}, is the product of the molality of the solute, m_{solute}, and a constant characteristic of the solvent, K_{fp}.

$$\text{Freezing point depression} = \Delta T_{fp} = K_{fp}m_{solute}$$

Equation 14.8 (page 637) The osmotic pressure, Π, is the product of the solute concentration c (in mol/L), the universal gas constant R (0.082057 L · atm/K · mol), and the temperature T (in kelvins).

$$\Pi = cRT$$

Equation 14.9 (page 639) This modified equation for freezing point depression accounts for the possible dissociation of a solute. The van't Hoff factor, i, the ratio of the measured freezing point depression and the freezing point depression calculated assuming no solute dissociation, is related to the relative number of particles produced by a dissolved solute.

$$\Delta T_{fp} \text{ measured} = K_{fp} \times m \times i$$

STUDY QUESTIONS

OWL Online homework for this chapter may be assigned in OWL.

▲ denotes challenging questions.

■ denotes questions assignable in OWL.

Blue-numbered questions have answers in Appendix O and fully-worked solutions in the *Student Solutions Manual*.

Practicing Skills

Concentration
(See Examples 14.1 and 14.2 and ChemistryNow Screen 14.2.)

1. Suppose you dissolve 2.56 g of succinic acid, $C_2H_4(CO_2H)_2$, in 500. mL of water. Assuming that the density of water is 1.00 g/cm³, calculate the molality, mole fraction, and weight percentage of acid in the solution.

2. ■ Assume you dissolve 45.0 g of camphor, $C_{10}H_{16}O$, in 425 mL of ethanol, C_2H_5OH. Calculate the molality, mole fraction, and weight percent of camphor in this solution. (The density of ethanol is 0.785 g/mL.)

3. Fill in the blanks in the table. Aqueous solutions are assumed.

Compound	Molality	Weight Percent	Mole Fraction
NaI	0.15	_____	_____
C_2H_5OH	_____	5.0	_____
$C_{12}H_{22}O_{11}$	0.15	_____	_____

4. Fill in the blanks in the table. Aqueous solutions are assumed.

Compound	Molality	Weight Percent	Mole Fraction
KNO_3	_____	10.0	_____
CH_3CO_2H	0.0183	_____	_____
$HOCH_2CH_2OH$	_____	18.0	_____

5. What mass of Na_2CO_3 must you add to 125 g of water to prepare 0.200 m Na_2CO_3? What is the mole fraction of Na_2CO_3 in the resulting solution?

6. ■ You want to prepare a solution that is 0.0512 m in $NaNO_3$. What mass of $NaNO_3$ must be added to 500. g of water? What is the mole fraction of $NaNO_3$ in the solution?

7. You wish to prepare an aqueous solution of glycerol, $C_3H_5(OH)_3$, in which the mole fraction of the solute is 0.093. What mass of glycerol must you add to 425 g of water to make this solution? What is the molality of the solution?

8. You want to prepare an aqueous solution of ethylene glycol, $HOCH_2CH_2OH$, in which the mole fraction of solute is 0.125. What mass of ethylene glycol, in grams, should you combine with 955 g of water? What is the molality of the solution?

9. ■ Hydrochloric acid is sold as a concentrated aqueous solution. If the molarity of commercial HCl is 12.0 and its density is 1.18 g/cm^3, calculate the following:
   (a) the molality of the solution
   (b) the weight percent of HCl in the solution

10. ■ Concentrated sulfuric acid has a density of 1.84 g/cm^3 and is 95.0% by weight H_2SO_4. What is the molality of this acid? What is its molarity?

11. The average lithium ion concentration in sea water is 0.18 ppm. What is the molality of Li^+ in sea water?

12. ■ Silver ion has an average concentration of 28 ppb (parts per billion) in U.S. water supplies.
   (a) What is the molality of the silver ion?
   (b) If you wanted 1.0×10^2 g of silver and could recover it chemically from water supplies, what volume of water in liters, would you have to treat? (Assume the density of water is 1.0 g/cm^3.)

The Solution Process
(See Example 14.3 and ChemistryNow Screens 14.3 and 14.4.)

13. ■ Which pairs of liquids will be miscible?
   (a) H_2O and $CH_3CH_2CH_2CH_3$
   (b) C_6H_6 (benzene) and CCl_4
   (c) H_2O and CH_3CO_2H

14. Acetone, CH_3COCH_3, is quite soluble in water. Explain why this should be so.

15. Use the data of Table 14.1 to calculate the enthalpy of solution of LiCl.

16. ■ Use the following data to calculate the enthalpy of solution of sodium perchlorate, $NaClO_4$:

$\Delta_f H°(s) = -382.9 \text{ kJ/mol}$ and
$\Delta_f H°(aq, 1 \text{ } m) = -369.5 \text{ kJ/mol}$

17. You make a saturated solution of NaCl at 25 °C. No solid is present in the beaker holding the solution. What can be done to increase the amount of dissolved NaCl in this solution? (See Figure 14.11.)
   (a) Add more solid NaCl.
   (b) Raise the temperature of the solution.

   (c) Raise the temperature of the solution, and add some NaCl.
   (d) Lower the temperature of the solution, and add some NaCl.

18. Some lithium chloride, LiCl, is dissolved in 100 mL of water in one beaker, and some Li_2SO_4 is dissolved in 100 mL of water in another beaker. Both are at 10 °C, and both are saturated solutions; some solid remains undissolved in each beaker. Describe what you would observe as the temperature is raised. The following data are available to you from a handbook of chemistry:

	Solubility (g/100 mL)	
Compound	10 °C	40 °C
Li_2SO_4	35.5	33.7
LiCl	74.5	89.8

Henry's Law
(See Example 14.4 and ChemistryNow Screen 14.5.)

19. The partial pressure of O_2 in your lungs varies from 25 mm Hg to 40 mm Hg. What mass of O_2 can dissolve in 1.0 L of water at 25 °C if the partial pressure of O_2 is 40 mm Hg?

20. ■ The Henry's law constant for O_2 in water at 25 °C is given in Table 14.2. Which of the following is a reasonable constant when the temperature is 50 °C? Explain the reason for your choice.
   (a) $6.7 \times 10^{-4} \text{ mol/kg} \cdot \text{bar}$ (c) $1.3 \times 10^{-3} \text{ mol/kg} \cdot \text{bar}$
   (b) $2.6 \times 10^{-3} \text{ mol/kg} \cdot \text{bar}$ (d) $6.4 \times 10^{-2} \text{ mol/kg} \cdot \text{bar}$

21. An unopened soda can has an aqueous CO_2 concentration of 0.0506 m at 25 °C. What is the pressure of CO_2 gas in the can?

22. ■ Hydrogen gas has a Henry's law constant of $7.8 \times 10^{-4} \text{ mol/kg} \cdot \text{bar}$ at 25 °C when dissolving in water. If the total pressure of gas (H_2 gas plus water vapor) over water is 1.0 bar, what is the concentration of H_2 in the water in grams per milliliter? (See Appendix G for the vapor pressure of water.)

Raoult's Law
(See Example 14.5 and ChemistryNow Screen 14.7.)

23. A 35.0-g sample of ethylene glycol, $HOCH_2CH_2OH$, is dissolved in 500.0 g of water. The vapor pressure of water at 32 °C is 35.7 mm Hg. What is the vapor pressure of the water–ethylene glycol solution at 32 °C? (Ethylene glycol is nonvolatile.)

24. ■ Urea, $(NH_2)_2CO$, which is widely used in fertilizers and plastics, is quite soluble in water. If you dissolve 9.00 g of urea in 10.0 mL of water, what is the vapor pressure of the solution at 24 °C? Assume the density of water is 1.00 g/mL.

25. Pure ethylene glycol, $HOCH_2CH_2OH$, is added to 2.00 kg of water in the cooling system of a car. The vapor pressure of the water in the system when the temperature is 90 °C is 457 mm Hg. What mass of glycol was added? (Assume the solution is ideal. See Appendix G for the vapor pressure of water.)

26. Pure iodine (105 g) is dissolved in 325 g of CCl_4 at 65 °C. Given that the vapor pressure of CCl_4 at this temperature is 531 mm Hg, what is the vapor pressure of the CCl_4–I_2 solution at 65 °C? (Assume that I_2 does not contribute to the vapor pressure.)

Boiling Point Elevation
(See Example 14.6 and ChemistryNow Screen 14.8.)

27. Verify that 0.200 mol of a nonvolatile solute in 125 g of benzene (C_6H_6) produces a solution whose boiling point is 84.2 °C.

28. ■ What is the boiling point of a solution composed of 15.0 g of urea, $(NH_2)_2CO$, in 0.500 kg of water?

29. What is the boiling point of a solution composed of 15.0 g of $CHCl_3$ and 0.515 g of the nonvolatile solute acenaphthene, $C_{12}H_{10}$, a component of coal tar?

30. ■ A solution of glycerol, $C_3H_5(OH)_3$, in 735 g of water has a boiling point of 104.4 °C at a pressure of 760 mm Hg. What is the mass of glycerol in the solution? What is the mole fraction of the solute?

Freezing Point Depression
(See Example 14.7 and ChemistryNow Screen 14.8.)

31. A mixture of ethanol, C_2H_5OH, and water has a freezing point of −16.0 °C.
    (a) What is the molality of the alcohol?
    (b) What is the weight percent of alcohol in the solution?

32. ■ Some ethylene glycol, $HOCH_2CH_2OH$, is added to your car's cooling system along with 5.0 kg of water. If the freezing point of the water–glycol solution is −15.0 °C, what mass of $HOCH_2CH_2OH$ must have been added?

33. You dissolve 15.0 g of sucrose, $C_{12}H_{22}O_{11}$, in a cup of water (225 g). What is the freezing point of the solution?

34. Assume a bottle of wine consists of an 11 weight percent solution of ethanol (C_2H_5OH) in water. If the bottle of wine is chilled to −20 °C, will the solution begin to freeze?

Colligative Properties and Molar Mass Determination
(See Example 14.8.)

35. ■ You add 0.255 g of an orange, crystalline compound whose empirical formula is $C_{10}H_8Fe$ to 11.12 g of benzene. The boiling point of the benzene rises from 80.10 °C to 80.26 °C. What are the molar mass and molecular formula of the compound?

36. Butylated hydroxyanisole (BHA) is used as an antioxidant in margarine and other fats and oils. (It prevents oxidation and prolongs the shelf-life of the food.) What is the molar mass of BHA if 0.640 g of the compound, dissolved in 25.0 g of chloroform, produces a solution whose boiling point is 62.22 °C?

37. Benzyl acetate is one of the active components of oil of jasmine. If 0.125 g of the compound is added to 25.0 g of chloroform ($CHCl_3$), the boiling point of the solution is 61.82 °C. What is the molar mass of benzyl acetate?

38. Anthracene, a hydrocarbon obtained from coal, has an empirical formula of C_7H_5. To find its molecular formula, you dissolve 0.500 g in 30.0 g of benzene. The boiling point of pure benzene is 80.10 °C, whereas the solution has a boiling point of 80.34 °C. What is the molecular formula of anthracene?

39. ■ An aqueous solution contains 0.180 g of an unknown, nonionic solute in 50.0 g of water. The solution freezes at −0.040 °C. What is the molar mass of the solute?

40. The organic compound called aluminon is used as a reagent to test for the presence of the aluminum ion in aqueous solution. A solution of 2.50 g of aluminon in 50.0 g of water freezes at −0.197 °C. What is the molar mass of aluminon?

Colligative Properties of Ionic Compounds
(See Example 14.9 and ChemistryNow Screen 14.8.)

41. ■ If 52.5 g of LiF is dissolved in 306 g of water, what is the expected freezing point of the solution? (Assume the van't Hoff factor, i, for LiF is 2.)

42. To make homemade ice cream, you cool the milk and cream by immersing the container in ice and a concentrated solution of rock salt (NaCl) in water. If you want to have a water–salt solution that freezes at −10. °C, what mass of NaCl must you add to 3.0 kg of water? (Assume the van't Hoff factor, i, for NaCl is 1.85.)

43. ■ List the following aqueous solutions in order of increasing melting point. (The last three are all assumed to dissociate completely into ions in water.)
    (a) 0.1 m sugar   (c) 0.08 m $CaCl_2$
    (b) 0.1 m NaCl   (d) 0.04 m Na_2SO_4

44. Arrange the following aqueous solutions in order of decreasing freezing point. (The last three are all assumed to dissociate completely into ions in water.)
    (a) 0.20 m ethylene glycol (nonvolatile, nonelectrolyte)
    (b) 0.12 m K_2SO_4
    (c) 0.10 m $MgCl_2$
    (d) 0.12 m KBr

▲ more challenging   ■ in OWL   Blue-numbered questions answered in Appendix O

Osmosis
(See Example 14.10 and ChemistryNow Screen 14.9.)

45. ■ An aqueous solution contains 3.00% phenylalanine $(C_9H_{11}NO_2)$ by mass. Assume the phenylalanine is nonionic and nonvolatile. Find the following:
    (a) the freezing point of the solution
    (b) the boiling point of the solution
    (c) the osmotic pressure of the solution at 25 °C

    In your view, which of these values is most easily measurable in the laboratory?

46. Estimate the osmotic pressure of human blood at 37 °C. Assume blood is isotonic with a 0.154 M NaCl solution, and assume the van't Hoff factor, i, is 1.90 for NaCl.

47. ■ An aqueous solution containing 1.00 g of bovine insulin (a protein, not ionized) per liter has an osmotic pressure of 3.1 mm Hg at 25 °C. Calculate the molar mass of bovine insulin.

48. Calculate the osmotic pressure of a 0.0120 M solution of NaCl in water at 0 °C. Assume the van't Hoff factor, i, is 1.94 for this solution.

Colloids
(See Section 14.5 and ChemistryNow Screen 14.10.)

49. When solutions of $BaCl_2$ and Na_2SO_4 are mixed, the mixture becomes cloudy. After a few days, a white solid is observed on the bottom of the beaker with a clear liquid above it.
    (a) Write a balanced equation for the reaction that occurs.
    (b) Why is the solution cloudy at first?
    (c) What happens during the few days of waiting?

50. ■ The dispersed phase of a certain colloidal dispersion consists of spheres of diameter 1.0×10^2 nm.
    (a) What are the volume ($V = \frac{4}{3}\pi r^3$) and surface area ($A = 4\pi r^2$) of each sphere?
    (b) How many spheres are required to give a total volume of 1.0 cm³? What is the total surface area of these spheres in square meters?

General Questions

These questions are not designated as to type or location in the chapter. They may combine several concepts.

51. Phenylcarbinol is used in nasal sprays as a preservative. A solution of 0.52 g of the compound in 25.0 g of water has a melting point of −0.36 °C. What is the molar mass of phenylcarbinol?

52. (a) Which aqueous solution is expected to have the higher boiling point: 0.10 m Na_2SO_4 or 0.15 m sugar?
    (b) For which aqueous solution is the vapor pressure of water higher: 0.30 m NH_4NO_3 or 0.15 m Na_2SO_4?

53. ■ Arrange the following aqueous solutions in order of (i) increasing vapor pressure of water and (ii) increasing boiling point.
    (a) 0.35 m $HOCH_2CH_2OH$ (a nonvolatile solute)
    (b) 0.50 m sugar
    (c) 0.20 m KBr (a strong electrolyte)
    (d) 0.20 m Na_2SO_4 (a strong electrolyte)

54. Making homemade ice cream is one of life's great pleasures. Fresh milk and cream, sugar, and flavorings are churned in a bucket suspended in an ice–water mixture, the freezing point of which has been lowered by adding rock salt. One manufacturer of home ice cream freezers recommends adding 2.50 lb (1130 g) of rock salt (NaCl) to 16.0 lb of ice (7250 g) in a 4-qt freezer. For the solution when this mixture melts, calculate the following:
    (a) the weight percent of NaCl
    (b) the mole fraction of NaCl
    (c) the molality of the solution

55. Dimethylglyoxime [DMG, $(CH_3CNOH)_2$] is used as a reagent to precipitate nickel ion. Assume that 53.0 g of DMG has been dissolved in 525 g of ethanol (C_2H_5OH).

The red, insoluble compound formed between nickel(II) ion and dimethylglyoxime (DMG) is precipitated when DMG is added to a basic solution of Ni^{2+}(aq).

    (a) What is the mole fraction of DMG?
    (b) What is the molality of the solution?
    (c) What is the vapor pressure of the ethanol over the solution at ethanol's normal boiling point of 78.4 °C?
    (d) What is the boiling point of the solution? (DMG does not produce ions in solution.) (K_{bp} for ethanol = +1.22 °C/m)

56. ■ A 10.7 m solution of NaOH has a density of 1.33 g/cm³ at 20 °C. Calculate the following:
    (a) the mole fraction of NaOH
    (b) the weight percent of NaOH
    (c) the molarity of the solution

57. Concentrated aqueous ammonia has a molarity of 14.8 mol/L and a density of 0.90 g/cm³. What is the molality of the solution? Calculate the mole fraction and weight percent of NH_3.

58. ■ If you dissolve 2.00 g of $Ca(NO_3)_2$ in 750 g of water, what is the molality of $Ca(NO_3)_2$? What is the total molality of ions in solution? (Assume total dissociation of the ionic solid.)

59. If you want a solution that is 0.100 m in ions, what mass of Na_2SO_4 must you dissolve in 125 g of water? (Assume total dissociation of the ionic solid.)

60. ■ Consider the following aqueous solutions: (i) 0.20 m $HOCH_2CH_2OH$ (nonvolatile, nonelectrolyte); (ii) 0.10 m $CaCl_2$; (iii) 0.12 m KBr; and (iv) 0.12 m Na_2SO_4.
  (a) Which solution has the highest boiling point?
  (b) Which solution has the lowest freezing point?
  (c) Which solution has the highest water vapor pressure?

61. ■ (a) Which solution is expected to have the higher boiling point: 0.20 m KBr or 0.30 m sugar?
  (b) Which aqueous solution has the lower freezing point: 0.12 m NH_4NO_3 or 0.10 m Na_2CO_3?

62. The solubility of NaCl in water at 100 °C is 39.1 g/100. g of water. Calculate the boiling point of this solution. (Assume i = 1.85 for NaCl.)

63. Instead of using NaCl to melt the ice on your sidewalk, you decide to use $CaCl_2$. If you add 35.0 g of $CaCl_2$ to 150. g of water, what is the freezing point of the solution? (Assume i = 2.7 for $CaCl_2$.)

64. ■ The smell of ripe raspberries is due to 4-(p-hydroxyphenyl)-2-butanone, which has the empirical formula C_5H_6O. To find its molecular formula, you dissolve 0.135 g in 25.0 g of chloroform, $CHCl_3$. The boiling point of the solution is 61.82 °C. What is the molecular formula of the solute?

65. Hexachlorophene has been used in germicidal soap. What is its molar mass if 0.640 g of the compound, dissolved in 25.0 g of chloroform, produces a solution whose boiling point is 61.93 °C?

66. The solubility of ammonium formate, NH_4CHO_2, in 100 g of water is 102 g at 0 °C and 546 g at 80 °C. A solution is prepared by dissolving NH_4CHO_2 in 200 g of water until no more will dissolve at 80 °C. The solution is then cooled to 0 °C. What mass of NH_4CHO_2 precipitates? (Assume that no water evaporates and that the solution is not supersaturated.)

67. ■ How much N_2 can dissolve in water at 25 °C if the N_2 partial pressure is 585 mm Hg?

68. Cigars are best stored in a "humidor" at 18 °C and 55% relative humidity. This means the pressure of water vapor should be 55% of the vapor pressure of pure water at the same temperature. The proper humidity can be maintained by placing a solution of glycerol $[C_3H_5(OH)_3]$ and water in the humidor. Calculate the percent by mass of glycerol that will lower the vapor pressure of water to the desired value. (The vapor pressure of glycerol is negligible.)

69. An aqueous solution containing 10.0 g of starch per liter has an osmotic pressure of 3.8 mm Hg at 25 °C.
  (a) What is the average molar mass of starch? (Because not all starch molecules are identical, the result will be an average.)
  (b) What is the freezing point of the solution? Would it be easy to determine the molecular weight of starch by measuring the freezing point depression? (Assume that the molarity and molality are the same for this solution.)

70. Vinegar is a 5% solution (by weight) of acetic acid in water. Determine the mole fraction and molality of acetic acid. What is the concentration of acetic acid in parts per million (ppm)? Explain why it is not possible to calculate the molarity of this solution from the information provided.

71. ■ Calculate the enthalpies of solution for Li_2SO_4 and K_2SO_4. Are the solution processes exothermic or endothermic? Compare them with LiCl and KCl. What similarities or differences do you find?

Compound	$\Delta_f H°(s)$ (kJ/mol)	$\Delta_f H°(aq, 1\ m)$ (kJ/mol)
Li_2SO_4	−1436.4	−1464.4
K_2SO_4	−1437.7	−1414.0

72. ▲ Water at 25 °C has a density of 0.997 g/cm³. Calculate the molality and molarity of pure water at this temperature.

73. ▲ If a volatile solute is added to a volatile solvent, both substances contribute to the vapor pressure over the solution. Assuming an ideal solution, the vapor pressure of each is given by Raoult's law, and the total vapor pressure is the sum of the vapor pressures for each component. A solution, assumed to be ideal, is made from 1.0 mol of toluene ($C_6H_5CH_3$) and 2.0 mol of benzene (C_6H_6). The vapor pressures of the pure solvents are 22 mm Hg and 75 mm Hg, respectively, at 20 °C. What is the total vapor pressure of the mixture? What is the mole fraction of each component in the liquid and in the vapor?

74. ■ A solution is made by adding 50.0 mL of ethanol (C_2H_5OH, d = 0.789 g/ml) to 50.0 mL of water (d = 0.998 g/mL). What is the total vapor pressure over the solution at 20 °C? (See Study Question 73.) The vapor pressure of ethanol at 20 °C is 43.6 mm Hg.

75. A 2.0% (by mass) aqueous solution of novocainium chloride ($C_{13}H_{21}ClN_2O_2$) freezes at −0.237 °C. Calculate the van't Hoff factor, i. How many moles of ions are in the solution per mole of compound?

76. A solution is 4.00% (by mass) maltose and 96.00% water. It freezes at −0.229 °C.
  (a) Calculate the molar mass of maltose (which is not an ionic compound).
  (b) The density of the solution is 1.014 g/mL. Calculate the osmotic pressure of the solution.

▲ more challenging   ■ in OWL   Blue-numbered questions answered in Appendix O

77. ▲ The following table lists the concentrations of the principal ions in sea water:

Concentration

Ion	(ppm)
Cl^-	1.95×10^4
Na^+	1.08×10^4
Mg^{2+}	1.29×10^3
SO_4^{2-}	9.05×10^2
Ca^{2+}	4.12×10^2
K^+	3.80×10^2
Br^-	67

(a) Calculate the freezing point of water.
(b) Calculate the osmotic pressure of sea water at 25 °C. What is the minimum pressure needed to purify sea water by reverse osmosis?

78. ■ ▲ A tree is exactly 10 m tall.
(a) What must be the total molarity of the solutes if sap rises to the top of the tree by osmotic pressure at 20 °C? Assume the groundwater outside the tree is pure water and that the density of the sap is 1.0 g/mL. (1 mm Hg = 13.6 mm H_2O.)
(b) If the only solute in the sap is sucrose, $C_{12}H_{22}O_{11}$, what is its percent by mass?

79. ■ A 2.00% solution of H_2SO_4 in water freezes at −0.796 °C.
(a) Calculate the van't Hoff factor, i.
(b) Which of the following best represents sulfuric acid in a dilute aqueous solution: H_2SO_4, $H_3O^+ + HSO_4^-$, or $2 H_3O^+ + SO_4^{2-}$?

80. ■ A compound is known to be a potassium halide, KX. If 4.00 g of the salt is dissolved in exactly 100 g of water, the solution freezes at −1.28 °C. Identify the halide ion in this formula.

In the Laboratory

81. ▲ A solution of benzoic acid in benzene has a freezing point of 3.1 °C and a boiling point of 82.6 °C. (The freezing point of pure benzene is 5.50 °C, and its boiling point is 80.1 °C.) The structure of benzoic acid is

What can you conclude about the state of the benzoic acid molecules at the two different temperatures? Recall the discussion of hydrogen bonding in Section 12.2, and see Figure 12.7.

82. ▲ ■ You dissolve 5.0 mg of iodine, I_2, in 25 mL of water. You then add 10.0 mL of CCl_4 and shake the mixture. If I_2 is 85 times more soluble in CCl_4 than in H_2O (on a volume basis), what are the masses of I_2 in the water and CCl_4 layers after shaking? (See Figure 14.6.)

83. ▲ A solution of 5.00 g of acetic acid in 100. g of benzene freezes at 3.37 °C. A solution of 5.00 g of acetic acid in 100. g of water freezes at −1.49 °C. Find the molar mass of acetic acid from each of these experiments. What can you conclude about the state of the acetic acid molecules dissolved in each of these solvents? Recall the discussion of hydrogen bonding in Section 12.2 (and see Figure 12.7), and propose a structure for the species in benzene solution.

84. ▲ ■ In a police forensics lab, you examine a package that may contain heroin. However, you find the white powder is not pure heroin but a mixture of heroin ($C_{21}H_{23}O_5N$) and lactose ($C_{12}H_{22}O_{11}$). To determine the amount of heroin in the mixture, you dissolve 1.00 g of the white powdery mixture in water in a 100.0-mL volumetric flask. You find that the solution has an osmotic pressure of 539 mm Hg at 25 °C. What is the composition of the mixture?

85. ■ A newly synthesized compound containing boron and fluorine is 22.1% boron. Dissolving 0.146 g of the compound in 10.0 g of benzene gives a solution with a vapor pressure of 94.16 mm Hg at 25 °C. (The vapor pressure of pure benzene at this temperature is 95.26 mm Hg.) In a separate experiment, it is found that the compound does not have a dipole moment.
(a) What is the molecular formula for the compound?
(b) Draw a Lewis structure for the molecule, and suggest a possible molecular structure. Give the bond angles in the molecule and the hybridization of the boron atom.

86. In chemical research we often send newly synthesized compounds to commercial laboratories for analysis. These laboratories determine the weight percent of C and H by burning the compound and collecting the evolved CO_2 and H_2O. They determine the molar mass by measuring the osmotic pressure of a solution of the compound. Calculate the empirical and molecular formulas of a compound, C_xH_yCr, given the following information:
(a) The compound contains 73.94% C and 8.27% H; the remainder is chromium.
(b) At 25 °C, the osmotic pressure of a solution containing 5.00 mg of the unknown dissolved in exactly 100 mL of chloroform solution is 3.17 mm Hg.

Summary and Conceptual Questions

The following questions may use concepts from this and previous chapters.

87. In each pair of ionic compounds, which is more likely to have the more negative enthalpy of hydration? Briefly explain your reasoning in each case.
    (a) LiF or RbF
    (b) KNO_3 or $Ca(NO_3)_2$
    (c) CsBr or $CuBr_2$

88. ■ When salts of Mg^{2+}, Ca^{2+}, and Be^{2+} are placed in water, the positive ion is hydrated (as is the negative ion). Which of these three cations is most strongly hydrated? Which one is least strongly hydrated?

89. Which salt, Li_2SO_4 or Cs_2SO_4, is expected to have the more exothermic enthalpy of hydration? Explain briefly.

90. Explain why a cucumber shrivels up when it is placed in a concentrated solution of salt.

91. If you dissolve equal molar amounts of NaCl and $CaCl_2$ in water, the $CaCl_2$ lowers the freezing point of the water almost 1.5 times as much as the NaCl. Why?

92. A 100.-gram sample of sodium chloride (NaCl) is added to 100. mL of water at 0 °C. After equilibrium is reached, about 64 g of solid remains undissolved. Describe the equilibrium that exists in this system at the particulate level.

93. ■ Which of the following substances is/are likely to dissolve in water, and which is/are likely to dissolve in benzene (C_6H_6)?
    (a) $NaNO_3$
    (b) diethyl ether, $CH_3CH_2OCH_2CH_3$
    (c) naphthalene, $C_{10}H_8$ (see page 458 for structure)
    (d) NH_4Cl

94. Account for the fact that alcohols such as methanol (CH_3OH) and ethanol (C_2H_5OH) are quite miscible with water, whereas an alcohol with a long-carbon chain, such as octanol ($C_8H_{17}OH$), is poorly soluble in water.

95. Starch contains C—C, C—H, C—O, and O—H bonds. Hydrocarbons have only C—C and C—H bonds. Both starch and hydrocarbons can form colloidal dispersions in water. Which dispersion is classified as hydrophobic? Which is hydrophilic? Explain briefly.

96. ■ Which substance would have the greater influence on the vapor pressure of water when added to 1000. g of the liquid: 10.0 g of sucrose ($C_{12}H_{22}O_{11}$) or 10.0 g of ethylene glycol [$HOCH_2CH_2OH$]?

97. ■ Suppose you have two aqueous solutions separated by a semipermeable membrane. One contains 5.85 g of NaCl dissolved in 100. mL of solution, and the other contains 8.88 g of KNO_3 dissolved in 100. mL of solution. In which direction will solvent flow: from the NaCl solution to the KNO_3 solution, or from KNO_3 to NaCl? Explain briefly.

98. A protozoan (single-celled animal) that normally lives in the ocean is placed in fresh water. Will it shrivel or burst? Explain briefly.

99. In the process of distillation, a mixture of two (or more) volatile liquids is first heated to convert the volatile materials to the vapor state. Then the vapor is condensed, reforming the liquid. The net result of this liquid→ vapor→ liquid conversion is to enrich the fraction of a more volatile component in the mixture in the condensate. We can describe how this occurs using Raoult's law. Imagine that you have a mixture of 12% (by weight) ethanol and water (as formed, for example, by fermentation of grapes.)
    (a) What are the mole fractions of ethanol and water in this mixture?
    (b) This mixture is heated to 78.5 °C (the normal boiling point of ethanol). What are the equilibrium vapor pressures of ethanol and water at this temperature, assuming Raoult's Law (ideal) behavior? (You will need to derive the equilibrium vapor pressure of water at 78.5 °C from data in Appendix G.)
    (c) What are the mole fractions of ethanol and water in the vapor?
    (d) After this vapor is condensed to a liquid, to what extent has the mole fraction of ethanol been enriched? What is the mass fraction of ethanol in the condensate?

100. Sodium chloride (NaCl) is commonly used to melt ice on roads during the winter. Calcium chloride ($CaCl_2$) is sometimes used for this purpose too. Let us compare the effectiveness of equal masses of these two compounds in lowering the freezing point of water, by calculating the freezing point lowering of solutions containing 200 g of each salt in 1.00 kg of water. (An advantage of $CaCl_2$ is that it acts more quickly because it is hygroscopic, that is, it absorbs moisture from the air to give a solution and begin the process. A disadvantage is that this compound is more costly).

101. Review the trend in values of the van't Hoff factor i as a function of concentration (Table 14.4). Use the following data to calculate the van't Hoff factor for a NaCl concentration of 5.0 mass % (for which $\Delta T = -3.05$ °C) and a Na_2SO_4 concentration of 5.0 mass % (for which $\Delta T = -1.36$ °C). Are these values in line with your expectations based on the trend in the values given in Table 14.4? Speculate on why this trend is seen.

▲ more challenging   ■ in OWL   Blue-numbered questions answered in Appendix O

102. The table below give experimentally determined values for freezing points of 1.00% solutions (mass %) of a series of acids.

(a) Calculate the molality of each solution, determine the calculated freezing points, and then calculate the values of the van't Hoff factor i. Fill these values into the table.

Acid, (1.00 mass %)	molality (mol/kg H_2O)	$T_{measured}$ (°C)	$T_{calculated}$ (°C)	i
HNO_3		0.56		
CH_3CO_2H		0.32		
H_2SO_4		0.42		
$H_2C_2O_4$		0.30		
HCO_2H		0.42		
CCl_3CO_2H		0.21		

(b) Analyze the results, comparing the values of i for the various acids. How does this data relate to acid strengths? (The discussion of strong and weak acids on pages 132 and 133 will assist you to answer this question.)

103. It is interesting how the Fahrenheit temperature scale was established. One report, given by Fahrenheit in a paper in 1724, stated that the value of 0 °F was established as the freezing temperature of saturated solutions of sea salt. From the literature we find that the freezing point of a 20% by mass solution of NaCl is −16.46 °C (This is the lowest freezing temperature reported for solutions of NaCl). Does this value lend credence to this story of the establishment of the Fahrenheit scale?

104. The osmotic pressure exerted by seawater at 25 °C is about 27 atm. Calculate the concentration of ions dissolved in seawater that is needed to give an osmotic pressure of this magnitude. (Desalinization of sea water is accomplished by reverse osmosis. In this process an applied pressure forces water through a membrane against a concentration gradient. The minimum external force needed for this process will be 27 atm. Actually, to accomplish the process at a reasonable rate, the applied pressure needs to be about twice this value.)

Let's Review | Chapters 11–14

Many of us love the beach, and of course there are things of interest in chemistry there. The sand on the beach consists of many different substances, among them pulverized corals and sea shells. Another ingredient is quartz sand. A tiny portion of the structure of quartz is shown in the inset in the photograph. The water washing onto the sand is a most peculiar substance. One of its properties is that it can dissolve substances of many kinds—ionic salts and gases, among others. Water does not dissolve the sand itself, although the sand does become wet, and wet sand makes wonderful sand castles. And the ocean itself is a solution of sodium chloride plus many other dissolved salts.

THE PURPOSE OF *LET'S REVIEW*

- *Let's Review* provides additional questions for Chapters 11 through 14. Routine questions covering the concepts in a chapter are in the Study Questions at the end of that chapter and are usually identified by topic. In contrast, *Let's Review* questions combine several concepts from one or more chapters. Many come from the examinations given by the authors and others are based on actual experiments or processes in chemical research or in the chemical industries.

- *Let's Review* provides guidance for Chapters 11 through 14 as you prepare for an exam on these chapters. Although this is designated for Chapters 11 through 14 you may choose only material appropriate to the exam in your course.

- To direct your review, **Comprehensive Questions** are correlated with relevant chapter sections and with the OWL online homework system to which you may have purchased access. Some questions may include a screen shot from one of these tools so you see what resources are available to help you review.

PREPARING FOR AN EXAMINATION ON CHAPTERS 11–14

1. Review **Go Chemistry** modules for these chapters. Go Chemistry modules are available at **www.cengage.com/chemistry/kotz** or **www.ichapters.com**.

2. Take the ChemistryNow **Pre-Test** and work through your **Personalized Learning Plan.** Work through ChemistryNow **Exercises, Guided Simulations,** and **Intelligent Tutors.**

3. **OWL** If you subscribe to OWL, use the **Tutorials** in that system.

4. Work on the questions below that are relevant to a particular chapter or chapters. See the solutions to those questions at the end of this section.

5. For background and help answering a question, use the Go Chemistry and OWL questions correlated with it.

KEY POINTS TO KNOW FOR CHAPTERS 11–14

Here are some of the key points you must know to be successful in Chapters 11–14.

- The gas laws: Boyle's and Charles's laws and Avogadro's hypothesis.
- The ideal gas law, $PV = nRT$.
- Reaction stoichiometry and the gas laws.
- Kinetic-molecular theory and its connection to the gas laws and gas behavior.
- The non-ideal behavior of gases.
- Intermolecular forces and their effects.
- The importance of hydrogen bonding and the circumstances under which it occurs.
- The properties of liquids (such as melting and boiling point, vapor pressure, critical temperature and pressure).
- Unit cells of solids, especially cubic unit cells.
- Lattice energy and physical properties of solids.
- Interpretation of phase diagrams.
- Solution concentration.
- Solubility and the process of dissolving.
- Colligative properties of solutions (melting point depression, boiling point elevation, osmotic pressure).

EXAMINATION PREPARATION QUESTIONS

▲ denotes more challenging questions.

Important information about the questions that follow:

- See the Study Questions in each chapter for questions on basic concepts.
- Some of these questions arise from recent research in chemistry and the other sciences. They often involve concepts from more than one chapter and may be more challenging than those in earlier chapters. Not all chapter goals or concepts are necessarily addressed in these questions.
- **Assessing Key Points** are short-answer questions covering the Key Points to Know on this page.
- **Comprehensive Questions** bring together concepts from multiple chapters and are correlated with text sections covering that topic, with Go Chemistry modules, and with questions in OWL that may provide additional background.
- The screens shots are largely taken from Go Chemistry modules available at **www.cengage.com/chemistry/kotz** or **www.ichapters.com.**

Assessing Key Points

1. (Chapter 11) You have a 5.0 L flask filled with N_2 at a pressure of 735 mm Hg at 21 °C.
   (a) How many N_2 molecules are in the flask?
   (b) If the N_2 originally in the 5.0-L flask is placed in a 2.5-L flask and cooled to 0.0 °C, what is the pressure under the new conditions?

2. (Chapter 11) Consider the following gases: He, SO_2, CO_2, and Cl_2.
   (a) Which has the largest density (assuming that all gases are at the same T and P)?
   (b) Which gas will effuse fastest through a porous plate?

3. (Chapter 11) What volume (in liters) of O_2, measured at standard temperature and pressure, is required to oxidize 0.400 mol of phosphorus (P_4)?

$$P_4(s) + 5\ O_2(g) \rightarrow P_4O_{10}(s)$$

4. (Chapter 11) Several small molecules (besides water) are important in biochemical systems: O_2, CO, CO_2, and NO. You have isolated one of these, and to identify it you determine its molar mass. You release 0.37 g of the gas into an evacuated flask with a volume of 732 mL at 21 °C. The gas pressure in the flask is 209 mm Hg. What is the unknown gas?

5. (Chapter 11) Under which set of conditions will CO_2 deviate most from ideal gas behavior?
   (a) 1 atm, 0 °C   (c) 10 atm, 0 °C
   (b) 0.1 atm, 100 °C   (d) 1 atm, 100 °C

6. (Chapter 11) A 10.0-L flask contains the following mixture of gases at 25 °C: 16 g of O_2, 28 g of N_2, 2.0 g of He, and 4.0 g of H_2.
   (a) What is the total pressure in the flask?
   (b) Which gas exerts the largest partial pressure?

7. (Chapter 11) Air contains 21 mol % O_2. If the pressure of air in a room is 745 mm Hg, what is the partial pressure of O_2?

8. (Chapter 11) Two flasks, each with a volume of 1.00 L, contain O_2 with a pressure of 380 mm Hg. Flask A is inside the Chemistry Building where the temperature is 25 °C. Flask B is outside in the cold winter air at 0 °C.
   (a) Which flask contains the greater number of O_2 molecules?
   (b) Which flask contains O_2 molecules with greater average speed? With greater average kinetic energy?

9. (Chapter 11) Rank the following gases in order of increasing average molecular speed at a given temperature: CO, CO_2, O_2, and NH_3. (The relation between molar mass and molecular speed can be explored using Go Chemistry module 16 on the Gas Laws and the Kinetic-Molecular Theory.)

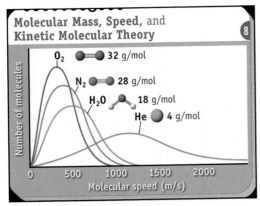

Molecular Mass, Speed, and Kinetic Molecular Theory

8

O_2 ●=● 32 g/mol
N_2 ●=● 28 g/mol
H_2O ● 18 g/mol
He ● 4 g/mol

Number of molecules

0   500   1000   1500   2000
Molecular speed (m/s)

Screen from Go Chemistry module 16 on
the gas laws and kinetic-molecular theory

10. (Chapter 11) Propane reacts with O_2 according to the equation

$$C_3H_8(g) + 5 O_2(g) \rightarrow 3 CO_2(g) + 4 H_2O(g)$$

You mix C_3H_8 with O_2 in the correct stoichiometric ratio, and the total pressure of the mixture is 120 mm Hg at some temperature.
(a) What are the partial pressures of C_3H_8 and O_2?
(b) What will be the partial pressure of water vapor, at the same temperature, after complete reaction?

11. (Chapter 12) In samples of which of the following pure substances will there be hydrogen bonding between molecules: H_2O, CH_3OCH_3, CH_3OH, CH_4, H_2, HNO_3?

12. (Chapter 12) Which of the following compounds would be expected to form intermolecular hydrogen bonds with water?
(a) CH_3OCH_3 (dimethyl ether)

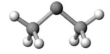

(b) C_3H_8 (propane)

(c) CH_3CO_2H (acetic acid)

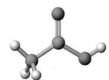

(d) Aspirin $C_6H_4(CO_2H)(CO_2CH_3)$

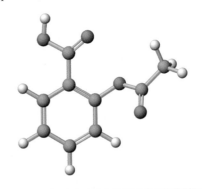

INTERMOLECULAR FORCES
Example

14

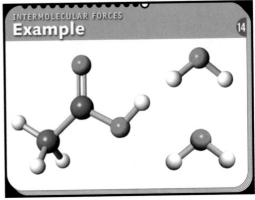

Screen from Go Chemistry module 17
on intermolecular forces.

13. (Chapter 12) Rank the following compounds in terms of increasing strength of intermolecular forces in the pure substance: Ar, CH_3OH, CO_2, NH_3

14. (Chapter 12) The following types of intermolecular forces are generally found to be important:

(i) ion-dipole
(ii) dipole-induced dipole
(iii) dipole-dipole
(iv) induced dipole-induced dipole
(v) hydrogen bonds

Decide which type of intermolecular force is most important for each of the following systems.
(a) Between methane (CH_4) molecules in liquid methane.
(b) Between H_2O and CH_3OH molecules in a mixture of the liquids.
(c) Between Li^+ and Cl^- ions and water in aqueous lithium chloride.
(d) Between O_2 and H_2O molecules when O_2 is dissolved in water.

15. (Chapter 12) Rank the following substances in order of increasing boiling point: (a) Ne, (b) CH_3OH, and (c) SO_2.

16. (Chapter 12) Use the vapor pressure curves for carbon disulfide (CS_2), ethanol (CH_3CH_2OH), and heptane (C_7H_{16}) below to answer the following questions:

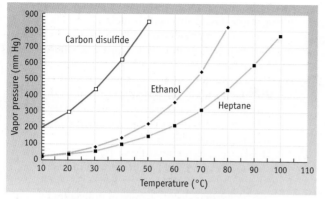

Vapor pressure curves for carbon disulfide (CS_2), ethanol (CH_3CH_2OH), and heptane (C_7H_{16})

(a) What is the vapor pressure of heptane at 70 °C?
(b) What is the normal boiling point of ethanol?
(c) What types of intermolecular forces exist
  (i) between two CS_2 molecules?
  (ii) between two heptane molecules?
  (iii) between two ethanol molecules?
(d) Decide if each substance is a liquid or vapor when the pressure is 600 mm Hg and the temperature is 50 °C.
(e) Which of these molecules is expected to dissolve readily in water?
(f) Which has the higher normal boiling point, ethanol or CS_2? Explain.
(g) Which has the higher normal boiling point, heptane or CS_2? Explain.

17. (Chapter 13) Types of solids include molecular solids, metallic solids, network solids, amorphous solids, and ionic solids. Classify each of the following solids:
(a) $CaCO_3$
(b) polyethylene
(c) tungsten
(d) solid CO_2 (dry ice)

18. (Chapter 13) Magnesium oxide has a NaCl-like crystal structure.

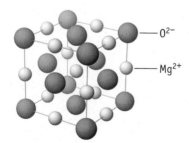

Unit cell of MgO

(a) In which type of unit cell are the O^{2-} ions arranged?
(b) How many Mg^{2+} ions are there per unit cell?

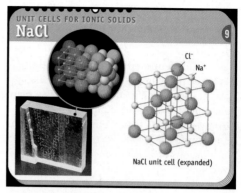

Screen from Go Chemistry module 18 on unit cells

19. (Chapter 12) List the compounds in each set in order of increasing boiling point, then explain your choice in terms of intermolecular forces.
(a) CH_3CO_2H, CH_3OCH_3, CH_3CH_2OH
(b) hexane (C_6H_{14}), octane (C_8H_{18}), propane (C_3H_8)

20. (Chapter 13) The following data are available for methane at the NIST website (National Institutes for Standards and Technology, http://webbook.nist.gov/chemistry/):

Triple point = 90.67 K at 0.117 bar
Normal melting point = 90.69 K
Normal boiling point = 111.2 K
Critical T = 190.6 K at critical P = 46.1 bar

(a) Is solid methane more or less dense than liquid methane?
(b) Can methane be liquefied at 0 °C?

21. (Chapter 14) At 20 °C you dissolve 45.0 g of dimethylglyoxime (DMG) ($C_4H_8N_2O_2$) in 500. mL of ethanol, C_2H_5OH (density of ethanol at 20 °C = 0.790 g/mL). Calculate the molality and weight percent of DMG.

22. (Chapter 14) Which of the following aqueous solutions has the highest boiling point? The lowest freezing point? The highest vapor pressure? The highest osmotic pressure?
(a) 0.20 m $C_2H_4(OH)_2$ (nonvolatile, nonelectrolyte)
(b) 0.10 m $MgCl_2$
(c) 0.12 m KBr
(d) 0.12 m K_2SO_4

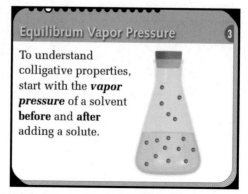

Screen from Go Chemistry module 19 on colligative properties

23. (Chapter 14) Which of the following ions should have the most negative enthalpy of hydration: Rb^+, Mg^{2+}, Na^+, or Ba^{2+}?

24. (Chapter 14) Concentrated salt solutions have boiling points lower than those calculated using the equation $\Delta T_{bp} = K_{bp} \cdot m$. Which of the following is a reasonable explanation of this observation?
(a) Positive ions repel each other more at high concentration.
(b) In solutions of higher concentration there is ion pairing.
(c) The water molecules will have a greater attraction for each other.
(d) Concentrated solutions contain small particles of nondissolved salt, thus lowering the molality.

25. (Chapter 14) You dissolve 29.3 g of NaCl in 500. g water. What is the freezing point of this solution?

26. (Chapter 14) Erythritol is a compound that occurs naturally in algae and fungi. It is about twice as sweet as sucrose. A solution of 2.50 g of erythritol in 50.0 g of water freezes at $-0.762\ °C$. What is the molar mass of the compound?

27. (Chapter 12) Below you see the OWL Simulation (12.4c) on vapor pressures. Here you can observe the behavior of the vapor pressure of pentane (C_5H_{12}) and hexane (C_6H_{14}) at various temperatures.
(a) Which has the higher vapor pressure at all temperatures and why?
(b) Vapor pressure data for hexane at two temperatures are given below. Use these to calculate the molar enthalpy of vaporization of hexane.

Temperature (K)	Vapor Pressure (mm Hg)
273	48.3
323	399.2

(c) Use the calculated $\Delta_{vap}H°$ from part (b) to estimate the normal boiling point of hexane.

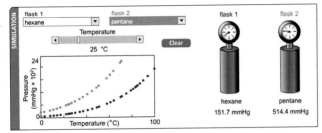

OWL Simulation 12.4c: Vapor Pressure

Comprehensive Questions

28. (Chapters 11 and 12) Researchers at the Fred Hutchison Cancer Research Center in Seattle discovered that mice can be put into a state of suspended animation by applying a low dose of hydrogen sulfide, H_2S. The breathing rate of the mice fell from 120 to 10 breaths a minute and their temperature fell to just $2\ °C$ above ambient temperature. Six hours later the mice were revived and seemed to show no negative effects.
(a) Hydrogen sulfide is a gas at room temperature and normal atmospheric pressure whereas water is a liquid with a low vapor pressure under the same conditions. Explain this difference.
(b) The H_2S gas in the mixture of H_2S and air delivered to the mice had a concentration of 80. ppm. (A concentration of 1 ppm is 1 part per million, or one molecule in every 1 million molecules.) If you deliver 1.0 L of gas (a mixture of O_2, N_2, and H_2S) at a total pressure of 725 mm Hg at a temperature of $22\ °C$, what is the partial pressure of the H_2S gas?
(c) Hydrogen sulfide can be converted to sulfuric acid. If 5.2 L of H_2S gas at 130 mm Hg pressure and $25\ °C$ is allowed to react with O_2 gas, how many liters of O_2 gas, also at 130 mm Hg pressure and $25\ °C$, are required for complete reaction? Assume the following reaction occurs.

$$H_2S(g) + 2\ O_2(g) \rightarrow H_2SO_4(\ell)$$

Text Sections: 11.2–11.5 and 12.2–12.4
OWL Questions: 11.4b, 11.5, 12.2-3c, 12.2–3e

29. (Chapter 11) A common industrial chemical, butyl acrylate, is made by combining acetylene (C_2H_2), butanol (C_4H_9OH), and CO in the presence of a catalyst. If you release 25.7 mg of the volatile liquid product of the reaction into a flask with a volume of 732 mL at $25\ °C$, the pressure is 5.10 mm Hg. What is the molar mass of the gas? Based on the reactants in the reaction, what is its formula?
Text Section: 11.3
OWL Question: 11.3f

30. (Chapters 4 and 12) Jacques Charles used 225 kg of H_2SO_4 and 450. kg of Fe to prepare H_2 gas for one of his earliest lighter-than-air balloon flights (August 1783; see text page 533). Assume that the atmospheric pressure that day was 735 mm Hg, and the temperature was $18\ °C$. What was the volume of the balloon (that is, the volume needed to contain this gas)? The hydrogen-forming reaction is

$$Fe(s) + H_2SO_4(aq) \rightarrow FeSO_4(s) + H_2(g)$$

Text Sections: 4.2 and 11.3
OWL Questions: 4.2f, 11.3b

31. (Chapter 11) Mercury has been poured into the U-tube, shown below, trapping air in the right side. What is the pressure of the trapped air? The (external) atmospheric pressure is 743 mm Hg.

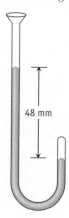

48 mm

Text Section: 11.1
OWL Question: 11.1

32. (Chapter 11) Unlike balloons made of rubber, balloons made of Mylar do not stretch. If you add gas to a Mylar balloon, the volume increases and, while filling, the pressure inside equals the pressure outside. This persists until the balloon is filled. After that, addition of gas will cause the pressure inside the balloon to increase above that of the outside atmosphere, and the volume won't change. At some point, you will exceed the tensile strength of the plastic film and the balloon will break.

(a) You place 4.8 g of dry ice [$CO_2(s)$] in a Mylar balloon whose volume when filled is 2.33 L. The dry ice sublimes and the gaseous CO_2 warms to room temperature, 18 °C. Atmospheric pressure that day is 0.98 atm. Assume there is no air inside the balloon at the start of this experiment. First, determine if the balloon is underfilled and the pressure inside is 0.98 atm or if the balloon is overfilled and the pressure inside is greater than 0.98 atm. Then, determine the actual pressure of gas inside the balloon.

(b) Compare the number of molecules of CO_2 used to fill the balloon in part (a) with the number of atoms of helium needed to fill the same balloon to the pressure calculated in (a).

(c) In which balloon (the one with He or the one with CO_2) are the gas molecules or atoms traveling at a greater average speed? Compare their relative average kinetic energies at 18 °C?

Text Sections: 11.2, 11.3, and 11.6
OWL Questions: 11.3b, 11.6e

33. (Chapter 11) Carbon dioxide, CO_2, was determined to effuse through a porous plate at the rate of 0.0330 mol/min. The same amount of an unknown gas, 0.0330 moles, is found to effuse through the same porous barrier in 104 seconds. Calculate the molar mass of the unknown gas.

Text Section: 11.7
OWL Question: 11.7c

34. (Chapters 8, 9, and 12) Bonding, structure, and properties of formamide, $HCONH_2$.

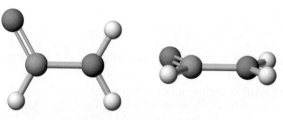

Front and side views of formamide, $HCONH_2$

(a) Draw an electron dot structure for formamide, Include all resonance structures.

(b) What is the C atom hybridization?

(c) Is the molecule polar?

(d) Can two formamide molecules interact by hydrogen bonding? Can formamide interact with water by hydrogen bonding?

(e) As indicated in the molecular model, the molecule is flat. Suggest a reason for the planar structure of the molecule.

(f) The enthalpy of vaporization of formamide at 25 °C is 60.15 kJ/mol. What is the enthalpy change for the vaporization of 10.0 g of the compound at 25 °C?

Text Sections: 8.2, 8.4, 8.8, 9.2, 12.2, and 12.4
OWL Questions: 8.4b, 8.5d, 8.8b, 9.2f, 9.2h, 12.2–3c, 12.4b

35. (Chapters 11 and 12) Acetone is a common solvent.

Acetone, $(CH_3)_2CO$

(a) Allyl alcohol, $CH_2=CH—CH_2OH$, is an isomer of acetone. Acetone has a vapor pressure of 100 mm Hg at +7.7 °C. Predict whether the vapor pressure of allyl alcohol is higher or lower than 100 mm Hg at this temperature. Explain.

(b) Use the Clausius-Clapeyron equation to calculate the enthalpy of vaporization of acetone from the following data.

Temperature (°C)	Vapor Pressure (mm Hg)
−9.4	40.
+7.7	100.
39.5	400.
56.5	760.

(c) Fluorination of acetone, C_3H_6O, by substituting fluorine atoms for some or all of the H atoms, produces a gaseous compound with the formula $C_3H_{6-x}F_xO$. To identify this compound its molar mass was determined by measuring gas density. The following data were obtained: Mass of gas, 1.53 g;

volume of flask = 264 mL; pressure exerted by gas, 722 mm Hg; temperature, 22 °C. Calculate the molar mass, then identify the molecular formula.

Text Sections: 11.3, 12.2, and 12.4
OWL Questions: 11.3b, 11.3f, 12.2–3c, 12.4g

36. (Chapter 13) Butane, the fuel in lighters and camping stoves, has the following physical properties:

Normal melting point = 136 K
Normal boiling point = 273 K
Triple point = 134.6 K at 7×10^{-6} bar

Construct a phase diagram for butane based on this information. Be sure to label the axes. Use S, L, and G to represent conditions for the three states of matter. Finally, use this drawing to answer the following questions:
(a) Is butane is a gas, liquid or solid at 0 °C and 400 mm Hg?
(b) Will an increase in pressure result in an increase, a decrease, or no change in the melting point of butane from its normal melting point?
(c) Between what temperatures is butane a liquid at 1.0 atm pressure?

Text Section: 13.6
OWL Question: 13.6c

37. (Chapter 13) The unit cell of one of several known molybdenum fluorides is pictured here.

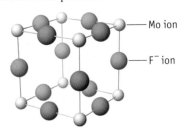

A unit cell of a molybdenum fluoride

How many molybdenum ions and how many fluoride ions are in each unit cell? What is the formula and name of this molybdenum fluoride?

Text Section: 13.2
OWL Question: 13.2c

38. (Chapter 13) The unit cell of sodium chloride is pictured below. The length of each side of the unit cell is 562.8 pm.

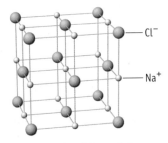

NaCl unit cell (expanded)

(a) What is the mass of one unit cell?
(b) What is the volume of one unit cell?
(c) What is the density of NaCl based on the mass and volume of the unit cell? (Compare the calculated value with a literature density of 2.17 g/cm³.)

Text Sections: 13.1 and 13.2
OWL Question: 13.2c

39. (Chapter 13) The unit cell of silver iodide is illustrated below.

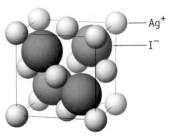

Silver iodide unit cell

(a) How many silver ions and how many iodide ions are there per unit cell?
(b) Sides of the unit cell are 649.6 pm. The density is 5.68 g/cm³. What is the mass of one unit cell?
(c) Based on the unit cell mass, what is the mass of one silver iodide formula unit and what is its molar mass? Compare this with the molar mass of silver iodide calculated from atomic weights.

Text Sections: 13.1 and 13.2
OWL Question: 13.2c

40. ▲ (Chapter 13) Units cells and close packing. Prove that the atoms packed in an idealized face-centered cubic unit cell occupy about 74% of the available space.

Text Section: 13.1
OWL Question: 13.1b

41. (Chapters 12 and 13) See the structure of quartz on page 656.
(a) What are some interesting structural features of quartz? What kind of solid does it represent?
(b) How does water interact with ordinary salt and oxygen gas so that they dissolve?
(c) Why does water have such peculiar properties? For example, for such a small molecule it has very high melting and boiling points.
(d) The quartz structure on page 656 shows the interior of the crystal. However, there are OH groups on the surface of the crystal that are attached to only one Si atom. Knowing this, explain why water can interact with sand—the sand gets wet—but it does not dissolve the sand.

Text Sections: 12.2, 12.3, 13.4, and 14.2
OWL Questions: 12.2–3c, 12.2–3e

42. (Chapters 12 and 14) Arrange the following aqueous solutions in order of (a) increasing boiling point and (b) increasing vapor pressure at 25 °C:

(i) 0.30 m $C_2H_4(OH)_2$ (ethylene glycol, nonvolatile solute)

(ii) 0.20 m CH_3CO_2H (acetic acid)

(iii) 0.20 m HNO_3

(iv) 0.20 m Na_2SO_4

Text Section: 14.4
OWL Questions: 14.4c, 14.4l

43. (Chapter 14) You have isolated a nonionic unknown compound from treated wastewater, and to help identify the compound you determine its molar mass. A solution of 0.238 g of the compound in 25.0 g of benzene freezes at 5.11 °C. What is the molar mass of the compound?

Text Sections: 14.4
OWL Questions: 14.4l

44. (Chapters 11 and 12) Naphthalene, $C_{10}H_8$, is a white solid that sublimes readily at room temperature and above.

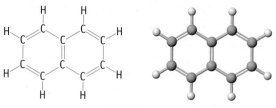

Naphthalene, $C_{10}H_8$

(a) If you place 1.05 g of napthalene in a 112 mL flask at 100 °C, where the vapor pressure is 18.8 mm Hg, how many molecules of the compound are in the vapor phase.

(b) Using data below, calculate the enthalpy of sublimation of the compound using the Clausius-Clapeyron equation.

Temperature (K)	Vapor Pressure (bar)
360.3	0.0142
392.7	0.0554

Text Sections: 11.3 and 12.4
OWL Questions: 11.3b, 12.4g

45. ▲ (Chapters 11 and 14) You have 2.25 g of a mixture of the organic liquids benzene and toluene in a 125 mL flask at 25 °C. Both are volatile liquids. Pure benzene has a vapor pressure of 95 mm Hg (at 25 °C), whereas that of toluene is 28 mm Hg (at 25 °C). This particular mixture of the two, however, has a total vapor pressure of 63 mm Hg.

(a) What is the mole fraction of each substance in the vapor phase?

(b) What is the mass of each substance in the vapor phase in this flask at 25 °C?

Benzene   Toluene

Text Sections: 11.5 and 14.4
OWL Questions: 11.5c, 14.4c

46. (Chapter 13) Titanium crystallizes in a face-centered cubic lattice. The metal reacts with hydrogen and carbon by allowing these elements to occupy holes in the lattice. Hydrogen atoms occupy tetrahedral holes, whereas carbon atoms occupy octahedral holes. What are the formulas of titanium hydride and titanium carbide, assuming that hydrogen atoms or carbon atoms, respectively, fill all of the appropriate holes in the lattice?

Text Section: 13.2
OWL Question: 13.2c

47. ▲ (Chapter 13) The structures of ionic solids can often be predicted by knowing the relative number of ions and their relative sizes. We begin by assuming cations are smaller than anions, and so lattices are built of anions with cations in the holes or interstices. (This is not always the case, of course, in compounds such as CsF where the cation is the larger of the two ions.) Nonetheless, the following *radius ratio rules* give reasonable predictions; that is, for a given range of cation to anion sizes, a particular coordination geometry is predicted for the cation.

Value of r_+/r_-	Coordination Geometry of the Cation
0.22–0.41	tetrahedral (Zn^{2+} in ZnS)
0.41–0.73	octahedral (Na^+ in NaCl)
>0.73	cubic (Cs^+ in CsCl)

Let us take an ionic compound MX as an example. Assume that the X anions form a primative cubic lattice and that they just touch along the edges of the lattice. Also assume the M cation in the center of the lattice touches all eight of the surrounding anions. What is the radius ratio r_+/r_- for this structure? (See Figure 13.8, but note that we assume X^- ions at cube corners touch along the cube edges.)

Text Section: 13.2
OWL Question: 13.2c

Answers to Assessing Key Points Questions

1. (a) Number of N_2 molecules

   Amount of $N_2 = n = PV/RT$

   $$= \frac{735 \text{ mm Hg} \left(\dfrac{1 \text{ atm}}{760 \text{ mm Hg}} \right) (5.0 \text{ L})}{(0.08206 \dfrac{\text{L} \cdot \text{atm}}{\text{K} \cdot \text{mol}}) (294 \text{ K})}$$

   $= 0.20$ mol

   Number of molecules =

   $= (0.20 \text{ mol}) \left(\dfrac{6.022 \times 10^{23} \text{ molecules}}{\text{mol}} \right)$

   $= 1.2 \times 10^{23}$ molecules

   (b) Pressure under new conditions. Use the general gas law, Equation 11.3, on page 521.

   $$P_{\text{new}} = 735 \text{ mm Hg} \left(\frac{5.0 \text{ L}}{2.5 \text{ L}} \right) \left(\frac{273 \text{ K}}{294 \text{ K}} \right) = 1400 \text{ mm Hg}$$

2. (a) Equation 11.5 (page 525) states that the density of a gas is proportional to the molar mass at a given P and T. The masses are in the order He $<$ CO_2 $<$ SO_2 $<$ Cl_2. Therefore, Cl_2 has the greatest density.
   (b) The rate of effusion is inversely proportional to the square root of the molar mass (page 538). Therefore, He will diffuse most rapidly.

3. Amount of O_2 required

   $0.400 \text{ mol P}_4 \left(\dfrac{5 \text{ mol O}_2}{1 \text{ mol P}_4} \right) = 2.00 \text{ mol O}_2$

   Volume of O_2 required.

   $V = nRT/P$

   $$= \frac{(2.00 \text{ mol O}_2) \left(0.08206 \dfrac{\text{L} \cdot \text{atm}}{\text{K} \cdot \text{mol}} \right) (273 \text{ K})}{1.00 \text{ atm}}$$

   $= 44.8$ L

   This could also have been solved using the molar volume of an ideal gas: 22.4 L/mol at STP. Thus, 2.00 mol O_2 at STP occupy twice the molar volume or 44.8 L.

4. Calculate the molar mass.

   Amount of gas $= n = \dfrac{PV}{RT}$

   $$= \frac{(209 \text{ mm Hg}) \left(\dfrac{1 \text{ atm}}{760 \text{ mm Hg}} \right) (0.732 \text{ L})}{\left(0.08206 \dfrac{\text{L} \cdot \text{atm}}{\text{K} \cdot \text{mol}} \right) (294 \text{ K})}$$

   $= 0.00834$ mol

   Molar mass $= \dfrac{0.37 \text{ g}}{0.00834 \text{ mol}} = 44$ g/mol

   The gas is CO_2.

5. (c) Gases at higher pressures and lower temperatures deviate most from ideality.

6. (a) The total pressure depends on the total number of molecules (moles) of gas in the flask (and T and V).

   $n(O_2) = 0.50$ mol
   $n(N_2) = 1.0$ mol
   $n(He) = 0.50$ mol
   $n(H_2) = 2.0$ mol

   Total amount $= n_{\text{total}} = 4.0$ mol

   $$P = \frac{n_{\text{total}} RT}{V} = \frac{(4.0 \text{ mol}) \left(0.08206 \dfrac{\text{L} \cdot \text{atm}}{\text{K} \cdot \text{mol}} \right) (298 \text{ K})}{10.0 \text{ L}}$$

   $= 9.8$ atm

   See Equation 11.7 on page 531.
   (b) The gas with the highest partial pressure is that present in the largest amount, here H_2.

7. The partial pressure of a gas depends on its mole fraction, here 0.21 for O_2. (See Equation 11.8 on page 531.) Thus, the O_2 partial pressure is 160 mm Hg ($= 0.21 \times 745$ mm Hg).

8. (a) Both flasks have the same P and same V, but B has a lower T. Therefore, B must have more molecules because more molecules are needed to produce the same P at a lower T. That is, given that $n = PV/RT$, when P, V, and R are constant, n must be greater for a lower T.
   (b) Flask A contains molecules with a greater average speed and greater average kinetic energy.

9. Molecules in order of decreasing molar mass and increasing speed: CO_2 ($M = 44$ g/mol), O_2 ($M = 32$ g/mol), CO ($M = 28$ g/mol), NH_3 ($M = 17$ g/mol).

10. (a) C_3H_8 and O_2 are mixed in a ratio of 1 mol to 5 mol.
    $X_{\text{propane}} = 1 \text{ mol}/(1 \text{ mol} + 5 \text{ mol}) = 1/6$
    $P_{\text{propane}} = X_{\text{propane}} P_{\text{total}} = (1/6)(120 \text{ mm Hg}) = 20.$ mm Hg
    $P_{\text{oxygen}} = (120 - 20.)$ mm Hg $= 100$ mm Hg
    The pressure of O_2 is 5 times that of C_3H_8 as required by stoichiometry.
    (b) Pressure of water vapor

    $$P_{H_2O} = P_{\text{propane}} \left(\frac{4 \text{ mol H}_2\text{O}}{1 \text{ mol propane}} \right) = 80. \text{ mm Hg}$$

11. H_2O, CH_3OH, and HNO_3. Note that HNO_3 has an OH bond and can H-bond to neighboring nitric acid molecules.

12. A H-bond could form between H_2O and the O atom of the polar molecule CH_3OCH_3. Both acetic acid and aspirin, with OH bonds, can H-bond to water.

13. Intermolecular forces: Atoms of Ar $<$ nonpolar CO_2 $<$ polar NH_3 (with weak H-bonding) $<$ polar CH_3OH (with significant H-bonding). See pages 561–563.

14. (a) induced dipole-induced dipole forces between nonpolar CH_4 molecules.

(b) dipole-dipole and hydrogen bonding between H_2O and CH_3OH (along with induced dipole-induced dipole forces).

(c) ion-dipole forces between Li^+ and Cl^- ions and water.

(d) dipole-induced dipole forces between nonpolar O_2 and polar water.

15. Ne $(-246 \ °C)$ < SO_2 $(-10.05 \ °C)$ < CH_3OH $(+64.6 \ °C)$

Neon atoms attract only by induced dipole-induced dipole forces, whereas SO_2 is weakly polar. Methanol molecules interact largely by dipole-dipole forces and hydrogen bonding (although induced dipole-induced dipole forces are also present).

16. (a) 300 mm Hg

(b) About 75 °C (literature value, 78.3 °C)

(c) Nonpolar CS_2 and heptane molecules interact by induced dipole-induced dipole forces. Ethanol molecules interact through dipole-dipole forces and hydrogen bonds. (Induced dipole-induced dipole forces are also present.)

(d) CS_2 is a vapor whereas both ethanol and heptane are liquids.

(e) Ethanol can interact strongly with water through both dipole-dipole forces and hydrogen bonding, so it dissolves readily in water. Neither of the nonpolar molecules, CS_2 or heptane, is miscible with water.

(f) The vapor pressure curve indicates CS_2 has a normal boiling point of about 45 °C, whereas that of ethanol is 78 °C. This makes sense because we predict that ethanol molecules interact through dipole-dipole forces and extensive hydrogen bonding, whereas CS_2 molecules interact through much weaker induced dipole-induced dipole forces.

(g) Both CS_2 and heptane are nonpolar, but heptane molecules are significantly heavier than CS_2 molecules (100.2 u versus 76.1 u) so its boiling point is predicted to be much higher. This is confirmed by the vapor pressure curves, which indicate that heptane has a normal boiling point of about 100 °C while the CS_2 normal boiling point is only about 45 °C.

17. (a) $CaCO_3$ is an ionic solid.

(b) Polyethylene is an amorphous solid (although partially crystalline polyethylene does exist).

(c) Tungsten is a metallic solid.

(d) Solid CO_2 is a molecular solid.

18. (a) The oxide ions are arranged in a face-centered cubic unit cell.

(b) There are four Mg^{2+} (and four O^{2-} ions) per unit cell.

19. (a) CH_3OCH_3 < CH_3CH_2OH < CH_3CO_2H

All three molecules are polar but only CH_3CH_2OH and CH_3CO_2H can interact through hydrogen

bonds. Hydrogen bonding is especially strong in CH_3CO_2H (acetic acid), which has not only an OH group but also a polar C=O group. (See Figure 12.7 on page 562.)

(b) propane (C_3H_8) < hexane (C_6H_{14}) < octane (C_8H_{18})

The boiling points of the nonpolar alkanes (a class of hydrocarbons with the general formula C_nH_{2n+2}) increase with increasing molar mass.

20. Phase diagram for methane, CH_4.

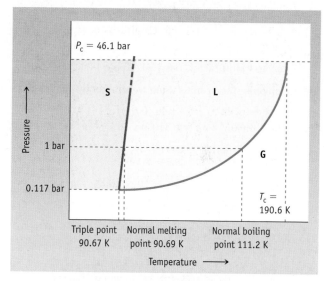

(a) Solid methane is more dense than liquid methane.

(b) No, this is above the critical temperature.

21. Molality and weight percent of dimethylglyoxime (DMG)

$$\text{Amount of DMG} = 45.0 \ \text{g DMG} \left(\frac{1 \ \text{mol DMG}}{116.1 \ \text{g DMG}} \right)$$
$$= 0.388 \ \text{mol DMG}$$

$$\text{Mass of ethanol} = 500. \ \text{mL} \left(\frac{0.790 \ \text{g ethanol}}{1 \ \text{mL ethanol}} \right)$$
$$= 395 \ \text{g ethanol}$$

$$\text{Molality } (m) = \frac{0.388 \ \text{mol DMG}}{0.395 \ \text{kg ethanol}} = 0.982 \ m$$

$$\text{Weight percent} = \left(\frac{45.0 \ \text{g DMG}}{45.0 \ \text{g} + 395 \ \text{g}} \right) 100\% = 10.2\%$$

22. The solution with the largest concentration of solute particles, 0.12 m K_2SO_4, has the highest boiling point, the lowest freezing point, and the highest osmotic pressure. The solution with the smallest concentration of solute particles, 0.20 m $C_2H_4(OH)_2$, has the highest vapor pressure.

23. The answer is Mg^{2+}. The enthalpy of hydration depends directly on the charge on the ion and inversely on its size. Thus, the smallest, most highly charged ion

will interact most strongly with water. Ion sizes are in the order $Rb^+ > Ba^{2+} > Na^+ > Mg^{2+}$ (Figure 7.12). (See pages 557–558 and 623–625.)

24. (b). See pages 640–641.

25. Freezing point depression. See Example 14.9.

$$\text{Mass \% NaCl} = \left(\frac{29.5 \text{ g}}{500 + 29.5 \text{ g}}\right)100\%$$
$$= 5.6\%$$

Estimate $i = 1.8$ (Table 14.4)

$$\Delta T_{fp} = K_{fp} \cdot m \cdot i = (-1.86 \text{ °C}/m)(1.00 \ m)(1.8) = -3.3 \text{ °C}$$

The van't Hoff factor, i, is 1.84 (Table 14.4, page 640).

26. Calculating molar mass using freezing point depression:

$$\Delta T_{fp} = -0.762 \text{ °C} = (-1.86 \text{ °C}/m)(c_m)$$

Concentration $= c_m = 0.410 \ m$

$$\left(0.410 \ \frac{\text{mol}}{\text{kg}}\right)0.0500 \text{ kg} = 0.0205 \text{ mol}$$

$$\text{Molar mass} = \frac{2.50 \text{ g}}{0.0205 \text{ mol}} = 122 \text{ g/mol}$$

Erythritol is $C_4H_{10}O_4$

27. (a) Pentane has the higher vapor pressure because it has the smaller molar mass.
   (b) At $T_1 = 0$ °C or 273 K, $P_1 = 48.3$ mm Hg
       At $T_2 = 50$ °C or 323 K, $P_2 = 399.20$ mm Hg

$$\ln \frac{P_2}{P_1} = -\frac{\Delta_{vap}H°}{R}\left[\frac{1}{T_2} - \frac{1}{T_1}\right]$$

$$\ln \frac{399.2}{48.3} = -\frac{\Delta_{vap}H°}{8.314 \text{ J/K} \cdot \text{mol}}\left[\frac{1}{323 \text{ K}} - \frac{1}{273 \text{ K}}\right]$$

$$\ln 8.265 = -\frac{\Delta_{vap}H°}{8.314 \text{ J/K} \cdot \text{mol}}\left[-5.67 \times 10^{-4}\right]1/\text{K}$$

$$\Delta_{vap}H° = 3.10 \times 10^4 \text{ J/mol or } 31.0 \text{ kJ/mol}$$

   (c) Use the Clausius-Clapeyron equation with $T_1 = 323$ K and $P_1 = 399.2$ mm Hg
       $T_2 =$ boiling point of hexane and $P_2 = 760.$ mm Hg

$$\ln \frac{760}{399.2} = -\frac{3.10 \times 10^4 \text{ J/mol}}{8.314 \text{ J/K} \cdot \text{mol}}\left[\frac{1}{T_2} - \frac{1}{323 \text{ K}}\right]$$

   Solving, we find $T_2 = 342$ K or 69 °C.

Solutions to Comprehensive Questions

28. (a) Water exhibits significant hydrogen bonding. Hydrogen sulfide, H_2S, does not.
   (b) Partial pressure of H_2S depends on the mole fraction of H_2S in the mixture (Equation 11.8). Here the mole fraction is the amount (moles) of H_2S divided by total amount (moles) of all gases, which is the same as the ratio of H_2S molecules relative to the total number of molecules.

$$P_{H_2S} = (\text{mole fraction } H_2S)(P_{total})$$
$$= \left(\frac{80. \text{ molecules}}{1.0 \times 10^6 \text{ molecules}}\right)(725 \text{ mm Hg})$$
$$= 0.058 \text{ mm Hg}$$

   (c) For gases at the same T and P, their volumes are directly proportional to the amount of gas. (This is Avogadro's Hypothesis; page 522. See also Example 11.5.)

$$5.2 \text{ L } H_2S \left(\frac{2 \text{ L } O_2}{1 \text{ L } H_2S}\right) = 10. \text{ L } O_2 \text{ required}$$

29. This is similar to Example 11.8, page 526.

$$n = \frac{PV}{RT} = \frac{5.10 \text{ mm Hg}\left(\dfrac{1 \text{ atm}}{760 \text{ mm Hg}}\right)(0.732 \text{ L})}{\left(0.08206 \ \dfrac{\text{L} \cdot \text{atm}}{\text{K} \cdot \text{mol}}\right)298 \text{ K}}$$

$$n = 2.01 \times 10^{-4} \text{ mol}$$

$$\text{Molar mass} = \frac{0.0257 \text{ g}}{2.01 \times 10^4 \text{ mol}} = 128 \text{ g/mol}$$

The product of the reaction, butyl acrylate, has a formula of $C_7H_{12}O_2$, formed by combining the reactants in a 1:1:1 ratio.

30. The volume of H_2 depends on its amount, and that in turn depends on which is the limiting reactant, Fe or H_2SO_4.

$$450. \times 10^3 \text{ g Fe}\left(\frac{1 \text{ mol Fe}}{55.85 \text{ g Fe}}\right) = 8.06 \times 10^3 \text{ mol Fe}$$

$$225 \times 10^3 \text{ g } H_2SO_4\left(\frac{1 \text{ mol } H_2SO_4}{98.08 \text{ g } H_2SO_4}\right)$$
$$= 2.29 \times 10^3 \text{ mol } H_2SO_4$$

The limiting reactant is H_2SO_4, which produces 2.29×10^3 mol H_2.

$$V = \frac{nRT}{P}$$

$$= \frac{(2.29 \times 10^3 \text{ mol } H_2)\left(0.08206 \ \dfrac{\text{L} \cdot \text{atm}}{\text{K} \cdot \text{mol}}\right)(291 \text{ K})}{735 \text{ mm Hg}\left(\dfrac{1 \text{ atm}}{760 \text{ mm Hg}}\right)}$$

$$V = 5.65 \times 10^4 \text{ L}$$

31. Pressure = 743 mm Hg + 48 mm Hg = 791 mm Hg

32. (a) Amount of CO_2 in the balloon:

$$\text{Amount of } CO_2 = 4.8 \text{ g } CO_2\left(\frac{1 \text{ mol } CO_2}{44.0 \text{ g } CO_2}\right)$$
$$= 0.11 \text{ mol}$$

Pressure in the balloon with $n = 0.11$ mol, $T = 291$ K, and $V = 2.33$ L.

$$P = \frac{(0.11 \text{ mol})\left(0.08206 \dfrac{\text{L} \cdot \text{atm}}{\text{K} \cdot \text{mol}}\right)(291 \text{ K})}{2.33 \text{ L}} = 1.1 \text{ atm}$$

The balloon is overfilled because the pressure generated by 0.11 mol of gas under these conditions is greater than the atmospheric pressure. The actual pressure in the balloon is 1.1 atm.

(b) The number of molecules is the same. The pressure of a gas (at a given T and V) depends only on the number of particles, not their identity.

(c) He atoms travel faster at a given T than CO_2 molecules (see Figure 11.15 and Screen 8 in Go Chemistry module 16) but their average kinetic energies are identical.

33. This problem on gas effusion uses Graham's law, Equation 11.10, page 538.

$$\frac{\text{Rate of effusion of } CO_2}{\text{Rate of effusion of unknown}} = \sqrt{\frac{\text{Molar mass unknown}}{\text{Molar mass } CO_2}}$$

$$\frac{0.0330 \text{ mol/min}}{0.0330 \text{ mol}/1.73 \text{ min}} = \sqrt{\frac{\text{Unknown}}{44.0 \text{ g/mol}}}$$

$$1.73 = \sqrt{\frac{\text{Unknown}}{44.0 \text{ g/mol}}}$$

$$2.99 = \frac{\text{Unknown}}{44.0 \text{ g/mol}}$$

Unknown = 132 g/mol

34. (a) Electron dot structure

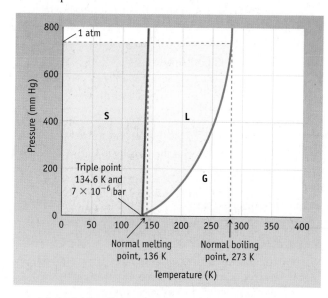

(b) The C atom is sp^2 hybridized.
(c) The molecule is polar.
(d) Yes, the N—H of one molecule could interact with an N atom or O atom on a neighboring molecule. The formamide molecule can also hydrogen bond to water.
(e) The molecule is flat due to the resonance structure with a N=C double bond.
(f) Vaporizing 10.0 g of formamide:

Energy required as heat =

$$10.0 \text{ g HCONH}_2 \left(\frac{1 \text{ mol HCONH}_2}{45.04 \text{ g HCONH}_2}\right)\left(\frac{60.15 \text{ kJ}}{1 \text{ mol HCONH}_2}\right)$$

= 13.4 kJ

35. (a) Allyl alcohol is an alcohol (like ethanol) and has an OH group capable of hydrogen bonding. This should lower its vapor pressure at a given temperature relative to that of acetone, which, while polar, is not capable of hydrogen bonding to another acetone molecule.

(b) One can choose any two sets of temperature and pressures and use Equation 12.2. Alternatively, it is better to plot the data (as in Figure 12.18, page 575) and derive the heat of vaporization from the slope of the line. A plot of ln P versus $1/T$ gives a slope of -3875.3.

$$\text{Slope} = -3875.3 = -\Delta_{\text{vap}}H°/R$$

Using $R = 8.314 \times 10^{-3}$ kJ/K·mol, and converting to kilojoules, we obtain $\Delta_{\text{vap}}H° = 32.2$ kJ/mol. (A similar result is obtained using Equation 12.2, page 576.)

(c) Calculate the molar mass of the fluorination product.

$$n = \frac{PV}{RT} = \frac{722 \text{ mm Hg}\left(\dfrac{1 \text{ atm}}{760 \text{ mm Hg}}\right)(0.264 \text{ L})}{\left(0.08206 \dfrac{\text{L} \cdot \text{atm}}{\text{K} \cdot \text{mol}}\right)295 \text{ K}}$$

$n = 0.0104$ mol

$$\text{Molar mass} = \frac{1.53 \text{ g}}{0.0104 \text{ mol}} = 148 \text{ g/mol}$$

The formula of the product must be C_3HF_5O. (The 3 C atoms and 1 O atom account for a mass of 52 g/mol of the 148 g/mol. The difference, 96, must be due to five F atoms and one H atom.)

36. The approximate phase diagram for butane is illustrated here. Also note that the triple point is at a very low pressure.

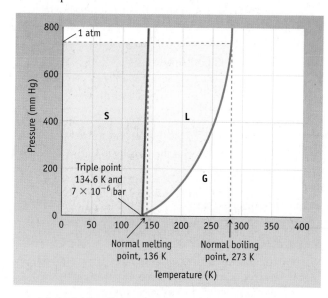

(a) At 0 °C and 400 mm Hg butane is a gas.
(b) An increase in pressure will result in an increase in melting point.

(c) Between the melting point (136 K) and the boiling point (273 K).

37. Fluoride ions occupy each of 12 edges and contribute ¼ of each ion to the unit cell for a total of three F^- ions. Mo ions are located at each corner and contribute a net of one Mo ion to the unit cell. Therefore, the formula is MoF_3 and its name is molybdenum(III) fluoride.

38. Sodium chloride unit cell.
   (a) Mass of one unit cell (which contains 4 NaCl units).

$$\left(\frac{58.44 \text{ g NaCl}}{1 \text{ mol NaCl}}\right)\left(\frac{1 \text{ mol NaCl}}{6.022 \times 10^{23} \text{ formula units}}\right)$$
$$\left(\frac{4 \text{ NaCl formula units}}{1 \text{ unit cell}}\right)$$
$$= 3.882 \times 10^{-22} \text{ g NaCl/unit cell}$$

   (b) Volume of one unit cell

   Length of unit cell edge =
$$562.8 \text{ pm}\left(\frac{1 \text{ m}}{1 \times 10^{12} \text{ pm}}\right)\left(\frac{100 \text{ cm}}{1 \text{ m}}\right)$$
$$= 5.628 \times 10^{-8} \text{ cm}$$
$$\text{Volume} = \left(5.628 \times 10^{-8} \text{ cm}\right)^3 = 1.783 \times 10^{-22} \text{ cm}^3$$

   (c) Density of NaCl

$$\text{Density} = \frac{3.882 \times 10^{-22} \text{ g NaCl}}{1.783 \times 10^{-22} \text{ cm}^3} = 2.178 \text{ g/cm}^3$$

   This calculated value agrees with the literature value.

39. (a) There are 4 Ag^+ ions (as a face-centered cube) in the unit cell. There are 4 I^- ions in tetrahedral holes.
   (b) First find the volume of the unit cell.

   Length of unit cell edge =
$$\left(649.6 \text{ pm}\right)\left(\frac{1 \text{ m}}{1 \times 10^{12} \text{ pm}}\right)\left(\frac{100 \text{ cm}}{1 \text{ m}}\right)$$
$$= 6.496 \times 10^{-8} \text{ cm}$$
$$\text{Volume} = \left(6.496 \times 10^{-8} \text{ cm}\right)^3 = 2.741 \times 10^{-22} \text{ cm}^3$$

   Use this volume with the density to derive the mass of the unit cell.

$$\left(\frac{2.741 \times 10^{-22} \text{ cm}^3}{1 \text{ unit cell}}\right)\left(\frac{5.68 \text{ g}}{1 \text{ cm}^3}\right) = \frac{1.557 \times 10^{-21} \text{ g}}{\text{unit cell}}$$

   (c) There are 4 AgI units per unit cell, so the mass of 1 AgI is ¼ of 1.557×10^{-21} g or 3.893×10^{-22} g. Multiplying by Avogadro's number gives 234.4 g/mol, very close to the value from atomic weights (234.8 g/mol).

40. The key assumption here is that the atoms in a face-centered cube just touch along the diagonal dimension in each face.

Atoms of a face-centered unit cell just touch along the face diagonal.

Let us assume the cell has an edge dimension of e, so the volume of the unit cell is e^3

Now solve for the volume of an individual atom.

Length of face diagonal $= \sqrt{2}\, e$
Face diagonal $= 4 \times$ radius of an atom

$$\text{Radius of an atom} = \frac{\sqrt{2}}{4}\, e$$

$$\text{Volume of an atom} = \frac{4}{3}\pi\left(\frac{\sqrt{2}}{4}\, e\right)^3$$
$$= 0.1851\, e^3$$

There are four atoms in each unit cell, so the total volume of the atoms is $4 \times 0.1851\, e^3 = 0.7405\, e^3$. This is equivalent to 74% of the volume of the unit cell.

41. (a) The quartz structure consists of tetrahedral sp^3 hybridized Si atoms bridged by O atoms. Also notice that Si and O form six-member rings. Quartz is a covalent, network solid.
   (b) The significant polarity of water molecules allows them to interact with the cations and anions of salts and bring the ions into solution. (See pages 557–558 and Figures 12.3 and 14.9.) Water molecules can also induce a dipole in nonpolar molecules such as O_2 and N_2, allowing them to dissolve to a small extent in water. (See pages 565–566.)
   (c) For such a small molecule, water has unusual properties (such as its high boiling point, low vapor pressure, and high specific heat capacity). Also, it is one of only two or three substances known to have a solid phase of lower density than the liquid phase. Much of this can be explained by the hydrogen bonding capability of the molecule (see pages 561–564.)
   (d) Polar water molecules interact with the OH groups on the surface of sand particles and wet the sand. However, the interaction is not strong enough to break down Si—O covalent bonds, and so the quartz sand does not dissolve in water.

42. Boiling points increase in order of increasing concentration of particles in the solution: $CH_3CO_2H <$ $C_2H_4(OH)_2 < HNO_3 < Na_2SO_4$. The vapor pressure increase is the opposite order. That is, the most concen-

trated solution will have the lowest vapor pressure (and thus the highest boiling point).

43. Freezing point depression. Use Equation 14.7

$$\Delta T_{fp} = (5.11\ ^\circ C - 5.50\ ^\circ C) = -0.39\ ^\circ C$$

Solute concentration (m) =
$\Delta T_{fp}/K_{fp} = -0.39\ ^\circ C/(-5.12\ ^\circ C/m) = 0.076\ m$

Amount of solute = $(0.076\ mol/1.00\ kg)(0.0250\ kg)$
$= 1.9 \times 10^{-3}$ mol

Molar mass $= 0.238\ g/1.9 \times 10^{-3}\ mol = 1.2 \times 10^2\ g/mol$

44. (a) n = amount of $C_{10}H_8$ in gas phase = PV/RT
When $P = 0.0247$ atm, $T = 373$, and $V = 0.112$ L,
$n = 9.05 \times 10^{-5}$ mol. So, number of molecules is
5.45×10^{19}

(b)

$$\ln \frac{P_2}{P_1} = -\frac{\Delta_{subl}H^\circ}{R}\left[\frac{1}{T_2} - \frac{1}{T_1}\right]$$

$$\ln \frac{0.0554}{0.0142} = -\frac{\Delta_{subl}H^\circ}{8.314\ J/K \cdot mol}\left[\frac{1}{392.7\ K} - \frac{1}{360.3\ K}\right]$$

$$\ln 3.90 = -\frac{\Delta_{subl}H^\circ}{8.314\ J/K \cdot mol}[-2.290 \times 10^{-4}]1/K$$

$$\Delta_{subl}H^\circ = 4.94 \times 10^4\ J/mol\ \text{or}\ 49.4\ kJ/mol$$

45. (a) P_{total} in gas phase = 63 mm Hg
$= X_{toluene}(28\ mm\ Hg) + X_{benzene}(95\ mm\ Hg)$

Because $X_{benzene} + X_{toluene} = 1$, we have
63 mm Hg
$= (1 - X_{benzene})(28\ mm\ Hg) + X_{benzene}(95\ mm\ Hg)$

Solving, we find $X_{benzene} = 0.52$. Therefore, $X_{toluene}$
$= 0.48$.

(b) $P = 0.0829$ atm, $V = 0.125$ L, $T = 298$ K
$n = PV/RT = 4.24 \times 10^{-4}$ mol

Composition of the vapor:
$(0.52)(4.24 \times 10^{-4}\ mol) = 2.2 \times 10^{-4}$ mol benzene
$(0.48)(4.24 \times 10^{-4}\ mol) = 2.0 \times 10^{-4}$ mol toluene

Mass of benzene
$= (2.2 \times 10^{-4}\ mol)(78.1\ g/mol) = 0.017\ g$

Mass of toluene
$= (2.0 \times 10^{-4}\ mol)(92.1\ g/mol) = 0.019\ g$

46. A fcc lattice has a net of four Ti atoms. If all eight tetrahedral holes are filled with H atoms, this leads to a formula of TiH_2. There are only four octahedral holes in a fcc lattice, so titanium carbide is TiC.

47. In the diagram below, focus on the X^- ion in red. The distance along the cube edge, where X^- ions just touch, is $2r_-$. An X^- ions lies diagonally across the cube face at a distance of $2(2^{1/2})r_-$. (This is derived from the fact that the distance along all cube edges is $2r_-$, so the diagonal distance across a cube face must be $2(2^{1/2})r_-$.)

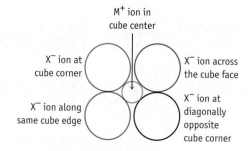

M$^+$ ion in cube center
X^- ion at cube corner
X^- ion across the cube face
X^- ion along same cube edge
X^- ion at diagonally opposite cube corner

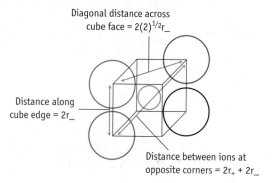

Diagonal distance across cube face = $2(2)^{1/2}r_-$
Distance along cube edge = $2r_-$
Distance between ions at opposite corners = $2r_+ + 2r_-$

Using the Pythagorean theorem, the diagonal distance across the cube (from the X^- ion in one corner to the X^- ion in the opposite corner) is $(12)^{1/2}r_-$.

(Diagonal across the cube)^2 = $(2r_-)^2 + [2(2^{1/2})r_-]^2$
$= 4r_-^2 + 8r_-^2 = 12r_-^2$

This distance is also $2r_+ + 2r_-$:

$(12)^{1/2}r_- = 2r_+ + 2r_-$

$3.464r_- = 2r_+ + 2r_-$

$1.464r_- = 2r_+$

Therefore, $r_+/r_- = 0.732$

The radius ratio indicates that the coordination geometry of the cation is cubic.

15 | Chemical Kinetics: The Rates of Chemical Reactions

Charles D. Winters

Fading of the color of phenolphthalein with time

(elapsed time about 3 minutes)

Where Did the Indicator Go?

The indicator phenolphthalein is often used for the titration of a weak acid using a strong base. A change from colorless to pale pink indicates that the equivalence point in the reaction has been reached (◄ page 184). If more base is added to the solution, the color of the indicator intensifies to a bright red color.

If the solution containing phenolphthalein has a pH higher than about 12, another phenomenon is observed. Slowly, the red color fades, and the solution becomes colorless. This is due to a chemical reaction of the anion of phenolphthalein with hydroxide ion, as shown in the equation. The reaction is slow, and it is easy to measure the rate of this reaction by monitoring the intensity of color of the solution.

This chapter is about one of the fundamental areas of chemistry: the rate of reactions and how they occur. In Study Question 71, you will see some data that will allow you to discover how the rate of the phenolphthalein reaction depends on the hydroxide ion concentration, and you will derive an equation that will allow you to predict the results under other conditions.

The reaction of phenolphthalein and hydroxide ion.

When carrying out a chemical reaction, chemists are concerned with two issues: the *rate* at which the reaction proceeds and the *extent* to which the reaction is product-favored. Chapter 5 began to address the second question, and Chapters 16 and 19 will develop that topic further. In this chapter, we turn to the other part of our question, **chemical kinetics,** a study of the rates of chemical reactions.

The study of kinetics is divided into two parts. The first part is at the *macroscopic level*, which addresses rates of reactions: what reaction rate means, how to determine a reaction rate experimentally, and how factors such as temperature and the concentrations of reactants influence rates. The second part of this subject considers chemical reactions at the *particulate level*. Here, the concern is with the **reaction mechanism,** the detailed pathway taken by atoms and molecules as a reaction proceeds. The goal is to reconcile data in the macroscopic world of chemistry with an understanding of how and why chemical reactions occur at the particulate level— and then to apply this information to control important reactions.

Chemistry.ꝏ.Now™

Throughout the text this icon introduces an opportunity for self-study or to explore interactive tutorials by signing in at **www.cengage.com/login**.

■ **Macroscopic–Particulate Connections** Recall the statement from page 10 that "Chemists carry out experiments on the macroscopic level, but they think about chemistry at the particulate level."

15.1 Rates of Chemical Reactions

The concept of rate is encountered in many nonchemical circumstances. Common examples are the speed of an automobile, given in terms of the distance traveled per unit time (for example, kilometers per hour) and the rate of flow of water from a faucet, given as volume per unit time (perhaps liters per minute). In each case, a change is measured over an interval of time. Similarly, the rate of a chemical reaction refers to the change in concentration of a reactant or product per unit of time.

$$\text{Rate of reaction} = \frac{\text{change in concentration}}{\text{change in time}}$$

Two measurements are made to determine the average speed of an automobile: distance traveled and time elapsed. Average speed is the distance traveled divided by the time elapsed, or $\Delta(\text{distance})/\Delta(\text{time})$. If an automobile travels 3.9 km in 4.5 min (0.075 h), its average speed is (3.9 km/0.075 h), or 52 kph (or 32 mph).

Average rates of chemical reactions can be determined similarly. Two quantities, concentration and time, are measured. Concentrations can be determined in a variety of ways, sometimes directly (using a pH meter for example), sometimes by measuring a property such as absorbance of light that can be related to concentration (Figure 15.1). The average rate of the reaction is the change in the concentration per unit time—that is, $\Delta(\text{concentration})/\Delta(\text{time})$.

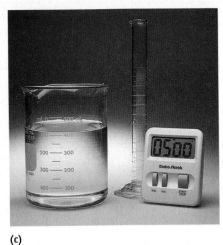

(a)   (b)   (c)

Photos: Charles D. Winters

FIGURE 15.1 An experiment to measure rate of reaction. (a) A few drops of blue food dye were added to water, followed by a solution of bleach. Initially, the concentration of dye was about 3.4×10^{-5} M, and the bleach (NaOCl) concentration was about 0.034 M. (b and c) The dye faded as it reacted with the bleach. The absorbance of the solution can be measured at various times using a spectrophotometer, and these values can be used to determine the concentration of the dye.

Let's consider an example, the decomposition of N_2O_5 in a solvent. This reaction occurs according to the following equation:

$$N_2O_5 \rightarrow 2\ NO_2 + \tfrac{1}{2}\ O_2$$

Concentrations and time elapsed for a typical experiment done at 30.0 °C are presented as a graph in Figure 15.2.

Active Figure 15.2 A plot of reactant concentration versus time for the decomposition of N_2O_5. The average rate for a 15-min interval from 45 min to 1 h is 0.0080 mol/L·min. The instantaneous rate calculated when $[N_2O_5]$ = 0.34 M is 0.0014 mol/L·min.

Chemistry‧ Now™ Sign in at www.cengage.com/login and go to the Chapter Contents menu to explore an interactive version of this figure accompanied by an exercise.

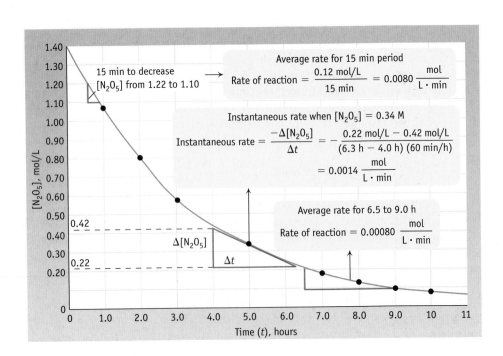

The rate of this reaction for any interval of time can be expressed as the change in concentration of N_2O_5 divided by the change in time:

$$\text{Rate of reaction} = \frac{\text{change in } \left[N_2O_5\right]}{\text{change in time}} = -\frac{\Delta\left[N_2O_5\right]}{\Delta t}$$

■ **Representing Concentration** Recall that square brackets around a formula indicate its concentrations in mol/L (Section 4.5).

The minus sign is required because the concentration of N_2O_5 decreases with time (that is, $\Delta[N_2O_5] = [N_2O_5](\text{final}) - [N_2O_5](\text{initial})$ is negative), and rate is always expressed as a positive quantity. Using data from Figure 15.2, the rate of disappearance of N_2O_5 between 40 min and 55 min is given by

$$\text{Rate} = -\frac{\Delta\left[N_2O_5\right]}{\Delta t} = -\frac{(1.10 \text{ mol/L}) - (1.22 \text{ mol/L})}{55 \text{ min} - 40 \text{ min}} = +\frac{0.12 \text{ mol/L}}{15 \text{ min}}$$

$$\text{Rate} = 0.0080 \frac{\text{mol } N_2O_5 \text{ consumed}}{\text{L} \cdot \text{min}}$$

■ **Calculating Changes** Recall that when we calculate a change in a quantity, we always do so by subtracting the initial quantity from the final quantity: $\Delta c = c_{\text{final}} - c_{\text{initial}}$.

Note the units for reaction rates; if concentration is expressed in mol/L, the units for rate will be mol/L · time.

During a chemical reaction, amounts of reactants decrease with time, and amounts of products increase. For the decomposition of N_2O_5, we could also express the rate either as $\Delta[NO_2]/\Delta t$ or as $\Delta[O_2]/\Delta t$. Rates based on changes in concentrations of products will have a positive sign because the concentration is increasing. Furthermore, the numerical values of rates defined in these ways will be different from value of $\Delta[N_2O_5]/\Delta t$. Note that the rate of decomposition of N_2O_5 is one half the rate of formation of NO_2 and twice the rate of formation of O_2. The relationship between these rate expressions is determined from the coefficients in the chemical equation.

$$\text{Rate of reaction} = -\frac{\Delta\left[N_2O_5\right]}{\Delta t} = +\frac{1}{2}\frac{\Delta\left[NO_2\right]}{\Delta t} = +2\frac{\Delta\left[O_2\right]}{\Delta t}$$

For the 15-minute interval between 40 and 55 minutes, the rates for the formation of NO_2 and O_2 are

$$\text{Rate} = \frac{\Delta\left[NO_2\right]}{\Delta t} = \frac{0.0080 \text{ mol } N_2O_5 \text{ consumed}}{\text{L} \cdot \text{min}} \times \frac{2 \text{ mol } NO_2 \text{ formed}}{1 \text{ mol } N_2O_5 \text{ consumed}}$$

$$= 0.016 \frac{\text{mol } NO_2 \text{ formed}}{\text{L} \cdot \text{min}}$$

$$\text{Rate} = \frac{\Delta\left[O_2\right]}{\Delta t} = \frac{0.0080 \text{ mol } N_2O_5 \text{ consumed}}{\text{L} \cdot \text{min}} \times \frac{\frac{1}{2} \text{ mol } O_2 \text{ formed}}{1 \text{ mol } N_2O_5 \text{ consumed}}$$

$$= 0.0040 \frac{\text{mol } O_2 \text{ formed}}{\text{L} \cdot \text{min}}$$

The graph of $[N_2O_5]$ versus time in Figure 15.2 does not give a straight line because the rate of the reaction changes during the course of the reaction. The concentration of N_2O_5 decreases rapidly at the beginning of the reaction but more slowly near the end. We can verify this by comparing the rate of disappearance of N_2O_5 calculated previously (the concentration decreased by 0.12 mol/L in 15 min) to the rate of reaction calculated for the time interval from 6.5 h to 9.0 h (when the concentration drops by 0.12 mol/L in 150 min). The rate in this later stage of this reaction is only one tenth of the previous value.

$$-\frac{\Delta[N_2O_5]}{\Delta t} = -\frac{(0.10\ \text{mol/L}) - (0.22\ \text{mol/L})}{540\ \text{min} - 390\ \text{min}} = +\frac{0.12\ \text{mol/L}}{150\ \text{min}}$$

$$= 0.00080\ \frac{\text{mol}}{\text{L} \cdot \text{min}}$$

The procedure we have used to calculate the reaction rate gives the average rate over the chosen time interval.

We might also ask what the instantaneous rate is at a single point in time. In an automobile, the instantaneous rate can be read from the speedometer. For a chemical reaction, we can extract the instantaneous rate from the concentration–time graph by drawing a line tangent to the concentration–time curve at a particular time (see Figure 15.2). The instantaneous rate is obtained from the slope of this line. For example, when $[N_2O_5] = 0.34$ mol/L and $t = 5.0$ h, the rate is

■ **The Slope of a Line** The instantaneous rate in Figure 15.2 can be determined from an analysis of the slope of the line. See pages 39–41 for more on finding the slope of a line.

$$\text{Rate when } [N_2O_5] \text{ is 0.34 M} = -\frac{\Delta[N_2O_5]}{\Delta t} = +\frac{0.20\ \text{mol/L}}{140\ \text{min}}$$

$$= 1.4 \times 10^{-3}\ \frac{\text{mol}}{\text{L} \cdot \text{min}}$$

At that particular moment in time, ($t = 5.0$ h), N_2O_5 is being consumed at a rate of 0.0014 mol/L · min.

Chemistry Ꭴ Now™

Sign in at **www.cengage.com/login** and go to Chapter 15 Contents to see Screen 15.2 for a visualization of ways to express reaction rates.

■ **Reaction Rates and Stoichiometry**
For the general reaction $a\ A + b\ B \rightarrow c\ C + d\ D$, the international convention defines the reaction rate as

$$\text{Rate} = -\frac{1}{a}\frac{\Delta[A]}{\Delta t} = -\frac{1}{b}\frac{\Delta[B]}{\Delta t}$$
$$= +\frac{1}{c}\frac{\Delta[C]}{\Delta t} = +\frac{1}{d}\frac{\Delta[D]}{\Delta t}$$

EXAMPLE 15.1 **Relative Rates and Stoichiometry**

Problem Relate the rates for the disappearance of reactants and formation of products for the following reaction:

$$4\ PH_3(g) \rightarrow P_4(g) + 6\ H_2(g)$$

Strategy In this reaction, PH_3 disappears, and P_4 and H_2 are formed. Consequently, the value of $\Delta[PH_3]/\Delta t$ will be negative, whereas $\Delta[P_4]/\Delta t$ and $\Delta[H_2]/\Delta t$ will be positive. To relate the rates to each other, we divide $\Delta[\text{reagent}]/\Delta t$ by its stoichiometric coefficient in the balanced equation.

Solution Because four moles of PH_3 disappear for every one mole of P_4 formed, the numerical value of the rate of formation of P_4 is one fourth of the rate of disappearance of PH_3. Similarly, P_4 is formed at only one sixth of the rate that H_2 is formed.

$$-\frac{1}{4}\left(\frac{\Delta[PH_3]}{\Delta t}\right) = +\frac{\Delta[P_4]}{\Delta t} = +\frac{1}{6}\left(\frac{\Delta[H_2]}{\Delta t}\right)$$

EXAMPLE 15.2 **Rate of Reaction**

Problem Data collected on the concentration of dye as a function of time (see Figure 15.1) are given in the graph below. What is the average rate of change of the dye concentration over the first 2 min? What is the average rate of change during the fifth minute (from $t = 4$ min to $t = 5$ min)? Estimate the instantaneous rate at 4 min.

Strategy To find the average rate, calculate the difference in concentration at the beginning and end of a time period ($\Delta c = c_{final} - c_{initial}$) and divide by the elapsed time. To find the instantaneous rate at 4 minutes, draw a line tangent to the graph at the specified time. The negative of the slope of the line is the instantaneous rate.

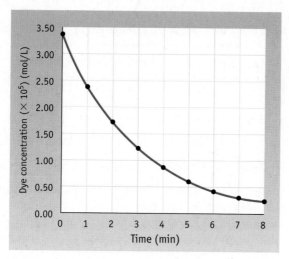

Solution The concentration of dye decreases from 3.4×10^{-5} mol/L at $t = 0$ min to 1.7×10^{-5} mol/L at $t = 2.0$ min. The average rate of the reaction in this interval of time is

$$\text{Average rate} = -\frac{\Delta[\text{Dye}]}{\Delta t} = -\frac{(1.7 \times 10^{-5} \text{ mol/L}) - (3.4 \times 10^{-5} \text{ mol/L})}{2.0 \text{ mol}}$$

$$\text{Average rate} = +\frac{8.5 \times 10^{-6} \text{ mol}}{\text{L} \cdot \text{min}}$$

The concentration of dye decreases from 0.90×10^{-5} mol/L at $t = 4.0$ min to 0.60×10^{-5} mol/L at $t = 5.0$ min. The average rate of the reaction in this interval of time is

$$\text{Average rate} = -\frac{\Delta[\text{Dye}]}{\Delta t} = -\frac{(0.60 \times 10^{-5} \text{ mol/L}) - (0.90 \times 10^{-5} \text{ mol/L})}{1.0 \text{ mol}}$$

$$\text{Average rate} = +\frac{3.0 \times 10^{-6} \text{ mol}}{\text{L} \cdot \text{min}}$$

From the slope of the line tangent to the curve, the instantaneous rate at 4 min is found to be $+3.5 \times 10^{-6}$ mol/L $\cdot$ min.

EXERCISE 15.1 Reaction Rates and Stoichiometry

What are the relative rates of appearance or disappearance of each product and reactant, respectively, in the decomposition of nitrosyl chloride, NOCl?

$$2 \text{ NOCl}(g) \rightarrow 2 \text{ NO}(g) + \text{Cl}_2(g)$$

EXERCISE 15.2 Rate of Reaction

Sucrose decomposes to fructose and glucose in acid solution. A plot of the concentration of sucrose as a function of time is given here. What is the rate of change of the sucrose concentration over the first 2 h? What is the rate of change over the last 2 h? Estimate the instantaneous rate at 4 h.

Chemistry ⚗ Now™

Sign in at **www.cengage.com/login** and go to Chapter 15 Contents to see Screen 15.2 for a self-study module on **rate of reaction**.

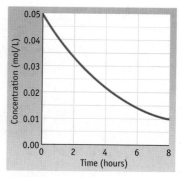

Concentration versus time for the decomposition of sucrose. (See Exercise 15.2.)

15.2 Reaction Conditions and Rate

Several factors—reactant concentrations, temperature, and presence of catalysts—affect the rate of a reaction. If the reactant is a solid, the surface area available for reaction is also a factor.

The "iodine clock reaction" (Figure 15.3) illustrates the effect of concentration and temperature. The reaction mixture contains hydrogen peroxide (H_2O_2), iodide ion (I^-), vitamin C (ascorbic acid), and starch (which is an indicator of the presence of iodine, I_2). A sequence of reactions begins with the slow oxidation of iodide ion to I_2 by H_2O_2.

$$H_2O_2(aq) + 2\ I^-(aq) + 2\ H_3O^+(aq) \rightarrow 4\ H_2O(\ell) + I_2(aq)$$

As soon as I_2 is formed in the solution, vitamin C rapidly reduces it to I^-.

$$2\ H_2O(\ell) + I_2(aq) + C_6H_8O_6(aq) \rightarrow C_6H_6O_6(aq) + 2\ H_3O^+(aq) + 2\ I^-(aq)$$

When all of the vitamin C has been consumed, I_2 remains in solution and forms a blue–black complex with starch. The time measured represents how long it has taken for the given amount of iodide ion to react. For the first experiment (A in Figure 15.3) the time required is 51 seconds. When the concentration of iodide ion is smaller (B), the time required for the vitamin C to be consumed is longer, 1 minute and 33 seconds. Finally, when the concentrations are again the same as in experiment B but the reaction mixture is heated, the reaction occurs more rapidly (56 seconds).

■ **Effect of Temperature on Reaction Rate** Cooking involves chemical reactions, and a higher temperature results in foods cooking faster. In the laboratory, reaction mixtures are often heated to make reactions occur faster.

(a) Initial Experiment.
The blue color of the starch–iodine complex develops in 51 seconds.

(b) Change Concentration.
The blue color of starch–iodine complex develops in 1 minute, 33 seconds when the solution is less concentrated than A.

(c) Change Temperature.
The blue color of the starch–iodine complex develops in 56 seconds when the solution is the same concentration as in B but at a higher temperature.

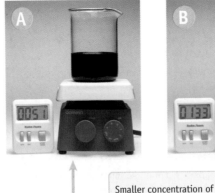

Solutions containing vitamin C, H_2O_2, I^-, and starch are mixed.

Smaller concentration of I^- than in Experiment A.

Hot bath

Same concentrations as in Experiment B, but at a higher temperature.

FIGURE 15.3 The iodine clock reaction. This reaction illustrates the effects of concentration and temperature on reaction rate. (You can do these experiments yourself with reagents available in the supermarket. For details, see S. W. Wright: "The vitamin C clock reaction," *Journal of Chemical Education*, Vol. 79, p. 41, 2002.) See ChemistryNow Screen 15.11 for a video of the iodine clock reaction.

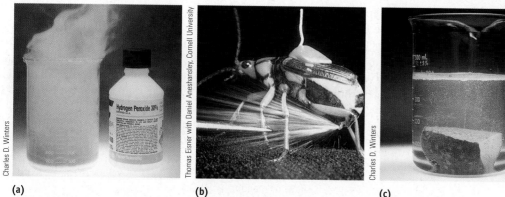

(a)   (b)   (c)

FIGURE 15.4 Catalyzed decomposition of H_2O_2. (a) The rate of decomposition of hydrogen peroxide is increased by the catalyst MnO_2. Here, H_2O_2 (as a 30% aqueous solution) is poured onto the black solid MnO_2 and rapidly decomposes to O_2 and H_2O. Steam forms because of the high heat of reaction. (b) A bombardier beetle uses the catalyzed decomposition of H_2O_2 as a defense mechanism. The heat of the reaction lets the insect eject hot water and other irritating chemicals with explosive force. (c) A naturally occurring catalyst, called an enzyme, decomposes hydrogen peroxide. Here, the enzyme found in a potato is used to catalyze H_2O_2 decomposition, and bubbles of O_2 gas are seen rising in the solution.

Catalysts are substances that accelerate chemical reactions but are not themselves consumed. Consider the effect of a catalyst on the decomposition of hydrogen peroxide, H_2O_2, to form water and oxygen.

$$2\ H_2O_2(aq) \rightarrow O_2(g) + 2\ H_2O(\ell)$$

This decomposition is very slow; a solution of H_2O_2 can be stored for many months with only minimal change in concentration. Adding a manganese salt, an iodide-containing salt, or a biological substance called an *enzyme* causes this reaction to occur rapidly, as shown by vigorous bubbling as gaseous oxygen escapes from the solution (Figure 15.4).

The surface area of a solid reactant can also affect the reaction rate. Only molecules at the surface of a solid can come in contact with other reactants. The smaller the particles of a solid, the more molecules are found on the solid's surface. With very small particles, the effect of surface area on rate can be quite dramatic (Figure 15.5). Farmers know that explosions of fine dust particles (suspended in the air in an enclosed silo or at a feed mill) represent a major hazard.

Chemistry ·Ò· Now™

Sign in at **www.cengage.com/login** and go to Chapter 15 Contents to see:
- Screen 15.3 for a visualization of **the factors controlling rates**
- Screen 15.4 for a simulation of the **effect of concentration on rate**

15.3 Effect of Concentration on Reaction Rate

One important goal in studying the kinetics of a reaction is to determine its mechanism; that is, how the reaction occurs at the molecular level. The place to begin is to learn how concentrations of reactants affect the reaction rate.

The effect of concentration can be determined by evaluating the rate of a reaction using different concentrations of each reactant (with the temperature held constant).

(a)

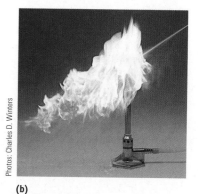

(b)

FIGURE 15.5 The combustion of lycopodium powder. (a) The spores of this common fern burn only with difficulty when piled in a dish. (b) If the spores are ground to a fine powder and sprayed into a flame, combustion is rapid.

Consider, for example, the decomposition of N_2O_5 to NO_2 and O_2. Figure 15.2 presented data on the concentration of N_2O_5 as a function of time. We previously calculated that, when $[N_2O_5] = 0.34$ mol/L, the instantaneous rate of disappearance of N_2O_5 is 0.0014 mol/L · min. An evaluation of the instantaneous rate of the reaction when $[N_2O_5] = 0.68$ mol/L reveals a rate of 0.0028 mol/L · min. That is, doubling the concentration of N_2O_5 doubles the reaction rate. A similar exercise shows that if $[N_2O_5]$ is 0.17 mol/L (half of 0.34 mol/L), the reaction rate is also halved. From these results, we know that the reaction rate must be directly proportional to the reactant concentration for this reaction:

$$N_2O_5 \rightarrow 2\ NO_2 + \tfrac{1}{2}\ O_2$$

$$\text{Rate of reaction} \propto [N_2O_5]$$

where the symbol $\propto$ means "proportional to."

Different relationships between reaction rate and reactant concentration are encountered in other reactions. For example, the reaction rate could be independent of concentration, or it may depend on the reactant concentration raised to some power (that is, $[\text{reactant}]^n$). If the reaction involves several reactants, the reaction rate may depend on the concentrations of each of them or on only one of them. Finally, if a catalyst is involved, its concentration may also affect the rate, as can the concentrations of products.

Rate Equations

The relationship between reactant concentration and reaction rate is expressed by an equation called a **rate equation**, or **rate law**. For the decomposition of N_2O_5 the rate equation is

$$N_2O_5(g) \rightarrow 2\ NO_2(g) + \tfrac{1}{2}\ O_2$$

$$\text{Rate of reaction} = k[N_2O_5]$$

where the proportionality constant, k, is called the **rate constant**. This rate equation tells us that this reaction rate is proportional to the concentration of the reactant. Based on this equation, we can determine that when $[N_2O_5]$ is doubled, the reaction rate doubles.

Generally, for a reaction such as

$$a\ A + b\ B \rightarrow x\ X$$

■ **Exponents on Reactant Concentrations and Reaction Stoichiometry** It is important to recognize that the exponents m and n are not necessarily the stoichiometric coefficients (a and b) for the balanced chemical equation.

the rate equation has the form

$$\text{Rate of reaction} = k[A]^m[B]^n$$

The rate equation expresses the fact that the rate of reaction is proportional to the reactant concentrations, each concentration being raised to some power. The exponents in this equation are often positive whole numbers, but they can also be negative numbers, fractions, or zero and they are determined by experiment.

If a homogeneous catalyst is present, its concentration might also be included in the rate equation, even though the catalytic species in not a product or reactant in the equation for the reaction. Consider, for example, the decomposition of hydrogen peroxide in the presence of a catalyst such as iodide ion.

$$H_2O_2(aq) \xrightarrow{\ I^-\,(aq)\ } H_2O(\ell) + \tfrac{1}{2}\ O_2(g)$$

Experiments show that this reaction has the following rate equation:

$$\text{Reaction rate} = k[H_2O_2][I^-]$$

Here, the concentration of I^- appears in the rate law, even though it is not involved in the balanced equation.

The Order of a Reaction

The **order** of a reaction with respect to a particular reactant is the exponent of its concentration term in the rate expression, and the **overall reaction order** is the sum of the exponents on all concentration terms. Consider, for example, the reaction of NO and Cl_2:

$$2 \text{ NO(g)} + Cl_2(g) \rightarrow 2 \text{ NOCl(g)}$$

The experimentally determined rate equation for this reaction is

$$\text{Rate} = k[\text{NO}]^2[Cl_2]$$

This reaction is second order in NO, first order in Cl_2, and third order overall. How is this related to the experimental data for the rate of disappearance of NO?

Experiment	[NO] mol/L	[Cl_2] mol/L	Rate mol/L · s
1	0.250	0.250	1.43×10^{-6}
	$\downarrow \times 2$	$\downarrow$ no change	$\downarrow \times 4$
2	0.500	0.250	5.72×10^{-6}
3	0.250	0.500	2.86×10^{-6}
4	0.500	0.500	11.4×10^{-6}

- *Compare Experiments 1 and 2:* Here, [Cl_2] is held constant, and [NO] is doubled. The change in [NO] leads to a reaction rate increase by a factor of 4; that is, the rate is proportional to the *square* of the NO concentration.
- *Compare Experiments 1 and 3:* In experiments 1 and 3, [NO] is held constant, and [Cl_2] is doubled, causing the rate to double. That is, the rate is proportional to [Cl_2].
- *Compare Experiments 1 and 4:* Both [NO] and [Cl_2] are doubled from 0.250 M to 0.500 M. From previous experiments, we know that doubling [NO] should cause a four-fold increase, and doubling [Cl_2] causes a two-fold increase. Therefore, doubling both concentrations should cause an eight-fold increase, as is observed ($1.43 \times 10^{-6} \times 8 = 11.4 \times 10^{-6}$ mol/L · s).

The decomposition of ammonia on a platinum surface at 856 °C is a zero order reaction.

$$NH_3(g) \rightarrow \tfrac{1}{2} N_2(g) + \tfrac{3}{2} H_2(g)$$

This means that the reaction rate is independent of NH_3 concentration.

$$\text{Rate} = k[NH_3]^0 = k$$

Reaction order is important because it gives some insight into the most interesting question of all—how the reaction occurs. This is described further in Section 15.6.

The Rate Constant, k

The rate constant, k, is a proportionality constant that relates rate and concentration at a given temperature. It is an important quantity because it enables you to find the reaction rate for a new set of concentrations. To see how to use k, consider

■ **Time and Rate Constants** The time in a rate constant can be seconds, minutes, hours, days, years, or whatever time unit is appropriate. The fraction 1/time can also be written as time^{-1}. For example, $1/y$ is equivalent to y^{-1}, and $1/s$ is equivalent to s^{-1}.

the substitution of Cl$^-$ ion by water in the cancer chemotherapy agent cisplatin, $Pt(NH_3)_2Cl_2$.

$$Pt(NH_3)_2Cl_2(aq) \quad + \quad H_2O(\ell) \quad \longrightarrow \quad [Pt(NH_3)_2(H_2O)Cl]^+(aq) \quad + \quad Cl^-(aq)$$

The rate law for this reaction is

$$\text{Rate} = k[Pt(NH_3)_2Cl_2]$$

and the rate constant, k, is 0.27/h at 25 °C. Knowing k allows you to calculate the rate at a particular reactant concentration—for example, when $[Pt(NH_3)_2Cl_2]$ = 0.018 mol/L:

$$\text{Rate} = (0.27/h)(0.018 \text{ mol/L}) = 0.0049 \text{ mol/L} \cdot h$$

As noted, earlier, reaction rates have units of mol/L · time when concentrations are given as moles per liter. Rate constants must have units consistent with the units for the other terms in the rate equation.

- First-order reactions: the units of k are 1/time.
- Second-order reactions: the units of k are L/mol · time.
- Zero-order reaction: the units of k are mol/L · time.

■ **Some Rate Constants**

First Order	$k(1/s)$
2 N$_2$O$_5$(g) → 4 NO$_2$(g) + O$_2$(g)	3.38 × 10^{-5} at 25 °C
C$_2$H$_6$(g) → 2 CH$_3$(g)	5.36 × 10^{-4} at 700 °C
Sucrose(aq, H$_3$O$^+$) → fructose(aq) + glucose(aq)	6.0 × 10^{-5} at 25 °C

Second Order	$k(L/mol \cdot s)$
2 NOBr(g) → 2 NO(g) + Br$_2$(g)	0.80 at 10 °C
H$_2$(g) + I$_2$(g) → 2 HI(g)	0.0242 at 400 °C

Determining a Rate Equation

One way to determine a rate equation is by using the "method of initial rates." The initial rate is the instantaneous reaction rate at the start of the reaction (the rate at $t = 0$). An approximate value of the initial rate can be obtained by mixing the reactants and determining $\Delta[\text{product}]/\Delta t$ or $-\Delta[\text{reactant}]/\Delta t$ after 1% to 2% of the limiting reactant has been consumed. Measuring the rate during the initial stage of a reaction is convenient because initial concentrations are known.

As an example of the determination of a reaction rate by the method of initial rates, let us consider the reaction of sodium hydroxide with methyl acetate to produce acetate ion and methanol.

$$CH_3CO_2CH_3(aq) \quad + \quad OH^-(aq) \quad \longrightarrow \quad CH_3CO_2^-(aq) \quad + \quad CH_3OH(aq)$$

Reactant concentrations and initial rates for this reaction for several experiments at 25 °C are collected in the table below.

Experiment	Initial Concentrations (mol/L)		Initial Reaction Rate
	[CH₃CO₂CH₃]	[OH⁻]	(mol/L · s) at 25 °C
1	0.050	0.050	0.00034
	↓ no change	↓ × 2	↓ × 2
2	0.050	0.10	0.00069
	↓ × 2	↓ no change	↓ × 2
3	0.10	0.10	0.00137

As noted in the table, when the initial concentration of one reactant (either $CH_3CO_2CH_3$ or OH^-) is doubled while the concentration of the other reactant is held constant, the initial reaction rate doubles. This rate doubling shows that the reaction rate is directly proportional to the concentrations of both $CH_3CO_2CH_3$ and OH^-; thus, the reaction is first order in each of these reactants and second order overall. The rate law that reflects these experimental observations is

$$\text{Rate} = k[CH_3CO_2CH_3][OH^-]$$

Using this equation, we can predict that doubling both concentrations at the same time should cause the rate to go up by a factor of 4. What happens, however, if one concentration is doubled and the other is halved? The rate equation tells us the rate should not change!

If the rate equation is known, the value of k, the rate constant, can be found by substituting values for the rate and concentration into the rate equation. Using the data for the methyl acetate/hydroxide ion reaction from the first experiment, we have

$$\text{Rate} = 0.00034 \text{ mol/L} \cdot \text{s} = k(0.050 \text{ mol/L})(0.050 \text{ mol/L})$$

$$k = \frac{0.00034 \text{ mol/L} \cdot \text{s}}{(0.050 \text{ mol/L})(0.050 \text{ mol/L})} = 0.14 \text{ L/mol} \cdot \text{s}$$

Chemistry ⚛ Now™

Sign in at **www.cengage.com/login** and go to Chapter 15 Contents to see:
- Screen 15.4 for a self-study module on **control of reaction rates**
- Screen 15.5 for a simulation, a tutorial, and an exercise on **determining rate equations from a study of the effect of concentration on reaction rate**

■ EXAMPLE 15.3 Determining a Rate Equation

Problem The rate of the reaction between CO and NO_2 at 540 K

$$CO(g) + NO_2(g) \rightarrow CO_2(g) + NO(g)$$

was measured starting with various concentrations of CO and NO_2. Determine the rate equation and the value of the rate constant.

Experiment	Initial Concentrations		Initial Rate
	[CO], mol/L	[NO₂], mol/L	(mol/L · h)
1	5.10×10^{-4}	0.350×10^{-4}	3.4×10^{-8}
2	5.10×10^{-4}	0.700×10^{-4}	6.8×10^{-8}
3	5.10×10^{-4}	0.175×10^{-4}	1.7×10^{-8}
4	1.02×10^{-3}	0.350×10^{-4}	6.8×10^{-8}
5	1.53×10^{-3}	0.350×10^{-4}	10.2×10^{-8}

Strategy For a reaction involving several reactants, the general approach is to keep the concentration of one reactant constant and then decide how the rate of reaction changes as the concentration of the other reagent is varied. Because the rate is proportional to the concentration of a reactant, say A, raised to some power n (the reaction order)

$$\text{Rate} \propto [A]^n$$

we can write the general equation

$$\frac{\text{Rate in experiment 2}}{\text{Rate in experiment 1}} = \frac{[A_2]^n}{[A_1]^n} = \left(\frac{[A_2]}{[A_1]}\right)^n$$

If [A] is doubled and the rate doubles from experiment 1 to experiment 2, then $n = 1$. If [A] doubles and the rate goes up by 4, then $n = 2$.

Solution In the first three experiments, the concentration of CO is held constant. In the second experiment, the NO_2 concentration has been doubled relative to Experiment 1, leading to a twofold increase in the rate. Thus, $n = 1$ and the reaction is first order in NO_2.

$$\frac{\text{Rate in experiment 2}}{\text{Rate in experiment 1}} = \frac{6.8 \times 10^{-8} \text{ mol/L} \cdot \text{h}}{3.4 \times 10^{-8} \text{ mol/L} \cdot \text{h}} = \left(\frac{0.700 \times 10^{-4}}{0.350 \times 10^{-4}}\right)^n$$

$$2 = (2)^n$$

and so $n = 1$.

This finding is confirmed by experiment 3. Decreasing $[NO_2]$ to half its original value in experiment 3 causes the rate to decrease by half.

The data in experiments 1 and 4 (with constant $[NO_2]$) show that doubling [CO] doubles the rate, and the data from experiments 1 and 5 show that tripling the concentration of CO triples the rate. These results mean that the reaction is first order in [CO]. We now know the rate equation is

$$\text{Rate} = k[CO][NO_2]$$

The rate constant, k, can be found by inserting data for one of the experiments into the rate equation. Using data from experiment 1, for example,

$$\text{Rate} = 3.4 \times 10^{-8} \text{ mol/L} \cdot \text{h} = k(5.10 \times 10^{-4} \text{ mol/L})(0.350 \times 10^{-4} \text{ mol/L})$$

$$k = 1.9 \text{ L/mol} \cdot \text{h}$$

EXAMPLE 15.4 Using a Rate Equation to Determine Rates

Problem Using the rate equation and rate constant determined for the reaction of CO and NO_2 at 540 K in Example 15.3, determine the initial rate of the reaction when $[CO] = 3.8 \times 10^{-4}$ mol/L and $[NO_2] = 0.650 \times 10^{-4}$ mol/L.

Strategy A rate equation consists of three parts: a rate, a rate constant (k), and the concentration terms. If two of these parts are known (here k and the concentrations), the third can be calculated.

Solution Substitute k ($= 1.9$ L/mol $\cdot$ h) and the concentration of each reactant into the rate law determined in Example 15.3.

$$\text{Rate} = k[CO][NO_2] = (1.9 \text{ L/mol} \cdot \text{h})(3.8 \times 10^{-4} \text{ mol/L})(0.650 \times 10^{-4} \text{ mol/L})$$

$$\text{Rate} = 4.7 \times 10^{-8} \text{ mol/L} \cdot \text{h}$$

Comment As a check on the calculated result, it is sometimes useful to make an educated guess at the answer before carrying out the mathematical solution. We know that the reaction here is first order in both reactants. Comparing the concentration values given in this problem with the concentration values in found experiment 1 in Example 15.3, we notice that [CO] is about three fourths of the concentration value, whereas $[NO_2]$ is almost twice the value. The effects do not precisely offset each other, but we might predict that the difference in rates between this experiment and experiment 1 will be fairly small, with the rate of this experiment being just a little greater. The calculated value bears this out.

EXERCISE 15.3 Determining a Rate Equation

The initial rate of the reaction of nitrogen monoxide and oxygen

$$2\ NO(g) + O_2(g) \rightarrow 2\ NO_2(g)$$

was measured at 25 °C for various initial concentrations of NO and O_2. Determine the rate equation from these data. What is the value of the rate constant, k, and what are its units?

Experiment	Initial Concentrations (mol/L)		Initial Rate
	[NO]	[O₂]	(mol/L · s)
1	0.020	0.010	0.028
2	0.020	0.020	0.057
3	0.020	0.040	0.114
4	0.040	0.020	0.227
5	0.010	0.020	0.014

EXERCISE 15.4 Using Rate Laws

The rate constant, k, at 25 °C is 0.27/h for the reaction

$$Pt(NH_3)_2Cl_2(aq) + H_2O(\ell) \rightarrow [Pt(NH_3)_2(H_2O)Cl]^+(aq) + Cl^-(aq)$$

and the rate equation is

$$Rate = k[Pt(NH_3)_2Cl_2]$$

Calculate the rate of reaction when the concentration of $Pt(NH_3)_2Cl_2$ is 0.020 M.

15.4 Concentration–Time Relationships: Integrated Rate Laws

 Module 20

It is often important for a chemist to know how long a reaction must proceed to reach a predetermined concentration of some reactant or product, or what the reactant and product concentrations will be after some time has elapsed. A mathematical equation that relates time and concentration—that is, an equation that describes concentration–time curves like the one shown in Figure 15.2—can be used to determine this information. With such an equation, we could calculate the concentration at any given time or the length of time needed for a given amount of reactant to react.

First-Order Reactions

Suppose the reaction "R → products" is first order. This means the reaction rate is directly proportional to the concentration of R raised to the first power, or, mathematically,

$$-\frac{\Delta[R]}{\Delta t} = k[R]$$

Using calculus, this relationship can be transformed into a very useful equation called an **integrated rate equation** (because integral calculus is used in its derivation).

$$\ln \frac{[R]_t}{[R]_0} = -kt \qquad\qquad (15.1)$$

Qualitatively, the rate of a reaction is easy to understand: it represents the change in concentration of the reactants and products. When we deal with rates of reaction quantitatively, however, we need to be specific about the reaction stoichiometry.

Consider the first order decomposition of N_2O_5, a reaction that we mentioned earlier

$$2 N_2O_5 \rightarrow 4 NO_2 + O_2(g)$$

The rate of the reaction can be expressed (and measured in lab) as the change in concentration of either reactants or products as a function of time. The numerical values of the rates of formation of reactants and products are related, but they are different because of the reaction stoichiometry. If we equate the rate of reaction to the rate of appearance of O_2, we would write

$$\text{Rate} = \frac{\Delta[O_2]}{\Delta t} = -\frac{1}{2}\frac{\Delta[N_2O_5]}{\Delta t} = +\frac{1}{4}\frac{\Delta[NO_2]}{\Delta t}$$

This relation is written by dividing each rate by its stoichiometric coefficient (◀ page 674).

There are two different pieces of information in the equation above. First, it gives the relationship between the rates of change of concentrations of reactants and products. Based on the reaction stoichiometry, we know that the rate of appearance of O_2 is one half the rate of disappearance of N_2O_5 and one fourth the rate of NO_2 appearance.

Second, this equation specifically defines what we mean by rate; it provides a single, numerical values for this parameter; and it tells us how to calculate the value of reaction rate from experimental data. If we were to follow the disappearance of N_2O_5 as a measure of reaction rate and base our definition of rate on the stoichiometry above, we should write the following differential form of the rate law.

$$\text{Rate} = -\frac{1}{2}\frac{\Delta[N_2O_5]}{\Delta t} = k[N_2O_5]$$

From this definition, it follows that the differential rate equation is

$$\text{Rate} = -\frac{\Delta[N_2O_5]}{\Delta t} = 2k[N_2O_5]$$

the integrated rate equation is (see page 683),

$$\ln\frac{[N_2O_5]_t}{[N_2O_5]_0} = -2kt$$

and the half-life equation is

$$t_{1/2} = 0.693/2k$$

We can also write the equation for N_2O_5 decomposition as follows:

$$N_2O_5 \rightarrow 2 NO_2 + \tfrac{1}{2} O_2(g)$$

Following the reasoning above, the rate laws for the reaction written this way would be:

Differential rate equation:

$$-\frac{\Delta[N_2O_5]}{\Delta t} = k'[N_2O_5]$$

Integrated rate equation:

$$\ln\frac{[N_2O_5]_t}{[N_2O_5]_0} = -k't$$

Half-life equation:

$$t_{1/2} = 0.693/k'$$

Note that the differential and integrated rate laws derived based on the two different chemical equations have the same form, but k and k' do not have the same values. In this case, $2k = k'$.

For more on this issue, see K. T. Quisenberry and J. Tellinghuisen, *Journal of Chemical Education*, Vol. 83, pp. 510–512, 2006.

■ **Initial and Final Time, t** The time $t = 0$ does not need to correspond to the actual beginning of the experiment. It can be the time when instrument readings were started, for example, even though the reaction may have already begun.

Here, $[R]_0$ and $[R]_t$ are concentrations of the reactant at time $t = 0$ and at a later time, t, respectively. The ratio of concentrations, $[R]_t/[R]_0$, is the fraction of reactant that remains after a given time has elapsed. In words, the equation says

$$\text{Natural logarithm}\left(\frac{\text{concentration of R after some time}}{\text{concentration of R at start of experiment}}\right)$$
$$= \ln(\text{fraction of R remaining at time, } t)$$
$$= -(\text{rate constant})(\text{elapsed time})$$

Notice the negative sign in the equation. The ratio $[R]_t/[R]_0$ is less than 1 because $[R]_t$ is always less than $[R]_0$; the reactant R is consumed during the reaction. This means the logarithm of $[R]_t/[R]_0$ is negative, so the other side of the equation must also bear a negative sign.

Equation 15.1 can be used to carry out the following calculations:

- If $[R]_t/[R]_0$ is measured in the laboratory after some amount of time has elapsed, then k can be calculated.
- If $[R]_0$ and k are known, then the concentration of material remaining after a given amount of time ($[R]_t$) can be calculated.
- If k is known, then the time elapsed until a specific fraction ($[R]_t/[R]_0$) remains can be calculated.

Finally, notice that k for a first-order reaction is independent of concentration; k has units of time^{-1} (y^{-1} or s^{-1}, for example). This means we can choose any convenient unit for $[R]_t$ and $[R]_0$: moles per liter, moles, grams, number of atoms, number of molecules, or gas pressure.

Chemistry ☼ Now™

Sign in at **www.cengage.com/login** and go to Chapter 15 Contents to see Screen 15.6 for a tutorial on **the use of the integrated first-order rate equation.**

EXAMPLE 15.5 The First-Order Rate Equation

Problem In the past, cyclopropane, C_3H_6, was used in a mixture with oxygen as an anesthetic. (This practice has almost ceased today, because the compound is flammable.) When heated, cyclopropane rearranges to propene in a first-order process.

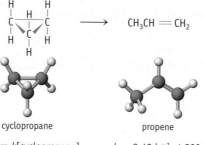

$$\longrightarrow \quad CH_3CH = CH_2$$

cyclopropane   propene

Rate $= k[\text{cyclopropane}]$ $k = 2.42\ h^{-1}$ at 500 °C

If the initial concentration of cyclopropane is 0.050 mol/L, how much time (in hours) must elapse for its concentration to drop to 0.010 mol/L?

Strategy The reaction is first order in cyclopropane. You know the rate constant, k, and the initial and final concentrations. Use Equation 15.1 to calculate the time (t) elapsed to reach a concentration of 0.010 mol/L.

Solution Values for $[\text{cyclopropane}]_t$, $[\text{cyclopropane}]_0$, and k are substituted into Equation 15.1; t (time) is the unknown:

$$\ln \frac{[0.010]}{[0.050]} = (2.42\ h^{-1})t$$

$$t = \frac{-\ln(0.20)}{2.42\ h^{-1}} = \frac{-(-1.61)}{2.42\ h^{-1}} = \boxed{0.665\ h}$$

Comment Cycloalkanes with fewer than five carbon atoms are strained because the C—C—C bond angles cannot match the preferred 109.5°. Because of ring strain, the cyclopropane ring opens readily to form propene.

EXAMPLE 15.6 Using the First-Order Rate Equation

Problem Hydrogen peroxide decomposes in a dilute sodium hydroxide solution at 20 °C in a first-order reaction:

$H_2O_2(aq) \rightarrow H_2O(\ell) + \frac{1}{2}\ O_2(g)$

Rate $= k[H_2O_2]$ with $k = 1.06 \times 10^{-3}\ min^{-1}$

What is the fraction remaining after 100. min if the initial concentration of H_2O_2 is 0.020 mol/L? What is the concentration of the peroxide after 100. min?

Strategy Because the reaction is first order in H_2O_2, we use Equation 15.1. Here, $[H_2O_2]_0$, k, and t are known, and we are asked to find the value of $[H_2O_2]_t$ and the fraction remaining. Recall that

$$\frac{[R]_t}{[R]_0} = \text{fraction remaining}$$

Once this value is known, and knowing $[H_2O_2]_0$, we can calculate $[H_2O_2]_t$.

Solution Substitute the known values into Equation 15.1.

$$\ln \frac{[H_2O_2]_t}{[H_2O_2]_0} = -kt = -(1.06 \times 10^{-3}\ \text{min}^{-1})(100.\ \text{min})$$

$$\ln \frac{[H_2O_2]_t}{[H_2O_2]_0} = -0.106$$

Taking the antilogarithm of -0.106 [i.e., the inverse of $\ln(-0.106)$ or $e^{-0.106}$], we find the fraction remaining to be 0.90.

$$\text{Fraction remaining} = \frac{[H_2O_2]_t}{[H_2O_2]_0} = \boxed{0.90}$$

Because $[H_2O_2]_0 = 0.020$ mol/L, this gives $\boxed{[H_2O_2]_t = 0.018\ \text{mol/L}}$.

EXERCISE 15.5 Using the First-Order Rate Equation

Sucrose, a sugar, decomposes in acid solution to give glucose and fructose. The reaction is first order in sucrose, and the rate constant at 25 °C is $k = 0.21\ \text{h}^{-1}$. If the initial concentration of sucrose is 0.010 mol/L, what is its concentration after 5.0 h?

EXERCISE 15.6 Using the First-Order Rate Equation

Gaseous azomethane ($CH_3N_2CH_3$) decomposes to ethane and nitrogen when heated:

$$CH_3N_2CH_3g) \rightarrow CH_3CH_3(g) + N_2(g)$$

The disappearance of azomethane is a first-order reaction with $k = 3.6 \times 10^{-4}\ \text{s}^{-1}$ at 600 K.

(a) A sample of gaseous $CH_3N_2CH_3$ is placed in a flask and heated at 600 K for 150 s. What fraction of the initial sample remains after this time?

(b) How long must a sample be heated so that 99% of the sample has decomposed?

Chemistry ⚛ Now™

Sign in at **www.cengage.com/login** and go to Chapter 15 Contents to see Screen 15.6 for a self-study module on the **first-order rate equation.**

Second-Order Reactions

Suppose the reaction "R → products" is second order. The rate equation is

$$-\frac{\Delta[R]}{\Delta t} = k[R]^2$$

Using calculus, this relationship can be transformed into the following equation that relates reactant concentration and time:

$$\frac{1}{[R]_t} - \frac{1}{[R]_0} = kt \qquad \text{(15.2)}$$

The same symbolism used with first-order reactions applies: $[R]_0$ is the concentration of reactant at the time $t = 0$; $[R]_t$ is the concentration at a later time; and k is the second-order rate constant which has the units of L/mol · time.

Problem The gas-phase decomposition of HI

$$HI(g) \rightarrow \tfrac{1}{2}\, H_2(g) + \tfrac{1}{2}\, I_2(g)$$

has the rate equation

$$-\frac{\Delta[HI]}{\Delta t} = k[HI]^2$$

where $k = 30.$ L/mol · min at 443 °C. How much time does it take for the concentration of HI to drop from 0.010 mol/L to 0.0050 mol/L at 443 °C?

Strategy Substitute the values of $[HI]_0$, $[HI]_t$, and k into Equation 15.2, and solve for the unknown, t.

Solution Here, $[HI]_0 = 0.010$ mol/L and $[HI]_t = 0.0050$ mol/L. Using Equation 15.2, we have

$$\frac{1}{0.0050 \text{ mol/L}} - \frac{1}{0.010 \text{ mol/L}} = (30. \text{ L/mol} \cdot \text{min})t$$

$$(2.0 \times 10^2 \text{ L/mol}) - (1.0 \times 10^2 \text{ L/mol}) = (30. \text{ L/mol} \cdot \text{min})t$$

$$t = \boxed{3.3 \text{ min}}$$

EXERCISE 15.7 **Using the Second-Order Integrated Rate Law Equation**

Using the rate constant for HI decomposition given in Example 15.7, calculate the concentration of HI after 12 min if $[HI]_0 = 0.010$ mol/L.

Zero-Order Reactions

If a reaction (R → products) is zero order, the rate equation is

$$-\frac{\Delta[R]}{\Delta t} = k[R]^0$$

This equation leads to the integrated rate equation

$$[R]_0 - [R]_t = kt \qquad\qquad \textbf{(15.3)}$$

where the units of k are mol/L · s.

Graphical Methods for Determining Reaction Order and the Rate Constant

We can derive a convenient way to determine the order of a reaction and its rate constant using graphical methods. Equations 15.1, 15.2, and 15.3, if rearranged slightly, have the form $y = mx + b$. This is the equation for a straight line, where m is the slope of the line and b is the y-intercept. In these equations, $x = t$ in each case.

Zero order	First order	Second order
$[R]_t = -kt + [R]_0$	$\ln [R]_t = -kt + \ln [R]_0$	$\dfrac{1}{[R]_t} = +kt + \dfrac{1}{[R]_0}$
$y \quad mx \quad b$	$y \quad mx \quad b$	$y \quad mx \quad b$

■ **Finding the Slope of a Line** See pages 39–41 for a description of methods for finding the slope of a line.

$t(s)$	$P \times 10^2$ atm	ln P
0	8.20	−2.50
1000	5.72	−2.86
2000	3.99	−3.22
3000	2.78	−3.58
4000	1.94	−3.94

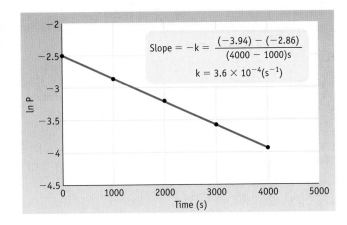

As an example of the graphical method for determining reaction order, consider the decomposition of azomethane.

$$CH_3N_2CH_3(g) \rightarrow CH_3CH_3(g) + N_2(g)$$

The decomposition of azomethane was followed at 600 K by observing the decrease in its partial pressure with time (Figure 15.6). (Recall from Chapter 11 that pressure is proportional to concentration at a given temperature and volume.) The third column lists values of ln $P(CH_3N_2CH_3)$. A plot of pressure vs. time for a first-order reaction is a curved line (see Figure 15.2). As shown in Figure 15.6, however, a graph of ln $P(CH_3N_2CH_3)$ versus time produces a straight line, showing that the reaction is first order in $CH_3N_2CH_3$. The slope of the line can be measured, and the negative of the slope equals the rate constant for the reaction, 3.6×10^{-4} s^{-1}.

The decomposition of NO_2 is a second-order process.

$$NO_2(g) \rightarrow NO(g) + \tfrac{1}{2} O_2(g)$$

$$\text{Rate} = k[NO_2]^2$$

This fact can be verified by showing that a plot of $1/[NO_2]$ versus time is a straight line (Figure 15.7). Here, the slope of the line is equal to k.

For a zero-order reaction (Figure 15.8), a plot of concentration vs. time gives a straight line with a slope equal to the negative of the rate constant.

FIGURE 15.7 A second-order reaction. A plot of $1/[NO_2]$ versus time for the decomposition of NO_2,

$$NO_2(g) \rightarrow NO(g) + \tfrac{1}{2} O_2(g)$$

results in a straight line. This confirms that this is a second-order reaction. The slope of the line equals the rate constant for this reaction.

Time (min)	$[NO_2]$ (mol/L)	$1/[NO_2]$ (L/mol)
0	0.020	50
0.50	0.015	67
1.0	0.012	83
1.5	0.010	100
2.0	0.0087	115

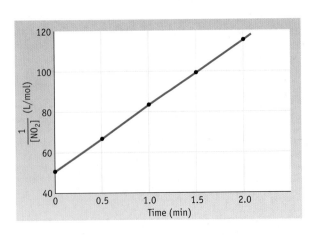

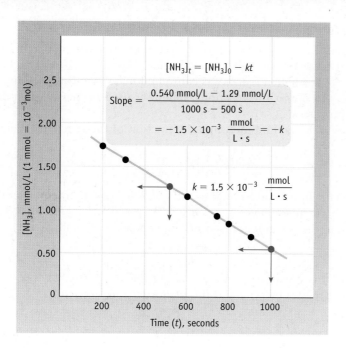

$$[NH_3]_t = [NH_3]_0 - kt$$

Slope $= \dfrac{0.540\ mmol/L - 1.29\ mmol/L}{1000\ s - 500\ s}$

$= -1.5 \times 10^{-3}\ \dfrac{mmol}{L \cdot s} = -k$

$k = 1.5 \times 10^{-3}\ \dfrac{mmol}{L \cdot s}$

FIGURE 15.8 Plot of a zero-order reaction. A graph of the concentration of ammonia, $[NH_3]_t$, against time for the decomposition of NH_3.

$$2\ NH_3(g) \rightarrow N_2(g) + 3\ H_2(g)$$

on a metal surface at 856 °C is a straight line, indicating that this is a zero-order reaction. The rate constant, k, for this reaction is found from the slope of the line; $k = -$slope. (The points chosen to calculate the slope are given in red.)

Table 15.1 summarizes the relationships between concentration and time for first-, second-, and zero-order processes.

Chemistry⚛Now™

Sign in at **www.cengage.com/login** and go to Chapter 15 Contents to see Screen 15.7 for a tutorial on **graphical methods.**

EXERCISE 15.8 Using Graphical Methods

Data for the decomposition of N_2O_5 in a particular solvent at 45 °C are as follows:

$[N_2O_5]$, mol/L	t, min
2.08	3.07
1.67	8.77
1.36	14.45
0.72	31.28

Plot $[N_2O_5]$, $\ln [N_2O_5]$, and $1/[N_2O_5]$ versus time, t. What is the order of the reaction? What is the rate constant for the reaction?

TABLE 15.1 Characteristic Properties of Reactions of the Type "R $\longrightarrow$ Products"

Order	Rate Equation	Integrated Rate Equation	Straight-Line Plot	Slope	k Units
0	$-\Delta[R]/\Delta t = k[R]^0$	$[R]_0 - [R]_t = kt$	$[R]_t$ vs. t	$-k$	mol/L · time
1	$-\Delta[R]/\Delta t = k[R]^1$	$\ln ([R]_t/[R]_0) = -kt$	$\ln [R]_t$ vs. t	$-k$	time^{-1}
2	$-\Delta[R]/\Delta t = k[R]^2$	$(1/[R]_t) - (1/[R]_0) = kt$	$1/[R]_t$ vs. t	k	L/mol · time

Half-Life and First-Order Reactions

The **half-life, $t_{1/2}$,** of a reaction is the time required for the concentration of a reactant to decrease to one half its initial value. Half-life is a convenient way to describe the rate at which a reactant is consumed in a chemical reaction: The longer the half-life, the slower the reaction. Half-life is used primarily when dealing with first-order processes.

The half-life, $t_{1/2}$, is the time when the fraction of the reactant R remaining is

$$[R]_t = \tfrac{1}{2}[R]_0 \quad \text{or} \quad \frac{[R]_t}{[R]_0} = \tfrac{1}{2}$$

Here, $[R]_0$ is the initial concentration, and $[R]_t$ is the concentration after the reaction is half completed. To evaluate $t_{1/2}$ for a first-order reaction, we substitute $[R]_t/[R]_0 = \tfrac{1}{2}$ and $t = t_{1/2}$ into the integrated first-order rate equation (Equation 15.1),

$$\ln\left(\tfrac{1}{2}\right) = -kt_{1/2} \quad \text{or} \quad \ln 2 = kt_{1/2}$$

Rearranging this equation (and calculating that $\ln 2 = 0.693$) provides a useful equation that relates half-life and the first-order rate constant:

$$t_{1/2} = \frac{0.693}{k} \tag{15.4}$$

This equation identifies an important feature of first-order reactions: $t_{1/2}$ is *independent of concentration.*

To illustrate the concept of half-life, consider again the first-order decomposition of azomethane, $CH_3N_2CH_3$.

$$CH_3N_2CH_3(g) \rightarrow CH_3CH_3(g) + N_2(g)$$

$$\text{Rate} = k[CH_3N_2CH_3] \text{ with } k = 3.6 \times 10^{-4} \text{ s}^{-1} \text{ at 600 K}$$

Given a rate constant of 3.6×10^{-4} s^{-1}, we calculate a half-life of 1.9×10^3 s or 32 min.

$$t_{1/2} = \frac{0.693}{3.6 \times 10^{-4} \text{ s}^{-1}} = 1.9 \times 10^3 \text{ s}$$

The partial pressure of azomethane has been plotted as a function of time in Figure 15.9, and this graph shows that P(azomethane) decreases by half every 32 minutes. The initial pressure was 820 mm Hg, but it dropped to 410 mm Hg in 32 minutes, and then dropped to 205 mm Hg in another 32 minutes. That is, after two half-lives (64 min), the pressure is $(\tfrac{1}{2}) \times (\tfrac{1}{2}) = (\tfrac{1}{2})^2 = \tfrac{1}{4}$ or 25% of the initial pressure. After three half-lives, the pressure has dropped further to 102 mm Hg or 12.5% of the initial value and equal to $(\tfrac{1}{2}) \times (\tfrac{1}{2}) \times (\tfrac{1}{2}) = (\tfrac{1}{2})^3 = \tfrac{1}{8}$ of the initial value.

It can be hard to visualize whether a reaction is fast or slow from the rate constant value. Can you tell from the rate constant, $k = 3.6 \times 10^{-4}$ s^{-1}, whether the azomethane decomposition will take seconds, hours, or days to reach completion? Probably not, but this is easily assessed from the value of the half-life for the reaction (32 min). Now we know that we would only have to wait a few hours for the reactant to be essentially consumed.

■ **Half-Life and Radioactivity** Half-life is a term often encountered when dealing with radioactive elements. Radioactive decay is a first-order process, and half-life is commonly used to describe how rapidly a radioactive element decays. See Chapter 23 and Example 15.9.

■ **Half-Life Equations for Other Reaction Orders**
For a zero-order reaction, R → products

$$t_{1/2} = \frac{[R]_0}{2k}$$

For a second-order reaction, R → products

$$t_{1/2} = \frac{1}{k[R]_0}$$

Note that in both cases the half-life depends on the initial concentration.

Chemistry ☼ Now™

Sign in at **www.cengage.com/login** and go to Chapter 15 Contents to see Screen 15.8 for tutorials on **using half-life.**

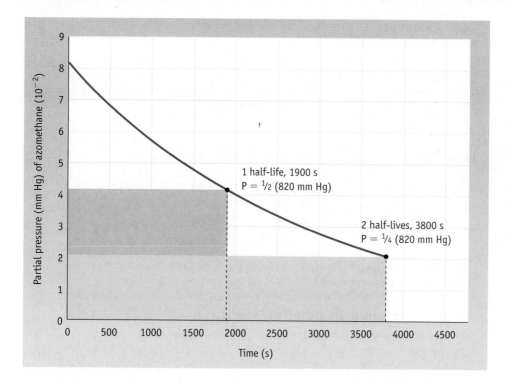

Active Figure 15.9 **Half-life of a first-order reaction.** The curve is a plot of the pressure of $CH_3N_2CH_3$ as a function of time. (The compound decomposes to CH_3CH_3 and N_2 with $k = 3.6 \times 10^{-4}$ s^{-1}). The pressure of $CH_3N_2CH_3$ is halved every 1900 s (32 min). (This plot of pressure versus time is similar in shape to plots of concentration versus time for all other first-order reactions.)

Chemistry.Now™ Sign in at www.cengage.com/login and go to the Chapter Contents menu to explore an interactive version of this figure accompanied by an exercise.

EXAMPLE 15.8 Half-Life and a First-Order Process

Problem Sucrose, $C_{12}H_{22}O_{11}$, decomposes to fructose and glucose in acid solution with the rate law

$$\text{Rate} = k[C_{12}H_{22}O_{11}] \qquad k = 0.216 \text{ h}^{-1} \text{ at } 25\ °C$$

(a) What is the half-life of $C_{12}H_{22}O_{11}$ at this temperature?

(b) What amount of time is required for 87.5% of the initial concentration of $C_{12}H_{22}O_{11}$ to decompose?

Strategy (a) The decomposition of $C_{12}H_{22}O_{11}$ is first order in this compound, so Equation 15.4 can be used to calculate the half-life. (b) After 87.5% of the $C_{12}H_{22}O_{11}$ has decomposed, 12.5% (or one-eighth of the sample) remains. To reach this point, three half-lives are required.

Half-Life	Fraction Remaining
1	0.5
2	0.25
3	0.125

Therefore, we calculate the half-life from Equation 15.4 and then multiply by 3.

Solution

(a) The half-life for the reaction is

$$t_{1/2} = 0.693/k = 0.693/(0.216 \text{ h}^{-1}) = 3.21 \text{ h}$$

(b) Three half-lives must elapse before the fraction remaining is 0.125, so

$$\text{Time elapsed} = 3 \times 3.21 \text{ h} = \boxed{9.63 \text{ h}}$$

EXAMPLE 15.9 Half-Life and First-Order Processes

Problem Radioactive radon-222 gas (^{222}Rn) from natural sources can seep into the basement of a home. The half-life of ^{222}Rn is 3.8 days. Assume that the radon gas is trapped in the basement and cannot escape. If a basement has 4.0×10^{13} atoms of ^{222}Rn per liter of air initially, how many atoms of ^{222}Rn per liter will remain after one month (30 days)?

Strategy Using Equation 15.1, and knowing the number of atoms at the beginning ($[R]_0$), the elapsed time (30 days), and the rate constant, we can calculate the number of atoms remaining ($[R]_t$). First, the rate constant, k, must be found from the half-life using Equation 15.4.

Solution The rate constant, k, is

$$k = \frac{0.693}{t_{1/2}} = \frac{0.693}{3.8 \text{ d}} = 0.18 \text{ d}^{-1}$$

Now use Equation 15.1 to calculate the number of atoms remaining after 30. days.

$$\ln \frac{[Rn]_t}{4.0 \times 10^{13} \text{ atom/L}} = -(0.18 \text{ d}^{-1})(30. \text{ d}) = -5.5$$

$$\frac{[Rn]_t}{4.0 \times 10^{13} \text{ atom/L}} = e^{-5.5} = 0.0042$$

$$[Rn]_t = 1.7 \times 10^{11} \text{ atom/L}$$

Comment Thirty days is approximately 8 half-lives for this element. This means that the concentration at the end of the month is approximately $(1/2)^8$ or $1/256$th of the original concentration.

EXERCISE 15.9 Half-Life and a First-Order Process

Americium is used in smoke detectors and in medicine for the treatment of certain malignancies. One isotope of americium, ^{241}Am, has a rate constant, k, for radioactive decay of 0.0016 y^{-1}. In contrast, radioactive iodine-125, which is used for studies of thyroid functioning, has a rate constant for decay of 0.011 d^{-1}.

(a) What are the half-lives of these isotopes?

(b) Which isotope decays faster?

(c) If you are given a dose of iodine-125 containing 1.6×10^{15} atoms, how many atoms remain after 2.0 days?

15.5 A Microscopic View of Reaction Rates

Throughout this book, we have turned to the particulate level of chemistry to understand chemical phenomena. Rates of reaction are no exception. Looking at the way reactions occur at the atomic and molecular levels can provide some insight into the various influences on rates of reactions.

Let us review the macroscopic observations we have made so far concerning reaction rates. We know that there are wide differences in rates of reactions—from very fast reactions like the explosion that occurs when hydrogen and oxygen are exposed to a spark or flame (Figure 1.18), to slow reactions like the formation of rust that occur over days, weeks, or years. For a specific reaction, factors that influence reaction rate include the concentrations of the reactants, the temperature of the reaction system, and the presence of catalysts. Let us look at each of these influences in more depth.

Concentration, Reaction Rate, and Collision Theory

Consider the gas-phase reaction of nitric oxide and ozone:

$$NO(g) + O_3(g) \rightarrow NO_2(g) + O_2(g)$$

The rate law for this product-favored reaction is first order in each reactant: Rate = $k[NO][O_3]$. How can this reaction have this rate law?

Let us consider the reaction at the particulate level and imagine a flask containing a mixture of NO and O_3 molecules in the gas phase. Both kinds of molecules are in rapid and random motion within the flask. They strike the walls of the vessel and collide with other molecules. For this or any other reaction to occur, the **collision theory of reaction rates** states that three conditions must be met:

1. The reacting molecules must collide with one another.
2. The reacting molecules must collide with sufficient energy to initiate the process of breaking and forming bonds.
3. The molecules must collide in an orientation that can lead to rearrangement of the atoms and the formation of products.

We shall discuss each of these conditions within the context of the effects of concentration and temperature on reaction rate.

To react, molecules must collide with one another. It is reasonable to propose that the rate of their reaction be related to the number of collisions, which is in turn related to their concentrations (Figure 15.10). Doubling the concentration of one reagent in the NO + O_3 reaction, say NO, will lead to twice the number of molecular collisions. Figure 15.10a shows a single molecule of one of the reactants (NO) moving randomly among sixteen O_3 molecules. In a given time period, it might collide with two O_3 molecules. The number of NO—O_3 collisions will double, however, if the concentration of NO molecules is doubled (to 2, as shown in Figure 15.10b) or if the number of O_3 molecules is doubled (to 32, as in Figure 15.10c). Thus, we can explain the dependence of reaction rate on concentration: The number of collisions between the two reactant molecules is directly proportional to the concentration of each reactant, and the rate of the reaction shows a first-order dependence on each reactant.

Chemistry ⚛ Now™

Sign in at **www.cengage.com/login** and go to Chapter 15 Contents to see Screen 15.9 for a visualization of **collision theory** and for tutorials on **using half-life.**

Temperature, Reaction Rate, and Activation Energy

In a laboratory or in the chemical industry, a chemical reaction is often carried out at elevated temperature because this allows the reaction to occur more rapidly. Conversely, it is sometimes desirable to lower the temperature to slow down a chemical reaction (to avoid an uncontrollable reaction or a potentially dangerous explosion). Chemists are very aware of the effect of temperature on the rate of a reaction.

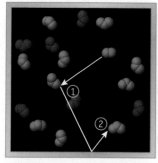

(a) 1 NO : 16 O_3 — *2 hits/second*

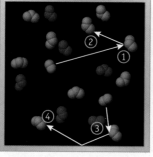

(b) 2 NO : 16 O_3 — *4 hits/second*

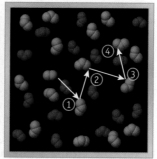

(c) 1 NO : 32 O_3 — *4 hits/second*

FIGURE 15.10 The effect of concentration on the frequency of molecular collisions. (a) A single NO molecule, moving among sixteen O_3 molecules, is shown colliding with two of them per second. (b) If two NO molecules move among 16 O_3 molecules, we would predict that four NO—O_3 collisions would occur per second. (c) If the number of O_3 molecules is doubled (to 32), the frequency of NO—O_3 collisions is also doubled, to four per second.

FIGURE 15.11 Energy distribution curve. The vertical axis gives the relative number of molecules possessing the energy indicated on the horizontal axis. The graph indicates the minimum energy required for an arbitrary reaction. At a higher temperature, a larger fraction of the molecules have sufficient energy to react. (Recall Figure 11.14, the Boltzmann distribution function, for a collection of gas molecules.)

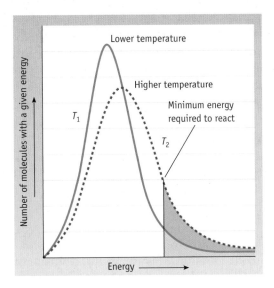

A discussion of the effect of temperature on reaction rate begins with reference to distribution of energies for molecules in a sample of a gas or liquid. Recall from studying gases and liquids that the molecules in a sample have a wide range of energies, described earlier as a Boltzmann distribution of energies (◄ Figure 11.14). In any sample of a gas or liquid, some molecules have very low energies; others have very high energies; but most have some intermediate energy. As the temperature increases, the average energy of the molecules in the sample increases, as does the fraction having higher energies (Figure 15.11).

Activation Energy

Molecules require some minimum energy to react. Chemists visualize this as an energy barrier that must be surmounted by the reactants for a reaction to occur (Figure 15.12). The energy required to surmount the barrier is called the **activation energy, E_a**. If the barrier is low, the energy required is low, and a high proportion of the molecules in a sample may have sufficient energy to react. In such a case, the reaction will be fast. If the barrier is high, the activation energy is high, and only a few reactant molecules in a sample may have sufficient energy. In this case, the reaction will be slow.

To illustrate an activation energy barrier, consider the conversion of NO_2 and CO to NO and CO_2 or the reverse reaction (Figure 15.13). At the molecular level, we imagine that the reaction involves the transfer of an O atom from an NO_2 molecule to a CO molecule (or, in the reverse reaction, the transfer of an O atom from CO_2 to NO).

$$NO_2(g) + CO(g) \rightleftharpoons NO(g) + CO_2(g)$$

We can describe this process by using an energy diagram or **reaction coordinate** diagram. The horizontal axis describes the reaction progress as the reaction proceeds, and the vertical axis represents the potential energy of the system during the reaction. When NO_2 and CO approach and O atom transfer begins, an N—O bond is being broken, and a C=O bond is forming. Energy input (the activation energy) is required for this to occur. The energy of the system reaches a maximum at the **transition state**. At the transition state, sufficient energy has been concentrated in the appropriate bonds; bonds in the reactants can now break, and new bonds can form

FIGURE 15.12 An analogy to chemical activation energy. For the volleyball to go over the net, the player must give it sufficient energy.

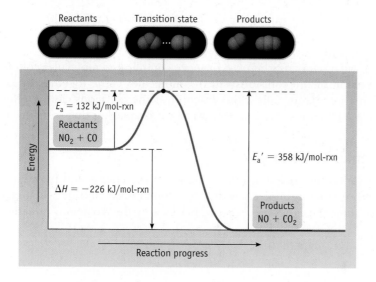

Reactants   Transition state   Products

Active Figure 15.13 **Activation Energy.** The reaction of NO_2 and CO (to give NO and CO_2) has an activation energy barrier of 132 kJ/mol-rxn. The reverse reaction (NO + $CO_2 \rightarrow NO_2$ + CO) requires 358 kJ/mol-rxn. The net energy change for the reaction of NO_2 and CO is −226 kJ/mol-rxn.

Chemistry **Now**™ Sign in at www.cengage.com/login and go to the Chapter Contents menu to explore an interactive version of this figure accompanied by an exercise.

to give products. The system is poised to go on to products. Alternatively, it can return to the reactants. Because the transition state is at a maximum in potential energy, it cannot be isolated. Using computer molecular modeling techniques, however, chemists can describe what the transition state must look like.

In the NO_2 + CO reaction, 132 kJ/mol is required to reach the transition state; that is, the top of the energy barrier. As the reaction continues toward the products—as the N—O bond is finally broken and a C=O bond forms—the reaction evolves energy, 358 kJ/mol-rxn. The net energy change involved in this exothermic reaction is −226 kJ/mol-rxn.

$$\Delta U = +132 \text{ kJ/mol-rxn} + (-358 \text{ kJ/mol-rxn}) = -226 \text{ kJ/mol-rxn}$$

What happens if NO and CO_2 are mixed to form NO_2 and CO? Now the reaction requires 358 kJ/mol-rxn to reach the transition state, and 132 kJ/mol-rxn is evolved on proceeding to the product, NO_2 and CO. The reaction in this direction is endothermic, requiring an input of +226 kJ/mol-rxn.

Chemistry **Now**™

Sign in at **www.cengage.com/login** and go to Chapter 15 Contents to see Screen 15.10 for a simulation of **reaction coordinate diagrams.**

Effect of a Temperature Increase

The conversion of NO_2 and CO to products at room temperature is slow because only a small fraction of the molecules have enough energy to reach the transition state. The rate can be increased by heating the sample. Raising the temperature increases the reaction rate by increasing the fraction of molecules with enough energy to surmount the activation energy barrier (Figure 15.11).

Effect of Molecular Orientation on Reaction Rate

Having a sufficiently high energy is necessary, but it is not sufficient to ensure that reactants will form products. The reactant molecules must also come together in the correct orientation. For the reaction of NO_2 and CO, we can imagine that the transition state structure has one of the O atoms of NO_2 beginning to bind to the

C atom of CO in preparation for O atom transfer (Figure 15.13). The lower the probability of achieving the proper alignment, the smaller the value of k, and the slower the reaction.

Imagine what happens when two or more complicated molecules collide. In only a small fraction of the collisions will the molecules come together in exactly the right orientation. Thus, only a tiny fraction of the collisions can be effective. No wonder some reactions are slow. Conversely, it is amazing that so many are fast!

The Arrhenius Equation

The observation that reaction rates depend on the energy and frequency of collisions between reacting molecules, on the temperature, and on whether the collisions have the correct geometry is summarized by the **Arrhenius equation**:

$$k = \text{rate constant} = A\underbrace{e^{-E_a/RT}}$$

Frequency factor ⟋   ⟍ Fraction of molecules with minimum energy for reaction

(15.5)

In this equation, k is the rate constant, where R is the gas constant with a value of 8.314510×10^{-3} kJ/K · mol, and T is the kelvin temperature. The parameter A is called the **frequency factor**, and it has units of L/mol · s. It is related to the number of collisions and to the fraction of collisions that have the correct geometry; A is specific to each reaction and is temperature dependent. The factor $e^{-E_a/RT}$ represents *the fraction of molecules having the minimum energy required for reaction*; its value is always less than 1. As the table in the margin shows, this fraction changes significantly with temperature.

The Arrhenius equation has significant uses.

- It can be used to calculate E_a from the temperature, dependence of the rate constant.
- It can be used to calculate the rate constant for a given temperature, if E_a and A are known.

If rate constants of a given reaction are measured at several temperatures then one can apply graphical techniques to determine the activation energy of a reaction. Taking the natural logarithm of each side of Equation 15.5, we have

$$\ln k = \ln A + \left(-\frac{E_a}{RT}\right)$$

Rearranging this expression slightly shows that $\ln k$ and $1/T$ are related linearly.

$$\ln k = -\frac{E_a}{R}\left(\frac{1}{T}\right) + \ln A \qquad \leftarrow \text{Arrhenius equation}$$

(15.6)

$$\downarrow \qquad \downarrow \qquad \downarrow$$
$$y \quad = \quad mx \quad + b \qquad \leftarrow \text{Equation for straight line}$$

This means that, if the natural logarithm of k ($\ln k$) is plotted versus $1/T$, the result is a downward-sloping straight line with a slope of $(-E_a/R)$. The activation energy, E_a, can be obtained from the slope of this line.

Chemistry. Now™

Sign in at **www.cengage.com/login** and go to Chapter 15 Contents to see Screen 15.11 for a simulation and tutorials on **the temperature dependence of reaction rates** and the **Arrhenius equation.**

■ **Interpreting the Arrhenius Equation**
(a) The exponential term. This gives the fraction of molecules having sufficient energy for reaction and is a function of T.

Temperature (K)	Value of $e^{-E_a/RT}$ for $E_a =$ 40 kJ/mol-rxn
298	9.7×10^{-8}
400	5.9×10^{-6}
600	3.3×10^{-4}

(b) Significance of A. Although a complete understanding of A goes beyond the level of this text, it can be noted that A becomes smaller as the reactants become larger. It reflects the fact that reacting molecules must come together in the appropriate geometry.

A Closer Look

Reaction Coordinate Diagrams

Reaction coordinate diagrams (Figure 15.13) convey a great deal of information. A reaction that would have an energy diagram like that in Figure 15.13 is the substitution of a halogen atom of CH_3Cl by an ion such as F^-. Here, the F^- ion attacks the molecule from the side opposite the Cl substituent. As F^- begins to form a bond to carbon, the C—Cl bond weakens, and the CH_3 portion of the molecule changes shape. As time progresses, the products CH_3F and Cl^- are formed.

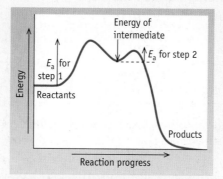

FIGURE A **A reaction coordinate diagram for a two-step reaction, a process involving an intermediate.**

The diagram in Figure A describes a reaction that occurs in two steps. An example of such a reaction is the substitution of the —OH group on methanol by a halide ion in the presence of acid. In the first step, an H^+ ion attaches to the O of the C—O—H group in a rapid, reversible reaction. The energy of this protonated species, $CH_3OH_2^+$, a reaction intermediate, is higher than the energies of the reactants and is represented by the dip in the curve shown in Figure A. In the second step, a halide ion, say Br^-, attacks the intermediate to produce methyl bromide, CH_3Br, and water. There is an activation energy barrier in both the first step and second step.

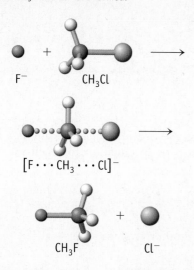

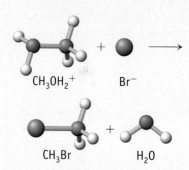

Notice in Figure A, as in Figure 15.13, that the energy of the products is lower than the energy of the reactants. The reaction is exothermic.

EXAMPLE 15.10 Determination of E_a from the Arrhenius Equation

Problem Using the experimental data shown in the table, calculate the activation energy E_a for the reaction

$$2\ N_2O(g) \rightarrow 2\ N_2(g) + O_2(g)$$

Experiment	Temperature (K)	k (L/mol · s)
1	1125	11.59
2	1053	1.67
3	1001	0.380
4	838	0.0011

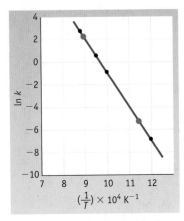

FIGURE 15.14 Arrhenius plot.
A plot of ln k versus $1/T$ for the reaction
$2\ N_2O(g) \rightarrow 2\ N_2(g) + O_2(g)$. The slope of
the line gives E_a. See Example 15.10.

Strategy To solve this problem graphically, we first need to calculate ln k and $1/T$ for each data point. These data are then plotted, and E_a is calculated from the resulting straight line (slope $= -E_a/R$).

Solution First, calculate $1/T$ and ln k.

Experiment	$1/T$ (K^{-1})	ln k
1	8.889×10^{-4}	2.4501
2	9.497×10^{-4}	0.513
3	9.990×10^{-4}	−0.968
4	11.9×10^{-4}	−6.81

Plotting these data gives the graph shown in Figure 15.14. Choosing the large blue points on the graph, the slope is found to be

$$\text{Slope} = \frac{\Delta \ln k}{\Delta(1/T)} = \frac{2.0 - (-5.6)}{(9.0 - 11.5)(10^{-4})K^{-1}} = -3.0 \times 10^4 \text{ K}$$

The activation energy is evaluated from the slope.

$$\text{Slope} = -\frac{E_a}{R} = -3.0 \times 10^4 \text{ K} = -\frac{E_a}{8.31 \times 10^{-3} \text{ kJ/K} \cdot \text{mol}}$$

$$E_a = 250 \text{ kJ/mol-rxn}$$

The activation energy, E_a, for a reaction can be obtained algebraically if k is known at two different temperatures. We can write an equation for each set of these conditions:

$$\ln k_1 = -\left(\frac{E_a}{RT_1}\right) + \ln A \quad \text{or} \quad \ln k_2 = -\left(\frac{E_a}{RT_2}\right) + \ln A$$

If one of these equations is subtracted from the other, we have

$$\ln k_2 - \ln k_1 = \ln \frac{k_2}{k_1} = -\frac{E_a}{R}\left[\frac{1}{T_2} - \frac{1}{T_1}\right] \tag{15.7}$$

Example 15.11 demonstrates the use of this equation.

■ **E_a, Reaction Rates, and Temperature**
A often-used rule of thumb is that reaction rates double for every 10 °C rise in temperature in the vicinity of room temperature.

■ **EXAMPLE 15.11 Calculating E_a Numerically**

Problem Use values of k determined at two different temperatures to calculate the value of E_a for the decomposition of HI:

$$2\ HI(g) \rightarrow H_2(g) + I_2(g)$$

$$k_1 = 2.15 \times 10^{-8} \text{ L/(mol} \cdot \text{s) at } 6.50 \times 10^2 \text{ K (T}_1)$$

$$k_2 = 2.39 \times 10^{-7} \text{ L/(mol} \cdot \text{s) at } 7.00 \times 10^2 \text{ K (T}_2)$$

Strategy Use Equation 15.7.

Solution

$$\ln \frac{2.39 \times 10^{-7} \text{ L/(mol} \cdot \text{s)}}{2.15 \times 10^{-8} \text{ L/(mol} \cdot \text{s)}} = -\frac{E_a}{8.315 \times 10^{-3} \text{ kJ/K} \cdot \text{mol}} \times \left[\frac{1}{7.00 \times 10^2 \text{ K}} - \frac{1}{6.50 \times 10^2 \text{ K}}\right]$$

Solving this equation gives $E_a = 180 \text{ kJ/mol-rxn}$.

Comment Another way to write the difference in fractions in brackets is

$$\left[\frac{1}{T_2} - \frac{1}{T_1}\right] = \frac{T_1 - T_2}{T_1 T_2}$$

This expression is often easier to use.

Effect of Catalysts on Reaction Rate

Catalysts are substances that speed up the rate of a chemical reaction. We have seen several examples of catalysts in earlier discussions in this chapter: MnO_2, iodide ion, an enzyme in a potato, and hydroxide ion all catalyze the decomposition of hydrogen peroxide (Figure 15.4). In biological systems, catalysts called enzymes influence the rates of most reactions (page 702).

Catalysts are not consumed in a chemical reaction. They are, however, intimately involved in the details of the reaction at the particulate level. Their function is to provide a different pathway with a lower activation energy for the reaction. To illustrate how a catalyst participates in a reaction, let us consider the isomerization of *cis*-2-butene, to the slightly more stable isomer, *trans*-2-butene.

cis-2-butene   Transition state   trans-2-butene

π bond breaks   End rotates

■ **Enzymes: Biological Catalysts** Catalase is an enzyme whose function is to speed up the decomposition of hydrogen peroxide. This enzyme ensures that hydrogen peroxide, which is highly toxic, does not build up in the body.

■ **Catalysts and the Economy** "One third of [the] material gross national product in the U.S. involves a catalytic process somewhere in the production chain." (Quoted in A. Bell, *Science*, Vol. 299, page 1688, 2003.)

The activation energy for the uncatalyzed conversion is relatively large—264 kJ/mol-rxn—because the π bond must be broken to allow one end of the molecule to rotate into a new position. Because of the high activation energy, this is a slow reaction, and rather high temperatures are required for it to occur at a reasonable rate.

The *cis*- to *trans*-2-butene reaction is greatly accelerated by a catalyst, iodine. In the presence of iodine, this reaction can be carried out at a temperature several hundred degrees lower than for the uncatalyzed reaction. Iodine is not consumed (nor is it a product), and it does not appear in the overall balanced equation. It does appear in the reaction rate law, however; the rate of the reaction depends on the square root of the iodine concentration:

$$\text{Rate} = k[\textit{cis}\text{-2-butene}][I_2]^{1/2}$$

The presence of I_2 changes the way the reaction occurs; that is, it changes the mechanism of the reaction (Figure 15.15). The best hypothesis is that iodine molecules first dissociate to form iodine atoms (Step 1). An iodine atom then adds to one of the C atoms of the C=C double bond (Step 2). This converts the double bond between the carbon atoms to a single bond (the π bond is broken) and allows the ends of the molecule to twist freely relative to each other (Step 3). If the iodine atom then dissociates from the intermediate, the double bond can re-form

■ **Butene Isomerization** Isomerization of *cis*-2-butene is a first order process with the rate law "Rate = k[*cis*-2-butene]." It is suggested to occur by rotation around the carbon–carbon double bond. The rate at which a molecule will isomerize is related to the fraction of molecules that have a high enough energy. (See ChemistryNow Screen 15.8 to view an animation of the interconversion of butene isomers and the energy barrier for the process.)

FIGURE 15.15 The mechanism of the iodine-catalyzed isomerization of *cis*-2-butene. *Cis*-2-butene is converted to *trans*-2-butene in the presence of a catalytic amount of iodine. Catalyzed reactions are often pictured in such diagrams to emphasize what chemists refer to as a "catalytic cycle."

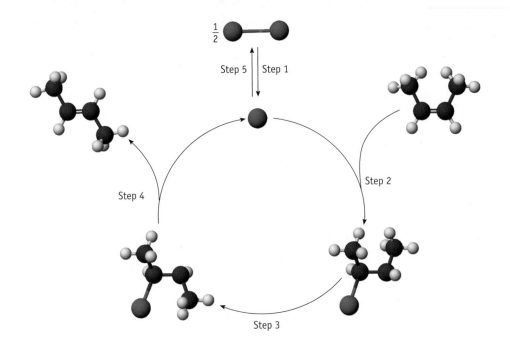

in the *trans* configuration (Step 4). The iodine atom catalyzing the rotation is now free to add to another molecule of *cis*-2-butene. The result is a kind of chain reaction, as one molecule of *cis*-2-butene after another is converted to the *trans* isomer. The chain is broken if the iodine atom recombines with another iodine atom to re-form molecular iodine.

An energy profile for the catalyzed reaction (Figure 15.16) shows that the overall energy barrier is much lower than for the uncatalyzed reaction. Five separate steps are identified for the mechanism in the energy profile. This proposed mechanism also includes a series of chemical species called **reaction intermediates,** species formed in one step of the reaction and consumed in a later step. Iodine atoms are intermediates, as are the free radical species formed when an iodine atom adds to *cis*-2-butene.

FIGURE 15.16 Energy profile for the iodine-catalyzed reaction of *cis*-2-butene. A catalyst accelerates a reaction by altering the mechanism so that the activation energy is lowered. With a smaller barrier to overcome, more reacting molecules have sufficient energy to surmount the barrier, and the reaction occurs more rapidly. The energy profile for the uncatalyzed conversion of *cis*-2-butene to *trans*-2-butene is shown by the black curve, and that for the iodine-catalyzed reaction is represented by the red curve. Notice that the shape of the barrier has changed because the mechanism has changed.

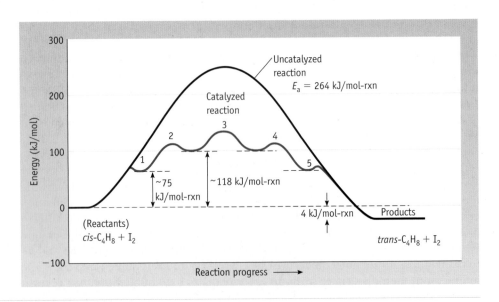

Five important points are associated with this mechanism:

- Iodine molecules, I_2, dissociate to atoms and then re-form. On the macroscopic level, the concentration of I_2 is unchanged. Iodine does not appear in the balanced, stoichiometric equation even though it appears in the rate equation. This is generally true of catalysts.
- Both the catalyst I_2 and the reactant *cis*-2-butene are in the gas phase. If a catalyst is present in the same phase as the reacting substance, it is called a *homogeneous catalyst.*
- Iodine atoms and the radical species formed by addition of an iodine atom to a 2-butene molecule are intermediates.
- The activation energy barrier to reaction is significantly lower because the mechanism changed. Dropping the activation energy from 264 kJ/mol-rxn for the uncatalyzed reaction to about 150 kJ/mol-rxn for the catalyzed process makes the catalyzed reaction 10^{15} times faster!
- The diagram of energy-versus-reaction progress has five energy barriers (five humps appear in the curve). This feature in the diagram means that the reaction occurs in a series of five steps.

What we have described here are reaction mechanisms. The uncatalyzed isomerization reaction of *cis*-2-butene is a one-step reaction mechanism, whereas the catalyzed mechanism involves a series of steps. We shall discuss reaction mechanisms in more detail in the next section.

Chemistry Now™

Sign in at **www.cengage.com/login** and go to Chapter 15 Contents to see Screen 15.14 for tutorials on **using half-life various catalysts,** a visualization of **the effect of a catalyst on activation energy,** an interview of a scientist describing **catalyst use in industry,** two exercises on **reaction mechanisms and the effect of catalysts,** and a video exercise on **catalysis.**

15.6 Reaction Mechanisms

Rate laws help us understand **reaction mechanisms**, the sequence of bond-making and bond-breaking steps that occurs during the conversion of reactants to products. We want to analyze the changes that molecules undergo when they react. We then want to relate this description back to the macroscopic world, to the experimental observations of reaction rates.

Based on the rate equation for a reaction, and by applying chemical intuition, chemists can often make an educated guess about the mechanism for a reaction. In some reactions, the conversion of reactants to products in a single step is envisioned as the logical mechanism. For example, the uncatalyzed isomerization of *cis*-2-butene to *trans*-2-butene is best described as a single-step reaction (Figure 15.16).

Most chemical reactions occur in a sequence of steps, however. A multiple-step mechanism was proposed for the iodine-catalyzed 2-butene isomerization reaction. Another example of a reaction that occurs in several steps is the reaction of bromine and NO:

$$Br_2(g) + 2\ NO \rightarrow 2\ BrNO(g)$$

A single-step reaction would require that three reactant molecules collide simultaneously in just the right orientation. The probability of this occurring is small; thus, it would be reasonable to look for a mechanism that occurs in a series of steps, with each step involving only one or two molecules. In one possible mechanism, Br_2 and NO might combine in an initial step to produce an intermediate species,

■ **Rate Laws and Mechanisms** Rate laws are derived by experiment; they are macroscopic observations. Mechanisms are schemes we propose that speculate on how reactions occur at the particulate level.

Within any living organism, there are untold numbers of chemical reactions occurring, many of them extremely rapidly. In many cases, enzymes, natural catalysts, speed up reactions that would normally move at a snail's pace from reactants to products. Typically, enzymes give reaction rates 10^7 to 10^{14} times faster than the uncatalyzed rate.

Enzymes are typically large proteins, often containing metal ions such as Zn^{2+}. They are thought to function by bringing the reactants together in just the right orientation in a site where specific bonds can be broken and/or made.

Carbonic anhydrase is one of many enzymes important in biological processes (Figure A). Carbon dioxide dissolves in water to a small extent to produce carbonic acid, which ionizes to give H_3O^+ and HCO_3^- ions.

$$CO_2(g) \rightleftharpoons CO_2(aq) \qquad (1)$$

$$CO_2(aq) + H_2O(\ell) \rightleftharpoons H_2CO_3(aq) \qquad (2)$$

$$H_2CO_3(aq) + H_2O(\ell)$$
$$\rightleftharpoons H_3O^+(aq) + HCO_3^-(aq) \qquad (3)$$

Carbonic anhydrase speeds up reactions 1 and 2. Many of the H_3O^+ ions produced by ionization of H_2CO_3 (reaction 3) are picked up by hemoglobin in the blood as hemoglobin loses O_2. The resulting HCO_3^- ions are transported back to the lungs. When hemoglobin again takes on O_2, it releases H_3O^+ ions. These ions and HCO_3^- re-form H_2CO_3, from which CO_2 is liberated and exhaled.

You can do an experiment that illustrates the effect of carbonic anhydrase. First, add a small amount of NaOH to a cold, aqueous solution of CO_2. The solution becomes basic immediately because there is not enough H_2CO_3 in the solution to use up the NaOH. After some seconds, however, dissolved CO_2 slowly produces more H_2CO_3, which consumes NaOH, and the solution is again acidic.

Now try the experiment again, this time adding a few drops of blood to the solution (Figure A). Carbonic anhydrase in blood speeds up reactions 1 and 2 by a factor of about 10^7, as evidenced by the more rapid reaction under these conditions.

In 1913, Leonor Michaelis and Maud L. Menten proposed a general theory of enzyme action based on kinetic observations. They assumed that the substrate, S (the reactant), and the enzyme, E, form a complex, ES. This complex then breaks down, releasing the enzyme and the product, P.

$$E + S \rightleftharpoons ES$$

$$ES \rightarrow P$$

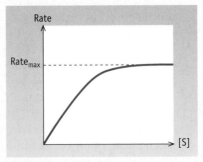

FIGURE B Rate of enzyme catalyzed reaction. This plot of substrate concentration [S] versus reaction velocity is typical of reactions catalyzed by enzymes and following the Michaelis–Menten model.

When the substrate concentration is low, the rate of the reaction is first order in S (Figure B). As [S] increases, however, the active sites in the enzyme become saturated with substrate, and the rate reaches its maximum value. Now the kinetics are zero order in substrate.

Questions:
1. *Catalase can decompose hydrogen peroxide to O_2 and water about 10^7 times faster than the uncatalyzed reaction. If the latter requires one year, how much time is required by the enzyme-catalyzed reaction?*
2. *According to the Michaelis–Menten model, if 1/Rate is plotted versus 1/[S], the intercept of the plot (when 1/[S] = 0) is 1/Rate$_{max}$. Find Rate$_{max}$ for a reaction involving carbonic anhydrase.*

[S], mol/L	Rate (millimoles/min)
2.500	0.588
1.00	0.500
0.714	0.417
0.526	0.370
0.250	0.256

Answers to these questions are in Appendix Q.

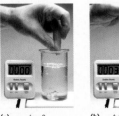

| (a) $t = 0$ | (b) $t = 3$ sec | (c) $t = 15$ sec | (d) $t = 17$ sec | (e) $t = 21$ sec |

Photos: Charles D. Winters

FIGURE A CO_2 in water. (a) A few drops of blood are added to a cold solution of CO_2 in water. (b) A few drops of a dye (bromthymol blue) are added to the solution, the yellow color indicating an acidic solution. (c and d) A less-than-stoichiometric amount of sodium hydroxide is added, converting the H_2CO_3 to HCO_3^- (and CO_3^{2-}). The blue color of the dye indicates a basic solution. (e) The blue color begins to fade after some seconds as CO_2 forms more H_2CO_3. The amount of H_2CO_3 formed is finally sufficient to consume the added NaOH, and the solution is again acidic. Blood is a source of the enzyme carbonic anhydrase, so the last steps are noticeably more rapid than the reaction in the absence of blood.

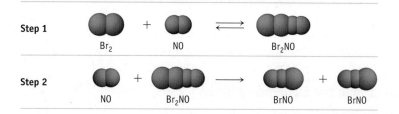

FIGURE 15.17 A reaction mechanism. A representation of the proposed two-step mechanism by which NO and Br_2 are converted to NOBr.

Br_2NO (Figure 15.17). This intermediate would then react with another NO molecule to give the reaction products. The equation for the overall reaction is obtained by adding the equations for these two steps:

Step 1. $Br_2(g) + NO(g) \rightleftharpoons Br_2NO(g)$
Step 2. $Br_2NO(g) + NO(g) \rightarrow 2\ BrNO(g)$
Overall Reaction: $Br_2(g) + 2\ NO(g) \rightarrow 2\ BrNO(g)$

Each step in a multistep reaction sequence is an **elementary step**, defined by a chemical equation that describes a single molecular event such as the formation or rupture of a chemical bond resulting from a molecular collision. Each step has its own activation energy, E_a, and rate constant, k. Adding the equations for each step must give the balanced equation for the overall reaction, and the time required to complete all of the steps defines the overall reaction rate. The series of steps constitutes a possible reaction mechanism.

Mechanisms of reactions are usually postulated starting with experimental data. To see how this is done, we first describe three types of elementary steps in terms of the concept of *molecularity*.

Molecularity of Elementary Steps

Elementary steps are classified by the number of reactant molecules (or ions, atoms, or free radicals) that come together. This whole, positive number is called the **molecularity** of the elementary step. When one molecule is the only reactant in an elementary step, the reaction is a **unimolecular** process. A **bimolecular** elementary process involves two molecules, which may be identical (A + A → products) or different (A + B → products). The mechanism proposed for the decomposition of ozone in the stratosphere illustrates the use of these terms.

Step 1.   Unimolecular $O_3(g) \rightarrow O_2(g) + O(g)$
Step 2.   Bimolecular $O_3(g) + O(g) \rightarrow 2\ O_2(g)$
Overall Reaction: $2\ O_3(g) \rightarrow 3\ O_2(g)$

A **termolecular** elementary step involves three molecules, which could be the same or different (3 A →products; 2 A + B → products; or A + B + C → products). Be aware, however, the simultaneous collision of three molecules has a low probability, unless one of the molecules involved is in high concentration, such as a solvent molecule. In fact, most termolecular processes involve the collision of two reactant molecules and a third, inert molecule. The function of the inert molecule is to absorb the excess energy produced when a new chemical bond is formed by the first two molecules. For example, N_2 is unchanged in a termolecular reaction between oxygen molecules and oxygen atoms that produces ozone in the upper atmosphere:

$$O(g) + O_2(g) + N_2(g) \rightarrow O_3(g) + \text{energetic } N_2(g)$$

The probability that four or more molecules will simultaneously collide with sufficient kinetic energy and proper orientation to react is so small that reaction molecularities greater than three are never proposed.

Rate Equations for Elementary Steps

The experimentally determined rate equation for a reaction cannot be predicted from its overall stoichiometry. In contrast, the rate equation for any elementary step is defined by the reaction stoichiometry. The rate equation of an elementary step is given by the product of the rate constant and the concentrations of the reactants in that step. We can therefore write the rate equation for any elementary step, as shown by examples in the following table:

Elementary Step	Molecularity	Rate Equation
A → product	unimolecular	Rate $= k[A]$
A + B → product	bimolecular	Rate $= k[A][B]$
A + A → product	bimolecular	Rate $= k[A]^2$
2 A + B → product	termolecular	Rate $= k[A]^2[B]$

For example, the rate laws for each of the two steps in the decomposition of ozone are

$$\text{Rate for (unimolecular) Step 1} = k[O_3]$$

$$\text{Rate for (bimolecular) Step 2} = k'[O_3][O]$$

When a reaction mechanism consists of two elementary steps, the two steps will likely occur at different rates. The two rate constants (k and k' in this example) are not expected to have the same value (nor the same units, if the two steps have different molecularities).

Molecularity and Reaction Order

A unimolecular elementary step must be first order; a bimolecular elementary step must be second order; and a termolecular elementary step must be third order. Such a direct relation between molecularity and order is emphatically not true for a multistep reaction. If you learn from an experiment that a reaction is first order, you cannot conclude that it occurs in a single, unimolecular elementary step. Similarly, a second-order rate equation does not imply that the reaction occurs in a single, bimolecular elementary step. An illustration of this is the decomposition of N_2O_5:

$$2\ N_2O_5(g) \rightarrow 4\ NO_2(g) + O_2(g)$$

Here, the rate law is "Rate $= k[N_2O_5]$," but chemists are fairly certain the mechanism involves a series of unimolecular and bimolecular steps.

To see how the experimentally observed rate equation for the overall reaction is connected with a possible mechanism or sequence of elementary steps requires some chemical intuition. We will provide only a glimpse of the subject in the next section.

N_2O_5 Decomposition. The first step in the decomposition of N_2O_5 is thought to be the cleavage of one of the N—O bonds in the N—O—N link to give the odd-electron molecules NO_2 and NO_3. These react further to give the final products.

EXAMPLE 15.12 Elementary Steps

Problem The hypochlorite ion undergoes self-oxidation–reduction to give chlorate, ClO_3^-, and chloride ions.

$$3\ ClO^-(aq) \rightarrow ClO_3^-(aq) + 2\ Cl^-(aq)$$

This reaction is thought to occur in two steps:

Step 1: $ClO^-(aq) + ClO^-(aq) \rightarrow ClO_2^-(aq) + Cl^-(aq)$

Step 2: $ClO_2^-(aq) + ClO^-(aq) \rightarrow ClO_3^-(aq) + Cl^-(aq)$

What is the molecularity of each step? Write the rate equation for each reaction step. Show that the sum of these reactions gives the equation for the net reaction.

Strategy The molecularity is the number of ions or molecules involved in a reaction step. The rate equation involves the concentration of each ion or molecule in an elementary step, raised to the power of its stoichiometric coefficient.

Solution Because two ions are involved in each elementary step, each step is bimolecular. The rate equation for any elementary step involves the product of the concentrations of the reactants. Thus, in this case, the rate equations are

Step 1:   Rate = $k[ClO^-]^2$

Step 2:   Rate = $k'[ClO_2^-][ClO^-]$

From the equations for the two elementary steps, we see that the ClO_2^- ion is an intermediate, a product of the first step and a reactant in the second step. It therefore cancels out, and we are left with the stoichiometric equation for the overall reaction:

Step 1: $ClO^-(aq) + ClO^-(aq) \rightarrow ClO_2^-(aq) + Cl^-(aq)$

Step 2: $ClO_2^-(aq) + ClO^-(aq) \rightarrow ClO_3^-(aq) + Cl^-(aq)$

Sum of steps: $3\ ClO^-(aq) \rightarrow ClO_3^-(aq) + 2\ Cl^-(aq)$

EXERCISE 15.11 Elementary Steps

Nitrogen monoxide is reduced by hydrogen to give nitrogen and water:

$$2\ NO(g) + 2\ H_2(g) \rightarrow N_2(g) + 2\ H_2O(g)$$

One possible mechanism for this reaction is

$$2\ NO(g) \rightarrow N_2O_2(g)$$

$$N_2O_2(g) + H_2(g) \rightarrow N_2O(g) + H_2O(g)$$

$$N_2O(g) + H_2(g) \rightarrow N_2(g) + H_2O(g)$$

What is the molecularity of each of the three steps? What is the rate equation for the third step? Identify the intermediates in this reaction; how many different intermediates are there? Show that the sum of these elementary steps gives the equation for the overall reaction.

Reaction Mechanisms and Rate Equations

The dependence of rate on concentration is an experimental fact. Mechanisms, by contrast, are constructs of our imagination, intuition, and good "chemical sense." To describe a mechanism, we need to make a guess (a good guess, we hope) about how the reaction occurs at the particulate level. Several mechanisms can always be proposed that correspond to the observed rate equation, and a postulated mechanism is often wrong. A good mechanism is a worthy goal because it allows us to understand the chemistry better. A practical consequence of a good mechanism is that it allows us to predict, for example, how to control a reaction better and how to design new experiments.

One of the important guidelines of kinetics is that *products of a reaction can never be produced at a rate faster than the rate of the slowest step.* If one step in a multistep reaction is slower than the others, then *the rate of the overall reaction is limited by the combined rates of all elementary steps up through the slowest step in the mechanism.* Often the overall reaction rate and the rate of the slow step are nearly the same. If the slow step determines the rate of the reaction, it is called the **rate-determining step,** or rate-limiting step.

Imagine that a reaction takes place with a mechanism involving two sequential steps, and assume that we know the rates of both steps. The first step is slow and the second is fast:

■ **Can You Derive a Mechanism?** At this introductory level, you cannot be expected to derive reaction mechanisms. Given a mechanism, however, you can decide whether it agrees with experimental rate laws.

Elementary Step 1 $A + B \xrightarrow[\text{Slow, } E_a \text{ large}]{k_1} X + M$

Elementary Step 2 $M + A \xrightarrow[\text{Fast, } E_a \text{ small}]{k_2} Y$

Overall Reaction $2A + B \longrightarrow X + Y$

In the first step, A and B come together and slowly react to form one of the products (X) plus another reactive species, M. Almost as soon as M is formed, however, it is rapidly consumed by reacting with another molecule of A to form the second product Y. The rate-determining elementary step in this example is the first step. That is, the rate of the first step is equal to the rate of the overall reaction. This step is bimolecular and so has the rate equation

$$\text{Rate} = k_1[A][B]$$

where k_1 is the rate constant for that step. The overall reaction is expected to have this same second-order rate equation.

Let us apply these ideas to the mechanism of a real reaction. Consider the reaction of nitrogen dioxide with fluorine which has a second-order rate equation:

Overall Reaction $2\,NO_2(g) + F_2(g) \rightarrow 2\,FNO_2(g)$

$$\text{Rate} = k[NO_2][F_2]$$

The rate equation immediately rules out the possibility that the reaction occurs in a single step. If the equation for the reaction represented an elementary step, the rate law would have a second-order dependence on $[NO_2]$. Because a single-step reaction is ruled out, the mechanism must include at least two steps. We can also conclude from the rate law that the rate-determining elementary step must involve NO_2 and F_2 in a 1:1 ratio. One possible mechanism proposes that molecules of NO_2 and F_2 first react to produce one molecule of the product (FNO_2) plus one F atom. In a second step, the fluorine atom produced in the first step reacts with additional NO_2 to give a second molecule of product. If the first, bimolecular step is rate determining, the rate equation would be "Rate = $k_1[NO_2][F_2]$," the same as the experimentally observed rate equation. The experimental rate constant would be the same as k_1.

Elementary Step 1   Slow $NO_2(g) + F_2(g) \xrightarrow{k_1} FNO_2(g) + F(g)$

Elementary Step 2   Fast $NO_2(g) + F(g) \xrightarrow{k_2} FNO_2(g)$

Overall Reaction $2\,NO_2(g) + F_2(g) \longrightarrow 2\,FNO_2(g)$

The fluorine atom formed in the first step of the NO_2/F_2 reaction is a reaction intermediate. It does not appear in the equation describing the overall reaction. Reaction intermediates usually have only a fleeting existence, but occasionally they have long enough lifetimes to be observed. The detection and identification of an intermediate are strong evidence for the proposed mechanism.

■ EXAMPLE 15.13 Elementary Steps and Reaction Mechanisms

Problem Oxygen atom transfer from NO_2 to CO produces nitrogen monoxide and carbon dioxide (Figure 15.13):

$$NO_2(g) + CO(g) \rightarrow NO(g) + CO_2(g)$$

The rate equation for this reaction at temperatures less than 500 K is:

$$Rate = k[NO_2]^2$$

Can this reaction occur in one bimolecular step?

Strategy Write the rate law based on the equation for the NO_2 + CO reaction occurring as if it were an elementary step. If this rate law corresponds to the observed rate law, then a one-step mechanism is possible.

Solution If the reaction occurs by the collision of one NO_2 molecule with one CO molecule, the rate equation would be

$$Rate = k[NO_2][CO]$$

This does not agree with experiment, so the mechanism must involve more than a single step. In one possible mechanism, the reaction occurs in two, bimolecular steps, the first one slow and the second one fast:

Elementary Step 1	Slow, rate-determining	$2\ NO_2(g) \longrightarrow NO_3(g) + NO(g)$

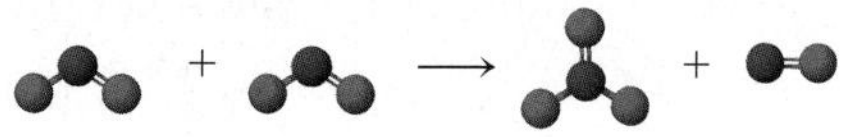

Elementary Step 2	Fast	$NO_3(g) + CO(g) \longrightarrow NO_2(g) + CO_2(g)$

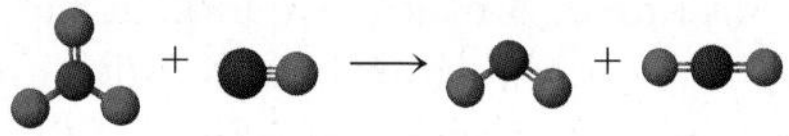

Overall Reaction	$NO_2(g) + CO(g) \longrightarrow NO(g) + CO_2(g)$

The first (rate-determining) step has a rate equation that agrees with experiment, so this is a possible mechanism.

EXERCISE 15.12 Elementary Steps and Reaction Mechanisms

The Raschig reaction produces hydrazine, N_2H_4, an industrially important reducing agent, from NH_3 and OCl^- in basic, aqueous solution. A proposed mechanism is

Step 1 Fast $NH_3(aq) + OCl^-(aq) \rightarrow NH_2Cl(aq) + OH^-(aq)$

Step 2 Slow $NH_2Cl(aq) + NH_3(aq) \rightarrow N_2H_5^+(aq) + Cl^-(aq)$

Step 3 Fast $N_2H_5^+(aq) + OH^-(aq) \rightarrow N_2H_4(aq) + H_2O(\ell)$

(a) What is the overall stoichiometric equation?

(b) Which step of the three is rate determining?

(c) Write the rate equation for the rate-determining elementary step.

(d) What reaction intermediates are involved?

A common two-step reaction mechanism involves an initial fast reaction that produces an intermediate, followed by a slower second step in which the intermediate is converted to the final product. The rate of the reaction is determined by the second step, for which a rate law can be written. The rate of that step, however, depends on the concentration of the intermediate. Remember, though, that the rate law must be written with respect to the reactants only. An intermediate, whose concentration will probably not be measurable, cannot appear as a term in the overall rate equation.

The reaction of nitrogen monoxide and oxygen is an example of a two-step reaction where the first step is fast and the second step is rate determining.

$$2\ NO(g) + O_2(g) \rightarrow 2\ NO_2(g)$$

$$\text{Rate} = k[NO]^2[O_2]$$

The experimentally determined rate law shows second-order dependence on NO and first-order dependence on O_2. Although this rate law would be correct for a termolecular reaction, experimental evidence indicates that an intermediate is formed in this reaction. A possible two-step mechanism that proceeds through an intermediate is

Elementary Step 1:   Fast, Equilibrium $NO(g) + O_2(g) \underset{k_{-1}}{\overset{k_1}{\rightleftarrows}} OONO(g)$ intermediate

Elementary Step 2:   Slow, Rate-determining $NO(g) + OONO(g) \overset{k_2}{\rightarrow} 2\ NO_2(g)$

Overall Reaction $2\ NO(g) + O_2(g) \rightarrow 2\ NO_2(g)$

The second step of this reaction is the slow step, and the overall rate depends on it. We can write a rate law for the second step:

$$\text{Rate} = k_2[NO][OONO]$$

This rate law cannot be compared directly with the experimental rate law because it contains the concentration of an intermediate, OONO. To eliminate the intermediate from this rate expression, we look at the rapid first step in this reaction sequence that involves an equilibrium between the intermediate species and the reactants.

At the beginning of the reaction, NO and O_2 react rapidly and produce the intermediate OONO. The rate of formation can be defined by a rate law with a rate constant k_1:

$$\text{Rate of production of OONO} = k_1[NO][O_2]$$

Because the intermediate is consumed only very slowly in the second step, it is possible for the OONO to revert to NO and O_2 before it reacts further:

$$\text{Rate of reverse reaction (OONO} \rightarrow NO + O_2) = k_{-1}[OONO]$$

As NO and O_2 form OONO, their concentrations drop, so the rate of the forward reaction decreases. At the same time, the concentration of OONO builds up, so the rate of the reverse reaction increases. At equilibrium, the rates of the forward and reverse reactions become the same.

$$\text{Rate of forward reaction} = \text{rate of reverse reaction}$$

$$k_1[NO][O_2] = k_{-1}[OONO]$$

Rearranging this equation, we find

$$\frac{k_1}{k_{-1}} = \frac{[N_2O_2]}{[NO][O_2]} = K$$

The connection between an experimental rate equation and the proposed reaction mechanism is important in chemistry.

1. Experiments must first be performed to determine the experimental rate equation.
2. A mechanism for the reaction is proposed on the basis of the experimental rate equation, the principles of stoichiometry

and molecular structure and bonding, general chemical experience, and intuition.
3. The proposed reaction mechanism is used to derive a rate equation. This rate equation can contain only those species present in the overall chemical reaction. If the derived and experimental rate equations

are the same, the postulated mechanism *may* be a reasonable hypothesis of the reaction sequence.
4. If more than one mechanism can be proposed, and they all predict derived rate equations in agreement with experiment, then more experiments must be done.

Both k_1 and k_{-1} are constants (they will change only if the temperature changes). We can define a new constant K equal to the ratio of these two constants and called the **equilibrium constant**, which is equal to the quotient $[OONO]/[NO][O_2]$. From this, we can derive an expression for the concentration of OONO:

$$[OONO] = K[NO][O_2]$$

If $K[NO][O_2]$ is substituted for $[OONO]$ in the rate law for the rate-determining elementary step, we have

$$\text{Rate} = k_2[NO][OONO] = k_2[NO]\{K[NO][O_2]\}$$

$$= k_2 K[NO]^2[O_2]$$

Because both k_2 and K are constants, their product is another constant k', and we have

$$\text{Rate} = k'[NO]^2[O_2]$$

This is exactly the rate law derived from experiment. Thus, the sequence of reactions on which the rate law is based may be a reasonable mechanism for this reaction. It is not the only possible mechanism, however. This rate equation is also consistent with the reaction occurring in a single termolecular step. Another possible mechanism is illustrated in Example 15.14.

■ **Equilibrium Constant** The important concept of chemical equilibrium was introduced in Chapter 3 and will be described in more detail in Chapters 16–19.

■ **Mechanisms with an Initial Equilibrium** In this mechanism, the forward and reverse reactions in the first elementary step are so much faster than the second elementary step that equilibrium is established before any significant amount of OONO is consumed by NO to give NO_2. The state of equilibrium for the first step remains throughout the lifetime of the overall reaction.

EXAMPLE 15.14 Reaction Mechanism Involving an Equilibrium Step

Problem The $NO + O_2$ reaction described in the text could also occur by the following mechanism:

Elementary Step 1: Fast, equilibrium

$$NO(g) + NO(g) \underset{k_{-1}}{\overset{k_1}{\rightleftharpoons}} N_2O_2(g) \text{ intermediate}$$

Elementary Step 2: Slow, rate-determining

$$N_2O_2(g) + O_2(g) \xrightarrow{k_2} 2\,NO_2(g)$$

Overall Reaction: $2\,NO(g) + O_2(g) \longrightarrow 2\,NO_2(g)$

Show that this mechanism leads to the following experimental rate law: Rate $= k[NO]^2[O_2]$.

Strategy The rate law for the rate-determining elementary step is

$$\text{Rate} = k_2[N_2O_2][O_2]$$

The intermediate N_2O_2 cannot appear in the final derived rate law. To obtain the rate law, we use the equilibrium constant expression for the first step.

Solution $[N_2O_2]$ and [NO] are related by the equilibrium constant.

$$\frac{k_1}{k_{-1}} = \frac{[N_2O_2]}{[NO]^2} = K$$

Solving this equation for $[N_2O_2]$ gives $[N_2O_2] = K[NO]^2$. When this is substituted into the derived rate law

$$\text{Rate} = k_2\{K[NO_2]^2\}[O_2]$$

the resulting equation is identical with the experimental rate law where $k_2K = k$.

Comment Three mechanisms have been proposed for the NO + O_2 reaction. The challenge for chemists is to decide which is correct. In this case, further experimentation detected the species OONO as a short-lived intermediate, confirming the mechanism involving this intermediate.

EXERCISE 15.13 Reaction Mechanism Involving a Fast Initial Step

One possible mechanism for the decomposition of nitryl chloride, NO_2Cl, is

Elementary Step 1: Fast, Equilibrium $$NO_2Cl(g) \underset{k_{-1}}{\overset{k_1}{\rightleftharpoons}} NO_2(g) + Cl(g)$$

Elementary Step 2: Slow $$NO_2Cl(g) + Cl(g) \xrightarrow{k_2} NO_2(g) + Cl_2(g)$$

What is the overall reaction? What rate law would be derived from this mechanism? What effect does increasing the concentration of the product NO_2 have on the reaction rate?

Chapter Goals Revisited

Chemistry Now™ Sign in at **www.cengage.com/login** to:

- Assess your understanding with Study Questions in OWL keyed to each goal in the Goals and Homework menu for this chapter
- For quick review, download Go Chemistry mini-lecture flashcard modules (or purchase them at **www.ichapters.com**)
- Check your readiness for an exam by taking the Pre-Test and exploring the modules recommended in your Personalized Study plan.

Access **How Do I Solve It?** tutorials on how to approach problem solving using concepts in this chapter.

For additional preparation for an examination on this chapter see the *Let's Review* section on pages 948–961.

Now that you have studied this chapter, you should ask whether you have met the chapter goals. In particular, you should be able to:

Understand rates of reaction and the conditions affecting rates

a. Explain the concept of reaction rate (Section 15.1).

b. Derive the average and instantaneous rates of a reaction from concentration–time data (Section 15.1). Study Question(s) assignable in OWL: 5.

c. Describe factors that affect reaction rate (i.e., reactant concentrations, temperature, presence of a catalyst, and the state of the reactants) (Section 15.2). Study Question(s) assignable in OWL: 8, 10, 62, 76, 77, 81.

Derive the rate equation, rate constant, and reaction order from experimental data

a. Define the various parts of a rate equation (the rate constant and order of reaction), and understand their significance (Section 15.3). Study Question(s) assignable in OWL: 12, 14, 68.

b. Derive a rate equation from experimental information (Section 15.3). Study Question(s) assignable in OWL: 12, 14, 48, 56, 58, 71.

Use integrated rate laws

a. Describe and use the relationships between reactant concentration and time for zero-order, first-order, and second-order reactions (Section 15.4 and Table 15.1). Study Question(s) assignable in OWL: 16, 18, 19, 20, 24; Go Chemistry Module 20.

b. Apply graphical methods for determining reaction order and the rate constant from experimental data (Section 15.4 and Table 15.1). Study Question(s) assignable in OWL: 28, 30.

c. Use the concept of half-life ($t_{1/2}$), especially for first-order reactions (Section 15.4). Study Question(s) assignable in OWL: 22, 24, 26, 60, 71.

Understand the collision theory of reaction rates and the role of activation energy
a. Describe the collision theory of reaction rates (Section 15.5).
b. Relate activation energy (E_a) to the rate and thermodynamics of a reaction (Section 15.5). Study Question(s) assignable in OWL: 36, 69, 83.
c. Use collision theory to describe the effect of reactant concentration on reaction rate (Section 15.5).
d. Understand the effect of molecular orientation on reaction rate (Section 15.5).
e. Describe the effect of temperature on reaction rate using the collision theory of reaction rates and the Arrhenius equation (Equation 15.7 and Section 15.5).
f. Use Equations 15.5, 15.6, and 15.7 to calculate the activation energy from rate constants at different temperatures (Section 15.5).

Relate reaction mechanisms and rate laws
a. Describe the functioning of a catalyst and its effect on the activation energy and mechanism of a reaction (Section 15.5).
b. Understand reaction coordinate diagrams (Section 15.5).
c. Understand the concept of a reaction mechanism (a proposed sequence of bond-making and bond-breaking steps that occurs during the conversion of reactants to products) and the relation of the mechanism to the overall, stoichiometric equation for a reaction (Section 15.6).
d. Describe the elementary steps of a mechanism, and give their molecularity (Section 15.6). Study Question(s) assignable in OWL: 40, 42, 44, 74.
e. Define the rate-determining step in a mechanism, and identify any reaction intermediates (Section 15.6). Study Question(s) assignable in OWL: 44, 69, 70, 78, 80.

KEY EQUATIONS

Equation 15.1 (page 683) Integrated rate equation for a first-order reaction (in which $-\Delta[R]/\Delta t = k[R]$).

$$\ln\frac{[R]_t}{[R]_0} = -kt$$

Here, $[R]_0$ and $[R]_t$ are concentrations of the reactant at time $t = 0$ and at a later time, t. The ratio of concentrations, $[R]_t/[R]_0$, is the fraction of reactant that remains after a given time has elapsed.

Equation 15.2 (page 686) Integrated rate equation for a second-order reaction (in which $-\Delta[R]/\Delta t = k[R]^2$).

$$\frac{1}{[R]_t} - \frac{1}{[R]_0} = kt$$

Equation 15.3 (page 687) Integrated rate equation for a zero-order reaction (in which $-\Delta[R]/\Delta t = k[R]^0$).

$$[R]_0 - [R]_t = kt$$

Equation 15.4 (page 690) The relation between the half-life ($t_{1/2}$) and the rate constant (k) for a first-order reaction.

$$t_{1/2} = \frac{0.693}{k}$$

Equation 15.5 (page 696) Arrhenius equation in exponential form

$$k = \text{rate constant} = Ae^{-E_a/RT}$$

Frequency factor

Fraction of molecules with minimum energy for reaction

A is the frequency factor; E_a is the activation energy; T is the temperature (in kelvins); and R is the gas constant ($= 8.314510 \times 10^{-3}$ kJ/K · mol).

Equation 15.6 (page 696) Expanded Arrhenius equation in logarithmic form.

$$\ln k = -\frac{E_a}{R}\left(\frac{1}{T}\right) + \ln A \quad \longleftarrow \text{Arrhenius equation}$$

$$\begin{array}{ccc} \downarrow & \downarrow & \downarrow \\ y & = mx & + b \longleftarrow \text{Equation for straight line} \end{array}$$

Equation 15.7 (page 698) A version of the Arrhenius equation used to calculate the activation energy for a reaction when you know the values of the rate constant at two temperatures (in kelvins).

$$\ln k_2 - \ln k_1 = \ln \frac{k_2}{k_1} = -\frac{E_a}{R}\left[\frac{1}{T_2} - \frac{1}{T_1}\right]$$

STUDY QUESTIONS

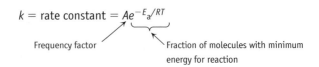 Online homework for this chapter may be assigned in OWL.

▲ denotes challenging questions.

■ denotes questions assignable in OWL.

Blue-numbered questions have answers in Appendix O and fully-worked solutions in the *Student Solutions Manual*.

Practicing Skills

Reaction Rates
(See Examples 15.1–15.2, Exercises 15.1–15.2, and ChemistryNow Screen 15.2.)

1. Give the relative rates of disappearance of reactants and formation of products for each of the following reactions.
   (a) $2 O_3(g) \longrightarrow 3 O_2(g)$
   (b) $2 HOF(g) \longrightarrow 2 HF(g) + O_2(g)$

2. Give the relative rates of disappearance of reactants and formation of products for each of the following reactions.
   (a) $2 NO(g) + Br_2(g) \longrightarrow 2 NOBr(g)$
   (b) $N_2(g) + 3 H_2(g) \longrightarrow 2 NH_3(g)$

3. In the reaction $2 O_3(g) \longrightarrow 3 O_2(g)$, the rate of formation of O_2 is 1.5×10^{-3} mol/L · s. What is the rate of decomposition of O_3?

4. In the synthesis of ammonia, if $-\Delta[H_2]/\Delta t = 4.5 \times 10^{-4}$ mol/L·min, what is $\Delta[NH_3]/\Delta t$?

$$N_2(g) + 3 H_2(g) \rightarrow 2 NH_3(g)$$

5. ■ Experimental data are listed here for the reaction $A \longrightarrow 2 B$.

Time (s)	[B] (mol/L)
0.00	0.000
10.0	0.326
20.0	0.572
30.0	0.750
40.0	0.890

   (a) Prepare a graph from these data; connect the points with a smooth line; and calculate the rate of change of [B] for each 10-s interval from 0.0 to 40.0 s. Does the rate of change decrease from one time interval to the next? Suggest a reason for this result.
   (b) How is the rate of change of [A] related to the rate of change of [B] in each time interval? Calculate the rate of change of [A] for the time interval from 10.0 to 20.0 s.
   (c) What is the instantaneous rate, $\Delta[B]/\Delta t$, when [B] = 0.750 mol/L?

6. Phenyl acetate, an ester, reacts with water according to the equation

$$\underset{\text{phenyl acetate}}{CH_3\overset{\displaystyle O}{\overset{\|}{C}}OC_6H_5} + H_2O \longrightarrow \underset{\text{acetic acid}}{CH_3\overset{\displaystyle O}{\overset{\|}{C}}OH} + \underset{\text{phenol}}{C_6H_5OH}$$

The data in the table were collected for this reaction at 5 °C.

Time (s)	[Phenyl acetate] (mol/L)
0	0.55
15.0	0.42
30.0	0.31
45.0	0.23
60.0	0.17
75.0	0.12
90.0	0.085

(a) Plot the phenyl acetate concentration versus time, and describe the shape of the curve observed.
(b) Calculate the rate of change of the phenyl acetate concentration during the period 15.0 s to 30.0 s and also during the period 75.0 s to 90.0 s. Why is one value smaller than the other?
(c) What is the rate of change of the phenol concentration during the time period 60.0 s to 75.0 s?
(d) What is the instantaneous rate at 15.0 s?

Concentration and Rate Equations

(See Examples 15.3–15.4, Exercises 15.3–15.4, and ChemistryNow Screens 15.4 and 15.5.)

7. Using the rate equation "Rate $= k[A]^2[B]$," define the order of the reaction with respect to A and B. What is the total order of the reaction?

8. ■ A reaction has the experimental rate equation Rate $= k[A]^2$. How will the rate change if the concentration of A is tripled? If the concentration of A is halved?

9. The reaction between ozone and nitrogen dioxide at 231 K is first order in both $[NO_2]$ and $[O_3]$.

$$2 NO_2(g) + O_3(g) \rightarrow N_2O_5(s) + O_2(g)$$

(a) Write the rate equation for the reaction.
(b) If the concentration of NO_2 is tripled (and $[O_3]$ is not changed), what is the change in the reaction rate?
(c) What is the effect on reaction rate if the concentration of O_3 is halved (no change in $[NO_2]$)?

10. ■ Nitrosyl bromide, NOBr, is formed from NO and Br_2:

$$2 NO(g) + Br_2(g) \rightarrow 2 NOBr(g)$$

Experiments show that this reaction is second order in NO and first order in Br_2.
(a) Write the rate equation for the reaction.
(b) How does the initial reaction rate change if the concentration of Br_2 is changed from 0.0022 mol/L to 0.0066 mol/L?
(c) What is the change in the initial rate if the concentration of NO is changed from 0.0024 mol/L to 0.0012 mol/L?

11. The data in the table are for the reaction of NO and O_2 at 660 K.

$$2 NO(g) + O_2(g) \rightarrow 2 NO_2(g)$$

Reactant Concentration (mol/L)		Rate of Disappearance of NO (mol/L · s)
[NO]	[O₂]	
0.010	0.010	2.5×10^{-5}
0.020	0.010	1.0×10^{-4}
0.010	0.020	5.0×10^{-5}

(a) Determine the order of the reaction for each reactant.
(b) Write the rate equation for the reaction.
(c) Calculate the rate constant.
(d) Calculate the rate (in mol/L · s) at the instant when $[NO] = 0.015$ mol/L and $[O_2] = 0.0050$ mol/L.
(e) At the instant when NO is reacting at the rate 1.0×10^{-4} mol/L · s, what is the rate at which O_2 is reacting and NO_2 is forming?

12. ■ The reaction

$$2 NO(g) + 2 H_2(g) \rightarrow N_2(g) + 2 H_2O(g)$$

was studied at 904 °C, and the data in the table were collected.

Reactant Concentration (mol/L)		Rate of Appearance of N₂ (mol/L · s)
[NO]	[H₂]	
0.420	0.122	0.136
0.210	0.122	0.0339
0.210	0.244	0.0678
0.105	0.488	0.0339

(a) Determine the order of the reaction for each reactant.
(b) Write the rate equation for the reaction.
(c) Calculate the rate constant for the reaction.
(d) Find the rate of appearance of N_2 at the instant when $[NO] = 0.350$ mol/L and $[H_2] = 0.205$ mol/L.

13. Data for the reaction $2\,NO(g) + O_2(g) \rightarrow 2\,NO_2(g)$ are given in the table.

	Concentration (mol/L)		Initial Rate
Experiment	[NO]	[O₂]	(mol/L · h)
1	3.6×10^{-4}	5.2×10^{-3}	3.4×10^{-8}
2	3.6×10^{-4}	1.04×10^{-2}	6.8×10^{-8}
3	1.8×10^{-4}	1.04×10^{-2}	1.7×10^{-8}
4	1.8×10^{-4}	5.2×10^{-3}	?

(a) What is the rate law for this reaction?
(b) What is the rate constant for the reaction?
(c) What is the initial rate of the reaction in experiment 4?

14. ■ Data for the following reaction are given in the table below.

$$CO(g) + NO_2(g) \rightarrow CO_2(g) + NO(g)$$

	Concentration (mol/L)		Initial Rate
Experiment	[CO]	[NO₂]	(mol/L · h)
1	5.0×10^{-4}	0.36×10^{-4}	3.4×10^{-8}
2	5.0×10^{-4}	0.18×10^{-4}	1.7×10^{-8}
3	1.0×10^{-3}	0.36×10^{-4}	6.8×10^{-8}
4	1.5×10^{-3}	0.72×10^{-4}	?

(a) What is the rate law for this reaction?
(b) What is the rate constant for the reaction?
(c) What is the initial rate of the reaction in experiment 4?

Concentration–Time Relationships
(See Examples 15.5–15.7, Exercises 15.5–15.7, and ChemistryNow Screen 15.6.)

15. The rate equation for the hydrolysis of sucrose to fructose and glucose

$$C_{12}H_{22}O_{11}(aq) + H_2O(\ell) \rightarrow 2\,C_6H_{12}O_6(aq)$$

is $-\Delta[\text{sucrose}]/\Delta t = k[C_{12}H_{22}O_{11}]$. After 27 min at 27 °C, the sucrose concentration decreased from 0.0146 M to 0.0132 M. Find the rate constant, k.

16. ■ The decomposition of N_2O_5 in CCl_4 is a first-order reaction. If 2.56 mg of N_2O_5 is present initially, and 2.50 mg is present after 4.26 min at 55 °C, what is the value of the rate constant, k?

17. The decomposition of SO_2Cl_2 is a first-order reaction:

$$SO_2Cl_2(g) \rightarrow SO_2(g) + Cl_2(g)$$

The rate constant for the reaction is 2.8×10^{-3} min^{-1} at 600 K. If the initial concentration of SO_2Cl_2 is 1.24×10^{-3} mol/L, how long will it take for the concentration to drop to 0.31×10^{-3} mol/L?

18. ■ The conversion of cyclopropane to propene (see Example 15.5) occurs with a first-order rate constant of 2.42×10^{-2} h^{-1}. How long will it take for the concentration of cyclopropane to decrease from an initial concentration 0.080 mol/L to 0.020 mol/L?

19. ■ Hydrogen peroxide, $H_2O_2(aq)$, decomposes to $H_2O(\ell)$ and $O_2(g)$ in a reaction that is first order in H_2O_2 and has a rate constant $k = 1.06 \times 10^{-3}$ min^{-1} at a given temperature.
(a) How long will it take for 15% of a sample of H_2O_2 to decompose?
(b) How long will it take for 85% of the sample to decompose?

20. ■ The decomposition of nitrogen dioxide at a high temperature

$$NO_2(g) \rightarrow NO(g) + \tfrac{1}{2}\,O_2(g)$$

is second order in this reactant. The rate constant for this reaction is 3.40 L/mol · min. Determine the time needed for the concentration of NO_2 to decrease from 2.00 mol/L to 1.50 mol/L.

Half-Life
(See Examples 15.8 and 15.9, Exercise 15.9, and ChemistryNow Screen 15.8.)

21. The rate equation for the decomposition of N_2O_5 (giving NO_2 and O_2) is Rate = $k[N_2O_5]$. The value of k is 6.7×10^{-5} s^{-1} for the reaction at a particular temperature.
(a) Calculate the half-life of N_2O_5.
(b) How long does it take for the N_2O_5 concentration to drop to one tenth of its original value?

22. ■ The decomposition of SO_2Cl_2

$$SO_2Cl_2(g) \rightarrow SO_2(g) + Cl_2(g)$$

is first order in SO_2Cl_2, and the reaction has a half-life of 245 min at 600 K. If you begin with 3.6×10^{-3} mol of SO_2Cl_2 in a 1.0-L flask, how long will it take for the amount of SO_2Cl_2 to decrease to 2.00×10^{-4} mol?

23. Gaseous azomethane, $CH_3N{=}NCH_3$, decomposes in a first-order reaction when heated:

$$CH_3N{=}NCH_3(g) \rightarrow N_2(g) + C_2H_6(g)$$

The rate constant for this reaction at 600 K is 0.0216 min^{-1}. If the initial quantity of azomethane in the flask is 2.00 g, how much remains after 0.0500 h? What quantity of N_2 is formed in this time?

24. ■ The compound $Xe(CF_3)_2$ decomposes in a first-order reaction to elemental Xe with a half-life of 30. min. If you place 7.50 mg of $Xe(CF_3)_2$ in a flask, how long must you wait until only 0.25 mg of $Xe(CF_3)_2$ remains?

25. The radioactive isotope ^{64}Cu is used in the form of copper(II) acetate to study Wilson's disease. The isotope has a half-life of 12.70 h. What fraction of radioactive copper(II) acetate remains after 64 h?

26. ■ Radioactive gold-198 is used in the diagnosis of liver problems. The half-life of this isotope is 2.7 days. If you begin with a 5.6-mg sample of the isotope, how much of this sample remains after 1.0 day?

Graphical Analysis: Rate Equations and *k*
(See Exercise 15.8 and ChemistryNow Screen 15.7.)

27. Data for the decomposition of dinitrogen oxide

$$2 N_2O(g) \rightarrow 2 N_2(g) + O_2(g)$$

on a gold surface at 900 °C are given below. Verify that the reaction is first order by preparing a graph of ln [N_2O] versus time. Derive the rate constant from the slope of the line in this graph. Using the rate law and value of *k*, determine the decomposition rate at 900 °C when [N_2O] = 0.035 mol/L.

Time (min)	[N₂0] (mol/L)
15.0	0.0835
30.0	0.0680
80.0	0.0350
120.0	0.0220

28. ■ Ammonia decomposes when heated according to the equation

$$NH_3(g) \rightarrow NH_2(g) + H(g)$$

The data in the table for this reaction were collected at a high temperature.

Time (h)	[NH₃] (mol/L)
0	8.00×10^{-7}
25	6.75×10^{-7}
50	5.84×10^{-7}
75	5.15×10^{-7}

Plot ln [NH_3] versus time and $1/[NH_3]$ versus time. What is the order of this reaction with respect to NH_3? Find the rate constant for the reaction from the slope.

29. Gaseous NO_2 decomposes at 573 K.

$$2 NO_2(g) \rightarrow 2 NO(g) + O_2(g)$$

The concentration of NO_2 was measured as a function of time. A graph of $1/[NO_2]$ versus time gives a straight line with a slope of 1.1 L/mol · s. What is the rate law for this reaction? What is the rate constant?

30. ■ The decomposition of HOF occurs at 25 °C.

$$2 HOF(g) \rightarrow 2 HF(g) + O_2(g)$$

Using the data in the table below, determine the rate law, and then calculate the rate constant.

[HOF] (mol/L)	Time (min)
0.850	0
0.810	2.00
0.754	5.00
0.526	20.0
0.243	50.0

31. For the reaction $2 C_2F_4 \rightarrow C_4F_8$, a graph of $1/[C_2F_4]$ versus time gives a straight line with a slope of +0.04 L/mol · s. What is the rate law for this reaction?

32. Butadiene, $C_4H_6(g)$, dimerizes when heated, forming 1,5-cyclooctadiene, C_8H_{12}. The data in the table were collected.

$$2 H_2C=CHCH=CH_2 \longrightarrow$$

1,3-butadiene

H₂C—CH₂
HC   CH
HC   CH
H₂C—CH₂

1,5-cyclooctadiene

[C₄H₆] (mol/L)	Time (s)
1.0×10^{-2}	0
8.7×10^{-3}	200.
7.7×10^{-3}	500.
6.9×10^{-3}	800.
5.8×10^{-3}	1200.

(a) Use a graphical method to verify that this is a second-order reaction.
(b) Calculate the rate constant for the reaction.

Kinetics and Energy
(See Examples 15.10 and 15.11, and ChemistryNow Screens 15.9 and 15.10.)

33. Calculate the activation energy, E_a, for the reaction

$$2 N_2O_5(g) \rightarrow 4 NO_2(g) + O_2(g)$$

from the observed rate constants: *k* at 25 °C = 3.46×10^{-5} s⁻¹ and *k* at 55 °C = 1.5×10^{-3} s⁻¹.

34. If the rate constant for a reaction triples when the temperature rises from 3.00×10^2 K to 3.10×10^2 K, what is the activation energy of the reaction?

35. When heated to a high temperature, cyclobutane, C_4H_8, decomposes to ethylene:

$$C_4H_8(g) \rightarrow 2 C_2H_4(g)$$

The activation energy, E_a, for this reaction is 260 kJ/mol-rxn. At 800 K, the rate constant $k = 0.0315$ s⁻¹. Determine the value of *k* at 850 K.

36. ■ When heated, cyclopropane is converted to propene (see Example 15.5). Rate constants for this reaction at 470 °C and 510 °C are $k = 1.10 \times 10^{-4}$ s⁻¹ and $k = 1.02 \times 10^{-3}$ s⁻¹, respectively. Determine the activation energy, E_a, from these data.

37. The reaction of H_2 molecules with F atoms

$$H_2(g) + F(g) \rightarrow HF(g) + H(g)$$

has an activation energy of 8 kJ/mol-rxn and an energy change of -133 kJ/mol-rxn. Draw a diagram similar to Figure 15.13 for this process. Indicate the activation energy and enthalpy change on this diagram.

38. Answer the following questions based on the diagram below.
(a) Is the reaction exothermic or endothermic?
(b) Does the reaction occur in more than one step? If so, how many?

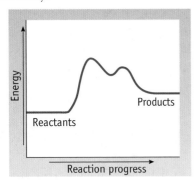

Reaction Mechanisms
(See Examples 15.12–15.14, Exercises 15.11–15.13, and ChemistryNow Screens 15.12 and 15.13.)

39. What is the rate law for each of the following elementary reactions?
(a) $NO(g) + NO_3(g) \rightarrow 2 NO_2(g)$
(b) $Cl(g) + H_2(g) \rightarrow HCl(g) + H(g)$
(c) $(CH_3)_3CBr(aq) \rightarrow (CH_3)_3C^+(aq) + Br^-(aq)$

40. ■ What is the rate law for each of the following elementary reactions?
(a) $Cl(g) + ICl(g) \rightarrow I(g) + Cl_2(g)$
(b) $O(g) + O_3(g) \rightarrow 2 O_2(g)$
(c) $2 NO_2(g) \rightarrow N_2O_4(g)$

41. Ozone, O_3, in the earth's upper atmosphere decomposes according to the equation

$$2 O_3(g) \rightarrow 3 O_2(g)$$

The mechanism of the reaction is thought to proceed through an initial fast, reversible step followed by a slow, second step.

Step 1   Fast, reversible $O_3(g) \rightleftharpoons O_2(g) + O(g)$

Step 2   Slow $O_3(g) + O(g) \rightarrow 2 O_2(g)$

(a) Which of the steps is rate-determining?
(b) Write the rate equation for the rate determining step.

42. ■ The reaction of $NO_2(g)$ and $CO(g)$ is thought to occur in two steps:

Step 1   Slow $NO_2(g) + NO_2(g) \rightarrow NO(g) + NO_3(g)$

Step 2   Fast $NO_3(g) + CO(g) \rightarrow NO_2(g) + CO_2(g)$

(a) Show that the elementary steps add up to give the overall, stoichiometric equation.
(b) What is the molecularity of each step?
(c) For this mechanism to be consistent with kinetic data, what must be the experimental rate equation?
(d) Identify any intermediates in this reaction.

43. A proposed mechanism for the reaction of NO_2 and CO is

Step 1 Slow, endothermic
$$2 NO_2(g) \rightarrow NO(g) + NO_3(g)$$

Step 2 Fast, exothermic
$$NO_3(g) + CO(g) \rightarrow NO_2(g) + CO_2(g)$$

Overall Reaction   Exothermic
$$NO_2(g) + CO(g) \rightarrow NO(g) + CO_2(g)$$

(a) Identify each of the following as a reactant, product, or intermediate: $NO_2(g)$, $CO(g)$, $NO_3(g)$, $CO_2(g)$, $NO(g)$.
(b) Draw a reaction coordinate diagram for this reaction. Indicate on this drawing the activation energy for each step and the overall enthalpy change.

44. ■ The mechanism for the reaction of CH_3OH and HBr is believed to involve two steps. The overall reaction is exothermic.

Step 1   Fast, endothermic
$$CH_3OH + H^+ \rightleftharpoons CH_3OH_2^+$$

Step 2   Slow
$$CH_3OH_2^+ + Br^- \rightarrow CH_3Br + H_2O$$

(a) Write an equation for the overall reaction.
(b) Draw a reaction coordinate diagram for this reaction.
(c) Show that the rate law for this reaction is Rate $= k[CH_3OH][H^+][Br^-]$.

General Questions
These questions are not designated as to type or location in the chapter. They may combine several concepts from this and other chapters.

45. A reaction has the following experimental rate equation: Rate $= k[A]^2[B]$. If the concentration of A is doubled and the concentration of B is halved, what happens to the reaction rate?

46. For a first-order reaction, what fraction of reactant remains after five half-lives have elapsed?

▲ more challenging   ■ in OWL   Blue-numbered questions answered in Appendix O

47. To determine the concentration dependence of the rate of the reaction

$$H_2PO_3^-(aq) + OH^-(aq) \rightarrow HPO_3^{2-}(aq) + H_2O(\ell)$$

you might measure $[OH^-]$ as a function of time using a pH meter. (To do so, you would set up conditions under which $[H_2PO_3^-]$ remains constant by using a large excess of this reactant.) How would you prove a second-order rate dependence for $[OH^-]$?

48. ■ Data for the following reaction are given in the table.

$$2\, NO(g) + Br_2(g) \rightarrow 2\, NOBr(g)$$

Experiment	[NO] (M)	[Br₂] (M)	Initial Rate (mol/L · s)
1	1.0×10^{-2}	2.0×10^{-2}	2.4×10^{-2}
2	4.0×10^{-2}	2.0×10^{-2}	0.384
3	1.0×10^{-2}	5.0×10^{-2}	6.0×10^{-2}

What is the order of the reaction with respect to [NO] and [Br₂], and what is the overall order of the reaction?

49. Formic acid decomposes at 550 °C according to the equation

$$HCO_2H(g) \rightarrow CO_2(g) + H_2(g)$$

The reaction follows first-order kinetics. In an experiment, it is determined that 75% of a sample of HCO_2H has decomposed in 72 seconds. Determine $t_{1/2}$ for this reaction.

50. Isomerization of CH_3NC occurs slowly when CH_3NC is heated.

$$CH_3NC(g) \rightarrow CH_3CN(g)$$

To study the rate of this reaction at 488 K, data on $[CH_3NC]$ were collected at various times. Analysis led to the graph below.
(a) What is the rate law for this reaction?
(b) What is the equation for the straight line in this graph?
(c) Calculate the rate constant for this reaction.
(d) How long does it take for half of the sample to isomerize?
(e) What is the concentration of CH_3NC after 1.0×10^4 s?

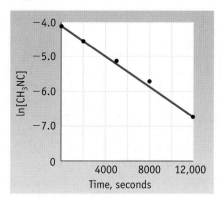

51. When heated, tetrafluoroethylene dimerizes to form octafluorocyclobutane.

$$2\, C_2F_4(g) \rightarrow C_4F_8(g)$$

To determine the rate of this reaction at 488 K, the data in the table were collected. Analysis was done graphically, as shown below:

[C₂F₄] (M)	Time (s)
0.100	0
0.080	56
0.060	150.
0.040	335
0.030	520.

(a) What is the rate law for this reaction?
(b) What is the value of the rate constant?
(c) What is the concentration of C_2F_4 after 600 s?
(d) How long will it take until the reaction is 90% complete?

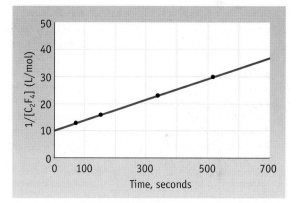

52. Data in the table were collected at 540 K for the following reaction:

$$CO(g) + NO_2(g) \rightarrow CO_2(g) + NO(g)$$

(a) Derive the rate equation.
(b) Determine the reaction order with respect to each reactant.
(c) Calculate the rate constant, giving the correct units for k.

Initial Concentration (mol/L)		Initial Rate (mol/L · h)
[CO]	[NO₂]	
5.1×10^{-4}	0.35×10^{-4}	3.4×10^{-8}
5.1×10^{-4}	0.70×10^{-4}	6.8×10^{-8}
5.1×10^{-4}	0.18×10^{-4}	1.7×10^{-8}
1.0×10^{-3}	0.35×10^{-4}	6.8×10^{-8}
1.5×10^{-3}	0.35×10^{-4}	10.2×10^{-8}

53. Ammonium cyanate, NH_4NCO, rearranges in water to give urea, $(NH_2)_2CO$.

$$NH_4NCO(aq) \rightarrow (NH_2)_2CO(aq)$$

Time (min)	[NH₄NCO] (mol/L)
0	0.458
4.50×10^1	0.370
1.07×10^2	0.292
2.30×10^2	0.212
6.00×10^2	0.114

Using the data in the table:
(a) Decide whether the reaction is first order or second order.
(b) Calculate k for this reaction.
(c) Calculate the half-life of ammonium cyanate under these conditions.
(d) Calculate the concentration of NH_4NCO after 12.0 h.

54. Nitrogen oxides, NO_x (a mixture of NO and NO_2 collectively designated as NO_x), play an essential role in the production of pollutants found in photochemical smog. The NO_x in the atmosphere is slowly broken down to N_2 and O_2 in a first-order reaction. The average half-life of NO_x in the smokestack emissions in a large city during daylight is 3.9 h.
(a) Starting with 1.50 mg in an experiment, what quantity of NO_x remains after 5.25 h?
(b) How many hours of daylight must have elapsed to decrease 1.50 mg of NO_x to 2.50×10^{-6} mg?

55. At temperatures below 500 K, the reaction between carbon monoxide and nitrogen dioxide

$$CO(g) + NO_2(g) \rightarrow CO_2(g) + NO(g)$$

has the following rate equation: Rate = $k[NO_2]^2$. Which of the three mechanisms suggested here best agrees with the experimentally observed rate equation?

Mechanism 1	Single, elementary step
	$NO_2 + CO \rightarrow CO_2 + NO$

Mechanism 2	Two steps
Slow	$NO_2 + NO_2 \rightarrow NO_3 + NO$
Fast	$NO_3 + CO \rightarrow NO_2 + CO_2$

Mechanism 3	Two steps
Slow	$NO_2 \rightarrow NO + O$
Fast	$CO + O \rightarrow CO_2$

56. ■ ▲ Nitryl fluoride can be made by treating nitrogen dioxide with fluorine:

$$2\ NO_2(g) + F_2(g) \rightarrow 2\ NO_2F(g)$$

Use the rate data in the table to do the following:
(a) Write the rate equation for the reaction.
(b) Indicate the order of reaction with respect to each component of the reaction.
(c) Find the numerical value of the rate constant, k.

Experiment	Initial Concentrations (mol/L) [NO₂]	[F₂]	[NO₂F]	Initial Rate (mol/L · s)
1	0.001	0.005	0.001	2.0×10^{-4}
2	0.002	0.005	0.001	4.0×10^{-4}
3	0.006	0.002	0.001	4.8×10^{-4}
4	0.006	0.004	0.001	9.6×10^{-4}
5	0.001	0.001	0.001	4.0×10^{-5}
6	0.001	0.001	0.002	4.0×10^{-5}

57. The decomposition of dinitrogen pentaoxide

$$2\ N_2O_5(g) \rightarrow 4\ NO_2(g) + O_2(g)$$

has the following rate equation: Rate = $k[N_2O_5]$. It has been found experimentally that the decomposition is 20.5 % complete in 13.0 h at 298 K. Calculate the rate constant and the half-life at 298 K.

58. ■ The data in the table give the temperature dependence of the rate constant for the reaction $N_2O_5(g)$ $\rightarrow 2\ NO_2(g) + \frac{1}{2}\ O_2(g)$. Plot these data in the appropriate way to derive the activation energy for the reaction.

T(K)	k (s⁻¹)
338	4.87×10^{-3}
328	1.50×10^{-3}
318	4.98×10^{-4}
308	1.35×10^{-4}
298	3.46×10^{-5}
273	7.87×10^{-7}

59. The decomposition of gaseous dimethyl ether at ordinary pressures is first order. Its half-life is 25.0 min at 500 °C:

$$CH_3OCH_3(g) \rightarrow CH_4(g) + CO(g) + H_2(g)$$

(a) Starting with 8.00 g of dimethyl ether, what mass remains (in grams) after 125 min and after 145 min?
(b) Calculate the time in minutes required to decrease 7.60 ng (nanograms) to 2.25 ng.
(c) What fraction of the original dimethyl ether remains after 150 min?

▲ more challenging ■ in OWL Blue-numbered questions answered in Appendix O

60. ■ The decomposition of phosphine, PH_3, proceeds according to the equation

$$4\,PH_3(g) \longrightarrow P_4(g) + 6\,H_2(g)$$

It is found that the reaction has the following rate equation: Rate = $k[PH_3]$. The half-life of PH_3 is 37.9 s at 120 °C.

(a) How much time is required for three-fourths of the PH_3 to decompose?

(b) What fraction of the original sample of PH_3 remains after 1.00 min?

61. The ozone in the earth's ozone layer decomposes according to the equation

$$2\,O_3(g) \longrightarrow 3\,O_2(g)$$

The mechanism of the reaction is thought to proceed through an initial fast equilibrium and a slow step:

Step 1 Fast, reversible $O_3(g) \rightleftharpoons O_2(g) + O(g)$

Step 2 Slow $O_3(g) + O(g) \longrightarrow 2\,O_2(g)$

Show that the mechanism agrees with this experimental rate law:

$$-\Delta[O_3]/\Delta t = k\,[O_3]^2/[O_2].$$

62. ■ Hundreds of different reactions can occur in the stratosphere, among them reactions that destroy the earth's ozone layer. The table below lists several (second-order) reactions of Cl atoms with ozone and organic compounds; each is given with its rate constant.

Reaction	Rate Constant (298 K, cm^3/molecule · s)
(a) $Cl + O_3 \rightarrow ClO + O_2$	1.2×10^{-11}
(b) $Cl + CH_4 \rightarrow HCl + CH_3$	1.0×10^{-13}
(c) $Cl + C_3H_8 \rightarrow HCl + C_3H_7$	1.4×10^{-10}
(d) $Cl + CH_2FCl \rightarrow HCl + CHFCl$	3.0×10^{-18}

For equal concentrations of Cl and the other reactant, which is the slowest reaction? Which is the fastest reaction?

63. Data for the reaction

$$[Mn(CO)_5(CH_3CN)]^+ + NC_5H_5$$
$$\longrightarrow [Mn(CO)_5(NC_5H_5)]^+ + CH_3CN$$

are given in the table. Calculate E_a from a plot of ln k versus $1/T$.

T(K)	k(min^{-1})
298	0.0409
308	0.0818
318	0.157

64. ■ The gas-phase reaction

$$2\,N_2O_5(g) \longrightarrow 4\,NO_2(g) + O_2(g)$$

has an activation energy of 103 kJ/mol-rxn, and the rate constant is 0.0900 min^{-1} at 328.0 K. Find the rate constant at 318.0 K.

65. ■ ▲ Egg protein albumin is precipitated when an egg is cooked in boiling (100 °C) water. E_a for this first-order reaction is 52.0 kJ/mol. Estimate the time to prepare a 3-min egg at an altitude at which water boils at 90 °C.

66. ■ ▲ Two molecules of 1,3-butadiene (C_4H_6) form 1,5-cyclooctadiene, C_8H_{12} at higher temperatures.

$$2\,C_4H_6(g) \longrightarrow C_8H_{12}(g)$$

Use the following data to determine the order of the reaction and the rate constant, k. (Note that the total pressure is the pressure of the unreacted C_4H_6 at any time and the pressure of the C_8H_{12}.)

Time (min)	Total Pressure (mm Hg)
0	436
3.5	428
11.5	413
18.3	401
25.0	391
32.0	382
41.2	371

67. ■ ▲ Hypofluorous acid, HOF, is very unstable, decomposing in a first-order reaction to give HF and O_2, with a half-life of 30. min at room temperature:

$$HOF(g) \longrightarrow HF(g) + \tfrac{1}{2}\,O_2(g)$$

If the partial pressure of HOF in a 1.00-L flask is initially 1.00×10^2 mm Hg at 25 °C, what are the total pressure in the flask and the partial pressure of HOF after exactly 30 min? After 45 min?

68. ■ ▲ We know that the decomposition of SO_2Cl_2 is first order in SO_2Cl_2,

$$SO_2Cl_2(g) \longrightarrow SO_2(g) + Cl_2(g)$$

with a half-life of 245 min at 600 K. If you begin with a partial pressure of SO_2Cl_2 of 25 mm Hg in a 1.0-L flask, what is the partial pressure of each reactant and product after 245 min? What is the partial pressure of each reactant after 12 h?

69. ■▲ Nitramide, NO_2NH_2, decomposes slowly in aqueous solution according to the following reaction:

$$NO_2NH_2(aq) \rightarrow N_2O(g) + H_2O(\ell)$$

The reaction follows the experimental rate law

$$Rate = \frac{k[NO_2NH_2]}{[H_3O^+]}$$

(a) What is the apparent order of the reaction in a buffered solution?

(b) Which of the following mechanisms is the most appropriate for the interpretation of this rate law? Explain.

Mechanism 1

$$NO_2NH_2 \xrightarrow{k_1} N_2O + H_2O$$

Mechanism 2

$$NO_2NH_2 + H_3O^+ \underset{k_2'}{\overset{k_2}{\rightleftharpoons}} NO_2NH_3^+ + H_2O$$
(rapid equilibrium)

$$NO_2NH_3^+ \xrightarrow{k_3} N_2O + H_3O^+ \quad \text{(rate limiting step)}$$

Mechanism 3

$$NO_2NH_2 + H_2O \underset{k_4'}{\overset{k_4}{\rightleftharpoons}} NO_2NH^- + H_3O^+$$
(rapid equilibrium)

$$NO_2NH^- \xrightarrow{k_5} N_2O + OH^- \quad \text{(rate limiting step)}$$

$$H_3O^+ + OH^- \xrightarrow{k_6} 2\,H_2O \quad \text{(very fast reaction)}$$

(c) Show the relationship between the experimentally observed rate constant, k, and the rate constants in the selected mechanism.

(d) Show that hydroxyl ions catalyze the decomposition of nitramide.

70. ■ Many biochemical reactions are catalyzed by acids. A typical mechanism consistent with the experimental results (in which HA is the acid and X is the reactant) is

Step 1 **Fast, reversible** $\quad HA \rightleftharpoons H^+ + A^-$

Step 2 **Fast, reversible** $\quad X + H^+ \rightleftharpoons XH^+$

Step 3 **Slow** $\quad XH^+ \rightarrow$ products

What rate law is derived from this mechanism? What is the order of the reaction with respect to HA? How would doubling the concentration of HA affect the reaction?

In the Laboratory

71. ■ The color change accompanying the reaction of phenolphthalein with strong base is illustrated on page 670. The change in concentration of the dye can be followed by spectrophotometry (page 190), and some data collected by that approach are given below. The initial concentrations were [phenolphthalein] = 0.0050 mol/L and [OH⁻] = 0.61 mol/L. (Data are taken from review materials for kinetics at chemed.chem.purdue.edu.)

(For more details on this reaction see L. Nicholson, *Journal of Chemical Education*, Vol. 66, page 725, 1989.)

Concentration of Phenolphthalein (mol/L)	Time (s)
0.0050	0.00
0.0045	10.5
0.0040	22.3
0.0035	35.7
0.0030	51.1
0.0025	69.3
0.0020	91.6
0.0015	120.4
0.0010	160.9
0.00050	230.3
0.00025	299.6

(a) Plot the data above as [phenolphthalein] versus time, and determine the average rate from $t = 0$ to $t = 15$ s and from $t = 100$ s to $t = 125$ s. Does the rate change? If so, why?

(b) What is the instantaneous rate at 50 s?

(c) Use a graphical method to determine the order of the reaction with respect to phenolphthalein. Write the rate law, and determine the rate constant.

(d) What is the half-life for the reaction?

72. ▲ We want to study the hydrolysis of the beautiful green, cobalt-based complex called *trans*-dichloro-bis (ethylenediamine)cobalt(III) ion,

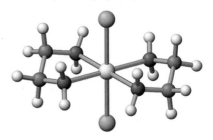

In this hydrolysis reaction, the green complex ion *trans*–$[Co(en)_2Cl_2]^+$ forms the red complex ion $[Co(en)_2(H_2O)Cl]^{2+}$ as a Cl^- ion is replaced with a water molecule on the Co^{3+} ion (en = $H_2NCH_2CH_2NH_2$).

$$trans\text{–}[Co(en)_2Cl_2]^+(aq) + H_2O(\ell) \rightarrow$$
green

$$[Co(en)_2(H_2O)Cl]^{2+}(aq) + Cl^-(aq)$$
red

The reaction progress is followed by observing the color of the solution. The original solution is green, and the final solution is red, but at some intermediate stage when both the reactant and product are present, the solution is gray.

Original solution

Intermediate solution

Final solution

Photos: Charles D. Winters

Reactions such as this have been studied extensively, and experiments suggest that the initial, slow step in the reaction is the breaking of the Co—Cl bond to give a five-coordinate intermediate. The intermediate is then attacked rapidly by water.

Slow: trans–$[Co(en)_2Cl_2]^+(aq) \rightarrow$
$$[Co(en)_2Cl]^{2+}(aq) + Cl^-(aq)$$

Fast: $[Co(en)_2Cl]^{2+}(aq) + H_2O(aq) \rightarrow$
$$[Co(en)_2(H_2O)Cl]^{2+}(aq)$$

(a) Based on the reaction mechanism, what is the predicted rate law?

(b) As the reaction proceeds, the color changes from green to red with an intermediate stage where the color is gray. The gray color is reached at the same time, no matter what the concentration of the green starting material (at the same temperature). How does this show the reaction is first order in the green form? Explain.

(c) The activation energy for a reaction can be found by plotting ln k versus $1/T$. However, here we do not need to measure k directly. Instead, because $k = -(1/t)\ln([R]/[R]_0)$, the time needed to achieve the gray color is a measure of k. Use the data below to find the activation energy.

Temperature °C	Time Needed to Achieve Gray Colors (for the same initial concentration)
56	156 s
60	114 s
65	88 s
75	47 s

73. The enzyme chymotrypsin catalyzes the hydrolysis of a peptide containing phenylalanine. Using the data below at a given temperature, calculate the maximum rate of the reaction, Rate$_{max}$. (For more information on enzyme catalysis and the Michaelis–Menten model, see page 702.)

Peptide Concentration (mol/L)	Reaction Rate (mol/L · min)
2.5×10^{-4}	2.2×10^{-6}
5.0×10^{-4}	3.8×10^{-6}
10.0×10^{-4}	5.9×10^{-6}
15.0×10^{-4}	7.1×10^{-6}

74. ■ The substitution of CO in $Ni(CO)_4$ by another molecule L [where L is an electron-pair donor such as $P(CH_3)_3$] was studied some years ago and led to an understanding of some of the general principles that govern the chemistry of compounds having metal–CO bonds. (See J. P. Day, F. Basolo, and R. G. Pearson: *Journal of the American Chemical Society*, Vol. 90, p. 6927, 1968.) A detailed study of the kinetics of the reaction led to the following mechanism:

Slow $\quad Ni(CO)_4 \rightarrow Ni(CO)_3 + CO$

Fast $\quad Ni(CO)_3 + L \rightarrow Ni(CO)_3L$

(a) What is the molecularity of each of the elementary reactions?

(b) Doubling the concentration of $Ni(CO)_4$ increased the reaction rate by a factor of 2. Doubling the concentration of L had no effect on the reaction rate. Based on this information, write the rate equation for the reaction. Does this agree with the mechanism described?

(c) The experimental rate constant for the reaction, when L = $P(C_6H_5)_3$, is 9.3×10^{-3} s^{-1} at 20 °C. If the initial concentration of $Ni(CO)_4$ is 0.025 M, what is the concentration of the product after 5.0 min?

Summary and Conceptual Questions

The following questions may use concepts from this and previous chapters.

75. Hydrogenation reactions, processes wherein H_2 is added to a molecule, are usually catalyzed. An excellent catalyst is a very finely divided metal suspended in the reaction solvent. Tell why finely divided rhodium, for example, is a much more efficient catalyst than a small block of the metal.

76. ■ ▲ Suppose you have 1000 blocks, each of which is 1.0 cm on a side. If all 1000 of these blocks are stacked to give a cube that is 10. cm on a side, what fraction of the 1000 blocks have at least one surface on the outside surface of the cube? Next, divide the 1000 blocks into eight equal piles of blocks and form them into eight cubes, 5.0 cm on a side. What fraction of the blocks now have at least one surface on the outside of the cubes? How does this mathematical model pertain to Study Question 75?

77. ■ The following statements relate to the reaction for the formation of HI:

$$H_2(g) + I_2(g) \rightarrow 2\,HI(g) \qquad Rate = k[H_2][I_2]$$

Determine which of the following statements are true. If a statement is false, indicate why it is incorrect.
(a) The reaction must occur in a single step.
(b) This is a second-order reaction overall.
(c) Raising the temperature will cause the value of k to decrease.
(d) Raising the temperature lowers the activation energy for this reaction.
(e) If the concentrations of both reactants are doubled, the rate will double.
(f) Adding a catalyst in the reaction will cause the initial rate to increase.

78. ■ Chlorine atoms contribute to the destruction of the earth's ozone layer by the following sequence of reactions:

$$Cl + O_3 \rightarrow ClO + O_2$$

$$ClO + O \rightarrow Cl + O_2$$

where the O atoms in the second step come from the decomposition of ozone by sunlight:

$$O_3(g) \rightarrow O(g) + O_2(g)$$

What is the net equation on summing these three equations? Why does this lead to ozone loss in the stratosphere? What is the role played by Cl in this sequence of reactions? What name is given to species such as ClO?

79. Describe each of the following statements as true or false. If false, rewrite the sentence to make it correct.
(a) The rate-determining elementary step in a reaction is the slowest step in a mechanism.
(b) It is possible to change the rate constant by changing the temperature.
(c) As a reaction proceeds at constant temperature, the rate remains constant.
(d) A reaction that is third order overall must involve more than one step.

80. ■ Identify which of the following statements are incorrect. If the statement is incorrect, rewrite it to be correct.
(a) Reactions are faster at a higher temperature because activation energies are lower.
(b) Rates increase with increasing concentration of reactants because there are more collisions between reactant molecules.
(c) At higher temperatures, a larger fraction of molecules have enough energy to get over the activation energy barrier.
(d) Catalyzed and uncatalyzed reactions have identical mechanisms.

81. ■ The reaction cyclopropane $\rightarrow$ propene occurs on a platinum metal surface at 200 °C. (The platinum is a catalyst.) The reaction is first order in cyclopropane. Indicate how the following quantities change (increase, decrease, or no change) as this reaction progresses, assuming constant temperature.
(a) [cyclopropane]
(b) [propene]
(c) [catalyst]
(d) the rate constant, k
(e) the order of the reaction
(f) the half-life of cyclopropane

82. Isotopes are often used as "tracers" to follow an atom through a chemical reaction, and the following is an example. Acetic acid reacts with methanol (Chapter 11).

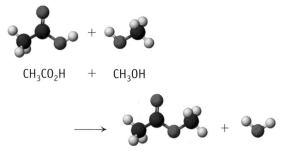

$$CH_3CO_2H \quad + \quad CH_3OH$$

$$CH_3CO_2CH_3 \quad + \quad H_2O$$

Explain how you could use the isotope ^{18}O to show whether the oxygen atom in the water comes from the —OH of the acid or the —OH of the alcohol.

83. ■ Examine the reaction coordinate diagram given here.

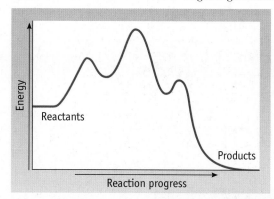

(a) How many steps are in the mechanism for the reaction described by this diagram?

(b) Is the reaction overall exothermic or endothermic?

84. Draw a reaction coordinate diagram for an exothermic reaction that occurs in a single step. Identify the activation energy and the net energy change for the reaction on this diagram. Draw a second diagram that represents the same reaction in the presence of a catalyst, assuming a single step reaction is involved here also. Identify the activation energy of this reaction and the energy change. Is the activation energy in the two drawings different? Does the energy evolved in the two reactions differ?

85. Screen 15.2 in ChemistryNow illustrates the rate at which a blue dye is bleached.

(a) What is the difference between an instantaneous rate and an average rate?

(b) Observe the graph of food dye concentration versus time on this screen. (Click the "tool" icon on this screen.) The plot shows the concentration of dye as the reaction progresses. What does the steepness of the plot at any particular time tell you about the rate of the reaction at that time?

(c) As the reaction progresses, the concentration of dye decreases as it is consumed. What happens to the reaction rate as this occurs? What is the relationship between reaction rate and dye concentration?

86. Watch the video on Screen 15.4 in ChemistryNow (Control of Reaction Rates—Concentration Dependence).

(a) How does an increase in HCl concentration affect the rate of the reaction of the acid with magnesium metal?

(b) On the second portion of this screen are data for the rate of decomposition of N_2O_5 (click "More"). The initial reaction rate is given for three separate experiments, each beginning with a different concentration of N_2O_5. How is the initial reaction rate related to $[N_2O_5]$?

87. The "Microscopic View of Reactions" is described on Screen 15.9 in ChemistryNow.

(a) According to collision theory, what three conditions must be met for two molecules to react?

(b) Examine the animations that play when numbers 1 and 2 are selected. One of these occurs at a higher temperature than the other. Which one? Explain briefly.

(c) Examine the animations that play when numbers 2 and 3 are selected. Would you expect the reaction of O_3 with N_2 to be more or less sensitive to proper orientation for reaction than the reaction displayed on this screen? Explain briefly.

88. "Reaction Mechanisms and Rate Equations" are described on Screen 15.13 in ChemistryNow.

(a) What is the relationship between the stoichiometric coefficients of the reactants in an elementary step and the rate law for that step?

(b) What is the rate law for Step 2 of mechanism 2?

(c) Examine the "Isotopic Labeling" sidebar to this screen. If the transfer of an oxygen atom from NO_2 to CO occurred in a single step, would any $N^{16}O^{18}O$ be found if the reaction is started using a mixture of $N^{16}O_2$ and $N^{18}O_2$? Why or why not?

89. The mechanism for the iodide ion–catalyzed decomposition of H_2O_2 is described on Screen 15.14 (Catalysis and Reaction Rate) in ChemistryNow.

(a) Examine the mechanism for the iodide ion–catalyzed decomposition of H_2O_2. Explain how the mechanism shows that I^- is a catalyst.

(b) How does the reaction coordinate diagram show that the catalyzed reaction is expected to be faster than the uncatalyzed reaction?

16 Principles of Reactivity: Chemical Equilibria

Photos: Charles D. Winters

Solution of cobalt(II) chloride in dilute hydrochloric acid.

Dynamic and Reversible!

Chemical reactions are dynamic, as proved by experiments in which reactants and products can be interconverted by making small changes in the conditions of the reaction. Dissolving cobalt(II) chloride in dilute hydrochloric acid demonstrates this very well.

Solution in an ice bath.

Solution in a boiling water bath.

Solution after adding excess hydrochloric acid.

Solution after adding excess water.

Reactions and equilibria involving cobalt (II) ions in aqueous solution.

$$[Co(H_2O)_6]^{2+}(aq) + 4\ Cl^-(aq) \rightleftharpoons [CoCl_4]^{2-}(aq) + 6\ H_2O(\ell)$$
red   blue

The solution in the top photo shows the system is a mixture of the red cation, $[Co(H_2O)_6]^{2+}$, and the blue anion, $[CoCl_4]^{2-}$. When the solution is placed in ice, the color changes to red, and when it is put in boiling water, the color is blue. Adding excess hydrochloric acid again changes the color as does adding water.

Questions:

1. Is the conversion of the red cation to the blue anion by changing the temperature exo- or endothermic?
2. Account for the effect of adding hydrochloric acid and excess water.
3. How do these observations prove the reaction is reversible?

Answers to these questions are in Appendix Q.

The concept of equilibrium is fundamental in chemistry. The general concept was introduced in Chapter 3, and you have already encountered its importance in explaining such phenomena as solubility, acid–base behavior, and changes of state. These preliminary discussions of equilibrium emphasized the following concepts: that chemical reactions are reversible, that in a closed system a state of equilibrium is achieved eventually between reactants and products, and that outside forces can affect the equilibrium. A major result of our further exploration of chemical equilibria in this and the next two chapters will be an ability to describe chemical reactions in more quantitative terms.

Chemistry.◯.Now™

Throughout the text this icon introduces an opportunity for self-study or to explore interactive tutorials by signing in at **www.cengage.com/login**.

16.1 Chemical Equilibrium: A Review

If you mix solutions of $CaCl_2$ and $NaHCO_3$, a chemical reaction is immediately detected: a gas (CO_2) bubbles from the mixture, and white solid (insoluble) $CaCO_3$ forms (Figure 16.1a). The reaction occurring is:

$$Ca^{2+}(aq) + 2\ HCO_3^-(aq) \rightarrow CaCO_3(s) + CO_2(g) + H_2O(\ell)$$

If you next add pieces of dry ice to the suspension of $CaCO_3$ (or if you bubble gaseous CO_2 into the mixture), you will observe that the solid $CaCO_3$ dissolves (Figure 16.1b). This happens because a reaction occurs that is the reverse of the reaction that led to precipitation of $CaCO_3$; that is:

$$CaCO_3(s) + CO_2(aq) + H_2O(\ell) \rightarrow Ca^{2+}(aq) + 2\ HCO_3^-(aq)$$

Now imagine what will happen if the solution of Ca^{2+} and HCO_3^- ions is in a *closed* container (unlike the reaction in Figure 16.1, which was done in an open container). As the reaction begins, Ca^{2+} and HCO_3^- react to give products at some rate. As the reactants are used up, the rate of this reaction slows. At the same time, however, the reaction products ($CaCO_3$, CO_2, and H_2O) begin to combine to reform Ca^{2+} and HCO_3^-, at a rate that increases as the amounts of $CaCO_3$ and CO_2 increase. Eventually, the rate of the forward reaction, the formation of $CaCO_3$, and the rate of the reverse reaction, the redissolving of $CaCO_3$, become equal. With $CaCO_3$ being formed and redissolving at the same rate, no further macroscopic change is observed. We have reached equilibrium, and no further *net* change is observed.

We describe an equilibrium system with an equation that connects reactants and products with double arrows. The double arrows, ⇌, indicate that the reaction

■ **Cave Chemistry** This same chemistry accounts for stalactites and stalagmites in caves. See page 119.

(a)   (b)   (c)

FIGURE 16.1 Equilibria in the CO₂/Ca²⁺/H₂O system. (a) Combining solution of $NaHCO_3$ and $CaCl_2$ produces solid $CaCO_3$. (b) If excess dry ice (the white solid) is added to the $CaCO_3$ precipitated in (a), the calcium carbonate dissolves to give Ca^{2+}(aq) and HCO_3^-(aq) (c). (See also Figure 3.6.)

■ **Reversibility of Reactions** All chemical reactions are reversible, in theory. You may see some of these in your laboratory. A few examples include

$NH_3(g) + HCl(g) \rightleftharpoons NH_4Cl(s)$

$CuSO_4 \cdot 5H_2O(s) \rightleftharpoons$

$\qquad\qquad CuSO_4(s) + 5\ H_2O(g)$

$(NH_4)_2CO_3(s) \rightleftharpoons$

$\qquad 2\ NH_3(g) + H_2O(g) + CO_2(g)$

Practically speaking, some reactions cannot be reversed. Frying an egg, for example, is not a reversible process in practical terms.

is reversible and that the reaction will be studied using the concepts of chemical equilibria.

$$Ca^{2+}(aq) + 2\ HCO_3^-(aq) \rightleftharpoons CaCO_3(s) + CO_2(g) + H_2O(\ell)$$

These experiments illustrate an important feature of chemical reactions: *All chemical reactions are reversible, at least in principle.* This was a key point in our earlier discussion of equilibrium (Chapter 3).

Our next step will be to move from a qualitative to a quantitative assessment of equilibrium systems. Among other things, this will lead us to the subject of product- and reactant-favored reactions (◄ page 121). Recall that a reaction that has a greater concentration of products than reactants once it has reached equilibrium is said to be *product-favored*. Similarly, a reaction that has a greater concentration of reactants than products at equilibrium is said to be *reactant-favored*.

Chemistry ⚛ Now™

Sign in at **www.cengage.com/login** and go to Chapter 16 Contents to see:
• Screen 16.2 to watch a video of **a reversible reaction**
• Screen 16.3 for a simulation of **a chemical equilibrium**

16.2 The Equilibrium Constant and Reaction Quotient

Chemical equilibria can also be described in a quantitative fashion. The concentrations of reactants and products when a reaction has reached equilibrium are related. For the reaction of hydrogen and iodine to produce hydrogen iodide, for example, a very large number of experiments have shown that at equilibrium the ratio of the square of the HI concentration to the product of the H_2 and I_2 concentrations is a constant.

$$H_2(g) + I_2(g) \rightleftharpoons 2\ HI(g)$$

$$\frac{[HI]^2}{[H_2][I_2]} = \text{constant }(K)\text{ at equilibrium}$$

This constant is always the same within experimental error for all experiments done at a given temperature. Suppose, for example, the concentrations of H_2 and I_2 in a

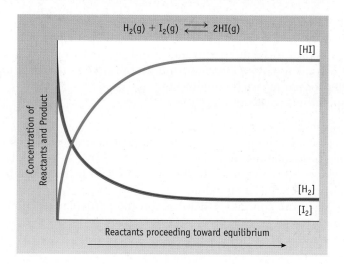

$$H_2(g) + I_2(g) \rightleftharpoons 2HI(g)$$

[HI]

[H₂]

[I₂]

Concentration of Reactants and Product

Reactants proceeding toward equilibrium

flask are each initially 0.0175 mol/L at 425 °C and that no HI is present. Over time, the concentrations of H_2 and I_2 will decrease, and the concentration of HI will increase until a state of equilibrium is reached (Figure 16.2). If the gases in the flask are then analyzed, the observed concentrations would be $[H_2] = [I_2] = 0.0037$ mol/L and $[HI] = 0.0276$ mol/L. The following table—which we call an **ICE table** for *initial, change,* and *equilibrium* concentrations—summarizes these results:

Equation	$H_2(g)$	$+$	$I_2(g)$	$\rightleftharpoons$	$2\ HI(g)$
I = *Initial* concentration (M)	0.0175		0.0175		0
C = *Change* in concentration as reaction proceeds to equilibrium	−0.0138		−0.0138		+0.0276
E = *Equilibrium* concentration (M)	0.0037		0.0037		0.0276

■ **ICE Table: Initial, Change, and Equilibrium** Throughout our discussions of chemical equilibria, we shall express the quantitative information for reactions in an amounts table or ICE table (see Chapter 4, page 159). These tables show what the initial (*I*) concentrations are, how those concentrations change (*C*) on proceeding to equilibrium, and what the concentrations are at equilibrium (*E*).

The second line in the table gives the change in concentration of reactants and products on proceeding to equilibrium. Changes are always equal to the difference between the experimentally observed equilibrium and initial concentrations.

Change in concentration = Equilibrium concentration − Initial concentration

Putting the equilibrium concentration values from the ICE table into the expression for the constant (*K*) gives a value of 56 (to two significant figures).

$$\frac{[HI]^2}{[H_2][I_2]} = \frac{(0.0276)^2}{(0.0037)(0.0037)} = 56$$

Other experiments can be done on the H_2/I_2 reaction with different concentrations of reactants, or done using mixtures of reactants and products. Regardless of the initial amounts, when equilibrium is achieved, the ratio $[HI]^2/[H_2][I_2]$ is always the same (at the same temperature).

The observation that the product and reactant concentrations for the H_2 and I_2 reaction are always in the same ratio can be generalized to other reactions. For the general chemical reaction

$$a\,A + b\,B \rightleftharpoons c\,C + d\,D$$

we can define the equilibrium constant, *K*.

When reaction is at equilibrium

$$\text{Equilibrium constant} = K = \frac{[C]^c[D]^d}{[A]^a[B]^b} \qquad \textbf{(16.1)}$$

Equation 16.1 is called the **equilibrium constant expression**. If the ratio of products to reactants as defined by Equation 16.1 matches the equilibrium constant value, the system is known to be at equilibrium. Conversely, if the ratio has a different value, the system is not at equilibrium, and we can predict in which direction the reaction will proceed to reach equilibrium.

In an equilibrium constant expression,

- All concentrations are equilibrium values.
- Product concentrations appear in the numerator, and reactant concentrations appear in the denominator.
- Each concentration is raised to the power of its stoichiometric coefficient in the balanced chemical equation.
- The value of the constant K depends on the particular reaction and on the temperature.
- Units are never given with K.

Chemistry.ᴏ̣.Now™

Sign in at **www.cengage.com/login** and go to Chapter 16 Contents to see Screen 16.4 for a simulation of **equilibrium and determination of the constant.**

Writing Equilibrium Constant Expressions

Reactions Involving Solids

The oxidation of solid, yellow sulfur produces colorless sulfur dioxide gas in a product-favored reaction (Figure 16.3).

$$S(s) + O_2(g) \rightleftharpoons SO_2(g)$$

The general principle when writing an equilibrium constant expression is to place product concentrations in the numerator and reactant concentrations in the denominator. In reactions involving solids, however, experiments show that the equilibrium concentrations of other reactants or products—here, O_2 and SO_2—do not depend on the amount of solid present (as long as some solid is present at equilibrium). The concentration of a solid such as sulfur is determined by its density, and the density is a fixed value. Therefore, the concentration of sulfur is essentially constant and is not included in the equilibrium constant expression.

$$K = \frac{[SO_2]}{[O_2]}$$

In general, *the concentrations of any solid reactants and products are not included in the equilibrium constant expression.*

Reactions in Aqueous Solutions

There are also special considerations for reactions occurring in aqueous solution in which water is either a reactant or a product. Consider ammonia, which is a weak base owing to its reaction with water.

$$NH_3(aq) + H_2O(\ell) \rightleftharpoons NH_4^+(aq) + OH^-(aq)$$

Because the water concentration is very high in a dilute ammonia solution, the concentration of water is essentially unchanged by the reaction. The general rule for such reactions in aqueous solution is that *the molar concentration of water is not included in the equilibrium constant expression.* Thus, for aqueous ammonia we write

$$K = \frac{[NH_4^+][OH^-]}{[NH_3]}$$

FIGURE 16.3 Burning sulfur.
Elemental sulfur burns in oxygen with a beautiful blue flame to give SO_2 gas.

Charles D. Winters

Reactions Involving Gases: K_c and K_p

Concentration data can be used to calculate equilibrium constants for both aqueous and gaseous systems. In these cases, the symbol K is sometimes given the subscript "c" for "concentration," as in K_c. For gases, however, equilibrium constant expressions can be written in another way—in terms of partial pressures of reactants and products. If you rearrange the ideal gas law, $[PV = nRT]$, and recognize that the "gas concentration," (n/V), is equivalent to P/RT, you see that the partial pressure of a gas is proportional to its concentration $[P = (n/V)RT]$. If reactant and product quantities are given in partial pressures (in atmospheres or, more properly, in bars), then K is given the subscript "p," as in K_p.

$$H_2(g) + I_2(g) \rightleftharpoons 2\ HI(g)$$

$$K_p = \frac{P_{HI}^2}{P_{H_2} P_{I_2}}$$

Notice that the basic form of the equilibrium constant expression is the same as for K_c. In some cases, the numerical values of K_c and K_p are the same, but they are different when the numbers of moles of gaseous reactants and products are different. *A Closer Look: Equilibrium Constant Expressions for Gases— K_c and K_p* shows how K_c and K_p are related and how to convert from one to the other.

■ K_c and K_p The subscript "c" (K_c) indicates that the numerical values of concentrations in the equilibrium constant expression have units of mol/L. A subscript "p" (K_p) indicates values in units of pressure. In this chapter, we will sometimes write simply K for K_c but will always write K_p to indicate that equilibrium values are in units of pressure.

Chemistry⚬Now™

Sign in at **www.cengage.com/login** and go to Chapter 16 Contents to see Screen 16.5 for a simulation and a tutorial on **writing equilibrium expressions.**

■ **EXAMPLE 16.1** Writing Equilibrium Constant Expressions

Problem Write the equilibrium constant expressions for the following reactions.

(a) $N_2(g) + 3\ H_2(g) \rightleftharpoons 2\ NH_3(g)$

(b) $H_2CO_3(aq) + H_2O(\ell) \rightleftharpoons HCO_3^-(aq) + H_3O^+(aq)$

Strategy Remember that product concentrations always appear in the numerator and reactant concentrations appear in the denominator. Each concentration should be raised to a power equal to the stoichiometric coefficient in the balanced equation. In reaction (b), the water concentration does not appear in the equilibrium constant expression.

Solution

(a) $\quad K = \dfrac{[NH_3]^2}{[N_2][H_2]^3}$ $\qquad$ (b) $\quad K = \dfrac{[HCO_3^-][H_3O^+]}{[H_2CO_3]}$

EXERCISE 16.1 Writing Equilibrium Constant Expressions

Write the equilibrium constant expression for each of the following reactions in terms of concentrations.

(a) $CO_2(g) + C(s) \rightleftharpoons 2\ CO(g)$

(b) $[Cu(NH_3)_4]^+(aq) \rightleftharpoons Cu^{2+}(aq) + 4\ NH_3(aq)$

(c) $CH_3CO_2H(aq) + H_2O(\ell) \rightleftharpoons CH_3CO_2^-(aq) + H_3O^+(aq)$

Equilibrium Constant Expressions for Gases—K_c and K_p

Many metal carbonates, such as limestone, decompose on heating to give the metal oxide and CO_2 gas.

$$CaCO_3(s) \rightleftharpoons CaO(s) + CO_2(g)$$

The equilibrium condition for this reaction can be expressed either in terms of the number of moles per liter of CO_2, $K_c = [CO_2]$ or in terms of the pressure of CO_2, $K_p = P_{CO_2}$. From the ideal gas law, you know that

$$P = (n/V)RT =$$
$$\text{(concentration in mol/L)} \times RT$$

For this reaction, we can therefore say that $P_{CO_2} = [CO_2]RT = K_p$. Because $K_c = [CO_2]$, we find that $K_p = K_c(RT)$. That is, the values of K_p and K_c are not the same; for the decomposition of calcium carbonate, K_p is the product of K_c and the factor RT.

Consider the equilibrium constant for the reaction of N_2 and H_2 to produce ammonia in terms of partial pressures, K_p.

$$N_2(g) + 3\,H_2(g) \rightleftharpoons 2\,NH_3(g)$$

$$K_p = \frac{(P_{NH_3})^2}{(P_{N_2})(P_{H_2})^3} = 5.8 \times 10^5$$

Does K_c, the equilibrium constant in terms of concentrations, have the same value as or a different value than K_p? We can answer this question by substituting for each pressure in K_p the equivalent expression $[C](RT)$. That is,

$$K_p = \frac{\{[NH_3](RT)\}^2}{\{[N_2](RT)\}\{[H_2](RT)\}^3} =$$
$$\frac{[NH_3]^2}{[N_2][H_2]^3} \times \frac{1}{(RT)^2} = \frac{K_c}{(RT)^2}$$

Solving for K_c we find

$$K_c = K_p(RT)^2$$
$$K_c = 5.8 \times 10^5 \,[(0.08206)(298)]^2 = 3.5 \times 10^8$$

Once again, you see that K_p and K_c are not the same but are related by some function of RT.

Looking carefully at these examples, we find that

$$K_p = K_c(RT)^{\Delta n}$$

where Δn is the change in the number of moles of gas on going from reactants to products.

$$\Delta n = \text{total moles of gaseous products} -$$
$$\text{total moles of gaseous reactants}$$

For the decomposition of $CaCO_3$,

$$\Delta n = 1 - 0 = 1$$

whereas the value of Δn for the ammonia synthesis is

$$\Delta n = 2 - 4 = -2$$

The Meaning of the Equilibrium Constant, K

Table 16.1 lists a few equilibrium constants for different kinds of reactants. A large value of K means that the concentration of the products is higher than the concentrations of the reactants at equilibrium. That is, the products are favored over the reactants at equilibrium.

$K > 1$: Reaction is product-favored at equilibrium. The concentrations of products are greater than the concentrations of the reactants at equilibrium.

An example is the reaction of nitrogen monoxide and ozone.

$$NO(g) + O_3(g) \rightleftharpoons NO_2(g) + O_2(g)$$

$$K = \frac{[NO_2][O_2]}{[NO][O_3]} = 6 \times 10^{34} \text{ at } 25\,°C$$

The very large value of K indicates that, at equilibrium, $[NO_2][O_2] \gg [NO][O_3]$. If stoichiometric amounts of NO and O_3 are mixed and allowed to come to equilibrium, virtually none of the reactants will be found (Figure 16.4a). Essentially, all will have been converted to NO_2 and O_2. A chemist would say that "the reaction has gone to completion."

Conversely, a small value of K means that very little of the products exist when equilibrium has been achieved (Figure 16.4b). That is, the reactants are favored over the products at equilibrium.

$K < 1$: Reaction is reactant-favored at equilibrium. Concentrations of reactants are greater than concentrations of products at equilibrium.

This is true for the formation of ozone from oxygen.

$$\tfrac{3}{2}\,O_2(g) \rightleftharpoons O_3(g)$$

$$K = \frac{[O_3]}{[O_2]^{3/2}} = 2.5 \times 10^{-29} \text{ at } 25\,°C$$

TABLE 16.1 Selected Equilibrium Constant Values

Reaction	Equilibrium Constant, K (at 25 °C)	Product- or Reactant-Favored
Combination Reaction of Nonmetals		
$S(s) + O_2(g) \rightleftharpoons SO_2(g)$	4.2×10^{52}	$K > 1$; product-favored
$2 H_2(g) + O_2(g) \rightleftharpoons 2 H_2O(g)$	3.2×10^{81}	$K > 1$; product-favored
$N_2(g) + 3 H_2(g) \rightleftharpoons 2 NH_3(g)$	3.5×10^8	$K > 1$; product-favored
$N_2(g) + O_2(g) \rightleftharpoons 2 NO(g)$	1.7×10^{-3} (at 2300 K)	$K < 1$; reactant-favored
Ionization of Weak Acids and Bases		
$HCO_2H(aq) + H_2O(\ell) \rightleftharpoons HCO_2^-(aq) + H_3O^+(aq)$ formic acid	1.8×10^{-4}	$K < 1$; reactant-favored
$CH_3CO_2H(aq) + H_2O(\ell) \rightleftharpoons CH_3CO_2^-(aq) + H_3O^+(aq)$ acetic acid	1.8×10^{-5}	$K < 1$; reactant-favored
$H_2CO_3(aq) + H_2O(\ell) \rightleftharpoons HCO_3^-(aq) + H_3O^+(aq)$ carbonic acid	4.2×10^{-7}	$K < 1$; reactant-favored
$NH_3(aq) + H_2O(\ell) \rightleftharpoons NH_4^+(aq) + OH^-(aq)$ ammonia	1.8×10^{-5}	$K < 1$; reactant-favored
Dissolution of "Insoluble" Solids		
$CaCO_3(s) \rightleftharpoons Ca^{2+}(aq) + CO_3^{2-}(aq)$	3.8×10^{-9}	$K < 1$; reactant-favored
$AgCl(s) \rightleftharpoons Ag^+(aq) + Cl^-(aq)$	1.8×10^{-10}	$K < 1$; reactant-favored

The very small value of K indicates that, at equilibrium, $[O_3] << [O_2]^{3/2}$. If O_2 is placed in a flask, very little O_2 will have been converted to O_3 when equilibrium has been achieved.

When K is close to 1, it may not be immediately clear whether the reactant concentrations are larger than the product concentrations, or *vice versa*. It will depend on the form of K and thus on the reaction stoichiometry. Calculations of the concentrations will have to be done.

Chemistry Now™

Sign in at **www.cengage.com/login** and go to Chapter 16 Contents to see Screen 16.6 for a simulation of **an equilibrium.**

(a)

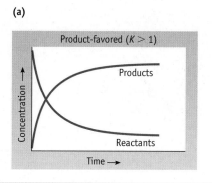

(b)

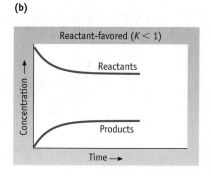

FIGURE 16.4 The difference between product- and reactant-favored reactions. In (a) the concentration of products exceeds the concentration of reactants, and the reaction is product-favored. In (b), the reactant concentrations exceed the product concentration, and the reaction is reactant-favored.

EXERCISE 16.2 The Equilibrium Constant and Extent of Reaction

Are the following reactions product- or reactant-favored at equilibrium?

(a) $[Cu(NH_3)_4]^{2+} \rightleftharpoons Cu^{2+}(aq) + 4\ NH_3(aq)$ $\quad K = 1.5 \times 10^{-13}$

(b) $[Cd(NH_3)_4]^{2+} \rightleftharpoons Cd^{2+}(aq) + 4\ NH_3(aq)$ $\quad K = 1.0 \times 10^{-7}$

If each reaction has a reactant concentration of 0.10 M, in which solution is the NH_3 concentration greater?

The Reaction Quotient, *Q*

The equilibrium constant, *K*, for a reaction has a particular numerical value when the reactants and products are at equilibrium. When the reactants and products in a reaction are not at equilibrium, however, it is convenient to calculate the reaction quotient, *Q*. For the general reaction of *A* and *B* to give *C* and *D*,

$$a\,A + b\,B \rightleftharpoons c\,C + d\,D$$

the reaction quotient is defined as

$$\text{Reaction quotient} = Q = \frac{[C]^c[D]^d}{[A]^a[B]^b} \qquad \textbf{(16.2)}$$

■ **Comparing *Q* and *K***

Relative Magnitude	Direction of Reaction
$Q < K$	Reactants → Products
$Q = K$	Reaction at equilibrium
$Q > K$	Reactants ← Products

This expression *appears* to be just like Equation 16.1, but it is not. The concentrations of reactants and products in the expression for *Q* are those that occur *at any point* as the reaction proceeds from reactants to an equilibrium mixture. *Only when the system is at equilibrium does* $Q = K$. For the reaction of H_2 and I_2 to give HI (Figure 16.2), any combination of reactant and product concentrations before equilibrium is achieved will give a value of *Q* different than *K*.

Determining a reaction quotient is useful for two reasons. First, it will tell you whether a system is at equilibrium (when $Q = K$) or is not at equilibrium (when $Q \neq K$). Second, by comparing *Q* and *K*, we can predict what changes will occur in reactant and product concentrations as the reaction proceeds to equilibrium.

- $\boldsymbol{Q < K}$ If *Q* is less than *K*, some reactants must be converted to products for the reaction to reach equilibrium. This will decrease the reactant concentrations and increase the product concentrations. (This is the case for the system in Figure 16.5a.)
- $\boldsymbol{Q > K}$ If *Q* is greater than *K*, some products must be converted to reactants for the reaction to reach equilibrium. This will increase the reactant concentrations and decrease the product concentrations. (See Figure 16.5c)

To illustrate these points, let us consider a reaction such as the transformation of butane to isobutane (2-methylpropane).

$$\text{Butane} \rightleftharpoons \text{Isobutane}$$

$$CH_3CH_2CH_2CH_3 \rightleftharpoons CH_3CH(CH_3)CH_3$$

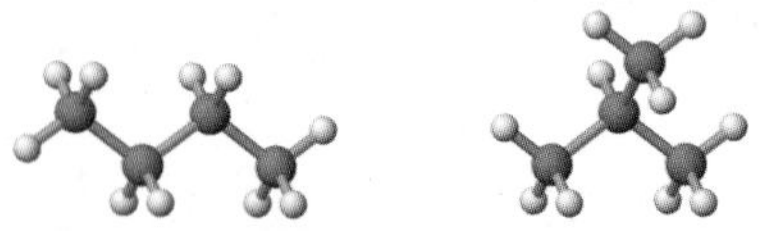

$$K_c = \frac{[\text{isobutane}]}{[\text{butane}]} = 2.50 \text{ at } 298\text{ K}$$

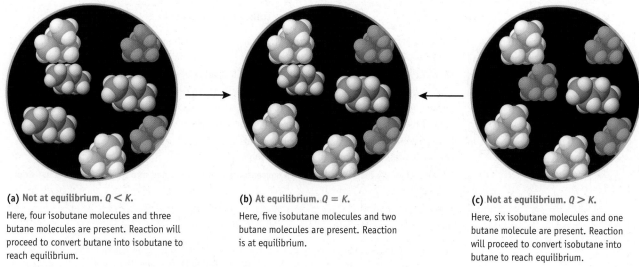

(a) Not at equilibrium. $Q < K$.

Here, four isobutane molecules and three butane molecules are present. Reaction will proceed to convert butane into isobutane to reach equilibrium.

(b) At equilibrium. $Q = K$.

Here, five isobutane molecules and two butane molecules are present. Reaction is at equilibrium.

(c) Not at equilibrium. $Q > K$.

Here, six isobutane molecules and one butane molecule are present. Reaction will proceed to convert isobutane into butane to reach equilibrium.

FIGURE 16.5 The interconversion of isobutane and butane. Only when the concentrations of isobutane and butane are in the ratio [isobutane/butane] = 2.5 is the system at equilibrium (b). With any other ratio of concentrations, there will be a net conversion of one compound into the other until equilibrium is achieved.

If the concentration of one of the compounds is known, then only one value of the other concentration will satisfy the equation for the equilibrium constant. For example, if [butane] is 1.0 mol/L, then the equilibrium concentration of isobutane, [isobutane], must be 2.5 mol/L. If [butane] is 0.63 mol/L at equilibrium, then [isobutane] is 1.6 mol/L.

$$[\text{isobutane}] = K[\text{butane}] = (2.50)(0.63 \text{ mol/L}) = 1.6 \text{ mol/L}$$

Any mixture of butane and isobutane, whether at equilibrium or not, can be represented by the reaction quotient Q (=[isobutane]/[butane]). Suppose you have a mixture composed of 3 mol/L of butane and 4 mol/L of isobutane (at 298 K) (Figure 16.5a). This means that the reaction quotient, Q, is

$$Q = \frac{\left[\text{isobutane}\right]}{\left[\text{butane}\right]} = \frac{4.0}{3.0} = 1.3$$

This set of concentrations clearly does not represent an equilibrium system because $Q < K$. To reach equilibrium, some butane molecules must be transformed into molecules of isobutane, thereby lowering [butane] and raising [isobutane]. This transformation will continue until the ratio [isobutane]/[butane] = 2.5; that is, until $Q = K$ (Figure 16.5b).

What happens when there is too much isobutane in the system relative to the amount of butane? Suppose [isobutane] = 6.0 mol/L but [butane] is only 1.0 mol/L (Figure 16.5c). Now the reaction quotient Q is greater than K ($Q > K$), and the system is again not at equilibrium. It will proceed to equilibrium by converting isobutane molecules to butane molecules.

Chemistry ‑̇Ọ̇‑ Now™

Sign in at **www.cengage.com/login** and go to Chapter 16 Contents to see Screen 16.9 for a simulation and tutorial on **Q, the reaction quotient.**

EXAMPLE 16.2 **The Reaction Quotient**

Problem The brown gas nitrogen dioxide, NO_2, can exist in equilibrium with the colorless gas N_2O_4. $K = 170$ at 298 K for the reaction

$$2\ NO_2(g) \rightleftharpoons N_2O_4(g)\quad K = 170$$

Suppose that, at a specific time, the concentration of NO_2 is 0.015 M and the concentration of N_2O_4 is 0.025 M. Is Q larger than, smaller than, or equal to K? If the system is not at equilibrium, in which direction will the reaction proceed to achieve equilibrium?

Strategy Write the expression for Q, and substitute the numerical values into the equation. Decide whether Q is less than, equal to, or greater than K.

Solution When the reactant and product concentrations are substituted into the reaction quotient expression, we have

$$Q = \frac{[N_2O_4]}{[NO_2]^2} = \frac{(0.025)}{(0.015)^2} = 110$$

The value of Q is less than the value of K ($Q < K$), so the reaction is not at equilibrium. The system proceeds to equilibrium by converting NO_2 to N_2O_4, increasing $[N_2O_4]$, and decreasing $[NO_2]$ until $Q = K$.

Comment When calculating Q, make sure that you raise each concentration to the power of the stoichiometric coefficient.

EXERCISE 16.3 **The Reaction Quotient**

Answer the following questions regarding the butane $\rightleftharpoons$ isobutane equilibrium ($K = 2.50$ at 298 K).

(a) Is the system at equilibrium when [butane] = 0.97 M and [isobutane] = 2.18 M? If it is not at equilibrium, in which direction will the reaction proceed to achieve equilibrium?

(b) Is the system at equilibrium when [butane] = 0.75 M and [isobutane] = 2.60 M? If it is not at equilibrium, in which direction will the reaction proceed to achieve equilibrium?

EXERCISE 16.4 **The Reaction Quotient**

At 2000 K the equilibrium constant for the formation of $NO(g)$ is 4.0×10^{-4}.

$$N_2(g) + O_2(g) \rightleftharpoons 2\ NO(g)$$

You have a flask in which, at 2000 K, the concentration of N_2 is 0.50 mol/L, that of O_2 is 0.25 mol/L, and that of NO is 4.2×10^{-3} mol/L. Is the system at equilibrium? If not, predict which way the reaction will proceed to achieve equilibrium.

16.3 Determining an Equilibrium Constant

When the experimental values of the concentrations of all of the reactants and products are known at equilibrium, an equilibrium constant can be calculated by substituting the data into the equilibrium constant expression. Consider this concept as it applies to the oxidation of sulfur dioxide.

$$2\ SO_2(g) + O_2(g) \rightleftharpoons 2\ SO_3(g)$$

In an experiment done at 852 K, the equilibrium concentrations are found to be $[SO_2] = 3.61 \times 10^{-3}$ mol/L, $[O_2] = 6.11 \times 10^{-4}$ mol/L, and $[SO_3] = 1.01 \times 10^{-2}$ mol/L. Substituting these data into the equilibrium constant expression, we can determine the value of K.

$$K = \frac{[SO_3]^2}{[SO_2]^2[O_2]} = \frac{(1.01 \times 10^{-2})^2}{(3.61 \times 10^{-3})^2(6.11 \times 10^{-4})} = 1.28 \times 10^4 \text{ at 852 K}$$

(Notice that K has a large value; at equilibrium, the oxidation of sulfur dioxide is product-favored at 852 K.)

More commonly, an experiment will provide information on the initial quantities of reactants and the concentration at equilibrium of only one of the reactants or of one of the products. The equilibrium concentrations of the rest of the reactants and products must then be inferred from the balanced chemical equation. As an example, consider again the oxidation of sulfur dioxide to sulfur trioxide. Suppose that 1.00 mol of SO_2 and 1.00 mol of O_2 are placed in a 1.00-L flask, this time at 1000 K. When equilibrium has been achieved, 0.925 mol of SO_3 has been formed. Let us use this information to calculate the equilibrium constant for the reaction. After writing the equilibrium constant expression in terms of concentrations, we set up an ICE table (page 727) showing the initial concentrations, the changes in those concentrations on proceeding to equilibrium, and the concentrations at equilibrium.

Equation	2 SO_2(g)	+	O_2(g)	$\rightleftharpoons$	2 SO_3(g)
Initial (M)	1.00		1.00		0
Change (M)	−0.925		−0.925/2		+0.925
Equilibrium (M)	1.00 − 0.925 = 0.075		1.00 − 0.925/2 = 0.54		0.925

The quantities in the ICE table result from the following analysis:

- The amount of SO_2 consumed on proceeding to equilibrium is equal to the amount of SO_3 produced (= 0.925 mol because the stoichiometric factor is [2 mol SO_2 consumed/2 mol SO_3 produced]). Because SO_2 is consumed, the change in SO_2 concentration is −0.925 M.
- The amount of O_2 consumed is half of the amount of SO_3 produced (= 0.463 mol because the stoichiometric factor is [1 mol O_2 consumed/2 mol SO_3 produced]). The amount of O_2 remaining is 0.54 M.
- The equilibrium concentration of a reactant is always the initial concentration minus the quantity consumed on proceeding to equilibrium. The equilibrium concentration of a product is always the initial concentration plus the quantity produced on proceeding to equilibrium.

With the equilibrium concentrations now known, it is possible to calculate K.

$$K = \frac{[SO_3]^2}{[SO_2]^2[O_2]} = \frac{(0.925)^2}{(0.075)^2(0.54)} = 2.8 \times 10^2 \text{ at } 1000 \text{ K}$$

Chemistry ⦾ Now™

Sign in at **www.cengage.com/login** and go to Chapter 16 Contents to see:
- Screen 16.8 for a simulation and a tutorial on **determining an equilibrium constant**
- Screen 16.9 for a simulation and a tutorial on **systems at equilibrium**

■ **EXAMPLE 16.3** Calculating an Equilibrium Constant

Problem An aqueous solution of ethanol and acetic acid, each with an initial concentration of 0.810 M, is heated to 100 °C. At equilibrium, the acetic acid concentration is 0.748 M. Calculate K for the reaction

C_2H_5OH(aq) + CH_3CO_2H(aq) $\rightleftharpoons$ $CH_3CO_2C_2H_5$(aq) + H_2O(ℓ)

ethanol   acetic acid   ethyl acetate

Strategy Always focus on defining equilibrium concentrations. The amount of acetic acid remaining is known, so the amount consumed is given by [initial concentration of reactant − concentration of reactant remaining]. Because the balanced chemical equation tells us 1 mol of ethanol reacts per mol of acetic acid, the concentration of ethanol is also known at equilibrium. Finally, the concentration of the product formed upon reaching equilibrium is calculated from the amount of reactant consumed.

■ Ester Preparation and Equilibrium

Esters are a common and important class of organic molecules (◄ page 729). The equilibrium constant for the reaction of an acid and an alcohol is not large, so chemists know that to achieve maximum yield of the ester they remove the water formed in the reaction. As explained in Section 16.6, this means that a larger concentration of ester can exist at equilibrium.

Solution The amount of acetic acid consumed is 0.810 M − 0.748 M = 0.062 M. This is the same as the amount of ethanol consumed and the same as the amount of ethyl acetate produced. The ICE table for this reaction is therefore

Equation	C_2H_5OH	+	CH_3CO_2H	⇌	$CH_3CO_2C_2H_5$	+	H_2O
Initial (M)	0.810		0.810		0		
Change (M)	−0.062		−0.062		+0.062		
Equilibrium (M)	0.748		0.748		0.062		

The concentration of each substance at equilibrium is now known, and K can be calculated.

$$K = \frac{[CH_3CO_2C_2H_5]}{[C_2H_5OH][CH_3CO_2H]} = \frac{0.062}{(0.748)(0.748)} = \boxed{0.11}$$

Comment Notice that water does not appear in the equilibrium expression.

■ **EXAMPLE 16.4 Calculating an Equilibrium Constant (K_p) Using Partial Pressures**

Problem Suppose a tank initially contains H_2S at a pressure of 10.00 atm and a temperature of 800 K. When the reaction

$$2\ H_2S(g) \rightleftharpoons 2\ H_2(g) + S_2(g)$$

has come to equilibrium, the partial pressure of S_2 vapor is 0.020 atm. Calculate K_p.

Strategy Recall from page 729 that the equilibrium constant expression can be written in terms of gas partial pressures or concentrations; here, the data are given in terms of partial pressures. In determining the value of an equilibrium constant, we again focus on defining equilibrium amounts. The partial pressure of $S_2(g)$ at equilibrium is known, so the amount produced in proceeding to equilibrium is given by [equilibrium partial pressure − initial partial pressure]. The balanced chemical equation tells us that 2 mol of $H_2(g)$ are produced per mole of $S_2(g)$ produced, so we can determine the partial pressure of $H_2(g)$ produced and then the partial pressure of $H_2(g)$ at equilibrium. Finally, the balanced equation also tells us that the partial pressure of $H_2S(g)$ consumed is twice the partial pressure of $S_2(g)$ produced. The equilibrium pressure of the $H_2S(g)$ is then given by $P_{initial} − P_{gas\ consumed}$.

Solution The equilibrium constant expression that we want to evaluate is

$$K_p = \frac{(P_{H_2})^2 P_{S_2}}{(P_{H_2S})^2}$$

We know that $P(H_2S)_{initial} = 10.00$ atm and that $P(S_2)_{equilibrium} = 0.020$ atm, so we can set up an ICE table that expresses the equilibrium partial pressures of each gas.

Equation	$2\ H_2S(g)$	⇌	$2\ H_2(g)$	+	$S_2(g)$
Initial (atm)	10.00		0		0
Change (atm)	−2(0.020)		+2(0.020)		+0.020
Equilibrium (atm)	9.96		0.040		0.020

Now that the partial pressures of all of the reactants and products are known, K_p can be calculated.

$$K_p = \frac{(P_{H_2})^2 P_{S_2}}{(P_{H_2S})^2} = \frac{(0.040)^2(0.020)}{(9.96)^2} = \boxed{3.2} \times \boxed{10^{-7}}$$

Comment The value of K_p will be the same as the value of K_c only when the number of moles of gaseous reactants is the same as the number of moles of gaseous products. This is not true here, so $K_p \neq K_c$. See *A Closer Look* (page 730).

$C_6H_{10}I_2$

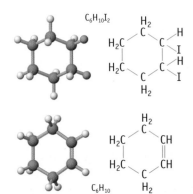

C_6H_{10}

EXERCISE 16.5 Calculating an Equilibrium Constant, K

A solution is prepared by dissolving 0.050 mol of diiodocyclohexane, $C_6H_{10}I_2$, in the solvent CCl_4. The total solution volume is 1.00 L. When the reaction

$$C_6H_{10}I_2 \rightleftharpoons C_6H_{10} + I_2$$

has come to equilibrium at 35 °C, the concentration of I_2 is 0.035 mol/L.

(a) What are the concentrations of $C_6H_{10}I_2$ and C_6H_{10} at equilibrium?

(b) Calculate K_c, the equilibrium constant.

16.4 Using Equilibrium Constants in Calculations

In many cases, the value of K and the initial amounts of reactants are known, and you want to know the amounts present at equilibrium. As we look at several examples of this situation, we will again use ICE tables that summarize initial conditions, final conditions, and changes on proceeding to equilibrium.

Chemistry ꞏ Now™

Sign in at **www.cengage.com/login** and go to Chapter 16 Contents to see Screen 16.10 for a tutorial on **determining equilibrium concentrations.**

■ **EXAMPLE 16.5 Calculating Equilibrium Concentrations**

Problem The equilibrium constant K_c (= 55.64) for

$$H_2(g) + I_2(g) \rightleftharpoons 2\ HI(g)$$

has been determined at 425 °C. If 1.00 mol each of H_2 and I_2 are placed in a 0.500-L flask at 425 °C, what are the concentrations of H_2, I_2, and HI when equilibrium has been achieved?

Strategy Because we know the value of K_c and the initial concentrations, we can set up the equilibrium constant expression and an ICE table. We will use the equilibrium constant expression to solve for the unknown values in the table.

Solution The first step is to write the equilibrium constant expression.

$$K = \frac{[HI]^2}{[H_2][I_2]} = 55.64$$

Next, set up an ICE table to express the concentrations of H_2, I_2, and HI before reaction and upon reaching equilibrium. Here, however, we do not know the numerical values of the changes in the H_2 and I_2 concentrations on proceeding to equilibrium. Because the change in $[H_2]$ is the same as the change in $[I_2]$ and because their coefficients in the balanced equation are each 1, we express these changes as the unknown quantity x. It follows that $2x$ is the quantity of HI produced (because the stoichiometric factor is [2 mol HI produced/1 mol H_2 consumed]).

Equation	$H_2(g)$	+	$I_2(g)$	$\rightleftharpoons$	$2\ HI(g)$
Initial (M)	1.00 mol/0.500 L = 2.00 M		1.00 mol/0.500 L = 2.00 M		0 0
Change (M)	$-x$		$-x$		$+2x$
Equilibrium (M)	$2.00 - x$		$2.00 - x$		$2x$

Now the expressions for the equilibrium concentrations can be substituted into the equilibrium constant expression.

$$55.64 = \frac{(2x)^2}{(2.00 - x)(2.00 - x)} = \frac{(2x)^2}{(2.00 - x)^2}$$

In this case, the unknown quantity x can be found by taking the square root of both sides of the equation,

$$\sqrt{K} = 7.459 = \frac{2x}{2.00 - x}$$

$$7.459\ (2.00 - x) = 14.9 - 7.459x = 2x$$

$$14.9 = 9.459x$$

$$x = 1.58$$

With x known, we can solve for the equilibrium concentrations of the reactants and products.

$$[H_2] = [I_2] = 2.00 - x = 0.42\ M$$

$$[HI] = 2x = 3.16\ M$$

Comment It is always wise to verify the answer by substituting the values back into the equilibrium expression to see if your calculated K agrees with the one given in the problem. In this case, $(3.16)^2/(0.42)^2 = 57$. The slight discrepancy with the given value, $K = 55.64$, occurs because we know $[H_2]$ and $[I_2]$ to only two significant figures.

EXERCISE 16.6 Calculating Equilibrium Concentrations

At some temperature, $K_c = 33$ for the reaction

$$H_2(g) + I_2(g) \rightleftharpoons 2\ HI(g)$$

Assume the initial concentrations of both H_2 and I_2 are 6.00×10^{-3} mol/L. Find the concentration of each reactant and product at equilibrium.

Calculations Where the Solution Involves a Quadratic Expression

Suppose you are studying the decomposition of PCl_5 to form PCl_3 and Cl_2. You know that $K = 1.20$ at a given temperature.

$$PCl_5(g) \rightleftharpoons PCl_3(g) + Cl_2(g)$$

If the initial concentration of PCl_5 is 1.60 M, what will be the concentrations of reactant and products when the system reaches equilibrium? Following the procedures outlined in Example 16.5, you would set up an ICE table to define the equilibrium concentrations of reactants and products.

Reaction	$PCl_5(g)$ $\rightleftharpoons$	$PCl_3(g)$ +	$Cl_2(g)$
Initial (M)	1.60	0	0
Change (M)	$-x$	$+x$	$+x$
Equilibrium (M)	$1.60 - x$	x	x

Substituting into the equilibrium constant expression, we have

$$K = 1.20 = \frac{[PCl_3][Cl_2]}{[PCl_5]} = \frac{(x)(x)}{1.60 - x}$$

Expanding the algebraic expression results in a quadratic equation,

$$x^2 + 1.20x - 1.92 = 0$$

Using the quadratic formula (Appendix A; $a = 1$, $b = 1.20$, and $c = -1.92$), we find two roots to the equation: $x = 0.91$ and -2.11. Because a negative value of x (which represents a negative concentration) is not chemically meaningful, the answer is $x = 0.91$. Therefore, we have, at equilibrium,

$$[PCl_5] = 1.60 - 0.91 = 0.69\ M$$

$$[PCl_3] = [Cl_2] = 0.91\ M$$

Although a solution to a quadratic equation can always be obtained using the quadratic formula, in many instances an acceptable answer can be obtained by using a realistic approximation to simplify the equation. To illustrate this, let us consider another equilibrium, the dissociation of I_2 molecules to form I atoms, for which $K = 5.6 \times 10^{-12}$ at 500 K.

$$I_2(g) \rightleftharpoons 2\ I(g)$$

$$K = \frac{[I]^2}{[I_2]} = 5.6 \times 10^{-12}$$

Assuming the initial I_2 concentration is 0.45 M, and setting up the ICE table in the usual manner, we have

Reaction	$I_2(g)$	$\rightleftharpoons$	2 I(g)
Initial (M)	0.45		0
Change (M)	$-x$		$+2x$
Equilibrium (M)	$0.45 - x$		$2x$

For the equilibrium constant expression, we again arrive at a quadratic equation.

$$K = 5.6 \times 10^{-12} = \frac{(2x)^2}{(0.45 - x)}$$

Although we could solve this equation using the quadratic formula, there is a simpler way to reach an answer. Notice that the value of K is very small, indicating that the amount of I_2 that will be dissociated ($= x$) is very small. In fact, K is so small that subtracting x from the original reactant concentration (0.45 mol/L) in the denominator of the equilibrium constant expression will leave the denominator essentially unchanged. That is, $(0.45 - x)$ is essentially equal to 0.45. Thus, we drop x in the denominator and have a simpler equation to solve.

$$K = 5.6 \times 10^{-12} = \frac{(2x)^2}{(0.45)}$$

The solution to this equation gives $x = 7.9 \times 10^{-7}$. From this value, we can determine that $[I_2] = 0.45 - x \approx 0.45$ mol/L and $[I] = 2x = 1.6 \times 10^{-6}$ mol/L. Notice that the answer to the I_2 dissociation problem confirms the assumption the dissociation of I_2 is so small that $[I_2]$ at equilibrium is essentially equal to the initial concentration.

When is it possible to simplify a quadratic equation? The decision depends on both the value of the initial concentration of the reactant and the value of x, which is in turn related to the value of K. Consider the general reaction

$$A \rightleftharpoons B + C$$

where $K = [B][C]/[A]$. Assume we know K and the initial concentration of A ($= [A]_0$) and wish to find the equilibrium concentrations of B and C ($= x$). The equilibrium constant expression now is

$$K = \frac{[B][C]}{[A]} = \frac{(x)(x)}{[A]_0 - x}$$

When K is very small, the value of x will be much less than $[A]_0$, so $[A]_0 - x \approx [A]_0$. Therefore, we can write the following expression.

$$K = \frac{[B][C]}{[A]} \approx \frac{(x)(x)}{[A]_0} \qquad (16.3)$$

If $100 \times K < [A]_0$, the approximate expression, Equation 16.3, will give acceptable values of equilibrium concentrations (to two significant figures). For more about this useful guideline, see Problem Solving Tip 16.1.

■ **Solving Quadratic Equations**
Quadratic equations are usually solved using the quadratic formula (Appendix A). An alternative is the *method of successive approximations*, also outlined in Appendix A. Most equilibrium expressions can be solved quickly by this method, and you are urged to try it. This will remove the uncertainty of whether K expressions need to be solved exactly. (There are, however, rare cases in which this does not work.)

When Do You Need to Use the Quadratic Formula?

In most equilibrium calculations, the quantity x may be neglected in the denominator of the equation $K = x^2/([A]_0 - x)$ if x is less than 10% of the quantity of reactant initially present. The guideline presented in the text for making the approximation that $[A]_0 - x \approx [A]_0$ when $100 \times K < [A]_0$ reflects this fact.

In general, when K is about 1 or greater, the approximation cannot be made. If K is much less than 1 and $100 \times K < [A]_0$ (you will see many such cases in Chapter 17), the approximate expression ($K = x^2/[A]_0$) gives an acceptable answer. If you are not certain, then first make the assumption that the

unknown (x) is small, and solve the approximate expression (Equation 16.3). Next, compare the "approximate" value of x with $[A]_0$. If x has a value equal to or less than 10% of $[A]_0$, then there is no need to solve the full equation using the quadratic formula.

EXAMPLE 16.6 Calculating Equilibrium Concentrations Using an Equilibrium Constant

Problem The reaction

$$N_2(g) + O_2(g) \rightleftharpoons 2\,NO(g)$$

contributes to air pollution whenever a fuel is burned in air at a high temperature, as in a gasoline engine. At 1500 K, $K = 1.0 \times 10^{-5}$. Suppose a sample of air has $[N_2] = 0.80$ mol/L and $[O_2] = 0.20$ mol/L before any reaction occurs. Calculate the equilibrium concentrations of reactants and products after the mixture has been heated to 1500 K.

Strategy Set up an ICE table of equilibrium concentrations, and then substitute these concentrations into the equilibrium constant expression. The result will be a quadratic equation. This expression can be solved using the methods outlined in Appendix A or by using the guideline in the text to derive an acceptable, approximate answer.

Solution We first set up an ICE table of equilibrium concentrations.

Equation	$N_2(g)$	+	$O_2(g)$	$\rightleftharpoons$	$2\,NO(g)$
Initial (M)	0.80		0.20		0
Change (M)	$-x$		$-x$		$+2x$
Equilibrium (M)	$0.80 - x$		$0.20 - x$		$2x$

Next, the equilibrium concentrations are substituted into the equilibrium constant expression.

$$K = 1.0 \times 10^{-5} = \frac{[NO]^2}{[N_2][O_2]} = \frac{[2x]^2}{(0.80 - x)(0.20 - x)}$$

We refer to the guideline (Equation 16.3) to decide whether an approximate solution is possible. Here, $100 \times K\,(= 1.0 \times 10^{-3})$ is smaller than either of the initial reactant concentrations (0.80 and 0.20). This means we can use the approximate expression

$$K = 1.0 \times 10^{-5} = \frac{[NO]^2}{[N_2][O_2]} = \frac{(2x)^2}{(0.80)(0.20)}$$

Solving this expression, we find

$$1.6 \times 10^{-6} = 4x^2$$

$$x = 6.3 \times 10^{-4}$$

Therefore, the reactant and product concentrations at equilibrium are

$$[N_2] = 0.80 - 6.3 \times 10^{-4} \approx 0.80\ M$$

$$[O_2] = 0.20 - 6.3 \times 10^{-4} \approx 0.20\ M$$

$$[NO] = 2x = 1.26 \times 10^{-3}\ M$$

Comment The value of x obtained using the approximation is the same as that obtained from the quadratic formula. If the full equilibrium constant expression is expanded, we have

$$(1.0 \times 10^{-5})(0.80 - x)(0.20 - x) = 4x^2$$

$$(1.0 \times 10^{-5})(0.16 - 1.00x + x^2) = 4x^2$$

$$\underset{ax^2}{(4 - 1.0 \times 10^{-5})x^2} + \underset{bx}{(1.0 \times 10^{-5})x} - \underset{c}{0.16 \times 10^{-5}} = 0$$

The two roots to this equation are:

$$x = 6.3 \times 10^{-4} \text{ or } x = -6.3 \times 10^{-4}$$

The only meaningful root is identical to the approximate answer obtained above. The approximation is indeed valid in this case.

EXERCISE 16.7 Calculating an Equilibrium Concentration Using an Equilibrium Constant

Graphite and carbon dioxide are kept at constant volume at 1000 K until the reaction

$$C(graphite) + CO_2 (g) \rightleftharpoons 2\ CO(g)$$

has come to equilibrium. At this temperature, $K = 0.021$. The initial concentration of CO_2 is 0.012 mol/L. Calculate the equilibrium concentration of CO.

16.5 More About Balanced Equations and Equilibrium Constants

Chemical equations can be balanced using different sets of stoichiometric coefficients. For example, the equation for the oxidation of carbon to give carbon monoxide can be written

$$C(s) + \tfrac{1}{2}\ O_2(g) \rightleftharpoons CO(g)$$

In this case, the equilibrium constant expression would be

$$K_1 = \frac{[CO]}{[O_2]^{1/2}} = 4.6 \times 10^{23} \text{ at } 25\ ^{\circ}C$$

You can write the chemical equation equally well, however, as

$$2\ C(s) + O_2(g) \rightleftharpoons 2\ CO(g)$$

and the equilibrium constant expression would now be

$$K_2 = \frac{[CO]^2}{[O_2]} = 2.1 \times 10^{47} \text{ at } 25\ ^{\circ}C$$

When you compare the two equilibrium constant expressions you find that $K_2 = (K_1)^2$; that is,

$$K_2 = \frac{[CO]^2}{[O_2]} = \left\{ \frac{[CO]}{[O_2]^{1/2}} \right\}^2 = K_1^{\ 2}$$

When the stoichiometric coefficients of a balanced equation are multiplied by some factor, the equilibrium constant for the new equation (K_{new}) is the old equilibrium constant (K_{old}) raised to the power of the multiplication factor.

In the case of the oxidation of carbon, the second equation was obtained by multiplying the first equation by two. Therefore, K_2 is the *square* of K_1 ($K_2 = K_1^{\ 2}$).

Let us consider what happens if a chemical equation is reversed. Here, we will compare the value of K for formic acid transferring an H^+ ion to water

$$HCO_2H(aq) + H_2O(\ell) \rightleftharpoons HCO_2^-(aq) + H_3O^+(aq)$$

$$K_1 = \frac{[HCO_2^-][H_3O^+]}{[HCO_2H]} = 1.8 \times 10^{-4} \text{ at } 25\ ^\circ C$$

with the opposite reaction, the gain of an H^+ ion by the formate ion, HCO_2^-.

$$HCO_2^-(aq) + H_3O^+(aq) \rightleftharpoons HCO_2H(aq) + H_2O(\ell)$$

$$K_2 = \frac{[HCO_2H]}{[HCO_2^-][H_3O^+]} = 5.6 \times 10^3 \text{ at } 25\ ^\circ C$$

Here, $K_2 = 1/K_1$.

The equilibrium constants for a reaction and its reverse are the reciprocals of one another.

It is often useful to add two equations to obtain the equation for a net process. As an example, consider the reactions that take place when silver chloride dissolves in water (to a *very* small extent) and ammonia is added to the solution. The ammonia reacts with the silver ion to form a water-soluble compound, $Ag(NH_3)_2Cl$ (Figure 16.6). Adding the equation for dissolving solid AgCl to the equation for the reaction of Ag^+ ion with ammonia gives the equation for net reaction, dissolving solid AgCl in aqueous ammonia. (All equilibrium constants are given at 25 °C.)

$$AgCl(s) \rightleftharpoons Ag^+(aq) + Cl^-(aq) \qquad\qquad K_1 = [Ag^+][Cl^-] = 1.8 \times 10^{-10}$$

$$Ag^+(aq) + 2\,NH_3(aq) \rightleftharpoons [Ag(NH_3)_2]^+(aq) \qquad\qquad K_2 = \frac{[Ag(NH_3)_2^+]}{[Ag^+][NH_3]^2} = 1.6 \times 10^7$$

Net reaction:

$$AgCl(s) + 2\,NH_3(aq) \rightleftharpoons [Ag(NH_3)_2]^+(aq) + Cl^-(aq)$$

To obtain the equilibrium constant for the net reaction, K_{net}, we *multiply* the equilibrium constants for the two reactions, K_1 by K_2.

$$K_{net} = K_1 \times K_2 = [Ag^+][Cl^-] \times \frac{[Ag(NH_3)_2^+]}{[Ag^+][NH_3]^2} = \frac{[Ag(NH_3)_2^+][Cl^-]}{[NH_3]^2}$$

$$K_{net} = K_1 \times K_2 = 2.9 \times 10^{-3}$$

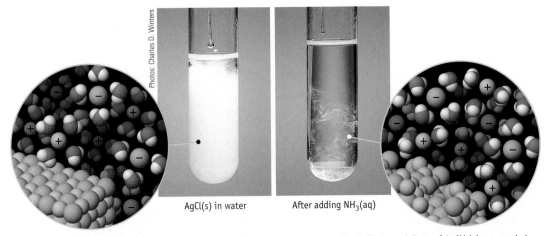

AgCl(s) in water   After adding NH₃(aq)

FIGURE 16.6 Dissolving silver chloride in aqueous ammonia. (left) A precipitate of AgCl(s) is suspended in water. (right) When aqueous ammonia is added, the ammonia reacts with the trace of silver ion in solution, the equilibrium shifts, and the silver chloride dissolves.

When two or more chemical equations are added to produce a net equation, the equilibrium constant for the net equation is the product of the equilibrium constants for the added equations.

■ **Complex Ions** This compound, $[Ag(NH_3)_2]Cl$, is made up of a cation (called a complex ion), $[Ag(NH_3)_2]^+$, and an anion, Cl^-. Square brackets are often used to indicate the cation is a single entity. We will discuss complex ions further in Chapters 18 and 22.

EXAMPLE 16.7 Balanced Equations and Equilibrium Constants

Problem A mixture of nitrogen, hydrogen, and ammonia is brought to equilibrium. When the equation is written using whole-number coefficients, as follows, the value of K is 3.5×10^8 at 25 °C.

Equation 1: $N_2(g) + 3 H_2(g) \rightleftharpoons 2 NH_3(g)$ $K_1 = 3.5 \times 10^8$

However, the equation can also be written as given in *Equation 2*. What is the value of K_2?

Equation 2: $\frac{1}{2} N_2(g) + \frac{3}{2} H_2(g) \rightleftharpoons NH_3(g)$ $K_2 = ?$

The decomposition of ammonia to the elements *(Equation 3)* is the reverse of its formation *(Equation 1)*. What is the value of K_3?

Equation 3: $2 NH_3(g) \rightleftharpoons N_2(g) + 3 H_2(g)$ $K_3 = ?$

Strategy Review what happens to the value of K when the stoichiometric coefficients are changed or the reaction is reversed. (See Problem Solving Tip 16.2.)

Solution To see the relation between K_1 and K_2, first write the equilibrium constant expressions for these two balanced equations.

$$K_1 = \frac{[NH_3]^2}{[N_2][H_2]^3} \qquad K_2 = \frac{[NH_3]}{[N_2]^{1/2}[H_2]^{3/2}}$$

Writing these expressions makes it clear that K_2 is the square root of K_1.

$$K_2 = (K_1)^{1/2} = \sqrt{K_1} = \sqrt{3.5 \times 10^8} = \boxed{1.9 \times 10^4}$$

Equation 3 is the reverse of *Equation 1*, and its equilibrium constant expression is

$$K_3 = \frac{[N_2][H_2]^3}{[NH_3]^2}$$

In this case, K_3 is the reciprocal of K_1. That is, $K_3 = 1/K_1$.

$$K_3 = \frac{1}{K_1} = \frac{1}{3.5 \times 10^8} = \boxed{2.9 \times 10^{-9}}$$

Comment As a final comment, notice that the production of ammonia from the elements has a large equilibrium constant and is product-favored (see Section 16.2). As expected, the reverse reaction, the decomposition of ammonia to its elements, has a small equilibrium constant and is reactant-favored.

EXERCISE 16.8 Manipulating Equilibrium Constant Expressions

The conversion of oxygen to ozone has a very small equilibrium constant.

$3/2 O_2(g) \rightleftharpoons O_3(g)$ $K = 2.5 \times 10^{-29}$

(a) What is the value of K when the equation is written using whole-number coefficients?

$3 O_2(g) \rightleftharpoons 2 O_3(g)$

(b) What is the value of K for the conversion of ozone to oxygen?

$2 O_3(g) \rightleftharpoons 3 O_2(g)$

EXERCISE 16.9 Manipulating Equilibrium Constant Expressions

The following equilibrium constants are given at 500 K:

$H_2(g) + Br_2(g) \rightleftharpoons 2 HBr(g)$ $K_p = 7.9 \times 10^{11}$

$H_2(g) \rightleftharpoons 2 H(g)$ $K_p = 4.8 \times 10^{-41}$

$Br_2(g) \rightleftharpoons 2 Br$ $K_p = 2.2 \times 10^{-15}$

Calculate K_p for the reaction of H and Br atoms to give HBr.

$H(g) + Br(g) \rightleftharpoons HBr(g)$ $K_p = ?$

16.6 Disturbing a Chemical Equilibrium

The equilibrium between reactants and products may be disturbed in three ways: (1) by changing the temperature, (2) by changing the concentration of a reactant or product, or (3) by changing the volume (for systems involving gases) (Table 16.2). *A change in any of the factors that determine the equilibrium conditions of a system will cause the system to change in such a manner as to reduce or counteract the effect of the change.* This statement is often referred to as *Le Chatelier's principle* (◄ page 627). It is a shorthand way of saying how a reaction will adjust the quantities of reactants and products so that equilibrium is restored, that is, so that the reaction quotient is once again equal to the equilibrium constant.

Chemistry₊ₒ₊Now™

Sign in at **www.cengage.com/login** and go to Chapter 16 Contents to see Screen 16.11 to view an animation of **Le Chatelier's principle**.

TABLE 16.2   Effects of Disturbances on Equilibrium Composition

Disturbance	Change as Mixture Returns to Equilibrium	Effect on Equilibrium	Effect on K
Reactions Involving Solids, Liquids, or Gases			
Rise in temperature	Heat energy is consumed by system	Shift in endothermic direction	Change
Drop in temperature	Heat energy is generated by system	Shift in exothermic direction	Change
Addition of reactant*	Some of added reactant is consumed	Product concentration increases	No change
Addition of product*	Some of added product is consumed	Reactant concentration increases	No change
Reactions Involving Gases			
Decrease in volume, increase in pressure	Pressure decreases	Composition changes to reduce total number of gas molecules	No change
Increase in volume, decrease in pressure	Pressure increases	Composition changes to increase total number of gas molecules	No change

* Does not apply when an insoluble solid reactant or product is added. Recall that their "concentrations" do not appear in the reaction quotient.

Effect of the Addition or Removal of a Reactant or Product

If the concentration of a reactant or product is changed from its equilibrium value *at a given temperature*, equilibrium will be reestablished eventually. The new equilibrium concentrations of reactants and products will be different, but the value of the equilibrium constant expression will still equal K (Table 16.1). To illustrate this, let us return to the butane/isobutane equilibrium (with $K = 2.5$).

$$CH_3CH_2CH_2CH_3 \rightleftharpoons \underset{\text{isobutane}}{CH_3\overset{\displaystyle \overset{CH_3}{|}}{C}HCH_3} \qquad K = 2.5$$

butane   isobutane

Suppose the equilibrium mixture consists of two molecules of butane and five molecules of isobutane (Figure 16.7). The reaction quotient, Q, is 5/2 (or 2.5/1), the value of the equilibrium constant for the reaction. Now we add seven more molecules of isobutane to the mixture to give a ratio of 12 isobutane molecules to two butane molecules. The reaction quotient is now 6/1. Q is greater than K, so the system will change to reestablish equilibrium. To do so, some molecules of isobutane must be changed into butane molecules, a process that continues until the ratio [isobutane]/[butane] is once again 2.5/1. In this particular case, if two of the 12 isobutane molecules change to butane, the ratio of isobutane to butane is again equal to K (= 10/4 = 2.5/1), and equilibrium is reestablished.

Chemistry ⚛ Now™

Sign in at **www.cengage.com/login** and go to Chapter 16 Contents to see Screen 16.13 for a simulation and a tutorial on **the effect of concentration changes on an equilibrium.**

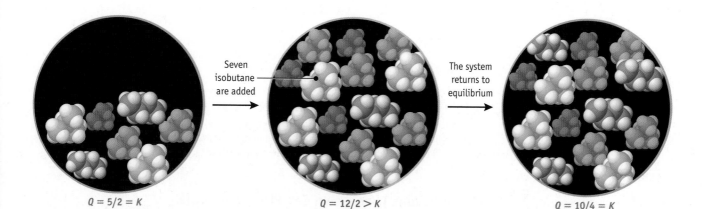

$Q = 5/2 = K$

$Q = 12/2 > K$

$Q = 10/4 = K$

An equilibrium mixture of five isobutane molecules and two butane molecules.

Seven isobutane molecules are added, so the system is no longer at equilibrium.

A net of two isobutane molecules has changed to butane molecules, to once again give an equilibrium mixture where the ratio of isobutane to butane is 5 to 2 (or 2.5/1).

Active Figure 16.7   Addition of more reactant or product to an equilibrium system.

Chemistry ⚛ Now™ Sign in at www.cengage.com/login and go to the Chapter Contents menu to explore an interactive version of this figure accompanied by an exercise.

■ EXAMPLE 16.8 Effect of Concentration Changes on Equilibrium

Problem Assume equilibrium has been established in a 1.00-L flask with [butane] = 0.500 mol/L and [isobutane] = 1.25 mol/L.

$$\text{Butane} \rightleftharpoons \text{Isobutane} \quad K = 2.50$$

Then 1.50 mol of butane is added. What are the concentrations of butane and isobutane when equilibrium is reestablished?

Strategy After adding excess butane, $Q < K$. To reestablish equilibrium, the concentration of butane must decrease, and that of isobutane must increase. Use an ICE table to track the changes. The decrease in butane concentration and the increase in isobutane concentration are both designated as x.

Solution First organize the information in a modified ICE table.

Equation	Butane	$\rightleftharpoons$	Isobutane
Initial (M)	0.500		1.25
Concentration immediately on adding butane (M)	0.500 + 1.50		1.25
Change in concentration to reestablish equilibrium (M)	$-x$		$+x$
Equilibrium (M)	0.500 + 1.50 − x		1.25 + x

The entries in this table were arrived at as follows:

(a) The concentration of butane when equilibrium is reestablished will be the original equilibrium concentration plus what was added (1.50 mol/L) minus the concentration of butane that is converted to isobutane to reestablish equilibrium. The quantity of butane converted to isobutane is unknown and so is designated as x.

(b) The concentration of isobutane when equilibrium is reestablished is the concentration that was already present (1.25 mol/L) plus the concentration formed (x mol/L) on reestablishing equilibrium.

Having defined [butane] and [isobutane] when equilibrium is reestablished and remembering that K is a constant (=2.50), we can write

$$K = 2.50 = \frac{[\text{isobutane}]}{[\text{butane}]}$$

We now calculate the new equilibrium composition:

$$2.50 = \frac{1.25 + x}{0.500 + 1.50 - x} = \frac{1.25 + x}{2.00 - x}$$

$$2.50\,(2.00 - x) = 1.25 + x$$

$$x = 1.07 \text{ mol/L}$$

$$[\text{butane}] = 0.500 + 1.50 - x = 0.93 \text{ M and } [\text{isobutane}] = 1.25 + x = 2.32 \text{ M}$$

Comment Check your answer to verify that [isobutane]/[butane] = 2.32/0.93 = 2.5.

EXERCISE 16.10 Effect of Concentration Changes on Equilibrium

Equilibrium exists between butane and isobutane when [butane] = 0.20 M and [isobutane] = 0.50 M. An additional 2.00 mol/L of isobutane is added to the mixture. What are the concentrations of butane and isobutane after equilibrium has again been attained?

Effect of Volume Changes on Gas-Phase Equilibria

For a reaction that involves gases, what happens to equilibrium concentrations or pressures if the size of the container is changed? (Such a change occurs, for example, when fuel and air are compressed in an automobile engine.) To answer this question, recall that concentrations are in moles per liter. If the volume of a gas changes, its concentration therefore must also change, and the equilibrium composition can change. As an example, consider the following equilibrium:

$$2\ NO_2(g) \rightleftharpoons N_2O_4(g)$$

brown gas   colorless gas

$$K = \frac{[N_2O_4]}{[NO_2]^2} = 170 \text{ at } 298\ K$$

What happens to this equilibrium if the volume of the flask holding the gases is suddenly halved? The immediate result is that the concentrations of both gases will double. For example, assume equilibrium is established when $[N_2O_4]$ is 0.0280 mol/L and $[NO_2]$ is 0.0128 mol/L. When the volume is halved, $[N_2O_4]$ becomes 0.0560 mol/L, and $[NO_2]$ is 0.0256 mol/L. The reaction quotient, Q, under these circumstances is $(0.0560)/(0.0256)^2 = 85.5$, a value less than K. Because Q is less than K, the quantity of product must increase at the expense of the reactants to return to equilibrium, and the new equilibrium composition will have a higher concentration of N_2O_4 than immediately after the volume change.

$$2\ NO_2(g) \rightleftharpoons N_2O_4(g)$$

decrease volume of container
———————————————→
new equilibrium favors product

The concentration of NO_2 decreases twice as much as the concentration of N_2O_4 increases because one molecule of N_2O_4 is formed by consuming two molecules of NO_2. This occurs until the reaction quotient, $Q = [N_2O_4]/[NO_2]^2$, is once again equal to K. The net effect of the volume decrease is to decrease the number of molecules in the gas phase.

The conclusions for the NO_2/N_2O_4 equilibrium can be generalized:

- For reactions involving gases, the stress of a volume decrease (a pressure increase) will be counterbalanced by a change in the equilibrium composition to one having a smaller number of gas molecules.
- For a volume increase (a pressure decrease), the equilibrium composition will favor the side of the reaction with the larger number of gas molecules.
- For a reaction in which there is no change in the number of gas molecules, such as in the reaction of H_2 and I_2 to produce HI $[H_2(g) + I_2(g) \rightleftharpoons 2\ HI(g)]$, a volume change will have no effect.

Chemistry.Now™

Sign in at **www.cengage.com/login** and go to Chapter 16 Contents to see Screen 16.14 for a simulation of **the effect of a volume change for a reaction involving gases.**

EXERCISE 16.11 Effect of Concentration and Volume Changes on Equilibria

The formation of ammonia from its elements is an important industrial process.

$$3\ H_2(g) + N_2(g) \rightleftharpoons 2\ NH_3(g)$$

(a) How does the equilibrium composition change when extra H_2 is added? When extra NH_3 is added?

(b) What is the effect on the equilibrium when the volume of the system is increased?

Effect of Temperature Changes on Equilibrium Composition

The value of the equilibrium constant for a given reaction varies with temperature. Changing the temperature of a system at equilibrium is therefore different in some ways from the other means we have studied of disturbing a chemical equilibrium because the equilibrium constant itself will be different at the new temperature from what it was at the previous temperature. Predicting the exact changes in equilibrium compositions with temperature is beyond the scope of this text, but you can make a qualitative prediction about the effect if you know whether the reaction is exothermic or endothermic. As an example, consider the endothermic reaction of N_2 with O_2 to give NO.

■ ***K* for the N_2/O_2 Reaction** We are surrounded by N_2 and O_2, but you know that they do not react appreciably at room temperature. However, if a mixture of N_2 and O_2 is heated above 700 °C, as in an automobile engine, the equilibrium mixture will contain appreciable amounts of NO.

$$N_2(g) + O_2(g) \rightleftharpoons 2\ NO(g) \qquad \Delta_r H° = +180.6\ \text{kJ/mol-rxn}$$

$$K = \frac{[NO]^2}{[N_2][O_2]}$$

Le Chatelier's principle allows us to predict how the value of *K* will vary with temperature. The formation of NO from N_2 and O_2 is endothermic; that is, energy must be provided as heat for the reaction to occur. We might imagine that heat is a "reactant." If the system is at equilibrium and the temperature then increases, the system will adjust to alleviate this "stress." The way to counteract the energy input is to use up some of the energy added as heat by consuming N_2 and O_2 and producing more NO as the system returns to equilibrium. This raises the value of the numerator ($[NO]^2$) and lowers the value of the denominator ($[N_2][O_2]$) in the reaction quotient, *Q*, resulting in a higher value of *K*.

This prediction is borne out. The following table lists the equilibrium constant for this reaction at various temperatures. As predicted, the equilibrium constant and thus the proportion of NO in the equilibrium mixture increase with temperature.

Equilibrium Constant, *K*	Temperature (K)
4.5×10^{-31}	298
6.7×10^{-10}	900
1.7×10^{-3}	2300

As another example, consider the combination of molecules of the brown gas NO_2 to form colorless N_2O_4. An equilibrium between these compounds is readily achieved in a closed system (Figure 16.8).

$$2\ NO_2(g) \rightleftharpoons N_2O_4(g) \qquad \Delta_r H° = -57.1\ \text{kJ/mol-rxn}$$

$$K = \frac{[N_2O_4]}{[NO_2]^2}$$

Equilibrium Constant, *K*	Temperature (K)
1300	273
170	298

Here, the reaction is exothermic, so we might imagine heat as being a reaction "product." By lowering the temperature of the system, as in Figure 16.8, some energy is removed as heat. The removal of energy can be counteracted if the reaction produces energy as heat by the combination of NO_2 molecules to give more N_2O_4. Thus, the equilibrium concentration of NO_2 decreases; the concentration of N_2O_4 increases; and the value of *K* is larger at lower temperatures.

Nitrogen-containing substances are used around the world to stimulate the growth of field crops. Farmers from Portugal to Tibet have used animal waste for centuries as a "natural" fertilizer. In the 19th century, industrialized countries imported nitrogen-rich marine bird manure from Peru, Bolivia, and Chile, but the supply of this material was clearly limited. In 1898, William Ramsay (the discoverer of the noble gases) pointed out that the amount of "fixed nitrogen" in the world was being depleted and predicted that world food shortages would occur by the mid-20th century as a result. That Ramsay's prediction failed to materialize was due in part to the work of Fritz Haber (1868–1934). In about 1908, Haber developed a method making ammonia directly from the elements,

$$N_2(g) + 3\ H_2(g) \rightleftharpoons 2\ NH_3(g)$$

and, a few years later, Carl Bosch (1874–1940) perfected the industrial scale synthesis. Ammonia is now made for pennies per kilogram and is consistently ranked in the top five chemicals produced in the United States with 15–20 billion kilograms produced annually. Not only is ammonia used directly as a fertilizer, but it is also a starting material for making nitric acid and ammonium nitrate, among other things.

The manufacture of ammonia (Figure A) is a good example of the role that kinetics and chemical equilibria play in practical chemistry.

The $N_2 + H_2$ reaction is exothermic and product-favored ($K > 1$ at 25 °C).

At 25 °C, K (calc'd value) $= 3.5 \times 10^8$ and $\Delta_r H° = -92.2$ kJ/mol-rxn

Unfortunately, the reaction at 25 °C is slow, so it is carried out at a higher temperature to increase the reaction rate. The problem with this, however, is that the equilibrium constant declines with temperature, as predicted by Le Chatelier's Principle.

At 450 °C, K (experimental value) $= 0.16$ and $\Delta_r H° = -111.3$ kJ/mol-rxn

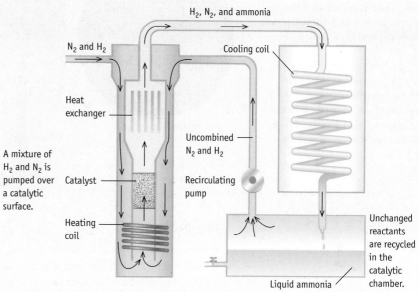

FIGURE A **The Haber process for ammonia synthesis.** A mixture of H_2 and N_2 is pumped over a catalytic surface. The NH_3 is collected as a liquid (at -33 °C), and unchanged reactants are recycled in the catalytic chamber.

Thus, the yield declines with increasing temperature.

There are two things that can be done. The first is to raise the pressure. This does not change the value of K, but an increase in pressure can be compensated by converting 4 mol of reactants to 2 mol of product.

In an industrial ammonia plant, it is necessary to balance reaction rate (improved at higher temperature) with product yield (K is smaller at higher temperatures). Therefore, catalysts are often used to accelerate reactions. An effective catalyst for the Haber process is Fe_3O_4 mixed with KOH, SiO_2, and Al_2O_3 (all inexpensive chemicals). Because the catalyst is not effective below 400 °C, the process is carried out at 450–500 °C and 250 atm pressure.

Questions:

1. *Anhydrous ammonia is used directly as a fertilizer, but much of it is also converted to other fertilizers, ammonium nitrate and urea.*

(a) *How is NH_3 converted to ammonium nitrate?*
(b) *Urea is formed in the reaction of ammonia and CO_2.*

$$2\ NH_3(g) + CO_2(g) \rightleftharpoons (NH_2)_2CO(s) + H_2O(g)$$

Which would favor urea production, high temperature or high pressure? ($\Delta_f H°$ for solid urea $= -333.1$ kJ/mol-rxn)

2. *One important aspect of the Haber process is the source of the hydrogen. This is made from natural gas in a process called steam reforming.*

$$CH_4(g) + H_2O(g) \rightarrow CO(g) + 3\ H_2(g)$$

$$CO(g) + H_2O(g) \rightarrow CO_2(g) + H_2(g)$$

(a) *Are the two reactions above endo- or exothermic?*
(b) *To manufacture 15 billion kilograms of NH_3, how much CH_4 is required, and what mass of CO_2 is produced as a by-product?*

Answers to these questions are in Appendix Q.

FIGURE 16.8 Effect of temperature on an equilibrium. The tubes in the photograph both contain gaseous NO_2 (brown) and N_2O_4 (colorless) at equilibrium. K is larger at the lower temperature because the equilibrium favors colorless N_2O_4. This is clearly seen in the tube at the right, where the gas in the ice bath at 0 °C is only slightly brown, which indicates a smaller concentration of the brown gas NO_2. At 50 °C (the tube at the left), the equilibrium is shifted toward NO_2, as indicated by the darker brown color.

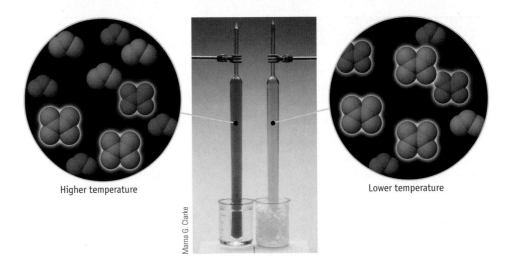

Higher temperature

Lower temperature

Marna G. Clarke

In summary,

- When the temperature of a system at equilibrium increases, the equilibrium will shift in the direction that absorbs energy as heat (Table 16.2)—that is, in the endothermic direction.
- If the temperature decreases, the equilibrium will shift in the direction that releases energy as heat—that is, in the exothermic direction.
- Changing the temperature changes the value of K.

Chemistry.☌.Now™

Sign in at **www.cengage.com/login** and go to Chapter 16 Contents to see Screen 16.12 for a tutorial on **the effect of temperature changes.**

EXERCISE 16.12 Disturbing a Chemical Equilibrium

Does the equilibrium concentration of NOCl increase or decrease as the temperature of the system is increased?

$$2\ NOCl(g) \rightleftharpoons 2\ NO(g) + Cl_2(g) \quad \Delta_r H° = +77.1\ kJ$$

Chapter Goals Revisited

Now that you have studied this chapter, you should ask whether you have met the chapter goals. In particular, you should be able to:

Understand the nature and characteristics of chemical equilibria

a. Chemical reactions are reversible and equilibria are dynamic (Section 16.1).

Understand the significance of the equilibrium constant, K, and reaction quotient, Q.

a. Write the reaction quotient, Q, for a chemical reaction (Section 16.2). When the system is at equilibrium, the reaction quotient is called the equilibrium constant expression and has a constant value called the equilibrium constant, which is symbolized by K (Equation 16.2). Study Question(s) assignable in OWL: 2,4.

b. Recognize that the concentrations of solids, pure liquids, and solvents (e.g., water) are not included in the equilibrium constant expression (Equation 16.1, Section 16.2).

c. Recognize that a large value of K ($K > 1$) means the reaction is product-favored, and the product concentrations are greater than the reactant concentrations at equilibrium. A small value of K ($K < 1$) indicates a reactant-favored reaction in which the product concentrations are smaller than the reactant concentrations at equilibrium (Section 16.2). Study Question(s) assignable in OWL: 66, 68, 70.

d. Appreciate the fact that equilibrium concentrations may be expressed in terms of reactant and product concentrations (in moles per liter) and that K is then sometimes designated as K_c. Alternatively, concentrations of gases may be represented by partial pressures, and K for such cases is designated K_p (Section 16.2).

Understand how to use *K* in quantitative studies of chemical equilibria

a. Use the reaction quotient (Q) to decide whether a reaction is at equilibrium ($Q = K$), or if there will be a net conversion of reactants to products ($Q < K$) or products to reactants ($Q > K$) to attain equilibrium (Section 16.2).

b. Calculate an equilibrium constant given the reactant and product concentrations at equilibrium (Section 16.3). Study Question(s) assignable in OWL: 8, 11, 29, 33, 34, 44, 61a.

c. Use equilibrium constants to calculate the concentration (or pressure) of a reactant or a product at equilibrium (Section 16.4). Study Question(s) assignable in OWL: 16, 17, 32, 36, 42, 46, 47, 50–54, 56, 58–62; Go Chemistry Module 21.

d. Know how K changes as different stoichiometric coefficients are used in a balanced equation, if the equation is reversed, or if several equations are added to give a new net equation (Section 16.5). Study Question(s) assignable in OWL: 21, 31, 37.

e. Know how to predict, using Le Chatelier's principle, the effect of a disturbance on a chemical equilibrium—a change in temperature, a change in concentrations, or a change in volume or pressure for a reaction involving gases (Section 16.6 and Table 16.2). Study Question(s) assignable in OWL: 25, 26, 28, 39, 41, 54, 62.

Chemistry ⚛ Now™ Sign in at www. cengage.com/login to:

- Assess your understanding with Study Questions in OWL keyed to each goal in the Goals and Homework menu for this chapter
- For quick review, download Go Chemistry mini-lecture flashcard modules (or purchase them at **www.ichapters.com**)
- Check your readiness for an exam by taking the Pre-Test and exploring the modules recommended in your Personalized Study plan.

❓ Access **How Do I Solve It?** tutorials on how to approach problem solving using concepts in this chapter.

For additional preparation for an examination on this chapter see the *Let's Review* section on pages 948–961.

KEY EQUATIONS

Equation 16.1 (page 727) The equilibrium constant expression. At equilibrium, the ratio of products to reactants has a constant value, K (at a particular temperature). For the general reaction $aA + bB \rightleftharpoons cC + dD$,

$$\text{Equilibrium constant} = K = \frac{[C]^c[D]^d}{[A]^a[B]^b}$$

Equation 16.2 (page 732) For the general reaction $aA + bB \rightleftharpoons cC + dD$, the ratio of product to reactant concentrations at any point in the reaction is the reaction quotient.

$$\text{Reaction quotient} = Q = \frac{[C]^c[D]^d}{[A]^a[B]^b}$$

STUDY QUESTIONS

Practicing Skills

Writing Equilibrium Constant Expressions
(See Example 16.1 and ChemistryNow Screens 16.3, 16.4, and 16.5.)

1. Write equilibrium constant expressions for the following reactions. For gases, use either pressures or concentrations.
   (a) $2 H_2O_2(g) \rightleftharpoons 2 H_2O(g) + O_2(g)$
   (b) $CO(g) + \frac{1}{2} O_2(g) \rightleftharpoons CO_2(g)$
   (c) $C(s) + CO_2(g) \rightleftharpoons 2 CO(g)$
   (d) $NiO(s) + CO(g) \rightleftharpoons Ni(s) + CO_2(g)$

2. ■ Write equilibrium constant expressions for the following reactions. For gases, use either pressures or concentrations.
   (a) $3 O_2(g) \rightleftharpoons 2 O_3(g)$
   (b) $Fe(s) + 5 CO(g) \rightleftharpoons Fe(CO)_5(g)$
   (c) $(NH_4)_2CO_3(s) \rightleftharpoons 2 NH_3(g) + CO_2(g) + H_2O(g)$
   (d) $Ag_2SO_4(s) \rightleftharpoons 2 Ag^+(aq) + SO_4^{2-}(aq)$

The Equilibrium Constant and Reaction Quotient
(See Example 16.2 and ChemistryNow Screen 16.9.)

3. $K = 5.6 \times 10^{-12}$ at 500 K for the dissociation of iodine molecules to iodine atoms.

$$I_2(g) \rightleftharpoons 2 I(g)$$

   A mixture has $[I_2] = 0.020$ mol/L and $[I] = 2.0 \times 10^{-8}$ mol/L. Is the reaction at equilibrium (at 500 K)? If not, which way must the reaction proceed to reach equilibrium?

4. ■ The reaction

$$2 NO_2(g) \rightleftharpoons N_2O_4(g)$$

   has an equilibrium constant, K_c, of 170 at 25 °C. If 2.0×10^{-3} mol of NO_2 is present in a 10.-L flask along with 1.5×10^{-3} mol of N_2O_4, is the system at equilibrium? If it is not at equilibrium, does the concentration of NO_2 increase or decrease as the system proceeds to equilibrium?

5. A mixture of SO_2, O_2, and SO_3 at 1000 K contains the gases at the following concentrations: $[SO_2] = 5.0 \times 10^{-3}$ mol/L, $[O_2] = 1.9 \times 10^{-3}$ mol/L, and $[SO_3] = 6.9 \times 10^{-3}$ mol/L. Is the reaction at equilibrium? If not, which way will the reaction proceed to reach equilibrium?

$$2 SO_2(g) + O_2(g) \rightleftharpoons 2 SO_3(g) \quad K = 279$$

6. The equilibrium constant, K_c, for the reaction

$$2 NOCl(g) \rightleftharpoons 2 NO(g) + Cl_2(g)$$

   is 3.9×10^{-3} at 300 °C. A mixture contains the gases at the following concentrations: $[NOCl] = 5.0 \times 10^{-3}$ mol/L, $[NO] = 2.5 \times 10^{-3}$ mol/L, and $[Cl_2] = 2.0 \times 10^{-3}$ mol/L. Is the reaction at equilibrium at 300 °C? If not, in which direction does the reaction proceed to come to equilibrium?

Calculating an Equilibrium Constant
(See Examples 16.3 and 16.4 and ChemistryNow Screens 16.4 and 16.8.)

7. The reaction

$$PCl_5(g) \rightleftharpoons PCl_3(g) + Cl_2(g)$$

   was examined at 250 °C. At equilibrium, $[PCl_5] = 4.2 \times 10^{-5}$ mol/L, $[PCl_3] = 1.3 \times 10^{-2}$ mol/L, and $[Cl_2] = 3.9 \times 10^{-3}$ mol/L. Calculate K for the reaction.

8. ■ An equilibrium mixture of SO_2, O_2, and SO_3 at a high temperature contains the gases at the following concentrations: $[SO_2] = 3.77 \times 10^{-3}$ mol/L, $[O_2] = 4.30 \times 10^{-3}$ mol/L, and $[SO_3] = 4.13 \times 10^{-3}$ mol/L. Calculate the equilibrium constant, K, for the reaction.

$$2 SO_2(g) + O_2(g) \rightleftharpoons 2 SO_3(g)$$

9. The reaction

$$C(s) + CO_2(g) \rightleftharpoons 2 CO(g)$$

   occurs at high temperatures. At 700 °C, a 2.0-L flask contains 0.10 mol of CO, 0.20 mol of CO_2, and 0.40 mol of C at equilibrium.
   (a) Calculate K for the reaction at 700 °C.
   (b) Calculate K for the reaction, also at 700 °C, if the amounts at equilibrium in the 2.0-L flask are 0.10 mol of CO, 0.20 mol of CO_2, and 0.80 mol of C.
   (c) Compare the results of (a) and (b). Does the quantity of carbon affect the value of K? Explain.

10. Hydrogen and carbon dioxide react at a high temperature to give water and carbon monoxide.

$$H_2(g) + CO_2(g) \rightleftharpoons H_2O(g) + CO(g)$$

   (a) Laboratory measurements at 986 °C show that there are 0.11 mol each of CO and H_2O vapor and 0.087 mol each of H_2 and CO_2 at equilibrium in a 1.0-L container. Calculate the equilibrium constant for the reaction at 986 °C.
   (b) Suppose 0.050 mol each of H_2 and CO_2 are placed in a 2.0-L container. When equilibrium is achieved at 986 °C, what amounts of CO(g) and $H_2O(g)$, in moles, would be present? [Use the value of K from part (a).]

11. ■ A mixture of CO and Cl_2 is placed in a reaction flask: [CO] = 0.0102 mol/L and $[Cl_2]$ = 0.00609 mol/L. When the reaction

$$CO(g) + Cl_2(g) \rightleftharpoons COCl_2(g)$$

has come to equilibrium at 600 K, $[Cl_2]$ = 0.00301 mol/L.
(a) Calculate the concentrations of CO and $COCl_2$ at equilibrium.
(b) Calculate K_c.

12. You place 3.00 mol of pure SO_3 in an 8.00-L flask at 1150 K. At equilibrium, 0.58 mol of O_2 has been formed. Calculate K for the reaction at 1150 K.

$$2\ SO_3(g) \rightleftharpoons 2\ SO_2(g) + O_2(g)$$

Using Equilibrium Constants
(See Examples 16.5 and 16.6 and ChemistryNow Screen 16.10.)

13. The value of K_c for the interconversion of butane and isobutane is 2.5 at 25 °C.

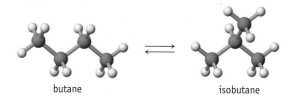

butane   isobutane

If you place 0.017 mol of butane in a 0.50-L flask at 25 °C and allow equilibrium to be established, what will be the equilibrium concentrations of the two forms of butane?

14. Cyclohexane, C_6H_{12}, a hydrocarbon, can isomerize or change into methylcyclopentane, a compound of the same formula ($C_5H_9CH_3$) but with a different molecular structure.

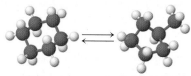

cyclohexane   methylcyclopentane

The equilibrium constant has been estimated to be 0.12 at 25 °C. If you had originally placed 0.045 mol of cyclohexane in a 2.8-L flask, what would be the concentrations of cyclohexane and methylcyclopentane when equilibrium is established?

15. The equilibrium constant for the dissociation of iodine molecules to iodine atoms

$$I_2(g) \rightleftharpoons 2\ I(g)$$

is 3.76×10^{-3} at 1000 K. Suppose 0.105 mol of I_2 is placed in a 12.3-L flask at 1000 K. What are the concentrations of I_2 and I when the system comes to equilibrium?

16. ■ The equilibrium constant for the reaction

$$N_2O_4(g) \rightleftharpoons 2\ NO_2(g)$$

at 25 °C is 5.88×10^{-3}. Suppose 15.6 g of N_2O_4 is placed in a 5.00-L flask at 25 °C. Calculate the following:
(a) the amount of NO_2 (mol) present at equilibrium;
(b) the percentage of the original N_2O_4 that is dissociated.

17. ■ Carbonyl bromide decomposes to carbon monoxide and bromine.

$$COBr_2(g) \rightleftharpoons CO(g) + Br_2(g)$$

K_c is 0.190 at 73 °C. If you place 0.500 mol of $COBr_2$ in a 2.00-L flask and heat it to 73 °C, what are the equilibrium concentrations of $COBr_2$, CO, and Br_2? What percentage of the original $COBr_2$ decomposed at this temperature?

18. Iodine dissolves in water, but its solubility in a nonpolar solvent such as CCl_4 is greater.

Nonpolar I_2
Polar H_2O

Nonpolar CCl_4

Shake the test tube

Polar H_2O

Nonpolar CCl_4 and I_2

Extracting iodine (I_2) from water with the nonpolar solvent CCl_4. I_2 is more soluble in CCl_4 and, after shaking a mixture of water and CCl_4, the I_2 has accumulated in the more dense CCl_4 layer.

The equilibrium constant is 85.0 for the reaction

$$I_2(aq) \rightleftharpoons I_2(CCl_4)$$

You place 0.0340 g of I_2 in 100.0 mL of water. After shaking it with 10.0 mL of CCl_4, how much I_2 remains in the water layer?

Manipulating Equilibrium Constant Expressions
(See Example 16.7 and ChemistryNow Screen 16.7.)

19. Which of the following correctly relates the equilibrium constants for the two reactions shown?

$$A + B \rightleftharpoons 2\ C \quad K_1$$
$$2\ A + 2\ B \rightleftharpoons 4\ C \quad K_2$$

(a) $K_2 = 2K_1$ (c) $K_2 = 1/K_1$
(b) $K_2 = K_1^2$ (d) $K_2 = 1/K_1^2$

Photos: Charles D. Winters

20. Which of the following correctly relates the equilibrium constants for the two reactions shown?

$$A + B \rightleftharpoons 2 C \quad K_1$$

$$C \rightleftharpoons \tfrac{1}{2} A + \tfrac{1}{2} B \quad K_2$$

(a) $K_2 = 1/(K_1)^{1/2}$ (c) $K_2 = K_1^2$
(b) $K_2 = 1/K_1$ (d) $K_2 = -K_1^{1/2}$

21. ■ Consider the following equilibria involving $SO_2(g)$ and their corresponding equilibrium constants.

$$SO_2(g) + \tfrac{1}{2} O_2(g) \rightleftharpoons SO_3(g) \quad K_1$$

$$2 SO_3(g) \rightleftharpoons 2 SO_2(g) + O_2(g) \quad K_2$$

Which of the following expressions relates K_1 to K_2?
(a) $K_2 = K_1^2$ (d) $K_2 = 1/K_1$
(b) $K_2^2 = K_1$ (e) $K_2 = 1/K_1^2$
(c) $K_2 = K_1$

22. The equilibrium constant K for the reaction

$$CO_2(g) \rightleftharpoons CO(g) + \tfrac{1}{2} O_2(g)$$

is 6.66×10^{-12} at 1000 K. Calculate K for the reaction

$$2 CO(g) + O_2(g) \rightleftharpoons 2 CO_2(g)$$

23. Calculate K for the reaction

$$SnO_2(s) + 2 CO(g) \rightleftharpoons Sn(s) + 2 CO_2(g)$$

given the following information:

$$SnO_2(s) + 2 H_2(g) \rightleftharpoons Sn(s) + 2 H_2O(g) \quad K = 8.12$$

$$H_2(g) + CO_2(g) \rightleftharpoons H_2O(g) + CO(g) \quad K = 0.771$$

24. Calculate K for the reaction

$$Fe(s) + H_2O(g) \rightleftharpoons FeO(s) + H_2(g)$$

given the following information:

$$H_2O(g) + CO(g) \rightleftharpoons H_2(g) + CO_2(g) \quad K = 1.6$$

$$FeO(s) + CO(g) \rightleftharpoons Fe(s) + CO_2(g) \quad K = 0.67$$

Disturbing a Chemical Equilibrium
(See Example 16.8 and ChemistryNow Screens 16.11–16.14.)

25. ■ Dinitrogen trioxide decomposes to NO and NO_2 in an endothermic process ($\Delta_r H = 40.5$ kJ/mol-rxn).

$$N_2O_3(g) \rightleftharpoons \text{`NO}(g) + NO_2(g)$$

Predict the effect of the following changes on the position of the equilibrium; that is, state which way the equilibrium will shift (left, right, or no change) when each of the following changes is made.
(a) adding more $N_2O_3(g)$
(b) adding more $NO_2(g)$
(c) increasing the volume of the reaction flask
(d) lowering the temperature

26. ■ K_p for the following reaction is 0.16 at 25 °C:

$$2 NOBr(g) \rightleftharpoons 2 NO(g) + Br_2(g)$$

The enthalpy change for the reaction at standard conditions is +16.3 k/mol-rxn. Predict the effect of the following changes on the position of the equilibrium; that is, state which way the equilibrium will shift (left, right, or no change) when each of the following changes is made.
(a) adding more $Br_2(g)$
(b) removing some $NOBr(g)$
(c) decreasing the temperature
(d) increasing the container volume

27. Consider the isomerization of butane with an equilibrium constant of $K = 2.5$. (See Study Question 13.) The system is originally at equilibrium with [butane] = 1.0 M and [isobutane] = 2.5 M.
(a) If 0.50 mol/L of isobutane is suddenly added and the system shifts to a new equilibrium position, what is the equilibrium concentration of each gas?
(b) If 0.50 mol/L of butane is added and the system shifts to a new equilibrium position, what is the equilibrium concentration of each gas?

28. ■ The decomposition of NH_4HS

$$NH_4HS(s) \rightleftharpoons NH_3(g) + H_2S(g)$$

is an endothermic process. Using Le Chatelier's principle, explain how increasing the temperature would affect the equilibrium. If more NH_4HS is added to a flask in which this equilibrium exists, how is the equilibrium affected? What if some additional NH_3 is placed in the flask? What will happen to the pressure of NH_3 if some H_2S is removed from the flask?

General Questions
These questions are not designated as to type or location in the chapter. They may combine several concepts from this and other chapters.

29. ■ Suppose 0.086 mol of Br_2 is placed in a 1.26-L flask and heated to 1756 K, a temperature at which the halogen dissociates to atoms

$$Br_2(g) \rightleftharpoons 2 Br(g)$$

If Br_2 is 3.7% dissociated at this temperature, calculate K_c.

30. The equilibrium constant for the reaction

$$N_2(g) + O_2(g) \rightleftharpoons 2 NO(g)$$

is 1.7×10^{-3} at 2300 K.
(a) What is K for the reaction when written as follows?

$$\tfrac{1}{2} N_2(g) + \tfrac{1}{2} O_2(g) \rightleftharpoons NO(g)$$

(b) What is K for the following reaction?

$$2 NO(g) \rightleftharpoons N_2(g) + O_2(g)$$

▲ more challenging   ■ in OWL   Blue-numbered questions answered in Appendix 0

31. ■ K_p for the formation of phosgene, $COCl_2$, is 6.5×10^{11} at 25 °C.

$$CO(g) + Cl_2(g) \rightleftharpoons COCl_2(g)$$

What is the value of K_p for the dissociation of phosgene?

$$COCl_2(g) \rightleftharpoons CO(g) + Cl_2(g)$$

32. ■ The equilibrium constant, K_c, for the following reaction is 1.05 at 350 K.

$$2\ CH_2Cl_2(g) \rightleftharpoons CH_4(g) + CCl_4(g)$$

If an equilibrium mixture of the three gases at 350 K contains 0.0206 M $CH_2Cl_2(g)$ and 0.0163 M CH_4, what is the equilibrium concentration of CCl_4?

33. ■ Carbon tetrachloride can be produced by the following reaction:

$$CS_2(g) + 3\ Cl_2(g) \rightleftharpoons S_2Cl_2(g) + CCl_4(g)$$

Suppose 1.2 mol of CS_2 and 3.6 mol of Cl_2 are placed in a 1.00-L flask. After equilibrium has been achieved, the mixture contains 0.90 mol CCl_4. Calculate K_c.

34. ■ Equal numbers of moles of H_2 gas and I_2 vapor are mixed in a flask and heated to 700 °C. The initial concentration of each gas is 0.0088 mol/L, and 78.6% of the I_2 is consumed when equilibrium is achieved according to the equation

$$H_2(g) + I_2(g) \rightleftharpoons 2\ HI(g)$$

Calculate K_c for this reaction.

35. The equilibrium constant for the butane $\rightleftharpoons$ isobutane isomerization reaction is 2.5 at 25 °C. If 1.75 mol of butane and 1.25 mol of isobutane are mixed, is the system at equilibrium? If not, when it proceeds to equilibrium, which reagent increases in concentration? Calculate the concentrations of the two compounds when the system reaches equilibrium.

36. ■ At 2300 K the equilibrium constant for the formation of NO(g) is 1.7×10^{-3}.

$$N_2(g) + O_2(g) \rightleftharpoons 2\ NO(g)$$

(a) Analysis shows that the concentrations of N_2 and O_2 are both 0.25 M, and that of NO is 0.0042 M under certain conditions. Is the system at equilibrium?

(b) If the system is not at equilibrium, in which direction does the reaction proceed?

(c) When the system is at equilibrium, what are the equilibrium concentrations?

37. ■ Which of the following correctly relates the two equilibrium constants for the two reactions shown?

$$NOCl(g) \rightleftharpoons NO(g) + \tfrac{1}{2}\ Cl_2(g) \qquad K_1$$

$$2\ NO(g) + Cl_2(g) \rightleftharpoons 2\ NOCl(g) \qquad K_2$$

(a) $K_2 = -K_1^2$ (c) $K_2 = 1/K_1^2$
(b) $K_2 = 1/(K_1)^{1/2}$ (d) $K_2 = 2K_1$

38. Sulfur dioxide is readily oxidized to sulfur trioxide.

$$2\ SO_2(g) + O_2(g) \rightleftharpoons 2\ SO_3(g) \qquad K_c = 279$$

If we add 3.00 g of SO_2 and 5.00 g of O_2 to a 1.0-L flask, approximately what quantity of SO_3 will be in the flask once the reactants and the product reach equilibrium?

(a) 2.21 g   (c) 3.61 g
(b) 4.56 g   (d) 8.00 g

(Note: The full solution to this problem results in a cubic equation. Do not try to solve it exactly. Decide only which of the answers is most reasonable.)

39. ■ Heating a metal carbonate leads to decomposition.

$$BaCO_3(s) \rightleftharpoons BaO(s) + CO_2(g)$$

Predict the effect on the equilibrium of each change listed below. Answer by choosing (i) no change, (ii) shifts left, or (iii) shifts right.

(a) add $BaCO_3$ (c) add BaO
(b) add CO_2 (d) raise the temperature
(e) increase the volume of the flask containing the reaction

40. Carbonyl bromide decomposes to carbon monoxide and bromine.

$$COBr_2(g) \rightleftharpoons CO(g) + Br_2(g)$$

K_c is 0.190 at 73 °C. Suppose you place 0.500 mol of $COBr_2$ in a 2.00-L flask and heat it to 73 °C (Study Question 17). After equilibrium has been achieved, you add an additional 2.00 mol of CO.

(a) How is the equilibrium mixture affected by adding more CO?

(b) When equilibrium *is* reestablished, what are the new equilibrium concentrations of $COBr_2$, CO, and Br_2?

(c) How has the addition of CO affected the percentage of $COBr_2$ that decomposed?

41. ■ Phosphorus pentachloride decomposes at higher temperatures.

$$PCl_5(g) \rightleftharpoons PCl_3(g) + Cl_2(g)$$

An equilibrium mixture at some temperature consists of 3.120 g of PCl_5, 3.845 g of PCl_3, and 1.787 g of Cl_2 in a 1.00-L flask. If you add 1.418 g of Cl_2, how will the equilibrium be affected? What will the concentrations of PCl_5, PCl_3, and Cl_2 be when equilibrium is reestablished?

42. ■ Ammonium hydrogen sulfide decomposes on heating.

$$NH_4HS(s) \rightleftharpoons NH_3(g) + H_2S(g)$$

If K_p for this reaction is 0.11 at 25 °C (when the partial pressures are measured in atmospheres), what is the total pressure in the flask at equilibrium?

---

43. ■ Ammonium iodide dissociates reversibly to ammonia and hydrogen iodide if the salt is heated to a sufficiently high temperature.

$$NH_4I(s) \rightleftharpoons NH_3(g) + HI(g)$$

Some ammonium iodide is placed in a flask, which is then heated to 400 °C. If the total pressure in the flask when equilibrium has been achieved is 705 mm Hg, what is the value of K_p (when partial pressures are in atmospheres)?

44. ■ When solid ammonium carbamate sublimes, it dissociates completely into ammonia and carbon dioxide according to the following equation:

$$(NH_4)(H_2NCO_2)(s) \rightleftharpoons 2\ NH_3(g) + CO_2(g)$$

At 25 °C, experiment shows that the total pressure of the gases in equilibrium with the solid is 0.116 atm. What is the equilibrium constant, K_p?

45. The equilibrium reaction $N_2O_4(g) \rightleftharpoons 2\ NO_2(g)$ has been thoroughly studied (see Figure 16.8).
 (a) If the total pressure in a flask containing NO_2 and N_2O_4 gas at 25 °C is 1.50 atm and the value of K_p at this temperature is 0.148, what fraction of the N_2O_4 has dissociated to NO_2?
 (b) What happens to the fraction dissociated if the volume of the container is increased so that the total equilibrium pressure falls to 1.00 atm?

46. ■ In the gas phase, acetic acid exists as an equilibrium of monomer and dimer molecules. (The dimer consists of two molecules linked through hydrogen bonds.)

The equilibrium constant, K_c, at 25 °C for the monomer–dimer equilibrium

$$2\ CH_3CO_2H \rightleftharpoons (CH_3CO_2H)_2$$

has been determined to be 3.2×10^4. Assume that acetic acid is present initially at a concentration of 5.4×10^{-4} mol/L at 25 °C and that no dimer is present initially.
 (a) What percentage of the acetic acid is converted to dimer?
 (b) As the temperature increases, in which direction does the equilibrium shift? (Recall that hydrogen-bond formation is an exothermic process.)

47. ■ Assume 3.60 mol of ammonia is placed in a 2.00-L vessel and allowed to decompose to the elements.

$$2\ NH_3(g) \rightleftharpoons N_2(g) + 3\ H_2(g)$$

If the experimental value of K is 6.3 for this reaction at the temperature in the reactor, calculate the equilibrium concentration of each reagent. What is the total pressure in the flask?

48. ■ The total pressure for a mixture of N_2O_4 and NO_2 is 1.5 atm. If $K_p = 6.75$ (at 25 °C), calculate the partial pressure of each gas in the mixture.

$$2\ NO_2(g) \rightleftharpoons N_2O_4(g)$$

49. K_c for the decomposition of ammonium hydrogen sulfide is 1.8×10^{-4} at 25 °C.

$$NH_4HS(s) \rightleftharpoons NH_3(g) + H_2S(g)$$

 (a) When the pure salt decomposes in a flask, what are the equilibrium concentrations of NH_3 and H_2S?
 (b) If NH_4HS is placed in a flask already containing 0.020 mol/L of NH_3 and then the system is allowed to come to equilibrium, what are the equilibrium concentrations of NH_3 and H_2S?

50. ■ The equilibrium constant, K_p, is 0.15 at 25 °C for the following reaction:

$$N_2O_4(g) \rightleftharpoons 2\ NO_2(g)$$

If the total pressure of the gas mixture is 2.5 atm at equilibrium, what is the partial pressure of each gas?

51. ■ ▲ A 15-L flask at 300 K contains 64.4 g of a mixture of NO_2 and N_2O_4 in equilibrium. What is the total pressure in the flask? (K_p for $2\ NO_2(g) \rightleftharpoons N_2O_4(g)$ is 6.67.)

52. ■ ▲ Lanthanum oxalate decomposes when heated to lanthanum oxide, CO, and CO_2.

$$La_2(C_2O_4)_3(s) \rightleftharpoons La_2O_3(s) + 3\ CO(g) + 3\ CO_2(g)$$

 (a) If, at equilibrium, the total pressure in a 10.0-L flask is 0.200 atm, what is the value of K_p?
 (b) Suppose 0.100 mol of $La_2(C_2O_4)_3$ was originally placed in the 10.0-L flask. What quantity of $La_2(C_2O_4)_3$ remains unreacted at equilibrium at 373 K?

53. ■ ▲ The reaction of hydrogen and iodine to give hydrogen iodide has an equilibrium constant, K_c, of 56 at 435 °C.
 (a) What is the value of K_p?
 (b) Suppose you mix 0.45 mol of H_2 and 0.45 mol of I_2 in a 10.0-L flask at 425 °C. What is the total pressure of the mixture before and after equilibrium is achieved?
 (c) What is the partial pressure of each gas at equilibrium?

▲ more challenging ■ in OWL Blue-numbered questions answered in Appendix O

54. ■ Sulfuryl chloride, SO_2Cl_2, is a compound with very irritating vapors; it is used as a reagent in the synthesis of organic compounds. When heated to a sufficiently high temperature, it decomposes to SO_2 and Cl_2.

$$SO_2Cl_2(g) \rightleftharpoons SO_2(g) + Cl_2(g) \qquad K_c = 0.045 \text{ at } 375 \text{ °C}$$

(a) A 1.00-L flask containing 6.70 g of SO_2Cl_2 is heated to 375 °C. What is the concentration of each of the compounds in the system when equilibrium is achieved? What fraction of SO_2Cl_2 has dissociated?

(b) What are the concentrations of SO_2Cl_2, SO_2, and Cl_2 at equilibrium in the 1.00-L flask at 375 °C if you begin with a mixture of SO_2Cl_2 (6.70 g) and Cl_2 (1.00 atm)? What fraction of SO_2Cl_2 has dissociated?

(c) Compare the fractions of SO_2Cl_2 in parts (a) and (b). Do they agree with your expectations based on Le Chatelier's principle?

55. ▲ Hemoglobin (Hb) can form a complex with both O_2 and CO. For the reaction

$$HbO_2(aq) + CO(g) \rightleftharpoons HbCO(aq) + O_2(g)$$

at body temperature, K is about 200. If the ratio $[HbCO]/[HbO_2]$ comes close to 1, death is probable. What partial pressure of CO in the air is likely to be fatal? Assume the partial pressure of O_2 is 0.20 atm.

56. ■ ▲ Limestone decomposes at high temperatures.

$$CaCO_3(s) \rightleftharpoons CaO(s) + CO_2(g)$$

At 1000 °C, $K_p = 3.87$. If pure $CaCO_3$ is placed in a 5.00-L flask and heated to 1000 °C, what quantity of $CaCO_3$ must decompose to achieve the equilibrium pressure of CO_2?

57. At 1800 K, oxygen dissociates very slightly into its atoms.

$$O_2(g) \rightleftharpoons 2 O(g) \qquad K_p = 1.2 \times 10^{-10}$$

If you place 1.0 mol of O_2 in a 10.-L vessel and heat it to 1800 K, how many O atoms are present in the flask?

58. ■ ▲ Nitrosyl bromide, NOBr, is prepared by the direct reaction of NO and Br_2.

$$2 NO(g) + Br_2(g) \rightarrow 2 NOBr(g)$$

The compound dissociates readily at room temperature, however.

$$NOBr(g) \rightleftharpoons NO(g) + \tfrac{1}{2} Br_2(g)$$

Some NOBr is placed in a flask at 25 °C and allowed to dissociate. The total pressure at equilibrium is 190 mm Hg and the compound is found to be 34% dissociated. What is the value of K_p?

59. ■ ▲ Boric acid and glycerin form a complex

$$B(OH)_3(aq) + \text{glycerin}(aq) \rightleftharpoons B(OH)_3 \cdot \text{glycerin}(aq)$$

with an equilibrium constant of 0.90. If the concentration of boric acid is 0.10 M, how much glycerin should be added, per liter, so that 60.% of the boric acid is in the form of the complex?

60. ■ ▲ The dissociation of calcium carbonate has an equilibrium constant of $K_p = 1.16$ at 800 °C.

$$CaCO_3(s) \rightleftharpoons CaO(s) + CO_2(g)$$

(a) What is K_c for the reaction?

(b) If you place 22.5 g of $CaCO_3$ in a 9.56-L container at 800 °C, what is the pressure of CO_2 in the container?

(c) What percentage of the original 22.5-g sample of $CaCO_3$ remains undecomposed at equilibrium?

61. ▲ A sample of N_2O_4 gas with a pressure of 1.00 atm is placed in a flask. When equilibrium is achieved, 20.0% of the N_2O_4 has been converted to NO_2 gas.

(a) ■ Calculate K_p.

(b) If the original pressure of N_2O_4 is 0.10 atm, what is the percent dissociation of the gas? Is the result in agreement with Le Chatelier's principle?

62. ■ ▲ A reaction important in smog formation is

$$O_3(g) + NO(g) \rightleftharpoons O_2(g) + NO_2(g) \qquad K = 6.0 \times 10^{34}$$

(a) If the initial concentrations are $[O_3] = 1.0 \times 10^{-6}$ M, $[NO] = 1.0 \times 10^{-5}$ M, $[NO_2] = 2.5 \times 10^{-4}$ M, and $[O_2] = 8.2 \times 10^{-3}$ M, is the system at equilibrium? If not, in which direction does the reaction proceed?

(b) If the temperature is increased, as on a very warm day, will the concentrations of the products increase or decrease? (*Hint:* You may have to calculate the enthalpy change for the reaction to find out if it is exothermic or endothermic.)

In the Laboratory

63. ▲ The ammonia complex of trimethylborane, $(NH_3)B(CH_3)_3$, dissociates at 100 °C to its components with $K_p = 4.62$ (when the pressures are in atmospheres).

$$(NH_3)B(CH_3)_3(g) \rightleftharpoons B(CH_3)_3(g) + NH_3(g)$$

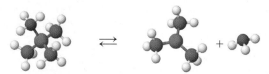

If NH_3 is changed to some other molecule, the equilibrium constant is different.

For $[(CH_3)_3P]B(CH_3)_3$ $K_p = 0.128$

For $[(CH_3)_3N]B(CH_3)_3$ $K_p = 0.472$

(a) If you begin an experiment by placing 0.010 mol of each complex in a flask, which would have the largest partial pressure of $B(CH_3)_3$ at 100 °C?

(b) If 0.73 g (0.010 mol) of $(NH_3)B(CH_3)_3$ is placed in a 100.-mL flask and heated to 100 °C, what is the partial pressure of each gas in the equilibrium mixture, and what is the total pressure? What is the percent dissociation of $(NH_3)B(CH_3)_3$?

64. The photographs below show what occurs when a solution of potassium chromate is treated with a few drops of concentrated hydrochloric acid. Some of the bright yellow chromate ion is converted to the orange dichromate ion.

$$2\ CrO_4^{2-}(aq) + 2\ H_3O^+(aq) \rightleftharpoons Cr_2O_7^{2-}(aq) + 3\ H_2O(\ell)$$

Charles D. Winters

(a) Explain this experimental observation in terms of Le Chatelier's principle.

(b) What would you observe if you treated the orange solution with sodium hydroxide? Explain your observation.

65. The photographs in (a) show what occurs when a solution of iron(III) nitrate is treated with a few drops of aqueous potassium thiocyanate. (See ChemistryNow, Screen 16.4.) The nearly colorless iron(III) ion is converted to a red $[Fe(H_2O)_5SCN]^{2+}$ ion. (This is a classic test for the presence of iron(III) ions in solution.)

$$[Fe(H_2O)_6]^{3+}(aq) + SCN^-(aq) \rightleftharpoons$$
$$[Fe(H_2O)_5SCN]^{2+}(aq) + H_2O(\ell)$$

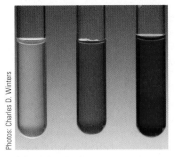

Photos: Charles D. Winters

(a) Adding KSCN **(b) Adding Ag⁺**

(a) As more KSCN is added to the solution, the color becomes even more red. Explain this observation.

(b) Silver ions form a white precipitate with SCN^- ions. What would you observe on adding a few drops of aqueous silver nitrate to a red solution of $[Fe(H_2O)_5SCN]^+$ ions? Explain your observation.

66. ■ ▲ The photographs at the bottom of the page show what occurs when you add ammonia to aqueous nickel(II) nitrate and then add ethylenediamine ($NH_2CH_2CH_2NH_2$) to the intermediate blue-purple solution.

$$[Ni(H_2O)_6]^{2+}(aq) + 6\ NH_3(aq)$$
green
$$\rightleftharpoons [Ni(NH_3)_6]^{2+}(aq) + 6\ H_2O(\ell) \qquad K_1$$
blue-purple

$$[Ni(NH_3)_6]^{2+}(aq) + 3\ NH_2CH_2CH_2NH_2(aq)$$
blue-purple
$$\rightleftharpoons [Ni(NH_2CH_2CH_2NH_2)_3]^{2+}(aq) + 6\ NH_3(aq)\ K_2$$
violet

Which equilibrium constant is greater, K_1 or K_2? Explain.

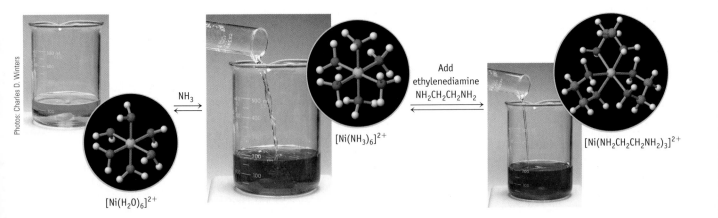

Photos: Charles D. Winters

$[Ni(H_2O)_6]^{2+}$

NH_3

$[Ni(NH_3)_6]^{2+}$

Add ethylenediamine $NH_2CH_2CH_2NH_2$

$[Ni(NH_2CH_2CH_2NH_2)_3]^{2+}$

▲ more challenging ■ in OWL Blue-numbered questions answered in Appendix O

Summary and Conceptual Questions

The following questions may use concepts from this and previous chapters.

67. Decide whether each of the following statements is true or false. If false, change the wording to make it true.
   (a) The magnitude of the equilibrium constant is always independent of temperature.
   (b) When two chemical equations are added to give a net equation, the equilibrium constant for the net equation is the product of the equilibrium constants of the summed equations.
   (c) The equilibrium constant for a reaction has the same value as K for the reverse reaction.
   (d) Only the concentration of CO_2 appears in the equilibrium constant expression for the reaction $CaCO_3(s) \rightleftharpoons CaO(s) + CO_2(g)$.
   (e) For the reaction $CaCO_3(s) \rightleftharpoons CaO(s) + CO_2(g)$, the value of K is numerically the same, whether the amount of CO_2 is expressed as moles/liter or as gas pressure.

68. ■ Neither $PbCl_2$ nor PbF_2 is appreciably soluble in water. If solid $PbCl_2$ and solid PbF_2 are placed in equal amounts of water in separate beakers, in which beaker is the concentration of Pb^{2+} greater? Equilibrium constants for these solids dissolving in water are as follows:

$$PbCl_2(s) \rightleftharpoons Pb^{2+}(aq) + 2\,Cl^-(aq) \quad K = 1.7 \times 10^{-5}$$

$$PbF_2(s) \rightleftharpoons Pb^{2+}(aq) + 2\,F^-(aq) \quad K = 3.7 \times 10^{-8}$$

69. Characterize each of the following as product- or reactant-favored.
   (a) $CO(g) + \frac{1}{2} O_2(g) \rightleftharpoons CO_2(g) \quad K_p = 1.2 \times 10^{45}$
   (b) $H_2O(g) \rightleftharpoons H_2(g) + \frac{1}{2} O_2(g) \quad K_p = 9.1 \times 10^{-41}$
   (c) $CO(g) + Cl_2(g) \rightleftharpoons COCl_2(g) \quad K_p = 6.5 \times 10^{11}$

70. ■ Consider a gas-phase reaction where a colorless compound C produces a blue compound B.

$$2\,C(g) \rightleftharpoons B(g)$$

After reaching equilibrium, the size of the flask is halved.
   (a) What color change (if any) is observed immediately upon halving the flask size?
   (b) What color change (if any) is observed after equilibrium has been reestablished in the flask?

71. An ice cube is placed in a beaker of water at 20 °C. The ice cube partially melts, and the temperature of the water is lowered to 0 °C. At this point, both ice and water are at 0 °C, and no further change is apparent. Is the system at equilibrium? Is this a dynamic equilibrium? That is, are events still occurring at the molecular level? Suggest an experiment to test whether this is so. (*Hint:* Consider using D_2O.)

72. See the simulation on ChemistryNow, Screen 16.4.
   (a) Set the concentration of Fe^{3+} at 0.0050 M and that of SCN^- at 0.0070 M. Click the "React" button. Does the concentration of Fe^{3+} go to zero? When equilibrium is reached, what are the concentrations of the reactants and the products? What is the equilibrium constant?
   (b) Begin with $[Fe^{3+}] = [SCN^-] = 0.0$ M and $[FeSCN^{2+}] = 0.0080$ M. When equilibrium is reached, which ion has the largest concentration in solution?
   (c) Begin with $[Fe^{3+}] = 0.0010$ M, $[SCN^-] = 0.0020$ M, and $[FeSCN^{2+}] = 0.0030$ M. Describe the result of allowing this system to come to equilibrium.

17 | The Chemistry of Acids and Bases

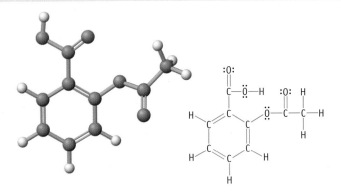

Photo of crystals of aspirin taken using a microscope and polarized light.

© Michael W. Davidson, 2007

Aspirin Is Over 100 Years Old!

Aspirin is one of the most successful non-prescription drugs ever made. Americans swallow more than 50 million aspirin tablets a day, mostly for the pain-relieving (analgesic) effects of the drug. Aspirin also wards off heart disease and thrombosis (blood clots), and it has even been suggested as a possible treatment for certain cancers and for senile dementia.

Hippocrates (460–370 BC), the ancient Greek physician, recommended an infusion of willow bark to ease the pain of childbirth. It was not until the 19th century that an Italian chemist, Raffaele Piria, isolated salicylic acid, the active compound in the bark. Soon thereafter, it was found that the acid could be extracted from a wild flower, *Spiraea ulmaria*. It is from the name of this plant that the name "aspirin" (a + spiraea) is derived.

Hippocrates's willow bark extract, salicylic acid, is an analgesic, but it is also very irritating to the stomach lining. It was therefore an important advance when chemists at Bayer Chemicals in Germany found, in 1897, that a derivative of salicylic acid, acetylsalicylic acid,

was also a useful drug and had fewer side effects. This is the compound we now call "aspirin."

Acetylsalicylic acid slowly reverts to salicylic acid, $C_6H_4(CO_2H)$ (OH), and acetic acid in the presence of moisture; therefore, if you smell the characteristic odor of acetic acid in an old bottle of aspirin tablets, they are too old and should be discarded.

Aspirin is a component of various over-the-counter medicines, such as Anacin, Ecotrin, Excedrin, and Alka-Seltzer. The latter is a combination of aspirin with citric acid and sodium bicarbonate. Sodium bicarbonate is a base and reacts with the acid to produce the sodium salt of acetylsalicylic acid, a form of aspirin that is water-soluble and quicker acting.

Questions:

1. Aspirin has a pK_a of 3.49, and that of acetic acid is 4.74. Which is the stronger acid?
2. Identify the acidic H atom in aspirin.
3. Write an equation for the ionization of aspirin.

Answers to these questions are in Appendix Q.

◉WL *See Chapter Goals Revisited (page 799) for Study Questions keyed to these goals and assignable in OWL.*

- Use the Brønsted–Lowry and Lewis theories of acids and bases.
- Apply the principles of chemical equilibrium to acids and bases in aqueous solution.
- Predict the outcome of reactions of acids and bases.
- Understand the influence of structure and bonding on acid–base properties.

Acids and bases are among the most common substances in nature. Amino acids are the building blocks of proteins. The pH of the lakes, rivers, and oceans is affected by dissolved acids and bases, and your bodily functions depend on acids and bases. You were introduced to the definitions of acids and bases and to some of their chemistry in Chapter 3, but this chapter and the next take up the detailed chemistry of this important class of substances.

Chemistry.◉.Now™

Throughout the text this icon introduces an opportunity for self-study or to explore interactive tutorials by signing in at **www.cengage.com/login**.

17.1 Acids and Bases: A Review

In Chapter 3, you were introduced to two definitions of acids and bases: the Arrhenius definition and the Brønsted–Lowry definition. According to the Arrhenius definition, an acid is any substance that, when dissolved in water, increases the concentration of hydrogen ions, H^+ (◄ page 132). An Arrhenius base is any substance that increases the concentration of hydroxide ions, OH^-, when dissolved in water. Based on the Arrhenius definition, hydrochloric acid was therefore classified as an acid, and sodium hydroxide was classified as a base.

$$HCl(aq) \rightarrow H^+(aq) + Cl^-(aq)$$

$$NaOH(aq) \rightarrow Na^+(aq) + OH^-(aq)$$

Using this definition, reactions between acids and bases involve the combination of H^+ and OH^- ions to form water (and a salt).

$$NaOH(aq) + HCl(aq) \rightarrow H_2O(\ell) + NaCl(aq)$$

The Brønsted–Lowry definition of acids and bases is more general and views acid–base behavior in terms of proton transfer from one substance to another. A Brønsted–Lowry acid is a proton (H^+) donor, and a Brønsted–Lowry base is a proton acceptor. The reaction between an acid and a base is viewed as involving an equilibrium in which a new acid and base (the conjugate base of the acid and the conjugate acid of the base) are formed. This definition extends the list of bases and the scope of acid–base reactions. In the following reaction, HCl acts as a

Brønsted–Lowry acid, and water acts as a Brønsted–Lowry base because HCl transfers a H^+ ion to H_2O to form the hydronium ion, H_3O^+.

$$HCl(aq) + H_2O(\ell) \rightleftharpoons H_3O^+(aq) + Cl^-(aq)$$

This equilibrium strongly favors formation of $H_3O^+(aq)$ and $Cl^-(aq)$; that is, HCl is a stronger acid than H_3O^+.

We will begin this chapter by looking at Brønsted–Lowry acid–base chemistry in more detail.

17.2 The Brønsted–Lowry Concept of Acids and Bases Extended

A wide variety of Brønsted–Lowry acids is known. These include some molecular compounds such as nitric acid,

$$HNO_3(aq) + H_2O(\ell) \rightleftharpoons NO_3^-(aq) + H_3O^+(aq)$$
Acid

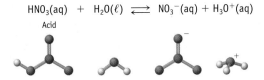

cations such as NH_4^+,

$$NH_4^+(aq) + H_2O(\ell) \rightleftharpoons NH_3(aq) + H_3O^+(aq)$$
Acid

and anions.

$$H_2PO_4^-(aq) + H_2O(\ell) \rightleftharpoons HPO_4^{2-}(aq) + H_3O^+(aq)$$

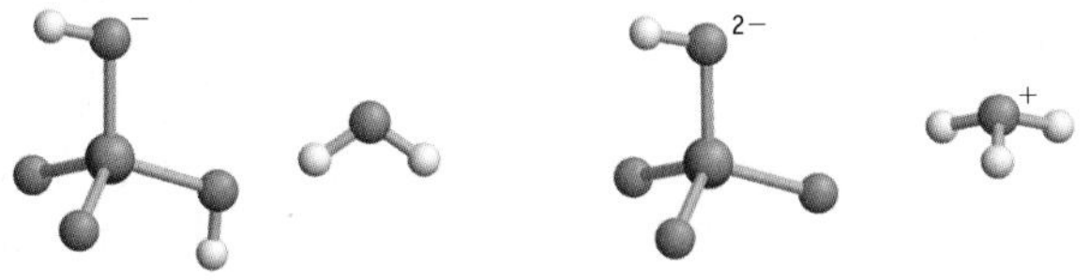

Similarly, many different types of species can act as Brønsted bases in their reactions with water. These include some molecular compounds,

$$NH_3(aq) + H_2O(\ell) \rightleftharpoons NH_4^+(aq) + OH^-(aq)$$
Base

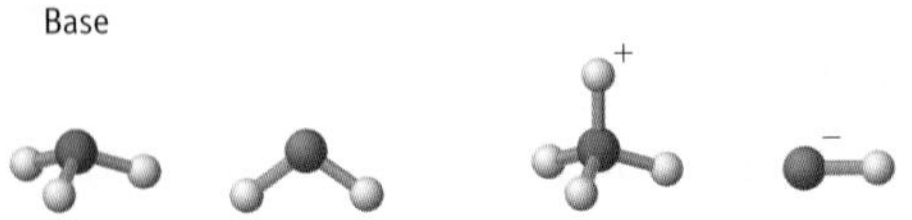

anions,

$$CO_3^{2-}(aq) + H_2O(\ell) \rightleftharpoons HCO_3^-(aq) + OH^-(aq)$$

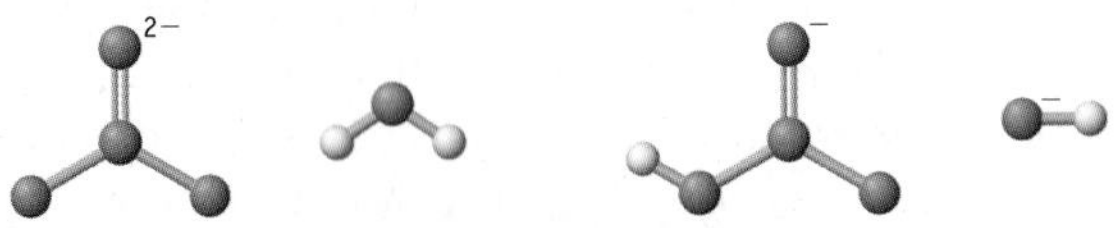

and hydrated metal cations. These cations can act as acids and bases.

$$[Fe(H_2O)_6]^{3+}(aq) + H_2O(\ell) \rightleftharpoons [Fe(H_2O)_6(OH)]^{2+}(aq) + H_3O^+(aq)$$

$$[Al(H_2O)_5(OH)]^{2+}(aq) + H_2O(\ell) \rightleftharpoons [Al(H_2O)_6]^{3+}(aq) + OH^-(aq)$$

Acids such as HF, HCl, HNO_3, and CH_3CO_2H (acetic acid) are all capable of donating one proton and so are called **monoprotic acids.** Other acids, called **polyprotic acids** (Table 17.1), are capable of donating two or more protons. A familiar example of a polyprotic acid is sulfuric acid.

$$H_2SO_4(aq) \quad + \quad H_2O(\ell) \rightleftharpoons HSO_4^-(aq) + H_3O^+(aq)$$

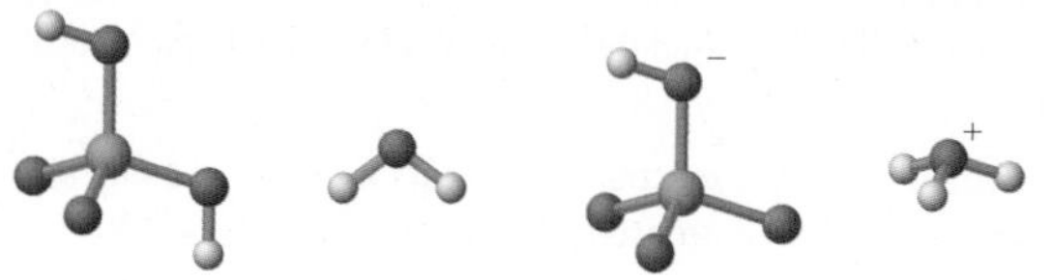

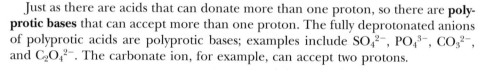

$$HSO_4^-(aq) \quad + \quad H_2O(\ell) \rightleftharpoons SO_4^{2-}(aq) + H_3O^+(aq)$$

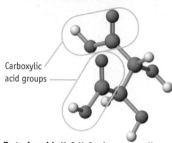

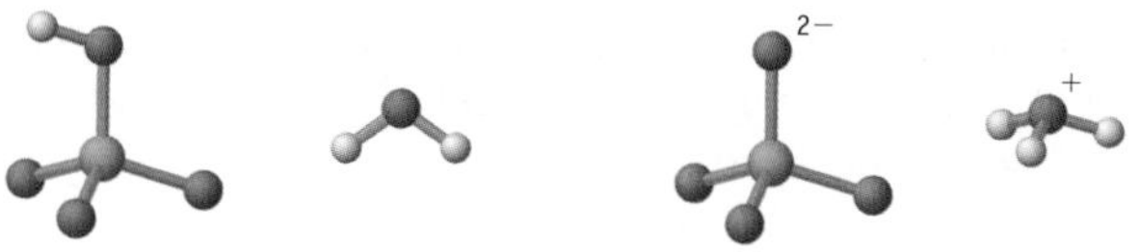

Tartaric acid, $H_2C_4H_4O_6$, is a naturally occurring diprotic acid. Tartaric acid and its potassium salt are found in many fruits. The acidic protons are the H atoms of the $-CO_2H$ or carboxylic acid groups.

Just as there are acids that can donate more than one proton, so there are **polyprotic bases** that can accept more than one proton. The fully deprotonated anions of polyprotic acids are polyprotic bases; examples include SO_4^{2-}, PO_4^{3-}, CO_3^{2-}, and $C_2O_4^{2-}$. The carbonate ion, for example, can accept two protons.

$$CO_3^{2-}(aq) + H_2O(\ell) \rightleftharpoons HCO_3^-(aq) + OH^-(aq)$$

Base

$$HCO_3^-(aq) + H_2O(\ell) \rightleftharpoons H_2CO_3(aq) + OH^-(aq)$$

Base

Some molecules (such as water) and ions can behave either as Brønsted acids or bases and are referred to as being **amphiprotic** (◄ page 136). An example of an

TABLE 17.1 Polyprotic Acids and Bases

Acid Form	Amphiprotic Form	Base Form
H_2S (hydrosulfuric acid or hydrogen sulfide)	HS^- (hydrogen sulfide ion)	S^{2-} (sulfide ion)
H_3PO_4 (phosphoric acid)	$H_2PO_4^-$ (dihydrogen phosphate ion) HPO_4^{2-} (hydrogen phosphate ion)	PO_4^{3-} (phosphate ion)
H_2CO_3 (carbonic acid)	HCO_3^- (hydrogen carbonate ion or bicarbonate ion)	CO_3^{2-} (carbonate ion)
$H_2C_2O_4$ (oxalic acid)	$HC_2O_4^-$ (hydrogen oxalate ion)	$C_2O_4^{2-}$ (oxalate ion)

amphiprotic anion that is particularly important in biochemical systems is the dihydrogen phosphate anion (Table 17.1).

$$H_2PO_4^-(aq) + H_2O(\ell) \rightleftharpoons H_3O^+(aq) + HPO_4^{2-}(aq)$$

Acid

$$H_2PO_4^{2-}(aq) + H_2O(\ell) \rightleftharpoons H_3PO_4(aq) + OH^-(aq)$$

Base

EXERCISE 17.1 Brønsted Acids and Bases

(a) Write a balanced equation for the reaction that occurs when H_3PO_4, phosphoric acid, donates a proton to water to form the dihydrogen phosphate ion. Is the dihydrogen phosphate ion an acid, a base, or amphiprotic?

(b) Write a balanced equation for the reaction that occurs when the cyanide ion, CN^-, accepts a proton from water to form HCN. Is CN^- a Brønsted acid or base?

Conjugate Acid–Base Pairs

A reaction important in the control of acidity in biological systems involves the hydrogen carbonate ion, which can act as a Brønsted base or acid in water. The equation for HCO_3^- functioning as an base exemplifies a feature of all reactions involving Brønsted acids and bases.

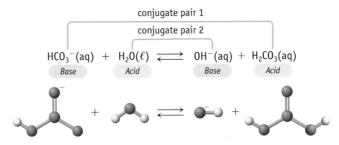

conjugate pair 1
conjugate pair 2

$$HCO_3^-(aq) + H_2O(\ell) \rightleftharpoons OH^-(aq) + H_2CO_3(aq)$$

Base · Acid · Base · Acid

In the forward direction, HCO_3^- is the Brønsted base because it captures H^+ from the Brønsted acid, H_2O. The reverse reaction, however, is also an acid–base reaction. In this case, the H_2CO_3 is the acid, and OH^- is the base.

A **conjugate acid–base pair** consists of two species that differ from each other by the presence of one hydrogen ion. Thus, H_2CO_3 and HCO_3^- comprise a conjugate acid–base pair. In this pair, HCO_3^- is the conjugate base of the acid H_2CO_3, and H_2CO_3 is the conjugate acid of the base HCO_3^-. There is a second conjugate acid–base pair in this reaction: H_2O and H_3O^+. In fact, *every reaction between a Brønsted acid and a Brønsted base involves two conjugate acid–base pairs* (Table 17.2).

Chemistry .ₒ. Now™

Sign in at **www.cengage.com/login** and go to Chapter 17 Contents to see Screen 17.2 for an exercise and tutorial on **acids, bases, and their conjugates.**

EXERCISE 17.2 Conjugate Acids and Bases

In the following reaction, identify the acid on the left and its conjugate base on the right. Similarly, identify the base on the left and its conjugate acid on the right.

$$HNO_3(aq) + NH_3(aq) \rightleftharpoons NH_4^+(aq) + NO_3^-(aq)$$

TABLE 17.2 Acid–Base Reactions and Conjugate Acid–Base Pairs*

Name	Acid 1		Base 2		Base 1		Acid 2
Hydrochloric acid	HCl	+	H_2O	$\rightleftharpoons$	Cl^-	+	H_3O^+
Nitric acid	HNO_3	+	H_2O	$\rightleftharpoons$	NO_3^-	+	H_3O^+
Carbonic acid	H_2CO_3	+	H_2O	$\rightleftharpoons$	HCO_3^-	+	H_3O^+
Acetic acid	CH_3CO_2H	+	H_2O	$\rightleftharpoons$	$CH_3CO_2^-$	+	H_3O^+
Hydrocyanic acid	HCN	+	H_2O	$\rightleftharpoons$	CN^-	+	H_3O^+
Hydrogen sulfide	H_2S	+	H_2O	$\rightleftharpoons$	HS^-	+	H_3O^+
Ammonia	H_2O	+	NH_3	$\rightleftharpoons$	OH^-	+	NH_4^+
Carbonate ion	H_2O	+	CO_3^{2-}	$\rightleftharpoons$	OH^-	+	HCO_3^-
Water	H_2O	+	H_2O	$\rightleftharpoons$	OH^-	+	H_3O^+

*Acid 1 and base 1 are a conjugate pair, as are base 2 and acid 2.

17.3 Water and the pH Scale

Because we generally use aqueous solutions of acids and bases, and because the acid–base reactions in your body occur in your aqueous interior, we want to consider the behavior of water in terms of chemical equilibria.

Water Autoionization and the Water Ionization Constant, K_w

An acid such as HCl does not need to be present for the hydronium ion to exist in water. In fact, two water molecules can interact with each other to produce a hydronium ion and a hydroxide ion by proton transfer from one water molecule to the other.

$$2\ H_2O(\ell) \rightleftharpoons H_3O^+(aq) + OH^-(aq)$$

This **autoionization** reaction of water was demonstrated many years ago by Friedrich Kohlrausch (1840–1910). He found that, even after water is painstakingly purified, it still conducts electricity to a very small extent because autoionization produces very low concentrations of H_3O^+ and OH^- ions. Water autoionization is the cornerstone of our concepts of aqueous acid–base behavior.

When water autoionizes, the equilibrium lies far to the left side. In fact, in pure water at 25 °C, only about two out of a billion (10^9) water molecules are ionized at any instant. To express this idea more quantitatively, we can write the equilibrium constant expression for autoionization.

$$K_w = [H_3O^+][OH^-] = 1.0 \times 10^{-14} \text{ at 25 °C} \qquad (17.1)$$

■ K_w **and Temperature** The equation $K_w = [H_3O^+][OH^-]$ is valid for pure water and for any aqueous solution. K_w is temperature dependent. Because the autoionization reaction is endothermic, K_w increases with temperature.

T (°C)	K_w
10	0.29×10^{-14}
15	0.45×10^{-14}
20	0.68×10^{-14}
25	1.01×10^{-14}
30	1.47×10^{-14}
50	5.48×10^{-14}

There are several important aspects of this equation.

- Based on the rules we have given for writing equilibrium constants, we would not include the concentration of water.
- The equilibrium constant is given a special symbol, K_w, and is known as the **autoionization constant for water.**
- Because the autoionization of water is the only source of hydronium and hydroxide ions in pure water, we know that $[H_3O^+]$ must equal $[OH^-]$ in pure water. Electrical conductivity measurements of pure water show that $[H_3O^+] = [OH^-] = 1.0 \times 10^{-7}$ M at 25 °C, so K_w has a value of 1.0×10^{-14} at 25 °C.

In pure water, the hydronium ion and hydroxide ion concentrations are equal, and the water is said to be neutral. If some acid or base is added to pure water, however, the equilibrium

$$2\ H_2O(\ell) \rightleftharpoons H_3O^+(aq) + OH^-(aq)$$

is disturbed. Adding acid raises the concentration of the H_3O^+ ions, so the solution is acidic. To oppose this increase, Le Chatelier's principle (◀ Section 16.6) predicts that a small fraction of the H_3O^+ ions will react with OH^- ions from water autoionization to form water. This lowers $[OH^-]$ until the product of $[H_3O^+]$ and $[OH^-]$ is again equal to 1.0×10^{-14} at 25 °C. Similarly, adding a base to pure water gives a basic solution because the OH^- ion concentration has increased. Le Chatelier's principle predicts that some of the added OH^- ions will react with H_3O^+ ions present in the solution from water autoionization, thereby lowering $[H_3O^+]$ until the value of the product $[H_3O^+]$ and $[OH^-]$ equals 1.0×10^{-14} at 25 °C.

Thus, for aqueous solutions at 25 °C, we can say that

- In a neutral solution, $[H_3O^+] = [OH^-]$.
  Both are equal to 1.0×10^{-7} M.

- In an acidic solution, $[H_3O^+] > [OH^-]$.
  $[H_3O^+] > 1.0 \times 10^{-7}$ M and $[OH^-] < 1.0 \times 10^{-7}$ M.

- In a basic solution, $[H_3O^+] < [OH^-]$.
  $[H_3O^+] < 1.0 \times 10^{-7}$ M and $[OH^-] > 1.0 \times 10^{-7}$ M.

Chemistry ⚛ Now™

Sign in at **www.cengage.com/login** and go to Chapter 17 Contents to see Screen 17.3 for a simulation of the effect of temperature on K_w.

■ **EXAMPLE 17.1 Ion Concentrations in a Solution of a Strong Base**

Problem What are the hydroxide and hydronium ion concentrations in a 0.0012 M solution of NaOH at 25 °C?

Strategy NaOH, a strong base, is 100% dissociated into ions in water, so we assume that the OH^- ion concentration is the same as the NaOH concentration. The H_3O^+ ion concentration can then be calculated using Equation 17.1.

Solution The initial concentration of OH^- is 0.0012 M.

$$0.0012\ \text{mol NaOH per liter} \rightarrow 0.0012\ \text{M Na}^+(aq) + 0.0012\ \text{M OH}^-(aq)$$

Substituting the OH^- concentration into Equation 17.1, we have

$$K_w = 1.0 \times 10^{-14} = [H_3O^+][OH^-] = [H_3O^+](0.0012)$$

and so

$$[H_3O^+] = \frac{1.0 \times 10^{-14}}{0.0012} = 8.3 \times 10^{-12} \text{ M}$$

Comment Why didn't we take into account the ions produced by water autoionization when we calculated the concentration of hydroxide ions? It should add OH^- and H_3O^+ ions to the solution. If x is equal to the concentration of OH^- ions generated by the autoionization of water, then, when equilibrium is achieved,

$[OH^-] = (0.0012 \text{ M} + OH^-$ from water autoionization)

$[OH^-] = (0.0012 \text{ M} + x)$

In pure water, the concentration of OH^- ion generated is 1.0×10^{-7} M. Le Chatelier's principle (◄ Section 16.6) suggests that the concentration should be even smaller when OH^- ions are already present in solution from NaOH; that is, x should be $<< 1.0 \times 10^{-7}$ M. This means x in the term $(0.0012 + x)$ is insignificant compared with 0.0012. (Following the rules for significant figures, the sum of 0.0012 and a number even smaller than 1.0×10^{-7} is 0.0012.) Thus, the equilibrium concentration of OH^- is equivalent to the concentration of NaOH in the solution.

Lastly, what about the Na^+ ion? As described later (page 774), alkali metal ions have no effect on the acidity or basicity of a solution.

EXERCISE 17.3 Hydronium Ion Concentration in a Solution of a Strong Acid

A solution of the strong acid HCl has $[HCl] = 4.0 \times 10^{-3}$ M. What are the concentrations of H_3O^+ and OH^- in this solution at 25 °C? (Recall that because HCl is a strong acid, it is 100% ionized in water.)

The pH Scale

The **pH** of a solution is defined as the negative of the base-10 logarithm (log) of the hydronium ion concentration (◄ Section 4.6, page 179).

$$pH = -\log[H_3O^+] \qquad \text{(4.3 and 17.2)}$$

In a similar way, we can define the pOH of a solution as the negative of the base-10 logarithm of the hydroxide ion concentration.

$$pOH = -\log[OH^-] \qquad \text{(17.3)}$$

In pure water, the hydronium and hydroxide ion concentrations are both 1.0×10^{-7} M. Therefore, for pure water at 25 °C

$$pH = -\log(1.0 \times 10^{-7}) = 7.00$$

In the same way, you can show that the pOH of pure water is also 7.00 at 25 °C.

If we take the negative logarithms of both sides of the expression $K_w = [H_3O^+][OH^-]$, we obtain another useful equation.

$$
\begin{aligned}
K_w = 1.0 \times 10^{-14} &= [H_3O^+][OH^-] \\
-\log K_w = -\log(1.0 \times 10^{-14}) &= -\log([H_3O^+][OH^-]) \\
pK_w = 14.00 &= -\log([H_3O^+]) + (-\log[OH^-]) \\
pK_w = 14.00 &= pH + pOH
\end{aligned}
\qquad \text{(17.4)}
$$

■ **The pX Scale**
In general, $-\log X = pX$, so $-\log K = pK$
$-\log[H_3O^+] = pH$
$-\log[OH^-] = pOH$

The sum of the pH and pOH of a solution must be equal to 14.00 at 25 °C.

As illustrated in Figures 4.11 and 17.1, solutions with pH less than 7.00 (at 25 °C) are acidic, whereas solutions with pH greater than 7.00 are basic. Solutions with pH = 7.00 at 25 °C are neutral.

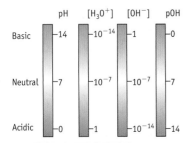

pH $[H_3O^+]$ $[OH^-]$ pOH

Basic   14 10^{-14} 1   0

Neutral   7 10^{-7} 10^{-7} 7

Acidic   0   1 10^{-14} 14

Active Figure 17.1 **pH and pOH.** This figure illustrates the relationship of hydronium ion and hydroxide ion concentrations and of pH and pOH.

Chemistry.ȯ.Now™ Sign in at www.cengage.com/login and go to the Chapter Contents menu to explore an interactive version of this figure accompanied by an exercise.

Calculating pH

The calculation of pH from the hydronium ion concentration, or the concentration of hydronium ion concentration from pH, was introduced in Chapter 4 (◄ page 179). Exercise 17.4 reviews those calculations.

Chemistry.ȯ.Now™

Sign in at **www.cengage.com/login** and go to Chapter 17 Contents to see Screen 17.4 for a simulation and tutorial on **using pH and pOH.**

EXERCISE 17.4 **Reviewing pH Calculations**

(a) What is the pH of a 0.0012 M NaOH solution at 25 °C?

(b) The pH of a diet soda is 4.32 at 25 °C. What are the hydronium and hydroxide ion concentrations in the soda?

(c) If the pH of a solution containing the strong base $Sr(OH)_2$ is 10.46 at 25 °C, what is the concentration of $Sr(OH)_2$?

17.4 Equilibrium Constants for Acids and Bases

In Chapter 3, it was stated that acids and bases can be divided roughly into those that are strong electrolytes (such as HCl, HNO_3, and NaOH) and those that are weak electrolytes (such as CH_3CO_2H and NH_3) (Figure 17.2) (◄ Table 3.2, Common Acids and Bases, page 132). Hydrochloric acid is a strong acid, so 100% of the acid ionizes to produce hydronium and chloride ions. In contrast, acetic acid and ammonia are weak electrolytes. They ionize to only a very small extent in water. For example, for acetic acid, the acid, its anion, and the hydronium ion are all present at equilibrium in solution, but the ions are present in very low concentration relative to the acid concentration.

One way to define the relative strengths of a series of acids would be to measure the pH of solutions of acids of equal concentration: The lower the pH, the greater the concentration of hydronium ion, the stronger the acid. Similarly, for a series

Strong Acid   **Weak Acid**   **Weak Base**

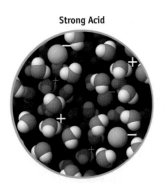 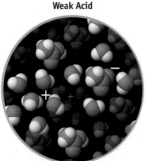 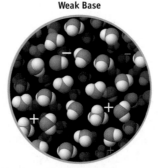 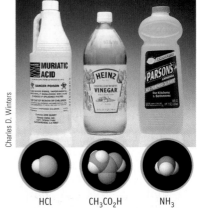

(a) HCl completely ionizes in aqueous solution.

(b) Acetic acid, CH_3CO_2H, ionizes only slightly in water.

(c) The weak base ammonia reacts to a small extent with water to give a weakly basic solution.

HCl CH_3CO_2H NH_3

Charles D. Winters

FIGURE 17.2 Strong and weak acids and bases. (a) Hydrochloric acid, a strong acid, is sold for household use as "muriatic acid." The acid completely ionizes in water. (b) Vinegar is a solution of acetic acid, a weak acid that ionizes only to a small extent in water. (c) Ammonia is a weak base, ionizing to a small extent in water.

of weak bases, [OH⁻] will increase, and the pH will increase as the bases become stronger.

- For a strong monoprotic acid, $[H_3O^+]$ in solution is equal to the original acid concentration. Similarly, for a strong monoprotic base, $[OH^-]$ will be equal to the original base concentration.
- For a weak acid, $[H_3O^+]$ will be much less than the original acid concentration. That is, $[H_3O^+]$ will be smaller than if the acid were a strong acid of the same concentration. Similarly, a weak base will give a smaller $[OH^-]$ than if the base were a strong base of the same concentration.
- For a series of weak monoprotic acids (of the type HA) of the same concentration, $[H_3O^+]$ will increase (and the pH will decline) as the acids become stronger. Similarly, for a series of weak bases, $[OH^-]$ will increase (and the pH will increase) as the bases become stronger.

The relative strength of an acid or base can also be expressed quantitatively with an equilibrium constant, often called an **ionization constant.** For the general acid HA, we can write

$$HA(aq) + H_2O(\ell) \rightleftharpoons H_3O^+(aq) + A^-(aq)$$

$$K_a = \frac{[H_3O^+][A^-]}{[HA]} \qquad\qquad \textbf{(17.5)}$$

where the equilibrium constant, K, has a subscript "a" to indicate that it is an equilibrium constant for an acid in water. For weak acids, the value of K_a is less than 1 because the product $[H_3O^+][A^-]$ is less than the equilibrium concentration of the weak acid [HA]. For a series of acids, the acid strength increases as the value of K_a increases.

Similarly, we can write the equilibrium expression for a weak base B in water. Here, we label K with a subscript "b." Its value is less than 1 for weak bases.

$$B(aq) + H_2O(\ell) \rightleftharpoons BH^+(aq) + OH^-(aq)$$

$$K_b = \frac{[BH^+][OH^-]}{[B]} \qquad\qquad \textbf{(17.6)}$$

Some acids and bases are listed in Table 17.3, each with its value of K_a or K_b. The following are important ideas concerning this table.

- Acids are listed in Table 17.3 at the left, and their conjugate bases are on the right.
- A large value of K indicates that ionization products are strongly favored, whereas a small value of K indicates that reactants are favored.
- The strongest acids are at the upper left. They have the largest K_a values. K_a values become smaller on descending the chart as the acid strength declines.
- The strongest bases are at the lower right. They have the largest K_b values. K_b values become larger on descending the chart as base strength increases.
- *The weaker the acid, the stronger its conjugate base.* That is, the smaller the value of K_a, the larger the value of K_b.
- Some acids or bases are listed as having K_a or K_b values that are large or very small. Acids that are stronger than H_3O^+ are completely ionized (HNO_3, for example), so their K_a values are "large." Their conjugate bases (such as NO_3^-) do not produce meaningful concentrations of OH^- ions, so their K_b values are "very small." Similar arguments follow for strong bases and their conjugate acids.

TABLE 17.3 Ionization Constants for Some Acids and Their Conjugate Bases at 25 °C

Acid Name	Acid	K_a	Base	K_b	Base Name
Perchloric acid	$HClO_4$	large	ClO_4^-	very small	perchlorate ion
Sulfuric acid	H_2SO_4	large	HSO_4^-	very small	hydrogen sulfate ion
Hydrochloric acid	HCl	large	Cl^-	very small	chloride ion
Nitric acid	HNO_3	large	NO_3^-	very small	nitrate ion
Hydronium ion	H_3O^+	1.0	H_2O	1.0×10^{-14}	water
Sulfurous acid	H_2SO_3	1.2×10^{-2}	HSO_3^-	8.3×10^{-13}	hydrogen sulfite ion
Hydrogen sulfate ion	HSO_4^-	1.2×10^{-2}	SO_4^{2-}	8.3×10^{-13}	sulfate ion
Phosphoric acid	H_3PO_4	7.5×10^{-3}	$H_2PO_4^-$	1.3×10^{-12}	dihydrogen phosphate ion
Hexaaquairon(III) ion	$[Fe(H_2O)_6]^{3+}$	6.3×10^{-3}	$[Fe(H_2O)_5OH]^{2+}$	1.6×10^{-12}	pentaaquahydroxoiron(III) ion
Hydrofluoric acid	HF	7.2×10^{-4}	F^-	1.4×10^{-11}	fluoride ion
Nitrous acid	HNO_2	4.5×10^{-4}	NO_2^-	2.2×10^{-11}	nitrite ion
Formic acid	HCO_2H	1.8×10^{-4}	HCO_2^-	5.6×10^{-11}	formate ion
Benzoic acid	$C_6H_5CO_2H$	6.3×10^{-5}	$C_6H_5CO_2^-$	1.6×10^{-10}	benzoate ion
Acetic acid	CH_3CO_2H	1.8×10^{-5}	$CH_3CO_2^-$	5.6×10^{-10}	acetate ion
Propanoic acid	$CH_3CH_2CO_2H$	1.3×10^{-5}	$CH_3CH_2CO_2^-$	7.7×10^{-10}	propanoate ion
Hexaaquaaluminum ion	$[Al(H_2O)_6]^{3+}$	7.9×10^{-6}	$[Al(H_2O)_5OH]^{2+}$	1.3×10^{-9}	pentaaquahydroxoaluminum ion
Carbonic acid	H_2CO_3	4.2×10^{-7}	HCO_3^-	2.4×10^{-8}	hydrogen carbonate ion
Hexaaquacopper(II) ion	$[Cu(H_2O)_6]^{2+}$	1.6×10^{-7}	$[Cu(H_2O)_5OH]^+$	6.3×10^{-8}	pentaaquahydroxocopper(II) ion
Hydrogen sulfide	H_2S	1×10^{-7}	HS^-	1×10^{-7}	hydrogen sulfide ion
Dihydrogen phosphate ion	$H_2PO_4^-$	6.2×10^{-8}	HPO_4^{2-}	1.6×10^{-7}	hydrogen phosphate ion
Hydrogen sulfite ion	HSO_3^-	6.2×10^{-8}	SO_3^{2-}	1.6×10^{-7}	sulfite ion
Hypochlorous acid	$HClO$	3.5×10^{-8}	ClO^-	2.9×10^{-7}	hypochlorite ion
Hexaaqualead(II) ion	$[Pb(H_2O)_6]^{2+}$	1.5×10^{-8}	$[Pb(H_2O)_5OH]^+$	6.7×10^{-7}	pentaaquahydroxolead(II) ion
Hexaaquacobalt(II) ion	$[Co(H_2O)_6]^{2+}$	1.3×10^{-9}	$[Co(H_2O)_5OH]^+$	7.7×10^{-6}	pentaaquahydroxocobalt(II) ion
Boric acid	$B(OH)_3(H_2O)$	7.3×10^{-10}	$B(OH)_4^-$	1.4×10^{-5}	tetrahydroxoborate ion
Ammonium ion	NH_4^+	5.6×10^{-10}	NH_3	1.8×10^{-5}	ammonia
Hydrocyanic acid	HCN	4.0×10^{-10}	CN^-	2.5×10^{-5}	cyanide ion
Hexaaquairon(II) ion	$[Fe(H_2O)_6]^{2+}$	3.2×10^{-10}	$[Fe(H_2O)_5OH]^+$	3.1×10^{-5}	pentaaquahydroxoiron(II) ion
Hydrogen carbonate ion	HCO_3^-	4.8×10^{-11}	CO_3^{2-}	2.1×10^{-4}	carbonate ion
Hexaaquanickel(II) ion	$[Ni(H_2O)_6]^{2+}$	2.5×10^{-11}	$[Ni(H_2O)_5OH]^+$	4.0×10^{-4}	pentaaquahydroxonickel(II) ion
Hydrogen phosphate ion	HPO_4^{2-}	3.6×10^{-13}	PO_4^{3-}	2.8×10^{-2}	phosphate ion
Water	H_2O	1.0×10^{-14}	OH^-	1.0	hydroxide ion
Hydrogen sulfide ion*	HS^-	1×10^{-19}	S^{2-}	1×10^5	sulfide ion
Ethanol	C_2H_5OH	very small	$C_2H_5O^-$	large	ethoxide ion
Ammonia	NH_3	very small	NH_2^-	large	amide ion
Hydrogen	H_2	very small	H^-	large	hydride ion

Increasing Acid Strength →

Increasing Base Strength →

*The values of K_a for HS^- and K_b for S^{2-} are estimates.

Problem Solving Tip 17.1 Strong or Weak?

How can you tell whether an acid or a base is weak? The easiest way is to remember those few that are strong. All others are probably weak.

Strong acids are:

Hydrohalic acids: HCl, HBr, and HI (but not HF)

Nitric acid: HNO_3

Sulfuric acid: H_2SO_4 (for loss of first H^+ only)

Perchloric acid: $HClO_4$

Some common strong bases include the following:

All Group 1A hydroxides: LiOH, NaOH, KOH, RbOH, CsOH

Group 2A hydroxides: $Sr(OH)_2$ and $Ba(OH)_2$ [$Mg(OH)_2$ and $Ca(OH)_2$ are not considered strong bases because they do not dissolve appreciably in water.]

To illustrate some of these ideas, let us compare some common acids and bases. For example, HF is a stronger acid than HClO, which is in turn stronger than HCO_3^-,

Decreasing acid strength →

HF	HClO	HCO_3^-
$K_a = 7.2 \times 10^{-4}$	$K_a = 3.5 \times 10^{-8}$	$K_a = 4.8 \times 10^{-11}$

and their conjugate bases become stronger from F^- to ClO^- to CO_3^{2-}.

Increasing base strength →

F^-	ClO^-	CO_3^{2-}
$K_b = 1.4 \times 10^{-11}$	$K_b = 2.9 \times 10^{-7}$	$K_b = 2.1 \times 10^{-4}$

Nature abounds in acids and bases (Figure 17.3). Many naturally occurring acids are based on the carboxyl group ($-CO_2H$), and a few are illustrated here. Notice that the organic portion of the *molecule* has an effect on its relative strength (as described further in Section 17.10).

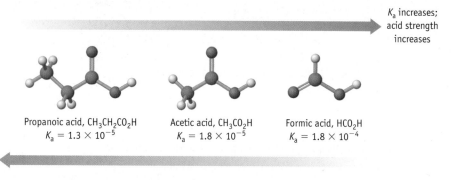

K_a increases; acid strength increases →

Propanoic acid, $CH_3CH_2CO_2H$ $K_a = 1.3 \times 10^{-5}$

Acetic acid, CH_3CO_2H $K_a = 1.8 \times 10^{-5}$

Formic acid, HCO_2H $K_a = 1.8 \times 10^{-4}$

← K_b of conjugate base increases

There are many naturally occurring weak bases as well as weak acids (Figure 17.3). Ammonia and its conjugate acid, the ammonium ion, are part of the nitrogen cycle in the environment (▶ page 951). Biological systems reduce nitrate ion to NH_3 and NH_4^+ and incorporate nitrogen into amino acids and proteins. Many bases are derived from NH_3 by replacement of the H atoms with organic groups.

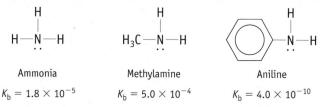

Ammonia $K_b = 1.8 \times 10^{-5}$

Methylamine $K_b = 5.0 \times 10^{-4}$

Aniline $K_b = 4.0 \times 10^{-10}$

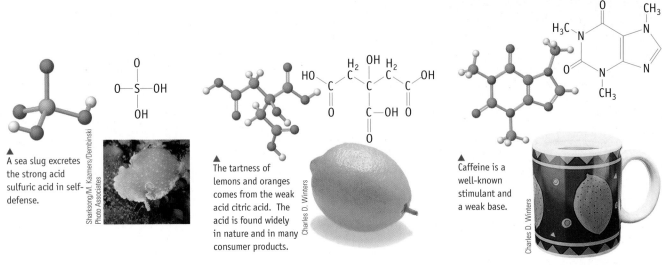

A sea slug excretes the strong acid sulfuric acid in self-defense.

Sharksong/M. Kazmers/Dembinski Photo Associates

The tartness of lemons and oranges comes from the weak acid citric acid. The acid is found widely in nature and in many consumer products.

Charles D. Winters

Caffeine is a well-known stimulant and a weak base.

Charles D. Winters

FIGURE 17.3 Natural acids and bases. Hundreds of acids and bases occur in nature. Our foods contain a wide variety, and biochemically important molecules are often acids and bases.

Ammonia is a weaker base than methylamine (K_b for $NH_3 < K_b$ for CH_3NH_2). This means that the conjugate acid of ammonia, NH_4^+ ($K_a = 5.6 \times 10^{-10}$) is stronger than the conjugate acid of methylamine ($CH_3NH_3^+$, $K_a = 2.0 \times 10^{-11}$).

Chemistry.ᐤ.Now™

Sign in at **www.cengage.com/login** and go to Chapter 17 Contents to see:
- Screen 17.5 for tutorials on **the pH of solutions of acids and bases**
- Screen 17.6 for a table of K_a and K_b values

EXERCISE 17.5 Strengths of Acids and Bases

Use Table 17.2 to answer the following questions.

(a) Which is the stronger acid, H_2SO_4 or H_2SO_3?

(b) Is benzoic acid, $C_6H_5CO_2H$, stronger or weaker than acetic acid?

(c) Which has the stronger conjugate base, acetic acid or boric acid?

(d) Which is the stronger base, ammonia or the acetate ion?

(e) Which has the stronger conjugate acid, ammonia or the acetate ion?

K_a Values for Polyprotic Acids

Like all polyprotic acids, phosphoric acid ionizes in a series of steps, three in this case.

First ionization step: $K_{a1} = 7.5 \times 10^{-3}$

$$H_3PO_4(aq) + H_2O(\ell) \rightleftharpoons H_2PO_4^-(aq) + H_3O^+(aq)$$

Second ionization step: $K_{a2} = 6.2 \times 10^{-8}$

$$H_2PO_4^-(aq) + H_2O(\ell) \rightleftharpoons HPO_4^{2-}(aq) + H_3O^+(aq)$$

Third ionization step: $K_{a3} = 3.6 \times 10^{-13}$

$$HPO_4^{2-}(aq) + H_2O(\ell) \rightleftharpoons PO_4^{3-}(aq) + H_3O^+(aq)$$

Notice that the K_a value for each successive step becomes smaller and smaller because it is more difficult to remove H^+ from a negatively charged ion, such as $H_2PO_4^-$, than from a neutral molecule, such as H_3PO_4. Similarly, the larger the negative charge of the anionic acid, the more difficult it is to remove H^+. Finally, also notice that for many inorganic polyprotic acids, K_a values become smaller by about 10^{-5} for each proton removed.

Aqueous Solutions of Salts

A number of the acids and bases listed in Table 17.2 are cations or anions. As described earlier, anions can act as Brønsted bases because they can accept a proton from an acid to form the conjugate acid of the base.

$$CO_3^{2-}(aq) + H_2O(\ell) \rightleftharpoons HCO_3^-(aq) + OH^-(aq)$$

$$K_b = 2.1 \times 10^{-4}$$

You should also notice that many metal cations in water are Brønsted acids.

$$[Al(H_2O)_6]^{3+}(aq) + H_2O(\ell) \rightleftharpoons [Al(H_2O)_5(OH)]^{2+}(aq) + H_3O^+(aq)$$

$$K_a = 7.9 \times 10^{-6}$$

Table 17.4 summarizes the acid–base properties of some of the common cations and anions. As you look over this table, notice the following points:

- Anions that are conjugate bases of strong acids (for example, Cl^- and NO_3^-) are such weak bases that they have no effect on solution pH.
- There are numerous basic anions (such as CO_3^{2-}). All are the conjugate bases of weak acids.
- The acid–base behavior of anions of polyprotic acids depends on the extent of deprotonation. For example, a fully deprotonated anion (such as CO_3^{2-}) will be basic. A partially deprotonated anion (such as HCO_3^-) is amphiprotic. Its behavior will depend on the other species in the reaction.
- Alkali metal and alkaline earth cations have no measurable effect on solution pH.
- Basic cations are conjugate bases of acidic cations such as $[Al(H_2O)_6]^{3+}$.
- Acidic cations are limited to metal cations with 2+ and 3+ charges and to ammonium ions (and their organic derivatives).
- All metal cations are hydrated in water. That is, they form ions such as $[M(H_2O)_6]^{n+}$. However, only when M is a 2+ or 3+ ion, particularly a transition metal ion, does the ion act as an acid.

Chemistry.⚛.Now™

Sign in at **www.cengage.com/login** and go to Chapter 17 Contents to see Screen 17.11 for a simulation showing **the pH of a number of cation/anion combinations.**

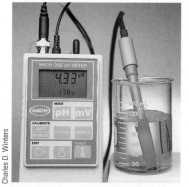

Charles D. Winters

Many aqueous metal cations are Brønsted acids. A pH measurement of a dilute solution of copper(II) sulfate shows that the solution is clearly acidic. Among the common cations, Al^{3+} and transition metal ions form acidic solutions in water.

TABLE 17.4 Acid and Base Properties of Some Ions in Aqueous Solution

	Neutral		Basic			Acidic
Anions	Cl^-	NO_3^-	$CH_3CO_2^-$	CN^-	SO_4^{2-}	HSO_4^-
	Br^-	ClO_4^-	HCO_2^-	PO_4^{3-}	HPO_4^{2-}	$H_2PO_4^-$
	I^-		CO_3^{2-}	HCO_3^-	SO_3^{2-}	HSO_3^-
			S^{2-}	HS^-	OCl^-	
			F^-	NO_2^-		
Cations	Li^+		$[Al(H_2O)_5(OH)]^{2+}$ (for example)			$[Al(H_2O)_6]^{3+}$ and hydrated transition metal cations (such as $[Fe(H_2O)_6]^{3+}$)
	Na^+	Ca^{2+}				
	K^+	Ba^{2+}				NH_4^+

■ **EXAMPLE 17.2 Acid–Base Properties of Salts**

Problem Decide whether each of the following will give rise to an acidic, basic, or neutral solution in water.

(a) $NaNO_3$ (d) $NaHCO_3$

(b) K_3PO_4 (e) NH_4F

(c) $FeCl_2$

Strategy First, decide on the cation and anion in each salt. Next, use Tables 17.3 and 17.4 to describe the properties of each ion.

Solution

(a) $NaNO_3$: This salt gives a neutral, aqueous solution (pH = 7). Neither the sodium ion, Na^+, nor the nitrate ion, NO_3^- (the very weak conjugate base of a strong acid), affects the solution pH.

(b) K_3PO_4: An aqueous solution of K_3PO_4 should be basic (pH > 7) because PO_4^{3-} is the conjugate base of the weak acid HPO_4^{2-}. The K^+ ion, like the Na^+ ion, does not affect the solution pH.

(c) $FeCl_2$: An aqueous solution of $FeCl_2$ should be weakly acidic (pH < 7). The Fe^{2+} ion in water, $[Fe(H_2O)_6]^{2+}$, is a Brønsted acid. In contrast, Cl^- is the very weak conjugate base of the strong acid HCl, so it does not contribute excess OH^- ions to the solution.

(d) $NaHCO_3$: Some additional information is needed concerning salts of amphiprotic anions such as HCO_3^-. Because they have an ionizable hydrogen, they can act as acids.

$$HCO_3^-(aq) + H_2O(\ell) \rightleftharpoons CO_3^{2-}(aq) + H_3O^+(aq) \qquad\qquad K_a = 4.8 \times 10^{-11}$$

They are also the conjugate bases of weak acids.

$$HCO_3^-(aq) + H_2O(\ell) \rightleftharpoons H_2CO_3(aq) + OH^-(aq) \qquad\qquad K_b = 2.4 \times 10^{-8}$$

Whether the solution is acidic or basic will depend on the relative magnitude of K_a and K_b. In the case of the hydrogen carbonate anion, K_b is larger than K_a, so $[OH^-]$ is larger than $[H_3O^+]$, and an aqueous solution of $NaHCO_3$ will be slightly basic.

(e) NH_4F: What happens if you have a salt based on an acidic cation and a basic anion? One example is ammonium fluoride. Here, the ammonium ion would decrease the pH, and the fluoride ion would increase the pH.

$$NH_4^+(aq) + H_2O(\ell) \rightleftharpoons H_3O^+(aq) + NH_3(aq) \qquad\qquad K_a(NH_4^+) = 5.6 \times 10^{-10}$$

$$F^-(aq) + H_2O(\ell) \rightleftharpoons HF(aq) + OH^-(aq) \qquad\qquad K_b(F^-) = 1.4 \times 10^{-11}$$

Because K_a (NH_4^+) > K_b (F^-), the ammonium ion is a stronger acid than the fluoride ion is a base. The resulting solution should be slightly acidic.

Comment There are two important points to notice here:

• Anions that are conjugate bases of strong acids—such as Cl^- and NO_3^-—have no effect on solution pH.

• For a salt that has an acidic cation and a basic anion, the pH of the solution will be determined by the ion that is the stronger acid or base of the two.

Problem Solving Tip 17.2   Aqueous Solutions of Salts

Because aqueous solutions of salts are found in our bodies and throughout our economy and environment, it is important to know how to predict their acid and base properties. Information on the pH of an aqueous solution of a salt is summarized in Table 17.4. Consider also the following examples:

Cation	Anion	pH of the Solution
From strong base (Na^+)	From strong acid (Cl^-)	= 7 (neutral)
From strong base (K^+)	From weak acid ($CH_3CO_2^-$)	> 7 (basic)
From weak base (NH_4^+)	From strong acid (Cl^-)	< 7 (acidic)
From any weak base (BH^+)	From any weak acid (A^-)	Depends on relative strengths of BH^+ and A^-

---

EXERCISE 17.6 Acid–Base Properties of Salts in Aqueous Solution

For each of the following salts in water, predict whether the pH will be greater than, less than, or equal to 7.

(a) KBr   (b) NH_4NO_3 (c) $AlCl_3$ (d) Na_2HPO_4

A Logarithmic Scale of Relative Acid Strength, pK_a

Many chemists and biochemists use a logarithmic scale to report and compare relative acid strengths.

$$pK_a = -\log K_a \qquad (17.7)$$

The pK_a of an acid is the negative log of the K_a value (just as pH is the negative log of the hydronium ion concentration). For example, acetic acid has a pK_a value of 4.74.

$$pK_a = -\log (1.8 \times 10^{-5}) = 4.74$$

The pK_a value becomes smaller as the acid strength increases.

—— Acid strength increases ⟶

Propanoic acid	Acetic acid	Formic acid
$CH_3CH_2CO_2H$	CH_3CO_2H	HCO_2H
$K_a = 1.3 \times 10^{-5}$	$K_a = 1.8 \times 10^{-5}$	$K_a = 1.8 \times 10^{-4}$
$pK_a = 4.89$	$pK_a = 4.74$	$pK_a = 3.74$

⟵ pK_a increases ——

EXERCISE 17.7 A Logarithmic Scale for Acid Strength, pK_a

(a) What is the pK_a value for benzoic acid, $C_6H_5CO_2H$?

(b) Is chloroacetic acid ($ClCH_2CO_2H$), $pK_a = 2.87$, a stronger or weaker acid than benzoic acid?

(c) What is the pK_a for the conjugate acid of ammonia? Is this acid stronger or weaker than acetic acid?

Relating the Ionization Constants for an Acid and Its Conjugate Base

Let us look again at Table 17.3. From the top of the table to the bottom, the strengths of the acids decline (K_a becomes smaller), and the strengths of their conjugate bases increase (the values of K_b increase). Examining a few cases shows that the product of K_a for an acid and K_b for its conjugate base is equal to a constant, specifically K_w.

$$K_a \times K_b = K_w \tag{17.8}$$

■ **A Relation Among pK Values** A useful relationship for an acid–conjugate base pair can be derived from Equation 17.8.

$$pK_w = pK_a + pK_b$$

Consider the specific case of the ionization of a weak acid, say HCN, and the interaction of its conjugate base, CN^-, with H_2O.

Weak acid:	$HCN(aq) + H_2O(\ell) \rightleftharpoons H_3O^+(aq) + CN^-(aq)$	$K_a = 4.0 \times 10^{-10}$
Conjugate base:	$CN^-(aq) + H_2O(\ell) \rightleftharpoons HCN(aq) + OH^-(aq)$	$K_b = 2.5 \times 10^{-5}$
	$2\ H_2O(\ell) \rightleftharpoons H_3O^+(aq) + OH^-(aq)$	$K_w = 1.0 \times 10^{-14}$

Adding the equations gives the chemical equation for the autoionization of water, and the numerical value is indeed 1.0×10^{-14}. That is,

$$K_a \times K_b = \left(\frac{[H_3O^+][\cancel{CN^-}]}{[\cancel{HCN}]} \right) \left(\frac{[\cancel{HCN}][OH^-]}{[\cancel{CN^-}]} \right) = [H_3O^+][OH^-] = K_w$$

Equation 17.8 is useful because K_b can be calculated from K_a. The value of K_b for the cyanide ion, for example, is

$$K_b \text{ for } CN^- = \frac{K_w}{K_a \text{ for HCN}} = \frac{1.0 \times 10^{-14}}{4.0 \times 10^{-10}} = 2.5 \times 10^{-5}$$

EXERCISE 17.8 Using the Equation $K_a \times K_b = K_w$

K_a for lactic acid, $CH_3CHOHCO_2H$, is 1.4×10^{-4}. What is K_b for the conjugate base of this acid, $CH_3CHOHCO_2^-$? Where does this base fit in Table 17.3?

17.5 Predicting the Direction of Acid–Base Reactions

According to the Brønsted–Lowry theory, all acid–base reactions can be written as equilibria involving the acid and base and their conjugates.

$$\text{Acid} + \text{Base} \rightleftharpoons \text{Conjugate base of the acid} + \text{Conjugate acid of the base}$$

In Section 17.4, we used equilibrium constants to provide quantitative information about the relative strengths of acids and bases. Now we want to show how the constants can be used to decide whether a particular acid–base reaction is product- or reactant-favored at equilibrium.

Hydrochloric acid is a strong acid. Its equilibrium constant for reaction with water is very large, with the equilibrium effectively lying completely to the right.

$$HCl(aq) + H_2O(\ell) \rightleftharpoons H_3O^+(aq) + Cl^-(aq)$$
$$\text{Strong acid } (\approx 100\% \text{ ionized}), K \gg 1$$
$$[H_3O^+] \approx \text{initial concentration of the acid}$$

■ **K and Product- and Reactant-Favored Reactions** Reactions with an equilibrium constant greater than 1 are said to be product-favored at equilibrium. Those with $K < 1$ are reactant-favored at equilibrium.

Of the two acids here, HCl is stronger than H_3O^+. Of the two bases, H_2O and Cl^-, water is the stronger base and wins out in the competition for the proton. Thus, the equilibrium lies to the side of the chemical equation having the weaker acid and base.

In contrast to HCl and other strong acids, acetic acid, a *weak* acid, ionizes to only a very small extent (Table 17.3).

$$CH_3CO_2H(aq) + H_2O(\ell) \rightleftharpoons H_3O^+(aq) + CH_3CO_2^-(aq)$$

Weak acid (< 100% ionized), $K = 1.8 \times 10^{-5}$

$[H_3O^+] \ll$ initial concentration of the acid

When equilibrium is achieved in a 0.1 M aqueous solution of CH_3CO_2H, the concentrations of $H_3O^+(aq)$ and $CH_3CO_2^-(aq)$ are each only about 0.001 M. Approximately 99% of the acetic acid is not ionized.

conjugate pair 1

conjugate pair 2

$CH_3CO_2H(aq)$	+	$H_2O(\ell)$	$\rightleftharpoons$ $K < 1$	$H_3O^+(aq)$	+	$CH_3CO_2^-(aq)$
Weaker acid than H_3O^+		Weaker base than $CH_3CO_2^-$		Stronger acid than CH_3CO_2H		Stronger base than H_2O

Again, the equilibrium lies toward the side of the reaction having the weaker acid and base.

These two examples of the relative extent of acid–base reactions illustrate a general principle: *All proton transfer reactions proceed from the stronger acid and base to the weaker acid and base.* Using this principle and Table 17.3, you can predict which reactions are product-favored and which are reactant-favored. Consider the possible reaction of phosphoric acid and acetate ion to give acetic acid and the dihydrogen phosphate ion. Table 17.3 informs us that H_3PO_4 is a stronger acid ($K_a = 7.5 \times 10^{-3}$) than acetic acid ($K_a = 1.8 \times 10^{-5}$), and the acetate ion ($K_b = 5.6 \times 10^{-10}$) is a stronger base than the dihydrogen phosphate ion ($K_b = 1.3 \times 10^{-12}$).

Brønsted acids

Brønsted bases

$H_3PO_4(aq)$	+	$CH_3CO_2^-(aq)$	$\rightleftharpoons$	$H_2PO_4^-(aq)$	+	$CH_3CO_2H(aq)$
Stronger acid than CH_3CO_2H		Stronger base than $H_2PO_4^-$		Weaker base than $CH_3CO_2^-$		Weaker acid than H_3PO_4

Thus, mixing phosphoric acid with sodium acetate would produce a significant amount of dihydrogen phosphate ion and acetic acid. That is, the equilibrium is predicted to lie to the right because the reaction proceeds from the stronger acid–base combination to the weaker acid–base combination.

Chemistry.Now™

Sign in at **www.cengage.com/login** and go to Chapter 17 Contents to see Screen 17.7 for a simulation on **predicting the direction of acid–base reactions.**

■ **EXAMPLE 17.3** **Reactions of Acids and Bases**

Problem Write a balanced, net ionic equation for the reaction that occurs between acetic acid and sodium bicarbonate. Decide whether the equilibrium lies predominantly to the left or to the right.

Strategy First, identify the products of the acid–base reaction (which arise by H^+ transfer from the acid to the base). Next, identify the two acids (or the two bases) in the reaction. Finally, use Table 17.3 to decide which is the weaker of the two acids (or the weaker of the two bases). The reaction will proceed from the stronger acid (or base) to the weaker acid (or base).

Reaction of vinegar and baking soda. This reaction involves the weak acid acetic acid and the weak base HCO_3^- from sodium hydrogen carbonate. Based on the values of the equilibrium constants, the reaction is predicted to proceed to the right to produce acetate ion, CO_2, and water.

Charles D. Winters

Solution Acetic acid is clearly one acid involved (and its conjugate base is the acetate ion, $CH_3CO_2^-$). The other reactant, $NaHCO_3$, is a water-soluble salt that forms Na^+ and HCO_3^- ions in water. Because acetic acid can function only as an acid, the HCO_3^- ion in this case must be the Brønsted base. Thus, hydrogen ion transfer from the acid to the base (HCO_3^- ion) could lead to the following net ionic equation:

$$CH_3CO_2H(aq) + HCO_3^-(aq) \rightleftharpoons CH_3CO_2^-(aq) + H_2CO_3(aq)$$

According to Table 17.3, H_2CO_3 is a weaker acid ($K_a = 4.2 \times 10^{-7}$) than CH_3CO_2H ($K_a = 1.8 \times 10^{-5}$), and $CH_3CO_2^-$ is a weaker base ($K_b = 5.6 \times 10^{-10}$) than HCO_3^- ($K_b = 2.4 \times 10^{-8}$). The reaction favors the side having the weaker acid and base—that is, the right side.

Comment The reaction of acetic acid and $NaHCO_3$ favors the weaker acid (H_2CO_3) and base ($CH_3CO_2^-$). In the photograph in the margin, you see that the product, H_2CO_3, also dissociates into CO_2 and H_2O because the CO_2 bubbles out of the solution: the equilibrium lies far to the right.

$$H_2CO_3(aq) \rightleftharpoons CO_2(g) + H_2O(\ell)$$

See the discussion of gas-forming reactions in Chapter 3 and of Le Chatelier's principle in Section 14.3.

EXERCISE 17.9 Predicting the Direction of an Acid–Base Reaction

(a) Which is the stronger Brønsted acid, HCO_3^- or NH_4^+? Which has the stronger conjugate base?

(b) Is a reaction between HCO_3^- ions and NH_3 product- or reactant-favored?

$$HCO_3^-(aq) + NH_3(aq) \rightleftharpoons CO_3^{2-}(aq) + NH_4^+(aq)$$

(c) You mix solutions of sodium hydrogen phosphate and ammonia. The net ionic equation for a possible reaction is

$$HPO_4^{2-}(aq) + NH_3(aq) \rightleftharpoons PO_4^{3-}(aq) + NH_4^+(aq)$$

Does the equilibrium lie to the left or to the right in this reaction?

17.6 Types of Acid–Base Reactions

The reaction of hydrochloric acid and sodium hydroxide is the classic example of a strong acid–strong base reaction, whereas the reaction of citric acid and bicarbonate ion represents the reaction of a weak acid and weak base (Figure 17.4). There are four general types of acid–base reactions.

Type of Acid–Base Reaction	Example
Strong acid + strong base	HCl and NaOH
Strong acid + weak base	HCl and NH_3
Weak acid + strong base	CH_3CO_2H and NaOH
Weak acid + weak base	Citric acid and HCO_3^-

Because acid–base reactions are among the most important classes of chemical reactions, it is useful for you to know the outcome of the various types of these reactions (Table 17.5).

TABLE 17.5 Characteristics of Acid–Base Reactions

Type	Example	Net Ionic Equation	Species Present after Equal Molar Amounts Are Mixed; pH
Strong acid + strong base	HCl + NaOH	$H_3O^+(aq) + OH^-(aq) \rightleftharpoons 2\ H_2O(\ell)$	Cl^-, Na^+, pH = 7
Strong acid + weak base	HCl + NH_3	$H_3O^+(aq) + NH_3(aq) \rightleftharpoons NH_4^+(aq) + H_2O(\ell)$	Cl^-, NH_4^+, pH < 7
Weak acid + strong base	HCO_2H + NaOH	$HCO_2H(aq) + OH^-(aq) \rightleftharpoons HCO_2^-(aq) + H_2O(\ell)$	HCO_2^-, Na^+, pH > 7
Weak acid + weak base	HCO_2H + NH_3	$HCO_2H(aq) + NH_3(aq) \rightleftharpoons HCO_2^-(aq) + NH_4^+(aq)$	HCO_2^-, NH_4^+, pH dependent on K_a and K_b of conjugate acid and base

The Reaction of a Strong Acid with a Strong Base

Strong acids and bases are effectively 100% ionized in solution. Therefore, the total ionic equation for the reaction of HCl (strong acid) and NaOH (strong base) is

$$H_3O^+(aq) + Cl^-(aq) + Na^+(aq) + OH^-(aq) \rightleftharpoons 2\ H_2O(\ell) + Na^+(aq) + Cl^-(aq)$$

which leads to the following net ionic equation

$$H_3O^+(aq) + OH^-(aq) \rightleftharpoons 2\ H_2O(\ell) \qquad K = 1/K_w = 1.0 \times 10^{14}$$

The net ionic equation for the reaction of any strong acid with any strong base is always simply the union of hydronium ion and hydroxide ion to give water (◀ Section 3.7). Because this reaction is the reverse of the autoionization of water, it has an equilibrium constant of $1/K_w$. This very large value of K shows that, for all practical purposes, the reactants are completely consumed to form products. Thus, if equal numbers of moles of NaOH and HCl are mixed, the result is just a solution of NaCl in water. The constituents of NaCl, Na^+ and Cl^- ions, which arise from a strong base and a strong acid, respectively, produce a neutral aqueous solution. For this reason, reactions of strong acids and bases are often called "neutralizations."

> Mixing equal amounts (moles) of a strong base with a strong acid produces a neutral solution (pH = 7.00 at 25 °C).

The Reaction of a Weak Acid with a Strong Base

Consider the reaction of the naturally occurring weak acid formic acid, HCO_2H, with sodium hydroxide. The net ionic equation is

$$HCO_2H(aq) + OH^-(aq) \rightleftharpoons H_2O(\ell) + HCO_2^-(aq)$$

In the reaction of formic acid with NaOH, OH^- is a much stronger base than HCO_2^- ($K_b = 5.6 \times 10^{-11}$), and the reaction is predicted to proceed to the right. If equal amounts of weak acid and base are mixed, the final solution will contain sodium formate ($NaHCO_2$), a salt that is 100% dissociated in water. The Na^+ ion is the cation of a strong base and so gives a neutral solution. The formate ion, however, is the conjugate base of a weak acid (Table 17.3), so the solution is basic. This example leads to a useful general conclusion:

> Mixing equal amounts (moles) of a strong base with a weak acid produces a salt whose anion is the conjugate base of the weak acid. The solution is basic, with the pH depending on K_b for the anion.

The Reaction of a Strong Acid with a Weak Base

The net ionic equation for the reaction of the strong acid HCl and the weak base NH_3 is

$$H_3O^+(aq) + NH_3(aq) \rightleftharpoons H_2O(\ell) + NH_4^+(aq)$$

The hydronium ion, H_3O^+, is a much stronger acid than NH_4^+ ($K_a = 5.6 \times 10^{-10}$), and NH_3 is a stronger base ($K_b = 1.8 \times 10^{-5}$) than H_2O. Therefore, reaction is predicted to proceed to the right and essentially to completion. Thus, after mixing equal amounts of HCl and NH_3, the solution contains the salt ammonium chloride, NH_4Cl. The Cl^- ion has no effect on the solution pH (Tables 17.3 and 17.4). However, the NH_4^+ ion is the conjugate acid of the weak base NH_3, so the solution at the conclusion of the reaction is acidic. In general, we can conclude that

> Mixing equal amounts (moles) of a strong acid and a weak base produces a salt whose cation is the conjugate acid of the weak base. The solution is acidic, with the pH depending on K_a for the cation.

FIGURE 17.4 Reaction of a weak acid with a weak base. The bubbles coming from the tablet are carbon dioxide. This arises from the reaction of a weak Brønsted acid (citric acid) with a weak Brønsted base (HCO_3^-). The reaction is driven to completion by gas evolution.

■ **Formic Acid + NaOH** The equilibrium constant for the reaction of formic acid and sodium hydroxide is 1.8×10^{10}. Can you confirm this? (See Study Question 17.97.)

■ **Ammonia + HCl** The equilibrium constant for the reaction of a strong acid with aqueous ammonia is 1.8×10^9. Can you confirm this? (See Study Question 17.96.)

A weak acid reacting with a weak base. Baking powder contains the weak acid calcium dihydrogen phosphate, $Ca(H_2PO_4)_2$. This can react with the basic HCO_3^- ion in baking soda to give HPO_4^{2-}, CO_2 gas, and water.

■ *K* for Reaction of Weak Acid and Weak Base The equilibrium constant for the reaction between a weak acid and a weak base is $K_{net} = (K_a \cdot K_b)/K_w$. Can you confirm this? (See Study Question 17.121.)

 Module 22

The Reaction of a Weak Acid with a Weak Base

If acetic acid, a weak acid, is mixed with ammonia, a weak base, the following reaction occurs.

$$CH_3CO_2H(aq) + NH_3(aq) \rightleftharpoons NH_4^+(aq) + CH_3CO_2^-(aq)$$

You know that the reaction is product-favored because CH_3CO_2H is a stronger acid than NH_4^+ and NH_3 is a stronger base than $CH_3CO_2^-$ (Table 17.3). Thus, if equal amounts of the acid and base are mixed, the resulting solution contains ammonium acetate, $NH_4CH_3CO_2$. Is this solution acidic or basic? On page 775 you learned that this depends on the relative values of K_a for the conjugate acid (here, NH_4^+; $K_a = 5.6 \times 10^{-10}$) and K_b for the conjugate base (here, $CH_3CO_2^-$; $K_b = 5.6 \times 10^{-10}$). In this case, the values of K_a and K_b are the same, so the solution is predicted to be neutral.

Mixing equal amounts (moles) of a weak acid and a weak base produces a salt whose cation is the conjugate acid of the weak base and whose anion is the conjugate base of the weak acid. The solution pH depends on the relative K_a and K_b values.

EXERCISE 17.10 Acid–Base Reactions

(a) Equal amounts (moles) of HCl(aq) and NaCN(aq) are mixed. Is the resulting solution acidic, basic, or neutral?

(b) Equal amounts (moles) of acetic acid and sodium sulfite, Na_2SO_3, are mixed. Is the resulting solution acidic, basic, or neutral?

17.7 Calculations with Equilibrium Constants

Determining *K* from Initial Concentrations and Measured pH

The K_a and K_b values found in Table 17.3 and in the more extensive tables in Appendices H and I were all determined by experiment. There are several experimental methods available, but one approach, illustrated by the following example, is to determine the pH of the solution.

Chemistry.⚛.Now™

Sign in at **www.cengage.com/login** and go to Chapter 17 Contents to see Screen 17.8 for a tutorial on determining K_a and K_b values.

■ EXAMPLE 17.4 Calculating a K_a Value from a Measured pH

Problem A 0.10 M aqueous solution of lactic acid, $CH_3CHOHCO_2H$, has a pH of 2.43. What is the value of K_a for lactic acid?

Strategy To calculate K_a, we must know the equilibrium concentration of each species. The pH of the solution directly tells us the equilibrium concentration of H_3O^+, and we can derive the other equilibrium concentrations from this. These are used to calculate K_a.

Solution The equation for the equilibrium interaction of lactic acid with water is

$$CH_3CHOHCO_2H(aq) + H_2O(\ell) \rightleftharpoons CH_3CHOHCO_2^-(aq) + H_3O^+(aq)$$

    Lactic acid   Lactate ion

and the equilibrium constant expression is

$$K_a \text{ (lactic acid)} = \frac{[H_3O^+][CH_3CHOHCO_2^-]}{[CH_3CHOHCO_2H]}$$

    Sign in at **www.cengage.com/login** to download the Go Chemistry module for this section or go to **www.ichapters.com** to purchase modules.

We begin by converting the pH to $[H_3O^+]$.

$$[H_3O^+] = 10^{-pH} = 10^{-2.43} = 3.7 \times 10^{-3} \text{ M}$$

Next, prepare an ICE table of the concentrations in the solution before equilibrium is established, the change that occurs as the reaction proceeds to equilibrium, and the concentrations when equilibrium has been achieved. (See Examples 16.2–16.5.)

Equilibrium	$CH_3CHOHCO_2H + H_2O \rightleftharpoons CH_3CHOHCO_2^- + H_3O^+$		
Initial (M)	0.10	0	0
Change (M)	$-x$	$+x$	$+x$
Equilibrium (M)	$(0.10 - x)$	x	x

Lactic acid, $CH_3CHOHCO_2H$

Lactic acid, $CH_3CHOHCO_2H$. Lactic acid is a weak monoprotic acid that occurs naturally in sour milk and arises from metabolism in the human body.

The following points can be made concerning the ICE table.

- The quantity x represents the equilibrium concentrations of hydronium ion and lactate ion. That is, at equilibrium $x = [H_3O^+] = [CH_3CHOHCO_2^-] = 3.7 \times 10^{-3}$ M.

- By stoichiometry, x is also the quantity of acid that ionized on proceeding to equilibrium. With these points in mind, we can calculate K_a for lactic acid.

$$K_a \text{ (lactic acid)} = \frac{[H_3O^+][CH_3CHOHCO_2^-]}{[CH_3CHOHCO_2H]}$$

$$= \frac{(3.7 \times 10^{-3})(3.7 \times 10^{-3})}{0.10 - 0.0037} = 1.4 \times 10^{-4}$$

Comparing this value of K_a with others in Table 17.3, we see it is similar to formic acid in its strength.

Comment Hydronium ion, H_3O^+, is present in solution from lactic acid ionization and from water autoionization. Le Chatelier's principle informs us that the H_3O^+ added to the water by lactic acid will suppress the H_3O^+ coming from the water autoionization. However, because $[H_3O^+]$ from water must be less than 10^{-7} M, the pH is almost completely a reflection of H_3O^+ from lactic acid. (See Example 17.1.)

EXERCISE 17.11 Calculating a K_a Value from a Measured pH

A solution prepared from 0.055 mol of butanoic acid dissolved in sufficient water to give 1.0 L of solution has a pH of 2.72. Determine K_a for butanoic acid. The acid ionizes according to the balanced equation

$$CH_3CH_2CH_2CO_2H(aq) + H_2O(\ell) \rightleftharpoons H_3O^+(aq) + CH_3CH_2CH_2CO_2^-(aq)$$

There is an important point to notice in Example 17.4. The lactic acid concentration at equilibrium was given by $(0.10 - x)$ where x was found to be 3.7×10^{-3} M. By the usual rules governing significant figures $(0.10 - 0.0037)$ is equal to 0.10. The acid is weak, so very little of it ionizes (approximately 4%), and the equilibrium concentration of lactic acid is essentially equal to the initial acid concentration. Neglecting to subtract 0.0037 from 0.10 has no effect on the answer to two significant figures.

Like lactic acid, most weak acids (HA) are so weak that the equilibrium concentration of the acid, [HA], is effectively its initial concentration (= $[HA]_0$). This leads to the useful conclusion that the denominator in the equilibrium constant expression for dilute solutions of most weak acids is simply $[HA]_0$, the original or initial concentration of the weak acid.

$$HA(aq) + H_2O(\ell) \rightleftharpoons H_3O^+(aq) + A^-(aq)$$

$$K_a = \frac{[H_3O^+][A^-]}{[HA]_0 - [H_3O^+]} \approx \frac{[H_3O^+][A^-]}{[HA]_0}$$

Analysis shows that

> The approximation that $[HA]_{equilibrium}$ is effectively equal to $[HA]_0$
> $([HA]_{equilibrium} = [HA]_0 - [H_3O^+] \approx [HA]_0)$
> is valid whenever $[HA]_0$ is greater than or equal to $100 \cdot K_a$.

This is the same approximation we derived in Chapter 16 when deciding whether we needed to solve quadratic equations exactly (◄ Problem Solving Tip 16.1).

What Is the pH of an Aqueous Solution of a Weak Acid or Base?

Knowing values of the equilibrium constants for weak acids and bases enables us to calculate the pH of a solution of a weak acid or base.

Chemistry.Now™

Sign in at **www.cengage.com/login** and go to Chapter 17 Contents to see Screen 17.9 for a tutorial on **estimating the pH of weak acid solutions.**

EXAMPLE 17.5 Calculating Equilibrium Concentrations and pH from K_a

Problem Calculate the pH of a 0.020 M solution of benzoic acid ($C_6H_5CO_2H$) if $K_a = 6.3 \times 10^{-5}$ for the acid.

$$C_6H_5CO_2H(aq) + H_2O(\ell) \rightleftharpoons H_3O^+(aq) + C_6H_5CO_2^-(aq)$$

Strategy This is similar to Examples 16.5 and 16.6, where we wanted to find the concentration of a reaction product. The strategy is the same: designate the quantity of product (here $[H_3O^+]$) by x, and derive the other concentrations from that starting point.

Solution Organize the information in an ICE table

Equilibrium	$C_6H_5CO_2H + H_2O \rightleftharpoons C_6H_5CO_2^- + H_3O^+$		
Initial (M)	0.020	0	0
Change (M)	$-x$	$+x$	$+x$
Equilibrium (M)	$(0.020 - x)$	x	x

According to reaction stoichiometry,

$$[H_3O^+] = [C_6H_5CO_2^-] = x \text{ at equilibrium}$$

Stoichiometry also tells us that the quantity of acid ionized is x. Thus, the benzoic acid concentration at equilibrium is

$$[C_6H_5CO_2H] = \text{initial acid quantity} - \text{quantity of acid that ionized}$$
$$[C_6H_5CO_2H] = [C_6H_5CO_2H]_0 - x$$
$$[C_6H_5CO_2H] = 0.020 - x$$

Substituting these equilibrium concentrations into the K_a expression, we have

$$K_a = \frac{[H_3O^+][C_6H_5CO_2^-]}{[C_6H_5CO_2H]}$$
$$6.3 \times 10^{-5} = \frac{(x)(x)}{0.020 - x}$$

The value of x is small compared with 0.020 (because $[HA]_0 > 100 \cdot K_a$; 0.020 M $> 6.3 \times 10^{-3}$). Therefore,

$$K_a = 6.3 \times 10^{-5} = \frac{x^2}{0.020}$$

Solving for x, we have

$$x = \sqrt{K_a \times (0.020)} = 0.0011 \text{ M}$$

and we find that

$$[H_3O^+] = [C_6H_5CO_2^-] = 0.0011 \text{ M}$$

and

$$[C_6H_5CO_2H] = (0.020 - x) = 0.019 \text{ M}$$

Finally, the pH of the solution is found to be

$$\text{pH} = -\log(1.1 \times 10^{-3}) = \boxed{2.96}$$

Comment Let us think again about the result. Because benzoic acid is weak, we made the approximation that $(0.020 - x) \approx 0.020$. If we do not make the approximation and instead solve the exact expression, $x = [H_3O^+] = 1.1 \times 10^{-3}$ M. This is the same answer to two significant figures that we obtained from the "approximate" expression. Finally, notice that we again ignored any H_3O^+ that arises from water ionization.

■ **EXAMPLE 17.6 Calculating Equilibrium Concentrations and pH from K_a and Using the Method of Successive Approximations**

Problem What is the pH of a 0.0010 M solution of formic acid? What is the concentration of formic acid at equilibrium? The acid is moderately weak, with $K_a = 1.8 \times 10^{-4}$.

$$HCO_2H(aq) + H_2O(\ell) \rightleftharpoons HCO_2^-(aq) + H_3O^+(aq)$$

Strategy This is similar to Example 17.5, except that an approximate solution will not be possible.

Solution The ICE table is shown here.

Equilibrium	$HCO_2H + H_2O \rightleftharpoons HCO_2^- + H_3O^+$		
Initial (M)	0.0010	0	0
Change (M)	$-x$	$+x$	$+x$
Equilibrium (M)	$(0.0010 - x)$	x	x

Substituting the values in the table into the K_a expression we have

$$K_a = \frac{[H_3O^+][HCO_2^-]}{[HCO_2H]} = 1.8 \times 10^{-4} = \frac{(x)(x)}{0.0010 - x}$$

Formic acid is a weak acid because it has a value of K_a much less than 1. In this example, however, $[HA]_0$ ($= 0.0010$ M) is *not* greater than $100 \cdot K_a$ ($= 1.8 \times 10^{-2}$), so the usual approximation is not reasonable. Thus, we have to find the equilibrium concentrations by solving the "exact" expression. This can be solved with the quadratic formula (page 740) or by successive approximations (Appendix A). Let us use the successive approximation method here.

To use the successive approximations approach, begin by solving the approximate expression for x.

$$1.8 \times 10^{-4} = \frac{(x)(x)}{0.0010}$$

Solving this, we find $x = 4.2 \times 10^{-4}$. Put this value into the expression for x in the denominator of the exact expression.

$$1.8 \times 10^{-4} = \frac{(x)(x)}{0.0010 - x} = \frac{(x)(x)}{0.0010 - 4.2 \times 10^{-4}}$$

Solving this equation for x, we now find $x = 3.2 \times 10^{-4}$. Again, put this value into the denominator, and solve for x.

$$1.8 \times 10^{-4} = \frac{(x)(x)}{0.0010 - x} = \frac{(x)(x)}{0.0010 - 3.2 \times 10^{-4}}$$

Continue this procedure until the value of x does not change from one cycle to the next. In this case, two more steps give us the result that

$$x = [H_3O^+] = [HCO_2^-] = 3.4 \times 10^{-4} \text{ M}$$

Thus,

$$[HCO_2H] = 0.0010 - x \approx 0.0007 \text{ M}$$

and the pH of the formic acid solution is

$$pH = -\log (3.4 \times 10^{-4}) = \boxed{3.47}$$

Comment If we would have used the approximate expression to find the H_3O^+ concentration, we would have obtained a value of $[H_3O^+] = 4.2 \times 10^{-4}$ M. A simplifying assumption led to a large error, about 24%. The approximate solution fails in this case because (a) the acid concentration is small and (b) the acid is not all that weak. These made invalid the approximation that $[HA]_{equilibrium} \approx [HA]_0$.

EXERCISE 17.12 Calculating Equilibrium Concentrations and pH from K_a

What are the equilibrium concentrations of acetic acid, the acetate ion, and H_3O^+ for a 0.10 M solution of acetic acid ($K_a = 1.8 \times 10^{-5}$)? What is the pH of the solution?

EXERCISE 17.13 Calculating Equilibrium Concentrations and pH from K_a

What are the equilibrium concentrations of HF, F^- ion, and H_3O^+ ion in a 0.015 M solution of HF? What is the pH of the solution?

Just as acids can be molecular species or ions, so too can bases be molecular or ionic (Figures 17.3–17.5). Many molecular bases are based on nitrogen, with ammonia being the simplest. Many other nitrogen-containing bases occur naturally; caffeine and nicotine are two that are well known. The anionic conjugate bases of weak acids make up another group of bases. The following example describes the calculation of the pH for a solution of sodium acetate.

Chemistry.Now™

Sign in at **www.cengage.com/login** and go to Chapter 17 Contents to see:
- Screen 17.7 for a simulation of **the prediction of the direction of a number of acid–base reactions**
- Screen 17.11 for a simulation **of acid–base properties of salts**

FIGURE 17.5 Examples of weak bases. Weak bases in water include molecules having one or more N atoms capable of accepting an H^+ ion. Anionic bases such as benzoate and phosphate are conjugate bases of weak acids.

Benzoate ion, $C_6H_5CO_2^-$
$K_b = 1.6 \times 10^{-10}$

Phosphate ion, PO_4^{3-}
$K_b = 2.8 \times 10^{-2}$

Ammonia, NH_3
$K_b = 1.8 \times 10^{-5}$

Caffeine, $C_8H_{10}N_4O_2$
$K_b = 2.5 \times 10^{-4}$

Charles D. Winters

Problem What is the pH of a 0.015 M solution of sodium acetate, $NaCH_3CO_2$?

Strategy Sodium acetate will be basic in water because the acetate ion, the conjugate base of a weak acid, acetic acid, reacts with water to form OH^- (Tables 17.3 and 17.4). (Note that the sodium ion of sodium acetate does not affect the solution pH.) We shall calculate the hydroxide ion concentration in manner parallel with that in Example 17.5.

Solution The value of K_b for the acetate ion is 5.6×10^{-10} (Table 17.3).

$$CH_3CO_2^-(aq) + H_2O(\ell) \rightleftharpoons CH_3CO_2H(aq) + OH^-(aq)$$

Set up an ICE table to summarize the initial and equilibrium concentrations of the species in solution.

Equilibrium	$CH_3CO_2^- + H_2O$ $\rightleftharpoons$	CH_3CO_2H +	OH^-
Initial (M)	0.015	0	0
Change (M)	$-x$	$+x$	$+x$
Equilibrium (M)	$(0.015 - x)$	x	x

Next, substitute the values in the table into the K_b expression.

$$K_b = 5.6 \times 10^{-10} = \frac{[CH_3CO_2H][OH^-]}{[CH_3CO_2^-]} = \frac{x^2}{0.015 - x}$$

The acetate ion is a weak base, as reflected by the very small value of K_b. Therefore, we assume that x, the concentration of hydroxide ion generated by reaction of acetate ion with water, is very small, and we use the approximate expression to solve for x.

$$K_b = 5.6 \times 10^{-10} = \frac{x^2}{0.015}$$
$$x = [OH^-] = [CH_3CO_2H] = \sqrt{(5.6 \times 10^{-10})(0.015)} = 2.9 \times 10^{-6} \ M$$

To calculate the pH of the solution, we need the hydronium ion concentration. In aqueous solutions, it is always true that, at 25 °C,

$$K_w = 1.0 \times 10^{-14} = [H_3O^+][OH^-]$$

Therefore,

$$[H_3O^+] = \frac{K_w}{[OH^-]} = \frac{1.0 \times 10^{-14}}{2.9 \times 10^{-6}} = 3.5 \times 10^{-9} \ M$$
$$pH = -\log(3.5 \times 10^{-9}) = 8.46$$

The acetate ion gives rise to a weakly basic solution.

Comment The hydroxide ion concentration (x) is indeed quite small relative to the initial acetate ion concentration. (We would have predicted this from our "rule of thumb": that $100 \cdot K_b$ should be less than the initial base concentration if we wish to use the approximate expression.)

EXERCISE 17.14 The pH of the Solution of the Conjugate Base of a Weak Acid

Sodium hypochlorite, NaClO, is used as a disinfectant in swimming pools and water treatment plants. What are the concentrations of HClO and OH^- and the pH of a 0.015 M solution of NaClO?

Chemistry ⚛ Now™

Sign in at **www.cengage.com/login** and go to Chapter 17 Contents to see Screen 17.10 for a tutorial on **estimating the pH following an acid–base reaction.**

EXAMPLE 17.8 Calculating the pH After the Reaction of a Base with an Acid

Problem What is the pH of the solution that results from mixing 25 mL of 0.016 M NH_3 and 25 mL of 0.016 M HCl?

Strategy This question involves three problems in one:

(a) *Writing a Balanced Equation:* We first have to write a balanced equation for the reaction that occurs and then decide whether the reaction products are acids or bases. Here, NH_4^+ is the product of interest, and it is a weak acid.

(b) *Stoichiometry Problem:* To find the "initial" NH_4^+ concentration is a stoichiometry problem: What amount of NH_4^+ (in moles) is produced in the HCl + NH_3 reaction, and in what volume of solution is the NH_4^+ ion found?

(c) *Equilibrium Problem:* Calculating the pH involves solving an equilibrium problem. The crucial piece of information needed here is the "initial" concentration of NH_4^+ from part (b).

Solution If equal amounts (moles) of base (NH_3) and acid (HCl) are mixed, the result should be an acidic solution because the significant species remaining in solution upon completion of the reaction is NH_4^+, the conjugate acid of the weak base ammonia (see Tables 17.3 and 17.5). The chemistry can be summarized by the following net ionic equations.

(a) *Writing Balanced Equations*

Reaction of HCl (the supplier of hydronium ion) with NH_3 to give NH_4^+:

$$NH_3(aq) + H_3O^+(aq) \rightarrow NH_4^+(aq) + H_2O(\ell)$$

The reaction of NH_4^+, the product, with water:

$$NH_4^+(aq) + H_2O(\ell) \rightleftharpoons H_3O^+(aq) + NH_3(aq)$$

(b) *Stoichiometry Problem*

Amount of HCl and NH_3 consumed:

$$(0.025 \text{ L HCl})(0.016 \text{ mol/L}) = 4.0 \times 10^{-4} \text{ mol HCl}$$

$$(0.025 \text{ L NH}_3)(0.016 \text{ mol/L}) = 4.0 \times 10^{-4} \text{ mol NH}_3$$

Amount of NH_4^+ produced upon completion of the reaction:

$$4.0 \times 10^{-4} \text{ mol NH}_3\left(\frac{1 \text{ mol NH}_4^+}{1 \text{ mol NH}_3}\right) = 4.0 \times 10^{-4} \text{ mol NH}_4^+$$

Concentration of NH_4^+: Combining 25 mL each of HCl and NH_3 gives a total solution volume of 50. mL. Therefore, the concentration of NH_4^+ is

$$[NH_4^+] = \frac{4.0 \times 10^{-4} \text{ mol}}{0.050 \text{ L}} = 8.0 \times 10^{-3} \text{ M}$$

(c) *Acid–Base Equilibrium Problem*

With the initial concentration of ammonium ion known, set up an ICE table to find the equilibrium concentration of hydronium ion.

Equilibrium	**NH_4^+ + H_2O**	$\rightleftharpoons$	**NH_3**	+	**H_3O^+**
Initial (M)	0.0080		0		0
Change	$-x$		$+x$		$+x$
Equilibrium (M)	$(0.0080 - x)$		x		x

Next, substitute the values in the table into the K_a expression for the ammonium ion. Thus, we have

$$K_a = 5.6 \times 10^{-10} = \frac{[H_3O^+][NH_3]}{[NH_4^+]} = \frac{(x)(x)}{0.0080 - x}$$

Table 17.5 summarizes the outcome of mixing various types of acids and bases. But how do you calculate a numerical value for the pH, particularly in the case of mixing a weak acid with a strong base or a weak base with a strong acid? The strategy (Example 17.8) is to recognize that this involves two related calculations: a stoichiometry calculation and an equilibrium calculation. The key to this is that

you need to know the concentration of the weak acid or weak base produced when the acid and base are mixed. You should ask yourself the following questions:

(a) What amounts of acid and base are used (in moles)? (This is a stoichiometry problem.)

(b) What is the total volume of the solution after mixing the acid and base solutions?

(c) What is the concentration of the weak acid or base produced on mixing the acid and base solutions?

(d) Using the concentration found in Step (c), what is the hydronium ion concentration in the solution? (This is an equilibrium problem.)

(e) Calculate the pH of the solution from $[H_3O^+]$.

The ammonium ion is a very weak acid, as reflected by the very small value of K_a. Therefore, x, the concentration of hydronium ion generated by reaction of ammonium ion with water, is assumed to be very small, and the approximate expression is used to solve for x. (Here $100 \cdot K_a$ is much less than the original acid concentration.)

$$K_a = 5.6 \times 10^{-10} \approx \frac{x^2}{0.0080}$$

$$x = \sqrt{(5.6 \times 10^{-10})(0.0080)}$$

$$= [H_3O^+] = [NH_3] = 2.1 \times 10^{-6} \text{ M}$$

$$pH = -\log(2.1 \times 10^{-6}) = 5.67$$

Comment As predicted (Table 17.5), the solution after mixing equal amounts of a strong acid and weak base is weakly acidic.

EXERCISE 17.15 What is the pH After the Reaction of a Weak Acid and Strong Base?

Calculate the pH after mixing 15 mL of 0.12 M acetic acid with 15 mL of 0.12 M NaOH. What are the major species in solution at equilibrium (besides water), and what are their concentrations?

17.8 Polyprotic Acids and Bases

Because polyprotic acids are capable of donating more than one proton (Table 17.1), they present us with additional problems when predicting the pH of their solutions. For many inorganic polyprotic acids, such as phosphoric acid, carbonic acid, and hydrogen sulfide, each successive loss of a proton is about 10^4 to 10^6 more difficult than the previous ionization step. This means that the first ionization step of a polyprotic acid produces up to about a million times more H_3O^+ ions than the second step. For this reason, *the pH of many inorganic polyprotic acids depends primarily on the hydronium ion generated in the first ionization step; the hydronium ion produced in the second step can be neglected.* The same principle applies to the conjugate bases of polyprotic acids. This is illustrated by the calculation of the pH of a solution of carbonate ion, an important base in our environment (Example 17.9).

Charles D. Winters

A polyprotic acid. Malic acid is a diprotic acid occurring in apples. It is also classified as an alpha-hydroxy acid because it has an OH group on the C atom next to the CO_2H (in the alpha position). It is one of a larger group of natural acids such as lactic acid, citric acid, and ascorbic acid. Alpha-hydroxy acids have been touted as an ingredient in "anti-aging" skin creams. They work by accelerating the natural process by which skin replaces the outer layer of cells with new cells.

EXAMPLE 17.9 Calculating the pH of the Solution of a Polyprotic Base

Problem The carbonate ion, CO_3^{2-}, is a base in water, forming the hydrogen carbonate ion, which in turn can form carbonic acid.

$$CO_3^{2-}(aq) + H_2O(\ell) \rightleftharpoons HCO_3^-(aq) + OH^-(aq) \qquad K_{b1} = 2.1 \times 10^{-4}$$

$$HCO_3^-(aq) + H_2O(\ell) \rightleftharpoons H_2CO_3(aq) + OH^-(aq) \qquad K_{b2} = 2.4 \times 10^{-8}$$

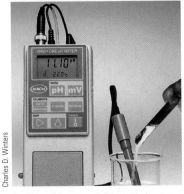

Charles D. Winters

Sodium carbonate, a polyprotic base.
This common substance is a base in aqueous solution. Its primary use is in the glass industry. Although it used to be manufactured, it is now mined as the mineral trona, $Na_2CO_3 \cdot NaHCO_3 \cdot 2\ H_2O$.

What is the pH of a 0.10 M solution of Na_2CO_3?

Strategy The second ionization constant, K_{b2}, is much smaller than the first, K_{b1}, so the hydroxide ion concentration in the solution results almost entirely from the first step. Therefore, let us calculate the OH^- concentration produced in the first ionization step but test the conclusion that OH^- produced in the second step is negligible.

Solution Set up an ICE table for the reaction of the carbonate ion (Equilibrium Table 1).

Equilibrium Table 1—Reaction of CO_3^{2-} Ion

Equilibrium	CO_3^{2-}	+	H_2O	$\rightleftharpoons$	HCO_3^-	+	OH^-
Initial (M)	0.10				0		0
Change	$-x$				$+x$		$+x$
Equilibrium (M)	$(0.10 - x)$				x		x

Based on this table, the equilibrium concentration of OH^- ($= x$) can then be calculated.

$$K_{b1} = 2.1 \times 10^{-4} = \frac{[HCO_3^-][OH^-]}{[CO_3^{2-}]} = \frac{x^2}{0.10 - x}$$

Because K_{b1} is relatively small, it is reasonable to make the approximation that $(0.10 - x) \approx 0.10$. Therefore,

$$x = [HCO_3^-] = [OH^-] = \sqrt{(2.1 \times 10^{-4})(0.10)} = 4.6 \times 10^{-3}\ M$$

Using this value of $[OH^-]$, we first calculate the pOH of the solution,

$$pOH = -\log(4.6 \times 10^{-3}) = 2.34$$

and then use the relationship pH + pOH = 14 to calculate the pH.

$$pH = 14 - pOH = \boxed{11.66}$$

Finally, we see that the concentration of the carbonate ion is, to a good approximation, 0.10 M.

$$[CO_3^{2-}] = 0.10 - 0.0046 \approx 0.10\ M$$

Comment It is instructive to ask what the concentration of H_2CO_3 in the solution might be. If HCO_3^- were to react significantly with water to produce H_2CO_3, the pH of the solution would be affected. Let us set up a second ICE Table.

Equilibrium Table 2—Reaction of HCO_3^- Ion

Equilibrium	HCO_3^-	+	H_2O	$\rightleftharpoons$	H_2CO_3	+	OH^-
Initial (M)	4.6×10^{-3}				0		4.6×10^{-3}
Change	$-y$				$+y$		$+y$
Equilibrium (M)	$(4.6 \times 10^{-3} - y)$				y		$(4.6 \times 10^{-3} + y)$

Because K_{b2} is so small, the second step occurs to a much smaller extent than the first step. This means the amount of H_2CO_3 and OH^- produced in the second step ($= y$) is much smaller than $10^{-3}\ M$. Therefore, it is reasonable that both $[HCO_3^-]$ and $[OH^-]$ are very close to $4.6 \times 10^{-3}\ M$.

$$K_{b2} = 2.4 \times 10^{-8} = \frac{[H_2CO_3][OH^-]}{[HCO_3^-]} = \frac{(y)(4.6 \times 10^{-3})}{4.6 \times 10^{-3}}$$

Because $[HCO_3^-]$ and $[OH^-]$ have nearly identical values, they cancel from the expression, and we find that $[H_2CO_3]$ is simply equal to K_{b2}.

$$y = [H_2CO_3] = K_{b2} = 2.4 \times 10^{-8}\ M$$

For the carbonate ion, where K_1 and K_2 differ by about 10^4, the hydroxide ion is essentially all produced in the first equilibrium process.

EXERCISE 17.16 Calculating the pH of the Solution of a Polyprotic Acid

What is the pH of a 0.10 M solution of oxalic acid, $H_2C_2O_4$? What are the concentrations of H_3O^+, $HC_2O_4^-$, and the oxalate ion, $C_2O_4^{2-}$? (See Appendix H for K_a values.)

17.9 The Lewis Concept of Acids and Bases

The concept of acid–base behavior advanced by Brønsted and Lowry in the 1920s works well for reactions involving proton transfer. A more general acid–base concept, however, was developed by Gilbert N. Lewis in the 1930s (◀ page 352). This concept is based on the sharing of electrons pairs between an acid and a base. A **Lewis acid** is a substance that can accept a pair of electrons from another atom to form a new bond, and a **Lewis base** is a substance that can donate a pair of electrons to another atom to form a new bond. This means that an acid–base reaction in the Lewis sense occurs when a molecule (or ion) donates a pair of electrons to another molecule (or ion).

$$
\begin{array}{ccccc}
\text{A} & + & \text{B:} & \rightarrow & \text{B}{\rightarrow}\text{A} \\
\text{Acid} & & \text{Base} & & \text{Adduct}
\end{array}
$$

The product is often called an **acid–base adduct.** In Section 8.3, this type of chemical bond was called a *coordinate covalent bond.*

Case Study — Uric Acid, Gout, and Bird Droppings

All living creatures metabolize food and dispose of the waste products, many of which contain nitrogen. Ammonia is the end product of this metabolic chain for fish and marine invertebrates, for example. And fish sometimes produce the Lewis and Brønsted base trimethylamine, $N(CH_3)_3$, a water-soluble compound and the source of the characteristic "fish odor."

Unlike fish, most terrestrial animals do not have an "infinite" supply of water. Mammals have a bladder and usually live in conditions where adequate water is available. Their mechanism of disposal for most toxins is to prepare a water-soluble compound and then excrete it through the urine. Thus, urea, NH_2CONH_2, is a major by-product of nitrogen metabolism in mammals. Reptiles and desert animals do not usually have much water available, and birds cannot afford the luxury of the weight of a bladder. These animals do not make urea; rather, they convert all of their nitrogen waste to uric acid, the concentrated white solid so familiar in bird droppings.

John Katz

Uric acid in bird droppings. Birds excrete uric acid, which you see as the white solid in their feces. The acidic material can cause severe environmental damage.

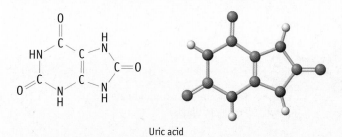

Uric acid

Uric acid can cause problems in primates because of its low water solubility. Deposits of uric acid in the joints and extremities can cause a very painful condition called *gout* or gouty arthritis. Chronic gout can also lead to lumps of uric acid around and in joints, to decreased kidney function, and to kidney stones.

You know you have gout if you experience excruciating and sudden pain with swelling and redness in a joint. Often, the first attack occurs in a big toe, but other joints such as those in the ankle, knee, wrist, fingers, and elbow can be affected as well.

Although gout may be a hereditary disease, you can help avoid the problem by eating smaller amounts of foods with high levels of the purines, which are metabolized to uric acid. These include meat, fish, dry beans, mushrooms, spinach, and asparagus. On the other hand, eating fresh fruit (especially cherries and strawberries) and most fresh vegetables can help lower uric acid levels.

Finally, gout is one of the most frequently recorded medical conditions throughout history. People such as Henry VIII, Isaac Newton, Thomas Jefferson, Benjamin Franklin, John Hancock, and Karl Marx have suffered from the condition.

Questions:

1. *A diagnosis of hyperuricemia will be made when the uric acid blood level is greater than 420 μmol/L. What is this level in milligrams of uric acid per liter?*
2. *Uric acid is a polyprotic acid with one pK_a of 5.40 and a second pK_a of 5.53. Considering only the loss of the first proton, what acid in Table 17.3 has a similar acid strength?*

Answers to these questions are in Appendix Q.

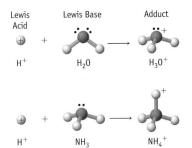

Lewis Acid   Lewis Base   Adduct

H^+ H_2O H_3O^+

H^+ NH_3 NH_4^+

FIGURE 17.6 Protonation of water and ammonia are examples of Lewis acid–base reactions.

Formation of a hydronium ion from H^+ and water is a good example of a Lewis acid–base reaction (Figure 17.6). The H^+ ion has no electrons in its valence ($1s$) shell, and the water molecule has two unshared pairs of electrons (located in sp^3 hybrid orbitals). One of the O atom lone pairs of a water molecule can be shared with an H^+ ion, thus forming an O—H bond in an H_3O^+ ion. A similar interaction occurs between H^+ and the Lewis base ammonia to form the ammonium ion. Such reactions are very common. In general, they involve Lewis acids that are cations or neutral molecules with an available, empty valence orbital and bases that are anions or neutral molecules with a lone electron pair.

Cationic Lewis Acids

Just as H^+ and water form a Lewis acid–base adduct, metal cations interact with water molecules to form hydrated cations (Figure 17.7 and page 557). In these species, coordinate covalent bonds form between the metal cation and a lone pair of electrons on the O atom of each water. For example, an iron(II) ion, Fe^{2+}, forms six coordinate covalent bonds to water.

$$Fe^{2+}(aq) + 6\ H_2O(\ell) \rightarrow [Fe(H_2O)_6]^{2+}(aq)$$

Similar structures formed by transition metal cations are generally very colorful (Figures 17.7 and 17.8 and Section 22.3). Chemists call these **complex ions** or, because of the coordinate covalent bond, **coordination complexes.** Several are listed in Table 17.3 as acids, and their behavior is described further in Section 17.10 and Chapter 22.

Like water, ammonia is an excellent Lewis base and combines with metal cations to give adducts (complex ions), which are often very colorful. For example, copper(II) ions, light blue in aqueous solution (Figure 17.7), react with ammonia to give a deep blue adduct with four ammonia molecules surrounding each Cu^{2+} ion.

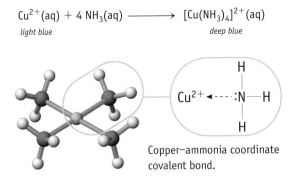

$$Cu^{2+}(aq) + 4\ NH_3(aq) \longrightarrow [Cu(NH_3)_4]^{2+}(aq)$$
light blue   *deep blue*

Copper–ammonia coordinate covalent bond.

FIGURE 17.7 The Lewis acid–base complex ion $[Cu(NH_3)_4]^{2+}$. Here, aqueous ammonia was added to aqueous $CuSO_4$ (the light blue solution at the bottom of the beaker). The small concentration of OH^- in $NH_3(aq)$ first formed insoluble blue-white $Cu(OH)_2$ (the solid in the middle of the beaker). With additional NH_3, however, the deep blue, soluble complex ion formed (the solution at the top of the beaker). The model in the text shows the copper(II)–ammonia complex ion.

Hydroxide ion, OH^-, is an excellent Lewis base and binds readily to metal cations to give metal hydroxides. An important feature of the chemistry of some metal hydroxides is that they are **amphoteric.** An amphoteric metal hydroxide can behave as an acid or a base (Table 17.6). One of the best examples of this behavior is provided by aluminum hydroxide, $Al(OH)_3$ (Figure 17.9). Adding OH^- to a precipitate of $Al(OH)_3$ produces the water-soluble $[Al(OH)_4]^-$ ion.

$$Al(OH)_3(s) + OH^-(aq) \rightarrow [Al(OH)_4]^-(aq)$$
Acid   Base

Charles D. Winters

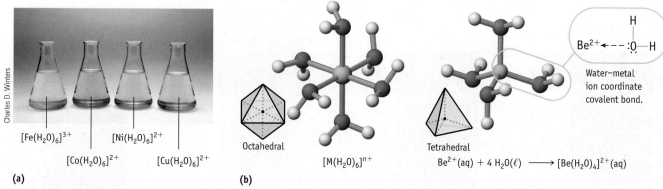

[Fe(H₂O)₆]³⁺   [Ni(H₂O)₆]²⁺

[Co(H₂O)₆]²⁺   [Cu(H₂O)₆]²⁺

Octahedral $[M(H_2O)_6]^{n+}$

Tetrahedral

Water–metal ion coordinate covalent bond.

$Be^{2+}(aq) + 4 H_2O(\ell) \longrightarrow [Be(H_2O)_4]^{2+}(aq)$

(a)   (b)

FIGURE 17.8 Metal cations in water. (a) Solutions of the nitrate salts of iron(III), cobalt(II), nickel(II), and copper(II) all have characteristic colors. (b) Models of complex ions (Lewis acid–base adducts) formed between a metal cation and water molecules. Such complexes often have six water molecules arranged octahedrally around the metal cation.

If acid is added to the $Al(OH)_3$ precipitate, it again dissolves. This time, however, aluminum hydroxide is acting as a base.

$$Al(OH)_3(s) + 3 H_3O^+(aq) \rightarrow Al^{3+}(aq) + 6 H_2O(\ell)$$
$$\text{Base} \qquad\quad \text{Acid}$$

Molecular Lewis Acids

Lewis's acid–base concept also accounts for the fact that oxides of nonmetals such as CO_2 and SO_2 behave as acids (◀ Section 3.7). Because oxygen is more electronegative than C, the C—O bonding electrons in CO_2 are polarized away from carbon and toward oxygen. This causes the carbon atom to be slightly positive, and it is this atom that the negatively charged Lewis base OH^- can attack to give, ultimately, the bicarbonate ion.

■ **CO_2 in Basic Solution** This reaction of CO_2 with OH^- is the first step in the precipitation of $CaCO_3$ when CO_2 is bubbled into a solution of $Ca(OH)_2$ (Figure 3.6, page 120).

Similarly, SO_2 reacts with aqueous OH^- to form the HSO_3^- ion.

Compounds based on the Group 3A elements boron and aluminum are among the most-studied Lewis acids. One example is a reaction in organic chemistry that is catalyzed by the Lewis acid $AlCl_3$. The mechanism of this important reaction—called the Friedel–Crafts reaction—is illustrated here. In the first step, a Lewis base,

TABLE 17.6 Some Common Amphoteric Metal Hydroxides*

Hydroxide	Reaction as a Base	Reaction as an Acid
$Al(OH)_3$	$Al(OH)_3(s) + 3 H_3O^+(aq) \rightleftharpoons Al^{3+}(aq) + 6 H_2O(\ell)$	$Al(OH)_3(s) + OH^-(aq) \rightleftharpoons [Al(OH)_4]^-(aq)$
$Zn(OH)_2$	$Zn(OH)_2(s) + 2 H_3O^+(aq) \rightleftharpoons Zn^{2+}(aq) + 4 H_2O(\ell)$	$Zn(OH)_2(s) + 2 OH^-(aq) \rightleftharpoons [Zn(OH)_4]^{2-}(aq)$
$Sn(OH)_4$	$Sn(OH)_4(s) + 4 H_3O^+(aq) \rightleftharpoons Sn^{4+}(aq) + 8 H_2O(\ell)$	$Sn(OH)_4(s) + 2 OH^-(aq) \rightleftharpoons [Sn(OH)_6]^{2-}(aq)$
$Cr(OH)_3$	$Cr(OH)_3(s) + 3 H_3O^+(aq) \rightleftharpoons Cr^{3+}(aq) + 6 H_2O(\ell)$	$Cr(OH)_3(s) + OH^-(aq) \rightleftharpoons [Cr(OH)_4]^-(aq)$

* The aqueous metal cations are best described as $[M(H_2O)_6]^{n+}$.

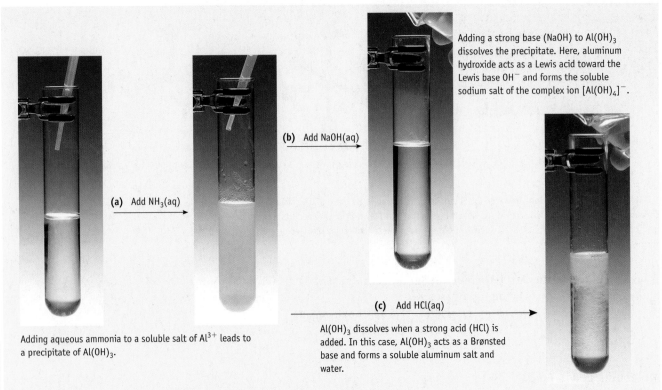

Adding a strong base (NaOH) to Al(OH)₃ dissolves the precipitate. Here, aluminum hydroxide acts as a Lewis acid toward the Lewis base OH⁻ and forms the soluble sodium salt of the complex ion $[Al(OH)_4]^-$.

(b) Add NaOH(aq)

(c) Add HCl(aq)

$Al(OH)_3$ dissolves when a strong acid (HCl) is added. In this case, $Al(OH)_3$ acts as a Brønsted base and forms a soluble aluminum salt and water.

Adding aqueous ammonia to a soluble salt of Al^{3+} leads to a precipitate of $Al(OH)_3$.

(a) Add NH₃(aq)

FIGURE 17.9 The amphoteric nature of Al(OH)₃. Aluminum hydroxide is formed by the reaction of aqueous Al^{3+} and ammonia.

$$Al^{3+}(aq) + 3\ NH_3(aq) + 3\ H_2O(\ell) \rightleftharpoons Al(OH)_3(s) + 3\ NH_4^+(aq)$$

Reactions of solid Al(OH)₃ with aqueous NaOH and HCl demonstrate that aluminum hydroxide is amphoteric.

the Cl⁻ ion, transfers from the reactant, here CH₃COCl, to the Lewis acid to give $[AlCl_4]^-$ and an organic cation (that is stabilized by resonance). The organic cation attacks a benzene molecule to give a cationic intermediate, and this then interacts with $[AlCl_4]^-$ to produce HCl and the final organic product.

Molecular Lewis Bases

Ammonia is widely distributed in nature and is involved as a Lewis base in numerous reactions. One example where this is important is in the conversion of ammonia to urea (NH_2CONH_2) in natural systems. The process begins with the reaction of bicarbonate ion with ATP (adenosine triphosphate), and a subsequent step in the mechanism is the following:

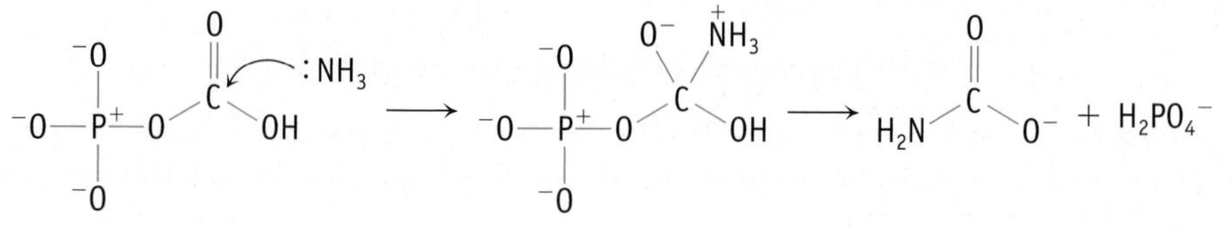

intermediate

Here, the Lewis base ammonia attacks a carbon atom with a partial positive charge. The dihydrogen phosphate ion is then released, yielding the $NH_2CO_2^-$ ion, which eventually forms urea in another step in this reaction mechanism.

Chemistry Now™

Sign in at **www.cengage.com/login** and go to Chapter 17 Contents to see:
• Screen 17.12 for a tutorial on **Lewis acids and bases**
• Screen 17.13 for a description of **cationic Lewis acids**
• Screen 17.14 for a tutorial on **neutral Lewis acids**

EXERCISE 17.17 Lewis Acids and Bases

Describe each of the following as a Lewis acid or a Lewis base.

(a) PH_3 (c) H_2S

(b) BCl_3 (d) HS^-

Hint: In each case, draw the Lewis electron dot structure of the molecule or ion. Are there lone pairs of electrons on the central atom? If so, it can be a Lewis base. Does the central atom lack an electron pair? If so, it can behave as a Lewis acid.

17.10 Molecular Structure, Bonding, and Acid–Base Behavior

One of the most interesting aspects of chemistry is the correlation between a molecule's structure and bonding and its chemical properties. Because so many compounds are acids and bases, and play such a key role in chemistry, it is especially useful to see if there are some general principles governing acid–base behavior.

Chemistry Now™

Sign in at **www.cengage.com/login** and go to Chapter 17 Contents to see Screen 17.15 for a self-study module on **molecular interpretation of acid–base behavior.**

Acid Strength of the Hydrogen Halides, HX

Aqueous HF is a weak Brønsted acid in water, whereas the other hydrohalic acids— aqueous HCl, HBr, and HI—are all strong acids. Experiments show that the acid strength increases in the order HF << HCl < HBr < HI. A detailed analysis of

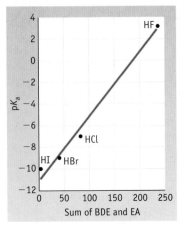

FIGURE 17.10 The effect of H—X bond energy and X electron affinity on acid strength. Stronger acids have weaker H—X bonds and more electronegative A atoms. (BDE is the bond dissociation enthalpy of the H—X bond, and EA is the electron affinity of the halogen atom.) See M. Moran, *Journal of Chemical Education*, Vol, 83, pages 800–803, 2006.

the factors that lead to these differences in acid strength in this group is complex (see *A Closer Look, Acid and Base Strength*). However, predictions about relative acid strength can be made based on the sum of two energy quantities, the energy required to break the H—X bond and the electron affinity of the halogen. That is, when a hydrohalic acid HX ionizes in water,

$$HX(aq) + H_2O(\ell) \rightarrow H_3O^+(aq) + X^-(aq)$$

the sum of the two energy terms

$$\Delta U \propto \text{HX bond breaking enthalpy} + \text{electron affinity of X}$$

correlates with acid strength. Specifically, the more easily the H—X bond is broken and the more negative the electron affinity of X, the greater the relative strength of the acid.

The bond enthalpy and electron affinity effects can work together (a weak H—X bond and a large electron affinity of the X group) to produce a strong acid, but they can also work in opposite directions. The balance of the two effects is thus important. Let us examine some data for the Group 7A binary acids, HX.

	HF	HCl	HBr	HI
		Increasing acid strength ⟶		
pK_a	+3.14	−7	−9	−10
H—X bond strength (kJ/mol)	.565	432	366	299
Electron affinity of X (kJ/mol)	−328	−349	−325	−295
Sum (kJ/mol)	237	83	41	4

In this series of acids, the bond enthalpy factor dominates, the weakest acid, HF, has the strongest H—X bond, and the strongest acid, HI, has the weakest H—X bond. However, the electron affinity of X becomes less negative from F to I. A low electron affinity should lead to a weaker acid, but it is the *sum* of the two effects that leads to the observation that HI is the strongest acid. In Figure 17.10, you see there is a good correlation between an acid's pK_a and the *sum* of the bond breaking enthalpy and electron affinity.

TABLE 17.7 Oxoacids

Acid	pK_a
Cl-Based Oxoacids	
HOCl	7.46
HOClO (HClO$_2$)	~ 2
HOClO$_2$ (HClO$_3$)	~ −3
HOClO$_3$ (HClO$_4$)	~ −8
S-Based Oxoacids	
(HO)$_2$SO [H$_2$SO$_3$]	1.92, 7.21
(HO)$_2$SO$_2$ [H$_2$SO$_4$]	~ −3, 1.92

According to Linus Pauling, for oxoacids with the general formula (HO)$_n$E(O)$_m$, the value of pK_a is about 8–5m. When $n > 1$, the pK_a increases by about 5 for each successive loss of a proton.

Comparing Oxoacids: HNO$_2$ and HNO$_3$

Nitrous acid (HNO$_2$) and nitric acid (HNO$_3$) are representative of several series of **oxoacids.** Oxoacids contain an atom (usually a nonmetal atom) bonded to one or more oxygen atoms, some with hydrogen atoms attached. Besides those based on N, you are familiar with the sulfur- and chlorine-based oxoacids (Table 17.7). In all these series of related compounds, the acid strength increases as the number of oxygen atoms bonded to the central element increases. Thus, nitric acid (HNO$_3$) is a stronger acid than nitrous acid (HNO$_2$).

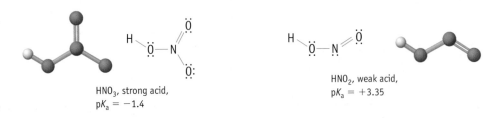

HNO$_3$, strong acid, pK_a = −1.4

HNO$_2$, weak acid, pK_a = +3.35

Acid Strengths and Molecular Structure

Although predictions about acid strength in aqueous solution are fairly simple to make, explanations are in fact quite complicated.

Acid strength is sometimes correlated with the strength and the polarity of the H—X bond, readily identifiable characteristics derived from the structure of the acid, the reactant in the ionization process. We need to point out, however, that when one is assessing any chemical reaction, it is necessary to consider both reactants and products. Looking only at the reactant when dealing with acid dissociation only takes you halfway.

When evaluating the strength of an acid HX(aq), we are looking at the following reaction

$$HX(aq) + H_2O(\ell) \rightleftharpoons H_3O^+(aq) + X^-(aq)$$

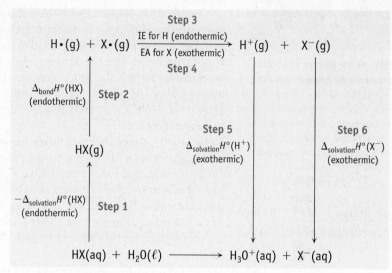

An energy diagram for the ionization of an acid HX in aqueous solution.

To fully explain the extent of ionization, we must consider characteristics of both the acid and the anion. The ability of the anion to spread out the negative charge across the ion, for example, and the solvation of the anion by the solvent are among the issues that must have some relevance in an explanation of the strength of the acid.

How enthalpy changes contribute to acid strength can be assessed using a thermochemical cycle (such as the one used to evaluate a lattice enthalpy, page 599). Consider the relative acid strengths of the hydrogen halides. The enthalpy change for the ionization of an acid in water can be related to other enthalpy changes as shown in the diagram. The solvation of H^+ (Step 5) and the ionization energy of H(g) (Step 3) are common to all of the hydrogen halides and do not contribute to the differences among hydrogen halides, but the four remaining terms are dif-

ferent. For the hydrogen halides, the bond dissociation enthalpy (Step 2) of HF is much larger than the dissociation enthalpies of the other hydrogen halides. However, it is compensated for significantly by the enthalpy of solvation of the anion (Step 6), which for the fluoride ion is much more exothermic than the solvation energies of the other halide ions. The electron affinity is also a contributor to the differences in overall enthalpy changes. Electron affinity values vary among the halogens, but to a smaller extent than the variation in bond energy and the enthalpy of solvation of the halide ion. Differences in solvation energy for the molecular species (Step 1) are minimal.

A complete analysis of strengths of acids in aqueous solution will include consideration of both enthalpies and entropies. Entropy has

yet to be discussed in this text in detail (► Chapter 19) but we have noted earlier (◄ page 621) that entropy plays an important role in solution chemistry, specifically in determining solubilities. It is not surprising that entropy has a role in determining acid strength, too. Indeed, differences in entropy changes are significant in accounting for the differences in acid strength of the hydrogen halides.

Although all of these terms contribute to acid strength, acid strength can often be correlated with a subset of this information, as can be seen by the examples presented in this section. We point out, however, that correlations, while highly useful to a chemist because they can be used to make important predictions, are at best only partial explanations.

Let's apply the bond enthalpy/electron affinity analysis to HNO_3 and HNO_2.

	Increasing acid strength ⟶	
	HNO₂	HNO₃
pK_a	+3.35	−1.4
H—O bond strength (kJ/mol)	328	423
Electron affinity of X (kJ/mol)	−219	−377
Sum (kJ/mol)	109	46

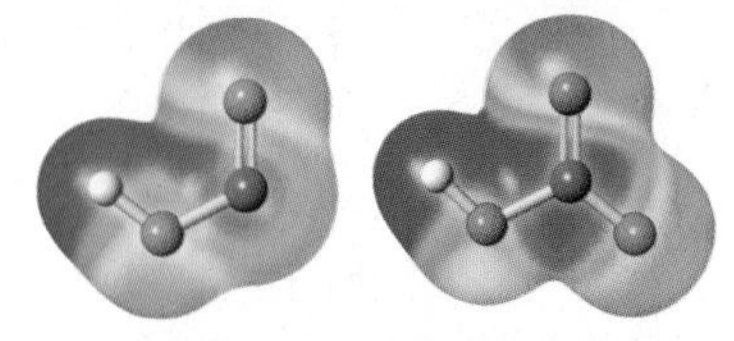

Nitrous acid, HNO_2 Nitric acid, HNO_3

FIGURE 17.11 Electrostatic potential surfaces for the nitrogen oxoacids. Both surfaces show the O—H bond is quite polar. More importantly, calculations show that the H atom becomes more positive as more O atoms are added to N, and the O—H bond becomes even more polar.

Partial Charges

Molecule	H atom	O atom of OH	N atom
HNO_2	+0.23	−0.28	+0.34
HNO_3	+0.27	−0.37	+0.66

TABLE 17.8 Correlation of Atom Formal Charge and pK_a

	Central atom formal charge	pK_a

:O—H
    |
:O—S—O:
    |
:O—H
	+2	−3

H :O—H | | :O—S—O:	+1	1.92
:O—Cl—O—H	+1	2
:Cl—O—H	0	7.46

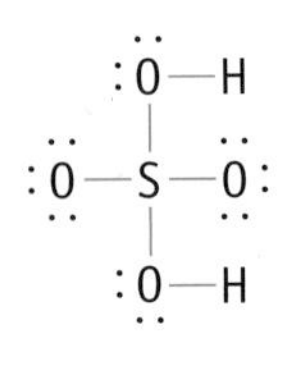

As in the case of the Group 7A acids, we again see that acid strength correlates with the sum of the bond breaking energy and X group (NO_2 or NO_3) electron affinity.

Our analysis of the Group 7A acids showed that, in this series, the H—X bond strength was the more important factor; as the H—X bond became stronger, the acid became weaker. However, a glance at the data for HNO_3 and HNO_2 shows this is not true here. The O—H bond is stronger in the stronger acid HNO_3. The electron affinity term is the more important term in this correlation. These same effects are observed for other oxyacids such as the chlorine-based oxoacids $HOCl <$ $HOClO < HOClO_2 < HOClO_3$ and the S-based oxoacids (Table 17.7). How is this to be interpreted?

In HNO_3, there are two other oxygen atoms bonded to the central nitrogen atom, whereas in HNO_2 only one other oxygen is bonded to the nitrogen atom. By attaching more electronegative O atoms to nitrogen, we are increasing the electron affinity of the group attached to hydrogen, and anything that increases the electron affinity of the X group should also make HX a stronger acid and X^- a weaker conjugate base. This is another way of saying that if X^- has a way to accommodate and stabilize a negative charge, it will be a weaker conjugate base. In the case of oxoacids, additional oxygen atoms have the effect of stabilizing the anion because the negative charge on the anion can be dispersed over more atoms. In the nitrate ion, for example, the negative charge is shared equally over the three oxygen atoms. This is represented symbolically in the three resonance structures for this ion.

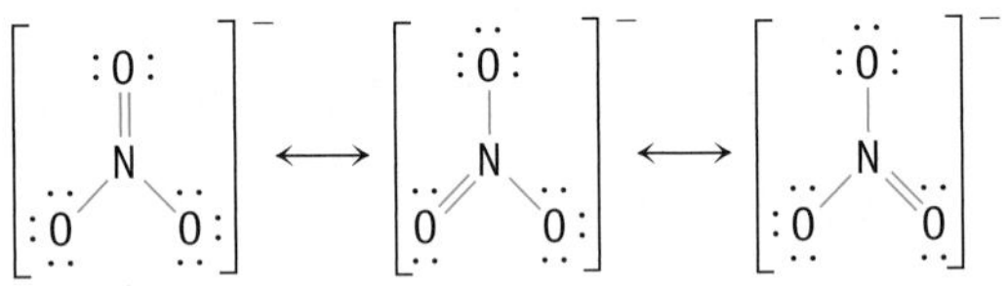

$$\left[\begin{array}{c}:O:\\ \| \\ N \\ :O \quad O:\end{array}\right]^- \longleftrightarrow \left[\begin{array}{c}:O:\\ N \\ :O \quad O:\end{array}\right]^- \longleftrightarrow \left[\begin{array}{c}:O:\\ N \\ :O \quad O\end{array}\right]^-$$

In nitrite ion, only two atoms share the negative charge. Therefore, NO_2^- is a stronger conjugate base than NO_3^-. In general, greater stabilization of the products formed by ionizing the acid contributes to increased acidity.

A glance at Table 17.7 and Figure 17.11 shows that another empirical correlation can be made between the structure of an acid and its acidity: In a series of related acids, the larger the formal charge on the central atom, the stronger the acid (Table 17.8). For example, the N atom formal charge in the weak acid HNO_2 is 0, whereas it is +1 in the strong acid HNO_3, and these are reflected by the results of theoretical calculations cited in Figure 17.11.

In summary, molecules such as the oxoacids can behave as stronger Brønsted acids when the anion created by loss of H^+ is stable and able to accommodate the negative charge. These conditions are promoted by

- the presence of electronegative atoms attached to the central atom.
- the possibility of resonance structures for the anion, which lead to delocalization of the negative charge over the anion and thus to a stable ion.

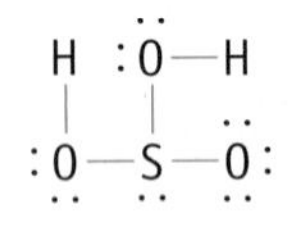

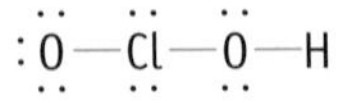

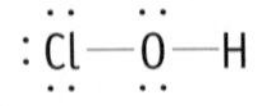

Why Are Carboxylic Acids Brønsted Acids?

There is a large class of organic acids, typified by acetic acid (CH_3CO_2H) (Figure 17.12), called carboxylic acids because all have the carboxylic acid group, $-CO_2H$. The arguments used to explain the acidity of oxoacids can also be applied to carboxylic acids. The O—H bond in these compounds is polar, a prerequisite for ionization.

C—H bonds not broken in water

Polar O—H bond broken by interaction of positively charged H atom with hydrogen-bonded H_2O

FIGURE 17.12 Electrostatic potential surface and partial charges for acetic acid. The H atoms of the molecule are all positively charged, but the H atom of the OH is much more highly charged. As expected, both of the electronegative O atoms have a partial negative charge. The table below gives the computer-calculated partial charges on the acid.

Atom or Group	Calc'd Partial Charge
H of OH	+0.24
O of OH	−0.32
H of CH_3	+0.12

In addition, carboxylate anions are stabilized by delocalizing the negative charge over the two oxygen atoms.

The simple carboxylic acids, RCO_2H in which R is a hydrocarbon group (◄ Section 10.4), do not differ markedly in acid strength (compare acetic acid, $pK_a = 4.74$, and propanoic acid, $pK_a = 4.89$, Table 17.3). The acidity of carboxylic acids is enhanced, however, if electronegative substituents replace the hydrogens in the alkyl group. Compare, for example, the pK_a values of a series of acetic acids in which hydrogen is replaced sequentially by the more electronegative element chlorine.

Acid		pK_a Value	
CH_3CO_2H	Acetic acid	4.74	
$ClCH_2CO_2H$	Chloroacetic acid	2.85	*increasing acid*
Cl_2CHCO_2H	Dichloroacetic acid	1.49	*strength*
Cl_3CCO_2H	Trichloroacetic acid	0.7	

As in the nitrogen oxoacids, increasingly electronegative substituents lead to an increase in acid strength. Indeed, recent research has found that a key role of electronegative substituents is to stabilize the negative charge of the anion. That is, compared with $CH_3CO_2^-$, the $Cl_3CCO_2^-$ anion is stabilized by the presence of the three Cl atoms, and $Cl_3CCO_2^-$ is a weaker base than $CH_3CO_2^-$.

Finally, why are the C—H hydrogens of carboxylic acids not dissociated as H^+ instead of (or in addition to) the O—H hydrogen atom? The calculated partial positive charges listed in Figure 17.12 show that the H atoms of the CH_3 group have a much smaller positive partial charge than the O—H hydrogen atom. Furthermore, in carboxylic acids, the C atom of the CH_3 group is not sufficiently electronegative to accommodate the negative charge left if the bond breaks as $C—H \rightarrow C{:}^- + H^+$, and the product anion is not well stabilized.

Why Are Hydrated Metal Cations Brønsted Acids?

When a coordinate covalent bond is formed between a metal cation (a Lewis acid) and a water molecule (a Lewis base), the positive charge of the metal ion and its small size means that the electrons of the $H_2O—M^{n+}$ bond are very strongly at-

■ **Polarization of O—H Bonds** Water molecules attached to a metal cation have strongly polarized O—H bonds.

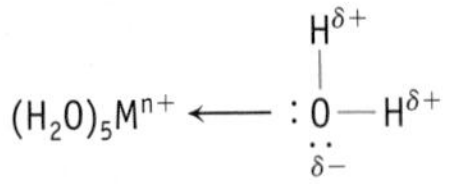

$$(H_2O)_5M^{n+} \longleftarrow :\overset{H^{\delta+}}{\underset{\delta-}{O}}-H^{\delta+}$$

tracted to the metal. As a result, the O—H bonds of the bound water molecules are polarized, just as in oxoacids and carboxylic acids. The net effect is that a H atom of a coordinated water molecule is removed as H^+ more readily than in an uncoordinated water molecule. Thus, a hydrated metal cation functions as a Brønsted acid or proton donor (Figure 17.8).

$$[Cu(H_2O)_6]^{2+} + H_2O(\ell) \rightleftharpoons [Cu(H_2O)_5(OH)]^+(aq) + H_3O^+(aq)$$

The effect of the metal ion increases with increasing charge. Consulting Table 17.3, you see that the Brønsted acidity of +3 ions (for example Al^{3+} and Fe^{3+}) is greater than for +2 cations (Cu^{2+}, Pb^{2+}, Co^{2+}, Fe^{2+}, Ni^{2+}). Ions with a single positive charge such as Na^+ and K^+ are not acidic. (This is similar to the effect of central atom formal charge in a series of related acids. See Table 17.8.)

Why Are Anions Brønsted Bases?

Anions, particularly oxoanions such as PO_4^{3-}, are Brønsted bases. The negatively charged anion interacts with the positively charged H atom of a polar water molecule, and an H^+ ion is transferred to the anion.

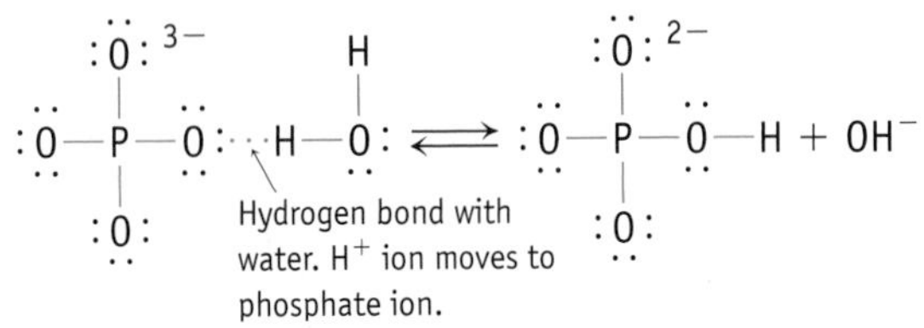

$$:\overset{:\ddot{O}:^{3-}}{\underset{:\ddot{O}:}{\ddot{O}-P-\ddot{O}:}} \quad \overset{H}{\underset{}{\ddot{O}:}} \quad H-\ddot{O}: \rightleftharpoons :\overset{:\ddot{O}:^{2-}}{\underset{:\ddot{O}:}{\ddot{O}-P-\ddot{O}}}-H + OH^-$$

Hydrogen bond with water. H^+ ion moves to phosphate ion.

The data in Table 17.9 show that, in a series of related anions, the basicity of an anionic base increases as the negative charge of the anion increases.

Anion	pK_b
PO_4^{3-}	1.55
HPO_4^{2-}	6.80
$H_2PO_4^{-}$	11.89
CO_3^{2-}	3.68
HCO_3^{-}	7.62
SO_3^{2-}	6.80
HSO_3^{-}	12.08

TABLE 17.9 Basic Oxoanions

Why Are Ammonia and Its Derivatives Brønsted and Lewis Bases?

Ammonia is the parent compound of an enormous number of compounds that behave as Brønsted and Lewis bases (Figure 17.13). These molecules all have an electronegative N atom with a partial negative charge surrounded by three bonds and a lone pair of electrons. Owing to this negatively charged N atom, they can extract a proton from water.

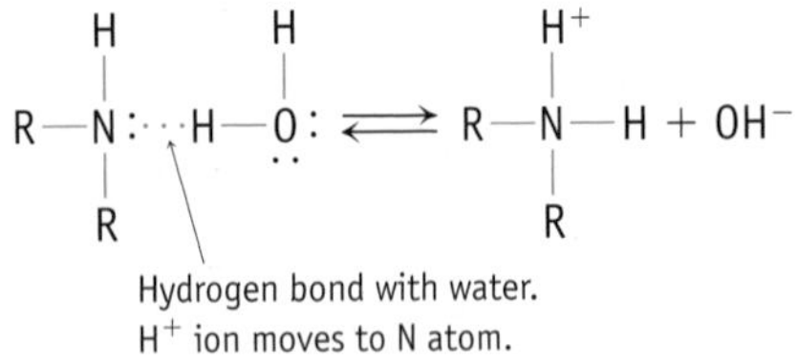

$$R-\overset{H}{\underset{R}{N}}: \quad H-\ddot{O}: \rightleftharpoons R-\overset{H}{\underset{R}{N}}-H + OH^-$$

Hydrogen bond with water. H^+ ion moves to N atom.

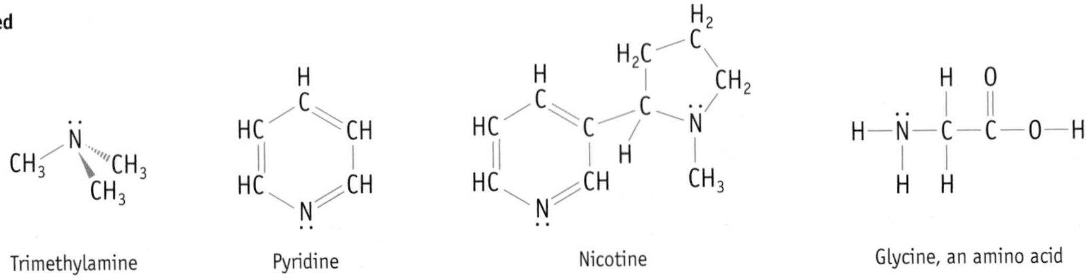

FIGURE 17.13 Nitrogen-based Lewis and Brønsted bases. All have an N atom surrounded by three bonds and a lone pair of electrons.

Trimethylamine

Pyridine

Nicotine

Glycine, an amino acid

In addition, the lone pair can be used to form a coordinate covalent bond to Lewis acids such as a metal cation (◀ page 790).

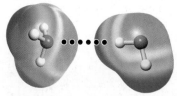

EXERCISE 17.18 Molecular Structure, Acids, and Bases

(a) Which should be the stronger acid, H_2SeO_4 or H_2SeO_3?

(b) Which should be the stronger acid, $[Fe(H_2O)_6]^{2+}$ or $[Fe(H_2O)_6]^{3+}$?

(c) Which should be the stronger acid, HOCl or HOBr?

(d) The molecule whose structure is illustrated here is amphetamine, a stimulant. Is the compound a Brønsted acid, a Lewis acid, a Brønsted base, a Lewis base, or some combination of these?

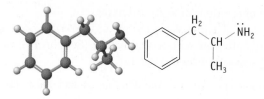

Electrostatic potential surfaces for NH₃ and H₂O. The red or negative region of these surfaces corresponds to the lone pair of electrons on N or the two pairs on O. The N atom of NH_3 has a calculated partial charge of -0.40, and the H atoms have a charge of $+0.13$. The N atom lone pair of NH_3 is involved in forming a hydrogen bond with the polar O—H bond of water. The NH_3 is both a Lewis and a Brønsted base and can remove the proton from water to form NH_4^+ and OH^-.

Chapter Goals Revisited

Now that you have studied this chapter, you should ask whether you have met the chapter goals. In particular, you should be able to:

Use the Brønsted–Lowry and Lewis theories of acids and bases

a. Define and use the Brønsted concept of acids and bases (Sections 17.1 and 17.2).

b. Recognize common monoprotic and polyprotic acids and bases, and write balanced equations for their ionization in water (Section 17.2).

c. Appreciate when a substance can be amphiprotic (Section 17.2).

d. Recognize the Brønsted acid and base in a reaction, and identify the conjugate partner of each (Section 17.2). Study Question(s) assignable in OWL: 2, 4, 8.

e. Understand the concept of water autoionization and its role in Brønsted acid–base chemistry. Use the water ionization constant, K_w (Section 17.3).

f. Use the pH concept (Section 17.3). Study Question(s) assignable in OWL: 10, 12.

g. Identify common strong acids and bases (Tables 3.2 and 17.3).

h. Recognize some common weak acids and understand that they can be neutral molecules (such as acetic acid), cations (NH_4^+ or hydrated metal ions such as $[Fe(H_2O)_6]^{2+}$, or anions (such as HCO_3^-) (Table 17.3).

Apply the principles of chemical equilibrium to acids and bases in aqueous solution

a. Write equilibrium constant expressions for weak acids and bases (Section 17.4).

b. Calculate pK_a from K_a (or K_a from pK_a), and understand how pK_a is correlated with acid strength (Section 17.4). Study Question(s) assignable in OWL: 26, 28, 30, 104, 106.

c. Understand the relationship between K_a for a weak acid and K_b for its conjugate base (Section 17.4). Study Question(s) assignable in OWL: 15, 18.

d. Write equations for acid–base reactions, and decide whether they are product- or reactant-favored at equilibrium (Section 17.5 and Table 17.5). Study Question(s) assignable in OWL: 36, 38.

e. Calculate the equilibrium constant for a weak acid (K_a) or a weak base (K_b) from experimental information (such as pH, [H_3O^+], or [OH^-]) (Section 17.7 and Example 17.4). Study Question(s) assignable in OWL: 42, 44, 85, 107.

f. Use the equilibrium constant and other information to calculate the pH of a solution of a weak acid or weak base (Section 17.7 and Examples 17.5 and 13.7). Study Question(s) assignable in OWL: 48, 52, 56, 65, 66, 89, 91, 99; Go Chemistry Module 22.

g. Describe the acid–base properties of salts, and calculate the pH of a solution of a salt of a weak acid or of a weak base (Section 17.7 and Example 17.7). Study Question(s) assignable in OWL: 84, 92, 93, 103, 121.

Predict the outcome of reactions of acids and bases

a. Recognize the type of acid–base reaction, and describe its result (Section 17.6).

b. Calculate the pH after an acid–base reaction (Section 17.7 and Example 17.8). Study Question(s) assignable in OWL: 62, 98, 101, 102.

Understand the influence of structure and bonding on acid–base properties

a. Characterize a compound as a Lewis base (an electron-pair donor) or a Lewis acid (an electron-pair acceptor) (Section 17.9). Study Question(s) assignable in OWL: 70, 72, 108.

b. Appreciate the connection between the structure of a compound and its acidity or basicity (Section 17.10). Study Question(s) assignable in OWL: 74.

KEY EQUATIONS

Equation 17.1 (page 765): Water ionization constant.

$$K_w = [H_3O^+][OH^-] = 1.0 \times 10^{-14} \text{ at 25 °C}$$

Equation 17.2 (page 767): Definition of pH (see also Equation 4.3).

$$pH = -\log[H_3O^+]$$

Equation 17.3 (page 767): Definition of pOH

$$pOH = -\log[OH^-]$$

Equation 17.4 (page 767): Definition of pK_w = pH + pOH (= 14.00 at 25 °C)

$$pK_w = 14.00 = pH + pOH$$

Equation 17.5 (page 769): Equilibrium expression for a general acid, HA, in water.

$$K_a = \frac{[H_3O^+][A^-]}{[HA]}$$

Equation 17.6 (page 769): Equilibrium expression for a general base, B, in water.

$$K_b = \frac{[BH^+][OH^-]}{[B]}$$

Equation 17.7 (page 775): Definition of pK_a.

$$pK_a = -\log K_a$$

Equation 17.8 (page 776): Relationship of K_a, K_b, and K_w, where K_a and K_b are for a conjugate acid–base pair.

$$K_a \times K_b = K_w$$

STUDY QUESTIONS

$\overline{\text{U}}$WL Online homework for this chapter may be assigned in OWL.

▲ denotes challenging questions.

■ denotes questions assignable in OWL.

Blue-numbered questions have answers in Appendix O and fully-worked solutions in the *Student Solutions Manual*.

Practicing Skills

The Brønsted Concept
(See Exercises 17.1 and 17.2 and ChemistryNow Screen 17.2.)

1. Write the formula and give the name of the conjugate base of each of the following acids.
   (a) HCN   (b) HSO_4^- (c) HF

2. ■ Write the formula and give the name of the conjugate acid of each of the following bases.
   (a) NH_3 (b) HCO_3^- (c) Br^-

3. What are the products of each of the following acid–base reactions? Indicate the acid and its conjugate base and the base and its conjugate acid.
   (a) $HNO_3 + H_2O \rightarrow$
   (b) $HSO_4^- + H_2O \rightarrow$
   (c) $H_3O^+ + F^- \rightarrow$

4. ■ What are the products of each of the following acid–base reactions? Indicate the acid and its conjugate base and the base and its conjugate acid.
   (a) $HClO_4 + H_2O \rightarrow$
   (b) $NH_4^+ + H_2O \rightarrow$
   (c) $HCO_3^- + OH^- \rightarrow$

5. Write balanced equations showing how the hydrogen oxalate ion, $HC_2O_4^-$, can be both a Brønsted acid and a Brønsted base.

6. Write balanced equations showing how the HPO_4^{2-} ion of sodium hydrogen phosphate, Na_2HPO_4, can be a Brønsted acid or a Brønsted base.

7. In each of the following acid–base reactions, identify the Brønsted acid and base on the left and their conjugate partners on the right.
   (a) $HCO_2H(aq) + H_2O(\ell) \rightleftharpoons HCO_2^-(aq) + H_3O^+(aq)$
   (b) $NH_3(aq) + H_2S(aq) \rightleftharpoons NH_4^+(aq) + HS^-(aq)$
   (c) $HSO_4^-(aq) + OH^-(aq) \rightleftharpoons SO_4^{2-}(aq) + H_2O(\ell)$

8. ■ In each of the following acid–base reactions, identify the Brønsted acid and base on the left and their conjugate partners on the right.
   (a) $C_5H_5N(aq) + CH_3CO_2H(aq) \rightleftharpoons$
       $C_5H_5NH^+(aq) + CH_3CO_2^-(aq)$
   (b) $N_2H_4(aq) + HSO_4^-(aq) \rightleftharpoons$
       $N_2H_5^+(aq) + SO_4^{2-}(aq)$
   (c) $[Al(H_2O)_6]^{3+}(aq) + OH^-(aq) \rightleftharpoons$
       $[Al(H_2O)_5OH]^{2+}(aq) + H_2O(\ell)$

pH Calculations
(See Examples 4.7 and 17.1, Exercise 17.4, and ChemistryNow Screens 4.11 and 17.3–17.4.)

9. An aqueous solution has a pH of 3.75. What is the hydronium ion concentration of the solution? Is it acidic or basic?

10. ■ A saturated solution of milk of magnesia, $Mg(OH)_2$, has a pH of 10.52. What is the hydronium ion concentration of the solution? What is the hydroxide ion concentration? Is the solution acidic or basic?

11. What is the pH of a 0.0075 M solution of HCl? What is the hydroxide ion concentration of the solution?

12. ■ What is the pH of a 1.2×10^{-4} M solution of KOH? What is the hydronium ion concentration of the solution?

13. What is the pH of a 0.0015 M solution of $Ba(OH)_2$?

14. The pH of a solution of $Ba(OH)_2$ is 10.66 at 25 °C. What is the hydroxide ion concentration in the solution? If the solution volume is 125 mL, what mass of $Ba(OH)_2$ must have been dissolved?

Equilibrium Constants for Acids and Bases
(See Example 17.2, Exercise 17.5, and ChemistryNow Screen 17.6.)

15. ■ Several acids are listed here with their respective equilibrium constants:

$$C_6H_5OH(aq) + H_2O(\ell) \rightleftharpoons H_3O^+(aq) + C_6H_5O^-(aq)$$
$$K_a = 1.3 \times 10^{-10}$$

$$HCO_2H(aq) + H_2O(\ell) \rightleftharpoons H_3O^+(aq) + HCO_2^-(aq)$$
$$K_a = 1.8 \times 10^{-4}$$

$$HC_2O_4^-(aq) + H_2O(\ell) \rightleftharpoons H_3O^+(aq) + C_2O_4^{2-}(aq)$$
$$K_a = 6.4 \times 10^{-5}$$

   (a) Which is the strongest acid? Which is the weakest acid?
   (b) Which acid has the weakest conjugate base?
   (c) Which acid has the strongest conjugate base?

16. Several acids are listed here with their respective equilibrium constants.

$$HF(aq) + H_2O(\ell) \rightleftharpoons H_3O^+(aq) + F^-(aq)$$
$$K_a = 7.2 \times 10^{-4}$$

$$HPO_4^-(aq) + H_2O(\ell) \rightleftharpoons H_3O^+(aq) + PO_4^{3-}(aq)$$
$$K_a = 3.6 \times 10^{-13}$$

$$CH_3CO_2H(aq) + H_2O(\ell) \rightleftharpoons H_3O^+(aq) + CH_3CO_2^-(aq)$$
$$K_a = 1.8 \times 10^{-5}$$

   (a) Which is the strongest acid? Which is the weakest acid?
   (b) What is the conjugate base of the acid HF?
   (c) Which acid has the weakest conjugate base?
   (d) Which acid has the strongest conjugate base?

17. State which of the following ions or compounds has the strongest conjugate base, and briefly explain your choice.
    (a) HSO_4^- (b) CH_3CO_2H (c) $HOCl$

18. ■ Which of the following compounds or ions has the strongest conjugate acid? Briefly explain your choice.
    (a) CN^- (b) NH_3 (c) SO_4^{2-}

19. Dissolving K_2CO_3 in water gives a basic solution. Write a balanced equation showing how this salt can produce a basic solution.

20. Dissolving ammonium bromide in water gives an acidic solution. Write a balanced equation showing how this can occur.

21. If each of the salts listed here were dissolved in water to give a 0.10 M solution, which solution would have the highest pH? Which would have the lowest pH?
    (a) Na_2S (d) NaF
    (b) Na_3PO_4 (e) $NaCH_3CO_2$
    (c) NaH_2PO_4 (f) $AlCl_3$

22. Which of the following common food additives would give a basic solution when dissolved in water?
    (a) $NaNO_3$ (used as a meat preservative)
    (b) $NaC_6H_5CO_2$ (sodium benzoate; used as a soft-drink preservative)
    (c) Na_2HPO_4 (used as an emulsifier in the manufacture of pasteurized cheese)

pK_a: A Logarithmic Scale of Acid Strength

(See Exercise 17.7 and ChemistryNow Screen 17.6.)

23. A weak acid has a K_a of 6.5×10^{-5}. What is the value of pK_a for the acid?

24. If K_a for a weak acid is 2.4×10^{-11}, what is the value of pK_a?

25. Epinephrine hydrochloride has a pK_a value of 9.53. What is the value of K_a? Where does the acid fit in Table 17.3?

26. ■ An organic acid has pK_a = 8.95. What is its K_a value? Where does the acid fit in Table 17.3?

27. Which is the stronger of the following two acids?
    (a) benzoic acid, $C_6H_5CO_2H$, pK_a = 4.20
    (b) 2-chlorobenzoic acid, $ClC_6H_4CO_2H$, pK_a = 2.88

28. ■ Which is the stronger of the following two acids?
    (a) acetic acid, CH_3CO_2H, K_a = 1.8×10^{-5}
    (b) chloroacetic acid, $ClCH_2CO_2H$, pK_a = 2.87

Ionization Constants for Weak Acids and Their Conjugate Bases
(See Exercise 17.8 and ChemistryNow Screen 17.6.)

29. Chloroacetic acid ($ClCH_2CO_2H$) has K_a = 1.41×10^{-3}. What is the value of K_b for the chloroacetate ion ($ClCH_2CO_2^-$)?

30. ■ A weak base has K_b = 1.5×10^{-9}. What is the value of K_a for the conjugate acid?

31. The trimethylammonium ion, $(CH_3)_3NH^+$, is the conjugate acid of the weak base trimethylamine, $(CH_3)_3N$. A chemical handbook gives 9.80 as the pK_a value for $(CH_3)_3NH^+$. What is the value of K_b for $(CH_3)_3N$?

32. The chromium(III) ion in water, $[Cr(H_2O)_6]^{3+}$, is a weak acid with pK_a = 3.95. What is the value of K_b for its conjugate base, $[Cr(H_2O)_5OH]^{2+}$?

Predicting the Direction of Acid–Base Reactions
(See Example 17.3 and ChemistryNow Screen 17.7.)

33. Acetic acid and sodium hydrogen carbonate, $NaHCO_3$, are mixed in water. Write a balanced equation for the acid–base reaction that could, in principle, occur. Using Table 17.3, decide whether the equilibrium lies predominantly to the right or to the left.

34. Ammonium chloride and sodium dihydrogen phosphate, NaH_2PO_4, are mixed in water. Write a balanced equation for the acid–base reaction that could, in principle, occur. Using Table 17.3, decide whether the equilibrium lies predominantly to the right or to the left.

35. For each of the following reactions, predict whether the equilibrium lies predominantly to the left or to the right. Explain your predictions briefly.
    (a) $NH_4^+(aq) + Br^-(aq) \rightleftharpoons NH_3(aq) + HBr(aq)$
    (b) $HPO_4^{2-}(aq) + CH_3CO_2^-(aq) \rightleftharpoons$
        $PO_4^{3-}(aq) + CH_3CO_2H(aq)$
    (c) $[Fe(H_2O)_6]^{3+}(aq) + HCO_3^-(aq) \rightleftharpoons$
        $[Fe(H_2O)_5(OH)]^{2+}(aq) + H_2CO_3(aq)$

36. ■ For each of the following reactions, predict whether the equilibrium lies predominantly to the left or to the right. Explain your predictions briefly.
    (a) $H_2S(aq) + CO_3^{2-}(aq) \rightleftharpoons HS^-(aq) + HCO_3^-(aq)$
    (b) $HCN(aq) + SO_4^{2-}(aq) \rightleftharpoons CN^-(aq) + HSO_4^-(aq)$
    (c) $SO_4^{2-}(aq) + CH_3CO_2H(aq) \rightleftharpoons$
        $HSO_4^-(aq) + CH_3CO_2^-(aq)$

Types of Acid–Base Reactions
(See Exercise 17.10 and ChemistryNow Screen 17.7.)

37. Equal molar quantities of sodium hydroxide and sodium hydrogen phosphate (Na_2HPO_4) are mixed.
    (a) Write the balanced, net ionic equation for the acid–base reaction that can, in principle, occur.
    (b) Does the equilibrium lie to the right or left?

38. ■ Equal molar quantities of hydrochloric acid and sodium hypochlorite (NaClO) are mixed.
    (a) Write the balanced, net ionic equation for the acid–base reaction that can, in principle, occur.
    (b) Does the equilibrium lie to the right or left?

39. Equal molar quantities of acetic acid and sodium hydrogen phosphate (Na_2HPO_4) are mixed.
    (a) Write a balanced, net ionic equation for the acid–base reaction that can, in principle, occur.
    (b) Does the equilibrium lie to the right or left?

▲ more challenging   ■ in OWL   Blue-numbered questions answered in Appendix O

40. Equal molar quantities of ammonia and sodium dihydrogen phosphate (NaH_2PO_4) are mixed.
(a) Write a balanced, net ionic equation for the acid–base reaction that can, in principle, occur.
(b) Does the equilibrium lie to the right or left?

Using pH to Calculate Ionization Constants
(See Example 17.4 and ChemistryNow Screen 17.8.)

41. A 0.015 M solution of hydrogen cyanate, HOCN, has a pH of 2.67.
(a) What is the hydronium ion concentration in the solution?
(b) What is the ionization constant, K_a, for the acid?

42. ■ A 0.10 M solution of chloroacetic acid, $ClCH_2CO_2H$, has a pH of 1.95. Calculate K_a for the acid.

43. A 0.025 M solution of hydroxylamine has a pH of 9.11. What is the value of K_b for this weak base?

$$H_2NOH(aq) + H_2O(\ell) \rightleftharpoons H_3NOH^+(aq) + OH^-(aq)$$

44. ■ Methylamine, CH_3NH_2, is a weak base.

$$CH_3NH_2(aq) + H_2O(\ell) \rightleftharpoons CH_3NH_3^+(aq) + OH^-(aq)$$

If the pH of a 0.065 M solution of the amine is 11.70, what is the value of K_b?

45. A 2.5×10^{-3} M solution of an unknown acid has a pH of 3.80 at 25 °C.
(a) What is the hydronium ion concentration of the solution?
(b) Is the acid a strong acid, a moderately weak acid (K_a of about 10^{-5}), or a very weak acid (K_a of about 10^{-10})?

46. A 0.015 M solution of a base has a pH of 10.09.
(a) What are the hydronium and hydroxide ion concentrations of this solution?
(b) Is the base a strong base, a moderately weak base (K_b of about 10^{-5}), or a very weak base (K_b of about 10^{-10})?

Using Ionization Constants
(See Examples 17.5–17.7 and ChemistryNow Screens 17.9–17.11.)

47. What are the equilibrium concentrations of hydronium ion, acetate ion, and acetic acid in a 0.20 M aqueous solution of acetic acid?

48. ■ The ionization constant of a very weak acid, HA, is 4.0×10^{-9}. Calculate the equilibrium concentrations of H_3O^+, A^-, and HA in a 0.040 M solution of the acid.

49. What are the equilibrium concentrations of H_3O^+, CN^-, and HCN in a 0.025 M solution of HCN? What is the pH of the solution?

50. Phenol (C_6H_5OH), commonly called carbolic acid, is a weak organic acid.

$$C_6H_5OH(aq) + H_2O(\ell) \rightleftharpoons C_6H_5O^-(aq) + H_3O^+(aq)$$
$$K_a = 1.3 \times 10^{-10}$$

If you dissolve 0.195 g of the acid in enough water to make 125 mL of solution, what is the equilibrium hydronium ion concentration? What is the pH of the solution?

51. What are the equilibrium concentrations of NH_3, NH_4^+, and OH^- in a 0.15 M solution of ammonia? What is the pH of the solution?

52. ■ A hypothetical weak base has $K_b = 5.0 \times 10^{-4}$. Calculate the equilibrium concentrations of the base, its conjugate acid, and OH^- in a 0.15 M solution of the base.

53. The weak base methylamine, CH_3NH_2, has $K_b = 4.2 \times 10^{-4}$. It reacts with water according to the equation

$$CH_3NH_2(aq) + H_2O(\ell) \rightleftharpoons CH_3NH_3^+(aq) + OH^-(aq)$$

Calculate the equilibrium hydroxide ion concentration in a 0.25 M solution of the base. What are the pH and pOH of the solution?

54. Calculate the pH of a 0.12 M aqueous solution of the base aniline, $C_6H_5NH_2$ ($K_b = 4.0 \times 10^{-10}$).

$$C_6H_5NH_2(aq) + H_2O(\ell) \rightleftharpoons C_6H_5NH_3^+(aq) + OH^-(aq)$$

55. Calculate the pH of a 0.0010 M aqueous solution of HF.

56. ■ A solution of hydrofluoric acid, HF, has a pH of 2.30. Calculate the equilibrium concentrations of HF, F^-, and H_3O^+, and calculate the amount of HF originally dissolved per liter.

Acid–Base Properties of Salts
(See Example 17.7 and ChemistryNow Screen 17.11.)

57. Calculate the hydronium ion concentration and pH in a 0.20 M solution of ammonium chloride, NH_4Cl.

58. ▲ Calculate the hydronium ion concentration and pH for a 0.015 M solution of sodium formate, $NaHCO_2$.

59. Sodium cyanide is the salt of the weak acid HCN. Calculate the concentrations of H_3O^+, OH^-, HCN, and Na^+ in a solution prepared by dissolving 10.8 g of NaCN in enough water to make 5.00×10^2 mL of solution at 25 °C.

60. The sodium salt of propanoic acid, $NaCH_3CH_2CO_2$, is used as an antifungal agent by veterinarians. Calculate the equilibrium concentrations of H_3O^+ and OH^-, and the pH, for a solution of 0.10 M $NaCH_3CH_2CO_2$.

pH after an Acid–Base Reaction
(See Example 17.8 and ChemistryNow Screens 17.7 and 17.10.)

61. Calculate the hydronium ion concentration and pH of the solution that results when 22.0 mL of 0.15 M acetic acid, CH_3CO_2H, is mixed with 22.0 mL of 0.15 M NaOH.

62. ■ Calculate the hydronium ion concentration and the pH when 50.0 mL of 0.40 M NH_3 is mixed with 50.0 mL of 0.40 M HCl.

63. For each of the following cases, decide whether the pH is less than 7, equal to 7, or greater than 7.
 (a) Equal volumes of 0.10 M acetic acid, CH_3CO_2H, and 0.10 M KOH are mixed.
 (b) 25 mL of 0.015 M NH_3 is mixed with 25 mL of 0.015 M HCl.
 (c) 150 mL of 0.20 M HNO_3 is mixed with 75 mL of 0.40 M NaOH.

64. For each of the following cases, decide whether the pH is less than 7, equal to 7, or greater than 7.
 (a) 25 mL of 0.45 M H_2SO_4 is mixed with 25 mL of 0.90 M NaOH.
 (b) 15 mL of 0.050 M formic acid, HCO_2H, is mixed with 15 mL of 0.050 M NaOH.
 (c) 25 mL of 0.15 M $H_2C_2O_4$ (oxalic acid) is mixed with 25 mL of 0.30 M NaOH. (Both H^+ ions of oxalic acid are removed with NaOH.)

Polyprotic Acids and Bases
(See Example 17.9.)

65. ■ Sulfurous acid, H_2SO_3, is a weak acid capable of providing two H^+ ions.
 (a) What is the pH of a 0.45 M solution of H_2SO_3?
 (b) What is the equilibrium concentration of the sulfite ion, SO_3^{2-}, in the 0.45 M solution of H_2SO_3?

66. ■ Ascorbic acid (vitamin C, $C_6H_8O_6$) is a diprotic acid ($K_{a1} = 6.8 \times 10^{-5}$ and $K_{a2} = 2.7 \times 10^{-12}$). What is the pH of a solution that contains 5.0 mg of acid per milliliter of solution?

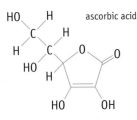
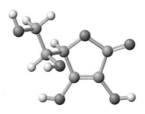

ascorbic acid

67. Hydrazine, N_2H_4, can interact with water in two steps.

$$N_2H_4(aq) + H_2O(\ell) \rightleftharpoons N_2H_5^+(aq) + OH^-(aq)$$
$$K_{b1} = 8.5 \times 10^{-7}$$

$$N_2H_5^+(aq) + H_2O(\ell) \rightleftharpoons N_2H_6^{2+}(aq) + OH^-(aq)$$
$$K_{b2} = 8.9 \times 10^{-16}$$

 (a) What is the concentration of OH^-, $N_2H_5^+$, and $N_2H_6^{2+}$ in a 0.010 M aqueous solution of hydrazine?
 (b) What is the pH of the 0.010 M solution of hydrazine?

68. Ethylenediamine, $H_2NCH_2CH_2NH_2$, can interact with water in two steps, forming OH^- in each step (see Appendix I). If you have a 0.15 M aqueous solution of the amine, calculate the concentrations of $[H_3NCH_2CH_2NH_3]^{2+}$ and OH^-.

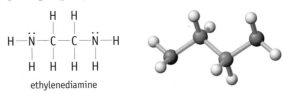

ethylenediamine

Lewis Acids and Bases
(See Exercise 17.17 and ChemistryNow Screens 17.12–17.14.)

69. Decide whether each of the following substances should be classified as a Lewis acid or a Lewis base.
 (a) H_2NOH in the reaction

$$H_2NOH(aq) + HCl(aq) \longrightarrow [H_3NOH]Cl(aq)$$

 (b) Fe^{2+}
 (c) CH_3NH_2 (Hint: Draw the electron dot structure.)

70. ■ Decide whether each of the following substances should be classified as a Lewis acid or a Lewis base.
 (a) BCl_3 (Hint: Draw the electron dot structure.)
 (b) H_2NNH_2, hydrazine (Hint: Draw the electron dot structure.)
 (c) the reactants in the reaction

$$Ag^+(aq) + 2\ NH_3(aq) \rightleftharpoons [Ag(NH_3)_2]^+(aq)$$

71. Carbon monoxide forms complexes with low-valent metals. For example, $Ni(CO)_4$ and $Fe(CO)_5$ are well known. CO also forms complexes with the iron(II) ion in hemoglobin, which prevents the hemoglobin from acting in its normal way. Is CO a Lewis acid or a Lewis base?

72. ■ Trimethylamine, $(CH_3)_3N$, is a common reagent. It interacts readily with diborane gas, B_2H_6. The latter dissociates to BH_3, and this forms a complex with the amine, $(CH_3)_3N \rightarrow BH_3$. Is the BH_3 fragment a Lewis acid or a Lewis base?

Molecular Structure, Bonding, and Acid–Base Behavior
(See Section 17.10 and Exercise 17.18.)

73. Which should be the stronger acid, HOCN or HCN? Explain briefly. (In HOCN, the H^+ ion is attached to the O atom of the OCN^- ion.)

74. ■ Which should be the stronger Brønsted acid, $[V(H_2O)_6]^{2+}$ or $[V(H_2O)_6]^{3+}$?

75. Explain why benzenesulfonic acid is a Brønsted acid.

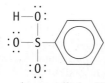

benzenesulfonic acid

76. The structure of ethylenediamine is illustrated in Study Question 68. Is this compound a Brønsted acid, a Brønsted base, a Lewis acid, or a Lewis base, or some combination of these?

General Questions on Acids and Bases

These questions are not designated as to type or location in the chapter. They may combine several concepts.

77. About this time, you may be wishing you had an aspirin. Aspirin is an organic acid (page 760) with a K_a of 3.27×10^{-4} for the reaction

$$HC_9H_7O_4(aq) + H_2O(\ell) \rightleftharpoons C_9H_7O_4^-(aq) + H_3O^+(aq)$$

If you have two tablets, each containing 0.325 g of aspirin (mixed with a neutral "binder" to hold the tablet together), and you dissolve them in a glass of water to give 225 mL of solution, what is the pH of the solution?

78. Consider the following ions: NH_4^+, CO_3^{2-}, Br^-, S^{2-}, and ClO_4^-.
(a) Which of these ions might lead to an acidic solution, and which might lead to a basic solution?
(b) Which of these anions will have no effect on the pH of an aqueous solution?
(c) Which ion is the strongest base?
(d) Write a chemical equation for the reaction of each basic anion with water.

79. A 2.50-g sample of a solid that could be $Ba(OH)_2$ or $Sr(OH)_2$ was dissolved in enough water to make 1.00 L of solution. If the pH of the solution is 12.61, what is the identity of the solid?

80. ▲ In a particular solution, acetic acid is 11% ionized at 25 °C. Calculate the pH of the solution and the mass of acetic acid dissolved to yield 1.00 L of solution.

81. Hydrogen sulfide, H_2S, and sodium acetate, $NaCH_3CO_2$, are mixed in water. Using Table 17.3, write a balanced equation for the acid–base reaction that could, in principle, occur. Does the equilibrium lie toward the products or the reactants?

82. For each of the following reactions, predict whether the equilibrium lies predominantly to the left or to the right. Explain your prediction briefly.
(a) $HCO_3^-(aq) + SO_4^{2-}(aq) \rightleftharpoons$
$$CO_3^{2-}(aq) + HSO_4^-(aq)$$
(b) $HSO_4^-(aq) + CH_3CO_2^-(aq) \rightleftharpoons$
$$SO_4^{2-}(aq) + CH_3CO_2H(aq)$$
(c) $[Co(H_2O)_6]^{2+}(aq) + CH_3CO_2^-(aq) \rightleftharpoons$
$$[Co(H_2O)_5(OH)]^+(aq) + CH_3CO_2H(aq)$$

83. A monoprotic acid HX has $K_a = 1.3 \times 10^{-3}$. Calculate the equilibrium concentrations of HX and H_3O^+ and the pH for a 0.010 M solution of the acid.

84. ■ Arrange the following 0.10 M solutions in order of increasing pH.
(a) NaCl   (d) $NaCH_3CO_2$
(b) NH_4Cl (e) KOH
(c) HCl

85. ■ *m*-Nitrophenol, a weak acid, can be used as a pH indicator because it is yellow at a pH above 8.6 and colorless at a pH below 6.8. If the pH of a 0.010 M solution of the compound is 3.44, calculate its pK_a.

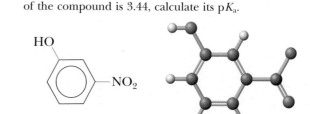

m-nitrophenol

86. The butylammonium ion, $C_4H_9NH_3^+$, has a K_a of 2.3×10^{-11}.

$$C_4H_9NH_3^+(aq) + H_2O(\ell) \rightleftharpoons H_3O^+(aq) + C_4H_9NH_2(aq)$$

(a) Calculate K_b for the conjugate base, $C_4H_9NH_2$ (butylamine).
(b) Place the butylammonium ion and its conjugate base in Table 17.3. Name an acid weaker than $C_4H_9NH_3^+$ and a base stronger than $C_4H_9NH_2$.
(c) What is the pH of a 0.015 M solution of the butylammonium chloride?

87. The local anesthetic novocaine is the hydrogen chloride salt of an organic base, procaine.

$$C_{13}H_{20}N_2O_2(aq) + HCl(aq) \longrightarrow [HC_{13}H_{20}N_2O_2]^+Cl^-(aq)$$
procaine   novocaine

The pK_a for novocaine is 8.85. What is the pH of a 0.0015 M solution of novocaine?

88. Pyridine is a weak organic base and readily forms a salt with hydrochloric acid.

$$C_5H_5N(aq) + HCl(aq) \longrightarrow C_5H_5NH^+(aq) + Cl^-(aq)$$
$$\text{pyridine} \qquad\qquad \text{pyridinium ion}$$

What is the pH of a 0.025 M solution of pyridinium hydrochloride, $[C_5H_5NH^+]Cl^-$?

89. ■ The base ethylamine $(CH_3CH_2NH_2)$ has a K_b of 4.3×10^{-4}. A closely related base, ethanolamine $(HOCH_2CH_2NH_2)$, has a K_b of 3.2×10^{-5}.
(a) Which of the two bases is stronger?
(b) Calculate the pH of a 0.10 M solution of the stronger base.

90. Chloroacetic acid, $ClCH_2CO_2H$, is a moderately weak acid ($K_a = 1.40 \times 10^{-3}$). If you dissolve 94.5 mg of the acid in water to give 125 mL of solution, what is the pH of the solution?

91. ■ Saccharin $(HC_7H_4NO_3S)$ is a weak acid with $pK_a = 2.32$ at 25 °C. It is used in the form of sodium saccharide, $NaC_7H_4NO_3S$. What is the pH of a 0.10 M solution of sodium saccharide at 25 °C?

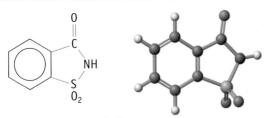

saccharin

92. ■ Given the following solutions:
(a) 0.1 M NH_3
(b) 0.1 M Na_2CO_3
(c) 0.1 M NaCl
(d) 0.1 M CH_3CO_2H
(e) 0.1 M NH_4Cl
(f) 0.1 M $NaCH_3CO_2$
(g) 0.1 M $NH_4CH_3CO_2$
(i) Which of the solutions are acidic?
(ii) Which of the solutions are basic?
(iii) Which of the solutions is most acidic?

93. ■ For each of the following salts, predict whether a 0.10 M solution has a pH less than, equal to, or greater than 7.
(a) $NaHSO_4$
(b) NH_4Br
(c) $KClO_4$
(d) Na_2CO_3
(e) $(NH_4)_2S$
(f) $NaNO_3$
(g) Na_2HPO_4
(h) LiBr
(i) $FeCl_3$
Which solution has the highest pH? The lowest pH?

94. Nicotine, $C_{10}H_{14}N_2$, has two basic nitrogen atoms (page 798), and both can react with water.

$$Nic(aq) + H_2O(\ell) \rightleftharpoons NicH^+(aq) + OH^-(aq)$$

$$NicH^+(aq) + H_2O(\ell) \rightleftharpoons NicH_2^{2+}(aq) + OH^-(aq)$$

K_{b1} is 7.0×10^{-7} and K_{b2} is 1.1×10^{-10}. Calculate the approximate pH of a 0.020 M solution.

95. ■ Oxalic acid is a relatively weak diprotic acid. Calculate the equilibrium constant for the reaction shown below from K_{a1} and K_{a2}. (See Appendix H for the required K_a values.)

$$H_2C_2O_4(aq) + 2 H_2O(\ell) \rightleftharpoons C_2O_4^{2-}(aq) + 2 H_3O^+(aq)$$

96. ▲ The equilibrium constant for the reaction of hydrochloric acid and ammonia is 1.8×10^9 (page 779). Confirm this value.

97. ▲ The equilibrium constant for the reaction of formic acid and sodium hydroxide is 1.8×10^{10} (page 779). Confirm this value.

98. ■ ▲ Calculate the pH of the solution that results from mixing 25.0 mL of 0.14 M formic acid and 50.0 mL of 0.070 M sodium hydroxide.

99. ■ ▲ To what volume should 1.00×10^2 mL of any weak acid, HA, with a concentration 0.20 M be diluted to double the percentage ionization?

100. ▲ The hydrogen phthalate ion, $C_8H_5O_4^-$, is a weak acid with $K_a = 3.91 \times 10^{-6}$.

$$C_8H_5O_4^-(aq) + H_2O(\ell) \rightleftharpoons C_8H_4O_4^{2-}(aq) + H_3O^+(aq)$$

What is the pH of a 0.050 M solution of potassium hydrogen phthalate, $KC_8H_5O_4$? *Note:* To find the pH for a solution of the anion, we must take into account that the ion is amphiprotic. It can be shown that, for most cases of amphiprotic ions, the H_3O^+ concentration is

$$[H_3O^+] = \sqrt{K_1 \times K_2}$$

For phthalic acid, $C_8H_6O_4$, K_1 is 1.12×10^{-3}, and K_2 is 3.91×10^{-6}.

101. ■ ▲ You prepare a 0.10 M solution of oxalic acid, $H_2C_2O_4$. What molecules and ions exist in this solution? List them in order of decreasing concentration.

102. ■ ▲ You mix 30.0 mL of 0.15 M NaOH with 30.0 mL of 0.15 M acetic acid. What molecules and ions exist in this solution? List them in order of decreasing concentration.

In the Laboratory

103. ■ Describe an experiment that will allow you to place the following three bases in order of increasing base strength: NaCN, CH_3NH_2, Na_2CO_3.

▲ more challenging   ■ in OWL   Blue-numbered questions answered in Appendix O

104. ■ The data below compare the strength of acetic acid with a related series of acids, where the H atoms of the CH_3 group in acetic acid are successively replaced by Br.

Acid	pK_a
CH_3CO_2H	4.74
$BrCH_2CO_2H$	2.90
Br_2CHCO_2H	1.39
Br_3CCO_2H	−0.147

(a) What trend in acid strength do you observe as H is successively replaced by Br? Can you suggest a reason for this trend?

(b) Suppose each of the acids above were present as a 0.10 M aqueous solution. Which would have the highest pH? The lowest pH?

105. ▲ You have three solutions labeled A, B, and C. You know only that each contains a different cation—Na^+, NH_4^+, or H^+. Each has an anion that does not contribute to the solution pH (e.g., Cl^-). You also have two other solutions, Y and Z, each containing a different anion, Cl^- or OH^-, with a cation that does not influence solution pH (e.g., K^+). If equal amounts of B and Y are mixed, the result is an acidic solution. Mixing A and Z gives a neutral solution, whereas B and Z give a basic solution. Identify the five unknown solutions. (Adapted from D. H. Barouch: *Voyages in Conceptual Chemistry*, Boston, Jones and Bartlett, 1997.)

	Y	**Z**
A		neutral
B	acidic	basic
C		

106. ■ A hydrogen atom in the organic base pyridine, C_5H_5N, can be substituted by various atoms or groups to give XC_5H_4N, where X is an atom such as Cl or a group such as CH_3. The following table gives K_a values for the conjugate acids of a variety of substituted pyridines.

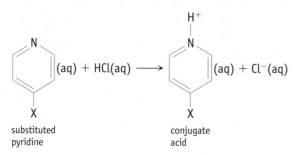

substituted   conjugate
pyridine   acid

Atom or Group X	K_a of Conjugate Acid
NO_2	5.9×10^{-2}
Cl	1.5×10^{-4}
H	6.8×10^{-6}
CH_3	1.0×10^{-6}

(a) Suppose each conjugate acid is dissolved in sufficient water to give a 0.050 M solution. Which solution would have the highest pH? The lowest pH?

(b) Which of the substituted pyridines is the strongest Brønsted base? Which is the weakest Brønsted base?

107. ■ Nicotinic acid, $C_6H_5NO_2$, is found in minute amounts in all living cells, but appreciable amounts occur in liver, yeast, milk, adrenal glands, white meat, and corn. Whole-wheat flour contains about 60. μg per 1g of flour. One gram (1.00 g) of the acid dissolves in water to give 60. mL of solution having a pH of 2.70. What is the approximate value of K_a for the acid?

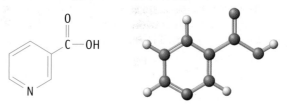

nicotinic acid

108. ■▲ Equilibrium constants can be measured for the dissociation of Lewis acid–base complexes such as the dimethyl ether complex of BF_3, $(CH_3)_2O \rightarrow BF_3$. The value of K (here K_p) for the reaction is 0.17.

$$(CH_3)_2O \rightarrow BF_3(g) \rightleftharpoons BF_3(g) + (CH_3)_2O(g)$$

(a) Describe each product as a Lewis acid or a Lewis base.

(b) If you place 1.00 g of the complex in a 565-mL flask at 25 °C, what is the total pressure in the flask? What are the partial pressures of the Lewis acid, the Lewis base, and the complex?

109. ▲ Sulfanilic acid, which is used in making dyes, is made by reacting aniline with sulfuric acid.

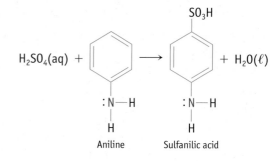

Aniline   Sulfanilic acid

(a) Is aniline a Brønsted base, a Lewis base, or both? Explain, using its possible reactions with HCl, BF_3, or other acid.

(b) Sulfanilic acid has a pK_a value of 3.23. The sodium salt of the acid, $Na(H_2NC_6H_4SO_3)$, is quite soluble in water. If you dissolve 1.25 g of the salt in water to give 125 mL of solution, what is the pH of the solution?

110. Amino acids are an important group of compounds (see page 498). At low pH, both the carboxylic acid group (—CO_2H) and the amine group (—NHR) are protonated. However, as the pH of the solution increases (say by adding base), the carboxylic acid proton is removed, usually at a pH between 2 and 3. In a middle range of pHs, the amine group is protonated, but the carboxylic acid group has lost the proton. (This is called a *zwitterion*.) At more basic pH values, the amine proton is dissociated.

$$
\underset{\substack{\text{Alanine}\\\text{Cationic form}}}{\overset{\text{O}}{\underset{\text{CH}_3}{\overset{\|}{\text{H}_3\overset{+}{\text{N}}-\text{CH}-\text{C}-\text{OH}}}}} \xrightleftharpoons{pK_a = 2.4} \underset{\substack{\text{Zwitterionic form}}}{\overset{\text{O}}{\underset{\text{CH}_3}{\overset{\|}{\text{H}_3\overset{+}{\text{N}}-\text{CH}-\text{C}-\text{O}^-}}}}
$$

$$
\xrightleftharpoons{pK_a = 9.7} \underset{\substack{\text{Anionic form}}}{\overset{\text{O}}{\underset{\text{CH}_3}{\overset{\|}{\text{H}_2\text{N}-\text{CH}-\text{C}-\text{O}^-}}}}
$$

What is the pH of a 0.20 M solution of alanine hydrochloride, $[NH_3CHCH_3CO_2H]Cl$?

Summary and Conceptual Questions

The following questions may use concepts from this and previous chapters.

111. How can water be both a Brønsted base and a Lewis base? Can water be a Brønsted acid? A Lewis acid?

112. The nickel(II) ion exists as $[Ni(H_2O)_6]^{2+}$ in aqueous solution. Why is such a solution acidic? As part of your answer, include a balanced equation depicting what happens when $[Ni(H_2O)_6]^{2+}$ interacts with water.

113. The halogens form three stable, weak acids HOX.

Acid	pK_a
HOCl	7.46
HOBr	8.7
HOI	10.6

(a) Which is the strongest of these acids?

(b) Explain why the acid strength changes as the halogen atom is changed.

114. The acidity of the oxoacids was described on page 794, and a larger number of acids are listed in the table below.

$E(OH)_m$	pK_a	$EO(OH)_m$	pK_a	$EO_2(OH)_m$	pK_a	$EO_3(OH)_m$	pK_a
Very weak		**Weak**		**Strong**		**Very strong**	
Cl(OH)	7.5	ClO(OH)	2	$ClO_2(OH)$	−3	$ClO_3(OH)$	−10
Br(OH)	8.7	NO(OH)	3.4	$NO_2(OH)$	−1.4		
I(OH)	10.6	IO(OH)	1.6	$IO_2(OH)$	0.8		
$Si(OH)_4$	9.7	$SO(OH)_2$	1.8	$SO_2(OH)_2$	−3		
$Sb(OH)_4$	11.0	$SeO(OH)_2$	2.5	$SeO_2(OH)_2$	−3		
$As(OH)_3$	9.2	$AsO(OH)_3$	2.3				
		$PO(OH)_3$	2.1				
		$HPO(OH)_2$	1.8				
		$H_2PO(OH)$	2.0				

(a) What general trends do you see in these data?

(b) What has a greater effect on acidity, the number of O atoms bonded directly to the central atom E or the number of OH groups?

(c) Look at the acids based on Cl, N, and S. Is there a correlation of acidity with the formal charge on the central atom, E?

(d) The acid H_3PO_3 has a pK_a of 1.8, and this led to some insight into its structure. If the structure of the acid were $P(OH)_3$, what would be its predicted pK_a value? Given that this is a diprotic acid, which H atoms are lost as H^+ ions?

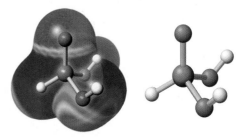

115. Perchloric acid behaves as an acid, even when it is dissolved in sulfuric acid.

(a) Write a balanced equation showing how perchloric acid can transfer a proton to sulfuric acid.

(b) Draw a Lewis electron dot structure for sulfuric acid. How can sulfuric acid function as a base?

116. You purchase a bottle of water. On checking its pH, you find that it is not neutral, as you might have expected. Instead, it is slightly acidic. Why?

117. Iodine, I_2, is much more soluble in a water solution of potassium iodide, KI, than it is in pure water. The anion found in solution is I_3^-.

(a) Draw an electron dot structure for I_3^-.

(b) Write an equation for this reaction, indicating the Lewis acid and the Lewis base.

OWL *See Chapter Goals Revisited (page 849) for Study Questions keyed to these goals and assignable in OWL.*

- Understand the common ion effect.
- Understand the control of pH in aqueous solution with buffers.
- Evaluate the pH in the course of acid–base titrations.
- Apply chemical equilibrium concepts to the solubility of ionic compounds.

In Chapter 3, we described four fundamental types of chemical reactions: acid–base reactions, precipitation reactions, gas-forming reactions, and oxidation-reduction reactions. In the present chapter, we want to apply the principles of chemical equilibria to an understanding of the first two of these kinds of reactions.

With regard to acid–base reactions, we are looking for answers to the following questions:

- How can we control the pH in a solution?
- What happens when an acid and base are mixed in any amount?

Precipitation reactions can also be understood in terms of chemical equilibria. The following questions are discussed in this chapter:

- If aqueous solutions of two ionic compounds are mixed, will precipitation occur?
- To what extent does an insoluble substance actually dissolve?
- What chemical reactions can be used to redissolve a precipitate?

Chemistry.Now™

Throughout the text this icon introduces an opportunity for self-study or to explore interactive tutorials by signing in at **www.cengage.com/login**.

18.1 The Common Ion Effect

In the previous chapter, we examined the behavior of weak acids and bases in aqueous solution. There are many cases, however, where the weak acid solution also contains a significant concentration of its conjugate base or where a weak base solution has a significant concentration of conjugate acid. The pH of such solutions will be different than those of solutions of a weak acid or base with very small amounts of conjugate bases or acids produced by ionization. The effect of a significant concentration of conjugate base on the pH of a weak acid solution, for example, is called the **common ion effect**, and it is particularly important in buffer solutions, as we shall see in Section 18.2.

Let us see how the common ion effect works. If 1.0 L of a 0.25 M acetic acid solution has a pH of 2.67, what is the pH after adding 0.10 mol of sodium acetate? Sodium acetate, $NaCH_3CO_2$, is 100% dissociated into its ions, Na^+ and $CH_3CO_2^-$, in water. Sodium ion has no effect on the pH of a solution (◄ Table 17.4 and Example 17.2). Thus, the important components of the solution are a weak acid (CH_3CO_2H) and its conjugate base ($CH_3CO_2^-$); the added acetate ion is "common" to the ionization equilibrium reaction of acetic acid.

$$CH_3CO_2H(aq) + H_2O(\ell) \Longrightarrow H_3O^+(aq) + CH_3CO_2^-(aq)$$

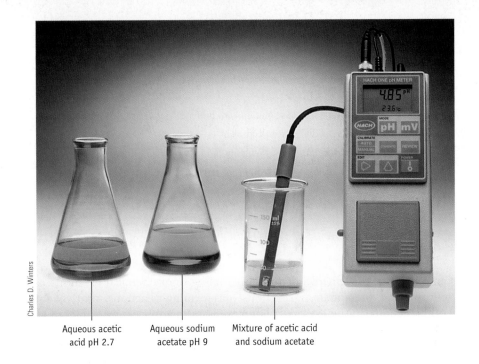

Aqueous acetic   Aqueous sodium   Mixture of acetic acid
acid pH 2.7   acetate pH 9   and sodium acetate

Assume the acid ionizes to give H_3O^+ and $CH_3CO_2^-$, both in the amount x. This means that, relative to their initial concentrations, CH_3CO_2H decreases in concentration slightly (by an amount x) and $CH_3CO_2^-$ increases slightly (by an amount x).

■ **The Common Ion Effect** In this ICE
table, the first row (Initial) reflects the
assumption that no ionization (or hydrolysis of the conjugate base) has yet occurred. Ionization of the acid in the presence of the conjugate base then produces
x mol/L of hydronium ion and x mol/L
more of the conjugate base.

Equation	CH_3CO_2H	$+$	$H_2O \rightleftharpoons$	H_3O^+	$+$	$CH_3CO_2^-$
Initial (M)	0.25			0		0.10
Change (M)	$-x$			$+x$		$+x$
Equilibrium (M)	$(0.25 - x)$			x		$0.10 + x$

Because we have been able to define the equilibrium concentrations of acid and conjugate base and we know K_a, the hydronium ion concentration ($= x$) can be calculated from the usual equilibrium constant expression.

$$K_a = 1.8 \times 10^{-5} = \frac{[H_3O^+][CH_3CO_2^-]}{[CH_3CO_2H]} = \frac{(x)(0.10 + x)}{0.25 - x}$$

Now, because acetic acid is a weak acid and because it is ionizing in the presence of a significant concentration of its conjugate base, let us assume x is quite small. That is, it is reasonable to assume that $(0.10 + x)M \approx 0.10$ M and that $(0.25 - x)M \approx 0.25$ M. This leads to the "approximate" expression.

$$K_a = 1.8 \times 10^{-5} = \frac{[H_3O^+][CH_3CO_2^-]}{[CH_3CO_2H]} = \frac{(x)(0.10)}{0.25}$$

■ **Equilibrium Constants and**
Temperature Unless specified otherwise,
all equilibrium constants and all calculations in this chapter are at 25 °C.

Solving this, we find that $x = [H_3O^+] = 4.5 \times 10^{-5}$ M and the pH is 4.35.

Without added $NaCH_3CO_2$, which provides the "common ion" $CH_3CO_2^-$, ioniza-
tion of 0.25 M acetic acid will produce H_3O^+ and $CH_3CO_2^-$ ions in a concentration of 0.0021 M (to give a pH of 2.68). Le Chatelier's principle, however, predicts that the added common ion causes the reaction to proceed less far to the right. Hence, as we have found, $x = [H_3O^+]$ is less than 0.0021 M in the presence of added acetate ion.

Sign in at **www.cengage.com/login** and go to Chapter 18 Contents to see Screen 18.2 for a simulation of the **common ion effect**.

■ **EXAMPLE 18.1** **Reaction of Lactic Acid with a Deficiency of Sodium Hydroxide**

Problem What is the pH of the solution that results from adding 25.0 mL of 0.0500 M NaOH to 25.0 mL of 0.100 M lactic acid? (K_a for lactic acid $= 1.4 \times 10^{-4}$)

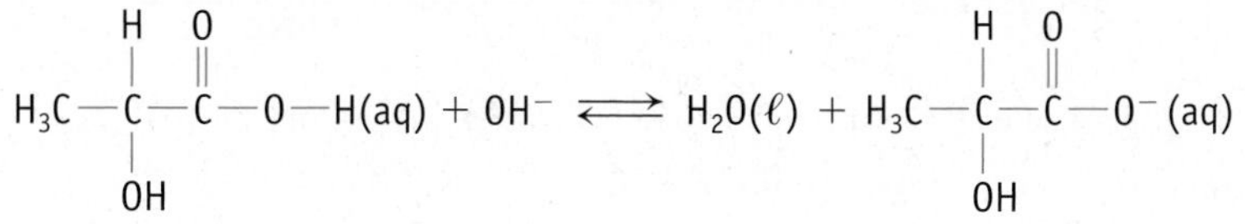

$$H_3C-\overset{\displaystyle H}{\underset{\displaystyle OH}{C}}-\overset{\displaystyle O}{C}-O-H(aq) + OH^- \rightleftharpoons H_2O(\ell) + H_3C-\overset{\displaystyle H}{\underset{\displaystyle OH}{C}}-\overset{\displaystyle O}{C}-O^- (aq)$$

lactic acid ($HC_3H_5O_3$)
$K_a = 1.4 \times 10^{-4}$

lactate ion ($C_3H_5O_3^-$)

Strategy There are two parts to this problem: a stoichiometry problem followed by an equilibrium problem. We first calculate the concentrations of lactic acid and lactate ion that are present following the reaction of lactic acid with NaOH. Then, with the acid and conjugate base concentrations known, we follow the strategy in the text above to determine the pH.

Solution

Part 1: *Stoichiometry Problem*

First, consider what species remain in solution after the acid–base reaction and what the concentrations of those species are.

(a) Amounts of NaOH and lactic acid used in the reaction

$$(0.0250 \text{ L NaOH})(0.0500 \text{ mol/L}) = 1.25 \times 10^{-3} \text{ mol NaOH}$$

$$(0.0250 \text{ L lactic acid})(0.100 \text{ mol/L}) = 2.50 \times 10^{-3} \text{ mol lactic acid}$$

(b) Amount of lactate ion produced by the acid-base reaction
Recognizing that NaOH is the limiting reactant, we have

$$(1.25 \times 10^{-3} \text{ mol NaOH})\left(\frac{1 \text{ mol lactate ion}}{1 \text{ mol NaOH}}\right) = 1.25 \times 10^{-3} \text{ mol lactate ion produced}$$

(c) Amount of lactic acid consumed

$$(1.25 \times 10^{-3} \text{ mol NaOH})\left(\frac{1 \text{ mol lactic acid}}{1 \text{ mol NaOH}}\right) = 1.25 \times 10^{-3} \text{ mol lactic acid consumed}$$

(d) Amount of lactic acid remaining when reaction is complete.
$$2.50 \times 10^{-3} \text{ mol lactic acid available} - 1.25 \times 10^{-3} \text{ mol lactic acid consumed}$$
$$= 1.25 \times 10^{-3} \text{ mol lactic acid remaining}$$

(e) Concentrations of lactic acid and lactate ion after reaction. Note that the total solution volume after reaction is 50.0 mL or 0.050 L.

$$[\text{lactic acid}] = \frac{1.25 \times 10^{-3} \text{ mol lactic acid}}{0.0500 \text{ L}} = 2.50 \times 10^{-2} \text{ M}$$

Because the amount of lactic acid remaining is the same as the amount of lactate ion produced, we have

$$[\text{lactic acid}] = [\text{lactate ion}] = 2.50 \times 10^{-2} \text{ M}$$

Part 2: *Equilibrium Calculation*

With the "initial" concentrations known, construct a table summarizing the equilibrium concentrations.

Equilibrium	$HC_3H_5O_3 + H_2O$	$\rightleftharpoons$	H_3O^+	$+$	$C_3H_5O_3^-$
Initial (M)	0.0250		0		0.0250
Change (M)	$-x$		$+x$		$+x$
Equilibrium (M)	$(0.0250 - x)$		x		$(0.0250 + x)$

Substituting the concentrations into the equilibrium expression, we have

$$K_a \text{ (lactic acid)} = 1.4 \times 10^{-4} = \frac{[H_3O^+][C_3H_5O_2^-]}{[HC_3H_5O_2]} = \frac{(x)(0.0250 + x)}{0.0250 - x}$$

Making the assumption that x is small with respect to 0.0250 M, we see that

$$x = [H_3O^+] = K_a = 1.4 \times 10^{-4} \text{ M}$$

which gives a pH of 3.85.

Comment There are two final points to be made:

- Our assumption that $x \ll 0.0250$ is valid.
- The pH of a solution containing only 0.100 M lactic acid solution is 2.43. Adding a base (lactate ion) increases the pH.

EXERCISE 18.1 Common Ion Effect

Assume you have a 0.30 M solution of formic acid (HCO_2H) and have added enough sodium formate ($NaHCO_2$) to make the solution 0.10 M in the salt. Calculate the pH of the formic acid solution before and after adding solid sodium formate.

EXERCISE 18.2 Mixing an Acid and a Base

What is the pH of the solution that results from adding 30.0 mL of 0.100 M NaOH to 45.0 mL of 0.100 M acetic acid?

Module 23

18.2 Controlling pH: Buffer Solutions

The normal pH of human blood is 7.4. However, the addition of a small quantity of strong acid or base, say 0.010 mol, to a liter of blood leads to a change in pH of only about 0.1 pH units. In comparison, if you add 0.010 mol of HCl to 1.0 L of pure water, the pH drops from 7 to 2. Addition of 0.010 mol of NaOH to pure water increases the pH from 7 to 12. Blood, and many other body fluids, are said to be buffered. A **buffer** causes solutions to be resistant to a change in pH when a strong acid or base is added (Figure 18.2).

There are two requirements for a buffer:

- Two substances are needed: an acid capable of reacting with added OH^- ions and a base that can consume added H_3O^+ ions.
- The acid and base must not react with each another.

These requirements mean a buffer is usually prepared from a conjugate acid–base pair: (1) a weak acid and its conjugate base (acetic and acetate ion, for example), or (2) a weak base and its conjugate acid (ammonia and ammonium ion, for example). Some buffers commonly used in the laboratory are given in Table 18.1.

Sign in at **www.cengage.com/login** to download the Go Chemistry module for this section or go to **www.ichapters.com** to purchase modules.

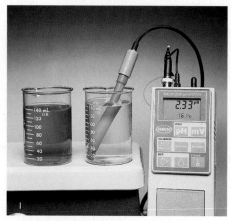

Before

After adding 0.10 M HCl

Charles D. Winters

Buffered   Not buffered

(a) The pH electrode is indicating the pH of water that contains a trace of acid (and bromphenol blue acid–base indicator). The solution at the left is a buffer solution with a pH of about 7. (It also contains bromphenol blue dye.)

(b) When 5 mL of 0.10 M HCl is added to each solution, the pH of the water drops several units, whereas the pH of the buffer stays constant, as implied by the fact that the indicator color did not change.

Active Figure 18.2
Buffer solutions.
Chemistry ⚛ Now™ Sign in at www.cengage.com/login and go to the Chapter Contents menu to explore an interactive version of this figure accompanied by an exercise.

To see how a buffer works, let us consider an acetic acid/acetate ion buffer. Acetic acid, a weak acid, is needed to consume any added hydroxide ions.

$$CH_3CO_2H(aq) + OH^-(aq) \rightleftharpoons CH_3CO_2^-(aq) + H_2O(\ell) \qquad K = 1.8 \times 10^9$$

The equilibrium constant for the reaction is very large because OH^- is a much stronger base than acetate ion, $CH_3CO_2^-$ (see Section 17.6 and Table 17.3). This means that any OH^- entering the solution from an outside source is consumed completely. In a similar way, any hydronium ion added to the solution reacts with the acetate ion present in the buffer.

$$H_3O^+(aq) + CH_3CO_2^-(aq) \rightleftharpoons H_2O(\ell) + CH_3CO_2H(aq) \qquad K = 5.6 \times 10^4$$

The equilibrium constant for this reaction is also quite large because H_3O^+ is a much stronger acid than CH_3CO_2H.

The next several examples illustrate how to calculate the pH of a buffer solution, how to prepare a buffer, and how a buffer can control the pH of a solution.

■ **Buffers and the Common Ion Effect** The common ion effect is observed for an acid (or base) ionizing in the presence of its conjugate base (or acid). A buffer is a solution of an acid, for example, and its conjugate base.

Chemistry ⚛ Now™

Sign in at **www.cengage.com/login** and go to Chapter 18 Contents to see:
- Screen 18.3 for a simulation and tutorials on **buffer solutions**
- Screen 18.4 for a simulation and tutorials on **pH of buffer solutions**

TABLE 18.1   Some Commonly Used Buffer Systems

Weak Acid	Conjugate Base	Acid K_a (pK_a)	Useful pH Range
Phthalic acid, $C_6H_4(CO_2H)_2$	Hydrogen phthalate ion, $C_6H_4(CO_2H)(CO_2)^-$	1.3×10^{-3} (2.89)	1.9–3.9
Acetic acid, CH_3CO_2H	Acetate ion, $CH_3CO_2^-$	1.8×10^{-5} (4.74)	3.7–5.8
Dihydrogen phosphate ion, $H_2PO_4^-$	Hydrogen phosphate ion, HPO_4^{2-}	6.2×10^{-8} (7.21)	6.2–8.2
Hydrogen phosphate ion, HPO_4^{2-}	Phosphate ion, PO_4^{3-}	3.6×10^{-13} (12.44)	11.3–13.3

Problem What is the pH of an acetic acid/sodium acetate buffer with $[CH_3CO_2H] = 0.700$ M and $[CH_3CO_2^-] = 0.600$ M?

Strategy The concentrations of the weak acid, its conjugate base, and K_a are all known, so we can use the usual equilibrium expression to calculate the hydronium ion concentration.

Solution Write a balanced equation for the ionization of acetic acid and set up an ICE table.

Equilibrium	$CH_3CO_2H + H_2O \rightleftharpoons$	H_3O^+ +	$CH_3CO_2^-$
Initial (M)	0.700	0	0.600
Change (M)	$-x$	$+x$	$+x$
Equilibrium (M)	$0.700 - x$	x	$0.600 + x$

The appropriate equilibrium constant expression is

$$K_a = 1.8 \times 10^{-5} = \frac{[H_3O^+][CH_3CO_2^-]}{[CH_3CO_2H]} = \frac{(x)(0.600 + x)}{0.700 - x}$$

As explained on page 814, the value of x will be very small with respect to 0.700 or 0.600, so we can use the "approximate expression" to find x, the hydronium ion concentration.

$$K_a = 1.8 \times 10^{-5} = \frac{[H_3O^+][CH_3CO_2^-]}{[CH_3CO_2H]} = \frac{(x)(0.600)}{0.700}$$

$$x = 2.1 \times 10^{-5} \text{ M}$$

$$pH = -\log(2.1 \times 10^{-5}) = \boxed{4.68}$$

Comment The pH of the buffer has a value between the pH of 0.700 M acetic acid (2.45) and 0.600 M sodium acetate (9.26).

EXERCISE 18.3 pH of a Buffer Solution

What is the pH of a buffer solution composed of 0.50 M formic acid (HCO_2H) and 0.70 M sodium formate ($NaHCO_2$)?

General Expressions for Buffer Solutions

In Example 18.2, we found the hydronium ion concentration of the acetic acid/acetate ion buffer solution by solving for x in the equation

$$K_a = 1.8 \times 10^{-5} = \frac{[H_3O^+][CH_3CO_2^-]}{[CH_3CO_2H]} = \frac{(x)(0.600)}{0.700}$$

If this equation is rearranged, we have a very useful equation that can help you better understand how a buffer works.

$$[H_3O^+] = \frac{[CH_3CO_2H]}{[CH_3CO_2^-]} \times K_a$$

That is, the hydrogen ion concentration in the acetic acid/acetate ion buffer is given by the ratio of the acid and conjugate base concentrations times the acid ionization constant. Indeed, this is true for all solutions of *a weak acid and its conjugate base.*

■ **Buffer Solutions** You will find it generally useful to consider all buffer solutions as composed of a weak acid and its conjugate base. Suppose, for example, a buffer is composed of the weak base ammonia and its conjugate acid ammonium ion. The hydronium ion concentration can be found from Equation 18.1 by assuming the buffer is composed of the weak acid NH_4^+ and its conjugate base, NH_3.

$$[H_3O^+] = \frac{[acid]}{[conjugate\ base]} \times K_a \qquad (18.1)$$

It is often convenient to use Equation 18.1 in a different form. If we take the negative logarithm of each side of the equation, we have

$$-\log[H_3O^+] = \left\{-\log\frac{[acid]}{[conjugate\ base]}\right\} + \left(-\log K_a\right)$$

You know that $-\log[H_3O^+]$ is defined as pH, and $-\log K_a$ is defined as pK_a (◄ Sections 17.3 and 17.4). Furthermore, because

$$-\log\frac{[\text{acid}]}{[\text{conjugate base}]} = +\log\frac{[\text{conjugate base}]}{[\text{acid}]}$$

the preceding equation can be rewritten as

$$pH = pK_a + \log\frac{[\text{conjugate base}]}{[\text{acid}]} \qquad (18.2)$$

This equation is known as the **Henderson–Hasselbalch equation.**

Both Equations 18.1 and 18.2 show that the pH of a buffer solution is controlled by two factors: the strength of the acid (as expressed by K_a or pK_a) and the relative amounts of acid and conjugate base. The solution pH is established primarily by the value of K_a or pK_a, and the pH is fine-tuned by adjusting the acid-to-conjugate base ratio.

When the concentrations of conjugate base and acid are the same in a solution, the ratio [conjugate base]/[acid] is 1. The log of 1 is zero, so $pH = pK_a$ under these circumstances. If there is more of the conjugate base in the solution than acid, for example, then $pH > pK_a$. Conversely, if there is more acid than conjugate base in solution, then $pH < pK_a$.

■ **The Henderson–Hasselbalch Equation** Many handbooks of chemistry list acid ionization constants in terms of pK_a values, so the approximate pH values of possible buffer solutions are readily apparent.

Chemistry.⊙.Now™

Sign in at **www.cengage.com/login** and go to Chapter 18 Contents to see Screen 18.4 for a simulation and tutorial on **the Henderson–Hasselbalch equation.**

■ **EXAMPLE 18.3** **Using the Henderson–Hasselbalch Equation**

Problem Benzoic acid ($C_6H_5CO_2H$, 2.00 g) and sodium benzoate ($NaC_6H_5CO_2$, 2.00 g) are dissolved in enough water to make 1.00 L of solution. Calculate the pH of the solution using the Henderson–Hasselbalch equation.

Strategy The Henderson–Hasselbalch equation requires the pK_a of the acid, and this is obtained from the K_a for the acid (see Table 17.3 or Appendix H). You will also need the acid and conjugate base concentrations.

Solution K_a for benzoic acid as 6.3×10^{-5}. Therefore,

$$pK_a = -\log(6.3 \times 10^{-5}) = 4.20$$

Next, we need the concentrations of the acid (benzoic acid) and its conjugate base (benzoate ion).

$$2.00 \text{ g benzoic acid} \left(\frac{1 \text{ mol}}{122.1 \text{ g}}\right) = 0.0164 \text{ mol benzoic acid}$$

$$2.00 \text{ g sodium benzoate} \left(\frac{1 \text{ mol}}{144.1 \text{ g}}\right) = 0.0139 \text{ mol sodium benzoate}$$

Because the solution volume is 1.00 L, the concentrations are [benzoic acid] = 0.0164 M and [sodium benzoate] = 0.0139 M. Therefore, using Equation 18.2, we have

$$pH = 4.20 + \log\frac{0.0139}{0.0164} = 4.20 + \log(0.848) = \boxed{4.13}$$

Comment Notice that the pH is less than the pK_a because the concentration of acid is greater than the concentration of the conjugate base (the ratio of conjugate base to acid concentration is less than 1).

> **EXERCISE 18.4 Using the Henderson–Hasselbalch Equation**
>
> Use the Henderson–Hasselbalch equation to calculate the pH of 1.00 L of a buffer solution containing 15.0 g of $NaHCO_3$ and 18.0 g of Na_2CO_3. (Consider this buffer as a solution of the weak acid HCO_3^- with CO_3^{2-} as its conjugate base.)

Preparing Buffer Solutions

To be useful, a buffer solution must have two characteristics:

- *pH Control:* It should control the pH at the desired value. The Henderson–Hasselbalch equation shows us how this can be done.

$$pH = pK_a + \log \frac{[\text{conjugate base}]}{[\text{acid}]}$$

First, an acid is chosen whose pK_a (or K_a) is near the intended value of pH (or $[H_3O^+]$). Second, the exact value of pH (or $[H_3O^+]$) is then achieved by adjusting the acid-to-conjugate base ratio. (Example 18.4 illustrates this approach.)

- *Buffer capacity:* The buffer should have the ability to keep the pH approximately constant after the addition of reasonable amounts of acid and base. For example, the concentration of acetic acid in an acetic acid/acetate ion buffer must be sufficient to consume all the hydroxide ion that may be added and still control the pH (see Example 18.4). Buffers are usually prepared as 0.10 M to 1.0 M solutions of reagents. However, any buffer will lose its capacity if too much strong acid or base is added.

Chemistry ·Now™

Sign in at **www.cengage.com/login** and go to Chapter 18 Contents to see Screen 18.5 for a simulation and tutorials on **preparing buffer solutions.**

EXAMPLE 18.4 Preparing a Buffer Solution

Problem You wish to prepare 1.0 L of a buffer solution with a pH of 4.30. A list of possible acids (and their conjugate bases) follows:

Acid	Conjugate Base	K_a	pK_a
HSO_4^-	SO_4^{2-}	1.2×10^{-2}	1.92
CH_3CO_2H	$CH_3CO_2^-$	1.8×10^{-5}	4.75
HCO_3^-	CO_3^{2-}	4.8×10^{-11}	10.32

Which combination should be selected, and what should the ratio of acid to conjugate base be?

Strategy Use either the general equation for a buffer (Equation 18.1) or the Henderson–Hasselbalch equation (Equation 18.2). Equation 18.1 informs you that $[H_3O^+]$ should be close to the acid K_a value, and Equation 18.2 tells you that pH should be close to the acid pK_a value. This will establish which acid you will use.

Having decided which acid to use, convert pH to $[H_3O^+]$ to use Equation 18.1. If you use Equation 18.2, use the pK_a value in the table. Finally, calculate the ratio of acid to conjugate base.

Solution The hydronium ion concentration for the buffer is found from the targeted pH.

$$pH = 4.30, \text{ so } [H_3O^+] = 10^{-pH} = 10^{-4.30} = 5.0 \times 10^{-5} \text{ M}$$

Of the acids given, only acetic acid (CH_3CO_2H) has a K_a value close to that of the desired $[H_3O^+]$ (or a pK_a close to a pH of 4.30). Now you need only to adjust the ratio $[CH_3CO_2H]/[CH_3CO_2^-]$ to achieve the desired hydronium ion concentration.

$$[H_3O^+] = 5.0 \times 10^{-5} \text{ M} = \frac{[CH_3CO_2H]}{[CH_3CO_2^-]}(1.8 \times 10^{-5})$$

Rearrange this equation to find the ratio $[CH_3CO_2H]/[CH_3CO_2^-]$.

$$\frac{[CH_3CO_2H]}{[CH_3CO_2^-]} = \frac{K_a}{[H_3O^+]} = \frac{5.0 \times 10^{-5}}{1.8 \times 10^{-5}} = \frac{2.8 \text{ mol/L}}{1.0 \text{ mol/L}}$$

Therefore, if you add 0.28 mol of acetic acid and 0.10 mol of sodium acetate (or any other pair of molar quantities in the ratio 2.8/1) to enough water to make 1.0 L of solution, the buffer solution will have a pH of 4.30.

Comment If you prefer to use the Henderson–Hasselbalch equation, you would have

$$pH = 4.30 = 4.74 + \log\frac{[CH_3CO_2^-]}{[CH_3CO_2H]}$$

$$\log\frac{[CH_3CO_2^-]}{[CH_3CO_2H]} = 4.30 - 4.74 = -0.44$$

$$\frac{[CH_3CO_2^-]}{[CH_3CO_2H]} = 10^{-0.44} = 0.36$$

The ratio of conjugate base to acid, $[CH_3CO_2^-]/[CH_3CO_2H]$, is 0.36. The reciprocal of this ratio $\{= [CH_3CO_2H]/[CH_3CO_2^-] = 1/0.36)\}$ is 2.8/1. This is the same result obtained previously using Equation 18.1.

EXERCISE 18.5 Preparing a Buffer Solution

Using an acetic acid/sodium acetate buffer solution, what ratio of acid to conjugate base will you need to maintain the pH at 5.00? Describe how you would make up such a solution.

Example 18.4 illustrates several important points concerning buffer solutions. The hydronium ion concentration depends not only on the K_a value of the acid but also on the ratio of acid and conjugate base concentrations. However, even though we write these ratios in terms of reagent concentrations, it is *the relative number of moles of acid and conjugate base that is important in determining the pH of a buffer solution*. Because both reagents are dissolved in the same solution, their concentrations depend on the same solution volume. In Example 18.4, the ratio 2.8/1 for acetic acid and sodium acetate implies that 2.8 times as many moles of acid were dissolved per liter as moles of sodium acetate.

$$\frac{[CH_3CO_2H]}{[CH_3CO_2^-]} = \frac{2.8 \text{ mol } CH_3CO_2H/L}{1.0 \text{ mol } CH_3CO_2^-/L} = \frac{2.8 \text{ mol } CH_3CO_2H}{1.0 \text{ mol } CH_3CO_2^-}$$

Notice that on dividing one concentration by the other, the volumes "cancel." This means that we only need to ensure that the ratio of moles of acid to moles of conjugate base is 2.8 to 1 in this example. The acid and its conjugate base could have been dissolved in any reasonable amount of water. This also means that *diluting a buffer solution will not change its pH*. Commercially available buffer solutions are often sold as premixed, dry ingredients. To use them, you only need to mix the ingredients in some volume of pure water (Figure 18.3).

FIGURE 18.3 A commercial buffer solution. The solid acid and conjugate base in the packet are mixed with water to give a solution with the indicated pH. The quantity of water used does not matter because the ratio [acid]/[conjugate base] does not depend on the solution volume. (However, if too much water is added, the acid and conjugate base concentrations will be too low, and the buffer capacity could be exceeded. Again, buffer solutions usually have solute concentrations around 0.1 M to 1.0 M.)

Problem Solving Tip 18.1   Buffer Solutions

The following is a summary of important aspects of buffer solutions.

- A buffer resists changes in pH on adding small quantities of strong acid or base.
- A buffer contains a weak acid and its conjugate base.
- The hydronium ion concentration of a buffer solution can be calculated from Equation 18.1,

$$[H_3O^+] = \frac{[acid]}{[conjugate\ base]} \times K_a$$

or the pH can be calculated from the Henderson–Hasselbalch equation (Equation 18.2).

$$pH = pK_a + \log\frac{[conjugate\ base]}{[acid]}$$

- The pH depends primarily on the K_a of the weak acid and secondarily on the relative amounts of acid and conjugate base.
- The function of the weak acid of a buffer is to consume added base, and the conju-

gate base consumes added acid. Such reactions affect the relative quantities of weak acid and its conjugate base. Because this ratio of acid to its conjugate base has only a secondary effect on the pH, the pH can be maintained relatively constant.

- The buffer must have sufficient capacity to react with reasonable quantities of added acid or base.

How Does a Buffer Maintain pH?

Now let us explore quantitatively how a given buffer solution can maintain the pH of a solution on adding a small amount of strong acid.

Chemistry⚛Now™

Sign in at **www.cengage.com/login** and go to Chapter 18 Contents to see Screen 18.6 for a tutorial on **adding reagents to a buffer solution.**

■ **EXAMPLE 18.5** **How Does a Buffer Maintain a Constant pH?**

Problem What is the change in pH when 1.00 mL of 1.00 M HCl is added to (1) 1.000 L of pure water and to (2) 1.000 L of acetic acid/sodium acetate buffer with $[CH_3CO_2H] = 0.700$ M and $[CH_3CO_2^-] = 0.600$ M? (See Example 18.2, where the pH of this acetic acid/acetate ion buffer was found to be 4.68.)

Strategy HCl is a strong acid and therefore ionizes completely to supply H_3O^+ ions. Part 1 involves two steps: (a) Find the H_3O^+ concentration when diluting 1.00 mL of acid to 1.00 L. (b) Convert the value of $[H_3O^+]$ for the dilute solution to pH.

Part 2 involves three steps: (a) A stoichiometry calculation to find how the concentrations of acid and conjugate base change on adding H_3O^+. (b) An equilibrium calculation to find $[H_3O^+]$ for a buffer solution where the concentrations of CH_3CO_2H and $CH_3CO_2^-$ are slightly altered owing to the reaction of $CH_3CO_2^-$ with added H_3O^+. (c) Conversion of $[H_3O^+]$ to pH.

Solution

Part 1: Adding Acid to Pure Water

1.00 mL of 1.00 M HCl represents 0.00100 mol of acid. If this is added to 1.000 L of pure water, the H_3O^+ concentration of the water changes from 10^{-7} to 10^{-3},

$$c_1 \times V_1 = c_2 \times V_2$$
$$(1.00\ M)(0.00100\ L) = c_2 \times (1.001\ L)$$
$$c_2 = [H_3O^+]\ in\ diluted\ solution = 1.00 \times 10^{-3}\ M$$

and so the   pH falls from 7.00 to 3.00.

Part 2: Adding Acid to an Acetic Acid/Acetate Buffer Solution

HCl is a strong acid that is 100% ionized in water and supplies H_3O^+, which reacts completely with the base (acetate ion) in the buffer solution according to the following equation:

$$H_3O^+(aq) + CH_3CO_2^-(aq) \rightleftharpoons H_2O(\ell) + CH_3CO_2H(aq)$$

	[H₃O⁺] from Added HCl	[CH₃CO₂⁻] from Buffer	[CH₃CO₂H] from Buffer
Initial amount of acid or base (mol = $c \times V$)	0.00100	0.600	0.700
Change (mol)	−0.00100	−0.00100	+0.00100
Equilibrium (mol)	0	0.599	0.700
Concentrations after reaction (c = mol/V)	0	0.598	0.700

Because the added HCl reacts completely with acetate ion to produce acetic acid, the solution after this reaction (with V = 1.001 L) is once again a buffer containing only the weak acid and its salt. Now we only need to use Equation 18.1 (or the Henderson–Hasselbalch equation) to find [H₃O⁺] and the pH in the buffer solution as in Examples 18.2 and 18.3.

Equilibrium	CH₃CO₂H	+	H₂O	⇌	H₃O⁺	+	CH₃CO₂⁻
Initial (M)	0.700				0		0.598
Change (M)	−x				+x		+x
Equilibrium (M)	0.700 − x				x		0.598 + x

As usual, we make the approximation that x, the amount of H₃O⁺ formed by ionizing acetic acid in the presence of acetate ion, is very small compared with 0.700 M or 0.598 M. Using Equation 18.1, we calculate a pH of 4.68.

$$[H_3O^+] = x = \frac{[CH_3CO_2H]}{[CH_3CO_2^-]} \times K_a = \left(\frac{0.700 \text{ mol}}{0.598 \text{ mol}}\right)(1.8 \times 10^{-5}) = 2.1 \times 10^{-5} \text{ M}$$

$$pH = 4.68$$

Comment Within the number of significant figures allowed, the pH of the buffer solution does not change after adding HCl. The buffer solution contains the conjugate base of the weak acid, and the base consumed the added HCl. In contrast, pH changed by 4 units when 1 mL of 1.0 M HCl was added to 1.0 L of pure water.

EXERCISE 18.6 Buffer Solutions

Calculate the pH of 0.500 L of a buffer solution composed of 0.50 M formic acid (HCO₂H) and 0.70 M sodium formate (NaHCO₂) before and after adding 10.0 mL of 1.0 M HCl.

18.3 Acid–Base Titrations

A titration is one of the most important ways of determining accurately the quantity of an acid, a base, or some other substance in a mixture or of ascertaining the purity of a substance. You learned how to perform the stoichiometry calculations involved in titrations in Chapter 4 (◄ Section 4.7). In Chapter 17, we described the following important points regarding acid–base reactions (◄ Section 17.6):

- The pH at the equivalence point of a strong acid–strong base titration is 7. The solution at the equivalence point is truly "neutral" *only* when a strong acid is titrated with a strong base and vice versa.
- If the substance being titrated is a weak acid or base, then the pH at the equivalence point is not 7 (see Table 17.5).
  - (a) A weak acid titrated with strong base leads to pH > 7 at the equivalence point due to the conjugate base of the weak acid.
  - (b) A weak base titrated with strong acid leads to pH < 7 at the equivalence point due to the conjugate acid of the weak base.

A knowledge of buffer solutions and how they work will now allow us to more fully understand how the pH changes in the course of an acid–base reaction.

■ **Equivalence Point** The equivalence point for a reaction is the point at which one reactant has been completely consumed by addition of another reactant. See page 185.

■ **Weak Acid–Weak Base Titrations** Titrations combining a weak acid and weak base are generally not done because the equivalence point often cannot be accurately judged.

Take a Deep Breath!

Maintenance of pH is vital to the cells of all living organisms because enzyme activity is influenced by pH. The primary protection against harmful pH changes in cells is provided by buffer systems. The intracellular pH of most cells is maintained in a range between 6.9 and 7.4. Two important biological buffer systems control pH in this range: the bicarbonate/carbonic acid system (HCO_3^-/H_2CO_3) and the phosphate system ($HPO_4^{2-}/H_2PO_4^-$).

The bicarbonate/carbonic acid buffer is important in blood plasma. Three equilibria are important here.

$$CO_2(g) \rightleftharpoons CO_2(\text{dissolved})$$

$$CO_2(\text{dissolved}) + H_2O(\ell) \rightleftharpoons H_2CO_3(aq)$$

$$H_2CO_3(aq) + H_2O(\ell) \rightleftharpoons$$
$$H_3O^+(aq) + HCO_3^-(aq)$$

The overall equilibrium constant for the second and third steps is $pK_{\text{overall}} = 6.3$ at 37 °C, the temperature of the human body. Thus,

$$7.4 = 6.3 + \log \frac{[HCO_3^-]}{[CO_2(\text{dissolved})]}$$

Although the value of pK_{overall} is about 1 pH unit away from the blood pH, the natural partial pressure of CO_2 in the alveoli of the lungs (about 40 mm Hg) is sufficient to keep [CO_2(dissolved)] at about 1.2×10^{-3} M and [HCO_3^-] at about 1.5×10^{-2} M.

If blood pH rises above about 7.45, you can suffer from a condition called *alkalosis*. *Respiratory alkalosis* can arise from hyperventilation when a person breathes quickly to expel CO_2 from the lungs. This has the effect of lowering the CO_2 concentration, which in turn leads to a lower H_3O^+ concentration and a higher pH. This same condition can also arise from severe anxiety or from an oxygen defi-

Alkalosis. If blood pH is too high, alkalosis results. Respiratory alkalosis can be reversed by breathing into a bag, an action that recycles exhaled CO_2. This affects the carbonic acid buffer system in the body, raising the blood hydronium ion concentration. The blood pH drops back to a more normal level of 7.4.

ciency at high altitude. It can ultimately lead to overexcitability of the central nervous system, muscle spasms, convulsions, and death. One way to treat acute respiratory alkalosis is to breathe into a paper bag. The CO_2 you exhale is recycled. This raises the blood CO_2 level and causes the equilibria above to shift to the right, thus raising the hydronium ion concentration and lowering the pH.

Metabolic alkalosis can occur if you take large amounts of sodium bicarbonate to treat stomach acid (which is mostly HCl at a pH of about 4). It also commonly occurs when a person vomits profusely. This depletes the body of hydrogen ions, which leads to an increase in bicarbonate ion concentration.

Athletes can use the H_2CO_3/HCO_3^- equilibrium to enhance their performance. Strenuous activity produces high levels of lactic acid, and this can lower blood pH and cause muscle cramps. To counteract this, athletes will prepare before the race by hyperventilating for

some seconds to raise blood pH, thereby helping to neutralize the acidity from the lactic acid.

Acidosis is the opposite of alkalosis. A toddler who came to the hospital with viral gastroenteritis had *metabolic acidosis*. He had severe diarrhea, was dehydrated, and had a high rate of respiration. One function of the bicarbonate ion is to neutralize stomach acid in the intestines. However, because of his diarrhea, the toddler was losing bicarbonate ions in his stool, and his blood pH was too low. To compensate, the toddler was breathing rapidly and blowing off CO_2 through the lungs (the effect of which is to lower [H_3O^+] and raise the pH).

Respiratory acidosis results from a buildup of CO_2 in the body. This can be caused by pulmonary problems, by head injuries, or by drugs such as anesthetics and sedatives. It can be reversed by breathing rapidly and deeply. Doubling the breathing rate increases the blood pH by about 0.23 units.

Questions:

Phosphate ions are abundant in cells, both as the ions themselves and as important substituents on organic molecules. Most importantly, the pK_a for the $H_2PO_4^-$ ion is 7.20, which is very close to the high end of the normal pH range in the body.

$$H_2PO_4^-(aq) + H_2O(\ell) \rightleftharpoons$$
$$H_3O^+(aq) + HPO_4^{2-}(aq)$$

1. *What should the ratio $[HPO_4^{2-}]/[H_2PO_4^-]$ be to control the pH at 7.4?*
2. *A typical total phosphate concentration in a cell, $[HPO_4^{2-}] + [H_2PO_4^-]$, is 2.0×10^{-2} M. What are the concentrations of HPO_4^{2-} and $H_2PO_4^-$?*

Answers to these questions are in Appendix Q.

Titration of a Strong Acid with a Strong Base

Figure 18.4 illustrates what happens to the pH as 0.100 M NaOH is slowly added to 50.0 mL of 0.100 M HCl.

$$HCl(aq) + NaOH(aq) \rightarrow NaCl(aq) + H_2O(\ell)$$

Net ionic equation: $H_3O^+(aq) + OH^-(aq) \rightarrow 2\,H_2O(\ell)$

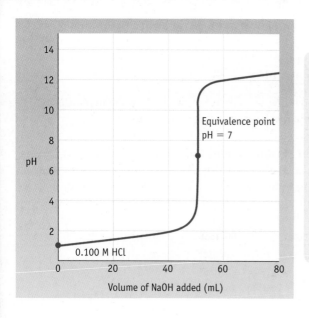

| 50.0 mL of 0.100 M HCl titrated with 0.100 M NaOH ||
Volume of base added	pH
0.0	1.00
10.0	1.18
20.0	1.37
40.0	1.95
45.0	2.28
48.0	2.69
49.0	3.00
50.0	7.00
51.0	11.00
55.0	11.68
60.0	11.96
80.0	12.36
100.0	12.52
very large amount	13.00 (maximum)

FIGURE 18.4 The change in pH as a strong acid is titrated with a strong base. In this case, 50.0 mL of 0.100 M HCl is titrated with 0.100 M NaOH. The pH at the equivalence point is 7.0 for the reaction of a strong acid with a strong base.

Let us focus on four regions on this plot.

- pH of the initial solution
- pH as NaOH is added to the HCl solution before the equivalence point
- pH at the equivalence point
- pH after the equivalence point

Before beginning the titration, the 0.100 M solution of HCl has a pH of 1.00. As NaOH is added to the acid solution, the amount of HCl declines, and the acid remaining is dissolved in an ever-increasing volume of solution. Thus, $[H_3O^+]$ decreases, and the pH slowly increases. As an example, let us find the pH of the solution after 10.0 mL of 0.100 M NaOH has been added to 50.0 mL of 0.100 M HCl. Here, we set up a table to list the amounts of acid and base before reaction, the changes in those amounts, and the amounts remaining after reaction. Be sure to notice that the volume of the solution after reaction is the sum of the combined volumes of NaOH and HCl (60.0 mL or 0.0600 L in this case).

	$H_3O^+(aq)$	+	$OH^-(aq)$	$\rightarrow$	$2 H_2O(\ell)$
Initial amount (mol = $c \times V$)	0.00500		0.00100		
Change (mol)	−0.00100		−0.00100		
After reaction (mol)	0.00400		0		
After reaction ($c = $ mol/V)	0.00400 mol/0.0600 L = 0.0667 M		0		

After addition of 10.0 mL of NaOH, the final solution has a hydronium ion concentration of 0.0667 M, and so the pH is

$$pH = -\log[H_3O^+] = -\log(0.0667) = 1.176$$

After 49.5 mL of base has been added—that is, just before the equivalence point—we can use the same approach to show that the pH is 3.3. The solution being titrated is still quite acidic, even very close to the equivalence point.

The pH of the equivalence point in an acid–base titration is taken as the midpoint in the vertical portion of the pH versus volume of titrant curve. (The **titrant** is the substance being added during the titration.) In the HCl/NaOH titration illustrated in Figure 18.4, you see that the pH increases very rapidly near the equivalence point. In fact, in this case the pH rises 7 units (the H_3O^+ concentration increases by a factor of 10 million!) when only a drop or two of the NaOH solution is added, and the midpoint of the vertical portion of the curve is a pH of 7.00.

> The pH of the solution at the equivalence point in a strong acid–strong base reaction is always 7.00 (at 25 °C) because the solution contains a neutral salt.

After all of the HCl has been consumed and the slightest excess of NaOH has been added, the solution will be basic, and the pH will continue to increase as more NaOH is added (and the solution volume increases). For example, if we calculate the pH of the solution after 55.0 mL of 0.100 M NaOH has been added to 50.0 mL of 0.100 M HCl, we find

	$H_3O^+(aq)$	+	$OH^-(aq)$	$\rightarrow$	$2\ H_2O(\ell)$
Initial amount (mol = $c \times V$)	0.00500		0.00550		
Change (mol)	−0.00500		−0.00500		
After reaction (mol)	0		0.00050		
After reaction (c = mol/V)	0		0.00050 mol/0.1050 L = 0.0048 M		

At this point, the solution has a hydroxide ion concentration of 0.0048 M. Calculate the pOH from this value, then use this to calculate pH.

$$pOH = -\log[OH^-] = -\log(0.0048) = 2.32$$

$$pH = 14.00 - pOH = 11.68$$

EXERCISE 18.7 Titration of a Strong Acid with a Strong Base

What is the pH after 25.0 mL of 0.100 M NaOH has been added to 50.0 mL of 0.100 M HCl? What is the pH after 50.50 mL of NaOH has been added?

Titration of a Weak Acid with a Strong Base

The titration of a weak acid with a strong base is somewhat different from the strong acid–strong base titration. Look carefully at the curve for the titration of 100.0 mL of 0.100 M acetic acid with 0.100 M NaOH (Figure 18.5).

$$CH_3CO_2H(aq) + NaOH(aq) \rightarrow NaCH_3CO_2(aq) + H_2O(\ell)$$

Let us focus on three important points on this curve:

- *The pH before titration begins.* The pH before any base is added can be calculated from the weak acid K_a value and the acid concentration (◄ Example 17.5).
- *The pH at the equivalence point.* At the equivalence point, the solution contains only sodium acetate, the CH_3CO_2H and NaOH having been consumed. The pH is controlled by the acetate ion, the conjugate base of acetic acid (◄ Table 17.5, page 728).
- *The pH at the halfway point (half-equivalence point) of the titration.* Here, the pH is equal to the pK_a of the weak acid, a conclusion that is discussed in more detail below.

As NaOH is added to acetic acid the base is consumed and sodium acetate is produced. Thus, at every point between the beginning of the titration (when only acetic acid is present) and the equivalence point (when only sodium acetate is present), the solution contains both acetic acid and its salt, sodium acetate. These

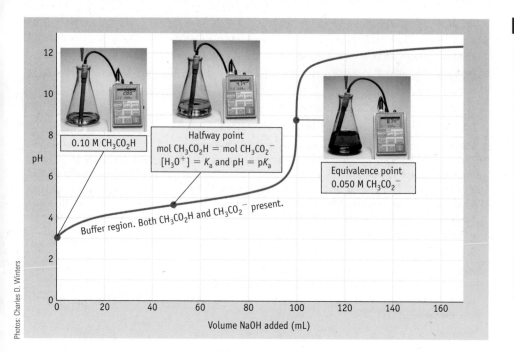

Active Figure 18.5 The change in pH during the titration of a weak acid with a strong base. Here, 100.0 mL of 0.100 M acetic acid is titrated with 0.100 M NaOH. Note especially the following: (a) Acetic acid is a weak acid, so the pH of the original solution is 2.87. (b) The pH at the point at which half the acid has reacted with base is equal to the pK_a for the acid ($pH = pK_a = 4.74$). (c) At the equivalence point, the solution contains the acetate ion, a weak base. Therefore, the solution is basic, with a pH of 8.72.

Chemistry_.⚬_.Now™ Sign in at www.cengage.com/login and go to the Chapter Contents menu to explore an interactive version of this figure accompanied by an exercise.

are the components of a *buffer solution*, and the hydronium ion concentration can be calculated from Equation 18.3 or 18.4.

$$[H_3O^+] = \frac{[\text{weak acid remaining}]}{[\text{conjugate base produced}]} \times K_a \tag{18.3}$$

or

$$pH = pK_a + \log \frac{[\text{conjugate base produced}]}{[\text{weak acid remaining}]} \tag{18.4}$$

The fact that a buffer is present at any point between the beginning of the titration and the equivalence point is the reason that the pH of the solution only rises slowly after a few milliliters of titrant has been added.

What happens when *exactly* half of the acid has been consumed by base? Half of the acid (CH_3CO_2H) has been converted to the conjugate base ($CH_3CO_2^-$), and half remains. Therefore, the concentration of weak acid remaining is equal to the concentration of conjugate base produced ($[CH_3CO_2H] = [CH_3CO_2^-]$). Using Equations 18.3 or 18.4, we see that

$$[H_3O^+] = (1) \times K_a \qquad \text{or} \qquad pH = pK_a + \log(1)$$

Because $\log(1) = 0$, we come to the following general conclusion:

At the halfway point in the titration of a weak acid with a strong base

$$[H_3O^+] = K_a \text{ and } pH = pK_a \tag{18.5}$$

In the particular case of the titration of acetic acid with a strong base, $[H_3O^+] = 1.8 \times 10^{-5}$ M at the halfway point, and so the pH is 4.74. This is equal to the pK_a of acetic acid.

Chemistry_.⚬_.Now™

Sign in at **www.cengage.com/login** and go to Chapter 18 Contents to see Screen 18.7 for a simulation and tutorial on **titration curves**.

Problem Consider the titration of 100.0 mL of 0.100 M acetic acid with 0.100 M NaOH (see Figure 18.5).

(a) What is the pH of the solution when 90.0 mL of 0.100 M NaOH has been added to 100.0 mL of 0.100 M acetic acid?

(b) What is the pH at the equivalence point?

(c) What is the pH after 110.0 mL of NaOH has been added?

Strategy The problem generally involves two major steps: (1) A stoichiometry calculation to find the quantity of acid remaining, if any, and quantity of conjugate base formed after adding NaOH. (2) Before the equivalence point, in the "buffer region," you will do an equilibrium calculation to find $[H_3O^+]$ for a buffer solution where the quantities of CH_3CO_2H and $CH_3CO_2^-$ are known from the first part of the calculation. At the equivalence point, only the conjugate base will remain, so the calculation resembles Example 17.7. After the equivalence point, the solution contains both the conjugate base of the weak acid and excess NaOH, but the latter controls the pH.

Solution

Part a: *pH before the equivalence point.* Let us first calculate the amounts of reactants before reaction (= concentration × volume) and then use the principles of stoichiometry to calculate the amounts of reactants and products after reaction. The limiting reactant is NaOH, so some CH_3CO_2H remains along with the product, $CH_3CO_2^-$.

Equation	CH_3CO_2H	+	OH^-	⇌	$CH_3CO_2^-$	+	H_2O
Initial (mol)	0.0100		0.00900		0		
Change (mol)	−0.00900		−0.00900		+0.00900		
After reaction (mol)	0.0010		0		0.00900		

The ratio of amounts (moles) of acid to conjugate base is the same as the ratio of their concentrations. Therefore, we can use the amounts of weak acid remaining and conjugate base formed to find the pH from Equation 18.3 (where we use amounts and not concentrations).

$$[H_3O^+] = \frac{mol\ CH_3CO_2H}{mol\ CH_3CO_2^-} \times K_a = \left(\frac{0.0010\ mol}{0.0090\ mol}\right)(1.8 \times 10^{-5}) = 2.0 \times 10^{-6}\ M$$

$$pH = -log(2.0 \times 10^{-6}) = 5.70$$

The pH is 5.70, in agreement with Figure 18.5. Notice that this pH is appropriate for a point after the halfway point (4.74) but before the equivalence point (8.72).

Part b: *pH at the equivalence point.* To reach the equivalence point, 0.0100 mol of NaOH has been added to 0.0100 mol of CH_3CO_2H and 0.0100 mol of $CH_3CO_2^-$ has been formed.

Equation	CH_3CO_2H	+	OH^-	⇌	$CH_3CO_2^-$	+	H_2O
Initial (mol)	0.0100		0.0100		0		
Change (mol)	−0.0100		−0.0100		+0.0100		
After reaction (mol)	0		0		0.0100		

Because two solutions, each with a volume of 100.0 mL, have been combined, the concentration of $CH_3CO_2^-$ at the equivalence point is (0.0100 mol/0.200 L) = 0.0050 M. Next, we set up an ICE table for the hydrolysis of this weak base,

Equation	$CH_3CO_2^-$	+	H_2O	⇌	CH_3CO_2H	+	OH^-
Initial (M)	0.00500				0		0
Change (M)	−x				+x		+x
After reaction (M)	0.00500 − x				x		x

and calculate the concentration of OH^- ion using K_b for the weak base.

$$K_b\ for\ CH_3CO_2^- = 5.6 \times 10^{-10} = \frac{[CH_3CO_2H][OH^-]}{[CH_3CO_2^-]} = \frac{(x)(x)}{0.00500 - x}$$

Making the usual assumption that x is small with respect to 0.00500 M,

$$x = [OH^-] = 1.7 \times 10^{-6} \text{ M (pOH = 5.78)}$$

$$pH = 14.00 - 5.78 = 8.22$$

Part c: *pH after the equivalence point.* Now the limiting reactant is the CH_3CO_2H, and the solution contains excess OH^- ion from the unused NaOH as well as from the hydrolysis of $CH_3CO_2^-$.

Equation	CH_3CO_2H	+	OH^-	$\rightleftharpoons$	$CH_3CO_2^-$	+	H_2O
Initial (mol)	0.0100		0.0110		0		
Change (mol)	−0.0100		−0.0100		+0.0100		
After reaction (mol)	0		0.0010		0.0100		

The amount of OH^- produced by $CH_3CO_2^-$ hydrolysis is very small (see part b), so the pH of the solution after the equivalence point is determined by the excess NaOH (in 210 mL of solution).

$$[OH^-] = 0.0010 \text{ mol/0.210 L} = 4.8 \times 10^{-3} \text{ M (pOH = 2.32)}$$

$$pH = 14.00 - 2.32 = 11.68$$

EXERCISE 18.8 Titration of a Weak Acid with a Strong Base

The titration of 0.100 acetic acid with 0.100 M NaOH is described in the text. What is the pH of the solution when 35.0 mL of the base has been added to 100.0 mL of 0.100 M acetic acid?

Titration of Weak Polyprotic Acids

The titrations illustrated thus far have been for the reaction of a monoprotic acid (HA) with a base such as NaOH. It is possible to extend the discussion of titrations to polyprotic acids such as oxalic acid, $H_2C_2O_4$.

$$H_2C_2O_4(aq) + H_2O(\ell) \rightleftharpoons HC_2O_4^-(aq) + H_3O^+(aq) \qquad K_{a1} = 5.9 \times 10^{-2}$$

$$HC_2O_4^-(aq) + H_2O(\ell) \rightleftharpoons C_2O_4^-(aq) + H_3O^+(aq) \qquad K_{a2} = 6.4 \times 10^{-5}$$

Figure 18.6 illustrates the curve for the titration of 100 mL of 0.100 M oxalic acid with 0.100 M NaOH. The first significant rise in pH is experienced after 100 mL of base has been added, indicating that the first proton of the acid has been titrated.

$$H_2C_2O_4(aq) + OH^-(aq) \rightleftharpoons HC_2O_4^-(aq) + H_2O(aq)$$

When the second proton of oxalic acid is titrated, the pH again rises significantly.

$$HC_2O_4^-(aq) + OH^-(aq) \rightleftharpoons C_2O_4^{2-}(aq) + H_2O(\ell)$$

The pH at this second equivalence point is controlled by the oxalate ion, $C_2O_4^{2-}$.

$$C_2O_4^{2-}(aq) + H_2O(\ell) \rightleftharpoons HC_2O_4^-(aq) + OH^-(aq)$$

$$K_b = K_w/K_{a2} = 1.6 \times 10^{-10}$$

Calculation of the pH at the equivalence point indicates that it should be about 8.4, as observed.

Chemistry⚛Now™

Sign in at **www.cengage.com/login** and go to Chapter 18 Contents to see Screen 18.8 for a simulation on **titration of a weak polyprotic acid.**

FIGURE 18.6 Titration curve for a diprotic acid. The curve for the titration of 100.0 mL of 0.100 M oxalic acid ($H_2C_2O_4$, a weak diprotic acid) with 0.100 M NaOH. The first equivalence point (at 100 mL) occurs when the first hydrogen ion of $H_2C_2O_4$ is titrated, and the second (at 200 mL) occurs at the completion of the reaction. The curve for pH versus volume of NaOH added shows an initial rise at the first equivalence point and then another rise at the second equivalence point.

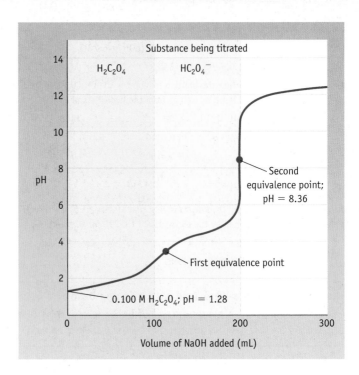

Substance being titrated

$H_2C_2O_4$ $HC_2O_4^-$

Second equivalence point; pH = 8.36

First equivalence point

0.100 M $H_2C_2O_4$; pH = 1.28

Volume of NaOH added (mL)

Titration of a Weak Base with a Strong Acid

Finally, it is useful to consider the titration of a weak base with a strong acid. Figure 18.7 illustrates the pH curve for the titration of 100.0 mL of 0.100 M NH_3 with 0.100 M HCl.

$$NH_3(aq) + H_3O^+(aq) \rightleftharpoons NH_4^+(aq) + H_2O(\ell)$$

The initial pH for a 0.100 M NH_3 solution is 11.12. As the titration progresses, the important species in solution are the weak acid NH_4^+ and its conjugate base, NH_3.

$$NH_4^+(aq) + H_2O(\ell) \rightleftharpoons NH_3(aq) + H_3O^+(aq) \qquad K_a = 5.6 \times 10^{-10}$$

FIGURE 18.7 Titration of a weak base with a strong acid. The change in pH during the titration of a weak base (100.0 mL of 0.100 M NH_3) with a strong acid (0.100 M HCl). The pH at the half-neutralization point is equal to the pK_a for the conjugate acid (NH_4^+) of the weak base (NH_3) (pH = pK_a = 9.26). At the equivalence point, the solution contains the NH_4^+ ion, a weak acid, so the pH is about 5.

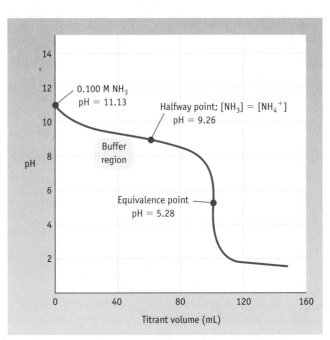

0.100 M NH_3
pH = 11.13

Halfway point; $[NH_3] = [NH_4^+]$
pH = 9.26

Buffer region

Equivalence point
pH = 5.28

Titrant volume (mL)

Calculating the pH at Various Stages of an Acid–Base Reaction

Finding the pH at or before the equivalence point for an acid–base reaction always involves several calculation steps. There are no shortcuts. Consider the *titration of a weak base, B, with a strong acid* as in Example 18.7. (The same principles apply to other acid–base reactions.)

$$H_3O^+(aq) + B(aq) \rightleftharpoons BH^+(aq) + H_2O(\ell)$$

Step 1. *Solve the stoichiometry problem.* Up to the equivalence point, acid is consumed completely to leave a solution containing some base (B) and its conjugate acid (BH⁺). Use the principles of stoichiometry to calcu-

late (a) the amount of acid added, (b) the amount of base consumed, and (c) the amount of conjugate base (BH⁺) formed.
Step 2. *Calculate the concentrations of base, [B], and conjugate acid, [BH⁺].* Recognize that the volume of the solution at any point is the sum of the original volume of base solution plus the volume of acid solution added.
Step 3. *Calculate the pH before the equivalence point.* At any point before the equivalence point, the solution is a buffer solution because both the base and its conjugate acid are present. Calculate [H₃O⁺] using the con-

centrations of Step 2 and the value of K_a for the conjugate acid of the weak base.
Step 4. *Calculate the pH at the equivalence point.* Calculate the concentration of the conjugate acid using the procedure of Steps 1 and 2. Use the value of K_a for the conjugate acid of the weak base and the procedure outlined in Example 18.7 (or in Example 18.6 for a weak acid). (For a titration of a weak acid with a strong base, use the value of K_b for the conjugate base of the acid and follow the procedure outlined in Example 18.6.)

At the halfway point, the concentrations of NH_4^+ and NH_3 are the same, so

$$[H_3O^+] = \frac{[NH_4^+]}{[NH_3]} \times K_a = 5.6 \times 10^{-10}$$

$$[H_3O^+] = K_a$$

$$pH = pK_a = -\log(5.6 \times 10^{-10}) = 9.25$$

As the addition of HCl to NH_3 continues, the pH declines slowly because of the buffering action of the NH_3/NH_4^+ combination. Near the equivalence point, however, the pH drops rapidly. At the equivalence point, the solution contains only ammonium chloride, a weak Brønsted acid, and the solution is weakly acidic.

Chemistry．Now™

Sign in at **www.cengage.com/login** and go to Chapter 18 Contents to see Screen 18.9 for a simulation on **titration of a weak base with a strong acid.**

EXAMPLE 18.7 Titration of Ammonia with HCl

Problem What is the pH of the solution at the equivalence point in the titration of 100.0 mL of 0.100 M ammonia with 0.100 M HCl (see Figure 18.7)?

Strategy This problem has two steps: (a) A stoichiometry calculation to find the concentration of NH_4^+ at the equivalence point. (b) An equilibrium calculation to find [H₃O⁺] for a solution of the weak acid NH_4^+.

Solution

Part 1: Stoichiometry Problem

Here, we are titrating 0.0100 mol of NH_3 ($= c \times V$), so 0.0100 mol of HCl is required. Thus, 100.0 mL of 0.100 M HCl ($= 0.0100$ mol HCl) must be used in the titration.

Equation	NH_3	+	H_3O^+	$\rightleftharpoons$	NH_4^+	+	H_2O
Initial (mol = $c \times V$)	0.0100		0.0100		0		
Change on reaction (mol)	−0.0100		−0.0100		+0.0100		
After reaction (mol)	0		0		0.0100		
Concentration (M)	0		0		0.0100 mol (in 0.200L)		
					= 0.0500 M		

Part 2: Equilibrium Problem

When the equivalence point is reached, the solution consists of 0.0500 M NH_4^+. The pH is determined by the hydrolysis of the acid.

Equation	NH_4^+	+	H_2O	$\rightleftharpoons$	NH_3	+	H_3O^+
Initial (M)	0.0500				0		0
Change (M)	$-x$				$+x$		$+x$
Equilibrium (M)	$0.0500 - x$				x		x

Using K_a for the weak acid NH_4^+, we have

$$K_a = 5.6 \times 10^{-10} = \frac{[NH_3][H_3O^+]}{[NH_4^+]} = \frac{x}{0.0500 - x}$$

$$\text{Simplifying, } x = [H_3O^+] = \sqrt{(5.6 \times 10^{-10})(0.0500)} = 5.3 \times 10^{-6} \text{ M}$$

$$\boxed{pH = 5.28}$$

The pH at the equivalence point in this weak base–strong acid titration is indeed slightly acidic, as expected.

EXERCISE 18.9 Titration of a Weak Base with a Strong Acid

Calculate the pH after 75.0 mL of 0.100 M HCl has been added to 100.0 mL of 0.100 M NH_3. See Figure 18.7.

---

pH Indicators

Many organic compounds, both natural and synthetic, have a color that changes with pH (Figure 18.8). Not only does this add beauty and variety to our world, but it is also a useful property in chemistry.

FIGURE 18.8 Phenolphthalein, a common acid–base indicator. Phenolphthalein, a weak acid, is colorless. As the pH increases, the pink conjugate base form predominates, and the color of the solution changes. The change in color is most noticeable around pH 9. The dye is commonly used for strong acid + strong base or weak acid + strong base titrations because the pH changes from 3–4 to 10–12 in these cases. For other suitable indicator dyes, see Figure 18.10.

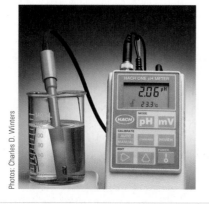

You have likely carried out an acid–base titration in the laboratory, and, before starting the titration, you would have added an **indicator.** The acid–base indicator is usually an organic compound that is itself a weak acid or weak base (similar to the compounds that give the color to flowers). In aqueous solution, the acid form is in equilibrium with its conjugate base. Abbreviating the indicator's acid formula as HInd and the formula of its conjugate base as Ind⁻, we can write the equilibrium equation

$$HInd(aq) + H_2O(\ell) \rightleftharpoons H_3O^+(aq) + Ind^-(aq)$$

The important characteristic of acid–base indicators is that the acid form of the compound (HInd) has one color and the conjugate base (Ind⁻) has another. To see how such compounds can be used as equivalence point indicators, let us write the usual equilibrium constant expressions for the dependence of hydronium ion concentration or pH on the indicator's ionization constant (K_a) and on the relative quantities of the acid and conjugate base.

$$[H_3O^+] = \frac{[HInd]}{[Ind^-]} \times K_a \quad \text{or} \quad pH = pK_a + \log\frac{[Ind^-]}{[HInd]} \tag{18.6}$$

These equations inform us that

- when the hydronium ion concentration is equivalent to the value of K_a (or when $pH = pK_a$), then $[HInd] = [Ind^-]$
- when $[H_3O^+] > K_a$ (or $pH < pK_a$), then $[HInd] > [Ind^-]$
- when $[H_3O^+] < K_a$ (or $pH > pK_a$), then $[HInd] < [Ind^-]$

Now let us apply these conclusions to, for example, the titration of an acid with a base using an indicator whose pK_a value is nearly the same as the pH at the equivalence point (Figure 18.9). At the beginning of the titration, the pH is low and $[H_3O^+]$ is high; the acid form of the indicator (HInd) predominates. Its color is the one observed. As the titration progresses and the pH increases ($[H_3O^+]$ decreases), less of the acid HInd and more of its conjugate base exist in solution. Finally, just after we reach the equivalence point, $[Ind^-]$ is much larger than $[HInd]$, and the color of $[Ind^-]$ is observed.

Several obvious questions remain to be answered. If you are trying to analyze for an acid and add an indicator that is a weak acid, won't this affect the analysis? Recall that you use only a tiny amount of an indicator in a titration. Although the acidic indicator molecules also react with the base as the titration progresses, so little indicator is present that the analysis is not in error.

Another question is whether you could accurately determine the pH by observing the color change of an indicator. In practice, your eyes are not quite that good. Usually, you see the color of HInd when $[HInd]/[Ind^-]$ is about 10/1, and the color of Ind⁻ when $[HInd]/[Ind^-]$ is about 1/10. This means the color change is observed over a hydronium ion concentration interval of about 2 pH units. However, as you can see in Figures 18.4–18.7, on passing through the equivalence point of these titrations, the pH changes by as many as 7 units.

As Figure 18.10 shows, a variety of indicators are available, each changing color in a different pH range. If you are analyzing a weak acid or base by titration, you must choose an indicator that changes color in a range that includes the pH to be observed at the equivalence point. This means that an indicator that changes color in the pH range 7 ± 2 should be used for a strong acid–strong base titration. On the other hand, the pH at the equivalence point in the titration of a weak acid with a strong base is greater than 7, and you should choose an indicator that changes color at a pH near the anticipated equivalence point.

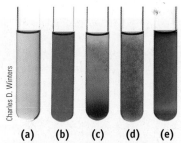

Charles D. Winters

(a)   (b)   (c)   (d)   (e)

Extract of red rose at various pH's.
(a) The pigment in red rose petals was extracted with ethanol; the extract was a faint red. (b) After adding one drop of 6 M HCl, the color changed to a vivid red. (c) Adding two drops of 6 M NH₃ produced a green color, and (d) adding 1 drop each of HCl and NH₃ (to give a buffer solution) gave a blue solution. (e) Finally, adding a few milligrams of Al(NO₃)₃ turned the solution deep purple. (The deep purple color with aluminum ions was so intense that the solution had to be diluted significantly to take the photo.)

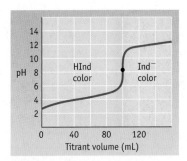

FIGURE 18.9 Indicator color changes in the course of a titration when the pK_a of the indicator HInd is about 8.

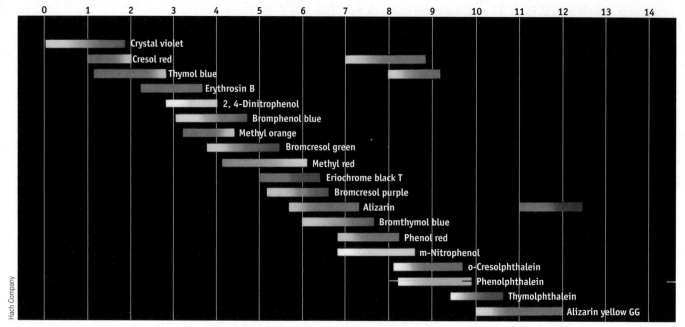

FIGURE 18.10 Common acid–base indicators. The color changes occur over a range of pH values. Notice that a few indicators have color changes over two different pH ranges.

Chemistry .ọ. Now™

Sign in at **www.cengage.com/login** and go to Chapter 18 Contents to see Screen 18.10 for a simulation on **acid–base indicators.**

EXERCISE 18.10 Indicators

Use Figure 18.10 to decide which indicator is best to use in the titration of NH_3 with HCl shown in Figure 18.7.

18.4 Solubility of Salts

Precipitation reactions (◀ Section 3.6) are exchange reactions in which one of the products is a water-insoluble compound such as $CaCO_3$,

$$CaCl_2(aq) + Na_2CO_3(aq) \rightarrow CaCO_3(s) + 2\ NaCl(aq)$$

that is, a compound having a water solubility of less than about 0.01 mole of dissolved material per liter of solution (Figure 18.11).

How do you know when to predict an insoluble compound as the product of a reaction? In Chapter 3, we listed some guidelines for predicting solubility (Figure 3.10) and mentioned a few important minerals that are insoluble in water. Now we want to make our estimates of solubility more quantitative and to explore conditions under which some compounds precipitate and others do not.

The Solubility Product Constant, K_{sp}

Silver bromide, AgBr, is used in photographic film (Figure 18.11c). If some AgBr is placed in pure water, a tiny amount of the compound dissolves, and an equilibrium is established.

$$AgBr(s) \rightleftharpoons Ag^+(aq, 7.35 \times 10^{-7}\ M) + Br^-(aq, 7.35 \times 10^{-7}\ M)$$

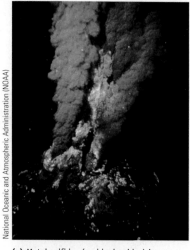

(a) Metal sulfides (and hydroxides) in a black smoker (◄ page 140).

(b) CaCO₃ stalactites.

(c) Black-and-white film is coated with water-insoluble silver bromide. The image is formed by metallic silver particles.

FIGURE 18.11 Some insoluble substances.

When sufficient AgBr has dissolved and equilibrium is attained, the solution is said to be **saturated** (◄ Section 14.2), and experiments show that the concentrations of the silver and bromide ions in the solution are each about 7.35×10^{-7} M at 25 °C. The extent to which an insoluble salt dissolves can be expressed in terms of the equilibrium constant for the dissolving process. In this case, the appropriate expression is

$$K_{sp} = [Ag^+][Br^-]$$

The value of the equilibrium constant that reflects the solubility of a compound is often referred to as its **solubility product constant.** Chemists often use the notation **K_{sp}** for such constants, the subscript "sp" denoting a "solubility product."

The water solubility of a compound, and thus its K_{sp} value, can be estimated by determining the concentration of the cation or anion when the compound dissolves. For example, if we find that AgBr dissolves to give a silver ion concentration of 7.35×10^{-7} mol/L, we know that 7.35×10^{-7} mol of AgBr must have dissolved per liter of solution (and that the bromide ion concentration also equals 7.35×10^{-7} M). Therefore, the calculated value of the equilibrium constant for the dissolving process is

$$K_{sp} = [Ag^+][Br^-] = (7.35 \times 10^{-7})(7.35 \times 10^{-7}) = 5.40 \times 10^{-13} \text{ (at 25 °C)}$$

Equilibrium constants for the dissolving of other insoluble salts can be calculated in the same manner.

The solubility product constant, K_{sp}, for any salt always has the form

$$A_xB_y(s) \rightleftharpoons x\, A^{y+}(aq) + y\, B^{x-}(aq) \qquad K_{sp} = [A^{y+}]^x[B^{x-}]^y$$

For example,

$$CaF_2(s) \rightleftharpoons Ca^{2+}(aq) + 2\, F^-(aq) \qquad K_{sp} = [Ca^{2+}][F^-]^2 = 5.3 \times 10^{-11}$$

$$Ag_2SO_4(s) \rightleftharpoons 2\, Ag^+(aq) + SO_4{}^{2-}(aq) \qquad K_{sp} = [Ag^+]^2[SO_4{}^{2-}] = 1.2 \times 10^{-5}$$

The numerical values of K_{sp} for a few salts are given in Table 18.2, and more values are collected in Appendix J.

■ **Writing Equilibrium Constant Expressions** Solids are not included in these equations. See page 728.

TABLE 18.2 Some Common Insoluble Compounds and Their K_{sp} Values*

Formula	Name	K_{sp} (25 °C)	Common Names/Uses
$CaCO_3$	Calcium carbonate	3.4×10^{-9}	Calcite, iceland spar
$MnCO_3$	Manganese(II) carbonate	2.3×10^{-11}	Rhodochrosite (forms rose-colored crystals)
$FeCO_3$	Iron(II) carbonate	3.1×10^{-11}	Siderite
CaF_2	Calcium fluoride	5.3×10^{-11}	Fluorite (source of HF and other inorganic fluorides)
$AgCl$	Silver chloride	1.8×10^{-10}	Chlorargyrite
$AgBr$	Silver bromide	5.4×10^{-13}	Used in photographic film
$CaSO_4$	Calcium sulfate	4.9×10^{-5}	The hydrated form is commonly called gypsum
$BaSO_4$	Barium sulfate	1.1×10^{-10}	Barite (used in "drilling mud" and as a component of paints)
$SrSO_4$	Strontium sulfate	3.4×10^{-7}	Celestite
$Ca(OH)_2$	Calcium hydroxide	5.5×10^{-5}	Slaked lime

* The values in this table were taken from *Lange's Handbook of Chemistry*, 15th edition, McGraw-Hill Publishers, New York, NY (1999). Additional K_{sp} values are given in Appendix J.

Do not confuse the *solubility* of a compound with its *solubility product constant*. The *solubility* of a salt is the quantity present in some volume of a saturated solution, expressed in moles per liter, grams per 100 mL, or other units. The *solubility product constant* is an equilibrium constant. Nonetheless, there is a connection between them: If one is known, the other can be calculated.

Chemistry.Now™

Sign in at **www.cengage.com/login** and go to Chapter 18 Contents to see:
- Screen 18.11 for a review of **precipitation reactions**
- Screen 18.12 for a simulation on **solubility product constant**

EXERCISE 18.11 Writing K_{sp} Expressions

Write K_{sp} expressions for the following insoluble salts and look up numerical values for the constant in Appendix J.

(a) AgI   (b) BaF_2 (c) Ag_2CO_3

Relating Solubility and K_{sp}

Solubility product constants are determined by careful laboratory measurements of the concentrations of ions in solution.

Chemistry.Now™

Sign in at **www.cengage.com/login** and go to Chapter 18 Contents to see Screen 18.13 for a tutorial on **determining K_{sp} experimentally**.

Fluorite. The mineral fluorite is water-insoluble calcium fluoride. The mineral can vary widely in color from purple to green and to colorless. The colors are likely due to impurities.

Charles D. Winters

■ **EXAMPLE 18.8 K_{sp} from Solubility Measurements**

Problem Calcium fluoride, the main component of the mineral fluorite, dissolves to a slight extent in water.

$$CaF_2(s) \rightleftharpoons Ca^{2+}(aq) + 2\ F^-(aq) \qquad K_{sp} = [Ca^{2+}]\ [F^-]^2$$

Calculate the K_{sp} value for CaF_2 if the calcium ion concentration has been found to be 2.3×10^{-4} mol/L.

Strategy We first write the K_{sp} expression for CaF_2 and then substitute the numerical values for the equilibrium concentrations of the ions.

Solution When CaF_2 dissolves to a small extent in water, the balanced equation shows that the concentration of F^- ion must be twice the Ca^{2+} ion concentration.

If $[Ca^{2+}] = 2.3 \times 10^{-4}$ M, then $[F^-] = 2 \times [Ca^{2+}] = 4.6 \times 10^{-4}$ M

This means the solubility product constant is

$$K_{sp} = [Ca^{2+}][F^-]^2 = (2.3 \times 10^{-4})(4.6 \times 10^{-4})^2 = \boxed{4.9 \times 10^{-11}}$$

EXERCISE 18.12 K_{sp} from Solubility Measurements

The barium ion concentration, $[Ba^{2+}]$, in a saturated solution of barium fluoride is 7.5×10^{-3} M. Calculate the value of the K_{sp} for BaF_2.

$$BaF_2(s) \rightleftharpoons Ba^{2+}(aq) + 2\ F^-(aq)$$

K_{sp} values for insoluble salts can be used to estimate the solubility of a solid salt or to determine whether a solid will precipitate when solutions of its anion and cation are mixed. Let us first look at an example of the estimation of the solubility of a salt from its K_{sp} value.

Chemistry Now™

Sign in at **www.cengage.com/login** and go to Chapter 18 Contents to see Screen 18.14 for a tutorial on **estimating salt solubility using K_{sp}.**

■ **EXAMPLE 18.9** Solubility from K_{sp}

Problem The K_{sp} for $BaSO_4$ (as the mineral barite, Figure 18.12) is 1.1×10^{-10} at 25 °C. Calculate the solubility of barium sulfate in pure water in (a) moles per liter and (b) grams per liter.

Strategy When 1 mol of $BaSO_4$ dissolves, 1 mol of Ba^{2+} ions and 1 mol of SO_4^{2-} ions are produced. Thus, the solubility of $BaSO_4$ can be estimated by calculating the concentration of either Ba^{2+} or SO_4^{2-} from the solubility product constant.

Solution The equation for the solubility of $BaSO_4$ is

$$BaSO_4(s) \rightleftharpoons Ba^{2+}(aq) + SO_4^{2-}(aq) \qquad K_{sp} = [Ba^{2+}][SO_4^{2-}] = 1.1 \times 10^{-10}$$

Let us denote the solubility of $BaSO_4$ (in mol/L) by x; that is, x moles of $BaSO_4$ dissolve per liter. Therefore, both $[Ba^{2+}]$ and $[SO_4^{2-}]$ must also equal x at equilibrium.

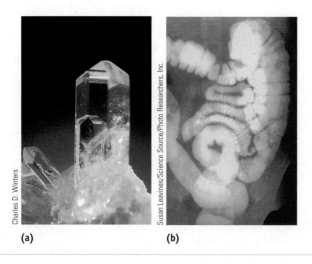

(a)　　　　　(b)

Charles D. Winters

Susan Leavines/Science Source/Photo Researchers, Inc.

FIGURE 18.12 Barium sulfate.
Barium sulfate, a white solid, is quite insoluble in water ($K_{sp} = 1.1 \times 10^{-10}$) (see Example 18.9). (a) A sample of the mineral barite, which is mostly barium sulfate. (b) Barium sulfate is opaque to x-rays, so it is used by physicians to examine the digestive tract. A patient drinks a "cocktail" containing $BaSO_4$, and the progress of the $BaSO_4$ through the digestive organs can be followed by x-ray analysis. This photo is an x-ray of a gastrointestinal tract after a person ingested barium sulfate. It is fortunate that $BaSO_4$ is so insoluble, because water- and acid-soluble barium salts are toxic.

Equation	$BaSO_4(s)$	$\rightleftharpoons$	$Ba^{2+}(aq)$	+	$SO_4^{2-}(aq)$
Initial (M)			0		0
Change (M)			$+x$		$+x$
Equilibrium (M)			x		x

Because K_{sp} is the product of the barium and sulfate ion concentrations, K_{sp} is the square of the solubility, x,

$$K_{sp} = [Ba^{2+}][SO_4^{2-}] = 1.1 \times 10^{-10} = (x)(x) = x^2$$

and so the value of x is

$$x = [Ba^{2+}] = [SO_4^{2-}] = \sqrt{1.1 \times 10^{-10}} = 1.0 \times 10^{-5}\ M$$

The solubility of $BaSO_4$ in pure water is 1.0×10^{-5} mol/L. To find its solubility in g/L, we need only multiply by the molar mass of $BaSO_4$.

$$\text{Solubility in g/L} = (1.0 \times 10^{-5}\ \text{mol/L})(233\ \text{g/mol}) = 0.0024\ \text{g/L}$$

■ EXAMPLE 18.10 Solubility from K_{sp}

Problem Knowing that the K_{sp} value for MgF_2 is 5.2×10^{-11}, calculate the solubility of the salt in (a) moles per liter and (b) grams per liter.

Strategy The problem is to define the salt solubility in terms that will allow us to solve the K_{sp} expression for this value. We know that, if 1 mol of MgF_2 dissolves, 1 mol of Mg^{2+} and 2 mol of F^- appear in the solution. This means the MgF_2 solubility (in moles dissolved per liter) is equivalent to the concentration of Mg^{2+} ions in the solution. Thus, if the solubility of MgF_2 is x mol/L, then $[Mg^{2+}] = x$ and $[F^-] = 2x$.

Solution We begin by writing the equilibrium equation and the K_{sp} expression,

$$MgF_2(s) \rightleftharpoons Mg^{2+}(aq) + 2\ F^-(aq) \qquad K_{sp} = [Mg^{2+}][F^-]^2 = 5.2 \times 10^{-11}$$

and then set up an ICE table.

Equation	$MgF_2(s)$	$\rightleftharpoons$	$Mg^{2+}(aq)$	+	$2\ F^-(aq)$
Initial (M)			0		0
Change (M)			$+x$		$+2x$
Equilibrium (M)			x		$2x$

Substituting these values into the K_{sp} expression, we find

$$K_{sp} = [Mg^{2+}][F^-]^2 = (x)(2x)^2 = 4x^3$$

Solving the equation for x,

$$x = \sqrt[3]{\frac{K_{sp}}{4}} = \sqrt[3]{\frac{5.2 \times 10^{-11}}{4}} = 2.4 \times 10^{-4}$$

we find that 2.4×10^{-4} moles of MgF_2 dissolve per liter. The solubility of MgF_2 in grams per liter is

$$(2.4 \times 10^{-4}\ \text{mol/L})(62.3\ \text{g/mol}) = 0.015\ \text{g}\ MgF_2/L$$

Comment Problems like this one often provoke our students to ask such questions as, "Aren't you counting things twice when you multiply x by 2 and then square it as well?" in the expression $K_{sp} = (x)(2x)^2$. The answer is no. The 2 in the $2x$ term is based on the stoichiometry of the compound. The exponent of 2 on the F^- ion concentration arises from the rules for writing equilibrium expressions.

EXERCISE 18.13 Salt Solubility from K_{sp}

Calculate the solubility of $Ca(OH)_2$ in mol/L and g/L using the value of K_{sp} in Appendix J.

The K_{sp} value reported for lead(II) chloride, $PbCl_2$, is 1.7×10^{-5}. If we assume the appropriate equilibrium in solution is

$$PbCl_2(s) \rightleftharpoons Pb^{2+}(aq) + 2\ Cl^-(aq)$$

the calculated solubility of $PbCl_2$ is 0.016 M. The experimental value for the solubility of the salt, however, is 0.036 M, more than twice the calculated value! What is the problem? There are several, as summarized by the diagram below.

The main problem in the lead(II) chloride case, and in many others, is that the compound dissolves but is not 100% dissociated into its constituent ions. Instead, it dissolves as the undissociated salt or forms ion pairs.

Other problems that lead to discrepancies between calculated and experimental solubilities are the reactions of ions (particularly anions) with water and complex ion formation. An example of the former effect is the reaction of sulfide ion with water, that is, hydrolysis.

$$S^{2-}(aq) + H_2O(\ell) \rightleftharpoons HS^-(aq) + OH^-(aq)$$

This means that the solubility of a metal sulfide is better described by a chemical equation such as

$$NiS(s) + H_2O(\ell) \rightleftharpoons Ni^{2+}(aq) + HS^-(aq) + OH^-(aq)$$

Complex ion formation is illustrated by the fact that lead chloride is more soluble in the presence of excess chloride ion, owing to the formation of the complex ion $PbCl_4^{2-}$.

$$PbCl_2(s) + 2\ Cl^-(aq) \rightleftharpoons PbCl_4^{2-}(aq)$$

Hydrolysis and complex ion formation are discussed further on pages 840–841 and 847–848, respectively.

For further information on these issues see:
(a) L. Meites, J. S. F. Pode, and H. C. Thomas: *Journal of Chemical Education*, Vol. 43, pp. 667–672, 1966.
(b) S. J. Hawkes: *Journal of Chemical Education*, Vol. 75, pp. 1179–1181, 1998.
(c) R. W. Clark and J. M. Bonicamp: *Journal of Chemical Education*, Vol. 75, pp. 1182–1185, 1998.
(d) R. J. Myers: *Journal of Chemical Education*, Vol. 63, pp. 687–690, 1986.

The *relative* solubilities of salts can often be deduced by comparing values of solubility product constants, but you must be careful! For example, the K_{sp} for silver chloride is

$$AgCl(s) \rightleftharpoons Ag^+(aq) + Cl^-(aq) \qquad K_{sp} = 1.8 \times 10^{-10}$$

whereas that for silver chromate is

$$Ag_2CrO_4(s) \rightleftharpoons 2\ Ag^+(aq) + CrO_4^{2-}(aq) \qquad K_{sp} = 9.0 \times 10^{-12}$$

In spite of the fact that Ag_2CrO_4 has a numerically smaller K_{sp} value than AgCl, the chromate salt is about 10 times *more* soluble than the chloride salt. If you determine solubilities from K_{sp} values as in the examples above, you would find the solubility of AgCl is 1.3×10^{-5} mol/L, whereas that of Ag_2CrO_4 is 1.3×10^{-4} mol/L. From this example and countless others, we conclude that

> Direct comparisons of the solubility of two salts on the basis of their K_{sp} values can be made only for salts having the same cation-to-anion ratio.

This means, for example, that you can directly compare solubilities of 1:1 salts such as the silver halides by comparing their K_{sp} values.

$$AgI\ (K_{sp} = 8.5 \times 10^{-17}) < AgBr\ (K_{sp} = 5.4 \times 10^{-13}) < AgCl\ (K_{sp} = 1.8 \times 10^{-10})$$

— increasing K_{sp} and increasing solubility ⟶

Similarly, you could compare 1:2 salts such as the lead halides.

$$PbI_2 \ (K_{sp} = 9.8 \times 10^{-9}) < PbBr_2 \ (K_{sp} = 6.6 \times 10^{-6}) < PbCl_2 \ (K_{sp} = 1.7 \times 10^{-5})$$

——— increasing K_{sp} and increasing solubility ———→

but you cannot directly compare a 1:1 salt (AgCl) with a 2:1 salt (Ag_2CrO_4).

EXERCISE 18.14 Comparing Solubilities

Using K_{sp} values, predict which salt in each pair is more soluble in water.

(a) AgCl or AgCN

(b) $Mg(OH)_2$ or $Ca(OH)_2$

(c) $Ca(OH)_2$ or $CaSO_4$

Solubility and the Common Ion Effect

The test tube on the left in Figure 18.13 contains a precipitate of silver acetate, $AgCH_3CO_2$, in water. The solution is saturated, and the silver ions and acetate ions in the solution are in equilibrium with solid silver acetate.

$$AgCH_3CO_2(s) \rightleftharpoons Ag^+(aq) + CH_3CO_2^-(aq)$$

But what would happen if the silver ion concentration is increased, say by adding silver nitrate? Le Chatelier's principle (◄ Section 16.6) suggests—and we observe —that more silver acetate precipitate should form because a product ion has been added, causing the equilibrium to shift to form more silver acetate.

The ionization of weak acids and bases is affected by the presence of an ion common to the equilibrium process (Section 18.1), and the effect of adding silver ions to a saturated silver acetate solution is another example of the common ion effect. Adding a common ion to a saturated solution of a salt will lower the salt solubility.

Chemistry.ᐡ.Now™

Sign in at **www.cengage.com/login** and go to Chapter 18 Contents to see Screen 18.15 for a simulation and tutorial on the **common ion effect.**

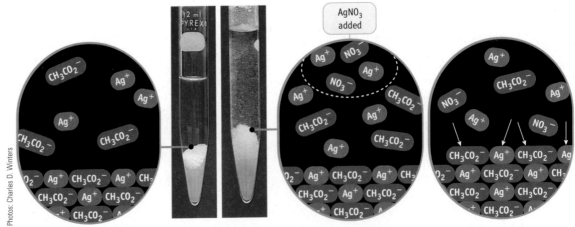

Photos: Charles D. Winters

FIGURE 18.13 The common ion effect. The tube at the left contains a saturated solution of silver acetate, $AgCH_3CO_2$. When 1.0 M $AgNO_3$ is added to the tube (right), more solid silver acetate forms.

EXAMPLE 18.11 The Common Ion Effect and Salt Solubility

Problem If solid AgCl is placed in 1.00 L of 0.55 M NaCl, what mass of AgCl will dissolve?

Strategy The presence of an ion common to the equilibrium suppresses the solubility of a salt. To determine the solubility of the salt under these circumstances, calculate the concentration of the ion (Ag^+ ion in this case) other than the common ion (here Cl^-).

Solution In pure water, the solubility of AgCl is equal to either $[Ag^+]$ or $[Cl^-]$.

$$AgCl(s) \rightleftharpoons Ag^+(aq) + Cl^-(aq)$$

Solubility of AgCl in pure water $= [Ag^+]$ or $[Cl^-] = \sqrt{K_{sp}} = 1.3 \times 10^{-5}$ mol/L or 0.0019 g/L

However, in water already containing a common ion, here the Cl^- ion, Le Chatelier's principle predicts that the solubility is less than 1.3×10^{-5} mol/L. In this case, the solubility of AgCl is equivalent to the concentration of Ag^+ ion in solution, so we set up an ICE table to show the concentrations of Ag^+ and Cl^- when equilibrium is attained.

Equation	AgCl(s) $\rightleftharpoons$	Ag$^+$(aq)	+	Cl$^-$(aq)
Initial (M)		0		0.55
Change (M)		$+x$		$+x$
Equilibrium (M)		x		$0.55 + x$

Some AgCl dissolves in the presence of chloride ion and produces Ag^+ and Cl^- ion concentrations of x mol/L. Because some chloride ion was already present, the total chloride ion concentration is what was already there (0.55 M) plus the amount supplied by AgCl dissociation ($= x$).

The equilibrium concentrations from the table are substituted into the K_{sp} expression,

$$K_{sp} = 1.8 \times 10^{-10} = [Ag^+][Cl^-] = (x)(0.55 + x)$$

and rearranged to

$$x^2 + 0.55x - K_{sp} = 0$$

This is a quadratic equation and can be solved by the methods in Appendix A. An easier approach, however, is to make the approximation that x is very small with respect to 0.55 [and so $(0.55 + x) \approx 0.55$]. This is a reasonable assumption because we know that the solubility equals 1.3×10^{-5} M without the common ion Cl^- and that it will be even smaller in the presence of added Cl^-. Therefore,

$$K_{sp} = 1.8 \times 10^{-10} = (x)(0.55)$$
$$x = [Ag^+] = 3.3 \times 10^{-10} \text{ M}$$

The solubility in grams per liter is then

$$(3.3 \times 10^{-10} \text{ mol/L})(143 \text{ g/mol}) = \boxed{4.7 \times 10^{-8} \text{ g/L}}$$

As predicted by Le Chatelier's principle, the solubility of AgCl in the presence of added Cl^- is less (3.3×10^{-10} M) than in pure water (1.3×10^{-5} M).

Comment As a final step, check the approximation by substituting the calculated value of x into the exact expression $K_{sp} = (x)(0.55 + x)$. If the product $(x)(0.55 + x)$ is the same as the given value of K_{sp}, the approximation is valid.

$$K_{sp} = (x)(0.55 + x) = (3.3 \times 10^{-10})(0.55 + 3.3 \times 10^{-10}) = 1.8 \times 10^{-10}$$

The approximation we made here is similar to the approximations we make in acid–base equilibrium problems.

EXAMPLE 18.12 The Common Ion Effect and Salt Solubility

Problem Calculate the solubility of silver chromate, Ag_2CrO_4, at 25 °C in the presence of 0.0050 M K_2CrO_4 solution.

$$Ag_2CrO_4(s) \rightleftharpoons 2 Ag^+(aq) + CrO_4^{2-}(aq)$$
$$K_{sp} = [Ag^+]^2[CrO_4^{2-}] = 9.0 \times 10^{-12}$$

For comparison, the solubility of Ag_2CrO_4 in pure water is 1.3×10^{-4} mol/L.

Strategy In the presence of chromate ion from the water-soluble salt K_2CrO_4, the concentration of Ag^+ ions produced by Ag_2CrO_4 will be less than in pure water. Assume the solubility of Ag_2CrO_4 is x mol/L. This means the concentration of Ag^+ ions will be $2x$ mol/L, whereas the concentration of CrO_4^{2-} ions will be x mol/L plus the amount of CrO_4^{2-} already in the solution.

Solution

Equation	$Ag_2CrO_4(s) \rightleftharpoons 2\ Ag^+(aq)\ +$	$CrO_4^{2-}(aq)$
Initial (M)	0	0.0050
Change	$+2x$	$+x$
Equilibrium (M)	$2x$	$0.0050 + x$

Substituting the equilibrium amounts into the K_{sp} expression, we have

$$K_{sp} = 9.0 \times 10^{-12} = [Ag^+]^2[CrO_4^{2-}]$$

$$K_{sp} = (2x)^2(0.0050 + x)$$

As in Example 18.11, you can make the approximation that x is very small with respect to 0.0050, and so $(0.0050 + x) \approx 0.0050$. (This is reasonable because $[CrO_4^{2-}]$ is 0.00013 M without added chromate ion, and it is certain that x is even smaller in the presence of extra chromate ion.) Therefore, the approximate expression is

$$K_{sp} = 9.0 \times 10^{-12} = [Ag^+]^2[CrO_4^{2-}] = (2x)^2(0.0050)$$

Solving, we find x, the solubility of silver chromate in the presence of excess chromate ion, is

$$x = \text{Solubility of } Ag_2CrO_4 = \boxed{2.1 \times 10^{-5}\ M}$$

Comment The silver ion concentration in the presence of the common ion is

$$[Ag^+] = 2x = 4.2 \times 10^{-5}\ M$$

This silver ion concentration is indeed less than its value in pure water (2.6×10^{-4} M), owing to the presence of an ion "common" to the equilibrium.

EXERCISE 18.15 The Common Ion Effect and Salt Solubility

Calculate the solubility of $BaSO_4$ (a) in pure water and (b) in the presence of 0.010 M $Ba(NO_3)_2$. K_{sp} for $BaSO_4$ is 1.1×10^{-10}.

EXERCISE 18.16 The Common Ion Effect and Salt Solubility

Calculate the solubility of $Zn(CN)_2$ at 25 °C (a) in pure water and (b) in the presence of 0.10 M $Zn(NO_3)_2$. (K_{sp} for $Zn(CN)_2$ is 8.0×10^{-12}.)

Examples 18.11 and 18.12 allow us to propose two important general ideas:

- The solubility of a salt will be reduced by the presence of a common ion, in accordance with Le Chatelier's principle.
- We made the approximation that the amount of common ion added to the solution was very large in comparison with the amount of that ion coming from the insoluble salt, and this allowed us to simplify our calculations. This is almost always the case, but you should check to be sure.

The Effect of Basic Anions on Salt Solubility

The next time you are tempted to wash a supposedly insoluble salt down the kitchen or laboratory drain, stop and consider the consequences. Many metal ions such as lead, chromium, and mercury are toxic in the environment. Even if a so-called insoluble salt of one of these cations does not appear to dissolve, its solubility in water may be greater than you think, in part owing to the possibility that the anion of the salt is a weak base or the cation is a weak acid.

Lead sulfide, PbS, which is found in nature as the mineral galena (Figure 18.14), provides an example of the effect of the acid–base properties of an ion on salt solubility. When placed in water, a trace amount dissolves,

$$PbS(s) \rightleftharpoons Pb^{2+}(aq) + S^{2-}(aq)$$

and one product of the reaction is the sulfide ion. This anion is a strong base,

$$S^{2-}(aq) + H_2O(\ell) \rightleftharpoons HS^-(aq) + OH^-(aq) \qquad K_b = 1 \times 10^5$$

and it undergoes extensive hydrolysis (reaction with water) (◀ Table 17.3). The equilibrium process for dissolving PbS thus shifts to the right, and the lead ion concentration in solution is greater than expected from the simple ionization of the salt.

The lead sulfide example leads to the following general observation:

> Any salt containing an anion that is the conjugate base of a weak acid will dissolve in water to a greater extent than given by K_{sp}.

This means that salts of phosphate, acetate, carbonate, and cyanide, as well as sulfide, can be affected, because all of these anions undergo the general hydrolysis reaction

$$X^-(aq) + H_2O(\ell) \rightleftharpoons HX(aq) + OH^-(aq)$$

The observation that ions from insoluble salts can undergo hydrolysis is related to another useful, general conclusion:

> Insoluble salts in which the anion is the conjugate base of a weak acid dissolve in strong acids.

Insoluble salts containing such anions as acetate, carbonate, hydroxide, phosphate, and sulfide dissolve in strong acids. For example, you know that if a strong acid is added to a water-insoluble metal carbonate such as $CaCO_3$, the salt dissolves (◀ Section 3.4).

$$CaCO_3(s) + 2\ H_3O^+(aq) \rightarrow Ca^{2+}(aq) + 3\ H_2O(\ell) + CO_2(g)$$

You can think of this as the result of a series of reactions.

$CaCO_3(s) \rightleftharpoons Ca^{2+}(aq) + CO_3^{2-}(aq)$ $\qquad K_{sp} = 3.4 \times 10^{-9}$

$CO_3^{2-}(aq) + H_3O^+(aq) \rightleftharpoons HCO_3^-(aq) + H_2O(\ell)$ $\qquad 1/K_{a2} = 1/4.8 \times 10^{-11} = 2.1 \times 10^{10}$

$HCO_3^-(aq) + H_3O^+(aq) \rightleftharpoons H_2CO_3(aq) + H_2O(\ell)$ $\qquad 1/K_{a1} = 1/4.2 \times 10^{-7} = 2.4 \times 10^6$

Overall: $CaCO_3(s) + 2\ H_3O^+(aq) \rightleftharpoons Ca^{2+}(aq) + 2\ H_2O(\ell) + H_2CO_3(aq)$

$K_{net} = (K_{sp})(1/K_{a2})(1/K_{a1}) = 1.7 \times 10^8$

Carbonic acid, a product of this reaction, is not stable,

$$H_2CO_3(aq) \rightleftharpoons CO_2(g) + H_2O(\ell) \qquad\qquad K \approx 10^5$$

and you see CO_2 bubbling out of the solution, a process that moves the $CaCO_3 + H_3O^+$ equilibrium even further to the right. Calcium carbonate dissolves completely in strong acid!

Charles D. Winters

FIGURE 18.14 Lead sulfide (galena). This and other metal sulfides dissolve in water to a greater extent than expected because the sulfide ion reacts with water to form the very stable species HS^- and OH^-.

$PbS(s) + H_2O(\ell) \rightleftharpoons$
$\qquad Pb^{2+}(aq) + HS^-(aq) + OH^-(aq)$

The model of PbS shows that the unit cell is cubic, a feature reflected by the cubic crystals of the mineral galena.

■ **Metal Sulfide Solubility** The true solubility of a metal sulfide is better represented by a modified solubility product constant, K_{spa}, which is defined as follows:

$MS(s) \rightleftharpoons M^{2+}(aq) + S^{2-}(aq)$
$\qquad\qquad K_{sp} = [M^{2+}][S^{2-}]$

$S^{2-}(aq) + H_2O(\ell) \rightleftharpoons$
$\qquad HS^-(aq) + OH^-(aq)$
$\qquad\qquad K_b = [HS^-][OH^-]/[S^{2-}]$

Net reaction:

$MS(s) + H_2O(\ell) \rightleftharpoons$
$\qquad HS^-(aq) + M^{2+}(aq) + OH^-(aq)$
$\qquad K_{spa} = [M^{2+}][HS^-][OH^-] = K_{sp} \times K_b$

Values for K_{spa} for several metal sulfides are included in Appendix J.

FIGURE 18.15 The effect of the anion on salt solubility in acid. (left) A precipitate of AgCl (white) and Ag_3PO_4 (yellow). (right) Adding a strong acid (HNO_3) dissolves Ag_3PO_4 (and leaves insoluble AgCl). The basic anion PO_4^{3-} reacts with acid to give H_3PO_4, whereas Cl^- is too weakly basic to form HCl.

Photos: Charles D. Winters

Add strong acid

Precipitate of
AgCl and Ag_3PO_4

Precipitate of
AgCl

Many metal sulfides are also soluble in strong acids

$$FeS(s) + 2\ H_3O^+(aq) \rightleftharpoons Fe^{2+}(aq) + H_2S(aq) + 2\ H_2O(\ell)$$

as are metal phosphates (Figure 18.15),

$$Ag_3PO_4(s) + 3\ H_3O^+(aq) \rightleftharpoons 3\ Ag^+(aq) + H_3PO_4(aq) + 3\ H_2O(\ell)$$

and metal hydroxides.

$$Mg(OH)_2(s) + 2\ H_3O^+(aq) \rightleftharpoons Mg^{2+}(aq) + 4\ H_2O(\ell)$$

In general, the solubility of a salt containing the conjugate base of a weak acid is increased by addition of a stronger acid to the solution. In contrast, salts are not soluble in strong acid if the anion is the conjugate base of a strong acid. For example, AgCl is not soluble in strong acid

$$AgCl(s) \rightleftharpoons Ag^+(aq) + Cl^-(aq) \qquad\qquad K_{sp} = 1.8 \times 10^{-10}$$

$$H_3O^+(aq) + Cl^-(aq) \rightleftharpoons HCl(aq) + H_2O(\ell) \qquad\qquad K << 1$$

because Cl^- is a very weak base (◄ Table 17.3), and so its concentration is not lowered by a reaction with the strong acid H_3O^+ (Figure 18.15). This same conclusion would also apply to insoluble salts of Br^- and I^-.

Chemistry Now™

Sign in at **www.cengage.com/login** and go to Chapter 18 Contents to see Screen 18.16 for a self-study module on **solubility and pH.**

18.5 Precipitation Reactions

Metal-bearing ores contain the metal in the form of an insoluble salt (Figure 18.16), and, to complicate matters, ores often contain several such metal salts. Many industrial methods for separating metals from their ores involve dissolving metal salts to obtain the metal ion or ions in solution. The solution is then concentrated in some manner, and a precipitating agent is added to precipitate selectively only one type of metal ion as an insoluble salt. In the case of nickel, for example, the Ni^{2+} ion can be precipitated as insoluble nickel(II) sulfide or nickel(II) carbonate.

$$Ni^{2+}(aq) + HS^-(aq) + H_2O(\ell) \rightleftharpoons NiS(s) + H_3O^+(aq) \qquad K = 1.7 \times 10^{18}$$

$$Ni^{2+}(aq) + CO_3^{2-}(aq) \rightleftharpoons NiCO_3(s) \qquad\qquad K = 3.2 \times 10^{10}$$

Charles D. Winters

FIGURE 18.16 Minerals. Minerals are insoluble salts. The minerals shown here are light purple fluorite (calcium fluoride), black hematite [iron(III) oxide], and rust brown goethite, a mixture of iron(III) oxide and iron(III) hydroxide.

The final step in obtaining the metal itself is to reduce the metal cation to the metal either chemically or electrochemically (▶ Chapter 20).

Our immediate goal is to work out methods to determine whether a precipitate will form under a given set of conditions. For example, if Ag^+ and Cl^- are present at some given concentrations, will AgCl precipitate from the solution?

K_{sp} and the Reaction Quotient, Q

Silver chloride, like silver bromide, is used in photographic films. It dissolves to a very small extent in water and has a correspondingly small value of K_{sp}.

$$AgCl(s) \rightleftharpoons Ag^+(aq) + Cl^-(aq) \qquad\qquad K_{sp} = [Ag^+][Cl^-] = 1.8 \times 10^{-10}$$

But let us look at the problem from the other direction: If a solution contains Ag^+ and Cl^- ions at some concentration, will AgCl precipitate from solution? This is the same question we asked in Section 16.3 when we wanted to know if a given mixture of reactants and products was an equilibrium mixture, if the reactants continued to form products, or if products would revert to reactants. The procedure there was to calculate the reaction quotient, Q.

For silver chloride, the expression for the reaction quotient, Q, is

$$Q = [Ag^+][Cl^-]$$

Recall that *the difference between Q and K is that the concentrations in the reaction quotient expression may or may not be those at equilibrium.* For the case of a slightly soluble salt such as AgCl, we can reach the following conclusions (◀ Section 16.3).

1. If $Q = K_{sp}$, the solution is saturated.

When the product of the ion concentrations is equal to K_{sp}, the ion concentrations have reached their maximum value.

2. If $Q < K_{sp}$, the solution is not saturated.

This can mean two things: (i) If solid AgCl is present, more will dissolve until equilibrium is achieved (when $Q = K_{sp}$). (ii) If solid AgCl is not already present, more $Ag^+(aq)$ or more $Cl^-(aq)$ (or both) could be added to the solution until precipitation of solid AgCl begins (when $Q > K_{sp}$).

3. If $Q > K_{sp}$, the system is not at equilibrium; precipitation will occur.

The concentrations of Ag^+ and Cl^- in solution are too high, and AgCl will precipitate until $Q = K_{sp}$.

Chemistry ⚛ Now™

Sign in at **www.cengage.com/login** and go to Chapter 18 Contents to see Screen 18.17 for a simulation and tutorial on **when a precipitation reaction can occur.**

▪ **EXAMPLE 18.13 Solubility and the Reaction Quotient**

Problem Solid AgCl has been placed in a beaker of water. After some time, the concentrations of Ag^+ and Cl^- are each 1.2×10^{-5} mol/L. Has the system reached equilibrium? If not, will more AgCl dissolve?

Strategy Use the experimental ion concentrations to calculate the reaction quotient Q. Compare Q and K_{sp} to decide if the system is at equilibrium (if $Q = K_{sp}$).

Solution For this AgCl case,

$$Q = [Ag^+][Cl^-] = (1.2 \times 10^{-5})(1.2 \times 10^{-5}) = 1.4 \times 10^{-10}$$

Here, Q is less than K_{sp} (1.8×10^{-10}). The solution is not yet saturated, and AgCl will continue to dissolve until $Q = K_{sp}$, at which point $[Ag^+] = [Cl^-] = 1.3 \times 10^{-5}$ M. That is, an additional 0.1×10^{-5} mol of AgCl (about 1.9 mg) will dissolve per liter.

EXERCISE 18.17 Solubility and the Reaction Quotient

Solid PbI_2 $(K_{sp} = 9.8 \times 10^{-9})$ is placed in a beaker of water. After a period of time, the lead(II) concentration is measured and found to be 1.1×10^{-3} M. Has the system yet reached equilibrium? That is, is the solution saturated? If not, will more PbI_2 dissolve?

K_{sp}, the Reaction Quotient, and Precipitation Reactions

With some knowledge of the reaction quotient, we can decide (1) if a precipitate will form when the ion concentrations are known or (2) what concentrations of ions are required to begin the precipitation of an insoluble salt.

Suppose the concentration of aqueous magnesium ion in a solution is 1.5×10^{-6} M. If enough NaOH is added to make the solution 1.0×10^{-4} M in hydroxide ion, OH^-, will precipitation of $Mg(OH)_2$ occur $(K_{sp} = 5.6 \times 10^{-12})$? If not, will it occur if the concentration of OH^- is increased to 1.0×10^{-2} M?

Our strategy will be as in Example 18.13. That is, use the ion concentrations to calculate the value of Q and then compare Q with K_{sp} to decide if the system is at equilibrium. Let us begin with the equation for the dissolution of insoluble $Mg(OH)_2$.

$$Mg(OH)_2(s) \rightleftharpoons Mg^{2+}(aq) + 2\,OH^-(aq)$$

When the concentrations of magnesium and hydroxide ions are those stated above, we find that Q is less than K_{sp}.

$$Q = [Mg^{2+}][OH^-]^2 = (1.5 \times 10^{-6})(1.0 \times 10^{-4})^2 = 1.5 \times 10^{-14}$$

$$Q\,(1.5 \times 10^{-14}) < K_{sp}\,(5.6 \times 10^{-12})$$

This means the solution is not yet saturated, and precipitation does not occur.

When $[OH^-]$ is increased to 1.0×10^{-2} M, the reaction quotient is 1.5×10^{-10},

$$Q = (1.5 \times 10^{-6})(1.0 \times 10^{-2})^2$$

$$Q = 1.5 \times 10^{-10} > K_{sp}\,(5.6 \times 10^{-12})$$

The reaction quotient is now *larger* than K_{sp}. Precipitation of $Mg(OH)_2$ occurs and will continue until the Mg^{2+} and OH^- ion concentrations have declined to the point where their product is equal to K_{sp}.

EXERCISE 18.18 Deciding Whether a Precipitate Will Form

Will $SrSO_4$ precipitate from a solution containing 2.5×10^{-4} M strontium ion, Sr^{2+}, if enough of the soluble salt Na_2SO_4 is added to make the solution 2.5×10^{-4} M in SO_4^{2-}? K_{sp} for $SrSO_4$ is 3.4×10^{-7}.

Now that we know how to decide if a precipitate will form when the concentration of each ion is known, let us turn to the problem of deciding how much of the precipitating agent is required to begin the precipitation of an ion at a given concentration level.

EXAMPLE 18.14 Ion Concentrations Required to Begin Precipitation

Problem The concentration of barium ion, Ba^{2+}, in a solution is 0.010 M.

(a) What concentration of sulfate ion, SO_4^{2-}, is required once $BaSO_4$ has started to precipitate?

(b) When the concentration of sulfate ion in the solution reaches 0.015 M, what concentration of barium ion will remain in solution?

Strategy There are three variables in the K_{sp} expression: K_{sp} and the anion and cation concentrations. Here, we know K_{sp} (1.1×10^{-10}) and one of the ion concentrations. We can then calculate the other ion concentration.

Solution Let us begin by writing the balanced equation for the equilibrium that will exist when $BaSO_4$ has been precipitated.

$$BaSO_4(s) \rightleftharpoons Ba^{2+}(aq) + SO_4^{2-}(aq) \qquad K_{sp} = [Ba^{2+}][SO_4^{2-}] = 1.1 \times 10^{-10}$$

(a) When the product of the ion concentrations exceeds the K_{sp} ($= 1.1 \times 10^{-10}$)—that is, when $Q > K_{sp}$—precipitation will occur. The Ba^{2+} ion concentration is known (0.010 M), so the SO_4^{2-} ion concentration necessary for precipitation can be calculated.

$$[SO_4^{2-}] = \frac{K_{sp}}{[Ba^{2+}]} = \frac{1.1 \times 10^{-10}}{0.010} = \boxed{1.1 \times 10^{-8} \text{ M}}$$

The result tells us that if the sulfate ion is just slightly greater than 1.1×10^{-8} M, $BaSO_4$ will begin to precipitate; $Q = [Ba^{2+}][SO_4^{2-}]$ would then be greater than K_{sp}.

(b) If the sulfate ion concentration is increased to 0.015 M, the maximum concentration of Ba^{2+} ion that can exist in solution (in equilibrium with $BaSO_4$) is

$$[Ba^{2+}] = \frac{K_{sp}}{[SO_4^{2-}]} = \frac{1.1 \times 10^{-10}}{0.015} = \boxed{7.3 \times 10^{-9} \text{ M}}$$

Comment The fact that the barium ion concentration is so small under these circumstances means that the Ba^{2+} ion has been essentially completely removed from solution. (It began at 0.010 M and has dropped by a factor of about 10 million.) The Ba^{2+} ion precipitation is, for all practical purposes, complete.

EXAMPLE 18.15 K_{sp} and Precipitations

Problem Suppose you mix 100.0 mL of 0.0200 M $BaCl_2$ with 50.0 mL of 0.0300 M Na_2SO_4. Will $BaSO_4$ ($K_{sp} = 1.1 \times 10^{-10}$) precipitate?

Strategy Here, we mix two solutions, one containing Ba^{2+} ions and the other SO_4^{2-} ions. First, find the concentration of each of these ions after mixing. Then, knowing the ion concentrations in the diluted solution, calculate Q and compare it with the K_{sp} value for $BaSO_4$.

Solution First, use the equation $c_1V_1 = c_2V_2$ (◀ Section 4.5) to calculate c_2, the concentration of the Ba^{2+} or SO_4^{2-} ions after mixing, to give a new solution with a volume of 150.0 mL ($= V_2$).

$$[Ba^{2+}] \text{ after mixing} = \frac{(0.0200 \text{ mol/L})(0.1000 \text{ L})}{0.1500 \text{ L}} = 0.0133 \text{ M}$$

$$[SO_4^{2-}] \text{ after mixing} = \frac{(0.0300 \text{ mol/L})(0.0500 \text{ L})}{0.1500 \text{ L}} = 0.0100 \text{ M}$$

Now the reaction quotient can be calculated.

$$Q = [Ba^{2+}][SO_4^{2-}] = (0.0133)(0.0100) = 1.33 \times 10^{-4}$$

Q is much larger than K_{sp}, so $BaSO_4$ precipitates.

EXERCISE 18.19 Ion Concentrations Required to Begin Precipitation

What is the minimum concentration of I^- that can cause precipitation of PbI_2 from a 0.050 M solution of $Pb(NO_3)_2$? K_{sp} for PbI_2 is 8.7×10^{-9}. What concentration of Pb^{2+} ions remains in solution when the concentration of I^- is 0.0015 M?

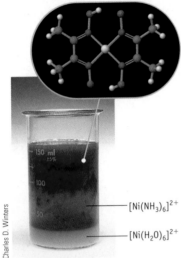

Dimethylglyoximate complex of Ni^{2+} ion

FIGURE 18.17 Complex ions.
The green solution contains soluble $Ni(H_2O)_6^{2+}$ ions in which water molecules are bound to Ni^{2+} ions by ion–dipole forces. This complex ion gives the solution its green color. The Ni^{2+}-ammonia complex ion is purple. The red, insoluble solid is the dimethylglyoximate complex of the Ni^{2+} ion [$Ni(C_4H_7O_2N_2)_2$] (model at top). Formation of this beautiful red insoluble compound is the classical test for the presence of the aqueous Ni^{2+} ion.

$[Ni(NH_3)_6]^{2+}$

$[Ni(H_2O)_6]^{2+}$

Charles D. Winters

■ **Complex Ions** Complex ions are prevalent in chemistry and are the basis of such biologically important substances as hemoglobin and vitamin B_{12}. They are described in more detail in Chapter 22.

EXERCISE 18.20 K_{sp} and Precipitation

You have 100.0 mL of 0.0010 M silver nitrate. Will AgCl precipitate if you add 5.0 mL of 0.025 M HCl?

18.6 Equilibria Involving Complex Ions

Metal ions exist in aqueous solution as complex ions (◀ Section 17.10) (Figure 18.17). Complex ions consist of the metal ion and other molecules or ions bound into a single entity. In water, metal ions are always surrounded by water molecules, with the negative end of the polar water molecule, the oxygen atom, attracted to the positive metal ion. In the case of Ni^{2+}, the ion exists as $[Ni(H_2O)_6]^{2+}$ in water. On adding ammonia, water molecules are displaced successively, and in the presence of a high enough concentration of ammonia, the complex ion $[Ni(NH_3)_6]^{2+}$ exists. Many organic molecules also form complex ions with metal ions, one example being the complex with the dimethylglyoximate ion in Figure 18.17.

The molecules or ions that bind to metal ions are called **ligands** (▶ Chapter 22). In aqueous solution, metal ions and ligands exist in equilibrium, and the equilibrium constants for these reactions are referred to as **formation constants, K_f** (Appendix K). For example,

$$Cu^{2+}(aq) + NH_3(aq) \rightleftharpoons [Cu(NH_3)]^{2+}(aq) \qquad K_{f1} = 2.0 \times 10^4$$

$$[Cu(NH_3)]^{2+}(aq) + NH_3(aq) \rightleftharpoons [Cu(NH_3)_2]^{2+}(aq) \qquad K_{f2} = 4.7 \times 10^3$$

$$[Cu(NH_3)_2]^{2+}(aq) + NH_3(aq) \rightleftharpoons [Cu(NH_3)_3]^{2+}(aq) \qquad K_{f3} = 1.1 \times 10^3$$

$$[Cu(NH_3)_3]^{2+}(aq) + NH_3(aq) \rightleftharpoons [Cu(NH_3)_4]^{2+}(aq) \qquad K_{f4} = 2.0 \times 10^2$$

(In these reactions, Cu^{2+} begins as $[Cu(H_2O)_4]^{2+}$. Ammonia successively displaces the water molecules.) Overall, the formation of the tetraammine copper(II) complex ion has an equilibrium constant of 2.1×10^{13} ($= K_{f1} \times K_{f2} \times K_{f3} \times K_{f4}$).

$$Cu^{2+}(aq) + 4\, NH_3(aq) \rightleftharpoons [Cu(NH_3)_4]^{2+}(aq) \qquad K_f = 2.1 \times 10^{13}$$

■ **EXAMPLE 8.16 Complex Ion Equilibria**

Problem What is the concentration of Cd^{2+} ions in a solution prepared by adding 0.00100 mol of $Cd(NO_3)_2$ to 1.00 L of 1.50 M NH_3? K_f for complex ion $[Cd(NH_3)_4]^{2+}$ is 1.3×10^7.

Strategy The formation constant for the complex ion is very large, so we can assume nearly all of the Cd^{2+} ions are in that form. That is, the initial concentration of the complex ion, $[Cd(NH_3)_4]^{2+}$, is 0.00100 M. This then dissociates to produce Cd^{2+} ions in solution.

Solution Let us set up an ICE table for the dissociation of $[Cd(NH_3)_4]^{2+}$.

Equation	$[Cd(NH_3)_4]^{2+}(aq)$	$\rightleftharpoons$	$Cd^{2+}(aq)$	$+$	$4\, NH_3(aq)$
Initial (M)	0.00100		0		1.50 − 0.00400 M
Change	$-x$		$+x$		$+4x$
Equilibrium (M)	$0.00100 - x \approx 0.00100$		x		$1.50 - 0.00400 + 4x \approx 1.50$

$$K = \frac{1}{K_f} = \frac{1}{1.3 \times 10^7} = \frac{[Cd^{2+}][NH_3]^4}{\{[Cd(NH_3)_4]^{2+}\}} = \frac{(x)(1.50)}{0.000100}$$

$$x = [Cd^{2+}] = 5.1 \times 10^{-11}\ M$$

18.7 Solubility and Complex Ions

Silver chloride dissolves neither in water nor in strong acid, but it does dissolve in ammonia because it forms a water-soluble complex ion, $[Ag(NH_3)_2]^+$ (Figure 18.18).

$$AgCl(s) + 2\ NH_3(aq) \rightleftharpoons [Ag(NH_3)_2]^+(aq) + Cl^-(aq)$$

We can view dissolving $AgCl(s)$ in this way as a two-step process. First, AgCl dissolves minimally in water, giving $Ag^+(aq)$ and $Cl^-(aq)$ ion. Then, the $Ag^+(aq)$ ion combines with NH_3 to give the ammonia complex. Lowering the $Ag^+(aq)$ concentration through complexation with NH_3 shifts the solubility equilibrium to the right, and more solid AgCl dissolves.

$$AgCl(s) \rightleftharpoons Ag^+(aq) + Cl^-(aq) \qquad\qquad K_{sp} = 1.8 \times 10^{-10}$$

$$Ag^+(aq) + 2\ NH_3(aq) \rightleftharpoons [Ag(NH_3)_2]^+(aq) \qquad K_f = 1.6 \times 10^7$$

This is an example of combining or "coupling" two (or more) equilibria where one is a product-favored reaction and the other is reactant-favored.

The large value of the formation constant for $[Ag(NH_3)_2]^+$ means that the equilibrium lies well to the right, and AgCl dissolves in the presence of NH_3. If we combine K_f with K_{sp}, we obtain the net equilibrium constant for the interaction of AgCl and aqueous ammonia.

$$K_{net} = K_{sp} \times K_f = (1.8 \times 10^{-10})(1.6 \times 10^7) = 2.9 \times 10^{-3}$$

$$K_{net} = 2.9 \times 10^{-3} = \frac{\{[Ag(NH_3)_2]^+\}[Cl^-]}{[NH_3]^2}$$

Even though the value of K_{net} seems small, if we use a large concentration of NH_3, the concentration of $[Ag(NH_3)_2]^+$ in solution can be high. Silver chloride is thus much more soluble in the presence of ammonia than in pure water.

The stabilities of various complex ions involving silver(I) can be compared by comparing values of their formation constants.

Formation Equilibrium	K_f
$Ag^+(aq) + 2\ Cl^-(aq) \rightleftharpoons [AgCl_2]^-(aq)$	2.5×10^5
$Ag^+(aq) + 2\ S_2O_3^{2-}(aq) \rightleftharpoons [Ag(S_2O_3)_2]^{3-}(aq)$	2.0×10^{13}
$Ag^+(aq) + 2\ CN^-(aq) \rightleftharpoons [Ag(CN)_2]^-(aq)$	5.6×10^{18}

The formation of all three silver complexes is strongly product-favored. The cyanide complex ion $[Ag(CN)_2]^-$ is the most stable of the three.

Figure 18.18 shows what happens as complex ions are formed. Beginning with a precipitate of AgCl, adding aqueous ammonia dissolves the precipitate to give the soluble complex ion $[Ag(NH_3)_2]^+$. Silver bromide is even more stable than $[Ag(NH_3)_2]^+$, so AgBr ($K_{sp} = 5.4 \times 10^{-13}$) forms in preference to the complex ion on adding bromide ion. If thiosulfate ion, $S_2O_3^{2-}$, is then added, AgBr dissolves due to the formation of $[Ag(S_2O_3)_2]^{3-}$, a complex ion with a large formation constant (2.0×10^{13}).

AgCl(s),
$K_{sp} = 1.8 \times 10^{-10}$

(a) AgCl precipitates on adding NaCl(aq) to AgNO₃(aq) (see Figure 3.7).

→ NH₃(aq) →

$[Ag(NH_3)_2]^+$(aq)

(b) The precipitate of AgCl dissolves on adding aqueous NH₃ to give water-soluble $[Ag(NH_3)_2]^+$.

→ NaBr(aq) →

AgBr(s),
$K_{sp} = 5.4 \times 10^{-13}$

(c) The silver-ammonia complex ion is changed to insoluble AgBr on adding NaBr(aq).

→ Na₂S₂O₃(aq) →

$[Ag(S_2O_3)_2]^{3-}$(aq)

(d) Solid AgBr is dissolved on adding Na₂S₂O₃(aq). The product is the water-soluble complex ion $[Ag(S_2O_3)_2]^{3-}$.

FIGURE 18.18 Forming and dissolving precipitates. Insoluble compounds often dissolve upon addition of a complexing agent.

Chemistry.⚛.Now™

Sign in at **www.cengage.com/login** and go to Chapter 18 Contents to see:
• Screen 18.18 for more information on **combining equilibria**
• Screen 18.19 for a tutorial on **complex ion formation and solubility**

■ **EXAMPLE 18.17 Complex Ions and Solubility**

Problem What is the value of the equilibrium constant, K_{net}, for dissolving AgBr in a solution containing the thiosulfate ion, $S_2O_3^{2-}$ (Figure 18.18)? Explain why AgBr dissolves readily on adding aqueous sodium thiosulfate to the solid.

Strategy Summing several equilibrium processes gives the net chemical equation. K_{net} is the product of the values of K of the summed chemical equations. (See the preceding text and Section 16.10.)

Solution The overall reaction for dissolving AgBr in the presence of the thiosulfate anion is the sum of two equilibrium processes.

AgBr(s) $\rightleftharpoons$ Ag⁺(aq) + Br⁻(aq) $K_{sp} = 5.0 \times 10^{-13}$

Ag⁺(aq) + 2 $S_2O_3^{2-}$(aq) $\rightleftharpoons$ $[Ag(S_2O_3)_2]^{3-}$(aq) $K_f = 2.0 \times 10^{13}$

Net chemical equation:

AgBr(aq) + 2 $S_2O_3^{2-}$(aq) $\rightleftharpoons$ $[Ag(S_2O_3)_2]^{3-}$(aq) + Br⁻(aq) $K_{net} = K_{sp} \times K_f = 1.0 \times 10^1$

The value of K_{net} is greater than 1, indicating a product-favored reaction. AgBr is predicted to dissolve readily in aqueous Na₂S₂O₃, as observed (Figure 18.18).

EXERCISE 18.22 Complex Ions and Solubility

Calculate the value of the equilibrium constant, K_{net}, for dissolving Cu(OH)₂ in aqueous ammonia (to form the complex ion $[Cu(NH_3)_4]^{2+}$) (see Figure 17.7).

Photos: Charles D. Winters

Chapter Goals Revisited

Now that you have studied this chapter, you should ask whether you have met the chapter goals. In particular, you should be able to:

Understand the common ion effect

(a) Predict the effect of the addition of a "common ion" on the pH of the solution of a weak acid or base (Section 18.1). **Study Question(s) assignable in OWL: 2, 4, 109.**

Understand the control of pH in aqueous solutions with buffers

(a) Describe the functioning of buffer solutions. (Section 18.2) **Go Chemistry Module 23.**

(b) Use the Henderson–Hasselbalch equation (Equation 18.2) to calculate the pH of a buffer solution of given composition. **Study Question(s) assignable in OWL: 6, 7, 14.**

(c) Describe how a buffer solution of a given pH can be prepared. **Study Question(s) assignable in OWL: 9, 16, 83, 90, 101, 102, 109.**

(d) Calculate the pH of a buffer solution before and after adding acid or base. **Study Question(s) assignable in OWL: 20, 22, 74, 76, 82.**

Evaluate the pH in the course of acid–base titrations

(a) Predict the pH of an acid–base reaction at its equivalence point (Section 18.3; see also Sections 17.5 and 17.6).

Acid	Base	pH at Equivalence Point
Strong	Strong	$= 7$ (neutral)
Strong	Weak	< 7 (acidic)
Weak	Strong	> 7 (basic)

Study Question(s) assignable in OWL: 24, 74, 76, 98, 108.

(b) Understand the differences between the titration curves for a strong acid–strong base titration and titrations in which one of the substances is weak.

(c) Describe how an indicator functions in an acid–base titration. **Study Question(s) assignable in OWL: 32, 72, 80, 96, 105.**

Apply chemical equilibrium concepts to the solubility of ionic compounds

(a) Write the equilibrium constant expression—relating concentrations of ions in solutions to K_{sp}—for any insoluble salt (Section 18.4).

(b) Calculate K_{sp} values from experimental data (Section 18.4). **Study Question(s) assignable in OWL: 40, 42.**

(c) Estimate the solubility of a salt from the value of K_{sp} (Section 18.4). **Study Question(s) assignable in OWL: 46, 48, 72, 80, 96, 105.**

(d) Calculate the solubility of a salt in the presence of a common ion (Section 18.4). **Study Question(s) assignable in OWL: 54.**

(e) Understand how hydrolysis of basic anions affects the solubility of a salt (Section 18.4). **Study Question(s) assignable in OWL: 58.**

(f) Decide if a precipitate will form when the ion concentrations are known Section 18.5). **Study Question(s) assignable in OWL: 36, 60, 64, 70, 88, 89.**

(g) Calculate the ion concentrations that are required to begin the precipitation of an insoluble salt (Section 18.5).

(h) Understand that the formation of a complex ion can increase the solubility of an insoluble salt (Section 18.6). **Study Question(s) assignable in OWL: 66, 70, 92.**

Chemistry.Now™ Sign in at **www.cengage.com/login** to:

- Assess your understanding with Study Questions in OWL keyed to each goal in the Goals and Homework menu for this chapter
- For quick review, download Go Chemistry mini-lecture flashcard modules (or purchase them at **www.ichapters.com**)
- Check your readiness for an exam by taking the Pre-Test and exploring the modules recommended in your Personalized Study plan.

Access **How Do I Solve It?** tutorials on how to approach problem solving using concepts in this chapter.

For additional preparation for an examination on this chapter see the *Let's Review* section on pages 948–961.

KEY EQUATIONS

Equation 18.1 (page 816) Hydronium ion concentration in a buffer solution composed of a weak acid and its conjugate base.

$$[H_3O^+] = \frac{[acid]}{[conjugate\ base]} \times K_a$$

Equation 18.2 (page 817) Henderson–Hasselbalch equation. To calculate the pH of a buffer solution composed of a weak acid and its conjugate base.

$$pH = pK_a + log\frac{[conjugate\ base]}{[acid]}$$

Equation 18.3 (page 825) Equation to calculate the hydronium ion concentration before the equivalence point in the titration of a weak acid with a strong base. See also Equation 18.4 for the version of the equation based on the Henderson–Hasselbalch equation.

$$[H_3O^+] = \frac{[weak\ acid\ remaining]}{[conjugate\ base\ produced]} \times K_a$$

Equation 18.5 (page 825) The relationship between the pH of the solution and the pK_a of the weak acid (or $[H_3O^+]$ and K_a) at the halfway or half-neutralization point in the titration of a weak acid with a strong base (or of a weak base with a strong acid).

$$[H_3O^+] = K_a \text{ and } pH = pK_a$$

STUDY QUESTIONS

⦿WL Online homework for this chapter may be assigned in OWL.

▲ denotes challenging questions.

■ denotes questions assignable in OWL.

Blue-numbered questions have answers in Appendix O and fully-worked solutions in the *Student Solutions Manual*.

Practicing Skills

The Common Ion Effect and Buffer Solutions
(See Examples 18.1 and 18.2 and ChemistryNow Screens 18.2–18.4.)

1. Does the pH of the solution increase, decrease, or stay the same when you
   (a) Add solid ammonium chloride to a dilute aqueous solution of NH_3?
   (b) Add solid sodium acetate to a dilute aqueous solution of acetic acid?
   (c) Add solid NaCl to a dilute aqueous solution of NaOH?

2. ■ Does the pH of the solution increase, decrease, or stay the same when you
   (a) Add solid sodium oxalate, $Na_2C_2O_4$, to 50.0 mL of 0.015 M oxalic acid, $H_2C_2O_4$?
   (b) Add solid ammonium chloride to 75 mL of 0.016 M HCl?
   (c) Add 20.0 g of NaCl to 1.0 L of 0.10 M sodium acetate, $NaCH_3CO_2$?

3. What is the pH of a solution that consists of 0.20 M ammonia, NH_3, and 0.20 M ammonium chloride, NH_4Cl?

4. ■ What is the pH of 0.15 M acetic acid to which 1.56 g of sodium acetate, $NaCH_3CO_2$, has been added?

5. What is the pH of the solution that results from adding 30.0 mL of 0.015 M KOH to 50.0 mL of 0.015 M benzoic acid?

6. ■ What is the pH of the solution that results from adding 25.0 mL of 0.12 M HCl to 25.0 mL of 0.43 M NH_3?

7. ■ What is the pH of the buffer solution that contains 2.2 g of NH_4Cl in 250 mL of 0.12 M NH_3? Is the final pH lower or higher than the pH of the 0.12 M ammonia solution?

8. Lactic acid ($CH_3CHOHCO_2H$) is found in sour milk, in sauerkraut, and in muscles after activity. (K_a for lactic acid = 1.4×10^{-4}.)
   (a) If 2.75 g of $NaCH_3CHOHCO_2$, sodium lactate, is added to 5.00×10^2 mL of 0.100 M lactic acid, what is the pH of the resulting buffer solution?
   (b) Is the pH of the buffered solution lower or higher than the pH of the lactic acid solution?

9. ■ What mass of sodium acetate, $NaCH_3CO_2$, must be added to 1.00 L of 0.10 M acetic acid to give a solution with a pH of 4.50?

10. What mass of ammonium chloride, NH_4Cl, must be added to exactly 5.00×10^2 mL of 0.10 M NH_3 solution to give a solution with a pH of 9.00?

Using the Henderson–Hasselbalch Equation
(See Example 18.3 and ChemistryNow Screen 18.4.)

11. Calculate the pH of a solution that has an acetic acid concentration of 0.050 M and a sodium acetate concentration of 0.075 M.

12. Calculate the pH of a solution that has an ammonium chloride concentration of 0.050 M and an ammonia concentration of 0.045 M.

13. A buffer is composed of formic acid and its conjugate base, the formate ion.
   (a) What is the pH of a solution that has a formic acid concentration of 0.050 M and a sodium formate concentration of 0.035 M?
   (b) What must the ratio of acid to conjugate base be to increase the pH by 0.5 unit from the value calculated in part (a)?

14. ■ A buffer solution is composed of 1.360 g of KH_2PO_4 and 5.677 g of Na_2HPO_4.
   (a) What is the pH of the buffer solution?
   (b) What mass of KH_2PO_4 must be added to decrease the buffer solution pH by 0.5 unit from the value calculated in part (a)?

Preparing a Buffer Solution
(See Example 18.4 and ChemistryNow Screen 18.5.)

15. Which of the following combinations would be the best to buffer the pH of a solution at approximately 9?
   (a) HCl and NaCl
   (b) NH_3 and NH_4Cl
   (c) CH_3CO_2H and $NaCH_3CO_2$

16. ■ Which of the following combinations would be the best choice to buffer the pH of a solution at approximately 7?
   (a) H_3PO_4 and NaH_2PO_4
   (b) NaH_2PO_4 and Na_2HPO_4
   (c) Na_2HPO_4 and Na_3PO_4

17. Describe how to prepare a buffer solution from NaH_2PO_4 and Na_2HPO_4 to have a pH of 7.5.

18. Describe how to prepare a buffer solution from NH_3 and NH_4Cl to have a pH of 9.5.

Adding an Acid or a Base to a Buffer Solution
(See Example 18.5 and ChemistryNow Screen 18.6.)

19. A buffer solution was prepared by adding 4.95 g of sodium acetate, $NaCH_3CO_2$, to 2.50×10^2 mL of 0.150 M acetic acid, CH_3CO_2H.
   (a) What is the pH of the buffer?
   (b) What is the pH of 1.00×10^2 mL of the buffer solution if you add 82 mg of NaOH to the solution?

20. ■ You dissolve 0.425 g of NaOH in 2.00 L of a buffer solution that has $[H_2PO_4^-] = [HPO_4^{2-}] = 0.132$ M. What is the pH of the solution before adding NaOH? After adding NaOH?

21. A buffer solution is prepared by adding 0.125 mol of ammonium chloride to 5.00×10^2 mL of 0.500 M solution of ammonia.
   (a) What is the pH of the buffer?
   (b) If 0.0100 mol of HCl gas is bubbled into 5.00×10^2 mL of the buffer, what is the new pH of the solution?

22. ■ What will be the pH change when 20.0 mL of 0.100 M NaOH is added to 80.0 mL of a buffer solution consisting of 0.169 M NH_3 and 0.183 M NH_4Cl?

More about Acid–Base Reactions: Titrations
(See Examples 18.6 and 18.7 and ChemistryNow Screen 18.7.)

23. Phenol, C_6H_5OH, is a weak organic acid. Suppose 0.515 g of the compound is dissolved in exactly 125 mL of water. The resulting solution is titrated with 0.123 M NaOH.

   $$C_6H_5OH(aq) + OH^-(aq) \rightleftharpoons C_6H_5O^-(aq) + H_2O(\ell)$$

   (a) What is the pH of the original solution of phenol?
   (b) What are the concentrations of all of the following ions at the equivalence point: Na^+, H_3O^+, OH^-, and $C_6H_5O^-$?
   (c) What is the pH of the solution at the equivalence point?

24. ■ Assume you dissolve 0.235 g of the weak acid benzoic acid, $C_6H_5CO_2H$, in enough water to make 1.00×10^2 mL of solution and then titrate the solution with 0.108 M NaOH.

   $$C_6H_5CO_2H(aq) + OH^-(aq) \rightleftharpoons C_6H_5CO_2^-(aq) + H_2O(\ell)$$

   (a) What was the pH of the original benzoic acid solution?
   (b) What are the concentrations of all of the following ions at the equivalence point: Na^+, H_3O^+, OH^-, and $C_6H_5CO_2^-$?
   (c) What is the pH of the solution at the equivalence point?

25. You require 36.78 mL of 0.0105 M HCl to reach the equivalence point in the titration of 25.0 mL of aqueous ammonia.
    (a) What was the concentration of NH_3 in the original ammonia solution?
    (b) What are the concentrations of H_3O^+, OH^-, and NH_4^+ at the equivalence point?
    (c) What is the pH of the solution at the equivalence point?

26. A solution of the weak base aniline, $C_6H_5NH_2$, in 25.0 mL of water requires 25.67 mL of 0.175 M HCl to reach the equivalence point.

$$C_6H_5NH_2(aq) + H_3O^+(aq) \rightleftharpoons$$
$$C_6H_5NH_3^+(aq) + H_2O(\ell)$$

    (a) What was the concentration of aniline in the original solution?
    (b) What are the concentrations of H_3O^+, OH^-, and $C_6H_5NH_3^+$ at the equivalence point?
    (c) What is the pH of the solution at the equivalence point?

Titration Curves and Indicators
(See Figures 18.4–18.10 and ChemistryNow Screen 18.7.)

27. Without doing detailed calculations, sketch the curve for the titration of 30.0 mL of 0.10 M NaOH with 0.10 M HCl. Indicate the approximate pH at the beginning of the titration and at the equivalence point. What is the total solution volume at the equivalence point?

28. Without doing detailed calculations, sketch the curve for the titration of 50 mL of 0.050 M pyridine, C_5H_5N (a weak base), with 0.10 M HCl. Indicate the approximate pH at the beginning of the titration and at the equivalence point. What is the total solution volume at the equivalence point?

29. You titrate 25.0 mL of 0.10 M NH_3 with 0.10 M HCl.
    (a) What is the pH of the NH_3 solution before the titration begins?
    (b) What is the pH at the equivalence point?
    (c) What is the pH at the halfway point of the titration?
    (d) What indicator in Figure 18.10 could be used to detect the equivalence point?
    (e) Calculate the pH of the solution after adding 5.00, 15.0, 20.0, 22.0, and 30.0 mL of the acid. Combine this information with that in parts (a)–(c) and plot the titration curve.

30. Construct a rough plot of pH versus volume of base for the titration of 25.0 mL of 0.050 M HCN with 0.075 M NaOH.
    (a) What is the pH before any NaOH is added?
    (b) What is the pH at the halfway point of the titration?
    (c) What is the pH when 95% of the required NaOH has been added?

    (d) What volume of base, in milliliters, is required to reach the equivalence point?
    (e) What is the pH at the equivalence point?
    (f) What indicator would be most suitable for this titration? (See Figure 18.10.)
    (g) What is the pH when 105% of the required base has been added?

31. Using Figure 18.10, suggest an indicator to use in each of the following titrations:
    (a) The weak base pyridine is titrated with HCl.
    (b) Formic acid is titrated with NaOH.
    (c) Ethylenediamine, a weak diprotic base, is titrated with HCl.

32. ■ Using Figure 18.10, suggest an indicator to use in each of the following titrations.
    (a) $NaHCO_3$ is titrated to CO_3^{2-} with NaOH.
    (b) Hypochlorous acid is titrated with NaOH.
    (c) Trimethylamine is titrated with HCl.

Solubility Guidelines
(Review Section 3.5, Figure 3.10, and Example 3.2; also see ChemistryNow.)

33. Name two insoluble salts of each of the following ions.
    (a) Cl^-
    (b) Zn^{2+}
    (c) Fe^{2+}

34. Name two insoluble salts of each of the following ions.
    (a) SO_4^{2-}
    (b) Ni^{2+}
    (c) Br^-

35. Using the solubility guidelines (Figure 3.10), predict whether each of the following is insoluble or soluble in water.
    (a) $(NH_4)_2CO_3$
    (b) $ZnSO_4$
    (c) NiS
    (d) $BaSO_4$

36. ■ Predict whether each of the following is insoluble or soluble in water.
    (a) $Pb(NO_3)_2$
    (b) $Fe(OH)_3$
    (c) $ZnCl_2$
    (d) CuS

Writing Solubility Product Constant Expressions
(See Exercise 18.11 and ChemistryNow Screen 18.9.)

37. For each of the following insoluble salts, (1) write a balanced equation showing the equilibrium occurring when the salt is added to water, and (2) write the K_{sp} expression.
    (a) AgCN
    (b) $NiCO_3$
    (c) $AuBr_3$

▲ more challenging ■ in OWL Blue-numbered questions answered in Appendix O

38. For each of the following insoluble salts, (1) write a balanced equation showing the equilibrium occurring when the salt is added to water, and (2) write the K_{sp} expression.
    (a) $PbSO_4$
    (b) BaF_2
    (c) Ag_3PO_4

Calculating K_{sp}
(See Example 18.8 and ChemistryNow Screen 18.10.)

39. When 1.55 g of solid thallium(I) bromide is added to 1.00 L of water, the salt dissolves to a small extent.

$$TlBr(s) \rightleftharpoons Tl^+(aq) + Br^-(aq)$$

The thallium(I) and bromide ions in equilibrium with TlBr each have a concentration of 1.9×10^{-3} M. What is the value of K_{sp} for TlBr?

40. ■ At 20 °C, a saturated aqueous solution of silver acetate, $AgCH_3CO_2$, contains 1.0 g of the silver compound dissolved in 100.0 mL of solution. Calculate K_{sp} for silver acetate.

$$AgCH_3CO_2(s) \rightleftharpoons Ag^+(aq) + CH_3CO_2^-(aq)$$

41. When 250 mg of SrF_2, strontium fluoride, is added to 1.00 L of water, the salt dissolves to a very small extent.

$$SrF_2(s) \rightleftharpoons Sr^{2+}(aq) + 2 F^-(aq)$$

At equilibrium, the concentration of Sr^{2+} is found to be 1.03×10^{-3} M. What is the value of K_{sp} for SrF_2?

42. ■ Calcium hydroxide, $Ca(OH)_2$, dissolves in water to the extent of 1.3 g per liter. What is the value of K_{sp} for $Ca(OH)_2$?

$$Ca(OH)_2(s) \rightleftharpoons Ca^{2+}(aq) + 2 OH^-(aq)$$

43. You add 0.979 g of $Pb(OH)_2$ to 1.00 L of pure water at 25 °C. The pH is 9.15. Estimate the value of K_{sp} for $Pb(OH)_2$.

44. You place 1.234 g of solid $Ca(OH)_2$ in 1.00 L of pure water at 25 °C. The pH of the solution is found to be 12.68. Estimate the value of K_{sp} for $Ca(OH)_2$.

Estimating Salt Solubility from K_{sp}
(See Examples 18.9 and 18.10, Exercise 8.14, and ChemistryNow Screen 18.11.)

45. Estimate the solubility of silver iodide in pure water at 25 °C (a) in moles per liter and (b) in grams per liter.

$$AgI(s) \rightleftharpoons Ag^+(aq) + I^-(aq)$$

46. ■ What is the molar concentration of $Au^+(aq)$ in a saturated solution of AuCl in pure water at 25 °C?

$$AuCl(s) \rightleftharpoons Au^+(aq) + Cl^-(aq)$$

47. Estimate the solubility of calcium fluoride, CaF_2, (a) in moles per liter and (b) in grams per liter of pure water.

$$CaF_2(s) \rightleftharpoons Ca^{2+}(aq) + 2 F^-(aq)$$

48. ■ Estimate the solubility of lead(II) bromide (a) in moles per liter and (b) in grams per liter of pure water.

49. The K_{sp} value for radium sulfate, $RaSO_4$, is 4.2×10^{-11}. If 25 mg of radium sulfate is placed in 1.00×10^2 mL of water, does all of it dissolve? If not, how much dissolves?

50. If 55 mg of lead(II) sulfate is placed in 250 mL of pure water, does all of it dissolve? If not, how much dissolves?

51. Use K_{sp} values to decide which compound in each of the following pairs is the more soluble.
    (a) $PbCl_2$ or $PbBr_2$
    (b) HgS or FeS
    (c) $Fe(OH)_2$ or $Zn(OH)_2$

52. Use K_{sp} values to decide which compound in each of the following pairs is the more soluble.
    (a) AgBr or AgSCN
    (b) $SrCO_3$ or $SrSO_4$
    (c) AgI or PbI_2
    (d) MgF_2 or CaF_2

The Common Ion Effect and Salt Solubility
(See Examples 18.11 and 18.12 and ChemistryNow Screen 18.12.)

53. Calculate the molar solubility of silver thiocyanate, AgSCN, in pure water and in water containing 0.010 M NaSCN.

54. ■ Calculate the solubility of silver bromide, AgBr, in moles per liter, in pure water. Compare this value with the molar solubility of AgBr in 225 mL of water to which 0.15 g of NaBr has been added.

55. Compare the solubility, in milligrams per milliliter, of silver iodide, AgI, (a) in pure water and (b) in water that is 0.020 M in $AgNO_3$.

56. What is the solubility, in milligrams per milliliter, of BaF_2, (a) in pure water and (b) in water containing 5.0 mg/mL KF?

The Effect of Basic Anions on Salt Solubility
(See pages 882–883 and ChemistryNow Screen 18.13.)

57. Which insoluble compound in each pair should be more soluble in nitric acid than in pure water?
    (a) $PbCl_2$ or PbS
    (b) Ag_2CO_3 or AgI
    (c) $Al(OH)_3$ or AgCl

58. ■ Which compound in each pair is more soluble in water than is predicted by a calculation from K_{sp}?
    (a) AgI or Ag_2CO_3
    (b) $PbCO_3$ or $PbCl_2$
    (c) AgCl or AgCN

Precipitation Reactions
(See Examples 18.13–18.15 and ChemistryNow Screen 18.14.)

59. You have a solution that has a lead(II) ion concentration of 0.0012 M.

$$PbCl_2(s) \rightleftharpoons Pb^{2+}(aq) + 2\ Cl^-(aq)$$

If enough soluble chloride-containing salt is added so that the Cl^- concentration is 0.010 M, will $PbCl_2$ precipitate?

60. ■ Sodium carbonate is added to a solution in which the concentration of Ni^{2+} ion is 0.0024 M.

$$NiCO_3(s) \rightleftharpoons Ni^{2+}(aq) + CO_3^{2-}(aq)$$

Will precipitation of $NiCO_3$ occur (a) when the concentration of the carbonate ion is 1.0×10^{-6} M or (b) when it is 100 times greater (or 1.0×10^{-4} M)?

61. If the concentration of Zn^{2+} in 10.0 mL of water is 1.63×10^{-4} M, will zinc hydroxide, $Zn(OH)_2$, precipitate when 4.0 mg of NaOH is added?

62. You have 95 mL of a solution that has a lead(II) concentration of 0.0012 M. Will $PbCl_2$ precipitate when 1.20 g of solid NaCl is added?

63. If the concentration of Mg^{2+} ion in seawater is 1350 mg per liter, what OH^- concentration is required to precipitate $Mg(OH)_2$?

64. ■ Will a precipitate of $Mg(OH)_2$ form when 25.0 mL of 0.010 M NaOH is combined with 75.0 mL of a 0.10 M solution of magnesium chloride?

Equilibria Involving Complex Ions
(See Examples 18.16 and 18.17 and ChemistryNow Screen 18.16.)

65. Zinc hydroxide is amphoteric (page 791). Use equilibrium constants to show that, given sufficient OH^-, $Zn(OH)_2$ can dissolve in NaOH.

66. ■ Solid silver iodide, AgI, can be dissolved by adding aqueous sodium cyanide to it. Calculate K_{net} for the following reaction.

$$AgI(s) + 2\ CN^-(aq) \rightleftharpoons [Ag(CN)_2]^-(aq) + I^-(aq)$$

67. ▲ What amount of ammonia (moles) must be added to dissolve 0.050 mol of AgCl suspended in 1.0 L of water?

68. Can you dissolve 15.0 mg of AuCl in 100.0 mL of water if you add 15.0 mL of 6.00 M NaCN?

69. What is the solubility of AgCl (a) in pure water and (b) in 1.0 M NH_3?

70. ■ ▲ Suppose you mix 50.0 mL of 0.200 M NaCN with 10.0 mL of 0.100 M $AgNO_3$. Will the compound $Ag[Ag(CN)_2]$ precipitate? The equilibria involved are:

$$Ag[Ag(CN)_2](s) \rightleftharpoons Ag^+(aq) + [Ag(CN)_2]^-(aq)$$
$$K_{sp} = 5.0 \times 10^{-12}$$

$$Ag^+(aq) + 2\ CN^-(aq) \rightleftharpoons [Ag(CN)_2]^-(aq)$$
$$K_f = 5.0 \times 10^{21}$$

General Questions
These questions are not designated as to type or location in the chapter. They may combine several concepts.

71. In each of the following cases, decide whether a precipitate will form when mixing the indicated reagents, and write a balanced equation for the reaction.
    (a) $NaBr(aq) + AgNO_3(aq)$
    (b) $KCl(aq) + Pb(NO_3)_2(aq)$

72. ■ In each of the following cases, decide whether a precipitate will form when mixing the indicated reagents, and write a balanced equation for the reaction.
    (a) $Na_2SO_4(aq) + Mg(NO_3)_2(aq)$
    (b) $K_3PO_4(aq) + FeCl_3(aq)$

73. If you mix 48 mL of 0.0012 M $BaCl_2$ with 24 mL of 1.0×10^{-6} M Na_2SO_4, will a precipitate of $BaSO_4$ form?

74. ■ Calculate the hydronium ion concentration and the pH of the solution that results when 20.0 mL of 0.15 M acetic acid, CH_3CO_2H, is mixed with 5.0 mL of 0.17 M NaOH.

75. Calculate the hydronium ion concentration and the pH of the solution that results when 50.0 mL of 0.40 M NH_3 is mixed with 25.0 mL of 0.20 M HCl.

76. ■ For each of the following cases, decide whether the pH is less than 7, equal to 7, or greater than 7.
    (a) Equal volumes of 0.10 M acetic acid, CH_3CO_2H, and 0.10 M KOH are mixed.
    (b) 25 mL of 0.015 M NH_3 is mixed with 12 mL of 0.015 M HCl.
    (c) 150 mL of 0.20 M HNO_3 is mixed with 75 mL of 0.40 M NaOH.
    (d) 25 mL of 0.45 M H_2SO_4 is mixed with 25 mL of 0.90 M NaOH.

77. Rank the following compounds in order of increasing solubility in water: Na_2CO_3, $BaCO_3$, Ag_2CO_3.

78. A sample of hard water contains about 2.0×10^{-3} M Ca^{2+}. A soluble fluoride-containing salt such as NaF is added to "fluoridate" the water (to aid in the prevention of dental caries). What is the maximum concentration of F^- that can be present without precipitating CaF_2?

Dietary sources of fluoride ion. Adding fluoride ion to drinking water (or toothpaste) prevents the formation of dental caries.

Charles D. Winters

▲ more challenging   ■ in OWL   Blue-numbered questions answered in Appendix O

79. What is the pH of a buffer solution prepared from 5.15 g of NH_4NO_3 and 0.10 L of 0.15 M NH_3? What is the new pH if the solution is diluted with pure water to a volume of 5.00×10^2 mL?

80. ■ If you place 5.0 mg of $SrSO_4$ in 1.0 L of pure water, will all of the salt dissolve before equilibrium is established, or will some salt remain undissolved?

Celestite, $SrSO_4$
Strontium sulfate

SO_4^{2-}

81. Describe the effect on the pH of the following actions:
    (a) Adding sodium acetate, $NaCH_3CO_2$, to 0.100 M CH_3CO_2H
    (b) Adding $NaNO_3$ to 0.100 M HNO_3
    (c) Explain why there is or is not an effect in each case.

82. ■ What volume of 0.120 M NaOH must be added to 100. mL of 0.100 M $NaHC_2O_4$ to reach a pH of 4.70?

83. ■ ▲ A buffer solution is prepared by dissolving 1.50 g each of benzoic acid, $C_6H_5CO_2H$, and sodium benzoate, $NaC_6H_5CO_2$, in 150.0 mL of solution.
    (a) What is the pH of this buffer solution?
    (b) Which buffer component must be added, and what quantity is needed to change the pH to 4.00?
    (c) What quantity of 2.0 M NaOH or 2.0 M HCl must be added to the buffer to change the pH to 4.00?

84. What volume of 0.200 M HCl must be added to 500.0 mL of 0.250 M NH_3 to have a buffer with a pH of 9.00?

85. What is the equilibrium constant for the following reaction?

$$AgCl(s) + I^-(aq) \rightleftharpoons AgI(s) + Cl^-(aq)$$

Does the equilibrium lie predominantly to the left or to the right? Will AgI form if iodide ion, I^-, is added to a saturated solution of AgCl?

86. Calculate the equilibrium constant for the following reaction.

$$Zn(OH)_2(s) + 2\ CN^-(aq) \rightleftharpoons$$
$$Zn(CN)_2(s) + 2\ OH^-(aq)$$

Does the equilibrium lie predominantly to the left or to the right? Can zinc hydroxide be transformed into zinc cyanide by adding a soluble salt of the cyanide ion?

87. ▲ In principle, the ions Ba^{2+} and Ca^{2+} can be separated by the difference in solubility of their fluorides, BaF_2 and CaF_2. If you have a solution that is 0.10 M in both Ba^{2+} and Ca^{2+}, CaF_2 will begin to precipitate first as fluoride ion is added slowly to the solution.
    (a) What concentration of fluoride ion will precipitate the maximum amount of Ca^{2+} ion without precipitating BaF_2?
    (b) What concentration of Ca^{2+} remains in solution when BaF_2 just begins to precipitate?

88. ■ ▲ A solution contains 0.10 M iodide ion, I^-, and 0.10 M carbonate ion, CO_3^{2-}.
    (a) If solid $Pb(NO_3)_2$ is slowly added to the solution, which salt will precipitate first, PbI_2 or $PbCO_3$?
    (b) What will be the concentration of the first ion that precipitates (CO_3^{2-} or I^-) when the second, more soluble salt begins to precipitate?

Lead iodide ($K_{sp} = 9.8 \times 10^{-9}$) is a bright yellow solid.

89. ■ ▲ A solution contains Ca^{2+} and Pb^{2+} ions, both at a concentration of 0.010 M. You wish to separate the two ions from each other as completely as possible by precipitating one but not the other using aqueous Na_2SO_4 as the precipitating agent.
    (a) Which will precipitate first as sodium sulfate is added, $CaSO_4$ or $PbSO_4$?
    (b) What will be the concentration of the first ion that precipitates (Ca^{2+} or Pb^{2+}) when the second, more soluble salt begins to precipitate?

90. ■ Buffer capacity is defined as the number of moles of a strong acid or strong base that are required to change the pH of one liter of the buffer solution by one unit. What is the buffer capacity of a solution that is 0.10 M in acetic acid and 0.10 M in sodium acetate?

91. The Ca^{2+} ion in hard water can be precipitated as $CaCO_3$ by adding soda ash, Na_2CO_3. If the calcium ion concentration in hard water is 0.010 M and if the Na_2CO_3 is added until the carbonate ion concentration is 0.050 M, what percentage of the calcium ions have been removed from the water? (You may neglect carbonate ion hydrolysis.)

This sample of calcium carbonate ($K_{sp} = 3.4 \times 10^{-9}$) was deposited in a cave formation.

92. ■ Some photographic film is coated with crystals of AgBr suspended in gelatin. Some of the silver ions are reduced to silver metal on exposure to light. Unexposed AgBr is then dissolved with sodium thiosulfate in the "fixing" step.

$$AgBr(s) + 2\,S_2O_3^{2-}(aq) \rightleftharpoons$$
$$[Ag(S_2O_3)_2]^{3-}(aq) + Br^-(aq)$$

(a) What is the equilibrium constant for the reaction above?
(b) What mass of $Na_2S_2O_3$ must be added to dissolve 1.00 g of AgBr suspended in 1.00 L of water?

In the Laboratory

93. Each pair of ions below is found together in aqueous solution. Using the table of solubility product constants in Appendix J, devise a way to separate these ions by precipitating one of them as an insoluble salt and leaving the other in solution.
(a) Ba^{2+} and Na^+
(b) Ni^{2+} and Pb^{2+}

94. ■ Each pair of ions below is found together in aqueous solution. Using the table of solubility product constants in Appendix J, devise a way to separate these ions by adding one reagent to precipitate one of them as an insoluble salt and leave the other in solution.
(a) Cu^{2+} and Ag^+
(b) Al^{3+} and Fe^{3+}

95. ▲ The cations Ba^{2+} and Sr^{2+} can be precipitated as very insoluble sulfates.
(a) If you add sodium sulfate to a solution containing these metal cations, each with a concentration of 0.10 M, which is precipitated first, $BaSO_4$ or $SrSO_4$?
(b) What will be the concentration of the first ion that precipitates (Ba^{2+} or Sr^{2+}) when the second, more soluble salt begins to precipitate?

96. ■ ▲ You will often work with salts of Fe^{3+}, Pb^{2+}, and Al^{3+} in the laboratory. (All are found in nature, and all are important economically.) If you have a solution containing these three ions, each at a concentration of 0.10 M, what is the order in which their hydroxides precipitate as aqueous NaOH is slowly added to the solution?

97. Aniline hydrochloride, $(C_6H_5NH_3)Cl$, is a weak acid. (Its conjugate base is the weak base aniline, $C_6H_5NH_2$.) The acid can be titrated with a strong base such as NaOH.

$$C_6H_5NH_3^+(aq) + OH^-(aq) \rightleftharpoons$$
$$C_6H_5NH_2(aq) + H_2O(\ell)$$

Assume 50.0 mL of 0.100 M aniline hydrochloride is titrated with 0.185 M NaOH. (K_a for aniline hydrochloride is 2.4×10^{-5}.)
(a) What is the pH of the $(C_6H_5NH_3)Cl$ solution before the titration begins?
(b) What is the pH at the equivalence point?
(c) What is the pH at the halfway point of the titration?
(d) Which indicator in Figure 18.10 could be used to detect the equivalence point?
(e) Calculate the pH of the solution after adding 10.0, 20.0, and 30.0 mL of base.
(f) Combine the information in parts (a), (b), and (e), and plot an approximate titration curve.

▲ more challenging   ■ in OWL   Blue-numbered questions answered in Appendix O

Charles D. Winters

98. ■ The weak base ethanolamine, $HOCH_2CH_2NH_2$, can be titrated with HCl.

$$HOCH_2CH_2NH_2(aq) + H_3O^+(aq) \rightleftharpoons$$
$$HOCH_2CH_2NH_3^+(aq) + H_2O(\ell)$$

Assume you have 25.0 mL of a 0.010 M solution of ethanolamine and titrate it with 0.0095 M HCl. (K_b for ethanolamine is 3.2×10^{-5}.)

(a) What is the pH of the ethanolamine solution before the titration begins?

(b) What is the pH at the equivalence point?

(c) What is the pH at the halfway point of the titration?

(d) Which indicator in Figure 18.10 would be the best choice to detect the equivalence point?

(e) Calculate the pH of the solution after adding 5.00, 10.0, 20.0, and 30.0 mL of the acid.

(f) Combine the information in parts (a), (b), and (e), and plot an approximate titration curve.

99. For the titration of 50.0 mL of 0.150 M ethylamine, $C_2H_5NH_2$, with 0.100 M HCl, find the pH at each of the following points, and then use that information to sketch the titration curve and decide on an appropriate indicator.

(a) At the beginning, before HCl is added

(b) At the halfway point in the titration

(c) When 75% of the required acid has been added

(d) At the equivalence point

(e) When 10.0 mL more HCl has been added than is required

(f) Sketch the titration curve.

(g) Suggest an appropriate indicator for this titration.

100. A buffer solution with a pH of 12.00 consists of Na_3PO_4 and Na_2HPO_4. The volume of solution is 200.0 mL.

(a) Which component of the buffer is present in a larger amount?

(b) If the concentration of Na_3PO_4 is 0.400 M, what mass of Na_2HPO_4 is present?

(c) Which component of the buffer must be added to change the pH to 12.25? What mass of that component is required?

101. ■ To have a buffer with a pH of 2.50, what volume of 0.150 M NaOH must be added to 100. mL of 0.230 M H_3PO_4?

102. ■ ▲ What mass of Na_3PO_4 must be added to 80.0 mL of 0.200 M HCl to obtain a buffer with a pH of 7.75?

103. You have a solution that contains $AgNO_3$, $Pb(NO_3)_2$, and $Cu(NO_3)_2$. Devise a separation method that results in having Ag^+ in one test tube, Pb^{2+} ions in another, and Cu^{2+} in a third test tube. Use solubility guidelines and K_{sp} and K_f values.

104. Once you have separated the three salts in Study Question 103 into three test tubes, you now need to confirm their presence.

(a) For Pb^{2+} ion, one way to do this is to treat a precipitate of $PbCl_2$ with K_2CrO_4 to produce $PbCrO_4$. Using K_{sp} values, confirm that the chloride salt should be converted to the chromate salt.

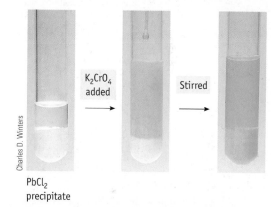

White $PbCl_2$ is converted to yellow $PbCrO_4$ on adding K_2CrO_4.

(b) Suggest a method of confirming the presence of Ag^+ and Cu^{2+} ions using complex ions.

Summary and Conceptual Questions

The following questions may use concepts from this and previous chapters.

105. ■ Suggest a method for separating a precipitate consisting of a mixture of solid CuS and solid $Cu(OH)_2$.

106. Which of the following barium salts should dissolve in a strong acid such as HCl: $Ba(OH)_2$, $BaSO_4$, or $BaCO_3$?

107. Explain why the solubility of Ag_3PO_4 can be greater in water than is calculated from the K_{sp} value of the salt.

108. ■ Two acids, each approximately 0.01 M in concentration, are titrated separately with a strong base. The acids show the following pH values at the equivalence point: HA, pH = 9.5, and HB, pH = 8.5.
(a) Which is the stronger acid, HA or HB?
(b) Which of the conjugate bases, A⁻ or B⁻, is the stronger base?

109. ■ Composition diagrams, commonly known as "alpha plots," are often used to visualize the species in a solution of an acid or base as the pH is varied. The diagram for 0.100 M acetic acid is shown here.

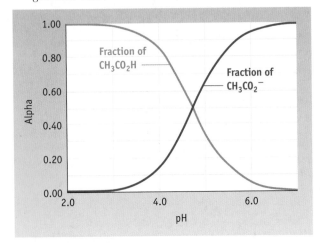

The plot shows how the fraction [= alpha (α)] of acetic acid in solution,

$$\alpha = \frac{[CH_3CO_2H]}{[CH_3CO_2H] + [CH_3CO_2^-]}$$

changes as the pH increases (blue curve). (The red curve shows how the fraction of acetate ion, $CH_3CO_2^-$, changes as the pH increases.) Alpha plots are another way of viewing the relative concentrations of acetic acid and acetate ion as a strong base is added to a solution of acetic acid in the course of a titration.
(a) Explain why the fraction of acetic acid declines and that of acetate ion increases as the pH increases.
(b) Which species predominates at a pH of 4, acetic acid or acetate ion? What is the situation at a pH of 6?
(c) Consider the point where the two lines cross. The fraction of acetic acid in the solution is 0.5, and so is that of acetate ion. That is, the solution is half acid and half conjugate base; their concentrations are equal. At this point, the graph shows the pH is 4.74. Explain why the pH at this point is 4.74.

110. The composition diagram, or alpha plot, for the important acid–base system of carbonic acid, H_2CO_3, is illustrated below. (See Study Question 109 for more information on such diagrams.)

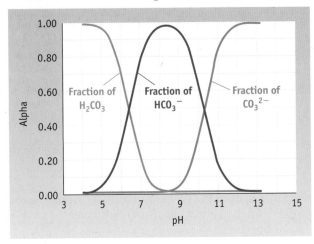

(a) Explain why the fraction of bicarbonate ion, HCO_3^-, rises and then falls as the pH increases.
(b) What is the composition of the solution when the pH is 6.0? When the pH is 10.0?
(c) If you wanted to buffer a solution at a pH of 11.0, what should be the ratio of HCO_3^- to CO_3^{2-}?

111. The chemical name for aspirin is acetylsalicylic acid. It is believed that the analgesic and other desirable properties of aspirin are due not to the aspirin itself but rather to the simpler compound salicylic acid, $C_6H_4(OH)CO_2H$, that results from the breakdown of aspirin in the stomach.

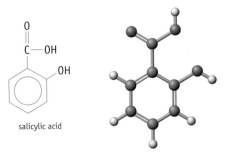

salicylic acid

(a) Give approximate values for the following bond angles in the acid: (i) C—C—C in the ring; (ii) O—C=O; (iii) either of the C—O—H angles; and (iv) C—C—H.
(b) What is the hybridization of the C atoms of the ring? Of the C atom in the —CO₂H group?
(c) Experiment shows that 1.00 g of the acid will dissolve in 460 mL of water. If the pH of this solution is 2.4, what is K_a for the acid?

▲ more challenging ■ in OWL Blue-numbered questions answered in Appendix O

(d) If you have salicylic acid in your stomach and if the pH of gastric juice is 2.0, calculate the percentage of salicylic acid that will be present in the stomach in the form of the salicylate ion, $C_6H_4(OH)CO_2^-$.

(e) Assume you have 25.0 mL of a 0.014 M solution of salicylic acid and titrate it with 0.010 M NaOH. What is the pH at the halfway point of the titration? What is the pH at the equivalence point?

112. Aluminum chloride reacts with phosphoric acid to give $AlPO_4$. The substance is used industrially as adhesives, binders, and cements.

(a) Write the balanced equation for the preparation of $AlPO_4$ from aluminum chloride and phosphoric acid.

(b) If you begin with 152 g of aluminum chloride and 3.00 L of 0.750 M phosphoric acid, what is the theoretical yield of $AlPO_4$?

(c) If you place 25.0 g of $AlPO_4$ in 1.00 L of water, what are the concentrations of Al^{3+} and PO_4^{3-} at equilibrium? (Neglect hydrolysis of aqueous Al^{3+} and PO_4^{3-} ion.) K_{sp} for $AlPO_4$ is 1.3×10^{-20}.

(d) Does the solubility of $AlPO_4$ increase or decrease on adding HCl? Explain.

Charles D. Winters

This is a sample of hydrated aluminum phosphate, a mineral known as augelite.

19 | Principles of Reactivity: Entropy and Free Energy

Charles D. Winters

Thus far, the ethanol used as a fuel in the United States is largely derived from corn.

Can Ethanol Contribute to Energy and Environmental Goals?

About 3.4 billion gallons of ethanol were blended into gasoline in 2004. According to A. E. Farrell, et al. (*Science*, Vol. 311, pp. 506–508, 2006), this amounted to about 2% of all gasoline sold by volume and 1.3% of its energy content. This is a significant contribution to the energy used in the United States, and it promises to be larger in the future. Therefore, the use of ethanol as a substitute for gasoline has been widely discussed in the popular press and in the scientific literature.

Let us focus on two points at the beginning of this chapter: the energetics of ethanol combustion and the production of the greenhouse gas, CO_2. Let us compare the energy and amount of CO_2 released by burning 1.00 kg of liquid ethanol (C_2H_5OH) and, to represent gasoline, 1.00 kg of liquid octane (C_8H_{18}).

Questions:
1. Calculate $\Delta_r H°$ and $\Delta_r G°$ for the combustion of 1.00 kg each of liquid ethanol and liquid octane. Which fuel releases more energy per kilogram? [Values for $\Delta_f H°$ and $S°$ are located in Appendix L. In addition, for liquid octane at 298 K, $\Delta_f H° = -250.0$ kJ/mol and $S° = 361.2$ J/K·mol.]

2. Compare the two fuels on the basis of the release of CO_2, a common greenhouse gas. Which fuel produces more CO_2 per kilogram?
3. On the basis of this simple comparison and neglecting the energy costs involved in producing 1.00 kg each of ethanol and octane, which is the better fuel in terms of energy production and greenhouse gases?

Answers to these questions are in Appendix Q.

Chapter Goals

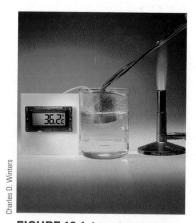
Chapter Outline

Change is central to chemistry, so it is important to understand the factors that determine whether a change will occur. In chemistry, we encounter many examples of chemical change (chemical reactions) and physical change (the formation of mixtures, expansion of gases, and changes of state, to name a few). Chemists use the term **spontaneous** to represent a change that occurs without outside intervention. *Spontaneous changes occur only in the direction that leads to equilibrium.* Whether or not the process is spontaneous does not tell us anything about the rate of the change or the extent to which a process will occur before equilibrium is reached. It says only that the change will occur in a specific direction (toward equilibrium) and will occur naturally and unaided.

If a piece of hot metal is placed in a beaker of cold water, energy is transferred spontaneously as heat from the hot metal to the cooler water (Figure 19.1), and energy transfer will continue until the two objects are at the same temperature and thermal equilibrium is attained. Similarly, chemical reactions proceed spontaneously until equilibrium is reached, regardless of whether the position of the equilibrium favors products or reactants. We readily recognize that, starting with pure reactants, all product-favored reactions must be spontaneous, such as the formation of water from gaseous hydrogen and oxygen and the neutralization of $H_3O^+(aq)$ and $OH^-(aq)$ (◄ Chapter 3). Notice, however, that reactant-favored reactions are also spontaneous until equilibrium is achieved. Even though the dissolution of $CaCO_3$ is reactant-favored at equilibrium, if you place a handful of $CaCO_3$ in water, the process of dissolving will proceed spontaneously until equilibrium is reached.

All physical and chemical changes occur in a direction toward achieving equilibrium. Systems never change spontaneously in a direction that takes them farther from equilibrium. Given two objects at the same temperature, in contact but thermally isolated from their surroundings, it will never happen that one will heat up while the other becomes colder. Gas molecules will never spontaneously congregate at one end of a flask. Similarly, once equilibrium is established, the small amount of dissolved $CaCO_3$ in equilibrium with solid $CaCO_3$ will not spontaneously precipitate from solution.

The factors that determine the directionality and extent of change are among the topics of this chapter.

Chemistry⚛Now™

Throughout the text this icon introduces an opportunity for self-study or to explore interactive tutorials by signing in at **www.cengage.com/login**.

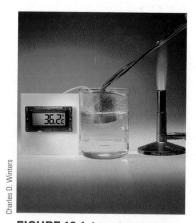

Charles D. Winters

FIGURE 19.1 A spontaneous process. The heated metal cylinder is placed in water. Energy transfers as heat spontaneously from the metal to water, that is, from the hotter object to the cooler object.

A Review of Concepts of Thermodynamics

To understand the thermodynamic concepts introduced in this chapter, be sure to review the ideas of Chapter 5.

System: The part of the universe under study.

Surroundings: The rest of the universe exclusive of the system, capable of exchanging energy and/or matter with the system.

Exothermic: Energy transfers as heat from the system to the surroundings.

Endothermic: Energy transfers as heat from the surroundings to the system.

First law of thermodynamics: The law of conservation of energy, $\Delta U = q + w$. The change in internal energy of a system is the sum of energy transferred as heat to or from the system and the work done on or by the system. The first law states that energy cannot be created or destroyed.

Enthalpy change: The energy transferred as heat at constant pressure.

State function: A quantity whose value depends only on the state of the system;

changes in a state function can be calculated by taking into account the initial and final states of a system.

Standard conditions: Pressure of 1 bar (1 bar = 0.98692 atm) and solution concentration of 1 m.

Standard enthalpy of formation, $\Delta_f H°$: The enthalpy change occurring when a compound is formed from its elements in their standard states.

19.1 Spontaneity and Energy Transfer as Heat

■ **Spontaneous Processes** A spontaneous physical or chemical change proceeds to equilibrium without outside intervention. Such a process may or may not be product-favored at equilibrium.

We can readily recognize many chemical reactions that are spontaneous, such as hydrogen and oxygen combining to form water, methane burning to give CO_2 and H_2O, Na and Cl_2 reacting to form NaCl, HCl(aq), and NaOH(aq), reacting to form H_2O and NaCl(aq). A common feature of these reactions is that they are exothermic, so it would be tempting to conclude that evolution of energy as heat is the criterion that determines whether a reaction or process is spontaneous. Further inspection, however, reveals significant flaws in this reasoning. This is especially evident with the inclusion of some common spontaneous changes that are endothermic or energy neutral:

- *Dissolving NH_4NO_3.* The ionic compound NH_4NO_3 dissolves spontaneously in water. The process is endothermic ($\Delta_r H° = +25.7$ kJ/mol).
- *Expansion of a gas into a vacuum.* A system is set up with two flasks connected by a valve (Figure 19.2). One flask is filled with a gas, and the other is evacuated. When the valve is opened, the gas will flow spontaneously from one flask to the other until the pressure is the same throughout. The expansion of an ideal gas is energy neutral (although expansion of most real gases is endothermic).
- *Phase changes.* Melting of ice is an endothermic process. Above 0 °C, the melting of ice is spontaneous. Below 0 °C, melting of ice is not spontaneous. At 0 °C, no net change will occur; liquid water and ice coexist at equilibrium. This example illustrates that temperature can have a role in determining spontaneity and that equilibrium is somehow an important aspect of the problem.
- *Energy transfer as heat.* The temperature of a cold soft drink sitting in a warm environment will rise until the beverage reaches the ambient temperature. The energy required for this process comes from the surroundings. Energy transfer as heat from a hotter object (the surroundings) to a cooler object (the soft drink) is spontaneous.
- The reaction of H_2 and I_2 to form HI is endothermic, and the reverse reaction, the decomposition of HI to form H_2 and I_2, is exothermic. If $H_2(g)$ and $I_2(g)$ are mixed, a reaction forming HI will occur [$H_2(g) + I_2(g) \rightleftharpoons 2\ HI(g)$] until equilibrium is reached. Furthermore, if HI(g) is placed in a container, there will also be a reaction, but in the reverse direction, until equilibrium is achieved. Notice that approach to equilibrium occurs spontaneously from either direction.

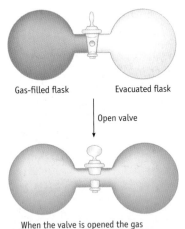

Gas-filled flask   Evacuated flask

Open valve

When the valve is opened the gas expands irreversibly to fill both flasks.

FIGURE 19.2 Spontaneous expansion of a gas. (See ChemistryNow Screen 19.3 to view an animation of this figure.)

On further reflection, it is logical to conclude that evolution of heat cannot be a sufficient criterion in determining spontaneity. The first law of thermodynamics tells us that in any process energy must be conserved. If energy is transferred out of a system, then the same amount of energy must be transferred to the surroundings. Exothermicity of the system is always accompanied by an endothermic change in the surroundings. If energy evolution were the only factor determining whether a change is spontaneous, then for every spontaneous process there would be a corresponding nonspontaneous change in the surroundings. We must search further than the first law of thermodynamics to determine whether a change is spontaneous.

19.2 Dispersal of Energy: Entropy

We have shown that we cannot use energy itself as an indicator of spontaneity because energy is conserved in any process; we always end up with the same amount of energy as we had at the beginning. Imagine dropping this book on the floor. (But don't actually do it!) It would fall spontaneously. The initial potential energy it has from being a certain distance above the floor is converted to kinetic energy. When the book hits the floor, the kinetic energy of the book is converted into other forms of kinetic energy: acoustic energy and thermal energy of the book, floor, and air, since these are all heated up somewhat. Through all of these processes, the total energy is conserved. There is a directionality to this process, however. The book will spontaneously fall to the ground, but we will not observe a book on its own jump spontaneously from the floor up to a desk. Is there a way to predict this directionality?

Let us consider the initial and final states for this process. Initially, the energy is concentrated in the book—the book has a certain potential energy as it is held above the floor. At the end of the process, the energy has been dispersed to the air, floor, and book. The energy has gone from being concentrated to being more dispersed. This is the indicator for which we have been searching. *In a spontaneous process, energy goes from being more concentrated to being more dispersed.*

There is a state function (◄ Section 5.4) called **entropy (S)** that allows us to quantify this. The **second law of thermodynamics** states that *a spontaneous process is one that results in an increase of the entropy of the universe.* In a spontaneous process, therefore, ΔS(universe) is greater than zero; this corresponds to energy being dispersed in the process.

Because thermal energy is caused by the random motion of particles, potential energy is dispersed when it is converted to thermal energy. This conversion occurs when energy is transferred as heat, q. It is therefore not surprising that q is a part of the mathematical definition of ΔS. This is not the whole picture, however, in part because q is not a state function. In addition, the effect of a given quantity of energy transferred as heat on energy dispersal is different at different temperatures. It turns out that a given q has a greater effect at a lower temperature than at a higher temperature; that is, the extent of energy dispersal is inversely proportional to the temperature.

Our proposed definition for ΔS is thus q/T, but this is still not quite correct. We must be a little more specific about q. The value of q used in the calculation of an entropy change must be the energy transferred as heat under what are called *reversible conditions*, q_{rev} (see *A Closer Look: Reversible and Irreversible Processes*). Adding energy by heating an object slowly (adding energy in very small increments) approximates a reversible process. Our mathematical definition of ΔS is therefore q_{rev} divided by the absolute (Kelvin) temperature:

$$\Delta S = \frac{q_{rev}}{T} \tag{19.1}$$

As this equation predicts, the units for entropy are J/K.

■ **Entropy** For a more complete discussion of entropy, see the papers by F. L. Lambert, such as "Entropy Is Simple, Qualitatively," *Journal of Chemical Education*, Vol. 79, pp. 1241–1246, 2002, and references therein. See also Lambert's site: **www.entropysite.com.** Finally, see A. H. Jungermann, "Entropy and the Shelf Model," *Journal of Chemical Education*, Vol. 83, pp. 1686–1694, 2006.

To determine entropy changes experimentally, the energy transferred by heating and cooling must be measured for a reversible process. But what is a reversible process?

The test for reversibility is that after carrying out a change along a given path (for example, energy added as heat), it must be possible to return to the starting point by the same path (energy taken away as heat) without altering the surroundings. Melting of ice and freezing of water at 0 °C are examples of reversible processes. Given a mixture of ice and water at equilibrium, adding energy as heat in small increments will convert ice to water; removing energy as heat in small increments will convert water back to ice.

Reversibility is closely associated with equilibrium. Assume that we have a system at equilibrium. Reversible changes can then be made by very slightly perturbing the equilibrium and letting the system readjust.

Spontaneous processes are often not reversible. Suppose a gas is allowed to expand into a vacuum. No work is done in this process because there is no force to resist expansion. To return the system to its original state, it is necessary to compress the gas. Doing so means doing work on the system, however, because the system will not return to its original state on its own. In this process, the energy content of the surroundings decreases by the amount of work expended by

the surroundings. The system can be restored to its original state, but the surroundings will be altered in the process.

In summary, there are two important points concerning reversibility:

- At every step along a reversible pathway between two states, the system remains at equilibrium.
- Spontaneous processes often follow irreversible pathways and involve nonequilibrium conditions.

To determine the entropy change for a process, it is necessary to identify a reversible pathway. Only then can an entropy change for the process be calculated from q_{rev} and the Kelvin temperature.

19.3 Entropy: A Microscopic Understanding

We have stated that entropy is a measure of the extent of energy dispersal. In all spontaneous physical and chemical changes, energy changes from being localized or concentrated in a system to becoming dispersed or spread out in the system and its surroundings. In a spontaneous process, the change in entropy, ΔS, of the universe indicates the extent to which energy is dispersed in a process carried out at a temperature T. So far, however, we have not explained why dispersal of energy occurs, nor have we given an equation for entropy itself. In order to do this, we will need to consider energy in its quantized form and matter on the atomic level.

Dispersal of Energy

We can explore the dispersal of energy using a simple example: energy being transferred as heat between hot and cold gaseous atoms. Consider an experiment involving two containers, one holding hot atoms and the other with cold atoms (Figure 19.3). Because they have translational energy, the atoms move randomly in each container and collide with the walls. When the containers are in contact, energy is transferred through the container walls. Eventually, both containers will be at the same temperature; the energy originally localized in the hotter atoms is distributed over a greater number of atoms; and the atoms in each container will have the same distribution of energies.

For further insight, let us look at a statistical explanation to show why energy is dispersed in a system. With statistical arguments, systems must include large numbers of particles for the arguments to be accurate. It will be easiest, however, if we look first at simple examples to understand the underlying concept and then extrapolate our conclusions to larger systems.

Consider a simple system in which, initially, there is one atom (1) with two discrete packets, or quanta, of energy and three other atoms (2, 3, and 4) with no energy (Figure 19.4). When these four atoms are brought together, the total energy in the system is 2 quanta. Collisions among the atoms allow energy to be transferred so that,

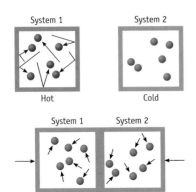

FIGURE 19.3 Energy transfer between molecules in the gas phase.

Possible distribution of energy packets

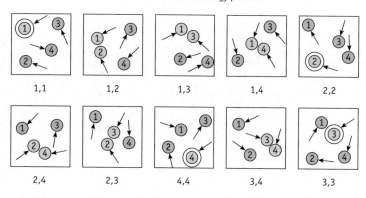

FIGURE 19.4 Energy dispersal.
Possible ways of distributing two packets of energy among four atoms. To keep our analysis simple, we assume that initially there is one atom with two quanta of energy and three atoms (2, 3 and 4) with no energy. The figure shows that there are 10 different ways to distribute the two quanta of energy over four atoms.

over time, all distributions of the two packets of energy over the four atoms are seen. There are 10 different ways to distribute these 2 quanta of energy over the four atoms. Each of these 10 different ways to distribute the energy is called a **microstate.** In only one of the microstates do the 2 quanta remain on atom 1. In fact, only in 4 of the 10 microstates [1, 1; 2, 2; 3, 3; and 4, 4] is the energy concentrated on a single atom. In the majority of cases, 6 out of 10, the energy is distributed to two different atoms. Even in a small sample (four atoms) with only two packets of energy, it is more likely that at any given time the energy will be distributed to two atoms rather than concentrated on a single atom. There is a distinct preference that the energy will be dispersed over a greater number of atoms.

Let us now add more atoms to our system. We again consider one atom (1) with 2 quanta of energy present but now have five other atoms (2, 3, 4, 5, and 6) with no energy initially. Collisions let the energy be transferred between the atoms, and we now find there are 21 possible microstates (Figure 19.5). There are six microstates in which the energy is concentrated on one atom, including one in which the energy is still on atom 1, but there are now 15 microstates in which the energy is present on two atoms. As the number of particles increases, the number of microstates available increases dramatically, and the fraction of microstates in which the energy is concentrated rather than dispersed goes down dramatically. It is much more likely that the energy will be dispersed than concentrated.

Now let us return to an example using a total of four atoms, but in which we have increased the quantity of energy from 2 quanta to 6 quanta. Assume that we start with two atoms having 3 quanta of energy each. The other two atoms initially have zero energy (Figure 19.6). Through collisions, energy can be transferred to achieve different distributions of energy among the four atoms. In all, there are 84 microstates, falling into nine basic patterns. For example, one possible arrangement has one atom with 3 quanta of energy, and three atoms with 1 quantum each. There are four microstates in which this is true (Figure 19.6c). Increasing the number of quanta from 2 to 6 with the same number of atoms increased the num-

Number of Microstates	Distribution of 2 Quanta of Energy Among Six Atoms					
6	1:1	2:2	3:3	4:4	5:5	6:6
5	1:2	2:3	3:4	4:5	5:6	
4	1:3	2:4	3:5	4:6		
3	1:4	2:5	3:6			
2	1:5	2:6				
1	1:6					

FIGURE 19.5 Distributing 2 quanta of energy among six atoms. The result is a total of 21 ways—21 microstates—of distributing 2 quanta of energy among six atoms.

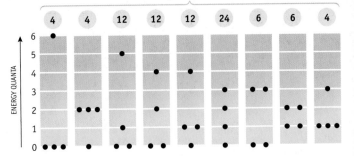

FIGURE 19.6 Energy dispersal.
Possible ways of distributing 6 quanta of energy among four atoms. A total of 84 microstates is possible.

Number of different ways to achieve this arrangement

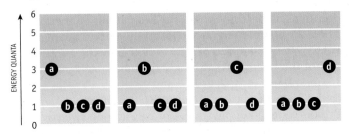

(a) Initially, four particles are separated from each other. Two particles each have 3 quanta of energy, and the other two have none. A total of 6 quanta of energy will be distributed once the particles interact.

(b) Once the particles begin to interact, there are nine ways to distribute the 6 available quanta. Each of these arrangements will have multiple ways of distributing the energy among the four atoms. Part (c) shows how the arrangement on the right can be achieved four ways.

(c) There are four different ways to have four particles (a, b, c, and d) such that one particle has 3 quanta of energy and the other three each have 1 quantum of energy.

Ludwig Boltzmann (1844–1906).
Engraved on his tombstone in Vienna, Austria, is his equation defining entropy. The constant k is now known as Boltzmann's constant.

Oesper Collection in the History of Chemistry, University of Cincinnati

■ **How Many Microstates?** To give you a sense of the number of microstates available to a substance, consider a mole of ice at 273 K, where $S° = 41.3$ J/K · mol. Using Boltzmann's equation, we find that $W = 10^{1,299,000,000,000,000,000,000,000}$. That is, there are many, many more microstates for 1 mol of ice than there are atoms in the universe (about 10^{80}).

ber of possible microstates from 10 to 84. In this case, the amount of energy that is dispersed resulted in an increase in the number of microstates.

A statistical analysis for larger aggregates of atoms and energy quanta is increasingly complex, but the conclusions are even more compelling. As the number of particles and/or quanta increases, the number of energy microstates grows rapidly. These allow the extent over which the energy is dispersed and/or the amount of the energy dispersed to increase. Ludwig Boltzmann proposed that the entropy of a system (the dispersal of energy at a given temperature) results from the number of microstates available. *As the number of microstates increases, so does the entropy of the system.* He enunciated this idea over 100 years ago in the equation

$$S = k \ln W \qquad (19.2)$$

which states that the entropy of a system, S, is proportional to the natural logarithm of the number of accessible microstates, W, that belong to a given energy of a system or substance. (The proportionality constant, k, is now known as the **Boltzmann's constant.**) Within these microstates, it turns out that those states that disperse energy over the largest number of atoms are vastly more probable than the others.

Dispersal of Matter: Dispersal of Energy Revisited

In many processes, it appears that the dispersal of matter also contributes to spontaneity. We shall see, however, that these effects can also be explained in terms of energy dispersal. Let us examine a specific case. Matter dispersal was illustrated in

Figure 19.2 by the expansion of a gas into a vacuum. How is this spontaneous expansion of a gas related to energy dispersal and entropy?

We begin with the premise that all energy is quantized and that this applies to any system, including gas molecules in a room or in a reaction flask. You know from the previous discussion of kinetic molecular theory that the molecules in a gas sample have a distribution of energies (◀ Figure 11.14) (often referred to as a Boltzmann distribution). The molecules are assigned to (or "occupy") quantized microstates, most of them in states near the average energy of the system, but fewer of them in states of high or low energy. (For a gas in a laboratory-sized container, the energy levels are so closely spaced that, for most purposes, there is a continuum of energy states.)

When the gas expands to fill a larger container, the average energy of the sample and the energy for the particles in a given energy range are constant. However, quantum mechanics shows (for now, you will have to take our word for it) that as a consequence of having a larger volume in which the molecules can move in the expanded state, there is an increase in the number of microstates and that those microstates are even more closely spaced than before (Figure 19.7). The result of this greater density of microstates is that the number of microstates available to the gas particles increases when the gas expands. Gas expansion, a dispersal of matter, leads to the dispersal of energy over a larger number of more closely spaced microstates and thus to an increase in entropy.

The logic applied to the expansion of a gas into a vacuum can be used to rationalize the mixing of two gases, the mixing of two liquids, or the dissolution of a solid in a liquid (Figure 19.8). For example, if flasks containing O_2 and N_2 are connected (in an experimental setup like that in Figure 19.2), the two gases diffuse together, eventually leading to a mixture in which O_2 and N_2 molecules are evenly distributed throughout the total volume. A mixture of O_2 and N_2 will never separate into samples of each component of its own accord. The gases spontaneously move toward a situation in which each gas and its energy are maximally dispersed. The energy of the system is dispersed over a larger number of microstates, and the entropy of the system increases. Indeed, this is a large part of the explanation for the fact that similar liquids (such as oil and gasoline or water and ethanol) will readily form homogeneous solutions. Recall the rule of thumb that "like dissolves like" (◀ Chapter 14).

■ **Statistical Thermodynamics** The arguments presented here come from a branch of chemistry called statistical thermodynamics. For an accessible treatment see H. Jungermann, *Journal of Chemical Education*, Vol. 83, pp. 1686–1694, 2006.

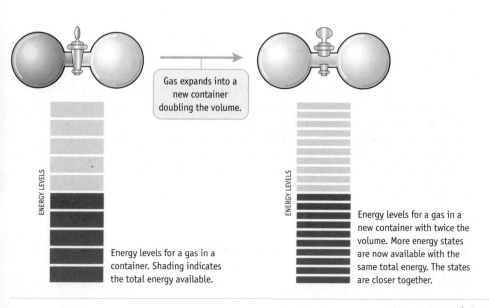

Gas expands into a new container doubling the volume.

ENERGY LEVELS

Energy levels for a gas in a container. Shading indicates the total energy available.

ENERGY LEVELS

Energy levels for a gas in a new container with twice the volume. More energy states are now available with the same total energy. The states are closer together.

FIGURE 19.7 Energy (and matter) dispersal. As the size of the container for the chemical or physical change increases, the number of microstates accessible to the atoms or molecules of the system increases, and the density of states increases. A consequence of the distribution of molecules over a greater number of microstates is an increase in entropy.

Note that for a gas in a container of the size likely to be found in a laboratory, the energy levels are so closely spaced that we do not need to think in terms of quantization of energy levels. For most purposes, the system can be regarded as having a continuum of energy levels.

Photos: Charles D. Winters

Time

FIGURE 19.8 Dissolving KMnO₄ in water. A small quantity of solid, purple KMnO₄ is added to water (left). With time, the solid dissolves, and the highly colored MnO₄⁻ ions (and the K⁺ ions) become dispersed throughout the solution. Entropy makes a large contribution to the mixing of liquids and solutions.

■ **Entropy Change on Gas Expansion** The entropy change for a gas expansion can be calculated from

$$\Delta S = nR\ln(V_{\text{final}}/V_{\text{initial}})$$

At a given temperature, V is proportional to the number of microstates, so the equation is related to $k \ln(W_{\text{final}}/W_{\text{initial}})$.

■ **Negative Entropy Values** A glance at thermodynamic tables indicates that ions in aqueous solution can and do have negative entropy values listed. However, these are not absolute entropies. For ions, the entropy of H⁺(aq) is arbitrarily assigned a standard entropy of zero.

A Summary: Entropy, Entropy Change, and Energy Dispersal

According to Boltzmann's equation for entropy, entropy is proportional to the number of ways that energy can be dispersed in a substance, that is, to the number of microstates available to the system (W). Thus, there will be a change in entropy, ΔS, if there is a change in the number of microstates over which energy can be dispersed.

$$\Delta S = S_{\text{final}} - S_{\text{initial}} = k\,(\ln W_{\text{final}} - \ln W_{\text{initial}}) = k \ln(W_{\text{final}}/W_{\text{initial}})$$

Our focus as chemists is on ΔS, and we shall be mainly concerned with the dispersion of energy in systems and surroundings during a physical or chemical change.

19.4 Entropy Measurement and Values

For any substance under a given set of conditions, a numerical value for entropy can be determined. The greater the dispersal of energy, the greater the entropy and the larger the value of S. The point of reference for entropy values is established by the **third law of thermodynamics.** Defined by Ludwig Boltzmann, the third law states that *a perfect crystal at 0 K has zero entropy; that is, S = 0.* The entropy of an element or compound under any other set of conditions is the entropy gained by converting the substance from 0 K to those conditions.

To determine the value of S, it is necessary to measure the energy transferred as heat under reversible conditions for the conversion from 0 K to the defined conditions and then to use Equation 19.1 ($\Delta S = q_{\text{rev}}/T$). Because it is necessary to add energy as heat to raise the temperature, all substances have positive entropy values at temperatures above 0 K. Negative values of entropy cannot occur. Recognizing that entropy is directly related to energy added as heat allows us to predict several general features of entropy values:

• Raising the temperature of a substance corresponds to adding energy as heat. Thus, the entropy of a substance will increase with an increase in temperature.
• Conversions from solid to liquid and from liquid to gas typically require large inputs of energy as heat. Consequently, there is a large increase in entropy in conversions involving changes of state (Figure 19.9).

Standard Entropy Values, $S°$

The standard state of a substance is its state under a pressure of 1 bar (approximately 1 atmosphere) and at the temperature under consideration. We introduced the concept of standard states into the earlier discussion of enthalpy (◄ Chapter 5), and we can similarly define the entropy of any substance in its standard state.

(a) **(b)**

FIGURE 19.9 Entropy and states of matter. (a) The entropy of liquid bromine, $Br_2(\ell)$, is 152.2 J/K · mol, and that for bromine vapor is 245.47 J/K · mol. (b) The entropy of ice, which has a highly ordered molecular arrangement, is smaller than the entropy of liquid water. (Sign in at **www.cengage.com/login** and go to Chapter 19 Contents to see Screen 19.4 for a self-study module on entropy.)

Photos: Charles D. Winters

The standard entropy, $S°$, of a substance is the entropy gained by converting it from a perfect crystal at 0 K to standard state conditions (1 bar, 1 molal for a solution). The units for standard entropy values are J/K · mol. Generally, values of $S°$ found in tables of data refer to a temperature of 298 K. Standard entropies at 298 K for a few substances are given in Table 19.1, and many more are available in Appendix L. More extensive lists of $S°$ values can be found in standard reference sources such as the NIST tables (**webbook.nist.gov**).

Scanning a list of standard entropies (such as those in Appendix L) will show that *large molecules generally have larger entropies than small molecules.* This seems reasonable; with a larger molecule, there are more ways for the molecule to rotate and vibrate, which provides a larger number of energy microstates over which energy can be distributed. As an example, consider the standard entropies for methane (CH_4), ethane (C_2H_6), and propane (C_3H_8), whose values are 186.3, 229.2, and 270.3 J/K · mol, respectively. Also, *molecules with more complex structures have larger entropies than molecules with simpler structures.* The effect of molecular structure can also be seen when comparing atoms or molecules of similar molar mass: Gaseous argon, CO_2, and C_3H_8 have entropies of 154.9, 213.7, and 270.3 J/K · mol, respectively.

Tables of entropy values also confirm the hypothesis that *entropies of gases are larger than those for liquids, and entropies of liquids are larger than those for solids.* In a solid, the particles have fixed positions in the solid lattice. When a solid melts, these particles have more freedom to assume different positions, resulting in an increase in the number of microstates available and an increase in entropy. When a liquid evaporates, constraints due to forces between the particles nearly disappear; the volume increases greatly; and a large entropy increase occurs. For example, the standard entropies of $I_2(s)$, $Br_2(\ell)$, and $Cl_2(g)$ are 116.1, 152.2, and 223.1 J/K · mol, respectively.

Finally, as illustrated in Figure 19.9, *for a given substance, a large increase in entropy accompanies changes of state,* reflecting the relatively large energy transfer as heat required to carry out these processes (as well as the dispersion of energy over a larger number of available microstates). For example, the entropies of liquid and gaseous water are 65.95 and 188.84 J/K · mol.

TABLE 19.1 Standard Molar Entropy Values at 298 K

Substance	Entropy, $S°$ (J/K · mol)
C(graphite)	5.6
C(diamond)	2.377
C(vapor)	158.1
$H_2(g)$	130.7
$O_2(g)$	205.1
$H_2O(g)$	188.84
$H_2O(\ell)$	69.95

$S°$ (J/K · mol)

186.3

methane

229.2

ethane

270.3

propane

Problem Which substance has the higher entropy under standard conditions? Explain your reasoning. Check your answer against data in Appendix L.

(a) $NO_2(g)$ or $N_2O_4(g)$

(b) $I_2(g)$ or $I_2(s)$

Strategy Entropy decreases in the order gas > liquid > solid, and larger molecules of related substances have greater entropy than smaller molecules.

Solution

(a) Both NO_2 and N_2O_4 are gases. N_2O_4 is a larger molecule than NO_2 and so is expected to have the higher standard entropy. $S°$ values in Appendix L confirm this prediction: $S°$ for $NO_2(g)$ is 240.04 J/K · mol, and $S°$ for $N_2O_4(g)$ is 304.38 J/K · mol.

(b) For a given substance, gases have higher entropies than solids. $S°$ for $I_2(g)$ is 260.69 J/K · mol; $S°$ for $I_2(s)$ is 116.135 J/K · mol.

EXERCISE 19.1 Entropy Comparisons

Predict which substance has the higher entropy and explain your reasoning.

(a) $O_2(g)$ or $O_3(g)$

(b) $SnCl_4(\ell)$ or $SnCl_4(g)$

Determining Entropy Changes in Physical and Chemical Processes

It is also possible to use standard entropy values quantitatively to calculate the change in entropy that occurs in various processes under standard conditions. The standard entropy change is the sum of the standard entropies of the products minus the sum of the standard entropies of the reactants.

$$\Delta_r S° = \Sigma S°(\text{products}) - \Sigma S°(\text{reactants}) \qquad (19.3)$$

This equation allows us to calculate entropy changes for a *system* in which reactants are completely converted to products, under standard conditions. To illustrate, let us calculate $\Delta_r S°$ for the oxidation of NO with O_2.

$$2\ NO(g) + O_2(g) \rightarrow 2\ NO_2(g)$$

Here, we subtract the entropies of the reactants (2 mol NO and 1 mol O_2) from the entropy of the products (2 mol NO_2).

$$\begin{aligned}\Delta_r S° = {}& (2\ \text{mol}\ NO_2/\text{mol-rxn})(240.0\ \text{J/K} \cdot \text{mol}) - \\ & [(2\ \text{mol}\ NO(g)/\text{mol-rxn})(210.8\ \text{J/K} \cdot \text{mol}) + (1\ \text{mol}\ O_2/\text{mol-rxn})(205.1\ \text{J/K} \cdot \text{mol})] \\ = {}& -146.7\ \text{J/K} \cdot \text{mol-rxn}\end{aligned}$$

The entropy of the system decreases, as is generally observed when some number of gaseous reactants has been converted to fewer molecules of gaseous products.

The reaction of NO with O₂. The entropy of the system decreases when two molecules of gas are produced from three molecules of gaseous reactants.

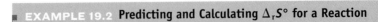

Problem Calculate the standard entropy changes for the following processes. Do the calculations match predictions?

(a) Evaporation of 1.00 mol of liquid ethanol to ethanol vapor

$$C_2H_5OH(\ell) \rightarrow C_2H_5OH(g)$$

(b) Formation of ammonia from hydrogen and nitrogen.

$$N_2(g) + 3\ H_2(g) \rightarrow 2\ NH_3(g)$$

The discussion to this point, along with the examples and exercises, allows the listing of several general principles involving entropy changes:

- The entropy of a substance will increase in going from a solid to a liquid to a gas.
- The entropy of any substance increases as the temperature is raised. Energy must be

added to a system to increase its temperature (that is, $q > 0$), so q_{rev}/T is necessarily positive.

- The entropy of a gas increases with an increase in volume. A larger volume pro-

vides a larger number of energy states over which to disperse energy.

- Reactions that increase the number of moles of gases in a system are accompanied by an increase in entropy.

Strategy Entropy changes for each system can be calculated from values of standard entropies (Appendix L) using Equation 19.3. Predictions are made using the guidelines given in the text: An entropy increase is predicted going from solid to liquid to gas and if there is an increase in the number of moles of gas.

Solution

(a) Evaporation of ethanol

$\Delta_r S° = \Sigma S°(\text{products}) - \Sigma S°(\text{reactants})$

$= (1 \text{ mol } C_2H_5OH(g)/\text{mol-rxn})\{S°[C_2H_5OH(g)]\} - (1 \text{ mol } C_2H_5OH(\ell)/\text{mol-rxn})\{S°[C_2H_5OH(\ell)]\}$

$= (1 \text{ mol } C_2H_5OH(g)/\text{mol-rxn})(282.70 \text{ J/K} \cdot \text{mol}) - (1 \text{ mol } C_2H_5OH(\ell)/\text{mol-rxn})(160.7 \text{ J/K} \cdot \text{mol})$

$= +122.0 \text{ J/K} \cdot \text{mol-rxn}$

A large positive value for the entropy change is expected because the process converts ethanol from a liquid to a vapor.

(b) Formation of ammonia

$\Delta_r S° = \Sigma S°(\text{products}) - \Sigma S°(\text{reactants})$

$= (2 \text{ mol } NH_3(g)/\text{mol-rxn})\{S°[NH_3(g)]\} -$
$\qquad [(1 \text{ mol } N_2(g)/\text{mol-rxn})\{S°[N_2(g)]\} + (3 \text{ mol } H_2(g)/\text{mol-rxn})\{S°[H_2(g)]\}]$

$= (2 \text{ mol } NH_3(g)/\text{mol-rxn})(192.77 \text{ J/K} \cdot \text{mol}) -$
$\qquad [(1 \text{ mol } N_2(g)/\text{mol-rxn})(191.56 \text{ J/K} \cdot \text{mol}) + (3 \text{ mol } H_2(g)/\text{mol-rxn})(130.7 \text{ J/K} \cdot \text{mol})]$

$= -198.12 \text{ J/K} \cdot \text{mol-rxn}$

A decrease in entropy is predicted for this reaction because the number of moles of gases decreases from four to two.

Comment Values of entropies in tables are based on 1 mol of the compound. In part (b), the number of moles of reactants and products per mole of reaction is defined by the stoichiometric coefficients in the balanced chemical equation.

■ **Amount of Substance and Thermodynamic Calculations** In the calculation here and in all others in this chapter, when we write, for example,

282.70 J/K · mol

for the standard entropy of ethanol at 298 K, we mean

282.70 J/K · mol $C_2H_5OH(\ell)$

The identifying formula has been left off for the sake of simplicity.

EXERCISE 19.2 Calculating the Entropy Change for a Reaction, $\Delta_r S°$

Calculate the standard entropy changes for the following processes using the entropy values in Appendix L. Is the sign of the calculated values of $\Delta_r S°$ in accord with predictions?

(a) Dissolving 1 mol of $NH_4Cl(s)$ in water: $NH_4Cl(s) \rightarrow NH_4Cl(aq)$

(b) Oxidation of ethanol: $C_2H_5OH(g) + 3 O_2(g) \rightarrow 2 CO_2(g) + 3 H_2O(g)$

19.5 Entropy Changes and Spontaneity

As illustrated by Example 19.2, the standard entropy change *for the system* in a physical or chemical change can be either positive (evaporation of ethanol) or negative (synthesis of ammonia from nitrogen and hydrogen). How does this information contribute to determining the spontaneity of the process?

As discussed previously (page 863), spontaneity is determined by the *second law of thermodynamics*, which states that *a spontaneous process is one that results in an increase of entropy in the universe.* The universe has two parts: the system and its surroundings (◄ Section 5.1), and it makes sense that the entropy change for the universe is the sum of the entropy changes for the system and the surroundings. Under standard conditions, the entropy change for the universe, $\Delta S°$(universe) is

$$\Delta S°(\text{universe}) = \Delta S°(\text{system}) + \Delta S°(\text{surroundings}) \qquad (19.4)$$

The calculation in Example 19.2 gave us the entropy change under standard conditions for a system, only half of the information needed. Now we will have to determine how the change being studied affects the entropy of the surroundings so that we can then find the entropy change for the universe.

The value of $\Delta S°$(universe) calculated from Equation 19.4 is the entropy change when reactants are converted *completely* to products, with all species at standard conditions. *A process is spontaneous under standard conditions if $\Delta S°$ (universe) is greater than zero.* As an example of the determination of reaction spontaneity, let us calculate $\Delta S°$(universe) for the reaction currently used to manufacture methanol, CH_3OH.

$$CO(g) + 2\ H_2(g) \rightarrow CH_3OH(\ell)$$

If $\Delta S°$(universe) is positive, the conversion of 1 mol of CO(g) and 2 mol of H_2(g) to 1 mol of $CH_3OH(\ell)$ will be spontaneous under standard conditions.

■ **Using $\Delta S°$(universe)** For a process that is spontaneous under standard conditions:

$$\Delta S°(\text{universe}) > 0$$

For a process at equilibrium under standard conditions:

$$\Delta S°(\text{universe}) = 0$$

For a process that is not spontaneous under standard conditions:

$$\Delta S°(\text{universe}) < 0$$

Note that these conclusions refer to the complete conversion of reactants to products.

Calculating $\Delta S°$(system) To calculate $\Delta S°$(system), we start by defining the system to include the reactants and products. This means that $\Delta S°$(system) corresponds to the entropy change for the reaction, $\Delta_r S°$. Calculation of this entropy change follows the procedure given in Example 19.2.

$$\Delta S°(\text{system}) = \Delta_r S° = \Sigma \Delta S°(\text{products}) - \Sigma \Delta S°(\text{reactants})$$

$$= (1\ \text{mol}\ CH_3OH(\ell)/\text{mol-rxn})\{S°[CH_3OH(\ell)]\} -$$
$$[(1\ \text{mol}\ CO(g)/\text{mol-rxn})\{S°[CO(g)]\} + (2\ \text{mol}\ H_2(g)/\text{mol-rxn})\{S°[H_2(g)]\}]$$

$$= (1\ \text{mol}\ CH_3OH(\ell)/\text{mol-rxn})(127.2\ \text{J/K}\cdot\text{mol}) -$$
$$[(1\ \text{mol}\ CO(g)/\text{mol-rxn})(197.7\ \text{J/K}\cdot\text{mol}) + (2\ \text{mol}\ H_2(g)/\text{mol-rxn})(130.7\ \text{J/K}\cdot\text{mol})]$$

$$= -331.9\ \text{J/K}\cdot\text{mol-rxn}$$

A decrease in entropy for the system is expected because three moles of gaseous reactants are converted to one mole of a liquid product.

Calculating $\Delta S°$(surroundings) We now need to calculate the entropy change for the surroundings. Recall from Equation 19.1 that for a reversible change, ΔS is equal to q_{rev}/T. Under constant pressure conditions and assuming a reversible process, the entropy change in the surroundings results from the fact that the enthalpy change for the reaction ($q_p = \Delta H$) affects the surroundings. That is, the energy associated with an exothermic chemical reaction is dispersed into the surroundings. Recognizing that $\Delta H°$(surroundings) $= -\Delta_r H°$(system), the entropy change for the surroundings can be calculated by the equation

$$\Delta S°(\text{surroundings}) = \Delta H°(\text{surroundings})/T = -\Delta_r H°(\text{system})/T$$

For the synthesis of methanol by the reaction given, the enthalpy change is -127.9 kJ/mol-rxn, calculated from enthalpy of formation data.

$$\Delta H°(\text{system}) = \Sigma \Delta_f H°(\text{products}) - \Sigma \Delta_f H°(\text{reactants})$$

$$= (1 \text{ mol } CH_3OH(\ell)/\text{mol-rxn})\{\Delta_f H°[CH_3OH(\ell)]\} -$$
$$[(1 \text{ mol } CO(g)/\text{mol-rxn})\{\Delta_f H°[CO(g)]\} +$$
$$(2 \text{ mol } H_2(g)/\text{mol-rxn})\{\Delta_f H°[H_2(g)]\}]$$

$$= (1 \text{ mol } CH_3OH(\ell)/\text{mol-rxn})(-238.4 \text{ kJ/mol}) -$$
$$[(1 \text{ mol } CO(g)/\text{mol-rxn})(-110.5 \text{ kJ/mol}) +$$
$$(2 \text{ mol } H_2(g)/\text{mol-rxn})(0 \text{ kJ/ mol})]$$

$$= -127.9 \text{ kJ/mol-rxn}$$

Assuming that the process is reversible and occurs at a constant temperature and pressure, the entropy change for the surroundings in the methanol synthesis is $+429.2$ J/K · mol-rxn, calculated as follows.

$$\Delta S°(\text{surroundings}) = -\Delta_r H°(\text{system})/T$$

$$= -[(-127.9 \text{ kJ/mol-rxn})/298 \text{ K})](1000 \text{ J/kJ})$$

$$= +429.2 \text{ J/K} \cdot \text{mol-rxn}$$

Calculating $\Delta S°$(universe), the Entropy Change for the System and Surroundings

The pieces are now in place to calculate the entropy change in the universe. For the formation of $CH_3OH(\ell)$ from $CO(g)$ and $H_2(g)$, $\Delta S°$(universe), is

$$\Delta S°(\text{universe}) = \Delta S°(\text{system}) + \Delta S°(\text{surroundings})$$

$$= -331.9 \text{ J/K} \cdot \text{mol-rxn} + 429.2 \text{ J/K} \cdot \text{mol-rxn}$$

$$= +97.3 \text{ J/K} \cdot \text{mol-rxn}$$

The positive value indicates an increase in the entropy of the universe. It follows from the second law of thermodynamics that this reaction is spontaneous.

Chemistry.Now™

Sign in at **www.cengage.com/login** and go to Chapter 19 Contents to see:
- Screen 19.5 for a simulation and tutorial on **calculating ΔS for a reaction**
- Screen 19.6 for a simulation and tutorial on **the second law of thermodynamics**

EXAMPLE 19.3 Determining Whether a Process Is Spontaneous

Problem Show that $\Delta S°$(universe) is positive for the process of dissolving NaCl in water at 298 K.

Strategy The process occurring is NaCl(s) → NaCl(aq). The entropy change for the system, $\Delta S°$(system), can be calculated from values of $S°$ for the two species using Equation 19.3. $\Delta S°$(surroundings) is determined by dividing $-\Delta_r H°$ for the process by the Kelvin temperature. The sum of these two entropy changes is $\Delta S°$(universe). Values of $\Delta_f H°$ and $S°$ for NaCl(s) and NaCl(aq) are obtained from Appendix L.

Solution

Calculate $\Delta S°$(system)

$$\Delta S°(\text{system}) = \Sigma S°(\text{products}) - \Sigma S°(\text{reactants})$$

$$= (1 \text{ mol } NaCl(aq)/\text{mol-rxn})\{S°[NaCl(aq)]\} - (1 \text{ mol } NaCl(s)/\text{mol-rxn})\{S°[NaCl(s)]\}$$

$$= (1 \text{ mol } NaCl(aq)/\text{mol-rxn})(115.5 \text{ J/K} \cdot \text{mol}) - (1 \text{ mol } NaCl(s)/\text{mol-rxn})(72.11 \text{ J/K} \cdot \text{mol})$$

$$= +43.4 \text{ J/K} \cdot \text{mol-rxn}$$

◾ $\Delta S°$(universe), Spontaneity, and Standard Conditions

It is important to reiterate that when we calculate $\Delta H°$ or $\Delta S°$ for a reaction, this is the value for the complete conversion of reactants to products under standard conditions. If $\Delta S°$(universe) is > 0, the reaction as written is spontaneous *under standard conditions*. However, one can calculate values for ΔS(universe) (without the superscript zero) for *nonstandard* conditions. If ΔS(universe) > 0, the reaction is spontaneous under those conditions. However, it is possible that this same reaction under standard conditions is not spontaneous [$\Delta S°$(universe) < 0]. We will return to this point in Sections 19.6 and 19.7.

Calculate $\Delta S°$(surroundings)

$$\Delta_r H°(\text{system}) = \Sigma \Delta_f H°(\text{products}) - \Sigma \Delta_f H°(\text{reactants})$$
$$= (1 \text{ mol NaCl(aq)/mol-rxn})\{\Delta_f H°[\text{NaCl(aq)}]\} - (1 \text{ mol NaCl(s)/mol-rxn})\{\Delta_f H°[\text{NaCl(s)}]\}$$
$$= (1 \text{ mol NaCl(aq)/mol-rxn})(-407.27 \text{ kJ/mol}) - (1 \text{ mol NaCl(s)/mol-rxn})(-411.12 \text{ kJ/mol})$$
$$= +3.85 \text{ kJ/mol-rxn}$$

The entropy change of the surroundings is determined by dividing $-\Delta_r H°(\text{system})$ by the Kelvin temperature.

$$\Delta S°(\text{surroundings}) = -\Delta_r H°(\text{system})/T$$
$$= [(-3.85 \text{ kJ/mol-rxn}/298 \text{ K})](1000 \text{ J/1 kJ})$$
$$= -12.9 \text{ J/K} \cdot \text{mol-rxn}$$

Calculate $\Delta S°$(universe)

The overall entropy change—the change of entropy in the universe—is the sum of the values for the system and the surroundings.

$$\Delta S°(\text{universe}) = \Delta S°(\text{system}) + \Delta S°(\text{surroundings})$$
$$= +43.4 \text{ J/K} \cdot \text{mol-rxn} - 12.9 \text{ J/K} \cdot \text{mol-rxn}$$
$$= +30.5 \text{ J/K} \cdot \text{mol-rxn}$$

Comment The sum of the two entropy quantities is positive, indicating that the entropy in the universe increases; thus, the process is spontaneous under standard conditions. Notice, however, that the spontaneity of the process results from $\Delta S°$(system) and not from $\Delta S°$(surroundings).

In Summary: Spontaneous or Not?

In the preceding examples, predictions about the spontaneity of a process under standard conditions were made using values of $\Delta S°$(system) and $\Delta H°$(system) calculated from tables of thermodynamic data. It will be useful to look at all possibilities that result from the interplay of these two quantities. There are four possible outcomes when these two quantities are paired (Table 19.2). In two, $\Delta H°$(system) and $\Delta S°$(system) work in concert (Types 1 and 4 in Table 19.2). In the other two, the two quantities are opposed (Types 2 and 3).

Processes in which both the standard enthalpy and entropy changes favor energy dispersal (Type 1) are always spontaneous under standard conditions. Processes disfavored by both their standard enthalpy and entropy changes in the system (Type 4) can *never* be spontaneous under standard conditions. Let us consider examples that illustrate each situation.

Combustion reactions are always exothermic and often produce a larger number of product molecules from a few reactant molecules. They are Type 1 reactions. The equation for the combustion of butane is an example.

$$2 \text{ C}_4\text{H}_{10}(\text{g}) + 13 \text{ O}_2(\text{g}) \rightarrow 8 \text{ CO}_2(\text{g}) + 10 \text{ H}_2\text{O}(\text{g})$$

TABLE 19.2   Predicting Whether a Reaction Will Be Spontaneous Under Standard Conditions

Reaction Type	$\Delta H°$(system)	$\Delta S°$(system)	Spontaneous Process (Standard Conditions)
1	Exothermic, < 0	Positive, > 0	Spontaneous at all temperatures. $\Delta S°$(universe) > 0.
2	Exothermic, < 0	Negative, < 0	Depends on relative magnitudes of $\Delta H°$ and $\Delta S°$. Spontaneous at lower temperatures.
3	Endothermic, > 0	Positive, > 0	Depends on relative magnitudes of $\Delta H°$ and $\Delta S°$. Spontaneous at higher temperatures.
4	Endothermic, > 0	Negative, < 0	Not spontaneous at any temperature. $\Delta S°$(universe) < 0.

For this reaction, $\Delta_r H° = -5315.1$ kJ, and $\Delta_r S° = 312.4$ J/K. Both contribute to this reaction's being spontaneous under standard conditions.

Hydrazine, N_2H_4, is used as a high-energy rocket fuel. Synthesis of N_2H_4 from gaseous N_2 and H_2 would be attractive because these reactants are inexpensive.

$$N_2(g) + 2\,H_2(g) \rightarrow N_2H_4(\ell)$$

However, this reaction fits into the Type 4 category. The reaction is endothermic ($\Delta_r H° = +50.63$ kJ/mol-rxn), and the entropy change is negative ($\Delta_r S° = -331.4$ J/K·mol-rxn) (1 mol of liquid is produced from 3 mol of gases), so the reaction is not spontaneous under standard conditions, and complete conversion of reactants to products will not occur without outside intervention.

In the two other possible outcomes, entropy and enthalpy changes oppose each other. A process could be favored by the enthalpy change but disfavored by the entropy change (Type 2), or vice versa (Type 3). In either instance, whether a process is spontaneous depends on which factor is more important.

Temperature also influences the value of $\Delta S°$(universe). Because the enthalpy change for the surroundings is divided by the temperature to obtain $\Delta S°$(surroundings), the numerical value of $\Delta S°$(surroundings) will be smaller (either less positive or less negative) at higher temperatures. In contrast, $\Delta S°$(system) and $\Delta H°$(system) do not vary much with temperature. Thus, the effect of $\Delta S°$(surroundings) relative to $\Delta S°$(system) is diminished at higher temperature. Stated another way, at higher temperature, the enthalpy change becomes a less important factor in determining the overall entropy change. Consider the two cases where $\Delta H°$(system) and $\Delta S°$(system) are in opposition (Table 19.2):

- Type 2: Exothermic processes with $\Delta S°$(system) < 0. Such processes become less favorable with an increase in temperature.
- Type 3: Endothermic processes with $\Delta S°$(system) > 0. These processes become more favorable as the temperature increases.

The effect of temperature is illustrated by two examples. The first is the reaction of N_2 and H_2 to form NH_3. The reaction is exothermic, and thus it is favored by energy dispersal to the surroundings. The entropy change for the system is unfavorable, however, because the reaction, $N_2(g) + 3\,H_2(g) \rightarrow 2\,NH_3(g)$, converts four moles of gaseous reactants to two moles of gaseous products. The favorable enthalpy effect [$\Delta_r S°$(surroundings) $= -\Delta_r H°$(system)$/T$] becomes less important at higher temperatures. Furthermore, it is reasonable to expect that the reaction will not be spontaneous if the temperature is high enough.

The second example considers the thermal decomposition of NH_4Cl (Figure 19.10). At room temperature, NH_4Cl is a stable, white, crystalline salt. When heated strongly, it decomposes to $NH_3(g)$ and $HCl(g)$. The reaction is endothermic (enthalpy-disfavored) but entropy-favored because of the formation of two moles of gas from one mole of a solid reactant. The reaction is increasingly favored at higher temperatures.

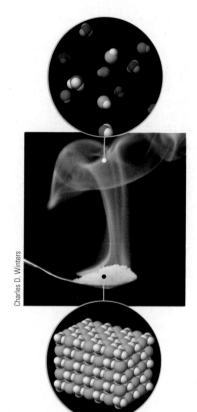

Charles D. Winters

FIGURE 19.10 Thermal decomposition of $NH_4Cl(s)$. White, solid ammonium chloride, $NH_4Cl(s)$, is heated in a spoon. At high temperatures, decomposition to form $NH_3(g)$ and $HCl(g)$ is spontaneous. At lower temperatures, the reverse reaction, forming $NH_4Cl(s)$, is spontaneous. As gaseous $HCl(g)$ and $NH_3(g)$ cool, they recombine to form solid NH_4Cl, the white "smoke" seen in this photo.

EXERCISE 19.3 Is a Reaction Spontaneous?

Classify the following reactions as one of the four types of reactions summarized in Table 19.2.

Reaction	$\Delta_r H°$ (at 298 K) (kJ/mol-rxn)	$\Delta_r S°$ (at 298 K) (J/K · mol-rxn)
(a) $CH_4(g) + 2\,O_2(g) \rightarrow 2\,H_2O(\ell) + CO_2(g)$	-890.6	-242.8
(b) $2\,Fe_2O_3(s) + 3\,C(graphite) \rightarrow 4\,Fe(s) + 3\,CO_2(g)$	$+467.9$	$+560.7$
(c) $C(graphite) + O_2(g) \rightarrow CO_2(g)$	-393.5	$+3.1$
(d) $N_2(g) + 3\,F_2(g) \rightarrow 2\,NF_3(g)$	-264.2	-277.8

Module 24

■ **J. Willard Gibbs (1839–1903)** Gibbs received a Ph.D. from Yale University in 1863. His was the first Ph.D. in science awarded from an American university.

Burndy Library/Courtesy Emilio Segre Visual Archives

19.6 Gibbs Free Energy

The method used so far to determine whether a process is spontaneous required evaluation of two quantities, $\Delta S°(system)$ and $\Delta S°(surroundings)$. Wouldn't it be convenient to have a single thermodynamic function that serves the same purpose? A function associated with the system only—one that does not require assessment of the surroundings—would be even better. Such a function exists. It is called the **Gibbs free energy**, with the name honoring J. Willard Gibbs (1839–1903). Gibbs free energy, G, often referred to simply as "free energy," is defined mathematically as

$$G = H - TS$$

where H is enthalpy, T is the Kelvin temperature, and S is entropy. In this equation, G, H, and S all refer to the system. Because enthalpy and entropy are state functions (◄ Section 5.4), free energy is also a state function.

Every substance possesses free energy, but the actual quantity is seldom known. Instead, just as with enthalpy (H) and internal energy (U), we are concerned with *changes* in free energy, ΔG, that occur in chemical and physical processes.

Let us first see how to use free energy as a way to determine whether a reaction is spontaneous. We can then ask further questions about the meaning of the term "free energy" and its use in deciding whether a reaction is product- or reactant-favored.

The Change in the Gibbs Free Energy, ΔG

Recall the equation defining the entropy change for the universe:

$$\Delta S(universe) = \Delta S(surroundings) + \Delta S(system)$$

The entropy change of the surroundings equals the negative of the change in enthalpy of the system divided by T. Thus,

$$\Delta S(universe) = -\Delta H(system)/T + \Delta S(system)$$

Multiplying through this equation by $-T$, gives the equation

$$-T\Delta S(universe) = \Delta H(system) - T\Delta S(system)$$

Gibbs defined the free energy function so that $\Delta G(system) = -T\Delta S(universe)$. Combining terms and simplifying give the general expression relating changes in free energy to the enthalpy and entropy changes in the system.

$$\Delta G = \Delta H - T\Delta S$$

Under standard conditions, we can rewrite the Gibbs free energy equation as

$$\Delta G° = \Delta H° - T\Delta S° \qquad\qquad \textbf{(19.5)}$$

Gibbs Free Energy, Spontaneity, and Chemical Equilibrium

Because $\Delta_r G°$ is related directly to $\Delta S°$(universe), the Gibbs free energy can be used as a criterion of spontaneity for physical and chemical changes. As shown earlier, the signs of $\Delta_r G°$ and $\Delta S°$(universe) will be opposites [$\Delta_r G°$ (system) $= -T\Delta S°$(universe)]. Therefore, we find the following relationships:

$\Delta_r G° < 0$ The process is spontaneous in the direction written under standard conditions.

$\Delta_r G° = 0$ The process is at equilibrium under standard conditions.

$\Delta_r G° > 0$ The process is not spontaneous in the direction written under standard conditions.

To better understand the Gibbs function, let us examine the diagrams in Figure 19.11. The free energy of pure reactants is plotted on the left, and the free energy of the pure products on the right. The extent of reaction, plotted on the *x*-axis, goes from zero (pure reactants) to one (pure products). In both cases in Figure 19.11, the free energy initially declines as reactants begin to form products; it reaches a minimum at equilibrium and then increases again as we move from the equilibrium position to pure products. *The free energy at equilibrium, where there is a mixture of reactants and products, is always lower than the free energy of the pure reactants and of the pure products. A reaction proceeds spontaneously toward the minimum in free energy, which corresponds to equilibrium.*

$\Delta_r G°$ is the change in free energy accompanying the chemical reaction in which the reactants are converted completely to the products under standard

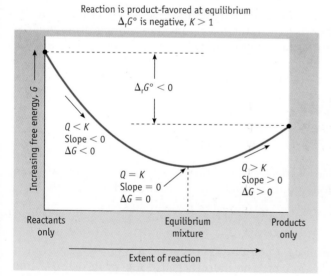

(a)

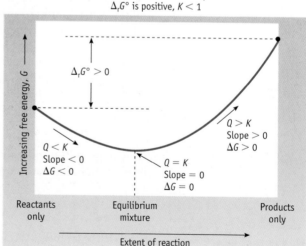

(b)

FIGURE 19.11 Free energy changes in the course of a reaction. The difference in free energy between the pure reactants in their standard states and the pure products in their standard states is $\Delta_r G°$. Here, Q is the reaction quotient, and K is the equilibrium constant.

conditions. Mathematically, it is the difference in free energy between the products and the reactants under standard conditions. If the free energy of the products is less than that of the reactants, then $\Delta_r G° < 0$, and the reaction is spontaneous under standard conditions (Figure 19.11a). Conversely, if the free energy of the products is greater than that of the reactants, then $\Delta_r G°$ is positive ($\Delta_r G° > 0$), and the reaction is not spontaneous under standard conditions (Figure 19.11b).

Finally, notice that in Figure 19.11a, the equilibrium position occurs closer to the product side than to the reactant side. This is a product-favored reaction at equilibrium. In Figure 19.11b, we find the opposite. The reaction is reactant-favored at equilibrium. It is no accident that the reaction with a negative $\Delta_r G°$ is product-favored, whereas the one with the positive $\Delta_r G°$ is reactant-favored at equilibrium. It turns out that this is always true as the discussion below will show.

Now let us now consider what happens to the instantaneous slope of the curve in Figure 19.11 as the reaction proceeds. Initially, this slope is negative, corresponding to a negative ΔG in moving from point to point. Eventually, however, the free energy reaches a minimum. At this point, the instantaneous slope of the graph is zero ($\Delta G = 0$) and the reaction has reached equilibrium. If we move past the equilibrium point, the instantaneous slope is positive ($\Delta G > 0$); proceeding further to products is not spontaneous. In fact, the reverse reaction will occur spontaneously; the reaction will once again proceed toward equilibrium.

The relationship of $\Delta_r G°$ (the value of $\Delta_r G$ under standard conditions) and the value of $\Delta_r G$ under nonstandard conditions is given by Equation 19.6

$$\Delta_r G = \Delta_r G° + RT \ln Q \qquad \text{(19.6)}$$

where R is the universal gas constant, T is the temperature in kelvins, and Q is the reaction quotient (◀ Section 16.2).

$$Q = \frac{[C]^c[D]^d}{[A]^a[B]^b} \text{ for } aA + bB \rightarrow cC + dD$$

Equation 19.6 informs us that, at a given temperature, $\Delta_r G$ is determined by the values of $\Delta_r G°$ and Q. Further, as long as the reaction is "descending" from the free energy of the pure reactants to the equilibrium position, $\Delta_r G$ is negative, and the reaction is spontaneous in the forward direction (and $Q < K$).

When the system reaches equilibrium, no further net change in concentration of reactants and products will occur, and $\Delta_r G = 0$ and $Q = K$. Substituting these values into Equation 19.6 gives

$$0 = \Delta_r G° + RT \ln K \text{ (at equilibrium)}$$

Rearranging this equation leads to a useful relationship between the standard free energy change for a reaction and the equilibrium constant, K, Equation 19.7:

$$\Delta_r G° = -RT \ln K \qquad \text{(19.7)}$$

From this equation, we learn that, when $\Delta_r G°$ is negative, K is greater than 1, and we say the reaction is *product-favored*. The more negative the value of $\Delta_r G°$, the larger the equilibrium constant. This makes sense because, as described in Chapter 16, large equilibrium constants are associated with product-favored reactions. The converse is also true: For *reactant-favored* reactions, $\Delta_r G°$ is positive, and K is less than 1. Finally, if $K = 1$ (a special set of conditions), then $\Delta_r G° = 0$.

A Summary: Gibbs Free Energy ($\Delta_r G$ and $\Delta_r G°$), the Reaction Quotient (Q) and Equilibrium Constant (K), and Reaction Favorability

Let us now summarize the relationships among $\Delta_r G°$, $\Delta_r G$, Q, and K.

- In Figure 19.11, you see that free energy decreases to a minimum as a system approaches equilibrium. The free energy of the mixture of reactants and products at equilibrium is always lower than the free energy of the pure reactants or of the pure products.
- When $\Delta_r G < 0$, the reaction is proceeding spontaneously toward equilibrium and $Q < K$.
- When $\Delta_r G > 0$, the reaction is beyond the equilibrium point and is not spontaneous in the forward direction. It will be spontaneous in the reverse direction; $Q > K$.
- When $\Delta_r G = 0$, the reaction is at equilibrium; $Q = K$.
- When $\Delta_r G° < 0$, the reaction is *spontaneous under standard conditions*. The system will proceed to an equilibrium position at which point the products will dominate in the reaction mixture because $K > 1$. That is, the reaction is product-favored at equilibrium.
- When $\Delta_r G° > 0$, the reaction is *not spontaneous under standard conditions*. The system will proceed to the equilibrium position at which the reactants will dominate in the equilibrium mixture because $K < 1$. That is, the reaction is *reactant-favored*.
- For the special condition where $\Delta_r G° = 0$, the reaction is at equilibrium at standard conditions, with $K = 1$.

A reactant-favored process. If a sample of yellow lead iodide is placed in pure water, a small amount of the compound will dissolve spontaneously ($\Delta_r G < 0$ and $Q < K$) until equilibrium is reached. Because PbI_2 is quite insoluble ($K_{sp} = 9.8 \times 10^{-9}$), however, the process of dissolving the compound is reactant-favored. We may conclude, therefore, that the value of $\Delta_r G°$ is positive.

What Is "Free" Energy?

The term "free energy" was not arbitrarily chosen. In any given process, the free energy represents the maximum energy available to do useful work (mathematically, $\Delta G = w_{max}$). In this context, the word "free" means "available."

To illustrate the reasoning behind this relationship, consider a reaction carried out under standard conditions and in which energy is evolved as heat ($\Delta_r H° < 0$) and entropy decreases ($\Delta_r S° < 0$).

$$2 H_2(g) + O_2(g) \rightarrow 2 H_2O(g)$$

$\Delta_r H° = -483.6$ kJ/mol-rxn and $\Delta_r S° = -88.8$ J/K · mol-rxn

$\Delta_r G° = -483.6$ kJ/mol-rxn $- (298 \text{ K})(-0.0888$ kJ/mol-rxn$) = -457.2$ kJ/mol-rxn

At first glance, it might seem reasonable that all the energy released as heat (-483.6 kJ/mol-rxn) would be available. This energy could be transferred to the surroundings and would thus be available to do work. This is not the case, however. A negative entropy change in this reaction means that energy is less dispersed in the products than in the reactants. A portion of the energy released as heat from the reaction must be used to reverse energy dispersal in the system; that is, to concentrate energy in the product. The energy left over is "free," or available to perform work. Here, the free energy change amounts to -457.2 kJ/mol-rxn.

19.7 Calculating and Using Free Energy

Standard Free Energy of Formation

The standard free energy of formation of a compound, $\Delta_f G°$, is the free energy change that occurs to form one mole of the compound from the component elements, with products and reactants in their standard states. By defining $\Delta_f G°$ in this way, *the free energy of formation of an element in its standard state is zero.*

Just as the standard enthalpy or entropy change for a reaction can be calculated using values of $\Delta_f H°$ (Equation 5.6) or $S°$ (Equation 19.3), the standard free energy change for a reaction can be calculated from values of $\Delta_f G°$:

$$\Delta_r G° = \Sigma\Delta_f G°(\text{products}) - \Sigma\Delta_f G°(\text{reactants})$$ (19.8)

Calculating $\Delta_r G°$, the Free Energy Change for a Reaction Under Standard Conditions

The free energy change for a reaction under standard conditions can be calculated from thermodynamic data in two ways, either from standard enthalpy and entropy changes using values of $\Delta_f H°$ and $S°$ (as we did for the formation of H_2O just above) or directly from values of $\Delta_f G°$ found in tables. These calculations are illustrated in the following two examples.

Chemistry.ᓂ.Now™

■ **EXAMPLE 19.4 Calculating $\Delta_r G°$ from $\Delta_r H°$ and $\Delta_r S°$**

Problem Calculate the standard free energy change, $\Delta_r G°$, for the formation of methane from carbon and hydrogen at 298 K, using tabulated values of $\Delta_f H°$ and $\Delta S°$. Is the reaction spontaneous under standard conditions? Is it product-favored or reactant-favored at equilibrium?

$$C(\text{graphite}) + 2\ H_2(g) \rightarrow CH_4(g)$$

Strategy The values of $\Delta_f H°$ and $S°$ needed in this problem are found in Appendix L. These are first combined to find $\Delta_r H°$ and $\Delta_r S°$. With these values known, $\Delta_r G°$ can be calculated using Equation 19.5. When doing the calculation, remember that $S°$ values are given in units of J/K · mol, whereas $\Delta_f H°$ values are given in units of kJ/mol.

Solution

	C(graphite)	$H_2(g)$	$CH_4(g)$
$\Delta_f H°$ (kJ/mol)	0	0	−74.9
$S°$ (J/K·mol)	+5.6	+130.7	+186.3

From these values, we can find both $\Delta_r H°$ and $\Delta_r S°$ for the reaction:

$\Delta_r H° = \Sigma\Delta_f H°(\text{products}) - \Sigma\Delta_f H°(\text{reactants})$

$= (1\text{ mol }CH_4(g)/\text{mol-rxn})\{\Delta_f H°[CH_4(g)]\} - [(1\text{ mol }C(\text{graphite})/\text{mol-rxn})\{\Delta_f H°[C(\text{graphite})]\} + (2\text{ mol }H_2(g)/\text{mol-rxn})\{\Delta_f H°[H_2(g)]\}]$

$= (1\text{ mol }CH_4(g)/\text{mol-rxn})(-74.9\text{ kJ/mol}) - [(1\text{ mol }C(\text{graphite})/\text{mol-rxn})(0\text{ kJ/mol}) + (2\text{ mol }H_2(g)/\text{mol-rxn})(0\text{ kJ/mol})]$

$= -74.9\text{ kJ/mol-rxn}$

$\Delta_r S° = \Sigma\Delta S°(\text{products}) - \Sigma\Delta S°(\text{reactants})$

$= (1\text{ mol }CH_4(g)/\text{mol-rxn})\{S°[CH_4(g)]\} - [(1\text{ mol }C(\text{graphite})/\text{mol-rxn})\{S°[C(\text{graphite})]\} + (2\text{ mol }H_2(g)/\text{mol-rxn})\{S°[H_2(g)]\}]$

$= (1\text{ mol }CH_4(g)/\text{mol-rxn})(186.3\text{ J/K}\cdot\text{mol}) - [1\text{ mol }C(\text{graphite})/\text{mol-rxn}](5.6\text{ J/K}\cdot\text{mol}) + (2\text{ mol }H_2(g)/\text{mol-rxn})(130.7\text{ J/K}\cdot\text{mol})]$

$= -80.7\text{ J/K}\cdot\text{mol-rxn}$

Combining the values of $\Delta_rH°$ and $\Delta_rS°$ using Equation 19.5 gives $\Delta_rG°$.

$$\Delta_rG° = \Delta_rH° - T\Delta_rS°$$

$$= -74.9 \text{ kJ/mol-rxn} - [(298 \text{ K})(-80.7 \text{ J/K} \cdot \text{mol-rxn})](1 \text{ kJ/1000 J})$$

$$= \boxed{-50.9 \text{ kJ/mol-rxn}}$$

$\Delta_rG°$ is negative at 298 K, so the reaction is predicted to be spontaneous under standard conditions at this temperature. It is also predicted to be product-favored at equilibrium.

■ **Enthalpy- and Entropy-Driven Reactions** In Example 19.4, the product $T\Delta_rS°$ is negative (-24.0 J/mol-rxn) and disfavors the reaction. However, the entropy change is relatively small, and $\Delta_rH° = -74.9$ kJ/mol-rxn) is the dominant term. Chemists call this an "enthalpy-driven reaction."

■ EXAMPLE 19.5 Calculating $\Delta_rG°$ Using Free Energies of Formation

Problem Calculate the standard free energy change for the combustion of one mole of methane using values for standard free energies of formation of the products and reactants. Is the reaction spontaneous under standard conditions? Is it product-favored or reactant-favored at equilibrium?

Strategy Write a balanced equation for the reaction. Then, use Equation 19.8 with values of $\Delta_fG°$ obtained from Appendix L.

Solution The balanced equation and values of $\Delta_fG°$ for each reactant and product are:

$$CH_4(g) + 2 O_2(g) \rightarrow 2 H_2O(g) + CO_2(g)$$

$\Delta_fG°$(kJ/mol)	-50.8	0	-228.6	-394.4

Because $\Delta_fG°$ values are given for 1 mol of each substance (the units are kJ/mol), each value of $\Delta_fG°$ must be multiplied by the number of moles defined by the stoichiometric coefficient in the balanced chemical equation.

$$\Delta_rG°(\text{system}) = \Sigma\Delta_fG°(\text{products}) - \Sigma\Delta_fG°(\text{reactants})$$

$$= [(2 \text{ mol } H_2O(g)/\text{mol-rxn})\{\Delta_fG°[H_2O(g)]\} + (1 \text{ mol } CO_2(g)/\text{mol-rxn})\{\Delta_fG°[CO_2(g)]\}]$$

$$- [(1 \text{ mol } CH_4(g)/\text{mol-rxn})\{\Delta_fG°[CH_4(g)]\} + (2 \text{ mol } O_2(g)/\text{mol-rxn})\{\Delta_fG°[O_2(g)]\}]$$

$$= [(2 \text{ mol } H_2O(g)/\text{mol-rxn})(-228.6 \text{ kJ/mol}) + (1 \text{ mol } CO_2(g)/\text{mol-rxn})(-394.4 \text{ kJ/mol})\}$$

$$- [(1 \text{ mol } CH_4(g)/\text{mol-rxn})(-50.8 \text{ kJ/mol}) - (2 \text{ mol } O_2(g)/\text{mol-rxn})(0 \text{ kJ/mol})]$$

$$= \boxed{-800.8 \text{ kJ/mol-rxn}}$$

The large negative value of $\Delta_rG°$ indicates that the reaction is spontaneous under standard conditions and that it is product-favored at equilibrium.

Comment Common errors made by students in this calculation are (1) overlooking the stoichiometric coefficients in the equation and (2) confusing the signs for the terms when using Equation 19.8.

EXERCISE 19.6 Calculating $\Delta_rG°$ from $\Delta_rH°$ and $\Delta_rS°$

Using values of $\Delta_fH°$ and $S°$ to find $\Delta_rH°$ and $\Delta_rS°$, calculate the free energy change, $\Delta_rG°$, for the formation of 2 mol of $NH_3(g)$ from the elements at standard conditions and 25 °C. $N_2(g) + 3 H_2(g) \rightarrow 2 NH_3(g)$.

EXERCISE 19.7 Calculating $\Delta_rG°$ from $\Delta_fG°$

Calculate the standard free energy change for the oxidation of 1.00 mol of $SO_2(g)$ to form $SO_3(g)$ using values of $\Delta_fG°$.

Free Energy and Temperature

The definition for free energy, $G = H - TS$, informs us that free energy is a function of temperature, so $\Delta_rG°$ will change as the temperature changes (Figure 19.12). A consequence of this dependence on temperature is that, in certain instances, reactions can be product-favored at equilibrium at one temperature

■ **Entropy- or Enthalpy-Favored** Table 19.2 describes the balance of $\Delta H°$ and $\Delta S°$ and the effect of temperature on reaction spontaneity.

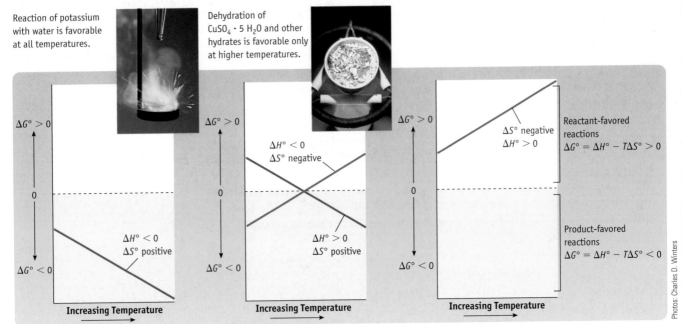

Reaction of potassium with water is favorable at all temperatures.

Dehydration of $CuSO_4 \cdot 5\ H_2O$ and other hydrates is favorable only at higher temperatures.

$\Delta G° > 0$

$\Delta H° < 0$ $\Delta S°$ positive

$\Delta G° < 0$

Increasing Temperature

$\Delta H° < 0$ and $\Delta S° > 0$. Product-favored at all temperatures.

$\Delta G° > 0$

$\Delta H° < 0$ $\Delta S°$ negative

$\Delta H° > 0$ $\Delta S°$ positive

$\Delta G° < 0$

Increasing Temperature

Blue line: $\Delta H° < 0$ and $\Delta S° < 0$. Favored at low T. Red line: $\Delta H° > 0$ and $\Delta S° > 0$. Favored at high T.

$\Delta G° > 0$

$\Delta S°$ negative $\Delta H° > 0$

$\Delta G° < 0$

Increasing Temperature

$\Delta H° > 0$ and $\Delta S° < 0$. Reactant-favored at all temperatures.

Reactant-favored reactions $\Delta G° = \Delta H° - T\Delta S° > 0$

Product-favored reactions $\Delta G° = \Delta H° - T\Delta S° < 0$

Photos: Charles D. Winters

Active Figure 19.12 The variation in $\Delta_r G°$ with temperature.

Chemistry ⦶ Now™ Sign in at www.cengage.com/login and go to the Chapter Contents menu to explore an interactive version of this figure accompanied by an exercise.

and reactant-favored at another. Those instances arise when the $\Delta_r H°$ and $T\Delta_r S°$ terms work in opposite directions:

- Processes that are entropy-favored ($\Delta_r S° > 0$) and enthalpy-disfavored ($\Delta_r H° > 0$)
- Processes that are enthalpy-favored ($\Delta_r H° < 0$) and entropy-disfavored ($\Delta_r S° < 0$)

Let us explore the relationship of $\Delta G°$ and T further and illustrate how it can be used to advantage.

Calcium carbonate is the primary component of limestone, marble, and seashells. Heating $CaCO_3$ produces lime, CaO, an important chemical, along with gaseous CO_2. The data below from Appendix L are at 298 K (25 °C).

	$CaCO_3(s)$	$\rightarrow$	$CaO(s)$	$+$	$CO_2(g)$
$\Delta_f G°$ (kJ/mol)	−1129.16		−603.42		−394.36
$\Delta_f H°$ (kJ/mol)	−1207.6		−635.09		−393.51
$S°$ (J/K · mol)	91.7		38.2		213.74

For the conversion of 1 mol of $CaCO_3(s)$ to 1 mol of $CaO(s)$ under standard conditions, $\Delta_r G° = +131.38$ kJ, $\Delta_r H° = +179.0$ kJ, and $\Delta_r S° = +160.2$ J/K. Although the reaction is entropy-favored, the large positive and unfavorable enthalpy change dominates at 298 K. Thus, the standard free energy change is positive at 298 K and 1 bar, indicating that the reaction is reactant-favored at equilibrium under the given conditions.

The temperature dependence of $\Delta_r G°$ provides a means to turn the $CaCO_3$ decomposition into a product-favored reaction. Notice that the entropy change in the reaction is positive as a result of the formation of CO_2 gas in the reaction. Thus, raising the temperature results in the value of $T\Delta_r S°$ becoming increasingly large. At a high enough temperature, $T\Delta_r S°$ will outweigh the enthalpy effect, and the process will become product-favored at equilibrium.

How high must the temperature be for this reaction to become product-favored? An estimate of the temperature can be obtained using Equation 19.5, by calculating the temperature at which $\Delta_r G° = 0$. Above that temperature, $\Delta_r G°$ will have a negative value.

$$\Delta_r G° = \Delta_r H° - T\Delta_r S°$$

$$0 = (179.0 \text{ kJ/mol-rxn})(1000 \text{ J/kJ}) - T(160.2 \text{ J/K} \cdot \text{mol-rxn})$$

$$T = 1117 \text{ K (or 844 °C)}$$

How accurate is this result? As noted earlier, we can obtain only an approximate answer from this calculation. One source of error is the assumption that $\Delta_r H°$ and $\Delta S°$ do not vary with temperature, which is not strictly true. There is always a small variation in these values when the temperature changes—not large enough to be important if the temperature range is narrow, but potentially a problem over wider temperature ranges such as seen in this example. As an estimate, however, a temperature in the range of 850 °C for this reaction is reasonable.

■ **$CaCO_3$ Decomposition** Experiments show that the pressure of CO_2 in an equilibrium system [$CaCO_3(s) \rightleftharpoons CaO(s) + CO_2(g)$; $\Delta G° = 0$] is 1 bar at about 900 °C, close to our estimated temperature.

Chemistry.ⓐ.Now™

Sign in at **www.cengage.com/login** and go to Chapter 19 Contents to see Screen 19.8 for a simulation and tutorial on **the relationship of $\Delta H°$, $\Delta S°$, and T.**

■ **EXAMPLE 19.6 Effect of Temperature on $\Delta_r G°$**

Problem The decomposition of liquid $Ni(CO)_4$ to produce nickel metal and carbon monoxide has a $\Delta_r G°$ value of 40 kJ/mol-rxn at 25 °C.

$$Ni(CO)_4(\ell) \rightarrow Ni(s) + 4 CO(g)$$

Use values of $\Delta_f H°$ and $S°$ for the reactant and products to estimate the temperature at which the reaction becomes product-favored at equilibrium.

Strategy The reaction is reactant-favored at equilibrium at 298 K. However, if the entropy change is positive for the reaction and the reaction is endothermic (with a positive value of $\Delta_r H°$), then a higher temperature may allow the reaction to become product-favored at equilibrium. Therefore, we first find $\Delta_r H°$ and $\Delta_r S°$ to see if their values meet our criteria for spontaneity at a higher temperature, and then we calculate the temperature at which the following condition is met: $0 = \Delta_r H° - T\Delta_r S°$.

Solution Values for $\Delta_f H°$ and $S°$ are obtained from the chemical literature for the substances involved.

	$Ni(CO)_4(\ell)$	→	Ni(s)	+	4 CO(g)
$\Delta_f H°$(kJ/mol)	−632.0		0		−110.525
$S°$(J/K · mol)	320.1		29.87		197.67

For a process in which 1 mol of liquid $Ni(CO)_4$ is converted to 1 mol of Ni(s) and 4 mol of CO(g), we find

$$\Delta_r H° = +189.9 \text{ kJ/mol-rxn}$$

$$\Delta_r S° = +500.5 \text{ J/K mol-rxn}$$

At 298 K, the reaction is reactant-favored at equilibrium largely because it is quite endothermic. However, a positive entropy change should allow the reaction to be product-favored at equilibrium at a higher temperature. Therefore, we use the values of $\Delta_r H°$ and $\Delta_r S°$ to find the temperature at which $\Delta_r G° = 0$.

$$\Delta_r G° = \Delta_r H° - T\Delta_r S°$$
$$0 = (189.9 \text{ kJ/mol-rxn})(1000 \text{ J/kJ}) - T(500.5 \text{ J/K} \cdot \text{mol-rxn})$$
$$T = \boxed{379.4 \text{ K (or 106.2 °C)}}$$

Case Study

Thermodynamics and Living Things

The laws of thermodynamics apply to all chemical reactions. It should come as no surprise, therefore, that issues of spontaneity and ΔG arise in studies of biochemical reactions. For biochemical processes, however, a different standard state is often used. Most of the usual definition is retained: 1 bar pressure for gases and 1 m concentration for aqueous solutes with the exception of one very important solute. Rather than using a standard state of 1 molal for hydronium ions (corresponding to a pH of about 0), biochemists use a hydronium concentration of 1×10^{-7} M, corresponding to a pH of 7. This pH is much more useful for biochemical reactions. When biochemists use this as the standard state, they write the symbol ' next to the thermodynamic function. For example, they would write $\Delta G°'$ (pronounced *delta G zero prime*).

Living things require energy to perform their many functions. One of the main reactions involved in providing this energy is the reaction of adenosine triphosphate (ATP) with water, a reaction for which $\Delta_r G°' = -30.5$ kJ/mol-rxn (◄ *The Chemistry of Life: Biochemistry*).

ATP, adenosine triphosphate

One of the key functions of the process of respiration is to produce molecules of ATP for our bodies to use. ATP is produced in the reaction of adenosine diphosphate (ADP) with hydrogen phosphate (HP$_i$ = HPO$_4^{2-}$),

$$\text{ADP} + \text{HP}_i + \text{H}^+ \rightarrow \text{ATP} + \text{H}_2\text{O}$$
$$\Delta_r G°' = + 30.5 \text{ kJ/mol}$$

a reaction that is reactant-favored at equilibrium. How then do our bodies get this reaction to occur? The answer is to couple the production of ATP with another reaction that is even more product-favored than ATP production is reactant-favored. For example, organisms carry out the oxidation of carbohydrates in a multistep process, producing energy. One of the compounds produced in the process called *glycolysis* is phosphoenolpyruvate (PEP).

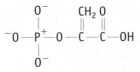

PEP, phosphoenolpyruvate

Its reaction with water is product-favored at equilibrium

$$\text{PEP} + \text{H}_2\text{O} \rightarrow \text{Pyruvate} + \text{HP}_i$$
$$\Delta_r G°' = - 61.9 \text{ kJ/mol}$$

This reaction and the ATP formation are linked through the HP$_i$ that is produced in the PEP reaction. If both reactions are carried out, we obtain the following

$$\text{PEP} + \text{H}_2\text{O} \rightarrow \text{Pyruvate} + \text{HP}_i$$
$$\Delta_r G°' = -61.9 \text{ kJ/mol}$$

$$\text{ADP} + \text{HP}_i + \text{H}^+ \rightarrow \text{ATP} + \text{H}_2\text{O}$$
$$\Delta_r G°' = + 30.5 \text{ kJ/mol}$$

$$\text{PEP} + \text{ADP} + \text{H}^+ \rightarrow \text{Pyruvate} + \text{ATP}$$
$$\Delta_r G°' = -31.4 \text{ kJ/mol}$$

The overall reaction has a negative value for $\Delta_r G°'$ and thus is product-favored at equilibrium. ATP is formed in this process.

The coupling of reactions to produce a system that is product-favored is used in a multitude of reactions that occur in our bodies.

John Kotz

Living things use ATP to produce energy.

Questions:

1. *Consider the hydrolysis reactions of cre* phosphate *and adenosine-5'-monophc*

   Creatine Phosphate + H_2O
   $\rightarrow$ *Creatin*
   $$\Delta_r G°' = -43.3 \text{ kJ/mol}$$

   Adenosine-5'-Monophosphate + H_2O
   $\rightarrow$ *adenosine* + *H*
   $$\Delta_r G°' = -9.2 \text{ kJ/mol}$$

   In which direction does a reaction th product-favored at equilibrium resul creatine phosphate to transfer phosp to adenosine or for adenosine-5'-mc phosphate to transfer phosphate to atine?

2. *Assume the reaction* $A(aq) + B(aq)$
   $\rightarrow C(aq) + H_3O^+(aq)$ *produces one* nium *ion. What is the mathematical tionship between* $\Delta G°'$ *and* $\Delta G°$ *at (Hint: Use the equation* $\Delta G = \Delta G°$ ln$Q$ *and substitute* $\Delta G°'$ *for* ΔG.)

Answers to these questions are in Append

Oxygen was first prepared by Joseph Priestley (1733–1804) by heating HgO. Use data in Appendix L to estimate the temperature required to decompose HgO(s) into Hg(ℓ) and O_2(g).

Using the Relationship Between $\Delta_r G°$ and K

Equation 19.7 provides a direct route to determine the standard free energy change from experimentally determined equilibrium constants. Alternatively, it allows calculation of an equilibrium constant from thermochemical data contained in tables or obtained from an experiment.

Chemistry◌̇Now™

Sign in at **www.cengage.com/login** and go to Chapter 19 Contents to see Screen 19.9 for a simulation and tutorial on $\Delta G°$ and K.

EXAMPLE 19.7 **Calculating K_p from $\Delta_r G°$**

Problem Determine the standard free energy change, $\Delta_r G°$, for the formation of 1.00 mol of NH_3(g) from nitrogen and hydrogen, and use this value to calculate the equilibrium constant for this reaction at 25 °C.

Strategy The free energy of formation of ammonia represents the free energy change to form 1.00 mol of NH_3(g) from the elements. The equilibrium constant for this reaction is calculated from $\Delta_r G°$ using Equation 19.7. Because the reactants and products are gases, the calculated value will be K_p.

Solution Begin by specifying a balanced equation for the chemical reaction under investigation.

$$\tfrac{1}{2} N_2(g) + \tfrac{3}{2} H_2(g) \rightleftharpoons NH_3(g)$$

The free energy change for this reaction is −16.37 kJ/mol-rxn ($\Delta_r G° = \Delta_f G°$ for NH_3(g); Appendix L). In a calculation of K_p using Equation 19.7, we will need consistent units. The gas constant, R, is 8.3145 J/ K·mol, so the value of $\Delta_r G°$ must be in J/mol-rxn (and not kJ/mol-rxn). The temperature is 298 K.

$$\Delta_r G° = -RT \ln K$$

$$-16{,}370 \text{ J/mol-rxn} = (-8.3145 \text{ J/K·mol-rxn})(298.15 \text{ K}) \ln K_p$$

$$\ln K_p = 6.604$$

$$\boxed{K_p = 7.38 \times 10^2}$$

Comment This example illustrates how to calculate equilibrium constants from thermodynamic data. In fact, many equilibrium constants you find in the chemical literature are not experimentally determined but are instead calculated from thermodynamic data in this way.

EXAMPLE 19.8 **Calculating $\Delta_r G°$ from K_{sp} for an Insoluble Solid**

Problem The value of K_{sp} for AgCl(s) at 25 °C is 1.8×10^{-10}. Use this value in Equation 19.7 to determine $\Delta_r G°$ for the process Ag^+(aq) + Cl^-(aq) $\rightleftharpoons$ AgCl(s) at 25 °C.

Strategy The chemical equation given is the opposite of the equation used to define K_{sp}; therefore, the equilibrium constant for this reaction is $1/K_{sp}$. This value is used to calculate $\Delta_r G°$.

Solution For Ag^+(aq) + Cl^-(aq) $\rightleftharpoons$ AgCl(s),

$$K = 1/K_{sp} = 1/ 1.8 \times 10^{-10} = 5.6 \times 10^9$$

$$\Delta_r G° = -RT \ln K = -(8.3145 \text{ J/K·mol-rxn})(298.15 \text{ K}) \ln(5.6 \times 10^9)$$

$$= \boxed{-56 \text{ kJ/mol-rxn}}$$

Comment The negative value of $\Delta_r G°$ indicates that the precipitation of AgCl from Ag^+(aq) and Cl^-(aq) is product-favored at equilibrium.

Chapter Goals Revisited

Now that you have studied this chapter, you should ask whether you have met the chapter goals. In particular, you should be able to:

Understand the concept of entropy and its relationship to reaction spontaneity

a. Understand that entropy is a measure of energy dispersal (Section 19.2). Study Question(s) assignable in OWL: 2.

b. Recognize that an entropy change can be determined experimentally as the energy transferred as heat for a reversible process divided by the Kelvin temperature. (*A Closer Look*, Section 19.3.) Study Question(s) assignable in OWL: 40.

c. Identify common processes that are entropy favored (Section 19.4).

Calculate the change in entropy for system, surroundings, and the universe to determine whether a process is spontaneous

a. Calculate entropy changes from tables of standard entropy values for compounds (Section 19.4). Study Question(s) assignable in OWL: 4, 6, 11.

b. Use standard entropy and enthalpy changes to predict whether a reaction will be spontaneous under standard conditions (Section 19.5 and Table 19.2). Study Question(s) assignable in OWL: 10, 12, 33, 35, 47, 55, 67, 72.

c. Recognize how temperature influences whether a reaction is spontaneous (Section 19.5). Study Question(s) assignable in OWL: 14, 25, 26.

Understand and use the Gibbs free energy

a. Understand the connection between enthalpy and entropy changes and the Gibbs free energy change for a process (Section 19.6).

b. Understand the relationship of $\Delta_r G$, $\Delta_r G°$, Q, K, reaction spontaneity, and product- or reactant-favorability (Section 19.6).

Q	ΔG	Spontaneous?
$Q < K$	$\Delta G < 0$	Spontaneous to the right as the equation is written
$Q = K$	$\Delta G = 0$	Reaction is at equilibrium
$Q > K$	$\Delta G > 0$	Not spontaneous to the right; spontaneous to the left

K	$\Delta G°$	Reactant-Favored or Product-Favored at Equilibrium?	Spontaneous Under Standard Conditions?
$K \gg 1$	$\Delta G° < 0$	Product-favored	Spontaneous under standard conditions
$K = 1$	$\Delta G° = 0$	$[C]^c[D]^d = [A]^a[B]^b$ at equilibrium	At equilibrium under standard conditions
$K \ll 1$	$\Delta G° > 0$	Reactant-favored	Not spontaneous under standard conditions

c. Describe and use the relationship between the free energy change under standard conditions and equilibrium constants, and calculate K from $\Delta_r G°$ (Sections 19.6 and 19.7). Study Question(s) assignable in OWL: 28, 30, 44, 48, 50, 61; Go Chemistry Module 24.

d. Calculate the change in free energy at standard conditions for a reaction from the enthalpy and entropy changes under standard conditions or from the standard free energy of formation of reactants and products ($\Delta_f G°$) (Section 19.7). Study Question(s) assignable in OWL: 16, 18, 20, 22, 46, 56, 75, 79.

e. Know how free energy changes with temperature (Section 19.7). Study Question(s) assignable in OWL: 24, 57, 59, 60, 63, 65, 70.

KEY EQUATIONS

Equation 19.1 (page 863): Calculate the entropy change from the energy transferred as heat for a reversible process and the temperature at which it occurs.

$$\Delta S = \frac{q_{rev}}{T}$$

Equation 19.2 (page 866) The Boltzmann equation: The entropy of a system, S, is proportional to the number of accessible microstates, W, belonging to a given energy of a system or substance.

$$S = k \ln W$$

Equation 19.3 (page 870): Calculate the standard entropy change under standard conditions for a process from the tabulated entropies of the products and reactants.

$$\Delta_r S° = \Sigma S°(\text{products}) - \Sigma S°(\text{reactants})$$

Equation 19.4 (page 872): Calculate the total entropy change for a system and its surroundings, to determine whether a process is spontaneous under standard conditions.

$$\Delta S°(\text{universe}) = \Delta S°(\text{system}) + \Delta S°(\text{surroundings})$$

Equation 19.5 (page 877): Calculate the free energy change for a process from enthalpy and entropy changes.

$$\Delta_r G° = \Delta_r H° - T\Delta_r S°$$

Equation 19.6 (page 878): Relates the free energy change under nonstandard conditions ($\Delta_r G$) to the standard free energy change ($\Delta_r G°$) and the reaction quotient Q.

$$\Delta_r G = \Delta_r G° + RT \ln Q$$

Equation 19.7 (page 878): Relates the standard free energy change for a reaction and its equilibrium constant.

$$\Delta_r G° = -RT \ln K$$

Equation 19.8 (page 880): Calculate the standard free energy change for a reaction using tabulated values of $\Delta_f G°$.

$$\Delta_r G° = \Sigma \Delta_f G°(\text{products}) - \Sigma \Delta_f G°(\text{reactants})$$

STUDY QUESTIONS

OWL Online homework for this chapter may be assigned in OWL.

▲ denotes challenging questions.

■ denotes questions assignable in OWL.

Blue-numbered questions have answers in Appendix O and fully-worked solutions in the *Student Solutions Manual*.

Practicing Skills

Entropy
(See Examples 19.1 and 19.2 and ChemistryNow Screens 19.4 and 19.5.)

1. Which substance has the higher entropy?
   (a) dry ice (solid CO_2) at -78 °C or $CO_2(g)$ at 0 °C
   (b) liquid water at 25 °C or liquid water at 50 °C
   (c) pure alumina, $Al_2O_3(s)$, or ruby (Ruby is Al_2O_3 in which some Al^{3+} ions in the crystalline lattice are replaced with Cr^{3+} ions.)
   (d) one mole of $N_2(g)$ at 1 bar pressure or one mole of $N_2(g)$ at 10 bar pressure (both at 298 K)

2. ■ Which substance has the higher entropy?
   (a) a sample of pure silicon (to be used in a computer chip) or a piece of silicon containing a trace of another element such as boron or phosphorus
   (b) $O_2(g)$ at 0 °C or $O_2(g)$ at −50 °C
   (c) $I_2(s)$ or $I_2(g)$, both at room temperature
   (d) one mole of $O_2(g)$ at 1 bar pressure or one mole of $O_2(g)$ at 0.01 bar pressure (both at 298 K)

3. Use $S°$ values to calculate the standard entropy change, $\Delta_r S°$, for each of the following processes and comment on the sign of the change.
   (a) $KOH(s) \rightarrow KOH(aq)$
   (b) $Na(g) \rightarrow Na(s)$
   (c) $Br_2(\ell) \rightarrow Br_2(g)$
   (d) $HCl(g) \rightarrow HCl(aq)$

4. ■ Use $S°$ values to calculate the standard entropy change, $\Delta_r S°$, for each of the following changes, and comment on the sign of the change.
   (a) $NH_4Cl(s) \rightarrow NH_4Cl(aq)$
   (b) $CH_3OH(\ell) \rightarrow CH_3OH(g)$
   (c) $CCl_4(g) \rightarrow CCl_4(\ell)$
   (d) $NaCl(s) \rightarrow NaCl(g)$

5. Calculate the standard entropy change for the formation of 1.0 mol of the following compounds from the elements at 25 °C.
   (a) $HCl(g)$ (b) $Ca(OH)_2(s)$

6. ■ Calculate the standard entropy change for the formation of 1.0 mol of the following compounds from the elements at 25 °C.
   (a) $H_2S(g)$ (b) $MgCO_3(s)$

7. ■ Calculate the standard entropy change for each of the following reactions at 25 °C. Comment on the sign of $\Delta_r S°$.
   (a) $2 Al(s) + 3 Cl_2(g) \rightarrow 2 AlCl_3(s)$
   (b) $2 CH_3OH(\ell) + 3 O_2(g) \rightarrow 2 CO_2(g) + 4 H_2O(g)$

8. Calculate the standard entropy change for each of the following reactions at 25 °C. Comment on the sign of $\Delta_r S°$.
   (a) $2 Na(s) + 2 H_2O(\ell) \rightarrow 2 NaOH(aq) + H_2(g)$
   (b) $Na_2CO_3(s) + 2 HCl(aq) \rightarrow 2 NaCl(aq) + H_2O(\ell) + CO_2(g)$

$\Delta_r S°$(universe) and Spontaneity
(See Example 19.3 and ChemistryNow Screen 19.6.)

9. Is the reaction $Si(s) + 2 Cl_2(g) \rightarrow SiCl_4(g)$ spontaneous under standard conditions at 298 K? Answer this question by calculating $\Delta S°$(system), $\Delta S°$(surroundings), and $\Delta S°$(universe). (Define reactants and products as the system.)

10. ■ Is the reaction $Si(s) + 2 H_2(g) \rightarrow SiH_4(g)$ spontaneous under standard conditions at 298 K? Answer this question by calculating calculating $\Delta S°$(system), $\Delta S°$(surroundings), and $\Delta S°$(universe). (Define reactants and products as the system.)

11. Calculate $\Delta S°$(universe) for the decomposition of 1 mol of liquid water to form gaseous hydrogen and oxygen. Is this reaction spontaneous under these conditions at 25 °C? Explain your answer briefly.

12. ■ Calculate $\Delta S°$(universe) for the formation of 1 mol $HCl(g)$ from gaseous hydrogen and chlorine. Is this reaction spontaneous under these conditions at 25 °C? Explain your answer briefly.

13. Classify each of the reactions according to one of the four reaction types summarized in Table 19.2.
   (a) $Fe_2O_3(s) + 2 Al(s) \rightarrow 2 Fe(s) + Al_2O_3(s)$

   $\Delta_r H° = -851.5$ kJ/mol-rxn
   $$\Delta_r S° = -375.2 \text{ J/K} \cdot \text{mol-rxn}$$

   (b) $N_2(g) + 2 O_2(g) \rightarrow 2 NO_2(g)$

   $\Delta_r H° = 66.2$ kJ/mol-rxn
   $$\Delta_r S° = -121.6 \text{ J/K} \cdot \text{mol-rxn}$$

14. ■ Classify each of the reactions according to one of the four reaction types summarized in Table 19.2.
   (a) $C_6H_{12}O_6(s) + 6 O_2(g) \rightarrow 6 CO_2(g) + 6 H_2O(\ell)$

   $\Delta_r H° = -673$ kJ/mol-rxn
   $$\Delta_r S° = 60.4 \text{ J/K} \cdot \text{mol-rxn}$$

   (b) $MgO(s) + C(graphite) \rightarrow Mg(s) + CO(g)$

   $\Delta_r H° = 490.7$ kJ/mol-rxn
   $$\Delta_r S° = 197.9 \text{ J/K} \cdot \text{mol-rxn}$$

Gibbs Free Energy
(See Example 19.4; see ChemistryNow Screen 19.7.)

15. Using values of $\Delta_f H°$ and $S°$, calculate $\Delta_r G°$ for each of the following reactions at 25 °C.
   (a) $2 Pb(s) + O_2(g) \rightarrow 2 PbO(s)$
   (b) $NH_3(g) + HNO_3(aq) \rightarrow NH_4NO_3(aq)$

   Which of these reactions is (are) predicted to be product-favored at equilibrium? Are the reactions enthalpy- or entropy-driven?

16. ■ Using values of $\Delta_f H°$ and $S°$, calculate $\Delta_r G°$ for each of the following reactions at 25 °C.
   (a) $2 Na(s) + 2 H_2O(\ell) \rightarrow 2 NaOH(aq) + H_2(g)$
   (b) $6 C(graphite) + 3 H_2(g) \rightarrow C_6H_6(\ell)$

   Which of these reactions is (are) predicted to be product-favored at equilibrium? Are the reactions enthalpy- or entropy-driven?

17. Using values of $\Delta_f H°$ and $S°$, calculate the standard molar free energy of formation, $\Delta_f G°$, for each of the following compounds:
   (a) $CS_2(g)$
   (b) $NaOH(s)$
   (c) $ICl(g)$

   Compare your calculated values of $\Delta_f G°$ with those listed in Appendix L. Which of these formation reactions are predicted to be spontaneous under standard conditions at 25 °C?

▲ more challenging   ■ in OWL   Blue-numbered questions answered in Appendix O

18. ■ Using values of $\Delta_f H°$ and $S°$, calculate the standard molar free energy of formation, $\Delta_f G°$, for each of the following:
   (a) $Ca(OH)_2(s)$
   (b) $Cl(g)$
   (c) $Na_2CO_3(s)$

   Compare your calculated values of $\Delta_f G°$ with those listed in Appendix L. Which of these formation reactions are predicted to be spontaneous under standard conditions at 25 °C?

Free Energy of Formation
(See Example 19.5; see ChemistryNow Screen 19.7.)

19. Using values of $\Delta_f G°$, calculate $\Delta_r G°$ for each of the following reactions at 25 °C. Which are product-favored at equilibrium?
   (a) $2\ K(s) + Cl_2(g) \rightarrow 2\ KCl(s)$
   (b) $2\ CuO(s) \rightarrow 2\ Cu(s) + O_2(g)$
   (c) $4\ NH_3(g) + 7\ O_2(g) \rightarrow 4\ NO_2(g) + 6\ H_2O(g)$

20. ■ Using values of $\Delta_f G°$, calculate $\Delta_r G°$ for each of the following reactions at 25 °C. Which are product-favored at equilibrium?
   (a) $HgS(s) + O_2(g) \rightarrow Hg(\ell) + SO_2(g)$
   (b) $2\ H_2S(g) + 3\ O_2(g) \rightarrow 2\ H_2O(g) + 2\ SO_2(g)$
   (c) $SiCl_4(g) + 2\ Mg(s) \rightarrow 2\ MgCl_2(s) + Si(s)$

21. For the reaction $BaCO_3(s) \rightarrow BaO(s) + CO_2(g)$, $\Delta_r G° = +219.7$ kJ. Using this value and other data available in Appendix L, calculate the value of $\Delta_f G°$ for $BaCO_3(s)$.

22. ■ For the reaction $TiCl_2(s) + Cl_2(g) \rightarrow TiCl_4(\ell)$, $\Delta_r G° = -272.8$ kJ. Using this value and other data available in Appendix L, calculate the value of $\Delta_f G°$ for $TiCl_2(s)$.

Effect of Temperature on ΔG
(See Example 19.6 and ChemistryNow Screen 19.8.)

23. Determine whether the reactions listed below are entropy-favored or disfavored under standard conditions. Predict how an increase in temperature will affect the value of $\Delta_r G°$.
   (a) $N_2(g) + 2\ O_2(g) \rightarrow 2\ NO_2(g)$
   (b) $2\ C(s) + O_2(g) \rightarrow 2\ CO(g)$
   (c) $CaO(s) + CO_2(g) \rightarrow CaCO_3(s)$
   (d) $2\ NaCl(s) \rightarrow 2\ Na(s) + Cl_2(g)$

24. ■ Determine whether the reactions listed below are entropy-favored or disfavored under standard conditions. Predict how an increase in temperature will affect the value of $\Delta_r G°$.
   (a) $I_2(g) \rightarrow 2\ I(g)$
   (b) $2\ SO_2(g) + O_2(g) \rightarrow 2\ SO_3(g)$
   (c) $SiCl_4(g) + 2\ H_2O(\ell) \rightarrow SiO_2(s) + 4\ HCl(g)$
   (d) $P_4(s, \text{white}) + 6\ H_2(g) \rightarrow 4\ PH_3(g)$

25. ■ Heating some metal carbonates, among them magnesium carbonate, leads to their decomposition.

$$MgCO_3(s) \rightarrow MgO(s) + CO_2(g)$$

   (a) Calculate $\Delta_r H°$ and $\Delta_r S°$ for the reaction.
   (b) Is the reaction spontaneous under standard conditions at 298 K?
   (c) Is the reaction predicted to be spontaneous at higher temperatures?

26. ■ Calculate $\Delta_r H°$ and $\Delta_r S°$ for the reaction of tin(IV) oxide with carbon.

$$SnO_2(s) + C(s) \rightarrow Sn(s) + CO_2(g)$$

   (a) Is the reaction spontaneous under standard conditions at 298 K?
   (b) Is the reaction predicted to be spontaneous at higher temperatures?

Free Energy and Equilibrium Constants
(See Example 19.7; use $\Delta G° = -RT \ln K$; see ChemistryNow Screen 19.9.)

27. The standard free energy change, $\Delta_r G°$, for the formation of $NO(g)$ from its elements is $+86.58$ kJ/mol at 25 °C. Calculate K_p at this temperature for the equilibrium

$$\tfrac{1}{2} N_2(g) + \tfrac{1}{2} O_2(g) \rightleftharpoons NO(g)$$

   Comment on the sign of $\Delta G°$ and the magnitude of K_p.

28. ■ The standard free energy change, $\Delta_r G°$, for the formation of $O_3(g)$ from $O_2(g)$ is $+163.2$ kJ/mol at 25 °C. Calculate K_p at this temperature for the equilibrium

$$3\ O_2(g) \rightleftharpoons 2\ O_3(g)$$

   Comment on the sign of $\Delta G°$ and the magnitude of K_p.

29. Calculate $\Delta_r G°$ at 25 °C for the formation of one mol of $C_2H_6(g)$ from $C_2H_4(g)$ and $H_2(g)$. Use this value to calculate K_p for the equilibrium.

$$C_2H_4(g) + H_2(g) \rightleftharpoons C_2H_6(g)$$

   Comment on the sign of $\Delta_r G°$ and the magnitude of K_p.

30. ■ Calculate $\Delta_r G°$ at 25 °C for the formation of 1 mol of $C_2H_5OH(g)$ from $C_2H_4(g)$ and $H_2O(g)$. Use this value to calculate K_p for the equilibrium.

$$C_2H_4(g) + H_2O(g) \rightleftharpoons C_2H_5OH(g)$$

   Comment on the sign of $\Delta_r G°$ and the magnitude of K_p.

General Questions

These questions are not designated as to type or location in the chapter. They may combine several concepts.

31. Compare the formulas in each set of compounds, and decide which is expected to have the higher entropy. Assume all are at the same temperature. Check your answers using data in Appendix L.
    (a) $HF(g)$, $HCl(g)$, or $HBr(g)$
    (b) $NH_4Cl(s)$ or $NH_4Cl(aq)$
    (c) $C_2H_4(g)$ or $N_2(g)$ (two substances with the same molar mass)
    (a) $NaCl(s)$ or $NaCl(g)$

32. Using standard entropy values, calculate $\Delta_rS°$ for the formation of 1.0 mol of $NH_3(g)$ from $N_2(g)$ and $H_2(g)$ at 25 °C.

33. ■ About 5 billion kilograms of benzene, C_6H_6, are made each year. Benzene is used as a starting material for many other compounds and as a solvent (although it is also a carcinogen, and its use is restricted). One compound that can be made from benzene is cyclohexane, C_6H_{12}.

    $$C_6H_6(\ell) + 3\ H_2(g) \rightarrow C_6H_{12}(\ell)$$

    $$\Delta_rH° = -206.7\ kJ;\ \Delta_rS° = -361.5\ J/K$$

    Is this reaction predicted to be product-favored at equilibrium at 25 °C? Is the reaction enthalpy- or entropy-driven?

34. Hydrogenation, the addition of hydrogen to an organic compound, is an industrially important reaction. Calculate $\Delta_rH°$, $\Delta_rS°$, and $\Delta_rG°$ for the hydrogenation of octene, C_8H_{16}, to give octane, C_8H_{18}, at 25 °C. Is the reaction product- or reactant-favored at equilibrium?

    $$C_8H_{16}(g) + H_2(g) \rightarrow C_8H_{18}(g)$$

    Along with data in Appendix L, the following information is needed for this calculation.

Compound	$\Delta_fH°$ (kJ/mol)	$S°$ (J/K · mol)
Octene	−82.93	462.8
Octane	−208.45	463.639

35. ■ Is the combustion of ethane, C_2H_6, product-favored at equilibrium at 25 °C?

    $$C_2H_6(g) + \tfrac{7}{2}\ O_2(g) \rightarrow 2CO_2(g) + 3\ H_2O(g)$$

    Answer the question by calculating the value of $\Delta S°$ (universe) at 298 K, using values of $\Delta_fH°$ and $S°$ in Appendix L. Does the answer agree with your preconceived idea of this reaction?

36. Write a balanced equation that depicts the formation of 1 mol of $Fe_2O_3(s)$ from its elements. What is the standard free energy of formation of 1.00 mol of $Fe_2O_3(s)$? What is the value of $\Delta G°$ when 454 g (1 lb) of $Fe_2O_3(s)$ is formed from the elements?

37. When vapors from hydrochloric acid and aqueous ammonia come in contact, they react, producing a white "cloud" of solid NH_4Cl (Figure 19.10).

    $$HCl(g) + NH_3(g) \rightleftharpoons NH_4Cl(s)$$

    Defining the reactants and products as the system under study:
    (a) Predict whether $\Delta S°$(system), $\Delta S°$(surroundings), $\Delta S°$(universe), $\Delta_rH°$, and $\Delta_rG°$ (at 298 K) are greater than zero, equal to zero, or less than zero; and explain your prediction. Verify your predictions by calculating values for each of these quantities.
    (b) Calculate the value of K_p for this reaction at 298 K.

38. Calculate $\Delta S°$(system), $\Delta S°$(surroundings), $\Delta S°$(universe) for each of the following processes at 298 K, and comment on how these systems differ.
    (a) $HNO_3(g) \rightarrow HNO_3(aq)$
    (b) $NaOH(s) \rightarrow NaOH(aq)$

39. Methanol is now widely used as a fuel in race cars. Consider the following reaction as a possible synthetic route to methanol.

    $$C(graphite) + \tfrac{1}{2}\ O_2(g) + 2\ H_2(g) \rightleftharpoons CH_3OH(\ell)$$

    Calculate K_p for the formation of methanol at 298 K using this reaction. Would a different temperature be better suited to this reaction?

40. ■ The enthalpy of vaporization of liquid diethyl ether, $(C_2H_5)_2O$, is 26.0 kJ/mol at the boiling point of 35.0 °C. Calculate $\Delta S°$ for a vapor-to-liquid transformation at 35.0 °C.

41. Calculate the entropy change, $\Delta S°$, for the vaporization of ethanol, C_2H_5OH, at its normal boiling point, 78.0 °C. The enthalpy of vaporization of ethanol is 39.3 kJ/mol.

42. Using thermodynamic data, estimate the normal boiling point of ethanol. (Recall that liquid and vapor are in equilibrium at 1.0 atm pressure at the normal boiling point.) The actual normal boiling point is 78 °C. How well does your calculated result agree with the actual value?

43. The following reaction is reactant-favored at equilibrium at room temperature.

    $$COCl_2(g) \rightarrow CO(g) + Cl_2(g)$$

    Will raising or lowering the temperature make it product-favored?

44. ■ When calcium carbonate is heated strongly, CO_2 gas is evolved. The equilibrium pressure of CO_2 is 1.00 bar at 897 °C, and $\Delta_rH°$ at 298 K is 179.0 kJ.

    $$CaCO_3(s) \rightarrow CaO(s) + CO_2(g)$$

    Estimate the value of $\Delta_rS°$ at 897 °C for the reaction.

▲ more challenging ■ in OWL Blue-numbered questions answered in Appendix O

45. Sodium reacts violently with water according to the equation

$$Na(s) + H_2O(\ell) \rightarrow NaOH(aq) + \tfrac{1}{2} H_2(g)$$

Without doing calculations, predict the signs of $\Delta_r H°$ and $\Delta_r S°$ for the reaction. Verify your prediction with a calculation.

46. ■ Yeast can produce ethanol by the fermentation of glucose ($C_6H_{12}O_6$), which is the basis for the production of most alcoholic beverages.

$$C_6H_{12}O_6(aq) \rightarrow 2\ C_2H_5OH(\ell) + 2\ CO_2(g)$$

Calculate $\Delta_r H°$, $\Delta_r S°$, and $\Delta_r G°$ for the reaction at 25 °C. Is the reaction product- or reactant-favored? In addition to the thermodynamic values in Appendix L, you will need the following data for $C_6H_{12}O_6(aq)$:

$\Delta_f H° = -1260.0$ kJ/mol; $S° = 289$ J/K · mol; and $\Delta_f G° = -918.8$ kJ/mol.

47. ■ Elemental boron, in the form of thin fibers, can be made by reducing a boron halide with H_2.

$$BCl_3(g) + \tfrac{3}{2} H_2(g) \rightarrow B(s) + 3HCl(g)$$

Calculate $\Delta_r H°$, $\Delta_r S°$, and $\Delta_r G°$ at 25 °C for this reaction. Is the reaction predicted to be product-favored at equilibrium at 25 °C? If so, is it enthalpy- or entropy-driven? [$S°$ for B(s) is 5.86 J/K · mol.]

48. ■ ▲ Estimate the vapor pressure of ethanol at 37 °C using thermodynamic data. Express the result in mm of mercury.

49. The equilibrium constant, K_p, for $N_2O_4(g) \rightleftharpoons$ $2\ NO_2(g)$ is 0.14 at 25 °C. Calculate $\Delta_r G°$ for the conversion of $N_2O_4(g)$ to $NO_2(g)$ from this constant, and compare this value with that determined from the $\Delta_f G°$ values in Appendix L.

50. ■ ▲ Estimate the boiling point of water in Denver, Colorado (where the altitude is 1.60 km and the atmospheric pressure is 630 mm Hg or 0.840 bar).

51. The equilibrium constant for the butane $\rightleftharpoons$ isobutane equilibrium at 25 °C is 2.50. Calculate $\Delta_r G°$ at this temperature in units of kJ/mol.

$$\text{butane} \quad \rightleftharpoons \quad \text{isobutane}$$

$$CH_3CH_2CH_2CH_3 \quad \rightleftharpoons \quad \underset{\displaystyle CH_3CHCH_3}{\overset{\displaystyle CH_3}{}}$$

$$K_c = \frac{[\text{isobutane}]}{[\text{butane}]} = 2.50 \text{ at } 298 \text{ K}$$

52. ■ A crucial reaction for the production of synthetic fuels is the conversion of coal to H_2 with steam. The chemical reaction is

$$C(s) + H_2O(g) \rightarrow CO(g) + H_2(g)$$

(a) Calculate $\Delta_r G°$ for this reaction at 25 °C, assuming C(s) is graphite.
(b) Calculate K_p for the reaction at 25 °C.
(c) Is the reaction predicted to be product-favored at equilibrium at 25 °C? If not, at what temperature will it become so?

53. Calculate $\Delta_r G°$ for the decomposition of sulfur trioxide to sulfur dioxide and oxygen.

$$2\ SO_3(g) \rightleftharpoons 2\ SO_2(g) + O_2(g)$$

(a) Is the reaction product-favored at equilibrium at 25 °C?
(b) If the reaction is not product-favored at 25 °C, is there a temperature at which it will become so? Estimate this temperature.
(c) What is the equilibrium constant for the reaction at 1500 °C?

54. Methanol can be made by partial oxidation of methane by $O_2(g)$.

$$CH_4(g) + \tfrac{1}{2} O_2(g) \rightleftharpoons CH_3OH(\ell)$$

(a) Determine $\Delta S°$(system), $\Delta S°$ (surroundings), and $\Delta S°$ (universe) for this process.
(b) Is this reaction product-favored at equilibrium at 25 °C?

55. ■ A cave in Mexico was recently discovered to have some interesting chemistry. Hydrogen sulfide, H_2S, reacts with oxygen in the cave to give sulfuric acid, which drips from the ceiling in droplets with a pH less than 1. The reaction occurring is

$$H_2S(g) + 2\ O_2(g) \rightarrow H_2SO_4(\ell)$$

Calculate $\Delta_r H°$, $\Delta_r S°$, and $\Delta_r G°$. Is the reaction product-favored at equilibrium at 25 °C? Is it enthalpy- or entropy-driven?

56. ■ Wet limestone is used to scrub SO_2 gas from the exhaust gases of power plants. One possible reaction gives hydrated calcium sulfite:

$$CaCO_3(s) + SO_2(g) + \tfrac{1}{2} H_2O(\ell) \rightleftharpoons$$
$$CaSO_3 \cdot \tfrac{1}{2} H_2O(s) + CO_2(g)$$

Another reaction gives hydrated calcium sulfate:

$$CaCO_3(s) + SO_2(g) + \tfrac{1}{2} H_2O(\ell) + \tfrac{1}{2} O_2(g) \rightleftharpoons$$
$$CaSO_4 \cdot \tfrac{1}{2} H_2O(s) + CO_2(g)$$

(a) Which is the more product-favored reaction? Use the data in the table on the next page and any other information needed in Appendix L to calculate $\Delta_r G°$ for each reaction at 25 °C.

	CaSO$_3$ · ½ H$_2$O(s)	CaSO$_4$ · ½ H$_2$O(s)
$\Delta_f H°$ (kJ/mol)	−1311.7	−1574.65
$S°$ (J/K · mol)	121.3	134.8

(b) Calculate $\Delta_r G°$ for the reaction

CaSO$_3$ · ½ H$_2$O(s) + ½ O$_2$(g) $\rightleftharpoons$ CaSO$_4$ · ½ H$_2$O(s)

Is this reaction product- or reactant-favored at equilibrium?

57. ■ Sulfur undergoes a phase transition between 80 and 100 °C.

$$S_8(\text{rhombic}) \rightarrow S_8(\text{monoclinic})$$

$\Delta_r H° = 3.213$ kJ/mol-rxn $\Delta_r S° = 8.7$ J/K · mol-rxn

(a) Estimate $\Delta_r G°$ for the transition at 80.0 °C and 110.0 °C. What do these results tell you about the stability of the two forms of sulfur at each of these temperatures?
(b) Calculate the temperature at which $\Delta_r G° = 0$. What is the significance of this temperature?

58. Calculate the entropy change for dissolving HCl gas in water at 25 °C. Is the sign of $\Delta S°$ what you expected? Why or why not?

In the Laboratory

59. ■ Some metal oxides can be decomposed to the metal and oxygen under reasonable conditions. Is the decomposition of silver(I) oxide product-favored at 25 °C?

$$2 \text{ Ag}_2\text{O(s)} \rightarrow 4 \text{ Ag(s)} + \text{O}_2(\text{g})$$

If not, can it become so if the temperature is raised? At what temperature does the reaction become product-favored?

60. ■ Copper(II) oxide, CuO, can be reduced to copper metal with hydrogen at higher temperatures.

$$\text{CuO(s)} + \text{H}_2(\text{g}) \rightarrow \text{Cu(s)} + \text{H}_2\text{O(g)}$$

Is this reaction product- or reactant-favored at equilibrium at 298 K?

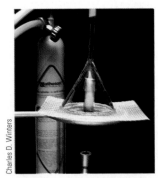

If copper metal is heated in air, a black film of CuO forms on the surface. In this photo, the heated bar, covered with a black CuO film, has been bathed in hydrogen gas. Black, solid CuO is reduced rapidly to copper at higher temperatures.

61. ■ Calculate $\Delta_f G°$ for HI(g) at 350 °C, given the following equilibrium partial pressures: $P(\text{H}_2) = 0.132$ bar, $P(\text{I}_2) = 0.295$ bar, and $P(\text{HI}) = 1.61$ bar. At 350 °C and 1 bar, I$_2$ is a gas.

$$\text{½ H}_2(\text{g}) + \text{½ I}_2(\text{g}) \rightleftharpoons \text{HI(g)}$$

62. ■ Calculate the equilibrium constant for the formation of NiO at 1627 °C. Can the reaction proceed in the forward direction if the initial pressure of O$_2$ is below 1.00 mm Hg? {$\Delta_f G°$ [NiO(s)] = −72.1 kJ/mol at 1627 °C}

$$\text{Ni(s)} + \text{½ O}_2(\text{g}) \rightleftharpoons \text{NiO(s)}$$

63. ■ Titanium(IV) oxide is converted to titanium carbide with carbon at a high temperature.

$$\text{TiO}_2(\text{s}) + 3 \text{ C(s)} \rightarrow 2 \text{ CO(g)} + \text{TiC(s)}$$

Compound	Free Energies of Formation at 727 °C, kJ/mol
TiO$_2$(s)	−757.8
TiC(s)	−162.6
CO(g)	−200.2

(a) Calculate $\Delta_r G°$ and K at 727 °C
(b) Is the reaction product-favored at equilibrium at this temperature?
(c) How can the reactant or product concentrations be adjusted for the reaction to be product-favored at 727 °C?

64. Cisplatin [*cis*-diamminedichloroplatinum(II)] is a potent treatment for certain types of cancers, but the *trans* isomer is not effective. (They are called *isomers* because the two compounds have the same formula but a different arrangement of atoms.) What is the equilibrium constant at 298 K for the transformation of the *cis* to the *trans* isomer? Which is more thermodynamically stable, the *cis* or the *trans* isomer?

Compound	$\Delta_f H°$ (kJ/mol, 298 K)	$\Delta_f G°$ (kJ/mol, 298 K)
Cis-Pt(NH$_3$)$_2$Cl$_2$	−467.4	−228.7
Trans-Pt(NH$_3$)$_2$Cl$_2$	−480.3	−222.8

cis isomer   trans isomer

▲ more challenging ■ in OWL Blue-numbered questions answered in Appendix O

Summary and Conceptual Questions

The following questions may use concepts from this and previous chapters.

65. ■ ▲ Mercury vapor is dangerous because it can be breathed into the lungs. We wish to estimate the vapor pressure of mercury at two different temperatures from the following data:

	$\Delta_f H°$ (kJ/mol)	$S°$ (J/K · mol)	$\Delta_f G°$ (kJ/mol)
Hg(ℓ)	0	76.02	0
Hg(g)	61.38	174.97	31.88

Estimate the temperature at which K_p for the process Hg(ℓ) $\rightleftharpoons$ Hg(g) is equal to (a) 1.00 and (b) 1/760. What is the vapor pressure at each of these temperatures? (Experimental vapor pressures are 1.00 mm Hg at 126.2 °C and 1.00 bar at 356.6 °C.) (Note: The temperature at which $P = 1.00$ bar can be calculated from thermodynamic data. To find the other temperature, you will need to use the temperature for $P = 1.00$ bar and the Clausius–Clapeyron equation on page 576.)

66. Explain why each of the following statements is incorrect.
    (a) Entropy increases in all spontaneous reactions.
    (b) Reactions with a negative free energy change ($\Delta_r G° < 0$) are product-favored and occur with rapid transformation of reactants to products.
    (c) All spontaneous processes are exothermic.
    (d) Endothermic processes are never spontaneous.

67. ■ Decide whether each of the following statements is true or false. If false, rewrite it to make it true.
    (a) The entropy of a substance increases on going from the liquid to the vapor state at any temperature.
    (b) An exothermic reaction will always be spontaneous.
    (c) Reactions with a positive $\Delta_r H°$ and a positive $\Delta_r S°$ can never be product-favored.
    (d) If $\Delta_r G°$ for a reaction is negative, the reaction will have an equilibrium constant greater than 1.

68. Under what conditions is the entropy of a pure substance 0 J/K · mol? Could a substance at standard conditions have a value of 0 J/K · mol? A negative entropy value? Are there any conditions under which a substance will have negative entropy? Explain your answer.

69. In Chapter 14, you learned that entropy, as well as enthalpy, plays a role in the solution process. If $\Delta H°$ for the solution process is zero, explain how the process can be driven by entropy.

70. ■ ▲ Consider the formation of NO(g) from its elements.

$$N_2(g) + O_2(g) \rightleftharpoons 2 \text{ NO}(g)$$

(a) Calculate K_p at 25 °C. Is the reaction product-favored at this temperature?
(b) Assuming $\Delta_r H°$ and $\Delta_r S°$ are nearly constant with temperature, calculate $\Delta_r G°$ at 700 °C. Estimate K_p from the new value of $\Delta_r G°$ at 700 °C. Is the reaction product-favored at 700 °C?
(c) Using K_p at 700 °C, calculate the equilibrium partial pressures of the three gases if you mix 1.00 bar each of N_2 and O_2.

71. Write a chemical equation for the oxidation of $C_2H_6(g)$ by $O_2(g)$ to form $CO_2(g)$ and $H_2O(g)$. Defining this as the system:
    (a) Predict whether the signs of $\Delta S°$ (system), $\Delta S°$ (surroundings), and $\Delta S°$ (universe) will be greater than zero, equal to zero, or less than zero. Explain your prediction.
    (b) Predict the signs of $\Delta_r H°$ and $\Delta_r G°$. Explain how you made this prediction.
    (c) Will the value of K_p be very large, very small, or near 1? Will the equilibrium constant, K_p, for this system be larger or smaller at temperatures greater than 298 K? Explain how you made this prediction.

72. ■ The normal melting point of benzene, C_6H_6, is 5.5 °C. For the process of melting, what is the sign of each of the following?
    (a) $\Delta H°$ (c) $\Delta G°$ at 5.5 °C   (e) $\Delta G°$ at 25.0 °C
    (b) $\Delta S°$ (d) $\Delta G°$ at 0.0 °C

73. Calculate the standard molar entropy change, $\Delta_r S°$, for each of the following reactions at 25 °C:

    1. $C(s) + 2 H_2(g) \rightarrow CH_4(g)$

    2. $CH_4(g) + \frac{1}{2} O_2(g) \rightarrow CH_3OH(\ell)$

    3. $C(s) + 2 H_2(g) + \frac{1}{2} O_2(g) \rightarrow CH_3OH(\ell)$

    Verify that these values are related by the equation $\Delta_r S°_1 + \Delta_r S°_2 = \Delta_r S°_3$. What general principle is illustrated here?

74. For each of the following processes, predict the algebraic sign of $\Delta_r H°$, $\Delta_r S°$, and $\Delta_r G°$. No calculations are necessary; use your common sense.
    (a) The decomposition of liquid water to give gaseous oxygen and hydrogen, a process that requires a considerable amount of energy.
    (b) Dynamite is a mixture of nitroglycerin, $C_3H_5N_3O_9$, and diatomaceous earth. The explosive decomposition of nitroglycerin gives gaseous products such as water, CO_2, and others; much heat is evolved.
    (c) The combustion of gasoline in the engine of your car, as exemplified by the combustion of octane.

    $$2 \text{ } C_8H_{18}(g) + 25 \text{ } O_2(g) \rightarrow 16 \text{ } CO_2(g) + 18 \text{ } H_2O(g)$$

75. ■ "Heater Meals" are food packages that contain their own heat source. Just pour water into the heater unit, wait a few minutes, and voilà! You have a hot meal.

$$Mg(s) + 2\,H_2O(\ell) \rightarrow Mg(OH)_2(s) + H_2(g)$$

Charles D. Winters

The heat for the heater unit is produced by the reaction of magnesium with water.

(a) Confirm that this is a spontaneous reaction under standard conditions.
(b) What mass of magnesium is required to produce sufficient energy to heat 225 mL of water (density = 0.995 g/mL) from 25 °C to the boiling point?

76. *Abba's Refrigerator* was described on page 222 is an example of the validity of the second law of thermodynamics. Explain how the second law applies to this simple but useful device.

77. Oxygen dissolved in water can cause corrosion in hot-water heating systems. To remove oxygen, hydrazine (N_2H_4) is often added. Hydrazine reacts with dissolved O_2 to form water and N_2.
(a) Write a balanced chemical equation for the reaction of hydrazine and oxygen. Identify the oxidizing and reducing agents in this redox reaction.
(b) Calculate $\Delta_r H°$, $\Delta_r S°$, and $\Delta_r G°$ for this reaction involving 1 mol of N_2H_4 at 25 °C.
(c) Because this is an exothermic reaction, energy is evolved as heat. What temperature change is expected in a heating system containing 5.5×10^4 L of water? (Assume no energy is lost to the surroundings.)
(d) The mass of a hot-water heating system is 5.5×10^4 kg. What amount of O_2 (in moles) would be present in this system if it is filled with water saturated with O_2? (The solubility of O_2 in water at 25 °C is 0.000434 g per 100 g of water.)
(e) Assume hydrazine is available as a 5.0% solution in water. What mass of this solution should be added to totally consume the dissolved O_2 [described in part (d)]?
(f) Assuming the N_2 escapes as a gas, calculate the volume of $N_2(g)$ (measured at 273 K and 1.00 bar) that will be produced.

78. The formation of diamond from graphite is a process of considerable importance.

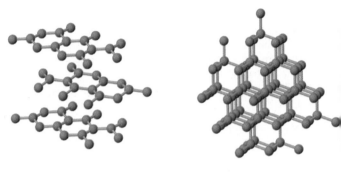

graphite   diamond

(a) Using data in Appendix L, calculate $\Delta_r S°$, $\Delta_r H°$, and $\Delta_r G°$ for this process at 25 °C.
(b) The calculations will suggest that this process is not possible at any temperature. However, the synthesis of diamonds by this reaction is a commercial process. How can this contradiction be rationalized? (Note: In the industrial synthesis, high pressure and high temperatures are used.)

79. ■ Iodine, I_2, dissolves readily in carbon tetrachloride. For this process, $\Delta H° = 0$ kJ/mol.

$$I_2(s) \rightarrow I_2 \text{ (in } CCl_4 \text{ solution)}$$

What is the sign of $\Delta_r G°$? Is the dissolving process entropy driven or enthalpy driven? Explain briefly.

80. Use the simulation on Screen 19.8 of ChemistryNow to answer the following questions.
(a) Consider the reaction of Fe_2O_3 and C. How does $\Delta_r G°$ vary with temperature? Is there a temperature at which the reaction is spontaneous?
(b) Consider the reaction of HCl and Na_2CO_3. Is there a temperature at which the reaction is no longer spontaneous?
(c) Is the spontaneity of a reaction dependent on or independent of temperature?

81. Use the simulation on Screen 19.6 of ChemistryNow to answer the following questions.
(a) Does the spontaneity of the decomposition of CH_3OH to the elements change as the temperature increases?
(b) Is there a temperature between 400 K and 1000 K at which the decomposition is spontaneous?

82. Use the simulation on Screen 19.6 of ChemistryNow to answer the following questions regarding the reaction of NO and Cl_2 to produce NOCl.
(a) What is $\Delta S°$ (system) at 400 K for this reaction?
(b) Does $\Delta S°$ (system) change with temperature?
(c) Does $\Delta S°$ (surroundings) change with temperature?

▲ more challenging   ■ in OWL   Blue-numbered questions answered in Appendix O

(d) Does $\Delta S°$(universe) always change with an increase in temperature?

(e) Do exothermic reactions always lead to positive values of $\Delta S°$(universe)?

(f) Is the NO + Cl$_2$ reaction spontaneous at 400 K? At 700 K?

83. ■ ▲ The Haber–Bosch process for the production of ammonia is one of the key processes in industrialized countries.

$$N_2(g) + 3\ H_2(g) \rightleftharpoons 2\ NH_3(g)$$

(a) Calculate $\Delta_r G°$ for the reaction at 298 K, 800 K, and 1300 K. Data at 298 K are in Appendix L. Data for the other temperatures are as follows:

Temperature	$\Delta_r H°$ (kJ/mol)	$\Delta_r S°$ (J/K · mol)
800 K	−107.4	−225.4
1300 K	−112.4	−228.0

How does the free energy change for the reaction change with temperature?

(b) Calculate the equilibrium constant for the reaction at 298 K, 800 K, and 1300 K.

(c) Calculate the mole fraction of ammonia in the equilibrium mixture at each of the temperatures. At what temperature is the mole fraction of NH$_3$ the largest?

84. ▲ Muscle cells need energy to contract. One biochemical pathway for energy transfer is the breakdown of glucose to pyruvate in a process called glycolysis. In the presence of sufficient oxygen in the cell, pyruvate is oxidized to CO$_2$ and H$_2$O to make further energy available. However, under extreme conditions not enough oxygen can be supplied to the cells, so muscle cells produce lactate ion according to the reaction

where $\Delta_r G°' = -25.1$ kJ/mol. In living cells, the pH value is about 7. The hydronium ion concentration is constant and is included in $\Delta G°$, which is then called $\Delta_r G°'$ (as explained on page 884). (This problem is taken from the problems for the 36th International Chemistry Olympiad for high school students held in Kiel, Germany in 2004.)

(a) Calculate $\Delta_r G°$ for the reaction at 25 °C.

(b) Calculate the equilibrium constant K'. (The hydronium ion concentration is included in the constant. That is, $K' = K \cdot [\text{H}_3\text{O}^+]$ for the reaction at 25 °C and pH = 7.0.)

(c) $\Delta_r G°'$ is the free energy change under standard conditions; that is, the concentrations of all reactants (except H$_3$O$^+$) are 1.00 mol/L. Calculate $\Delta_r G'$ at 25 °C, assuming the following concentrations in the cell: pyruvate, 380 μmol/L; NADH, 50 μmol/L; lactate ion, 3700 μmol/L; and NAD$^+$ ion, 540 μmol/L.

20 Principles of Reactivity: Electron Transfer Reactions

New euro coins that use different metal alloys.

Don't Hold onto That Money!

Nickel Allergy from Coins

Shortly after the new euro coins were introduced in European countries in 2002, people showed up in hospitals with strange allergies. These allergic reactions were soon identified as arising from nickel, presumably from the coins.

The surface of the 1- and 2-euro coins consists of a white Cu-Ni alloy (75% Cu and 25% Ni) and a yellow nickel-brass (75% Cu, 20% Zn, and 5% Ni). Skin tests with these coins showed that patients did get a rash from the coins, so there was initially quite a controversy about the coins. More extensive testing, however, showed that the euro coins did not release any more nickel than other coins with a similar composition.

Nickel allergy, caused by nickel(II) ions, is one of the most common causes of contact dermatitis, a skin inflammation that results in swollen, reddened, and itchy skin. Up to 15% of women are allergic to nickel, probably from nickel in less expensive costume jewelry. Unfortunately, there is no cure. One can only prevent it by staying away from nickel-containing objects, which is not easy to do because so many articles (such as watchbands, hairpins, eyeglass frames, paper clips, keys, and tools) contain nickel.

Questions:

Experiments show that metal ions, Ni^{2+} and Cu^{2+}, are present on the surface of coins, presumably from corrosion. In one experiment, the bimetallic euro coins were put in salty "artificial sweat," and the coins showed signs of significant corrosion. Under these conditions, the yellow outer ring of the 1-euro coin had a tiny negative charge, and the white inner portion had a slight positive charge.

1. What electrochemical reactions are possible that could involve Cu^{2+} and Ni or Ni^{2+} and Cu?
2. Could either reaction produce an electric current?
3. If such a reaction occurs under standard conditions, what is the value of the electric potential, $E°_{cell}$?

Answers to these questions are in Appendix Q.

Chapter Goals

OWL *See Chapter Goals Revisited (page 939) for Study Questions keyed to these goals and assignable in OWL.*

• Balance equations for oxidation–reduction reactions in acidic or basic solutions using the half-reaction approach.

• Understand the principles underlying voltaic cells.

• Understand how to use electrochemical potentials.

• Explore electrolysis, the use of electrical energy to produce chemical change.

Let us introduce you to electrochemistry and electron transfer reactions with a simple experiment. Place a piece of copper in an aqueous solution of silver nitrate. After a short time, metallic silver deposits on the copper, and the solution takes on the blue color typical of aqueous Cu^{2+} ions (Figure 20.1). The following oxidation–reduction (redox) reaction has occurred:

$$Cu(s) + 2\,Ag^{+}(aq) \rightarrow Cu^{2+}(aq) + 2\,Ag(s)$$

At the particulate level, Ag^{+} ions in solution come into direct contact with the copper surface where the transfer of electrons occurs. Two electrons are transferred

Chemistry ⚛ Now™

Throughout the text this icon introduces an opportunity for self-study or to explore interactive tutorials by signing in at **www.cengage.com/login**.

A clean piece of copper wire will be placed in a solution of silver nitrate, $AgNO_3$.

Add $AgNO_3$(aq)

With time, the copper reduces Ag^+ ions to silver metal crystals, and the copper metal is oxidized to copper ions, Cu^{2+}.

After several days

The blue color of the solution is due to the presence of aqueous copper(II) ions.

Silver ions in solution

Surface of copper wire

Cu^{2+}

Photos: Charles D. Winters

FIGURE 20.1 The oxidation of copper by silver ions. Note that water molecules are not shown for clarity. (See ChemistryNow for photographs of this reaction sequence.)

from a Cu atom to two Ag^+ ions. Copper ions, Cu^{2+}, enter the solution, and silver atoms are deposited on the copper surface. This product-favored reaction continues until one or both of the reactants is consumed.

The reaction between copper metal and silver ions can be used to generate an electric current if the experiment is carried out in a different way. If the reactants, $Cu(s)$ and $Ag^+(aq)$, are in direct contact, electrons will be transferred directly from copper atoms to silver ions, and an increase in temperature (heating) rather than electrical work will result. Instead, the reaction has to be done in an apparatus that allows electrons to be transferred from one reactant to the other through an electrical circuit. The movement of electrons through the circuit constitutes an electric current that can be used to light a light bulb or to run a motor.

Devices that use chemical reactions to produce an electric current are called **voltaic cells** or **galvanic cells**, names honoring Count Alessandro Volta (1745–1827) and Luigi Galvani (1737–1798). All voltaic cells work in the same general way. They use product-favored redox reactions composed of an oxidation and a reduction. The cell is constructed so that electrons produced by the reducing agent are transferred through an electric circuit to the oxidizing agent.

A voltaic cell converts chemical energy to electrical energy. The opposite process, the use of electric energy to effect a chemical change, occurs in **electrolysis**. An example is the electrolysis of water (Figure 1.12), in which electrical energy is used to split water into its component elements, hydrogen and oxygen. Electrolysis is also used to electroplate one metal onto another, to obtain aluminum from its common ore (bauxite, mostly Al_2O_3), and to prepare important chemicals such as chlorine.

Electrochemistry is the field of chemistry that considers chemical reactions that produce or are caused by electrical energy. Because all electrochemical reactions are oxidation–reduction (redox) reactions, we begin our exploration of this subject by first describing electron transfer reactions in more detail.

■ **Two Types of Electrochemical Processes**
• Chemical change can produce an electric current in a voltaic cell.
• Electric energy can cause chemical change in the process of electrolysis.

Module 25

20.1 Oxidation–Reduction Reactions

In an oxidation–reduction reaction, electron transfer occurs between a reducing agent and an oxidizing agent [see Section 3.9]. The essential features of all electron transfer reactions are as follows:

• One reactant is oxidized, and one is reduced.
• The extent of oxidation and reduction must balance.
• The oxidizing agent (the chemical species causing oxidation) is reduced.
• The reducing agent (the chemical species causing reduction) is oxidized.

These aspects of oxidation–reduction or redox reactions are illustrated for the reaction of copper metal and silver ion (Figure 20.1).

■ **Oxidation Numbers** Oxidation numbers (page 144) can be used to determine whether a substance is oxidized or reduced. An element is oxidized if its oxidation number increases. The oxidation number decreases in a reduction.

Cu oxidized, oxidation number increases;
Cu is the reducing agent.

$$Cu(s) + 2\,Ag^+(aq) \longrightarrow Cu^{2+}(aq) + 2\,Ag(s)$$

Ag^+ reduced, oxidation number decreases;
Ag^+ is the oxidizing agent.

Balancing Oxidation–Reduction Equations

All equations for oxidation–reduction reactions must be balanced for both mass and charge. The same number of atoms appear in the products and reactants of an equation, and the sum of electric charges of all the species on each side of the equation arrow must be the same. Charge balance guarantees that the number of electrons produced in oxidation equals the number of electrons consumed in reduction.

Balancing some redox equations can be complicated, but fortunately some systematic procedures can be used in these cases. Here, we describe the **half-reaction method**, a procedure that involves writing separate, balanced equations for the oxidation and reduction processes called half-reactions. One half-reaction describes the oxidation part of the reaction, and a second half-reaction describes the reduction part.

When a reaction has been determined to involve oxidation and reduction (by noting, for example, that oxidation state changes have occurred), the equation is separated into two half-reactions, which are then balanced for mass and charge. The equation for the overall reaction is then the sum of these two balanced half-reactions, after adjustments have been made (if necessary) in one or both half-reaction equations so that the numbers of electrons transferred from reducing agent to oxidizing agent balance. For example, the half-reactions for the reaction of copper metal with silver ions are

Reduction half-reaction: $Ag^+(aq) + e^- \rightarrow Ag(s)$

Oxidation half-reaction: $Cu(s) \rightarrow Cu^{2+}(aq) + 2\ e^-$

Notice that the equations for the half-reactions are themselves balanced for mass and charge. In the copper half-reaction, there is one Cu atom on each side of the equation (mass balance). The electric charge on the right side of the equation is 0 (the sum of $+2$ for the ion and -2 for two electrons), as it is on the left side (charge balance).

To produce the net chemical equation, we will add the two half-reactions. First, however, we must multiply the silver half-reaction by 2.

$$2\ Ag^+(aq) + 2\ e^- \rightarrow 2\ Ag(s)$$

Each mole of copper atoms produces two moles of electrons, and two moles of Ag^+ ions are required to consume those electrons.

Finally, adding the two half-reactions and canceling electrons from both sides leads to the net ionic equation for the reaction.

Reduction half-reaction: $2\ [Ag^+(aq) + e^- \rightarrow Ag(s)]$

Oxidation half-reaction: $Cu(s) \rightarrow Cu^{2+}(aq) + 2\ e^-$

Net ionic equation $Cu(s) + 2\ Ag^+(aq) \rightarrow Cu^{2+}(aq) + 2\ Ag(s)$

The resulting net ionic equation is balanced for mass and charge.

Chemistry ⚛ Now™

Sign in at **www.cengage.com/login** and go to Chapter 20 Contents to see:
- Screen 20.2 for a self-study module on various types of **oxidation–reduction reactions**
- Screen 20.3 for a self-study module on **methods of balancing redox reactions in acidic solution**

FIGURE 20.2 Reduction of Cu^{2+} by Al. (a) A ball of aluminum foil is added to a solution of $Cu(NO_3)_2$ and NaCl. (b) A coating of copper is soon seen on the surface of the aluminum, and the reaction generates a significant amount of heat. (Aluminum always has a thin coating of Al_2O_3 on the surface, which protects the metal from further reaction. However, in the presence of Cl^- ion, the coating is breached, and reaction occurs.) See Example 20.1.

Photos: Charles D. Winters

(a)　　　　　　　　(b)

■ **EXAMPLE 20.1 Balancing Oxidation–Reduction Equations**

Problem Balance the following net ionic equation

$$Al(s) + Cu^{2+}(aq) \rightarrow Al^{3+}(aq) + Cu(s)$$

Identify the oxidizing agent, the reducing agent, the substance oxidized, and the substance reduced. Write balanced half-reactions and the balanced net ionic equation. See Figure 20.2 for photographs of this reaction.

Strategy First, make sure the reaction is an oxidation–reduction reaction by checking each element to see whether the oxidation numbers change. Next, separate the equation into half-reactions, identifying what has been reduced (oxidizing agent) and what has been oxidized (reducing agent). Then balance the half-reactions, first for mass and then for charge. Finally, add the two half-reactions, after ensuring that the reducing agent half-reaction involves the same number of moles of electrons as the oxidizing agent half-reaction.

Solution

Step 1. Recognize the reaction as an oxidation–reduction reaction.

Here, the oxidation number for aluminum changes from 0 to +3, and the oxidation number of copper changes from +2 to 0. Aluminum is oxidized and serves as the reducing agent. Copper(II) ions are reduced, and Cu^{2+} is the oxidizing agent.

Step 2. Separate the process into half-reactions.

Reduction: $\qquad\qquad\qquad Cu^{2+}(aq) \rightarrow Cu(s)$
(Oxidation number of Cu decreases.)

Oxidation: $\qquad\qquad\qquad Al(s) \rightarrow Al^{3+}(aq)$
(Oxidation number of Al increases.)

Step 3. Balance each half-reaction for mass.

Both half-reactions are already balanced for mass.

Step 4. Balance each half-reaction for charge.

To balance the equations for charge, add electrons to the more positive side of each half-reaction.

Reduction: $\qquad\qquad 2\ e^- + Cu^{2+}(aq) \rightarrow Cu(s)$
Each Cu^{2+} ion requires two electrons.

Oxidation: $\qquad\qquad Al(s) \rightarrow Al^{3+}(aq) + 3\ e^-$
Each Al atom releases three electrons.

Step 5. Multiply each half-reaction by an appropriate factor.

The reducing agent must donate as many electrons as the oxidizing agent acquires. Three Cu^{2+} ions are required to take on the six electrons produced by two Al atoms. Thus, we multiply the Cu^{2+}/Cu half-reaction by 3 and the Al/Al^{3+} half-reaction by 2.

Reduction: $\qquad\qquad 3[2\ e^- + Cu^{2+}(aq) \rightarrow Cu(s)]$

Oxidation: $\qquad\qquad 2[Al(s) \rightarrow Al^{3+}(aq) + 3\ e^-]$

Step 6. Add the half-reactions to produce the overall balanced equation.

Reduction:	$6\,e^- + 3\,Cu^{2+}(aq) \rightarrow 3\,Cu(s)$
Oxidation:	$2\,Al(s) \rightarrow 2\,Al^{3+}(aq) + 6\,e^-$
Net ionic equation:	$3\,Cu^{2+}(aq) + 2\,Al(s) \rightarrow 3\,Cu(s) + 2\,Al^{3+}(aq)$

Step 7. Simplify by eliminating reactants and products that appear on both sides.

This step is not required here.

Comment You should always check the overall equation to ensure there is mass and charge balance. In this case, three Cu atoms and two Al atoms appear on each side. The net electric charge on each side is +6. The equation is balanced.

EXERCISE 20.1 Balancing Oxidation–Reduction Equations

Aluminum reacts with nonoxidizing acids to give $Al^{3+}(aq)$ and $H_2(g)$. The (unbalanced) equation is

$$Al(s) + H^+(aq) \rightarrow Al^{3+}(aq) + H_2(g)$$

Write balanced equations for the half-reactions and the balanced net ionic equation. Identify the oxidizing agent, the reducing agent, the substance oxidized, and the substance reduced.

■ **Balancing Equations in Acid Solution** To simplify equations, we shall use H^+ instead of H_3O^+ when balancing equations in acid solution.

Balancing Equations in Acid Solution

When balancing equations for redox reactions in aqueous solution, it is sometimes necessary to add water molecules (H_2O) and either $H^+(aq)$ in acidic solution or $OH^-(aq)$ in basic solution to the equation. Equations that include oxoanions such as SO_4^{2-}, NO_3^-, ClO^-, CrO_4^{2-}, and MnO_4^- and organic compounds fall into this category. The process is outlined in Example 20.2 for the reduction of an oxocation in acid solution and in Example 20.3 for a reaction in basic solution.

■ **EXAMPLE 20.2 Balancing Equations for Oxidation–Reduction Reactions in Acid Solution**

Problem Balance the net ionic equation for the reaction of the dioxovanadium(V) ion, VO_2^+, with zinc in acid solution to form VO^{2+} (see Figure 20.3).

$$VO_2^+(aq) + Zn(s) \rightarrow VO^{2+}(aq) + Zn^{2+}(aq)$$

Strategy Follow the strategy outlined in the text and Example 20.1. Note that water and H^+ ions will appear as product and reactant, respectively, in the half-reaction for the reduction of VO_2^+ ion. (But H_2O and H^+ will never appear on the same side of the balanced half-reaction.)

Solution

Step 1. Recognize the reaction as an oxidation–reduction reaction.

The oxidation number of V changes from +5 in VO_2^+ to +4 in VO^{2+}. The oxidation number of Zn changes from 0 in the metal to +2 in Zn^{2+}.

Step 2. Separate the process into half-reactions.

Oxidation:	$Zn(s) \rightarrow Zn^{2+}(aq)$
	Zn(s) is oxidized and is the reducing agent.
Reduction:	$VO_2^+(aq) \rightarrow VO^{2+}(aq)$
	$VO_2^+(aq)$ is reduced and is the oxidizing agent.

Step 3. Balance the half-reactions for mass.

Begin by balancing all atoms except H and O. (These atoms are always the last to be balanced because they often appear in more than one reactant or product.)

Zinc half-reaction:	$Zn(s) \rightarrow Zn^{2+}(aq)$

This half-reaction is already balanced for mass.

Vanadium half-reaction:	$VO_2^+(aq) \rightarrow VO^{2+}(aq)$

The VO_2^+ ion is yellow in acid solution.

VO_2^+

Add Zn →

Zn added. With time, the yellow VO_2^+ ion is reduced to blue VO^{2+} ion.

VO^{2+}

With time, the blue VO^{2+} ion is further reduced to green V^{3+} ion.

V^{3+}

Finally, green V^{3+} ion is reduced to violet V^{2+} ion.

V^{2+}

FIGURE 20.3 Reduction of vanadium(V) with zinc. See Example 20.2 for the balanced equation for the first stage of the reaction.

The V atoms in this half-reaction are already balanced. An oxygen-containing species must be added to the right side of the equation to achieve an O atom balance, however.

$$VO_2^+(aq) \rightarrow VO^{2+}(aq) + (\text{need 1 O atom})$$

In acid solution, add H_2O to the side requiring O atoms, one H_2O molecule for each O atom required.

$$VO_2^+(aq) \rightarrow VO^{2+}(aq) + H_2O(\ell)$$

There are now two unbalanced H atoms on the right. Because the reaction occurs in an acidic solution, H^+ ions are present. Therefore, a mass balance for H can be achieved by adding H^+ to the side of the equation deficient in H atoms. Here, two H^+ ions are added to the left side of the equation.

$$2\,H^+(aq) + VO_2^+(aq) \rightarrow VO^{2+}(aq) + H_2O(\ell)$$

Step 4. Balance the half-reactions for charge by adding electrons to the more positive side to make the charges equal on both sides.

Two electrons are added to the right side of the zinc half-reaction to bring its charge down to the same value as is present on the left side (in this case, zero).

 Zinc half-reaction: $Zn(s) \rightarrow Zn^{2+}(aq) + 2\,e^-$

The mass-balanced VO_2^+ equation has a net charge of $3+$ on the left side and $2+$ on the right. Therefore, $1\,e^-$ is added to the more positive left side.

 Vanadium half-reaction: $e^- + 2\,H^+(aq) + VO_2^+(aq) \rightarrow VO^{2+}(aq) + H_2O(\ell)$

As a check on your work, notice that the vanadium atom changes in oxidation number from $+5$ to $+4$ and so needs to acquire one electron.

Step 5. Multiply the half-reactions by appropriate factors so that the reducing agent donates as many electrons as the oxidizing agent consumes.

Here, the oxidation half-reaction supplies 2 mol of electrons per mol of Zn, and the reduction half-reaction consumes 1 mol of electrons per mol of VO_2^+. Therefore, the reduction half-reaction must be multiplied by 2. Now 2 mol of the oxidizing agent (VO_2^+) consumes the 2 mol of electrons provided per mole of the reducing agent (Zn).

$$Zn(s) \rightarrow Zn^{2+}(aq) + 2\,e^-$$
$$2[e^- + 2\,H^+(aq) + VO_2^+(aq) \rightarrow VO^{2+}(aq) + H_2O(\ell)]$$

Step 6. Add the half-reactions to give the balanced, overall equation.

Oxidation half-reaction: $Zn(s) \rightarrow Zn^{2+}(aq) + 2\ e^-$

Reduction half-reaction: $2\ e^- + 4\ H^+(aq) + 2\ VO_2{}^+(aq) \rightarrow 2\ VO^{2+}(aq) + 2\ H_2O(\ell)$

Net ionic equation: $Zn(s) + 4\ H^+(aq) + 2\ VO_2{}^+(aq) \rightarrow Zn^{2+}(aq) + 2\ VO^{2+}(aq) + 2\ H_2O(\ell)$

Step 7. Simplify by eliminating reactants and products that appear on both sides.

This step is not required here.

Comment Check the overall equation to ensure that there is a mass and charge balance.

Mass balance: 1 Zn, 2 V, 4 H, and 4 O

Charge balance: Each side has a net charge of 6+.

FIGURE 20.4 The reaction of purple permanganate ion ($MnO_4{}^-$) with iron(II) ions in acid solution. The products are the nearly colorless Mn^{2+} and Fe^{3+} ions.

Charles D. Winters

EXERCISE 20.2 Balancing Oxidation–Reduction Equations

The yellow dioxovanadium(V) ion, $VO_2{}^+(aq)$, is reduced by zinc metal in three steps. The first step reduces it to blue $VO^{2+}(aq)$ (Example 20.2). This ion is further reduced to green $V^{3+}(aq)$ in the second step, and V^{3+} can be reduced to violet $V^{2+}(aq)$ in a third step. In each step, zinc is oxidized to $Zn^{2+}(aq)$. Write balanced net ionic equations for Steps 2 and 3. (This reduction sequence is shown in Figure 20.3.)

EXERCISE 20.3 Balancing Equations for Oxidation–Reduction Reactions in Acid Solution

A common laboratory analysis for iron is to titrate aqueous iron(II) ion with a solution of potassium permanganate of precisely known concentration. Use the half-reaction method to write the balanced net ionic equation for the reaction in acid solution.

$$MnO_4{}^-(aq) + Fe^{2+}(aq) \rightarrow Mn^{2+}(aq) + Fe^{3+}(aq)$$

Identify the oxidizing agent, the reducing agent, the substance oxidized, and the substance reduced. See Figure 20.4.

Balancing Equations in Basic Solution

Example 20.2 and Exercises 20.2 and 20.3 illustrate the technique of balancing equations for redox reactions involving oxocations and oxoanions that occur in acid solution. Under these conditions, H^+ ion or the H^+/H_2O pair can be used to achieve a balanced equation if required. Conversely, in basic solution, only OH^- ion or the OH^-/H_2O pair can be used.

Problem Solving Tip 20.1

- Hydrogen balance can be achieved only with H^+/H_2O (in acid) or OH^-/H_2O (in base). Never add H or H_2 to balance hydrogen.
- Use H_2O or OH^- as appropriate to balance oxygen. Never add O atoms, O^{2-} ions, or O_2 for O balance.

Balancing Oxidation–Reduction Equations: A Summary

- Never include $H^+(aq)$ and $OH^-(aq)$ in the same equation. A solution can be either acidic or basic, never both.
- The number of electrons in a half-reaction reflects the change in oxidation number of the element being oxidized or reduced.
- Electrons are always a component of half-reactions but should never appear in the overall equation.

- Include charges in the formulas for ions. Omitting the charge, or writing the charge incorrectly, is one of the most common errors seen on student papers.
- The best way to become competent in balancing redox equations is to practice, practice, practice.

Problem Aluminum metal is oxidized in aqueous base, with water serving as the oxidizing agent. The products of the reaction are $[Al(OH)_4]^-(aq)$ and $H_2(g)$. Write a balanced net ionic equation for this reaction.

Strategy First, identify the oxidation and reduction half-reactions, and then balance them for mass and charge. Finally, add the balanced half-reactions to obtain the balanced net ionic equation for the reaction.

Solution

Step 1. Recognize the reaction as an oxidation–reduction reaction.

The unbalanced equation is

$$Al(s) + H_2O(\ell) \rightarrow [Al(OH)_4]^-(aq) + H_2(g)$$

Here, aluminum is oxidized, with its oxidation number changing from 0 to +3. Hydrogen is reduced, with its oxidation number decreasing from +1 to zero.

Step 2. Separate the process into half-reactions.

Oxidation half-reaction: $\qquad Al(s) \rightarrow [Al(OH)_4]^-(aq)$

(Al oxidation number increased from 0 to +3.)

Reduction half-reaction: $\qquad H_2O(\ell) \rightarrow H_2(g)$

(H oxidation number decreased from +1 to 0.)

Step 3. Balance the half-reactions for mass.

Addition of OH^- and/or H_2O is required for mass balance in both half-reactions. In the case of the aluminum half-reaction, we simply add OH^- ions to the left side.

Oxidation half-reaction: $\qquad Al(s) + 4\ OH^-(aq) \rightarrow [Al(OH)_4]^-(aq)$

To balance the half-reaction for water reduction, notice that an oxygen-containing species must appear on the right side of the equation. Because H_2O is a reactant, we use OH^-, which is present in this basic solution, as the other product.

Reduction half-reaction: $\qquad 2\ H_2O(\ell) \rightarrow H_2(g) + 2\ OH^-(aq)$

Step 4. Balance the half-reactions for charge.

Electrons are added to balance charge.

Oxidation half-reaction: $\qquad Al(s) + 4\ OH^-(aq) \rightarrow [Al(OH)_4]^-(aq) + 3\ e^-$

Reduction half-reaction: $\qquad 2\ H_2O(\ell) + 2\ e^- \rightarrow H_2(g) + 2\ OH^-(aq)$

Step 5. Multiply the half-reactions by appropriate factors so that the reducing agent donates as many electrons as the oxidizing agent consumes.

Here, electron balance is achieved by using 2 mol of Al to provide 6 mol of e^-, which are then acquired by 6 mol of H_2O.

Oxidation half-reaction: $\qquad 2[Al(s) + 4\ OH^-(aq) \rightarrow [Al(OH)_4]^-(aq) + 3\ e^-]$

Reduction half-reaction: $\qquad 3[2\ H_2O(\ell) + 2\ e^- \rightarrow H_2(g) + 2\ OH^-(aq)]$

Step 6. Add the half-reactions.

$$2\ Al(s) + 8\ OH^-(aq) \rightarrow 2\ [Al(OH)_4]^-(aq) + 6\ e^-$$
$$\underline{6\ H_2O(\ell) + 6\ e^- \rightarrow 3\ H_2(g) + 6\ OH^-(aq)]}$$

Net equation: $\qquad 2\ Al(s) + 8\ OH^-(aq) + 6\ H_2O(\ell) \rightarrow 2\ [Al(OH)_4]^-(aq) + 3\ H_2(g) + 6\ OH^-(aq)$

Step 7. Simplify by eliminating reactants and products that appear on both sides.

Six OH^- ions can be canceled from the two sides of the equation:

$$2\ Al(s) + 2\ OH^-(aq) + 6\ H_2O(\ell) \rightarrow 2\ [Al(OH)_4]^-(aq) + 3\ H_2(g)$$

Comment The final equation is balanced for mass and charge.

Mass balance: $\qquad\qquad\qquad$ 2 Al, 14 H, and 8 O

Charge balance: $\qquad\qquad\qquad$ There is a net −2 charge on each side.

An Alternative Method of Balancing Equations in Basic Solution

Balancing redox equations in basic solution, which may require you to use OH^- and H_2O, can sometimes be more challenging than doing so in acidic solution. One of the ways to balance such equations for reactions in basic solution is to first balance it as if it were in acidic solution and then add enough OH^- ions to both sides of the equation so that the H^+ ions are converted to water. Taking the half-reaction for the reduction of ClO^- ion to Cl_2, we have:

(a) Balance in acid

$$4\,H^+(aq) + 2\,ClO^-(aq) + 2\,e^- \rightarrow Cl_2(g) + 2\,H_2O(\ell)$$

(b) Add four OH^- ions to both sides

$$4\,OH^-\,(aq) + 4\,H^+(aq) + 2\,ClO^-(aq) + 2\,e^- \rightarrow$$
$$Cl_2(g) + 2\,H_2O(\ell) + 4\,OH^-(aq)$$

(c) Combine OH^- and H^+ to form water where appropriate

$$4\,H_2O(\ell) + 2\,ClO^-(aq) + 2\,e^- \rightarrow Cl_2(g) + 2\,H_2O(\ell) + 4\,OH^-(aq)$$

(d) Simplify

$$2\,H_2O(\ell) + 2\,ClO^-(aq) + 2\,e^- \rightarrow Cl_2(g) + 4\,OH^-(aq)$$

EXERCISE 20.4 Balancing Equations for Oxidation–Reduction Reactions in Basic Solution

Voltaic cells based on the reduction of sulfur are under development. One such cell involves the reaction of sulfur with aluminum under basic conditions.

$$Al(s) + S(s) \rightarrow Al(OH)_3(s) + HS^-(aq)$$

(a) Balance this equation, showing each balanced half-reaction.

(b) Identify the oxidizing and reducing agents, the substance oxidized, and the substance reduced.

20.2 Simple Voltaic Cells

Let us use the reaction of copper metal and silver ions (Figure 20.1) as the basis of a voltaic cell. To do so, we place the components of the two half-reactions in separate compartments (Figure 20.5). This prevents the copper metal from transferring electrons directly to silver ions. Instead, electrons will be transferred through an external circuit, and useful work can potentially be done.

The copper half-cell (on the left in Figure 20.5) holds copper metal that serves as one electrode and a solution containing copper(II) ions. The half-cell on the right uses a silver electrode and a solution containing silver(I) ions. Important features of this simple cell are as follows:

- *The two half-cells are connected with a **salt bridge** that allows cations and anions to move between the two half-cells.* The electrolyte chosen for the salt bridge should contain ions that will not react with chemical reagents in both half-cells. In the example in Figure 20.5, $NaNO_3$ is used.
- *In all electrochemical cells, the **anode** is the electrode at which oxidation occurs. The electrode at which reduction occurs is always the **cathode**.* (In Figure 20.5, the copper electrode is the anode, and the silver electrode is the cathode.)
- *A negative sign can be assigned to the anode in a voltaic cell, and the cathode is marked with a positive sign.* The chemical oxidation occurring at the anode, which produces electrons, gives it a negative charge. Electric current in the external circuit of a voltaic cell consists of electrons moving from the negative to the positive electrode.
- *In all electrochemical cells, electrons flow in the external circuit from the anode to the cathode.*

■ **Salt Bridges** A simple salt bridge can be made by adding gelatin to a solution of an electrolyte. Gelatin makes the contents semi-rigid so that the salt bridge is easier to handle. Porous glass disks and permeable membranes are alternatives to a salt bridge. These devices allow ions to traverse from one half-cell to the other while keeping the two solutions from mixing.

FIGURE 20.5 A voltaic cell using Cu(s) | Cu²⁺(aq) and Ag(s) | Ag⁺(aq) half cells. Electrons flow through the external circuit from the anode (the copper electrode) to the cathode (silver electrode). In the salt bridge, which contains aqueous NaNO₃, negative NO₃⁻(aq) ions migrate toward the copper half-cell, and positive Na⁺(aq) ions migrate toward the silver half-cell. Using 1.0 M Cu²⁺(aq) and 1.0 M Ag⁺(aq) solutions, this cell will generate 0.46 volts.

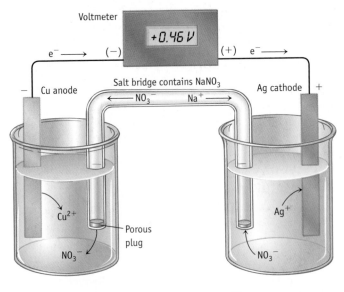

Net reaction: Cu(s) + 2 Ag⁺(aq) ⟶ Cu²⁺(aq) + 2 Ag(s)

The chemistry occurring in the cell pictured in Figure 20.5 is summarized by the following half-reactions and net ionic equation:

Cathode (reduction): $2 \; Ag^+(aq) + 2 \; e^- \rightarrow 2 \; Ag(s)$

Anode (oxidation): $Cu(s) \rightarrow Cu^{2+}(aq) + 2 \; e^-$

Net ionic equation: $Cu(s) + 2 \; Ag^+(aq) \rightarrow Cu^{2+}(aq) + 2 \; Ag(s)$

The salt bridge is required in a voltaic cell for the reaction to proceed. In the Cu/Ag⁺ voltaic cell, anions move in the salt bridge toward the copper half-cell, and cations move toward the silver half-cell (Figure 20.5). As $Cu^{2+}(aq)$ ions are formed in the copper half-cell by oxidation of copper metal, negative ions enter that cell from the salt bridge (and positive ions leave the cell), so that the numbers of positive and negative charges in the half-cell compartment remain in balance. Likewise, in the silver half-cell, negative ions move out of the half-cell into the salt bridge, and positive ions move into the cell as Ag^+ (aq) ions are reduced to silver metal. A complete circuit is required for current to flow. If the salt bridge is removed, reactions at the electrodes will cease.

In Figure 20.5, the electrodes are connected by wires to a voltmeter. In an alternative set-up, the connections might be to a light bulb or other device that uses electricity. Electrons are produced by oxidation of copper, and $Cu^{2+}(aq)$ ions enter the solution. The electrons traverse the external circuit to the silver electrode, where they reduce $Ag^+(aq)$ ions to silver metal. To balance the extent of oxidation and reduction, two $Ag^+(aq)$ ions are reduced for every $Cu^{2+}(aq)$ ion formed. The main features of this and of all other voltaic cells are summarized in Figure 20.6.

■ **Electron and Ion Flow** It is helpful to notice that in an electrochemical cell the negative electrons and negatively charged anions make a "circle." That is, electrons move from anode to cathode in the external circuit, and negative anions move from the cathode compartment, through the salt bridge, to the anode compartment.

Chemistry ⚛ Now™

Sign in at **www.cengage.com/login** and go to Chapter 20 Contents to see Screen 20.4 for an animation of **a cell based on zinc and copper.**

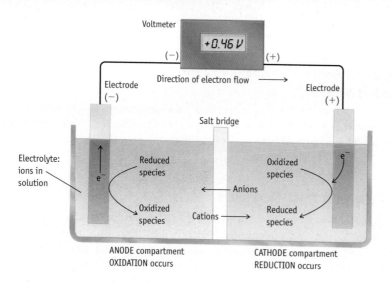

Voltmeter

+0.46 V

(−)   (+)

Direction of electron flow →

Electrode (−)   Electrode (+)

Salt bridge

Electrolyte: ions in solution

e^-

Reduced species

Oxidized species

← Anions

Cations →

Oxidized species

Reduced species

e^-

ANODE compartment
OXIDATION occurs

CATHODE compartment
REDUCTION occurs

FIGURE 20.6 Summary of terms used in a voltaic cell. Electrons move from the anode, the site of oxidation, through the external circuit to the cathode, the site of reduction. Charge balance in each half-cell is achieved by migration of ions through the salt bridge. Negative ions move from the reduction half-cell to the oxidation half-cell and positive ions move in the opposite direction.

EXAMPLE 20.4 Electrochemical Cells

Problem Describe how to set up a voltaic cell to generate an electric current using the reaction

$$Fe(s) + Cu^{2+}(aq) \rightarrow Cu(s) + Fe^{2+}(aq)$$

Which electrode is the anode, and which is the cathode? In which direction do electrons flow in the external circuit? In which direction do the positive and negative ions flow in the salt bridge? Write equations for the half-reactions that occur at each electrode.

Strategy First, identify the two different half-cells that make up the cell. Next, decide in which half-cell oxidation occurs and in which reduction occurs.

Solution This voltaic cell is similar to the one diagrammed in Figure 20.5. One half-cell contains an iron electrode and a solution of an iron(II) salt such as $Fe(NO_3)_2$. The other half-cell contains a copper electrode and a soluble copper(II) salt such as $Cu(NO_3)_2$. The two half-cells are linked with a salt bridge containing an electrolyte such as KNO_3. Iron is oxidized, so the iron electrode is the anode:

Oxidation, anode: $Fe(s) \rightarrow Fe^{2+}(aq) + 2\ e^-$

Because copper(II) ions are reduced, the copper electrode is the cathode. The cathodic half-reaction is

Reduction, cathode: $Cu^{2+}(aq) + 2\ e^- \rightarrow Cu(s)$

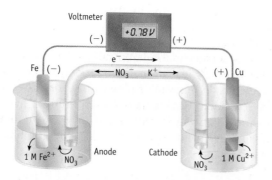

Voltmeter

+0.78 V

(−)   (+)

e^- →

Fe (−)   ← NO_3^- K^+ →   (+) Cu

1 M Fe^{2+} NO_3^- Anode   Cathode NO_3^- 1 M Cu^{2+}

In the external circuit, electrons flow from the iron electrode (anode) to the copper electrode (cathode). In the salt bridge, negative ions flow toward the Fe | Fe^{2+}(aq) half-cell, and positive ions flow in the opposite direction.

Voltaic Cells with Inert Electrodes

In the half-cells described so far, the metal used as an electrode is also a reactant or a product in the redox reaction. Not all half-reactions involve a metal as a reactant or product, however. With the exception of carbon in the form of graphite, most nonmetals are unsuitable as electrode materials because they do not conduct electricity. It is not possible to make an electrode from a gas, a liquid (except mercury), or a solution. Ionic solids do not make satisfactory electrodes because the ions are locked tightly in a crystal lattice, and these materials do not conduct electricity.

In situations where reactants and products cannot serve as the electrode material, an inert or chemically unreactive electrode must be used. Such electrodes are made of materials that conduct an electric current but that are neither oxidized nor reduced in the cell.

Consider constructing a voltaic cell to accommodate the following product-favored reaction:

$$2\,Fe^{3+}(aq) + H_2(g) \rightarrow 2\,Fe^{2+}(aq) + 2\,H^+(aq)$$

Reduction half reaction: $\qquad Fe^{3+}(aq) + e^- \rightarrow Fe^{2+}(aq)$

Oxidation half reaction: $\qquad H_2(g) \rightarrow 2\,H^+(aq) + 2\,e^-$

Neither the reactants nor the products can be used as an electrode material. Therefore, the two half-cells are set up so that the reactants and products come in contact with an electrode such as graphite where they can accept or give up electrons. Graphite is a commonly used electrode material: It is a conductor of electricity, and it is inexpensive (essential in commercial cells) and not readily oxidized under the conditions encountered in most cells. Mercury is used in certain types of cells. Platinum and gold are also commonly used because both are chemically inert under most circumstances, but they are generally too costly for commercial cells.

The *hydrogen electrode* is particularly important in the field of electrochemistry because it is used as a reference in assigning cell voltages (see Section 20.4) (Figure 20.7). The electrode material is platinum, chosen because hydrogen adsorbs on the metal's surface. In this half-cell's operation, hydrogen is bubbled over the electrode, and a large surface area maximizes the contact of the gas and the electrode. The aqueous solution contains $H^+(aq)$. The half-reactions involving $H^+(aq)$ and $H_2(g)$

$$2\,H^+(aq) + 2\,e^- \rightarrow H_2(g) \qquad \text{or} \qquad H_2(g) \rightarrow 2\,H^+(aq) + 2\,e^-$$

take place at the electrode surface, and the electrons involved in the reaction are conducted to or from the reaction site by the metal electrode.

A half-cell using the reduction of $Fe^{3+}(aq)$ to $Fe^{2+}(aq)$ can also be set up with a platinum electrode. In this case, the solution surrounding the electrode contains

Charles D. Winters

FIGURE 20.7 Hydrogen electrode.
Hydrogen gas is bubbled over a platinum electrode in a solution containing H^+ ions. Such electrodes function best if they have a large surface area. Often, platinum wires are woven into a gauze, or the metal surface is roughened either by abrasion or by chemical treatment to increase the surface area.

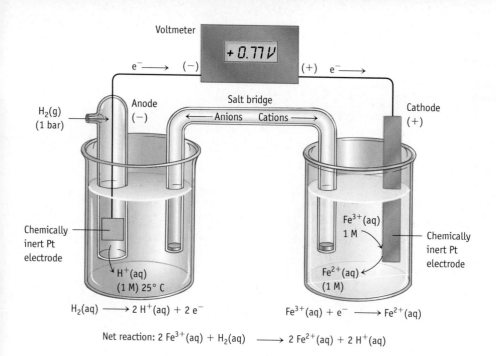

FIGURE 20.8 A voltaic cell with a hydrogen electrode. This cell has Fe^{2+}(aq, 1.0 M) and Fe^{3+}(aq, 1.0 M) in the cathode compartment and H_2(g) and H^+(aq, 1.0 M) in the anode compartment. At 25 °C, the cell generates 0.77 V.

iron ions in two different oxidation states. Transfer of electrons to or from the reactant occurs at the electrode surface.

A voltaic cell involving the reduction of Fe^{3+}(aq, 1.0 M) to Fe^{2+}(aq, 1.0 M) with H_2 gas is illustrated in Figure 20.8. In this cell, the hydrogen electrode is the anode (H_2 is oxidized to H^+), and the iron-containing compartment is the cathode (Fe^{3+} is reduced to Fe^{2+}). The cell produces 0.77 V.

Electrochemical Cell Notations

Chemists often use a shorthand notation to simplify cell descriptions. For example, the cell involving the reduction of silver ion with copper metal is written as

$$Cu(s) \,|\, Cu^{2+}(aq,\ 1.0\ M)\, ||\, Ag^+(aq,\ 1.0\ M)\, |\, Ag(s)$$

The cell using H_2 gas to reduce Fe^{3+} ions is written as

$$Pt \,|\, H_2(P = 1\ bar) \,|\, H^+(aq,\ 1.0\ M)\, ||\, Fe^{3+}(aq,\ 1.0\ M),\ Fe^{2+}(aq,\ 1.0\ M) \,|\, Pt$$

Anode information Cathode information

By convention, on the left we write the anode and information with respect to the solution with which it is in contact. A single vertical line (|) indicates a phase boundary, and double vertical lines (||) indicate a salt bridge.

20.3 Commercial Voltaic Cells

The cells described so far are unlikely to have practical use. They are neither compact nor robust, high priorities for most applications. In most situations, it is also important that the cell produce a constant voltage, but a problem with the cells described so far is that the voltage produced varies as the concentrations of ions in solution change (see Section 20.5). Also, the current production is low.

Voltaic cells are also called galvanic cells after an Italian physician Luigi Galvani (1737–1798), who carried out early studies of what he called "animal electricity," studies that brought new words into our language—among them "galvanic" and "galvanize."

Around 1780, Galvani observed that the electric current from a static electricity generator caused the contraction of the muscles in a frog's leg. Investigating further, he found he could induce contractions when the muscle was in contact with two different metals. Because no external source of electricity was applied to the muscles, Galvani concluded the frog's muscles were themselves generating electricity. This was evidence, he believed, of a kind of "vital energy" or "animal electricity," which was related to but different from "natural electricity" generated by machines or lightning.

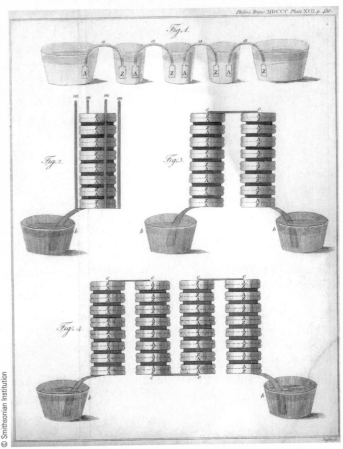

Volta's "voltaic pile." These drawings done by Volta show the arrangement of silver and zinc disks used to generate an electric current.

Alessandro Volta, 1745–1827.

Alessandro Volta repeated Galvani's experiments, with the same results, but he came to different conclusions. Volta proposed that an electric current was generated by the contact between two different metals—an explanation we now know to be correct—and that the frog muscle was simply detecting the small current generated.

To prove his hypothesis, Volta built the first "electric pile" in 1800. This was a series of metal disks of two kinds (silver and zinc), separated by paper disks soaked in acid or salt solutions. Soon after Volta announced his discovery, Carlisle and Nicholson in England used the electricity from a "pile" to decompose water into hydrogen and oxygen. Within a few years, the great English chemist Humphry Davy used a more powerful voltaic pile to isolate potassium and sodium metals by electrolysis.

■ **Cell Potentials and Reactant and Product Concentrations** Concentrations of species in a cell affect the potential, as discussed in Section 20.5.

Attempting to draw a large current results in a drop in voltage because the current depends on how fast ions in solution migrate to the electrode. Ion concentrations near the electrode become depleted if current is drawn rapidly, resulting in a decline in voltage.

The electrical work that can be drawn from a voltaic cell depends on the quantity of reagents consumed. A voltaic cell must have a large mass of reactants to produce current over a prolonged period. In addition, a voltaic cell that can be recharged is

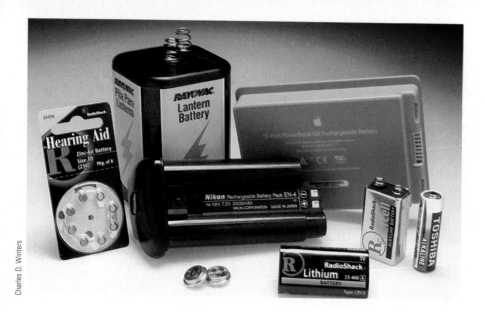

FIGURE 20.9 Some commercial voltaic cells. Commercial voltaic cells provide energy for a wide range of devices, come in a myriad of sizes and shapes, and produce different voltages. Some are rechargeable; others are discarded after use. One might think that there is nothing further to learn about batteries, but this is not true. Research on these devices is actively pursued in the chemical community.

attractive. Recharging a cell means returning the reagents to their original sites in the cell. In the cells described so far, the movement of ions in the cell mixes the reagents, and they cannot be "unmixed" after the cell has been running.

Batteries can be classified as primary and secondary. **Primary batteries** cannot be returned to their original state by recharging, so when the reactants are consumed, the battery is "dead" and must be discarded. **Secondary batteries** are often called **storage batteries** or **rechargeable batteries**. The reactions in these batteries can be reversed; thus, the batteries can be recharged.

Years of development have led to many different commercial voltaic cells to meet specific needs (Figure 20.9), and several common ones are described below. All adhere to the principles that have been developed in earlier discussions.

Primary Batteries: Dry Cells and Alkaline Batteries

If you buy an inexpensive flashlight battery or dry cell battery, it might be a modern version of a voltaic cell invented by George LeClanché in 1866 (Figure 20.10). Zinc serves as the anode, and the cathode is a graphite rod placed down the center of the device. These cells are often called "dry cells" because there is no visible liquid phase. However, water is present, so the cell contains a moist paste of NH_4Cl, $ZnCl_2$, and MnO_2. The moisture is necessary because the ions present must be in a medium in which they can migrate from one electrode to the other. The cell generates a potential of 1.5 V using the following half-reactions:

Cathode, reduction: $\quad 2\ NH_4^+(aq) + 2\ e^- \rightarrow 2\ NH_3(g) + H_2(g)$

Anode, oxidation: $\quad\quad\quad Zn(s) \rightarrow Zn^{2+}(aq) + 2\ e^-$

The two gases formed at the cathode will build up pressure and could cause the cell to rupture. This problem is avoided, however, by two other reactions that take place in the cell. Ammonia molecules bind to Zn^{2+} ions, and hydrogen gas is oxidized by MnO_2 to water.

$$Zn^{2+}(aq) + 2\ NH_3(g) + 2\ Cl^-(aq) \rightarrow Zn(NH_3)_2Cl_2(s)$$

$$2\ MnO_2(s) + H_2(g) \rightarrow Mn_2O_3(s) + H_2O(\ell)$$

FIGURE 20.10 The common LeClanché dry cell battery.

■ Batteries The word battery has become part of our common language, des-
ignating any self-contained device that
generates an electric current. The term
battery has a more precise scientific
meaning, however. It refers to a collection of two or more voltaic cells. For example, the 12-volt battery used in automobiles is made up of six voltaic cells.
Each voltaic cell develops a voltage of
2 volts. Six cells connected in series
produce 12 volts.

LeClanché cells were widely used because of their low cost, but they have several disadvantages. If current is drawn from the battery rapidly, the gaseous products cannot be consumed rapidly enough, so the cell resistance rises, and the voltage drops. In addition, the zinc electrode and ammonium ions are in contact in the cell, and these chemicals react slowly. Recall that zinc reacts with acid to form hydrogen. The ammonium ion, $NH_4^+(aq)$, is a weak Brønsted acid and reacts slowly with zinc. Because of this reaction, these voltaic cells cannot be stored indefinitely, a fact you may have learned from experience. When the zinc outer shell deterio-rates, the battery can leak acid and perhaps damage the appliance in which it is contained.

At the present time, you are more likely to use **alkaline batteries** in your camera or flashlight. They generate current up to 50% longer than a dry cell of the same size. The chemistry of alkaline cells is quite similar to that in a LeClanché cell, except that the material inside the cell is basic (alkaline). Alkaline cells use the oxidation of zinc and the reduction of MnO_2 to generate a current, but NaOH or KOH is used in the cell instead of the acidic salt NH_4Cl.

Cathode, reduction: $\quad 2\ MnO_2(s) + H_2O(\ell) + 2\ e^- \rightarrow Mn_2O_3(s) + 2\ OH^-(aq)$

Anode, oxidation: $\quad Zn(s) + 2\ OH^-(aq) \rightarrow ZnO(s) + H_2O(\ell) + 2\ e^-$

Alkaline cells, which produce 1.54 V (approximately the same voltage as the LeClanché cell), have the further advantage that the cell potential does not decline under high current loads because no gases are formed.

Prior to 2000, mercury-containing batteries were widely used in calculators, cam-eras, watches, heart pacemakers, and other devices. However, these small batteries were banned in the United States in the 1990s because of environmental problems. They have been replaced by several other types of batteries, such as silver oxide batteries and zinc-oxygen batteries. Both operate under alkaline conditions, and both have zinc anodes. In the silver oxide battery, which produces a voltage of about 1.5 V, the cell reactions are

Cathode, reduction: $\quad Ag_2O(s) + H_2O(\ell) + 2\ e^- \rightarrow 2\ Ag(s) + 2\ OH^-(aq)$

Anode, oxidation: $\quad Zn(s) + 2\ OH^-(aq) \rightarrow ZnO(s) + H_2O(\ell) + 2\ e^-$

The zinc-oxygen battery, which produces about 1.15–1.35 V, is unique in that at-mospheric oxygen and not a metal oxide is the oxidizing agent.

Cathode, reduction: $\quad O_2(g) + 2\ H_2O(\ell) + 4\ e^- \rightarrow 4\ OH^-(aq)$

Anode, oxidation: $\quad Zn(s) + 2\ OH^-(aq) \rightarrow ZnO(s) + H_2O(\ell) + 2\ e^-$

These batteries have found use in hearing aids, pagers, and medical devices.

Secondary or Rechargeable Batteries

When a LeClanché cell or an alkaline cell ceases to produce a usable electric cur-rent, it is discarded. In contrast, some types of cells can be recharged, often hun-dreds of times. Recharging requires applying an electric current from an external source to restore the cell to its original state.

An automobile battery—the **lead storage battery**—is probably the best-known rechargeable battery (Figure 20.11). The 12-V version of this battery contains six voltaic cells, each generating about 2 V. The lead storage battery can produce a large initial current, an essential feature when starting an automobile engine.

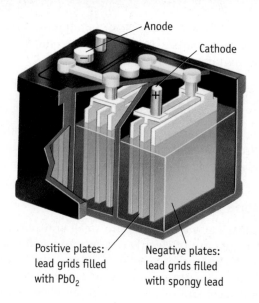

Anode

Cathode

Positive plates: lead grids filled with PbO_2

Negative plates: lead grids filled with spongy lead

FIGURE 20.11 Lead storage battery, a secondary or rechargeable battery. The negative plates (anode) are lead grids filled with spongy lead. The positive plates (cathode) are lead grids filled with lead(IV) oxide, PbO_2. Each cell of the battery generates 2 V.

The anode of a lead storage battery is metallic lead. The cathode is also made of lead, but it is covered with a layer of compressed, insoluble lead(IV) oxide, PbO_2. The electrodes, arranged alternately in a stack and separated by thin fiberglass sheets, are immersed in aqueous sulfuric acid. When the cell supplies electrical energy, the lead anode is oxidized to lead(II) sulfate, an insoluble substance that adheres to the electrode surface. The two electrons produced per lead atom move through the external circuit to the cathode, where PbO_2 is reduced to Pb^{2+} ions that, in the presence of H_2SO_4, also form lead(II) sulfate.

Cathode, reduction:	$PbO_2(s) + 4\ H^+(aq) + SO_4{}^{2-}(aq) + 2\ e^- \rightarrow PbSO_4(s) + 2\ H_2O(\ell)$
Anode, oxidation:	$Pb(s) + SO_4{}^{2-}(aq) \rightarrow PbSO_4(s) + 2\ e^-$
Net ionic equation:	$Pb(s) + PbO_2(s) + 2\ H_2SO_4(aq) \rightarrow 2\ PbSO_4(s) + 2\ H_2O(\ell)$

When current is generated, sulfuric acid is consumed and water is formed. Because water is less dense than sulfuric acid, the density of the solution decreases during this process. Therefore, one way to determine whether a lead storage battery needs to be recharged is to measure the density of the solution.

A lead storage battery is recharged by supplying electrical energy. The $PbSO_4$ coating the surfaces of the electrodes is converted back to metallic lead and PbO_2, and sulfuric acid is regenerated. Recharging this battery is possible because the reactants and products remain attached to the electrode surface. The lifetime of a lead storage battery is limited, however, because, with time, the coatings of PbO_2 and $PbSO_4$ flake off of the surface and fall to the bottom of the battery case.

Scientists and engineers would like to find an alternative to lead storage batteries, especially for use in cars. Lead storage batteries have the disadvantage of being large and heavy. In addition, lead and its compounds are toxic and their disposal adds a further complication. Nevertheless, at this time, the advantages of lead storage batteries outweigh their disadvantages.

Nickel-cadmium ("Ni-cad") batteries, used in a variety of cordless appliances such as telephones, video camcorders, and cordless power tools, are lightweight and rechargeable. The chemistry of the cell utilizes the oxidation of cadmium and the reduction of nickel(III) oxide under basic conditions. As with the lead storage battery, the reactants and products formed when producing a current are solids that adhere to the electrodes.

Cathode, reduction: $\qquad$ $NiO(OH)(s) + H_2O(\ell) + e^- \rightarrow Ni(OH)_2(s) + OH^-(aq)$

Anode, oxidation: $\qquad$ $Cd(s) + 2\ OH^-(aq) \rightarrow Cd(OH)_2(s) + 2\ e^-$

Ni-cad batteries produce a nearly constant voltage. However, their cost is relatively high, and there are restrictions on their disposal because cadmium compounds are toxic and present an environmental hazard.

Fuel Cells and Hybrid Cars

An advantage of voltaic cells is that they are small and portable, but their size is also a limitation. The amount of electric current produced is limited by the quantity of reagents contained in the cell. When one of the reactants is completely consumed, the cell will no longer generate a current. Fuel cells avoid this limitation because the reactants (fuel and oxidant) can be supplied continuously to the cell from an external reservoir.

Although the first fuel cells were constructed more than 150 years ago, little was done to develop this technology until the space program rekindled interest in these devices. Hydrogen-oxygen fuel cells have been used in NASA's Gemini, Apollo, and Space Shuttle programs. Not only are they lightweight and efficient, but they also have the added benefit that they generate drinking water for the ship's crew. The fuel cells on board the Space Shuttle deliver the same power as batteries weighing 10 times as much.

In a hydrogen-oxygen fuel cell (Figure 20.12), hydrogen is pumped onto the anode of the cell, and O_2 (or air) is directed to the cathode where the following reactions occur:

Cathode, reduction: $\qquad$ $O_2(g) + 2\ H_2O(\ell) + 4\ e^- \rightarrow 4\ OH^-(aq)$

Anode, oxidation: $\qquad$ $H_2(g) \rightarrow 2\ H^+(aq) + 2\ e^-$

■ **Energy for Automobiles** Energy available from systems that can be used to power an automobile.

Chemical System	W · h/kg* (1 W · h = 3600 J)
Lead-acid battery	18–56
Nickel-cadmium battery	33–70
Sodium-sulfur battery	80–140
Lithium polymer battery	150
Gasoline-air combustion engine	12,200

* watt-hour/kilogram

FIGURE 20.12 Fuel cell design. Hydrogen gas is oxidized to $H^+(aq)$ at the anode surface. On the other side of the proton exchange membrane (PEM), oxygen gas is reduced to $OH^-(aq)$. The $H^+(aq)$ ions travel through the PEM and combine with $OH^-(aq)$, forming water.

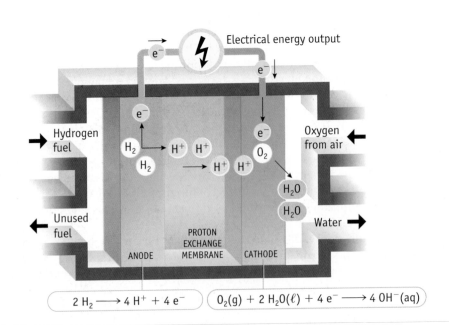

The two halves of the cell are separated by a special material called a proton exchange membrane (PEM). Protons, $H^+(aq)$, formed at the anode traverse the PEM and react with the hydroxide ions produced at the cathode, forming water. The net reaction in the cell is thus the formation of water from H_2 and O_2. Cells currently in use run at temperatures of 70–140 °C and produce about 0.9 V.

Hydrogen-oxygen fuel cells operate at 40–60% efficiency and meet most of the requirements for use in automobiles: they operate at room temperature or slightly above, start rapidly, and develop a high current density. Cost is a serious problem, however, and it appears that a substantial shift away from the internal combustion engine remains a long way off. For this reason, several major car manufacturers have designed electric cars that use various types of batteries to provide the power to drive the car. The most commonly employed type for automotive use is the lead storage battery, but these devices are problematic, owing to their mass. To produce one mole of electrons requires 321 g of reactants in lead storage batteries. As a result, these batteries rank very low among various options in power per kilogram of battery weight. In fact, the power available from any type of battery is much less than that available from an equivalent mass of gasoline.

Hybrid cars appear to offer an interim solution. These vehicles combine a small gasoline-fueled engine with an electric motor and batteries for storage of electric energy. Currently, hybrid cars use rechargeable nickel-metal hydride batteries. Electrons are generated when H atoms interact with OH^- ions at the metal alloy anode.

$$\text{Alloy(H)} + OH^- \rightarrow \text{Alloy} + H_2O + e^-$$

The reaction at the cathode is the same as in Ni-cad batteries.

$$\text{NiOOH} + H_2O + e^- \rightarrow \text{Ni(OH)}_2 + OH^-$$

©AP Photo/Shizuo Kambayashi, File

Hybrid car. This car combines a gasoline-fueled engine with an electric motor and rechargable batteries. Its fuel efficiency is about double that of the current generation of cars using only gasoline engines.

Chemistry ⚛ Now™

Sign in at **www.cengage.com/login** and go to Chapter 20 Contents to see Screen 20.5 to view animations of **various types of batteries.**

20.4 Standard Electrochemical Potentials

Different electrochemical cells produce different voltages: 1.5 V for the LeClanché and alkaline cells, about 1.25 V for a Ni-Cd battery, and about 2.0 V for the individual cells in a lead storage battery. In this section, we want to identify the various factors affecting cell voltages and develop procedures to calculate the voltage of a cell based on the chemistry in the cell and the conditions used.

Electromotive Force

Electrons generated at the anode of an electrochemical cell move through the external circuit toward the cathode, and the force needed to move the electrons arises from a difference in the potential energy of electrons at the two electrodes. This difference in potential energy per electrical charge is called the **electromotive force** or **emf**, for which the literal meaning is "force causing electrons to move." Emf has units of volts (V); 1 volt is the potential difference needed to impart one joule of energy to an electric charge of one coulomb $(1\,J = 1\,V \times 1\,C)$. *One coulomb is the quantity of charge that passes a point in an electric circuit when a current of 1 ampere flows for 1 second $(1\,C = 1\,A \times 1\,s)$.*

■ **Electrochemical Units**
- The coulomb (abbreviated C) is the standard (SI) unit of electrical charge (Appendix C.3).
- 1 joule = 1 volt × 1 coulomb.
- 1 coulomb = 1 ampere × 1 second.

Measuring Standard Potentials

Imagine you planned to study cell voltages in a laboratory with two objectives: (1) to understand the factors that affect these values and (2) to be able to predict the potential of a voltaic cell. You might construct a number of different half-cells, link them together in various combinations to form voltaic cells (as in Figure 20.13), and measure the cell potentials. After a few experiments, it would become apparent that cell voltages depend on a number of factors: the half-cells used (i.e., the reaction in each half-cell and the overall or net reaction in the cell), the concentrations of reactants and products in solution, the pressure of gaseous reactants, and the temperature.

So that we can later compare the potential of one half-cell with another, let us measure all cell voltages under **standard conditions**:

- Reactants and products are present in their standard states.
- Solutes in aqueous solution have a concentration of 1.0 M.
- Gaseous reactants or products have a pressure of 1.0 bar.

A cell potential measured under these conditions is called the **standard potential** and is denoted by $E°_{cell}$. Unless otherwise specified, all values of $E°_{cell}$ refer to measurements at 298 K (25 °C).

Suppose you set up a number of standard half-cells and connect each in turn to a **standard hydrogen electrode (SHE)**. Your apparatus would look like the voltaic cell in Figure 20.13. For now, we will concentrate on three aspects of this cell:

1. *The reaction that occurs.* The reaction occurring in the cell pictured in Figure 20.13 could be *either* the reduction of Zn^{2+} ions with H_2 gas

$$Zn^{2+}(aq) + H_2(g) \rightarrow Zn(s) + 2\,H^+(aq)$$

$Zn^{2+}(aq)$ is the oxidizing agent, and H_2 is the reducing agent.

Standard hydrogen electrode would be the anode (negative electrode).

or the reduction of $H^+(aq)$ ions by $Zn(s)$.

$$Zn(s) + 2\,H^+(aq) \rightarrow Zn^{2+}(aq) + H_2(g)$$

Zn is the reducing agent, and $H^+(aq)$ is the oxidizing agent.

Standard hydrogen electrode would be the cathode (positive electrode).

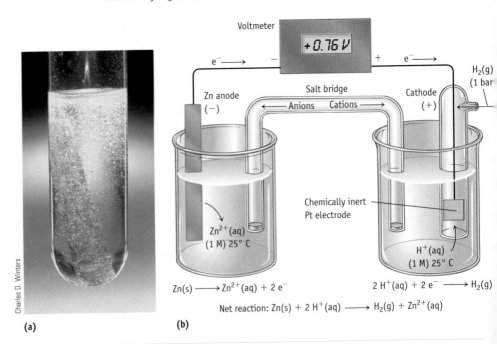

Active Figure 20.13 A voltaic cell using $Zn|Zn^{2+}(aq, 1.0\ M)$ and $H_2|H^+(aq, 1.0\ M)$ half cells. (a) Zinc metal reacts readily with aqueous HCl. (b) When zinc and acid are combined in an electrochemical cell, the cell generates a potential of 0.76 V under standard conditions. The electrode in the $H_2|H^+(aq, 1.0\ M)$ half-cell is the cathode, and the Zn electrode is the anode. Electrons flow in the external circuit to the hydrogen half-cell from the zinc half-cell. The positive sign of the measured voltage indicates that the hydrogen electrode is the cathode or positive electrode.

Chemistry ⚛ Now™ Sign in at www.cengage.com/login and go to the Chapter Contents menu to explore an interactive version of this figure accompanied by an exercise.

(a)

Charles D. Winters

(b)

All the substances named in these equations are present in the cell. The reaction that actually occurs is the one that is product-favored. That is, the reaction occurring is the one in which the reactants are the stronger reducing and oxidizing agents.

2. *Direction of electron flow in the external circuit.* In a voltaic cell, electrons always flow from the anode (negative electrode) to the cathode (positive electrode). That is, *electrons move from the electrode of higher potential energy to the one of lower potential energy.* We can tell the direction of electron movement by placing a voltmeter in the circuit. A positive potential is observed if the voltmeter terminal with a plus sign (+) is connected to the positive electrode [and the terminal with the minus sign (−) is connected to the negative electrode]. Connected in the opposite way (plus to minus and minus to plus), the voltmeter will show a negative value on the digital readout.

3. *Cell potential.* In Figure 20.13, the voltmeter is hooked up with its positive terminal connected to the hydrogen half-cell, and a reading of +0.76 V is observed. The hydrogen electrode is thus the positive electrode or cathode, and the reactions occurring in this cell must be

Reduction, cathode:	$2 \, H^+(aq) + 2 \, e^- \rightarrow H_2(g)$
Oxidation, anode:	$Zn(s) \rightarrow Zn^{2+}(aq) + 2 \, e^-$
Net cell reaction:	$Zn(s) + 2 \, H^+(aq) \rightarrow Zn^{2+}(aq) + H_2(g)$

This result confirms that, of the two oxidizing agents present in the cell, $H^+(aq)$ is better than $Zn^{2+}(aq)$ and that Zn metal is a better reducing agent than H_2 gas.

A potential of +0.76 V is measured for the oxidation of zinc with hydrogen ion. This value reflects the difference in potential energy of an electron at each electrode. From the direction of flow of electrons in the external circuit (Zn electrode → H_2 electrode), we conclude that the potential energy of an electron at the zinc electrode is higher than the potential energy of the electron at the hydrogen electrode.

Hundreds of electrochemical cells like that shown in Figure 20.13 can be set up, allowing us to determine the relative oxidizing or reducing ability of various chemical species and to determine the electrical potential generated by the reaction under standard conditions. A few results are given in Figure 20.14, where half-reactions are listed as reductions. That is, the chemical species on the left are oxidizing agents and are listed in descending oxidizing ability.

Standard Reduction Potentials

By doing experiments such as that illustrated by Figure 20.13, we not only have a notion of the relative oxidizing and reducing abilities of various chemical species, but we can also rank them quantitatively.

If $E^°_{cell}$ is a measure of the standard potential for the cell, then $E^°_{cathode}$ and $E^°_{anode}$ can be taken as measures of electrode potential. Because $E^°_{cell}$ reflects the difference in electrode potentials, $E^°_{cell}$ must be the difference between $E^°_{cathode}$ and $E^°_{anode}$.

$$E^°_{cell} = E^°_{cathode} - E^°_{anode} \tag{20.1}$$

Here, $E^°_{cathode}$ and $E^°_{anode}$ are the standard *reduction* potentials for the half-cell reactions that occur at the cathode and anode, respectively. Equation 20.1 is important for three reasons:

• If we have values for $E^°_{cathode}$ and $E^°_{anode}$, we can calculate the standard potential, $E^°_{cell}$, for a voltaic cell.

■ **Equation 20.1** Equation 20.1 is another example of calculating a change from $X_{final} - X_{initial}$. Electrons move to the cathode (the "final" state) from the anode (the "initial" state). Thus, Equation 20.1 resembles equations you have seen previously in this book (such as Equations 5.6 and 6.5).

Emf and cell potential (E_{cell}) are often used synonymously, but the two are subtly different. E_{cell} is a measured quantity, so its value is affected by how the measurement is made. To understand this point, consider as an analogy water in a pipe under pressure. Water pressure can be viewed as analogous to emf; it represents a force that will cause water in the pipe to move. If we open a faucet, water will flow. Opening the faucet will, however, decrease the pressure in the system.

Emf is the potential difference when no current flows. To measure E_{cell}, a voltmeter is placed in the external circuit. Although voltmeters have high internal resistance to minimize current flow, a small current flows nonetheless. As a result, the value of E_{cell} will be slightly different than the emf.

Finally, there is a difference between a potential and a voltage. The voltage of a cell has a magnitude but no sign. In contrast, the potential of a half-reaction or a cell has a sign ($+$ or $-$) and a magnitude.

- *When the calculated value of $E°_{cell}$ is positive, the reaction as written is predicted to be product-favored at equilibrium.* Conversely, if the calculated value of $E°_{cell}$ is negative, the reaction is predicted to be reactant-favored at equilibrium. Such a reaction will be product-favored at equilibrium in a direction opposite to the way it is written.
- If we measure $E°_{cell}$ and know either $E°_{cathode}$ or $E°_{anode}$, we can calculate the other value. This value would tell us how one half-cell reaction compares with others in terms of relative oxidizing or reducing ability.

But here is a dilemma. One cannot measure individual half-cell potentials. Just as values for $\Delta_f H°$ and $\Delta_f G°$ were established by choosing a reference point (the elements in their standard states), scientists have selected a reference point for half-reactions. We assign a potential of exactly 0 V to the half-reaction that occurs at a standard hydrogen electrode (SHE).

$$2\ H^+(aq,\ 1\ M) + 2\ e^- \rightarrow H_2(g,\ 1\ bar) \quad E° = 0.00\ V$$

With this standard, we can now determine $E°$ values for half-cells by measuring $E°_{cell}$ in experiments such as those described in Figures 20.8 and 20.13, where one of the electrodes is the standard hydrogen electrode. We can then quantify the information with reduction potential tables such as Figure 20.14 and use these values to make predictions about $E°_{cell}$ for new voltaic cells.

Tables of Standard Reduction Potentials

The experimental approach just described leads to lists of $E°$ values such as seen in Figure 20.14, Table 20.1, and Appendix M. Let us list some important points concerning these tables and then illustrate them in the discussion and examples that follow.

1. Reactions are written as "oxidized form + electrons → reduced form." The species on the left side of the reaction arrow is an oxidizing agent, and the species on the right side of the reaction arrow is a reducing agent. Therefore, *all potentials are for reduction reactions.*
2. The more positive the value of $E°$ for the reactions in Figure 20.14, Table 20.1, and similar tables, the better the oxidizing ability of the ion or compound on the left side of the reaction. This means $F_2(g)$ *is the best oxidizing agent in the table.* Lithium ion at the lower-left corner of Table 20.1 is the poorest oxidizing agent because its $E°$ value is the most negative.

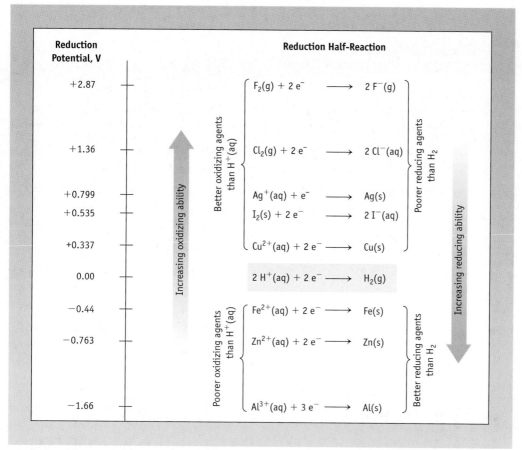

FIGURE 20.14 A potential ladder for reduction half-reactions. The relative position of a half-reaction on this potential ladder reflects the relative ability of the species at the left to act as an oxidizing agent. The higher the compound or ion is in list, the better it is as an oxidizing agent. Conversely, the atoms or ions on the right are reducing agents. The lower they are in the list, the better they are as a reducing agent. The potential for each half-reaction is given with its reduction potential, $E°_{cathode}$. (For more information see J. R. Runo and D. G. Peters, *Journal of Chemical Education*, Volume 70, page 708, 1993.)

3. The more negative the value of the reduction potential, $E°$, the less likely the half-reaction will occur as a reduction, and the more likely the reverse half-reaction will occur (as an oxidation). Thus, Li(s) is the strongest reducing agent in the table, and F^- is the weakest reducing agent. The reducing agents in the table (the ions, elements, and compounds at the right) increase in strength from the top to the bottom.

4. When a reaction is reversed (to give "reduced form → oxidized form + electrons"), the sign of $E°$ is reversed, but the magnitude of $E°$ is unaffected.

$$Fe^{3+}(aq, 1\ M) + e^- \rightarrow Fe^{2+}(aq, 1\ M) \qquad E° = +0.771\ V$$

$$Fe^{2+}(aq, 1\ M) \rightarrow Fe^{3+}(aq, 1\ M) + e^- \qquad E° = -0.771\ V$$

5. The reaction between any substance on the left in this table (an oxidizing agent) with any substance *lower* than it on the right (a reducing agent) is product-favored at equilibrium. This has been called the *northwest–southeast*

■ *E°* **Values** An extensive listing of $E°$ values is found in Appendix M, and still larger tables of data can be found in chemistry reference books. A common convention, used in Appendix M, lists standard reduction potentials in two groups, one for acid and neutral solutions and the other for basic solutions.

TABLE 20.1 Standard Reduction Potentials in Aqueous Solution at 25 °C*

Reduction Half-Reaction		$E°$ (V)
$F_2(g) + 2\ e^-$	$\rightarrow 2\ F^-(aq)$	+2.87
$H_2O_2(aq) + 2\ H^+(aq) + 2\ e^-$	$\rightarrow 2\ H_2O(\ell)$	+1.77
$PbO_2(s) + SO_4^{2-}(aq) + 4\ H^+(aq) + 2\ e^-$	$\rightarrow PbSO_4(s) + 2\ H_2O(\ell)$	+1.685
$MnO_4^-(aq) + 8\ H^+(aq) + 5\ e^-$	$\rightarrow Mn^{2+}(aq) + 4\ H_2O(\ell)$	+1.51
$Au^{3+}(aq) + 3\ e^-$	$\rightarrow Au(s)$	+1.50
$Cl_2(g) + 2\ e^-$	$\rightarrow 2\ Cl^-(aq)$	+1.36
$Cr_2O_7^{2-}(aq) + 14\ H^+(aq) + 6\ e^-$	$\rightarrow 2\ Cr^{3+}(aq) + 7\ H_2O(\ell)$	+1.33
$O_2(g) + 4\ H^+(aq) + 4\ e^-$	$\rightarrow 2\ H_2O(\ell)$	+1.229
$Br_2(\ell) + 2\ e^-$	$\rightarrow 2\ Br^-(aq)$	+1.08
$NO_3^-(aq) + 4\ H^+(aq) + 3\ e^-$	$\rightarrow NO(g) + 2\ H_2O(\ell)$	+0.96
$OCl^-(aq) + H_2O(\ell) + 2\ e^-$	$\rightarrow Cl^-(aq) + 2\ OH^-(aq)$	+0.89
$Hg^{2+}(aq) + 2\ e^-$	$\rightarrow Hg(\ell)$	+0.855
$Ag^+(aq) + e^-$	$\rightarrow Ag(s)$	+0.799
$Hg_2^{2+}(aq) + 2\ e^-$	$\rightarrow 2\ Hg(\ell)$	+0.789
$Fe^{3+}(aq) + e^-$	$\rightarrow Fe^{2+}(aq)$	+0.771
$I_2(s) + 2\ e^-$	$\rightarrow 2\ I^-(aq)$	+0.535
$O_2(g) + 2\ H_2O(\ell) + 4\ e^-$	$\rightarrow 4\ OH^-(aq)$	+0.40
$Cu^{2+}(aq) + 2\ e^-$	$\rightarrow Cu(s)$	+0.337
$Sn^{4+}(aq) + 2\ e^-$	$\rightarrow Sn^{2+}(aq)$	+0.15
$2\ H^+(aq) + 2\ e^-$	$\rightarrow H_2(g)$	0.00
$Sn^{2+}(aq) + 2\ e^-$	$\rightarrow Sn(s)$	−0.14
$Ni^{2+}(aq) + 2\ e^-$	$\rightarrow Ni(s)$	−0.25
$V^{3+}(aq) + e^-$	$\rightarrow V^{2+}(aq)$	−0.255
$PbSO_4(s) + 2\ e^-$	$\rightarrow Pb(s) + SO_4^{2-}(aq)$	−0.356
$Cd^{2+}(aq) + 2\ e^-$	$\rightarrow Cd(s)$	−0.40
$Fe^{2+}(aq) + 2\ e^-$	$\rightarrow Fe(s)$	−0.44
$Zn^{2+}(aq) + 2\ e^-$	$\rightarrow Zn(s)$	−0.763
$2\ H_2O(\ell) + 2\ e^-$	$\rightarrow H_2(g) + 2\ OH^-(aq)$	−0.8277
$Al^{3+}(aq) + 3\ e^-$	$\rightarrow Al(s)$	−1.66
$Mg^{2+}(aq) + 2\ e^-$	$\rightarrow Mg(s)$	−2.37
$Na^+(aq) + e^-$	$\rightarrow Na(s)$	−2.714
$K^+(aq) + e^-$	$\rightarrow K(s)$	−2.925
$Li^+(aq) + e^-$	$\rightarrow Li(s)$	−3.045

Increasing strength of oxidizing agents (left vertical arrow, pointing up)

Increasing strength of reducing agents (right vertical arrow, pointing down)

* In volts (V) versus the standard hydrogen electrode.

rule: Product-favored reactions will always involve a reducing agent that is "southeast" of the proposed oxidizing agent.

■ Northwest–Southeast Rule This guideline is a reflection of the idea of moving down a potential energy "ladder" in a product-favored reaction.

Reduction Half-Reaction

$$I_2(s) + 2\,e^- \longrightarrow 2\,I^-(aq)$$
$$Cu^{2+}(aq) + 2\,e^- \longrightarrow Cu(s)$$
$$2\,H^+(aq) + 2\,e^- \longrightarrow H_2(g)$$
$$Fe^{2+}(aq) + 2\,e^- \longrightarrow Fe(s)$$
$$Zn^{2+}(aq) + 2\,e^- \longrightarrow Zn(s)$$

The northwest–southeast rule: The reducing agent always lies to the southeast of the oxidizing agent in a product-favored reaction.

For example, Zn can reduce Fe^{2+}, H^+, Cu^{2+}, and I_2, but, of the species on this list, Cu can reduce only I_2.

6. The algebraic sign of the half-reaction reduction potential is the sign of the electrode when it is attached to the H_2/H^+ standard cell (see Figures 20.8 and 20.13).

7. Electrochemical potentials depend on the nature of the reactants and products and their concentrations, not on the quantities of material used. Therefore, changing the stoichiometric coefficients for a half-reaction does not change the value of $E°$. For example, the reduction of Fe^{3+} has an $E°$ of $+0.771$ V, whether the reaction is written as

$$Fe^{3+}(aq, 1\,M) + e^- \rightarrow Fe^{2+}(aq, 1\,M) \qquad E° = +0.771\ V$$

or as

$$2\,Fe^{3+}(aq, 1\,M) + 2\,e^- \rightarrow 2\,Fe^{2+}(aq, 1\,M) \qquad E° = +0.771\ V$$

■ Changing Stoichiometric Coefficients The volt is defined as "energy/charge" (V = J/C). Multiplying a reaction by some number causes both the energy and the charge to be multiplied by that number. Thus, the ratio "energy/charge = volt" does not change.

Using Tables of Standard Reduction Potentials

Tables or "ladders" of standard reduction potentials are immensely useful. They allow you to predict the potential of a new voltaic cell, provide information that can be used to balance redox equations, and help predict which redox reactions are product-favored.

Calculating Standard Cell Potentials, $E°_{cell}$

The standard reduction potentials for half-reactions were obtained by measuring cell potentials. It makes sense, therefore, that these values can be combined to give the potential of some new cell.

The net reaction occurring in a voltaic cell using silver and copper half-cells is

$$2\,Ag^+(aq) + Cu(s) \rightarrow 2\,Ag(s) + Cu^{2+}(aq)$$

The silver electrode is the cathode, and the copper electrode is the anode. We know this because silver ion is reduced (to silver metal) and copper metal is oxidized (to Cu^{2+} ions). (Recall that oxidations always occur at the anode and reductions at the cathode.) Also notice that the $Cu^{2+}|Cu$ half-reaction is "southeast" of the $Ag^+|Ag$ half-reaction in the potential ladder (Figure 20.14 and Table 20.1).

$E°_{cathode} = +0.799\ V \qquad Ag^+(aq) + e^- \longrightarrow Ag(s)$

"Distance" from $E°_{cathode}$ to $E°_{anode}$ is $0.799\ V - 0.337\ V = 0.462\ V.$

Cu is "southeast" of Ag^+

$E°_{anode} = +0.337\ V \qquad Cu^{2+}(aq) + 2\,e^- \longrightarrow Cu(s)$

20.4 | Standard Electrochemical Potentials **921**

The potential for the voltaic cell is the difference between the standard reduction potentials for the two half-reactions.

$$E°_{cell} = E°_{cathode} - E°_{anode}$$

$$E°_{cell} = (+0.799 \text{ V}) - (+0.337 \text{ V})$$

$$E°_{cell} = +0.462 \text{ V}$$

Notice that the value of $E°_{cell}$ is related to the "distance" between the cathode and anode reactions on the potential ladder. The products have a lower potential energy than the reactants, and the cell potential, $E°_{cell}$, has a positive value.

A positive potential calculated for the $Ag^+|Ag$ and $Cu^{2+}|Cu$ cell ($E°_{cell} = +0.462$ V) confirms that the reduction of silver ions in water with copper metal is product-favored at equilibrium (Figure 20.1). We might ask, however, about the value of $E°_{cell}$ if a reactant-favored equation had been selected. For example, what is $E°_{cell}$ for the reduction of copper ions with silver metal?

Cathode, reduction:	$Cu^{2+}(aq) + 2\ e^- \rightarrow Cu(s)$
Anode, oxidation:	$2\ Ag(s) \rightarrow 2\ Ag^+(aq) + 2\ e^-$
Net ionic equation:	$2\ Ag\ (s) + Cu^{2+}(aq) \rightarrow 2\ Ag^+(aq) + Cu(s)$

Cell Voltage Calculation

$$E°_{cathode} = +\ 0.337 \text{ V and } E°_{anode} = +\ 0.799 \text{ V}$$

$$E°_{cell} = E°_{cathode} - E°_{anode} = (+0.337 \text{ V}) - (0.799 \text{ V})$$

$$E°_{cell} = -\ 0.462 \text{ V}$$

The negative sign for $E°_{cell}$ indicates that the reaction as written is reactant-favored at equilibrium. The products of the reaction (Ag^+ and Cu) have a higher potential energy than the reactants (Ag and Cu^{2+}). For the indicated reaction to occur, a potential of at least 0.462 V would have to be imposed on the system by an external source of electricity (see Section 20.7).

Chemistry ⚛ Now™

Sign in at **www.cengage.com/login** and go to Chapter 20 Contents to see:
- Screen 20.5 for demonstration of **the potentials of various cells**
- Screen 20.6 for a simulation and tutorial on **standard potentials**

EXERCISE 20.6 Calculating Standard Cell Potentials

The net reaction that occurs in a voltaic cell is

$$Zn(s) + 2\ Ag^+(aq) \rightarrow Zn^{2+}(aq) + 2\ Ag(s)$$

Identify the half-reactions that occur at the anode and the cathode, and calculate a potential for the cell assuming standard conditions.

Relative Strengths of Oxidizing and Reducing Agents

Five half-reactions, selected from Appendix M, are arranged from the half-reaction with the highest (most positive) $E°$ value to the one with the lowest (most negative) value.

$E°$, V		Reduction Half-Reaction
+1.36		$Cl_2(g) + 2\ e^- \longrightarrow 2\ Cl^-(aq)$
+0.80		$Ag^+(aq) + e^- \longrightarrow Ag(s)$
+0.00	Increasing strength as oxidizing agents	$2\ H^+(aq) + 2\ e^- \longrightarrow H_2(g)$
−0.25		$Ni^{2+}(aq) + 2\ e^- \longrightarrow Ni(s)$
−0.76		$Zn^{2+}(aq) + 2\ e^- \longrightarrow Zn(s)$

- The list on the left is headed by Cl_2, an element that is a strong oxidizing agent and thus is easily reduced. At the bottom of the list is $Zn^{2+}(aq)$, an ion not easily reduced and thus a poor oxidizing agent.
- On the right, the list is headed by $Cl^-(aq)$, an ion that can be oxidized to Cl_2 only with difficulty. It is a very poor reducing agent. At the bottom of the list is zinc metal, which is quite easy to oxidize and a good reducing agent.

By arranging these half-reactions based on $E°$ values, we have also arranged the chemical species on the two sides of the equation in order of their strengths as oxidizing or reducing agents. In this list, from strongest to weakest, the order is

Oxidizing agents: $Cl_2 > Ag^+ > H^+ > Ni^{2+} > Zn^{2+}$

strong $\longrightarrow$ weak

Reducing agents: $Zn > Ni > H_2 > Ag > Cl^-$

strong $\longrightarrow$ weak

Finally, notice that the value of $E°_{cell}$ is greater the farther apart the oxidizing and reducing agents are on the potential ladder. For example,

$$Zn(s) + Cl_2(g) \rightarrow Zn^{2+}(aq) + 2\ Cl^-(aq) \qquad E° = +2.12\ V$$

is more strongly product-favored than the reduction of hydrogen ions with nickel metal

$$Ni(s) + 2\ H^+(aq) \rightarrow Ni^{2+}(aq) + H_2(g) \qquad E° = +0.25\ V$$

EXAMPLE 20.5 Ranking Oxidizing and Reducing Agents

Problem Use the table of standard reduction potentials (Table 20.1) to do the following:

(a) Rank the halogens in order of their strength as oxidizing agents.

(b) Decide whether hydrogen peroxide (H_2O_2) in acid solution is a stronger oxidizing agent than Cl_2.

(c) Decide which of the halogens is capable of oxidizing gold metal to $Au^{3+}(aq)$.

Strategy The ability of a species on the left side of a reduction potential table to function as an oxidizing agent declines on descending the list (see points 2 and 3, pages 918–919).

Solution

(a) Ranking halogens according to oxidizing ability. The halogens (F_2, Cl_2, Br_2, and I_2) appear in the upper-left portion of the table, with F_2 being highest, followed in order by the other three species. Their strengths as oxidizing agents are $F_2 > Cl_2 > Br_2 > I_2$. (The ability of bromine to oxidize iodide ions to molecular iodine is illustrated in Figure 20.15.)

FIGURE 20.15 The reaction of bromine and iodide ion. This experiment proves that Br_2 is a better oxidizing agent than I_2. The presence of I_2 in the bottom layer in the photo on the right indicates that the added Br_2 was able to oxidize the iodide ions originally present to molecular iodine (I_2).

The test tube contains an aqueous solution of KI (top layer) and immiscible CCl_4 (bottom layer).

Add Br_2 to solution of KI, and shake.

After adding a few drops of Br_2 in water, the I_2 produced collects in the bottom CCl_4 layer and gives it a purple color. (The top layer contains excess Br_2 in water.)

Photos: Charles D. Winters

(b) Comparing hydrogen peroxide and chlorine. H_2O_2 lies just below F_2 but well above Cl_2 in the potential ladder (Table 20.1). Thus, H_2O_2 is a weaker oxidizing agent than F_2 but a stronger one than Cl_2. (Note that the $E°$ value for H_2O_2 refers to an acidic solution and standard conditions.)

(c) Which halogen will oxidize gold metal to gold(III) ions? The $Au^{3+}\,|\,Au$ half-reaction is listed below the $F_2\,|\,F^-$ half-reaction and just above the $Cl_2\,|\,Cl^-$ half-reaction. This tells us that, among the halogens, only F_2 is capable of oxidizing Au to Au^{3+} under standard conditions. That is, for the reaction of Au and F_2,

Oxidation, anode:	$Au(s) \rightarrow Au^{3+}(aq) + 3\ e^-$
Reduction, cathode:	$F_2(g) + 2\ e^- \rightarrow 2\ F^-(aq)$
Net ionic equation:	$3\ F_2(g) + 2\ Au(s) \rightarrow 6\ F^-(aq) + 2\ Au^{3+}(aq)$

$$E°_{cell} = E°_{cathode} - E°_{anode} = +2.87\ V - (+1.50\ V) = +1.37\ V$$

F_2 is a stronger oxidizing agent than Au^{3+}, so the reaction proceeds from left to right as written. (This is confirmed by a positive value of $E°_{cell}$.) For the reaction of Cl_2 and Au, Table 20.1 shows us that Cl_2 is a weaker oxidizing agent than Au^{3+}, so the reaction would be expected to proceed in the opposite direction.

Oxidation, anode:	$Au(s) \rightarrow Au^{3+}(aq) + 3\ e^-$
Reduction, cathode:	$Cl_2(aq) + 2\ e^- \rightarrow 2\ Cl^-(aq)$
Net ionic equation:	$3\ Cl_2(aq) + 2\ Au(s) \rightarrow 6\ Cl^-(aq) + 2\ Au^{3+}(aq)$

$$E°_{cell} = E°_{cathode} - E°_{anode} = +1.36\ V - (+1.50\ V) = -0.14\ V$$

This is confirmed by the negative value for $E°_{cell}$.

Comment In part (c), we calculated $E°_{cell}$ for two reactions. To achieve a balanced net ionic equation, we added the half-reactions, but only after multiplying the gold half-reaction by 2 and the halogen, half-reaction by 3. (This means 6 mol of electrons was transferred from 2 mol Au to 3 mol Cl_2.) Notice that this multiplication does not change the value of $E°$ for the half-reactions because cell potentials do not depend on the quantity of material.

EXERCISE 20.7 Relative Oxidizing and Reducing Ability

Which metal in the following list is easiest to oxidize: Fe, Ag, Zn, Mg, Au? Which metal is the most difficult to oxidize?

EXERCISE 20.8 Using a Table of Standard Reduction Potentials to Predict Chemical Reactions

Determine whether the following redox equations are product-favored at equilibrium.

(a) $Ni^{2+}(aq) + H_2(g) \rightarrow Ni(s) + 2\ H^+(aq)$

(b) $2\ Fe^{3+}(aq) + 2\ I^-(aq) \rightarrow 2\ Fe^{2+}(aq) + I_2(s)$

(c) $Br_2(\ell) + 2\ Cl^-(aq) \rightarrow 2\ Br^-(aq) + Cl_2(g)$

(d) $Cr_2O_7^{2-}(aq) + 6\ Fe^{2+}(aq) + 14\ H^+(aq) \rightarrow 2\ Cr^{3+}(aq) + 6\ Fe^{3+}(aq) + 7\ H_2O(\ell)$

20.5 Electrochemical Cells Under Nonstandard Conditions

Electrochemical cells seldom operate under standard conditions in the real world. Even if the cell is constructed with all dissolved species at 1 M, reactant concentra-tions decrease and product concentrations increase in the course of the reaction. Changing concentrations of reactants and products will affect the cell voltage. Thus, we need to ask what happens to cell potentials under nonstandard conditions.

The Nernst Equation

Based on both theory and experimental results, it has been determined that cell potentials are related to concentrations of reactants and products and to tempera-ture, as follows:

$$E = E° - (RT/nF) \ln Q \tag{20.2}$$

In this equation, which is known as the **Nernst equation**, R is the gas constant (8.314472 J/K · mol); T is the temperature (K); and n is the number of moles of electrons transferred between oxidizing and reducing agents (as determined by the balanced equation for the reaction). The symbol F represents the **Faraday constant** (9.6485338×10^4 C/mol). *One Faraday is the quantity of electric charge carried by one mole of electrons.* The term Q is the reaction quotient, an expression relating the concentrations of the products and reactants raised to an appropriate power as defined by the stoichiometric coefficients in the balanced, net equation [see Equation 16.2, Section 16.2]. Substituting values for the constants in Equation 20.2, and using 298 K as the temperature, gives

$$E = E° - \frac{0.0257}{n} \ln Q \quad \text{at 25 °C} \tag{20.3}$$

or, in a commonly used form using base-10 logarithms,

$$E = E° - \frac{0.0591}{n} \log Q$$

In essence, the term $(RT/nF)\ln Q$ "corrects" the standard potential $E°$ for nonstan-dard conditions or concentrations.

■ **Walther Nernst (1864–1941)** Nernst was a German physicist and chemist known for his work relating to the third law of thermodynamics.

■ **Units of R and F** The gas constant R has units of J/K · mol, and F has units of coulombs per mol (C/mol). Because 1 J $= 1$ C · V, the factor RT/nF has units of volts.

Chemistry ⚛ Now™

Sign in at **www.cengage.com/login** and go to Chapter 20 Contents to see Screen 20.8 for a tutorial on **the Nernst equation.**

Problem A voltaic cell is set up at 25 °C with the half-cells: $Al^{3+}(0.0010\ M)\ |\ Al$ and $Ni^{2+}(0.50\ M)\ |\ Ni$. Write an equation for the reaction that occurs when the cell generates an electric current, and determine the cell potential.

Strategy The first step is to determine which substance is oxidized (Al or Ni) by looking at the appropriate half-reactions in Table 20.1 and deciding which is the better reducing agent (Example 20.5). Next, add the half-reactions to determine the net ionic equation, and calculate $E°$. Finally, use the Nernst equation to calculate E, the nonstandard potential.

Solution Aluminum metal is a stronger reducing agent than Ni metal. (Conversely, Ni^{2+} is a better oxidizing agent than Al^{3+}.) Therefore, Al is oxidized, and the $Al^{3+}\ |\ Al$ compartment is the anode.

Cathode, reduction:	$Ni^{2+}(aq) + 2\ e^- \rightarrow Ni(s)$
Anode, oxidation:	$Al(s) \rightarrow Al^{3+}(aq) + 3\ e^-$
Net ionic equation:	$2\ Al(s) + 3\ Ni^{2+}(aq) \rightarrow 2\ Al^{3+}(aq) + 3\ Ni(s)$

$E°_{cell} = E°_{cathode} - E°_{anode}$

$E°_{cell} = (-0.25\ V) - (-1.66\ V) = 1.41\ V$

The expression for Q is written based on the cell reaction. In the net reaction, $Al^{3+}(aq)$ has a coefficient of 2, so this concentration is squared. Similarly, $[Ni^{2+}(aq)]$ is cubed. Solids are not included in the expression for Q (◀ Section 16.1).

$$Q = \frac{[Al^{3+}]^2}{[Ni^{2+}]^3}$$

The net equation requires transfer of six electrons from two Al atoms to three Ni^{2+} ions, so $n = 6$. Substituting for $E°$, n and Q in the Nernst equation gives

$$E_{cell} = E°_{cell} - \frac{0.0257}{n} \ln \frac{[Al^{3+}]^2}{[Ni^{2+}]^3}$$

$$= +1.41\ V - \frac{0.0257}{6} \ln \frac{[0.0010]^2}{[0.50]^3}$$

$$= +1.41\ V - 0.00428 \ln (8.0 \times 10^{-6})$$

$$= +1.41\ V - 0.00428\ (-11.7)$$

$$= 1.46\ V$$

Comment Notice that E_{cell} is larger than $E°_{cell}$ because the product concentration, $[Al^{3+}]$, is much smaller than 1.0 M. Generally, when product concentrations are smaller initially than the reactant concentrations in a product-favored reaction, the cell potential is more positive than $E°$.

EXERCISE 20.9 Variation of E_{cell} with Concentration

A voltaic cell is set up with an aluminum electrode in a 0.025 M $Al(NO_3)_3(aq)$ solution and an iron electrode in a 0.50 M $Fe(NO_3)_2(aq)$ solution. Determine the cell potential, E_{cell}, at 298 K.

Example 20.6 demonstrates the calculation of a cell potential if concentrations are known. It is also useful to apply the Nernst equation in the opposite sense, using a measured cell potential to determine an unknown concentration. A device that does just this is the pH meter (Figure 20.16). In an electrochemical cell in which $H^+(aq)$ is a reactant or product, the cell voltage will vary predictably with the hydrogen ion concentration. The cell voltage is measured and the value used to calculate pH. Example 20.7 illustrates how E_{cell} varies with the hydrogen ion concentration in a simple cell.

EXAMPLE 20.7 Variation of E_{cell} with Concentration

Problem A voltaic cell is set up with copper and hydrogen half-cells. Standard conditions are employed in the copper half-cell, Cu^{2+}(aq, 1.00 M)|Cu(s). The hydrogen gas pressure is 1.00 bar, and [H^+(aq)] in the hydrogen half-cell is the unknown. A value of 0.490 V is recorded for E_{cell} at 298 K. Determine the pH of the solution.

Strategy We first decide which is the better oxidizing and reducing agent so as to decide what net reaction is occurring in the cell. With this known, $E°_{cell}$ can be calculated. The only unknown quantity in the Nernst equation is the concentration of hydrogen ion, from which we can calculate the solution pH.

Solution Hydrogen is a better reducing agent than copper metal, so Cu(s)|Cu^{2+}(aq, 1.00 M) is the cathode, and H_2(g, 1.00 bar)|H^+(aq, ? M) is the anode.

Cathode, reduction:	Cu^{2+}(aq) + 2 e^- → Cu(s)
Anode, oxidation:	H_2(g) → 2 H^+(aq) + 2 e^-
Net ionic equation:	H_2(g) + Cu^{2+}(aq) → Cu(s) + 2 H^+(aq)

$E°_{cell} = E°_{cathode} - E°_{anode}$

$E°_{cell} = (+0.337\ V) - (0.00\ V) = +0.337\ V$

The reaction quotient, Q, is derived from the balanced net ionic equation.

$$Q = \frac{[H^+]^2}{[Cu^{2+}]P_{H_2}}$$

The net equation requires the transfer of two electrons, so $n = 2$. The value of [Cu^{2+}] is 1.00 M, but [H^+] is unknown. Substitute this information into the Nernst equation (and don't overlook the fact that [H^+] is squared in the expression for Q).

$$E = E° - \frac{0.0257}{n}\ln\frac{[H^+]^2}{[Cu^{2+}]P_{H_2}}$$

$$0.490\ V = 0.337\ V - \frac{0.0257}{2}\ln\frac{[H^+]^2}{(1.00)(1.00)}$$

$$-11.9 = \ln\ [H^+]^2$$

$$[H^+] = 2.6 \times 10^{-3}\ M$$

$$pH = 2.59$$

EXERCISE 20.10 Using the Nernst Equation

The half-cells Fe^{2+}(aq, 0.024 M)|Fe(s) and H^+(aq, 0.056 M)|H_2(1.0 bar) are linked by a salt bridge to create a voltaic cell. Determine the cell potential, E_{cell}, at 298 K.

In the real world, using a hydrogen electrode in a pH meter is not practical. The apparatus is clumsy; it is anything but robust; and platinum (for the electrode) is costly. Common pH meters use a glass electrode, so called because it contains a thin glass membrane separating the cell from the solution whose pH is to be measured (Figure 20.16). Inside the glass electrode is a silver wire coated with AgCl and a solution of HCl; outside is the solution of unknown pH to be evaluated. A Ag/AgCl or calomel electrode—a common reference electrode using a mercury(I)–mercury redox couple (Hg_2Cl_2|Hg)—serves as the second electrode of the cell. The potential across the glass membrane depends on [H^+]. Common pH meters give a direct readout of pH.

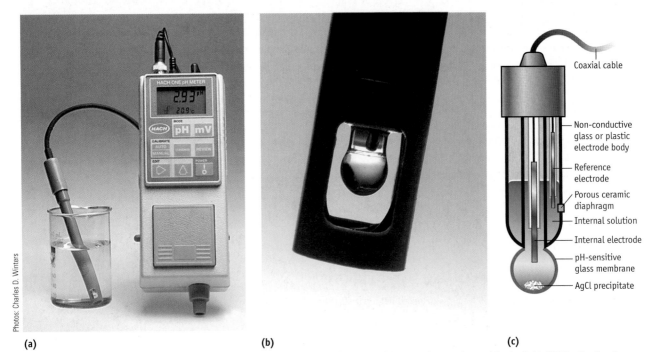

(a)   (b)   (c)

FIGURE 20.16 Measuring pH. (a) A pH portable meter that can be used in the field. (b) The tip of a glass electrode for measuring pH. (c) A schematic diagram of a glass electrode. (See ChemistryNow Screen 17.4 for an animation of the operation of a glass electrode for pH measurement.)

20.6 Electrochemistry and Thermodynamics

Work and Free Energy

The first law of thermodynamics [Section 5.4] states that the internal energy change in a system (ΔU) is related to two quantities, heat (q) and work (w): $\Delta U = q + w$. This equation also applies to chemical changes that occur in a voltaic cell. As current flows, energy is transferred from the system (the voltaic cell) to the surroundings.

In a voltaic cell, the decrease in internal energy in the system will manifest itself ideally as electrical work done on the surroundings by the system. In practice, however, some energy is usually evolved as heat by the voltaic cell. The maximum work done by an electrochemical system (ideally, assuming no heat is generated) is proportional to the potential difference (volts) and the quantity of charge (coulombs):

$$w_{max} = nFE \tag{20.4}$$

In this equation, E is the cell voltage, and nF is the quantity of electric charge transferred from anode to cathode.

The free energy change for a process is, by definition, the maximum amount of work that can be obtained [Section 19.6]. Because the maximum work and the cell potential are related, $E°$ and $\Delta_r G°$ can be related mathematically (taking care to assign signs correctly). The maximum work done on the surroundings when electricity is produced by a voltaic cell is $+nFE$, with the positive sign denoting an increase in energy in the surroundings. The energy content of the cell decreases by this amount. Thus, $\Delta_r G$ for the voltaic cell has the opposite sign.

$$\Delta_r G = -nFE \tag{20.5}$$

Under standard conditions, the appropriate equation is

$$\Delta_r G^\circ = -nFE^\circ \qquad (20.6)$$

This expression shows that, the more positive the value of E°, the larger and more negative the value of $\Delta_r G^\circ$ for the reaction. Also, because of the relationship between $\Delta_r G^\circ$ and K, the farther apart the half-reactions on the potential ladder, the more strongly product-favored the reaction is at equilibrium.

■ **Units in Equation 20.6** n has units of mol e^-, and F has units of (C/mol e^-). Therefore, nF has units of coulombs (C). Because 1 J = 1 C · V, the product nFE will have units of energy (J).

■ **EXAMPLE 20.8 The Relation Between E° and $\Delta_r G^\circ$**

Problem The standard cell potential, $E^\circ{}_{cell}$ for the reduction of silver ions with copper metal (Figure 20.5) is +0.462 V at 25 °C. Calculate $\Delta_r G^\circ$ for this reaction.

Strategy We use Equation 20.6, where F is a constant and $E^\circ{}_{cell}$ is given. The only problem here is to determine the value of n, the number of moles of electrons transferred between copper metal and silver ions in the balanced equation.

Solution In this cell, copper is the anode, and silver is the cathode. The overall cell reaction is

$$Cu(s) + 2\ Ag^+(aq) \rightarrow Cu^{2+}(aq) + 2\ Ag(s)$$

which means that each mole of copper transfers two moles of electrons to two moles of Ag^+ ions. That is, $n = 2$. Now use Equation 20.6.

$$\Delta_r G^\circ = -nFE^\circ = -(2\ \text{mol}\ e^-)(96{,}485\ \text{C/mol}\ e^-)(0.462\ V) = -89{,}200\ C \cdot V$$

Because 1 C · V = 1 J, we have

$$\Delta_r G^\circ = -89{,}200\ J\ \text{or}\ -89.2\ kJ$$

Comment This example demonstrates a very effective method of obtaining thermodynamic values from relatively simple electrochemical experiments.

EXERCISE 20.11 The Relationship Between E° and $\Delta_r G^\circ$

The following reaction has an E° value of −0.76 V:

$$H_2(g) + Zn^{2+}(aq) \rightarrow Zn(s) + 2\ H^+(aq)$$

Calculate $\Delta_r G^\circ$ for this reaction. Is the reaction product- or reactant-favored at equilibrium?

E° and the Equilibrium Constant

When a voltaic cell produces an electric current, the reactant concentrations decrease, and the product concentrations increase. The cell voltage also changes; as reactants are converted to products, the value of E_{cell} decreases. Eventually, the cell potential reaches zero; no further net reaction occurs; and equilibrium is achieved.

This situation can be analyzed using the Nernst equation. When $E_{cell} = 0$, the reactants and products are at equilibrium, and the reaction quotient, Q, is equal to the equilibrium constant, K. Substituting the appropriate symbols and values into the Nernst equation,

$$E = 0 = E^\circ - \frac{0.0257}{n} \ln K$$

and collecting terms gives an equation that relates the cell potential and equilibrium constant:

$$\ln K = \frac{nE^\circ}{0.0257} \quad \text{at 25 °C} \qquad (20.7)$$

■ **K and E°** The farther apart half-reactions for a product-favored reaction are on the potential ladder, the larger the value of K.

Equation 20.7 can be used to determine values for equilibrium constants, as illustrated in Example 20.9 and Exercise 20.12.

EXAMPLE 20.9 $E°$ and Equilibrium Constants

Problem Calculate the equilibrium constant for the reaction

$$Fe(s) + Cd^{2+}(aq) \rightleftharpoons Fe^{2+}(aq) + Cd(s)$$

Strategy First, determine $E°_{cell}$ from $E°$ values for the two half-reactions (see Example 20.5) and from those the value of n, the other parameter required in Equation 20.7.

Solution The half-reactions and $E°$ values are

Cathode, reduction:	$Cd^{2+}(aq) + 2\ e^- \rightarrow Cd(s)$
Anode, oxidation:	$Fe(s) \rightarrow Fe^{2+}(aq) + 2\ e^-$
Net ionic equation:	$Fe(s) + Cd^{2+}(aq) \rightleftharpoons Fe^{2+}(aq) + Cd(s)$

$E°_{cell} = E°_{cathode} - E°_{anode}$

$E°_{cell} = (-0.40\ V) - (-0.44\ V) = +0.04\ V$

Now substitute $n = 2$ and $E°_{cell}$ into Equation 20.7.

$$\ln K = \frac{nE°}{0.0257} = \frac{(2)(0.04\ V)}{0.0257} = 3.1$$

$$K = 20$$

Comment The relatively small positive voltage (0.04 V) for the cell indicates that the cell reaction is only mildly product-favored. A value of 20 for the equilibrium constant is in accord with this observation.

EXERCISE 20.12 $E°$ and Equilibrium Constants

Calculate the equilibrium constant at 25 °C for the reaction

$$2\ Ag^+(aq) + Hg(\ell) \rightleftharpoons 2\ Ag(s) + Hg^{2+}(aq)$$

The relationships between $E°$, K, and $\Delta_r G°$, which is summarized in Table 20.2, can be used to obtain equilibrium constants for many different chemical systems. For example, let us construct an electrode in which an insoluble ionic compound (such as AgCl) is a component of the half-cell. For this purpose, a silver electrode with a surface layer of AgCl can be prepared. The reaction occurring at this electrode is then

$$AgCl(s) + e^- \rightarrow Ag(s) + Cl^-(aq)$$

The standard reduction potential for this half-cell (Appendix M) is +0.222 V. When this half-reaction is paired with a standard silver electrode in an electrochemical cell, the cell reactions are

Cathode, reduction:	$AgCl(s) + e^- \rightarrow Ag(s) + Cl^-(aq)$
Anode, oxidation:	$Ag(s) \rightarrow Ag^+(aq) + e^-$
Net ionic equation:	$AgCl(s) \rightarrow Ag^+(aq) + Cl^-(aq)$

$$E°_{cell} = E°_{cathode} - E°_{anode} = (+0.222\ V) - (+0.799\ V) = -0.577\ V$$

TABLE 20.2 Summary of the Relationship of K, $\Delta_r G°$, and $E°$

K	$\Delta_r G°$	$E°$	Reactant-Favored or Product-Favored at Equilibrium?	Spontaneous under Standard Conditions?
$K \gg 1$	$\Delta_r G° < 0$	$E° > 0$	Product-favored	Spontaneous under standard conditions
$K = 1$	$\Delta_r G° = 0$	$E° = 0$	$[C]^c[D]^d = [A]^a[B]^b$ at equilibrium	At equilibrium under standard conditions
$K \ll 1$	$\Delta_r G° > 0$	$E° < 0$	Reactant-favored	Not spontaneous under standard conditions.

The equation for the net reaction represents the equilibrium of solid AgCl and its ions. The cell potential is negative, indicating a reactant-favored process, as would be expected based on the low solubility of AgCl. Using Equation 20.7, the value of the equilibrium constant [K_{sp}, Section 18.4] can be obtained from $E°_{cell}$.

$$\ln K = \frac{nE°}{0.0257} = \frac{(1)(-0.577\ V)}{0.0257} = -22.5$$

$$K_{sp} = e^{-22.5} = 2 \times 10^{-10}$$

EXERCISE 20.13 Determining an Equilibrium Constant

In Appendix M, the following standard reduction potential is reported:

$$[Zn(CN)_4]^{2-}(aq) + 2\ e^- \rightarrow Zn(s) + 4\ CN^-(aq) \qquad E° = -1.26\ V$$

Use this information, along with the data on the $Zn^{2+}(aq)|Zn$ half-cell, to calculate the equilibrium constant for the reaction

$$Zn^{2+}(aq) + 4\ CN^-(aq) \rightarrow [Zn(CN)_4]^{2-}(aq)$$

The value calculated is the formation constant for this complex ion at 25 °C.

20.7 Electrolysis: Chemical Change Using Electrical Energy

Thus far, we have described electrochemical cells that use product-favored redox reactions to generate an electric current. Equally important, however, is the opposite process, **electrolysis**, the use of electrical energy to bring about chemical change.

Electrolysis of water is a classic chemistry experiment, and the electroplating of metals is another example of electrolysis (Figure 20.17). In electroplating, an electric current is passed through a solution containing a salt of the metal to be plated. The object to be plated is the cathode. When metal ions in solution are reduced, the metal deposits on the object's surface.

Electrolysis is an important procedure because it is widely used in the refining of metals such as aluminum and in the production of chemicals such as chlorine.

O₂ gas   H₂ gas

(a)

(b)

FIGURE 20.17 Electrolysis.
(a) Electrolysis of water produces hydrogen and oxygen gas. (b) Electroplating adds a layer of metal to the surface of an object, either to protect the object from corrosion or to improve its physical appearance. The procedure uses an electrolysis cell, set up with the object to be plated as the cathode and a solution containing a salt of the metal to be plated.

Manganese is a key component of some oxidation–reduction cycles in the oceans. According to an article in the journal *Science*, it "can perform this role because it exists in multiple oxidation states and is recycled rapidly between these states by bacterial processes."

Figure A shows how this cycle was thought to work. Manganese(II) ions in subsurface water are oxidized to form manganese(IV) oxide, MnO_2. Particles of this insoluble solid sink toward the ocean floor. However, some encounter hydrogen sulfide, which is produced in the ocean depths, rising toward the surface. Another redox reaction occurs, producing sulfur and manganese(II) ions. The newly formed Mn^{2+} ions diffuse upward, where they are again oxidized.

The manganese cycle had been thought to involve only the +2 and +4 oxidation states of manganese, and analyses of water samples assumed the dissolved manganese existed only as Mn^{2+} ions. One reason for this is that the intermediate oxidation state, Mn^{3+}, is not predicted to be stable in water. It should disproportionate to the +2 and +4 states.

$$2\ Mn^{3+}(aq) + 2\ H_2O(\ell) \rightarrow$$
$$Mn^{2+}(aq) + MnO_2(s) + 4\ H^+(aq)$$

It is known, however, that Mn^{3+} can exist when complexed with species such as pyrophosphate ions, $P_2O_7^{4-}$.

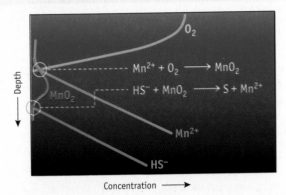

Figure A Manganese chemistry in the oceans. Relative concentrations of important species as a function of depth in the oceans. See K. S. Johnson, *Science*, Vol. 313, p. 1896, 2006 and R. E. Trouwborst, et al., *Science*, Vol. 313, pp. 1955–1957, 2006.

Several years ago, geochemists suggested that Mn^{3+} ions could exist in natural water. They could be produced by bacterial action and stabilized by phosphate from ATP or ADP. They speculated that the Mn^{3+} ion could play an important part of the natural manganese cycle.

Now, other researchers have indeed discovered that, in oxygen-poor waters, the manganese(III) ion, Mn^{3+}, can persist. These ions were found in anoxic zones (zones without dissolved oxygen) below 100 m in the Black Sea and below about 15 m in the Chesapeake Bay. It is now clear that Mn^{3+} ions, which had previously been known only in the laboratory, can exist in natural waters under the right circumstances and that the manganese cycle may have to be revised.

Questions:

1. *Given the following reduction potentials, show that Mn^{3+} should disproportionate to Mn^{2+} and MnO_2 at standard conditions.*
$$4\ H^+(aq) + MnO_2(s) + e^- \rightarrow$$
$$Mn^{3+}(aq) + 2\ H_2O(\ell)$$
$E° = 0.95\ V$
$$Mn^{3+}(aq) + e^- \rightarrow Mn^{2+}(aq)$$
$E° = 1.50\ V$

2. *Balance the following equations in acid solution.*
   (a) Reduction of MnO_2 with HS^- to Mn^{2+} and S
   (b) Oxidation of Mn^{2+} with O_2 to MnO_2

3. *Calculate $E°$ for the oxidation of Mn^{2+} with O_2 to MnO_2.*

Answers to these questions are in Appendix Q.

Electrolysis of Molten Salts

All electrolysis experiments are set up in a similar manner. The material to be electrolyzed, either a molten salt or a solution, is contained in an electrolysis cell. As was the case with voltaic cells, ions must be present in the liquid or solution for a current to flow. The movement of ions constitutes the electric current within the cell. The cell has two electrodes that are connected to a source of DC (direct-current) voltage. If a high enough voltage is applied, chemical reactions occur at the two electrodes. Reduction occurs at the negatively charged cathode, with electrons being transferred from that electrode to a chemical species in the cell. Oxidation occurs at the positive anode, with electrons from a chemical species being transferred to that electrode.

Let us first focus our attention on the chemical reactions that occur at each electrode in the electrolysis of a molten salt. Sodium chloride melts at about 800 °C, and in the molten state sodium ions (Na^+) and chloride ions (Cl^-) are freed from their rigid arrangement in the crystalline lattice. Therefore, if a poten-

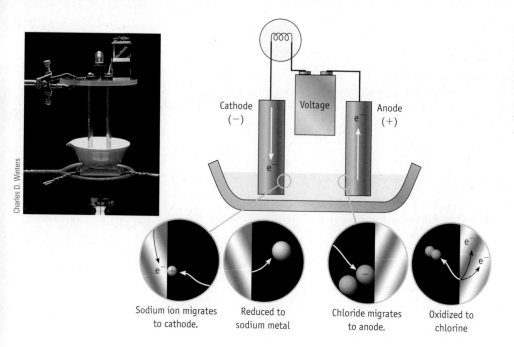

FIGURE 20.18 The preparation of sodium and chlorine by the electrolysis of molten NaCl. In the molten state, sodium ions migrate to the negative cathode, where they are reduced to sodium metal. Chloride ions migrate to the positive anode, where they are oxidized to elemental chlorine.

Cathode (−) Voltage Anode (+)

Sodium ion migrates to cathode.

Reduced to sodium metal

Chloride migrates to anode.

Oxidized to chlorine

Charles D. Winters

tial is applied to the electrodes, sodium ions are attracted to the negative electrode, and chloride ions are attracted to the positive electrode (Figure 20.18). If the potential is high enough, chemical reactions occur at each electrode. At the negative cathode, Na^+ ions accept electrons and are reduced to sodium metal (a liquid at this temperature). Simultaneously, at the positive anode, chloride ions give up electrons and form elemental chlorine.

Cathode (−), reduction:	$2\ Na^+ + 2\ e^- \rightarrow 2\ Na(\ell)$
Anode (+), oxidation:	$2\ Cl^- \rightarrow Cl_2(g) + 2\ e^-$
Net ionic equation:	$2\ Na^+ + 2\ Cl^- \rightarrow 2\ Na(\ell) + Cl_2(g)$

Electrons move through the external circuit under the force exerted by the applied potential, and the movement of positive and negative ions in the molten salt constitutes the current within the cell. Finally, it is important to recognize that the reaction is not spontaneous. The energy required for this reaction to occur has been provided by the electric current.

Electrolysis of Aqueous Solutions

Sodium ions (Na^+) and chloride ions (Cl^-) are the primary species present in molten NaCl. Only chloride ions can be oxidized, and only sodium ions can be reduced. Electrolyses of aqueous solutions are more complicated than electrolyses of molten salts, however, because water is now present. Water is an *electroactive* substance; that is, it can be oxidized or reduced in an electrochemical process.

Consider the electrolysis of aqueous sodium iodide (Figure 20.19). In this experiment, the electrolysis cell contains $Na^+(aq)$, $I^-(aq)$, and H_2O molecules. Possible *reduction reactions* at the *negative cathode* include

$$Na^+(aq) + e^- \rightarrow Na(s)$$

$$2\ H_2O(\ell) + 2\ e^- \rightarrow H_2(g) + 2\ OH^-(aq)$$

Whether you are describing a voltaic cell or an electrolysis cell, the terms "anode" and "cathode" always refer to the electrodes at which oxidation and reduction occur, respectively. The polarity of the electrodes is reversed, however.

Type of Cell	Electrode	Function	Polarity
Voltaic	Anode	Oxidation	−
	Cathode	Reduction	+
Electrolysis	Anode	Oxidation	+
	Cathode	Reduction	−

Possible *oxidation reactions* at the *positive anode* are

$$2\ I^-(aq) \rightarrow I_2(aq) + 2\ e^-$$

$$2\ H_2O(\ell) \rightarrow O_2(g) + 4\ H^+(aq) + 4\ e^-$$

In the electrolysis of aqueous NaI, experiment shows that $H_2(g)$ and $OH^-(aq)$ are formed by water reduction at the cathode, and iodine is formed at the anode (Figure 20.19). Thus, the overall cell process can be summarized by the following equations:

Cathode (−), reduction: $2\ H_2O(\ell) + 2\ e^- \rightarrow H_2(g) + 2\ OH^-(aq)$

Anode (+), oxidation: $\underline{2\ I^-(aq) \rightarrow I_2(aq) + 2\ e^-}$

Net ionic equation: $2\ H_2O(\ell) + 2\ I^-(aq) \rightarrow H_2(g) + 2\ OH^-(aq) + I_2(aq)$

where E°_{cell} has a negative value.

$$E^\circ_{cell} = E^\circ_{cathode} - E^\circ_{anode} = (-0.8277\ V) - (+0.621\ V) = -1.449\ V$$

This process is not spontaneous under standard conditions, and a potential of *at least* 1.45 V must be *applied* to the cell for these reactions to occur. If the process had involved the oxidation of water instead of iodide ion at the anode, the required potential would be $-2.057\ V$ [$E^\circ_{cathode} - E^\circ_{anode} = (-0.8277\ V) - (+1.229\ V)$], and if the reaction involving the reduction of Na^+ and the oxidation of I^- had occurred, the

FIGURE 20.19 Electrolysis of aqueous NaI. A solution of NaI(aq) is electrolyzed, a potential applied using an external source of electricity. A drop of phenolphthalein has been added to the solution in this experiment so that the formation of $OH^-(aq)$ can be detected (by the red color of the indicator in basic solution). Iodine forms at the anode, and H_2 and OH^- form at the cathode.

Photos: Charles D. Winters

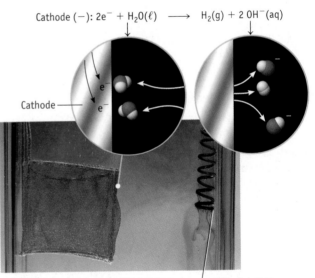

Cathode (−): $2e^- + H_2O(\ell) \longrightarrow H_2(g) + 2\ OH^-(aq)$

Anode (+): $2\ I^-(aq) \longrightarrow I_2(aq) + 2e^-$

required potential would be -3.335 V $[E°_{cathode} - E°_{anode} = (-2.714 \text{ V}) - (+0.621 \text{ V})]$. The reaction occurring is the one requiring the smaller applied potential, so the net cell reaction in the electrolysis of NaI(aq) is the oxidation of iodide and reduction of water.

What happens if an aqueous solution of some other metal halide such as $SnCl_2$ is electrolyzed? As before, consult Appendix M, and consider all possible half-reactions. In this case, aqueous Sn^{2+} ion is much more easily reduced ($E° = -0.14$ V) than water ($E° = -0.83$ V) at the cathode, so tin metal is produced. At the anode, two oxidations are possible: Cl^-(aq) to Cl_2(g) or H_2O to O_2(g). Experiments show that chloride ion is generally oxidized in preference to water, so the reactions occurring on electrolysis of aqueous tin(II) chloride are (Figure 20.20)

■ **Overvoltage** Voltages higher than the minimum are typically used to speed up reactions that would otherwise be slow. The term overvoltage is often used when describing experiments; this refers to the voltage needed to make a reaction occur at a reasonable rate.

Cathode (−), reduction: Sn^{2+}(aq) + 2 e^- → Sn(s)

Anode (+), oxidation: 2 Cl^-(aq) → Cl_2(g) + 2 e^-

Net ionic equation: Sn^{2+}(aq) + 2 Cl^-(aq) → Sn(s) + Cl_2(g)

$$E°_{cell} = E°_{cathode} - E°_{anode} = (-0.14 \text{ V}) - (+1.36 \text{ V}) = -1.50 \text{ V}$$

Formation of Cl_2 at the anode in the electrolysis of $SnCl_2$(aq) is contrary to a prediction based on $E°$ values. If the electrode reactions were

Cathode (−), reduction: Sn^{2+}(aq) + 2 e^- → Sn(s)

Anode (+), oxidation: 2 H_2O(ℓ) → O_2(g) + 4 H^+(aq) + 4 e^-

$$E°_{cell} = (-0.14 \text{ V}) - (+1.23 \text{ V}) = -1.37 \text{ V}$$

a smaller applied potential would seemingly be required. To explain the formation of chlorine instead of oxygen, we must take into account rates of reaction. This problem occurs in the commercially important electrolysis of aqueous NaCl, where a voltage high enough to oxidize both Cl^- and H_2O is used. However, because chloride ion is oxidized much faster than H_2O, the result is that Cl_2 is the major product in this electrolysis.

Another instance in which rates are important concerns electrode materials. Graphite, commonly used to make inert electrodes, can be oxidized. For the half-reaction CO_2(g) + 4 H^+(aq) + 4 e^- → C(s) + 2 H_2O(ℓ), $E°$ is +0.20 V, indicating that carbon is slightly easier to oxidize than copper ($E° = +0.34$ V). Based on this value, oxidation of a graphite electrode might reasonably be expected to occur during an electrolysis. And indeed it does, albeit slowly; graphite electrodes used in electrolysis cells slowly deteriorate and eventually have to be replaced.

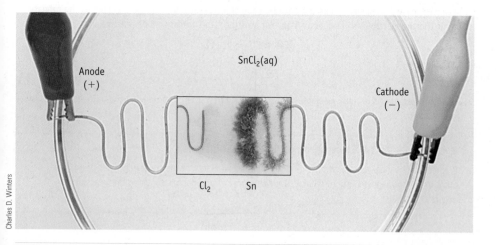

Anode (+)   SnCl$_2$(aq)   Cathode (−)

Cl$_2$ Sn

FIGURE 20.20 Electrolysis of aqueous tin(II) chloride. Tin metal collects at the negative cathode. Chlorine gas is formed at the positive anode. Elemental chlorine is formed in the cell, in spite of the fact that the potential for the oxidation of Cl^- is more negative than that for oxidation of water. (That is, chlorine should be less readily oxidized than water.) This is the result of chemical kinetics and illustrates the complexity of some aqueous electrochemistry.

Charles D. Winters

One other factor—the concentration of electroactive species in solution—must be taken into account when discussing electrolyses. As shown in Section 20.6, the potential at which a species in solution is oxidized or reduced depends on concentration. Unless standard conditions are used, predictions based on $E°$ values are merely qualitative. In addition, the rate of a half-reaction depends on the concentration of the electroactive substance at the electrode surface. At a very low concentration, the rate of the redox reaction may depend on the rate at which an ion diffuses from the solution to the electrode surface.

Chemistry ⚬ Now™

Sign in at **www.cengage.com/login** and go to Chapter 20 Contents to see Screen 20.11 for an illustration of water electrolysis.

■ **EXAMPLE 20.10 Electrolysis of Aqueous Solutions**

Problem Predict how products of electrolyses of aqueous solutions of NaF, NaCl, NaBr, and NaI are likely to be different. (The electrolysis of NaI is illustrated in Figure 20.19.)

Strategy The main criterion used to predict the chemistry in an electrolytic cell should be the ease of oxidation and reduction, an assessment based on $E°$ values.

Solution The cathode reaction in all four examples presents no problem—water is reduced to hydroxide ion and H_2 gas in preference to reduction of $Na^+(aq)$ (as in the electrolysis of aqueous NaI). Thus, the primary cathode reaction in all cases is

$$2 H_2O(\ell) + 2 e^- \rightarrow H_2(g) + 2 OH^-(aq)$$

$$E°_{cathode} = -0.83 \text{ V}$$

At the anode, we need to assess the ease of oxidation of the halide ions relative to water. Based on $E°$ values, the ease of oxidation of halide ions is $I^-(aq) > Br^-(aq) > Cl^-(aq) >> F^-(aq)$. Fluoride ion is much more difficult to oxidize than water, and electrolysis of an aqueous solution containing this ion results exclusively in O_2 formation. The primary anode reaction for NaF(aq) is

$$2 H_2O(\ell) \rightarrow O_2(g) + 4 H^+(aq) + 4 e^-$$

Therefore, in this case,

$$E°_{cell} = (-0.83 \text{ V}) - (+1.23 \text{ V}) = -2.06 \text{ V}$$

Recall that chlorine is the primary product at the anode in the electrolysis of aqueous solutions of chloride salts. Therefore, the anode reaction is

$$2 Cl^-(aq) \rightarrow Cl_2(g) + 2 e^-$$

$$E°_{cell} = (-0.83 \text{ V}) - (+1.36 \text{ V}) = -2.19 \text{ V}$$

Bromide ions are considerably easier to oxidize than chloride ions. Br_2 may be expected as the primary product in the electrolysis of aqueous NaBr. For NaBr(aq), the primary anode reaction is

$$2 Br^-(aq) \rightarrow Br_2(\ell) + 2 e^-$$

so $E°_{cell}$ is

$$E°_{cell} = (-0.83 \text{ V}) - (+1.08 \text{ V}) = -1.91 \text{ V}$$

Thus, the electrolysis of NaBr resembles that of NaI (Figure 20.19) in producing the halogen, hydrogen, and hydroxide ion.

EXERCISE 20.14 Electrolysis of Aqueous Solutions

Predict the chemical reactions that will occur at the two electrodes in the electrolysis of an aqueous sodium hydroxide solution. What is the minimum voltage needed to cause this reaction to occur?

20.8 Counting Electrons

Metallic silver is produced at the cathode in the electrolysis of aqueous $AgNO_3$ in which one mole of electrons is required to produce one mole of silver. In contrast, two moles of electrons are required to produce one mole of tin (Figure 20.20):

$$Sn^{2+}(aq) + 2\,e^- \rightarrow Sn(s)$$

It follows that if the number of moles of electrons flowing through the electrolysis cell could be measured, the number of moles of silver or tin produced could be calculated. Conversely, if the amount of silver or tin produced is known, then the number of moles of electrons moving through the circuit could be calculated.

The number of moles of electrons consumed or produced in an electron transfer reaction is obtained by measuring the current flowing in the external electric circuit in a given time. The **current** flowing in an electrical circuit is the amount of charge (in units of coulombs, C) per unit time, and the usual unit for current is the ampere (A). (One ampere equals the passage of one coulomb of charge per second.)

$$\text{Current (amperes, A)} = \frac{\text{electric charge (coulombs, C)}}{\text{time, } t \text{ (seconds, s)}} \quad \textbf{(20.8)}$$

The current passing through an electrochemical cell and the time for which the current flows are easily measured quantities. Therefore, the charge (in coulombs) that passes through a cell can be obtained by multiplying the current (in amperes) by the time (in seconds). Knowing the charge and using the Faraday constant as a conversion factor, we can calculate the number of moles of electrons that passed through an electrochemical cell. In turn, we can use this quantity to calculate the quantities of reactants and products. The following example illustrates this type of calculation.

Chemistry.᛭.Now™

Sign in at **www.cengage.com/login** and go to Chapter 20 Contents to see Screen 20.12 for a tutorial on **quantitative aspects of electrochemistry.**

Historical Perspectives   Electrochemistry and Michael Faraday

The terms anion, cation, electrode, and electrolyte originated with Michael Faraday (1791–1867), one of the most influential people in the history of chemistry. Faraday was apprenticed to a bookbinder in London when he was 13. This situation suited him perfectly, as he enjoyed reading the books sent to the shop for binding. By chance, one of these volumes was a small book on chemistry, which whetted his appetite for science, and he began performing experiments on electricity. In 1812, a patron of the shop invited Faraday to accompany him to the Royal Institute to attend a lecture by one of the most famous chemists of the day, Sir Humphry Davy. Faraday was so intrigued by Davy's lecture that he wrote to ask Davy for a

position as an assistant. He was accepted and began work in 1813. Faraday was so talented that his work proved extraordinarily fruitful, and he was made the director of the laboratory of the Royal Institute about 12 years later.

It has been said that Faraday's contributions were so enormous that, had there been Nobel Prizes when he was alive, he would have received at least six. These prizes could have been awarded for discoveries such as the following:

- Electromagnetic induction, which led to the first transformer and electric motor
- The laws of electrolysis (the effect of electric current on chemicals)
- The magnetic properties of matter

- Benzene and other organic chemicals (which led to important chemical industries)
- The "Faraday effect" (the rotation of the plane of polarized light by a magnetic field)
- The introduction of the concept of electric and magnetic fields

Michael Faraday (1791–1867)

Oesper Collection in the History of Chemistry, University of Cincinnati

In addition to making discoveries that had profound effects on science, Faraday was an educator. He wrote and spoke about his work in memorable ways, especially in lectures to the general public that helped to popularize science.

Problem A current of 2.40 A is passed through a solution containing $Cu^{2+}(aq)$ for 30.0 minutes, with copper metal being deposited at the cathode. What mass of copper, in grams, is deposited?

Strategy A roadmap for this calculation is as follows:

Solution

1. Calculate the charge (number of coulombs) passing through the cell in 30.0 min.

$$\text{Charge (C)} = \text{current (A)} \times \text{time (s)}$$
$$= (2.40 \text{ A})(30.0 \text{ min})(60.0 \text{ s/min})$$
$$= 4.32 \times 10^3 \text{ C}$$

2. Calculate the number of moles of electrons (i.e., the number of Faradays of electricity).

$$(4.32 \times 10^3 \text{ C})\left(\frac{1 \text{ mol } e^-}{96{,}485 \text{ C}}\right) = 4.48 \times 10^{-2} \text{ mol } e^-$$

■ **Faraday Constant** The Faraday constant is the charge carried by 1 mol of electrons:

$$9.6485338 \times 10^4 \text{ C/mol } e^-$$

3. Calculate the amount of copper and, from this, the mass of copper.

$$\text{mass of copper} = (4.48 \times 10^{-2} \text{ mol } e^-)\left(\frac{1 \text{ mol Cu}}{2 \text{ mol } e^-}\right)\left(\frac{63.55 \text{ g Cu}}{1 \text{ mol Cu}}\right) = \boxed{1.42 \text{ g}}$$

Comment The key relation in this calculation is current = charge/time. Most situations will involve knowing two of these three quantities from experiment and calculating the third.

EXERCISE 20.15 Using the Faraday Constant

Calculate the mass of O_2 produced in the electrolysis of water, using a current of 0.445 A for a period of 45 minutes.

EXERCISE 20.16 Using the Faraday Constant

In the commercial production of sodium by electrolysis, the cell operates at 7.0 V and a current of 25×10^3 A. What mass of sodium can be produced in one hour?

Chapter Goals Revisited

Now that you have studied this chapter, you should ask whether you have met the chapter goals. In particular, you should be able to:

Balance equations for oxidation–reduction reactions in acidic or basic solutions using the half-reaction approach Study Question(s) assignable in OWL: 2, 4-6, 16; Go Chemistry Module 25.

Understand the principles underlying voltaic cells

a. In a voltaic cell, identify the half-reactions occurring at the anode and the cathode, the polarity of the electrodes, the direction of electron flow in the external circuit, and the direction of ion flow in the salt bridge (Section 20.2). Study Question(s) assignable in OWL: 8, 10, 16, 51.

b. Appreciate the chemistry and advantages and disadvantages of dry cells, alkaline batteries, lead storage batteries, and Ni-cad batteries (Section 20.3).

c. Understand how fuel cells work, and recognize the difference between batteries and fuel cells (Section 20.3).

Understand how to use electrochemical potentials

a. Understand the process by which standard reduction potentials are determined, and identify standard conditions as applied to electrochemistry (Section 20.4).

b. Describe the standard hydrogen electrode ($E° = 0.00$ V), and explain how it is used as the standard to determine the standard potentials of half-reactions (Section 20.4).

c. Know how to use standard reduction potentials to determine cell voltages for cells under standard conditions (Equation 20.1). Study Question(s) assignable in OWL: 14, 16, 18, 56, 57.

d. Know how to use a table of standard reduction potentials (Table 20.1 and Appendix M) to rank the strengths of oxidizing and reducing agents, to predict which substances can reduce or oxidize another species, and to predict whether redox reactions will be product-favored or reactant-favored (Sections 20.4 and 20.5). Study Question(s) assignable in OWL: 20, 22, 24, 55, 56, 82.

e. Use the Nernst equation (Equations 20.2 and 20.3) to calculate the cell potential under nonstandard conditions (Section 20.5). Study Question(s) assignable in OWL: 26, 28, 30, 36.

f. Explain how cell voltage relates to ion concentration, and explain how this allows the determination of pH (Section 20.5) and other ion concentrations.

g. Use the relationships between cell voltage ($E°_{cell}$) and free energy ($\Delta_r G°$) (Equations 20.5 and 20.6) and between $E°_{cell}$ and an equilibrium constant for the cell reaction (Equation 20.7) (Section 20.6 and Table 20.2). Study Question(s) assignable in OWL: 32, 34, 60, 61, 63, 78, 86, 88.

Explore electrolysis, the use of electrical energy to produce chemical change

a. Describe the chemical processes occurring in an electrolysis. Recognize the factors that determine which substances are oxidized and reduced at the electrodes (Section 20.7). Study Question(s) assignable in OWL: 40, 41.

b. Relate the amount of a substance oxidized or reduced to the amount of current and the time the current flows (Section 20.8). Study Question(s) assignable in OWL: 44, 46, 48, 64-66, 73, 81.

Chemistry ⚛ Now™ Sign in at
www.cengage.com/login to:

• Assess your understanding with Study Questions in OWL keyed to each goal in the Goals and Homework menu for this chapter

• For quick review, download Go Chemistry mini-lecture flashcard modules (or purchase them at **www.ichapters.com**)

• Check your readiness for an exam by taking the Pre-Test and exploring the modules recommended in your Personalized Study plan.

❓ Access **How Do I Solve It?** tutorials on how to approach problem solving using concepts in this chapter.

For additional preparation for an examination on this chapter see the *Let's Review* section on pages 948–961.

KEY EQUATIONS

Equation 20.1 (page 917): Calculating a standard cell potential, $E°_{cell}$, from standard half-cell potentials.

$$E°_{cell} = E°_{cathode} - E°_{anode}$$

Equation 20.3 (page 925): Nernst equation (at 298 K).

$$E = E° - \frac{0.0257}{n}\ln Q$$

E is the cell potential under nonstandard conditions; n is the number of electrons transferred from the reducing agent to the oxidizing agent (according to the balanced equation); and Q is the reaction quotient.

Equation 20.6 (page 929): Relationship between standard free energy change and the standard cell potential.

$$\Delta G° = -nFE°$$

F is the Faraday constant, 96,485 C/mol e^-.

Equation 20.7 (page 929): Relationship between the equilibrium constant and the standard cell potential for a reaction (at 298 K).

$$\ln K = \frac{nE°}{0.0257}$$

Equation 20.8 (page 937): Relationship between current, electric charge, and time.

$$\text{Current (amperes, A)} = \frac{\text{electric charge (coulombs, C)}}{\text{time, } t \text{ (seconds, s)}}$$

STUDY QUESTIONS

OWL Online homework for this chapter may be assigned in OWL.

▲ denotes challenging questions.

■ denotes questions assignable in OWL.

Blue-numbered questions have answers in Appendix O and fully-worked solutions in the *Student Solutions Manual*.

Practicing Skills

Balancing Equations for Oxidation–Reduction Reactions
(See Examples 20.1–20.3 and ChemistryNow Screen 20.3.)

When balancing the following redox equations, it may be necessary to add $H^+(aq)$ or $H^+(aq)$ plus H_2O for reactions in acid, and $OH^-(aq)$ or $OH^-(aq)$ plus H_2O for reactions in base.

1. Write balanced equations for the following half-reactions. Specify whether each is an oxidation or reduction.
   (a) $Cr(s) \rightarrow Cr^{3+}(aq)$ (in acid)
   (b) $AsH_3(g) \rightarrow As(s)$ (in acid)
   (c) $VO_3^-(aq) \rightarrow V^{2+}(aq)$ (in acid)
   (d) $Ag(s) \rightarrow Ag_2O(s)$ (in base)

2. ■ Write balanced equations for the following half-reactions. Specify whether each is an oxidation or reduction.
   (a) $H_2O_2(aq) \rightarrow O_2(g)$ (in acid)
   (b) $H_2C_2O_4(aq) \rightarrow CO_2(g)$ (in acid)
   (c) $NO_3^-(aq) \rightarrow NO(g)$ (in acid)
   (d) $MnO_4^-(aq) \rightarrow MnO_2(s)$ (in base)

3. Balance the following redox equations. All occur in acid solution.
   (a) $Ag(s) + NO_3^-(aq) \rightarrow NO_2(g) + Ag^+(aq)$
   (b) $MnO_4^-(aq) + HSO_3^-(aq) \rightarrow Mn^{2+}(aq) + SO_4^{2-}(aq)$
   (c) $Zn(s) + NO_3^-(aq) \rightarrow Zn^{2+}(aq) + N_2O(g)$
   (d) $Cr(s) + NO_3^-(aq) \rightarrow Cr^{3+}(aq) + NO(g)$

4. ■ Balance the following redox equations. All occur in acid solution.
   (a) $Sn(s) + H^+(aq) \rightarrow Sn^{2+}(aq) + H_2(g)$
   (b) $Cr_2O_7^{2-}(aq) + Fe^{2+}(aq) \rightarrow Cr^{3+}(aq) + Fe^{3+}(aq)$
   (c) $MnO_2(s) + Cl^-(aq) \rightarrow Mn^{2+}(aq) + Cl_2(g)$
   (d) $CH_2O(aq) + Ag^+(aq) \rightarrow HCO_2H(aq) + Ag(s)$

5. ■ Balance the following redox equations. All occur in basic solution.
   (a) $Al(s) + H_2O(\ell) \rightarrow Al(OH)_4^-(aq) + H_2(g)$
   (b) $CrO_4^{2-}(aq) + SO_3^{2-}(aq) \rightarrow Cr(OH)_3(s) + SO_4^{2-}(aq)$
   (c) $Zn(s) + Cu(OH)_2(s) \rightarrow [Zn(OH)_4]^{2-}(aq) + Cu(s)$
   (d) $HS^-(aq) + ClO_3^-(aq) \rightarrow S(s) + Cl^-(aq)$

6. ■ Balance the following redox equations. All occur in basic solution.
(a) $Fe(OH)_3(s) + Cr(s) \rightarrow Cr(OH)_3(s) + Fe(OH)_2(s)$
(b) $NiO_2(s) + Zn(s) \rightarrow Ni(OH)_2(s) + Zn(OH)_2(s)$
(c) $Fe(OH)_2(s) + CrO_4^{2-}(aq) \rightarrow$
$$Fe(OH)_3(s) + [Cr(OH)_4]^-(aq)$$
(d) $N_2H_4(aq) + Ag_2O(s) \rightarrow N_2(g) + Ag(s)$

Constructing Voltaic Cells
(See Example 20.4 and ChemistryNow Screen 20.4.)

7. A voltaic cell is constructed using the reaction of chromium metal and iron(II) ion.

$$2\ Cr(s) + 3\ Fe^{2+}(aq) \rightarrow 2\ Cr^{3+}(aq) + 3\ Fe(s)$$

Complete the following sentences: Electrons in the external circuit flow from the ___ electrode to the ___ electrode. Negative ions move in the salt bridge from the ___ half-cell to the ___ half-cell. The half-reaction at the anode is ___, and that at the cathode is ___.

8. ■ A voltaic cell is constructed using the reaction

$$Mg(s) + 2\ H^+(aq) \rightarrow Mg^{2+}(aq) + H_2(g)$$

(a) Write equations for the oxidation and reduction half-reactions.
(b) Which half-reaction occurs in the anode compartment, and which occurs in the cathode compartment?
(c) Complete the following sentences: Electrons in the external circuit flow from the ___ electrode to the ___ electrode. Negative ions move in the salt bridge from the ___ half-cell to the ___ half-cell. The half-reaction at the anode is ___, and that at the cathode is ___.

9. The half-cells $Fe^{2+}(aq) \mid Fe(s)$ and $O_2(g) \mid H_2O$ (in acid solution) are linked to create a voltaic cell.
(a) Write equations for the oxidation and reduction half-reactions and for the overall (cell) reaction.
(b) Which half-reaction occurs in the anode compartment, and which occurs in the cathode compartment?
(c) Complete the following sentences: Electrons in the external circuit flow from the ___ electrode to the ___ electrode. Negative ions move in the salt bridge from the ___ half-cell to the ___ half-cell.

10. ■ The half-cells $Sn^2(aq) \mid Sn(s)$ and $Cl_2(g) \mid Cl^-(aq)$ are linked to create a voltaic cell.
(a) Write equations for the oxidation and reduction half-reactions and for the overall (cell) reaction.
(b) Which half-reaction occurs in the anode compartment, and which occurs in the cathode compartment?

(c) Complete the following sentences: Electrons in the external circuit flow from the ___ electrode to the ___ electrode. Negative ions move in the salt bridge from the ___ half-cell to the ___ half-cell.

Commercial Cells

11. What are the similarities and differences between dry cells, alkaline batteries, and Ni-cad batteries?

12. What reactions occur when a lead storage battery is re-charged?

Standard Electrochemical Potentials
(See Example 20.5 and ChemistryNow Screens 20.6 and 20.7.)

13. Calculate the value of $E°$ for each of the following reactions. Decide whether each is product-favored in the direction written.
(a) $2\ I^-(aq) + Zn^{2+}(aq) \rightarrow I_2(s) + Zn(s)$
(b) $Zn^{2+}(aq) + Ni(s) \rightarrow Zn(s) + Ni^{2+}(aq)$
(c) $2\ Cl^-(aq) + Cu^{2+}(aq) \rightarrow Cu(s) + Cl_2(g)$
(d) $Fe^{2+}(aq) + Ag^+(aq) \rightarrow Fe^{3+}(aq) + Ag(s)$

14. ■ Calculate the value of $E°$ for each of the following reactions. Decide whether each is product-favored in the direction written. [Reaction (d) occurs in basic solution.]
(a) $Br_2(\ell) + Mg(s) \rightarrow Mg^{2+}(aq) + 2\ Br^-(aq)$
(b) $Zn^{2+}(aq) + Mg(s) \rightarrow Zn(s) + Mg^{2+}(aq)$
(c) $Sn^{2+}(aq) + 2\ Ag^+(aq) \rightarrow Sn^{4+}(aq) + 2\ Ag(s)$
(d) $2\ Zn(s) + O_2(g) + 2\ H_2O(\ell) + 4\ OH^-(aq) \rightarrow$
$$2\ [Zn(OH)_4]^{2-}(aq)$$

15. Balance each of the following unbalanced equations; then calculate the standard potential, $E°$, and decide whether each is product-favored as written. (All reactions occur in acid solution.)
(a) $Sn^{2+}(aq) + Ag(s) \rightarrow Sn(s) + Ag^+(aq)$
(b) $Al(s) + Sn^{4+}(aq) \rightarrow Sn^{2+}(aq) + Al^{3+}(aq)$
(c) $ClO_3^-(aq) + Ce^{3+}(aq) \rightarrow Cl_2(g) + Ce^{4+}(aq)$
(d) $Cu(s) + NO_3^-(aq) \rightarrow Cu^{2+}(aq) + NO(g)$

16. ■ Balance each of the following unbalanced equations; then calculate the standard potential, $E°$, and decide whether each is product-favored as written. (All reactions occur in acid solution.)
(a) $I_2(s) + Br^-(aq) \rightarrow I^-(aq) + Br_2(\ell)$
(b) $Fe^{2+}(aq) + Cu^{2+}(aq) \rightarrow Cu(s) + Fe^{3+}(aq)$
(c) $Fe^{2+}(aq) + Cr_2O_7^{2-}(aq) \rightarrow Fe^{3+}(aq) + Cr^{3+}(aq)$
(d) $MnO_4^-(aq) + HNO_2(aq) \rightarrow Mn^{2+}(aq) + NO_3^-(aq)$

17. Consider the following half-reactions:

Half-Reaction	$E°$ (V)
$Cu^{2+}(aq) + 2\ e^- \rightarrow Cu(s)$	$+0.34$
$Sn^{2+}(aq) + 2\ e^- \rightarrow Sn(s)$	-0.14
$Fe^{2+}(aq) + 2\ e^- \rightarrow Fe(s)$	-0.44
$Zn^{2+}(aq) + 2\ e^- \rightarrow Zn(s)$	-0.76
$Al^{3+}(aq) + 3\ e^- \rightarrow Al(s)$	-1.66

(a) Based on $E°$ values, which metal is the most easily oxidized?

(b) Which metals on this list are capable of reducing $Fe^{2+}(aq)$ to $Fe(s)$?

(c) Write a balanced chemical equation for the reaction of $Fe^{2+}(aq)$ with $Sn(s)$. Is this reaction product-favored or reactant-favored?

(d) Write a balanced chemical equation for the reaction of $Zn^{2+}(aq)$ with $Sn(s)$. Is this reaction product-favored or reactant-favored?

18. ■ Consider the following half-reactions:

Half-Reaction	$E°$ (V)
$MnO_4^-(aq) + 8\ H^+(aq) + 5\ e^- \rightarrow Mn^{2+}(aq) + 4\ H_2O(\ell)$	$+1.51$
$BrO_3^-(aq) + 6\ H^+(aq) + 6\ e^- \rightarrow Br^-(aq) + 3\ H_2O(\ell)$	$+1.47$
$Cr_2O_7^{2-}(aq) + 14\ H^+(aq) + 6\ e^- \rightarrow 2\ Cr^{3+}(aq) + 7\ H_2O(\ell)$	$+1.33$
$NO_3^-(aq) + 4\ H^+(aq) + 3\ e^- \rightarrow NO(g) + 2\ H_2O(\ell)$	$+0.96$
$SO_4^{2-}(aq) + 4\ H^+(aq) + 2\ e^- \rightarrow SO_2(g) + 2\ H_2O(\ell)$	$+0.20$

(a) Choosing from among the reactants in these half-reactions, identify the strongest and weakest oxidizing agents.

(b) Which of the oxidizing agents listed is (are) capable of oxidizing $Br^-(aq)$ to $BrO_3^-(aq)$ (in acid solution)?

(c) Write a balanced chemical equation for the reaction of $Cr_2O_7^{2-}(aq)$ with $SO_2(g)$ in acid solution. Is this reaction product-favored or reactant-favored?

(d) Write a balanced chemical equation for the reaction of $Cr_2O_7^{2-}(aq)$ with $Mn^{2+}(aq)$. Is this reaction product-favored or reactant-favored?

Ranking Oxidizing and Reducing Agents

(See Example 20.5 and ChemistryNow Screen 20.7.) Use a table of standard reduction potentials (Table 20.1 or Appendix M) to answer Study Questions 19–24.

19. Which of the following elements is the best reducing agent under standard conditions?
(a) Cu
(b) Zn
(c) Fe
(d) Ag
(e) Cr

20. ■ From the following list, identify those elements that are easier to oxidize than $H_2(g)$.
(a) Cu
(b) Zn
(c) Fe
(d) Ag
(e) Cr

21. Which of the following ions is most easily reduced?
(a) $Cu^{2+}(aq)$
(b) $Zn^{2+}(aq)$
(c) $Fe^{2+}(aq)$
(d) $Ag^+(aq)$
(e) $Al^{3+}(aq)$

22. ■ From the following list, identify the ions that are more easily reduced than $H^+(aq)$.
(a) $Cu^{2+}(aq)$
(b) $Zn^{2+}(aq)$
(c) $Fe^{2+}(aq)$
(d) $Ag^+(aq)$
(e) $Al^{3+}(aq)$

23. (a) Which halogen is most easily reduced: F_2, Cl_2, Br_2, or I_2 in acidic solution?

(b) Identify the halogens that are better oxidizing agents than $MnO_2(s)$ in acidic solution.

24. ■ (a) Which ion is most easily oxidized to the elemental halogen: F^-, Cl^-, Br^-, or I^- in acidic solution?

(b) Identify the halide ions that are more easily oxidized than $H_2O(\ell)$ in acidic solution.

Electrochemical Cells Under Nonstandard Conditions

(See Examples 20.6 and 20.7 and ChemistryNow Screen 20.8.)

25. Calculate the potential delivered by a voltaic cell using the following reaction if all dissolved species are 2.5×10^{-2} M and the pressure of H_2 is 1.0 bar.

$$Zn(s) + 2\ H_2O(\ell) + 2\ OH^-(aq) \rightarrow [Zn(OH)_4]^{2-}(aq) + H_2\ (g)$$

26. ■ Calculate the potential developed by a voltaic cell using the following reaction if all dissolved species are 0.015 M.

$$2\ Fe^{2+}(aq) + H_2O_2(aq) + 2\ H^+(aq) \rightarrow 2\ Fe^{3+}(aq) + 2\ H_2O(\ell)$$

27. One half-cell in a voltaic cell is constructed from a silver wire dipped into a 0.25 M solution of $AgNO_3$. The other half-cell consists of a zinc electrode in a 0.010 M solution of $Zn(NO_3)_2$. Calculate the cell potential.

28. ■ One half-cell in a voltaic cell is constructed from a copper wire dipped into a 4.8×10^{-3} M solution of $Cu(NO_3)_2$. The other half-cell consists of a zinc electrode in a 0.40 M solution of $Zn(NO_3)_2$. Calculate the cell potential.

29. One half-cell in a voltaic cell is constructed from a silver wire dipped into a $AgNO_3$ solution of unknown concentration. The other half-cell consists of a zinc electrode in a 1.0 M solution of $Zn(NO_3)_2$. A potential of 1.48 V is measured for this cell. Use this information to calculate the concentration of $Ag^+(aq)$.

30. ■ One half-cell in a voltaic cell is constructed from an iron wire dipped into an $Fe(NO_3)_2$ solution of unknown concentration. The other half-cell is a standard hydrogen electrode. A potential of 0.49 V is measured for this cell. Use this information to calculate the concentration of $Fe^{2+}(aq)$.

▲ more challenging   ■ in OWL   Blue-numbered questions answered in Appendix O

Electrochemistry, Thermodynamics, and Equilibrium
(See Examples 20.8 and 20.9 and ChemistryNow Screen 20.9.)

31. Calculate $\Delta_r G°$ and the equilibrium constant for the following reactions.
    (a) $2\ Fe^{3+}(aq) + 2\ I^-(aq) \rightleftharpoons 2\ Fe^{2+}(aq) + I_2(aq)$
    (b) $I_2(aq) + 2\ Br^-(aq) \rightleftharpoons 2\ I^-(aq) + Br_2(aq)$

32. ■ Calculate $\Delta_r G°$ and the equilibrium constant for the following reactions.
    (a) $Zn^{2+}(aq) + Ni(s) \rightleftharpoons Zn(s) + Ni^{2+}(aq)$
    (b) $Cu(s) + 2\ Ag^+(aq) \rightleftharpoons Cu^{2+}(aq) + 2\ Ag(s)$

33. Use standard reduction potentials (Appendix M) for the half-reactions $AgBr(s) + e^- \rightarrow Ag(s) + Br^-(aq)$ and $Ag^+(aq) + e^- \rightarrow Ag(s)$ to calculate the value of K_{sp} for AgBr.

34. ■ Use the standard reduction potentials (Appendix M) for the half-reactions $Hg_2Cl_2(s) + 2\ e^- \rightarrow 2\ Hg(\ell) + 2\ Cl^-(aq)$ and $Hg_2^{2+}(aq) + 2\ e^- \rightarrow 2\ Hg(\ell)$ to calculate the value of K_{sp} for Hg_2Cl_2.

35. Use the standard reduction potentials (Appendix M) for the half-reactions $[AuCl_4]^-(aq) + 3\ e^- \rightarrow Au(s) + 4\ Cl^-(aq)$ and $Au^{3+}(aq) + 3\ e^- \rightarrow Au(s)$ to calculate the value of $K_{formation}$ for the complex ion $[AuCl_4]^-(aq)$.

36. ■ Use the standard reduction potentials (Appendix M) for the half-reactions $[Zn(OH)_4]^{2-}(aq) + 2\ e^- \rightarrow Zn(s) + 4\ OH^-(aq)$ and $Zn^{2+}(aq) + 2\ e^- \rightarrow Zn(s)$ to calculate the value of $K_{formation}$ for the complex ion $[Zn(OH)_4]^{2-}$.

Electrolysis
(See Section 20.7, Example 20.10, and ChemistryNow Screen 20.10.)

37. Diagram the apparatus used to electrolyze molten NaCl. Identify the anode and the cathode. Trace the movement of electrons through the external circuit and the movement of ions in the electrolysis cell.

38. Diagram the apparatus used to electrolyze aqueous $CuCl_2$. Identify the reaction products, the anode, and the cathode. Trace the movement of electrons through the external circuit and the movement of ions in the electrolysis cell.

39. Which product, O_2 or F_2, is more likely to form at the anode in the electrolysis of an aqueous solution of KF? Explain your reasoning.

40. ■ Which product, Ca or H_2, is more likely to form at the cathode in the electrolysis of $CaCl_2$? Explain your reasoning.

41. ■ An aqueous solution of KBr is placed in a beaker with two inert platinum electrodes. When the cell is attached to an external source of electrical energy, electrolysis occurs.
    (a) Hydrogen gas and hydroxide ion form at the cathode. Write an equation for the half-reaction that occurs at this electrode.
    (b) Bromine is the primary product at the anode. Write an equation for its formation.

42. An aqueous solution of Na_2S is placed in a beaker with two inert platinum electrodes. When the cell is attached to an external battery, electrolysis occurs.
    (a) Hydrogen gas and hydroxide ion form at the cathode. Write an equation for the half-reaction that occurs at this electrode.
    (b) Sulfur is the primary product at the anode. Write an equation for its formation.

Counting Electrons
(See Example 20.11 and ChemistryNow Screen 20.12.)

43. In the electrolysis of a solution containing $Ni^{2+}(aq)$, metallic Ni(s) deposits on the cathode. Using a current of 0.150 A for 12.2 min, what mass of nickel will form?

44. ■ In the electrolysis of a solution containing $Ag^+(aq)$, metallic Ag(s) deposits on the cathode. Using a current of 1.12 A for 2.40 h, what mass of silver forms?

45. Electrolysis of a solution of $CuSO_4(aq)$ to give copper metal is carried out using a current of 0.66 A. How long should electrolysis continue to produce 0.50 g of copper?

46. ■ Electrolysis of a solution of $Zn(NO_3)_2(aq)$ to give zinc metal is carried out using a current of 2.12 A. How long should electrolysis continue in order to prepare 2.5 g of zinc?

47. A voltaic cell can be built using the reaction between Al metal and O_2 from the air. If the Al anode of this cell consists of 84 g of aluminum, how many hours can the cell produce 1.0 A of electricity, assuming an unlimited supply of O_2?

48. ■ Assume the specifications of a Ni-Cd voltaic cell include delivery of 0.25 A of current for 1.00 h. What is the minimum mass of the cadmium that must be used to make the anode in this cell?

General Questions
These questions are not designated as to type or location in the chapter. They may combine several concepts.

49. Write balanced equations for the following half-reactions.
    (a) $UO_2^+(aq) \rightarrow U^{4+}(aq)$ (acid solution)
    (b) $ClO_3^-(aq) \rightarrow Cl^-(aq)$ (acid solution)
    (c) $N_2H_4(aq) \rightarrow N_2(g)$ (basic solution)
    (d) $ClO^-(aq) \rightarrow Cl^-(aq)$ (basic solution)

50. Balance the following equations.
(a) $Zn(s) + VO^{2+}(aq) \rightarrow$
$\qquad Zn^{2+}(aq) + V^{3+}(aq)$ (acid solution)
(b) $Zn(s) + VO_3^-(aq) \rightarrow$
$\qquad V^{2+}(aq) + Zn^{2+}(aq)$ (acid solution)
(c) $Zn(s) + ClO^-(aq) \rightarrow$
$\qquad Zn(OH)_2(s) + Cl^-(aq)$ (basic solution)
(d) $ClO^-(aq) + [Cr(OH)_4]^-(aq) \rightarrow$
$\qquad Cl^-(aq) + CrO_4^{2-}(aq)$ (basic solution)

51. ■ Magnesium metal is oxidized, and silver ions are reduced in a voltaic cell using $Mg^{2+}(aq, 1 \text{ M}) \mid Mg$ and
$Ag^+(aq, 1 \text{ M}) \mid Ag$ half-cells.

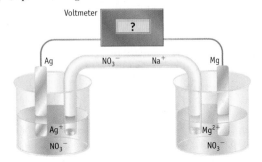

Voltmeter

?

Ag NO_3^- Na^+ Mg

Ag^+ Mg^{2+}
NO_3^- NO_3^-

(a) Label each part of the cell.
(b) Write equations for the half-reactions occurring at
the anode and the cathode, and write an equation
for the net reaction in the cell.
(c) Trace the movement of electrons in the external
circuit. Assuming the salt bridge contains $NaNO_3$,
trace the movement of the Na^+ and NO_3^- ions in
the salt bridge that occurs when a voltaic cell produces current. Why is a salt bridge required in a
cell?

52. You want to set up a series of voltaic cells with specific
cell voltages. A $Zn^{2+}(aq, 1.0 \text{ M}) \mid Zn(s)$ half-cell is in
one compartment. Identify several half-cells that you
could use so that the cell potential will be close to
(a) 1.1 V and (b) 0.50 V. Consider cells in which zinc
can be either the cathode or the anode.

53. You want to set up a series of voltaic cells with specific
cell potentials. The $Ag^+(aq, 1.0 \text{ M}) \mid Ag(s)$ half-cell is
one of the compartments. Identify several half-cells that
you could use so that the cell potential will be close to
(a) 1.7 V and (b) 0.50 V. Consider cells in which silver
can be either the cathode or the anode.

54. Which of the following reactions is (are) product-
favored?
(a) $Zn(s) + I_2(s) \rightarrow Zn^{2+}(aq) + 2 I^-(aq)$
(b) $2 Cl^-(aq) + I_2(s) \rightarrow Cl_2(g) + 2 I^-(aq)$
(c) $2 Na^+(aq) + 2 Cl^-(aq) \rightarrow 2 Na(s) + Cl_2(g)$
(d) $2 K(s) + H_2O(\ell) \rightarrow$
$\qquad 2 K^+(aq) + H_2(g) + 2 OH^-(aq)$

55. ■ In the table of standard reduction potentials, locate
the half-reactions for the reductions of the following
metal ions to the metal: $Sn^{2+}(aq)$, $Au^+(aq)$, $Zn^{2+}(aq)$,
$Co^{2+}(aq)$, $Ag^+(aq)$, $Cu^{2+}(aq)$. Among the metal ions
and metals that make up these half-reactions:
(a) Which metal ion is the weakest oxidizing agent?
(b) Which metal ion is the strongest oxidizing agent?
(c) Which metal is the strongest reducing agent?
(d) Which metal is the weakest reducing agent?
(e) Will $Sn(s)$ reduce $Cu^{2+}(aq)$ to $Cu(s)$?
(f) Will $Ag(s)$ reduce $Co^{2+}(aq)$ to $Co(s)$?
(g) Which metal ions on the list can be reduced
by $Sn(s)$?
(h) What metals can be oxidized by $Ag^+(aq)$?

56. ■ ▲ In the table of standard reduction potentials, locate the half-reactions for the reductions of the following nonmetals: F_2, Cl_2, Br_2, I_2 (reduction to halide
ions), and O_2, S, Se (reduction to H_2X in aqueous
acid). Among the elements, ions, and compounds that
make up these half-reactions:
(a) Which element is the weakest oxidizing agent?
(b) Which element is the weakest reducing agent?
(c) Which of the elements listed is (are) capable of
oxidizing H_2O to O_2?
(d) Which of these elements listed is (are) capable of
oxidizing H_2S to S?
(e) Is O_2 capable of oxidizing I^- to I_2, in acid solution?
(f) Is S capable of oxidizing I^- to I_2?
(g) Is the reaction $H_2S(aq) + Se(s) \rightarrow H_2Se(aq) + S(s)$
product-favored?
(h) Is the reaction $H_2S(aq) + I_2(s) \rightarrow 2 H^+(aq) +$
$2 I^-(aq) + S(s)$ product-favored?

57. ■ Four voltaic cells are set up. In each, one half-cell
contains a standard hydrogen electrode. The second
half-cell is one of the following: $Cr^{3+}(aq, 1.0 \text{ M}) \mid Cr(s)$,
$Fe^{2+}(aq, 1.0 \text{ M}) \mid Fe(s)$, $Cu^{2+}(aq, 1.0 \text{ M}) \mid Cu(s)$, or
$Mg^{2+}(aq, 1.0 \text{ M}) \mid Mg(s)$.
(a) In which of the voltaic cells does the hydrogen
electrode serve as the cathode?
(b) Which voltaic cell produces the highest voltage?
Which produces the lowest voltage?

58. The following half-cells are available: $Ag^+(aq, 1.0 \text{ M}) \mid$
$Ag(s)$, $Zn^{2+}(aq, 1.0 \text{ M}) \mid Zn(s)$, $Cu^{2+}(aq, 1.0 \text{ M}) \mid Cu(s)$,
and $Co^{2+}(aq, 1.0 \text{ M}) \mid Co(s)$. Linking any two half-cells
makes a voltaic cell. Given four different half-cells, six
voltaic cells are possible. These are labeled, for simplicity, Ag-Zn, Ag-Cu, Ag-Co, Zn-Cu, Zn-Co, and Cu-Co.
(a) In which of the voltaic cells does the copper electrode serve as the cathode? In which of the voltaic
cells does the cobalt electrode serve as the anode?
(b) Which combination of half-cells generates the highest potential? Which combination generates the
lowest potential?

59. The reaction occurring in the cell in which Al_2O_3 and aluminum salts are electrolyzed is $Al^{3+}(aq) + 3\ e^- \rightarrow Al(s)$. If the electrolysis cell operates at 5.0 V and 1.0×10^5 A, what mass of aluminum metal can be produced in a 24-h day?

60. ■ ▲ A cell is constructed using the following half-reactions:

$Ag^+(aq) + e^- \rightarrow Ag(s)$

$Ag_2SO_4(s) + 2\ e^- \rightarrow$
$$2\ Ag(s) + SO_4^{2-}(aq) \quad E° = 0.653\ V$$

(a) What reactions should be observed at the anode and cathode?
(b) Calculate the solubility product constant, K_{sp}, for Ag_2SO_4.

61. ■ ▲ A potential of 0.142 V is recorded (under standard conditions) for a voltaic cell constructed using the following half reactions:

Cathode: $\quad Pb^{2+}(aq) + 2\ e^- \rightarrow Pb(s)$

Anode: $\quad PbCl_2(s) + 2\ e^- \rightarrow Pb(s) + 2\ Cl^-(aq)$

Net: $\quad Pb^{2+}(aq) + 2\ Cl^-(aq) \rightarrow PbCl_2(s)$

(a) What is the standard reduction potential for the anode reaction?
(b) Estimate the solubility product, K_{sp}, for $PbCl_2$.

62. What is the value of $E°$ for the following half-reaction?

$$Ag_2CrO_4(s) + 2\ e^- \rightarrow 2\ Ag(s) + CrO_4^{2-}(aq)$$

63. ■ The standard voltage, $E°$, for the reaction of $Zn(s)$ and $Cl_2(g)$ is +2.12 V. What is the standard free energy change, $\Delta_r G°$, for the reaction?

64. ■ ▲ An electrolysis cell for aluminum production operates at 5.0 V and a current of 1.0×10^5 A. Calculate the number of kilowatt-hours of energy required to produce 1 metric ton (1.0×10^3 kg) of aluminum. (1 kWh = 3.6×10^6 J and 1 J = 1 C · V.)

65. ■ ▲ Electrolysis of molten NaCl is done in cells operating at 7.0 V and 4.0×10^4 A. What mass of $Na(s)$ and $Cl_2(g)$ can be produced in one day in such a cell? What is the energy consumption in kilowatt-hours? (1 kWh = 3.6×10^6 J and 1 J = 1 C · V.)

66. ■ ▲ A current of 0.0100 A is passed through a solution of rhodium sulfate, causing reduction of the metal ion to the metal. After 3.00 h, 0.038 g of Rh has been deposited. What is the charge on the rhodium ion, Rh^{n+}? What is the formula for rhodium sulfate?

67. ▲ A current of 0.44 A is passed through a solution of ruthenium nitrate causing reduction of the metal ion to the metal. After 25.0 min, 0.345 g of Ru has been deposited. What is the charge on the ruthenium ion, Ru^{n+}? What is the formula for ruthenium nitrate?

68. The total charge that can be delivered by a large dry cell battery before its voltage drops too low is usually about 35 amp-hours. (One amp-hour is the charge that passes through a circuit when 1 A flows for 1 h.) What mass of Zn is consumed when 35 amp-hours are drawn from the cell?

69. Chlorine gas is obtained commercially by electrolysis of brine (a concentrated aqueous solution of NaCl). If the electrolysis cells operate at 4.6 V and 3.0×10^5 A, what mass of chlorine can be produced in a 24-h day?

70. ▲ Write balanced equations for the following reduction half-reactions involving organic compounds.
(a) $HCO_2H \rightarrow CH_2O$ (acid solution)
(b) $C_6H_5CO_2H \rightarrow C_6H_5CH_3$ (acid solution)
(c) $CH_3CH_2CHO \rightarrow CH_3CH_2CH_2OH$ (acid solution)
(d) $CH_3OH \rightarrow CH_4$ (acid solution)

71. ▲ Balance the following equations involving organic compounds.
(a) $Ag^+(aq) + C_6H_5CHO(aq) \rightarrow$
$$Ag(s) + C_6H_5CO_2H(aq) \quad \text{(acid solution)}$$
(b) $CH_3CH_2OH + Cr_2O_7^{2-}(aq) \rightarrow$
$$CH_3CO_2H(aq) + Cr^{3+}(aq) \quad \text{(acid solution)}$$

72. A voltaic cell is constructed in which one half-cell consists of a silver wire in an aqueous solution of $AgNO_3$. The other half-cell consists of an inert platinum wire in an aqueous solution containing $Fe^{2+}(aq)$ and $Fe^{3+}(aq)$.
(a) Calculate the cell potential, assuming standard conditions.
(b) Write the net ionic equation for the reaction occurring in the cell.
(c) In this voltaic cell, which electrode is the anode, and which is the cathode?
(d) If $[Ag^+]$ is 0.10 M, and $[Fe^{2+}]$ and $[Fe^{3+}]$ are both 1.0 M, what is the cell potential? Is the net cell reaction still that used in part (a)? If not, what is the net reaction under the new conditions?

73. ■ An expensive but lighter alternative to the lead storage battery is the silver-zinc battery.

$$Ag_2O(s) + Zn(s) + H_2O(\ell) \rightarrow Zn(OH)_2(s) + 2\ Ag(s)$$

The electrolyte is 40% KOH, and silver–silver oxide electrodes are separated from zinc–zinc hydroxide electrodes by a plastic sheet that is permeable to hydroxide ions. Under normal operating conditions, the battery has a potential of 1.59 V.
(a) How much energy can be produced per gram of reactants in the silver-zinc battery? Assume the battery produces a current of 0.10 A.
(b) How much energy can be produced per gram of reactants in the standard lead storage battery? Assume the battery produces a current of 0.10 A at 2.0 V.
(c) Which battery (silver-zinc or lead storage) produces the greater energy per gram of reactants?

▲ more challenging   ■ in OWL   Blue-numbered questions answered in Appendix O

74. The specifications for a lead storage battery include delivery of a steady 1.5 A of current for 15 h.
  (a) What is the minimum mass of lead that will be used in the anode?
  (b) What mass of PbO_2 must be used in the cathode?
  (c) Assume that the volume of the battery is 0.50 L. What is the minimum molarity of H_2SO_4 necessary?

75. Manganese may play an important role in chemical cycles in the oceans (page 932). Two reactions involving manganese are the reduction of nitrate ions (to NO) with Mn^{2+} ions and the oxidation of ammonia (to N_2) with MnO_2.
  (a) Write balanced chemical equations for these reactions (in acid solution).
  (b) Calculate $E°_{cell}$ for the reactions. (One half-reaction potential you need is for reduction of N_2 to NH_4^+, $E° = -0.272$ V.)

76. ▲ You want to use electrolysis to plate a cylindrical object (radius = 2.50 and length = 20.00 cm) with a coating of nickel metal, 4.0 mm thick. You place the object in a bath containing a salt (Na_2SO_4). One electrode is impure nickel, and the other is the object to be plated. The electrolyzing potential is 2.50 V.
  (a) Which is the anode, and which is the cathode in the experiment? What half-reaction occurs at each electrode?
  (b) Calculate the number of kilowatt-hours (kWh) of energy required to carry out the electrolysis. (1 kWh = 3.6×10^6 J and 1 J = 1 C $\times$ 1 V).

77. ▲ Iron(II) ion undergoes a disproportionation reaction to give Fe(s) and the iron(III) ion. That is, iron(II) ion is both oxidized and reduced within the same reaction.

$$3\ Fe^{2+}(aq) \rightarrow Fe(s) + 2\ Fe^{3+}(aq)$$

  (a) What two half-reactions make up the disproportionation reaction?
  (b) Use the values of the standard reduction potentials for the two half-reactions in part (a) to determine whether this disproportionation reaction is product-favored.
  (c) What is the equilibrium constant for this reaction?

78. ■ ▲ Copper(I) ion disproportionates to copper metal and copper(II) ion. (See Study Question 77.)

$$2\ Cu^+(aq) \rightarrow Cu(s) + Cu^{2+}(aq)$$

  (a) What two half-reactions make up the disproportionation reaction?
  (b) Use values of the standard reduction potentials for the two half-reactions in part (a) to determine whether this disproportionation reaction is spontaneous.
  (c) What is the equilibrium constant for this reaction? If you have a solution that initially contains 0.10 mol of Cu^+ in 1.0 L of water, what are the concentrations of Cu^+ and Cu^{2+} at equilibrium?

In the Laboratory

79. Consider an electrochemical cell based on the half-reactions $Ni^{2+}(aq) + 2\ e^- \rightarrow Ni(s)$ and $Cd^{2+}(aq) + 2\ e^- \rightarrow Cd(s)$.
  (a) Diagram the cell, and label each of the components (including the anode, cathode, and salt bridge).
  (b) Use the equations for the half-reactions to write a balanced, net ionic equation for the overall cell reaction.
  (c) What is the polarity of each electrode?
  (d) What is the value of $E°_{cell}$?
  (e) In which direction do electrons flow in the external circuit?
  (f) Assume that a salt bridge containing $NaNO_3$ connects the two half-cells. In which direction do the $Na^+(aq)$ ions move? In which direction do the $NO_3^-(aq)$ ions move?
  (g) Calculate the equilibrium constant for the reaction.
  (h) If the concentration of Cd^{2+} is reduced to 0.010 M and $[Ni^{2+}] = 1.0$ M, what is the value of E_{cell}? Is the net reaction still the reaction given in part (b)?
  (i) If 0.050 A is drawn from the battery, how long can it last if you begin with 1.0 L of each of the solutions and each was initially 1.0 M in dissolved species? Each electrode weighs 50.0 g in the beginning.

80. An old method of measuring the current flowing in a circuit was to use a "silver coulometer." The current passed first through a solution of $Ag^+(aq)$ and then into another solution containing an electroactive species. The amount of silver metal deposited at the cathode was weighed. From the mass of silver, the number of atoms of silver was calculated. Since the reduction of a silver ion requires one electron, this value equalled the number of electrons passing through the circuit. If the time was noted, the average current could be calculated. If, in such an experiment, 0.052 g of Ag is deposited during 450 s, what was the current flowing in the circuit?

81. ■ A "silver coulometer" (Study Question 80) was used in the past to measure the current flowing in an electrochemical cell. Suppose you found that the current flowing through an electrolysis cell deposited 0.089 g of Ag metal at the cathode after exactly 10 min. If this same current then passed through a cell containing gold(III) ion in the form of $[AuCl_4]^-$, how much gold was deposited at the cathode in that electrolysis cell?

82. ■ ▲ Four metals, A, B, C, and D, exhibit the following properties:
  (a) Only A and C react with 1.0 M hydrochloric acid to give $H_2(g)$.
  (b) When C is added to solutions of the ions of the other metals, metallic B, D, and A are formed.
  (c) Metal D reduces B^{n+} to give metallic B and D^{n+}.

Based on this information, arrange the four metals in order of increasing ability to act as reducing agents.

| ▲ more challenging ■ in OWL Blue-numbered questions answered in Appendix O

83. ▲ A solution of KI is added dropwise to a pale blue solution of $Cu(NO_3)_2$. The solution changes to a brown color, and a precipitate of CuI forms. In contrast, no change is observed if solutions of KCl and KBr are added to aqueous $Cu(NO_3)_2$. Consult the table of standard reduction potentials to explain the dissimilar results seen with the different halides. Write an equation for the reaction that occurs when solutions of KI and $Cu(NO_3)_2$ are mixed.

84. ▲ The amount of oxygen, O_2, dissolved in a water sample at 25 °C can be determined by titration. The first step is to add solutions of $MnSO_4$ and NaOH to the water to convert the dissolved oxygen to MnO_2. A solution of H_2SO_4 and KI is then added to convert the MnO_2 to Mn^{2+}, and the iodide ion is converted to I_2. The I_2 is then titrated with standardized $Na_2S_2O_3$.
    (a) Balance the equation for the reaction of Mn^{2+} ions with O_2 in basic solution.
    (b) Balance the equation for the reaction of MnO_2 with I^- in acid solution.
    (c) Balance the equation for the reaction of $S_2O_3^{2-}$ with I_2.
    (d) Calculate the amount of O_2 in 25.0 mL of water if the titration requires 2.45 mL of 0.0112 M $Na_2S_2O_3$ solution.

Summary and Conceptual Questions

The following questions may use concepts from this and previous chapters.

85. Fluorinated organic compounds are important commercially, since they are used as herbicides, flame retardants, and fire-extinguishing agents, among other things. A reaction such as

$$CH_3SO_2F + 3\ HF \rightarrow CF_3SO_2F + 3\ H_2$$

is carried out electrochemically in liquid HF as the solvent.
    (a) If you electrolyze 150 g of CH_3SO_2F, what mass of HF is required, and what mass of each product can be isolated?
    (b) Is H_2 produced at the anode or the cathode of the electrolysis cell?
    (c) A typical electrolysis cell operates at 8.0 V and 250 A. How many kilowatt-hours of energy does one such cell consume in 24 h?

86. ■ ▲ The free energy change for a reaction, $\Delta_r G°$, is the maximum energy that can be extracted from the process, whereas $\Delta_r H°$ is the total chemical potential energy change. The efficiency of a fuel cell is the ratio of these two quantities.

$$\text{Efficiency} = \frac{\Delta_r G°}{\Delta_r H°} \times 100\%$$

Consider the hydrogen-oxygen fuel cell, where the net reaction is

$$H_2(g) + \tfrac{1}{2}\ O_2(g) \rightarrow H_2O(\ell)$$

    (a) Calculate the efficiency of the fuel cell under standard conditions.
    (b) Calculate the efficiency of the fuel cell if the product is water vapor instead of liquid water.
    (c) Does the efficiency depend on the state of the reaction product? Why or why not?

87. A hydrogen-oxygen fuel cell operates on the simple reaction

$$H_2(g) + \tfrac{1}{2}\ O_2(g) \rightarrow H_2O(\ell)$$

If the cell is designed to produce 1.5 A of current and if the hydrogen is contained in a 1.0-L tank at 200 atm pressure at 25 °C, how long can the fuel cell operate before the hydrogen runs out? (Assume there is an unlimited supply of O_2.)

88. ■ ▲ (a) Is it easier to reduce water in acid or base? To evaluate this, consider the half-reaction

$$2\ H_2O(\ell) + 2\ e^- \rightarrow 2\ OH^-(aq) + H_2(g)$$
$$E° = -0.83\ V$$

    (b) What is the reduction potential for water for solutions at pH = 7 (neutral) and pH = 1 (acid)? Comment on the value of $E°$ at pH = 1.

89. ▲ Living organisms derive energy from the oxidation of food, typified by glucose.

$$C_6H_{12}O_6(aq) + 6\ O_2(g) \rightarrow 6\ CO_2(g) + 6\ H_2O(\ell)$$

Electrons in this redox process are transferred from glucose to oxygen in a series of at least 25 steps. It is instructive to calculate the total daily current flow in a typical organism and the rate of energy expenditure (power). (See T. P. Chirpich: *Journal of Chemical Education*, Vol. 52, p. 99, 1975.)
    (a) The molar enthalpy of combustion of glucose is -2800 kJ/mol-rxn. If you are on a typical daily diet of 2400 Cal (kilocalories), what amount of glucose (in moles) must be consumed in a day if glucose is the only source of energy? What amount of O_2 must be consumed in the oxidation process?
    (b) How many moles of electrons must be supplied to reduce the amount of O_2 calculated in part (a)?
    (c) Based on the answer in part (b), calculate the current flowing, per second, in your body from the combustion of glucose.
    (d) If the average standard potential in the electron transport chain is 1.0 V, what is the rate of energy expenditure in watts?

Let's Review | Chapters 15–20

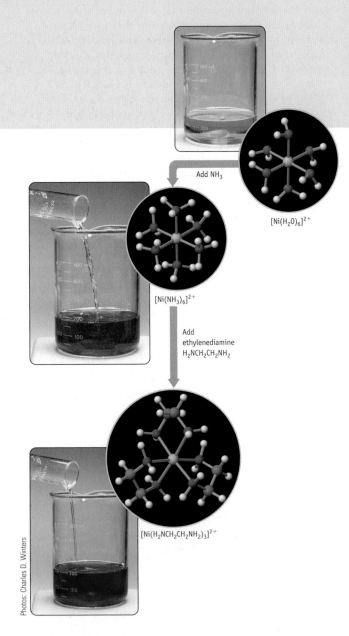

Add NH$_3$

$[Ni(H_2O)_6]^{2+}$

$[Ni(NH_3)_6]^{2+}$

Add ethylenediamine H$_2$NCH$_2$CH$_2$NH$_2$

$[Ni(H_2NCH_2CH_2NH_2)_3]^{2+}$

Photos: Charles D. Winters

Chemists and non-chemists alike are drawn to the wonderful colors of many chemical compounds. Here you see an aqueous solution of nickel(II) chloride. When the nickel(II) salt dissolves, a green solution is obtained, owing to the presence of the complex ion $[Ni(H_2O)_6]^{2+}$ in solution.

As aqueous ammonia, NH$_3$(aq), is added to the green solution it turns a characteristic blue color. The color arises from another complex ion, $[Ni(NH_3)_6]^{2+}$, in which ammonia molecules have taken the place of water molecules.

Interestingly, when we add another compound—ethylenediamine, H$_2$NCH$_2$CH$_2$NH$_2$—the blue color of the ammonia-containing ion is replaced by the purple color of the complex ion, $[Ni(H_2NCH_2CH_2NH_2)_3]^{2+}$.

In this series of chapters you have learned more about the reactivity of molecules and how to predict when one compound can be transformed into another.

THE PURPOSE OF *LET'S REVIEW*

- *Let's Review* provides additional questions for Chapters 15 through 20. Routine questions covering the concepts in a chapter are in the Study Questions at the end of that chapter and are usually identified by topic. In contrast, *Let's Review* questions combine several concepts from one or more chapters. Many come from the examinations given by the authors and others are based on actual experiments or processes in chemical research or in the chemical industries.

- *Let's Review* provides guidance for Chapters 15 through 20 as you prepare for an exam on these chapters. Although this is designated for Chapters 15 through 20 you may choose only material appropriate to the exam in your course.

- To direct your review, **Comprehensive Questions** are correlated with relevant chapter sections and with the OWL online homework

system to which you may have purchased access. Some questions may include a screen shot from one of these tools so you see what resources are available to help you review.

PREPARING FOR AN EXAMINATION ON CHAPTERS 15–20

1. Review **Go Chemistry** modules for these chapters. Go Chemistry modules are available at **www.cengage.com/chemistry/kotz** or **www.ichapters.com.**
2. Take the ChemistryNow **Pre-Test** and work through your **Personalized Learning Plan.** Work through ChemistryNow **Exercises, Guided Simulations,** and **Intelligent Tutors.**
3. **OWL** If you subscribe to OWL, use the **Tutorials** in that system.
4. Work on the questions below that are relevant to a particular chapter or chapters. See the solutions to those questions at the end of this section.
5. For background and help answering a question, use the Go Chemistry and OWL questions correlated with it.

KEY POINTS TO KNOW FOR CHAPTERS 15–20

Here are some of the key points you must know to be successful in Chapters 15–20.

- Rates of reaction and factors affecting reaction rates.
- Rate equations and integrated rate laws.
- Collision theory of reaction rates and activation energy.
- Reaction mechanisms.
- The nature of chemical equilibria.
- The reaction quotient (Q) and equilibrium constant (K).
- The Brønsted-Lowry and Lewis theories of acids and bases.
- Chemical equilibria involving acids, bases, and insoluble salts in aqueous solution, and pH calculations for acids, bases, and salts.
- Factors affecting the strengths of acids and bases.
- The nature of buffer solutions.
- The outcome of acid-base reactions (including titrations).
- Reaction spontaneity, free energy, and entropy.
- The relationship of free energy changes and equilibrium constants and whether a reaction is product- or reactant-favored.
- Balancing equations for redox reactions.
- Voltaic cells and electrochemical potentials under standard and nonstandard conditions.
- Electrolysis and electrical energy.

EXAMINATION PREPARATION QUESTIONS

▲ denotes more challenging questions.

Important information about the questions that follow:

- See the Study Questions in each chapter for questions on basic concepts.
- Some of these questions arise from recent research in chemistry and the other sciences. They often involve concepts from more than one chapter and may be more challenging than those in earlier chapters. Not all chapter goals or concepts are necessarily addressed in these questions.
- **Assessing Key Points** are short-answer questions covering the Key Points to Know on this page.
- **Comprehensive Questions** bring together concepts from multiple chapters and are correlated with text sections covering that topic, with Go Chemistry modules, and with questions in OWL that may provide additional background.
- The screen shots are largely taken from Go Chemistry modules available at **www.cengage.com/chemistry/kotz** or **www.ichapters.com.**

Assessing Key Points

1. (Chapter 15) A few drops of blue food dye were added to water followed by a solution of bleach. (Initially, the concentration of dye was about 3.4×10^{-5} M, and the bleach (NaOCl) concentration was about 0.034 M.) The dye faded as it reacted with the bleach. The color change was followed by a spectrophotometer, and the data are plotted below. (See ChemistryNow, Screen 15.2)

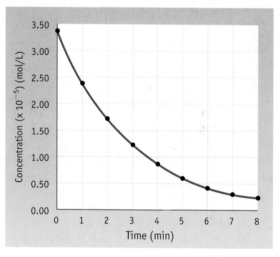

(a) What is the average rate of reaction over the first 2 minutes?
(b) What is the approximate half-life of the reaction?
(c) Does the rate of reaction decline, stay the same, or increase with time?

2. (Chapter 15) The reduction of NO with hydrogen produces nitrogen and water.

$$2\,NO(g) \,+\, 2\,H_2(g) \,\rightarrow\, N_2(g) \,+\, 2\,H_2O(g)$$

(a) The reaction is second order in NO and third order overall. What is the rate law for the reaction?
(b) If [NO] is increased by a factor of 5, how does the rate of the reaction change?
(c) If [H_2] is increased by a factor of 5, how does the rate of the reaction change?

3. (Chapter 15) Given the initial rate data for the reaction $A + B \rightarrow C$, determine the rate expression for the reaction. (The reaction is catalyzed by molecule D.)

[A], M	[B], M	[D], M	$\Delta[C]/\Delta t$ (mol/L·s)
0.10	0.20	0.10	2.58
0.10	0.10	0.10	1.29
0.24	0.10	0.20	2.58
0.10	0.20	0.20	5.16

(a) $\Delta[C]/\Delta t = k[A][D]^2$
(b) $\Delta[C]/\Delta t = k[A][B][D]$
(c) $\Delta[C]/\Delta t = k[B][D]$
(d) $\Delta[C]/\Delta t = k[A][B]$

4. (Chapter 15) Three reactions have the rate law Rate = $k[\text{Reactant}]^m$ where m is the order of reaction. (For assistance, see the OWL Simulation 15.3c.)

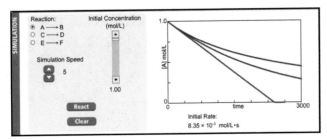

OWL Simulation 15.3c: Concentration Dependence of Rates

(a) For $A \rightarrow B$, when [A] = 0.5 M, Rate = 4.18×10^{-3} mol/L·s. When [A] = 1.0 M, Rate = 8.35×10^{-3} mol/L·s. Is m is 0, 1, or 2?
(b) For $C \rightarrow D$, when [C] = 0.5 M Rate = 2.09×10^{-3} mol/L·s. When [C] = 1.0 M, Rate = 8.35×10^{-3} mol/L·s. Is m is 0, 1, or 2?
(c) For $E \rightarrow F$, when [E] = 0.5 M Rate = 8.35×10^{-3} mol/L·s. When [E] = 1.0 M, Rate = 8.35×10^{-3} mol/L·s. Is m is 0, 1, or 2?
(d) Which of the three curves in the figure—top, middle, or bottom—corresponds to the reaction $E \rightarrow F$?

5. (Chapter 15) A reaction that occurs in our environment is the oxidation of NO to the brown gas NO_2.

$$2\ NO(g) + O_2(g) \rightarrow 2\ NO_2(g)$$

The mechanism of the reaction is thought to be

Step 1 $2\ NO(g) \rightleftharpoons N_2O_2(g)$
                                        rapidly established equilibrium

Step 2 $N_2O_2(g) + O_2(g) \rightarrow 2\ NO_2(g)$ slow

Which is the rate determining step? Is there an intermediate in the reaction?

6. (Chapter 15) The decomposition of SO_2Cl_2 to SO_2 and Cl_2 is first order in SO_2Cl_2.

$$SO_2Cl_2(g) \rightarrow SO_2(g) + Cl_2(g)$$

$$\text{Rate} = k\ [SO_2Cl_2] \text{ where } k = 0.17/\text{hr}$$

(a) What is the rate of decomposition when $[SO_2Cl_2]$ = 0.010 M?
(b) What is the half-life of the reaction?
(c) If the initial pressure of SO_2Cl_2 in a flask is 0.050 atm, what is the pressure of all gases (i.e., the total pressure) in the flask after the reaction has proceeded for one half-life period?

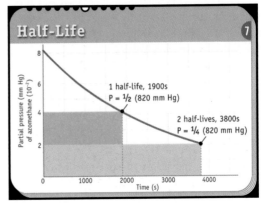

Screen from Go Chemistry module 20 on kinetics

7. (Chapter 16) A mixture of SO_2, O_2, and SO_3 at 1000 K contains the gases at the following concentrations: $[SO_2] = 5.0 \times 10^{-3}$ mol/L, $[O_2] = 1.9 \times 10^{-3}$ mol/L, and $[SO_3] = 6.9 \times 10^{-3}$ mol/L. Which way will the reaction proceed to reach equilibrium?

$$2\ SO_2(g) + O_2(g) \rightleftharpoons 2\ SO_3(g)\quad K_c = 279$$

8. (Chapter 16) You place 0.010 mol of $N_2O_4(g)$ in a 2.0 L flask at 200 °C. After reaching equilibrium, $[N_2O_4]$ = 0.0042 M.

$$N_2O_4(g) \rightleftharpoons 2\ NO_2(g)$$

Fill in the table below and then calculate K_c for the reaction at 200 °C.

	$N_2O_4(g) \rightleftharpoons$	$2\ NO_2(g)$
Initial concentration (M)	____	0
Change in concentration (M)	____	____
Equilibrium concentration (M)	0.0042	____

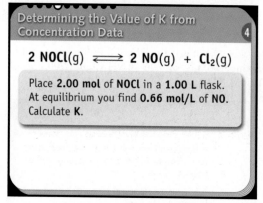

9. (Chapter 16) Nitrosyl bromide, $NOBr(g)$, decomposes according to the equation

$$NOBr(g) \rightleftharpoons NO(g) + 1/2 \text{ Br}_2(g)$$
$$K_c = 0.021 \text{ at } 350 \text{ °C}$$

If 1.5 mol of NOBr, 0.40 mol of NO, and 0.40 mol of Br_2 are mixed in a 1.0 L flask at 350 °C, will any net reaction occur? If a net reaction is observed, will NO be formed or consumed?

10. (Chapter 16) Samples of NO_2 and N_2O_4 are in equilibrium at some temperature. If $[N_2O_4] = 4.6 \times 10^{-5}$ M, what is $[NO_2]$?

$$2 \text{ NO}_2(g) \rightleftharpoons N_2O_4(g) \quad K_c = 240$$

11. (Chapter 16) Calculate K_c for the reaction

$$SnO_2(s) + 2 \text{ CO}(g) \rightleftharpoons Sn(s) + 2 \text{ CO}_2(g)$$

given the following information:

$$SnO_2(s) + 2 \text{ H}_2(g) \rightleftharpoons Sn(s) + 2 \text{ H}_2O(g) \quad K_c = 8.12$$
$$H_2(g) + CO_2(g) \rightleftharpoons CO(g) + H_2O(g) \quad K_c = 0.771$$

12. (Chapter 16) Heating ammonium hydrogen sulfide leads to decomposition.

$$\text{heat} + NH_4HS(s) \rightleftharpoons NH_3(g) + H_2S(g)$$

Predict the effect on the equilibrium of each change listed below. Answer by choosing (1) no change, (2) shifts left, or (3) shifts right.
(a) Add solid NH_4HS
(b) Add NH_3 gas
(c) Add H_2S gas
(d) Raise the temperature
(e) Increase the volume of the flask containing the reaction

13. (Chapter 17) What is the pH of a 0.020 M NaOH solution?

14. (Chapter 17) Conjugate acids and bases:
(a) What is the conjugate base of formic acid, HCO_2H?
(b) What is the conjugate base of the $H_2PO_4^-$ ion?
(c) What is the conjugate acid of the HCO_3^- ion?

15. (Chapter 17) Which of the following is NOT an acid-base conjugate pair?
(a) HClO and Cl^-
(b) HF and F^-
(c) HNO_2 and NO_2^-
(d) CO_3^{2-} and HCO_3^-

16. (Chapter 17) For each solution below, decide if the pH is less than 7, equal to 7, or greater than 7 at 25 °C.
(a) 0.10 M HNO_3
(b) 0.012 M KOH
(c) 0.15 M formic acid
(d) 0.45 M KBr
(e) 0.25 M Na_3PO_4
(f) 0.095 M $AlCl_3$

17. (Chapter 17) What is the pH of a 0.020 M solution of NH_3 (at 25 °C)?

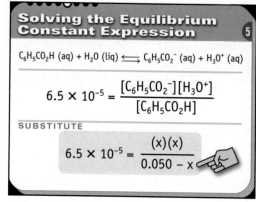

18. (Chapter 17) A 0.040 M solution of a weak acid has a pH of 3.02 at 25 °C. What is the value of K_a for the acid?

19. (Chapter 17) What are the concentrations of H_3O^+ and OH^- and what is the pH of a 0.15 M solution of Na_2CO_3 (at 25 °C)?

20. (Chapter 17) What is the pH of the solution obtained when 12.5 mL of 0.40 M NaOH is added to 40.0 mL of 0.125 M HCl (at 25 °C)?

21. (Chapter 17) Lewis acids and bases. The presence of iron(III) ion in aqueous solution can be detected by adding thiocyanate ion, SCN^- to give a deep red complex ion. Identify the Lewis acids and bases in the following equation.

$$Fe^{3+} + 5 \text{ H}_2O + \left[:\overset{..}{\underset{..}{S}} - C \equiv N: \right]^-$$

Deep red ion

22. (Chapter 18) Titrations. What is the pH at the half-neutralization point in a titration of formic acid (HCO_2H) with NaOH?

23. (Chapter 18) For each of the following cases, decide whether the pH is less than, equal to, or greater than 7 (at 25 °C).
(a) Equal volumes of 0.10 M acetic acid, CH_3CO_2H, and 0.10 M KOH are mixed.
(b) 25 mL of 0.015 M NH_3 is mixed with 25 mL of 0.015 M HCl
(c) 100. mL of 0.0020 M HNO_3 is mixed with 50. mL of 0.0040 M NaOH.

24. (Chapter 18) Decide which compound in each of the following pairs of salts is the more soluble in water.
(a) AgBr or AgSCN   (b) AgCl or Ag_2CO_3

25. (Chapter 18) Rank the following compounds in order of increasing molar solubility in water: Na_2CO_3, CaF_2, $BaCO_3$, Ag_2CO_3

26. (Chapter 18) Milk of magnesia is an aqueous suspension of $Mg(OH)_2$. What are the concentrations of H_3O^+ and OH^- in solution (at 25 °C)?

27. (Chapter 18) Which of the following insoluble compounds—MnS, $Al(OH)_3$, $Ca_3(PO_4)_2$, $MgCO_3$, AgCl, PbI_2—will not dissolve in 6 M HCl? List all correct answers.

28. (Chapter 18) You have a solution of NH_4Cl. Will the addition of NH_3 increase or decrease the pH or have no effect?

29. (Chapter 18) Suppose that in a 0.10 M $HClO_2$ solution, about 29% of the molecules have been converted to H_3O^+ and ClO_2^- ions. In this solution $[HClO_2] = 0.071$ M, $[H_3O^+] = 0.029$ M, and $[ClO_2^-] = 0.029$ M. (OWL Simulation 18.1 explores this common ion effect.)

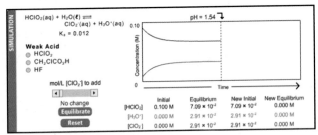

OWL Simulation 18.1: Common Ion Effect

(a) If more ClO_2^- ions are added to the solution described above (by adding $NaClO_2$), will the percentage ionization of $HClO_2$ be larger or smaller than 29% or will there be no change? Will the pH increase, decrease, or stay the same?
(b) ▲ Now take 1.00 L of the solution described above (in which $[HClO_2] = 0.071$ M, $[H_3O^+] = 0.029$ M, and $[ClO_2^-] = 0.029$ M) and add 0.010 mol of

$NaClO_2$. Determine the concentration of each species in the new solution. ($K_a = 0.012$ at 25 °C)

30. (Chapter 18) What is the pH of a buffer prepared by mixing 100. mL of 0.20 M NH_4Cl and 200. mL of 0.10 M NH_3?

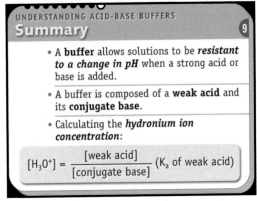

Screen from Go Chemistry module 23 on buffers

31. (Chapter 19) Calculate the standard entropy change for the following reaction using data in Appendix L.

$$F_2(g) + H_2(g) \rightarrow 2\,HF(g)$$

32. (Chapter 19) Which of the following do you expect to have the largest molar entropy at 25 °C?
(a) $H_2O(\ell)$ (c) $O_2(g)$
(b) $H_2O(s)$ (d) $CCl_4(g)$

33. (Chapter 19) In which of the following physical or chemical changes do you expect to have an increase in entropy?
(a) $Fe(s) \rightarrow Fe(\ell)$
(b) $NH_3(g) + HCl(g) \rightarrow NH_4Cl(s)$
(c) $2\,Fe(s) + 3/2\,O_2(g) \rightarrow Fe_2O_3(s)$
(d) $HF(\ell) \rightarrow HF(g)$

34. (Chapter 19) Calculate $\Delta_r G°$ for the following reaction using data in Appendix L.

$$N_2(g) + 3\,H_2O(\ell) \rightarrow 2\,NH_3(g) + 3/2\,O_2(g)$$

35. (Chapter 19) For the following general reaction, what can be said about the spontaneity at different temperatures?

$$A + B \rightarrow C + D; \Delta_r H° \text{ is positive and } \Delta_r S° \text{ is negative}$$

(a) Spontaneous at all temperatures
(b) Spontaneous only at high temperature
(c) Spontaneous only at low temperature
(d) Not spontaneous at any temperature

36. (Chapter 19) Given the following information, calculate $\Delta_r G°$ for the reaction below at 25 °C. Is the reaction spontaneous under standard conditions?

$$NiO(s) + 2\,HCl(g) \rightarrow NiCl_2(s) + H_2O(g)$$

$\Delta_r H° = -122.8$ kJ/mol-rxn

and $\Delta_r S° = -123.9$ J/K·mol-rxn

37. (Chapter 19) When sodium is added to water, the following reaction takes place readily.

$$Na(s) + H_2O(\ell) \rightarrow NaOH(aq) + 1/2\ H_2(g)\quad \Delta_r H° < 0$$

What can be said about this reaction?
(a) $\Delta_r G°$ is positive.
(b) $\Delta_r S°$ is negative.
(c) $\Delta_r G°$ will become less negative with increasing temperature.
(d) $\Delta_r G°$ will become more negative with increasing temperature.

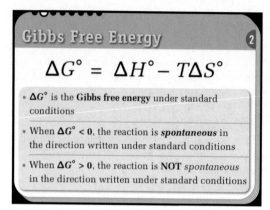

Gibbs Free Energy   2

$$\Delta G° = \Delta H° - T\Delta S°$$

- $\Delta G°$ is the **Gibbs free energy** under standard conditions
- When $\Delta G° < 0$, the reaction is **spontaneous** in the direction written under standard conditions
- When $\Delta G° > 0$, the reaction is **NOT** *spontaneous* in the direction written under standard conditions

Screen from Go Chemistry module 24 on free energy

38. (Chapter 19) Acetic acid has an ionization constant of 1.8×10^{-5}. What is the predicted sign for $\Delta_r G°$ for the ionization of acetic acid at 25 °C? What is the value of $\Delta_r G°$?

39. (Chapter 19) In the reaction of two Cl atoms to give a Cl_2 molecule $[2\ Cl(g) \rightarrow Cl_2(g)]$, decide if the sign of the enthalpy and entropy changes are positive or negative.

40. (Chapter 20) Balance the following oxidation-reduction reaction in acid solution. Designate the oxidizing and reducing agents and the substances oxidized and reduced.

$$MnO_4^-(aq) + C_2O_4^{2-}(aq) \rightarrow Mn^{2+}(aq) + CO_2(g)$$

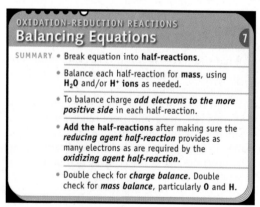

OXIDATION-REDUCTION REACTIONS
Balancing Equations   7

SUMMARY
- Break equation into **half-reactions**.
- Balance each half-reaction for **mass**, using H_2O and/or H^+ **ions** as needed.
- To balance charge **add electrons to the more positive side** in each half-reaction.
- **Add the half-reactions** after making sure the **reducing agent half-reaction** provides as many electrons as are required by the **oxidizing agent half-reaction**.
- Double check for **charge balance**. Double check for **mass balance**, particularly O and H.

Screen from Go Chemistry module 25 on balancing equations

41. (Chapter 20) Use the small table of reduction potentials below to answer the questions that follow.

Half Reaction			$E°$ (volts)
$Cl_2(g) + 2e^-$	$\rightarrow$	$2\ Cl^-(aq)$	+1.36
$Ag^+(aq) + e^-$	$\rightarrow$	$Ag(s)$	+0.80
$I_2(s) + 2e^-$	$\rightarrow$	$2\ I^-(aq)$	+0.535
$Cu^{2+}(aq) + 2e^-$	$\rightarrow$	$Cu(s)$	+0.34
$Pb^{2+}(aq) + 2e^-$	$\rightarrow$	$Pb(s)$	−0.126
$Ni^{2+}(aq) + 2e^-$	$\rightarrow$	$Ni(s)$	−0.25
$Zn^{2+}(aq) + 2e^-$	$\rightarrow$	$Zn(s)$	−0.76
$V^{2+}(aq) + 2e^-$	$\rightarrow$	$V(s)$	−1.18
$Al^{3+}(aq) + 3e^-$	$\rightarrow$	$Al(s)$	−1.66

(a) What is the weakest oxidizing agent in the list?
(b) What is the strongest oxidizing agent?
(c) What is the strongest reducing agent?
(d) What is the weakest reducing agent?
(e) Will Pb(s) reduce $V^{2+}(aq)$ to V(s)?
(f) Will $I_2(s)$ oxidize Cl^- to $Cl_2(g)$?
(g) Identify the ions or compounds that can be reduced by Pb(s)

42. (Chapter 20) Consider the electrochemical cell diagrammed below.

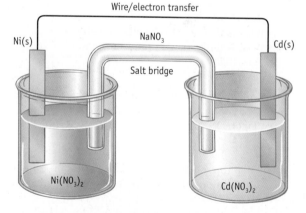

(a) Write the balanced net ionic equation for the reaction occurring in the cell.
(b) Indicate the direction of electron transfer.
(c) Which electrode is the anode and which is the cathode? Indicate the signs of the electrodes.
(d) Indicate the substance oxidized and the substance reduced.
(e) Calculate the standard cell potential, $E°$.
(f) Tell in which direction the Na^+ and NO_3^- ions flow in the salt bridge.

43. (Chapter 20) Consider the reaction

$$Cu(s) + 2\,Ag^+(aq) \rightarrow Cu^{2+}(aq) + 2\,Ag(s)$$

If $[Ag^+] = 1.0$ M and $[Cu^{2+}] = 0.020$ M, is the cell potential E (a) greater than $E°$; (b) less than $E°$; or (c) equal to $E°$?

44. (Chapter 20) If you electrolyze a solution of $Ni^{2+}(aq)$ to form $Ni(s)$ and use a current of 0.15 amps for 10. minutes, what mass of $Ni(s)$ is produced?

45. (Chapter 20) Permanganate ions and copper react in acid solution to give manganese(II) and copper(II) ions.
(a) Balance the net ionic equation for this reaction.
(b) Calculate $E°$ for the reaction.
(c) Calculate the cell potential under the following conditions: $[MnO_4^-] = 1.00$ M; $[Mn^{2+}] = 0.100$ M; $[Cu^{2+}] = 0.100$ M; and $[H_3O^+] = 0.500$ M.

Comprehensive Questions

46. (Chapter 15) Data in the table refers to the reaction

$$2\,NO(g) + H_2(g) \rightarrow N_2O(g) + H_2O(g)$$

Experiment	Initial [NO] (mol/L)	Initial [H₂] (mol/L)	Rate (mol/L·s)
1	2.16×10^{-2}	1.4×10^{-2}	1.2×10^{-2}
2	6.48×10^{-2}	1.4×10^{-2}	1.08×10^{-1}
3	4.32×10^{-2}	2.8×10^{-2}	9.6×10^{-2}

(a) What is the rate law equation for this reaction?
(b) What is the value and units of the rate constant k?
Text Section: 15.3
OWL Question: 15.3e

47. (Chapters 16 and 19) Heating ammonium chloride causes it to decompose to ammonia and hydrogen chloride. (See Figure 19.10, page 875).

$$NH_4Cl(s) \rightleftharpoons NH_3(g) + HCl(g)$$

(a) When the system has reached equilibrium, what is the effect on the equilibrium of adding more solid NH_4Cl? Of adding NH_3 gas?
(b) Predict the signs of $\Delta_r H°$ and $\Delta_r S°$ for NH_4Cl decomposition. Verify by calculating the enthalpy and entropy changes for the decomposition reaction from data in Appendix L.
(c) Is the reaction predicted to be product- or reactant-favored at 400 °C? Verify the prediction by calculating $\Delta_r G°$ and then calculate the pressure of ammonia in a flask at this temperature.
Text Sections: 16.4, 16.6, and 19.4–19.7
OWL Questions: 16.3b, 16.4b, 16.6d, 16.6m, 19.4c, 19.7c, 19.7f, 19.7i

48. (Chapter 17) A 0.44 M solution of hydroxyacetic acid, $HOCH_2CO_2H$, is 1.8% ionized. Calculate the pH of the solution and the value of the acid ionization equilibrium constant, K_a.
Text Section: 17.7
OWL Questions: 17.4a, 17.7b, 17.7d, 17.7e

49. (Chapter 17) Acid-base chemistry
(a) List the following acids in order of increasing acid strength: HF, NH_4^+, H_3PO_4, CH_3CO_2H, HNO_3.
(b) Use the ranking of relative acid strength to predict whether the equilibrium $HF(aq) + CH_3CO_2^-(aq) \rightleftharpoons F^-(aq) + CH_3CO_2H(aq)$ is product-favored or reactant-favored.
Text Sections: 17.4–17.5
OWL Questions: 17.4b, 17.4c

50. (Chapter 18) Refer to the Table of K_{sp} values in Appendix J and identify the most and least soluble silver salt, from among the following: $AgCl$, AgI, $AgCH_3CO_2$, $AgCN$, $AgBr$, and $AgSCN$.
Text Section: 18.4
OWL Question: 18.4d

51. (Chapter 18) You have been given solutions containing the compounds listed below. All concentrations are assumed to be 0.50 M.
  (i) $NH_3 + NH_4Cl$
  (ii) $Na_2HPO_4 + NaH_2PO_4$
  (iii) $HNO_3 + NaNO_3$
  (iv) $H_3PO_4 + NaH_2PO_4$
  (v) $NaF + HF$
(a) Which are buffer solutions?
(b) Which solution, among those listed, has the highest pH? The lowest pH?
(c) Assume you need a solution buffered at pH = 7.4. Select one of the solutions from the list, then describe how you would adjust its pH to achieve the desired value.
Text Section: 18.2
OWL Questions: 18.2d, 18.2j

52. (Chapter 18) Titration of chloroacetic acid in water with aqueous NaOH:
(a) Chloroacetic acid, $ClCH_2CO_2H$, has a pK_a of 2.867. What is the value of K_a?
(b) Write the net ionic equation for the reaction of chloroacetic acid with NaOH.
(c) What volume of 0.128 M NaOH solution is required to titrate 50.0 mL of 0.154 M acid to the equivalence point?
(d) Which of the following indicators: phenolphthalein, methyl red, or bromthymol blue, would be most suitable for this titration?
(e) What is the pH at the half-neutralization point?
(f) What is the pH at the equivalence point?
Text Section: 18.3
OWL Questions: 17.7i, 18.3e, 18.3f, 18.3h

53. (Chapter 20) Write balanced chemical equations for the following:

(a) $Cr_2O_7^{2-} + I^- \rightarrow Cr^{3+} + I_2$ (in acid).

(b) $MnO_4^- + HS^- \rightarrow MnO_2 + SO_4^{2-}$ (in base)

In each case identify the substance reduced, the reducing agent, and the change in oxidation state of chromium and manganese in these reactions.

Text Section: 20.1
OWL Questions: 20.1b, 20.1d, 20.1e

54. (Chapter 20) Electrochemical cells:

(a) Sketch a picture of the voltaic cell $Zn(s) \mid Zn^{2+}$ (1.0 M) $\parallel Sn^{4+}$(1.0 M) $\mid Sn^{2+}$(1.0 M) $\mid Pt(s)$. On the drawing, identify the anode, cathode, and the direction of flow of electrons in the external circuit.

(b) Assume the cell has a salt bridge containing $NaNO_3$. In what direction does each ion in the salt bridge flow?

(c) Write a balanced chemical equation for the overall cell reaction.

(d) What is $E°$ for this cell?

Text Sections: 20.2 and 20.4
OWL Questions: 20.2b, 20.4c

55. (Chapter 20) Refer to the table of standard reduction potentials to answer this question. Questions can have more than one correct answer. List all correct answers.

(a) Which of the following metals react with $H^+(aq)$ to produce H_2: Ag, Mn, Sn, Cu, Mg?

(b) Which of the following metal ions is most easily reduced: Li^+, Mg^{2+}, Sn^{2+}, Fe^{2+}?

(c) Which of the following metal ions can be reduced to the metal by Sn: Ag^+, Ni^{2+}, Mg^{2+}, Fe^{2+}?

(d) Which of the species listed below is the strongest reducing agent: Cl^-, H_2, Mg^{2+}, Br^-?

Text Section: 20.4
OWL Questions: 20.2b, 20.4c

56. (Chapter 20) In the electrolysis of a solution containing Cr^{3+}, how long should one run a current of 2.50 amperes to obtain 5.00 g of Cr?

Text Section: 20.8
OWL Question: 20.8b

57. (Chapter 18) The curve of pH versus volume of HCl added for the titration of 50.0 mL of 0.10 M diethylamine with 0.10 M aqueous HCl is shown below.

(a) Is diethylamine, $(C_2H_5)_2NH$, a weak acid or weak base in water?

(b) Write a balanced equation for the reaction of the amine with HCl.

(c) Use the graph of pH versus added HCl to determine the approximate pH at the half-neutralization point? Use this value to estimate the value of K_b for the hydrolysis of diethylamine.

(d) What is the approximate pH of the solution at the equivalence point? Verify your observation on the graph with a calculation.

(e) Explain briefly why this solution is acidic or basic at the equivalence point.

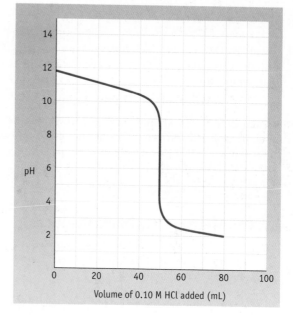

Text Section: 18.3
OWL Question: 18.3g

58. (Chapter 18) On page 948 you see photos of the reaction of aqueous nickel(II) ion with ammonia to give a complex ion,

$[Ni(H_2O)_6]^{2+}(aq) + 6\ NH_3(aq)$
$\rightleftharpoons [Ni(NH_3)_6]^{2+}(aq) + 6\ H_2O(aq)$

and then the reaction of that complex ion with the organic compound ethylenediamine to give another colorful complex ion.

$[Ni(NH_3)_6]^{2+}(aq) + 3\ H_2NCH_2CH_2NH_2(aq)$
$\rightleftharpoons [Ni(H_2NCH_2CH_2NH_2)_3]^{2+}(aq) + 6\ NH_3(aq)$

(a) What is the pH of a 0.10 M aqueous solution of nickel(II) chloride? (See Table 17.3, page 770.)

(b) What is the approximate pH of a 0.025 M aqueous solution of ethylenediamine? (See Appendix I for the K_b value.)

(c) In forming the complex ion $[Ni(NH_3)_6]^{2+}$ what is the Lewis acid and what is the Lewis base?

(d) Is the reaction of $Ni^{2+}(aq)$ with ammonia product- or reactant-favored at equilibrium? (See the discussion of formation constants on page 846 and Appendix K.)

(e) Given the formation constants below, calculate the equilibrium constant and $\Delta_r G°$ for the reaction of $[Ni(NH_3)_6]^{2+}(aq)$ with ethylenediamine at 25 °C.

Complex Ion	Formation Constant
$[Ni(NH_3)_6]^{2+}(aq)$	5.5×10^8
$[Ni(H_2NCH_2CH_2NH_2)_3]^{2+}(aq)$	1.9×10^{18}

Comment on what thermodynamic function controls the outcome of the reaction, $\Delta_rH°$ or $\Delta_rS°$.

Text Sections: 16.5, 17.3, 17.7, 17.9, and 19.7
OWL Questions: 16.5a, 16.5b, 17.3f, 17.7e, 17.7g, 17.7h, 17.9e,
18.7c, 19.7i

59. (Chapter 19) One way in which hydrogen gas is produced is to dehydrogenate ethane over a suitable catalyst at a high temperature.

$$C_2H_6(g) \rightleftharpoons C_2H_4(g) + H_2(g)$$

Assume $\Delta_rG°$ is 22.4 kJ/mol-rxn at 900 K. What is the mole percent of hydrogen at equilibrium if this process is carried out at 900 K and with an initial partial pressure of C_2H_6 of 1.00 atm?

Text Sections: 16.4 and 19.7
OWL Questions: 16.3b, 16.4b, 19.7i

Answers to Assessing Key Points Questions

1. (a) 0.85×10^{-5} mol/L·min. Divide the change in concentration by the time period over which it occurs.
    (b) Approximately 2 minutes
    (c) The rate depends on the dye concentration. Therefore, the rate declines with time because the concentration of the dye declines with time.

2. (a) Rate = $k[NO]^2[H_2]$. The sum of the exponents is 3.
    (b) The rate will increase 25-fold (5^2).
    (c) The rate increases by a factor of 5.

3. (c) $\Delta C/\Delta t = k[B][D]$. Comparing lines 1 and 2 of the data you see that the rate doubles when [B] doubles. Therefore, the reaction is 1st order in B. Comparing lines 1 and 4 you find that the rate doubles when [D] doubles, so the reaction is 1st order in D. Comparing lines 3 and 4 shows that the rate doubles with a doubling of [B], as expected, but the increase in [A] has no effect.

4. (a) $m = 1$; the rate doubles when concentration of A doubles.
    (b) $m = 2$; the rate increases by a factor of 4 when concentration of C doubles.
    (c) $m = 0$; there is no change in rate when the concentration of E changes.
    (d) Bottom. For a zero order reaction Rate = k. The concentration versus time curve is a straight line with a slope equal to $-k$.

5. Step 2 is rate determining and N_2O_2 is an intermediate.

6. (a) Rate = $(0.17/\text{hr})(0.010 \text{ mol/L}) = 0.0017$ mol/L·h
    (b) $t_{1/2} = 0.693/k = 4.1$ hr
    (c)

	SO_2Cl_2 $\rightleftharpoons$	SO_2 +	Cl_2
initial P (atm)	0.050	0	0
change in P (atm)	−0.025	+0.025	+0.025
final P (atm)	0.025	0.025	0.025

Total final pressure = 0.075 atm

7. Calculate Q, the reaction quotient.

$$Q_c = \frac{[SO_3]^2}{[SO_2]^2[O_2]} = \frac{(6.9 \times 10^{-3})^2}{(5.0 \times 10^{-3})^2(1.9 \times 10^{-3})}$$

$$Q_c = 1.0 \times 10^3$$

Because $Q > K$, the concentration of product is too large and that of the reactants is too small. The reaction will proceed to the left to attain equilibrium.

8.

	N_2O_4	$\rightleftharpoons$ 2 NO_2
Initial (M)	0.0050	0
Change (M)	−0.0008	+2 × 0.0008
Equilibrium (M)	0.0042	0.0016

The additions to the table are in bold. The final concentration of NO_2 is derived from the change in N_2O_4 concentration.

$$K_c = \frac{[NO_2]^2}{[N_2O_4]} = \frac{(0.0016)^2}{0.0042} = 6.1 \times 10^{-4}$$

9. $Q = \dfrac{[NO][Br_2]^{1/2}}{[NOBr]} = \dfrac{(0.40)(0.40)^{1/2}}{1.5} = 0.17$

    $Q > K_c$. Therefore, reaction is the reverse of the equation as written. and NO is consumed.

10. $K_c = 240 = \dfrac{[N_2O_4]}{[NO_2]^2} = \dfrac{(4.6 \times 10^{-5})}{[NO_2]^2}$

    $[NO_2] = 4.4 \times 10^{-4}$ M

11. See Section 16.5 and Problem-Solving Tip 16.2.

    $SnO_2(s) + 2 H_2(g) \rightleftharpoons Sn(s) + 2 H_2O(g)$
    $K_c = K_1 = 8.12$

    $2 [CO(g) + H_2O(g) \rightleftharpoons H_2(g) + CO_2(g)]$
    $K_c = (1/K_2)^2 = (1/0.771)^2$

    Summed equations:

    $SnO_2(s) + 2 CO(g) \rightleftharpoons Sn(s) + 2 CO_2(g)$
    $K_{net} = K_1 \times (1/K_2)^2 = 13.7$

12. (a) No change   (d) Shifts right
    (b) Shifts left   (e) Shifts right
    (c) Shifts left

13. NaOH is a strong base so [NaOH] = [OH⁻]

    pOH = $-\log$ [OH⁻] = $-\log$ (0.020) = 1.70
    pH + pOH = 14.00, so pH = 12.30

    Alternatively, we first solve for [H_3O^+]

    $K_w = [H_3O^+][OH^-] = 1.00 \times 10^{-14}$
    $[H_3O^+] = 5.0 \times 10^{-13}$ M

    and this gives a pH of 12.30.

14. See Table 17.3 on page 770.
    (a) HCO_2^- (b) HPO_4^{2-} (c) H_2CO_3

15. (a)

16. (a) Strong acid. pH < 7.
    (b) Strong base. pH > 7
    (c) Weak acid. pH < 7
    (d) Neutral salt. pH = 7
    (e) PO_4^{3-} is a relatively strong weak base ($K_b = 2.8 \times 10^{-2}$). pH > 7. See Problem-Solving Tip 17.2, page 775.
    (f) Al^{3+} is a weak acid. pH < 7

17. Set up an ICE table for the weak base, NH_3

	$NH_3(aq) + H_2O(\ell) \rightleftharpoons$	$NH_4^+(aq) +$	$OH^-(aq)$
Initial	0.020	0	0
Change	−x	+x	+x
Equilibrium	0.020 − x	x	x

$$K_b = 1.8 \times 10^{-5} = \frac{[NH_4^+][OH^-]}{[NH_3]}$$

$$1.8 \times 10^{-5} = \frac{[x]^2}{0.020 - x}$$

Assuming x is << 0.020
$x = [OH^-] = 6.0 \times 10^{-4}$ M
$pOH = -\log [OH^-] = 3.22$
$pH + pOH = 14.00$
$pH = 10.78$

18. Set up an ICE table for a weak acid HA where $[H_3O^+] = 10^{-pH} = 9.5 \times 10^{-4}$ M

	$HA(aq) + H_2O(\ell) \rightleftharpoons$	$H_3O^+(aq) +$	$A^-(aq)$
Initial	0.040	0	0
Change	−x	+x	+x
Equilibrium	0.040 − x	x	x

where $x = 9.5 \times 10^{-4}$ M

$$K_a = \frac{[H_3O^+][A^-]}{[HA]} = \frac{(9.5 \times 10^{-4})^2}{0.040 - 9.5 \times 10^{-4}} = 2.3 \times 10^{-5}$$

19. Set up an ICE table for the CO_3^{2-} ion behaving as a weak, monoprotic base.

	$CO_3^{2-}(aq) + H_2O(\ell) \rightleftharpoons$	$HCO_3^-(aq) +$	$OH^-(aq)$
Initial	0.15	0	0
Change	−x	+x	+x
Equilibrium	0.15 − x	x	x

$$K_b = \frac{[HCO_3^-][OH^-]}{[CO_3^{2-}]}$$

$$2.1 \times 10^{-4} = \frac{x^2}{0.15 - x}$$

Assuming x << 0.15 M
$x = [OH^-] = 5.6 \times 10^{-3}$ M
$pOH = 2.25$ and so $pH = 11.75$
$[H_3O^+] = 10^{-pH} = 1.8 \times 10^{-12}$

The small concentration of the product of CO_3^{2-} hydrolysis, HCO_3^-, does not affect the pH significantly.

20. Amount of NaOH used = $c \cdot V = 5.0 \times 10^{-3}$ mol
Amount of HCl used = $c \cdot V = 5.0 \times 10^{-3}$ mol
All of the NaOH and HCl are consumed in the reaction leaving only water and the neutral salt NaCl. The pH of the solution must be 7.00 (at 25 °C).

21. Fe^{3+} is a Lewis acid, an electron pair acceptor (as are all aqueous transition metal cations). Water and SCN^- ion are both electron pair donors, Lewis bases. See Section 17.9.

22. $HCO_2H(aq) + OH^-(aq) \rightleftharpoons HCO_2^-(aq) + H_2O(\ell)$
At the half-neutralization point of a titration of a weak acid with a strong base the solution contains half of the original acid and an equal amount of weak conjugate base. The solution is a buffer with $[H_3O^+] = K_a$ (and $pH = pK_a$). Here $[H_3O^+] = 1.8 \times 10^{-4}$ M and pH = 3.74. See Equation 18.5, page 825.

23. (a) $CH_3CO_2H(aq) + OH^-(aq)$
           $\rightleftharpoons CH_3CO_2^-(aq) + H_2O(\ell)$
    This is the reaction of a weak acid with an equal amount of a strong base. The product is the weak conjugate base of the acid, so the pH is greater than 7 after reaction is complete.
    (b) $NH_3(aq) + H_3O^+(aq) \rightleftharpoons NH_4^+(aq) + H_2O(\ell)$
    This is the reaction of a weak base with an equal amount of a strong acid. The product is the weak conjugate acid of the base, so the pH is less than 7 after reaction is complete.
    (c) $H_3O^+(aq) + OH^-(aq) \rightleftharpoons 2 H_2O(\ell)$
    This is the reaction of a strong acid with an equal amount of strong base. The solution consists of a neutral salt in water; pH = 7.0.

24. See Section 18.4 and page 834 in particular.
    (a) When two salts have the same formula type (for example, both have one cation and one anion) we can directly compare K_{sp} values to judge their relative solubility.
        AgSCN (1.0×10^{-12}) > AgBr (5.4×10^{-13})
    AgSCN is more soluble.

(b) For AgCl and Ag_2CO_3 we have to calculate their solubilities.

Solubility of AgCl = $(K_{sp})^{1/2} = (1.8 \times 10^{-10})^{1/2}$
$$= 1.3 \times 10^{-5} \text{ M}$$

Solubility of Ag_2CO_3

$Ag_2CO_3(s) \rightleftharpoons 2 \text{ Ag}^+(aq) + CO_3^{2-}(aq)$

$K_{sp} = [\text{Ag}^+]^2[CO_3^{2-}] = (2x)^2(x) = 8.5 \times 10^{-12}$

where $x = [CO_3^{2-}]$ and is equivalent to the molar solubility of the salt.

$[CO_3^{2-}] = 1.3 \times 10^{-4}$ M = molar solubility of Ag_2CO_3

Even though Ag_2CO_3 has a smaller K_{sp} value than AgCl, its molar solubility is greater.

25. Na_2CO_3 is a soluble salt.
$BaCO_3$. Solubility from $K_{sp} = 5.1 \times 10^{-5}$ M
CaF_2. Solubility from $K_{sp} = 2.4 \times 10^{-4}$ M
Ag_2CO_3. Solubility from $K_{sp} = 1.3 \times 10^{-4}$ M

Order of increasing molar solubility:
$BaCO_3 < Ag_2CO_3 < CaF_2 < Na_2CO_3$

26. $Mg(OH)_2(s) \rightleftharpoons Mg^{2+}(aq) + 2 \text{ OH}^-(aq)$
$K_{sp} = 5.6 \times 10^{-12} = [Mg^{2+}][\text{OH}^-]^2 = (x)(2x)^2$
$x = 1.1 \times 10^{-4}$ M
$[\text{OH}^-] = 2x = 2.2 \times 10^{-4}$ M
$[H_3O^+] = K_w/[\text{OH}^-] = 4.5 \times 10^{-11}$ M

27. Dissolve in 6 M HCl: MnS, $Ca_3(PO_4)_2$, $Al(OH)_3$, $MgCO_3$. Only these salts contain basic anions (which are conjugate bases of weak acids). The other two salts (AgCl and PbI_2) will not dissolve in 6 M HCl.

28. $NH_4^+(aq) + H_2O(\ell) \rightleftharpoons NH_3(aq) + H_3O^+(aq)$
Ammonium ion is in equilibrium with a small amount of NH_3. Adding the weak base NH_3 shifts the equilibrium to the left and raises the pH.

29. The results of this question can be confirmed using the OWL Simulation.
(a) Adding ClO_2^- leads to a lower percent ionization. The pH increases (as expected when a weak base is added).
(b)

	$HClO_2(aq) + H_2O(\ell) \rightleftharpoons H_3O^+(aq) + ClO_2^-(aq)$		
Initial	0.071	0.029	0.039
Change	$-x$	$+x$	$+x$
Equilibrium	$0.071 - x$	$0.029 + x$	$0.039 + x$

$$K_a = 0.012 = \frac{(0.029 + x)(0.039 + x)}{0.071 - x}$$

Solving this quadratic equation, we find $x = -0.0037$, which leads to $[HClO_2] = 0.075$ M, $[H_3O^+] = 0.025$ M, and $[ClO_2^-] = 0.035$ M.

30. Use Equation 18.1 to calculate the hydronium ion concentration and then calculate the pH.

$$[H_3O^+] = \frac{[NH_4^+]}{[NH_3]}K_a$$
$$= \left(\frac{0.020 \text{ mol } NH_4^+}{0.020 \text{ mol } NH_3}\right)5.6 \times 10^{-10} = 5.6 \times 10^{-10} \text{ M}$$

pH = 9.25.

31. Equation 19.3, page 870
$\Delta_r S^\circ = \Sigma S^\circ(\text{product}) - \Sigma S^\circ(\text{reactants})$
$\Delta_r S^\circ = 2 S^\circ(HF) - [S^\circ(H_2) + S^\circ(F_2)]$
$\Delta_r S^\circ = (2 \text{ mol HF}/1 \text{ mol-rxn})(173.78 \text{ J/K} \cdot \text{mol})$
$\quad - [(1 \text{ mol } H_2/1 \text{ mol-rxn})(130.7 \text{ J/K} \cdot \text{mol})$
$\quad + (1 \text{ mol } F_2/1 \text{ mol-rxn})(202.8 \text{ J/K} \cdot \text{mol})]$
$\Delta_r S^\circ = 14.1 \text{ J/K} \cdot \text{mol-rxn}$

32. (d). CCl_4 has more atoms in the molecule than the others and is in the gas phase.

33. (a) and (d)

34. See Equation 19.8, page 880.
$\Delta_r G^\circ = \Sigma \Delta_f G^\circ(\text{products}) - \Sigma \Delta_f G^\circ(\text{reactants})$
$\Delta_r G^\circ = 2 \Delta_f G^\circ [NH_3(g)] - 3 \Delta_f G^\circ [H_2O(\ell)]$
$\quad = (2 \text{ mol } NH_3/1 \text{ mol-rxn})(-16.37 \text{ kJ/mol})$
$\quad - (3 \text{ mol } H_2O(\ell)/1 \text{ mol-rxn})(-237.15 \text{ kJ/mol})$
$\quad = +678.71 \text{ kJ/mol-rxn}$

35. (d), not spontaneous at any temperature. See Table 19.2, page 874.

36. $\Delta_r G^\circ = \Delta_r H^\circ - T\Delta_r S^\circ$
$\Delta_r G^\circ = -122.8 \text{ kJ} - (298 \text{ K})(-0.1239 \text{ kJ/K})$
$\Delta_r G^\circ = -85.9 \text{ kJ}$

The reaction is spontaneous.

37. (d) $\Delta_r G^\circ$ becomes more negative with increasing T because $\Delta_r S$ is positive (and $\Delta_r H^\circ$ is negative). See the left-most panel in Figure 19.12, page 882.

38. (a) The sign of $\Delta_r G^\circ$ is predicted to be positive for a reaction for which K is less than 1.
(b) $\Delta_r G^\circ = -RT\ln K$
$\quad = -(8.3145 \text{ J/K} \cdot \text{mol})(298 \text{ K}) \ln(1.8 \times 10^{-5})$
$\quad \Delta_r G^\circ = 2.71 \times 10^4 \text{ J/mol-rxn}$

39. Both $\Delta_r H$ and $\Delta_r S$ are predicted to be negative. The combination of two atoms to form one molecule is always an exothermic process. In addition, when two atoms combine to form one molecule, $\Delta_r S < 0$.

40. MnO_4^- is the oxidizing agent and is reduced
$MnO_4^-(aq) + 8 \text{ H}^+(aq) + 5 e^- \rightarrow Mn^{2+}(aq) + 4 H_2O(\ell)$

$C_2O_4^{2-}$ is the reducing agent and is oxidized
$C_2O_4^{2-}(aq) \rightarrow 2 CO_2(g) + 2 e^-$

Complete equation:
$2 MnO_4^-(aq) + 16 \text{ H}^+(aq) + 5 C_2O_4^{2-}(aq)$
$\quad \rightleftharpoons 2 Mn^{2+}(aq) + 8 H_2O(\ell) + 10 CO_2(g)$

41. (a) Al^{3+}

(b) Cl_2

(c) Al

(d) Cl^-

(e) No, Pb will not reduce V^{2+}

(f) No, I_2 will not oxidize Cl^-

(g) Cl_2, Ag^+, I_2, and Cu^{2+}

42. (a) From Table 20.1, page 920, we know that Cd will reduce Ni^{2+} to Ni. Therefore,

$$Cd(s) + Ni^{2+}(aq) \rightarrow Cd^{2+}(aq) + Ni(s)$$

(b) Electrons transfer in the external wire from Cd to Ni.

(c) Cd is the site of oxidation, is the anode, and is labeled negative. The Ni electrode is the cathode and is labeled positive.

(d) Cd is oxidized to Cd^{2+} and Ni^{2+} is reduced to Ni.

(e) $E°_{cell} = E°_{cathode} - E°_{anode} = -0.25\ V - (-0.40\ V)$
$E°_{cell} = +0.15\ V$

(f) Anions flow into the Cd cell (to balance the charge of the Cd^{2+} ions being generated), and the cations flow into the Ni cell.

43. Using the Nernst equation, we have

$$E = E° - \frac{0.0257}{2} \ln \frac{[Cu^{2+}]}{[Ag^+]^2}$$

$$E = +0.462\ V - 0.0129 \ln \frac{0.020}{(1.0)^2}$$

$$E = 0.512\ V$$

The electrochemical potential is more positive than $E°$.

44. The charge passed in the 10.-minute (600 second) time period is:

$$(0.15\ amp)(600\ s) = 90.\ coulombs$$

$$\text{Amount of charge} = 90.\ C \left(\frac{1\ mol\ electrons}{96500\ C} \right)$$

$$= 9.3 \times 10^{-4}\ mol\ e^-$$

$$9.3 \times 10^{-4}\ mol\ e^- \left(\frac{1\ mol\ Ni\ deposited}{2\ mol\ e^-} \right)$$

$$= 4.7 \times 10^{-4}\ mol\ Ni$$

$$4.7 \times 10^{-4}\ mol\ Ni \left(\frac{58.7\ g\ Ni}{1\ mol\ Ni} \right) = 0.027\ g\ Ni$$

45. (a) $MnO_4^-(aq) + 8\ H^+(aq) + 5\ e^- \rightarrow$
$$Mn^{2+}(aq) + 4\ H_2O(\ell)$$
$$\underline{Cu(s) \rightarrow Cu^{2+}(aq) + 2\ e^-}$$
$$2\ MnO_4^-(aq) + 5\ Cu(s) + 16\ H^+(aq) \rightarrow$$
$$2\ Mn^{2+}(aq) + 5\ Cu^{2+}(aq) + 8\ H_2O(\ell)$$

(b) $E°_{cell} = E°_{cathode} - E°_{anode}$
$E°_{cell} = +1.51\ V - (0.34\ V) = +1.17\ V$

(c) $E = E° - \left(\dfrac{0.0257}{10} \right) \ln \dfrac{(0.100)^2(0.100)^5}{(1.00)^2(0.500)^{16}} = 1.18\ V$

Solutions to Comprehensive Questions

46. (a) Rate $= k[NO]^2[H_2]$. Compare experiments 1 and 2: tripling $[NO]$ increases the rate by a factor of 9, indicating the reaction is second order in $[NO]$. Compare experiments 1 and 3: doubling $[NO]$ and $[H_2]$ increases the rate by a factor of 8. You know that doubling $[NO]$ increases the rate by 4-fold. To achieve an increase by a factor of 8 after doubling both $[NO]$ and $[H_2]$ must mean the reaction is first-order in H_2.

(b) Using the first set of data to calculate k:

$$k = \frac{\text{Rate}}{[NO]^2[H_2]}$$

$$= \frac{1.2 \times 10^{-2}\ mol/L}{(2.16 \times 10^{-2}\ mol/L)^2(1.4 \times 10^{-2}\ mol/L)}$$

$$= 1.8 \times 10^3\ L^2/mol^2 \cdot s$$

47. (a) Addition of solid NH_4Cl has no effect. Addition of gaseous NH_3 will cause the equilibrium to shift to the left, forming more solid NH_4Cl and consuming some of the HCl and NH_3. The final concentration of $NH_3(g)$ will be greater than the original, whereas the final concentration of $HCl(g)$ will be less than the original.

(b) Predictions: $\Delta_r H°$: positive (heat must be added). $\Delta_r S°$: positive (conversion of 1 mole of solid to 2 moles of gases).

$\Delta_r H° = \Delta_f H°[NH_3(g)] + \Delta_f H°[HCl(g)]$
$$- \Delta_f H°[NH_4Cl(s)]$$
$= (1\ mol\ NH_3/1\ mol\text{-rxn})(-45.90\ kJ/mol)$
$+ (1\ mol\ HCl/1\ mol\text{-rxn})(-92.31\ kJ/mol)$
$- (1\ mol\ NH_4Cl/1\ mol\text{-rxn})(-314.55\ kJ/mol)$
$= 176.34\ kJ/mol\text{-rxn}$

$\Delta_r S° = S°[NH_3(g)] + S°[HCl(g)] - S°[NH_4Cl(s)]$
$= (1\ mol\ NH_3/1\ mol\text{-rxn})(192.77\ J/mol \cdot K)$
$+ (1\ mol\ HCl/1\ mol\text{-rxn})(186.2\ J/mol \cdot K)$
$- (1\ mol\ NH_4Cl/1\ mol\text{-rxn})(94.85\ J/mol \cdot K)$
$= 284.1\ J/K \cdot mol\text{-rxn}$

(c) Prediction: because of the favorable entropy term, this reaction will become product-favored at equilibrium at higher temperatures. A calculation is needed to determine if 400 °C is a high enough temperature. (Note that 400 °C = 673 K. Also note that we assume $\Delta_r H°$ and $\Delta_r S°$ do not change significantly with temperature.)

$\Delta_r G° = \Delta_r H° - T\Delta_r S°$
$= 176.34\ kJ/mol\text{-rxn}$
$$- (673\ K)(0.2841\ kJ/K \cdot mol\text{-rxn})$$
$= -14.9\ kJ/mol\text{-rxn}$

The negative sign indicates that the reaction is product-favored at this temperature.

To calculate $P(NH_3)$, first determine the equilibrium constant K_p for this reaction, then use this in an equilibrium calculation.

$\Delta_r G° = -RT \ln K$

$\ln K_p = -\dfrac{(-14900 \text{ J/mol})}{(8.3145 \text{ J/K} \cdot \text{mol})(673 \text{ K})} = 2.66$

$K_p = 14.3$

$K_p = P_{NH_3} P_{HCl}$

If $P_{NH_3} = P_{HCl} = x$

then $K_p = 14.3 = x^2$ and $x = 3.8$

$P_{NH_3} = P_{HCl} = 3.8$ atm

48. Set up an ICE table. Here the acid is ionized to the extent of 1.8% or $(0.018)(0.44 \text{ M}) = 0.0079$ M

	$HOCH_2CO_2H \rightleftharpoons H_3O^+ +$		$HOCH_2CO_2^-$
Initial (M)	0.44	0	0
Change (M)	−0.0079	+0.0079	+0.0079
Equilib. (M)	0.43	0.0079	0.0079

Because $[H_3O^+] = 0.0079$ M, pH = 2.10

$K_a = \dfrac{[H_3O^+][HOCH_2CO_2^-]}{[HOCH_2CO_2H]}$

$K_a = \dfrac{(0.0079)^2}{0.43} = 1.5 \times 10^{-4}$

49. Refer to K_a values in Table 17.3, page 770.
   (a) Acid strength:
   $NH_4^+ < CH_3CO_2H < HF < H_3PO_4 < HNO_3$
   (b) Product-favored. (Brønsted acid–base reactions favor the weaker acid and weaker base.)

50. Most soluble: $AgCH_3CO_2$, least soluble: AgCN

51. (a) Combinations (i), (ii), (iv), and (v) contain a weak acid and its weak conjugate base and are buffer solutions.
   (b) If the concentrations of the two species in the buffer are equal, pH = pK_a. The solution with highest pH is (i) and the solution with the lowest pH is (iii).
   (c) Select the buffer system for which the pK_a is closest to 7.40. This is (ii) for which $pK_a = 7.21$. To adjust the pH to 7.40, add base (either additional Na_2HPO_4 or NaOH, which would convert some of the NaH_2PO_4 to Na_2HPO_4).

52. (a) $K_a = 10^{-pK_a} = 10^{-2.867} = 1.36 \times 10^{-3}$
   (b) $ClCH_2CO_2H(aq) + OH^-(aq)$
   $\rightleftharpoons H_2O(\ell) + ClCH_2CO_2^-(aq)$
   (c) moles acid ($c_{acid} \times V_{acid}$)
   $= $ moles base ($c_{base} \times V_{base}$)
   $(0.154 \text{ mol/L})(0.0500 \text{ L}) = (0.128 \text{ mol/L})(V_{base})$
   $V_{base} = 0.0602$ L (= 60.2 mL)
   (d) Phenolphthalein. Choose an indicator that changes color near the pH at the equivalence point of the titration. In this case, the pH at the equivalence point is slightly basic. (Figure 18.10, page 832, shows the ranges of color changes for indicators.)
   (e) pH = $pK_a = 2.867$

(f) At the equivalence point, the solution contains 0.00770 moles $ClCH_2CO_2^-$ in a total volume of 0.1102 L (0.0602 + 0.0500 L). The concentration of this anion is 0.0699 M (0.0077 mol/0.1102 L). The anion is weakly basic:

$ClCH_2CO_2^-(aq) + H_2O(\ell)$
$\rightleftharpoons ClCH_2CO_2H(aq) + OH^-(aq)$

For this equilibrium

$K_b = K_w/K_a = (1.0 \times 10^{-14})/(1.36 \times 10^{-3})$
$= 7.4 \times 10^{-12}$

$K_b = \dfrac{[ClCH_2CO_2H][OH^-]}{[ClCH_2CO_2^-]}$

$7.4 \times 10^{-12} = \dfrac{(x)(x)}{0.0699 - x}$

$x = [OH^-] = 7.2 \times 10^{-7}$ M

pOH = 6.14

and so pH = $14.00 - 6.14 = 7.86$

53. (a) $Cr_2O_7{}^{2-} + 14 \text{ H}^+ + 6 \text{ } e^- \rightarrow 2 \text{ Cr}^{3+} + 7 \text{ H}_2O$
   $3[2 \text{ I}^- \rightarrow I_2 + 2 \text{ } e^-]$

   $\overline{Cr_2O_7{}^{2-} + 14 \text{ H}^+ + 6 \text{ I}^- \rightarrow 2 \text{ Cr}^{3+} + 7 \text{ H}_2O + 3 \text{ I}_2}$

   $Cr_2O_7{}^{2-}$ is reduced, I^- is the reducing agent, and the oxidation state of chromium changes from +6 to +3.
   (b) $8[MnO_4^- + 2 \text{ H}_2O + 3 \text{ } e^- \rightarrow MnO_2 + 4 \text{ OH}^-]$
   $3[HS^- + 9 \text{ OH}^- \rightarrow SO_4{}^{2-} + 5 \text{ H}_2O + 8 \text{ } e^-]$

   $\overline{8 \text{ MnO}_4^- + 3 \text{ HS}^- + H_2O}$
   $\rightarrow 8 \text{ MnO}_2 + 5 \text{ OH}^- + 3 \text{ SO}_4{}^{2-}$

   MnO_4^- is reduced, HS^- is the reducing agent, and the oxidation state of the manganese changes from +7 to +4.

54. (a) Cell using Zn as the anode and a chemically inert Pt electrode as the cathode.

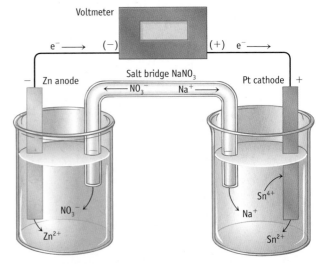

(b) The Na^+ ions move toward the $Sn^{4+} \mid Sn^{2+}$ (Pt) half-cell. The NO_3^- ions move toward the $Zn \mid Zn^{2+}$ half-cell.

(c) $Zn + Sn^{4+} \rightarrow Zn^{2+} + Sn^{2+}$

(d) $E°_{cell} = E°_{cathode} - E°_{anode}$
$= +0.15\ V - (-0.76\ V) = 0.91\ V$

55. For discussion of methodology for part (a) see "Northwest-southeast rule," page 921:

(a) Sn, Mg, and Mn

(b) Sn^{2+}

(c) Ag^+

(d) H_2

56. First, calculate moles of electrons required, next calculate the quantity of charge, and then use charge and current to calculate time required. (See Example 20.11.)

$$Mol\ e^- = (5.00\ g\ Cr)\left(\frac{1\ mol\ Cr}{52.0\ g\ Cr}\right)\left(\frac{3\ mol\ e^-}{1\ mol\ Cr}\right)$$
$$= 0.288\ mol\ e^-$$

$$Charge\ (C) = (0.288\ mol\ e^-)\left(\frac{96{,}500\ C}{mol\ e^-}\right)$$
$$= 2.78 \times 10^4\ C$$

Charge (C) = current (A) × time (s)
time = $(2.78 \times 10^4\ C/2.50\ A)$
$$= 1.11 \times 10^4\ s\ (=186\ min)$$

57. (a) The pH of the original solution is almost 12, so diethylamine is a weak base. Note that $[OH^-]$ for a 0.10 M solution is a little less than 0.010 M, indicating less than 10% of the base reacts with H_2O to form OH^-.

(b) $(C_2H_5)_2NH(aq) + HCl(aq)$
$$\rightleftharpoons (C_2H_5)_2NH_2^+(aq) + Cl^-(aq)$$

(c) At the half-neutralization point (after 25 mL of 0.10 M HCl has been added), pOH = 3.0. (pOH = 14.00 − pH where the pH = 11.0). pK_b = pOH, so $K_b = 1.0 \times 10^{-3}$. (Literature value = 6.3×10^{-4})

(d) The equivalence point occurs when exactly the amount of acid required has been added. Here 50.0 mL of a 0.10 M solution of the weak base requires 50.0 mL of 0.10 M HCl, and you observe a significant drop in the pH at this volume of acid. The pH at the mid-point of the vertical portion of the curve is the pH at the equivalence point, here about 6.2. The solution should be slightly acidic, as observed. At the equivalence point the solution contains the weak acid $(C_2H_5)_2NH_2^+$. The calculation of the equivalence point pH is outlined as follows:

Amount of $(C_2H_5)_2NH$ titrated = 0.0050 mol
Amount of $(C_2H_5)_2NH_2^+$ produced = 0.0050 mol
$[(C_2H_5)_2NH_2^+]$ at equivalence point
$$= (0.0050\ mol/0.100\ L) = 0.050\ M$$
K_b for $(C_2H_5)_2NH_2$ (from part c) = 1.0×10^{-3} so
K_a for $(C_2H_5)_2NH_2^+ = K_w/K_b = 1.0 \times 10^{-11}$

$$K_a = 1.0 \times 10^{-11} = \frac{[H_3O^+][(C_2H_5)_2NH]}{[(C_2H_5)_2NH_2^+]} = \frac{[H_3O^+]^2}{0.050}$$

$[H_3O^+] = 7.1 \times 10^{-7}\ M$ so pH = 6.15

(e) The solution contains $(C_2H_5)_2NH_2^+(aq)$, a weak acid.

58. (a) K_a for $Ni^{2+}(aq) = 2.5 \times 10^{-11}$. Use Equation 17.5 (page 769) to calculate the hydronium ion concentration. From $[H_3O^+]$ we find pH = 5.80.

(b) K_{b1} for ethylenediamine = 8.5×10^{-5}. Use Equation 17.6 to calculate $[OH^-]$ (= 1.5×10^{-3} M). Based on this we calculate a pOH of 2.84, which leads to a pH of 11.16 ($14.00 - 2.84 = 11.16$). (Note that ethylenediamine can undergo a second ionization ($K_{b2} = 2.7 \times 10^{-8}$), which will have only a minimal effect on pH.)

(c) Ni^{2+} is an electron-pair acceptor, a Lewis acid. NH_3, with its lone pair, is a Lewis base. (See Section 17.9.)

(d) K_f for the formation of $[Ni(NH_3)_6]^{2+}(aq)$ is 5.6×10^8. The reaction is product-favored at equilibrium.

(e) Calculating K_{net}.

$[Ni(NH_3)_6]^{2+}(aq) + 6\ H_2O(\ell)$
$\rightleftharpoons [Ni(H_2O)_6]^{2+}(aq) + 6\ NH_3(aq)$
$$1/K_{f1} = 1/5.5 \times 10^8$$

$[Ni(H_2O)_6]^{2+}(aq) + 3\ H_2NCH_2CH_2NH_2(aq)$
$\rightleftharpoons [Ni(H_2NCH_2CH_2NH_2)_3]^{2+}(aq) + 6\ H_2O(\ell)$
$$K_{f2} = 1.9 \times 10^{18}$$

$[Ni(NH_3)_6]^{2+}(aq) + 3\ H_2NCH_2CH_2NH_2(aq)$
$\rightleftharpoons [Ni(H_2NCH_2CH_2NH_2)_3]^{2+}(aq) + 6\ NH_3(aq)$
$$K_{net} = ?$$

$K_{net} = (1/K_{f1})K_{f2} = 3.5 \times 10^9$
$\Delta_r G° = -RT \ln K = -54\ kJ/mol$ at 298 K

This spontaneous (and product-favored) reaction is largely controlled by $\Delta_r S°$. $\Delta_r H°$ is probably about 0 because 6 Ni-NH_3 bonds are exchanged for bonds between Ni and the 6 N atoms of the three ethylenediamine molecules. $\Delta_r S°$ is expected to be large and positive because four ions or molecules are replaced by seven product ions or molecules.

59. From $\Delta_r G°$ we use Equation 19.7 (page 878) to calculate $K_p = 5.0 \times 10^{-2}$.

	$C_2H_6(g) \rightleftharpoons C_2H_4(g) + H_2(g)$		
Initial	1.00 atm	0	0
Change	−x	+x	+x
Equilibrium	1.00 − x	x	x

$K_p = (x^2)/(1.00 - x)$

Solving this quadratic expression, we find x = 0.20 atm. Therefore, at equilibrium $P(C_2H_4) = P(H_2) = 0.20$ atm and $P(C_2H_6) = 0.80$ atm. This means $P(total) = 1.20$ atm.

Mol % $H_2 = [P(H_2)/P(total)]100\%$
$= [(0.20\ atm)/(1.20\ atm)]100\% = 17\%\ H_2$

21 | The Chemistry of the Main Group Elements

Quartz (SiO$_2$), dry ice (solid CO$_2$), and pure silicon.

Charles D. Winters

Carbon and Silicon

Carbon and silicon are both highly signifi-cant elements in the earth's crust. Men-deleev placed them in the same periodic group based on the similarity in stoichi-ometry of their simple compounds such as their oxides (CO$_2$ and SiO$_2$). We know now that carbon is the back-bone of millions of organic compounds. As we will see in this chapter, silicon, the second most abundant element in the earth's crust, is vitally important in the structures of a large number of minerals.

Probe a bit further into silicon chemistry, however, and what emerges are the surprising differences between these elements. We get a hint of this when we compare the two oxides, CO$_2$, a gas above −78 °C and 1 atm pressure, and SiO$_2$, a rock hard solid with a very high melting point. Another interesting contrast can be made between the reactions of the two simple hydrogen compounds, CH$_4$ and SiH$_4$, with water. The reaction of methane with water is reactant-favored, whereas silane will explode on contact with water.

In this chapter, we will evaluate and summarize the inorganic chemistry of the main group elements and explore the similarities and differences between elements in each periodic group.

Questions:

1. Write balanced chemical equations for the reactions of water with CH$_4$ (forming CO$_2$ and H$_2$O) and SiH$_4$ (forming SiO$_2$ and H$_2$).
2. Using enthalpy of formation data, calculate the standard enthalpy change for the reactions in Question 1.
3. Look up the electronegativities of carbon, silicon, and hydro-gen. What conclusion can you draw concerning the polarity of C—H and Si—H bonds?
4. Carbon and silicon compounds with the empirical formulas (CH$_3$)$_2$CO (acetone) and (CH$_3$)$_2$SiO (a silicone polymer) also have quite different structures (Chapter 10). Draw Lewis struc-tures for these species. This difference, along with the differ-ence between structures of CO$_2$ and SiO$_2$, suggests a general observation about silicon compounds. Based on that observa-tion, do you expect that a silicon compound with a structure similar to ethene (C$_2$H$_4$) exists?

Answers to these questions are in Appendix Q.

Chapter Goals

◉WL *See Chapter Goals Revisited (page 1010) for Study Questions keyed to these goals and assignable in OWL.*

- Relate the formulas and properties of compounds to the periodic table.
- Describe the chemistry of the main group or A-Group elements, particularly H; Na and K; Mg and Ca; B and Al; Si; N and P; O and S; and F and Cl.
- Apply the principles of stoichiometry, thermodynamics, and electrochemistry to the chemistry of the main group elements.

The main group or A-Group elements occupy an important place in the world of chemistry. Eight of the 10 most abundant elements on the earth are in these groups. Likewise, the top 10 chemicals produced by the U.S. chemical industry are all main group elements or their compounds.

Because main group elements and their compounds are economically important—and because they have interesting chemistries—we devote this chapter to a brief survey of these elements.

Chemistry.◌.Now™

Throughout the text this icon introduces an opportunity for self-study or to explore interactive tutorials by signing in at **www.cengage.com/login**.

21.1 Element Abundances

The abundance of the first 18 elements in the solar system is plotted against their atomic numbers in Figure 21.1. As you can see, hydrogen and helium are the most abundant by a wide margin because most of the mass of the solar system resides in the sun, and these elements are the sun's primary components. Lithium, beryllium, and boron are low in abundance, but carbon's abundance is very high. From this point on, with the exception of iron and nickel, elemental abundances gradually decline as the atomic number increases.

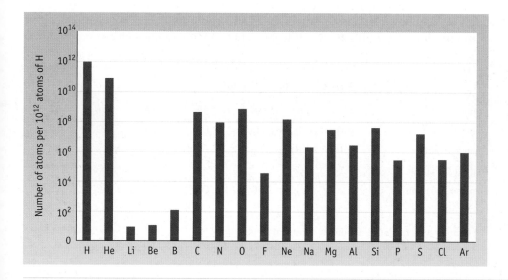

FIGURE 21.1 Abundance of elements 1–18. Li, Be, and B have relatively low abundances because they are circumvented when elements are made in stars. The common elements such as C, O, and Ne are made in stars by the accretion of alpha particles (helium nuclei). Helium has an atomic number of 2. If three He atoms combine, they produce an atom with atomic number 6 (carbon). Adding yet another He atom gives an atom with atomic number 8 (oxygen), and so on. (Notice that the vertical axis uses a logarithmic scale. This means, for example, there are 10^{12} H atoms for every 100 B atoms.)

TABLE 21.1 The 10 Most Abundant Elements in Earth's Crust

Rank	Element	Abundance (ppm)*
1	Oxygen	474,000
2	Silicon	277,000
3	Aluminum	82,000
4	Iron	56,300
5	Calcium	41,000
6	Sodium	23,600
7	Magnesium	23,300
8	Potassium	21,000
9	Titanium	5,600
10	Hydrogen	1,520

*ppm = g per 1000 kg. Most abundance data taken from J. Emsley: *The Elements*, New York, Oxford University Press, 3rd edition, 1998.

Ten elements account for 99% of the aggregate mass of our planet (Table 21.1). Oxygen, silicon, and aluminum represent more than 80% of this mass. Oxygen and nitrogen are the primary components of the atmosphere, and oxygen-containing water is highly abundant on the surface, underground, and as a vapor in the atmosphere. Many common minerals also contain these elements, including limestone ($CaCO_3$) and quartz or sand (SiO_2, Figure 2.8). Aluminum and silicon occur together in many minerals; among the more common ones are feldspar, granite, and clay.

21.2 The Periodic Table: A Guide to the Elements

The similarities in the properties of certain elements guided Mendeleev when he created the first periodic table (◀ page 59). He placed elements in groups based partly on the composition of their common compounds with oxygen and hydrogen (see Table 21.2). We now understand that the elements are grouped according to the arrangements of their valence electrons.

Recall that the metallic character of the elements declines on moving from left to right in the periodic table. Elements in Group 1A, the alkali metals, are the most metallic elements in the periodic table. Elements on the far right are nonmetals, and in between are the metalloids. Metallic character also increases from the top of a group to the bottom. This is especially well illustrated by Group 4A. Carbon, at the top of the group, is a nonmetal; silicon and germanium are metalloids; and tin and lead are metals (Figure 21.2). The significance of metallic character in a discussion of the chemistry of the elements is readily apparent; metals typically form ionic compounds, whereas compounds composed only of nonmetals are covalent. Typically, ionic compounds are crystalline solids that have high melting points and conduct electricity in the molten state. Covalent compounds, on the other hand, can be gases, liquids, or solids and have low melting and boiling points.

Valence Electrons

The ns and np electrons are the valence electrons for main group elements (where n is the period in which the element is found) (◀ Section 7.4). The chemical behavior of an element is determined by the valence electrons.

When considering electronic structure, a useful reference point is the noble gases (Group 8A), elements having filled electron subshells. Helium has an electron configuration of $1s^2$; the other noble gases have ns^2np^6 valence electron configura-

Charles D. Winters

FIGURE 21.2 Group 4A elements. A nonmetal, carbon (graphite crucible); a metalloid, silicon (round, lustrous bar); and metals tin (chips of metal) and lead (a bullet, a toy, and a sphere).

TABLE 21.2 Similarities within Periodic Groups*

Group	1A	2A	3A	4A	5A	6A	7A
Common oxide	M_2O	MO	M_2O_3	EO_2	E_4O_{10}	EO_3	E_2O_7
Common hydride	MH	MH_2	MH_3	EH_4	EH_3	EH_2	EH
Highest oxidation state	+1	+2	+3	+4	+5	+6	+7
Common oxoanion			BO_3^{3-}	CO_3^{2-}	NO_3^-	SO_4^{2-}	ClO_4^-
				SiO_4^{4-}	PO_4^{3-}		

*M denotes a metal and E denotes a nonmetal or metalloid.

tions. The dominant characteristic of the noble gases is their lack of reactivity. Indeed, the first two elements in the group do not form any compounds that can be isolated. The other four elements are now known to have limited chemistry, however, and the discovery of xenon compounds in the 1960s ranks as one of the most interesting developments in modern chemistry.

Ionic Compounds of Main Group Elements

Ions of main group elements having filled s and p subshells are very common—justifying the often-seen statement that elements react in ways that achieve a "noble gas configuration." The elements in Groups 1A and 2A form 1+ and 2+ ions with electron configurations that are the same as those for the previous noble gases. All common compounds of these elements (e.g., NaCl, $CaCO_3$) are ionic. The metallic elements in Group 3A (aluminum, gallium, indium, and thallium, but not the metalloid boron) form compounds containing 3+ ions.

Elements of Groups 6A and 7A can also achieve a noble gas configuration by adding electrons. The Group 7A elements (halogens) form anions with a 1− charge (the halide ions, F^-, Cl^-, Br^-, I^-), and the Group 6A elements form anions with a 2− charge (O^{2-}, S^{2-}, Se^{2-}, Te^{2-}). In Group 5A chemistry, 3− ions with a noble gas configuration (such as the nitride ion, N^{3-}) are also known. The energy required to form highly charged anions is large, however, which means that other types of chemical behavior will usually take precedence.

■ **EXAMPLE 21.1 Reactions of Group 1A–3A Elements**

Problem Give the formula and name for the product in each of the following reactions. Write a balanced chemical equation for the reaction.

(a) $Ca(s) + S_8(s)$

(b) $Rb(s) + I_2(s)$

(c) lithium and chlorine

(d) aluminum and oxygen

Strategy Predictions are based on the assumption that ions are formed with the electron configuration of the nearest noble gas. Group 1A elements form 1+ ions; Group 2A elements form 2+ ions; and metals in Group 3A form 3+ ions. In their reactions with metals, halogen atoms typically add a single electron to give anions with a 1− charge; Group 6A elements add two electrons to form anions with a 2− charge. For names of products, refer to the nomenclature discussion on page 77.

Solution

	Balanced Equation	Product Name
(a)	$8\ Ca(s) + S_8(s) \rightarrow 8\ CaS(s)$	Calcium sulfide
(b)	$2\ Rb(s) + I_2(s) \rightarrow 2\ RbI(s)$	Rubidium iodide
(c)	$2\ Li(s) + Cl_2(g) \rightarrow 2\ LiCl(s)$	Lithium chloride
(d)	$4\ Al(s) + 3\ O_2(g) \rightarrow 2\ Al_2O_3(s)$	Aluminum oxide

---

EXERCISE 21.1 Main Group Element Chemistry

Write a balanced chemical equation for a reaction forming the following compounds from the elements.

(a) NaBr   **(c)** PbO

(b) CaSe   **(d)** $AlCl_3$

Molecular Compounds of Main Group Elements

Many avenues of reactivity are open to nonmetallic main group elements. Reactions with metals generally result in formation of ionic compounds, whereas compounds containing only metalloids and nonmetallic elements are generally molecular in nature.

Molecular compounds are encountered with the Group 3A element boron (Figure 21.3), and the chemistry of carbon in Group 4A is dominated by molecular compounds with covalent bonds (◀ Chapters 8 and 10). Similarly, nitrogen chemistry is dominated by molecular compounds. Consider ammonia, NH_3; the various nitrogen oxides; and nitric acid, HNO_3. In each of these species, nitrogen bonds covalently to another nonmetallic element. Also in Group 5A, phosphorus reacts with chlorine to produce the molecular compounds PCl_3 and PCl_5 (◀ page 113).

The valence electron configurations of an element determine the composition of its molecular compounds. Involving all the valence electrons in the formation of a compound is a frequent occurrence in main group element chemistry. We should not be surprised to discover compounds in which the central element has the highest possible oxidation number (such as P in PF_5). The highest oxidation number is readily apparent: it equals the group number. Thus, the highest (and only) oxidation number of sodium in its compounds is +1; the highest oxidation number of C is +4; and the highest oxidation number of phosphorus is +5 (Tables 21.2 and 21.3).

Charles D. Winters

FIGURE 21.3 Boron halides. Liquid BBr_3 (left) and solid BI_3 (right). Formed from a metalloid and a nonmetal, both are molecular compounds. Both are sealed in glass ampules to prevent these boron compounds from reacting with H_2O in the air.

TABLE 21.3 Fluorine Compounds Formed by Main Group Elements

Group	Compound	Bonding
1A	NaF	Ionic
2A	MgF_2	Ionic
3A	AlF_3	Ionic
4A	SiF_4	Covalent
5A	PF_5	Covalent
6A	SF_6	Covalent
7A	IF_7	Covalent
8A	XeF_4	Covalent

■ **EXAMPLE 21.2 Predicting Formulas for Compounds of Main Group Elements**

Problem Predict the formula for each of the following:

(a) the product of the reaction between germanium and excess oxygen

(b) the product of the reaction of arsenic and fluorine

(c) a compound formed from phosphorus and excess chlorine

(d) an anion of selenic acid

Strategy We will predict that in each reaction the element other than the halogen or oxygen in each product achieves its most positive oxidation number, a value equal to the number of its periodic group.

Solution

(a) The Group 4A element germanium should have a maximum oxidation number of +4. Thus, its oxide has the formula GeO_2.

(b) Arsenic, in Group 5A, reacts vigorously with fluorine to form AsF_5, in which arsenic has an oxidation number of +5.

(c) PCl_5 is formed when the Group 5A element phosphorus reacts with excess chlorine.

(d) The chemistries of S and Se are similar. Sulfur, in Group 6A, has a maximum oxidation number of +6, so it forms SO_3 and sulfuric acid, H_2SO_4. Selenium, also in Group 6A, has analogous chemistry, forming SeO_3 and selenic acid, H_2SeO_4. The anion of this acid is the selenate ion, SeO_4^{2-}.

EXERCISE 21.2 Predicting Formulas for Main Group Compounds

Write the formula for each of the following:

(a) hydrogen telluride   **(c)** selenium hexachloride

(b) sodium arsenate   **(d)** perbromic acid

There are many similarities among elements in the same periodic group. This means you can use compounds of more common elements as examples when you encounter compounds of elements with which you are not familiar. For example, water, H_2O, is the simplest hydrogen compound of oxygen. You can reasonably expect the hydrogen compounds of other Group 6A elements to be H_2S, H_2Se, and H_2Te; all are well known.

■ **EXAMPLE 21.3 Predicting Formulas**

Problem Predict the formula for each of the following:

(a) a compound of hydrogen and phosphorus

(b) the hypobromite ion

(c) germane (the simplest hydrogen compound of germanium)

(d) two oxides of tellurium

Strategy Recall as examples some of the compounds of lighter elements in a group, and then assume other elements in that group will form analogous compounds.

Solution

(a) Phosphine, PH_3, has a composition analogous to ammonia, NH_3.

(b) Hypobromite ion, BrO^-, is similar to the hypochlorite ion, ClO^-, the anion of hypochlorous acid ($HClO$).

(c) GeH_4 is analogous to CH_4 and SiH_4, other Group 4A hydrogen compounds.

(d) Te and S are in Group 6A. TeO_2 and TeO_3 are analogs of the oxides of sulfur, SO_2 and SO_3.

■ **EXAMPLE 21.4 Recognizing Incorrect Formulas**

Problem One formula is incorrect in each of the following groups. Pick out the incorrect formula, and indicate why it is incorrect.

(a) $CsSO_4$, KCl, $NaNO_3$, Li_2O

(b) MgO, CaI_2, $BaPO_4$, $CaCO_3$

(c) CO, CO_2, CO_3

(d) PF_5, PF_4^+, PF_2, PF_6^-

Strategy Look for errors such as incorrect charges on ions or an oxidation number exceeding the maximum possible for the periodic group.

Solution

(a) $CsSO_4$. Sulfate ion has a $2-$ charge, so this formula would require a Cs^{2+} ion. Cesium, in Group 1A, forms only $1+$ ions. The formula of cesium sulfate is Cs_2SO_4.

(b) $BaPO_4$. This formula implies a Ba^{3+} ion (because the phosphate anion is PO_4^{3-}). The cation charge does not equal the group number. The formula of barium phosphate is $Ba_3(PO_4)_2$.

(c) CO_3. Given that O has an oxidation number of -2, carbon would have an oxidation number of $+6$. Carbon is in Group 4A, however, and can have a maximum oxidation number of $+4$.

(d) PF_2. This species has an odd number of electrons. Very few odd electron molecules are commonly seen. Examples include NO, NO_2, and ClO_2.

Comment To chemists, this exercise is second nature. Incorrect formulas stand out. You will find that your ability to write and recognize correct formulas will grow as you learn more chemistry.

EXERCISE 21.3 Predicting Formulas

Identify a compound or ion based on a second-period element that has a formula and Lewis structure analogous to each of the following:

(a) PH_4^+

(b) S_2^{2-}

(c) P_2H_4

(d) PF_3

Hydrogen, Helium, and Balloons

In 1783, Jacques Charles first used hydrogen to fill a balloon large enough to float above the French countryside (◄ page 516), In World War I, hydrogen-filled observation balloons were used. The Graf Zeppelin, a passenger-carrying dirigible built in Germany in 1928, was also filled with hydrogen. It carried more than 13,000 people between Germany and the United States until 1937, when it was replaced by the Hindenburg. The Hindenburg was designed to be filled with helium. At that time, World War II was approaching, and the United States, which has much of the world's supply of helium, would not sell the gas to Germany. As a consequence, the Hindenburg had to use hydrogen. The Hindenburg exploded and burned when landing in Lakehurst, New Jersey, in May 1937. Of the 62 people on board, only about half escaped uninjured. As a result of this disaster, hydrogen has acquired a reputation as being a very dangerous substance. Actually, it is as safe to handle as any other fuel, as evidenced by the large quantities used in rockets today.

Mary Evans Picture Library/Photo Researchers, Inc.

The Hindenburg. This hydrogen-filled dirigible crashed in Lakehurst, New Jersey, in May 1937. Some have speculated that the aluminum paint coating the skin of the dirigible was involved in sparking the fire.

EXERCISE 21.4 Recognizing Incorrect Formulas

Explain why compounds with the following formulas would not be expected to exist: ClO, Na_2Cl, $CaCH_3CO_2$, C_3H_7.

21.3 Hydrogen

Chemical and Physical Properties of Hydrogen

Hydrogen has three isotopes, two of them stable (protium and deuterium) and one radioactive (tritium).

Isotopes of Hydrogen

Isotope Mass (u)	Symbol	Name
1.0078	^1H (H)	Hydrogen (protium)
2.0141	^2H (D)	Deuterium
3.0160	^3H (T)	Tritium

Of the three isotopes, only H and D are found in nature in significant quantities. Tritium, which is produced by cosmic ray bombardment of nitrogen in the atmosphere, is found to the extent of 1 atom per 10^{18} atoms of ordinary hydrogen. Tritium has a half-life of 12.26 years.

Under standard conditions, hydrogen is a colorless gas. Its very low boiling point, 20.7 K, reflects its nonpolar character and low molar mass. As the least dense gas known, it is ideal for filling lighter-than-air craft.

Deuterium compounds have been the subject of much research. One important observation is that, because D has twice the mass of H, reactions involving D atom transfer are slightly slower than those involving H atoms. This knowledge led to a way to produce D_2O or "heavy water." Hydrogen can be produced, albeit expensively, by electrolysis of water (Figure 21.4).

$$2 \ H_2O(\ell) + \text{electrical energy} \rightarrow 2 \ H_2(g) + O_2(g)$$

Any sample of natural water always contains a tiny concentration of D_2O. When electrolyzed, H_2O is electrolyzed more rapidly than D_2O. Thus, as the electrolysis proceeds, the liquid remaining is enriched in D_2O. Repeating this process many times will eventually give pure D_2O, often called "heavy water." Large amounts of D_2O are now produced because this compound is used as a moderator in some nuclear reactors that are used for power generation.

Hydrogen combines chemically with virtually every other element, except the noble gases. There are three different types of binary hydrogen-containing compounds.

Ionic metal hydrides are formed in the reaction of H_2 with a Group 1A or 2A metal.

$$2 \ Na(s) + H_2(g) \rightarrow 2 \ NaH(s)$$

$$Ca(s) + H_2(g) \rightarrow CaH_2(s)$$

These compounds contain the hydride ion, H^-, in which hydrogen has a -1 oxidation number.

Molecular compounds (such as H_2O, HF, and NH_3) are generally formed by direct combination of hydrogen with nonmetallic elements (Figure 21.5). The oxidation number of the hydrogen atom in these compounds is $+1$, but covalent bonds to hydrogen are the rule.

$$N_2(g) + 3 \ H_2(g) \rightarrow 2 \ NH_3(g)$$

$$F_2(g) + H_2(g) \rightarrow 2 \ HF(g)$$

Hydrogen is absorbed by many metals to form *interstitial hydrides*, the third general class of hydrogen compounds. This name refers to the structures of these species, in which the hydrogen atoms reside in the spaces between the metal atoms (called *interstices*) in the crystal lattice. Palladium metal, for example, can soak up 1000 times its volume of hydrogen (at STP). Most interstitial hydrides are non-stoichiometric; that is, the ratio of metal and hydrogen is not a whole number. When interstitial metal hydrides are heated, H_2 is driven out. This phenomenon allows these materials to store H_2, just as a sponge can store water. It suggests one way to store hydrogen for use as a fuel in automobiles (◄ page 264).

Preparation of Hydrogen

About 300 billion liters (STP) of hydrogen gas are produced annually worldwide, and virtually all is used immediately in the manufacture of ammonia (► Section 21.8), methanol (◄ Section 10.3), or other chemicals.

Some hydrogen is made from coal and steam, a reaction that has been used for more than 100 years.

$$C(s) + H_2O(g) \longrightarrow \underbrace{H_2(g) + CO(g)}_{\text{water gas or synthesis gas}}$$

$$\Delta_r H^\circ = +131 \ \text{kJ/mol-rxn}$$

The reaction is carried out by injecting water into a bed of red-hot coke. The mixture of gases produced, called *water gas* or *synthesis gas*, was used until about 1950 as a fuel for cooking, heating, and lighting. However, it has serious drawbacks. It

FIGURE 21.4 Electrolysis of water. Electrolysis of water (containing dilute H_2SO_4 as an electrolyte) gives O_2 (left) and H_2 (right).

Charles D. Winters

Charles D. Winters

FIGURE 21.5 The reaction of H_2 and Br_2. Hydrogen gas burns in an atmosphere of bromine vapor to give hydrogen bromide.

Roger Ressmeyer/Corbis

FIGURE 21.6 Production of water gas. Water gas, also called synthesis gas, is a mixture of CO and H_2. It is produced by treating coal, coke, or a hydrocarbon like methane with steam at high temperatures in plants such as that pictured here. Methane has the advantage that it gives more total H_2 per gram than other hydrocarbons, and the ratio of the by-product CO_2 to H_2 is lower.

produces only about half as much heat as an equal amount of methane does, and the flame is nearly invisible. Moreover, because it contains carbon monoxide, water gas is toxic.

The largest quantity of hydrogen is now produced by the *catalytic steam reformation of hydrocarbons* such as methane in natural gas (Figure 21.6). Methane reacts with steam at high temperature to give H_2 and CO.

$$CH_4(g) + H_2O(g) \rightarrow 3\ H_2(g) + CO(g) \qquad \Delta_r H° = +206\ kJ/mol\text{-}rxn$$

The reaction is rapid at 900–1000 °C and goes nearly to completion. More hydrogen can be obtained in a second step in which the CO formed in the first step reacts with more water. This so-called *water gas shift reaction* is run at 400–500 °C and is slightly exothermic.

$$H_2O(g) + CO(g) \rightarrow H_2(g) + CO_2(g) \qquad \Delta_r H° = -41\ kJ/mol\text{-}rxn$$

The CO_2 formed in the process is removed by reaction with CaO (to give solid $CaCO_3$), leaving fairly pure hydrogen.

Perhaps the cleanest way to make hydrogen on a relatively large scale is the electrolysis of water (Figure 21.4). This approach provides not only hydrogen gas but also high-purity O_2. Because electricity is quite expensive, however, this method is not generally used commercially.

Table 21.4 and Figure 21.7 give examples of reactions used to produce H_2 gas in the laboratory. The most often used method is the reaction of a metal with an acid. Alternatively, the reaction of aluminum with aqueous NaOH (Figure 21.7b) also generates hydrogen. During World War II, this reaction was used to obtain hydrogen to inflate small balloons for weather observation and to raise radio antennas. Metallic aluminum was plentiful at the time because it came from damaged aircraft.

The combination of a metal hydride and water (Figure 21.7c) is an efficient but expensive way to synthesize H_2 in the laboratory. The reaction is more commonly used in laboratories to dry organic solvents because the metal hydride reacts with traces of water present in the solvent.

EXERCISE 21.5 Hydrogen Chemistry

Use bond enthalpies (page 389) to estimate the enthalpy change for the reaction of methane and water to give hydrogen and carbon monoxide (with all compounds in the gas phase).

FIGURE 21.7
Producing hydrogen gas.

Photos: Charles D. Winters

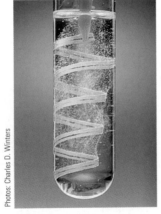

(a) The reaction of magnesium and acid. The products are hydrogen gas and a magnesium salt.

(b) The reaction of aluminum and NaOH. The products of this reaction are hydrogen gas and a solution of Na[Al(OH)$_4$].

(c) The reaction of CaH$_2$ and water. The products are hydrogen gas and Ca(OH)$_2$.

TABLE 21.4 Methods for Preparing H_2 in the Laboratory

1. Metal + Acid → metal salt + H_2

   $Mg(s) + 2\ HCl(aq) \rightarrow MgCl_2(aq) + H_2(g)$

2. Metal + H_2O → metal hydroxide or oxide + H_2

   $2\ Na(s) + 2\ H_2O(\ell) \rightarrow 2\ NaOH(aq) + H_2(g)$

   $2\ Fe(s) + 3\ H_2O(\ell) \rightarrow Fe_2O_3(s) + 3\ H_2(g)$

   $2\ Al(s) + 2\ KOH(aq) + 6\ H_2O(\ell) \rightarrow 2\ K[Al(OH)_4](aq) + 3\ H_2(g)$

3. Metal hydride + H_2O → metal hydroxide + H_2

   $CaH_2(s) + 2\ H_2O(\ell) \rightarrow Ca(OH)_2(s) + 2\ H_2(g)$

Charles D. Winters

FIGURE 21.8 The importance of salt. All animals, including humans, need a certain amount of salt in their diet. Sodium ions are important in maintaining electrolyte balance and in regulating osmotic pressure. For an interesting account of the importance of salt in society, culture, history, and economy, see *Salt, A World History*, by M. Kurlansky, New York, Penguin Books, 2002.

21.4 The Alkali Metals, Group 1A

Sodium and potassium are, respectively, the sixth and eighth most abundant elements in the earth's crust by mass. In contrast, lithium is relatively rare, as are rubidium and cesium. Only traces of radioactive francium occur in nature. Its longest-lived isotope (^{223}Fr) has a half-life of only 22 minutes.

The Group 1A elements are metals, and all are highly reactive with oxygen, water, and other oxidizing agents (see Figure 7.13, page 329). In all cases, compounds of the Group 1A metals contain the element as a 1+ ion. The free metal is never found in nature.

Most sodium and potassium compounds are water-soluble (◄ solubility guidelines, Figure 3.10), so it is not surprising that sodium and potassium compounds are found either in the oceans or in underground deposits that are the residue of ancient seas. To a much smaller extent, these elements are also found in minerals, such as Chilean saltpeter ($NaNO_3$).

Despite the fact that sodium is only slightly more abundant than potassium on the earth, sea water contains significantly more sodium than potassium (2.8% NaCl versus 0.8% KCl). Why the great difference? Most compounds of both elements are water-soluble, so why didn't rain dissolve Na- and K-containing minerals over the centuries and carry them down to the sea, so that they appear in the same proportions in the oceans as on land? The answer lies in the fact that potassium is an important factor in plant growth. Most plants contain four to six times as much combined potassium as sodium. Thus, most of the potassium ions in groundwater from dissolved minerals are taken up preferentially by plants, whereas sodium salts continue on to the oceans. (Because plants require potassium, commercial fertilizers usually contain a significant amount of potassium salts.)

Some NaCl is essential in the diet of humans and other animals because many biological functions are controlled by the concentrations of Na^+ and Cl^- ions (Figure 21.8). The fact that salt has long been recognized as important is evident in surprising ways. For example, we are paid a "salary" for work done. This word is derived from the Latin *salarium*, which meant "salt money" because Roman soldiers were paid in salt.

Preparation of Sodium and Potassium

Sodium is produced by reducing sodium ions in sodium salts. However, common chemical reducing agents are not powerful enough to convert sodium ions to sodium metal. Because of this, the metals are usually prepared by electrolysis.

Group 1A
Alkali metals

Lithium	3
Li	20 ppm
Sodium	11
Na	23,600 ppm
Potassium	19
K	21,000 ppm
Rubidium	37
Rb	90 ppm
Cesium	55
Cs	0.0003 ppm
Francium	87
Fr	trace

Element abundances are in parts per million in the earth's crust.

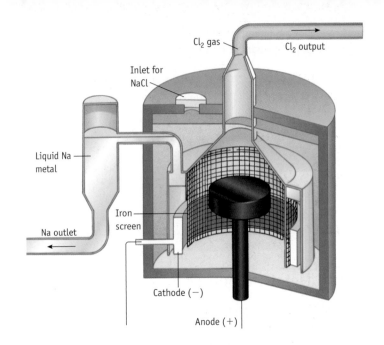

FIGURE 21.9. A Downs cell for preparing sodium. A circular iron cathode is separated from the graphite anode by an iron screen. At the temperature of the electrolysis, about 600 °C, sodium is a liquid. It floats to the top and is drawn off periodically. Chlorine gas is produced at the anode and collected inside the inverted cone in the center of the cell.

The English chemist Sir Humphry Davy first isolated sodium in 1807 by the electrolysis of molten sodium carbonate. However, the element remained a laboratory curiosity until 1824, when it was found sodium could be used to reduce aluminum chloride to aluminum metal. At that time, metallic aluminum was rare and very valuable, so this discovery inspired considerable interest in manufacturing sodium. By 1886, a practical method of sodium production had been devised (the reduction of NaOH with carbon). Unfortunately for sodium producers, in this same year Charles Hall and Paul Heroult invented the electrolytic method for aluminum production (▶ page 980), thereby eliminating this market for sodium.

Sodium is currently produced by the electrolysis of molten NaCl (◀ Section 20.7). The Downs cell for the electrolysis of molten NaCl operates at 7 to 8 V with currents of 25,000 to 40,000 amps (Figure 21.9). The cell is filled with a mixture of dry NaCl, $CaCl_2$, and $BaCl_2$. Adding other salts to NaCl lowers the melting point from that of pure NaCl (800.7 °C) to about 600 °C. [Recall that solutions have lower melting points than pure solvents (Chapter 14).] Sodium is produced at a copper or iron cathode that surrounds a circular graphite anode. Directly over the cathode is an inverted trough in which the low-density, molten sodium (melting point, 97.8 °C) collects. Chlorine, a valuable by-product, collects at the anode.

Potassium can also be made by electrolysis. Molten potassium is soluble in molten KCl, however, making separation of the metal difficult. The preferred method for preparation of potassium uses the reaction of sodium vapor with molten KCl, with potassium being continually removed from the equilibrium mixture.

$$Na(g) + KCl(\ell) \rightleftharpoons K(g) + NaCl(\ell)$$

Properties of Sodium and Potassium

Sodium and potassium are silvery metals that are soft and easily cut with a knife (see Figure 2.6). They are just a bit less dense than water. Their melting points are quite low, 97.8 °C for sodium and 63.7 °C for potassium.

All of the alkali metals are highly reactive. When exposed to moist air, the metal surface quickly becomes coated with a film of oxide or hydroxide. Consequently, the metals must be stored in a way that avoids contact with air, typically by placing them in kerosene or mineral oil.

■ **Alkali Metals React with Water—Thermodynamics and Kinetics** The alkali metals all react vigorously with water, and it is easily observed that the violence of the reaction increases with atomic number. This seems counter to the argument presented in *A Closer Look* that lithium is the best reducing agent. However, the reducing ability of a metal is a thermodynamic property, whereas the violence of the reaction is mainly a consequence of reaction rate.

The Reducing Ability of the Alkali Metals

The uses of the Group 1A metals depend on their reducing ability. The values of $E°$ reveal that Li is the best reducing agent in the group, whereas Na is the poorest; the remainder of these metals have roughly comparable reducing ability.

Reduction Potential

Element	$E°$ (V)
$Li^+ + e^- \rightarrow Li$	−3.045
$Na^+ + e^- \rightarrow Na$	−2.714
$K^+ + e^- \rightarrow K$	−2.925
$Rb^+ + e^- \rightarrow Rb$	−2.925
$Cs^+ + e^- \rightarrow Cs$	−2.92

Analysis of $E°$ is a thermodynamic problem, and to understand it better we can break the process of metal oxidation, $M(s) \rightarrow M^+(aq) + e^-$, into a series of steps. Here, we imagine that the metal sublimes to vapor, an electron is removed to form the gaseous cation, and the cation is hydrated. The first two steps require energy, but the last is exother-

$$M(g) \xrightarrow{IE \text{ (ionization energy)}} M^+(g) + e^-$$

with $\Delta_{sub}H$ on the left side and $\Delta_{hyd}H$ on the right side connecting to:

$$M(s) \xrightarrow{\Delta_rH_{net}} M^+(aq) + e^-$$

mic. From Hess's law (page 233), we know that the overall energy change should be

$$\Delta_rH_{net} = \Delta_{sub}H + IE + \Delta_{hyd}H$$

The element that is the best reducing agent should have the most negative (or least positive) value of ΔH. That is, the best reducing agent should be the metal that has the most exothermic value for its hydration energy because this can offset the energy of the endothermic steps ($\Delta_{sub}H$ and IE). For the alkali metals, enthalpies of hydration range from −506 kJ/mol for Li^+ to −180 kJ/mol for Cs^+. The fact that $\Delta_{hyd}H$ is so much greater for Li^+ than for Cs^+ largely accounts for the difference in reducing ability.

While this analysis of the problem gives us a reasonable explanation for the great reducing ability of lithium, recall that $E°$ is directly related to $\Delta_rG°$ and not to $\Delta H°$. However, $\Delta_rG°$ is largely determined by $\Delta_rH°$, so it is possible to relate variations in $E°$ to variations in $\Delta_rH°$.

Potassium is a very good reducing agent and reacts vigorously with water.

The high reactivity of Group 1A metals is exemplified by their reaction with water, which generates an aqueous solution of the metal hydroxide and hydrogen gas (Figure 7.13, page 329),

$$2 \, Na(s) + 2 \, H_2O(\ell) \rightarrow 2 \, Na^+(aq) + 2 \, OH^-(aq) + H_2(g)$$

and their reaction with any of the halogens to yield a metal halide (Figure 1.4),

$$2 \, Na(s) + Cl_2(g) \rightarrow 2 \, NaCl(s)$$

$$2 \, K(s) + Br_2(\ell) \rightarrow 2 \, KBr(s)$$

Chemistry often produces surprises. Group 1A metal oxides, M_2O, are known, but they are not the principal products of reactions between the Group 1A elements and oxygen. Instead, the primary product of the reaction of sodium and oxygen is sodium *peroxide*, Na_2O_2, whereas the principal product from the reaction of potassium and oxygen is KO_2, potassium *superoxide*.

$$2 \, Na(s) + O_2(g) \rightarrow Na_2O_2(s)$$

$$K(s) + O_2(g) \rightarrow KO_2(s)$$

Both Na_2O_2 and KO_2 are ionic compounds. The Group 1A cation is paired with either the peroxide ion (O_2^{2-}) or the superoxide ion (O_2^-). These compounds are not merely laboratory curiosities. They are used in oxygen generation devices in places where people are confined, such as submarines, aircraft, and spacecraft, or when an emergency supply is needed. When a person breathes, 0.82 L of CO_2 is exhaled for every 1 L of O_2 inhaled. Thus, a requirement of an O_2 generation system is that it should produce a larger volume of O_2 than the volume of CO_2

FIGURE 21.10. A closed-circuit breathing apparatus that generates its own oxygen. One source of oxygen is potassium superoxide (KO_2). Both carbon dioxide and moisture exhaled by the wearer into the breathing tube react with the KO_2 to generate oxygen. Because the rate of the chemical reaction is determined by the quantity of moisture and carbon dioxide exhaled, the production of oxygen is regulated automatically. With each exhalation, more oxygen is produced by volume than is required by the user.

taken in. This requirement is met with superoxides (Figure 21.10). With KO_2 the reaction is

$$4\ KO_2(s) + 2\ CO_2(g) \rightarrow 2\ K_2CO_3(s) + 3\ O_2(g)$$

Important Lithium, Sodium, and Potassium Compounds

Electrolysis of aqueous sodium chloride (*brine*) is the basis of one of the largest chemical industries in the United States.

$$2\ NaCl(aq) + 2\ H_2O(\ell) \rightarrow Cl_2(g) + 2\ NaOH(aq) + H_2(g)$$

Two of the products from this process—chlorine and sodium hydroxide—give the industry its name: the *chlor-alkali industry*. More than 10 billion kilograms of Cl_2 and NaOH is produced annually in the United States.

Sodium carbonate, Na_2CO_3, is another commercially important compound of sodium. It is also known by two common names, *soda ash* and *washing soda*. In the past, it was largely manufactured by combining NaCl, ammonia, and CO_2 in the *Solvay process* (which remains the method of choice in many countries). In the United States, however, sodium carbonate is obtained from naturally occurring deposits of the mineral *trona*, $Na_2CO_3 \cdot NaHCO_3 \cdot 2\ H_2O$ (Figure 21.11).

Owing to the environmental problems associated with the chlor-alkali process, considerable interest has arisen in the possibility of manufacturing sodium hydroxide by other methods. This has led to a revival of the old "soda-lime process," which produces NaOH from inexpensive lime (CaO) and soda ash (Na_2CO_3).

$$Na_2CO_3(aq) + CaO(s) + H_2O(\ell) \rightarrow 2\ NaOH(aq) + CaCO_3(s)$$

The insoluble calcium carbonate by-product is filtered off, then heated (calcining) to convert it to lime, which is recycled into the reaction system.

$$CaCO_3(s) \rightarrow CaO(s) + CO_2(g)$$

Sodium bicarbonate, $NaHCO_3$, also known as *baking soda*, is another common compound of sodium. Not only is $NaHCO_3$ used in cooking, but it is also added in small amounts to table salt. NaCl is often contaminated with small amounts of $MgCl_2$. The magnesium salt is hygroscopic; that is, it picks water up from the air

FIGURE 21.11 Producing soda ash. Trona mined in Wyoming and California is processed into soda ash (Na_2CO_3) and other sodium-based chemicals. Soda ash is the ninth most widely used chemical in the United States. Domestically, about half of all soda ash production is used in making glass. The remainder goes to make chemicals such as sodium silicate, sodium phosphate, and sodium cyanide. Some is also used to make detergents, in the pulp and paper industry, and in water treatment.

Jack Dermid/Photo Researchers, Inc.

(a) (Above) A mine in California. The mineral trona is taken from a mine 1600 feet deep.

Courtesy of FMC Wyoming Corp.

(b) (Right) Blocks of trona are cut from the face of the mine.

and, in doing so, causes the NaCl to clump. Adding $NaHCO_3$ converts $MgCl_2$ to magnesium carbonate, a nonhygroscopic salt.

$$MgCl_2(s) + 2\ NaHCO_3(s) \rightarrow MgCO_3(s) + 2\ NaCl(s) + H_2O(\ell) + CO_2(g)$$

Large deposits of sodium nitrate, $NaNO_3$, are found in Chile, which explains its common name of "Chile saltpeter." These deposits are thought to have formed by bacterial action on organisms in shallow seas. The initial product was ammonia, which was subsequently oxidized to nitrate ion; combination with sea salt led to sodium nitrate. Because nitrates in general, and alkali metal nitrates in particular, are highly water-soluble, deposits of $NaNO_3$ are found only in areas with very little rainfall.

Sodium nitrate is important because it can be converted to potassium nitrate by an exchange reaction.

$$NaNO_3(aq) + KCl(aq) \rightleftharpoons KNO_3(aq) + NaCl(s)$$

Equilibrium favors the products here because, of the four salts involved in this reaction, NaCl is least soluble in hot water. Sodium chloride precipitates, and the KNO_3 that remains in solution can be recovered by evaporating the water.

Potassium nitrate has been used for centuries as the oxidizing agent in gunpowder. A mixture of KNO_3, charcoal, and sulfur will spontaneously react when ignited.

$$2\ KNO_3(s) + 4\ C(s) \rightarrow K_2CO_3(s) + 3\ CO(g) + N_2(g)$$

$$2\ KNO_3(s) + 2\ S(s) \rightarrow K_2SO_4(s) + SO_2(g) + N_2(g)$$

Notice that both reactions (which are doubtless more complex than those written here) produce gases. These gases propel the bullet from a gun or cause a firecracker to explode.

Lithium carbonate, Li_2CO_3, has been used for more than 40 years as a treatment for bipolar disorder, an illness that involves alternating periods of depression or overexcitement that can extend over a few weeks to a year or more. Although the alkali metal salt is efficient in controlling the symptoms of bipolar disorder, its mechanism of action is not understood.

EXERCISE 21.6 Brine Electrolysis

What current must be used in a Downs cell operating at 7.0 V to produce 1.00 metric ton (exactly 1000 kg) of sodium per day? Assume 100% efficiency.

21.5 The Alkaline Earth Elements, Group 2A

The "earth" part of the name alkaline earth dates back to the days of medieval alchemy. To alchemists, any solid that did not melt and was not changed by fire into another substance was called an "earth." Compounds of the Group 2A elements, such as CaO, were alkaline according to experimental tests conducted by the alchemists: they had a bitter taste and neutralized acids. With very high melting points, these compounds were unaffected by fire.

Calcium and magnesium rank fifth and eighth, respectively, in abundance on the earth. Both elements form many commercially important compounds, and we shall focus our attention on these species.

Like the Group 1A elements, the Group 2A elements are very reactive, so they are found in nature as compounds. Unlike most of the compounds of the Group 1A metals, however, many compounds of the Group 2A elements have low water solubility, which explains their occurrence in various minerals (Figure 21.12).

Group 2A
Alkaline earths

| Beryllium |
| 4 |
| Be |
| 2.6 ppm |

| Magnesium |
| 12 |
| Mg |
| 23,300 ppm |

| Calcium |
| 20 |
| Ca |
| 41,000 ppm |

| Strontium |
| 38 |
| Sr |
| 370 ppm |

| Barium |
| 56 |
| Ba |
| 500 ppm |

| Radium |
| 88 |
| Ra |
| 6×10^{-7} ppm |

Element abundances are in parts per million in the earth's crust.

Limestone
CaCO₃

Gypsum
CaSO₄ · 2H₂O

Fluorite
CaF₂

Charles D. Winters

Common minerals of Group 2A elements.

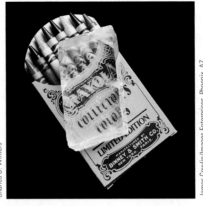

Charles D. Winters

Icelandic spar. This mineral, one of a number of crystalline forms of CaCO₃, displays birefringence, a property in which a double image is formed when light passes through the crystal.

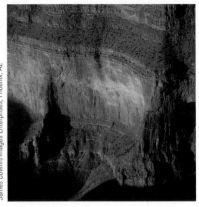

James Cowlin/Images Enterprises, Phoenix, AZ

The walls of the Grand Canyon in Arizona are largely limestone or dolomite.

FIGURE 21.12 Various minerals containing calcium and magnesium.

Calcium minerals include limestone ($CaCO_3$), gypsum ($CaSO_4 \cdot 2\,H_2O$), and fluorite (CaF_2). Magnesite ($MgCO_3$), talc or soapstone ($3\,MgO \cdot 4\,SiO_2 \cdot H_2O$), and asbestos ($3\,MgO \cdot 4\,SiO_2 \cdot 2\,H_2O$) are common magnesium-containing minerals. The mineral dolomite, $MgCa(CO_3)_2$, contains both magnesium and calcium.

Limestone, a sedimentary rock, is found widely on the earth's surface. Many of these deposits contain the fossilized remains of marine life. Other forms of calcium carbonate include marble and Icelandic spar, the latter occurring as large, clear crystals with the interesting optical property of birefringence.

Properties of Calcium and Magnesium

Calcium and magnesium are fairly high-melting, silvery metals. The chemical properties of these elements present few surprises. They are oxidized by a wide range of oxidizing agents to form ionic compounds that contain the M^{2+} ion. For example, these elements combine with halogens to form MX_2, with oxygen or sulfur to form MO or MS, and with water to form hydrogen and the metal hydroxide, $M(OH)_2$ (Figure 21.13). With acids, hydrogen is evolved (see Figure 21.6), and a salt of the metal cation and the anion of the acid results.

Metallurgy of Magnesium

Several hundred thousand tons of magnesium are produced annually, largely for use in lightweight alloys. (Magnesium has a very low density, 1.74 g/cm³.) Most aluminum used today contains about 5% magnesium to improve its mechanical properties and to make it more resistant to corrosion. Other alloys having more magnesium than aluminum are used when a high strength-to-weight ratio is needed and when corrosion resistance is important, such as in aircraft and automotive parts and in lightweight tools.

Interestingly, magnesium-containing minerals are not the source of this element. Most magnesium is obtained from sea water, in which Mg^{2+} ion is present in a concentration of about 0.05 M. To obtain magnesium metal, magnesium ions in sea water are first precipitated (Figure 21.14) as the relatively insoluble hydroxide [K_{sp} for $Mg(OH)_2 = 5.6 \times 10^{-12}$]. Calcium hydroxide, the source of OH^- in this reaction, is prepared in a sequence of reactions beginning with $CaCO_3$, which may be in the form of seashells. Heating $CaCO_3$ gives CO_2 and CaO, and addition of

Charles D. Winters

FIGURE 21.13 The reaction of calcium and warm water. Hydrogen bubbles are seen rising from the metal surface. The other reaction product is $Ca(OH)_2$. The inset is a model of hexagonal close-packed calcium metal (see page 595).

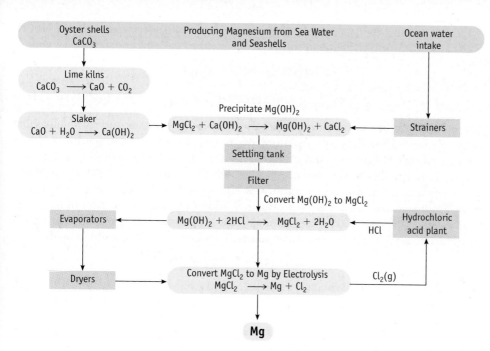

FIGURE 21.14 The process used to produce magnesium metal from the magnesium in sea water.

Producing Magnesium from Sea Water and Seashells

Oyster shells
CaCO₃

Lime kilns
$CaCO_3 \longrightarrow CaO + CO_2$

Slaker
$CaO + H_2O \longrightarrow Ca(OH)_2$

Ocean water intake

Strainers

Precipitate Mg(OH)₂
$MgCl_2 + Ca(OH)_2 \longrightarrow Mg(OH)_2 + CaCl_2$

Settling tank

Filter

Convert Mg(OH)₂ to MgCl₂

Evaporators

$Mg(OH)_2 + 2HCl \longrightarrow MgCl_2 + 2H_2O$

HCl

Hydrochloric acid plant

Dryers

Convert MgCl₂ to Mg by Electrolysis
$MgCl_2 \longrightarrow Mg + Cl_2$

$Cl_2(g)$

Mg

water to CaO gives calcium hydroxide. When $Ca(OH)_2$ is added to sea water, $Mg(OH)_2$ precipitates:

$$Mg^{2+}(aq) + Ca(OH)_2(s) \rightleftharpoons Mg(OH)_2(s) + Ca^{2+}(aq)$$

Magnesium hydroxide is isolated by filtration and then converted to magnesium chloride by reaction with hydrochloric acid.

$$Mg(OH)_2(s) + 2\,HCl(aq) \rightarrow MgCl_2(aq) + 2\,H_2O(\ell)$$

Chemical Perspectives

Alkaline Earth Metals and Biology

Plants and animals derive energy from the oxidation of a sugar, glucose, with oxygen. Plants are unique, however, in being able to synthesize glucose from CO_2 and H_2O by using sunlight as an energy source. This process is initiated by chlorophyll, a very large, magnesium-based molecule.

In your body, the metal ions Na^+, K^+, Mg^{2+}, and Ca^{2+} serve regulatory functions. Although the two alkaline earth metal ions are required by living systems, the other Group 2A elements are toxic. Beryllium compounds are carcinogenic, and soluble barium salts are poisons. You may be concerned if your physician asks you to drink a "barium cocktail" to check the condition of your digestive tract. Don't be afraid, because the "cocktail" contains very insoluble $BaSO_4$ ($K_{sp} = 1.1 \times 10^{-10}$), so it passes through your digestive tract without a significant amount being absorbed. Barium sulfate is opaque to x-rays, so its path through your organs appears on the developed x-ray.

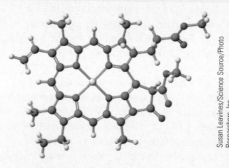

A molecule of chlorophyll. Magnesium is its central element.

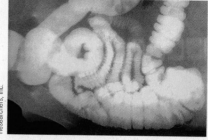

Susan Leavines/Science Source/Photo Researchers, Inc.

X-ray of a gastrointestinal tract using BaSO₄ to make the organs visible.

The calcium-containing compound hydroxyapatite is the main component of tooth enamel. Cavities in your teeth form when acids (such as soft drinks) decompose the weakly basic hydroxyapatite coating.

$$Ca_5(OH)(PO_4)_3(s) + 4\,H_3O^+(aq) \rightarrow$$
$$5\,Ca^{2+}(aq) + 3\,HPO_4^{2-}(aq) + 5\,H_2O(\ell)$$

This reaction can be prevented by converting hydroxyapatite to the much more acid-resistant coating of fluoroapatite.

$$Ca_5(OH)(PO_4)_3(s) + F^-(aq) \rightarrow$$
$$Ca_5F(PO_4)_3(s) + OH^-(aq)$$

The source of the fluoride ion can be sodium fluoride or sodium monofluorophosphate (Na_2FPO_3, commonly known as MFP) in your toothpaste.

After evaporating the water, anhydrous magnesium chloride remains. Solid $MgCl_2$ melts at 714 °C, and the molten salt is electrolyzed to give the metal and chlorine.

$$MgCl_2(\ell) \rightarrow Mg(s) + Cl_2(g)$$

Calcium Minerals and Their Applications

The most common calcium minerals are the fluoride, phosphate, and carbonate salts of the element. Fluorite, CaF_2, and fluoroapatite, $Ca_5F(PO_4)_3$, are important as commercial sources of fluorine. Almost half of the CaF_2 mined is used in the steel industry, where it is added to the mixture of materials that is melted to make crude iron. The CaF_2 acts to remove some impurities and improves the separation of molten metal from silicates and other by-products resulting from the reduction of iron ore to the metal (Chapter 22). A second major use of fluorite is in the manufacture of hydrofluoric acid by a reaction of the mineral with concentrated sulfuric acid.

$$CaF_2(s) + H_2SO_4(\ell) \rightarrow 2\ HF(g) + CaSO_4(s)$$

Hydrofluoric acid is used to make cryolite, Na_3AlF_6, a material needed in aluminum production (▶ Section 21.6) and in the manufacture of fluorocarbons such as tetrafluoroethylene, the precursor to Teflon (Table 10.12).

Apatites have the general formula $Ca_5X(PO_4)_3$ (X = F, Cl, OH). More than 100 million tons of apatite is mined annually, with Florida alone accounting for about one third of the world's output. Most of this material is converted to phosphoric acid by reaction with sulfuric acid. Phosphoric acid is needed in the manufacture of a multitude of products, including fertilizers and detergents, baking powder, and various food products (▶ Section 21.8.).

Chemical Perspectives

Of Romans, Limestone, and Champagne

The stones of the Appian Way in Italy, a road conceived by the Roman senate in about 310 B.C., are cemented with mortar made from limestone. The Appian Way was intended to serve as a military road linking Rome to seaports from which soldiers could embark to Greece and other Mediterranean ports. The road stretches 560 kilometers (350 miles) from Rome to Brindisi on the Adriatic Sea (at the heel of the Italian "boot"). It took almost 200 years to construct. The road had a standard width of 14 Roman feet, approximately 20 feet, large enough to allow two chariots to pass, and featured two sidewalks of 4 feet each. Every 10 miles or so, there were horse-changing stations with taverns, shops, and *latrinae*, the famous Roman restrooms.

All over the Roman Empire, buildings, temples, and aqueducts were constructed of blocks of limestone and marble, and the mortar to cement the blocks was made by heating the chips from stone cutting (to give CaO). In central France, the Romans dug chalk (also $CaCO_3$) from the ground for cementing sandstone blocks. This activity created huge caves that remain to this day and are used for aging and storing champagne.

The Appian Way in Italy.

Champagne in a limestone cave in France.

Calcium carbonate and calcium oxide (*lime*) are of special interest. The thermal decomposition of $CaCO_3$ to give lime (and CO_2) is one of the oldest chemical reactions known. Lime is one of the top 10 industrial chemicals produced today, with about 20 billion kilograms produced annually.

Limestone, which consists mostly of calcium carbonate, has been used in agriculture for centuries. It is spread on fields to neutralize acidic compounds in the soil and to supply Ca^{2+}, an essential nutrient. Because magnesium carbonate is often present in limestone, "liming" a field also supplies Mg^{2+}, another important nutrient for plants.

For several thousand years, lime has been used in *mortar* (a lime, sand, and water paste) to secure stones to one another in building houses, walls, and roads. The Chinese used it to set stones in the Great Wall. The Romans perfected its use, and the fact that many of their constructions still stand today is testament both to their skill and to the usefulness of lime. The famous Appian Way used lime mortar between several layers of its stones.

The utility of mortar depends on some simple chemistry. Mortar consists of one part lime to three parts sand, with water added to make a thick paste. The first reaction, referred to as *slaking*, occurs after the solids are mixed with water. This produces a slurry containing calcium hydroxide, which is known as *slaked lime*.

$$CaO(s) + H_2O(\ell) \rightleftharpoons Ca(OH)_2(s)$$

When the wet mortar mix is placed between bricks or stone blocks, it slowly reacts with CO_2 from the air, and the slaked lime is converted to calcium carbonate.

$$Ca(OH)_2(s) + CO_2(g) \rightleftharpoons CaCO_3(s) + H_2O(\ell)$$

The sand grains are bound together by the particles of calcium carbonate.

Charles D. Winters

Apatite. The mineral has the general formula of $Ca_5X(PO_4)_3$ (X = F, Cl, OH). (The apatite is the elongated crystal in the center of a matrix of other rock.)

■ **Dissolving Limestone** Figure 3.6 illustrates the equilibrium involving $CaCO_3$, CO_2, H_2O, Ca^{2+}, and HCO_3^-.

EXERCISE 21.7 Beryllium Chemistry

Beryllium, the lightest element in Group 2A, has some important industrial applications, but exposure (by breathing) to some of its compounds can cause berylliosis. Search the World Wide Web for the uses of the element and the causes and symptoms of berylliosis.

21.6 Boron, Aluminum, and the Group 3A Elements

With Group 3A, we see the first evidence of a change from metallic behavior of the elements at the left side of the periodic table to nonmetal behavior on the right side of the table. Boron is a metalloid, whereas all the other elements of Group 3A are metals.

The elements of Group 3A vary widely in their relative abundances on earth. Aluminum is the third most abundant element in the earth's crust (82,000 ppm), whereas the other elements of the group are relatively rare, and, except for boron, their compounds have limited commercial uses.

Chemistry of the Group 3A Elements

It is generally recognized that a chemical similarity exists between some elements diagonally situated in the periodic table. This diagonal relationship means that lithium and magnesium share some chemical properties, as do Be and Al, and B and Si. For example:

- Boric oxide, B_2O_3, and boric acid, $B(OH)_3$, are weakly acidic, as are SiO_2 and its acid, orthosilic acid (H_4SiO_4). Boron–oxygen compounds, borates, are often chemically similar to silicon–oxygen compounds, silicates.
- Both $Be(OH)_2$ and $Al(OH)_3$ are amphoteric, dissolving in a strong base such as aqueous NaOH (◄ page 791).

Group 3A

Boron
5
B
10 ppm

Aluminum
13
Al
82,000 ppm

Gallium
31
Ga
18 ppm

Indium
49
In
0.05 ppm

Thallium
81
Tl
0.6 ppm

Element abundances are in parts per million in the earth's crust.

No, hard water doesn't refer to ice. It is the name given to water containing high concentrations of Ca^{2+}(aq) and, in some instances, Mg^{2+}(aq) and other divalent metal cations. Accompanying these cations will be various anions, including in particular the hydrogen carbonate anion, HCO_3^-(aq).

Water obtained from reservoirs that store rainwater does not usually contain high concentrations of these ions, and so is not classified as being "hard water." In many parts of the country, however, the municipal water supply is obtained from aquifers deep underground. If rainwater, containing some dissolved CO_2, has to percolate down through layers of limestone ($CaCO_3$) to get into the aquifer, a small amount of the solid will dissolve because of the following equilibrium:

$$CaCO_3(s) + CO_2(aq) + H_2O(\ell) \rightleftharpoons$$
$$Ca^{2+}(aq) + 2\ HCO_3^-(aq)$$

If hard water containing Ca^{2+}(aq) and HCO_3^-(aq) is heated, or even if it is left to stand in an open vessel, CO_2 will be expelled, and the equilibrium will shift, precipitating $CaCO_3$(s) (◄ page 120). This can be a small problem in a teakettle but a bigger problem in an industrial setting, where the solid $CaCO_3$ can clog pipes. Another consequence of hard water is the formation of a scum when soaps are added to water. Recall that soap is made by hydrolysis of fats (saponification, page 476); soap scum is a precipitate of the calcium salt of a long chain carboxylic acid.

To avoid the problems associated with hard water, chemists and engineers have devised ways to soften water, that is, to decrease the concentration of the offending cations. In a water treatment plant for a municipality or a large industrial facility, most of the water hardness will be removed chemically, mainly by treatment with calcium oxide (lime, CaO). If HCO_3^- ions are present along with Ca^{2+} and/or Mg^{2+}, the following reactions occur:

$$Ca^{2+}(aq) + 2\ HCO_3^-(aq) + CaO(s) \rightarrow$$
$$2\ CaCO_3(s) + H_2O(\ell)$$

$$Mg^{2+}(aq) + 2\ HCO_3^-(aq) + CaO(s) \rightarrow$$
$$CaCO_3(s) + MgCO_3(s) + H_2O(\ell)$$

Although it seems odd to add CaO to remove calcium ions, notice that adding one mole of CaO leads to the precipitation of two moles of Ca^{2+} as $CaCO_3$.

On a smaller scale, most home water purification systems use ion exchange to soften water (Figure). This process involves the replacement of an ion adsorbed onto a solid ion-exchange resin by an ion in solution. Zeolites (▶ page 989), naturally occurring aluminosilicate minerals, were at one time used as ion exchange materials. Now, synthetic organic polymers with negatively charged functional groups (such as carboxylate groups, $-CO_2^-$) are the most commonly used resins for this purpose. Sodium ions, Na^+, are present in the resin to balance the negative charges of the carboxylate groups. The affinity of a surface for multicharged cations is greater than for monovalent cations. Therefore, when a solution of hard water is passed over the surface of the ion exchange resin, Ca^{2+} and Mg^{2+} (and other divalent ions if present) readily replace Na^+ ions in an ion exchange column. This process can be illustrated in a general way by the equilibrium

$$2\ NaX + Ca^{2+}(aq) \rightleftharpoons CaX_2 + 2\ Na^+(aq)$$

where X represents an adsorption site on the ion exchange resin. The equilibrium favors adsorption of Ca^{2+} and release of Na^+. However, the equilibrium is reversed if Na^+(aq) ions are present in high concentration, and this allows regeneration of the ion-exchange resin. A solution containing a high concentration of Na^+ (usually from salt, $NaCl$) is passed through the resin to convert the resin back to its initial form.

Questions:

1. *Assume that a sample of hard water contains 50 mg/L of Mg^{2+} and 150 mg/L of Ca^{2+}, with HCO_3^- as the accompanying anion. What mass of CaO should be added to 1.0 L of this aqueous solution to cause precipitation of $CaCO_3$ and $MgCO_3$? What is the total mass of the two solids formed?*

2. *One way to remove the calcium carbonate residue in a teakettle is to add vinegar (a dilute solution of acetic acid). Write a chemical equation to explain this process. What kind of a reaction is this?*

Answers to these questions are in Appendix Q.

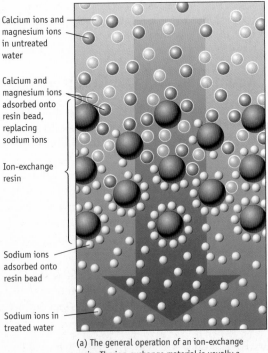

Calcium ions and magnesium ions in untreated water

Calcium and magnesium ions adsorbed onto resin bead, replacing sodium ions

Ion-exchange resin

Sodium ions adsorbed onto resin bead

Sodium ions in treated water

(a) The general operation of an ion-exchange resin. The ion-exchange material is usually a polymeric material formed into small beads.

Water softening by ion exchange in the home. The ion exchange resin is usually a polymeric material formed into small beads.

- Chlorides, bromides, and iodides of boron and silicon (such as BCl_3 and $SiCl_4$) react vigorously with water.
- The hydrides of boron and silicon are simple, molecular species; are volatile and flammable; and react readily with water.
- Beryllium hydride and aluminum hydride are colorless, nonvolatile solids that are extensively polymerized through Be—H—Be and Al—H—Al three-centered, two-electron bonds (see page 431).

Finally, the Group 3A elements are characterized by electron configurations of the type ns^2np^1. This means that each may lose three electrons to have a +3 oxidation number, although the heavier elements, especially thallium, also form compounds with an oxidation number of +1.

Boron Minerals and Production of the Element

Although boron has a low abundance on earth, its minerals are found in concentrated deposits. Large deposits of borax, $Na_2B_4O_7 \cdot 10\ H_2O$, are currently mined in the Mojave Desert near the town of Boron, California (Figure 21.15).

Isolation of pure, elemental boron from boron-containing minerals is extremely difficult and is done in small quantities. Like most metals and metalloids, boron can be obtained by chemically or electrolytically reducing an oxide or halide. Magnesium has often been used for chemical reductions, but the product of this reaction is a noncrystalline boron of low purity.

$$B_2O_3(s) + 3\ Mg(s) \rightarrow 2\ B(s) + 3\ MgO(s)$$

Boron has several allotropes, all characterized by having an icosahedron of boron atoms as one structural element (Figure 21.15c). Partly as a result of extended covalent bonding, elemental boron is a very hard and refractory (resistant to heat) semiconductor. In this regard, it differs from the other Group 3A elements; Al, Ga, In, and Tl are all relatively low-melting, rather soft metals with high electrical conductivity.

Metallic Aluminum and Its Production

The low cost of aluminum and the excellent characteristics of its alloys with other metals (low density, strength, ease of handling in fabrication, and inertness toward corrosion, among others), have led to its widespread use. You know it best in the form of aluminum foil, aluminum cans, and parts of aircraft.

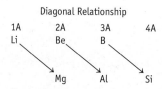

Diagonal Relationship

1A	2A	3A	4A
Li	Be	B	
	Mg	Al	Si

■ **Diagonal Relationship** The chemistries of elements diagonally situated in the periodic table are often quite similar.

Charles D. Winters

Gallium. Gallium, with a melting point of 29.8 °C, is one of the few metals that can be a liquid at or near room temperature. (Others are Hg and Cs.)

© George Gerster/Photo Researchers, Inc.

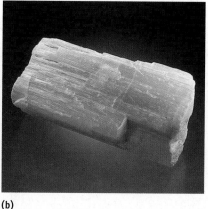

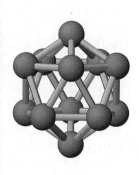

(a)   (b)   (c)

FIGURE 21.15 Boron. (a) A borax mine near the town of Boron, California. (b) Crystalline borax, $Na_2B_4O_7 \cdot 10\ H_2O$. (c) All allotropes of elemental boron have an icosahedron (a 20-sided polyhedron) of 12 covalently linked boron atoms as a structural element.

Pure aluminum is soft and weak; moreover, it loses strength rapidly at temperatures higher than 300 °C. What we call "aluminum" is actually aluminum alloyed with small amounts of other elements to strengthen the metal and improve its properties. A typical alloy may contain about 4% copper with smaller amounts of silicon, magnesium, and manganese. Softer, more corrosion-resistant alloys for window frames, furniture, highway signs, and cooking utensils may include only manganese.

The standard reduction potential of aluminum $[Al^{3+}(aq) + 3\ e^- \rightarrow Al(s)$; $E° = -1.66\ V]$ tells you that aluminum is easily oxidized. From this, we might expect aluminum to be highly susceptible to corrosion but, in fact, it is quite resistant. Aluminum's corrosion resistance is due to the formation of a thin, tough, and transparent skin of Al_2O_3 that adheres to the metal surface. An important feature of the protective oxide layer is that it rapidly self-repairs. If you penetrate the surface coating by scratching it or using some chemical agent, the exposed metal surface immediately reacts with oxygen (or another oxidizing agent) to form a new layer of oxide over the damaged area (Figure 21.16).

Aluminum was first prepared by reducing $AlCl_3$ using sodium or potassium. This was a costly process, and, in the 19th century, aluminum was a precious metal. At the 1855 Paris Exposition, in fact, a sample of aluminum was exhibited along with the crown jewels of France. In an interesting coincidence, in 1886 Frenchman Paul Heroult (1863–1914) and American Charles Hall (1863–1914) simultaneously and independently conceived of the electrochemical method used today. The Hall–Heroult method bears the names of the two discoverers.

Aluminum is found in nature as aluminosilicates, minerals such as clay that are based on aluminum, silicon, and oxygen. As these minerals weather, they break down to various forms of hydrated aluminum oxide, $Al_2O_3 \cdot n\ H_2O$, called *bauxite*. Mined in huge quantities, bauxite is the raw material from which aluminum is obtained. The first step is to purify the ore, separating Al_2O_3 from iron and silicon oxides. This is done by the *Bayer process*, which relies on the amphoteric, basic, or acidic nature of the various oxides. Silica, SiO_2, is an acidic oxide; Al_2O_3 is amphoteric; and Fe_2O_3 is a basic oxide. Silica and Al_2O_3 dissolve in a hot concentrated solution of caustic soda (NaOH), leaving insoluble Fe_2O_3 to be filtered out.

$$Al_2O_3(s) + 2\ NaOH(aq) + 3\ H_2O(\ell) \rightarrow 2\ Na[Al(OH)_4](aq)$$

$$SiO_2(s) + 2\ NaOH(aq) + 2\ H_2O(\ell) \rightarrow Na_2[Si(OH)_6](aq)$$

If a solution containing aluminate and silicate anions is treated with CO_2, Al_2O_3 precipitates, and the silicate ion remains in solution. Recall that CO_2 is an acidic

■ **Charles Martin Hall (1863–1914)**

Hall was only 22 years old when he worked out the electrolytic process for extracting aluminum from Al_2O_3 in a woodshed behind the family home in Oberlin, Ohio. He went on to found a company that eventually became ALCOA, the Aluminum Corporation of America.

Oesper Collection in the History of Chemistry/ University of Cincinnati

FIGURE 21.16 Corrosion of aluminum. (a) A ball of aluminum foil is added to a solution of copper(II) nitrate and sodium chloride. Normally, the coating of chemically inert Al_2O_3 on the surface of aluminum protects the metal from further oxidation. (b) In the presence of the Cl^- ion, the coating of Al_2O_3 is breached, and aluminum reduces copper(II) ions to copper metal. The reaction is rapid and so exothermic that the water can boil on the surface of the foil. [The blue color of aqueous copper(II) ions will fade as these ions are consumed in the reaction.]

Photos: Charles D. Winters

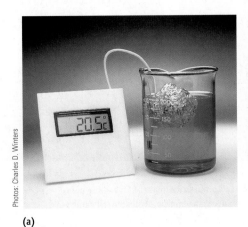

(a)

(b)

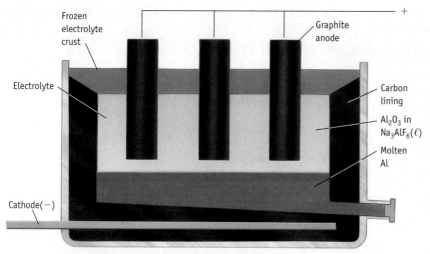

(a) Electrolysis of aluminum oxide to produce aluminum metal.

(b) Molten aluminum from recycled metal.

Active Figure 21.17 **Industrial production of aluminum.** (a) Purified aluminum-containing ore (bauxite), essentially Al_2O_3, is mixed with cryolite (Na_3AlF_6). Cryolite acts as a flux or solvent for the process, as it melts below 1173 K. The aluminum-containing substances are reduced at the graphite cathode to give molten aluminum. Oxygen is produced at the graphite anode, and the gas reacts slowly with the carbon to give CO_2, leading to eventual destruction of the electrode. (b) Molten aluminum alloy, produced from recycled metal, at 760 °C, in 1.6×10^4-kg capacity crucibles.

Chemistry.☉.Now™ Sign in at www.cengage.com/login and go to the Chapter Contents menu to explore an interactive version of this figure accompanied by an exercise.

oxide that forms the weak acid H_2CO_3 in water, so the Al_2O_3 precipitation in this step is an acid–base reaction.

$$H_2CO_3(aq) + 2\ Na[Al(OH)_4](aq) \rightarrow Na_2CO_3(aq) + Al_2O_3(s) + 5\ H_2O(\ell)$$

Metallic aluminum is obtained from purified bauxite by electrolysis (Figure 21.17). Bauxite is first mixed with cryolite, Na_3AlF_6, to give a lower-melting mixture (melting temperature = 980 °C) that is electrolyzed in a cell with graphite electrodes. The cell operates at a relatively low voltage (4.0–5.5 V) but with an extremely high current (50,000–150,000 A). Aluminum is produced at the cathode and oxygen at the anode. To produce 1 kg of aluminum requires 13 to 16 kilowatt-hours of energy plus the energy required to maintain the high temperature.

Boron Compounds

Borax, $Na_2B_4O_7 \cdot 10\ H_2O$, is the most important boron–oxygen compound and is the form of the element most often found in nature. It has been used for centuries in metallurgy because of the ability of molten borax to dissolve other metal oxides. That is, borax is used as a *flux* that cleans the surfaces of metals to be joined and permits a good metal-to-metal contact.

The formula for borax gives little information about its structure. The anion is better described by the formula $[B_4O_5(OH)_4]^{2-}$, the structure of which illustrates two commonly observed structural features in inorganic chemistry. First, many minerals consist of MO_n groups that share O atoms. Second, the sharing of O atoms between two metals or metalloids often leads to MO rings.

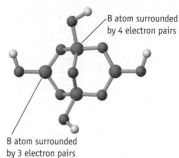

B atom surrounded by 4 electron pairs

B atom surrounded by 3 electron pairs

The borate ion of borax, $[B_4O_5(OH)_4]^{2-}$.

After refinement, borax can be treated with sulfuric acid to produce boric acid, $B(OH)_3$.

$$Na_2B_4O_7 \cdot 10\ H_2O(s) + H_2SO_4(aq) \rightarrow 4\ B(OH)_3(aq) + Na_2SO_4(aq) + 5\ H_2O(\ell)$$

The chemistry of boric acid incorporates both Lewis and Brønsted acid behavior. Hydronium ions are produced by a Lewis–acid base interaction between boric acid and water.

$$K_a = 7.3 \times 10^{-10}$$

Because of its weak acid properties and slight biological activity, boric acid has been used for many years as an antiseptic. Furthermore, because boric acid is a weak acid, salts of borate ions, such as the $[B_4O_5(OH)_4]^{2-}$ ion in borax, are weak bases.

Boric acid is dehydrated to boric oxide when strongly heated.

$$2\ B(OH)_3(s) \rightarrow B_2O_3(s) + 3\ H_2O(\ell)$$

By far the largest use for the oxide is in the manufacture of borosilicate glass. This type of glass is composed of 76% SiO_2, 13% B_2O_3, and much smaller amounts of Al_2O_3 and Na_2O. The presence of boric oxide gives the glass a higher softening temperature, imparts a better resistance to attack by acids, and makes the glass expand less on heating.

Like its metalloid neighbor silicon, boron forms a series of molecular compounds with hydrogen. Because boron is slightly less electronegative than hydrogen, these compounds are described as hydrides, in which the H atoms bear a partial negative charge. More than 20 neutral boron hydrides, or boranes, with the general formula B_xH_y are known. The simplest of these is diborane, B_2H_6, where x is 2 and y is 6. This colorless, gaseous compound has a boiling point of −92.6 °C. This molecule is described as electron deficient since there are apparently not enough electrons to attach all of the atoms using two-electron bonds. Instead, the description of bonding uses 3-center 2-electron bonds in the B-H-B bridges (◄ page 431).

Diborane has an endothermic enthalpy of formation ($\Delta_f H° = +41.0$ kJ/mol), which contributes to the high exothermicity of oxidation of the compound. Diborane burns in air to give boric oxide and water vapor in an extremely exothermic reaction. It is not surprising that diborane and other boron hydrides were once considered as possible rocket fuels.

$$B_2H_6(g) + 3\ O_2(g) \rightarrow B_2O_3(s) + 3\ H_2O(g) \qquad \Delta_r H° = -2038\ \text{kJ/mol-rxn}$$

Diborane can be synthesized from sodium borohydride, $NaBH_4$, the only B—H compound produced in ton quantities.

$$2\ NaBH_4(s) + I_2(s) \rightarrow B_2H_6(g) + 2\ NaI(s) + H_2(g)$$

Sodium borohydride, $NaBH_4$, a white, crystalline, water-soluble solid, is made from NaH and borate esters such as $B(OCH_3)_3$.

$$4\ NaH(s) + B(OCH_3)_3(g) \rightarrow NaBH_4(s) + 3\ NaOCH_3(s)$$

The main use of $NaBH_4$ is as a reducing agent in organic synthesis. We previously encountered its use to reduce aldehydes, carboxylic acids, and ketones in Chapter 10.

133 pm

119 pm

97°

122°

The structure of diborane, B_2H_6, the simplest member of a family of boron hydrides. See also page 431.

Charles D. Winters

Sodium borohydride, $NaBH_4$, is an excellent reducing agent. Here, silver ions are reduced to finely divided silver metal.

Aluminum Compounds

Aluminum is an excellent reducing agent, so it reacts readily with hydrochloric acid. In contrast, it does not react with nitric acid, a stronger oxidizing agent than hydrochloric acid. It turns out that nitric acid does rapidly oxidize the surface of aluminum, but the resulting film of Al_2O_3 that is produced protects the metal from further attack. This protection allows nitric acid to be shipped in aluminum tanks.

Various salts of aluminum dissolve in water, giving the hydrated Al^{3+}(aq) ion. These solutions are acidic (◀ Table 17.3, page 770) because the hydrated ion is a weak Brønsted acid.

$$[Al(H_2O)_6]^{3+}(aq) + H_2O(\ell) \rightleftharpoons [Al(H_2O)_5(OH)]^{2+}(aq) + H_3O^+(aq)$$

Adding acid shifts the equilibrium to the left, whereas adding base causes the equilibrium to shift to the right. Addition of sufficient hydroxide ion results ultimately in precipitation of the hydrated oxide $Al_2O_3 \cdot 3\ H_2O$.

Aluminum oxide, Al_2O_3, formed by dehydrating the hydrated oxide, is quite insoluble in water and generally resistant to chemical attack. In the crystalline form, aluminum oxide is known as *corundum*. This material is extraordinarily hard, a property that leads to its use as an abrasive in grinding wheels, "sandpaper," and toothpaste.

Some gems are impure aluminum oxide. Rubies, beautiful red crystals prized for jewelry and used in some lasers, are composed of Al_2O_3 contaminated with a small amount of Cr^{3+} (Figure 21.18). The Cr^{3+} ions replacing some of the Al^{3+} ions in the crystal lattice is the source of the red color. Synthetic rubies were first made in 1902, and the worldwide capacity is now about 200,000 kg/year; much of this production is used for jewel bearings in watches and instruments. Blue sapphires consist of Al_2O_3 with Fe^{2+} and Ti^{4+} impurities in place of Al^{3+} ions.

Boron forms halides such as gaseous BF_3 and BCl_3 that have the expected planar, trigonal molecular geometry of halogen atoms surrounding an sp^2 hybridized boron atom. In contrast, the aluminum halides are all solids and have more interesting structures. Aluminum bromide, which is made by the very exothermic reaction of aluminum metal and bromine (Figure 2.12, page 67),

$$2\ Al(s) + 3\ Br_2(\ell) \rightarrow Al_2Br_6(s)$$

is composed of two units of $AlBr_3$. That is, Al_2Br_6 is a dimer of $AlBr_3$ units. The structure resembles that of diborane in that bridging atoms appear between the two Al atoms. However, Al_2Br_6 is not electron deficient; the bridge is formed when a Br atom on one $AlBr_3$ uses a lone pair to form a coordinate covalent bond to a neighboring tetrahedral, sp^3-hybridized aluminum atom.

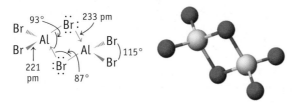

The structure of Al_2Br_6. The bonding in Al_2Br_6 is not unique to the aluminum halides. Metal–halogen–metal bridges are found in many other metal–halogen compounds.

Aluminum does not react with nitric acid. Nitric acid, a strongly oxidizing acid, reacts vigorously with copper (left), but aluminum (right) is untouched.

Charles D. Winters

Chip Clark, Smithsonian Museum of Natural History

FIGURE 21.18 Forms of corundum. Corundum is a crystalline form of aluminum oxide. Both rubies and sapphires are a form of corundum in which a few Al^{3+} ions have been replaced by ions such as Cr^{3+}, Fe^{2+} or Ti^{4+}. (*top*) The Star of Asia sapphire. (*middle*) Various sapphires. (*bottom*) Uncut corundum.

Both aluminum bromide and aluminum iodide have this structure. Aluminum chloride has a different solid state structure, but it exists as dimeric molecules in the vapor state.

Aluminum chloride can react with a chloride ion to form the anion $[AlCl_4]^-$. Aluminum fluoride, in contrast, can accommodate three additional F^- ions to form an octahedral $[AlF_6]^{3-}$ ion. This anion is found in cryolite, Na_3AlF_6, the compound added to aluminum oxide in the electrolytic production of aluminum metal. Apparently, the Al^{3+} ion can bind to six of the smaller F^- ions, whereas only four of the larger Cl^-, Br^-, or I^- ions can surround an Al^{3+} ion.

Chemistry.ọ̣.Now™

Sign in at **www.cengage.com/login** and go to Chapter 21 Contents to see Screen 21.5 for an exercise on **the chemistry of aluminum compounds.**

EXERCISE 21.8 Gallium Chemistry

(a) Gallium hydroxide, like aluminum hydroxide, is amphoteric. Write a balanced equation to show how this hydroxide can dissolve in both HCl(aq) and NaOH(aq).

(b) Gallium ion in water, Ga^{3+}(aq), has a K_a value of 1.2×10^{-3}. Is this ion a stronger or a weaker acid than Al^{3+}(aq)?

21.7 Silicon and the Group 4A Elements

Carbon is a nonmetal; silicon and germanium are classified as metalloids; tin and lead are metals. As a result, the elements of Group 4A have a broad range of chemical behavior.

The Group 4A elements are characterized by half-filled valence shells with two electrons in the ns orbital and two electrons in np orbitals. The bonding in carbon and silicon compounds is largely covalent and involves sharing four electron pairs with neighboring atoms. In germanium compounds, the $+4$ oxidation state is common (GeO_2 and $GeCl_4$), but some $+2$ oxidation state compounds exist (GeI_2). Oxidation numbers of both $+2$, and $+4$ are common in compounds of tin and lead (such as $SnCl_2$, $SnCl_4$, PbO, and PbO_2). Oxidation numbers two units less than the group number are often encountered for heavier elements in Groups 3A–7A.

Silicon

Silicon is second after oxygen in abundance in the earth's crust, so it is not surprising that we are surrounded by silicon-containing materials: bricks, pottery, porcelain, lubricants, sealants, computer chips, and solar cells. The computer revolution is based on the semiconducting properties of silicon.

Reasonably pure silicon can be made in large quantities by heating pure silica sand with purified coke to approximately 3000 °C in an electric furnace.

$$SiO_2(s) + 2\,C(s) \rightarrow Si(\ell) + 2\,CO(g)$$

The molten silicon is drawn off the bottom of the furnace and allowed to cool to a shiny blue-gray solid. Because extremely high-purity silicon is needed for the electronics industry, purifying raw silicon requires several steps. First, the silicon in the impure sample is allowed to react with chlorine to convert the silicon to liquid silicon tetrachloride.

$$Si(s) + 2\,Cl_2(g) \rightarrow SiCl_4(\ell)$$

Group 4A

Carbon
6
C
480 ppm

Silicon
14
Si
277,000 ppm

Germanium
32
Ge
1.8 ppm

Tin
50
Sn
2.2 ppm

Lead
82
Pb
14 ppm

Element abundances are in parts per million in the earth's crust.

Silicon tetrachloride (boiling point of 57.6 °C) is carefully purified by distillation and then reduced to silicon using magnesium.

$$SiCl_4(g) + 2\ Mg(s) \rightarrow 2\ MgCl_2(s) + Si(s)$$

The magnesium chloride is washed out with water, and the silicon is remelted and cast into bars. A final purification is carried out by zone refining, a process in which a special heating device is used to melt a narrow segment of the silicon rod. The heater is moved slowly down the rod. Impurities contained in the silicon tend to remain in the liquid phase because the melting point of a mixture is lower than that of the pure element (Chapter 14). The silicon that crystallizes above the heated zone is therefore of a higher purity (Figure 21.19).

Silicon Dioxide

The simplest oxide of silicon is SiO_2, commonly called *silica*, a constituent of many rocks such as granite and sandstone. Quartz is a pure crystalline form of silica, but impurities in quartz produce gemstones such as amethyst (Figure 21.20).

Silica and CO_2 are oxides of two elements in the same chemical group, so similarities between them might be expected. In fact, SiO_2 is a high-melting solid (quartz melts at 1610 °C), whereas CO_2 is a gas at room temperature and 1 bar. This great disparity arises from the different structures of the two oxides. Carbon dioxide is a molecular compound, with the carbon atom linked to each oxygen atom by a double bond. In contrast, SiO_2 is a network solid, which is the preferred structure because the bond energy of two Si=O double bonds is much less than the bond energy of four Si—O single bonds. The contrast between SiO_2 and CO_2 exemplifies a more general phenomenon. Multiple bonds, often encountered between second-period elements, are rare among elements in the third and higher periods. There are many compounds with multiple bonds to carbon but very few compounds featuring multiple bonds to silicon.

Quartz crystals are used to control the frequency of radio and television transmissions. Because these and related applications use so much quartz, there is not enough natural quartz to fulfill demand, and quartz is therefore synthesized. Noncrystalline, or vitreous, quartz, made by melting pure silica sand, is placed in a steel "bomb," and dilute aqueous NaOH is added. A "seed" crystal is placed in the mixture, just as you might use a seed crystal in a hot sugar solution to grow

FIGURE 21.19 Pure silicon. The manufacture of very pure silicon begins with producing the volatile liquid silanes $SiCl_4$ or $SiHCl_3$. After carefully purifying these by distillation, they are reduced to elemental silicon with extremely pure Mg or Zn. The resulting spongy silicon is purified by zone refining. The end result is a cylindrical rod of ultrapure silicon such as those seen in this photograph. Thin wafers of silicon are cut from the bars and are the basis for the semiconducting chips in computers and other devices.

FIGURE 21.20 Various forms of quartz.

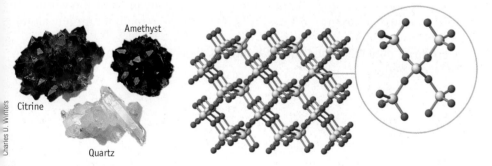

Amethyst

Citrine

Quartz

(a) Pure quartz is colorless, but the presence of small amounts of impurities adds color. Purple amethyst and brown citrine crystals are quartz with iron impurities.

(b) Quartz is a network solid in which each Si atom is bound tetrahedrally to four O atoms, each O atom linked to another Si atom. The basic structure consists of a lattice of Si and O atoms.

Synthetic quartz. These crystals were grown from silica in sodium hydroxide. The colors come from added Co^{2+} ions (blue) or Fe^{2+} ions (brown).

rock candy. When the mixture is heated above the critical temperature of water (above 400 °C and 1700 atm) over a period of days, pure quartz crystallizes.

Silicon dioxide is resistant to attack by all acids except HF, with which it reacts to give SiF_4 and H_2O.

$$SiO_2(s) + 4\ HF(\ell) \rightarrow SiF_4(g) + 2\ H_2O(\ell)$$

Silicon dioxide also dissolves slowly in hot, molten NaOH or Na_2CO_3 to give Na_4SiO_4, sodium silicate.

$$SiO_2(s) + 2\ Na_2CO_3(\ell) \rightarrow Na_4SiO_4(s) + 2\ CO_2(g)$$

After the molten mixture has cooled, hot water under pressure is added. This partially dissolves the material to give a solution of sodium silicate. After filtering off insoluble sand or glass, the solvent is evaporated to leave sodium silicate, called *water glass*. The biggest single use of this material is in household and industrial detergents, in which it is included because a sodium silicate solution maintains pH by its buffering ability. Additionally, sodium silicate is used in various adhesives and binders, especially for gluing corrugated cardboard boxes.

If sodium silicate is treated with acid, a gelatinous precipitate of SiO_2 called *silica gel* is obtained. Washed and dried, silica gel is a highly porous material with dozens of uses. It is a drying agent, readily absorbing up to 40% of its own weight of water. Small packets of silica gel are often placed in packing boxes of merchandise during storage. The material is frequently stained with $(NH_4)_2CoCl_4$, a humidity detector that is pink when hydrated and blue when dry.

Silicate Minerals with Chain and Ribbon Structures

The structure and chemistry of silicate minerals is an enormous topic in geology and chemistry. Although all silicates are built from tetrahedral SiO_4 units, they have different properties and a wide variety of structures because of the way these tetrahedral SiO_4 units link together.

The simplest silicates, *orthosilicates*, contain SiO_4^{4-} anions. The 4− charge of the anion is balanced by four M^+ ions, two M^{2+} ions, or a combination of ions. Olivine, an important mineral in the earth's mantle, contains Mg^{2+} and Fe^{2+}, with the Fe^{2+} ion giving the mineral its characteristic olive color, and gem-like zircons are $ZrSiO_4$. Calcium orthosilicate, Ca_2SiO_4, is a component of Portland cement, the most common type of cement used in many parts of the world. (It consists mostly of a mixture of CaO and SiO_2 with the remainder largely aluminum and iron oxides.)

A group of minerals called *pyroxenes* have as their basic structural unit a chain of SiO_4 tetrahedra.

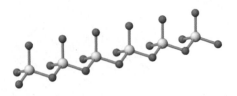

If two such chains are linked together by sharing oxygen atoms, the result is an *amphibole*, of which the asbestos minerals are one example. The molecular chain results in asbestos being a fibrous material.

Silica gel. Silica gel is solid, noncrystalline SiO_2. Packages of the material are often used to keep electronic equipment dry when stored. Silica gel is also used to clarify beer; passing beer through a bed of silica gel removes minute particles that would otherwise make the brew cloudy. Yet another use is in kitty litter.

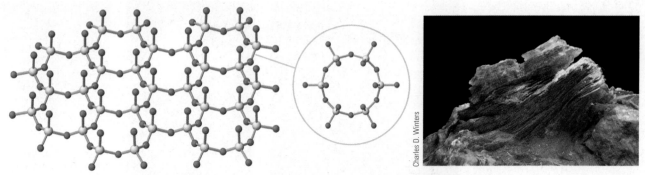

FIGURE 21.21 Mica, a sheet silicate. The sheet-like molecular structure of mica explains its physical appearance. As in the pyroxenes, each silicon is bonded to four oxygen atoms, but the Si and O atoms form a sheet of six-member rings of Si atoms with O atoms in each edge. The ratio of Si to O in this structure is 1 to 2.5. A formula of $SiO_{2.5}$ requires a positive ion, such as Na^+, to counterbalance the charge. Thus, mica and other sheet silicates, and aluminosilicates such as talc and many clays, have positive ions between the sheets. The sheet structure leads to the characteristic feature of mica, which is often found as "books" of thin, silicate sheets. Mica is used in furnace windows and as insulation, and flecks of mica give the glitter to "metallic" paints.

Silicates with Sheet Structures and Aluminosilicates

Linking many silicate chains together produces a sheet of SiO_4 tetrahedra (Figure 21.21). This sheet is the basic structural feature of some of the earth's most important minerals, particularly the clay minerals (such as china clay), mica, talc, and the chrysotile form of asbestos. However, these minerals do not contain just silicon and oxygen. Rather, they are often referred to as *aluminosilicates* because they frequently have Al^{3+} ions in place of Si^{4+} (which means that other positive ions such as Na^+, K^+, and Mg^{2+} must also be present in the lattice to balance the net negative and positive charges). In kaolinite clay, for example, the sheet of SiO_4 tetrahedra is bonded to a sheet of AlO_6 octahedra. In addition, some Si^{4+} ions can be replaced by Al^{3+} atoms. Another example is muscovite, a form of mica. Aluminum ions have replaced some Si^{4+} ions, and there are charge-balancing K^+ ions, so it is best represented by the formula $KAl_2(OH)_2(Si_3AlO_{10})$.

There are some interesting uses of clays, one being in medicine (Figure 21.22). In certain cultures, clay is eaten for medicinal purposes. Several remedies for the relief of upset stomach contain highly purified clays that absorb excess stomach acid as well as potentially harmful bacteria and their toxins by exchanging the intersheet cations in the clays for the toxins, which are often organic cations.

Other aluminosilicates include the feldspars, common minerals that make up about 60% of the earth's crust, and zeolites (Figure 21.22). Both materials are composed of SiO_4 tetrahedra in which some of the Si atoms have been replaced by Al atoms, along with alkali and alkaline earth metal ions for charge balance. The main feature of zeolite structures is their regularly shaped tunnels and cavities. Hole diameters are between 300 and 1000 pm, and small molecules such as water can fit into the cavities of the zeolite structure. As a result, zeolites can be used as drying agents to selectively absorb water from air or a solvent. Small amounts of zeolites are often sealed into multipane windows to keep the air dry between the panes.

Zeolites are also used as catalysts. ExxonMobil, for example, has patented a process in which methanol, CH_3OH, is converted to gasoline in the presence of specially tailored zeolites. In addition, zeolites are added to detergents, where they function as water-softening agents because the sodium ions of the zeolite can be exchanged for Ca^{2+} ions in hard water, effectively removing Ca^{2+} ions from the water.

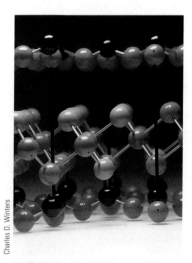

Kaolinite Clay. The basic structural feature of many clays, and kaolinite in particular, is a sheet of SiO_4 tetrahedra (black and red spheres) bonded to a sheet of AlO_6 octahedra (gray and green spheres).

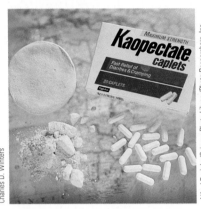

Charles D. Winters

(a) Remedies for stomach upset. One of the ingredients in Kaopectate is kaolin, one form of clay. The off-white objects are pieces of clay purchased in a market in Ghana, West Africa. This clay was made to be eaten as a remedy for stomach ailments. Eating clay is widespread among the world's different cultures.

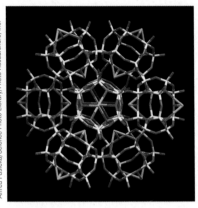

Alfred Pasieka/Science Photo Library/Photo Researchers, Inc.

(b) The stucture of a zeolite. Zeolites, which have Si, Al, and O linked in a polyhedral framework, are often portrayed in drawings like this. Each edge consists of a Si—O—Si, Al—O—Si, or Al—O—Al bond. The channels in the framework can selectively capture small molecules or ions or act as catalytic sites.

FIGURE 21.22. Aluminosilicates.

Charles D. Winters

(c) Apophyllite, a crystalline zeolite.

Charles D. Winters

(d) Consumer products that remove odor-causing molecules from the air often contain zeolites.

Chemistry ⚛ Now™

Sign in at **www.cengage.com/login** and go to Chapter 21 Contents to see Screen 21.6 for an exercise on **the structural chemistry of silicon–oxygen compounds.**

Silicone Polymers

Silicon and chloromethane (CH_3Cl) react at 300 °C in the presence of a catalyst, Cu powder. The primary product of this reaction is $(CH_3)_2SiCl_2$.

$$Si(s) + 2\ CH_3Cl(g) \rightarrow (CH_3)_2SiCl_2(\ell)$$

Halides of Group 4A elements other than carbon hydrolyze readily. Thus, the reaction of $(CH_3)_2SiCl_2$ with water initially produces $(CH_3)_2Si(OH)_2$. On standing, these molecules combine to form a condensation polymer by eliminating water. The polymer is called polydimethylsiloxane, a member of the *silicone* family of polymers.

$$(CH_3)_2SiCl_2 + 2\ H_2O \rightarrow (CH_3)_2Si(OH)_2 + 2\ HCl$$

$$n\ (CH_3)_2Si(OH)_2 \rightarrow [-(CH_3)_2SiO-]_n + n\ H_2O$$

Silicone polymers are nontoxic and have good stability to heat, light, and oxygen; they are chemically inert and have valuable antistick and antifoam properties. They can take the form of oils, greases, and resins. Some have rubber-like properties ("Silly Putty," for example, is a silicone polymer). More than 1 million tons of silicone polymers are made worldwide annually. These materials are used in a wide variety of products: lubricants, peel-off labels, lipstick, suntan lotion, car polish, and building caulk.

Charles D. Winters

Silicone. Some examples of products containing silicones, polymers with repeating —R_2Si—O— units.

> **EXERCISE 21.9 Silicon Chemistry**
>
> Silicon-oxygen rings are a common structural feature in silicate chemistry. Draw the structure for the anion $Si_3O_9^{6-}$, which is found in minerals such as benitoite. The ring has three Si atoms and three O atoms, and there are two other O atoms on each Si atom.

Lead anchors the bottom of Group 4A. One of a handful of elements known since ancient times, it has a variety of modern uses. It ranks fifth among metals in usage behind iron, copper, aluminum, and zinc. The major uses of the metal and its compounds are in storage batteries (page 913), pigments, ammunition, solders, plumbing, and bearings.

Unfortunately, lead and its compounds are cumulative poisons, particularly in children. At a blood level as low as 50 ppb (parts per billion), blood pressure is elevated; intelligence is affected at 100 ppb; and blood levels higher than 800 ppb can lead to coma and possible death. Health experts believe that more than 200,000 children become ill from lead poisoning annually, a problem caused chiefly by children eating paint containing lead-based pigments. Older homes often contain lead-based paint because white lead $[2\ PbCO_3 \cdot Pb(OH)_2]$ was the pigment used in white paint until about 40 years ago, when it was replaced by TiO_2. Lead salts have a sweet taste, which may contribute to the tendency of children to chew on painted objects.

The symptoms of lead poisoning are, among others, nausea, abdominal pain, irritability, headaches, and excess lethargy or hyperactivity. Indeed, these describe some of the symptoms of the illness that affected Ludwig van Beethoven. As a child, he was recognized as a musical prodigy and was thought to be the greatest pianist in Europe by the

Ludwig van Beethoven (1770–1827).

Erich Lessing/Art Resource, NY

time he was 19. But then he fell ill, and, by the time he was 29, he wrote to his brother to say he was considering suicide. By the time he died in 1827 at the age of 56, his belly, arms, and legs were swollen, and he complained constantly of pain in his joints and in his big toe. It is said he wandered the streets of Vienna with long, uncombed hair, dressed in a top hat and long coat, and scribbling in a notebook.

An autopsy at the time showed he died of kidney failure. Kidney stones had destroyed his kidneys, stones that presumably came from gout, the buildup of uric acid in his body. (Gout leads to joint pain, among other things. See the Case Study, page 789.) But why did he have gout?

It was well known in the time of the Roman Empire that lead and its salts are toxic. The Romans drank wine sweetened with

a very concentrated grape juice syrup that was prepared by boiling the juice in a lead kettle. The resulting syrup, called Sapa, had a very high concentration of lead, and many Romans contracted gout. So, if Beethoven enjoyed drinking wine, which was often kept in lead-glass decanters, he could have contracted gout and lead poisoning. One scientist has also noted that he may have been one of a small number of people who have a "metal metabolism disorder," a condition that prevents the excretion of toxic metals like lead.

In 2005, scientists at Argonne National Laboratory examined fragments of Beethoven's hair and skull and found both were extremely high in lead. The hair sample, for example, had 60 ppm lead, about 100 times higher than normal.

The mystery of what caused Beethoven's death has been solved. But what remains a mystery is how he contracted lead poisoning.

Questions:

1. *If blood contains 50 ppb lead, how many atoms of lead are there in 1.0 L of blood?*
2. *Research has found that port wine stored for a year in lead-glass decanters contains 2000 ppm lead. If the decanter contains 750 mL of wine (d = 1.0 g/mL), what mass of lead has been extracted into the wine?*

Answers to these question are in Appendix Q.

21.8 Nitrogen, Phosphorus, and the Group 5A Elements

Group 5A elements are characterized by the ns^2np^3 configuration with its half-filled np subshell. In compounds of the Group 5A elements, the primary oxidation numbers are +3 and +5, although common nitrogen compounds display a range of oxidation numbers from −3 to +3 and +5. Once again, as in Groups 3A and 4A, the most positive oxidation number is less common for the heavier elements. In many arsenic, antimony, and bismuth compounds, the element has an oxidation number of +3 state. Not surprisingly, compounds of these elements with oxidation numbers of +5 are powerful oxidizing agents.

This part of our tour of the main group elements will concentrate on the chemistries of nitrogen and phosphorus. Nitrogen is found primarily as N_2 in the atmosphere, where it constitutes 78.1% by volume (75.5% by weight). In contrast, phosphorus occurs in the earth's crust in solids. More than 200 different phosphorus-containing minerals are known; all contain the tetrahedral phosphate ion, PO_4^{3-}, or a derivative

Group 5A

Nitrogen
7
N
25 ppm

Phosphorus
15
P
1000 ppm

Arsenic
33
As
1.5 ppm

Antimony
51
Sb
0.2 ppm

Bismuth
83
Bi
0.048 ppm

Element abundances are in parts per million in the earth's crust.

of this ion. By far, the most abundant phosphorus-containing minerals are apatites (◀ page 978).

Nitrogen and its compounds play a key role in our economy, with ammonia making a particularly notable contribution. Phosphoric acid is an important commodity chemical, and it finds its greatest use in producing fertilizers.

Both phosphorus and nitrogen are part of every living organism. Phosphorus is contained in nucleic acids and phospholipids, and nitrogen occurs in proteins and nucleic acids (see *The Chemistry of Life: Biochemistry*, page 497).

Properties of Nitrogen and Phosphorus

Nitrogen (N_2) is a colorless gas that liquifies at 77 K ($-196\ °C$) (Figure 12.1, page 556). Its most notable feature is its reluctance to react with other elements or compounds because the N≡N triple bond has a large bond enthalpy (945 kJ/mol) and because the molecule is nonpolar. Nitrogen does, however, react with hydrogen to give ammonia in the presence of a catalyst (◀ Case Study, page 749) and with a few metals (notably lithium and magnesium) to give metal nitrides, compounds containing the N^{3-} ion.

$$3\ Mg(s) + N_2(g) \longrightarrow Mg_3N_2(s)$$
magnesium nitride

Elemental nitrogen is a very useful material. Because of its lack of reactivity, it is used to provide a nonoxidizing atmosphere for packaged foods and wine and to pressurize electric cables and telephone wires. Liquid nitrogen is valuable as a coolant in freezing biological samples such as blood and semen, in freeze-drying food, and for other applications that require extremely low temperatures.

Elemental phosphorus was first derived from human waste (see *A Closer Look: Making Phosphorus*, page 997), but it is now produced by the reduction of phosphate minerals in an electric furnace.

$$2\ Ca_3(PO_4)_2(s) + 10\ C(s) + 6\ SiO_2(s) \rightarrow P_4(g) + 6\ CaSiO_3(s) + 10\ CO(g)$$

White phosphorus is the most stable allotrope of phosphorus. Rather than occurring as a diatomic molecule with a triple bond, like its second-period relative nitrogen (N_2), phosphorus is made up of tetrahedral P_4 molecules in which each P atom is joined to three others via single bonds. Red phosphorus is a polymer of P_4 units.

White phosphorus, P_4

Polymeric red phosphorus

Nitrogen Compounds

A notable feature of the chemistry of nitrogen is the wide diversity of its compounds. Compounds with nitrogen in all oxidation numbers between -3 and $+5$ are known (Figure 21.23).

Charles D. Winters

The red and white allotropes of phosphorus.

Hydrogen Compounds of Nitrogen: Ammonia and Hydrazine

Ammonia is a gas at room temperature and pressure. It has a very penetrating odor and condenses to a liquid at -33 °C under 1 bar of pressure. Solutions in water, often referred to as ammonium hydroxide, are basic due to the reaction of ammonia with water (◄ Section 17.5 and Figure 3.13).

$$NH_3(aq) + H_2O(\ell) \rightleftharpoons NH_4^+(aq) + OH^-(aq) \quad K_b = 1.8 \times 10^{-5} \text{ at } 25 \text{ °C}$$

Ammonia is a major industrial chemical and is prepared by the Haber process (◄ page 749), largely for use as a fertilizer.

Hydrazine, N_2H_4, is a colorless, fuming liquid with an ammonia-like odor (mp, 2.0 °C; bp, 113.5 °C). Almost 1 million kilograms of hydrazine is produced annually by the Raschig process—the oxidation of ammonia with alkaline sodium hypochlorite in the presence of gelatin (which is added to suppress metal-catalyzed side reactions that lower the yield of hydrazine).

$$2 NH_3(aq) + NaClO(aq) \rightleftharpoons N_2H_4(aq) + NaCl(aq) + H_2O(\ell)$$

Hydrazine, like ammonia, is also a base,

$$N_2H_4(aq) + H_2O(\ell) \rightleftharpoons N_2H_5^+(aq) + OH^-(aq) \quad\quad K_b = 8.5 \times 10^{-7}$$

and it is a strong reducing agent, as reflected in the reduction potential for the following reaction of N_2 in basic solution:

$$N_2(g) + 4 H_2O(\ell) + 4 e^- \rightarrow N_2H_4(aq) + 4 OH^-(aq) \quad\quad E° = -1.15 \text{ V}$$

Hydrazine's reducing ability is exploited in its use in wastewater treatment for chemical plants. It removes oxidizing ions such as CrO_4^{2-} by reducing them, thus preventing them from entering the environment. A related use is the treatment of water boilers in large electric-generating plants. Oxygen dissolved in the water presents a serious problem in these plants because the dissolved gas can oxidize (corrode) the metal of the boiler and pipes. Hydrazine reduces the amount of dissolved oxygen in water.

$$N_2H_4(aq) + O_2(g) \rightarrow N_2(g) + 2 H_2O(\ell)$$

Oxides and Oxoacids of Nitrogen

Nitrogen is unique among all elements in the number of binary oxides it forms (Table 21.5). All are thermodynamically unstable with respect to decomposition to N_2 and O_2; that is, all have positive $\Delta_f G°$ values. Most are slow to decompose, however, and so are described as kinetically stable.

Dinitrogen monoxide, N_2O, commonly called *nitrous oxide*, is a nontoxic, odorless, and tasteless gas in which nitrogen has the lowest oxidation number ($+1$) among nitrogen oxides. It can be made by the careful decomposition of ammonium nitrate at 250 °C.

$$NH_4NO_3(s) \rightarrow N_2O(g) + 2 H_2O(g)$$

It is used as an anesthetic in minor surgery and has been called "laughing gas" because of its euphoriant effects. Because it is soluble in vegetable fats, the largest commercial use of N_2O is as a propellant and aerating agent in cans of whipped cream.

Nitrogen monoxide, NO, is an odd-electron molecule. It has 11 valence electrons, giving it one unpaired electron and making it a free radical. The compound has recently been the subject of intense research because it has been found to be important in a number of biochemical processes (◄ page 367).

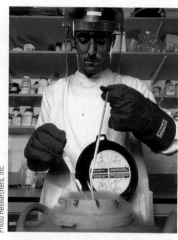

Liquid nitrogen. Biological samples—such as embryos or semen from animals or humans—can be stored in liquid nitrogen (at -196 °C) for long periods of time.

Compound & Oxidation Number of N

Ammonia, -3

Hydrazine, -2

Dinitrogen, 0

Dinitrogen oxide, $+1$

Nitrogen monoxide, $+2$

Nitrogen dioxide, $+4$

Nitric acid, $+5$

Active Figure 21.23

Compounds and oxidation numbers for nitrogen. In its compounds, the N atom can have oxidation states ranging from -3 to $+5$.

Chemistry ·ᐤ· Now™ Sign in at www.cengage.com/login and go to the Chapter 21 Contents menu to explore an interactive version of this figure accompanied by an exercise.

A Healthy Saltwater Aquarium and the Nitrogen Cycle

by Jeffrey Keaffaber, University of Florida

Large saltwater aquariums like Sea World in Florida, the Shedd Aquarium in Chicago, and the new Georgia Aquarium in Atlanta are a continual source of enjoyment. So are smaller aquariums in your home. Maintaining these facilities is not trivial, however; a healthy environment for its marine inhabitants is essential. For this, chemistry plays an important role.

A key part of aquarium maintenance involves control of the concentrations of various dissolved nitrogen-containing species, including ammonia, nitrite ion, and nitrate ion, all of which are stressful to fish at low concentrations and toxic in higher concentrations. The chemistry that relates to maintaining proper balance among these species is called the *nitrogen cycle*.

© Scripps Institution of Oceanography, UC San Diego. Used with permission.

Nitrification

The nitrogen cycle begins with the production of ammonia (and, in acid solution, its conjugate acid the ammonium ion, NH_4^+), fundamental waste products of protein metabolism in an aquarium habitat. Unless removed, the ammonia concentration will build up over time. To remove it, the aquarium water is cycled through sand filters infused with aerobic, oxygen-loving bacteria. These bacteria utilize enzymes that catalyze the oxidation of ammonia and ammonium ion by O_2 to form first nitrite ion and then nitrate ion. The overall process is called *nitrification*, and the saltwater bacteria that mediate each oxidation step are *Nitrosococcus sp.* and *Nitrococcus sp.*, respectively. Half-reactions representing this chemistry are:

Oxidation half-reactions:

$$NH_4^+(aq) + 8\ OH^-(aq) \rightarrow$$
$$NO_2^-(aq) + 6\ H_2O(\ell) + 6\ e^-$$

$$NO_2^-(aq) + 2\ OH^-(aq) \rightarrow$$
$$NO_3^-(aq) + H_2O(\ell) + 2\ e^-$$

Reduction half-reaction:

$$O_2(aq) + 2\ H_2O(\ell) + 4\ e^- \rightarrow 4\ OH^-(aq)$$

When setting up an aquarium at home, it is appropriate to monitor the concentrations of the various nitrogen species. Initially the NH_3/NH_4^+ concentration rises, but then it begins to fall as oxidation occurs. With time, the nitrite ion concentration builds up, peaks, and then decreases, with an accompanying increase in nitrate ion concentration. To reach a stable situation, as much as six weeks may be required.

Denitrification

Nitrate is much less toxic than ammonia and the nitrite ion, but its buildup must also be limited. In a small aquarium, nitrate ion concentration can be controlled by partial exchange of water. However, because of environmental restrictions this is not possible for large aquariums; they must use a closed water treatment process.

To remedy the build up the nitrate ion, another biologically catalyzed process is used that reduces the nitrate ion to nitrogen gas, N_2. A reducing agent is required, and early designs of denitrifying filters utilized methanol, CH_3OH, as the reducing agent. Among naturally occurring saltwater bacteria capable of nitrate reduction under low oxygen (anoxic) conditions, *Pseudomonas sp.*, is commonly used. The bacteria, utilizing enzymes to catalyze reaction of nitrate and methanol to form N_2 and CO_2, are introduced to sand filters where methanol is added.

A stable pH is also important to the health of aquarium fish. Therefore, the marine environment in a saltwater aquarium is maintained at a relatively constant pH of 8.0-8.2. To aid in this, the CO_2 produced by methanol oxidation remains dissolved in solution, and increases the buffer capacity of the seawater.

Questions:

1. *Write a balanced net ionic equation for the oxidation of NH_4^+ by O_2 to produce H_2O and NO_2^-.*

2. *Write half-reactions for the reduction of NO_3^- to N_2 and for the oxidation of CH_3OH to CO_2 in basic solution. Then, combine these half-reactions to obtain the balanced equation for the reduction of NO_3^- by CH_3OH.*

3. *Consider the carbon-containing species CO_2, H_2CO_3, HCO_3^-, and CO_3^{2-}. Which one is present in largest concentration at the pH conditions of the aquarium? Give a short explanation. K_a of $H_2CO_3 = 4.2 \times 10^{-7}$ and K_a of $HCO_3^- = 4.8 \times 10^{-11}$. (See Study Question 18-110.)*

4. *A large, 2.2×10^7 L, aquarium contains 1.7×10^4 kg of dissolved NO_3^-. Calculate nitrate concentrations in ppm (mg/L) N, ppm NO_3^-, and the molar concentration of NO_3^-.*

Answers to these questions are in Appendix Q.

TABLE 21.5 Some Oxides of Nitrogen

Formula	Name	Structure	Nitrogen Oxidation Number	Description
N_2O	Dinitrogen monoxide (nitrous oxide)	$:N\equiv N-\ddot{O}:$ linear	+1	Colorless gas (laughing gas)
NO	Nitrogen monoxide (nitric oxide)	*	+2	Colorless gas; odd-electron molecule (paramagnetic)
N_2O_3	Dinitrogen trioxide	planar	+3	Blue solid (mp, $-100.7\ ^\circ C$); reversibly dissociates to NO and NO_2
NO_2	Nitrogen dioxide		+4	Brown, paramagnetic gas; odd-electron molecule
N_2O_4	Dinitrogen tetraoxide	planar	+4	Colorless liquid/gas; dissociates to NO_2 (see Figure 16.8)
N_2O_5	Dinitrogen pentaoxide		+5	Colorless solid

*It is not possible to draw a Lewis structure that accurately represents the electronic structure of NO. See Chapter 8. Also note that only one resonance structure is shown for each structure.

Nitrogen dioxide, NO_2, is the brown gas you see when a bottle of nitric acid is allowed to stand in the sunlight.

$$2\ HNO_3(aq) \rightarrow 2\ NO_2(g) + H_2O(\ell) + \tfrac{1}{2}\ O_2(g)$$

Nitrogen dioxide is also a culprit in air pollution (◄ page 951). Nitrogen monoxide forms when atmospheric nitrogen and oxygen are heated in internal combustion engines. Released into the atmosphere, NO rapidly reacts with O_2 to form NO_2.

$$2\ NO(g) + O_2(g) \rightarrow 2\ NO_2(g)$$

Nitrogen dioxide has 17 valence electrons, so it is also an odd-electron molecule. Because the odd electron largely resides on the N atom, two NO_2 molecules can combine, forming an N—N bond and producing N_2O_4, *dinitrogen tetraoxide*.

$$2\ NO_2(g) \longrightarrow N_2O_4(g)$$
deep brown gas   colorless (mp, $-11.2\ ^\circ C$)

Solid N_2O_4 is colorless and consists entirely of N_2O_4 molecules. However, as the solid melts and the temperature increases to the boiling point, the color darkens as N_2O_4 dissociates to form brown NO_2. At the normal boiling point ($21.5\ ^\circ C$), the distinctly brown gas consists of 15.9% NO_2 and 84.1% N_2O_4.

Charles D. Winters

Nitrous oxide, N_2O. This oxide readily dissolves in fats, so the gas is added, under pressure, to cans of cream. When the valve is opened, the gas expands, whipping the cream. N_2O is also an anesthetic and is considered safe for medical uses. However, significant dangers arise from using it as a recreational drug. Long-term use can induce nerve damage and cause such problems as weakness and loss of feeling.

When NO_2 is bubbled into water, nitric acid and nitrous acid form.

$$2\ NO_2(g) + H_2O(\ell) \rightarrow HNO_3(aq) + HNO_2(aq)$$
$$\qquad\qquad\qquad\quad \text{nitric acid} \quad\ \text{nitrous acid}$$

Nitric acid has been known for centuries and has become an important compound in our modern economy. The oldest way to make the acid is to treat $NaNO_3$ with sulfuric acid (Figure 21.24).

$$2\ NaNO_3(s) + H_2SO_4(\ell) \rightarrow 2\ HNO_3(\ell) + Na_2SO_4(s)$$

Enormous quantities of nitric acid are now produced industrially by the oxidation of ammonia in the multistep *Ostwald process*. The acid has many applications, but by far the greatest amount is turned into ammonium nitrate (for use as a fertilizer) by the reaction of nitric acid and ammonia.

Nitric acid is a powerful oxidizing agent, as the large, positive E° values for the following half-reactions illustrate:

$$NO_3^-(aq) + 4\ H_3O^+(aq) + 3\ e^- \rightarrow NO(g) + 6\ H_2O(\ell) \qquad E^{\circ} = +0.96\ V$$

$$NO_3^-(aq) + 2\ H_3O^+(aq) + e^- \rightarrow NO_2(g) + 3\ H_2O(\ell) \qquad E^{\circ} = +0.80\ V$$

Concentrated nitric acid attacks and oxidizes most metals. (Aluminum is an exception; see page 985.) In this process, the nitrate ion is reduced to one of the nitrogen oxides. Which oxide is formed depends on the metal and on reaction conditions. In the case of copper, for example, either NO or NO_2 is produced, depending on the concentration of the acid (Figure 21.24b).

In dilute acid:

$$3\ Cu(s) + 8\ H_3O^+(aq) + 2\ NO_3^-(aq) \rightarrow 3\ Cu^{2+}(aq) + 12\ H_2O(\ell) + 2\ NO(g)$$

In concentrated acid:

$$Cu(s) + 4\ H_3O^+(aq) + 2\ NO_3^-(aq) \rightarrow Cu^{2+}(aq) + 6\ H_2O(\ell) + 2\ NO_2(g)$$

Four metals (Au, Pt, Rh, and Ir) that are not attacked by nitric acid are often described as the "noble metals." The alchemists of the 14th century, however, knew that if they mixed HNO_3 with HCl in a ratio of about $1:3$, this aqua regia, or "kingly water," would attack even gold, the noblest of metals.

$$10\ Au(s) + 6\ NO_3^-(aq) + 40\ Cl^-(aq) + 36\ H_3O^+(aq) \rightarrow$$
$$10\ [AuCl_4]^-(aq) + 3\ N_2(g) + 54\ H_2O(\ell)$$

FIGURE 21.24 The preparation and properties of nitric acid. (a) Nitric acid is prepared by the reaction of sulfuric acid and sodium nitrate. Pure HNO_3 is colorless, but samples of the acid are often brown because of NO_2 formed by decomposition of the acid. This gas fills the apparatus and colors the liquid in the distillation flask. (b) When concentrated nitric acid reacts with copper, the metal is oxidized to copper(II) ions, and NO_2 gas is a reaction product.

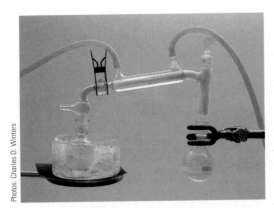

(a) Preparation of nitric acid.

(b) Reaction of HNO_3 with copper.

Photos: Charles D. Winters

Making Phosphorus

He stoked his small furnace with more charcoal and pumped the bellows until his retort glowed red hot. Suddenly something strange began to happen. Glowing fumes filled the vessel and from the end of the retort dripped a shining liquid that burst into flames.

J. Emsley: *The 13th Element*, p. 5.
New York, John Wiley, 2000.

John Emsley begins his story of phosphorus, its discovery, and its uses, by imagining what the German alchemist Hennig Brandt must have seen in his laboratory that day in 1669. (See page 338 for an artist's conception of the discovery of phosphorus by Brandt.) He was in search of the philosopher's stone, the magic elixir that would turn the crudest substance into gold.

Brandt was experimenting with urine, which had served as the source of useful chemicals since Roman times. It is not surprising that phosphorus could be extracted

from this source. Humans consume much more phosphorus, in the form of phosphate, than they require, and the excess phosphorus (about 1.4 g per day) is excreted in the urine. It is nonetheless extraordinary that Brandt was able to isolate the element. According to an 18th-century chemistry book, about 30 g of phosphorus could be obtained from 60 gallons of urine. And the process was not simple. Another 18th-century recipe states that "50 or 60 pails full" of urine was to be used. "Let it lie steeping . . . till it putrefy and breed worms." The chemist was then to reduce the whole to a paste and finally to heat the paste very strongly in a retort. After some days, phosphorus distilled from the mixture and was collected in water. (We know now that carbon from the organic compounds in the urine would have reduced the phosphate to phosphorus.) Phosphorus was made in this manner for more than 100 years.

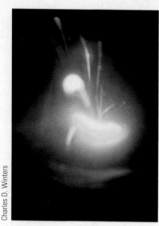

Charles D. Winters

The glow of phosphorus burning in air.

EXERCISE 21.10 Nitrogen Oxide Chemistry

Dinitrogen monoxide can be made by the decomposition of NH_4NO_3.

(a) A Lewis electron dot structure of N_2O is given in Table 21.5. Is it the only possible structure? If other structures are possible, is the one in Table 21.5 the most important?

(b) Is the decomposition of $NH_4NO_3(s)$ to give $N_2O(g)$ and $H_2O(g)$ endothermic or exothermic?

Hydrogen Compounds of Phosphorus and Other Group 5A Elements

The phosphorus analog of ammonia, phosphine (PH_3), is a poisonous, highly reactive gas with a faint garlic-like odor. Industrially, it is made by the reaction of white phosphorus and aqueous NaOH.

$$P_4(s) + 3\ KOH(aq) + 3\ H_2O(\ell) \rightarrow PH_3(g) + 3\ KH_2PO_2(aq)$$

The other hydrides of the heavier Group 5A elements are also toxic and become more unstable as the atomic number of the element increases. Nonetheless, arsine (AsH_3) is used in the semiconductor industry as a starting material in the preparation of gallium arsenide (GaAs) semiconductors.

Phosphorus Oxides and Sulfides

The most important compounds of phosphorus are those with oxygen, and there are at least six simple binary compounds containing just phosphorus and oxygen. All of them can be thought of as being derived structurally from the P_4 tetrahedron of white phosphorus. For example, if P_4 is carefully oxidized, P_4O_6 is formed; an O atom has been placed into each P—P bond in the tetrahedron (Figure 21.25).

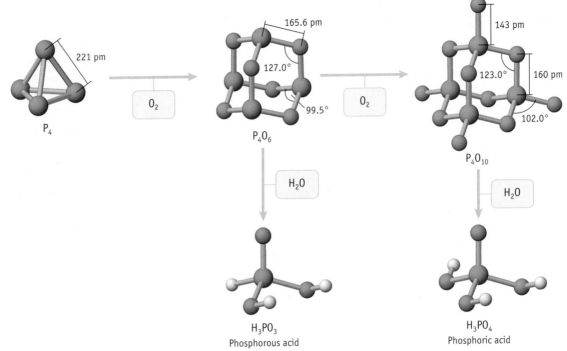

FIGURE 21.25 Phosphorus oxides. Other binary P—O compounds have formulas between P_4O_6 and P_4O_{10}. They are formed by starting with P_4O_6 and adding O atoms successively to the P atom vertices.

The most common and important phosphorus oxide is P_4O_{10}, a fine white powder commonly called "phosphorus pentaoxide" because its empirical formula is P_2O_5. In P_4O_{10}, each phosphorus atom is surrounded tetrahedrally by O atoms.

Phosphorus also forms a series of compounds with sulfur. Of these, the most important is P_4S_3.

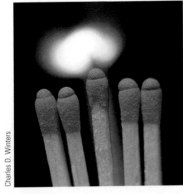

Matches. The head of a "strike anywhere" match contains P_4S_3 and the oxidizing agent $KClO_3$. (Other components are ground glass, Fe_2O_3, ZnO, and glue.) Safety matches have sulfur (3–5%) and $KClO_3$ (45–55%) in the match head and red phosphorus in the striking strip.

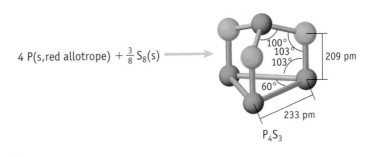

$$4\ P(\text{s, red allotrope}) + \tfrac{3}{8}S_8(\text{s}) \longrightarrow$$

In this phosphorus sulfide, S atoms are placed into only three of the P—P bonds. The principal use of P_4S_3 is in "strike anywhere" matches, the kind that light when you rub the head against a rough object. The active ingredients are P_4S_3 and the powerful oxidizing agent potassium chlorate, $KClO_3$. The "safety match" is now more common than the "strike anywhere" match. In safety matches, the head is predominantly $KClO_3$, and the material on the match book is red phosphorus (about 50%), Sb_2S_3, Fe_2O_3, and glue.

Phosphorus Oxoacids and Their Salts

A few of the many known phosphorus oxoacids are illustrated in Table 21.6. Indeed, there are so many acids and their salts in this category that structural principles have been developed to organize and understand them.

(a) All P atoms in the oxoacids and their anions (conjugate bases) are four-coordinate and tetrahedral.

(b) All the P atoms in the acids have at least one P—OH group (and this occurs often in the anions as well). In every case, the H atom is ionizable as H^+.

(c) Some oxoacids have one or more P—H bonds. This H atom is not ionizable as H^+.

(d) Polymerization can occur by P—O—P bond formation to give both linear and cyclic species. Two P atoms are never joined by more than one P—O—P bridge.

(e) When a P atom is surrounded only by O atoms (as in H_3PO_4), its oxidation number is +5. For each P—OH that is replaced by P—H, the oxidation number drops by 2 (because P is considered more electronegative than H). For example, the oxidation number of P in H_3PO_2 is +1.

FIGURE 21.26 Reaction of P_4O_{10} and water. The white solid oxide reacts vigorously with water to give orthophosphoric acid, H_3PO_4. (The heat generated vaporizes the water, so steam is visible.)

Orthophosphoric acid, H_3PO_4, and its salts are far more important commercially than other P—O acids. Millions of tons of phosphoric acid are made annually, some using white phosphorus as the starting material. The element is burned in oxygen to give P_4O_{10}, and the oxide reacts with water to produce the acid (Figure 21.26).

$$P_4O_{10}(s) + 6 H_2O(\ell) \rightarrow 4 H_3PO_4(aq)$$

TABLE 21.6 Phosphorus Oxoacids

Formula	Name	Structure
H_3PO_4	Orthophosphoric acid	
$H_4P_2O_7$	Pyrophosphoric acid (diphosphoric acid)	
$(HPO_3)_3$	Metaphosphoric acid	
H_3PO_3	Phosphorous acid (phosphonic acid)	
H_3PO_2	Hypophosphorous acid (phosphinic acid)	

(a) **Mining phosphate rock.** Phosphate rock is primarily $Ca_3(PO_4)_2$, and most mined in the United States comes from Florida.

© Nathan Benn/Corbis

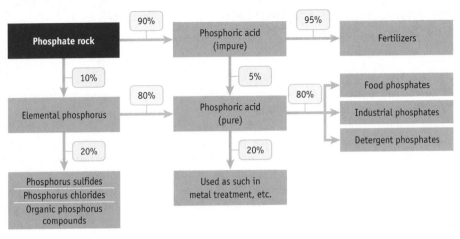

(b) **Uses of phosphorus and phosphoric acid.**

FIGURE 21.27 Uses of phosphate rock, phosphorus, and phosphoric acid.

This approach gives a pure product, so it is employed to make phosphoric acid for use in food products in particular. The acid is nontoxic, and it gives the tart or sour taste to carbonated "soft drinks," such as various colas (about 0.05% H_3PO_4) or root beer (about 0.01% H_3PO_4).

A major use for phosphoric acid is to impart corrosion resistance to metal objects such as nuts and bolts, tools, and car-engine parts by plunging the object into a hot acid bath. Car bodies are similarly treated with phosphoric acid containing metal ions such as Zn^{2+}, and aluminum trim is "polished" by treating it with the acid.

The reaction of H_3PO_4 with strong bases produces salts such as NaH_2PO_4, Na_2HPO_4, and Na_3PO_4. In industry, the monosodium and disodium salts are produced using Na_2CO_3 as the base, but an excess of the stronger (and more expensive) base NaOH is required to remove the third proton to give Na_3PO_4.

Sodium phosphate (Na_3PO_4) is used in scouring powders and paint strippers because the anion PO_4^{3-} is a relatively strong base in water ($K_b = 2.8 \times 10^{-2}$). Sodium monohydrogen phosphate, Na_2HPO_4, which has a less basic anion than PO_4^{3-}, is widely used in food products. Kraft has patented a process using the salt in the manufacture of pasteurized cheese, for example. Thousands of tons of Na_2HPO_4 are still used for this purpose, even though the function of the salt in this process is not completely understood. In addition, a small amount of Na_2HPO_4 in pudding mixes enables the mix to gel in cold water, and the basic anion raises the pH of cereals to provide "quick-cooking" breakfast cereal. (The OH^- ion from HPO_4^{2-} hydrolysis accelerates the breakdown of the cellulose material in the cereal.)

Calcium phosphates are used in a broad spectrum of products. For example, the weak acid $Ca(H_2PO_4)_2 \cdot H_2O$ is used as the acid leavening agent in baking powder. A typical baking powder contains (along with inert ingredients) 28% $NaHCO_3$, 10.7% $Ca(H_2PO_4)_2 \cdot H_2O$, and 21.4% $NaAl(SO_4)_2$ (also a weak acid). The weak acids react with sodium bicarbonate to produce CO_2 gas. For example,

$$Ca(H_2PO_4)_2 \cdot H_2O(s) + 2\ NaHCO_3(aq) \rightarrow 2\ CO_2(g) + 3\ H_2O(\ell) + Na_2HPO_4(aq) + CaHPO_4(aq)$$

Finally, calcium monohydrogen phosphate, $CaHPO_4$, is used as an abrasive and polishing agent in toothpaste.

21.9 Oxygen, Sulfur, and the Group 6A Elements

Oxygen is by far the most abundant element in the earth's crust, representing slightly less than 50% of it by weight. It is present as elemental oxygen in the atmosphere and is combined with other elements in water and in many minerals. Scientists believe that elemental oxygen did not appear on this planet until about 3.5 billion years ago, when it was formed on the planet by plants through the process of photosynthesis.

Sulfur, seventeenth in abundance in the earth's crust, is also found in its elemental form in nature, but only in certain concentrated deposits. Sulfur-containing compounds occur in natural gas and oil. In minerals, sulfur occurs as the sulfide ion (for example, in cinnabar, HgS, and galena, PbS), as the disulfide ion (in iron pyrite, FeS_2, or "fool's gold"), and as sulfate ion (e.g., in gypsum, $CaSO_4 \cdot 2\ H_2O$). Sulfur oxides (SO_2 and SO_3) also occur in nature, primarily as products of volcanic activity (Figure 21.28).

In the United States, most sulfur—about 10 million tons per year—is obtained from deposits of the element found along the Gulf of Mexico. These deposits occur typically at a depth of 150 to 750 m below the surface in layers about 30 m thick. They are thought to have been formed by anaerobic ("without elemental oxygen") bacteria acting on sedimentary sulfate deposits such as gypsum.

Preparation and Properties of the Elements

Pure oxygen is obtained by the fractional distillation of air and is among the top five industrial chemicals produced in the United States. Oxygen can be made in the laboratory by electrolysis of water (Figure 21.4) and by the catalyzed decomposition of metal chlorates such as $KClO_3$.

$$2\ KClO_3(s) \xrightarrow{\text{catalyst}} 2\ KCl(s) + 3\ O_2(g)$$

At room temperature and pressure, oxygen is a colorless gas, but it is pale blue when condensed to the liquid at $-183\ °C$ (◄ Figure 9.15). As described in Section 9.3, diatomic oxygen is paramagnetic because it has two unpaired electrons.

An allotrope of oxygen, ozone (O_3), is a blue, diamagnetic gas with an odor so strong that it can be detected in concentrations as low as 0.05 ppm. Ozone is synthesized by passing O_2 through an electric discharge or by irradiating O_2 with ultraviolet light. It is often in the news because of the realization that the earth's protective layer of ozone in the stratosphere is being disrupted by chlorofluorocarbons and other chemicals (◄ page 953).

Sulfur has numerous allotropes. The most common and most stable allotrope is the yellow, orthorhombic form, which consists of S_8 molecules with the sulfur atoms arranged in a crown-shaped ring (Figure 21.29a). Less stable allotropes are known that have rings of 6 to 20 sulfur atoms. Another form of sulfur, called plastic sulfur, has a molecular structure with chains of sulfur atoms (Figure 21.29b).

Sulfur is obtained from underground deposits by a process developed by Herman Frasch (1851–1914) about 1900. Superheated water (at 165 °C) and then air are forced into the deposit. The sulfur melts (mp, 113 °C) and is forced to the surface as a frothy, yellow stream, from which it solidifies.

Selenium and tellurium are comparatively rare on earth, having abundances about the same as those of silver and gold, respectively. Because their chemistry is similar to that of sulfur, they are often found in minerals associated with the sulfides of copper, silver, iron, and arsenic, and they are recovered as by-products of the industries devoted to those metals.

Group 6A

Oxygen	8
O	
474,000 ppm	
Sulfur	16
S	
260 ppm	
Selenium	34
Se	
0.5 ppm	
Tellurium	52
Te	
0.005 ppm	
Polonium	84
Po	
trace	

Element abundances are in parts per million in the earth's crust.

© Ludovic Maisant/Corbis

FIGURE 21.28 Sulfur spewing from a volcano in Indonesia.

FIGURE 21.29 Sulfur allotropes.
(a) At room temperature, sulfur exists as a bright yellow solid composed of S_8 rings. (b) When heated, the rings break open, and eventually form chains of S atoms in a material described as "plastic sulfur."

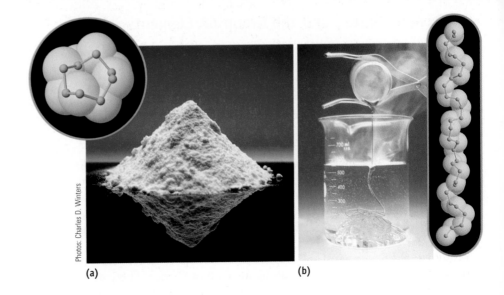

Photos: Charles D. Winters

(a)   (b)

Selenium has a range of uses, including in glass making. A cadmium sulfide/selenide mixture is added to glass to give it a brilliant red color (Figure 21.30a). The most familiar use of selenium is in xerography, a word meaning "dry printing" and a process at the heart of the modern copy machine. Most photocopy machines use an aluminum plate or roller coated with selenium. Light coming from the imaging lens selectively discharges a static electric charge on the selenium surface, and the black toner sticks only on the areas that remain charged. A copy is made when the toner is transferred to a sheet of plain paper.

The heaviest element of Group 6A, polonium, is radioactive and found only in trace amounts on earth. It was discovered in Paris, France, in 1898 by Marie Sklodowska Curie (1867–1934) and her husband Pierre Curie (1859-1906). The Curies painstakingly separated this element from a large quantity of pitchblende, a uranium-containing ore.

Chemistry ⚛ Now™

Sign in at **www.cengage.com/login** and go to Chapter 21 Contents to see Screen 21.8 for an exercise on **sulfur chemistry.**

FIGURE 21.30 Uses of selenium.
(a) Glass takes on a brilliant red color when a mixture of cadmium sulfide/selenide (CdS, CdSe) is added to it.
(b) These sample bottles hold suspensions of quantum dots, nanometer-sized crystals of CdSe dispersed in a polymer matrix. The crystals emit light in the visible range when excited by ultraviolet light. Light emission at different wavelengths is achieved by changing the particle size. Crystals of PbS and PbSe can be made that emit light in the infrared range.

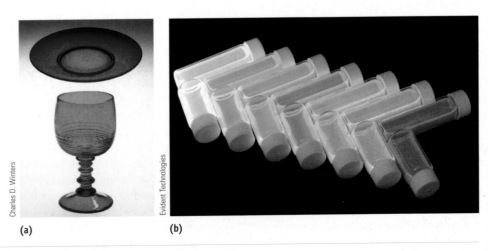

Charles D. Winters

Evident Technologies

(a)   (b)

Sulfur Compounds

Hydrogen sulfide, H_2S, has a bent molecular geometry, like water. Unlike water, however, H_2S is a gas under standard conditions (mp, -85.6 °C; bp, -60.3 °C) because its intermolecular forces are weak compared with the strong hydrogen bonding in water (see Figure 12.6). Hydrogen sulfide is poisonous, comparable in toxicity to hydrogen cyanide, but fortunately it has a terrible odor and is detectable in concentrations as low as 0.02 ppm. You must be careful with H_2S, though. Because it has an anesthetic effect, your nose rapidly loses its ability to detect it. Death occurs at H_2S concentrations of 100 ppm.

Sulfur is often found as the sulfide ion in conjunction with metals because all metal sulfides (except those based on Group 1A metals) are insoluble. The recovery of metals from their sulfide ores usually begins by heating the ore in air.

$$2\ PbS(s) + 3\ O_2(g) \rightarrow 2\ PbO(s) + 2\ SO_2(g)$$

Here, lead sulfide is converted to lead(II) oxide, and this is further reduced to lead using carbon or carbon monoxide in a blast furnace.

$$PbO(s) + CO(g) \rightarrow Pb(\ell) + CO_2(g)$$

Alternatively, the oxide can be reduced to elemental lead by combining it with fresh lead sulfide.

$$2\ PbO(s) + PbS(s) \rightarrow 3\ Pb(s) + SO_2(g)$$

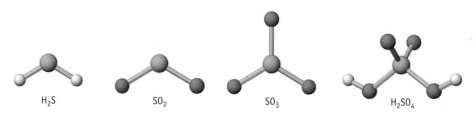

H_2S SO_2 SO_3 H_2SO_4

Models of some common sulfur-containing molecules: H_2S, SO_2, SO_3, and H_2SO_4.

Sulfur dioxide (SO_2), a colorless, toxic gas with a sharp odor, is produced on an enormous scale by the combustion of sulfur and by roasting sulfide ores in air. The combustion of sulfur in sulfur-containing coal and fuel oil creates particularly large environmental problems. It has been estimated that about 2.0×10^8 tons of sulfur oxides (primarily SO_2) are released into the atmosphere each year by human activities; this is more than half of the total emitted by all other natural sources of sulfur in the environment.

Sulfur dioxide readily dissolves in water. The most important reaction of this gas is its oxidation to SO_3.

$$SO_2(g) + \tfrac{1}{2} O_2(g) \rightarrow SO_3(g) \qquad \Delta_r H° = -98.9\ \text{kJ/mol-rxn}$$

Sulfur trioxide is almost never isolated but is converted directly to sulfuric acid by reaction with water in the "contact process."

The largest use of sulfur is the production of sulfuric acid, H_2SO_4, the compound produced in largest quantity by the chemical industry (◄ page 135). In the United States, roughly 70% of the acid is used to manufacture superphosphate fertilizer from phosphate rock. Plants need a soluble form of phosphorus for growth, but calcium phosphate and apatite [$Ca_5X(PO_4)_3$, X = F, OH, Cl] are insoluble. Treating phosphate-containing minerals with sulfuric acid produces a mixture of soluble

■ **Bad Breath** Halitosis or "bad breath" is due to three sulfur-containing compounds: H_2S, CH_3SH (methyl mercaptan), and $(CH_3)_2S$ (dimethyl sulfide). All three can be detected in very tiny concentrations. For example, your nose knows if as little as 0.2 microgram of CH_3SH is present per liter of air. The compounds result from bacteria's attack on the sulfur-containing amino acids cysteine and methionine in food particles in the mouth. A general rule: if something smells bad, it probably contains sulfur! (See Case Study, page 524.)

Common household products containing sulfur or sulfur-based compounds.

Snot-tites and Sulfur Chemistry

Sulfur chemistry can be important in cave formation, as a spectacular example in the jungles of southern Mexico amply demonstrates. Toxic hydrogen sulfide gas spews from the Cueva de Villa Luz along with water that is milky white with suspended sulfur particles. The cave can be followed downward to a large underground stream and a maze of actively enlarging cave passages. Water rises into the cave from underlying sulfur-bearing strata, releasing hydrogen sulfide at concentrations up to 150 ppm. Yellow sulfur crystallizes on the cave walls around the inlets. The sulfur and sulfuric acid are produced by the following reactions:

$$2\ H_2S(g) + O_2(g) \rightarrow 2\ S(s) + 2\ H_2O(\ell)$$
$$2\ S(s) + 2\ H_2O(\ell) + 3\ O_2(g) \rightarrow 2\ H_2SO_4(aq)$$

The cave atmosphere is poisonous to humans, so gas masks are essential for would-be explorers. But surprisingly, the cave is teeming with life. Several species of bacteria thrive on sulfur compounds in acidic environments. The chemical energy released in their metabolism is used to obtain carbon for their bodies from calcium carbonate and carbon dioxide, both of which are abundant in the cave. One result is that bacterial filaments hang from the walls and ceilings in bundles. Because the filaments look like something coming from a runny nose, cave explorers refer to them as "snot-tites." Other microbes feed on the bacteria, and so on up the food chain—which includes spiders, gnats, and pygmy snails—all the way to sardine-like fish that swim in the cave stream. This entire ecosystem is supported by reactions involving sulfur within the cave.

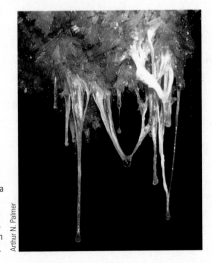

Snot-tites. Filaments of sulfur-oxidizing bacteria (dubbed "snot-tites") hang from the ceiling of a Mexican cave containing an atmosphere rich in hydrogen sulfide. The bacteria thrive on the energy released by oxidation of the hydrogen sulfide, forming the base of a complex food chain. Droplets of sulfuric acid on the filaments have an average pH of 1.4, with some as low as zero! Drops that landed on explorers in the cave burned their skin and disintegrated their clothing.

Arthur N. Palmer

---

phosphates. The balanced equation for the reaction of excess sulfuric acid and calcium phosphate, for example, is

$$Ca_3(PO_4)_2(s) + 3\ H_2SO_4(\ell) \rightarrow 2\ H_3PO_4(\ell) + 3\ CaSO_4(s)$$

but it does not tell the whole story. Concentrated superphosphate fertilizer is actually mostly $CaHPO_4$ or $Ca(H_2PO_4)_2$ plus some H_3PO_4 and $CaSO_4$. (Notice that the chemical principle behind this reaction is that sulfuric acid is a stronger acid than H_3PO_4 (Table 17.3), so the PO_4^{3-} ion is protonated by sulfuric acid.)

Smaller amounts of sulfuric acid are used in the conversion of ilmenite, a titanium-bearing ore, to TiO_2, which is then used as a white pigment in paint, plastics, and paper. The acid is also used to manufacture iron and steel as well as petroleum products, synthetic polymers, and paper.

Chemistry ⚛ Now™

Sign in at **www.cengage.com/login** and go to Chapter 21 Contents to see Screen 21.9 for an exercise on **the structural chemistry of sulfur compounds.**

EXERCISE 21.11 Sulfur Chemistry

Metal sulfides roasted in air produce metal oxides.

$$2\ ZnS(s) + 3\ O_2(g) \rightarrow 2\ ZnO(s) + 2\ SO_2(g)$$

Use thermodynamics to decide if the reaction is product- or reactant-favored at equilibrium at 298 K. Will the reaction be more or less product-favored at a high temperature?

21.10 The Halogens, Group 7A

Fluorine and chlorine are the most abundant halogens in the earth's crust, with fluorine somewhat more abundant than chlorine. If their abundance in sea water is measured, however, the situation is quite different. Chlorine has an abundance in sea water of 18,000 ppm, whereas the abundance of fluorine in the same source is only 1.3 ppm. This variation is a result of the differences in the solubility of their salts and plays a role in the methods used to recover the elements themselves.

Preparation of the Elements

Fluorine

The water-insoluble mineral fluorspar (calcium fluoride, CaF_2) is one of the many sources of fluorine. Because the mineral was originally used as a flux in metalworking, its name comes from the Latin word meaning "to flow." In the 17th century, it was discovered that solid CaF_2 would emit light when heated, and the phenomenon was called *fluorescence*. In the early 1800s, when it was recognized that a new element was contained in fluorspar, A. M. Ampère (1775–1836) suggested that the element be called fluorine.

Although fluorine was recognized as an element by 1812, it was not until 1886 that it was isolated by the French chemist Henri Moisson (1852–1907) in elemental form as a very pale yellow gas by the electrolysis of KF dissolved in anhydrous HF. Indeed, because F_2 is such a powerful oxidizing agent, chemical oxidation of F^- to F_2 is not feasible, and electrolysis is the only practical way to obtain gaseous F_2 (Figure 21.31).

The preparation of F_2 is difficult because F_2 is so reactive. It oxidizes (corrodes) the equipment and reacts violently with traces of grease or other contaminants. Furthermore, the products of electrolysis, F_2 and H_2, can recombine explosively, so they must not be allowed to come into contact with each other. (Compare with the reaction of H_2 and Br_2 in Figure 21.5.) Current U.S. production of fluorine is approximately 5000 metric tons per year.

Chlorine

Chlorine is a strong oxidizing agent, and to prepare this element from chloride ion by a chemical reaction requires a stronger oxidizing agent. Permanganate or dichromate ion in acid solution will serve this purpose (Figure 21.32). Elemental chlorine was first made by the Swedish chemist Karl Wilhelm Scheele (1742–1786) in 1774, who combined sodium chloride with an oxidizing agent in an acidic solution.

Industrially, chlorine is made by electrolysis of brine (concentrated aqueous NaCl). The other product of the electrolysis, NaOH, is also a valuable industrial chemical. About 80% of the chlorine produced is made using an electrochemical cell similar to the one depicted in Figure 21.33. Oxidation of chloride ion to Cl_2 gas occurs at the anode and reduction of water occurs at the cathode.

Anode reaction (oxidation)	$2\ Cl^-(aq) \rightarrow Cl_2(g) + 2\ e^-$
Cathode reaction (reduction)	$2\ H_2O(\ell) + 2\ e^- \rightarrow H_2(g) + 2\ OH^-(aq)$

Activated titanium is used for the anode, and stainless steel or nickel is preferred for the cathode in the electrolytic cell. The anode and cathode compartments are separated by a membrane that is not permeable to water but allows Na^+ ions to pass to maintain the charge balance. Thus, the membrane functions as a "salt" bridge between the anode and cathode compartments. The energy consumption of these cells is in the range of 2000–2500 kWh per ton of NaOH produced.

Group 7A
Halogens

Fluorine
9
F
950 ppm

Chlorine
17
Cl
130 ppm

Bromine
35
Br
0.37 ppm

Iodine
53
I
0.14 ppm

Astatine
85
At
trace

Element abundances are in parts per million in the earth's crust.

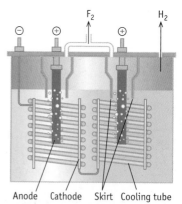

FIGURE 21.31 Schematic of an electrolysis cell for producing fluorine.

FIGURE 21.32 **Chlorine prepara-**
tion. Chlorine is prepared by oxidation
of chloride ion using a strong oxidizing
agent. Here, oxidation of NaCl is accomplished using $K_2Cr_2O_7$ in H_2SO_4. (The Cl_2
gas is bubbled into water in a receiving
flask.)

Charles D. Winters

Bromine

The standard reduction potentials of the halogens indicate that their strength as
oxidizing agents decreases going from F_2 to I_2.

Half-Reaction	Reduction Potential ($E°$, V)
$F_2(g) + 2\,e^- \rightarrow 2\,F^-(aq)$	2.87
$Cl_2(g) + 2\,e^- \rightarrow 2\,Cl^-(aq)$	1.36
$Br_2(\ell) + 2\,e^- \rightarrow 2\,Br^-(aq)$	1.08
$I_2(s) + 2\,e^- \rightarrow 2\,I^-(aq)$	0.535

This means that Cl_2 will oxidize Br^- ions to Br_2 in aqueous solution, for example.

$$Cl_2(aq) + 2\,Br^-(aq) \rightarrow 2\,Cl^-(aq) + Br_2(aq)$$

$$E°_{net} = E°_{cathode} - E°_{anode} = 1.36\ V - (1.08\ V) = +0.28\ V$$

In fact, this is the commercial method of preparing bromine when NaBr is obtained
from natural brine wells in Arkansas and Michigan.

Iodine

Iodine is a lustrous, purple-black solid, easily sublimed at room temperature and
atmospheric pressure (Figure 13.17). The element was first isolated in 1811 from
seaweed and kelp, extracts of which had long been used for treatment of goiter,
the enlargement of the thyroid gland. It is now known that the thyroid gland produces a growth-regulating hormone (thyroxine) that contains iodine. Consequently,
most table salt in the United States has 0.01% NaI added to provide the necessary
iodine in the diet.

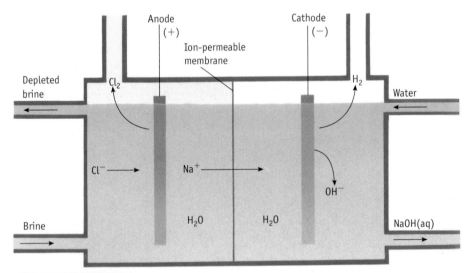

Active Figure 21.33 **A membrane cell for the production of NaOH and Cl_2 gas from a saturated, aque-**
ous solution of NaCl (brine). Here, the anode and cathode compartments are separated by a water-impermeable
but ion-conducting membrane. A widely used membrane is made of Nafion, a fluorine-containing polymer that is a
relative of polytetrafluoroethylene (Teflon). Brine is fed into the anode compartment and dilute sodium hydroxide or
water into the cathode compartment. Overflow pipes carry the evolved gases and NaOH away from the chambers of
the electrolysis cell.

Chemistry.⊙.Now™ **Sign in at www.cengage.com/login and go to the Chapter 21 Contents menu to**
explore an interactive version of this figure accompanied by an exercise.

FIGURE 21.34 The preparation of iodine. A mixture of sodium iodide and manganese(IV) oxide was placed in the flask (left). On adding concentrated sulfuric acid (right), brown iodine vapor is evolved.

$$2\ NaI(s) + 2\ H_2SO_4(aq) + MnO_2(s) \rightarrow$$
$$Na_2SO_4(aq) + MnSO_4(aq)$$
$$+ 2\ H_2O(\ell) + I_2(g)$$

A laboratory method for preparing I_2 is illustrated in Figure 21.34. The commercial preparation depends on the source of I^- and its concentration. One method is interesting because it involves some chemistry described earlier in this book. Iodide ions are first precipitated with silver ions to give insoluble AgI.

$$I^-(aq) + Ag^+(aq) \rightarrow AgI(s)$$

This is reduced by clean scrap iron to give iron(II) iodide and metallic silver.

$$2\ AgI(s) + Fe(s) \rightarrow FeI_2(aq) + 2\ Ag(s)$$

The silver is recycled by oxidizing it with nitric acid (forming silver nitrate) which is then reused. Finally, iodide ion from water-soluble FeI_2 is oxidized to iodine with chlorine [with iron(III) chloride as a by-product].

$$2\ FeI_2(aq) + 3\ Cl_2(aq) \rightarrow 2\ I_2(s) + 2\ FeCl_3(aq)$$

Fluorine Compounds

Fluorine is the most reactive of all of the elements, forming compounds with every element except He and Ne. In most cases, the elements combine directly, and some reactions can be so vigorous as to be explosive. This reactivity can be explained by at least two features of fluorine chemistry: the relatively weak F—F bond compared with chlorine and bromine, and, in particular, the relatively strong bonds formed by fluorine to other elements. This is illustrated by the table of bond dissociation enthalpies in the margin.

In addition to its oxidizing ability, another notable characteristic of fluorine is its small size. These properties lead to the formation of compounds where a number of F atoms can be bonded to a central element in a high oxidation state. Examples include PtF_6, UF_6, IF_7, and XeF_4.

Hydrogen fluoride is an important industrial chemical. More than 1 million tons of hydrogen fluoride is produced annually worldwide, almost all by the action of concentrated sulfuric acid on fluorspar.

$$CaF_2(s) + H_2SO_4(\ell) \rightarrow CaSO_4(s) + 2\ HF(g)$$

The U.S. capacity for HF production is approximately 210,000 metric tons, but currently demand is exceeding supply for this chemical. Anhydrous HF is used in

Bond Dissociation Enthalpies of Some Halogen Compounds (kJ/mol)

X	X—X	H—X	C—X (in CX_4)
F	155	565	485
Cl	242	432	339
Br	193	366	285
I	151	299	213

a broad range of industries: in the production of refrigerants, herbicides, pharmaceuticals, high-octane gasoline, aluminum, plastics, electrical components, and fluorescent lightbulbs.

The fluorspar used to produce HF must be very pure and free of SiO_2 because HF reacts readily with silicon dioxide.

$$SiO_2(s) + 4\ HF(aq) \rightarrow SiF_4(g) + 2\ H_2O(\ell)$$

$$SiF_4(g) + 2\ HF(aq) \rightarrow H_2SiF_6(aq)$$

This series of reactions explains why HF can be used to etch or frost glass (such as the inside of fluorescent light bulbs). It also explains why HF is not shipped in glass containers (unlike HCl, for example).

The aluminum industry consumes about 10–40 kg of cryolite, Na_3AlF_6, per metric ton of aluminum produced. The reason is that cryolite is added to aluminum oxide to produce a lower-melting mixture that can be electrolyzed. Cryolite is found in only small quantities in nature, so it is made in various ways, among them the following reaction:

$$6\ HF(aq) + Al(OH)_3(s) + 3\ NaOH(aq) \rightarrow Na_3AlF_6(s) + 6\ H_2O(\ell)$$

About 3% of the hydrofluoric acid produced is used in uranium fuel production. To separate uranium isotopes in a gas centrifuge (◄ page 523), the uranium must be in the form of a volatile compound. Naturally occurring uranium is processed to give UO_2. This oxide is treated with hydrogen fluoride to give UF_4, which is then reacted with F_2 to produce the volatile solid UF_6.

$$UO_2(s) + 4\ HF(aq) \rightarrow UF_4(s) + 2\ H_2O(\ell)$$

$$UF_4(s) + F_2(g) \rightarrow UF_6(s)$$

This last step consumes 70–80% of fluorine produced annually.

Chlorine Compounds

Hydrogen Chloride

Hydrochloric acid, an aqueous solution of hydrogen chloride, is a valuable industrial chemical. Hydrogen chloride gas can be prepared by the reaction of hydrogen and chlorine, but the rapid, exothermic reaction is difficult to control. The classical method of making HCl in the laboratory uses the reaction of NaCl and sulfuric acid, a procedure that takes advantage of the facts that HCl is a gas and that H_2SO_4 will not oxidize the chloride ion.

$$2\ NaCl(s) + H_2SO_4(\ell) \rightarrow Na_2SO_4(s) + 2\ HCl(g)$$

Hydrogen chloride gas has a sharp, irritating odor. Both gaseous and aqueous HCl react with metals and metal oxides to give metal chlorides and, depending on the reactant, hydrogen or water.

$$Mg(s) + 2\ HCl(aq) \rightarrow MgCl_2(aq) + H_2(g)$$

$$ZnO(s) + 2\ HCl(aq) \rightarrow ZnCl_2(aq) + H_2O(\ell)$$

Oxoacids of Chlorine

Oxoacids of chlorine range from HClO, in which chlorine has an oxidation number of +1, to $HClO_4$, in which the oxidation number is equal to the group number, +7. All are strong oxidizing agents.

Oxoacids of Chlorine

Acid	Name	Anion	Name
HClO	Hypochlorous	ClO^-	Hypochlorite
$HClO_2$	Chlorous	ClO_2^-	Chlorite
$HClO_3$	Chloric	ClO_3^-	Chlorate
$HClO_4$	Perchloric	ClO_4^-	Perchlorate

Hypochlorous acid, HClO, forms when chlorine dissolves in water. In this reaction, half of the chlorine is oxidized to hypochlorite ion and half is reduced to chloride ion in a **disproportionation reaction**.

$$Cl_2(g) + 2\ H_2O(\ell) \rightleftharpoons H_3O^+(aq) + HClO(aq) + Cl^-(aq)$$

If Cl_2 is dissolved in cold aqueous NaOH instead of in pure water, hypochlorite ion and chloride ion form.

$$Cl_2(g) + 2\ OH^-(aq) \rightleftharpoons ClO^-(aq) + Cl^-(aq) + H_2O(\ell)$$

Under basic conditions, the equilibrium lies far to the right. The resulting alkaline solution is the "liquid bleach" used in home laundries. The bleaching action of this solution is a result of the oxidizing ability of ClO^-. Most dyes are colored organic compounds, and hypochlorite ion oxidizes dyes to colorless products.

When calcium hydroxide is combined with Cl_2, solid $Ca(ClO)_2$ is the product. This compound is easily handled and is the "chlorine" that is sold for swimming pool disinfection.

When a basic solution of hypochlorite ion is heated, another disproportionation occurs, forming chlorate ion and chloride ion:

$$3\ ClO^-(aq) \rightarrow ClO_3^-(aq) + 2\ Cl^-(aq)$$

Sodium and potassium chlorates are made in large quantities this way. The sodium salt can be reduced to ClO_2, a compound used for bleaching paper pulp. Some $NaClO_3$ is also converted to potassium chlorate, $KClO_3$, the preferred oxidizing agent in fireworks and a component of safety matches.

Perchlorates, salts containing ClO_4^-, are powerful oxidants. Pure perchloric acid, $HClO_4$, is a colorless liquid that explodes if shocked. It explosively oxidizes organic materials and rapidly oxidizes silver and gold. Dilute aqueous solutions of the acid are safe to handle, however.

Perchlorate salts of most metals are usually relatively stable, albeit unpredictable. Great care should be used when handling any perchlorate salt. Ammonium perchlorate, for example, bursts into flame if heated above 200 °C.

$$2\ NH_4ClO_4(s) \rightarrow N_2(g) + Cl_2(g) + 2\ O_2(g) + 4\ H_2O(g)$$

The strong oxidizing ability of the ammonium salt accounts for its use as the oxidizer in the solid booster rockets for the Space Shuttle. The solid propellant in these rockets is largely NH_4ClO_4, the remainder being the reducing agent, powdered aluminum. Each launch requires about 750 tons of ammonium perchlorate, and more than half of the sodium perchlorate currently manufactured is converted to the ammonium salt. The process for making this conversion is an exchange reaction that takes advantage of the fact that ammonium perchlorate is less soluble in water than sodium perchlorate:

$$NaClO_4(aq) + NH_4Cl(aq) \rightleftharpoons NaCl(aq) + NH_4ClO_4(s)$$

■ **Disproportionation** A reaction in which an element or compound is simultaneously oxidized and reduced is called a disproportionation reaction. Here, Cl_2 is oxidized to ClO^- and reduced to Cl^-.

NASA

Use of a perchlorate salt. The solid-fuel booster rockets of the Space Shuttle utilize a mixture of NH_4ClO_4 (oxidizing agent) and Al powder (reducing agent).

Chapter Goals Revisited

Now that you have studied this chapter, you should ask whether you have met the chapter goals. In particular, you should be able to:

Relate the formulas and properties of compounds to the periodic table

a. Predict several chemical reactions of the Group A elements (Section 21.2). Study Question(s) assignable in OWL: 12.

b. Predict similarities and differences among the elements in a given group, based on the periodic properties (Section 21.2). Study Question(s) assignable in OWL: 22, 32, 34, 35.

c. Know which reactions produce ionic compounds, and predict formulas for common ions and common ionic compounds based on electron configurations (Section 21.2). Study Question(s) assignable in OWL: 14, 16, 26.

d. Recognize when a formula is incorrectly written, based on general principles governing electron configurations (Section 21.2).

Describe the chemistry of the main group or A-Group elements, particularly H; Na and K; Mg and Ca; B and Al; Si; N and P; O and S; and F and Cl

a. Identify the most abundant elements, know how they are obtained, and list some of their common chemical and physical properties.

b. Be able to summarize briefly a series of facts about the most common compounds of main group elements (ionic or covalent bonding, color, solubility, simple reaction chemistry) (Sections 21.3–21.10). Study Question(s) assignable in OWL: 86, 88.

c. Identify uses of common elements and compounds, and understand the chemistry that relates to their usage (Sections 21.3–21.10).

Apply the principles of stoichiometry, thermodynamics, and electrochemistry to the chemistry of the main group elements
Study Question(s) assignable in OWL: 18, 24, 29, 32, 34, 43, 48, 50, 54, 58, 61, 75, 86, 88.

STUDY QUESTIONS

OWL Online homework for this chapter may be assigned in OWL.

▲ denotes challenging questions.

■ denotes questions assignable in OWL.

Blue-numbered questions have answers in Appendix O and fully-worked solutions in the *Student Solutions Manual*.

Practicing Skills

Properties of the Elements

1. Give examples of two basic oxides. Write equations illustrating the formation of each oxide from its component elements. Write another chemical equation that illustrates the basic character of each oxide.

2. Give examples of two acidic oxides. Write equations illustrating the formation of each oxide from its component elements. Write another chemical equation that illustrates the acidic character of each oxide.

3. Give the name and symbol of each element having the valence configuration [noble gas] ns^2np^1.

4. Give symbols and names for four monatomic ions that have the same electron configuration as argon.

5. Select one of the alkali metals, and write a balanced chemical equation for its reaction with chlorine. Is the reaction likely to be exothermic or endothermic? Is the product ionic or molecular?

6. Select one of the alkaline earth metals and write a balanced chemical equation for its reaction with oxygen. Is the reaction likely to be exothermic or endothermic? Is the product ionic or molecular?

7. For the product of the reaction you selected in Study Question 5, predict the following physical properties: color, state of matter (s, ℓ, or g), solubility in water.

8. For the product of the reaction you selected in Study Question 6, predict the following physical properties: color, state of matter (s, ℓ, or g), solubility in water.

9. Would you expect to find calcium occurring naturally in the earth's crust as a free element? Why or why not?

10. Which of the first 10 elements in the periodic table are found as free elements in the earth's crust? Which elements in this group occur in the earth's crust only as part of a chemical compound?

11. Place the following oxides in order of increasing basicity: CO_2, SiO_2, SnO_2.

12. ■ Place the following oxides in order of increasing basicity: Na_2O, Al_2O_3, SiO_2, SO_3.

13. Complete and balance the equations for the following reactions. [Assume an excess of oxygen for (d).]
    (a) $Na(s) + Br_2(\ell) \rightarrow$
    (b) $Mg(s) + O_2(g) \rightarrow$
    (c) $Al(s) + F_2(g) \rightarrow$
    (d) $C(s) + O_2(g) \rightarrow$

14. ■ Complete and balance the equations for the following reactions:
    (a) $K(s) + I_2(g) \rightarrow$
    (b) $Ba(s) + O_2(g) \rightarrow$
    (c) $Al(s) + S_8(s) \rightarrow$
    (d) $Si(s) + Cl_2(g) \rightarrow$

Hydrogen

15. Write balanced chemical equations for the reaction of hydrogen gas with oxygen, chlorine, and nitrogen.

16. ■ Write an equation for the reaction of potassium and hydrogen. Name the product. Is it ionic or covalent? Predict one physical property and one chemical property of this compound.

17. Write a balanced chemical equation for the preparation of H_2 (and CO) by the reaction of CH_4 and water. Using data in Appendix L, calculate $\Delta_r H°$, $\Delta_r G°$, and $\Delta_r S°$ for this reaction.

18. ■ Using data in Appendix L, calculate $\Delta_r H°$, $\Delta_r G°$, and $\Delta_r S°$ for the reaction of carbon and water to give CO and H_2.

19. A method recently suggested for the preparation of hydrogen (and oxygen) from water proceeds as follows:
    (a) Sulfuric acid and hydrogen iodide are formed from sulfur dioxide, water, and iodine.
    (b) The sulfuric acid from the first step is decomposed by heat to water, sulfur dioxide, and oxygen.
    (c) The hydrogen iodide from the first step is decomposed with heat to hydrogen and iodine.

    Write a balanced equation for each of these steps, and show that their sum is the decomposition of water to form hydrogen and oxygen.

20. Compare the mass of H_2 expected from the reaction of steam (H_2O) per mole of methane, petroleum, and coal. (Assume complete reaction in each case. Use CH_2 and CH as representative formulas for petroleum and coal, respectively.)

Alkali Metals

21. Write equations for the reaction of sodium with each of the halogens. Predict at least two physical properties that are common to all of the alkali metal halides.

22. ■ Write balanced equations for the reaction of lithium, sodium, and potassium with O_2. Specify which metal forms an oxide, which forms a peroxide, and which forms a superoxide.

23. The electrolysis of aqueous NaCl gives NaOH, Cl_2, and H_2.
    (a) Write a balanced equation for the process.
    (b) In the United States, 1.19×10^{10} kg of NaOH and 1.14×10^{10} kg of Cl_2 were produced in a recent year. Does the ratio of masses of NaOH and Cl_2 produced agree with the ratio of masses expected from the balanced equation? If not, what does this tell you about the way in which NaOH and Cl_2 are actually produced? Is the electrolysis of aqueous NaCl the only source of these chemicals?

24. ■ (a) Write equations for the half-reactions that occur at the cathode and the anode when an aqueous solution of KCl is electrolyzed. Which chemical species is oxidized, and which chemical species is reduced in this reaction?
    (b) Predict the products formed when an aqueous solution of CsI is electrolyzed.

Alkaline Earth Elements

25. When magnesium burns in air, it forms both an oxide and a nitride. Write balanced equations for the formation of both compounds.

26. ■ Calcium reacts with hydrogen gas at 300–400 °C to form a hydride. This compound reacts readily with water, so it is an excellent drying agent for organic solvents.
    (a) Write a balanced equation showing the formation of calcium hydride from Ca and H_2.
    (b) Write a balanced equation for the reaction of calcium hydride with water (Figure 21.7).

27. Name three uses of limestone. Write a balanced equation for the reaction of limestone with CO_2 in water.

28. Explain what is meant by "hard water." What causes hard water, and what problems are associated with it?

29. ■ Calcium oxide, CaO, is used to remove SO_2 from power plant exhaust. These two compounds react to give solid $CaSO_3$. What mass of SO_2 can be removed using 1.2×10^3 kg of CaO?

30. $Ca(OH)_2$ has a K_{sp} of 5.5×10^{-5}, whereas K_{sp} for $Mg(OH)_2$ is 5.6×10^{-12}. Calculate the equilibrium constant for the reaction

    $$Ca(OH)_2(s) + Mg^{2+}(aq) \rightleftharpoons Ca^{2+}(aq) + Mg(OH)_2(s)$$

    Explain why this reaction can be used in the commercial isolation of magnesium from sea water.

Boron and Aluminum

31. Draw a possible structure for the cyclic anion in the salt $K_3B_3O_6$ and the anion in $Ca_2B_2O_5$.

32. ■ The boron trihalides (except BF_3) hydrolyze completely to boric acid and the acid HX.
    (a) Write a balanced equation for the reaction of BCl_3 with water.
    (b) Calculate $\Delta_rH°$ for the hydrolysis of BCl_3 using data in Appendix L and the following information: $\Delta_fH°$ [$BCl_3(g)$] = -403 kJ/mol; $\Delta_fH°$ [$B(OH)_3(s)$] = -1094 kJ/mol.

33. When boron hydrides burn in air, the reaction is very exothermic.
    (a) Write a balanced equation for the combustion of $B_5H_9(g)$ in air to give $B_2O_3(s)$ and $H_2O(\ell)$.
    (b) Calculate the enthalpy of combustion for $B_5H_9(g)$ ($\Delta_fH°$ = 73.2 kJ/mol), and compare it with the enthalpy of combustion of B_2H_6 on page 984. (The enthalpy of formation of $B_2O_3(s)$ is -1271.9 kJ/mol.)
    (c) Compare the enthalpy of combustion of $C_2H_6(g)$ with that of $B_2H_6(g)$. Which transfers more energy as heat per gram?

34. ■ Diborane can be prepared by the reaction of $NaBH_4$ and I_2. Which substance is oxidized, and which is reduced?

35. ■ Write balanced equations for the reactions of aluminum with HCl(aq), Cl_2, and O_2.

36. (a) Write a balanced equation for the reaction of Al and $H_2O(\ell)$ to produce H_2 and Al_2O_3.
    (b) Using thermodynamic data in Appendix L, calculate $\Delta_rH°$, $\Delta_rS°$, and $\Delta_rG°$ for this reaction. Do these data indicate that the reaction should favor the products?
    (c) Why is aluminum metal unaffected by water?

37. Aluminum dissolves readily in hot aqueous NaOH to give the aluminate ion, $[Al(OH)_4]^-$, and H_2. Write a balanced equation for this reaction. If you begin with 13.2 g of Al, what volume (in milliliters) of H_2 gas is produced when the gas is measured at 22.5 °C and a pressure of 735 mm Hg?

38. Alumina, Al_2O_3, is amphoteric. Among examples of its amphoteric character are the reactions that occur when Al_2O_3 is heated strongly or "fused" with acidic oxides and basic oxides.
    (a) Write a balanced equation for the reaction of alumina with silica, an acidic oxide, to give aluminum metasilicate, $Al_2(SiO_3)_3$.
    (b) Write a balanced equation for the reaction of alumina with the basic oxide CaO to give calcium aluminate, $Ca(AlO_2)_2$.

39. Aluminum sulfate is the most commercially important aluminum compound, after aluminum oxide and aluminum hydroxide. It is produced from the reaction of aluminum oxide and sulfuric acid. What mass (in kilograms) of aluminum oxide and sulfuric acid must be used to manufacture 1.00 kg of aluminum sulfate?

40. "Aerated" concrete bricks are widely used building materials. They are obtained by mixing gas-forming additives with a moist mixture of lime, cement, and possibly sand. Industrially, the following reaction is important:

$$2 \text{ Al(s)} + 3 \text{ Ca(OH)}_2(s) + 6 \text{ H}_2\text{O}(\ell) \rightarrow$$
$$3 \text{ CaO} \cdot \text{Al}_2\text{O}_3 \cdot 6 \text{ H}_2\text{O}(s) + 3 \text{ H}_2(g)$$

Assume that the mixture of reactants contains 0.56 g of Al (as well as excess calcium hydroxide and water) for each brick. What volume of hydrogen gas do you expect at 26 °C and a pressure of 745 mm Hg)?

Silicon

41. Describe the structure of pyroxenes (see page 988). What is the ratio of silicon to oxygen in this type of silicate?

42. Describe how ultrapure silicon can be produced from sand.

43. ■ Silicate structures: Draw a structure, and give the charge for a silicate anion with the formula $[\text{Si}_6\text{O}_{18}]^{n-}$.

44. Silicates often have chain, ribbon, or sheet structures. One of the simpler ribbon structures is $[\text{Si}_2\text{O}_5{}^{2-}]_n$. Draw a structure for this anionic material.

Nitrogen and Phosphorus

45. Consult the data in Appendix L. Are any of the nitrogen oxides listed there stable with respect to decomposition to N_2 and O_2?

46. Use data in Appendix L to calculate the enthalpy and free energy change for the reaction

$$2 \text{ NO}_2(g) \rightarrow \text{N}_2\text{O}_4(g)$$

Is this reaction exothermic or endothermic? Is the reaction product- or reactant-favored?

47. Use data in Appendix L to calculate the enthalpy and free energy change for the reaction

$$2 \text{ NO}(g) + \text{O}_2(g) \rightarrow 2 \text{ NO}_2(g)$$

Is this reaction exothermic or endothermic? Is the reaction product- or reactant-favored?

48. ■ The overall reaction involved in the industrial synthesis of nitric acid is

$$\text{NH}_3(g) + 2 \text{ O}_2(g) \rightarrow \text{HNO}_3(aq) + \text{H}_2\text{O}(\ell)$$

Calculate $\Delta_r G°$ for this reaction and its equilibrium constant at 25 °C.

49. A major use of hydrazine, N_2H_4, is in steam boilers in power plants.
(a) The reaction of hydrazine with O_2 dissolved in water gives N_2 and water. Write a balanced equation for this reaction.

(b) O_2 dissolves in water to the extent of 0.0044 g in 100. mL of water at 20 °C. To consume all of the dissolved O_2 in 3.00×10^4 L of water (enough to fill a small swimming pool), what mass of N_2H_4 is needed?

50. ■ Before hydrazine came into use to remove dissolved oxygen in the water in steam boilers, Na_2SO_3 was commonly used for this purpose:

$$2 \text{ Na}_2\text{SO}_3(aq) + \text{O}_2(aq) \rightarrow 2 \text{ Na}_2\text{SO}_4(aq)$$

What mass of Na_2SO_3 is required to remove O_2 from 3.00×10^4 L of water as outlined in Study Question 49?

51. Review the structure of phosphorous acid in Table 21.6.
(a) What is the oxidation number of the phosphorus atom in this acid?
(b) Draw the structure of diphosphorous acid, $\text{H}_4\text{P}_2\text{O}_5$. What is the maximum number of protons this acid can dissociate in water?

52. Unlike carbon, which can form extended chains of atoms, nitrogen can form chains of very limited length. Draw the Lewis electron dot structure of the azide ion, $\text{N}_3{}^-$. Is the ion linear or bent?

Oxygen and Sulfur

53. In the "contact process" for making sulfuric acid, sulfur is first burned to SO_2. Environmental restrictions allow no more than 0.30% of this SO_2 to be vented to the atmosphere.
(a) If enough sulfur is burned in a plant to produce 1.80×10^6 kg of pure, anhydrous H_2SO_4 per day, what is the maximum amount of SO_2 that is allowed to be exhausted to the atmosphere?
(b) One way to prevent any SO_2 from reaching the atmosphere is to "scrub" the exhaust gases with slaked lime, Ca(OH)_2:

$$\text{Ca(OH)}_2(s) + \text{SO}_2(g) \rightarrow \text{CaSO}_3(s) + \text{H}_2\text{O}(\ell)$$

$$2 \text{ CaSO}_3(s) + \text{O}_2(g) \rightarrow 2 \text{ CaSO}_4(s)$$

What mass of Ca(OH)_2 (in kilograms) is needed to remove the SO_2 calculated in part (a)?

54. ■ A sulfuric acid plant produces an enormous amount of heat. To keep costs as low as possible, much of this heat is used to make steam to generate electricity. Some of the electricity is used to run the plant, and the excess is sold to the local electrical utility. Three reactions are important in sulfuric acid production:
(1) burning S to SO_2; (2) oxidation of SO_2 to SO_3; and (3) reaction of SO_3 with H_2O:

$$\text{SO}_3(g) + \text{H}_2\text{O (in 98\% H}_2\text{SO}_4) \rightarrow \text{H}_2\text{SO}_4(\ell)$$

The enthalpy change of the third reaction is -130 kJ/mol. Estimate the enthalpy change when 1.00 mol of S is used to produce 1.00 mol of H_2SO_4. How much energy is produced per metric ton of H_2SO_4?

▲ more challenging   ■ in OWL   Blue-numbered questions answered in Appendix O

55. Sulfur forms anionic chains of S atoms called polysulfides. Draw a Lewis electron dot structure for the S_2^{2-} ion. The S_2^{2-} ion is the disulfide ion, an analogue of the peroxide ion. It occurs in iron pyrites, FeS_2.

56. Sulfur forms a range of compounds with fluorine. Draw Lewis electron dot structures for S_2F_2 (connectivity is FSSF), SF_2, SF_4, SF_6, and S_2F_{10}. What is the oxidation number of sulfur in each of these compounds?

Fluorine and Chlorine

57. The halogen oxides and oxoanions are good oxidizing agents. For example, the reduction of bromate ion has an $E°$ value of 1.44 V in acid solution:

$$2\ BrO_3^-(aq)\ +\ 12\ H^+(aq)\ +\ 10\ e^- \rightarrow$$
$$Br_2(aq)\ +\ 6\ H_2O(\ell)$$

Is it possible to oxidize aqueous 1.0 M Mn^{2+} to aqueous MnO_4^- with 1.0 M bromate ion?

58. ■ The hypohalite ions, XO^-, are the anions of weak acids. Calculate the pH of a 0.10 M solution of NaClO. What is the concentration of HClO in this solution?

59. Bromine is obtained from brine wells. The process involves treating water containing bromide ion with Cl_2 and extracting the Br_2 from the solution using an organic solvent. Write a balanced equation for the reaction of Cl_2 and Br^-. What are the oxidizing and reducing agents in this reaction? Using the table of standard reduction potentials (Appendix M), verify that this is a product-favored reaction.

60. To prepare chlorine from chloride ion a strong oxidizing agent is required. The dichromate ion, $Cr_2O_7^{2-}$, is one example (see Figure 21.32). Consult the table of standard reduction potentials (Appendix M), and identify several other oxidizing agents that may be suitable. Write balanced equations for the reactions of these substances with chloride ion.

61. ■ If an electrolytic cell for producing F_2 (Figure 21.31) operates at 5.00×10^3 A (at 10.0 V), what mass of F_2 can be produced per 24-hour day? Assume the conversion of F^- to F_2 is 100%.

62. Halogens combine with one another to produce *interhalogens* such as BrF_3. Sketch a possible molecular structure for this molecule, and decide if the F—Br—F bond angles will be less than or greater than ideal.

General Questions

The questions are not designated as to type or location in the chapter. They may combine several concepts.

63. For each of the third-period elements (Na through Ar), identify the following:
    (a) whether the element is a metal, nonmetal, or metalloid
    (b) the color and appearance of the element

(c) the state of the element (s, ℓ, or g) under standard conditions

For help in this question, consult Figure 2.4 or use the periodic table "tool" in ChemistryNow. The latter provides a picture of each element and a listing of its properties.

64. Consider the chemistries of C, Si, Ge, and Sn.
    (a) Write a balanced chemical equation to depict the reaction of each element with elemental chlorine.
    (b) Describe the bonding in each of the products of the reactions with chlorine as ionic or covalent.
    (c) Compare the reactions, if any, of some Group 4A chlorides —CCl_4, $SiCl_4$, and $SnCl_4$— with water.

65. Consider the chemistries of the elements potassium, calcium, gallium, germanium, and arsenic.
    (a) Write a balanced chemical equation depicting the reaction of each element with elemental chlorine.
    (b) Describe the bonding in each of the products of the reactions with chlorine as ionic or covalent.
    (c) Draw Lewis electron dot structures for the products of the reactions of gallium and arsenic with chlorine. What are their electron-pair and molecular geometries?

66. When BCl_3 gas is passed through an electric discharge, small amounts of the reactive molecule B_2Cl_4 are produced. (The molecule has a B—B covalent bond.)
    (a) Draw a Lewis electron dot structure for B_2Cl_4.
    (b) Describe the hybridization of the B atoms in the molecule and the geometry around each B atom.

67. Complete and balance the following equations.
    (a) $KClO_3$ + heat →
    (b) $H_2S(g)$ + $O_2(g)$ →
    (c) $Na(s)$ + $O_2(g)$ →
    (d) $P_4(s)$ + $KOH(aq)$ + $H_2O(\ell)$ →
    (e) $NH_4NO_3(s)$ + heat →
    (f) $In(s)$ + $Br_2(\ell)$ →
    (g) $SnCl_4(\ell)$ + $H_2O(\ell)$ →

68. (a) Heating barium oxide in pure oxygen gives barium peroxide. Write a balanced equation for this reaction.
    (b) Barium peroxide is an excellent oxidizing agent. Write a balanced equation for the reaction of iron with barium peroxide to give iron(III) oxide and barium oxide.

69. Worldwide production of silicon carbide, SiC, is several hundred thousand tons annually. If you want to produce 1.0×10^5 metric tons of SiC, what mass (metric tons) of silicon sand (SiO_2) will you use if 70% of the sand is converted to SiC?

70. To store 2.88 kg of gasoline with an energy equivalence of 1.43×10^8 J requires a volume of 4.1 L. In comparison, 1.0 kg of H_2 has the same energy equivalence. What volume is required if this quantity of H_2 is to be stored at 25 °C and 1.0 atm of pressure?

▲ more challenging   ■ in OWL   Blue-numbered questions answered in Appendix O

71. Using data in Appendix L, calculate $\Delta_r G°$ values for the decomposition of MCO_3 to MO and CO_2 where M = Mg, Ca, Ba. What is the relative tendency of these carbonates to decompose?

72. Ammonium perchlorate is used as the oxidizer in the solid-fuel booster rockets of the Space Shuttle. Assume that one launch requires 700 tons (6.35×10^5 kg) of the salt, and the salt decomposes according to the equation on page 1009.
    (a) What mass of water is produced? What mass of O_2 is produced?
    (b) If the O_2 produced is assumed to react with the powdered aluminum present in the rocket engine, what mass of aluminum is required to use up all of the O_2?
    (c) What mass of Al_2O_3 is produced?

73. ▲ Metals react with hydrogen halides (such as HCl) to give the metal halide and hydrogen:

$$M(s) + n\,HX(g) \rightarrow MX_n(s) + \tfrac{1}{2}n\,H_2(g)$$

The free energy change for the reaction is $\Delta_r G° = \Delta_f G° (MX_n) - n\,\Delta_f G° [HX(g)]$
    (a) $\Delta_f G°$ for HCl(g) is -95.1 kJ/mol. What must be the value for $\Delta_f G°$ for MX_n for the reaction to be product-favored?
    (b) Which of the following metals is (are) predicted to have product-favored reactions with HCl(g): Ba, Pb, Hg, Ti?

74. Halogens form polyhalide ions. Sketch Lewis electron dot structures and molecular structures for the following ions:
    (a) I_3^-
    (b) $BrCl_2^-$
    (c) ClF_2^+
    (d) An iodide ion and two iodine molecules form the I_5^- ion. Here, the ion has five I atoms in a row, but the ion is not linear. Draw the Lewis dot structure for the ion, and propose a structure for the ion.

75. ■ The standard enthalpy of formation of OF_2 gas is $+24.5$ kJ/mol. Calculate the average O—F bond enthalpy.

76. Calcium fluoride can be used in the fluoridation of municipal water supplies. If you want to achieve a fluoride ion concentration of 2.0×10^{-5} M, what mass of CaF_2 must you use for 1.0×10^6 L of water?

77. The steering rockets in the Space Shuttle use N_2O_4 and a derivative of hydrazine, 1,1-dimethylhydrazine (page 249). This mixture is called a *hypergolic fuel* because it ignites when the reactants come into contact:

$$H_2NN(CH_3)_2(\ell) + 2\,N_2O_4(\ell) \rightarrow$$
$$3\,N_2(g) + 4\,H_2O(g) + 2\,CO_2(g)$$

    (a) Identify the oxidizing agent and the reducing agent in this reaction.

(b) The same propulsion system was used by the Lunar Lander on moon missions in the 1970s. If the Lander used 4100 kg of $H_2NN(CH_3)_2$, what mass (in kilograms) of N_2O_4 was required to react with it? What mass (in kilograms) of each of the reaction products was generated?

78. ▲ Liquid HCN is dangerously unstable with respect to trimer formation—that is, formation of $(HCN)_3$ with a cyclic structure.
    (a) Propose a structure for this cyclic trimer.
    (b) Estimate the energy of the trimerization reaction using bond dissociation enthalpies (Table 8.10).

79. Use $\Delta_f H°$ data in Appendix L to calculate the enthalpy change of the reaction

$$2\,N_2(g) + 5\,O_2(g) + 2\,H_2O(\ell) \rightarrow 4\,HNO_3(aq)$$

Speculate on whether such a reaction could be used to "fix" nitrogen. Would research to find ways to accomplish this reaction be a useful endeavor?

80. ▲ Phosphorus forms an extensive series of oxoanions.
    (a) Draw a structure, and give the charge for an oxophosphate anion with the formula $[P_4O_{13}]^{n-}$. How many ionizable H atoms should the completely protonated acid have?
    (b) Draw a structure, and give the charge for an oxophosphate anion with the formula $[P_4O_{12}]^{n-}$. How many ionizable H atoms should the completely protonated acid have?

81. Boron and hydrogen form an extensive family of compounds, and the diagram below shows how they are related by reaction.

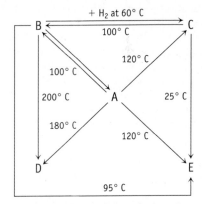

The following table gives the weight percent of boron in each of the compounds. Derive the empirical and molecular formulas of compounds A–D.

Substance	State (at STP)	Mass Percent B	Molar mass (g/mol)
A	Gas	78.3	27.7
B	Gas	81.2	53.3
C	Liquid	83.1	65.1
D	Liquid	85.7	63.1
E	Solid	88.5	122.2

82. ▲ In 1774, C. Scheele obtained a gas by reacting pyrolusite (MnO_2) with sulfuric acid. The gas, which had been obtained that same year by Joseph Priestley by a different method, was an element, **A**.
    (a) What is the element isolated by Scheele and Priestley?
    (b) Element **A** combines with almost all other elements. For example, with cesium it gives a compound in which the mass percent of **A** is 19.39%. The element combines with hydrogen to give a compound with a mass percent of element **A** of 94.12%. Determine the formulas of the cesium and hydrogen compounds.
    (c) The compounds of cesium and hydrogen with element **A** react with one another. Write a balanced equation for the reaction.

In the Laboratory

83. One material needed to make silicones is dichlorodimethylsilane, $(CH_3)_2SiCl_2$. It is made by treating silicon powder at about 300 °C with CH_3Cl in the presence of a copper-containing catalyst.
    (a) Write a balanced equation for the reaction.
    (b) Assume you carry out the reaction on a small scale with 2.65 g of silicon. To measure the CH_3Cl gas, you fill a 5.60-L flask at 24.5 °C. What pressure of CH_3Cl gas must you have in the flask to have the stoichiometrically correct amount of the compound?
    (c) What mass of $(CH_3)_2SiCl_2$ can be produced from 2.65 g of Si and excess CH_3Cl?

84. Sodium borohydride, $NaBH_4$, reduces many metal ions to the metal.
    (a) Write a balanced equation for the reaction of $NaBH_4$ with $AgNO_3$ in water to give silver metal, H_2 gas, boric acid, and sodium nitrate (page 984).
    (b) What mass of silver can be produced from 575 mL of 0.011 M $AgNO_3$ and 13.0 g of $NaBH_4$?

85. A common analytical method for hydrazine involves its oxidation with iodate ion, IO_3^-, in acid solution. In the process, hydrazine acts as a four-electron reducing agent.

$$N_2(g) + 5 H_3O^+(aq) + 4 e^- \rightarrow$$
$$N_2H_5^+(aq) + 5 H_2O(\ell) \quad E° = -0.23 \text{ V}$$

Write the balanced equation for the reaction of hydrazine in acid solution ($N_2H_5^+$) with $IO_3^-(aq)$ to give N_2 and I_2. Calculate $E°$ for this reaction.

86. ■ When 1.00 g of a white solid **A** is strongly heated, you obtain another white solid, **B**, and a gas. An experiment is carried out on the gas, showing that it exerts a pressure of 209 mm Hg in a 450-mL flask at 25 °C. Bubbling the gas into a solution of $Ca(OH)_2$ gives another white solid, **C**. If the white solid **B** is added to water, the resulting solution turns red litmus paper blue.

Addition of aqueous HCl to the solution of **B** and evaporation of the resulting solution to dryness yield 1.055 g of a white solid **D**. When **D** is placed in a Bunsen burner flame, it colors the flame green. Finally, if the aqueous solution of **B** is treated with sulfuric acid, a white precipitate, **E**, forms. Identify the lettered compounds in the reaction scheme.

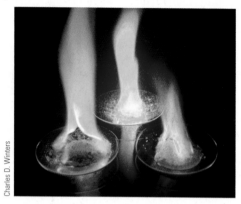

Charles D. Winters

The salts $CaCl_2$, $SrCl_2$, and $BaCl_2$ were suspended in methanol. When the methanol is set ablaze, the heat of combustion causes the salts to emit light of characteristic wavelengths: calcium salts are yellow; strontium salts are red; and barium salts are green-yellow.

87. ▲ In 1937, R. Schwartz and M. Schmiesser prepared a yellow-orange bromine oxide (BrO_2) by treating Br_2 with ozone in a fluorocarbon solvent. Many years later, J. Pascal found that, on heating, this oxide decomposed to two other oxides, a less volatile golden yellow oxide (**A**) and a more volatile deep-brown oxide (**B**). Oxide **B** was later identified as Br_2O. To determine the formula for oxide **A**, a sample was treated with iodide ion. The reaction liberated iodine, which was titrated to an equivalence point with 17.7 mL of 0.065 M sodium thiosulfate.

$$I_2(aq) + 2 S_2O_3^{2-}(aq) \rightarrow 2 I^-(aq) + S_4O_6^{2-}(aq)$$

Compound **A** was also treated with $AgNO_3$, and 14.4 mL of 0.020 M $AgNO_3$ was required to completely precipitate the bromine from the sample.
    (a) What is the formula of the unknown bromine oxide A?
    (b) Draw Lewis structures for **A** and Br_2O. Speculate on their molecular geometry.

88. ■ A mixture of PCl_5 (12.41 g) and excess NH_4Cl was heated at 145 °C for six hours. The two reacted in equimolar amounts and evolved 5.14 L of HCl (at STP). Three substances (**A**, **B**, and **C**) were isolated from the reaction mixture. The three substances had the same elemental composition but differed in their molar mass. Substance **A**, had a molar mass of 347.7 g/mol and **B** had a molar mass of 463.5 g/mol. Give the empirical and molecular formulas for **A** and **B** and draw a reasonable Lewis structure for **A**.

▲ more challenging ■ in OWL   Blue-numbered questions answered in Appendix O

Summary and Conceptual Questions

The following questions may use concepts from this and previous chapters.

89. Dinitrogen trioxide, N_2O_3, has the structure shown here.

The oxide is unstable, decomposing to NO and NO_2 in the gas phase at 25 °C.

$$N_2O_3(g) \rightarrow NO(g) + NO_2(g)$$

(a) Explain why one N—O bond distance in N_2O_3 is 114.2 pm, whereas the other two bonds are longer (121 pm) and nearly equal to each other.

(b) For the decomposition reaction, $\Delta_rH° = +40.5$ kJ/mol and $\Delta_rG° = -1.59$ kJ/mol. Calculate $\Delta S°$ and K for the reaction at 298 K.

(c) Calculate $\Delta_fH°$ for $N_2O_3(g)$.

90. ▲ The density of lead is 11.350 g/cm^3, and the metal crystallizes in a face-centered cubic unit cell. Estimate the radius of the lead atom.

91. You have a 1.0-L flask that contains a mixture of argon and hydrogen. The pressure inside the flask is 745 mm Hg, and the temperature is 22 °C. Describe an experiment that you could use to determine the percentage of hydrogen in this mixture.

92. The boron atom in boric acid, $B(OH)_3$, is bonded to three —OH groups. In the solid state, the —OH groups are in turn hydrogen-bonded to —OH groups in neighboring molecules.

(a) Draw the Lewis structure for boric acid.

(b) What is the hybridization of the boron atom in the acid?

(c) Sketch a picture showing how hydrogen bonding can occur between neighboring molecules.

93. How would you extinguish a sodium fire in the laboratory? What is the worst thing you could do?

94. Tin(IV) oxide, cassiterite, is the main ore of tin. It crystallizes in a rutile-like unit cell (Question 4, page 611).

(a) How many tin(IV) ions and oxide ions are there per unit cell of this oxide?

(b) Is it thermodynamically feasible to transform solid SnO_2 into liquid $SnCl_4$ by reaction of the oxide with gaseous HCl? What is the equilibrium constant for this reaction at 25 °C?

95. You are given a stoppered flask that contains hydrogen, nitrogen, or oxygen. Suggest an experiment to identify the gas.

96. The structure of nitric acid is illustrated on page 993.

(a) Why are the N—O bonds the same length, and why are both shorter than the N—OH bond length?

(b) Rationalize the bond angles in the molecule.

(c) What is the hybridization of the central N atom? Which orbitals overlap to form the N—O π bond?

97. Assume an electrolysis cell that produces chlorine from aqueous sodium chloride operates at 4.6 V (with a current of 3.0×10^5 A). Calculate the number of kilowatt-hours of energy required to produce 1.00 kg of chlorine (1 kWh = 1 kilowatt-hour = 3.6×10^6 J).

98. Sodium metal is produced by electrolysis of molten sodium chloride. The cell operates at 7.0 V with a current of 25×10^3 A.

(a) What mass of sodium can be produced in 1 h?

(b) How many kilowatt-hours of electricity are used to produce 1.00 kg of sodium metal (1 kWh = 3.6×10^6 J)?

99. The reduction potentials for the Group 3A metals, $E°$, are given below. What trend or trends do you observe in these data? What can you learn about the chemistry of the Group 3A elements from these data?

Half-Reaction	Reduction Potential ($E°$, V)
$Al^{3+}(aq) + 3 e^- \longrightarrow Al(s)$	−1.66
$Ga^{3+}(aq) + 3 e^- \longrightarrow Ga(s)$	−0.53
$In^{3+}(aq) + 3 e^- \longrightarrow In(s)$	−0.338
$Tl^{3+}(aq) + 3 e^- \longrightarrow Tl(s)$	+0.72

100. (a) Magnesium is obtained from sea water. If the concentration of Mg^{2+} in sea water is 0.050 M, what volume of sea water (in liters) must be treated to obtain 1.00 kg of magnesium metal? What mass of lime (CaO; in kilograms) must be used to precipitate the magnesium in this volume of sea water?

(b) When 1.2×10^3 kg of molten $MgCl_2$ is electrolyzed to produce magnesium, what mass (in kilograms) of metal is produced at the cathode? What is produced at the anode? What is the mass of this product? What is the total number of faradays of electricity used in the process?

(c) One industrial process has an energy consumption of 18.5 kWh/kg of Mg. How many joules are required per mole (1 kWh = 1 kilowatt-hour = 3.6×10^6 J)? How does this energy compare with the energy of the following process?

$$MgCl_2(s) \rightarrow Mg(s) + Cl_2(g)?$$

22 | The Chemistry of the Transition Elements

Memory Metal

In the 1960s, William J. Buehler, an engineer at the Naval Ordnance Laboratory in Maryland, was looking for a material for use in the nose cone of a Navy missile. It was important that the material be impact- and heat-resistant and not lose these properties when bent and shaped. He prepared long, thin strips of an alloy of nickel and titanium to demonstrate that it could be folded and unfolded many times without breaking. At a meeting to discuss this material, one of his associates held a cigarette lighter to a folded-up piece of metal and was amazed to observe that the metal strip immediately unfolded and assumed its original shape. Thus, memory metal was discovered. This unusual alloy is now called *nitinol*, a name constructed out of "nickel," "titanium," and "Naval Ordnance Laboratory."

Memory metal is an alloy with roughly the same number of Ni and Ti atoms. When the atoms are arranged in the highly symmetrical austenite phase, the alloy is relatively rigid. In this phase a specific shape is established that will be "remembered." If the alloy is cooled below

Nitinol frames for glasses. Can you do this with your eye glasses? If you can, it is likely they are made of nitinol, a nickel–titanium alloy. They snap back to the proper fit even after being twisted like a pretzel.

NASA/Science Source/Photo Researchers, Inc.

its "phase transition temperature," it enters a less symmetrical but flexible phase (martensite). Below this transition temperature, the metal is fairly soft and may be bent and twisted out of shape. When warmed above the phase transition temperature, nitinol returns to its original shape. The temperature at which the change in shape occurs varies with small differences in the nickel-to-titanium ratio.

Besides eye glasses frames, nitinol is now used in stents to reinforce blood vessels and in orthodontics.

Questions:

1. What are the dimensions of the austenite unit cell? Assume the Ti and Ni atoms are just touching along the unit cell diagonal. (Atom radii: Ti = 145 pm; Ni = 125 pm.)
2. Calculate the density of nitinol based on the austenite unit cell parameters. Does the calculated density of the austenite unit cell agree with the reported density of 6.5 g/cm³?
3. Are Ti and Ni atoms paramagnetic or diamagnetic?

Answers to these questions are in Appendix Q.

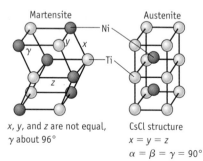

Martensite   Austenite

— Ni
— Ti

x, y, and z are not equal, γ about 96°

CsCl structure
$x = y = z$
$\alpha = \beta = \gamma = 90°$

Two phases of nitinol. The austenite form has a structure like CsCl (page 622).

The transition elements are the large block of elements in the central portion of the periodic table. All are metals and bridge the *s*-block elements at the left and the *p*-block elements on the right (Figure 22.1). The transition elements are often divided into two groups, depending on the valence electrons involved in their chemistry. The first group are the **d-block elements,** because their occurrence in the periodic table coincides with the filling of the *d* orbitals. The second group are the **f-block elements,** characterized by filling of the *f* orbitals. Contained within this group of elements are two subgroups: the *lanthanides,* elements that occur between La and Hf, and the *actinides,* elements that occur between Ac and Rf.

This chapter focuses primarily on the *d*-block elements, and within this group we concentrate mainly on the elements in the fourth period, that is, the elements of the first transition series, scandium to zinc.

Chemistry Now™

Throughout the text this icon introduces an opportunity for self-study or to explore interactive tutorials by signing in at **www.cengage.com/login**.

22.1 Properties of the Transition Elements

The *d*-block metals include elements with a wide range of properties. They encompass the most common metal used in construction and manufacturing (iron), metals that are valued for their beauty (gold, silver, and platinum), and metals used

Fourth-period transition metals:
left to right, Ti, V, Cr, Mn, Fe, Co, Ni, Cu

FIGURE 22.1 The transition metals. The *d*-block elements (transition elements) and *f*-block elements are highlighted in a darker shade of purple.

Group 8B: platinum (Pt)

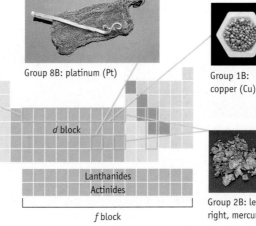

d block

Lanthanides
Actinides

f block

Group 1B: copper (Cu)

Group 1B: silver (Ag)

Group 1B: gold (Au)

Group 2B: left, zinc (Zn); right, mercury (Hg)

Photos: Charles D. Winters

in coins (nickel, copper, and zinc). There are metals used in modern technology (titanium) and metals known and used in early civilizations (copper, silver, gold, and iron). The d-block contains the densest elements (osmium, $d = 22.49$ g/cm^3, and iridium, $d = 22.41$ g/cm^3), the metals with the highest and lowest melting points (tungsten, mp = 3410 °C, and mercury, mp = -38.9 °C), and one of two radioactive elements with atomic numbers less than 83 [technetium (Tc), atomic number 43; the other is promethium (Pm), atomic number 61, in the f-block].

With the exception of mercury, the transition elements are solids, often with high melting and boiling points. They have a metallic sheen and conduct electricity and heat. They react with various oxidizing agents to give ionic compounds. There is considerable variation in such reactions among the elements, however. Because silver, gold, and platinum resist oxidation, for example, they are used for jewelry and decorative items.

Certain d-block elements are particularly important in living organisms. Cobalt is the crucial element in vitamin B$_{12}$, which is part of a catalyst essential for several biochemical reactions. Hemoglobin and myoglobin, oxygen-carrying and storage proteins, contain iron (see page 1033). Molybdenum and iron, together with sulfur, form the reactive portion of nitrogenase, a biological catalyst used by nitrogen-fixing organisms to convert atmospheric nitrogen into ammonia.

Many transition metal compounds are highly colored, which makes them useful as pigments in paints and dyes (Figure 22.2). Prussian blue, $Fe_4[Fe(CN)_6]_3 \cdot 14$ H$_2$O is a "bluing agent" used in engineering blueprints and in the laundry to brighten yellowed white cloth. A common pigment (artist's cadmium yellow) contains cadmium sulfide (CdS), and the white in most white paints is titanium(IV) oxide, TiO$_2$.

The presence of transition metal ions in crystalline silicates or alumina transforms these common materials into gemstones. Iron(II) ions cause the yellow color in citrine, and chromium(III) ions produce the red color of a ruby. Transition metal complexes in small quantities add color to glass. Blue glass contains a small amount of a cobalt(III) oxide, and addition of chromium(III) oxide to glass gives a green color. Old window panes sometimes take on a purple color over time as a

(a) Paint pigments: yellow, CdS; green, Cr$_2$O$_3$; white, TiO$_2$ and ZnO; purple, Mn$_3$(PO$_4$)$_2$; blue, Co$_2$O$_3$ and Al$_2$O$_3$; ochre, Fe$_2$O$_3$.

(b) Small amounts of transition metal compounds are used to color glass: blue, Co$_2$O$_3$; green, copper or chromium oxides; purple, nickel or cobalt oxides; red, copper oxide; iridescent green, uranium oxide.

(c) Traces of transition metal ions are responsible for the colors of green jade (iron), red corundum (chromium), blue azurite, blue-green turquoise (copper), and purple amethyst (iron).

FIGURE 22.2 Colorful chemistry. Transition metal compounds are often colored, a property that leads to specific uses.

consequence of oxidation of traces of manganese(II) ion present in the glass to permanganate ion (MnO_4^-).

In the next few pages, we will examine the properties of the transition elements, concentrating on the underlying principles that govern these properties.

Electron Configurations

Because chemical behavior is related to electron structure, it is important to know the electron configurations of the d-block elements (Table 22.1) and their common ions (◄ Section 7.4). Recall that the configuration of these metals has the general form [noble gas core]$(n - 1)d^b ns^a$; that is, valence electrons for the transition elements reside in the ns and $(n - 1)d$ subshells.

Oxidation and Reduction

A characteristic chemical property of all metals is that they undergo oxidation by a wide range of oxidizing agents such as oxygen, the halogens, and aqueous acids. Standard reduction potentials for the elements of the first transition series can be used to predict which elements will be oxidized by a given oxidizing agent. For example, all of these metals except vanadium and copper are oxidized by aqueous HCl (Table 22.2). This feature, which dominates the chemistry of these elements, is sometimes highly undesirable (see *Chemical Perspectives: Corrosion of Iron*, page 1023.)

When a transition metal is oxidized, the outermost s electrons are removed, followed by one or more d electrons. With a few exceptions, transition metal ions have the electron configuration [noble gas core]$(n - 1)d^x$. In contrast to ions formed by main group elements, transition metal cations often possess unpaired electrons, resulting in paramagnetism (◄ page 292). They are frequently colored as well, due to the absorption of light in the visible region of the electromagnetic spectrum. Color and magnetism figure prominently in a discussion of the properties and bonding of these elements, as you shall see shortly.

In the first transition series, the most commonly encountered metal ions have oxidation numbers of +2 and +3 (Table 22.2). With iron, for example, oxidation

TABLE 22.1 Electron Configurations of the Fourth-Period Transition Elements

	spdf Configuration	Box Notation (3d)	4s
Sc	[Ar]$3d^1 4s^2$	↑ _ _ _ _	↑↓
Ti	[Ar]$3d^2 4s^2$	↑ ↑ _ _ _	↑↓
V	[Ar]$3d^3 4s^2$	↑ ↑ ↑ _ _	↑↓
Cr	[Ar]$3d^5 4s^1$	↑ ↑ ↑ ↑ ↑	↑
Mn	[Ar]$3d^5 4s^2$	↑ ↑ ↑ ↑ ↑	↑↓
Fe	[Ar]$3d^6 4s^2$	↑↓ ↑ ↑ ↑ ↑	↑↓
Co	[Ar]$3d^7 4s^2$	↑↓ ↑↓ ↑ ↑ ↑	↑↓
Ni	[Ar]$3d^8 4s^2$	↑↓ ↑↓ ↑↓ ↑ ↑	↑↓
Cu	[Ar]$3d^{10} 4s^1$	↑↓ ↑↓ ↑↓ ↑↓ ↑↓	↑
Zn	[Ar]$3d^{10} 4s^2$	↑↓ ↑↓ ↑↓ ↑↓ ↑↓	↑↓

TABLE 22.2 Products from Reactions of the Elements in the First Transition Series with O_2, Cl_2, or Aqueous HCl

Element	Reaction with O_2*	Reaction with Cl_2	Reaction with Aqueous HCl
Scandium	Sc_2O_3	$ScCl_3$	$Sc^{3+}(aq)$
Titanium	TiO_2	$TiCl_4$	$Ti^{3+}(aq)$
Vanadium	V_2O_5	VCl_4	NR†
Chromium	Cr_2O_3	$CrCl_3$	$Cr^{2+}(aq)$
Manganese	MnO_2	$MnCl_2$	$Mn^{2+}(aq)$
Iron	Fe_2O_3	$FeCl_3$	$Fe^{2+}(aq)$
Cobalt	Co_2O_3	$CoCl_2$	$Co^{2+}(aq)$
Nickel	NiO	$NiCl_2$	$Ni^{2+}(aq)$
Copper	CuO	$CuCl_2$	NR†
Zinc	ZnO	$ZnCl_2$	$Zn^{2+}(aq)$

* Product obtained with excess oxygen.
† NR = no reaction.

Charles D. Winters

Prussian blue. When Fe^{3+} ions are added to $[Fe(CN)_6]^{4-}$ ions in water (or Fe^{2+} ions are added to $[Fe(CN)_6]^{3-}$ ions), a deep blue compound called Prussian blue forms. The formula of the compound is $Fe_4[Fe(CN)_6]_3 \cdot 14\ H_2O$. The color arises from electron transfer between the Fe(II) and Fe(III) ions in the compound.

FIGURE 22.3 Typical reactions of transition metals. These metals react with oxygen, with halogens, and with acids under appropriate conditions. (a) Steel wool reacts with O_2; (b) steel wool reacts with chlorine gas, Cl_2; and (c) iron chips react with aqueous HCl.

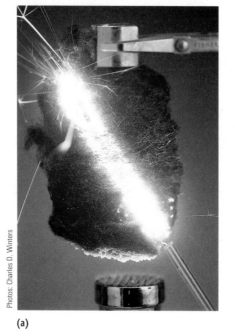

(a)

(b)

(c)

converts $Fe([Ar]3d^64s^2)$ to either $Fe^{2+}([Ar]3d^6)$ or $Fe^{3+}([Ar]3d^5)$. Iron reacts with chlorine to give $FeCl_3$, and it reacts with aqueous acids to produce $Fe^{2+}(aq)$ and H_2 (Figure 22.3). Despite the preponderance of 2+ and 3+ ions in compounds of the first transition metal series, the range of possible oxidation states for these compounds is broad (Figure 22.4). Earlier in this text, we encountered chromium with a +6 oxidation number (CrO_4^{2-}, $Cr_2O_7^{2-}$), manganese with an oxidation number of +7 (MnO_4^-), silver and copper as 1+ ions, and vanadium oxidation numbers that can range from +5 to +2 (Figure 20.3).

Higher oxidation numbers are more common in compounds of the elements in the second and third transition series. For example, the naturally occurring

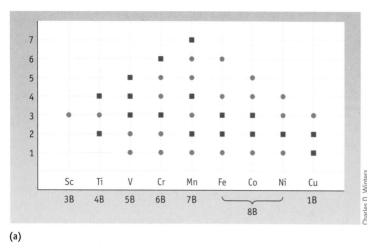

(a)

(b)

FIGURE 22.4 Oxidation states of the transition elements in the first transition series. (a) The most common oxidation states are indicated with red squares; less common oxidation states are indicated with blue dots. (b) Aqueous solutions of chromium compounds with two different oxidation numbers: +3 in $Cr(NO_3)_3$ (violet) and $CrCl_3$ (green), and +6 in K_2CrO_4 (yellow) and $K_2Cr_2O_7$ (orange).

1022 **Chapter 22** | The Chemistry of the Transition Elements

It is hard not to be aware of corrosion. Those of us who live in the northern part of the United States are well aware of the problems of rust on our automobiles. It is estimated that 20% of iron production each year goes solely to replace iron that has rusted away.

Qualitatively, we describe corrosion as the deterioration of metals by a product-favored oxidation reaction. The corrosion of iron, for example, converts iron metal to red-brown rust, which is hydrated iron(III) oxide, $Fe_2O_3 \cdot H_2O$. This process requires both air and water, and it is enhanced if the water contains dissolved ions and if the metal is stressed (e.g., if it has dents, cuts, and scrapes on the surface.)

The corrosion process occurs in what is essentially a small electrochemical cell. There is an anode and a cathode, an electrical connection between the two (the metal itself), and an electrolyte in contact with both anode and cathode. When a metal corrodes, the metal is oxidized on anodic areas of the metal surface.

Anode, oxidation $M(s) \longrightarrow M^{n+} + n\,e^-$

The electrons are consumed by several possible half-reactions in cathodic areas.

Cathode, reduction

$$2\,H_3O^+(aq) + 2\,e^- \longrightarrow H_2(g) + 2\,H_2O(\ell)$$

$$2\,H_2O(\ell) + 2\,e^- \longrightarrow H_2(g) + 2\,OH^-(aq)$$

$$O_2(g) + 2\,H_2O(\ell) + 4\,e^- \longrightarrow 4\,OH^-(aq)$$

The rate of iron corrosion is controlled by the rate of the cathodic process. Of the three possible cathodic reactions, the one that is fastest is determined by acidity and the amount of oxygen present. If little or no oxygen is present—as when a piece of iron is buried in soil such as moist clay—hydrogen ion or water is reduced, and $H_2(g)$ and hydroxide ions are

the products. Iron(II) hydroxide is relatively insoluble and will precipitate on the metal surface, inhibiting the further formation of Fe^{2+}.

Anode	$Fe(s) \longrightarrow Fe^{2+}(aq) + 2\,e^-$
Cathode	$2\,H_2O(\ell) + 2\,e^- \longrightarrow H_2(g) + 2\,OH^-(aq)$
Precipitation	$Fe^{2+}(aq) + 2\,OH^-(aq) \longrightarrow Fe(OH)_2(s)$
Net reaction	$Fe(s) + 2\,H_2O(\ell) \longrightarrow H_2(g) + Fe(OH)_2(s)$

If both water and O_2 are present, the chemistry of iron corrosion is somewhat different, and the corrosion reaction is about 100 times faster than without oxygen.

Anode	$2\,Fe(s) \longrightarrow 2\,Fe^{2+}(aq) + 4\,e^-$
Cathode	$O_2(g) + 2\,H_2O(\ell) + 4\,e^- \longrightarrow 4\,OH^-(aq)$
Precipitation	$2\,Fe^{2+}(aq) + 4\,OH^-(aq) \longrightarrow 2\,Fe(OH)_2(s)$
Net reaction	$2\,Fe(s) + 2\,H_2O(\ell) + O_2(g) \longrightarrow 2\,Fe(OH)_2(s)$

If oxygen is present but not in excess, further oxidation of the iron(II) hydroxide leads to the formation of magnetic iron oxide Fe_3O_4, (which can be thought of as a mixed oxide of Fe_2O_3 and FeO).

$$6\,Fe(OH)_2(s) + O_2(g) \longrightarrow 2\,Fe_3O_4 \cdot H_2O(s) + 4\,H_2O(\ell)$$
green hydrated magnetite

$$Fe_3O_4 \cdot H_2O(s) \longrightarrow H_2O(\ell) + Fe_3O_4(s)$$
black magnetite

It is the black magnetite that you find coating an iron object that has corroded by resting in moist soil.

If the iron object has free access to oxygen and water, as in the open or in flowing water, red-brown iron(III) oxide will form.

$$4\,Fe(OH)_2(s) + O_2(g) \longrightarrow 2\,Fe_2O_3 \cdot H_2O(s) + 2\,H_2O(\ell)$$
red-brown

This is the familiar rust you see on cars and buildings, and the substance that colors the water red in some mountain streams or in your home.

The corrosion or rusting of iron results in major economic loss.

Anode and cathode reactions in iron corrosion. Two iron nails were placed in an agar gel that contains phenolphthalein and $K_3[Fe(CN)_6]$. Iron(II) ion, formed at the tip and where the nail is bent, reacts with $[Fe(CN)_6]^{3-}$ to form blue-green $Fe_4[Fe(CN)_6]_3 \cdot 14\,H_2O$ (Prussian blue). Hydrogen and $OH^-(aq)$ are formed at the other parts of the surface of the nail, the latter being detected by the red color of the acid–dase indicator. In this electrochemical cell, regions of stress—the ends and the bent region of the nail—act as anodes, and the remainder of the surface serves as the cathode.

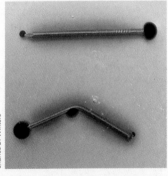

Charles D. Winters

sources of molybdenum and tungsten are the ores molybdenite (MoS_2) and wolframite (WO_3). This general trend is carried over in the f-block. The lanthanides form primarily 3+ ions. In contrast, actinide elements usually have higher oxidation numbers in their compounds; +4 and even +6 are typical. For example, UO_3 is a common oxide of uranium, and UF_6 is a compound important in processing uranium fuel for nuclear reactors [▶ Section 23.6].

Chemistry ⊙ Now™

Sign in at **www.cengage.com/login** and go to Chapter 22 Contents to see Screen 22.2 for an exercise on **transition metal compounds.**

Periodic Trends in the d-Block: Size, Density, Melting Point

The periodic table is the most useful single reference source for a chemist. Not only does it provide data that have everyday use, but it also organizes the elements with respect to their chemical and physical properties. Let us look at three physical properties of the transition elements that vary periodically: atomic radii, density and melting point.

Metal Atom Radii

The variation in atomic radii for the transition elements in the fourth, fifth, and sixth periods is illustrated in Figure 7.9. The radii of the transition elements vary over a fairly narrow range, with a small decrease to a minimum being observed around the middle of this group of elements. This similarity of radii can be understood based on electron configurations. Atom size is determined by the electrons in the outermost orbital, which for these elements is the ns orbital ($n = 4$, 5, or 6). Progressing from left to right in the periodic table, the size decline expected from increasing the number of protons in the nucleus is mostly canceled out by an opposing effect, repulsion from additional electrons in the $(n - 1)d$ orbitals.

The radii of the d-block elements in the fifth and sixth periods in each group are almost identical. The reason is that the lanthanide elements immediately precede the third series of d-block elements. The filling of 4f orbitals is accompanied by a steady contraction in size, consistent with the general trend of decreasing size from left to right in the periodic table. At the point where the 5d orbitals begin to fill again, the radii have decreased to a size similar to that of elements in the previous period. The decrease in size that results from the filling of the 4f orbitals is given a specific name, the **lanthanide contraction.**

The similar sizes of the second- and third-period d-block elements have significant consequences for their chemistry. For example, the "platinum group metals" (Ru, Os, Rh, Ir, Pd, and Pt) form similar compounds. Thus, it is not surprising that minerals containing these metals are found in the same geological zones on earth. Nor is it surprising that it is difficult to separate these elements from one another.

Density

The variation in metal radii causes the densities of the transition elements to first increase and then decrease across a period (Figure 22.5a). Although the overall change in radii among these elements is small, the effect is magnified because the volume is actually changing with the cube of the radius [$V = (4/3)\pi r^3$].

The lanthanide contraction explains why elements in the sixth period have the highest density. The relatively small radii of sixth-period transition metals, combined with the fact that their atomic masses are considerably larger than

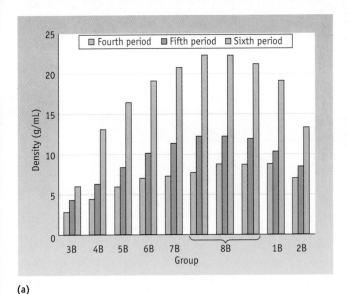

(a)

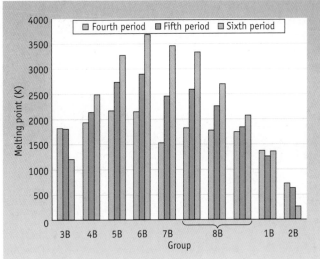

(b)

FIGURE 22.5 Periodic properties in the transition series. Density (a) and melting point (b) of the *d*-block elements.

their counterparts in the fifth period, causes sixth-period metal densities to be very large.

Melting Point

The melting point of any substance reflects the forces of attraction between the atoms, molecules, or ions that compose the solid. With transition elements, the melting points rise to a maximum around the middle of the series (Figure 22.5b), then descend. Again, these elements' electron configurations provide us with an explanation. The variation in melting point indicates that the strongest metallic bonds occur when the *d* subshell is about half filled. This is also the point at which the largest number of electrons occupy the bonding molecular orbitals in the metal. (See the discussion of bonding in metals on page 657.)

Chemistry‚Ó‚Now™

Sign in at **www.cengage.com/login** and go to Chapter 22 Contents to see Screen 22.3 for more on **transition metal chemistry.**

22.2 **Metallurgy**

A few metals occur in nature as the free elements. This group includes copper (Figure 22.6), silver, and gold. Most metals, however, are found as oxides, sulfides, halides, carbonates, or other ionic compounds (Figure 22.7). Some metal-containing mineral deposits have little economic value, either because the concentration of the metal is too low or because the metal is difficult to separate from impurities. The relatively few minerals from which elements can be obtained profitably are called *ores* (Figure 22.7). **Metallurgy** is the general name given to the process of obtaining metals from their ores.

Very few ores are chemically pure substances. Instead, the desired mineral is usually mixed with large quantities of impurities such as sand and clay, called **gangue** (pronounced "gang"). Generally, the first step in a metallurgical process is to sep-

Charles D. Winters

FIGURE 22.6 Naturally occurring copper. Copper occurs as the metal (native copper) and as minerals such as blue azurite [2 $CuCO_3 \cdot Cu(OH)_2$] and malachite [$CuCO_3 \cdot Cu(OH)_2$].

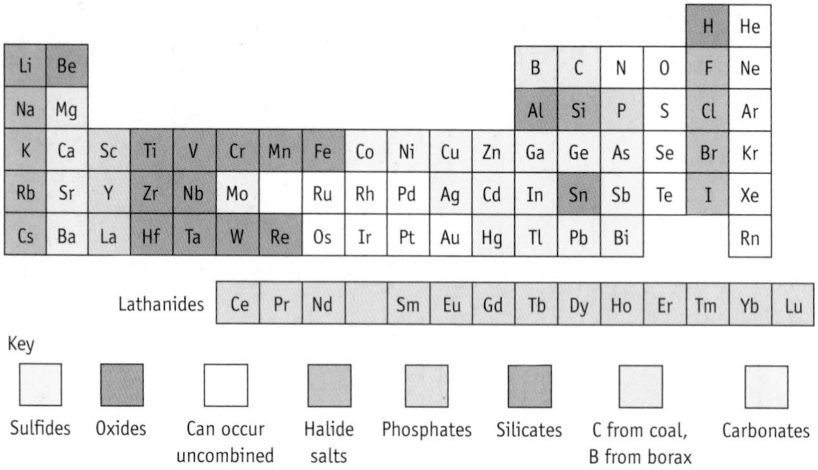

FIGURE 22.7 Major sources of the elements. A few transition metals, such as copper and gold, occur naturally as the metal. Most other elements are found naturally as oxides, sulfides, or other salts.

arate the mineral from the gangue. Then the ore is converted to the metal, a reduction process. Pyrometallurgy and hydrometallurgy are two methods of recovering metals from their ores. As the names imply, **pyrometallurgy** involves high temperatures and **hydrometallurgy** uses aqueous solutions (and thus is limited to the relatively low temperatures at which water is a liquid). Iron and copper metallurgy illustrate these two methods of metal production.

Pyrometallurgy: Iron Production

The production of iron from its ores is carried out in a blast furnace (Figure 22.8). The furnace is charged with a mixture of ore (usually hematite, Fe_2O_3), coke (which is primarily carbon), and limestone ($CaCO_3$). A blast of hot air forced in at the bottom of the furnace causes the coke to burn with such an intense heat that the temperature at the bottom is almost 1500 °C. The quantity of air input is controlled so that carbon monoxide is the primary product. Both carbon and carbon monoxide participate in the reduction of iron(III) oxide to give impure metal.

$$Fe_2O_3(s) + 3\ C(s) \longrightarrow 2\ Fe(\ell) + 3\ CO(g)$$

$$Fe_2O_3(s) + 3\ CO(g) \longrightarrow 2\ Fe(\ell) + 3\ CO_2(g)$$

■ **Coke: A Reducing Agent** Coke is made by heating coal in a tall, narrow oven that is sealed to keep out oxygen. Heating drives off volatile chemicals, including benzene and ammonia. What remains is nearly pure carbon.

Much of the carbon dioxide formed in the reduction process (and from heating the limestone) is reduced on contact with unburned coke and produces more reducing agent.

$$CO_2(g) + C(s) \longrightarrow 2\ CO(g)$$

The molten iron flows down through the furnace and collects at the bottom, where it is tapped off through an opening in the side. This impure iron is called *cast iron* or *pig iron*. Usually, the impure metal is either brittle or soft (undesirable properties for most uses) due to the presence of impurities such as elemental carbon, phosphorus, and sulfur.

Iron ores generally contain silicate minerals and silicon dioxide. Lime (CaO), formed when limestone is heated, reacts with these materials to give calcium silicate.

$$SiO_2(s) + CaO(s) \longrightarrow CaSiO_3(\ell)$$

This is an acid–base reaction because CaO is a basic oxide and SiO_2 is an acidic oxide. The calcium silicate, molten at the temperature of the blast furnace and less

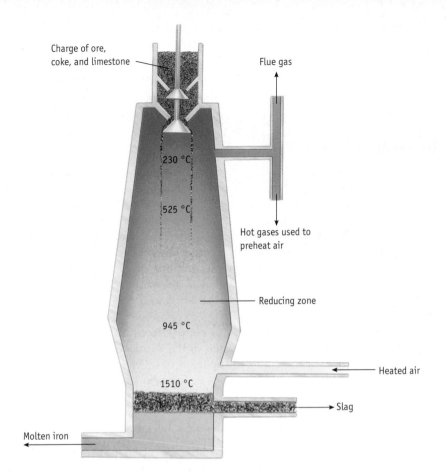

Charge of ore, coke, and limestone

Flue gas

230 °C

525 °C

Hot gases used to preheat air

Reducing zone

945 °C

1510 °C

Heated air

Slag

Molten iron

dense than molten iron, floats on the iron. Other nonmetal oxides dissolve in this layer and the mixture, called *slag*, is easily removed.

Pig iron from the blast furnace may contain as much as 4.5% carbon, 0.3% phosphorus, 0.04% sulfur, 1.5% silicon, and some other elements as well. The impure iron must be purified to remove these nonmetal components. Several processes are available to accomplish this task, but the most important uses the *basic oxygen furnace* (Figure 22.9). The process in the furnace removes much of the carbon and all of the phosphorus, sulfur, and silicon. Pure oxygen is blown into the molten pig iron and oxidizes phosphorus to P_4O_{10}, sulfur to SO_2, and carbon to CO_2. These nonmetal oxides either escape as gases or react with basic oxides such as CaO that are added or are used to line the furnace. For example,

$$P_4O_{10}(g) + 6\ CaO(s) \longrightarrow 2\ Ca_3(PO_4)_2(\ell)$$

The result is ordinary *carbon steel*. Almost any degree of flexibility, hardness, strength, and malleability can be achieved in carbon steel by reheating and cooling in a process called *tempering*. The resulting material can then be used in a wide variety of applications. The major disadvantages of carbon steel are that it corrodes easily and that it loses its properties when heated strongly.

Other transition metals, such as chromium, manganese, and nickel, can be added during the steel-making process, giving *alloys* (solid solutions of two or more metals; see *The Chemistry of Modern Materials*, page 656) that have

Bethlehem Steel Corp.

FIGURE 22.9 Molten iron being poured from a basic oxygen furnace.

FIGURE 22.10 Enriching copper ore by the flotation process. The less dense particles of Cu_2S are trapped in the soap bubbles and float. The denser gangue settles to the bottom.

specific physical, chemical, and mechanical properties. One well-known alloy is stainless steel, which contains 18% to 20% Cr and 8% to 12% Ni. Stainless steel is much more resistant to corrosion than carbon steel. Another alloy of iron is Alnico V. Used in loudspeaker magnets because of its permanent magnetism, it contains five elements: Al (8%), Ni (14%), Co (24%), Cu (3%), and Fe (51%).

Hydrometallurgy: Copper Production

In contrast to iron ores, which are mostly oxides, most copper minerals are sulfides. Copper-bearing minerals include chalcopyrite ($CuFeS_2$), chalcocite (Cu_2S), and covellite (CuS). Because ores containing these minerals generally have a very low percentage of copper, enrichment is necessary. This step is carried out by a process known as *flotation*. First, the ore is finely powdered. Next, oil is added and the mixture is agitated with soapy water in a large tank (Figure 22.10). At the same time, compressed air is forced through the mixture, so that the lightweight, oil-covered copper sulfide particles are carried to the top as a frothy mixture. The heavier gangue settles to the bottom of the tank, and the copper-laden froth is skimmed off.

Hydrometallurgy can be used to obtain copper from an enriched ore. In one method, enriched chalcopyrite ore is treated with a solution of copper(II) chloride. A reaction ensues that leaves copper in the form of solid, insoluble CuCl, which is easily separated from the iron that remains in solution as aqueous $FeCl_2$.

$$CuFeS_2(s) + 3\ CuCl_2(aq) \longrightarrow 4\ CuCl(s) + FeCl_2(aq) + 2\ S(s)$$

Aqueous NaCl is then added, and CuCl dissolves because of the formation of the complex ion $[CuCl_2]^-$.

$$CuCl(s) + Cl^-(aq) \longrightarrow [CuCl_2]^-(aq)$$

Copper(I) compounds in solution are unstable with respect to Cu(0) and Cu(II). Thus, $[CuCl_2]^-$ disproportionates to the metal and $CuCl_2$, and the latter is used to treat further ore.

$$2\ [CuCl_2]^-(aq) \longrightarrow Cu(s) + Cu^{2+}(aq) + 4\ Cl^-(aq)$$

Approximately 10% of the copper produced in the United States is obtained with the aid of bacteria. Acidified water is sprayed onto copper-mining wastes that contain low levels of copper. As the water trickles down through the crushed rock, the bacterium *Thiobacillus ferrooxidans* breaks down the iron sulfides in the rock and converts iron(II) to iron(III). Iron(III) ions oxidize the sulfide ion of copper sulfide to sulfate ions, leaving copper(II) ions in solution. Then the copper(II) ion is reduced to metallic copper by reaction with iron.

$$Cu^{2+}(aq) + Fe(s) \longrightarrow Cu(s) + Fe^{2+}(aq)$$

The purity of the copper obtained via these metallurgical processes is about 99%, but this is not acceptable because even traces of impurities greatly diminish the electrical conductivity of the metal. Consequently, a further purification step is needed—one involving electrolysis (Figure 22.11). Thin sheets of pure copper metal and slabs of impure copper are immersed in a solution containing $CuSO_4$ and H_2SO_4. The pure copper sheets serve as the cathode of an electrolysis cell, and the impure slabs are the anode. Copper in the impure sample is oxidized to copper(II) ions at the anode, and copper(II) ions in solution are reduced to pure copper at the cathode.

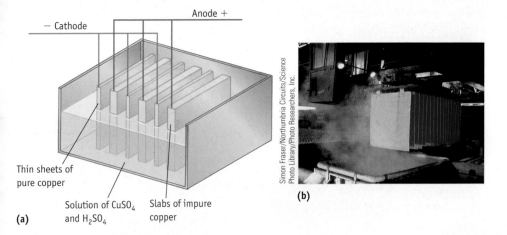

(b)

FIGURE 22.11 Electrolytic refining of copper. (a) Slabs of impure copper, called "blister copper," form the anode, and pure copper is deposited at the cathode. (b) The electrolysis cells at a copper refinery.

— Cathode

Anode +

Thin sheets of pure copper

Solution of $CuSO_4$ and H_2SO_4

Slabs of impure copper

(a)

22.3 Coordination Compounds

When metal salts dissolve, water molecules cluster around the ions (page 617). The negative end of each polar water molecule is attracted to the positively charged metal ion, and the positive end of the water molecule is attracted to the anion. As noted earlier (◀ Section 12.2), the energy of the ion–solvent interaction (solvation energy) is an important aspect of the solution process. But there is much more to this story.

Complexes and Ligands

A green solution formed by dissolving nickel(II) chloride in water contains Ni^{2+} (aq) and Cl^-(aq) ions (Figure 22.12). If the solvent is removed, a green crystalline solid is obtained. The formula of this solid is often written as $NiCl_2 \cdot 6\ H_2O$, and the compound is called nickel(II) chloride hexahydrate. Addition of ammonia to the aqueous nickel(II) chloride solution gives a lilac-colored solution from which another compound, $NiCl_2 \cdot 6\ NH_3$, can be isolated. This formula looks very similar to the formula for the hydrate, with ammonia substituted for water.

What are these two nickel species? The formulas identify the compositions of the compounds but fail to give information about their structures. Because properties of compounds derive from their structures, we need to evaluate the structures in more detail. Typically, metal compounds are ionic, and solid ionic compounds have structures with cations and anions arranged in a regular array. The structure of hydrated nickel chloride contains cations with the formula $[Ni(H_2O)_6]^{2+}$ and chloride anions. The structure of the ammonia-containing compound is similar to the hydrate; it is made up of $[Ni(NH_3)_6]^{2+}$ cations and chloride anions.

Ions such as $[Ni(H_2O)_6]^{2+}$ and $[Ni(NH_3)_6]^{2+}$, in which a metal ion and either water or ammonia molecules compose a single structural unit, are examples of **coordination complexes,** also known as **complex ions** (Figure 22.13). Compounds containing a coordination complex as part of the structure are called **coordination compounds,** and their chemistry is known as **coordination chemistry.** Although the older "hydrate" formulas are still used, the preferred method of writing the formula for coordination compounds places the metal atom or ion and the molecules or anions directly bonded to it within brackets to show that it is a single structural entity. Thus, the formula for the nickel(II)–ammonia compound is better written as $[Ni(NH_3)_6]Cl_2$.

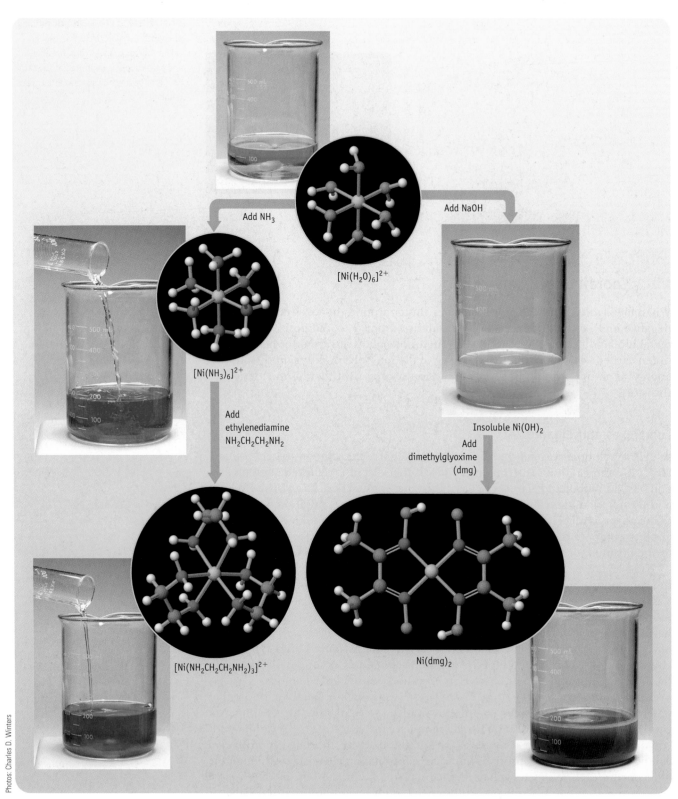

FIGURE 22.12 Coordination compounds of Ni²⁺ ion. The transition metals and their ions form a wide range of compounds, often with beautiful colors and interesting structures. One purpose of this chapter is to explore some commonly observed structures and explain how these compounds can be so colorful.

Add NH₃

Add NaOH

$[Ni(H_2O)_6]^{2+}$

$[Ni(NH_3)_6]^{2+}$

Add ethylenediamine $NH_2CH_2CH_2NH_2$

Insoluble $Ni(OH)_2$

Add dimethylglyoxime (dmg)

$[Ni(NH_2CH_2CH_2NH_2)_3]^{2+}$

$Ni(dmg)_2$

Photos: Charles D. Winters

All coordination complexes contain a metal atom or ion as the central part of the structure. Bonded to the metal are molecules or ions called **ligands** (from the Latin verb *ligare*, meaning "to bind"). In the preceding examples, water and ammonia are the ligands. The number of ligand atoms attached to the metal defines the **coordination number** of the metal. The geometry described by the attached ligands is called the **coordination geometry.** In the nickel complex ion $[Ni(NH_3)_6]^{2+}$ (Figure 22.12), the six ligands are arranged in a regular octahedral geometry around the central metal ion.

Ligands can be either neutral molecules or anions (or, in rare instances, cations). The characteristic feature of a ligand is that it contains a lone pair of electrons. In the classic description of bonding in a coordination complex, the lone pair of electrons on a ligand is shared with the metal ion. The attachment is a coordinate covalent bond (◀ Section 8.5), because the electron pair being shared was originally on the ligand. The name "coordination complex" derives from the name given to this kind of bonding.

The net charge on a coordination complex is the sum of the charges on the metal and its attached groups. Complexes can be cations (as in the two nickel complexes used as examples here), anions, or uncharged.

Ligands such as H_2O and NH_3, which coordinate to the metal via a single Lewis base atom, are termed **monodentate.** The word "dentate" comes from the Latin *dentis*, meaning "tooth," so NH_3 is a "one-toothed" ligand. Some ligands attach to the metal with more than one donor atom. These ligands are called **polydentate.** Ethylenediamine (1,2-diaminoethane), $H_2NCH_2CH_2NH_2$, often abbreviated as en; oxalate ion, $C_2O_4^{2-}$ (ox^{2-}); and phenanthroline, $C_{12}H_8N_2$ (phen), are examples of the wide variety of bidentate ligands (Figure 22.14). Structures and examples of some complex ions with **bidentate** ligands are shown in Figure 22.15.

Polydentate ligands are also called **chelating ligands,** or just chelates (pronounced "key-lates"). The name derives from the Greek *chele*, meaning "claw." Because two or more bonds are broken to separate the ligand from the metal, complexes with chelated ligands have greater stability than those with monodentate ligands. Chelated complexes are important in everyday life. One way to clean the rust out of water-cooled automobile engines and steam boilers is to add a solution of oxalic acid. Iron oxide reacts with oxalic acid to give a water-soluble iron oxalate complex ion:

$$3\ H_2O(\ell) + Fe_2O_3(s) + 6\ H_2C_2O_4(aq) \longrightarrow 2\ [Fe(C_2O_4)_3]^{3-}(aq) + 6\ H_3O^+(aq)$$

Ethylenediaminetetraacetate ion ($EDTA^{4-}$), a hexadentate ligand, is an excellent chelating ligand (Figure 22.16). It can wrap around a metal ion, encapsulating it. Salts of this anion are often added to commercial salad dressings to remove traces of free metal ions from solution; otherwise, these metal ions can act as catalysts for the oxidation of the oils in the dressing. Without $EDTA^{4-}$, the dressing would

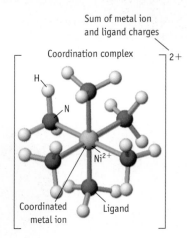

Sum of metal ion and ligand charges

Coordination complex — 2+

H

N

Ni^{2+}

Coordinated metal ion   Ligand

$[Ni(NH_3)_6]^{2+}$

FIGURE 22.13 A coordination complex. In the $[Ni(NH_3)_6]^{2+}$ ion, the ligands are NH_3 molecules. Because the metal has a 2+ charge and the ligands have no charge, the charge on the complex ion is 2+.

■ **Ligands Are Lewis Bases** Ligands are Lewis bases because they furnish the electron pair; the metal ion is a Lewis acid because it accepts electron pairs (see Section 17.9). Thus, the coordinate covalent bond between ligand and metal can be viewed as a Lewis acid–Lewis base interaction.

■ **Bidentate Ligands** All common bidentate ligands bind to *adjacent* sites on the metal.

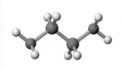

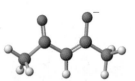

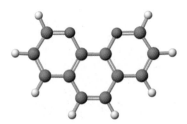

(a) $H_2NCH_2CH_2NH_2$, en   (b) $C_2O_4^{2-}$, ox   (c) $CH_3COCHCOCH_3^-$, acac$^-$ (d) $C_{12}H_8N_2$, phen

FIGURE 22.14 Common bidentate ligands. (a) Ethylenediamine, $H_2NCH_2CH_2NH_2$; (b) oxalate ion, $C_2O_4^{2-}$; (c) acetylacetonate ion, $CH_3COCHCOCH_3^-$; (d) phenanthroline, $C_{12}H_8N_2$. Coordination of these bidentate ligands to a transition metal ion results in five- or six-member metal-containing rings and no ring strain.

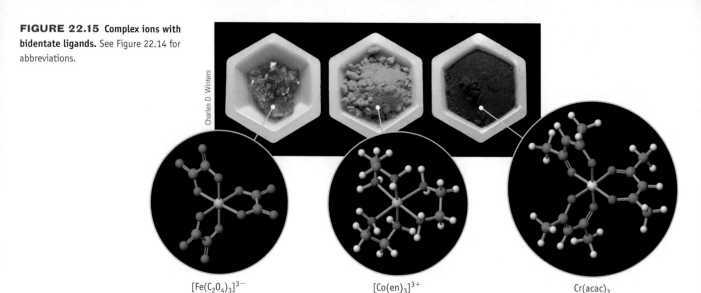

FIGURE 22.15 Complex ions with bidentate ligands. See Figure 22.14 for abbreviations.

Charles D. Winters

$[Fe(C_2O_4)_3]^{3-}$ $[Co(en)_3]^{3+}$ $Cr(acac)_3$

quickly become rancid. Another use is in bathroom cleansers. The $EDTA^{4-}$ ion removes deposits of $CaCO_3$ and $MgCO_3$ left by hard water by coordinating to Ca^{2+} or Mg^{2+} to create soluble complex ions.

Complexes with polydentate ligands play particularly important roles in biochemistry, one example of which is described in *A Closer Look: Hemoglobin*.

Formulas of Coordination Compounds

It is useful to be able to predict the formula of a coordination complex, given the metal ion and ligands, and to derive the oxidation number of the coordinated metal ion, given the formula in a coordination compound. The following examples explore these issues.

■ **EXAMPLE 22.1 Formulas of Coordination Complexes**

Problem Give the formulas of the following coordination complexes:

(a) A Ni^{2+} ion is bound to two water molecules and two bidentate oxalate ions.

(b) A Co^{3+} ion is bound to one Cl^- ion, one ammonia molecule, and two bidentate ethylenediamine (en) molecules.

Strategy The problem requires determining the net charge, which equals the sum of the charges of the various component parts of the complex ion. With that information, the metal and ligands can be assembled in the formula, which is placed in brackets, and the net charge indicated.

FIGURE 22.16 $EDTA^{4-}$, a hexadentate ligand. (a) Ethylenediaminetetraacetate, $EDTA^{4-}$. (b) $[Co(EDTA)]^-$. Notice the five- and six-member rings created when this ligand bonds to the metal.

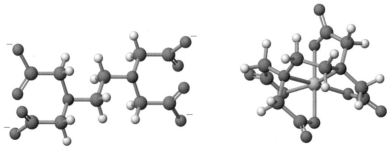

(a) Ethylenediaminetetraacetate, $EDTA^{4-}$ **(b)** $[Co(EDTA)]^-$

Metal-containing coordination compounds figure prominently in many biochemical reactions. Perhaps the best-known example is hemoglobin, the chemical in the blood responsible for O_2 transport. It is also one of the most thoroughly studied bioinorganic compounds.

As described in *The Chemistry of Life: Biochemistry* (page 496), hemoglobin (Hb) is a large iron-containing protein. It includes four polypeptide segments, each containing an iron(II) ion locked inside a porphyrin ring system and coordinated to a nitrogen atom

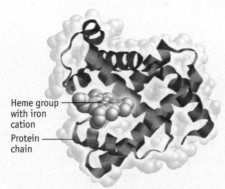

Heme group with iron cation
Protein chain

Myoglobin (Mb)

The heme group in myoglobin. This protein is a close relative of hemoglobin. The heme group with its iron ion is shown.

from another part of the protein. A sixth site is available to attach to oxygen.

One segment of the hemoglobin molecule resembles the myoglobin structure shown above. (Myoglobin, the oxygen-storage protein in muscle, has only one polypeptide chain with an enclosed heme group. It is the oxygen storage protein in muscle.) In this case, the iron-containing heme group is enclosed with a polypeptide chain. The iron ion in the porphyrin ring is shown. The first and sixth coordination positions are taken up by nitrogen atoms from amino acids of the polypeptide chain.

Hemoglobin functions by reversibly adding oxygen to the sixth coordination position of each iron, giving a complex called oxyhemoglobin.

Because hemoglobin features four iron centers, a maximum of four molecules of oxygen can bind to the molecule. The binding to oxygen is cooperative; that is, binding one molecule enhances the tendency to bind the second, third, and fourth molecules.

Formation of the oxygenated complex is favored, but not too highly, because oxygen must also be released by the molecule to body tissues. Interestingly, an increase in acidity leads to a decrease in the stability of the oxygenated complex. This phenomenon is known as the *Bohr effect*, named for Christian Bohr, Niels Bohr's father. Release of oxygen in tissues is facilitated by an increase in acidity that results from the presence of CO_2 formed by metabolism.

Among the notable properties of hemoglobin is its ability to form a complex with carbon monoxide. This complex is very stable, with the equilibrium constant for the following reaction being about 200 (where Hb is hemoglobin):

$$HbO_2(aq) + CO(g) \rightleftharpoons HbCO(aq) + O_2(g)$$

When CO complexes with iron, the oxygen-carrying capacity of hemoglobin is lost. Consequently, CO is highly toxic to humans. Exposure to even small amounts greatly reduces the capacity of the blood to transport oxygen.

Hemoglobin abnormalities are well known. One of the most common abnormalities causes sickle cell anemia and was described on page 500.

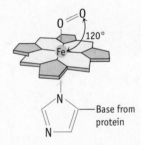

Base from protein

Oxygen binding. Oxygen binds to the iron of the heme group in oxyhemoglobin (and in myoglobin). Interestingly, the Fe—O—O angle is bent.

Porphyrin

$\downarrow$ $-2\,H^+$

Porphyrin^{2-}

Porphyrin ring of the heme group. The tetradentate ligand surrounding the iron(II) ion in hemoglobin is a dianion of a substituted molecule called a porphyrin. Because of the double bonds in this structure, all of the carbon and nitrogen atoms in the dianion of the porphyrin lie in a plane. In addition, the nitrogen lone pairs are directed toward the center of the molecule, and the molecular dimensions are such that a metal ion may fit nicely into the cavity.

Solution

(a) This complex ion is constructed from two neutral H_2O molecules, two $C_2O_4{}^{2-}$ ions, and one Ni^{2+} ion, so the net charge on the complex is $2-$. The formula for the complex ion is

$$[Ni(C_2O_4)_2(H_2O)_2]^{2-}$$

(b) This cobalt(III) complex combines two en molecules and one NH_3 molecule, both having no charge, as well as one Cl^- ion and a Co^{3+} ion. The net charge is $2+$. The formula for this complex (writing out the entire formula for ethylenediamine) is

$$[Co(H_2NCH_2CH_2NH_2)_2(NH_3)Cl]^{2+}$$

Problem In each of the following complexes, determine the metal's oxidation number and coordination number.

(a) $[Co(en)_2(NO_2)_2]Cl$

(b) $Pt(NH_3)_2(C_2O_4)$

(c) $Pt(NH_3)_2Cl_4$

(d) $[Co(NH_3)_5Cl]SO_4$

Strategy Each formula consists of a complex ion or molecule made up of the metal ion, neutral and/or anionic ligands (the part inside the square brackets), and a counterion (outside the brackets). The oxidation number of the metal is the charge necessary to balance the sum of the negative charges associated with the anionic ligands and counterion. The coordination number is the number of donor atoms in the ligands that are bonded to the metal. Remember that the bidentate ligands in these examples (en, oxalate ion) attach to the metal at two sites and that the counterion is not part of the complex ion—that is, it is not a ligand.

Solution

(a) The chloride ion with a 1− charge, outside the brackets, shows that the charge on the complex ion must be 1+. There are two nitrite ions (NO_2^-) and two neutral bidentate ethylenediamine ligands in the complex. To give a 1+ charge on the complex ion, the cobalt ion must have a charge of 3+; that is, the sum of 2− (two nitrites), 0 (two en ligands), and 3+ (the cobalt ion) equals 1+. Each en ligand fills two coordination positions, and the two nitrite ions fill two more positions. The coordination number of the metal is 6.

(b) There is an oxalate ion ($C_2O_4^{2-}$) and two neutral ammonia ligands. To balance the charge on the oxalate ion, platinum must have a 2+ charge; that is, it has an oxidation number of +2. The coordination number is 4, with an oxalate ligand filling two coordination positions and each ammonia molecule filling one.

(c) There are four chloride ions (Cl^-) and two neutral ammonia ligands. In this complex, the oxidation number of the metal is +4, and the coordination number is 6.

(d) There is one chloride ion (Cl^-) and five neutral ammonia ligands. The counter ion is sulfate with a 2− charge, so the overall charge on the complex is 2+. The oxidation number of the metal is +3 and the coordination number is 6 (sulfate is not coordinated to the metal).

EXERCISE 22.1 **Formulas of Coordination Compounds**

(a) What is the formula of a complex ion composed of one Co^{3+} ion, three ammonia molecules, and three Cl^- ions?

(b) Determine the metal's oxidation number and coordination number in (i) $K_3[Co(NO_2)_6]$ and in (ii) $Mn(NH_3)_4Cl_2$.

Naming Coordination Compounds

Just as rules govern naming of inorganic and organic compounds, coordination compounds are named according to an established system. The three compounds below are named according to the rules that follow.

Compound	Systematic Name
$[Ni(H_2O)_6]SO_4$	Hexaaquanickel(II) sulfate
$[Cr(en)_2(CN)_2]Cl$	Dicyanobis(ethylenediamine)chromium(III) chloride
$K[Pt(NH_3)Cl_3]$	Potassium amminetrichloroplatinate(II)

1. In naming a coordination compound that is a salt, name the cation first and then the anion. (This is how all salts are commonly named.)
2. When giving the name of the complex ion or molecule, name the ligands first, in alphabetical order, followed by the name of the metal. (When determining alphabetical order, the prefix is not considered part of the name.)

3. Ligands and their names:
   (a) If a ligand is an anion whose name ends in *-ite* or *-ate*, the final *e* is changed to *o* (sulfate $\longrightarrow$ sulfato or nitrite $\longrightarrow$ nitrito).
   (b) If the ligand is an anion whose name ends in *-ide*, the ending is changed to *o* (chloride $\longrightarrow$ chloro, cyanide $\longrightarrow$ cyano).
   (c) If the ligand is a neutral molecule, its common name is usually used with several important exceptions: Water as a ligand is referred to as *aqua;* ammonia is called *ammine;* and CO is called *carbonyl.*
   (d) When there is more than one of a particular monodentate ligand with a simple name, the number of ligands is designated by the appropriate prefix: *di, tri, tetra, penta,* or *hexa.* If the ligand name is complicated, the prefix changes to *bis, tris, tetrakis, pentakis,* or *hexakis,* followed by the ligand name in parentheses.
4. If the coordination complex is an anion, the suffix *-ate* is added to the metal name.
5. Following the name of the metal, the oxidation number of the metal is given in Roman numerals.

■ **EXAMPLE 22.3 Naming Coordination Compounds**

Problem Name the following compounds:

(a) $[Cu(NH_3)_4]SO_4$ **(c)** $Co(phen)_2Cl_2$

(b) $K_2[CoCl_4]$ **(d)** $[Co(en)_2(H_2O)Cl]Cl_2$

Strategy Apply the rules for nomenclature given above.

Solution

(a) The complex ion (in square brackets) is composed of four NH_3 molecules (named *ammine* in a complex) and the copper ion. To balance the 2− charge on the sulfate counterion, copper must have a 2+ charge. The compound's name is

> tetraamminecopper(II) sulfate

(b) The complex ion $[CoCl_4]^{2-}$ has a 2− charge. With four Cl^- ligands, the cobalt ion must have a +2 charge, so the sum of charges is 2−. The name of the compound is

> potassium tetrachlorocobaltate(II)

(c) This is a neutral coordination compound. The ligands include two Cl^- ions and two neutral bidentate *phen* (phenanthroline) ligands. The metal ion must have a 2+ charge (Co^{2+}). The name, listing ligands in alphabetical order, is

> dichlorobis(phenanthroline)cobalt(II)

(d) The complex ion has a 2− charge because it is paired with two uncoordinated Cl^- ions. The cobalt ion is Co^{3+} because it is bonded to two neutral en ligands, one neutral water, and one Cl^-. The name is

> aquachlorobis(ethylenediamine)cobalt(III) chloride

EXERCISE 22.2 Naming Coordination Compounds

Name the following coordination compounds.

(a) $[Ni(H_2O)_6]SO_4$ **(c)** $K[Pt(NH_3)Cl_3]$

(b) $[Cr(en)_2(CN)_2]Cl$ **(d)** $K[CuCl_2]$

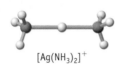

Linear

$[Ag(NH_3)_2]^+$

$Pt(NH_3)_2Cl_2$

Square planar

$[NiCl_4]^{2-}$

Tetrahedral

$[Ni(H_2O)_6]^{2+}$

Octahedral

22.4 Structures of Coordination Compounds

Common Coordination Geometries

The geometry of a coordination complex is defined by the arrangement of donor atoms of the ligands around the central metal ion. Metal ions in coordination compounds can have coordination numbers ranging from 2 to 12. Only complexes with coordination numbers of 2, 4, and 6 are common, however, so we will concentrate on species such as $[ML_2]^{n\pm}$, $[ML_4]^{n\pm}$, and $[ML_6]^{n\pm}$, where M is the metal ion and L is a monodentate ligand. Within these stoichiometries, the following geometries are encountered:

- All $[ML_2]^{n\pm}$ complexes are linear. The two ligands are on opposite sides of the metal, and the L—M—L bond angle is 180°. Common examples include $[Ag(NH_3)_2]^+$ and $[CuCl_2]^-$.
- Tetrahedral geometry occurs in many $[ML_4]^{n\pm}$ complexes. Examples include $TiCl_4$, $[CoCl_4]^{2-}$, $[NiCl_4]^{2-}$, and $[Zn(NH_3)_4]^{2+}$.
- Some $[ML_4]^{n\pm}$ complexes can have square planar geometry. This geometry is most often seen with metal ions that have eight d electrons. Examples include $Pt(NH_3)_2Cl_2$, $[Ni(CN)_4]^{2-}$, and the nickel complex with the dimethylglyoximate (dmg^-) ligand in Figure 22.12.
- Octahedral geometry is found in complexes with the stoichiometry $[ML_6]^{n\pm}$ (Figure 22.12).

Chemistry.ᐤ.Now™

Sign in at **www.cengage.com/login** and go to Chapter 22 Contents to see Screen 22.5 for an exercise on **compound geometries**.

Isomerism

Isomerism is one of the most interesting aspects of molecular structure. Recall that the chemistry of organic compounds is greatly enlivened by the multitude of isomeric compounds that are known.

Isomers are classified as follows:

- *Structural isomers* have the same molecular formula but different bonding arrangements of atoms.
- *Stereoisomers* have the same atom-to-atom bonding sequence, but the atoms differ in their arrangement in space. There are two types of stereoisomers: geometric isomers (such as *cis* and *trans* alkenes, page 421) and optical isomers (non-superimposable mirror images that have the unique property that they rotate planar polarized light, page 445).

All three types of isomerism, structural, geometric, and optical, are encountered in coordination chemistry.

Structural Isomerism

The two most important types of structural isomerism in coordination chemistry are coordination isomerism and linkage isomerism. **Coordination isomerism** occurs when it is possible to exchange a coordinated ligand and the uncoordinated counterion. For example, dark violet $[Co(NH_3)_5Br]SO_4$ and red $[Co(NH_3)_5SO_4]Br$ are coordination isomers. In the first compound, bromide ion is a ligand and sulfate is a counterion; in the second, sulfate is a ligand and bromide is the counterion. A diagnostic test for this kind of isomer is often made based on chemical reactions.

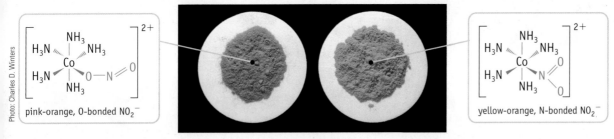

FIGURE 22.17 Linkage isomers, $[Co(NH_3)_5ONO]^{2+}$ and $[Co(NH_3)_5NO_2]^{2+}$. These complexes, whose systematic names are pentaamminenitritocobalt(III) and pentaamminenitrocobalt(III), were the first known examples of this type of isomerism.

For example, these two compounds can be distinguished by precipitation reactions. Addition of $Ba^{2+}(aq)$ to a solution of $[Co(NH_3)_5Br]SO_4$ gives a precipitate of $BaSO_4$, indicating the presence of sulfate ion in solution. In contrast, no reaction occurs if $Ba^{2+}(aq)$ is added to a solution of $[Co(NH_3)_5SO_4]Br$. In this complex, sulfate ion is attached to Co^{3+} and is not a free ion in solution.

$$[Co(NH_3)_5Br]SO_4 + Ba^{2+}(aq) \longrightarrow BaSO_4(s) + [CO(NH_3)_5Br]^{2+}(aq)$$

$$[Co(NH_3)_5SO_4]Br + Ba^{2+}(aq) \longrightarrow \text{no reaction}$$

Linkage isomerism occurs when it is possible to attach a ligand to the metal through different atoms. The two most common ligands with which linkage isomerism arises are thiocyanate, SCN^-, and nitrite, NO_2^-. The Lewis structure of the thiocyanate ion shows that there are lone pairs of electrons on sulfur and nitrogen. The ligand can attach to a metal either through sulfur (called S-bonded thiocyanate) or through nitrogen (called N-bonded thiocyanate). Nitrite ion can attach either at oxygen or at nitrogen. The former are called nitrito complexes; the latter are nitro complexes (Figure 22.17).

Ligands forming linkage isomers

:S̈—C≡N:

Bind to metal ion using either lone pair

:Ö=N—Ö:

Bind to metal ion using either lone pair

Geometric Isomerism

Geometric isomerism results when the atoms bonded directly to the metal have a different spatial arrangement. The simplest example of geometric isomerism in coordination chemistry is *cis-trans* isomerism, which occurs in both square-planar and octahedral complexes. An example of *cis-trans* isomerism is seen in the square-planar complex $Pt(NH_3)_2Cl_2$ (Figure 22.18a). In this complex, the two Cl^- ions can be either adjacent to each other (*cis*) or on opposite sides of the metal (*trans*). The *cis* isomer is effective in the treatment of testicular, ovarian, bladder, and osteogenic sarcoma cancers, but the *trans* isomer has no effect on these diseases.

Cis-trans isomerism in an octahedral complex is illustrated by a complex ion with two bidentate ethylenediamine ligands and two chloride ligands, $[Co(H_2NCH_2CH_2NH_2)_2Cl_2]^+$. In this complex, the two Cl^- ions occupy positions that are either adjacent (the purple *cis* isomer) or opposite (the green *trans* isomer) (Figure 22.18b).

■ ***Cis-Trans* Isomerism** *Cis-trans* isomerism is not possible for tetrahedral complexes. All L—M—L angles in tetrahedral geometry are 109.5°, and all positions are equivalent in this three-dimensional structure.

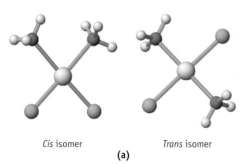
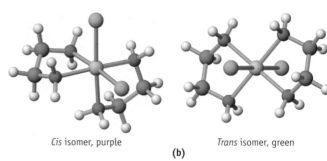

| *Cis* isomer | *Trans* isomer | *Cis* isomer, purple | *Trans* isomer, green |

(a)

(b)

FIGURE 22.18 *Cis-trans* isomers. (a) The square planar complex Pt(NH₃)₂Cl₂ can exist in two geometries, *cis* and *trans*. (b) Similarly, *cis* and *trans* octahedral isomers are possible for [Co(en)₂Cl₂]⁺.

Another common type of geometric isomerism occurs for octahedral complexes with the general formula MX₃Y₃. A *fac* isomer has three identical ligands lying at the corners of a triangular face of an octahedron defined by the ligands (*fac* = facial), whereas the ligands follow a meridian in the *mer* isomer (*mer* = meridional). *Fac* and *mer* isomers of Cr(NH₃)₃Cl₃ are shown in Figure 22.19.

Optical Isomerism

■ **Optical Isomerism** Square-planar complexes are incapable of optical isomerism based at the metal center; mirror images are always superimposable. Chiral tetrahedral complexes are possible, but examples of complexes with a metal bonded tetrahedrally to four different monodentate ligands are rare.

Optical isomerism (chirality) occurs for octahedral complexes when the metal ion coordinates to three bidentate ligands or when the metal ion coordinates to two bidentate ligands and two monodentate ligands in a *cis* position. The complexes [Co(en)₃]³⁺ and *cis*-[Co(en)₂Cl₂]⁺, illustrated in Figure 22.20, are examples of chiral complexes. The diagnostic test for chirality is met with both species: Mirror images of these molecules are not superimposable (page 446). Solutions of the optical isomers rotate plane-polarized light in opposite directions.

fac isomer

mer isomer

FIGURE 22.19 *Fac* and *mer* isomers of Cr(NH₃)₃Cl₃. In the *fac* isomer, the three chloride ligands (and the three ammonia ligands) are arranged at the corners of a triangular face. In the *mer* isomer, the three similar ligands follow a meridian.

Chemistry ⚛ Now™

Sign in at **www.cengage.com/login** and go to Chapter 22 Contents to see Screen 22.6 for an exercise on **isomerism in coordination chemistry.**

■ **EXAMPLE 22.4 Isomerism in Coordination Chemistry**

Problem For which of the following complexes do isomers exist? If isomers are possible, identify the type of isomerism (structural or geometric). Determine whether the coordination complex is capable of exhibiting optical isomerism.

(a) [Co(NH₃)₄Cl₂]⁺

(b) Pt(NH₃)₂(CN)₂ (square planar)

(c) Co(NH₃)₃Cl₃

(d) Zn(NH₃)₂Cl₂ (tetrahedral)

(e) K₃[Fe(C₂O₄)₃]

(f) [Co(NH₃)₅SCN]²⁺

Strategy Determine the number of ligands attached to the metal, and decide whether the ligands are monodentate or bidentate. Knowing how many donor atoms are coordinated to the metal (the coordination number) will allow you to establish the metal geometry. At that point, it is necessary to recall the possible types of isomers for each geometry. The only isomerism possible for square–planar complexes is geometric (*cis* and *trans*). Tetrahedral complexes do not have isomers. Six-coordinate metals of the formula MA₄B₂ can be either *cis* or *trans*. *Mer* and *fac* isomers are possible with a stoichiometry of MA₃B₃. Optical activity arises for metal complexes of the formula *cis*-M(bidentate)₂X₂ and M(bidentate)₃ (among others). Drawing pictures of the molecules will help you visualize the isomers.

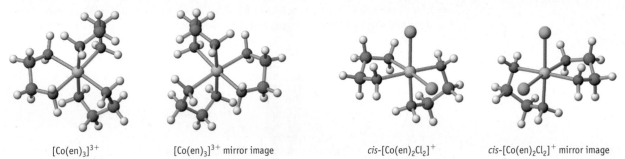

$[Co(en)_3]^{3+}$ $[Co(en)_3]^{3+}$ mirror image $cis\text{-}[Co(en)_2Cl_2]^+$ $cis\text{-}[Co(en)_2Cl_2]^+$ mirror image

FIGURE 22.20 Chiral metal complexes. Both $[Co(en)_3]^{3+}$ and $cis\text{-}[Co(en)_2Cl_2]^+$ are chiral. Notice that the mirror images of the two compounds are not superimposable.

Solution

(a) Two geometric isomers can be drawn for octahedral complexes with a formula of MA_4B_2, such as this one. One isomer has two Cl^- ions in *cis* positions (adjacent positions, at a 90° angle), and the other isomer has the Cl^- ligands in *trans* positions (with a 180° angle between the ligands). Optical isomers are not possible.

cis isomer   *trans* isomer

(b) In this square-planar complex, the two NH_3 ligands (and the two CN^- ligands) can be either *cis* or *trans*. These are geometric isomers. Optical isomers are not possible.

cis isomer   *trans* isomer

(c) Two geometric isomers of this octahedral complex, with chloride ligands either *fac* or *mer*, are possible. In the *fac* isomer, the three Cl^- ligands are all at 90° to each other; in the *mer* isomer, two Cl^- ligands are at 180°, and the third is 90° from the other two. Optical isomers are not possible.

fac isomer   *mer* isomer

(d) Only a single structure is possible for tetrahedral complexes such as $Zn(NH_3)_2Cl_2$.

(e) Ignore the counterions, K^+. The anion is an octahedral complex—remember that the bidentate oxalate ion occupies two coordination sites of the metal, and that three oxalate ligands means that the metal has a coordination number of 6. Mirror images of complexes of the stoichiometry M(bidentate)$_3$ are not superimposable; therefore, two optical isomers are possible. (Here the ligands, $C_2O_4^{2-}$, are drawn abbreviated as O—O.)

Nonsuperimposable mirror images of $[Fe(ox)_3]^{3-}$

(f) Only linkage isomerism (structural isomerism) is possible for this octahedral cobalt complex. Either the sulfur or the nitrogen of the SCN⁻ anion can be attached to the cobalt(III) ion in this complex.

$$\begin{bmatrix} & NH_3 & \\ H_3N\text{......} & | & \text{.....}NH_3 \\ & Co & \\ H_3N & | & SCN \\ & NH_3 & \end{bmatrix}^{2+} \qquad \begin{bmatrix} & NH_3 & \\ H_3N\text{......} & | & \text{.....}NH_3 \\ & Co & \\ H_3N & | & NCS \\ & NH_3 & \end{bmatrix}^{2+}$$

S-bonded SCN⁻   N-bonded SCN⁻

EXERCISE 22.3 Isomers in Coordination Complexes

What types of isomers are possible for the following complexes?

(a) $K[Co(NH_3)_2Cl_4]$

(b) $Pt(en)Cl_2$ (square planar)

(c) $[Co(NH_3)_5Cl]^{2+}$

(d) $[Ru(phen)_3]Cl_3$

(e) $Na_2[MnCl_4]$ (tetrahedral)

(f) $[Co(NH_3)_5NO_2]^{2+}$

22.5 Bonding in Coordination Compounds

Metal–ligand bonding in a coordination complex was described earlier in this chapter as being covalent, resulting from the sharing of an electron pair between the metal and the ligand donor atom. Although frequently used, this description is not capable of explaining the color and magnetic behavior of complexes. As a consequence, the covalent bonding picture has now largely been superseded by two other bonding models: molecular orbital theory and ligand field theory.

The bonding model based on molecular orbital theory assumes that the metal and the ligand bond through the molecular orbitals formed by atomic orbital overlap between metal and ligand. The **ligand field model,** in contrast, focuses on repulsion (and destabilization) of electrons in the metal coordination sphere. The ligand field model also assumes that the positive metal ion and the negative ligand lone pair are attracted electrostatically; that is, the bond arises when a positively charged metal ion attracts a negative ion or the negative end of a polar molecule. For the most part, the molecular orbital and ligand field models predict similar, qualitative results regarding color and magnetic behavior. Here, we will focus on the ligand field approach and illustrate how it explains color and magnetism of transition metal complexes.

The *d* Orbitals: Ligand Field Theory

To understand ligand field theory, it is necessary to look at the *d* orbitals, particularly with regard to their orientation relative to the positions of ligands in a metal complex.

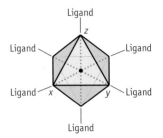

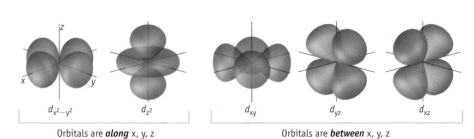

Orbitals are **along** x, y, z   Orbitals are **between** x, y, z

FIGURE 22.21 The *d* orbitals. The five *d* orbitals and their spatial relation to the ligands on the *x*-, *y*-, and *z*-axes.

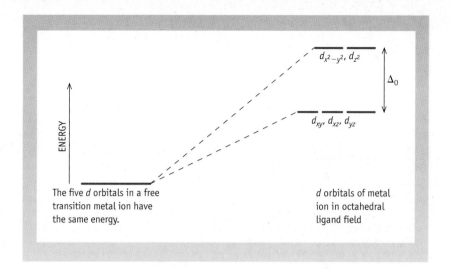

FIGURE 22.22 Ligand field splitting for an octahedral complex. The *d*-orbital energies increase as the ligands approach the metal along the *x*-, *y*-, and *z*-axes. The d_{xy}, d_{xz}, and d_{yz} orbitals, not pointed toward the ligands, are less destabilized than the $d_{x^2-y^2}$ and d_{z^2} orbitals. Thus, the d_{xy}, d_{xz}, and d_{yz} orbitals are at lower energy. (Δ_0 stands for the splitting in a octahedral ligand field.)

We look first at octahedral complexes. Assume the ligands in an octahedral complex lie along the *x*-, *y*-, and *z*-axes. This results in the five *d* orbitals (Figure 22.21) being subdivided into two sets: the $d_{x^2-y^2}$ and d_{z^2} orbitals in one set and the d_{xy}, d_{xz}, and d_{yz} orbitals in the second. The $d_{x^2-y^2}$ and d_{z^2} orbitals are directed along the *x*-, *y*-, and *z*-axes, whereas the orbitals of the second group are aligned between these axes.

In an isolated atom or ion, the five *d* orbitals have the same energy. For a metal atom or ion in a coordination complex, however, the *d* orbitals have different energies. According to the ligand field model, repulsion between *d* electrons on the metal and electron pairs of the ligands destabilizes electrons that reside in the *d* orbitals; that is, it causes their energy to increase. Electrons in the various *d* orbitals are not affected equally, however, because of their different orientations in space relative to the position of the ligand lone pairs (Figure 22.22). Electrons in the $d_{x^2-y^2}$ and d_{z^2} orbitals experience a larger repulsion because these orbitals point directly at the incoming ligand electron pairs. A smaller repulsive effect is experienced by electrons in the d_{xy}, d_{xz}, and d_{yz} orbitals. The difference in degree of repulsion means that an energy difference exists between the two sets of orbitals. This difference, called the **ligand field splitting** and denoted by the symbol Δ_0, is a function of the metal and the ligands and varies predictably from one complex to another.

A different splitting pattern is encountered with square-planar complexes (Figure 22.23). Assume that the four ligands are along the *x*- and *y*-axes. The $d_{x^2-y^2}$ orbital also points along these axes, so it has the highest energy. The d_{xy} orbital (which also lies in the *xy*-plane, but does not point at the ligands) is next highest in energy, followed by the d_{z^2} orbital. The d_{xz} and d_{yz} orbitals, both of which partially point in the *z*-direction, have the lowest energy.

The *d*-orbital splitting pattern for a tetrahedral complex is the reverse of the pattern observed for octahedral complexes. Three orbitals (d_{xz}, d_{xy}, d_{yz}) are higher in energy, whereas the $d_{x^2-y^2}$ and d_{z^2} orbitals are below them in energy (Figure 22.23).

Electron Configurations and Magnetic Properties

The *d*-orbital splitting in coordination complexes provides the means to explain both the magnetic behavior and the color of these complexes. To understand this explanation, however, we must first understand how to assign electrons to the various orbitals in each geometry.

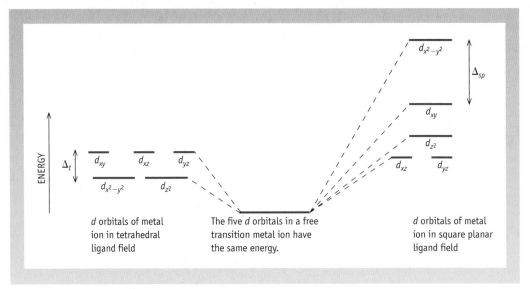

FIGURE 22.23 Splitting of the *d* orbitals in (*left*) tetrahedral and (*right*) square planar geometries. (Δ_t and Δ_{sp} are, respectively, the splitting in tetrahedral and square planar ligand fields.)

A gaseous Cr^{2+} ion has the electron configuration $[Ar]3d^4$. The term "gaseous" in this context is used to denote a single, isolated atom or ion with all other particles located an infinite distance away. In this situation, the five $3d$ orbitals have the same energy. The four electrons reside singly in different *d* orbitals, according to Hund's rule, and the Cr^{2+} ion has four unpaired electrons.

Cr(II) electron configuration

Cr^{2+} $[Ar]3d^4$ ⟨↑|↑|↑|↑| | ⟩ ⟨ ⟩
$3d$ $4s$

When the Cr^{2+} ion is part of an octahedral complex, the five *d* orbitals do not have identical energies. As illustrated in Figure 22.22, these orbitals divide into two sets, with the d_{xy}, d_{xz}, and d_{yz} orbitals having a lower energy than the $d_{x^2-y^2}$ and d_{z^2} orbitals. Having two sets of orbitals means that two different electron configurations are possible (Figure 22.24). Three of the four *d* electrons in Cr^{2+} are assigned to the lower-energy d_{xy}, d_{xz}, and d_{yz} orbitals. The fourth electron either can be assigned to an orbital in the higher-energy $d_{x^2-y^2}$ and d_{z^2} set or can pair up with an electron

FIGURE 22.24 High- and low-spin cases for an octahedral chromium(II) complex. (*left, high spin*) If the ligand field splitting (Δ_0) is smaller than the pairing energy (P), the electrons are placed in different orbitals, and the complex has four unpaired electrons. (*right, low spin*) If the splitting is larger than the pairing energy, all four electrons will be in the lower-energy orbital set. This requires pairing two electrons in one of the orbitals, so the complex will have two unpaired electrons.

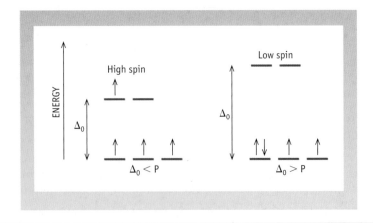

already in the lower-energy set. The first arrangement is called **high spin,** because it has the maximum number of unpaired electrons, four in the case of Cr^{2+}. The second arrangement is called **low spin,** because it has the minimum number of unpaired electrons possible.

At first glance, a high-spin configuration appears to contradict conventional thinking. It seems logical that the most stable situation would occur when electrons occupy the lowest-energy orbitals. A second factor intervenes, however. Because electrons are negatively charged, repulsion increases when they are assigned to the same orbital. This destabilizing effect bears the name **pairing energy.** The preference for an electron to be in the lowest-energy orbital and the pairing energy have opposing effects (Figure 22.24).

Low-spin complexes arise when the splitting of the d orbitals by the ligand field is large—that is, when Δ_0 has a large value. The energy gained by putting all of the electrons in the lowest-energy level is the dominant effect. In contrast, high-spin complexes occur if the value of Δ_0 is small.

For octahedral complexes, high- and low-spin complexes can occur only for configurations d^4 through d^7 (Figure 22.25). Complexes of the d^6 metal ion, Fe^{2+}, for example, can have either high spin or low spin. The complex formed when the Fe^{2+} ion is placed in water, $[Fe(H_2O)_6]^{2+}$, is high spin, whereas the $[Fe(CN)_6]^{4-}$ complex ion is low spin.

Electron configuration for Fe^{2+} in an octahedral complex

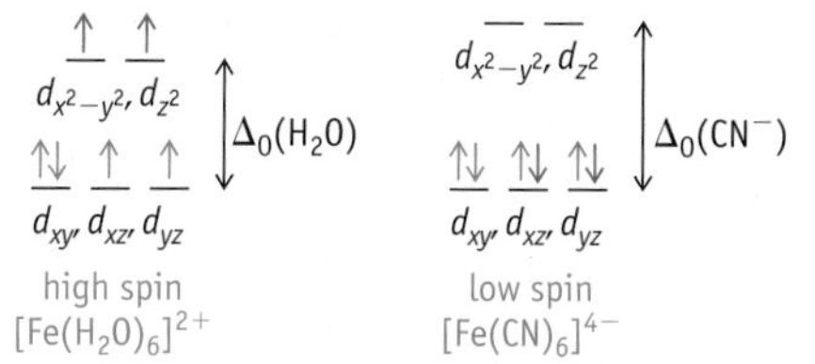

It is possible to tell whether a complex is high or low spin by examining its magnetic behavior. The high-spin complex $[Fe(H_2O)_6]^{2+}$ has four unpaired electrons and is *paramagnetic* (attracted by a magnet), whereas the low-spin $[Fe(CN)_6]^{4-}$ complex has no unpaired electrons and is *diamagnetic* (repelled by a magnet) (◄ page 293).

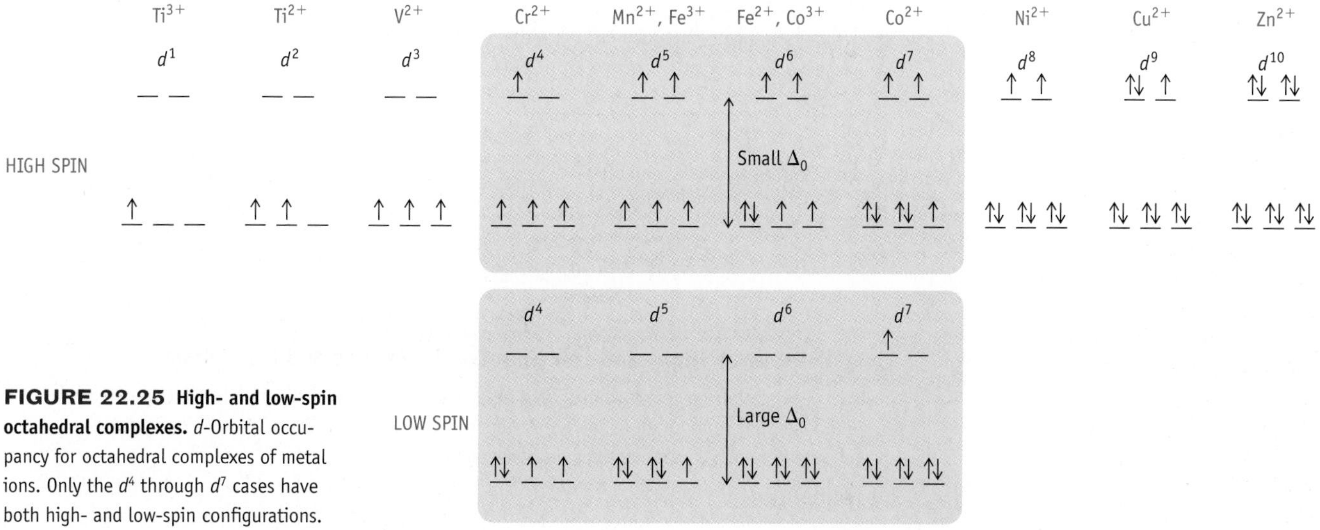

FIGURE 22.25 High- and low-spin octahedral complexes. *d*-Orbital occupancy for octahedral complexes of metal ions. Only the d^4 through d^7 cases have both high- and low-spin configurations.

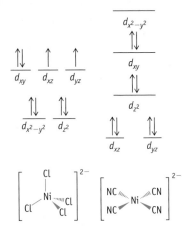

Nickel(II) complexes and magnetism. The anion $[NiCl_4]^{2-}$ is a paramagnetic tetrahedral complex. In contrast, $[Ni(CN)_4]^{2-}$ is a diamagnetic square-planar complex.

Most complexes of Pd^{2+} and Pt^{2+} ions are square planar, the electron configuration of these metals being [noble gas]$(n-1)d^8$. In a square-planar complex, there are four sets of orbitals (Figure 22.22). All except the highest-energy orbital are filled, and all electrons are paired, resulting in diamagnetic (low-spin) complexes.

Nickel, which is found above palladium in the periodic table, forms both square-planar and tetrahedral complexes. For example, the complex ion $[Ni(CN)_4]^{2-}$ is square planar, whereas the $[NiCl_4]^{2-}$ ion is tetrahedral. Magnetism allows us to differentiate between these two geometries. Based on the ligand field splitting pattern, the cyanide complex is expected to be diamagnetic, whereas the chloride complex is paramagnetic with two unpaired electrons.

Chemistry.Now™

■ **EXAMPLE 22.5** **High- and Low-Spin Complexes and Magnetism**

Problem Give the electron configuration for each of the following complexes. How many unpaired electrons are present in each complex? Are the complexes paramagnetic or diamagnetic?

(a) low-spin $[Co(NH_3)_6]^{3+}$ **(b)** high-spin $[CoF_6]^{3-}$

Strategy These ions are complexes of Co^{3+}, which has a d^6 valence electron configuration. Set up an energy-level diagram for an octahedral complex. In low-spin complexes, the electrons are added preferentially to the lower-energy set of orbitals. In high-spin complexes, the first five electrons are added singly to each of the five orbitals, then additional electrons are paired with electrons in orbitals in the lower-energy set.

Solution

(a) The six electrons of the Co^{3+} ion fill the lower-energy set of orbitals entirely. This d^6 complex ion has no unpaired electrons and is diamagnetic.

(b) To obtain the electron configuration in high-spin $[CoF_6]^{3-}$, place one electron in each of the five d orbitals, and then place the sixth electron in one of the lower-energy orbitals. The complex has four unpaired electrons and is paramagnetic.

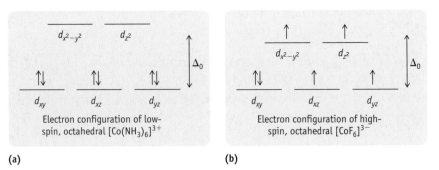

(a)   (b)

EXERCISE 22.4 **High- and Low-Spin Configurations and Magnetism**

For each of the following complex ions, give the oxidation number of the metal, depict possible low- and high-spin configurations, give the number of unpaired electrons in each configuration, and tell whether each is paramagnetic or diamagnetic.

(a) $[Ru(H_2O)_6]^{2+}$ **(b)** $[Ni(NH_3)_6]^{2+}$

FIGURE 22.26 Aqueous solutions of some transition metal ions. Compounds of transition metal elements are often colored, whereas those of main group metals are usually colorless. Pictured here, from left to right, are solutions of the nitrate salts of Fe^{3+}, Co^{2+}, Ni^{2+}, Cu^{2+}, and Zn^{2+}.

22.6 Colors of Coordination Compounds

One of the most interesting features of compounds of the transition elements is their colors (Figure 22.26). In contrast, compounds of main group metals are usually colorless. The color of transition metal compounds results from d-orbital splitting. Before discussing how d-orbital splitting is involved, we need to look more closely at what we mean by color.

Color

Visible light, consisting of radiation with wavelengths from 400 to 700 nm (◀ Section 6.1), represents a very small portion of the electromagnetic spectrum. Within this region are all the colors you see when white light passes through a prism: red, orange, yellow, green, blue, indigo, and violet (ROY G BIV). Each color is identified with a portion of the wavelength range.

Isaac Newton did experiments with light and established that the mind's perception of color requires only three colors! When we see white light, we are seeing a mixture of all of the colors—in other words, the superposition of red, green, and blue. If one or more of these colors is absent, the light of the other colors that reaches your eyes is interpreted by your mind as color.

Figure 22.27 will help you in analyzing perceived colors. This color wheel shows the three primary colors—red, green, and blue—as overlapping disks arranged in a triangle. The secondary colors—cyan, magenta, and yellow—appear where two disks overlap. The overlap of all three disks in the center produces white light.

The colors we perceive are determined as follows:

- Light of a single primary color is perceived as that color: Red light is perceived as red, green light as green, blue light as blue.
- Light made up of two primary colors is perceived as the color shown where the disks in Figure 22.27 overlap: Red and green light together appear yellow; green and blue light together are perceived as cyan; and red and blue light are perceived as magenta.
- Light made up of the three primary colors is white (colorless).

In discussing the color of a substance such as a coordination complex *in solution*, these guidelines are turned around.

- Red color is the result of the absence of green and blue light from white light.
- Green color results if red and blue light are absent from white light.
- Blue color results if red and green light are absent.

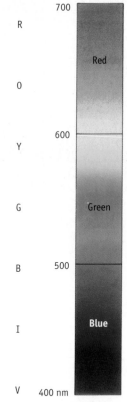

The ROY G BIV spectrum of colors of visible light. The colors used in printing this book are cyan, magenta, yellow, and black. The blue in ROY G BIV is actually cyan, according to color industry standards. Magenta doesn't have its own wavelength region. Rather, it is a mixture of blue and red.

FIGURE 22.27 Using color disks to analyze colors. The three primary colors are red, green, and blue. Adding light of two primary colors gives the secondary colors yellow (= red + green), cyan (= green + blue), and magenta (= red + blue). Adding all three primary colors results in white light.

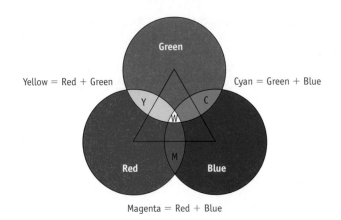

Yellow = Red + Green

Cyan = Green + Blue

Magenta = Red + Blue

Charles D. Winters

FIGURE 22.28 Light absorption and color. The color of a solution is due to the color of the light *not* absorbed by the solution. Here, a solution of Ni^{2+} ion in water absorbs red and blue light and so appears green. See also Figures 4.15–4.19.

■ **Spectrophotometry** See Section 4.8 for a description of spectrophotometry.

The secondary colors are rationalized similarly. Absorption of blue light gives yellow (the color across from it in Figure 22.27); absorption of red light results in cyan; and absorption of green light results in magenta.

Now we can apply these ideas to explain colors in transition metal complexes. Focus on what kind of light is *absorbed*. A solution of $[Ni(H_2O)_6]^{2+}$ is green. Green light is the result of removing red and blue light from white light. As white light passes through an aqueous solution of Ni^{2+}, red and blue light are absorbed, and green light is allowed to pass (Figure 22.28). Similarly, the $[Co(NH_3)_6]^{3+}$ ion is yellow because blue light has been absorbed and red and green light pass through.

The Spectrochemical Series

Recall that atomic spectra are obtained when electrons are excited from one energy level to another (◄ Section 6.3). The energy of the light absorbed or emitted is related to the energy levels of the atom or ion under study. The concept that light is absorbed when electrons move from lower to higher energy levels applies to all substances, not just atoms. It is the basic premise for the absorption of light for transition metal coordination complexes.

In coordination complexes, the splitting between d orbitals often corresponds to the energy of visible light, so light in the visible region of the spectrum is absorbed when electrons move from a lower-energy d orbital to a higher-energy d orbital. This change, as an electron moves between two orbitals having different energies in a complex, is called a **d-to-d transition.** Qualitatively, such a transition for $[Co(NH_3)_6]^{3+}$ might be represented using an energy-level diagram such as that shown here.

$$d_{x^2-y^2} \quad d_{z^2}$$

$$\Delta_0 \xrightarrow[\text{(light absorbed)}]{+ \text{energy} (\Delta_0)}$$

$$d_{x^2-y^2} \quad d_{z^2}$$

$\uparrow\downarrow$ $\uparrow\downarrow$ $\uparrow\downarrow$

d_{xy} d_{xz} d_{yz}

Ground state of low-spin, octahedral Co^{3+} complex

$\uparrow\downarrow$ $\uparrow\downarrow$ $\uparrow$

d_{xy} d_{xz} d_{yz}

Excited state

Experiments with coordination complexes reveal that, for a given metal ion, some ligands cause a small energy separation of the d orbitals, whereas others cause a large separation. In other words, some ligands create a small ligand field, and others create a large one. An example is seen in the spectroscopic data for several cobalt(III) complexes presented in Table 22.3.

- Both $[Co(NH_3)_6]^{3+}$ and $[Co(en)_3]^{3+}$ are yellow-orange, because they absorb light in the blue portion of the visible spectrum. These compounds have very similar spectra, to be expected because both have six amine-type donor atoms ($H—NH_2$ or $R—NH_2$).
- Although $[Co(CN)_6]^{3-}$ does not have an absorption band in the visible region, it is pale yellow. Light absorption occurs in the ultraviolet region, but the absorption is broad and extends minimally into the visible (blue) region.
- $[Co(C_2O_4)_3]^{3-}$ and $[Co(H_2O)_6]^{3+}$ have similar absorptions, in the yellow and violet regions. Their colors are shades of green with a small difference due to the relative amount of light of each color being absorbed.

The absorption maxima among the listed complexes range from 700 nm for $[CoF_6]^{3-}$ to 310 nm for $[Co(CN)_6]^{3-}$. The ligands change from member to member of this series, and we can conclude that the energy of the light absorbed by the complex is related to the different ligand field splittings, Δ_0, caused by the different ligands. Fluoride ion causes the smallest splitting of the d orbitals among the complexes listed in Table 22.3, whereas cyanide causes the largest splitting.

Spectra of complexes of other metals provide similar results. Based on this information, ligands can be listed in order of their ability to split the d orbitals. This list is called the **spectrochemical series** because it was determined by spectroscopy. A short list, with some of the more common ligands, follows:

$$F^-, Cl^-, Br^-, I^- < C_2O_4^{2-} < H_2O < NH_3 = en < phen < CN^-$$

small orbital splitting   large orbital splitting
small Δ_0 large Δ_0

The spectrochemical series is applicable to a wide range of metal complexes. Indeed, the ability of ligand field theory to explain the differences in the colors of the transition metal complexes is one of the strengths of this theory.

Based on the relative position of a ligand in the series, predictions can be made about a compound's magnetic behavior. Recall that d^4, d^5, d^6, and d^7 complexes can be high or low spin, depending on the ligand field splitting, Δ_0. Complexes

---

TABLE 22.3 The Colors of Some Co^{3+} Complexes*

Complex Ion	Wavelength of Light Absorbed (nm)	Color of Light Absorbed	Color of Complex
$[CoF_6]^{3-}$	700	Red	Green
$[Co(C_2O_4)_3]^{3-}$	600, 420	Yellow, violet	Dark green
$[Co(H_2O)_6]^{3+}$	600, 400	Yellow, violet	Blue-green
$[Co(NH_3)_6]^{3+}$	475, 340	Blue, ultraviolet	Yellow-orange
$[Co(en)_3]^{3+}$	470, 340	Blue, ultraviolet	Yellow-orange
$[Co(CN)_6]^{3-}$	310	Ultraviolet	Pale yellow

*The complex with fluoride ion, $[CoF_6]^{3-}$, is high spin and has one absorption band. The other complexes are low spin and have two absorption bands. In all but one case, one of these absorptions occurs in the visible region of the spectrum. The wavelengths are measured at the top of that absorption band.

formed with ligands near the left end of the spectrochemical series are expected to have small Δ_0 values and, therefore, are likely to be high spin. In contrast, complexes with ligands near the right end are expected to have large Δ_0 values and low-spin configurations. The complex $[CoF_6]^{3-}$ is high spin, whereas $[Co(NH_3)_6]^{3+}$ and the other complexes in Table 22.3 are low spin.

Chemistry .Ọ. Now™

Sign in at **www.cengage.com/login** and go to Chapter 22 Contents to see Screen 22.8 for a simulation on **the absorption and transmission of light by transition metal complexes.**

■ **EXAMPLE 22.6** Spectrochemical Series

Problem An aqueous solution of $[Fe(H_2O)_6]^{2+}$ is light blue-green. Do you expect the d^6 Fe^{2+} ion in this complex to have a high- or low-spin configuration? How would you make this determination by conducting an experiment?

Strategy Use the color wheel in Figure 22.27. The color of the complex, blue-green, tells us what kind of light is transmitted (blue and green), from which we learn what kind of light has been absorbed (red). Red light is at the low-energy end of the visible spectrum. From this fact, we can predict that the d-orbital splitting must be small. Our answer to the question derives from that conclusion.

Solution The low energy of the light absorbed suggests that $[Fe(H_2O)_6]^{2+}$ is likely to be a high-spin complex.

If the complex is high spin, it will have four unpaired electrons and be paramagnetic; if it is low spin, it will have no unpaired electrons and be diamagnetic. Identifying the presence of four unpaired electrons by measuring the compound's magnetism can be used to verify the high-spin configuration experimentally.

22.7 Organometallic Chemistry: The Chemistry of Low-Valent Metal–Organic Complexes

One of the largest and most active areas of chemistry over the past half-century has been the field of organometallic chemistry, the study of molecules having metal–carbon bonds. Thousands of such compounds have been made and characterized, and much of the activity has involved transition metals. Many have unique bonding modes and structures. In recent years, organometallic compounds have also found

There are many naturally occurring metal-based molecules such as heme, vitamin B_{12}, and the enzyme involved in fixing nitrogen (nitrogenase). Chemists have also synthesized various metal-based compounds for medical purposes. One of these, *cisplatin* [$PtCl_2(NH_3)_2$], was known for many years, but it was discovered serendipitously to be effective in treatment of certain kinds of cancers.

In 1965, Barnett Rosenberg, a biophysicist at Michigan State University, set out to study the effect of electric fields on living cells, but the results of his experiments were very different from his expectations. He and his students had placed an aqueous suspension of live *Escherichia coli* bacteria in an electric field between supposedly inert platinum electrodes. Much to their surprise, they found that cell growth was significantly affected. After careful experimentation, the effect on cell division was found to be due to a trace of the complex $PtCl_4(NH_3)_2$ formed by an electrolytic process involving the platinum electrode in the presence of ammonia in the growth medium.

To follow up on this interesting discovery, Rosenberg and his students tested the effect of *cis*- and *trans*-$PtCl_2(NH_3)_2$ on cell growth and found that only the *cis* isomer was effective. This led Rosenberg and others to study the effect of so-called *cisplatin* on cancer cell

growth, and the result is that cisplatin and similar compounds are now used to treat genitourinary tumors. In fact, testicular cancer in particular is now considered largely curable because of cisplatin chemotherapy.

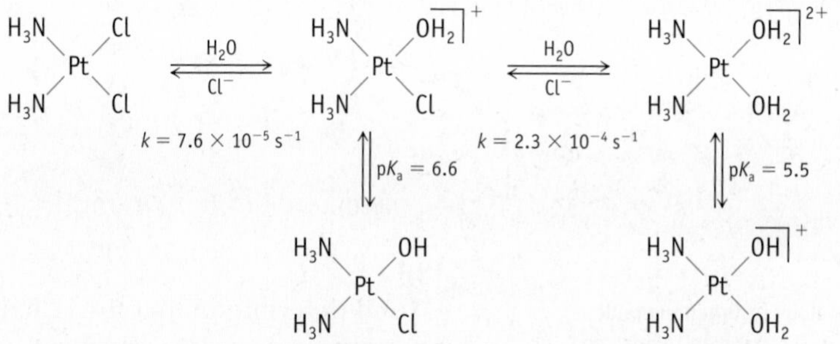

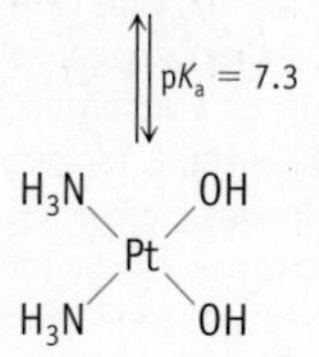

The chemistry of cisplatin has now been thoroughly studied and illustrates many of the principles of transition metal coordination chemistry. It has been found that cisplatin has a half-life of 2.5 h for the replacement of a Cl^- ligand by water at 310 K (in a first order reaction) and that the replacement of a second Cl^- ligand by water is slightly faster.

The aqua species are acidic and damaging to the kidneys, so cisplatin is generally used in a saline solution to prevent the hydrolysis reactions. It has been found that, in blood plasma at pH 7.4 and with a Cl^- ion concentration of about 1.04×10^{-5} M, $PtCl_2(NH_3)_2$

and $PtCl(OH)(NH_3)_2$ are the dominant species. In the cell nucleus, however, the Cl^- ion concentration is lower, and the aqua species are present in higher concentration.

Questions:
1. If a patient is given 10.0 mg of cisplatin, what quantity remains as cisplatin at 24 hours?
2. At a pH of 7.4, what is the ratio of concentrations of $[PtCl(NH_3)_2(H_2O)]^+$ and $PtCl(NH_3)_2(OH)$?

Answers to these questions are in Appendix Q.

The reaction scheme (top) shows, left to right:

$\begin{array}{c} H_3N \\ H_3N \end{array} Pt \begin{array}{c} Cl \\ Cl \end{array}$ $\xrightarrow[Cl^-]{H_2O}$ $\left[\begin{array}{c} H_3N \\ H_3N \end{array} Pt \begin{array}{c} \overline{OH_2} \\ Cl \end{array}\right]^+$ $\xrightarrow[Cl^-]{H_2O}$ $\left[\begin{array}{c} H_3N \\ H_3N \end{array} Pt \begin{array}{c} \overline{OH_2} \\ OH_2 \end{array}\right]^{2+}$

$k = 7.6 \times 10^{-5}\ s^{-1}$; $k = 2.3 \times 10^{-4}\ s^{-1}$

$pK_a = 6.6$; $pK_a = 5.5$

$\begin{array}{c} H_3N \\ H_3N \end{array} Pt \begin{array}{c} OH \\ Cl \end{array}$; $\left[\begin{array}{c} H_3N \\ H_3N \end{array} Pt \begin{array}{c} \overline{OH} \\ OH_2 \end{array}\right]^+$

$pK_a = 7.3$

$\begin{array}{c} H_3N \\ H_3N \end{array} Pt \begin{array}{c} OH \\ OH \end{array}$

particularly widespread use as reagents in organic synthesis and as catalysts for economically important chemical reactions.

Carbon Monoxide Complexes of Metals

In the earlier discussion of hemoglobin (page 1033), you learned that the iron in this biologically important complex binds not only to O_2 but also to CO. Our understanding of metal–CO complexes, however, emerged from the solution to a problem in industrial chemistry at the end of the 19th century.

The synthesis of sodium carbonate from NaCl, CO_2, NH_3, and H_2O by the Solvay process was an important chemical industry in the late 19th century (and remains so today in some parts of the world; page 974). In the late 1800s, a Solvay plant in England had a problem: the valves used to conduct the gaseous reactants and products rapidly corroded. A German chemist, Ludwig Mond (1839–1909), traced this problem to a small quantity of CO in the gas stream. Carbon monoxide gas reacted with nickel metal in the valves to form $Ni(CO)_4$ (Figure 22.29), tetracarbonyl nickel, a volatile liquid with a low boiling point (bp 47 °C). The deterioration of the valves occurred when the gaseous $Ni(CO)_4$ that formed was carried away in the effluent gas stream.

$$Ni(s) + 4\ CO(g) \rightleftharpoons Ni(CO)_4(g)$$

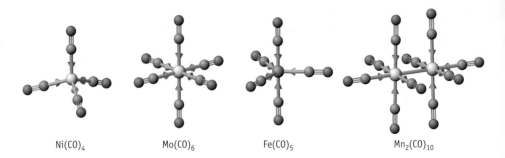

FIGURE 22.29 Metals carbonyls. $Ni(CO)_4$ is a tetrahedral molecule. Pentacarbonyliron(0) $[Fe(CO)_5]$ is trigonal bipyramidal, whereas $Mo(CO)_6$ is octahedral, and the geometry around the manganese atom in $Mn_2(CO)_{10}$ is likewise octahedral (with the sixth position being an Mn—Mn bond).

$Ni(CO)_4$ $Mo(CO)_6$ $Fe(CO)_5$ $Mn_2(CO)_{10}$

■ **Terminology in Organometallic Chemistry** The standard terminology of coordination chemistry applies to metal carbonyls. In tetracarbonylnickel(0), for example, the metal is formally zerovalent, and CO molecules are ligands. The metal has a coordination number of 4 and a tetrahedral coordination geometry.

Mond determined that the reaction forming $Ni(CO)_4$ is reversible; at moderate temperatures or at low pressures, CO is liberated, and nickel metal reforms. He then exploited the formation and decomposition reactions in a process to obtain pure nickel. Nickel and cobalt are generally found together in nature. Because of this, the two metals are obtained together when ores are refined, and they are difficult to separate. However, if a mixture of the metals is exposed to CO, nickel is converted to $Ni(CO)_4$ whereas cobalt is unchanged. Volatile $Ni(CO)_4$ is easily separated from solid cobalt metal. The $Ni(CO)_4$ can then be decomposed to give pure nickel. The Mond process, as it is now known, was the preferred procedure to obtain pure nickel for the first half of the 20th century.

Nickel is unique among metals in its facile reaction with CO, but many other transition metal carbonyl compounds are now known and can be synthesized by a variety of procedures. One of the most common is reductive carbonylation, in which a metal salt is reduced in the presence of CO, usually under high pressure. In effect, reduction of the metal salt gives metal atoms. Before these very reactive atoms aggregate to form the unreactive bulk metal, however, they react with CO. Metal carbonyls of most of the transition metals can be made by this route. Simple examples include hexacarbonyls of the Group 6B metals $[Cr(CO)_6, Mo(CO)_6,$ and $WCO)_6,]$ as well as $Fe(CO)_5$ and $Mn_2(CO)_{10}$ (Figure 22.29).

The Effective Atomic Number Rule and Bonding in Organometallic Compounds

An important observation has guided researchers studying these metal–CO complexes and other organometallic compounds. The **effective atomic number (EAN) rule,** now often referred to as the **18-electron rule,** states that compounds in which the sum of the metal valence electrons plus the electrons donated by the ligand groups totals 18 are likely to be stable. Thus, the 18-electron rule predicts the stoichiometry of a number of compounds. Iron(0), for example, which has eight valence electrons, would be expected to coordinate to five CO ligands. Each CO donates two electrons for a total of 10; adding these to the eight valence electrons on the metal gives 18 electrons around the Fe atom (Figure 22.30). We now recognize that the 18-electron rule is similar to the octet rule in main group chemistry, in that it defines the likely number of bonds to an element.

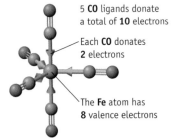

5 **CO** ligands donate a total of **10** electrons

Each **CO** donates 2 electrons

The **Fe** atom has 8 valence electrons

FIGURE 22.30 The EAN rule and $Fe(CO)_5$. The EAN or 18-electron rule states that stable organometallic compounds frequently have 18 valence electrons around the central metal. (There are also many 16-electron molecules, particularly of the heavier transition metals. See Study Question 22.34.) Here, the zerovalent Fe atom has the configuration $[Ar]3d^6 4s^2$, so eight valence electrons are available for bonding.

The bonding in traditional coordination compounds is described as being due to attractive forces between a positively charged metal ion and a polar molecule or an anion, and the properties of these species are in accord with substantial ionic character to the metal-ligand bond. In metal carbonyls, the zerovalent metal lacks a charge, and CO is only slightly polar. Both features argue against ionic bonding. The best model for these species instead describes the bonding between

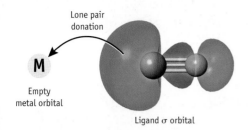

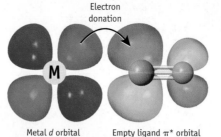

Lone pair donation

Empty metal orbital

Ligand σ orbital

Electron donation

Metal *d* orbital   Empty ligand π* orbital

Ligand to metal sigma bonding.
Donation of **CO** lone pair to empty orbital on **M**.

Metal to ligand pi bonding.
Donation of electrons from filled **M** *d* orbital to empty pi* antibonding orbital on **CO**.

FIGURE 22.31 Bonding in metal carbonyls. The current understanding is that the CO ligand donates a lone pair of electrons to the low-valent metal to form a sigma bond. The electron-rich metal then donates electrons from a *d* orbital to the antibonding π* orbital of the CO. There is a "synergistic" effect; the sigma and pi bonds complement each other.

the metal and CO as covalent. Each CO donates a C-atom lone pair to the metal atom to form a sigma bond (Figure 22.31). However, carbon monoxide is a very poor donor, and this alone would not lead to these species being stable. Rather, in conjunction with the sigma bond, the electron-rich metal donates a pair of electrons to form a π bond formed by overlap of a *d* orbital of the metal and a π* antibonding orbital of CO. The latter interaction is described as $d\pi-p\pi$ bonding. Based on this model of bonding, carbon monoxide in these compounds is best described as a σ donor and π acceptor ligand.

Ligands in Organometallic Compounds

The bonding model for metal–CO complexes leads to important conclusions: only metals of low charge and with filled or partially filled *d* orbitals can form stable bonds to CO, and only ligands capable of forming π bonds with the metal are capable of forming low-valent metal compounds. Thus, this area is dominated by low-valent metals and special types of ligands that are capable of π bonding.

Some of the most common ligands in coordination chemistry cannot engage in π bonding and thus cannot form low-valent compounds with transition metals. For example, low-valent metal complexes with NH_3 or amines (such as $N(CH_3)_3$) do not exist, but phosphine complexes of zerovalent metals are well known. Phosphines, such as $P(CH_3)_3$, are the phosphorus analogs of amines and so have a lone pair of electrons on the P atom. Thus, phosphines can donate this lone pair to a metal to form a sigma bond. In addition, phosphorus atoms have empty $3d$ orbitals, and these can form a $d\pi-p\pi$ bond with the filled *d*-orbitals of a low-valent metal. Ammonia, with no empty valence orbitals to overlap with a filled metal *d* orbitals, cannot form such π bonds.

Yet another class of molecules that can serve as ligands in organometallic compounds are organic species such as ethylene (C_2H_4) and benzene (C_6H_6). For example, in the anion of Zeise's salt, ethylene binds to a Pt^{2+} ion through donation of the two π electrons of the double bond (Figure 22.32). As in metal carbonyls, there is also a metal-to-ligand π bond formed by overlap of filled metal *d* orbitals with the antibonding π orbitals from the ligand. This combination of bonding modes strengthens the metal-ligand bond.

Benzene can be thought of as a tridentate ligand capable of donating three π electron pairs to a metal atom (which then donates *d* electrons back to the ligand in a π-type interaction). Such molecules also obey the 18-electron rule. For example, in dibenzenechromium (Figure 22.33), the Cr(0) atom with six valence electrons is bound to two ligands, each donating six electrons.

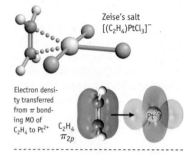

Zeise's salt
$[(C_2H_4)PtCl_3]^-$

Electron density transferred from π bonding MO of C_2H_4 to Pt^{2+} C_2H_4 π_{2p}

Electron density transferred from Pt^{2+} to π antibonding MO of C_2H_4 C_2H_4 π^*_{2p}

FIGURE 22.32 Bonding in the anion of Zeise's salt.

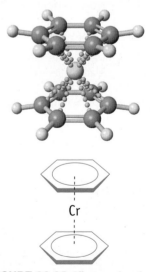

Cr

FIGURE 22.33 Dibenzenechromium. Two views of the molecule. Top: a computer-generated model. Bottom: a line drawing typically used by chemists.

Unexpected discoveries open up new areas of science. One example was the synthesis of compounds of Xe (page 405), a result that destroyed the myth that the noble gases were unreactive and led to a rich chemistry of these elements. At approximately the same time, another discovery, the synthesis of ferrocene, $Fe(C_5H_5)_2$, set the stage for the rapid and exciting growth of organometallic chemistry, the chemistry of compounds containing metal–carbon bonds. This destroyed another common myth of the time, that metal–carbon bonds are inherently unstable. Xenon compounds and ferrocene spearheaded a renaissance in inorganic chemistry that continues to this day.

The synthesis of ferrocene in two quite dissimilar research laboratories was accidental and unexpected. The first report, from an academic laboratory, described the reaction of the cyclopentadienide anion, $[C_5H_5]^-$ with $FeCl_2$. This reaction was intended to provide a precursor to an elusive organic compound fulvalene, $(C_5H_4)_2$ but a completely new substance—ferrocene—was obtained instead. The second report, from an industrial laboratory, described a high temperature process in which cyclopentadiene was passed over a liquid ammonia catalyst that contained, among other things, iron(II) oxide.

$$2\ C_5H_5MgCl + FeCl_2 \rightarrow Fe(\eta^5\text{-}C_5H_5)_2 + MgCl_2$$
(in diethyl ether)

$$2\ C_5H_6(g) + FeO(s) \rightarrow Fe(\eta^5\text{-}C_5H_5)_2(s) + H_2O(g)$$
(at high temperature)

The properties of ferrocene were unexpected. Ferrocene is a diamagnetic orange solid, has a relatively low melting (mp 173 °C), and is soluble in organic solvents but not in water. Most striking is its thermal and oxidative stability. Ferrocene is unaffected by oxygen,

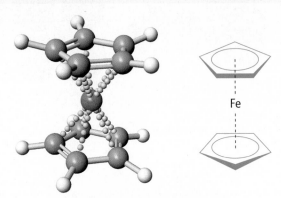

The structure of ferrocene, $Fe(\eta^5\text{-}C_5H_5)_2$

water, aqueous bases and nonoxidizing acids under ambient conditions, and can be heated to over 450 °C. These observations contradicted conventional wisdom that held that metal–carbon bonds were weak and unstable, hard to make, and reactive.

The structure of ferrocene was quickly established by x-ray crystallography. Like dibenzenechromium (Figure 22.23), ferrocene is a molecular "sandwich" compound, containing an iron atom sandwiched between two planar hydrocarbon rings (Figure). Iron(II), a d^6 metal ion, is in its low spin configuration. The cyclopentadienyl anions can be thought of as tridentate ligands with the six π electrons (three pairs) of each organic ring being donated to the metal ion.

Once the structure of ferrocene was known, the race was on to make other complexes with unsaturated hydrocarbon ligands. Synthesis of cyclopentadienyl compounds of other metals soon followed, and now hundreds are known in combination with CO, benzene, ethylene, and many other carbon-containing compounds. The

discovery of ferrocene was one of the keys that unlocked the field of organometallic chemistry.

Questions:

1. *Rationalize ferrocene's diamagnetism.*
2. *Dibenzenechromium is also a "sandwich" compound. What is the oxidation state of chromium in this compound? Is it diamagnetic or paramagnetic?*
3. *Do ferrocene and dibenzenechromium obey the 18-electron rule (page 1048)?*
4. *Ferrocene can be oxidized to form the ferrocenium cation, $[Fe(\eta\text{-}C_5H_5)_2]^+$. The standard reduction potential for the ferrocenium–ferrocene half-reaction is 0.400 V. Identify several oxidizing agents in Appendix M that are capable of oxidizing ferrocene. Is elemental chlorine, Cl_2, a sufficiently strong oxidizing agent to carry out this oxidation?*
5. *Write an equation for one way to synthesize nickelocene, $Ni(\eta^5\text{-}C_5H_5)_2$. Nickelocene is paramagnetic. Predict the number of unpaired electrons in this compound.*

Answers to these questions are in Appendix Q.

Dibenzenechromium is one of many organometallic compounds often referred to as "sandwich" compounds. (See *Case Study: Ferrocene.*) These are molecular compounds in which a low-valent metal atom is "sandwiched" between two organic ligands. In addition, they are often referred to as π complexes because the π electrons of the ligand are involved in bonding. Modern terminology uses the Greek letter eta (η) to indicate this type of attachment, so dibenzenechromium is properly symbolized as $Cr(\eta^6\text{-}C_6H_6)_2$ (where the superscript 6 indicates the number of carbon atoms involved in bonding on each ligand).

Problem Show that each of the following molecules or ions satisfies the EAN rule.

(a) $[Fe(CO)_2(\eta^5\text{-}C_5H_5)]^-$

(b) $[Mn(CO)_5]^-$

(c) $Co(C_2H_4)_2(\eta^5\text{-}C_5H_5)$

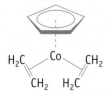

Strategy A complex obeys the EAN rule if the total number of electrons around the metal (valence electrons from the metal itself + electrons donated by the ligands) equals 18. Recognize that CO and C_2H_4 are both two-electron donors and that $C_5H_5^-$ is a six-electron donor. For the metal center, take its total number of valence electrons, and add or subtract electrons as necessary to adjust for negative or positive charges.

Solution

(a) The overall charge is 1−, which is equal to the charge on the $C_5H_5^-$ group. Thus, the Fe atom must have no charge.

6 electrons for $C_5H_5^-$ +8 electrons for Fe + 4 electrons for 2 CO groups = 18 electrons

(b) Because CO is neutral the Mn center must have a negative charge. This means the manganese center has effectively eight valence electrons. Together with the five CO groups, each donating two electrons, the total is 18 electrons.

(c) This is a neutral molecule, so the negative charge on the $C_5H_5^-$ group must be balanced by a positive charge on Co. The Co^+ ion has eight valence electrons. Each C_2H_4 molecule donates two electrons.

6 electrons for $C_5H_5^-$ +8 electrons for Co^+ +4 electrons for 2 C_2H_4 molecules = 18 electrons

---

EXERCISE 22.5 The Effective Atomic Number Rule

Show that the two molecules below satisfy the EAN rule.

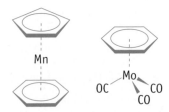

Chapter Goals Revisited

Now that you have studied this chapter, you should ask whether you have met the chapter goals. In particular, you should be able to:

Identify and explain the chemical and physical properties of the transition elements

a. Identify the general classes of transition elements (Section 22.1).

b. Identify the transition metals from their symbols and positions in the periodic table, and recall some physical and chemical properties (Section 22.1).

c. Understand the electrochemical nature of corrosion (Section 22.1).

d. Describe the metallurgy of iron and copper (Section 22.2).

Understand the composition, structure, and bonding in coordination compounds

a. Given the formula for a coordination complex, identify the metal and its oxidation state, the ligands, the coordination number and coordination geometry, and the overall charge on the complex (Section 22.3). Relate names and formulas of complexes. Study Question(s) assignable in OWL: 18, 20, 48, 57.

b. Given the formula for a complex, be able to recognize whether isomers will exist, and draw their structures (Section 22.4). Study Question(s) assignable in OWL: 28, 40, 48, 50.

c. Describe the bonding in coordination complexes (Section 22.5).

d. Apply the principles of stoichiometry, thermodynamics, and equilibrium to transition metal compounds. Study Question(s) assignable in OWL: 42, 55, 59, 64, 67, 68, 70.

Relate ligand field theory to the magnetic and spectroscopic properties of complexes

a. Understand why substances are colored (Section 22.6). Study Question(s) assignable in OWL: 32.

b. Understand the relationship between the ligand field splitting, magnetism, and color of complexes (Section 22.6). Study Question(s) assignable in OWL: 26, 28, 59, 60, 63.

Apply the effective atomic number rule to simple organometallic compounds of the transition metals.

a. Apply the EAN rule to molecules containing a low-valent metal and ligands such as C_6H_6, C_2H_4, and CO.

STUDY QUESTIONS

OWL Online homework for this chapter may be assigned in OWL.

▲ denotes challenging questions.

■ denotes questions assignable in OWL.

Blue-numbered questions have answers in Appendix O and fully-worked solutions in the *Student Solutions Manual*.

Practicing Skills

Properties of Transition Elements
(See Section 22.1 and Example 7.3.)

1. Give the electron configuration for each of the following ions, and tell whether each is paramagnetic or diamagnetic.
   (a) Cr^{3+} (b) V^{2+} (c) Ni^{2+} (d) Cu^+

2. Identify two transition metal cations with the following electron configurations.
   (a) $[Ar]3d^6$ (b) $[Ar]3d^{10}$ (c) $[Ar]3d^5$ (d) $[Ar]3d^8$

3. Identify a cation of a first series transition metal that is isoelectronic with each of the following.
   (a) Fe^{3+} (b) Zn^{2+} (c) Fe^{2+} (d) Cr^{3+}

4. Match up the isoelectronic ions on the following list.

   Cu^+ Mn^{2+} Fe^{2+} Co^{3+} Fe^{3+} Zn^{2+} Ti^{2+} V^{3+}

5. The following equations represent various ways of obtaining transition metals from their compounds. Balance each equation.
   (a) $Cr_2O_3(s) + Al(s) \longrightarrow Al_2O_3(s) + Cr(s)$
   (b) $TiCl_4(\ell) + Mg(s) \longrightarrow Ti(s) + MgCl_2(s)$
   (c) $[Ag(CN)_2]^-(aq) + Zn(s) \longrightarrow$
   $$Ag(s) + [Zn(CN)_4]^{2-}(aq)$$
   (d) $Mn_3O_4(s) + Al(s) \longrightarrow Mn(s) + Al_2O_3(s)$

6. Identify the products of each reaction, and balance the equation.
   (a) $CuSO_4(aq) + Zn(s) \longrightarrow$
   (b) $Zn(s) + HCl(aq) \longrightarrow$
   (c) $Fe(s) + Cl_2(g) \longrightarrow$
   (d) $V(s) + O_2(g) \longrightarrow$

Formulas of Coordination Compounds
(See Examples 22.1 and 22.2.)

7. Which of the following ligands is expected to be monodentate, and which might be polydentate?
   (a) CH_3NH_2 (d) en
   (b) CH_3CN (e) Br^-
   (c) N_3^- (f) phen

8. One of the following nitrogen compounds or ions is not capable of serving as a ligand: NH_4^+, NH_3, NH_2^-. Identify this species, and explain your answer.

9. Give the oxidation number of the metal ion in each of the following compounds.
   (a) $[Mn(NH_3)_6]SO_4$ (c) $[Co(NH_3)_4Cl_2]Cl$
   (b) $K_3[Co(CN)_6]$ (d) $Cr(en)_2Cl_2$

10. Give the oxidation number of the metal ion in each of the following complexes.
    (a) $[Fe(NH_3)_6]^{2+}$ (c) $[Co(NH_3)_5(NO_2)]^+$
    (b) $[Zn(CN)_4]^{2-}$ (d) $[Cu(en)_2]^{2+}$

11. Give the formula of a complex constructed from one Ni^{2+} ion, one ethylenediamine ligand, three ammonia molecules, and one water molecule. Is the complex neutral or is it charged? If charged, give the charge.

12. Give the formula of a complex constructed from one Cr^{3+} ion, two ethylenediamine ligands, and two ammonia molecules. Is the complex neutral or is it charged? If charged, give the charge.

Naming Coordination Compounds
(See Example 22.3.)

13. Write formulas for the following ions or compounds.
    (a) dichlorobis(ethylenediamine)nickel(II)
    (b) potassium tetrachloroplatinate(II)
    (c) potassium dicyanocuprate(I)
    (d) tetraamminediaquairon(II)

14. Write formulas for the following ions or compounds.
    (a) diamminetriaquahydroxochromium(II) nitrate
    (b) hexaammineiron(III) nitrate
    (c) pentacarbonyliron(0) (where the ligand is CO)
    (d) ammonium tetrachlorocuprate(II)

15. Name the following ions or compounds.
    (a) $[Ni(C_2O_4)_2(H_2O)_2]^{2-}$ (c) $[Co(en)_2(NH_3)Cl]^{2+}$
    (b) $[Co(en)_2Br_2]^+$ (d) $Pt(NH_3)_2(C_2O_4)$

16. Name the following ions or compounds.
    (a) $[Co(H_2O)_4Cl_2]^+$ (c) $[Pt(NH_3)Br_3]^-$
    (b) $Co(H_2O)_3F_3$ (d) $[Co(en)(NH_3)_3Cl]^{2+}$

17. Give the name or formula for each ion or compound, as appropriate.
    (a) pentaaquahydroxoiron(III) ion
    (b) $K_2[Ni(CN)_4]$
    (c) $K[Cr(C_2O_4)_2(H_2O)_2]$
    (d) ammonium tetrachloroplatinate(II)

18. ■ Give the name or formula for each ion or compound, as appropriate.
    (a) tetraaquadichlorochromium(III) chloride
    (b) $[Cr(NH_3)_5SO_4]Cl$
    (c) sodium tetrachlorocobaltate(II)
    (d) $[Fe(C_2O_4)_3]^{3-}$

Isomerism
(See Example 22.4.)

19. Draw all possible geometric isomers of the following.
    (a) $Fe(NH_3)_4Cl_2$
    (b) $Pt(NH_3)_2(SCN)(Br)$ (SCN^- is bonded to Pt^{2+} through S)
    (c) $Co(NH_3)_3(NO_2)_3$ (NO_2^- is bonded to Co^{3+} through N)
    (d) $[Co(en)Cl_4]^-$

20. ■ In which of the following complexes are geometric isomers possible? If isomers are possible, draw their structures and label them as *cis* or *trans,* or as *fac* or *mer.*
    (a) $[Co(H_2O)_4Cl_2]^+$ (c) $[Pt(NH_3)Br_3]^-$
    (b) $Co(NH_3)_3F_3$ (d) $[Co(en)_2(NH_3)Cl]^{2+}$

21. Determine whether the following complexes have a chiral metal center.
    (a) $[Fe(en)_3]^{2+}$
    (b) trans-$[Co(en)_2Br_2]^+$
    (c) *fac*-$[Co(en)(H_2O)Cl_3]$
    (d) square-planar $Pt(NH_3)(H_2O)(Cl)(NO_2)$

22. Four geometric isomers are possible for $[Co(en)(NH_3)_2(H_2O)Cl]^+$. Draw the structures of all four. (Two of the isomers are chiral, meaning that each has a non-superimposable mirror image.)

Magnetic Properties of Complexes
(See Example 22.5.)

23. The following are low-spin complexes. Use the ligand field model to find the electron configuration of each ion. Determine which are diamagnetic. Give the number of unpaired electrons for the paramagnetic complexes.
    (a) $[Mn(CN)_6]^{4-}$ (c) $[Fe(H_2O)_6]^{3+}$
    (b) $[Co(NH_3)_6]Cl_3$ (d) $[Cr(en)_3]SO_4$

24. The following are high-spin complexes. Use the ligand field model to find the electron configuration of each ion, and determine the number of unpaired electrons in each.
    (a) $K_4[FeF_6]$
    (b) $[MnF_6]^{4-}$
    (c) $[Cr(H_2O)_6]^{2+}$
    (d) $(NH_4)_3[FeF_6]$

25. Determine the number of unpaired electrons in the following tetrahedral complexes. All tetrahedral complexes are high spin.
    (a) $[FeCl_4]^{2-}$
    (b) $Na_2[CoCl_4]$
    (c) $[MnCl_4]^{2-}$
    (d) $(NH_4)_2[ZnCl_4]$

26. ■ Determine the number of unpaired electrons in the following tetrahedral complexes. All tetrahedral complexes are high spin.
    (a) $[Zn(H_2O)_4]^{2+}$
    (b) $VOCl_3$
    (c) $Mn(NH_3)_2Cl_2$
    (d) $[Cu(en)_2]^{2+}$

27. For the high-spin complex $[Fe(H_2O)_6]SO_4$, identify the following:
    (a) the coordination number of iron
    (b) the coordination geometry for iron
    (c) the oxidation number of iron
    (d) the number of unpaired electrons
    (e) whether the complex is diamagnetic or paramagnetic

28. ■ For the low-spin complex $[Co(en)(NH_3)_2Cl_2]ClO_4$, identify the following:
    (a) the coordination number of cobalt
    (b) the coordination geometry for cobalt
    (c) the oxidation number of cobalt
    (d) the number of unpaired electrons
    (e) whether the complex is diamagnetic or paramagnetic
    (f) Draw any geometric isomers.

29. The anion $[NiCl_4]^{2-}$ is paramagnetic, but when CN^- ions are added, the product, $[Ni(CN)_4]^{2-}$, is diamagnetic. Explain this observation.

$$[NiCl_4]^{2-}(aq) + 4\ CN^-(aq) \longrightarrow$$
paramagnetic
$$[Ni(CN)_4]^{2-}(aq) + 4\ Cl^-(aq)$$
diamagnetic

30. An aqueous solution of iron(II) sulfate is paramagnetic. If NH_3 is added, the solution becomes diamagnetic. Why does the magnetism change?

Spectroscopy of Complexes
(See Example 22.6.)

31. In water, the titanium(III) ion, $[Ti(H_2O)_6]^{3+}$, has a broad absorption band at about 500 nm. What color light is absorbed by the ion?

32. ■ In water, the chromium(II) ion, $[Cr(H_2O)_6]^{2+}$, absorbs light with a wavelength of about 700 nm. What color is the solution?

Organometallic Compounds
(See Example 22.7.)

33. Show that the molecules and ions below satisfy the EAN rule.
    (a) $[Mn(CO)_6]^+$ (b)   (c)

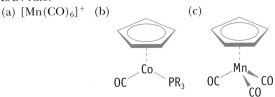

(In (b) PR_3 is a phosphine such as $P(C_6H_5)_3$, a two-electron donor ligand.)

34. Many organometallic compounds of the transition metals satisfy the 18-electron rule. However, there also are many other stable molecules that have only 16-valence electrons. These often have the capability of adding more ligands and function as catalysts in chemical reactions (see Study Question 71). (In the molecules below, PR_3 is a phosphine such as $P(C_6H_5)_3$, a two-electron donor ligand. For electron counting purposes, the CH_3 or methyl group is considered an anion, $(CH_3)^-$, and also a two-electron donor ligand.) Which molecules below have 18-valence electrons and which have 16?

General Questions
These questions are not designated as to type or location in the chapter. They may contain several concepts.

35. Describe an experiment that would determine whether nickel in $K_2[NiCl_4]$ is square planar or tetrahedral.

36. Which of the following low-spin complexes has the greatest number of unpaired electrons?
    (a) $[Cr(H_2O)_6]^{3+}$
    (b) $[Mn(H_2O)_6]^{2+}$
    (c) $[Fe(H_2O)_6]^{2+}$
    (d) $[Ni(H_2O)_6]^{2+}$

37. How many unpaired electrons are expected for high-spin and low-spin complexes of Fe^{2+}?

38. Excess silver nitrate is added to a solution containing 1.0 mol of $[Co(NH_3)_4Cl_2]Cl$. What amount of AgCl (in moles) will precipitate?

39. Which of the following complexes is (are) square planar?
    (a) $[Ti(CN)_4]^{2-}$
    (b) $[Ni(CN)_4]^{2-}$
    (c) $[Zn(CN)_4]^{2-}$
    (d) $[Pt(CN)_4]^{2-}$

▲ more challenging   ■ in OWL   Blue-numbered questions answered in Appendix O

40. ■ Which of the following complexes containing the oxalate ion is (are) chiral?
    (a) $[Fe(C_2O_4)Cl_4]^{2-}$
    (b) *cis*-$[Fe(C_2O_4)_2Cl_2]^{2-}$
    (c) *trans*-$[Fe(C_2O_4)_2Cl_2]^{2-}$

41. How many geometric isomers are possible for the square-planar complex $[Pt(NH_3)(CN)Cl_2]^-$?

42. ■ For a tetrahedral complex of a metal in the first transition series, which of the following statements concerning energies of the $3d$ orbitals is correct?
    (a) The five d orbitals have the same energy.
    (b) The $d_{x^2-y^2}$ and d_{z^2} orbitals are higher in energy than the d_{xz}, d_{yz}, and d_{xy} orbitals.
    (c) The d_{xz}, d_{yz}, and d_{xy} orbitals are higher in energy than the $d_{x^2-y^2}$ and d_{z^2} orbitals.
    (d) The d orbitals all have different energies.

43. A transition metal complex absorbs 425-nm light. What is its color?
    (a) red   (c) yellow
    (b) green   (d) blue

44. ■ For the low-spin complex $[Fe(en)_2Cl_2]Cl$, identify the following.
    (a) the oxidation number of iron
    (b) the coordination number for iron
    (c) the coordination geometry for iron
    (d) the number of unpaired electrons per metal atom
    (e) whether the complex is diamagnetic or paramagnetic
    (f) the number of geometric isomers

45. For the high-spin complex $Mn(NH_3)_4Cl_2$, identify the following.
    (a) the oxidation number of manganese
    (b) the coordination number for manganese
    (c) the coordination geometry for manganese
    (d) the number of unpaired electrons per metal atom
    (e) whether the complex is diamagnetic or paramagnetic
    (f) the number of geometric isomers

46. ■ A platinum-containing compound, known as Magnus's green salt, has the formula $[Pt(NH_3)_4][PtCl_4]$ (in which both platinum ions are Pt^{2+}). Name the cation and the anion.

47. Early in the 20th century, complexes sometimes were given names based on their colors. Two compounds with the formula $CoCl_3 \cdot 4\,NH_3$ were named praseo-cobalt chloride (*praseo* = green) and violio-cobalt chloride (violet color). We now know that these compounds are octahedral cobalt complexes and that they are *cis* and *trans* isomers. Draw the structures of these two compounds, and name them using systematic nomenclature.

48. ■ Give the formula and name of a square-planar complex of Pt^{2+} with one nitrite ion (NO_2^-, which binds to Pt^{2+} through N), one chloride ion, and two ammonia molecules as ligands. Are isomers possible? If so, draw the structure of each isomer, and tell what type of isomerism is observed.

49. Give the formula of the complex formed from one Co^{3+} ion, two ethylenediamine molecules, one water molecule, and one chloride ion. Is the complex neutral or charged? If charged, give the net charge on the ion.

50. ■ ▲ How many geometric isomers of the complex $[Cr(dmen)_3]^{3+}$ can exist? (dmen is the bidentate ligand 1,1-dimethylethylenediamine.)

$$(CH_3)_2\ddot{N}CH_2CH_2\ddot{N}H_2$$

1,1-Dimethylethylenediamine, dmen

51. ▲ Diethylenetriamine (dien) is capable of serving as a tridentate ligand.

$$H_2\ddot{N}CH_2CH_2-\overset{\displaystyle |}{\underset{\displaystyle H}{N}}-CH_2CH_2\ddot{N}H_2$$

Diethylenetriamine, dien

    (a) Draw the structures of *fac*-$Cr(dien)Cl_3$ and *mer*-$Cr(dien)Cl_3$.
    (b) Two different geometric isomers of *mer*-$Cr(dien)Cl_2Br$ are possible. Draw the structure for each.
    (c) Three different geometric isomers are possible for $[Cr(dien)_2]^{3+}$. Two have the dien ligand in a *fac* configuration, and one has the ligand in a *mer* orientation. Draw the structure of each isomer.

52. From experiment, we know that $[CoF_6]^{3-}$ is paramagnetic and $[Co(NH_3)_6]^{3+}$ is diamagnetic. Using the ligand field model, depict the electron configuration for each ion, and use this model to explain the magnetic property. What can you conclude about the effect of the ligand on the magnitude of Δ_0?

53. Three geometric isomers are possible for $[Co(en)(NH_3)_2(H_2O)_2]^{3+}$. One of the three is chiral; that is, it has a non-superimposable mirror image. Draw the structures of the three isomers. Which one is chiral?

54. The square-planar complex $Pt(en)Cl_2$ has chloride ligands in a *cis* configuration. No *trans* isomer is known. Based on the bond lengths and bond angles of carbon and nitrogen in the ethylenediamine ligand, explain why the *trans* compound is not possible.

55. ■ The complex $[Mn(H_2O)_6]^{2+}$ has five unpaired electrons, whereas $[Mn(CN)_6]^{4-}$ has only one. Using the ligand field model, depict the electron configuration for each ion. What can you conclude about the effects of the different ligands on the magnitude of Δ_0?

56. Experiments show that $K_4[Cr(CN)_6]$ is paramagnetic and has two unpaired electrons. The related complex $K_4[Cr(SCN)_6]$ is paramagnetic and has four unpaired electrons. Account for the magnetism of each compound using the ligand field model. Predict where the SCN^- ion occurs in the spectrochemical series relative to CN^-.

57. ■ Give a systematic name or the formula for the following:
(a) $(NH_4)_2[CuCl_4]$
(b) $Mo(CO)_6$
(c) tetraaquadichlorochromium(III) chloride
(d) aquabis(ethylenediamine)thiocyanatocobalt(III) nitrate

58. When $CrCl_3$ dissolves in water, three different species can be obtained.
(a) $[Cr(H_2O)_6]Cl_3$, violet
(b) $[Cr(H_2O)_5Cl]Cl_2$, pale green
(c) $[Cr(H_2O)_4Cl_2]Cl$, dark green

If diethyl ether is added, a fourth complex can be obtained: $Cr(H_2O)_3Cl_3$ (brown). Describe an experiment that will allow you to differentiate these complexes.

59. ■ ▲ The complex ion $[Co(CO_3)_3]^{3-}$, an octahedral complex with bidentate carbonate ions as ligands, has one absorption in the visible region of the spectrum at 640 nm. From this information:
(a) Predict the color of this complex, and explain your reasoning.
(b) Is the carbonate ion as weak- or strong-field ligand?
(c) Predict whether $[Co(CO_3)_3]^{3-}$ will be paramagnetic or diamagnetic.

60. ■ The glycinate ion, $H_2NCH_2CO_2^-$, formed by deprotonation of the amino acid glycine, can function as a bidentate ligand, coordinating to a metal through the nitrogen of the amino group and one of the oxygen atoms.

Glycinate ion, a bidentate ligand

Site of bonding to transition metal ion

A copper complex of this ligand has the formula $Cu(H_2NCH_2CO_2)_2(H_2O)_2$. For this complex, determine the following.
(a) the oxidation state of copper
(b) the coordination number of copper
(c) the number of unpaired electrons
(d) whether the complex is diamagnetic or paramagnetic

61. ▲ Draw structures for the five possible geometric isomers of $Cu(H_2NCH_2CO_2)_2(H_2O)_2$. Are any of these species chiral? (See the structure of the ligand in Study Question 60.)

62. Chromium forms two anionic carbonyls, $[Cr(CO)_5]^{x-}$ and $[Cr(CO)_4]^{y-}$. What are the values of x and y?

63. ■ Nickel and palladium both form complexes of the general formula $M(PR_3)_2Cl_2$ (where PR_3 is a phosphine such as $P(C_6H_5)_3$, triphenylphosphine). The nickel(II) compound is paramagnetic whereas the palladium(II) compound is diamagnetic.
(a) Explain the magnetic properties of these compounds.
(b) How many isomers of each compound are expected?

64. ■ ▲ The transition metals form a class of compounds called metal carbonyls, an example of which is the tetrahedral complex $Ni(CO)_4$. Given the following thermodynamic data (at 298 K):

	$\Delta_f H°$ (kJ/mol)	$S°$ (J/K · mol)
Ni(s)	0	29.87
CO(g)	-110.525	$+197.674$
Ni(CO)$_4$(g)	-602.9	$+410.6$

(a) Calculate the equilibrium constant for the formation of $Ni(CO)_4(g)$ from nickel metal and CO gas.
(b) Is the reaction of Ni(s) and CO(g) product- or reactant-favored?
(c) Is the reaction more or less product-favored at higher temperatures? How could this reaction be used in the purification of nickel metal?

In the Laboratory

65. Two different coordination compounds containing one cobalt(III) ion, five ammonia molecules, one bromide ion, and one sulfate ion exist. The dark violet form (A) gives a precipitate upon addition of aqueous $BaCl_2$. No reaction is seen upon addition of aqueous $BaCl_2$ to the violet-red form (B). Suggest structures for these two compounds, and write a chemical equation for the reaction of (A) with aqueous $BaCl_2$.

66. Three different compounds of chromium(III) with water and chloride ion have the same composition: 19.51% Cr, 39.92% Cl, and 40.57% H_2O. One of the compounds is violet and dissolves in water to give a complex ion with a 3+ charge and three chloride ions. All three chloride ions precipitate immediately as AgCl on adding $AgNO_3$. Draw the structure of the complex ion, and name the compound. Write a net ionic equation for the reaction of this compound with silver nitrate.

| ▲ more challenging ■ in OWL Blue-numbered questions answered in Appendix O

67. ■ ▲ A 0.213-g sample of uranyl(VI) nitrate, $UO_2(NO_3)_2$, is dissolved in 20.0 mL of 1.0 M H_2SO_4 and shaken with Zn. The zinc reduces the uranyl ion, UO_2^{2+}, to a uranium ion, U^{n+}. To determine the value of n, this solution is titrated with $KMnO_4$. Permanganate is reduced to Mn^{2+} and U^{n+} is oxidized back to UO_2^{2+}.
   (a) In the titration, 12.47 mL of 0.0173 M $KMnO_4$ was required to reach the equivalence point. Use this information to determine the charge on the ion U^{n+}.
   (b) With the identity of U^{n+} now established, write a balanced net ionic equation for the reduction of UO_2^{2+} by zinc (assume acidic conditions).
   (c) Write a balanced net ionic equation for the oxidation of U^{n+} to UO_2^{2+} by MnO_4^- in acid.

68. ■ ▲ You have isolated a solid organometallic compound containing manganese, some number of CO ligands, and one or more CH_3 ligands. To find the molecular formula of the compound, you burn 0.225 g of the solid in oxygen and isolate 0.283 g of CO_2 and 0.0290 g of H_2O. The molar mass of the compound is 210 g/mol. Suggest a plausible formula and structure for the molecule. (Make sure it satisfies the EAN rule. The CH_3 group can be thought of as a CH_3^- ion and is a two-electron donor ligand.)

Summary and Conceptual Questions

The following questions may use concepts from this and previous chapters.

69. The stability of analogous complexes $[ML_6]^{n+}$ (relative to ligand dissociation) is in the general order Mn^{2+}, Fe^{2+}, Co^{2+}, Ni^{2+}, Cu^{2+}, Zn^{2+}. This order of ions is called the Irving–Williams series. Look up the values of the formation constants for the ammonia complexes of Co^{2+}, Ni^{2+}, Cu^{2+}, and Zn^{2+} in Appendix K, and verify this statement.

70. ■ ▲ In this question, we explore the differences between metal coordination by monodentate and bidentate ligands. Formation constants, K_f, for $[Ni(NH_3)_6]^{2+}$(aq) and $[Ni(en)_3]^{2+}$(aq) are as follows:

$$Ni^{2+}(aq) + 6\ NH_3(aq) \longrightarrow [Ni(NH_3)_6]^{2+}(aq)$$
$$K_f = 10^8$$

$$Ni^{2+}(aq) + 3\ en(aq) \longrightarrow [Ni(en)_3]^{2+}(aq)$$
$$K_f = 10^{18}$$

The difference in K_f between these complexes indicates a higher thermodynamic stability for the chelated complex, caused by the *chelate effect*. Recall that K is related to the standard free energy of the reaction by $\Delta_r G° = -RT \ln K$ and $\Delta_r G° = \Delta_r H° - T\Delta S°$. We know from experiment that $\Delta_r H°$ for the NH_3 reaction is -109 kJ/mol-rxn, and $\Delta_r H°$ for the ethylenediamine reaction is -117 kJ/mol-rxn. Is the difference in $\Delta_r H°$ sufficient to account for the 10^{10} difference in K_f? Comment on the role of entropy in the second reaction.

71. As mentioned on page 1047, transition metal organometallic compounds have found use as catalysts. One example is Wilkinson's catalyst, a rhodium compound $[RhCl(PR_3)_3]$ used in the hydrogenation of alkenes. The steps involved in the catalytic process are outlined below.

Indicate whether the rhodium compounds in each step have 18- or 16-valence electrons. (See Study Question 34.)

Step 1—Addition of H_2 to the rhodium center of Wilkinson's catalyst. (For electron counting purposes H is considered a hydride ion, H^-, a two-electron donor.)

Step 2—Loss of a PR_3 ligand (a two-electron donor) to open a coordination site. (PR_3 is a phosphine such as $P(C_6H_5)_3$, triphenylphosphine.)

Step 3—Addition of the alkene to the open site.

Step 4—Rearrangement to add H to the double bond. (Here the $-CH_2CH_3$ group is a two-electron donor and can be thought of as a $[CH_2CH_3]^-$ anion for electron counting purposes.)

Step 5—Loss of the alkane

Step 6—Regeneration of the catalyst.

Net reaction: $CH_2{=}CH_2 + H_2 \longrightarrow CH_3CH_3$

---

23 | Nuclear Chemistry

A Primordial Nuclear Reactor

The natural nuclear reactors in West Africa have been called "one of the greatest natural phenomena that ever occurred." In 1972, a French scientist noticed that the uranium taken from a mine in Oklo, Gabon was strangely deficient in ^{235}U. Uranium exists in nature as two principal isotopes, ^{238}U (99.275% abundant) and ^{235}U (0.72% abundant). It is ^{235}U that most readily undergoes nuclear fission and is used to fuel nuclear power plants around the world. But the uranium found in the Oklo mines had an isotope ratio like that of the spent fuel that comes from modern reactors. On this and other evidence, scientists concluded that ^{235}U at the Oklo mine was once about 3% of the total and that a "natural" fission process occurred in the bed of uranium ore nearly 2 billion years ago.

The natural nuclear reactor in Oklo, Gabon (West Africa). Nearly two billion years ago, a natural formation containing uranium oxide (the yellow material) underwent fission that started and stopped over a period of a million years.

Courtesy of Francois Gauthier-Lafaye.

But intriguing questions can be raised: why fission could occur to a significant extent in this natural deposit of uranium and why the "reactor" didn't explode. Apparently, there must have been a moderator of neutron energy and a regulation mechanism. In a modern nuclear power reactor, control rods slow down the neutrons from nuclear fission so that they can induce fission in other ^{235}U nuclei; that is, they moderate the neutron energy. Without a moderator, the neutrons just fly off. In the Oklo reactors, water seeping into the bed of uranium ore could have acted as a moderator.

The reason the Oklo reactor did not explode is that water could have also been the regulator. As the fission process heated the water, it boiled off as steam. This caused the fission to stop, but it began again when more water seeped in. Scientists now believe this natural reactor

would turn on for about 30 minutes and then shut down for several hours before turning on again. There is evidence these natural reactors functioned intermittently for about 1 million years, until the concentration of uranium isotopes was too low to keep the reaction going.

Questions:

1. How many protons and neutrons are there in the ^{235}U and ^{238}U nuclei?
2. Although plutonium does not occur naturally on earth now, it is thought to have been produced in the Oklo reactor (and then decayed). Write balanced nuclear equations for:
   (a) the reaction of ^{238}U and a neutron to give ^{239}U
   (b) the decay of ^{239}Pu to ^{239}Np and then to ^{239}Pu by beta emission
   (c) the decay of ^{239}Pu to ^{235}U by alpha emission

Answers to these questions are in Appendix Q.

History of science scholars cite three pillars of modern chemistry: technology, medicine, and alchemy. The third of these pillars, alchemy, was pursued in many cultures on three continents for well over 1000 years. Simply stated, the goal of the ancient alchemists was to turn less valuable materials into gold. We now recognize the futility of these efforts, because this goal is not reachable by chemical processes. We also know that it *is* possible to transmute one element into another. This happens naturally in the decomposition of uranium and other radioactive elements, and scientists can intentionally carry out such reactions in the laboratory. The goal is no longer to make gold, however. Far more important and valuable products of nuclear reactions are possible.

Nuclear chemistry encompasses a wide range of topics that share one thing in common: they involve changes in the nucleus of an atom. While "chemistry" is a major focus in this chapter, the subject cuts across many areas of science. Radioactive isotopes are used in medicine. Nuclear power provides a sizable fraction of energy for modern society. And, then there are nuclear weapons. . . .

Chemistry.̣.Now™

Throughout the text this icon introduces an opportunity for self-study or to explore interactive tutorials by signing in at **www.cengage.com/login**.

23.1 Natural Radioactivity

In the late 19th century, while studying radiation emanating from uranium and thorium, Ernest Rutherford (1871–1937) stated, "There are present at least two distinct types of radiation—one that is readily absorbed, which will be termed for convenience **α (alpha) radiation,** and the other of a more penetrative character, which will be termed **β (beta) radiation."** Subsequently, charge-to-mass ratio measurements showed that α radiation is composed of helium nuclei (He^{2+}) and β radiation is composed of electrons (e^-) (Table 23.1).

Rutherford hedged his bet when he said at least two types of radiation existed. A third type was later discovered by the French scientist Paul Villard (1860–1934);

■ **Discovery of Radioactivity** The discovery of radioactivity by Henri Becquerel and the isolation of radium and polonium from pitchblende, a uranium ore, by Marie Curie were described in *Milestones in the Development of Chemistry*, page 338.

TABLE 23.1   Characteristics of α, β, and γ Radiation

Name	Symbols	Charge	Mass (g/particle)
Alpha	$_2^4He$, $_2^4\alpha$	2+	6.65×10^{-24}
Beta	$_{-1}^0e$, $_{-1}^0\beta$	1−	9.11×10^{-28}
Gamma	γ	0	0

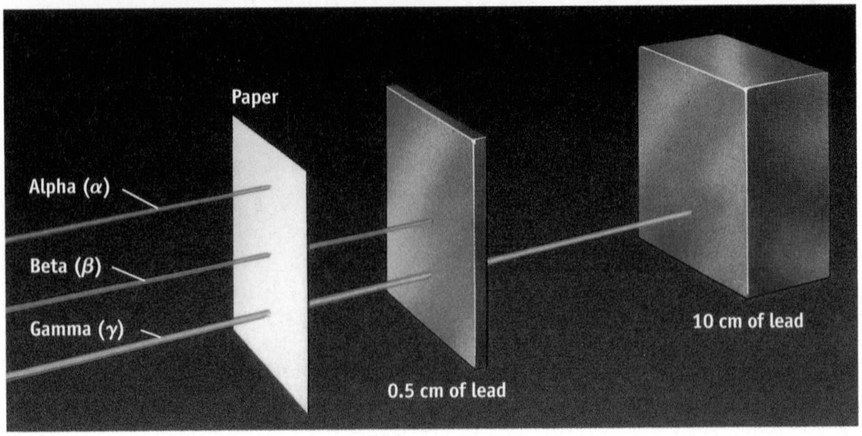

FIGURE 23.1 The relative penetrating ability of α, β, and γ radiation. Highly charged α particles interact strongly with matter and are stopped by a piece of paper. Beta particles, with less mass and a lower charge, interact to a lesser extent with matter and thus can penetrate farther. Gamma radiation is the most penetrating.

■ **Common Symbols: α and β** Symbols used to represent alpha and beta particles do not include a superscript to show that they have a charge.

he named it γ **(gamma) radiation,** using the third letter in the Greek alphabet in keeping with Rutherford's scheme. Unlike α and β radiation, γ radiation is not affected by electric and magnetic fields. Rather, it is a form of electromagnetic radiation like x-rays but even more energetic.

Early studies measured the penetrating power of the three types of radiation (Figure 23.1). Alpha radiation is the least penetrating; it can be stopped by several sheets of ordinary paper or clothing. Aluminum that is at least 0.5 cm thick is needed to stop β particles; they can penetrate several millimeters of living bone or tissue. Gamma radiation is the most penetrating. Thick layers of lead or concrete are required to shield the body from this radiation, and γ-rays can pass completely through the human body.

Alpha and β particles typically possess high kinetic energies. The energy of γ radiation is similarly very high. The energy associated with this radiation is transferred to any material used to stop the particle or absorb the radiation. This fact is important because the damage caused by radiation is related to the energy absorbed (see Section 23.8).

23.2 Nuclear Reactions and Radioactive Decay

Equations for Nuclear Reactions

In 1903, Rutherford and Frederick Soddy (1877–1956) proposed that radioactivity is the result of a natural change of an isotope of one element into an isotope of a different element. Such processes are called **nuclear reactions.**

Consider a reaction in which radium-226 (the isotope of radium with mass number 226) emits an α particle to form radon-222. The equation for this reaction is

$$^{226}_{88}\text{Ra} \rightarrow {}^{4}_{2}\alpha + {}^{222}_{86}\text{Rn}$$

■ **Symbols Used in Nuclear Equations** The mass number is included as a superscript, and the atomic number is included as a subscript preceding the symbols for reactants and products. This is done to facilitate balancing these equations.

In a nuclear reaction, the sum of the mass numbers of reacting particles must equal the sum of the mass numbers of products. Furthermore, to maintain nuclear charge balance, the sum of the atomic numbers of the products must equal the sum of the atomic numbers of the reactants. These principles are illustrated using the preceding nuclear equation:

	$^{226}_{88}\text{Ra}$	$\rightarrow$	$^{4}_{2}\alpha$	+	$^{222}_{86}\text{Rn}$
	radium-226	$\rightarrow$	α particle	+	radon-222
Mass number: (protons + neutrons)	226	=	4	+	222
Atomic number: (protons)	88	=	2	+	86

Alpha particle emission causes a decrease of two units in atomic number and four units in the mass number.

Similarly, nuclear mass and nuclear charge balance accompany β particle emission, as illustrated by the decomposition of uranium-239:

	$^{239}_{92}U$	$\rightarrow$	$^{0}_{-1}\beta$	$+$	$^{239}_{93}Np$
	uranium-239	$\rightarrow$	β particle	$+$	neptunium-239
Mass number: (protons + neutrons)	239	$=$	0	$+$	239
Atomic number: (protons)	92	$=$	-1	$+$	93

The β particle has a charge of $1-$. Charge balance requires that the atomic number of the product be one unit greater than the atomic number of the reacting nucleus. The mass number does not change in this process.

How does a nucleus, composed of protons and neutrons, eject an electron? It is a complex process, but the net result is the conversion within the nucleus of a neutron to a proton and an electron.

$$^{1}_{0}n \longrightarrow ^{0}_{-1}e + ^{1}_{1}p$$

neutron   electron   proton

Notice that the mass and charge numbers balance in this equation.

What is the origin of the gamma radiation that accompanies most nuclear reactions? Recall that a photon of visible light is emitted when an atom undergoes a transition from an excited electronic state to a lower energy state (◄ Section 6.3). Gamma radiation originates from transitions between nuclear energy levels. Nuclear reactions often result in the formation of a product nucleus in an excited nuclear state. One option is to return to the ground state by emitting the excess energy as a photon. The high energy of γ radiation is a measure of the large energy difference between the energy levels in the nucleus.

Chemistry.Now™

Sign in at **www.cengage.com/login** and go to Chapter 23 Contents to see:
- Screen 23.2 for a tutorial on **balancing equations for nuclear reactions**
- Screen 23.3 for a tutorial on **modes of radioactive decay**

EXERCISE 23.1 Mass and Charge Balance in Nuclear Reactions

Write equations for the following nuclear reactions, and confirm that they are balanced with respect to nuclear mass and nuclear charge.

(a) the emission of an α particle by radon-222 to form polonium-218

(b) the emission of a β particle by polonium-218 to form astatine-218

EXERCISE 23.2 Gamma Ray Energies

Calculate the energy per photon, and the energy per mole of photons, for γ radiation with a wavelength of 2.0×10^{-12} m. (*Hint:* Review similar calculations on the energy of photons of visible light, Section 6.2.)

■ **Energy Units** Gamma ray energies are often reported with the unit *MeV*, which stands for 1 million electron volts. One electron volt (1 eV) is the energy of an electron that has been accelerated by a potential of one volt. The conversion factor between electron volts and joules is 1 eV = 1.60218×10^{-19} J.

Radioactive Decay Series

Several naturally occurring radioactive isotopes are found to decay to form a product that is also radioactive. When this happens, the initial nuclear reaction is followed by a second nuclear reaction; if the situation is repeated, a third and a fourth nuclear reaction occur; and so on. Eventually, a nonradioactive isotope is formed to end the series. Such a sequence of nuclear reactions is called a **radioactive decay series.** In each step of this nuclear reaction sequence, the reactant nucleus is called the *parent,* and the product called the *daughter.*

Uranium-238, the most abundant of three naturally occurring uranium isotopes, heads one of four radioactive decay series. This series begins with the loss of an α particle from $^{238}_{92}U$ to form radioactive $^{234}_{90}Th$. Thorium-234 then decomposes by β emission to $^{234}_{91}Pa$, which emits a β particle to give $^{234}_{92}U$. Uranium-234 is an α emitter, forming $^{230}_{90}Th$. Further α and β emissions follow, until the series ends with formation of the stable, nonradioactive isotope, $^{206}_{82}Pb$. In all, this radioactive decay series converting $^{238}_{92}U$ to $^{206}_{82}Pb$ is made up of 14 reactions, with eight α and six β particles being emitted. The series is portrayed graphically by plotting atomic number versus mass number (Figure 23.2). An equation can be written for each step in the sequence. Equations for the first four steps in the uranium-238 radioactive decay series are:

Step 1. $^{238}_{92}U \rightarrow {}^{234}_{90}Th + {}^{4}_{2}\alpha$

Step 2. $^{234}_{90}Th \rightarrow {}^{234}_{91}Pa + {}^{0}_{-1}\beta$

Step 3. $^{234}_{91}Pa \rightarrow {}^{234}_{92}U + {}^{0}_{-1}\beta$

Step 4. $^{234}_{92}U \rightarrow {}^{230}_{90}Th + {}^{4}_{2}\alpha$

Uranium ore contains trace quantities of the radioactive elements formed in the radioactive decay series. A significant development in nuclear chemistry was Marie Curie's discovery in 1898 of radium and polonium as trace components of pitchblende, a uranium ore. The amount of each of these elements is small because the isotopes of these elements have short half-lives. Marie Curie isolated only a single gram of radium from 7 tons of ore. It is a credit to her skills as a chemist that she

FIGURE 23.2 The uranium-238 radioactive decay series. The steps in this radioactive decay series are shown graphically in this plot of mass number versus atomic number. Each α decay step lowers the atomic number by two units and the mass number by four units. Beta particle emission does not change the mass but raises the atomic number by one unit. Half-lives of the isotopes are included on the chart.

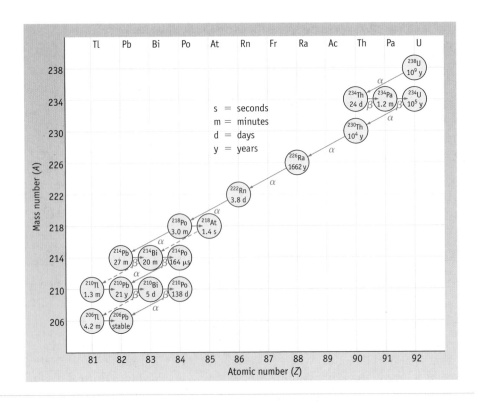

extracted sufficient amounts of radium and polonium from uranium ore to identify these elements.

The uranium-238 radioactive decay series is also the source of the environmental hazard radon. Trace quantities of uranium are often present naturally in the soil and rocks, and radon-222 is being continuously formed. Because radon is chemically inert, it is not trapped by chemical processes in soil or water and is free to seep into mines or into homes through pores in cement block walls, through cracks in the basement floor or walls, or around pipes. Because it is more dense than air, radon tends to collect in low spots, and its concentration can build up in a basement if steps are not taken to remove it.

The major health hazard from radon, when it is inhaled by humans, arises not from radon itself but from its decomposition product, polonium.

$$^{222}_{86}Rn \rightarrow ^{218}_{84}Po + ^{4}_{2}\alpha \qquad t_{1/2} = 3.82 \text{ days}$$

$$^{218}_{84}Po \rightarrow ^{214}_{82}Pb + ^{4}_{2}\alpha \qquad t_{1/2} = 3.04 \text{ minutes}$$

Radon does not undergo chemical reactions or form compounds that can be taken up in the body. Polonium, however, is not chemically inert. Polonium-218 can lodge in body tissues, where it undergoes α decay to give lead-214, another radioactive isotope. The range of an α particle in body tissue is quite small, perhaps 0.7 mm. This is approximately the thickness of the epithelial cells of the lungs, however, so α particle radiation can cause serious damage to lung tissues.

Virtually every home in the United States has some level of radon, and kits can be purchased to test for the presence of this gas. If radon gas is detected in your home, you should take corrective actions such as sealing cracks around the foundation and in the basement. It may be reassuring to know that the health risks associated with radon are low. The likelihood of getting lung cancer from exposure to radon is about the same as the likelihood of dying in an accident in your home.

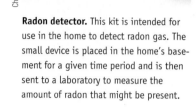

Charles D. Winters

Radon detector. This kit is intended for use in the home to detect radon gas. The small device is placed in the home's basement for a given time period and is then sent to a laboratory to measure the amount of radon that might be present.

■ **EXAMPLE 23.1 Radioactive Decay Series**

Problem A second radioactive decay series begins with $^{235}_{92}U$ and ends with $^{207}_{82}Pb$.

(a) How many α and β particles are emitted in this series?

(b) The first three steps of this series are (in order) α, β, and α emission. Write an equation for each of these steps.

Strategy First, find the total change in atomic number and mass number. A combination of α and β particles is required that will decrease the total nuclear mass by 28 (235 − 207) and at the same time decrease the atomic number by 10 (92 − 82).

Each equation must give symbols for the parent and daughter nuclei and the emitted particle. In the equations, the sums of the atomic numbers and mass numbers for reactants and products must be equal.

Solution

(a) Mass declines by 28 mass units (235 − 207). Because a decrease of 4 mass units occurs with each α emission, 7 α particles must be emitted. Also, for each α emission, the atomic number decreases by 2. Emission of 7 α particles would cause the atomic number to decrease by 14, but the actual decrease in atomic number is 10 (92 − 82). This means that 4 β particles must also have been emitted because each β emission *increases* the atomic number of the product by one unit. Thus, the radioactive decay sequence involves emission of 7 α and 4 β particles.

(b) Step 1. $^{235}_{92}U \rightarrow ^{231}_{90}Th + ^{4}_{2}\alpha$

Step 2. $^{231}_{90}Th \rightarrow ^{231}_{91}Pa + ^{0}_{-1}\beta$

Step 3. $^{231}_{91}Pa \rightarrow ^{227}_{89}Ac + ^{4}_{2}\alpha$

Comment Notice in Figure 23.2 that all daughter nuclei for the series beginning with $^{238}_{92}U$ have mass numbers differing by four units: 238, 234, 230, . . . , 206. This series is sometimes called the *4n + 2 series* because each mass number (M) fits the equation $4n + 2 = M$, where n is an integer (n is 59 for the first member of this series). For the series headed by $^{235}_{92}U$, the mass numbers are 235, 231, 227, . . . , 207; this is the *4n + 3 series*.

Two other decay series are possible. One, called the *4n* series and beginning with ^{232}Th, is found in nature; the other, the *4n + 1* series, is not. No member of this series has a very long half-life. During the 5 billion years since this planet was formed, all members of this series have completely decayed.

EXERCISE 23.3 Radioactive Decay Series

(a) Six α and four β particles are emitted in the thorium-232 radioactive decay series before a stable isotope is reached. What is the final product in this series?

(b) The first three steps in the thorium-232 decay series (in order) are α, β, and β emission. Write an equation for each step.

Other Types of Radioactive Decay

■ **Positrons** Positrons were discovered by Carl Anderson (1905–1991) in 1932. The positron is one of a group of particles that are known as *antimatter*. If matter and antimatter particles collide, mutual annihilation occurs, with energy being emitted.

■ **Neutrinos and Antineutrinos** Beta particles having a wide range of energies are emitted. To balance the energy associated with β decay, it is necessary to postulate the concurrent emission of another particle, the *antineutrino*. Similarly, neutrino emission accompanies positron emission. Much study has gone into detecting neutrinos and antineutrinos. These massless, chargeless particles are not included when writing nuclear equations.

Most naturally occurring radioactive elements decay by emission of α, β, and γ radiation. Other nuclear decay processes became known, however, when new radioactive elements were synthesized by artificial means. These include **positron ($^{0}_{+1}\beta$) emission** and **electron capture.**

Positrons ($^{0}_{+1}\beta$) and electrons have the same mass but opposite charge. The positron is the antimatter analogue to an electron. Positron emission by polonium-207, for example, results in the formation of bismuth-207.

	$^{207}_{84}Po$	$\rightarrow$	$^{0}_{+1}\beta$	$+$	$^{207}_{83}Bi$
	polonium-207	$\rightarrow$	positron	$+$	bismuth-207
Mass number: (protons + neutrons)	207	$=$	0	$+$	207
Atomic number: (protons)	84	$=$	1	$+$	83

To retain charge balance, positron decay results in a decrease in the atomic number.

In *electron capture,* an extranuclear electron is captured by the nucleus. The mass number is unchanged, and the atomic number is reduced by 1. (In an old nomenclature, the innermost electron shell was called the K shell, and electron capture was called *K capture.*)

	$^{7}_{4}Be$	$+$	$^{0}_{-1}e$	$\rightarrow$	$^{7}_{3}Li$
	beryllium-7	$+$	electron	$\rightarrow$	lithium-7
Mass number: (protons + neutrons)	7	$+$	0	$=$	7
Atomic number: (protons)	4	$+$	-1	$=$	3

In summary, most unstable nuclei decay by one of four paths: α or β decay, positron emission, or electron capture. Gamma radiation often accompanies these processes. Section 23.6 introduces a fifth way that nuclei decompose, *fission.*

■ **EXAMPLE 23.2 Nuclear Reactions**

Problem Complete the following equations. Give the symbol, mass number, and atomic number of the product species.

(a) $^{37}_{18}Ar + ^{0}_{-1}e \rightarrow ?$

(b) $^{11}_{6}C \rightarrow ^{11}_{5}B + ?$

(c) $^{35}_{16}S \rightarrow ^{35}_{17}Cl + ?$

(d) $^{30}_{15}P \rightarrow ^{0}_{+1}\beta + ?$

Strategy The missing product in each reaction can be determined by recognizing that the sums of mass numbers and atomic numbers for products and reactants must be equal. When you know the nuclear mass and nuclear charge of the product, you can identify it with the appropriate symbol.

Solution

(a) This is an electron capture reaction. The product has a mass number of $37 + 0 = 37$ and an atomic number of $18 - 1 = 17$. Therefore, the symbol for the product is $^{37}_{17}Cl$.

(b) This missing particle has a mass of zero and a charge of $1+$; these are the characteristics of a positron, $^{0}_{+1}\beta$. If this particle is included in the equation, the sums of the atomic numbers ($6 = 5 + 1$) and the mass numbers (11) on either side of the equation are equal.

(c) A beta particle, $^{0}_{-1}\beta$, is required to balance the mass numbers (35) and atomic numbers ($16 = 17 - 1$) in the equation.

(d) The product nucleus has mass number 30 and atomic number 14. This identifies the unknown as $^{30}_{14}Si$.

EXERCISE 23.4 Nuclear Reactions

Indicate the symbol, the mass number, and the atomic number of the missing product in each of the following nuclear reactions.

(a) $^{13}_{7}N \rightarrow ^{13}_{6}C + ?$ **(c)** $^{90}_{38}Sr \rightarrow ^{90}_{39}Y + ?$

(b) $^{41}_{20}Ca + ^{0}_{-1}e \rightarrow ?$ **(d)** $^{22}_{11}Na \rightarrow ? + ^{0}_{-1}\beta$

23.3 Stability of Atomic Nuclei

We can learn something about nuclear stability from Figure 23.3. In this plot, the horizontal axis represents the number of protons, and the vertical axis gives the number of neutrons for known isotopes. Each circle represents an isotope identified by the number of neutrons and protons contained in its nucleus. The black circles represent stable (nonradioactive) isotopes, about 300 in number, and the red circles represent some of the known radioactive isotopes. For example, the three isotopes of hydrogen are $^{1}_{1}H$ and $^{2}_{1}H$ (neither is radioactive) and $^{3}_{1}H$ (tritium, radioactive). For lithium, the third element, isotopes with mass numbers 4, 5, 6, and 7 are known. The isotopes with masses of 6 and 7 (shown in black) are stable, whereas the other two isotopes (in red) are radioactive.

Figure 23.3 contains the following information about nuclear stability:

- Stable isotopes fall in a very narrow range called the **band of stability.** It is remarkable how few isotopes are stable.
- Only two stable isotopes ($^{1}_{1}H$ and $^{3}_{2}He$) have more protons than neutrons.
- Up to calcium ($Z = 20$), stable isotopes often have equal numbers of protons and neutrons or only one or two more neutrons than protons.
- Beyond calcium, the neutron–proton ratio is always greater than 1. As the mass increases, the band of stable isotopes deviates more and more from a line in which $N = Z$.
- Beyond bismuth (83 protons and 126 neutrons), all isotopes are unstable and radioactive. There is apparently no nuclear "superglue" strong enough to hold heavy nuclei together.
- The lifetimes of unstable nuclei are shorter for the heaviest nuclei. For example, half of a sample of $^{238}_{92}U$ disintegrates in 4.5 billion years, whereas half of a sample of $^{257}_{103}Lr$ is gone in only 0.65 second. Isotopes that fall farther from the band of stability tend to have shorter half-lives than do unstable isotopes nearer to the band of stability.
- Elements of even atomic number have more stable isotopes than do those of odd atomic number. More stable isotopes have an even number of neutrons

FIGURE 23.3 **Stable and unstable**

isotopes. A graph of the number of neutrons (N) versus the number of protons (Z) for stable (black circles) and radioactive (red circles) isotopes from hydrogen to bismuth. This graph is used to assess criteria for nuclear stability and to predict modes of decay for unstable nuclei.

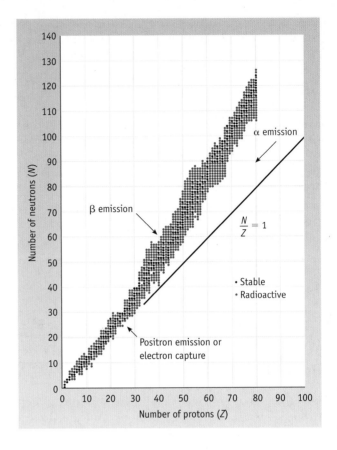

than have an odd number. Roughly 200 isotopes have an even number of neutrons and an even number of protons, whereas only about 120 isotopes have an odd number of either protons or neutrons. Only five stable isotopes (^1_1H, ^6_3Li, $^{10}_5B$, $^{14}_7N$, and $^{180}_{73}Ta$) have odd numbers of both protons and neutrons.

The Band of Stability and Radioactive Decay

Besides being a criterion for stability, the neutron–proton ratio can assist in predicting what type of radioactive decay will be observed. Unstable nuclei decay in a manner that brings them toward a stable neutron–proton ratio—that is, toward the band of stability.

- All elements beyond bismuth ($Z = 83$) are unstable. To reach the band of stability starting with these elements, a process that decreases the atomic number is needed. Alpha emission is an effective way to lower Z, the atomic number, because each emission decreases the atomic number by 2. For example, americium, the radioactive element used in smoke detectors, decays by α emission:

$$^{243}_{95}Am \rightarrow {}^4_2\alpha + {}^{239}_{93}Np$$

- Beta emission occurs for isotopes that have a high neutron–proton ratio—that is, isotopes above the band of stability. With β decay, the atomic number increases by 1, and the mass number remains constant, resulting in a lower n/p ratio.

$$^{60}_{27}Co \rightarrow {}^0_{-1}\beta + {}^{60}_{28}Ni$$

- Isotopes with a low neutron–proton ratio, below the band of stability, decay by positron emission or by electron capture. Both processes lead to product nuclei with a lower atomic number and the same mass number:

$$^{13}_{7}N \rightarrow {}^{0}_{+1}\beta + {}^{13}_{6}C$$

$$^{41}_{20}Ca + {}^{0}_{-1}e \rightarrow {}^{41}_{19}K$$

Chemistry .ᵔ. Now™

Sign in at **www.cengage.com/login** and go to Chapter 23 Contents to see Screen 23.3 for a tutorial on predicting modes of radioactive decay.

■ EXAMPLE 23.3 Predicting Modes of Radioactive Decay

Problem Identify probable mode(s) of decay for each isotope and write an equation for the decay process.

(a) oxygen-15, $^{15}_{8}O$ **(b)** uranium-234, $^{234}_{92}U$ **(c)** fluorine-20, $^{20}_{9}F$ **(d)** manganese-56, $^{56}_{25}Mn$

Strategy In parts (a), (c), and (d), compare the mass number with the atomic mass. If the mass number of the isotope is higher than the atomic weight, then there are too many neutrons, and β emission is likely. If the mass number is lower than the atomic weight, then there are too few neutrons, and positron emission or electron capture is the more likely process. It is not possible to choose between the latter two modes of decay without further information. For part (b), note that isotopes with atomic number greater than 83 are likely to be α emitters.

Solution

(a) Oxygen-15 has 7 neutrons and 8 protons, so the n/p ratio is less than 1—too low for ^{15}O to be stable. Nuclei with too few neutrons are expected to decay by either positron emission or electron capture. In this instance, the process is $^{0}_{+1}\beta$ emission, and the equation is $^{15}_{8}O \rightarrow {}^{0}_{+1}\beta + {}^{15}_{7}N$.

(b) Alpha emission is a common mode of decay for isotopes of elements with atomic numbers higher than 83. The decay of uranium-234 is one example:

$$^{234}_{92}U \rightarrow {}^{230}_{90}Th + {}^{4}_{2}\alpha$$

(c) Fluorine-20 has 11 neutrons and 9 protons, a high n/p ratio. The ratio is lowered by β emission :

$$^{20}_{9}F \rightarrow {}^{0}_{-1}\beta + {}^{20}_{10}Ne$$

(d) The atomic weight of manganese is 54.85. The higher mass number, 56, suggests that this radioactive isotope has an excess of neutrons, in which case it would be expected to decay by β emission :

$$^{56}_{25}Mn \rightarrow {}^{0}_{-1}\beta + {}^{56}_{26}Fe$$

Comment Be aware that predictions made in this manner will be right much of the time, but exceptions will sometimes occur.

EXERCISE 23.5 Predicting Modes of Radioactive Decay

Write an equation for the probable mode of decay for each of the following unstable isotopes, and write an equation for that nuclear reaction.

(a) silicon-32, $^{32}_{14}Si$ **(c)** plutonium-239, $^{239}_{94}Pu$

(b) titanium-45, $^{45}_{22}Ti$ **(d)** potassium-42, $^{42}_{19}K$

Nuclear Binding Energy

An atomic nucleus can contain as many as 83 protons and still be stable. For stability, nuclear binding (attractive) forces must be greater than the electrostatic repulsive forces between the closely packed protons in the nucleus. **Nuclear binding energy,** E_b, is defined as the energy required to separate the nucleus of an atom into protons and neutrons. For example, the nuclear binding energy for deuterium is the energy required to convert one mole of deuterium ($_1^2$H) nuclei into one mole of protons and one mole of neutrons.

$$_1^2H \rightarrow \, _1^1p + \, _0^1n \qquad E_b = 2.15 \times 10^8 \text{ kJ/mol}$$

The positive sign for E_b indicates that energy is required for this process. A deuterium nucleus is more stable than an isolated proton and an isolated neutron, just as the H_2 molecule is more stable than two isolated H atoms. Recall, however, that the H—H bond energy is only 436 kJ/mol. The energy holding a proton and a neutron together in a deuterium nucleus, 2.15×10^8 kJ/mol, is about 500,000 times larger than the typical covalent bond energies.

To further understand nuclear binding energy, we turn to an experimental observation and a theory. The experimental observation is that the mass of a nucleus is always less than the sum of the masses of its constituent protons and neutrons. The theory is that the "missing mass," called the **mass defect,** is equated with energy that holds the nuclear particles together.

The mass defect for deuterium is the difference between the mass of a deuterium nucleus and the sum of the masses of a proton and a neutron. Mass spectrometric measurements (◀ Section 2.3) give the accurate masses of these particles to a high level of precision, providing the numbers needed to carry out calculations of mass defects.

Masses of atomic nuclei are not generally listed in reference tables, but masses of atoms are. Calculation of the mass defect can be carried out using masses of atoms instead of masses of nuclei. By using atomic masses, we are including in this calculation the masses of extranuclear electrons in the reactants and the products. Because the same number of extranuclear electrons appears in products and reactants, this does not affect the result. Thus, for one mole of deuterium nuclei, the mass defect is found as follows:

$$
\begin{array}{ccccc}
_1^2H & \rightarrow & _1^1H & + & _0^1n \\
2.01410 \text{ g/mol} & & 1.007825 \text{ g/mol} & & 1.008665 \text{ g/mol}
\end{array}
$$

$$
\begin{aligned}
\text{Mass defect} = \Delta m &= \text{mass of products} - \text{mass of reactants} \\
&= [1.007825 \text{ g/mol} + 1.008665 \text{ g/mol}] - 2.01410 \text{ g/mol} \\
&= 0.00239 \text{ g/mol}
\end{aligned}
$$

The relationship between mass and energy is contained in Albert Einstein's 1905 theory of special relativity, which holds that mass and energy are different manifestations of the same quantity. Einstein defined the energy–mass relationship: energy is equivalent to mass times the square of the speed of light; that is, $E = mc^2$. In the case of atomic nuclei, it is assumed that the missing mass (the mass defect, Δm) is equated with the binding energy holding the nucleus together.

$$E_b = (\Delta m)c^2 \qquad \qquad (23.1)$$

If Δm is given in kilograms and the speed of light is given in meters per second, E_b will have units of joules (because $1 \text{ J} = 1 \text{ kg} \cdot \text{m}^2/\text{s}^2$). For the decomposition of one mole of deuterium nuclei to one mole of protons and one mole of neutrons, we have

$$E_b = (2.39 \times 10^{-6} \text{ kg/mol})(2.998 \times 10^8 \text{ m/s})^2$$

$$= 2.15 \times 10^{11} \text{ J/mol of } _1^2H \text{ nuclei} \ (= 2.15 \times 10^8 \text{ kJ/mol of } _1^2H \text{ nuclei})$$

The nuclear stabilities of different elements are compared using the **binding energy per mole of nucleons.** (**Nucleon** is the general name given to nuclear particles—that is, protons and neutrons.) A deuterium nucleus contains two nucle-

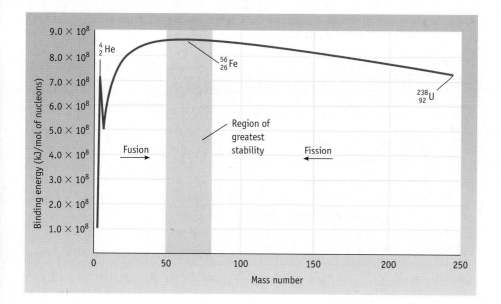

FIGURE 23.4 Relative stability of nuclei. Binding energy per nucleon for the most stable isotope of elements between hydrogen and uranium is plotted as a function of mass number. (Fission and fusion are discussed on pages 1080–1082.)

ons, so the binding energy per mole of nucleons, E_b/n, is 2.15×10^8 kJ/mol divided by 2, or 1.08×10^8 kJ/mol nucleon.

$$E_b/n = \left(\frac{2.15 \times 10^8 \text{ kJ}}{\text{mol } {}_1^2\text{H nuclei}} \right)\left(\frac{1 \text{ mol } {}_1^2\text{H nuclei}}{2 \text{ mol nucleons}} \right)$$

$$E_b/n = 1.08 \times 10^8 \text{ kJ/mol nucleons}$$

The binding energy per nucleon can be calculated for any atom whose mass is known. Then, to compare nuclear stabilities, binding energies per nucleon are plotted as a function of mass number (Figure 23.4). The greater the binding energy per nucleon, the greater the stability of the nucleus. From the graph in Figure 23.4, the point of maximum nuclear stability occurs at a mass of 56 (i.e., at iron in the periodic table).

Chemistry ⚛ Now™

Sign in at **www.cengage.com/login** and go to Chapter 23 Contents to see:
- Screen 23.4 for a simulation on **isotope stability**
- Screen 23.5 for a tutorial on **calculating binding energy**

■ **EXAMPLE 23.4 Nuclear Binding Energy**

Problem Calculate the binding energy, E_b (in kJ/mol), and the binding energy per nucleon, E_b/n (in kJ/mol nucleon), for carbon-12.

Strategy First, determine the mass defect, then use Equation 23.1 to determine the binding energy. There are 12 nuclear particles in carbon-12, so dividing the nuclear binding energy by 12 will give the binding energy per nucleon.

Solution The mass of ${}_1^1$H is 1.007825 g/mol, and the mass of ${}_0^1$n is 1.008665 g/mol. Carbon-12, ${}_6^{12}$C, is the standard for the atomic masses in the periodic table, and its mass is defined as exactly 12 g/mol

$$\Delta m = [(6 \times \text{mass } {}_1^1\text{H}) + (6 \times \text{mass } {}_0^1\text{n})] - \text{mass } {}_6^{12}\text{C}$$

$$= [(6 \times 1.007825 \text{ g/mol}) + (6 \times 1.008665 \text{ g/mol})] - 12.000000 \text{ g/mol}$$

$$= 9.8940 \times 10^{-2} \text{ g/mol nuclei}$$

The binding energy is calculated using Equation 23.1. Using the mass in kilograms and the speed of light in meters per second gives the binding energy in joules:

$$E_b = (\Delta m)c^2$$
$$= (9.8940 \times 10^{-5} \text{ kg/mol})(2.99792 \times 10^8 \text{ m/s})^2$$
$$= 8.89 \times 10^{12} \text{ J/mol nuclei} (= 8.89 \times 10^9 \text{ kJ/mol nuclei})$$

The binding energy per nucleon, E_b/n, is determined by dividing the binding energy by 12 (the number of nucleons)

$$\frac{E_b}{n} = \frac{8.89 \times 10^9 \text{ kJ/mol nuclei}}{12 \text{ mol nucleons/mol nuclei}}$$

$$= 7.41 \times 10^8 \text{ kJ/mol nucleons}$$

EXERCISE 23.6 Nuclear Binding Energy

Calculate the binding energy per nucleon, in kilojoules per mole, for lithium-6. The molar mass of ^6_3Li is 6.015125 g/mol.

23.4 Rates of Nuclear Decay

Half-Life

When a new radioactive isotope is identified, its *half-life* is usually measured. Half-life $(t_{1/2})$ is used in nuclear chemistry in the same way it is used when discussing the kinetics of first-order chemical reactions (◄ Section 15.4): It is the time required for half of a sample to decay to products (Figure 23.5). Recall that for first-order kinetics the half-life is independent of the amount of sample.

Half-lives for radioactive isotopes cover a wide range of values. Uranium-238 has one of the longer half-lives, 4.47×10^9 years, a length of time close to the age of the earth (estimated at 4.5–4.6×10^9 years). Roughly half of the uranium-238 present when the planet was formed is still around. At the other end of the range of half-lives are isotopes such as element 112, whose 277 isotope has a half-life of 240 microseconds (1 μs = 1×10^{-6} s).

Half-life provides an easy way to estimate the time required before a radioactive element is no longer a health hazard. Strontium-90, for example, is a β emitter

FIGURE 23.5 Decay of 20.0 mg of oxygen-15. After each half-life period of 2.0 min, the mass of oxygen-15 decreases by one half.

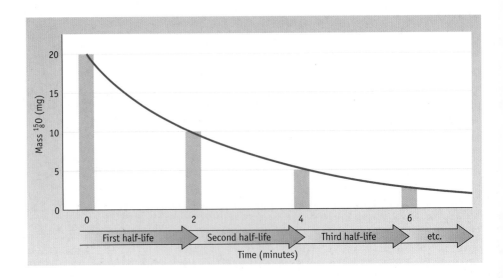

with a half-life of 29.1 years. Significant quantities of strontium-90 were dispersed into the environment in atmospheric nuclear bomb tests in the 1960s and 1970s, and from the half-life, we know that a little less than half is still around. The health problems associated with strontium-90 arise because calcium and strontium have similar chemical properties. Strontium-90 is taken into the body and deposited in bone, taking the place of calcium. Radiation damage by strontium-90 in bone has been directly linked to bone-related cancers.

■ **Half-Life and Temperature** Unlike what is observed in chemical kinetics, temperature does not affect the rate of nuclear decay.

■ **EXAMPLE 23.5 Using Half-Life**

Problem Radioactive iodine-131, used to treat hyperthyroidism, has a half-life of 8.04 days.

(a) If you have 8.8 μg (micrograms) of this isotope, what mass remains after 32.2 days?

(b) How long will it take for a sample of iodine-131 to decay to one eighth of its activity?

(c) Estimate the length of time necessary for the sample to decay to 10% of its original activity.

Strategy This problem asks you to use half-life to qualitatively assess the rate of decay. After one half-life, half of the sample remains. After another half-life, the amount of sample is again decreased by half to one fourth of its original value. (This situation is illustrated in Figure 23.5.) To answer these questions, assess the number of half-lives that have elapsed and use this information to determine the amount of sample remaining.

Solution

(a) The time elapsed, 32.2 days, is 4 half-lives (32.2/8.04 = 4). The amount of iodine-131 has decreased to 1/16 of the original amount [1/2 $\times$ 1/2 $\times$ 1/2 $\times$ 1/2 = $(1/2)^4$ = 1/16]. The amount of iodine remaining is 8.8 μg $\times$ $(1/2)^4$ or 0.55 μg .

(b) After 3 half-lives , the amount of iodine-131 remaining is 1/8 (= $(1/2)^3$) of the original amount. The amount remaining is 8.8 μg $\times$ $(1/2)^3$ = 1.1 μg.

(c) After 3 half-lives, 1/8 (12.5%) of the sample remains; after 4 half-lives, 1/16 (6.25%) remains. It will take between 3 and 4 half-lives, between 24.15 and 32.2 days, to decrease the amount of sample to 10% of its original value.

Comment You will find it useful to make approximations as we have done in (c). An exact time can be calculated from the first-order rate law (pages 683 and 1074).

EXERCISE 23.7 Using Half-Life

Tritium ($^3_1$H), a radioactive isotope of hydrogen has a half-life of 12.3 years.

(a) Starting with 1.5 mg of this isotope, how many milligrams remain after 49.2 years?

(b) How long will it take for a sample of tritium to decay to one eighth of its activity?

(c) Estimate the length of time necessary for the sample to decay to 1% of its original activity.

Kinetics of Nuclear Decay

The rate of nuclear decay is determined from measurements of the **activity** (A) of a sample. Activity refers to the number of disintegrations observed per unit time, a quantity that can be measured readily with devices such as a Geiger–Müller counter (Figure 23.6). *Activity is proportional to the number of radioactive atoms present (N).*

$$A \propto N \qquad \qquad \textbf{(23.2)}$$

If the number of radioactive nuclei N is reduced by half, the activity of the sample will be half as large. Doubling N will double the activity. This evidence indicates that the rate of decomposition is first order with respect to N. Consequently, the equations describing rates of radioactive decay are the same as those used to de-

■ **Ways of Expressing Activity** Common units for activity are dps (disintegrations per second) and dpm (disintegrations per minute).

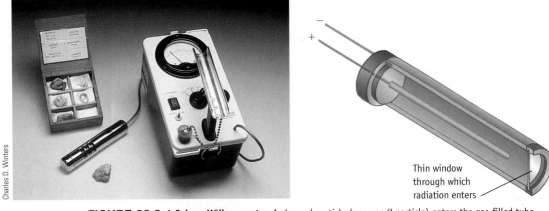

FIGURE 23.6 A Geiger–Müller counter. A charged particle (an α or β particle) enters the gas-filled tube (diagram at the right) and ionizes the gas. The gaseous ions migrate to electrically charged plates and are recorded as a pulse of electric current. The current is amplified and used to operate a counter. A sample of carnotite, a mineral containing uranium oxide, is also shown in the photograph.

Thin window through which radiation enters

scribe first-order chemical reactions; the change in the number of radioactive atoms N per unit of time is proportional to N:

$$\frac{\Delta N}{\Delta t} = -kN \tag{23.3}$$

The integrated rate equation can be written in two ways depending on the data used:

$$\ln\left(\frac{N}{N_0}\right) = -kt \tag{23.4}$$

or

$$\ln\left(\frac{A}{A_0}\right) = -kt \tag{23.5}$$

Here, N_0 and A_0 are the number of atoms and the activity of the sample initially, respectively, and N and A are the number of atoms and the activity of the sample after time t, respectively. Thus, N/N_0 is the fraction of atoms remaining after a given time (t), and A/A_0 is the fraction of the activity remaining after the same period. In these equations, k is the rate constant (decay constant) for the isotope in question. The relationship between half-life and the first-order rate constant is the same as seen with chemical kinetics (Equation 15.4, page 690):

$$t_{1/2} = \frac{0.693}{k} \tag{23.6}$$

Equations 23.3–23.6 are useful in several ways:

- If the activity (A) or the number of radioactive nuclei (N) is measured in the laboratory over some period t, then k can be calculated. The decay constant k can then be used to determine the half-life of the sample.
- If k is known, the fraction of a radioactive sample (N/N_0) still present after some time t has elapsed can be calculated.
- If k is known, the time required for that isotope to decay to a fraction of the original activity (A/A_0) can be calculated.

■ EXAMPLE 23.6 Determination of Half-Life

Problem A sample of radon-222 has an initial α particle activity (A_0) of 7.0×10^4 dps (disintegrations per second). After 6.6 days, its activity (A) is 2.1×10^4 dps. What is the half-life of radon-222?

Strategy Values for A, A_0, and t are given. The problem can be solved using Equation 23.5 with k as the unknown. Once k is found, the half-life can be calculated using Equation 23.6.

Solution

$$\ln (2.1 \times 10^4 \text{ dps}/7.0 \times 10^4 \text{ dps}) = -k \ (6.6 \text{ day})$$

$$\ln (0.30) = -k(6.6 \text{ day})$$

$$k = 0.18 \text{ days}^{-1}$$

From k we obtain $t_{1/2}$:

$$t_{1/2} = 0.693/0.18 \text{ days}^{-1} = \boxed{3.8 \text{ days}}$$

Comments Notice that the activity decreased to between one half and one fourth of its original value. The 6.6 days of elapsed time represents one full half-life and part of another half-life.

■ EXAMPLE 23.7 Time Required for a Radioactive Sample to Partially Decay

Problem Gallium citrate, containing the radioactive isotope gallium-67, is used medically as a tumor-seeking agent. It has a half-life of 78.2 h. How long will it take for a sample of gallium citrate to decay to 10.0% of its original activity?

Strategy Use Equation 23.5 to solve this problem. In this case, the unknown is the time t. The rate constant k is calculated from the half-life using Equation 23.6. Although we do not have specific values of activity, the value of A/A_0 is known. Because A is 10.0% of A_0, the value of A/A_0 is 0.100.

Solution First, determine k:

$$k = 0.693/t_{1/2} = 0.693/78.2 \text{ h}$$

$$k = 8.86 \times 10^{-3} \text{ h}^{-1}$$

Then substitute the given values of A/A_0 and k into Equation 23.5:

$$\ln (A/A_0) = -kt$$

$$\ln (0.100) = -(8.86 \times 10^{-3} \text{ h}^{-1})t$$

$$\boxed{t = 2.60 \times 10^2 \text{ h}}$$

Comments The time required is between three half-lives ($3 \times 78.2 \text{ h} = 235 \text{ h}$) and four half-lives ($4 \times 78.2 \text{ h} = 313 \text{ h}$).

EXERCISE 23.8 Determination of Half-Life

A sample of $Ca_3(PO_4)_2$ containing phosphorus-32 has an activity of 3.35×10^3 dpm. Two days later, the activity is 3.18×10^3 dpm. Calculate the half-life of phosphorus-32.

EXERCISE 23.9 Time Required for a Radioactive Sample to Partially Decay

A highly radioactive sample of nuclear waste products with a half-life of 200. years is stored in an underground tank. How long will it take for the activity to diminish from an initial activity of 6.50×10^{12} dpm to a fairly harmless activity of 3.00×10^3 dpm?

Radiocarbon Dating

In certain situations, the age of a material can be determined based on the rate of decay of a radioactive isotope. The best-known example of this procedure is the use of carbon-14 to date historical artifacts.

Carbon is primarily carbon-12 and carbon-13 with isotopic abundances of 98.9% and 1.1%, respectively. In addition, traces of a third isotope, carbon-14, are present to the extent of about 1 in 10^{12} atoms in atmospheric CO_2 and in living materials.

FIGURE 23.7 Variation of atmospheric carbon-14 activity. The amount of carbon-14 has varied with variation in cosmic ray activity. To obtain the data for the pre-1990 part of the curve shown in this graph, scientists carried out carbon-14 dating of artifacts for which the age was accurately known (often through written records). Similar results can be obtained using carbon-14 dating of tree rings.

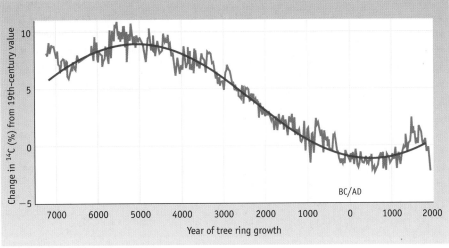

Source: Hans E. Suess, La Jolla Radiocarbon Laboratory

Oesper Collection in the History of Chemistry, University of Cincinnati

■ **Willard Libby (1908–1980)** Libby received the 1960 Nobel Prize in chemistry for developing carbon-14 dating techniques. Carbon-14 dating is widely used in fields such as anthropology.

Carbon-14 is a β emitter with a half-life of 5730 years. A 1-gram sample of carbon from living material will show about 14 disintegrations per minute, not a lot of radioactivity but nevertheless detectable by modern methods.

Carbon-14 is formed in the upper atmosphere by nuclear reactions initiated by neutrons in cosmic radiation:

$$^{14}_{7}N + ^{1}_{0}n \rightarrow ^{14}_{6}C + ^{1}_{1}H$$

Once formed, carbon-14 is oxidized to $^{14}CO_2$. This product enters the carbon cycle, circulating through the atmosphere, oceans, and biosphere.

The usefulness of carbon-14 for dating comes about in the following way. Plants absorb CO_2 and convert it to organic compounds, thereby incorporating carbon-14 into living tissue. As long as a plant remains alive, this process will continue, and the percentage of carbon that is carbon-14 in the plant will equal the percentage in the atmosphere. When the plant dies, carbon-14 will no longer be taken up. Radioactive decay continues, however, with the carbon-14 activity decreasing over time. After 5730 years, the activity will be 7 dpm/g; after 11,460 years, it will be 3.5 dpm/g; and so on. By measuring the activity of a sample, and knowing the half-life of carbon-14, it is possible to calculate when a plant (or an animal that was eating plants) died.

As with all experimental procedures, carbon-14 dating has limitations. The procedure assumes that the amount of carbon-14 in the atmosphere hundreds or thousands of years ago is the same as it is now. We know that this isn't exactly true; the percentage has varied by as much as 10% (Figure 23.7). Furthermore, it is not possible to use carbon-14 to date an object that is less than about 100 years old; the radiation level from carbon-14 will not change enough in this short time period to permit accurate detection of a difference from the initial value. In most instances, the accuracy of the measurement is, in fact, only about ± 100 years. Finally, it is not possible to determine ages of objects much older than about 40,000 years. By then, after nearly seven half-lives, the radioactivity will have decreased virtually to zero. But for the span of time between 100 and 40,000 years, this technique has provided important information (Figure 23.8).

FIGURE 23.8 The Ice Man. The world's oldest preserved human remains were discovered in the ice of a glacier high in the Alps. Carbon-14 dating techniques allowed scientists to determine that he lived about 5300 years ago.

Chemistry ⚛ Now™

Sign in at **www.cengage.com/login** and go to Chapter 23 Contents to see:
• Screen 23.3 for an exercise on **the Geiger counter**
• Screen 23.6 for a tutorial on **half-life and radiochemical dating**

EXAMPLE 23.8 **Radiochemical Dating**

Problem To test the concept of carbon-14 dating, J. R. Arnold and W. F. Libby applied this technique to analyze samples of acacia and cyprus wood whose ages were already known. (The acacia wood, which was supplied by the Metropolitan Museum of Art in New York, came from the tomb of Zoser, the first Egyptian pharaoh to be entombed in a pyramid. The cyprus wood was from the tomb of Sneferu.) The average activity based on five determinations was 7.04 dpm per gram of carbon. Assume (as Arnold and Libby did) that the activity of carbon-14, A_0, is 12.6 dpm per gram of carbon. Calculate the approximate age of the sample.

Strategy First, determine the rate constant for the decay of carbon-14 from its half-life ($t_{1/2}$ for ^{14}C is 5.73×10^3 years). Then, use Equation 23.5.

Solution

$$k = 0.693/t_{1/2} = 0.693/5730 \text{ yr}$$
$$= 1.21 \times 10^{-4} \text{ yr}^{-1}$$
$$\ln(A/A_0) = -kt$$
$$\ln\left(\frac{7.04 \text{ dpm/g}}{12.6 \text{ dpm/g}}\right) = (-1.21 \times 10^{-4} \text{ yr}^{-1})t$$
$$t = 4.8 \times 10^3 \text{ yr}$$

The wood is about 4800 years old.

Comment This problem uses real data from an early research paper in which the carbon-14 dating method was being tested. The age of the wood was known to be 4750 ± 250 years. (See J. R. Arnold and W. F. Libby: *Science,* Vol. 110, p. 678, 1949.)

EXERCISE 23.10 **Radiochemical Dating**

A sample of the inner part of a redwood tree felled in 1874 was shown to have ^{14}C activity of 9.32 dpm/g. Calculate the approximate age of the tree when it was cut down. Compare this age with that obtained from tree ring data, which estimated that the tree began to grow in 979 ± 52 BC. Use 13.4 dpm/g for the value of A_0.

23.5 Artificial Nuclear Reactions

How many different isotopes are found on earth? All of the stable isotopes occur naturally. A few unstable (radioactive) isotopes that have long half-lives are found in nature; the best-known examples are uranium-235, uranium-238, and thorium-232. Trace quantities of other radioactive isotopes with short half-lives are present because they are being formed continuously by nuclear reactions. They include isotopes of radium, polonium, and radon, along with other elements produced in various radioactive decay series, and carbon-14, formed in a nuclear reaction initiated by cosmic radiation.

Naturally occurring isotopes account for only a very small fraction of the currently known radioactive isotopes, however. The rest—several thousand—have been synthesized via artificial nuclear reactions, sometimes referred to as transmutation.

The first artificial nuclear reaction was identified by Rutherford about 80 years ago. Recall the classic experiment that led to the nuclear model of the atom (See *Milestones in the Development of Chemistry,* page 338) in which gold foil was bombarded with α particles. In the years following that experiment, Rutherford and his coworkers bombarded many other elements with α particles. In 1919, one of these experiments led to an unexpected result: when nitrogen atoms were bombarded with α particles, protons were detected among the products. Rutherford correctly concluded that a nuclear reaction had occurred. Nitrogen had undergone a *transmutation* to oxygen:

$$^{4}_{2}\text{He} + ^{14}_{7}\text{N} \rightarrow ^{17}_{8}\text{O} + ^{1}_{1}\text{H}$$

During the next decade, other nuclear reactions were discovered by bombarding other elements with α particles. Progress was slow, however, because in most cases α particles are simply scattered by target nuclei. The bombarding particles cannot get close enough to the nucleus to react because of the strong repulsive forces between the positively charged α particle and the positively charged atomic nucleus.

Two advances were made in 1932 that greatly extended nuclear reaction chemistry. The first involved the use of particle accelerators to create high-energy particles as projectiles. The second was the use of neutrons as the bombarding particles.

The α particles used in the early studies on nuclear reactions came from naturally radioactive materials such as uranium and had relatively low energies, at least by today's standards. Particles with higher energy were needed, so J. D. Cockcroft (1897–1967) and E. T. S. Walton (1903–1995), working in Rutherford's laboratory in Cambridge, England, turned to protons. Protons are formed when hydrogen atoms ionize in a cathode-ray tube, and it was known that they could be accelerated to higher energy by applying a high voltage. Cockcroft and Walton found that when energetic protons struck a lithium target, the following reaction occurs:

$$\ce{^7_3Li + ^1_1p -> 2 ^4_2He}$$

This was the first example of a reaction initiated by a particle that had been artificially accelerated to high energy. Since this experiment was conducted, the technique has been developed much further, and the use of particle accelerators in nuclear chemistry is now commonplace. Particle accelerators operate on the principle that a charged particle placed between charged plates will be accelerated to a high speed and high energy. Modern examples of this process are seen in the synthesis of the transuranium elements, several of which are described in more detail in *A Closer Look: The Search for New Elements.*

Experiments using neutrons as bombarding particles were first carried out in both the United States and Great Britain in 1932. Nitrogen, oxygen, fluorine, and neon were bombarded with energetic neutrons, and α particles were detected among the products. Using neutrons made sense: because neutrons have no charge, it was reasoned that these particles would not be repelled by the positively charged nucleus particles. Thus, neutrons did not need high energies to react.

In 1934, Enrico Fermi (1901–1954) and his coworkers showed that nuclear reactions using neutrons are more favorable if the neutrons have low energy. A low energy neutron is simply captured by the nucleus, giving a product in which the mass number is increased by one unit. Because of the low energy of the bombarding particle, the product nucleus does not have sufficient energy to fragment in these reactions. The new nucleus is produced in an excited state, however; when the nucleus returns to the ground state, a γ-ray is emitted. Reactions in which a neutron is captured and a γ-ray is emitted are called **(n, γ) reactions.**

The (n, γ) reactions are the source of many of the radioisotopes used in medicine and chemistry. An example is radioactive phosphorus, $\ce{^{32}_{15}P}$, which is used in chemical studies such as tracing the uptake of phosphorus in the body.

$$\ce{^{31}_{15}P + ^1_0n -> ^{32}_{15}P + \gamma}$$

Transuranium elements, elements with an atomic number greater than 92, were first made in a nuclear reaction sequence beginning with an (n, γ) reaction. Scientists at the University of California at Berkeley bombarded uranium-238 with neutrons. Among the products identified were neptunium-239 and plutonium-239. These new elements were formed when $^{239}\mathrm{U}$ decayed by β radiation.

$$\ce{^{238}_{92}U + ^1_0n -> ^{239}_{92}U}$$
$$\ce{^{239}_{92}U -> ^{239}_{93}Np + ^0_{-1}\beta}$$
$$\ce{^{239}_{93}Np -> ^{239}_{94}Pu + ^0_{-1}\beta}$$

■ **Discovery of Neutrons** Neutrons had been predicted to exist for more than a decade before they were identified in 1932 by James Chadwick (1891–1974). Chadwick produced neutrons in a nuclear reaction between α particles and beryllium: $\ce{^4_2\alpha + ^9_4Be -> ^{12}_6C + ^1_0n}$.

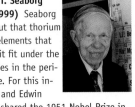

■ **Glenn T. Seaborg (1912–1999)** Seaborg figured out that thorium and the elements that followed it fit under the lanthanides in the periodic table. For this insight, he and Edwin McMillan shared the 1951 Nobel Prize in chemistry. Over a 21-year period, Seaborg and his colleagues synthesized 10 new transuranium elements (Pu through Lr). To honor Seaborg's scientific contributions, the name "seaborgium" was assigned to element 106. It marked the first time an element was named for a living person.

Lawrence Berkeley Laboratory

■ **Transuranium Elements in Nature** Neptunium, plutonium, and americium were unknown prior to their preparation via these nuclear reactions. Later, these elements were found to be present in trace quantities in uranium ores.

By 1936, guided first by Mendeleev's predictions and later by atomic theory, chemists had identified all but two of the elements with atomic numbers between 1 and 92. From this point onward, all new elements to be discovered came from artificial nuclear reactions. Two gaps in the periodic table were filled when radioactive technetium and promethium, the last two elements with atomic numbers less than 92, were identified in 1937 and 1942, respectively. The first success in the search for elements with atomic numbers higher than 92 came with the 1940 discovery of neptunium and plutonium.

Since 1950, laboratories in the United States (Lawrence Berkeley National Laboratory), Russia (Joint Institute for Nuclear Research at Dubna, near Moscow),

and Europe (Institute for Heavy Ion Research at Darmstadt, Germany) have competed to make new elements. Syntheses of new transuranium elements use a standard methodology. An element of fairly high atomic number is bombarded with a beam of high-energy particles. Initially, neutrons were used; later, helium nuclei and then larger nuclei such as ^{11}B and ^{12}C were employed; and, more recently, highly charged ions of elements such as calcium, chromium, cobalt, and zinc have been chosen. The bombarding particle fuses with the nucleus of the target atom, forming a new nucleus that lasts for a short time before decomposing. New elements are detected by their decomposition products, a signature of particles with specific masses and energies.

By using bigger particles and higher energies, the list of known elements reached 106 by the end of the 1970s. To further extend the search, Russian scientists employed a new idea, matching precisely the energy of the bombarding particle with the energy required to fuse the nuclei. This technique enabled the synthesis of elements 107, 108, and 109 in Darmstadt in the early 1980s, and the synthesis of elements 110, 111, and 112 in the following decade. Lifetimes of these elements were in the millisecond range; the 277 isotope of element 112, for example, mass has a half-life of 240 μs.

Yet another breakthrough was needed to extend the list further. Scientists have long known that isotopes with specific *magic numbers* of neutrons and protons are more stable. Elements with 2, 8, 20, 50, and 82 protons are members of this category, as are elements with 126 neutrons. The magic numbers correspond to filled shells in the nucleus. Their significance is analogous to the significance of filled shells for electronic structure. Theory had predicted that the next magic numbers would be 114 protons and 184 neutrons. Using this information, researchers discovered element 114 in early 1999. The Dubna group reporting this discovery found that the mass 289 isotope had an exceptionally long half-life, about 20 s.

At the time this book was written, 117 elements were known. Will research yield further new elements? It would be hard to say no, given past successes in this area of research, but the quest becomes ever more difficult as scientists venture to the very limits of nuclear stability.

Fermilab Visual Media Services, Batavia, IL

Fermilab. The tunnel housing the four-mile-long particle accelerator at Batavia, Illinois

---

Four years later, a similar reaction sequence was used to make americium-241. Plutonium-239 was found to add two neutrons to form plutonium-241, which decays by β emission to give americium-241.

EXAMPLE 23.9 Nuclear Reactions

Problem Write equations for the nuclear reactions described below.

(a) Fluorine-19 undergoes an (n, γ) reaction to give a radioactive product that decays by $_{-1}^{0}\beta$ emission. (Write equations for both nuclear reactions.)

(b) A common neutron source is a plutonium–beryllium alloy. Plutonium-239 is an α emitter. When beryllium-9 (the only stable isotope of beryllium) reacts with α particles emitted by plutonium, neutrons are ejected. (Write equations for both reactions.)

Strategy The equations are written so that both mass and charge are balanced.

Solution

(a) $^{19}_{9}F + ^{1}_{0}n \rightarrow ^{20}_{9}F + \gamma$

$^{20}_{9}F \rightarrow ^{20}_{10}Ne + ^{0}_{-1}\beta$

(b) $^{239}_{94}Pu \rightarrow ^{235}_{92}U + ^{4}_{2}\alpha$

$^{4}_{2}\alpha + ^{9}_{4}Be \rightarrow ^{12}_{6}C + ^{1}_{0}n$

23.6 Nuclear Fission

In 1938, two chemists, Otto Hahn (1879–1968) and Fritz Strassman (1902–1980), isolated and identified barium in a sample of uranium that had been bombarded with neutrons. How was barium formed? The answer to that question explained one of the most significant scientific discoveries of the 20th century. The uranium nucleus had split into smaller pieces in the process we now call **nuclear fission.**

The details of nuclear fission were unraveled through the work of a number of scientists. They determined that a uranium-235 nucleus initially captured a neutron to form uranium-236. This isotope underwent nuclear fission to produce two new nuclei, one with a mass number around 140 and the other with a mass around 90, along with several neutrons (Figure 23.9). The nuclear reactions that led to formation of barium when a sample of ^{235}U was bombarded with neutrons are

$$^{235}_{92}U + ^{1}_{0}n \rightarrow ^{236}_{92}U$$
$$^{236}_{92}U \rightarrow ^{141}_{56}Ba + ^{92}_{36}Kr + 3\ ^{1}_{0}n$$

An important aspect of fission reactions is that they produce more neutrons than are used to initiate the process. Under the right circumstances, these neutrons then serve to continue the reaction. If one or more of these neutrons are captured by another ^{235}U nucleus, then a further reaction can occur, releasing still more neutrons. This sequence repeats over and over. Such a mechanism, in which each step generates a reactant to continue the reaction, is called a **chain reaction.**

A nuclear fission chain reaction has three general steps:

1. *Initiation.* The reaction of a single atom is needed to start the chain. Fission of ^{235}U is initiated by the absorption of a neutron.
2. *Propagation.* This part of the process repeats itself over and over, with each step yielding more product. The fission of ^{236}U releases neutrons that initiate the fission of other uranium atoms.
3. *Termination.* Eventually, the chain will end. Termination could occur if the reactant (^{235}U) is used up, or if the neutrons that continue the chain escape from the sample without being captured by ^{235}U.

To harness the energy produced in a nuclear reaction, it is necessary to control the rate at which a fission reaction occurs. This is managed by balancing the propagation and termination steps by limiting the number of neutrons available. In a nuclear reactor, this balance is accomplished by using cadmium rods to absorb neutrons. By withdrawing or inserting the rods, the number of neutrons available to propagate the chain can be changed, and the rate of the fission reaction (and the rate of energy production) can be increased or decreased.

Uranium-235 and plutonium-239 are the fissionable isotopes most commonly used in power reactors. Natural uranium contains only 0.72% of uranium-235; more than 99% of the natural element is uranium-238. The percentage of uranium-235 in natural uranium is too small to sustain a chain reaction, however, so the uranium used for nuclear fuel must be enriched in this isotope. One way to do so is by

■ **Fission Reactions** In the fission of uranium-236, a large number of different fission products (elements) are formed. Barium was the element first identified, and its identification provided the key that led to recognition that fission had occurred.

■ **Lise Meitner (1878–1968)** Meitner's greatest contribution to 20th-century science was her explanation of the process of nuclear fission. She and her nephew, Otto Frisch, also a physicist,

AIP-Emilio Segré Visual Archives, Herzfeld Collection

published a paper in 1939 that was the first to use the term "nuclear fission." Element number 109 is named meitnerium to honor Meitner's contributions. The leader of the team that discovered this element said that "She should be honored as the most significant woman scientist of [the 20th] century."

■ **The Atomic Bomb** In an atomic bomb, each nuclear fission step produces 3 neutrons, which leads to about 3 more fissions and 9 more neutrons, which leads to 9 more fission steps and 27 more neutrons, and so on. The rate depends on the number of neutrons, so the nuclear reaction occurs faster and faster as more and more neutrons are formed, leading to an enormous output of energy in a short time span.

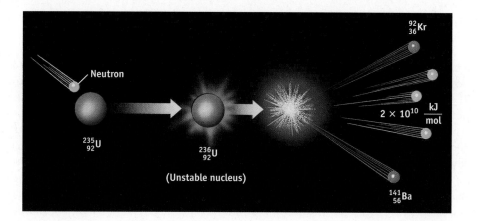

FIGURE 23.9 Nuclear fission.
Neutron capture by $^{235}_{92}$U produces $^{236}_{92}$U. This isotope undergoes fission, which yields several fragments along with several neutrons. These neutrons initiate further nuclear reactions by adding to other $^{235}_{92}$U nuclei. The process is highly exothermic, producing about 2×10^{10} kJ/mol.

gaseous diffusion (◄ Section 11.7). Plutonium, which occurs naturally in only trace quantities, must be made via a nuclear reaction. The raw material for this nuclear synthesis is the more abundant uranium isotope, ^{238}U. Addition of a neutron to ^{238}U gives ^{239}U, which, as noted earlier, undergoes two β emissions to form ^{239}Pu.

Currently, there are over 100 operating nuclear power plants in the United States and more than 400 worldwide. About 20% of this country's electricity (and 17% of the world's energy) comes from nuclear power (Table 23.2). Although one might imagine that nuclear energy would be called upon to meet the ever-increasing needs of society, no new nuclear power plants are under construction in the United States. Among other things, the disasters at Chernobyl (in the former Soviet Union) in 1986 and Three Mile Island (in Pennsylvania) in 1979 have sensitized the public to the issue of safety. The cost to construct a nuclear power plant (measured in terms of dollars per kilowatt-hour of power) is considerably more than the cost for a natural gas–powered facility, and the regulatory restrictions for nuclear power are burdensome. Disposal of highly radioactive nuclear waste is another thorny problem, with 20 metric tons of waste being generated per year at each reactor.

In addition to technical problems, nuclear energy production brings with it significant geopolitical security concerns. The process for enriching uranium for use in a reactor is the same process used for generating weapons-grade uranium. Also, some nuclear reactors are designed so that one by-product of their operation is the isotope plutonium-239, which can be removed and used in a nuclear weapon. Despite these problems, nuclear fission is an important part of the energy profile in a number of countries. For example, three fourths of power production in France and one third in Japan is nuclear generated.

TABLE 23.2 Percentage of Electricity Produced Using Nuclear Power Plants

Country (rank)	Total Power from Nuclear Energy (%)
1. France	75.0
2. Lithuania	73.1
3. Belgium	57.7
4. Bulgaria	47.1
5. Slovak Republic	47.0
6. Sweden	46.8
...	
19. United States	19.9
20. Russia	14.4
21. Canada	12.7

Source: Chemical and Engineering News, p. 42, Oct. 2, 2000.

23.7 Nuclear Fusion

In a **nuclear fusion** reaction, several small nuclei react to form a larger nucleus. Tremendous amounts of energy can be generated by such reactions. An example is the fusion of deuterium and tritium nuclei to form $^4_2$He and a neutron:

$$^2_1\text{H} + ^3_1\text{H} \rightarrow ^4_2\text{He} + ^1_0\text{n} \qquad \Delta E = -1.7 \times 10^9 \text{ kJ/mol}$$

Fusion reactions provide the energy of our sun and other stars. Scientists have long dreamed of being able to harness fusion to provide power. To do so, a temperature of 10^6 to 10^7 K, like that in the interior of the sun, would be required to bring the positively charged nuclei together with enough energy to overcome nuclear repulsions. At the very high temperatures needed for a fusion reaction, mat-

■ **Radon in Your Home** You should test your home for the presence of radon gas (◄ page 1065). The activity level should be less than 4 picocuries per liter of air.

ter does not exist as atoms or molecules; instead, matter is in the form of a *plasma* made up of unbound nuclei and electrons.

Three critical requirements must be met before nuclear fusion could represent a viable energy source. First, the temperature must be high enough for fusion to occur. The fusion of deuterium and tritium, for example, requires a temperature of 10^7 K or more. Second, the plasma must be confined long enough to release a net output of energy. Third, the energy must be recovered in some usable form.

Harnessing a nuclear fusion reaction for a peaceful use has not yet been achieved. Nevertheless, many attractive features encourage continuing research in this field. The hydrogen used as "fuel" is cheap and available in almost unlimited amounts. As a further benefit, most radioisotopes produced by fusion have short half-lives, so they remain a radiation hazard for only a short time.

23.8 Radiation Health and Safety

Units for Measuring Radiation

Several units of measurement are used to describe levels and doses of radioactivity. As is the case in everyday life, the units used in the United States are not the same as the SI units of measurement.

In the United States, the degree of radioactivity is often measured in **curies** (Ci). Less commonly used in the United States is the SI unit, the **becquerel** (Bq). Both units measure the number of disintegrations per second; 1 Ci is 3.7×10^{10} dps (disintegrations per second), while 1 Bq represents 1 dps. The curie and the becquerel are used to report the amount of radioactivity when multiple kinds of unstable nuclei are decaying and to report amounts necessary for medical purposes.

By itself, the degree of radioactivity does not provide a good measure of the amount of energy in the radiation or the amount of damage that the radiation can cause to living tissue. Two additional kinds of information are necessary. The first is the amount of energy absorbed; the second is the effectiveness of the particular kind of radiation in causing tissue damage. The amount of energy absorbed by living tissue is measured in **rads.** *Rad* is an acronym for "radiation absorbed dose." One rad represents 0.01 J of energy absorbed per kilogram of tissue. Its SI equivalent is the **gray** (Gy); 1 Gy denotes the absorption of 1 J per kilogram of tissue.

Different forms of radiation cause different amounts of biological damage. The amount of damage depends on how strongly a form of radiation interacts with matter. Alpha particles cannot penetrate the body any farther than the outer layer of skin. If α particles are emitted within the body, however, they will do between 10 and 20 times the amount of damage done by γ-rays, which can go entirely through a human body without being stopped. In determining the amount of biological damage to living tissue, differences in damaging power are accounted for using a "quality factor." This quality factor has been set at 1 for β and γ radiation, 5 for low-energy protons and neutrons, and 20 for α particles or high-energy protons and neutrons.

Biological damage is quantified in a unit called the **rem** (an acronym for "roentgen equivalent man"). A dose of radiation in rem is determined by multiplying the energy absorbed in rads by the quality factor for that kind of radiation. The rad and the rem are very large in comparison to normal exposures to radiation, so it is more common to express exposures in millirems (mrem). The SI equivalent of the rem is the **sievert** (Sv), determined by multiplying the dose in grays by the quality factor.

■ **The Roentgen** The roentgen (R) is an older unit of radiation exposure. It is defined as the amount of x-rays or γ radiation that will produce 2.08×10^9 ions in 1 cm³ of dry air. The roentgen and the rad are similar in size. Wilhelm Roentgen (1845–1923) first produced and detected x-radiation. Element 111 has been named roentgenium in his honor.

Radiation: Doses and Effects

Exposure to a small amount of radiation is unavoidable. Earth is constantly being bombarded with radioactive particles from outer space. There is also some exposure to radioactive elements that occur naturally on earth, including ^{14}C, ^{40}K (a radioactive isotope that occurs naturally in 0.0117% abundance), ^{238}U, and ^{232}Th. Radioactive elements in the environment that were created artificially (in the fallout from nuclear bomb tests, for example) also contribute to this exposure. For some people, medical procedures using radioisotopes are a major contributor.

The average dose of background radioactivity to which a person in the U.S. is exposed is about 200 mrem per year (Table 23.3). Well over half of that amount comes from natural sources over which we have no control. Of the 60–70 mrem per year exposure that comes from artificial sources, nearly 90% is delivered in medical procedures such as x-ray examinations and radiation therapy. Considering the controversy surrounding nuclear power, it is interesting to note that less than 0.5% of the total annual background dose of radiation that the average person receives can be attributed to the nuclear power industry.

Describing the biological effects of a dose of radiation precisely is not a simple matter. The amount of damage done depends not only on the kind of radiation and the amount of energy absorbed, but also on the particular tissues exposed and the rate at which the dose builds up. A great deal has been learned about the effects of radiation on the human body by studying the survivors of the bombs dropped over Japan in World War II and the workers exposed to radiation from

TABLE 23.3 Radiation Exposure of an Individual for One Year from Natural and Artificial Sources

	Millirem/Year	Percentage
Natural Sources		
Cosmic radiation	50.0	25.8
The earth	47.0	24.2
Building materials	3.0	1.5
Inhaled from the air	5.0	2.6
Elements found naturally in human tissue	21.0	10.8
Subtotal	**126.0**	**64.9**
Medical Sources		
Diagnostic x-rays	50.0	25.8
Radiotherapy	10.0	5.2
Internal diagnosis	1.0	0.5
Subtotal	**61.0**	**31.5**
Other Artificial Sources		
Nuclear power industry	0.85	0.4
Luminous watch dials, TV tubes	2.0	1.0
Fallout from nuclear tests	4.0	2.1
Subtotal	**6.9**	**3.5**
Total	**193.9**	**99.9**

What Is a Safe Exposure?

Is the exposure to natural background radiation totally without effect? Can you equate the effect of a single dose and the effect of cumulative, smaller doses that are spread out over a long period of time? The assumption generally made is that no "safe maximum dose," or level below which absolutely no damage will occur, exists. However, the accuracy of this assumption has come into question. These issues are not testable with human subjects, and tests based on animal studies are not completely reliable because of the uncertainty of species-to-species variations.

The model used by government regulators to set exposure limits assumes that the relationship between exposure to radiation and incidence of radiation-induced problems, such as cancer, anemia, and immune system problems, is linear. Under this assumption, if a dose of $2x$ rem causes damage in 20% of the population, then a dose of x rem will cause damage in 10% of the population. But is this true? Cells do possess mechanisms for repairing damage. Many scientists believe that this self-repair mechanism renders the human body less susceptible to damage from smaller doses of radiation, because the damage will be repaired as part of the normal course of events. They argue that, at extremely low doses of radiation, the self-repair response results in less damage.

The bottom line is that much still remains to be learned in this area. And the stakes are significant.

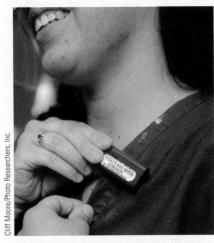

The film badge. These badges, worn by scientists using radioactive materials, are used to monitor cumulative exposure to radiation.

the reactor disaster at Chernobyl. From studies of the health of these survivors, we have learned that the effects of radiation are not generally observable below a single dose of 25 rem. At the other extreme, a single dose of >200 rem will be fatal to about half the population (Table 23.4).

Our information is more accurate when dealing with single, large doses than it is for the effects of chronic, smaller doses of radiation. One current issue of debate in the scientific community is how to judge the effects of multiple smaller doses or long-term exposure (see *A Closer Look: What Is A Safe Exposure?*).

23.9 Applications of Nuclear Chemistry

We tend to think about nuclear chemistry in terms of power plants and bombs. In truth, radioactive elements are now used in all areas of science and medicine, and they are of ever-increasing importance to our lives. Because describing all of their uses would take several books, we have selected just a few examples to illustrate the diversity of applications of radioactivity.

TABLE 23.4 Effects of a Single Dose of Radiation

Dose (rem)	Effect
0–25	No effect observed
26–50	Small decrease in white blood cell count
51–100	Significant decrease in white blood cell count, lesions
101–200	Loss of hair, nausea
201–500	Hemorrhaging, ulcers, death in 50% of population
500	Death

Nuclear Medicine: Medical Imaging

Diagnostic procedures using nuclear chemistry are essential in medical imaging, which entails the creation of images of specific parts of the body. There are three principal components to constructing a radioisotope-based image:

- A radioactive isotope, administered as the element or incorporated into a compound, that concentrates the radioactive isotope in the tissue to be imaged
- A method of detecting the type of radiation involved
- A computer to assemble the information from the detector into a meaningful image

The choice of a radioisotope and the manner in which it is administered are determined by the tissue in question. A compound containing the isotope must be absorbed more by the target tissue than by the rest of the body. Table 23.5 lists radioisotopes that are commonly used in nuclear imaging processes, their half-lives, and the tissues they are used to image. All of the isotopes in Table 23.5 are γ emitters; γ radiation is preferred for imaging because it is less damaging to the body in small doses than either α or β radiation.

Technetium-99m is used in more than 85% of the diagnostic scans done in hospitals each year (see *A Closer Look: Technetium-99m*). The "m" stands for *metastable*, a term used to identify an unstable state that exists for a finite period of time. Recall that atoms in excited electronic states emit visible, infrared, and ultraviolet radiation (◀ Chapter 6). Similarly, a nucleus in an excited state gives up its excess energy, but in this case a much higher energy is involved, and the emission occurs as γ radiation. The γ-rays given off by ^{99m}Tc are detected to produce the image (Figure 23.10).

Another medical imaging technique based on nuclear chemistry is positron emission tomography (PET). In PET, an isotope that decays by positron emission is incorporated into a carrier compound and given to the patient. When emitted, the positron travels no more than a few millimeters before undergoing matter–antimatter annihilation.

$$^{0}_{+1}\beta + \,^{0}_{-1}e \rightarrow 2\gamma$$

The two emitted γ-rays travel in opposite directions. By determining where high numbers of γ-rays are being emitted, one can construct a map showing where the positron emitter is located in the body.

An isotope often used in PET is ^{15}O. A patient is given gaseous O_2 that contains ^{15}O. This isotope travels throughout the body in the bloodstream, allowing images of the brain and bloodstream (Figure 23.11) to be obtained. Because positron emitters are typically very short-lived, PET facilities must be located near a cyclotron where the radioactive nuclei are prepared and then immediately incorporated into a carrier compound.

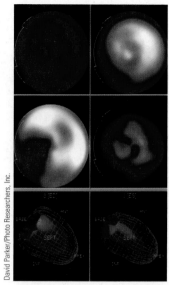

FIGURE 23.10 **Heart imaging with technetium-99m.** The radioactive element technetium-99m, a gamma emitter, is injected into a patient's vein in the form of the pertechnetate ion (TcO_4^{-}) or as a complex ion with an organic ligand. A series of scans of the gamma emissions of the isotope are made while the patient is resting and then again after strenuous exercise. Bright areas in the scans indicate that the isotope is binding to the tissue in that area. The scans in this figure show a normal heart function.

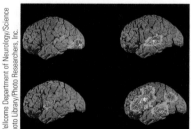

FIGURE 23.11 **PET scans of the brain.** These scans show the left side of the brain; red indicates an area of highest activity. (*upper left*) *Sight* activates the visual area in the occipital cortex at the back of the brain. (*upper right*) *Hearing* activates the auditory area in the superior temporal cortex of the brain. (*lower left*) *Speaking* activates the speech centers in the insula and motor cortex. (*lower right*) *Thinking* about verbs, and speaking them, generates high activity, including in the hearing, speaking, temporal, and parietal areas.

TABLE 23.5 **Radioisotopes Used in Medical Diagnostic Procedures**

Radioisotope	Half-Life (h)	Imaging
^{99m}Tc	6.0	Thyroid, brain, kidneys
^{201}Tl	73.0	Heart
^{123}I	13.2	Thyroid
^{67}Ga	78.2	Various tumors and abscesses
^{18}F	1.8	Brain, sites of metabolic activity

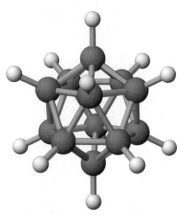

One of the compounds used in BNCT is $Na_2[B_{12}H_{12}]$. The structure of the $B_{12}H_{12}^{2-}$ anion is a regular polyhedron with 20 sides, called an icosahedron.

Nuclear Medicine: Radiation Therapy

To treat most cancers, it is necessary to use radiation that can penetrate the body to the location of the tumor. Gamma radiation from a cobalt-60 source is commonly used. Unfortunately, the penetrating ability of γ-rays makes it virtually impossible to destroy diseased tissue without also damaging healthy tissue in the process. Nevertheless, this technique is a regularly sanctioned procedure, and its successes are well known.

To avoid the side effects associated with more traditional forms of radiation therapy, a new form of treatment has been explored in the last 10 to 15 years, called *boron neutron capture therapy* (BNCT). BNCT is unusual in that boron-10, the isotope of boron used as part of the treatment, is not radioactive. Boron-10 is highly effective in capturing neutrons, however—2500 times better than boron-11, and eight times better than uranium-235. When the nucleus of a boron-10 atom captures a neutron, the resulting boron-11 nucleus has so much energy that it fragments to form an α particle and a lithium-7 atom. Although the α particles do a great deal of damage, because their penetrating power is so low, the damage remains confined to an area not much larger than one or two cells in diameter.

In a typical BNCT treatment, a solution of a boron compound is injected into the tumor. After a few hours, the tumor is bombarded with neutrons. The α particles are produced only at the site of the tumor, and the production stops when the neutron bombardment ends.

Analytical Methods: The Use of Radioactive Isotopes as Tracers

Radioactive isotopes can be used to help determine the fate of compounds in the body or in the environment. These studies begin with a compound that contains a radioactive isotope of one of its component elements. In biology, for example, scientists can use radioactive isotopes to measure the uptake of nutrients. Plants take up phosphorus-containing compounds from the soil through their roots. By adding a small amount of radioactive ^{32}P, a β emitter with a half-life of 14.3 days, to fertilizer and then measuring the rate at which the radioactivity appears in the leaves, plant biologists can determine the rate at which phosphorus is taken up. The outcome can assist scientists in identifying hybrid strains of plants that can absorb phosphorus quickly, resulting in faster-maturing crops, better yields per acre, and more food or fiber at less expense.

To measure pesticide levels, a pesticide can be tagged with a radioisotope and then applied to a test field. By counting the disintegrations of the radioactive tracer, information can be obtained about how much pesticide accumulates in the soil, is taken up by the plant, and is carried off in runoff surface water. After these tests are completed, the radioactive isotope decays to harmless levels in a few days or a few weeks because of the short half-lives of the isotopes used.

Analytical Methods: Isotope Dilution

Imagine, for the moment, that you wanted to estimate the volume of blood in an animal subject. How might you do this? Obviously, draining the blood and measuring its volume in volumetric glassware is not a desirable option.

One technique uses a method called isotope dilution. In this process, a small amount of radioactive isotope is injected into the bloodstream. After a period of time to allow the isotope to become distributed throughout the body, a blood sample is taken and its radioactivity measured. The calculation used to determine the total blood volume is illustrated in the next example.

A Closer Look

Technetium-99m

Technetium was the first new element to be made artificially. One might think that this element would be a chemical rarity, but this is not so: its importance in medical imaging has brought a great deal of attention to it. Although all the technetium in the world must be synthesized by nuclear reactions, the element is readily available and even inexpensive; its price in 1999 was $60 per gram, only about four times the price of gold.

Technetium-99m is formed when molybdenum-99 decays by β emission ($t_{1/2} = 6.01$h). Technetium-99m then decays to its ground state with a half-life of 6.01 h, giving off a 140-KeV γ-ray in the process. (Technetium-99 is itself unstable, decaying to stable ^{99}Ru with a half-life of 2.1×10^5 years.)

Technetium-99m is produced in hospitals using a molybdenum–technetium generator. Sheathed in lead shielding, the generator contains the artificially synthesized isotope ^{99}Mo in the form of molybdate ion, MoO_4^{2-}, adsorbed on a column of alumina, Al_2O_3. The MoO_4^{2-} is continually being converted into the pertechnate ion, $^{99m}TcO_4^-$ by β emission. When it is needed, the $^{99m}TcO_4^-$ is washed from the column using a saline solution. Technetium-99m may be used directly as the pertechnate ion or converted into other compounds. The pertechnate ion or radiopharmaceuticals made from it are administered intravenously to the patient. Such small quantities are needed that 1 μg (microgram) of technetium-99m is suffi-cient for the average hospital's daily imaging needs.

One use of ^{99m}Tc is for imaging the thyroid gland. Because I^-(aq) and TcO_4^-(aq) ions have very similar sizes, the thyroid will (mistakenly) take up TcO_4^-(aq) along with iodide ion. This uptake concentrates ^{99m}Tc in the thyroid and allows a physician to obtain images such as the one shown in the accompanying figure.

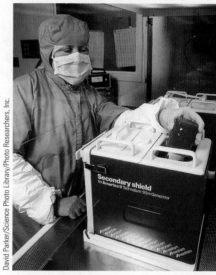

A **technetium-99m generator.** A technician is loading a sample containing the MoO_4^{2-} ion into the device that will convert molybdate ion to $^{99m}TcO_4^-$.

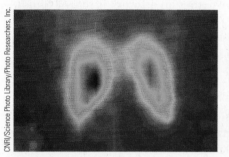

(a) Healthy human thyroid gland.

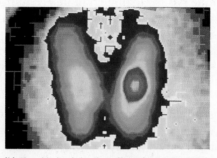

(b) Thyroid gland showing effect of hyperthyroidism.

Thyroid imaging. Technetium-99m concentrates in sites of high activity. Images of this gland, which is located at the base of the neck, were obtained by recording γ-ray emission after the patient was given radioactive technetium-99m. Current technology creates a computer color-enhanced scan.

■ EXAMPLE 23.10 Analysis Using Isotope Dilution

Problem A 1.00-mL solution containing 0.240 μCi of tritium is injected into a dog's bloodstream. After a period of time to allow the isotope to be dispersed, a 1.00-mL sample of blood is drawn. The radioactivity of this sample is found to be 4.3×10^{-4} μCi/mL. What is the total volume of blood in the dog?

Strategy For any solution, concentration equals the amount of solute divided by volume of solution. In this problem, we relate the activity of the sample (in Ci) to concentration. The total amount of solute is 0.240 μCi, and the concentration (measured on the small sample of blood) is 4.3×10^{-4} μCi/mL. The unknown is the volume.

Solution The blood contains a total of 0.240 μCi of the radioactive material. We can represent its concentration as 0.240 μCi/x, where x is the total blood volume. After dilution in the bloodstream, 1.00 mL of blood is found to have an activity of 4.3×10^{-4} μCi/mL.

$$0.240 \ \mu\text{Ci}/x \ \text{mL} = 4.3 \times 10^{-4} \ \mu\text{Ci}/1.00 \ \text{mL}$$

$$x = 560 \ \text{mL}$$

EXERCISE 23.11 Analysis by Isotope Dilution

Suppose you hydrolyze a 10.00-g sample of a protein. Next, you add to it a 3.00-mg sample of ^{14}C-labeled threonine, an amino acid with a specific activity of 3000 dpm. After mixing, part of the threonine (60.0 mg) is separated and isolated from the mixture. The activity of the isolated sample is 1200 dpm. How much threonine was present in the original sample?

TABLE 23.6 Rare Earth Analysis of Moon Rock Sample 10022 (a fine-grain igneous rock)

Element	Concentration (ppm)
La	26.4
Ce	68
Nd	66
Sm	21.2
Eu	2.04
Gd	25
Tb	4.7
Dy	31.2
Ho	5.5
Er	16
Yb	17.7
Lu	2.55

Source: L. A. Haskin, P. A, Helmke, and R. O. Allen: *Science,* Vol. 167, p. 487, 1970. The concentrations of rare earths in moon rocks were quite similar to the values in terrestrial rocks except that the europium concentration is much depleted. The January 30, 1970, issue of *Science* was devoted to analysis of moon rocks.

Space Science: Neutron Activation Analysis and the Moon Rocks

The first manned space mission to the moon brought back a number of samples of soil and rock—a treasure trove for scientists. One of their first tasks was to analyze these samples to determine their identity and composition. Most analytical methods require chemical reactions using at least a small amount of material; however, this was not a desirable option, considering that the moon rocks were at the time the most valuable rocks in the world.

A few scientists got a chance to work on this unique project, and one of the analytical tools they used was **neutron activation analysis.** In this nondestructive process, a sample is irradiated with neutrons. Most isotopes add a neutron to form a new isotope that is one mass unit higher in an excited nuclear state. When the nucleus decays to its ground state, it emits a γ-ray. The energy of the γ-ray identifies the element, and the number of γ-rays can be counted to determine the amount of the element in the sample. Using neutron activation analysis, it is possible to analyze for a number of elements in a single experiment (Table 23.6).

Neutron activation analysis has many other uses. This analytical procedure yields a kind of fingerprint that can be used to identify a substance. For example, this technique has been applied in determining whether an art work is real or fraudulent. Analysis of the pigments in paints on a painting can be carried out without damaging the painting to determine whether the composition resembles modern paints or paints used hundreds of years ago.

Food Science: Food Irradiation

Refrigeration, canning, and chemical additives provide significant protection in terms of food preservation, but in some parts of the world these procedures are unavailable, and stored-food spoilage may claim as much as 50% of the food crop. Irradiation with γ-rays from sources such as ^{60}Co and ^{137}Cs is an option for prolonging the shelf life of foods. Relatively low levels of radiation may retard the growth of organisms, such as bacteria, molds, and yeasts, that can cause food spoilage. After irradiation, milk in a sealed container has a minimum shelf life of 3 months without refrigeration. Chicken normally has a 3-day refrigerated shelf life; after irradiation, it may have a 3-week refrigerated shelf life.

Higher levels of radiation, in the 1- to 5-Mrad (1 Mrad = 1×10^6 rad) range, will kill every living organism. Foods irradiated at these levels will keep indefinitely when sealed in plastic or aluminum-foil packages. Ham, beef, turkey, and corned beef sterilized by radiation have been used on many Space Shuttle flights, for example. An astronaut said, "The beautiful thing was that it didn't disturb the taste, which made the meals much better than the freeze-dried and other types of foods we had."

These procedures are not without their opponents, and the public has not fully embraced irradiation of foods yet. An interesting argument favoring this technique is that radiation is less harmful than other methodologies for food preservation. This type of sterilization offers greater safety to food workers because it lessens chances of exposure to harmful chemicals, and it protects the environment by avoiding contamination of water supplies with toxic chemicals.

Food irradiation is commonly used in European countries, Canada, and Mexico. Its use in the United States is currently regulated by the U.S. Food and Drug Administration (FDA) and Department of Agriculture (USDA). In 1997, the FDA approved the irradiation of refrigerated and frozen uncooked meat to control pathogens and extend shelf-life, and in 2000 the USDA approved the irradiation of eggs to control *Salmonella* infection (Table 23.7).

The primary function of the thyroid gland, located in your neck, is the production of thyroxine (3,5,3′,5′-tetraiodothyronine) and 3,5,3′-triiodothyronine. These chemical compounds are hormones that help to regulate the rate of metabolism (page 510), a term that refers to all of the chemical reactions that take place in the body. In particular, the thyroid hormones play an important role in the processes that release energy from food.

Abnormally low levels of thyroxine result in a condition known as hypothyroidism. Its symptoms include lethargy and feeling cold much of the time. The remedy for this condition is medication, consisting of thyroxine pills. The opposite condition, hyperthyroidism, also occurs in some people. In this condition, the body produces too much of the hormone. Hyperthyroidism is diagnosed by symptoms such as nervousness, heat intolerance, increased appetite, and muscle weakness and fatigue when blood sugar is too rapidly depleted. The standard remedy for hyperthyroidism is to destroy part of the thyroid gland, and one way to do so is to use a compound containing radioactive iodine-123 or -131.

To understand this procedure, you need to know something about iodine in the body. Iodine is an essential element. Some diets provide iodine naturally (seaweed, for example, is a good source of iodine), but in the Western world most iodine taken up by the body comes from iodized salt, NaCl containing a few percent of NaI. An adult man or woman of average size should take in about 150 μg (micrograms) of iodine (1 μg = 10^{-6} g) in the daily diet. In the body, iodide ion is transported to the thyroid, where it serves as one of the raw materials in making thyroxine.

The fact that iodine concentrates in the thyroid tissue is essential to the procedure for using radioiodine therapy as a treatment for hyperthyroidism. Typically, an aqueous NaI solution in which a small fraction of iodide consists of the radioactive isotope iodine-131 or iodine-123, and the rest is nonradioactive iodine-127. The radioactivity destroys thyroid tissue, resulting in a decrease in thyroid activity.

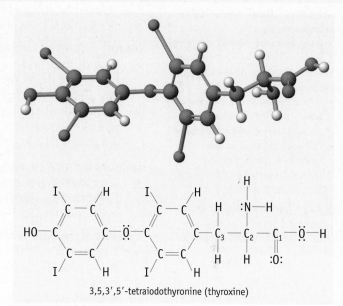

3,5,3′,5′-tetraiodothyronine (thyroxine)

Thyroxine. The hormone 3,5,3′,5′-tetraiodothyronine (thyroxine) exerts a stimulating effect on metabolism.

Questions:

1. ^{131}I decays by beta emission. What is the product of this decay? Write a balanced nuclear equation for this process.

2. The half-life of ^{131}I is 8.04 d, and that of ^{123}I is 13.3 h. If you begin with an equal number of moles of each isotope, at the end of 7 days what are their relative amounts?

Answers to these questions are in Appendix Q.

TABLE 23.7   Approvals of Food Irradiation

1963	FDA approves irradiation to control insects in wheat and flour.
1964	FDA approves irradiation to inhibit sprouting of white potatoes.
1985	FDA approves irradiation at specific doses to control *Trichinella spiralis* infection of pork.
1986	FDA approves irradiation at specific doses to delay maturation, inhibit growth, and disinfect foods including vegetables and spices.
1992	USDA approves irradiation of poultry to control infection by *Salmonella* and bacteria.
1997	FDA permits use of ionizing radiation to treat refrigerated and frozen meat and other meat products.
2000	USDA approves irradiation of eggs to control *Salmonella* infection.

Source: **www.foodsafety.gov/~fsg/irradiat.html.**

Chapter Goals Revisited

Now that you have studied this chapter, you should ask whether you have met the chapter goals. In particular, you should be able to:

Identify radioactive elements, and describe natural and artificial nuclear reactions

a. Identify α, β, and γ radiation, the three major types of radiation in natural radioactive decay (Section 23.1) and write balanced equations for nuclear reactions (Section 23.2). Study question(s) assignable in OWL: 12, 16, 32, 41.

b. Predict whether a radioactive isotope will decay by α or β emission, or by positron emission or electron capture (Sections 23.2 and 23.3). Study question(s) assignable in OWL: 17, 18, 20.

Calculate the binding energy and binding energy per nucleon for a particular isotope

a. Understand how binding energy per nucleon is defined (Section 23.3) and recognize the significance of a graph of binding energy per nucleon versus mass number (Section 23.3). Study question(s) assignable in OWL: 23, 52, 61, 62.

Understand the rates of radioactive decay

a. Understand and use mathematical equations that characterize the radioactive decay process (Section 23.4). Study question(s) assignable in OWL: 30, 32, 34, 36, 47, 50, 54, 58.

Understand artificial nuclear reactions

a. Describe nuclear chain reactions, nuclear fission, and nuclear fusion (Sections 23.6 and 23.7).

Understand issues of health and safety with respect to radioactivity

a. Describe the units used to measure intensity, and understand how they pertain to health issues (Section 23.8 and 23.9).

Be aware of some uses of radioactive isotopes in science and medicine

KEY EQUATIONS

Equation 23.1 (page 1070): The equation relating interconversion of mass (m) and energy (E). This equation is applied in the calculation of binding energy (E_b) for nuclei.

$$E_b = (\Delta m)c^2$$

Equation 23.2 (page 1073): The activity of a radioactive sample (A) is proportional to the number of radioactive atoms (N).

$$A \propto N$$

Equation 23.4 (page 1074): The rate law for nuclear decay based on number of radioactive atoms initially present (N_0) and the number N after time t.

$$\ln(N/N_0) = -kt$$

Equation 23.5 (page 1074): The rate law for nuclear decay based on the measured activity of a sample (A).

$$\ln(A/A_0) = -kt$$

Equation 23.6 (page 1074): The relationship between the half-life and the rate constant for a nuclear decay process.

$$t_{1/2} = 0.693/k$$

STUDY QUESTIONS

OWL Online homework for this chapter may be assigned in OWL.

▲ denotes challenging questions.

■ denotes questions assignable in OWL.

Blue-numbered questions have answers in Appendix O and fully-worked solutions in the *Student Solutions Manual*.

Practicing Skills

Important Concepts

1. Some important discoveries in scientific history that contributed to the development of nuclear chemistry are listed below. Briefly, describe each discovery, identify prominent scientists who contributed to it, and comment on the significance of the discovery to the development of this field.
   (a) 1896, the discovery of radioactivity
   (b) 1898, the identification of radium and polonium
   (c) 1918, the first artificial nuclear reaction
   (d) 1932, (n, γ) reactions
   (e) 1939, fission reactions

2. In Chapter 3, the law of conservation of mass was introduced as an important principle in chemistry. The discovery of nuclear reactions forced scientists to modify this law. Explain why, and give an example illustrating that mass is not conserved in a nuclear reaction.

3. A graph of binding energy per nucleon is shown in Figure 23.4. Explain how the data used to construct this graph were obtained.

4. How is Figure 23.3 used to predict the type of decomposition for unstable (radioactive) isotopes?

5. Outline how nuclear reactions are carried out in the laboratory. Describe the artificial nuclear reactions used to make an element with an atomic number greater than 92.

6. What mathematical equations define the rates of decay for radioactive elements?

7. Explain how carbon-14 is used to estimate the ages of archeological artifacts. What are the limitations for use of this technique?

8. Describe how the concept of half-life for nuclear decay is used.

9. What is a radioactive decay series? Explain why radium and polonium are found in uranium ores.

10. The interaction of radiation with matter has both positive and negative consequences. Discuss briefly the hazards of radiation and the way that radiation can be used in medicine.

Nuclear Reactions

(See Examples 23.1 and 23.2.)

11. Complete the following nuclear equations. Write the mass number and atomic number for the remaining particle, as well as its symbol.
    (a) $^{54}_{26}\text{Fe} + ^{4}_{2}\text{He} \longrightarrow 2\,^{1}_{0}\text{n} + ?$
    (b) $^{27}_{13}\text{Al} + ^{4}_{2}\text{He} \longrightarrow ^{30}_{15}\text{P} + ?$
    (c) $^{32}_{16}\text{S} + ^{1}_{0}\text{n} \longrightarrow ^{1}_{1}\text{H} + ?$
    (d) $^{96}_{42}\text{Mo} + ^{2}_{1}\text{H} \longrightarrow ^{1}_{0}\text{n} + ?$
    (e) $^{98}_{42}\text{Mo} + ^{1}_{0}\text{n} \longrightarrow ^{99}_{43}\text{Tc} + ?$
    (f) $^{18}_{9}\text{F} \longrightarrow ^{18}_{8}\text{O} + ?$

12. ■ Complete the following nuclear equations. Write the mass number, atomic number, and symbol for the remaining particle.
    (a) $^{9}_{4}\text{Be} + ? \longrightarrow ^{6}_{3}\text{Li} + ^{4}_{2}\text{He}$
    (b) $? + ^{1}_{0}\text{n} \longrightarrow ^{24}_{11}\text{Na} + ^{4}_{2}\text{He}$
    (c) $^{40}_{20}\text{Ca} + ? \longrightarrow ^{40}_{19}\text{K} + ^{1}_{1}\text{H}$
    (d) $^{241}_{95}\text{Am} + ^{4}_{2}\text{He} \longrightarrow ^{243}_{97}\text{Bk} + ?$
    (e) $^{246}_{96}\text{Cm} + ^{12}_{6}\text{C} \longrightarrow 4\,^{1}_{0}\text{n} + ?$
    (f) $^{238}_{92}\text{U} + ? \longrightarrow ^{249}_{100}\text{Fm} + 5\,^{1}_{0}\text{n}$

13. Complete the following nuclear equations. Write the mass number, atomic number, and symbol for the remaining particle.
    (a) $^{111}_{47}\text{Ag} \longrightarrow ^{111}_{48}\text{Cd} + ?$
    (b) $^{87}_{36}\text{Kr} \longrightarrow ^{0}_{-1}\beta + ?$
    (c) $^{231}_{91}\text{Pa} \longrightarrow ^{227}_{89}\text{Ac} + ?$
    (d) $^{230}_{90}\text{Th} \longrightarrow ^{4}_{2}\text{He} + ?$
    (e) $^{82}_{35}\text{Br} \longrightarrow ^{82}_{36}\text{Kr} + ?$
    (f) $? \longrightarrow ^{24}_{12}\text{Mg} + ^{0}_{-1}\beta$

14. Complete the following nuclear equations. Write the mass number, atomic number, and symbol for the remaining particle.
    (a) $^{19}_{10}\text{Ne} \longrightarrow ^{0}_{+1}\beta + ?$
    (b) $^{59}_{26}\text{Fe} \longrightarrow ^{0}_{-1}\beta + ?$
    (c) $^{40}_{19}\text{K} \longrightarrow ^{0}_{-1}\beta + ?$
    (d) $^{37}_{18}\text{Ar} + ^{0}_{-1}\text{e}$ (electron capture) $\longrightarrow ?$
    (e) $^{55}_{26}\text{Fe} + ^{0}_{-1}\text{e}$ (electron capture) $\longrightarrow ?$
    (f) $^{26}_{13}\text{Al} \longrightarrow ^{25}_{12}\text{Mg} + ?$

15. The uranium-235 radioactive decay series, beginning with $^{235}_{92}\text{U}$ and ending with $^{207}_{82}\text{Pb}$, occurs in the following sequence: $\alpha, \beta, \alpha, \beta, \alpha, \alpha, \alpha, \alpha, \beta, \beta, \alpha$. Write an equation for each step in this series.

16. ■ The thorium-232 radioactive decay series, beginning with $^{232}_{90}\text{Th}$ and ending with $^{208}_{82}\text{Pb}$, occurs in the following sequence: $\alpha, \beta, \beta, \alpha, \alpha, \alpha, \alpha, \beta, \beta, \alpha$. Write an equation for each step in this series.

Nuclear Stability and Nuclear Decay
(See Examples 23.3 and 23.4.)

17. ■ What particle is emitted in the following nuclear reactions? Write an equation for each reaction.
    (a) Gold-198 decays to mercury-198.
    (b) Radon-222 decays to polonium-218.
    (c) Cesium-137 decays to barium-137.
    (d) Indium-110 decays to cadmium-110.

18. ■ What is the product of the following nuclear decay processes? Write an equation for each process.
    (a) Gallium-67 decays by electron capture.
    (b) Potassium-38 decays with positron emission.
    (c) Technetium-99m decays with γ emission.
    (d) Manganese-56 decays by β emission.

19. Predict the probable mode of decay for each of the following radioactive isotopes, and write an equation to show the products of decay.
    (a) Bromine-80m   (c) Cobalt-61
    (b) Californium-240   (d) Carbon-11

20. ■ Predict the probable mode of decay for each of the following radioactive isotopes, and write an equation to show the products of decay.
    (a) Manganese-54   (c) Silver-110
    (b) Americium-241   (d) Mercury-197m

21. (a) Which of the following nuclei decay by $_{-1}^{0}\beta$ decay?

    $$^{3}\text{H} \quad ^{16}\text{O} \quad ^{20}\text{F} \quad ^{13}\text{N}$$

    (b) Which of the following nuclei decays by $_{+1}^{0}\beta$ decay?

    $$^{238}\text{U} \quad ^{19}\text{F} \quad ^{22}\text{Na} \quad ^{24}\text{Na}$$

22. (a) Which of the following nuclei decay by $_{-1}^{0}\beta$ decay?

    $$^{1}\text{H} \quad ^{23}\text{Mg} \quad ^{32}\text{P} \quad ^{20}\text{Ne}$$

    (b) Which of the following nuclei decay by $_{+1}^{0}\beta$ decay?

    $$^{235}\text{U} \quad ^{35}\text{Cl} \quad ^{38}\text{K} \quad ^{24}\text{Na}$$

23. ■ Boron has two stable isotopes, ^{10}B and ^{11}B. Calculate the binding energies per nucleon of these two nuclei. The required masses (in g/mol) are $_{1}^{1}\text{H} = 1.00783$, $_{0}^{1}\text{n} = 1.00867$, $_{5}^{10}\text{B} = 10.01294$, and $_{5}^{11}\text{B} = 11.00931$.

24. Calculate the binding energy in kilojoules per mole of nucleons of P for the formation of ^{30}P and ^{31}P. The required masses (in g/mol) are $_{1}^{1}\text{H} = 1.00783$, $_{0}^{1}\text{n} = 1.00867$, $_{15}^{30}\text{P} = 29.97832$, and $_{15}^{31}\text{P} = 30.97376$.

25. Calculate the binding energy per nucleon for calcium-40, and compare your result with the value in Figure 23.4. Masses needed for this calculation are (in g/mol) $_{1}^{1}\text{H} = 1.00783$, $_{0}^{1}\text{n} = 1.00867$, and $_{20}^{40}\text{Ca} = 39.96259$.

26. Calculate the binding energy per nucleon for iron-56. Masses needed for this calculation (in g/mol) are $_{1}^{1}\text{H} = 1.00783$, $_{0}^{1}\text{n} = 1.00867$, and $_{26}^{56}\text{Fe} = 55.9349$. Compare the result of your calculation to the value for iron-56 in the graph in Figure 23.4.

27. Calculate the binding energy per mole of nucleons for $_{8}^{16}\text{O}$. Masses needed for this calculations are $_{1}^{1}\text{H} = 1.00783$, $_{0}^{1}\text{n} = 1.00867$, and $_{8}^{16}\text{O} = 15.99492$.

28. Calculate the binding energy per nucleon for nitrogen-14. The mass of nitrogen-14 is 14.003074.

Rates of Radioactive Decay
(See Examples 23.5 and 23.6.)

29. Copper acetate containing ^{64}Cu is used to study brain tumors. This isotope has a half-life of 12.7 h. If you begin with 25.0 μg of ^{64}Cu, what mass in micrograms remains after 63.5 h?

30. ■ Gold-198 is used in the diagnosis of liver problems. The half-life of ^{198}Au is 2.69 days. If you begin with 2.8 μg of this gold isotope, what mass remains after 10.8 days?

31. Iodine-131 is used to treat thyroid cancer.
    (a) The isotope decays by β particle emission. Write a balanced equation for this process.
    (b) Iodine-131 has a half-life of 8.04 days. If you begin with 2.4 μg of radioactive ^{131}I, what mass remains after 40.2 days?

32. ■ Phosphorus-32 is used in the form of Na_2HPO_4 in the treatment of chronic myeloid leukemia, among other things.
    (a) The isotope decays by β particle emission. Write a balanced equation for this process.
    (b) The half-life of ^{32}P is 14.3 days. If you begin with 4.8 μg of radioactive ^{32}P in the form of Na_2HPO_4, what mass remains after 28.6 days (about one month)?

33. Gallium-67 ($t_{1/2} = 78.25$ h) is used in the medical diagnosis of certain kinds of tumors. If you ingest a compound containing 0.015 mg of this isotope, what mass (in milligrams) remains in your body after 13 days? (Assume none is excreted.)

34. ■ Iodine-131 ($t_{1/2} = 8.04$ days), a β emitter, is used to treat thyroid cancer.
    (a) Write an equation for the decomposition of ^{131}I.
    (b) If you ingest a sample of NaI containing ^{131}I, how much time is required for the activity to decrease to 35.0% of its original value?

35. Radon has been the focus of much attention recently because it is often found in homes. Radon-222 emits α particles and has a half-life of 3.82 d.
    (a) Write a balanced equation to show this process.
    (b) How long does it take for a sample of ^{222}Rn to decrease to 20.0% of its original activity?

36. ■ Strontium-90 is a hazardous radioactive isotope that resulted from atmospheric testing of nuclear weapons. A sample of strontium carbonate containing ^{90}Sr is found to have an activity of 1.0×10^{3} dpm. One year later, the activity of this sample is 975 dpm.

(a) Calculate the half-life of strontium-90 from this information.

(b) How long will it take for the activity of this sample to drop to 1.0% of the initial value?

37. Radioactive cobalt-60 is used extensively in nuclear medicine as a γ-ray source. It is made by a neutron capture reaction from cobalt-59 and is a β emitter; β emission is accompanied by strong γ radiation. The half-life of cobalt-60 is 5.27 years.

(a) How long will it take for a cobalt-60 source to decrease to one eighth of its original activity?

(b) What fraction of the activity of a cobalt-60 source remains after 1.0 year?

38. Scandium occurs in nature as a single isotope, scandium-45. Neutron irradiation produces scandium-46, a β emitter with a half-life of 83.8 days. If the initial activity is 7.0×10^4 dpm, draw a graph showing disintegrations per minute as a function of time during a period of one year.

Nuclear Reactions
(See Example 23.9.)

39. Americium-240 is made by bombarding plutonium-239 with α particles. In addition to ^{240}Am, the products are a proton and two neutrons. Write a balanced equation for this process.

40. There are two isotopes of americium, both with half-lives sufficiently long to allow the handling of large quantities. Americium-241, with a half-life of 432 years, is an α emitter. It is used in smoke detectors. The isotope is formed from ^{239}Pu by absorption of two neutrons followed by emission of a β particle. Write a balanced equation for this process.

41. ■ The superheavy element ^{287}Uuq was made by firing a beam of ^{48}Ca ions at ^{242}Pu. Three neutrons were ejected in the reaction. Write a balanced nuclear equation for the synthesis of ^{287}Uuq.

42. To synthesize the heavier transuranium elements, a nucleus must be bombarded with a relatively large particle. If you know the products are californium-246 and four neutrons, with what particle would you bombard uranium-238 atoms?

43. Deuterium nuclei ($^2_1$H) are particularly effective as bombarding particles to carry out nuclear reactions. Complete the following equations:

(A) $^{114}_{48}\text{Cd} + ^2_1\text{H} \longrightarrow ? + ^1_1\text{H}$

(B) $^6_3\text{Li} + ^2_1\text{H} \longrightarrow ? + ^1_0\text{n}$

(C) $^{40}_{20}\text{Ca} + ^2_1\text{H} \longrightarrow ^{38}_{19}\text{K} + ?$

(D) $? + ^2_1\text{H} \longrightarrow ^{65}_{30}\text{Zn} + \gamma$

44. Element ^{287}114 decayed by α emission with a half-life of about 5 s. Write an equation for this process.

45. Boron is an effective absorber of neutrons. When boron-10 adds a neutron, an α particle is emitted. Write an equation for this nuclear reaction.

46. Some of the reactions explored by Rutherford and others are listed below. Identify the unknown species in each reaction.

(a) $^{14}_7\text{N} + ^4_2\text{He} \longrightarrow ^{17}_8\text{O} + ?$

(b) $^9_4\text{Be} + ^4_2\text{He} \longrightarrow ? + ^1_0\text{n}$

(c) $? + ^4_2\text{He} \longrightarrow ^{30}_{15}\text{P} + ^1_0\text{n}$

(d) $^{239}_{94}\text{Pu} + ^4_2\text{He} \longrightarrow ? + ^1_0\text{n}$

General Questions
These questions are not designated as to type or location in the chapter. They may combine several concepts.

47. ■ ▲ A technique to date geological samples uses rubidium-87, a long-lived radioactive isotope of rubidium ($t_{1/2} = 4.8 \times 10^{10}$ years). Rubidium-87 decays by β emission to strontium-87. If the rubidium-87 is part of a rock or mineral, then strontium-87 will remain trapped within the crystalline structure of the rock. The age of the rock dates back to the time when the rock solidified. Chemical analysis of the rock gives the amounts of ^{87}Rb and ^{87}Sr. From these data, the fraction of ^{87}Rb that remains can be calculated.

Analysis of a stony meteorite determined that 1.8 mmol of ^{87}Rb and 1.6 mmol of ^{87}Sr were present. Estimate the age of the meteorite. (*Hint:* The amount of ^{87}Rb at t_0 is moles ^{87}Rb + moles ^{87}Sr.)

48. Tritium, $^3_1$H, is one of the nuclei used in fusion reactions. This isotope is radioactive, with a half-life of 12.3 years. Like carbon-14, tritium is formed in the upper atmosphere from cosmic radiation, and it is found in trace amounts on earth. To obtain the amounts required for a fusion reaction, however, it must be made via a nuclear reaction. The reaction of $^6_3$Li with a neutron produces tritium and an α particle. Write an equation for this nuclear reaction.

49. Phosphorus occurs in nature as a single isotope, phosphorus-31. Neutron irradiation of phosphorus-31 produces phosphorus-32, a β emitter with a half-life of 14.28 days. Assume you have a sample containing phosphorus-32 that has a rate of decay of 3.2×10^6 dpm. Draw a graph showing disintegrations per minute as a function of time during a period of one year.

50. ■ In June 1972, natural fission reactors, which operated billions of years ago, were discovered in Oklo, Gabon (page 1060). At present, natural uranium contains 0.72% ^{235}U. How many years ago did natural uranium contain 3.0% ^{235}U, the amount needed to sustain a natural reactor? ($t_{1/2}$ for ^{235}U is 7.04×10^8 years.)

51. If a shortage in worldwide supplies of fissionable uranium arose, it would be possible to use other fissionable nuclei. Plutonium, one such fuel, can be made in "breeder" reactors that manufacture more fuel than they consume. The sequence of reactions by which plutonium is made is as follows:

(a) A ^{238}U nucleus undergoes an (n, γ) to produce ^{239}U.

(b) ^{239}U decays by β emission ($t_{1/2} = 23.5$ min) to give an isotope of neptunium.

(c) This neptunium isotope decays by β emission to give a plutonium isotope.

(d) The plutonium isotope is fissionable. On collision of one of these plutonium isotopes with a neutron, fission occurs, with at least two neutrons and two other nuclei as products.

Write an equation for each of the nuclear reactions.

52. ■ When a neutron is captured by an atomic nucleus, energy is released as γ radiation. This energy can be calculated based on the change in mass in converting reactants to products.

For the nuclear reaction $^{6}_{3}Li + ^{1}_{0}n \longrightarrow ^{7}_{3}Li + \gamma$:

(a) Calculate the energy evolved in this reaction (per atom). Masses needed (in g/mol) are $^{6}_{3}Li = 6.01512$, $^{1}_{0}n = 1.00867$, and $^{7}_{3}Li = 7.01600$.

(b) Use the answer in part (a) to calculate the wavelength of the γ-rays emitted in the reaction.

In the Laboratory

53. A piece of charred bone found in the ruins of a Native American village has a $^{14}C : ^{12}C$ ratio that is 72% of the ratio found in living organisms. Calculate the age of the bone fragment ($t_{1/2}$ for ^{14}C is 5.73×10^3 y).

54. ■ A sample of wood from a Thracian chariot found in an excavation in Bulgaria has a ^{14}C activity of 11.2 dpm/g. Estimate the age of the chariot and the year it was made ($t_{1/2}$ for ^{14}C is 5.73×10^3 years, and the activity of ^{14}C in living material is 14.0 dpm/g).

55. The isotope of polonium that was most likely isolated by Marie Curie in her pioneering studies is polonium-210. A sample of this element was prepared in a nuclear reaction. Initially, its activity (α emission) was 7840 dpm. Measuring radioactivity over time produced the data below. Determine the half-life of polonium-210.

Activity (dpm)	Time (days)
7840	0
7570	7
7300	14
5920	56
5470	72

56. Sodium-23 (in a sample of NaCl) is subjected to neutron bombardment in a nuclear reactor to produce ^{24}Na. When removed from the reactor, the sample is radioactive, with β activity of 2.54×10^4 dpm. The decrease in radioactivity over time was studied, producing the following data:

Activity (dpm)	Time (h)
2.54×10^4	0
2.42×10^4	1
2.31×10^4	2
2.00×10^4	5
1.60×10^4	10
1.01×10^4	20

(a) Write equations for the neutron capture reaction and for the reaction in which the product of this reaction decays by β emission.

(b) Determine the half-life of sodium-24.

57. The age of minerals can sometimes be determined by measuring the amounts of ^{206}Pb and ^{238}U in a sample. This determination assumes that all of the ^{206}Pb in the sample comes from the decay of ^{238}U. The date obtained identifies when the rock solidified. Assume that the ratio of ^{206}Pb to ^{238}U in an igneous rock sample is 0.33. Calculate the age of the rock. ($t_{1/2}$ for ^{238}U is 4.5×10^9 y.)

58. ■ The oldest-known fossil found in South Africa has been dated based on the decay of Rb-87.

$$^{87}Rb \longrightarrow ^{87}Sr + ^{0}_{-1}\beta \qquad t_{1/2} = 4.8 \times 10^{10} \text{ y}$$

If the ratio of the present quantity of ^{87}Rb to the original quantity is 0.951, calculate the age of the fossil.

59. To measure the volume of the blood system of an animal, the following experiment was done. A 1.0-mL sample of an aqueous solution containing tritium, with an activity of 2.0×10^6 dps, was injected into the animal's bloodstream. After time was allowed for complete circulatory mixing, a 1.0-mL blood sample was withdrawn and found to have an activity of 1.5×10^4 dps. What was the volume of the circulatory system? (The half-life of tritium is 12.3 y, so this experiment assumes that only a negligible amount of tritium has decayed in the time of the experiment.)

60. Suppose that you hydrolyze 4.644 g of a protein to form a mixture of different amino acids. To this is added a 2.80-mg sample of ^{14}C-labeled threonine (one of the amino acids present). The activity of this small sample is 1950 dpm. A chromatographic separation of the amino acids is carried out, and a small sample of pure threonine is separated. This sample has an activity of 550 dpm. What fraction of the threonine present was separated? What is the total amount of threonine in the sample?

Summary and Conceptual Questions

The following questions may use concepts from this and previous chapters.

61. ■ The average energy output of a good grade of coal is 2.6×10^7 kJ/ton. Fission of 1 mol of ^{235}U releases 2.1×10^{10} kJ. Find the number of tons of coal needed to produce the same energy as 1 lb of ^{235}U. (See Appendix C for conversion factors.)

62. ■ Collision of an electron and a positron results in formation of two γ-rays. In the process, their masses are converted completely into energy.
    (a) Calculate the energy evolved from the annihilation of an electron and a positron, in kilojoules per mole.
    (b) Using Planck's equation (Equation 6.2), determine the frequency of the γ -rays emitted in this process.

63. The principle underlying the isotope dilution method can be applied to many kinds of problems. Suppose that you, a marine biologist, want to estimate the number of fish in a lake. You release 1000 tagged fish, and after allowing an adequate amount of time for the fish to disperse evenly in the lake, you catch 5250 fish and find that 27 of them have tags. How many fish are in the lake?

64. ▲ Radioactive isotopes are often used as "tracers" to follow an atom through a chemical reaction. The following is an example of this process: acetic acid reacts with methanol, CH_3OH, by eliminating a molecule of H_2O to form methyl acetate, $CH_3CO_2CH_3$. Explain how you would use the radioactive isotope ^{15}O to show whether the oxygen atom in the water product comes from the —OH of the acid or the —OH of the alcohol.

65. ▲ Radioactive decay series begin with a very long-lived isotope. For example, the half-life of ^{238}U is 4.5×10^9 y. Each series is identified by the name of the long-lived parent isotope of highest mass.
    (a) The uranium-238 radioactive decay series is sometimes referred to as the $4n + 2$ series because the masses of all 13 members of this series can be expressed by the equation $m = 4n + 2$, where m is the mass number and n is an integer. Explain why the masses are correlated in this way. (See the Comment in Example 23.1.)
    (b) Two other radioactive decay series identified in minerals in the earth's crust are the thorium-232 series and the uranium-235 series. Do the masses of the isotopes in these series conform to a simple mathematical equation? If so, identify the equation.
    (c) Identify the radioactive decay series to which each of the following isotopes belongs: $^{226}_{88}$Ra, $^{215}_{86}$At, $^{228}_{90}$Th, $^{210}_{83}$Bi.
    (d) Evaluation reveals that one series of elements, the $4n + 1$ series, is not present in the earth's crust. Speculate why.

66. ▲ The thorium decay series includes the isotope $^{228}_{90}$Th. Determine the sequence of nuclei on going from $^{232}_{90}$Th to $^{228}_{90}$Th.

67. ▲ The last unknown element between bismuth and uranium was discovered by Lise Meitner (1878–1968) and Otto Hahn (1879–1968) in 1918. They obtained ^{231}Pa by chemical extraction of pitchblende, in which its concentration is about 1 ppm. This isotope, an α emitter, has a half-life of 3.27×10^4 y.
    (a) Which radioactive decay series (the uranium-235, uranium-238, or thorium-232 series) contains ^{231}Pa as a member? (See the Comment in Example 23.1.)
    (b) Suggest a possible sequence of nuclear reactions starting with the long-lived isotope that eventually forms this isotope.
    (c) What quantity of ore would be required to isolate 1.0 g of ^{231}Pa, assuming 100% yield?
    (d) Write an equation for the radioactive decay process for ^{231}Pa.

68. ▲ You might wonder how it is possible to determine the half-life of long-lived radioactive isotopes such as ^{238}U. With a half-life of more than 10^9 y, the radioactivity of a sample of uranium will not measurably change in your lifetime. In fact, you can calculate the half-life using the mathematics governing first-order reactions.

    It can be shown that a 1.0-mg sample of ^{238}U decays at the rate of 12 α emissions per second. Set up a mathematical equation for the rate of decay, $\Delta N / \Delta t = -kN$, where N is the number of nuclei in the 1.0-mg sample and $\Delta N / \Delta t$ is 12 dps. Solve this equation for the rate constant for this process, and then relate the rate constant to the half-life of the reaction. Carry out this calculation, and compare your result with the literature value, 4.5×10^9 years.

69. ▲ Marie and Pierre Curie isolated radium and polonium from uranium ore (pitchblende, which contains ^{238}U and ^{235}U). Which of the following isotopes of radium and polonium can be found in the uranium ore? (Hint: consider both the isotope half lives and the decay series starting with ^{238}U and ^{235}U.)

Isotope	Half-life
^{226}Ra	1620 y
^{225}Ra	14.8 d
^{228}Ra	6.7 y
^{216}Po	0.15 s
^{210}Po	138.4 d

List of Appendices

A — Using Logarithms and the Quadratic Equation

An introductory chemistry course requires basic algebra plus a knowledge of (1) exponential (or scientific) notation, (2) logarithms, and (3) quadratic equations. The use of exponential notation was reviewed on pages 32–35, and this appendix reviews the last two topics.

A.1 Logarithms

Two types of logarithms are used in this text: (1) common logarithms (abbreviated log) whose base is 10 and (2) natural logarithms (abbreviated ln) whose base is e (= 2.71828):

$$\log x = n, \text{ where } x = 10^n$$
$$\ln x = m, \text{ where } x = e^m$$

Most equations in chemistry and physics were developed in natural, or base e, logarithms, and we follow this practice in this text. The relation between log and ln is

$$\ln x = 2.303 \log x$$

Despite the different bases of the two logarithms, they are used in the same manner. What follows is largely a description of the use of common logarithms.

A common logarithm is the power to which you must raise 10 to obtain the number. For example, the log of 100 is 2, since you must raise 10 to the second power to obtain 100. Other examples are

$$\log 1000 = \log (10^3) = 3$$
$$\log 10 = \log (10^1) = 1$$
$$\log 1 = \log (10^0) = 0$$
$$\log 0.1 = \log (10^{-1}) = -1$$
$$\log 0.0001 = \log (10^{-4}) = -4$$

To obtain the common logarithm of a number other than a simple power of 10, you must resort to a log table or an electronic calculator. For example,

$$\log 2.10 = 0.3222, \text{ which means that } 10^{0.3222} = 2.10$$
$$\log 5.16 = 0.7126, \text{ which means that } 10^{0.7126} = 5.16$$
$$\log 3.125 = 0.49485, \text{ which means that } 10^{0.49485} = 3.125$$

To check this on your calculator, enter the number, and then press the "log" ... y.

To obtain the natural logarithm ln of the numbers shown here, use a calculator ...ving this function. Enter each number, and press "ln:"

$$\ln 2.10 = 0.7419, \text{ which means that } e^{0.7419} = 2.10$$
$$\ln 5.16 = 1.6409, \text{ which means that } e^{1.6409} = 5.16$$

To find the common logarithm of a number greater than 10 or less than 1 with ...og table, first express the number in scientific notation. Then find the log of ...ch part of the number and add the logs. For example,

$$\log 241 = \log (2.41 \times 10^2) = \log 2.41 + \log 10^2$$
$$= 0.382 + 2 = 2.382$$
$$\log 0.00573 = \log (5.73 \times 10^{-3}) = \log 5.73 + \log 10^{-3}$$
$$= 0.758 + (-3) = -2.242$$

...gnificant Figures and Logarithms

...otice that the mantissa has as many significant figures as the number whose log ...s found. (So that you could more clearly see the result obtained with a calcula-...r or a table, this rule was not strictly followed until the last two examples.)

■ **Logarithms and Nomenclature**
The number to the left of the decimal in a logarithm is called the **characteristic,** and the number to the right of the decimal is the **mantissa.**

...taining Antilogarithms

...you are given the logarithm of a number, and find the number from it, you have ...tained the "antilogarithm," or "antilog," of the number. Two common procedures ...ed by electronic calculators to do this are:

...cedure A	Procedure B
...Enter the log or ln.	1. Enter the log or ln.
...Press 2ndF.	2. Press INV.
...Press 10^x or e^x.	3. Press log or ln x.

Test one or the other of these procedures with the following examples:
1. Find the number whose log is 5.234:
   Recall that log $x = n$, where $x = 10^n$. In this case, $n = 5.234$. Enter that number in your calculator, and find the value of 10^n, the antilog. In this case,

$$10^{5.234} = 10^{0.234} \times 10^5 = 1.71 \times 10^5$$

   Notice that the characteristic (5) sets the decimal point; it is the power of 10 in the exponential form. The mantissa (0.234) gives the value of the number x.
2. Find the number whose log is -3.456:

$$10^{-3.456} = 10^{0.544} \times 10^{-4} = 3.50 \times 10^{-4}$$

   Notice here that -3.456 must be expressed as the sum of -4 and $+0.544$.

Mathematical Operations Using Logarithms

Because logarithms are exponents, operations involving them follow the same ru[...]
used for exponents. Thus, multiplying two numbers can be done by adding lo[...]
rithms:

$$\log xy = \log x + \log y$$

For example, we multiply 563 by 125 by adding their logarithms and finding [...]
antilogarithm of the result:

$$\log 563 = 2.751$$
$$\log 125 = \underline{2.097}$$
$$\log xy = 4.848$$
$$xy = 10^{4.848} = 10^4 \times 10^{0.848} = 7.05 \times 10^4$$

One number (x) can be divided by another (y) by subtraction of their lo[...]
rithms:

$$\log \frac{x}{y} = \log x - \log y$$

For example, to divide 125 by 742,

$$\log 125 = 2.097$$
$$-\log 742 = \underline{2.870}$$

$$\log \frac{x}{y} = -0.773$$
$$\frac{x}{y} = 10^{-0.773} = 10^{0.227} \times 10^{-1} = 1.68 \times 10^{-1}$$

Similarly, powers and roots of numbers can be found using logarithms.

$$\log x^y = y(\log x)$$

$$\log \sqrt[y]{x} = \log x^{1/y} = \frac{1}{y} \log x$$

As an example, find the fourth power of 5.23. We first find the log of 5.23 a[...]
then multiply it by 4. The result, 2.874, is the log of the answer. Therefore, we fi[...]
the antilog of 2.874:

$$(5.23)^4 = ?$$
$$\log (5.23)^4 = 4 \log 5.23 = 4(0.719) = 2.874$$
$$(5.23)^4 = 10^{2.874} = 748$$

As another example, find the fifth root of 1.89×10^{-9}:

$$\sqrt[5]{1.89 \times 10^{-9}} = (1.89 \times 10^{-9})^{1/5} = ?$$
$$\log(1.89 \times 10^{-9})^{1/5} = \frac{1}{5}\log(1.89 \times 10^{-9}) = \frac{1}{5}(-8.724) = -1.745$$

The answer is the antilog of -1.745:

$$(1.89 \times 10^{-9})^{1/5} = 10^{-1.745} = 1.8 \times 10^{-2}$$

2 Quadratic Equations

Algebraic equations of the form $ax^2 + bx + c = 0$ are called **quadratic equations.** The coefficients a, b, and c may be either positive or negative. The two roots of the equation may be found using the *quadratic formula:*

$$x = \frac{-b \pm \sqrt{b^2 - 4ac}}{2a}$$

As an example, solve the equation $5x^2 - 3x - 2 = 0$. Here $a = 5$, $b = -3$, and $c = -2$. Therefore,

$$x = \frac{3 \pm \sqrt{(-3)^2 - 4(5)(-2)}}{2(5)}$$

$$= \frac{3 \pm [2(5) / \sqrt{9 - (-40)}]}{10} = \frac{3 \pm \sqrt{49}}{10} = \frac{3 \pm 7}{10}$$

$$= 1 \text{ and } -0.4$$

How do you know which of the two roots is the correct answer? You have to decide in each case which root has physical significance. It is *usually* true in this course, however, that negative values are not significant.

When you have solved a quadratic expression, you should always check your values by substitution into the original equation. In the previous example, we find that $5(1)^2 - 3(1) - 2 = 0$ and that $5(-0.4)^2 - 3(-0.4) - 2 = 0$.

The most likely place you will encounter quadratic equations is in the chapters on chemical equilibria, particularly in Chapters 16 through 18. Here, you will often be faced with solving an equation such as

$$1.8 \times 10^{-4} = \frac{x^2}{0.0010 - x}$$

This equation can certainly be solved using the quadratic equation (to give $x = 3.4 \times 10^{-4}$). You may find the **method of successive approximations** to be especially convenient, however. Here we begin by making a reasonable approximation of x. This approximate value is substituted into the original equation, which is then solved to give what is hoped to be a more correct value of x. This process is repeated until the answer converges on a particular value of x—that is, until the value of x derived from two successive approximations is the same.

Step 1: First, assume that x is so small that $(0.0010 - x) \approx 0.0010$. This means that

$$x^2 = 1.8 \times 10^{-4} (0.0010)$$
$$x = 4.2 \times 10^{-4} \text{ (to 2 significant figures)}$$

Step 2: Substitute the value of x from Step 1 into the denominator of the original equation, and again solve for x:

$$x^2 = 1.8 \times 10^{-4}(0.0010 - 0.00042)$$
$$x = 3.2 \times 10^{-4}$$

Step 3: Repeat Step 2 using the value of x found in that step:

$$x = \sqrt{1.8 \times 10^{-4}(0.0010 - 0.00032)} = 3.5 \times 10^{-4}$$

Step 4: Continue repeating the calculation, using the value of x found in the previous step:

$$x = \sqrt{1.8 \times 10^{-4}(0.0010 - 0.00035)} = 3.4 \times 10^{-4}$$

Step 5: $\qquad x = \sqrt{1.8 \times 10^{-4}(0.0010 - 0.00034)} = 3.4 \times 10^{-4}$

Here, we find that iterations after the fourth step give the same value for x, ind[...]ing that we have arrived at a valid answer (and the same one obtained from[...]quadratic formula).

Here are several final thoughts on using the method of successive approx[...]tions. First, in some cases the method does not work. Successive steps may[...]answers that are random or that diverge from the correct value. In Chapter[...]through 18, you confront quadratic equations of the form $K = x^2/(C - x)$.[...]method of approximations works as long as $K < 4C$ (assuming one begins[...]$x = 0$ as the first guess, that is, $K \approx x^2/C$). This is always going to be true for [...]acids and bases (the topic of Chapters 17 and 18), but it may *not* be the case[...]problems involving gas phase equilibria (Chapter 16), where K can be [...]large.

Second, values of K in the equation $K = x^2/(C - x)$ are usually known on[...]two significant figures. We are therefore justified in carrying out successive s[...]until two answers are the same to two significant figures.

Finally, we highly recommend this method of solving quadratic equations, e[...]cially those in Chapters 17 and 18. If your calculator has a memory function,[...]cessive approximations can be carried out easily and rapidly.

B* | Some Important Physical Concepts

B.1 Matter

The tendency to maintain a constant velocity is called inertia. Thus, unless acted on by an unbalanced force, a body at rest remains at rest, and a body in motion remains in motion with uniform velocity. Matter is anything that exhibits inertia; the quantity of matter is its mass.

B.2 Motion

Motion is the change of position or location in space. Objects can have the following classes of motion:

- Translation occurs when the center of mass of an object changes its location. Example: a car moving on the highway.
- Rotation occurs when each point of a moving object moves in a circle about an axis through the center of mass. Examples: a spinning top, a rotating molecule.
- Vibration is a periodic distortion of and then recovery of original shape. Examples: a struck tuning fork, a vibrating molecule.

B.3 Force and Weight

Force is that which changes the velocity of a body; it is defined as

$$\text{Force} = \text{mass} \times \text{acceleration}$$

The SI unit of force is the **newton,** N, whose dimensions are kilograms times meter per second squared ($kg \cdot m/s^2$). A newton is therefore the force needed to change the velocity of a mass of 1 kilogram by 1 meter per second in a time of 1 second.

Adapted from F. Brescia, J. Arents, H. Meislich, et al.: *General Chemistry,* 5th ed. Philadelphia, Harcourt Brace, 1988.

Because the earth's gravity is not the same everywhere, the weight correspond to a given mass is not a constant. At any given spot on earth, gravity is const however, and therefore weight is proportional to mass. When a balance tells us t a given sample (the "unknown") has the same weight as another sample (the "weigh as given by a scale reading or by a total of counterweights), it also tells us that two masses are equal. The balance is therefore a valid instrument for measuring mass of an object independently of slight variations in the force of gravity.

B.4 Pressure*

Pressure is force per unit area. The SI unit, called the pascal, Pa, is

$$1 \text{ pascal} = \frac{1 \text{ newton}}{\text{m}^2} = \frac{1 \text{ kg} \cdot \text{m/s}^2}{\text{m}^2} = \frac{1 \text{ kg}}{\text{m} \cdot \text{s}^2}$$

The International System of Units also recognizes the bar, which is 10^5 Pa a which is close to standard atmospheric pressure (Table 1).

TABLE 1 Pressure Conversions

From	To	Multiply By
atmosphere	mm Hg	760 mm Hg/atm (exactly)
atmosphere	lb/in²	14.6960 lb/(in² · atm)
atmosphere	kPa	101.325 kPa/atm
bar	Pa	10^5 Pa/bar (exactly)
bar	lb/in²	14.5038 lb/(in² · bar)
mm Hg	torr	1 torr/mm Hg (exactly)

Chemists also express pressure in terms of the heights of liquid columns, es cially water and mercury. This usage is not completely satisfactory, because t pressure exerted by a given column of a given liquid is not a constant but depen on the temperature (which influences the density of the liquid) and the locati (which influences gravity). Such units are therefore not part of the SI, and th use is now discouraged. The older units are still used in books and journals, ho ever, and chemists must be familiar with them.

The pressure of a liquid or a gas depends only on the depth (or height) and exerted equally in all directions. At sea level, the pressure exerted by the earth's mosphere supports a column of mercury about 0.76 m (76 cm, or 760 mm) high

One **standard atmosphere** (atm) is the pressure exerted by exactly 76 cm mercury at 0 °C (density, 13.5951 g/cm³) and at standard gravity, 9.80665 m/ The **bar** is equivalent to 0.9869 atm. One **torr** is the pressure exerted by exactly mm of mercury at 0 °C and standard gravity.

B.5 Energy and Power

The SI unit of energy is the product of the units of force and distance, or kilogram times meter per second squared (kg · m/s²) times meters (× m), which is kg m²/s²; this unit is called the **joule,** J. The joule is thus the work done when a forc of 1 newton acts through a distance of 1 meter.

*See Section 11.1.

Work may also be done by moving an electric charge in an electric field. When the charge being moved is 1 coulomb (C), and the potential difference between its initial and final positions is 1 volt (V), the work is 1 joule. Thus,

$$1 \text{ joule} = 1 \text{ coulomb volt (CV)}$$

Another unit of electric work that is not part of the International System of Units but is still in use is the **electron volt,** eV, which is the work required to move an electron against a potential difference of 1 volt. (It is also the kinetic energy acquired by an electron when it is accelerated by a potential difference of 1 volt.) Because the charge on an electron is 1.602×10^{-19} C, we have

$$1 \text{ eV} = 1.602 \times 10^{-19} \text{ CV} \times \frac{1 \text{ J}}{1 \text{ CV}} = 1.602 \times 10^{-19} \text{ J}$$

If this value is multiplied by Avogadro's number, we obtain the energy involved in moving 1 mole of electron charges (1 faraday) in a field produced by a potential difference of 1 volt:

$$1 \frac{\text{eV}}{\text{particle}} = \frac{1.602 \times 10^{-19} \text{ J}}{\text{particle}} \times \frac{6.022 \times 10^{23} \text{particles}}{\text{mol}} \cdot \frac{1 \text{ kJ}}{1000 \text{ J}} = 96.49 \text{ kJ/mol}$$

Power is the amount of energy delivered per unit time. The SI unit is the watt, W, which is 1 joule per second. One kilowatt, kW, is 1000 W. Watt hours and kilowatt hours are therefore units of energy (Table 2). For example, 1000 watts, or 1 kilowatt, is

$$1.0 \times 10^{3} \text{W} \times \frac{1 \text{ J}}{1 \text{ W} \cdot \text{s}} \cdot \frac{3.6 \times 10^{3} \text{ s}}{1 \text{ h}} = 3.6 \times 10^{6} \text{ J}$$

TABLE 2 Energy Conversions

From	To	Multiply By
calorie (cal)	joule	4.184 J/cal (exactly)
kilocalorie (kcal)	cal	10^{3} cal/kcal (exactly)
kilocalorie	joule	4.184×10^{3} J/kcal (exactly)
liter atmosphere (L · atm)	joule	101.325 J/L · atm
electron volt (eV)	joule	1.60218×10^{-19} J/eV
electron volt per particle	kilojoules per mole	96.485 kJ · particle/eV · mol
coulomb volt (CV)	joule	1 CV/J (exactly)
kilowatt hour (kWh)	kcal	860.4 kcal/kWh
kilowatt hour	joule	3.6×10^{6} J/kWh (exactly)
British thermal unit (Btu)	calorie	252 cal/Btu

c | Abbreviations and Useful Conversion Factors

TABLE 3 Some Common Abbreviations and Standard Symbols

Term	Abbreviation	Term	Abbreviation
Activation energy	E_a	Entropy	S
Ampere	A	Standard entropy	$S°$
Aqueous Solution	aq	Entropy change for reaction	$\Delta_r S°$
Atmosphere, unit of pressure	atm	Equilibrium constant	K
Atomic mass unit	u	Concentration basis	K_c
Avogadro's constant	N_A	Pressure basis	K_p
Bar, unit of pressure	bar	Ionization weak acid	K_a
Body-centered cubic	bcc	Ionization weak base	K_b
Bohr radius	a_0	Solubility product	K_{sp}
Boiling point	bp	Formation constant	K_{form}
Celsius temperature, °C	T	Ethylenediamine	en
Charge number of an ion	z	Face-centered cubic	fcc
Coulomb, electric charge	C	Faraday constant	F
Curie, radioactivity	Ci	Gas constant	R
Cycles per second, hertz	Hz	Gibbs free energy	G
Debye, unit of electric dipole	D	Standard free energy	$G°$
Electron	e^-	Standard free energy of formation	$\Delta_f G°$
Electron volt	eV	Free energy change for reaction	$\Delta_r G°$
Electronegativity	χ	Half-life	$t_{1/2}$
Energy	E	Heat	q
Enthalpy	H	Hertz	Hz
Standard enthalpy	$H°$	Hour	h
Standard enthalpy of formation	$\Delta_f H°$	Joule	J
Standard enthalpy of reaction	$\Delta_r H°$	Kelvin	K

TABLE 3   Some Common Abbreviations and Standard Symbols (continued)

Term	Abbreviation	Term	Abbreviation
kilocalorie	kcal	Pressure	
liquid	ℓ	Pascal, unit of pressure	Pa
logarithm, base 10	log	In atmospheres	atm
logarithm, base e	ln	In millimeters of mercury	mm Hg
minute	min	Proton number	Z
molar	M	Rate constant	k
molar mass	M	Primitive cubic (unit cell)	pc
mole	mol	Standard temperature and pressure	STP
osmotic pressure	Π	Volt	V
Planck's constant	h	Watt	W
pound	lb	Wavelength	λ

C.1 Fundamental Units of the SI System

The metric system was begun by the French National Assembly in 1790 and has undergone many modifications. The International System of Units or *Système International* (SI), which represents an extension of the metric system, was adopted by the 11th General Conference of Weights and Measures in 1960. It is constructed from seven base units, each of which represents a particular physical quantity (Table 4).

TABLE 4   SI Fundamental Units

Physical Quantity	Name of Unit	Symbol
length	meter	m
Mass	kilogram	kg
Time	second	s
Temperature	kelvin	K
Amount of substance	mole	mol
Electric current	ampere	A
Luminous intensity	candela	cd

The first five units listed in Table 4 are particularly useful in general chemistry and are defined as follows:

1. The *meter* was redefined in 1960 to be equal to 1,650,763.73 wavelengths of a certain line in the emission spectrum of krypton-86.
2. The *kilogram* represents the mass of a platinum–iridium block kept at the International Bureau of Weights and Measures at Sèvres, France.
3. The *second* was redefined in 1967 as the duration of 9,192,631,770 periods of a certain line in the microwave spectrum of cesium-133.

4. The *kelvin* is 1/273.15 of the temperature interval between absolute ze
   and the triple point of water.
5. The *mole* is the amount of substance that contains as many entities as th
   are atoms in exactly 0.012 kg of carbon-12 (12 g of ^{12}C atoms).

C.2 Prefixes Used with Traditional Metric Units and SI Units

Decimal fractions and multiples of metric and SI units are designated by using t
prefixes listed in Table 5. Those most commonly used in general chemistry app
in italics.

C.3 Derived SI Units

In the International System of Units, all physical quantities are represented by a
propriate combinations of the base units listed in Table 4. A list of the derived un
frequently used in general chemistry is given in Table 6.

TABLE 5   Traditional Metric and SI Prefixes

Factor	Prefix	Symbol	Factor	Prefix	Symbol
10^{12}	tera	T	10^{-1}	*deci*	d
10^9	giga	G	10^{-2}	*centi*	c
10^6	mega	M	10^{-3}	*milli*	m
10^3	*kilo*	k	10^{-6}	micro	μ
10^2	hecto	h	10^{-9}	*nano*	n
10^1	deka	da	10^{-12}	*pico*	p
			10^{-15}	femto	f
			10^{-18}	atto	a

TABLE 6   Derived SI Units

Physical Quantity	Name of Unit	Symbol	Definiti
Area	square meter	m^2	
Volume	cubic meter	m^3	
Density	kilogram per cubic meter	kg/m^3	
Force	newton	N	$kg \cdot m/s$
Pressure	pascal	Pa	N/m^2
Energy	joule	J	$kg \cdot m^2/s$
Electric charge	coulomb	C	$A \cdot s$
Electric potential difference	volt	V	$J/(A \cdot s)$

TABLE 7 Common Units of Mass and Weight

Pound = 453.39 Grams

kilogram = 1000 grams = 2.205 pounds

gram = 1000 milligrams

gram = 6.022×10^{23} atomic mass units

atomic mass unit = 1.6605×10^{-24} gram

short ton = 2000 pounds = 907.2 kilograms

long ton = 2240 pounds

metric tonne = 1000 kilograms = 2205 pounds

TABLE 8 Common Units of Length

inch = 2.54 centimeters (Exactly)

mile = 5280 feet = 1.609 kilometers

yard = 36 inches = 0.9144 meter

meter = 100 centimeters = 39.37 inches = 3.281 feet = 1.094 yards

kilometer = 1000 meters = 1094 yards = 0.6215 mile

Ångstrom = 1.0×10^{-8} centimeter = 0.10 nanometer = 100 picometers
 = 1.0×10^{-10} meter = 3.937×10^{-9} inch

TABLE 9 Common Units of Volume

quart = 0.9463 liter
liter = 1.0567 quarts

liter = 1 cubic decimeter = 1000 cubic centimeters = 0.001 cubic meter

milliliter = 1 cubic centimeter = 0.001 liter = 1.056×10^{-3} quart

cubic foot = 28.316 liters = 29.924 quarts = 7.481 gallons

D | Physical Constants

TABLE 10

Quantity	Symbol	Traditional Units	SI Units
Acceleration of gravity	g	980.6 cm/s	9.806 m/s
Atomic mass unit (1/12 the mass of ^{12}C atom)	u	1.6605×10^{-24} g	1.6605×10^{-27} kg
Avogadro's number	N	$6.02214179 \times 10^{23}$ particles/mol	$6.02214179 \times 10^{23}$ particles/mol
Bohr radius	a_0	0.052918 nm 5.2918×10^{-9} cm	5.2918×10^{-11} m
Boltzmann constant	k	1.3807×10^{-16} erg/K	1.3807×10^{-23} J/K
Charge-to-mass ratio of electron	e/m	1.7588×10^{8} C/g	1.7588×10^{11} C/kg
Electronic charge	e	1.6022×10^{-19} C 4.8033×10^{-10} esu	1.6022×10^{-19} C
Electron rest mass	m_e	9.1094×10^{-28} g 0.00054858 amu	9.1094×10^{-31} kg
Faraday constant	F	96,485 C/mol e$^-$ 23.06 kcal/V $\cdot$ mol e$^-$	96,485 C/mol e$^-$ 96,485 J/V $\cdot$ mol e$^-$
Gas constant	R	$0.082057 \dfrac{L \cdot atm}{mol \cdot K}$ $1.987 \dfrac{cal}{mol \cdot K}$	$8.3145 \dfrac{Pa \cdot dm^3}{mol \cdot K}$ 8.3145 J/mol $\cdot$ K
Molar volume (STP)	V_m	22.414 L/mol	22.414×10^{-3} m^3/mol 22.414 dm^3/mol
Neutron rest mass	m_n	1.67493×10^{-24} g 1.008665 amu	1.67493×10^{-27} kg
Planck's constant	h	6.6261×10^{-27} erg $\cdot$ s	$6.6260693 \times 10^{-34}$ J $\cdot$

ABLE 10 (continued)

uantity	Symbol	Traditional Units	SI Units
oton rest mass	m_p	1.6726×10^{-24} g	1.6726×10^{-27} kg
		1.007276 amu	
ydberg constant	R_a	3.289×10^{15} cycles/s	1.0974×10^7 m^{-1}
	Rhc		2.1799×10^{-18} J
elocity of light (in a vacuum)	c	2.9979×10^{10} cm/s	2.9979×10^8 m/s
		(186,282 miles/s)	

$= 3.1416$

$= 2.7183$

$X = 2.303 \log X$

ABLE 11 Specific Heats and Heat Capacities for Some Common Substances
25 °C

ubstance	Specific Heat (J/g · K)	Molar Heat Capacity (J/mol · K)
(s)	0.897	24.2
a(s)	0.646	25.9
u(s)	0.385	24.5
e(s)	0.449	25.1
g(ℓ)	0.140	28.0
$_2$O(s), ice	2.06	37.1
$_2$O(ℓ), water	4.184	75.4
$_2$O(g), steam	1.86	33.6
$_6$H$_6$(ℓ), benzene	1.74	136
$_6$H$_6$(g), benzene	1.06	82.4
$_2$H$_5$OH(ℓ), ethanol	2.44	112.3
$_2$H$_5$OH(g), ethanol	1.41	65.4
C$_2$H$_5$)$_2$O(ℓ), diethyl ether	2.33	172.6
C$_2$H$_5$)$_2$O(g), diethyl ether	1.61	119.5

TABLE 12 Heats of Transformation and Transformation Temperatures of Several Substances

Substance	MP (°C)	Heat of Fusion		BP (°C)	Heat of Vaporizat	
		J/g	kJ/mol		J/g	kJ/n
*Elements**						
Al	660	395	10.7	2518	12083	294
Ca	842	212	8.5	1484	3767	155
Cu	1085	209	13.3	2567	4720	300
Fe	1535	267	13.8	2861	6088	340
Hg	−38.8	11	2.29	357	295	59.
Compounds						
H_2O	0.00	333	6.01	100.0	2260	40.
CH_4	−182.5	58.6	0.94	−161.5	511	8.
C_2H_5OH	−114	109	5.02	78.3	838	38.
C_6H_6	5.48	127.4	9.95	80.0	393	30.
$(C_2H_5)_2O$	−116.3	98.1	7.27	34.6	357	26.

*Data for the elements are taken from J. A. Dean: *Lange's Handbook of Chemistry*, 15th Edition. New York, McGraw-Hill Publishers, 1999.

E A Brief Guide to Naming Organic Compounds

seems a daunting task—to devise a systematic procedure that gives each organic compound a unique name—but that is what has been done. A set of rules was developed to name organic compounds by the International Union of Pure and Applied Chemistry (IUPAC). The IUPAC nomenclature allows chemists to write a name for any compound based on its structure or to identify the formula and structure for a compound from its name. In this book, we have generally used the IUPAC nomenclature scheme when naming compounds.

In addition to the systematic names, many compounds have common names. The common names came into existence before the nomenclature rules were developed, and they have continued in use. For some compounds, these names are so well entrenched that they are used most of the time. One such compound is acetic acid, which is almost always referred to by that name and not by its systematic name, ethanoic acid.

The general procedure for systematic naming of organic compounds begins with the nomenclature for hydrocarbons. Other organic compounds are then named as derivatives of hydrocarbons. Nomenclature rules for simple organic compounds are given in the following section.

E.1 Hydrocarbons

Alkanes

The names of alkanes end in "-ane." When naming a specific alkane, the root of the name identifies the longest carbon chain in a compound. Specific substituent groups attached to this carbon chain are identified by name and position.

Alkanes with chains of from one to ten carbon atoms are given in Table 10.2. After the first four compounds, the names derive from Latin numbers—pentane, hexane, heptane, octane, nonane, decane—and this regular naming continues for higher alkanes. For substituted alkanes, the substituent groups on a hydrocarbon chain must be identified both by a name and by the position of substitution; this information precedes the root of the name. The position is indicated by a number that refers to the carbon atom to which the substituent is attached. (Numbering the carbon atoms in a chain should begin at the end of the carbon chain that allows the substituent groups to have the lowest numbers.)

Names of hydrocarbon substituents are derived from the name of the hydro[...] bon. The group —CH_3, derived by taking a hydrogen from methane, is called [...] methyl group; the C_2H_5 group is the ethyl group. The nomenclature schem[...] easily extended to derivatives of hydrocarbons with other substituent groups s[...] as —Cl (chloro), —NO_2 (nitro), —CN (cyano), —D (deuterio), and so on (T[...] 13). If two or more of the same substituent groups occur, the prefixes "di-," "[...] and "tetra-" are added. When different substituent groups are present, they [...] generally listed in alphabetical order.

TABLE 13   Names of Common Substituent Groups

Formula	Name	Formula	Nam[...]
—CH_3	methyl	—D	deut[...]
—C_2H_5	ethyl	—Cl	chlo[...]
—$CH_2CH_2CH_3$	1-propyl (*n*-propyl)	—Br	brom[...]
—$CH(CH_3)_2$	2-propyl (isopropyl)	—F	fluo[...]
—$CH=CH_2$	ethenyl (vinyl)	—CN	cyar[...]
—C_6H_5	phenyl	—NO_2	nitr[...]
—OH	hydroxo		
—NH_2	amino		

Example:

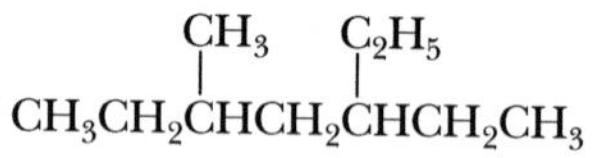

$$CH_3CH_2\overset{\overset{\displaystyle CH_3}{|}}{C}HCH_2\overset{\overset{\displaystyle C_2H_5}{|}}{C}HCH_2CH_3$$

Step	Information to include	Contribution to name
1.	An alkane	name will end in "-ane"
2.	Longest chain is 7 carbons	name as a *heptane*
3.	—CH_3 group at carbon 3	*3-methyl*
4.	—C_2H_5 group at carbon 5	*5-ethyl*
Name:		5-ethyl-3-methylheptane

Cycloalkanes are named based on the ring size and by adding the prefix "[...] clo"; for example, the cycloalkane with a six-member ring of carbons is call[...] cyclohexane.

Alkenes

Alkenes have names ending in "-ene." The name of an alkene must specify [...] length of the carbon chain and the position of the double bond (and when [...] propriate, the configuration, either *cis* or *trans*). As with alkanes, both identity a[...] position of substituent groups must be given. The carbon chain is numbered fr[...] the end that gives the double bond the lowest number.

Compounds with two double bonds are called dienes, and they are named si[...] ilarly—specifying the positions of the double bonds and the name and position [...] any substituent groups.

For example, the compound $H_2C{=}C(CH_3)CH(CH_3)CH_2CH_3$ has a five-carbon chain with a double bond between carbon atoms 1 and 2 and methyl groups on carbon atoms 2 and 3. Its name using IUPAC nomenclature is **2,3-dimethyl-1-pentene.** The compound $CH_3CH{=}CHCCl_3$ with a *cis* configuration around the double bond is named **1,1,1-trichloro-*cis*-2-butene.** The compound $H_2C{=}C(Cl)CH{=}CH_2$ is **2-chloro-1,3-butadiene.**

Alkynes

The naming of alkynes is similar to the naming of alkenes, except that *cis–trans* isomerism isn't a factor. The ending "-yne" on a name identifies a compound as an alkyne.

Benzene Derivatives

The carbon atoms in the six-member ring are numbered 1 through 6, and the name and position of substituent groups are given. The two examples shown here are **1-ethyl-3-methylbenzene** and **1,4-diaminobenzene.**

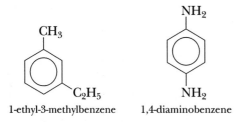

1-ethyl-3-methylbenzene   1,4-diaminobenzene

E.2 Derivatives of Hydrocarbons

The names for alcohols, aldehydes, ketones, and acids are based on the name of the hydrocarbon with an appropriate suffix to denote the class of compound, as follows:

- **Alcohols:** Substitute "-ol" for the final "-e" in the name of the hydrocarbon, and designate the position of the —OH group by the number of the carbon atom. For example, $CH_3CH_2CHOHCH_3$ is named as a derivative of the 4-carbon hydrocarbon butane. The —OH group is attached to the second carbon, so the name is 2-butanol.
- **Aldehydes:** Substitute "-al" for the final "-e" in the name of the hydrocarbon. The carbon atom of an aldehyde is, by definition, carbon-1 in the hydrocarbon chain. For example, the compound $CH_3CH(CH_3)CH_2CH_2CHO$ contains a 5-carbon chain with the aldehyde functional group being carbon-1 and the —CH_3 group at position 4; thus, the name is **4-methylpentanal.**
- **Ketones:** Substitute "-one" for the final "-e" in the name of the hydrocarbon. The position of the ketone functional group (the carbonyl group) is indicated by the number of the carbon atom. For example, the compound $CH_3COCH_2CH(C_2H_5)CH_2CH_3$ has the carbonyl group at the 2 position and an ethyl group at the 4 position of a 6-carbon chain; its name is **4-ethyl-2-hexanone.**
- **Carboxylic acids (organic acids):** Substitute "-oic" for the final "-e" in the name of the hydrocarbon. The carbon atoms in the longest chain are counted beginning with the carboxylic carbon atom. For example, *trans-*

$CH_3CH{=}CHCH_2CO_2H$ is named as a derivative of *trans*-3-pentene—that
trans-3-pentenoic acid.

An **ester** is named as a derivative of the alcohol and acid from which it is mad
The name of an ester is obtained by splitting the formula RCO_2R' into two par
the RCO_2- portion and the $-R'$ portion. The $-R'$ portion comes from the alc
hol and is identified by the hydrocarbon group name; derivatives of ethanol, f
example, are called *ethyl* esters. The acid part of the compound is named by dro
ping the "-oic" ending for the acid and replacing it by "-oate." The compoun
$CH_3CH_2CO_2CH_3$ is named **methyl propanoate.**

Notice that an anion derived from a carboxylic acid by loss of the acidic prot
is named the same way. Thus, $CH_3CH_2CO_2^-$ is the **propanoate anion,** and the s
dium salt of this anion, $Na(CH_3CH_2CO_2)$, is **sodium propanoate.**

F | Values for the Ionization Energies and Electron Affinities of the Elements

1A (1)																	8 (18)
H 1312	2A (2)											3A (13)	4A (14)	5A (15)	6A (16)	7A (17)	He 2371
Li 520	Be 899											B 801	C 1086	N 1402	O 1314	F 1681	Ne 2081
Na 496	Mg 738	3B (3)	4B (4)	5B (5)	6B (6)	7B (7)	⸺ 8B (8,9,10) ⸺			1B (11)	2B (12)	Al 578	Si 786	P 1012	S 1000	Cl 1251	Ar 1521
K 419	Ca 599	Sc 631	Ti 658	V 650	Cr 652	Mn 717	Fe 759	Co 758	Ni 757	Cu 745	Zn 906	Ga 579	Ge 762	As 947	Se 941	Br 1140	Kr 1351
Rb 403	Sr 550	Y 617	Zr 661	Nb 664	Mo 685	Tc 702	Ru 711	Rh 720	Pd 804	Ag 731	Cd 868	In 558	Sn 709	Sb 834	Te 869	I 1008	Xe 1170
Cs 377	Ba 503	La 538	Hf 681	Ta 761	W 770	Re 760	Os 840	Ir 880	Pt 870	Au 890	Hg 1007	Tl 589	Pb 715	Bi 703	Po 812	At 890	Rn 1037

BLE 14 Electron Affinity Values for Some Elements (kJ/mol)*

	Be	B	C	N	O	F
2.77						
9.63	0†	−26.7	−121.85	0	−140.98	−328.0
	Mg	Al	Si	P	S	Cl
2.87	0	−42.6	−133.6	−72.07	−200.41	−349.0
	Ca	Ga	Ge	As	Se	Br
8.39	0	−30	−120	−78	−194.97	−324.7
	Sr	In	Sn	Sb	Te	I
6.89	0	−30	−120	−103	−190.16	−295.16
	Ba	Tl	Pb	Bi	Po	At
5.51	0	−20	−35.1	−91.3	−180	−270

ata taken from H. Hotop and W. C. Lineberger: *Journal of Physical Chemistry, Reference Data*, Vol. , p. 731, 1985. (This paper also includes data for the transition metals.) Some values are known to ore than two decimal places.
lements with an electron affinity of zero indicate that a stable anion A⁻ of the element does not ist in the gas phase.

G | Vapor Pressure of Water at Various Temperatures

TABLE 15 Vapor Pressure of Water at Various Temperatures

Temperature (°C)	Vapor Pressure (torr)	Temperature (°C)	Vapor Pressure (torr)	Temperature (°C)	Vapor Pressure (torr)	Temperature (°C)	Vapor Pressure (to
−10	2.1	21	18.7	51	97.2	81	369
−9	2.3	22	19.8	52	102.1	82	384
−8	2.5	23	21.1	53	107.2	83	400
−7	2.7	24	22.4	54	112.5	84	416
−6	2.9	25	23.8	55	118.0	85	433
−5	3.2	26	25.2	56	123.8	86	450
−4	3.4	27	26.7	57	129.8	87	468
−3	3.7	28	28.3	58	136.1	88	487
−2	4.0	29	30.0	59	142.6	89	506
−1	4.3	30	31.8	60	149.4	90	525
0	4.6	31	33.7	61	156.4	91	546
1	4.9	32	35.7	62	163.8	92	567
2	5.3	33	37.7	63	171.4	93	588
3	5.7	34	39.9	64	179.3	94	610
4	6.1	35	42.2	65	187.5	95	633
5	6.5	36	44.6	66	196.1	96	657
6	7.0	37	47.1	67	205.0	97	682
7	7.5	38	49.7	68	214.2	98	707
8	8.0	39	52.4	69	223.7	99	733
9	8.6	40	55.3	70	233.7	100	760
10	9.2	41	58.3	71	243.9	101	787
11	9.8	42	61.5	72	254.6	102	815
12	10.5	43	64.8	73	265.7	103	845
13	11.2	44	68.3	74	277.2	104	875
14	12.0	45	71.9	75	289.1	105	906
15	12.8	46	75.7	76	301.4	106	937
16	13.6	47	79.6	77	314.1	107	970
17	14.5	48	83.7	78	327.3	108	1004
18	15.5	49	88.0	79	341.0	109	1038
19	16.5	50	92.5	80	355.1	110	1074
20	17.5						

H | Ionization Constants for Weak Acids at 25 °C

TABLE 16   Ionization Constants for Weak Acids at 25 °C

Acid	Formula and Ionization Equation	K_a
Acetic	$CH_3CO_2H \rightleftharpoons H^+ + CH_3CO_2^-$	1.8×10^{-5}
Arsenic	$H_3AsO_4 \rightleftharpoons H^+ + H_2AsO_4^-$	$K_1 = 2.5 \times 10^{-4}$
	$H_2AsO_4^- \rightleftharpoons H^+ + HAsO_4^{2-}$	$K_2 = 5.6 \times 10^{-3}$
	$HAsO_4^{2-} \rightleftharpoons H^+ + AsO_4^{3-}$	$K_3 = 3.0 \times 10^{-13}$
Arsenous	$H_3AsO_3 \rightleftharpoons H^+ + H_2AsO_3^-$	$K_1 = 6.0 \times 10^{-10}$
	$H_2AsO_3^- \rightleftharpoons H^+ + HAsO_3^{2-}$	$K_2 = 3.0 \times 10^{-14}$
Benzoic	$C_6H_5CO_2H \rightleftharpoons H^+ + C_6H_5CO_2^-$	6.3×10^{-5}
Boric	$H_3BO_3 \rightleftharpoons H^+ + H_2BO_3^-$	$K_1 = 7.3 \times 10^{-10}$
	$H_2BO_3^- \rightleftharpoons H^+ + HBO_3^{2-}$	$K_2 = 1.8 \times 10^{-13}$
	$HBO_3^{2-} \rightleftharpoons H^+ + BO_3^{3-}$	$K_3 = 1.6 \times 10^{-14}$
Carbonic	$H_2CO_3 \rightleftharpoons H^+ + HCO_3^-$	$K_1 = 4.2 \times 10^{-7}$
	$HCO_3^- \rightleftharpoons H^+ + CO_3^{2-}$	$K_2 = 4.8 \times 10^{-11}$
Citric	$H_3C_6H_5O_7 \rightleftharpoons H^+ + H_2C_6H_5O_7^-$	$K_1 = 7.4 \times 10^{-3}$
	$H_2C_6H_5O_7^- \rightleftharpoons H^+ + HC_6H_5O_7^{2-}$	$K_2 = 1.7 \times 10^{-5}$
	$HC_6H_5O_7^{2-} \rightleftharpoons H^+ + C_6H_5O_7^{3-}$	$K_3 = 4.0 \times 10^{-7}$
Cyanic	$HOCN \rightleftharpoons H^+ + OCN^-$	3.5×10^{-4}
Formic	$HCO_2H \rightleftharpoons H^+ + HCO_2^-$	1.8×10^{-4}
Hydrazoic	$HN_3 \rightleftharpoons H^+ + N_3^-$	1.9×10^{-5}
Hydrocyanic	$HCN \rightleftharpoons H^+ + CN^-$	4.0×10^{-10}
Hydrofluoric	$HF \rightleftharpoons H^+ + F^-$	7.2×10^{-4}
Hydrogen peroxide	$H_2O_2 \rightleftharpoons H^+ + HO_2^-$	2.4×10^{-12}
Hydrosulfuric	$H_2S \rightleftharpoons H^+ + HS^-$	$K_1 = 1 \times 10^{-7}$
	$HS^- \rightleftharpoons H^+ + S^{2-}$	$K_2 = 1 \times 10^{-19}$
Hypobromous	$HOBr \rightleftharpoons H^+ + OBr^-$	2.5×10^{-9}

(continued)

TABLE 16 Ionization Constants for Weak Acids at 25 °C *(continued)*

Acid	Formula and Ionization Equation	K_a
Hypochlorous	$HOCl \rightleftharpoons H^+ + OCl^-$	3.5×10^{-8}
Nitrous	$HNO_2 \rightleftharpoons H^+ + NO_2^-$	4.5×10^{-4}
Oxalic	$H_2C_2O_4 \rightleftharpoons H^+ + HC_2O_4^-$	$K_1 = 5.9 \times 1($
	$HC_2O_4^- \rightleftharpoons H^+ + C_2O_4^{2-}$	$K_2 = 6.4 \times 1($
Phenol	$C_6H_5OH \rightleftharpoons H^+ + C_6H_5O^-$	1.3×10^{-10}
Phosphoric	$H_3PO_4 \rightleftharpoons H^+ + H_2PO_4^-$	$K_1 = 7.5 \times 1($
	$H_2PO_4^- \rightleftharpoons H^+ + HPO_4^{2-}$	$K_2 = 6.2 \times 1($
	$HPO_4^{2-} \rightleftharpoons H^+ + PO_4^{3-}$	$K_3 = 3.6 \times 1($
Phosphorous	$H_3PO_3 \rightleftharpoons H^+ + H_2PO_3^-$	$K_1 = 1.6 \times 1($
	$H_2PO_3 \rightleftharpoons H^+ + HPO_3^{2-}$	$K_2 = 7.0 \times 10$
Selenic	$H_2SeO_4 \rightleftharpoons H^+ + HSeO_4^-$	$K_1 = $ very larg(
	$HSeO_4^- \rightleftharpoons H^+ + SeO_4^{2-}$	$K_2 = 1.2 \times 10$
Selenous	$HSeO_3 \rightleftharpoons H^+ + HSeO_3^-$	$K_1 = 2.7 \times 10$
	$HSeO_3^- \rightleftharpoons H^+ + SeO_3^{2-}$	$K_2 = 2.5 \times 10$
Sulfuric	$H_2SO_4 \rightleftharpoons H^+ + HSO_4^-$	$K_1 = $ very large
	$HSO_4^- \rightleftharpoons H^+ + SO_4^{2-}$	$K_2 = 1.2 \times 10$
Sulfurous	$H_2SO_3 \rightleftharpoons H^+ + HSO_3^-$	$K_1 = 1.2 \times 10($
	$HSO_3^- \rightleftharpoons H^+ + SO_3^{2-}$	$K_2 = 6.2 \times 10$
Tellurous	$H_2TeO_3 \rightleftharpoons H^+ + HTeO_3^-$	$K_1 = 2 \times 10^{-3}$
	$HTeO_3^- \rightleftharpoons H^+ + TeO_3^{2-}$	$K_2 = 1 \times 10^{-8}$

Ionization Constants for Weak Bases at 25 °C

TABLE 17   Ionization Constants for Weak Bases at 25 °C

Base	Formula and Ionization Equation	K_b
Ammonia	$NH_3 + H_2O \rightleftharpoons NH_4^+ + OH^-$	1.8×10^{-5}
Aniline	$C_6H_5NH_2 + H_2O \rightleftharpoons C_6H_5NH_3^+ + OH^-$	4.0×10^{-10}
Dimethylamine	$(CH_3)_2NH + H_2O \rightleftharpoons (CH_3)_2NH_2^+ + OH^-$	7.4×10^{-4}
Ethylenediamine	$H_2NCH_2CH_2NH_2 + H_2O \rightleftharpoons H_2NCH_2CH_2NH_3^+ \ OH^-$	$K_1 = 8.5 \times 10^{-5}$
	$H_2NCH_2CH_2NH_3^+ + H_2O \rightleftharpoons H_3NCH_2CH_2NH_3^{2+} \ OH^-$	$K_2 = 2.7 \times 10^{-8}$
Hydrazine	$N_2H_4 + H_2O \rightleftharpoons N_2H_5^+ + OH^-$	$K_1 = 8.5 \times 10^{-7}$
	$N_2H_5^+ + H_2O \rightleftharpoons N_2H_6^{2+} + OH^-$	$K_2 = 8.9 \times 10^{-16}$
Hydroxylamine	$NH_2OH + H_2O \rightleftharpoons NH_3OH^+ + OH^-$	6.6×10^{-9}
Methylamine	$CH_3NH_2 + H_2O \rightleftharpoons CH_3NH_3^+ + OH^-$	5.0×10^{-4}
Pyridine	$C_5H_5N + H_2O \rightleftharpoons C_5H_5NH^+ + OH^-$	1.5×10^{-9}
Trimethylamine	$(CH_3)_3N + H_2O \rightleftharpoons (CH_3)_3NH^+ + OH^-$	7.4×10^{-5}
Ethylamine	$C_2H_5NH_2 + H_2O \rightleftharpoons C_2H_5NH_3^+ + OH^-$	4.3×10^{-4}

J | Solubility Product Constants for Some Inorganic Compounds at 25 °C

TABLE 18A   Solubility Produce Constants (25 °C)

Cation	Compound	K_{sp}	Cation	Compound	K_{sp}
Ba^{2+}	*$BaCrO_4$	1.2×10^{-10}	Mg^{2+}	$MgCO_3$	$6.8 \times 10^-$
	$BaCO_3$	2.6×10^{-9}		MgF_2	$5.2 \times 10^-$
	BaF_2	1.8×10^{-7}		$Mg(OH)_2$	$5.6 \times 10^-$
	*$BaSO_4$	1.1×10^{-10}	Mn^{2+}	$MnCO_3$	$2.3 \times 10^-$
Ca^{2+}	$CaCO_3$ (calcite)	3.4×10^{-9}		*$Mn(OH)_2$	$1.9 \times 10^-$
	*CaF_2	5.3×10^{-11}	Hg_2^{2+}	*Hg_2Br_2	$6.4 \times 10^-$
	*$Ca(OH)_2$	5.5×10^{-5}		Hg_2Cl_2	$1.4 \times 10^-$
	$CaSO_4$	4.9×10^{-5}		*Hg_2I_2	$2.9 \times 10^-$
$Cu^{+,2+}$	$CuBr$	6.3×10^{-9}		Hg_2SO_4	$6.5 \times 10^-$
	CuI	1.3×10^{-12}	Ni^{2+}	$NiCO_3$	$1.4 \times 10^-$
	$Cu(OH)_2$	2.2×10^{-20}		$Ni(OH)_2$	$5.5 \times 10^-$
	$CuSCN$	1.8×10^{-13}	Ag^+	*$AgBr$	$5.4 \times 10^-$
Au^+	$AuCl$	2.0×10^{-13}		*$AgBrO_3$	$5.4 \times 10^-$
Fe^{2+}	$FeCO_3$	3.1×10^{-11}		$AgCH_3CO_2$	$1.9 \times 10^-$
	$Fe(OH)_2$	4.9×10^{-17}		$AgCN$	$6.0 \times 10^-$
Pb^{2+}	$PbBr_2$	6.6×10^{-6}		Ag_2CO_3	$8.5 \times 10^-$
	$PbCO_3$	7.4×10^{-14}		*$Ag_2C_2O_4$	$5.4 \times 10^-$
	$PbCl_2$	1.7×10^{-5}		*$AgCl$	$1.8 \times 10^-$
	$PbCrO_4$	2.8×10^{-13}		Ag_2CrO_4	$1.1 \times 10^-$
	PbF_2	3.3×10^{-8}		*AgI	$8.5 \times 10^-$
	PbI_2	9.8×10^{-9}		$AgSCN$	$1.0 \times 10^-$
	$Pb(OH)_2$	1.4×10^{-15}		*Ag_2SO_4	$1.2 \times 10^-$
	$PbSO_4$	2.5×10^{-8}			

(continue

ıtion	Compound	K_{sp}	Cation	Compound	K_{sp}
2+	$SrCO_3$	5.6×10^{-10}	Zn^{2+}	$Zn(OH)_2$	3×10^{-17}
	SrF_2	4.3×10^{-9}		$Zn(CN)_2$	8.0×10^{-12}
	$SrSO_4$	3.4×10^{-7}			
+	$TlBr$	3.7×10^{-6}			
	$TlCl$	1.9×10^{-4}			
	TlI	5.5×10^{-8}			

ne values reported in this table were taken from J. A. Dean: *Lange's Handbook of Chemistry,* 15th
dition. New York, McGraw-Hill Publishers, 1999. Values have been rounded off to two significant
 gures.
Calculated solubility from these K_{sp} values will match experimental solubility for this com-
ound within a factor of 2. Experimental values for solubilities are given in R. W. Clark and J. M.
onicamp: *Journal of Chemical Education,* Vol. 75, p. 1182, 1998.

**ABLE 18B K_{spa} Values* for Some
etal Sulfides (25 °C)**

ıbstance	K_{spa}
gS (red)	4×10^{-54}
gS (black)	2×10^{-53}
g₂S	6×10^{-51}
ıS	6×10^{-37}
ɔS	3×10^{-28}
ıS	8×10^{-28}
ıS	1×10^{-26}
ǝS	6×10^{-19}

The equilibrium constant value K_{spa} for
etal sulfides refers to the equilibrium
$MS(s) + H_2O(\ell) \rightleftharpoons M^{2+}(aq) + OH^-(a$
$+ HS^-(aq)$; see R. J. Myers, *Journal of
hemical Education,* Vol. 63, p. 687, 1986.

K Formation Constants for Some Complex Ions in Aqueous Solution

TABLE 19 Formation Constants for Some Complex Ions in Aqueous Solution*

Formation Equilibrium	K
$Ag^+ + 2\,Br^- \rightleftharpoons [AgBr_2]^-$	2.1×10^7
$Ag^+ + 2\,Cl^- \rightleftharpoons [AgCl_2]^-$	1.1×10^5
$Ag^+ + 2\,CN^- \rightleftharpoons [Ag(CN)_2]^-$	1.3×10^{21}
$Ag^+ + 2\,S_2O_3^{2-} \rightleftharpoons [Ag(S_2O_3)_2]^{3-}$	2.9×10^{13}
$Ag^+ + 2\,NH_3 \rightleftharpoons [Ag(NH_3)_2]^+$	1.1×10^7
$Al^{3+} + 6\,F^- \rightleftharpoons [AlF_6]^{3-}$	6.9×10^{19}
$Al^{3+} + 4\,OH^- \rightleftharpoons [Al(OH)_4]^-$	1.1×10^{33}
$Au^+ + 2\,CN^- \rightleftharpoons [Au(CN)_2]^-$	2.0×10^{38}
$Cd^{2+} + 4\,CN^- \rightleftharpoons [Cd(CN)_4]^{2-}$	6.0×10^{18}
$Cd^{2+} + 4\,NH_3 \rightleftharpoons [Cd(NH_3)_4]^{2+}$	1.3×10^7
$Co^{2+} + 6\,NH_3 \rightleftharpoons [Co(NH_3)_6]^{2+}$	1.3×10^5
$Cu^+ + 2\,CN^- \rightleftharpoons [Cu(CN)_2]^-$	1.0×10^{24}
$Cu^+ + 2\,Cl^- \rightleftharpoons [Cu(Cl)_2]^-$	3.2×10^5
$Cu^{2+} + 4\,NH_3 \rightleftharpoons [Cu(NH_3)_4]^{2+}$	2.1×10^{13}
$Fe^{2+} + 6\,CN^- \rightleftharpoons [Fe(CN)_6]^{4-}$	1.0×10^{35}
$Hg^{2+} + 4\,Cl^- \rightleftharpoons [HgCl_4]^{2-}$	1.2×10^{15}
$Ni^{2+} + 4\,CN^- \rightleftharpoons [Ni(CN)_4]^{2-}$	2.0×10^{31}
$Ni^{2+} + 6\,NH_3 \rightleftharpoons [Ni(NH_3)_6]^{2+}$	5.5×10^8
$Zn^{2+} + 4\,OH^- \rightleftharpoons [Zn(OH)_4]^{2-}$	4.6×10^{17}
$Zn^{2+} + 4\,NH_3 \rightleftharpoons [Zn(NH_3)_4]^{2+}$	2.9×10^9

*Data reported in this table are taken from J. A. Dean: *Lange's Handbook of Chemistry,* 15th Edition. New York, McGraw-Hill Publishers, 1999.

L | Selected Thermodynamic Values

TABLE 20 Selected Thermodynamic Values*

Species	ΔH_f° (298.15 K) (kJ/mol)	S° (298.15 K) (J/K · mol)	ΔG_f° (298.15 K) (kJ/mol)
Aluminum			
Al(s)	0	28.3	0
AlCl$_3$(s)	−705.63	109.29	−630.0
Al$_2$O$_3$(s)	−1675.7	50.92	−1582.3
Barium			
BaCl$_2$(s)	−858.6	123.68	−810.4
BaCO$_3$(s)	−1213	112.1	−1134.41
BaO(s)	−548.1	72.05	−520.38
BaSO$_4$(s)	−1473.2	132.2	−1362.2
Beryllium			
Be(s)	0	9.5	0
Be(OH)$_2$(s)	−902.5	51.9	−815.0
Boron			
BCl$_3$(g)	−402.96	290.17	−387.95
Bromine			
Br(g)	111.884	175.022	82.396
Br$_2$(ℓ)	0	152.2	0
Br$_2$(g)	30.91	245.47	3.12
BrF$_3$(g)	−255.60	292.53	−229.43
HBr(g)	−36.29	198.70	−53.45

(continued)

*Most thermodynamic data are taken from the NIST Webbook at **http://webbook.nist.gov**.

TABLE 20 Selected Thermodynamic Values* *(continued)*

Species	ΔH_f° (298.15 K) (kJ/mol)	S° (298.15 K) (J/K · mol)	ΔG_f° (298.15 K) (kJ/mol)
Calcium			
Ca(s)	0	41.59	0
Ca(g)	178.2	158.884	144.3
Ca^{2+}(g)	1925.90	—	—
CaC_2(s)	−59.8	70.	−64.93
$CaCO_3$(s, calcite)	−1207.6	91.7	−1129.16
$CaCl_2$(s)	−795.8	104.6	−748.1
CaF_2(s)	−1219.6	68.87	−1167.3
CaH_2(s)	−186.2	42	−147.2
CaO(s)	−635.09	38.2	−603.42
CaS(s)	−482.4	56.5	−477.4
$Ca(OH)_2$(s)	−986.09	83.39	−898.43
$Ca(OH)_2$(aq)	−1002.82		−868.07
$CaSO_4$(s)	−1434.52	106.5	−1322.02
Carbon			
C(s, graphite)	0	5.6	0
C(s, diamond)	1.8	2.377	2.900
C(g)	716.67	158.1	671.2
CCl_4(ℓ)	−128.4	214.39	−57.63
CCl_4(g)	−95.98	309.65	−53.61
$CHCl_3$(ℓ)	−134.47	201.7	−73.66
$CHCl_3$(g)	−103.18	295.61	−70.4
CH_4(g, methane)	−74.87	186.26	−50.8
C_2H_2(g, ethyne)	226.73	200.94	209.20
C_2H_4(g, ethene)	52.47	219.36	68.35
C_2H_6(g, ethane)	−83.85	229.2	−31.89
C_3H_8(g, propane)	−104.7	270.3	−24.4
C_6H_6(ℓ, benzene)	48.95	173.26	124.21
CH_3OH(ℓ, methanol)	−238.4	127.19	−166.14
CH_3OH(g, methanol)	−201.0	239.7	−162.5
C_2H_5OH(ℓ, ethanol)	−277.0	160.7	−174.7
C_2H_5OH(g, ethanol)	−235.3	282.70	−168.49
CO(g)	−110.525	197.674	−137.168
CO_2(g)	−393.509	213.74	−394.359
CS_2(ℓ)	89.41	151	65.2
CS_2(g)	116.7	237.8	66.61
$COCl_2$(g)	−218.8	283.53	−204.6

(continue

ecies	ΔH_f^o (298.15 K) (kJ/mol)	S^o (298.15 K) (J/K · mol)	ΔG_f^o (298.15 K) (kJ/mol)
sium			
Cs(s)	0	85.23	0
$Cs^+(g)$	457.964	—	—
CsCl(s)	−443.04	101.17	−414.53
lorine			
Cl(g)	121.3	165.19	105.3
$Cl^-(g)$	−233.13	—	—
$Cl_2(g)$	0	223.08	0
HCl(g)	−92.31	186.2	−95.09
HCl(aq)	−167.159	56.5	−131.26
romium			
Cr(s)	0	23.62	0
$Cr_2O_3(s)$	−1134.7	80.65	−1052.95
$CrCl_3(s)$	−556.5	123.0	−486.1
pper			
Cu(s)	0	33.17	0
CuO(s)	−156.06	42.59	−128.3
$CuCl_2(s)$	−220.1	108.07	−175.7
$CuSO_4(s)$	−769.98	109.05	−660.75
uorine			
$F_2(g)$	0	202.8	0
F(g)	78.99	158.754	61.91
$F^-(g)$	−255.39	—	—
$F^-(aq)$	−332.63		−278.79
HF(g)	−273.3	173.779	−273.2
HF(aq)	−332.63	88.7	−278.79
drogen			
$H_2(g)$	0	130.7	0
H(g)	217.965	114.713	203.247
$H^+(g)$	1536.202	—	—
$H_2O(\ell)$	−285.83	69.95	−237.15
$H_2O(g)$	−241.83	188.84	−228.59
$H_2O_2(\ell)$	−187.78	109.6	−120.35
dine			
$I_2(s)$	0	116.135	0
$I_2(g)$	62.438	260.69	19.327
I(g)	106.838	180.791	70.250

(continued)

TABLE 20 Selected Thermodynamic Values* (continued)

Species	ΔH_f° (298.15 K) (kJ/mol)	S° (298.15 K) (J/K · mol)	ΔG_f° (298.15 K) (kJ/mol)
$I^-(g)$	−197	—	—
$ICl(g)$	17.51	247.56	−5.73
Iron			
$Fe(s)$	0	27.78	0
$FeO(s)$	−272	—	—
$Fe_2O_3(s, hematite)$	−825.5	87.40	−742.2
$Fe_3O_4(s, magnetite)$	−1118.4	146.4	−1015.4
$FeCl_2(s)$	−341.79	117.95	−302.30
$FeCl_3(s)$	−399.49	142.3	−344.00
$FeS_2(s, pyrite)$	−178.2	52.93	−166.9
$Fe(CO)_5(\ell)$	−774.0	338.1	−705.3
Lead			
$Pb(s)$	0	64.81	0
$PbCl_2(s)$	−359.41	136.0	−314.10
$PbO(s, yellow)$	−219	66.5	−196
$PbO_2(s)$	−277.4	68.6	−217.39
$PbS(s)$	−100.4	91.2	−98.7
Lithium			
$Li(s)$	0	29.12	0
$Li^+(g)$	685.783	—	—
$LiOH(s)$	−484.93	42.81	−438.96
$LiOH(aq)$	−508.48	2.80	−450.58
$LiCl(s)$	−408.701	59.33	−384.37
Magnesium			
$Mg(s)$	0	32.67	0
$MgCl_2(s)$	−641.62	89.62	−592.09
$MgCO_3(s)$	−1111.69	65.84	−1028.2
$MgO(s)$	−601.24	26.85	−568.93
$Mg(OH)_2(s)$	−924.54	63.18	−833.51
$MgS(s)$	−346.0	50.33	−341.8
Mercury			
$Hg(\ell)$	0	76.02	0
$HgCl_2(s)$	−224.3	146.0	−178.6
$HgO(s, red)$	−90.83	70.29	−58.539
$HgS(s, red)$	−58.2	82.4	−50.6

(continue

pecies	ΔH_f° (298.15 K) (kJ/mol)	S° (298.15 K) (J/K · mol)	ΔG_f° (298.15 K) (kJ/mol)
ickel			
Ni(s)	0	29.87	0
NiO(s)	−239.7	37.99	−211.7
NiCl$_2$(s)	−305.332	97.65	−259.032
itrogen			
N$_2$(g)	0	191.56	0
N(g)	472.704	153.298	455.563
NH$_3$(g)	−45.90	192.77	−16.37
N$_2$H$_4$(ℓ)	50.63	121.52	149.45
NH$_4$Cl(s)	−314.55	94.85	−203.08
NH$_4$Cl(aq)	−299.66	169.9	−210.57
NH$_4$NO$_3$(s)	−365.56	151.08	−183.84
NH$_4$NO$_3$(aq)	−339.87	259.8	−190.57
NO(g)	90.29	210.76	86.58
NO$_2$(g)	33.1	240.04	51.23
N$_2$O(g)	82.05	219.85	104.20
N$_2$O$_4$(g)	9.08	304.38	97.73
NOCl(g)	51.71	261.8	66.08
HNO$_3$(ℓ)	−174.10	155.60	−80.71
HNO$_3$(g)	−135.06	266.38	−74.72
HNO$_3$(aq)	−207.36	146.4	−111.25
xygen			
O$_2$(g)	0	205.07	0
O(g)	249.170	161.055	231.731
O$_3$(g)	142.67	238.92	163.2
hosphorus			
P$_4$(s, white)	0	41.1	0
P$_4$(s, red)	−17.6	22.80	−12.1
P(g)	314.64	163.193	278.25
PH$_3$(g)	22.89	210.24	30.91
PCl$_3$(g)	−287.0	311.78	−267.8
P$_4$O$_{10}$(s)	−2984.0	228.86	−2697.7
H$_3$PO$_4$(ℓ)	−1279.0	110.5	−1119.1
otassium			
K(s)	0	64.63	0
KCl(s)	−436.68	82.56	−408.77
KClO$_3$(s)	−397.73	143.1	−296.25
KI(s)	−327.90	106.32	−324.892

(continued)

TABLE 20 Selected Thermodynamic Values* (continued)

Species	ΔH_f° (298.15 K) (kJ/mol)	S° (298.15 K) (J/K · mol)	ΔG_f° (298.15 (kJ/mol)
KOH(s)	−424.72	78.9	−378.92
KOH(aq)	−482.37	91.6	−440.50
Silicon			
Si(s)	0	18.82	0
SiBr₄(ℓ)	−457.3	277.8	−443.9
SiC(s)	−65.3	16.61	−62.8
SiCl₄(g)	−662.75	330.86	−622.76
SiH₄(g)	34.31	204.65	56.84
SiF₄(g)	−1614.94	282.49	−1572.65
SiO₂(s, quartz)	−910.86	41.46	−856.97
Silver			
Ag(s)	0	42.55	0
Ag₂O(s)	−31.1	121.3	−11.32
AgCl(s)	−127.01	96.25	−109.76
AgNO₃(s)	−124.39	140.92	−33.41
Sodium			
Na(s)	0	51.21	0
Na(g)	107.3	153.765	76.83
Na⁺(g)	609.358	—	—
NaBr(s)	−361.02	86.82	−348.983
NaCl(s)	−411.12	72.11	−384.04
NaCl(g)	−181.42	229.79	−201.33
NaCl(aq)	−407.27	115.5	−393.133
NaOH(s)	−425.93	64.46	−379.75
NaOH(aq)	−469.15	48.1	−418.09
Na₂CO₃(s)	−1130.77	134.79	−1048.08
Sulfur			
S(s, rhombic)	0	32.1	0
S(g)	278.98	167.83	236.51
S₂Cl₂(g)	−18.4	331.5	−31.8
SF₆(g)	−1209	291.82	−1105.3
H₂S(g)	−20.63	205.79	−33.56
SO₂(g)	−296.84	248.21	−300.13
SO₃(g)	−395.77	256.77	−371.04
SOCl₂(g)	−212.5	309.77	−198.3
H₂SO₄(ℓ)	−814	156.9	−689.96
H₂SO₄(aq)	−909.27	20.1	−744.53

(continued

TABLE 20 Selected Thermodynamic Values* *(continued)*

Species	ΔH_f° (298.15 K) (kJ/mol)	S° (298.15 K) (J/K · mol)	ΔG_f° (298.15 K) (kJ/mol)
Tin			
Sn(s, white)	0	51.08	0
Sn(s, gray)	−2.09	44.14	0.13
$SnCl_4(\ell)$	−511.3	258.6	−440.15
$SnCl_4(g)$	−471.5	365.8	−432.31
$SnO_2(s)$	−577.63	49.04	−515.88
Titanium			
Ti(s)	0	30.72	0
$TiCl_4(\ell)$	−804.2	252.34	−737.2
$TiCl_4(g)$	−763.16	354.84	−726.7
$TiO_2(s)$	−939.7	49.92	−884.5
Zinc			
Zn(s)	0	41.63	0
$ZnCl_2(s)$	−415.05	111.46	−369.398
ZnO(s)	−348.28	43.64	−318.30
ZnS(s, sphalerite)	−205.98	57.7	−201.29

M | Standard Reduction Potentials in Aqueous Solution at 25 °C

TABLE 21 Standard Reduction Potentials in Aqueous Solution at 25 °C

Acidic Solution	Standard Reduction Potential $E°$ (volt
$F_2(g) + 2\ e^- \longrightarrow 2\ F^-(aq)$	2.87
$Co^{3+}(aq) + e^- \longrightarrow Co^{2+}(aq)$	1.82
$Pb^{4+}(aq) + 2\ e^- \longrightarrow Pb^{2+}(aq)$	1.8
$H_2O_2(aq) + 2\ H^+(aq) + 2\ e^- \longrightarrow 2\ H_2O$	1.77
$NiO_2(s) + 4\ H^+(aq) + 2\ e^- \longrightarrow Ni^{2+}(aq) + 2\ H_2O$	1.7
$PbO_2(s) + SO_4^{2-}(aq) + 4\ H^+(aq) + 2\ e^- \longrightarrow PbSO_4(s) + 2\ H_2O$	1.685
$Au^+(aq) + e^- \longrightarrow Au(s)$	1.68
$2\ HClO(aq) + 2\ H^+(aq) + 2\ e^- \longrightarrow Cl_2(g) + 2\ H_2O$	1.63
$Ce^{4+}(aq) + e^- \longrightarrow Ce^{3+}(aq)$	1.61
$NaBiO_3(s) + 6\ H^+(aq) + 2\ e^- \longrightarrow Bi^{3+}(aq) + Na^+(aq) + 3\ H_2O$	≈ 1.6
$MnO_4^-(aq) + 8\ H^+(aq) + 5\ e^- \longrightarrow Mn^{2+}(aq) + 4\ H_2O$	1.51
$Au^{3+}(aq) + 3\ e^- \longrightarrow Au(s)$	1.50
$ClO_3^-(aq) + 6\ H^+(aq) + 5\ e^- \longrightarrow \frac{1}{2}\ Cl_2(g) + 3\ H_2O$	1.47
$BrO_3^-(aq) + 6\ H^+(aq) + 6\ e^- \longrightarrow Br^-(aq) + 3\ H_2O$	1.44
$Cl_2(g) + 2\ e^- \longrightarrow 2\ Cl^-(aq)$	1.36
$Cr_2O_7^{2-}(aq) + 14\ H^+(aq) + 6\ e^- \longrightarrow 2\ Cr^{3+}(aq) + 7\ H_2O$	1.33
$N_2H_5^+(aq) + 3\ H^+(aq) + 2\ e^- \longrightarrow 2\ NH_4^+(aq)$	1.24
$MnO_2(s) + 4\ H^+(aq) + 2\ e^- \longrightarrow Mn^{2+}(aq) + 2\ H_2O$	1.23
$O_2(g) + 4\ H^+(aq) + 4\ e^- \longrightarrow 2\ H_2O$	1.229
$Pt^{2+}(aq) + 2\ e^- \longrightarrow Pt(s)$	1.2
$IO_3^-(aq) + 6\ H^+(aq) + 5\ e^- \longrightarrow \frac{1}{2}\ I_2(aq) + 3\ H_2O$	1.195

(continued

idic Solution	Standard Reduction Potential $E°$ (volts)
$)_4^-(aq) + 2\ H^+(aq) + 2\ e^- \longrightarrow ClO_3^-(aq) + H_2O$	1.19
$_2(\ell) + 2\ e^- \longrightarrow 2\ Br^-(aq)$	1.08
$Cl_4^-(aq) + 3\ e^- \longrightarrow Au(s) + 4\ Cl^-(aq)$	1.00
$^{2+}(aq) + 2\ e^- \longrightarrow Pd(s)$	0.987
$)_3^-(aq) + 4\ H^+(aq) + 3\ e^- \longrightarrow NO(g) + 2\ H_2O$	0.96
$)_3^-(aq) + 3\ H^+(aq) + 2\ e^- \longrightarrow HNO_2(aq) + H_2O$	0.94
$Hg^+(aq) + 2\ e^- \longrightarrow Hg_2^{2+}(aq)$	0.920
$^{2+}(aq) + 2\ e^- \longrightarrow Hg(\ell)$	0.855
$^+(aq) + e^- \longrightarrow Ag(s)$	0.7994
$_2^{2+}(aq) + 2\ e^- \longrightarrow 2\ Hg(\ell)$	0.789
$^{3+}(aq) + e^- \longrightarrow Fe^{2+}(aq)$	0.771
$Cl_6^-(aq) + 2\ e^- \longrightarrow SbCl_4^-(aq) + 2\ Cl^-(aq)$	0.75
$tCl_4]^{2+}(aq) + 2\ e^- \longrightarrow Pt(s) + 4\ Cl^-(aq)$	0.73
$(g) + 2\ H^+(aq) + 2\ e^- \longrightarrow H_2O_2(aq)$	0.682
$tCl_6]^{2-}(aq) + 2\ e^- \longrightarrow [PtCl_4]^{2-}(aq) + 2\ Cl^-(aq)$	0.68
$(aq) + 2\ e^- \longrightarrow 2\ I^-(aq)$	0.621
$AsO_4(aq) + 2\ H^+(aq) + 2\ e^- \longrightarrow H_3AsO_3(aq) + H_2O$	0.58
$(s) + 2\ e^- \longrightarrow 2\ I^-(aq)$	0.535
$O_2(s) + 4\ H^+(aq) + 4\ e^- \longrightarrow Te(s) + 2\ H_2O$	0.529
$^+(aq) + e^- \longrightarrow Cu(s)$	0.521
$hCl_6]^{3-}(aq) + 3\ e^- \longrightarrow Rh(s) + 6\ Cl^-(aq)$	0.44
$^{2+}(aq) + 2\ e^- \longrightarrow Cu(s)$	0.337
$g_2Cl_2(s) + 2\ e^- \longrightarrow 2\ Hg(\ell) + 2\ Cl^-(aq)$	0.27
$Cl(s) + e^- \longrightarrow Ag(s) + Cl^-(aq)$	0.222
$)_4^{2-}(aq) + 4\ H^+(aq) + 2\ e^- \longrightarrow SO_2(g) + 2\ H_2O$	0.20
$)_4^{2-}(aq) + 4\ H^+(aq) + 2\ e^- \longrightarrow H_2SO_3(aq) + H_2O$	0.17
$^{2+}(aq) + e^- \longrightarrow Cu^+(aq)$	0.153
$^{4+}(aq) + 2\ e^- \longrightarrow Sn^{2+}(aq)$	0.15
$s) + 2\ H^+ + 2\ e^- \longrightarrow H_2S(aq)$	0.14
$gBr(s) + e^- \longrightarrow Ag(s) + Br^-(aq)$	0.0713
$H^+(aq) + 2\ e^- \longrightarrow H_2(g)\text{(reference electrode)}$	0.0000
$_2O(g) + 6\ H^+(aq) + H_2O + 4\ e^- \longrightarrow 2\ NH_3OH^+(aq)$	-0.05
$^{2+}(aq) + 2\ e^- \longrightarrow Pb(s)$	-0.126
$^{2+}(aq) + 2\ e^- \longrightarrow Sn(s)$	-0.14
$gI(s) + e^- \longrightarrow Ag(s) + I^-(aq)$	-0.15
$nF_6]^{2-}(aq) + 4\ e^- \longrightarrow Sn(s) + 6\ F^-(aq)$	-0.25
$^{2+}(aq) + 2\ e^- \longrightarrow Ni(s)$	-0.25
$^{2+}(aq) + 2\ e^- \longrightarrow Co(s)$	-0.28

(continued)

TABLE 21 Standard Reduction Potentials in Aqueous Solution at 25 °C *(continue*

Acidic Solution	Standard Reduct Potential $E°$ (vo
$Tl^+(aq) + e^- \longrightarrow Tl(s)$	−0.34
$PbSO_4(s) + 2\ e^- \longrightarrow Pb(s) + SO_4^{2-}(aq)$	−0.356
$Se(s) + 2\ H^+(aq) + 2\ e^- \longrightarrow H_2Se(aq)$	−0.40
$Cd^{2+}(aq) + 2\ e^- \longrightarrow Cd(s)$	−0.403
$Cr^{3+}(aq) + e^- \longrightarrow Cr^{2+}(aq)$	−0.41
$Fe^{2+}(aq) + 2\ e^- \longrightarrow Fe(s)$	−0.44
$2\ CO_2(g) + 2\ H^+(aq) + 2\ e^- \longrightarrow H_2C_2O_4(aq)$	−0.49
$Ga^{3+}(aq) + 3\ e^- \longrightarrow Ga(s)$	−0.53
$HgS(s) + 2\ H^+(aq) + 2\ e^- \longrightarrow Hg(\ell) + H_2S(g)$	−0.72
$Cr^{3+}(aq) + 3\ e^- \longrightarrow Cr(s)$	−0.74
$Zn^{2+}(aq) + 2\ e^- \longrightarrow Zn(s)$	−0.763
$Cr^{2+}(aq) + 2\ e^- \longrightarrow Cr(s)$	−0.91
$FeS(s) + 2\ e^- \longrightarrow Fe(s) + S^{2-}(aq)$	−1.01
$Mn^{2+}(aq) + 2\ e^- \longrightarrow Mn(s)$	−1.18
$V^{2+}(aq) + 2\ e^- \longrightarrow V(s)$	−1.18
$CdS(s) + 2\ e^- \longrightarrow Cd(s) + S^{2-}(aq)$	−1.21
$ZnS(s) + 2\ e^- \longrightarrow Zn(s) + S^{2-}(aq)$	−1.44
$Zr^{4+}(aq) + 4\ e^- \longrightarrow Zr(s)$	−1.53
$Al^{3+}(aq) + 3\ e^- \longrightarrow Al(s)$	−1.66
$Mg^{2+}(aq) + 2\ e^- \longrightarrow Mg(s)$	−2.37
$Na^+(aq) + e^- \longrightarrow Na(s)$	−2.714
$Ca^{2+}(aq) + 2\ e^- \longrightarrow Ca(s)$	−2.87
$Sr^{2+}(aq) + 2\ e^- \longrightarrow Sr(s)$	−2.89
$Ba^{2+}(aq) + 2\ e^- \longrightarrow Ba(s)$	−2.90
$Rb^+(aq) + e^- \longrightarrow Rb(s)$	−2.925
$K^+(aq) + e^- \longrightarrow K(s)$	−2.925
$Li^+(aq) + e^- \longrightarrow Li(s)$	−3.045

Basic Solution	
$ClO^-(aq) + H_2O + 2\ e^- \longrightarrow Cl^-(aq) + 2\ OH^-(aq)$	0.89
$OOH^-(aq) + H_2O + 2\ e^- \longrightarrow 3\ OH^-(aq)$	0.88
$2\ NH_2OH(aq) + 2\ e^- \longrightarrow N_2H_4(aq) + 2\ OH^-(aq)$	0.74
$ClO_3^-(aq) + 3\ H_2O + 6\ e^- \longrightarrow Cl^-(aq) + 6\ OH^-(aq)$	0.62
$MnO_4^-(aq) + 2\ H_2O + 3\ e^- \longrightarrow MnO_2(s) + 4\ OH^-(aq)$	0.588
$MnO_4^-(aq) + e^- \longrightarrow MnO_4^{2-}(aq)$	0.564
$NiO_2(s) + 2\ H_2O + 2\ e^- \longrightarrow Ni(OH)_2(s) + 2\ OH^-(aq)$	0.49
$Ag_2CrO_4(s) + 2\ e^- \longrightarrow 2\ Ag(s) + CrO_4^{2-}(aq)$	0.446
$O_2(g) + 2\ H_2O + 4\ e^- \longrightarrow 4\ OH^-(aq)$	0.40

(continue.

idic Solution	Standard Reduction Potential $E°$ (volts)
$)_4^-(aq) + H_2O + 2\ e^- \longrightarrow ClO_3^-(aq) + 2\ OH^-(aq)$	0.36
$_2O(s) + H_2O + 2\ e^- \longrightarrow 2\ Ag(s) + 2\ OH^-(aq)$	0.34
$NO_2^-(aq) + 3\ H_2O + 4\ e^- \longrightarrow N_2O(g) + 6\ OH^-(aq)$	0.15
$H_4(aq) + 2\ H_2O + 2\ e^- \longrightarrow 2\ NH_3(aq) + 2\ OH^-(aq)$	0.10
$o(NH_3)_6]^{3+}(aq) + e^- \longrightarrow [Co(NH_3)_6]^{2+}(aq)$	0.10
$)O(s) + H_2O + 2\ e^- \longrightarrow Hg(\ell) + 2\ OH^-(aq)$	0.0984
$(g) + H_2O + 2\ e^- \longrightarrow OOH^-(aq) + OH^-(aq)$	0.076
$)_3^-(aq) + H_2O + 2\ e^- \longrightarrow NO_2^-(aq) + 2\ OH^-(aq)$	0.01
$1O_2(s) + 2\ H_2O + 2\ e^- \longrightarrow Mn(OH)_2(s) + 2\ OH^-(aq)$	−0.05
$)_4^{2-}(aq) + 4\ H_2O + 3\ e^- \longrightarrow Cr(OH)_3(s) + 5\ OH^-(aq)$	−0.12
$(OH)_2(s) + 2\ e^- \longrightarrow Cu(s) + 2\ OH^-(aq)$	−0.36
$s) + 2\ e^- \longrightarrow S^{2-}(aq)$	−0.48
$(OH)_3(s) + e^- \longrightarrow Fe(OH)_2(s) + OH^-(aq)$	−0.56
$H_2O + 2\ e^- \longrightarrow H_2(g) + 2\ OH^-(aq)$	−0.8277
$NO_3^-(aq) + 2\ H_2O + 2\ e^- \longrightarrow N_2O_4(g) + 4\ OH^-(aq)$	−0.85
$(OH)_2(s) + 2\ e^- \longrightarrow Fe(s) + 2\ OH^-(aq)$	−0.877
$)_4^{2-}(aq) + H_2O + 2\ e^- \longrightarrow SO_3^{2-}(aq) + 2\ OH^-(aq)$	−0.93
$(g) + 4\ H_2O + 4\ e^- \longrightarrow N_2H_4(aq) + 4\ OH^-(aq)$	−1.15
$n(OH)_4]^{2-}(aq) + 2\ e^- \longrightarrow Zn(s) + 4\ OH^-(aq)$	−1.22
$(OH)_2(s) + 2\ e^- \longrightarrow Zn(s) + 2\ OH^-(aq)$	−1.245
$n(CN)_4]^{2-}(aq) + 2\ e^- \longrightarrow Zn(s) + 4\ CN^-(aq)$	−1.26
$(OH)_3(s) + 3\ e^- \longrightarrow Cr(s) + 3\ OH^-(aq)$	−1.30
$O_3^{2-}(aq) + 3\ H_2O + 4\ e^- \longrightarrow Si(s) + 6\ OH^-(aq)$	−1.70

N | Answers to Exercises

Chapter 1

1.1 (a) Na = sodium; Cl = chlorine; Cr = chromium
(b) Zinc = Zn; nickel = Ni; potassium = K

1.2 (a) Iron: lustrous solid, metallic, good conductor of heat and electricity, malleable, ductile, attracted to a magnet
(b) Water: colorless liquid (at room temperature); melting point is 0 °C, and boiling point is 100 °C, density ~ 1 g/cm^2
(c) Table salt: solid, white crystals, soluble in water
(d) Oxygen: colorless gas (at room temperature), low solubility in water

1.3 Chemical changes: the fuel in the campfire burns in air (combustion). Physical changes: water boils. Energy evolved in combustion is transferred to the water, to the water container, and to the surrounding air.

Let's Review

LR 1 [77 K − 273.15 K] (1 °C/K) = −196 °C

LR 2 Convert thickness to cm: 0.25 mm(1 cm/10 mm) = 0.025 cm

Volume = length × width × thickness

V = (2.50 cm)(2.50 cm)(0.025 cm) = 0.16 cm^3
(answer has 2 significant figures.)

LR 3 (a) (750 mL)(1 L/1000 mL) = 0.75 L
(0.75 L)(10 dL/L) = 7.5 dL
(b) 2.0 qt = 0.50 gal
(0.50 gal)(3.786 L/gal) = 1.9 L
(1.9 L)(1 dm^3/1 L) = 1.9 dm^3

LR 4 (a) Mass in kilograms = (5.59 g)(1 kg/1000 g) = 0.00559 kg
Mass in milligrams = 5.59 g (10^3 mg/g) = 5.59 × 10^3 mg
(b) (0.02 μg/L)(1 g/10^6 μg) = 2 × 10^{-8} g/L

LR 5 Student A: average = −0.1 °C; average deviation = 0.2 °C; error = −0.1 °C. Student B: average = +0.01 °C; average deviation = 0.02 °C; error = +0.01 °C. Student B's values are more accurate and less precise.

LR 6 (a) 2.33 × 10^7 has three significant figures; 50.5 has three significant figures; 200 has one significant figure. (200. or 2.00 × 10^2 would express this number with three significant figures.)
(b) The product of 10.26 and 0.063 is 0.65, a number with two significant figures. (10.26 has four significant figures, whereas 0.063 has two.)
The sum of 10.26 and 0.063 is 10.32. The number 10.26 has only two numbers to the right of the decimal, so the sum must also have two numbers after the decimal.
(c) x = 3.9 × 10^6. The difference between 110.7 and 64 is 47. Dividing 47 by 0.056 and 0.00216 gives an answer with two significant figures.

LR 7 (a) (198 cm)(1 m/100 cm) = 1.98 m;
(198 cm)(1 ft/30.48 cm) = 6.50 ft
(b) (2.33 × 10^7 m^2)(1 km^2/10^6 m^2) = 23.3 km^2
(c) (19,320 kg/m^3)(10^3 g/1 kg)(1 m^3/10^6 cm^3) = 19.32 g/cm^3
(d) (9.0 × 10^3 pc)(206,265 AU/1 pc)(1.496 × 10^8 km/1 AU) = 2.8 × 10^{17} km

8 Read from the graph, the mass of 50 beans is about 123 g.

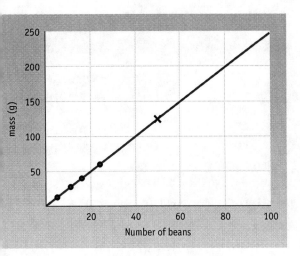

9 Change all dimensions to centimeters: 7.6 m = 760 cm; 2.74 m = 274 cm; 0.13 mm = 0.013 cm.

Volume of paint = (760 cm)(274 cm)(0.013 cm) = 2.7×10^3 cm³

Volume (L) = $(2.7 \times 10^3$ cm³)(1 L/10³ cm³) = 2.7 L

Mass = $(2.7 \times 10^3$ cm³)(0.914 g/cm³) = 2.5×10^3 g

Chapter 2

1 (a) Mass number with 26 protons and 30 neutrons is 56
(b) $(59.930788$ u)$(1.661 \times 10^{-24}$ g/u) = 9.955×10^{-23} g
(c) ^{64}Zn has 30 protons, 30 electrons, and $(64 - 30)$ = 34 neutrons.
(d) The mass of a ^{64}Zn atom is 63.929/12.0... . or 5.3274 times the mass of a ^{12}C atom. (Note that mass of ^{12}C is defined as an exact value.)

2 The mass number of the second silver isotope is 109 $(62 + 47)$. Symbol: ^{109}Ag, abundance = 48.161%.

3 Use Equation 2.2 for the calculation.
Atomic mass = $(34.96885)(75.77/100) + (36.96590)(24.23/100) = 35.45$. (Accuracy is limited by the value of the percent abundance to 4 significant figures.)

4 There are eight elements in the third period. Sodium (Na), magnesium (Mg), and aluminum (Al) are metals. Silicon (Si) is a metalloid. Phosphorus (P), sulfur (S), chlorine (Cl), and argon (Ar) are nonmetals.

5 The molecular formula is $C_3H_7NO_2S$. You will often see its formula written as $HSCH_2CH(N^+H_3)CO_2^-$ to better identify the molecule's structure.

6 (a) K^+ is formed if K loses one electron. K^+ has the same number of electrons as Ar.
(b) Se^{2-} is formed by adding two electrons to an atom of Se. It has the same number of electrons as Kr.

(c) Ba^{2+} is formed if Ba loses two electrons; Ba^{2+} has the same number of electrons as Xe.
(d) Cs^+ is formed if Cs loses one electron. It has the same number of electrons as Xe.

2.7 (a) (1) NaF: 1 Na^+ and 1 F^- ion. (2) $Cu(NO_3)_2$: 1 Cu^{2+} and 2 NO_3^- ions. (3) $NaCH_3CO_2$: 1 Na^+ and 1 $CH_3CO_2^-$ ion.
(b) $FeCl_2$, $FeCl_3$
(c) Na_2S, Na_3PO_4, BaS, $Ba_3(PO_4)_2$

2.8 (1) (a) NH_4NO_3; (b) $CoSO_4$; (c) $Ni(CN)_2$; (d) V_2O_3; (e) $Ba(CH_3CO_2)_2$; (f) $Ca(ClO)_2$
(2) (a) magnesium bromide; (b) lithium carbonate; (c) potassium hydrogen sulfite; (d) potassium permanganate; (e) ammonium sulfide; (f) copper(I) chloride and copper(II) chloride

2.9 The force of attraction between ions is proportional to the product of the ion charges (Coulomb's law). The force of attraction between Mg^{2+} and O^{2-} ions in MgO is approximately four times greater than the force of attraction between Na^+ and Cl^- ions in NaCl, so a much higher temperature is required to disrupt the orderly array of ions in crystalline MgO.

2.10 (1) (a) CO_2; (b) PI_3; (c) SCl_2; (d) BF_3; (e) O_2F_2; (f) XeO_3
(2) (a) dinitrogen tetrafluoride; (b) hydrogen bromide; (c) sulfur tetrafluoride; (d) boron trichloride; (e) tetraphosphorus decaoxide; (f) chlorine trifluoride

2.11 (a) (1.5 mol Si)(28.1 g/mol) = 42 g Si
(b) (454 g S)(1.00 mol S/32.07 g) = 14.2 mol S
(14.2 mol S)$(6.022 \times 10^{23}$ atoms/mol) = 8.53×10^{24} atoms S

2.12 $(2.6 \times 10^{24}$ atoms)(1.000 mol/6.022 $\times 10^{23}$ atoms)(197.0 g Au/1.000 mol) = 850 g Au

Volume = (850 g Au)(1.00 cm³/19.32 g) = 44 cm³

Volume = 44 cm³ = (thickness)(area) = (0.10 cm)(area)

Area = 440 cm²

Length = width = $\sqrt{440 \text{ cm}^2}$ = 21 cm

2.13 (a) Citric acid: 192.1 g/mol; magnesium carbonate: 84.3 g/mol
(b) 454 g citric acid (1.000 mol/192.1 g) = 2.36 mol citric acid
(c) 0.125 mol $MgCO_3$ (84.3 g/mol) = 10.5 g $MgCO_3$

2.14 (a) 1.00 mol $(NH_4)_2CO_3$ (molar mass 96.09 g/mol) has 28.0 g of N (29.2%), 8.06 g of H (8.39%), 12.0 g of C (12.5%), and 48.0 g of O (50.0%)
(b) 454 g C_8H_{18} (1 mol C_8H_{18}/114.2 g)(8 mol C/1 mol C_8H_{18})(12.01 g C/1 mol C) = 382 g C

2.15 (a) C_5H_4 (b) $C_2H_4O_2$

2.16 (88.17 g C)(1 mol C/12.011 g C) = 7.341 mol C

$(11.83 \text{ g H})(1 \text{ mol H}/1.008 \text{ g H}) = 11.74 \text{ mol H}$

$11.74 \text{ mol H}/7.341 \text{ mol C} = 1.6 \text{ mol H}/1 \text{ mol C}$
$= (8/5); (\text{mol H}/1 \text{ mol C}) = 8 \text{ mol H}/5 \text{ mol C}$

The empirical formula is C_5H_8. The molar mass, 68.11 g/mol, closely matches this formula, so C_5H_8 is also the molecular formula.

2.17 $(78.90 \text{ g C})(1 \text{ mol C}/12.011 \text{ g C}) = 6.569 \text{ mol C}$
$(10.59 \text{ g H})(1 \text{ mol H}/1.008 \text{ g H}) = 10.51 \text{ mol H}$
$(10.51 \text{ g O})(1 \text{ mol O}/16.00 \text{ g O}) = 0.6569 \text{ mol O}$

$10.51 \text{ mol H}/0.6569 \text{ mol O} = 16 \text{ mol H}/1 \text{ mol O}$

$6.569 \text{ mol C}/0.6569 \text{ mol O} = 10 \text{ mol C}/1 \text{ mol O}$

The empirical formula is $C_{10}H_{16}O$.

2.18 $(0.586 \text{ g K})(1 \text{ mol K}/39.10 \text{ g K}) = 0.0150 \text{ mol K}$
$(0.480 \text{ g O})(1 \text{ mol O}/16.00 \text{ g O}) = 0.0300 \text{ mol O}$

The ratio of moles K to moles O atoms is 1 to 2; the empirical formula is KO_2.

2.19 Mass of water lost on heating is $0.235 \text{ g} - 0.128 \text{ g}$ $= 0.107 \text{ g}$; 0.128 g NiCl_2 remain

$(0.107 \text{ g H}_2O)(1 \text{ mol H}_2O/18.016 \text{ g H}_2O)$
$= 0.00594 \text{ mol H}_2O$

$(0.128 \text{ g NiCl}_2)(1 \text{ mol NiCl}_2/129.6 \text{ g NiCl}_2)$
$= 0.000988 \text{ mol NiCl}_2$

Mole ratio $= 0.00594 \text{ mol H}_2O/0.000988 \text{ mol}$
$\text{NiCl}_2 = 6.01$: Therefore $x = 6$

The formula for the hydrate is $NiCl_2 \cdot 6 H_2O$.

Chapter 3

3.1 (a) Stoichiometric coefficients: 2 for Al, 3 for Br_2, and 1 for Al_2Br_6
(b) 8000 atoms of Al requires $(3/2)8000 = 12{,}000$ molecules of Br_2

3.2 (a) $2 C_4H_{10}(g) + 13 O_2(g) \longrightarrow$
$\qquad\qquad\qquad 8 CO_2(g) + 10 H_2O(\ell)$
(b) $2 Pb(C_2H_5)_4(\ell) + 27 O_2(g) \longrightarrow$
$\qquad\qquad 2 PbO(s) + 16 CO_2(g) + 20 H_2O(\ell)$

3.3 Epsom salt is an electrolyte, and methanol is a non-electrolyte.

3.4 (a) $LiNO_3$ is soluble and gives $Li^+(aq)$ and $NO_3^-(aq)$ ions.
(b) $CaCl_2$ is soluble and gives $Ca^{2+}(aq)$ and $Cl^-(aq)$ ions.
(c) CuO is not water-soluble.
(d) $NaCH_3CO_2$ is soluble and gives $Na^+(aq)$ and $CH_3CO_2^-(aq)$ ions.

3.5 (a) $Na_2CO_3(aq) + CuCl_2(aq) \longrightarrow$
$\qquad\qquad 2 NaCl(aq) + CuCO_3(s)$
(b) No reaction; no insoluble compound is produced.

(c) $NiCl_2(aq) + 2 KOH(aq) \longrightarrow$
$\qquad\qquad Ni(OH)_2(s) + 2 KCl(aq$

3.6 (a) $AlCl_3(aq) + Na_3PO_4(aq) \longrightarrow$
$\qquad\qquad\qquad AlPO_4(s) + 3 NaCl(aq$
$Al^{3+}(aq) + PO_4^{3-}(aq) \longrightarrow AlPO_4(s)$
(b) $FeCl_3(aq) + 3 KOH(aq) \longrightarrow$
$\qquad\qquad\qquad Fe(OH)_3(s) + 3 KCl(aq$
$Fe^{3+}(aq) + 3 OH^-(aq) \longrightarrow Fe(OH)_3(s)$
(c) $Pb(NO_3)_2(aq) + 2 KCl(aq) \longrightarrow$
$\qquad\qquad\qquad PbCl_2(s) + 2 KNO_3(aq$
$Pb^{2+}(aq) + 2 Cl^-(aq) \rightleftharpoons PbCl_2(s)$

3.7 (a) $H_3O(aq)$ and $NO_3^-(aq)$
(b) $Ba^{2+}(aq)$ and $2 OH^-(aq)$

3.8 (a) $H_3PO_4(aq) + H_2O(\ell) \rightleftharpoons$
$\qquad\qquad\qquad H_3O^+(aq) + H_2PO_4^-(aq$
(b) Acting as a base:
$H_2PO_4^-(aq) + H_2O(\ell) \rightleftharpoons$
$\qquad\qquad\qquad H_3PO_4(aq) + OH^-(aq$
Acting as an acid:
$H_2PO_4^-(aq) + H_2O(\ell) \rightleftharpoons$
$\qquad\qquad\qquad HPO_4^{2-}(aq) + H_3O^+$
Because $H_2PO_4^-(aq)$ can react as a Brønsted aci and as a base, it is said to be amphiprotic.
(c) $CN^-(aq) + H_2O(\ell) \rightleftharpoons HCN(aq) + OH^-(aq$ cyanide ion is a Brønsted base.

3.9 $Mg(OH)_2(s) + 2 HCl(aq) \longrightarrow$
$\qquad\qquad\qquad MgCl_2(aq) + 2 H_2O($
Net ionic equation: $Mg(OH)_2(s) + 2 H^+(aq) \longrightarrow$
$\qquad\qquad\qquad Mg^{2+}(aq) + 2 H_2O($

3.10 Metals form basic oxides; nonmetals form acidic oxides.
(a) SeO_2 is an acidic oxide; (b) MgO is a basic oxide and (c) P_4O_{10} is an acidic oxide.

3.11 (a) $BaCO_3(s) + 2 HNO_3(aq) \longrightarrow$
$\qquad\qquad Ba(NO_3)_2(aq) + CO_2(g) + H_2O($
Barium carbonate and nitric acid produce barium nitrate, carbon dioxide, and water.
(b) $(NH_4)_2SO_4(aq) + 2 NaOH(aq) \longrightarrow$
$\qquad\qquad 2 NH_3(g) + Na_2SO_4(aq) + 2 H_2O($

3.12 (a) Fe in Fe_2O_3, +3; (b) S in H_2SO_4, +6;
(c) C in CO_3^{2-}, +4; (d) N in NO_2^+, +5

3.13 Dichromate ion is the oxidizing agent and is reduce (Cr with a +6 oxidation number is reduced to Cr^{3+} with a +3 oxidation number.) Ethanol is the reducin agent and is oxidized. (The C atoms in ethanol have an oxidation number of −2. The oxidation number 0 in acetic acid.)

3.14 (b) Cu is the reducing agent and Cl_2 is the oxidizing agent.
(d) $S_2O_3^{2-}$ is the reducing agent and I_2 is the oxidizi agent.

15 (a) Gas-forming reaction:
$$CuCO_3(s) + H_2SO_4(aq) \longrightarrow$$
$$CuSO_4(aq) + H_2O(\ell) + CO_2(g)$$
Net ionic equation:
$$CuCO_3(s) + 2 H_3O(aq) \longrightarrow$$
$$Cu^{2+}(aq) + 3 H_2O(\ell) + CO_2(g)$$
(b) Oxidation-reduction: $Ga(s) + O_2(g) \longrightarrow$
$$Ga_2O_3(s)$$
(c) Acid–base reaction:
$$Ba(OH)_2(s) + 2 HNO_3(aq) \longrightarrow$$
$$Ba(NO_3)_2(aq) + 2 H_2O(\ell)$$
Net ionic equation:
$$Ba(OH)_2(s) + 2 H_3O(aq) \longrightarrow$$
$$Ba^{2+}(aq) + 4 H_2O(\ell)$$
(d) Precipitation reaction:
$$CuCl_2(aq) + (NH_4)_2S(aq) \longrightarrow$$
$$CuS(s) + 2 NH_4Cl(aq)$$
Net ionic equation:
$$Cu^{2+}(aq) + S^{2-}(aq) \longrightarrow CuS(s)$$

Chapter 4

4.1 $(454 \text{ g } C_3H_8)(1 \text{ mol } C_3H_8/44.10 \text{ g } C_3H_8)$
$= 10.3 \text{ mol } C_3H_8$

$10.3 \text{ mol } C_3H_8 (5 \text{ mol } O_2/1 \text{ mol } C_3H_8)$
$(32.00 \text{ g } O_2/1 \text{ mol } O_2) = 1650 \text{ g } O_2$

$(10.3 \text{ mol } C_3H_8)(3 \text{ mol } CO_2/1 \text{ mol } C_3H_8)$
$(44.01 \text{ g } CO_2/1 \text{ mol } CO_2) = 1360 \text{ g } CO_2$

$(10.3 \text{ mol } C_3H_8)(4 \text{ mol } H_2O/1 \text{ mol } C_3H_8)$
$(18.02 \text{ g } H_2O/1 \text{ mol } H_2O) = 742 \text{ g } H_2O$

4.2 (a) Amount Al $= (50.0 \text{ g Al})(1 \text{ mol Al}/26.98 \text{ g Al})$
$= 1.85 \text{ mol Al}$

Amount $Fe_2O_3 = (50.0 \text{ g } Fe_2O_3)(1 \text{ mol } Fe_2O_3/159.7 \text{ g } Fe_2O_3) = 0.313 \text{ mol } Fe_2O_3$

Mol Al/mol $Fe_2O_3 = 1.853/0.3131 = 5.92$

This is more than the 2:1 ratio required, so the limiting reactant is Fe_2O_3.

(b) Mass Fe $= (0.313 \text{ mol } Fe_2O_3)(2 \text{ mol Fe}/1 \text{ mol } Fe_2O_3) (55.85 \text{ g Fe}/1 \text{ mol Fe}) = 35.0 \text{ g Fe}$

4.3 Theoretical yield $= 125 \text{ g } Al_4C_3(1 \text{ mol } Al_4C_3/143.95 \text{ g } Al_4C_3)(3 \text{ mol } CH_4/1 \text{ mol } Al_4C_3)(16.04 \text{ g } CH_4/1 \text{ mol } CH_4) = 41.8 \text{ g } CH_4$

Percent yield $= (13.6 \text{ g}/41.8 \text{ g})(100\%) = 33.0\%$

4.4 $(0.143 \text{ g } O_2)(1 \text{ mol } O_2/32.00 \text{ g } O_2)(3 \text{ mol } TiO_2/ 3 \text{ mol } O_2)(79.88 \text{ g } TiO_2/1 \text{ mol } TiO_2) = 0.357 \text{ g } TiO_2$

Percent TiO_2 in sample $= (0.357 \text{ g}/2.367 \text{ g})(100\%)$
$= 15.1\%$

4.5 $(1.612 \text{ g } CO_2)(1 \text{ mol } CO_2/44.01 \text{ g } CO_2)(1 \text{ mol C}/ 1 \text{ mol } CO_2) = 0.03663 \text{ mol C}$

$(0.7425 \text{ g } H_2O)(1 \text{ mol } H_2O/18.01 \text{ g } H_2O)(2 \text{ mol H}/ 1 \text{ mol } H_2O) = 0.08243 \text{ mol H}$

$0.08243 \text{ mol H}/0.03663 \text{ mol} = 2.250 \text{ H}/1 \text{ C} = 9 \text{ H}/4 \text{ C}$

The empirical formula is C_4H_9, which has a molar mass of 57 g/mol. This is one half of the measured value of molar mass, so the molecular formula is C_8H_{18}.

4.6 $(0.240 \text{ g } CO_2)(1 \text{ mol } CO_2/44.01 \text{ g } CO_2) (1 \text{ mol C}/1 \text{ mol } CO_2)(12.01 \text{ g C}/1 \text{ mol C}) = 0.06549 \text{ g C}$

$(0.0982 \text{ g } H_2O)(1 \text{ mol } H_2O/18.02 \text{ g } H_2O)(2 \text{ mol H}/1 \text{ mol } H_2O)(1.008 \text{ g H}/1 \text{ mol H}) = 0.01099 \text{ g H}$

Mass O (by difference) $= 0.1342 \text{ g} - 0.06549 \text{ g} - 0.01099 \text{ g} = 0.05772 \text{ g}$

Amount C $= 0.06549 \text{ g}(1 \text{ mol C}/12.01 \text{ g C}) = 0.00545 \text{ mol C}$

Amount H $= 0.01099 \text{ g H}(1 \text{ mol H}/1.008 \text{ g H}) = 0.01090 \text{ mol H}$

Amount O $= 0.05772 \text{ g O}(1 \text{ mol O}/16.00 \text{ g O}) = 0.00361 \text{ mol O}$

To find a whole-number ratio, divide each value by 0.00361; this gives 1.51 mol C : 3.02 mol H : 1 mol O. Multiply each value by 2, and round off to 3 mol C : 6 mol H : 2 mol O. The empirical formula is $C_3H_6O_2$; given the molar mass of 74.1, this is also the molecular formula.

4.7 $(26.3 \text{ g})(1 \text{ mol } NaHCO_3/84.01 \text{ g } NaHCO_3) = 0.313 \text{ mol } NaHCO_3$

$0.313 \text{ mol } NaHCO_3/0.200 \text{ L} = 1.57 \text{ M}$

Ion concentrations: $[Na^+] = [HCO_3^-] = 1.57 \text{ M}$

4.8 First, determine the mass of $AgNO_3$ required.
Amount of $AgNO_3$ required $= (0.0200 \text{ M})(0.250 \text{ L})$
$= 5.00 \times 10^{-3} \text{ mol}$

Mass of $AgNO_3 = (5.00 \times 10^{-3} \text{ mol})(169.9 \text{ g/mol})$
$= 0.850 \text{ g } AgNO_3$

Weigh out 0.850 g $AgNO_3$. Then, dissolve it in a small amount of water in the volumetric flask. After the solid is dissolved, fill the flask to the mark.

4.9 $(2.00 \text{ M})(V_{\text{conc}}) = (1.00 \text{ M})(0.250 \text{ L}); V_{\text{conc}} = 0.125 \text{ L}$

To prepare the solution, measure accurately 125 mL of 2.00 M NaOH into a 250-mL volumetric flask, and add water to give a total volume of 250 mL.

4.10 (a) pH $= -\log (2.6 \times 10^{-2}) = 1.59$
(b) $-\log [H^+] = 3.80; [H^+] = 1.5 \times 10^{-4} \text{ M}$

4.11 HCl is the limiting reagent.

$(0.350 \text{ mol HCl}/1 \text{ L})(0.0750 \text{ L})(1 \text{ mol } CO_2/ 2 \text{ mol HCl})(44.01 \text{ g } CO_2/1 \text{ mol } CO_2) = 0.578 \text{ g } CO_2$

4.12 $(0.953 \text{ mol NaOH}/1 \text{ L})(0.02833 \text{ L NaOH}) = 0.0270 \text{ mol NaOH}$

$(0.0270 \text{ mol NaOH})(1 \text{ mol } CH_3CO_2H/1 \text{ mol NaOH}) = 0.0270 \text{ mol } CH_3CO_2H$

$(0.0270 \text{ mol } CH_3CO_2H)(60.05 \text{ g/mol}) = 1.62 \text{ g } CH_3CO_2H$

$0.0270 \text{ mol } CH_3CO_2H/0.0250 \text{ L} = 1.08 \text{ M}$

4.13 $(0.100 \text{ mol HCl}/1 \text{ L})(0.02967 \text{ L}) = 0.00297 \text{ mol HCl}$

$(0.00297 \text{ mol HCl})(1 \text{ mol NaOH}/1 \text{ mol HCl}) =$
0.00297 mol NaOH

$0.00297 \text{ mol NaOH}/0.0250 \text{ L} = 0.119 \text{ M NaOH}$

4.14 Mol acid $=$ mol base $= (0.323 \text{ mol/L})(0.03008 \text{ L}) =$
$9.716 \times 10^{-3} \text{ mol}$

Molar mass $= 0.856 \text{ g acid}/9.716 \times 10^{-3} \text{ mol}$
acid $= 88.1 \text{ g/mol}$

4.15 $(0.196 \text{ mol Na}_2\text{S}_2\text{O}_3/1 \text{ L})(0.02030 \text{ L}) = 0.00398 \text{ mol}$
$\text{Na}_2\text{S}_2\text{O}_3$

$(0.00398 \text{ mol Na}_2\text{S}_2\text{O}_3)(1 \text{ mol I}_2/2 \text{ mol Na}_2\text{S}_2\text{O}_3) =$
0.00199 mol I_2

0.00199 mol I_2 is in excess, and was not used in the
reaction with ascorbic acid.

I_2 originally added $= (0.0520 \text{ mol I}_2/1 \text{ L})(0.05000 \text{ L}) =$
0.00260 mol I_2

I_2 used in reaction with ascorbic acid $= 0.00260 \text{ mol}$
$- 0.00199 \text{ mol} = 6.1 \times 10^{-4} \text{ mol I}_2$

$(6.1 \times 10^{-4} \text{ mol I}_2)(1 \text{ mol C}_6\text{H}_8\text{O}_6/1 \text{ mol I}_2)$
$(176.1 \text{ g}/1 \text{ mol}) = 0.11 \text{ g C}_6\text{H}_8\text{O}_6$

Chapter 5

5.1 (a) $(3800 \text{ calories})(4.184 \text{ J/calorie}) = 1.6 \times 10^4 \text{ J}$
(b) $(250 \text{ calories})(1000 \text{ calories/calorie})(4.184 \text{ J/}$
$\text{calorie})(1 \text{ kJ}/1000 \text{ J}) = 1.0 \times 10^3 \text{ kJ}$

5.2 $C = 59.8 \text{ J}/[(25.0 \text{ g})(1.00 \text{ K})] = 2.39 \text{ J/g} \cdot \text{K}$

5.3 $(15.5 \text{ g})(C_{\text{metal}})(18.9 \text{ °C} - 100.0 \text{ °C}) + (55.5 \text{ g})$
$(4.184 \text{ J/g} \cdot \text{K})(18.9 \text{ °C} - 16.5 \text{ °C}) = 0$

$C_{\text{metal}} = 0.44 \text{ J/g} \cdot \text{K}$

5.4 Energy transferred as heat from tea $+$ energy as heat
expended to melt ice $= 0$

$(250 \text{ g})(4.2 \text{ J/g} \cdot \text{K})(273.2 \text{ K} - 291.4 \text{ K}) +$
$\qquad\qquad\qquad\qquad x \text{ g } (333 \text{ J/g}) = 0$

$x = 57 \text{ g}$

57 g of ice melts with energy as heat supplied by
cooling 250 g of tea from 18.2 °C (291.4 K) to 0 °C
(273.2 K)

Mass of ice remaining $=$ mass of ice initially $-$ mass of
ice melted

Mass of ice remaining $= 75 \text{ g} - 57 \text{ g} = 18 \text{ g}$

5.5 $(15.0 \text{ g C}_2\text{H}_6)(1 \text{ mol C}_2\text{H}_6/30.07 \text{ g C}_2\text{H}_6) = 0.4988$
$\text{mol C}_2\text{H}_6$

$\Delta_r H = 0.4988 \text{ mol C}_2\text{H}_6(1 \text{ mol-rxn}/2 \text{ mol C}_2\text{H}_6)$
$(-2857.3 \text{ kJ/mol-rxn})$

$= -713 \text{ kJ}$

5.6 Mass of final solution $= 400. \text{ g}$

$\Delta T = 27.78 \text{ °C} - 25.10 \text{ °C} = 2.68 \text{ °C} = 2.68 \text{ K}$

Amount of HCl used $=$ amount of NaOH used $=$
$C \times V = (0.400 \text{ mol/L}) \times 0.200 \text{ L} = 0.0800 \text{ mol}$

Energy transferred as heat by acid–base reaction $+$
energy gained as heat to warm solution $= 0$

$q_{\text{rxn}} + (4.20 \text{ J/g} \cdot \text{K})(400. \text{ g})(2.68 \text{ K}) = 0$

$q_{\text{rxn}} = -4.50 \times 10^3 \text{ J}$

This represents the energy transferred as heat in the
reaction of 0.0800 mol HCl.

Energy transferred as heat per mole $= \Delta_r H =$
$-4.50 \text{ kJ}/0.0800 \text{ mol HCl} = -56.3 \text{ kJ/mol HCl}$

5.7 (a) Energy evolved as heat in reaction $+$ energy as
heat absorbed by H_2O $+$ energy as heat absorbed
by bomb $= 0$

$q_{\text{rxn}} + (1.50 \times 10^3 \text{ g})(4.20 \text{ J/g} \cdot \text{K})(27.32 \text{ °C} -$
$25.00 \text{ °C}) + (837 \text{ J/K})(27.32 \text{ K} - 25.00 \text{ K}) = 0$

$q_{\text{rxn}} = -16,600 \text{ J}$ (energy as heat evolved in burning 1.0 g sucrose)

(b) Energy evolved as heat per mole $= (-16.6 \text{ kJ/g}$
$\text{sucrose})(342.2 \text{ g sucrose}/1 \text{ mol sucrose}) =$
$-5650 \text{ kJ/mol sucrose}$

5.8 $\text{C(s)} + \text{O}_2\text{(g)} \longrightarrow \text{CO}_2\text{(g)}$ $\qquad \Delta_r H_1^\circ = -393.5$
$2 [\text{S(s)} + \text{O}_2\text{(g)} \longrightarrow \text{SO}_2\text{(g)}]$

$\qquad\qquad\qquad\qquad \Delta_r H_2^\circ = 2(-296.8) = -593.6$

$\text{CO}_2\text{(g)} + 2 \text{ SO}_2\text{(g)} \longrightarrow \text{CS}_2\text{(g)} + 3 \text{ O}_2\text{(g)}$
$\qquad\qquad\qquad\qquad \Delta_r H_3^\circ = +1103.9$

Net: $\text{C(s)} + 2 \text{ S(s)} \longrightarrow \text{CS}_2\text{(g)}$
$\Delta_r H^\circ_{\text{net}} = \Delta_r H_1^\circ + \Delta_r H_2^\circ + \Delta_r H_3^\circ = +116.8 \text{ kJ}$

5.9 $\text{Fe(s)} + \tfrac{3}{2} \text{ Cl}_2\text{(g)} \longrightarrow \text{FeCl}_3\text{(s)}$

$12 \text{ C(s, graphite)} + 11 \text{ H}_2\text{(g)} + 11\tfrac{1}{2} \text{ O}_2\text{(g)} \longrightarrow$
$\qquad\qquad\qquad\qquad\qquad\qquad\qquad \text{C}_{12}\text{H}_{22}\text{O}_{11}($

5.10 $\Delta_r H^\circ = (6 \text{ mol/mol-rxn})\Delta_f H^\circ [\text{CO}_2\text{(g)}] + (3 \text{ mol/}$
$\text{mol-rxn})\Delta_f H^\circ[\text{H}_2\text{O(}\ell\text{)}] - \{(1 \text{ mol}/1 \text{ mol-rxn})\Delta_f H^\circ$
$[\text{C}_6\text{H}_6\text{(}\ell\text{)}] + (\tfrac{15}{2} \text{ mol/mol-rxn}) \Delta_f H^\circ [\text{O}_2\text{(g)}]\} =$
$(6 \text{ mol/mol-rxn})(-393.5 \text{ kJ/mol}) + (3 \text{ mol/}$
$\text{mol-rxn})(-285.8 \text{ J/mol}) - (1 \text{ mol/mol-rxn})$
$(+49.0 \text{ kJ/mol}) - 0$

$= -3267.4 \text{ kJ/mol-rxn}$

Chapter 6

6.1 (a) Highest frequency, violet; lowest frequency, red
(b) The FM radio frequency, 91.7 MHz, is lower than
the frequency of a microwave oven, 2.45 GHz.
(c) The wavelength of x-rays is shorter than the wavelength of ultraviolet light.

Orange light: 6.25×10^2 nm $= 6.25 \times 10^{-7}$ m

$\nu = (2.998 \times 10^8 \text{ m/s})/6.25 \times 10^{-7}$ m
$\qquad = 4.80 \times 10^{14} \text{ s}^{-1}$

$E = (6.626 \times 10^{-34} \text{ J} \cdot \text{s/photon})(4.80 \times 10^{14} \text{ s}^{-1})$
$\qquad\qquad\qquad (6.022 \times 10^{23} \text{ photons/mol})$

$\qquad = 1.92 \times 10^5$ J/mol

Microwave: $E = (6.626 \times 10^{-34} \text{ J} \cdot \text{s/photon})$
$\qquad\qquad (2.45 \times 10^9 \text{ s}^{-1})(6.022 \times$
$\qquad\qquad 10^{23} \text{ photons/mol})$

$\qquad\qquad = 0.978$ J/mol

Orange (625-nm) light is about 200,000 times more energetic than 2.45-GHz microwaves.

3 (a) E (per atom) $= -Rhc/n^2$
$\qquad\qquad\qquad = (-2.179 \times 10^{-18})/(3^2)$ J/atom
$\qquad\qquad\qquad = -2.421 \times 10^{-19}$ J/atom

(b) E (per mol) $= (-2.421 \times 10^{-19}$ J/atom$)$
$\qquad\qquad\qquad (6.022 \times 10^{23}$ atoms/mol$)$
$\qquad\qquad\qquad (1 \text{ kJ}/10^3 \text{ J})$
$\qquad\qquad\qquad = -145.8$ kJ/mol

4 The least energetic line is from the electron transition from $n = 2$ to $n = 1$.

$\Delta E = -Rhc[1/1^2 - 1/2^2]$
$\qquad = -(2.179 \times 10^{-18}$ J/atom$)(3/4)$
$\qquad = -1.634 \times 10^{-18}$ J/atom

$\nu = \Delta E/h$
$\qquad = (-1.634 \times 10^{-18} \text{ J/atom})/(6.626 \times 10^{-34} \text{ J} \cdot \text{s})$
$\qquad = 2.466 \times 10^{15} \text{ s}^{-1}$

$\lambda = c/\nu = (2.998 \times 10^8 \text{ m/s}^{-1})/(2.466 \times 10^{15} \text{ s}^{-1})$
$\qquad = 1.216 \times 10^{-7}$ m (or 121.6 nm)

5 Energy per atom $= \Delta E = -Rhc[1/\infty^2 - 1/1^2]$
$\qquad = 2.179 \times 10^{-18}$ J/atom

Energy per mole $= (2.179 \times 10^{-18}$ J/atom$)(6.022 \times 10^{23}$ atoms/mol$)$
$\qquad = 1.312 \times 10^6$ J/mol $(= 1312$ kJ/mol$)$

6 First, calculate the velocity of the neutron:
$v = [2E/m]^{1/2} = [2(6.21 \times 10^{-21} \text{ kg} \cdot \text{m}^2 \text{ s}^{-2})/(1.675$
$\qquad \times 10^{-27} \text{ kg})]^{1/2}$
$\qquad = 2720 \text{ m} \cdot \text{s}^{-1}$

Use this value in the de Broglie equation:
$\lambda = h/mv = (6.626 \times 10^{-34} \text{ kg} \cdot \text{m}^2 \text{ s}^{-2})/$
$\qquad\qquad (1.675 \times 10^{-31} \text{ kg})(2720 \text{ m s}^{-1})$
$\qquad = 1.45 \times 10^{-6}$ m

7 (a) $\ell = 0$ or 1; (b) $m_\ell = -1$, 0, or $+1$, p subshell; (c) d subshell; (d) $\ell = 0$ and $m_\ell = 0$; (e) 3 orbitals in the p subshell; (f) 7 values of m_ℓ and 7 orbitals

6.8 (a)

Orbital	n	ℓ
6s	6	0
4p	4	1
5d	5	2
4f	4	3

(b) A $4p$ orbital has one nodal plane; a $6d$ orbital has two nodal planes.

Chapter 7

7.1 (a) $4s$ $(n + \ell = 4)$ filled before $4p$ $(n + \ell = 5)$
(b) $6s$ $(n + \ell = 6)$ filled before $5d$ $(n + \ell = 7)$
(c) $5s$ $(n + \ell = 5)$ filled before $4f$ $(n + \ell = 7)$

7.2 (a) chlorine (Cl)
(b) $1s^2 2s^2 2p^6 3s^2 3p^3$

$$\qquad\qquad\quad 3s \qquad 3p$$
$$[\text{Ne}] \; \boxed{\uparrow\downarrow} \;\; \boxed{\uparrow\;\uparrow\;\uparrow}$$

(c) Calcium has two valence electrons in the 4s subshell. Quantum numbers for these two electrons are $n = 4$, $\ell = 0$, $m_\ell = 0$, and $m_s = \pm 1/2$

7.3 Obtain the answers from Table 7.3.

7.4
$$\qquad\qquad\qquad 3d \qquad\qquad 4s$$
$$\text{V}^{2+} \quad [\text{Ar}] \; \boxed{\uparrow\;\uparrow\;\uparrow\;\;\;\;\;} \; \boxed{\;}$$

$$\qquad\qquad\qquad 3d \qquad\qquad 4s$$
$$\text{V}^{3+} \quad [\text{Ar}] \; \boxed{\uparrow\;\uparrow\;\;\;\;\;\;\;} \; \boxed{\;}$$

$$\qquad\qquad\qquad 3d \qquad\qquad 4s$$
$$\text{Co}^{3+} \quad [\text{Ar}] \; \boxed{\uparrow\downarrow\;\uparrow\;\uparrow\;\uparrow\;\uparrow} \; \boxed{\;}$$

All three ions are paramagnetic with three, two, and four unpaired electrons, respectively.

7.5 Increasing atomic radius: C < Si < Al

7.6 (a) Increasing atomic radius: C < B < Al
(b) Increasing ionization energy: Al < B < C
(c) Carbon is predicted to have the most negative electron affinity.

7.7 Trend in ionic radii: $S^{2-} > Cl^- > K^+$. These ions are isoelectronic (they all have the Ar configuration). The size decreases with increased nuclear charge, the higher nuclear charge resulting in a greater force of attraction of the electrons by the nucleus.

7.8 $MgCl_3$, if it existed, would presumably contain one Mg^{3+} ion (and three Cl^- ions). The formation of Mg^{3+} is energetically unfavorable, with a huge input of energy being required to remove the third electron (a core electron).

Chapter 8

8.1

$$\left[\begin{array}{c} H \\ | \\ H-N-H \\ | \\ H \end{array}\right]^+ \quad :C\equiv O: \quad [:N\equiv O:]^+ \quad \left[\begin{array}{c} :\ddot{O}: \\ | \\ :\ddot{O}-S-\ddot{O}: \\ | \\ :\ddot{O}: \end{array}\right]^{2-}$$

8.2

$$\begin{array}{c} H \\ | \\ H-C-\ddot{O}-H \\ | \\ H \end{array} \qquad \begin{array}{c} H-\ddot{N}-\ddot{O}-H \\ | \\ H \end{array}$$

methanol   hydroxylamine

8.3

$$\left[\begin{array}{c} :\ddot{O}: \\ | \\ H-\ddot{O}-P-\ddot{O}-H \\ | \\ :\ddot{O}: \end{array}\right]^-$$

8.4 (a) The acetylide ion, C_2^{2-}, and the N_2 molecule have the same number of valence electrons (10) and identical electronic structures; that is, they are isoelectronic.

(b) Ozone, O_3, is isoelectronic with NO_2^-; hydroxide ion, OH^-, is isoelectronic with HF.

8.5 (a) CN^-: formal charge on C is -1; formal charge on N is 0.

(b) SO_3^{2-}: formal charge on S is $+2$; formal charge on each O is -1.

8.6 Resonance structures for the HCO_3^- ion:

$$\left[\begin{array}{c} \ddot{O}=C-\ddot{O}: \\ | \\ :\ddot{O}-H \end{array}\right]^- \longleftrightarrow \left[\begin{array}{c} :\ddot{O}-C=\ddot{O} \\ | \\ :\ddot{O}-H \end{array}\right]^-$$

(a) No. Three resonance structures are needed in the description of CO_3^{2-}; only two are needed to describe HCO_3^-.

(b) In each resonance structure, Carbon's formal charge is 0. The oxygen of the $-OH$ group and the double-bonded oxygen have a formal charge of zero; the singly bonded oxygen has a formal charge of -1. The average formal charge on the latter two oxygen atoms is $-\frac{1}{2}$. In the carbonate ion, the three oxygen atoms have an average formal charge of $-\frac{2}{3}$.

(c) H^+ would be expected to add to one of the oxygens with a negative formal charge; that is, one of the oxygens with formal charge of $-\frac{1}{2}$ in this structure.

8.7 $\left[:\ddot{F}-\ddot{Cl}-\ddot{F}:\right]^+$ ClF_2^+, 2 bond pairs and 2 lone pair

$\left[:\ddot{F}-\ddot{Cl}-\ddot{F}:\right]^-$ ClF_2^-, 2 bond pairs and 3 lone pairs

8.8 Tetrahedral geometry around carbon. The $Cl-C-$ bond angle will be close to $109.5°$.

8.9 For each species, the electron-pair geometry and the molecular shape are the same. BF_3: trigonal planar BF_4^-: tetrahedral. Adding F^- to BF_3 adds an electron pair to the central atom and changes the shape.

8.10 The electron-pair geometry around I is trigonal bipyramidal. The molecular geometry of the ion is linear

$$\left[\begin{array}{c} :\ddot{Cl}: \\ | \\ :-I< \\ | \\ :\ddot{Cl}: \end{array}\right]^-$$

8.11 (a) In PO_4^{3-}, there is tetrahedral electron-pair geometry. The molecular geometry is also tetrahedral.

$$\left[\begin{array}{c} :\ddot{O}: \\ | \\ :\ddot{O}-P-\ddot{O}: \\ | \\ :\ddot{O}: \end{array}\right]^{3-}$$

(b) In SO_3^{2-}, there is tetrahedral electron-pair geometry. The molecular geometry is trigonal pyramidal

$$\left[\begin{array}{c} :\ddot{O}-\ddot{S}-\ddot{O}: \\ | \\ :\ddot{O}: \end{array}\right]^{2-}$$

(c) In IF_5, there is octahedral electron-pair geometry. The molecular geometry is square pyramidal.

$$\begin{array}{c} F \\ F|F \\ \diagdown I \diagup \\ F\diagup|\diagdown F \end{array}$$

8.12 (a) The H atom is positive in each case. H—F ($\Delta\chi = 1.8$) is more polar than H—I ($\Delta\chi = 0.5$).

(b) B—F ($\Delta\chi = 2.0$) is more polar than B—C ($\Delta\chi = 0.5$). In B—F, F is the negative pole, and is the positive pole. In B—C, C is the negative pole, and B is the positive pole.

(c) C—Si ($\Delta\chi = 0.6$) is more polar than C—S ($\Delta\chi = 0.1$). In C—Si, C is the negative pole, and Si is the positive pole. In C—S, S is the negative pole, and C the positive pole.

13

$$\overset{-1\ +1\ 0}{:\ddot{O}-\ddot{S}=\ddot{O}} \longleftrightarrow \overset{0\ +1\ -1}{\ddot{O}=\ddot{S}-\ddot{O}:}$$

The S—O bonds are polar, with the negative end being the O atom. (The O atom is more electronegative than the S atom.) Formal charges show that these bonds are, in fact, polar, with the O atom being the more negative atom.

14 (a) $BFCl_2$, polar, negative side is the F atom because F is the most electronegative atom in the molecule.

(b) NH_2Cl, polar, negative side is the Cl atom.

(c) SCl_2, polar, Cl atoms are on the negative side.

15 (a)

Formal charges: S = +1, O = −1, Cl = 0
(Lewis structure of $SOCl_2$ with formal charges indicated)

(b) Geometry: trigonal pyramidal
(c) The molecule is polar. The positive charge is on sulfur, the negative charge on oxygen.

16 (a) C—N: bond order 1; C=N: bond order 2; C ≡ N: bond order 3. Bond length: C—N > C=N > C ≡ N

(b) $$\left[:\ddot{O}-\ddot{N}=\ddot{O}\right]^- \longleftrightarrow \left[\ddot{O}=\ddot{N}-\ddot{O}:\right]^-$$

The N-O bond order in NO_2^- is 1.5. Therefore, the NO bond length (124 pm) should be between the length of a N—O single bond (136 pm) and a N=O double bond (115 pm).

17 $CH_4(g) + 2\,O_2(g) \longrightarrow CO_2(g) + 2\,H_2O(g)$

Break 4 C—H bonds and 2 O=O bonds:
(4 mol)(413 kJ/mol) + (2 mol)(498 kJ/mol) = 2648 kJ

Make 2 C=O bonds and 4 H—O bonds:
(2 mol)(745 kJ/mol) + (4 mol)(463 kJ/mol) = 3342 kJ

$\Delta_r H° = 2648\ kJ - 3342\ kJ = -694\ kJ/mol\text{-rxn}$
(value calculated using enthalpies of formation
= −797 kJ/mol-rxn)

Chapter 9

9.1 The oxygen atom in H_3O^+ is sp^3 hybridized. The three O—H bonds are formed by overlap of oxygen sp^3 and hydrogen $1s$ orbitals. The fourth sp^3 orbital contains a lone pair of electrons.

The carbon and nitrogen atoms in CH_3NH_2 are sp^3 hybridized. The C—H bonds arise from overlap of carbon sp^3 orbitals and hydrogen $1s$ orbitals. The bond between C and N is formed by overlap of sp^3 orbitals from these atoms. Overlap of nitrogen sp^3 and hydrogen $1s$ orbitals gives the two N—H bonds, and there is a lone pair in the remaining sp^3 orbital on nitrogen.

9.2 (a) BH_4^-, tetrahedral electron-pair geometry, sp^3
(b) SF_5^-, octahedral electron-pair geometry, sp^3d^2
(c) SOF_4, trigonal-bipyramidal electron-pair geometry, sp^3d
(d) ClF_3, trigonal-bipyramidal electron-pair geometry, sp^3d
(e) BCl_3, trigonal-planar electron-pair geometry, sp^2
(f) XeO_6^{4-}, octahedral electron-pair geometry, sp^3d^2

9.3 The two CH_3 carbon atoms are sp^3 hybridized, and the center carbon atom is sp^2 hybridized. For each of the carbon atoms in the methyl groups, the sp^3 orbitals overlap with hydrogen $1s$ orbitals to form the three C—H bonds, and the fourth sp^3 orbital overlaps with an sp^2 orbital on the central carbon atom, forming a carbon–carbon sigma bond. Overlap of an sp^2 orbital on the central carbon and an oxygen sp^2 orbital gives the sigma bond between these elements. The pi bond between carbon and oxygen arises by overlap of a p orbital from each element.

9.4 A triple bond links the two nitrogen atoms, each of which also has one lone pair. Each nitrogen is sp hybridized. One sp orbital contains the lone pair; the other is used to form the sigma bond between the two atoms. Two pi bonds arise by overlap of p orbitals on the two atoms, perpendicular to the molecular axis.

9.5 Bond angles: H—C—H = 109.5°, H—C—C = 109.5°, C—C—N = 180°. Carbon in the CH_3 group is sp^3 hybridized; the central C and the N are sp hybridized. The three C—H bonds form by overlap of an H $1s$ orbital with one of the sp^3 orbitals of the CH_3 group; the fourth sp^3 orbital overlaps with an sp orbital on the central C to form a sigma bond. The triple bond between C and N is a combination of a sigma bond (the sp orbital on C overlaps with the sp orbital on N) and two pi bonds (overlap of two sets of p orbitals on these elements). The remaining sp orbital on N contains a lone pair.

9.6 H_2^+: $(\sigma_1 s)^1$ The ion has a bond order of ½ and is expected to exist. A bond order of ½ is predicted for He_2^+ and H_2^-, both of which are predicted to have electron configurations $(\sigma_1 s)^2 (\sigma^*_1 s)^1$.

9.7 Li_2^- is predicted to have an electron configuration $(\sigma_1 s)^2 (\sigma^*_1 s)^2 (\sigma_2 s)^2 (\sigma^*_2 s)^1$ and a bond order of $\frac{1}{2}$, the positive value implying that the ion might exist.

9.8 O_2^+: [core electrons] $(\sigma_2 s)^2 (\sigma^*_2 s)^2 (\pi_2 p)^4 (\sigma_2 p)^2 (\pi^*_2 p)^1$. The bond order is 2.5. The ion is paramagnetic with one unpaired electron.

Chapter 10

10.1 (a) Isomers of C_7H_{16}

$CH_3CH_2CH_2CH_2CH_2CH_2CH_3$ heptane

$CH_3CH_2CH_2CH_2\overset{\displaystyle CH_3}{\underset{\displaystyle |}{C}}HCH_3$ 2-methylhexane

$CH_3CH_2CH_2\overset{\displaystyle CH_3}{\underset{\displaystyle |}{C}}HCH_2CH_3$ 3-methylhexane

$CH_3CH_2\underset{\displaystyle \underset{\displaystyle CH_3}{|}}{\overset{\displaystyle \overset{\displaystyle CH_3}{|}}{C}}HCHCH_3$ 2,3-dimethylpentane

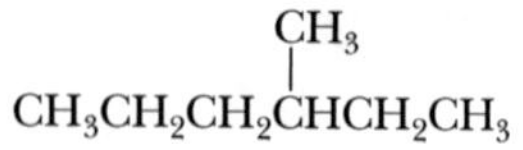

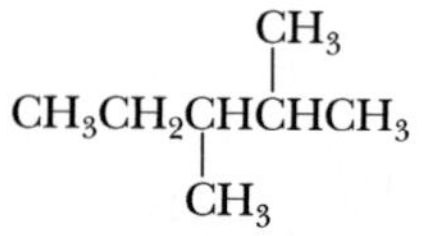

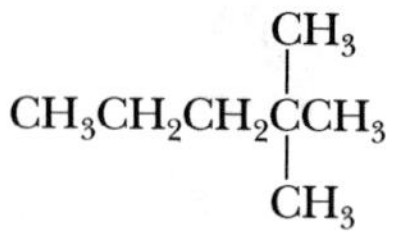

$CH_3CH_2CH_2\underset{\displaystyle \underset{\displaystyle CH_3}{|}}{\overset{\displaystyle \overset{\displaystyle CH_3}{|}}{C}}CH_3$ 2,2-dimethylpentane

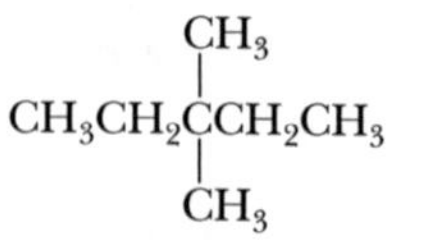

$CH_3CH_2\underset{\displaystyle \underset{\displaystyle CH_3}{|}}{\overset{\displaystyle \overset{\displaystyle CH_3}{|}}{C}}CH_2CH_3$ 3,3-dimethylpentane

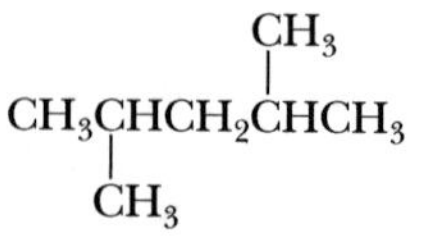

$CH_3\overset{\displaystyle CH_3}{\underset{\displaystyle |}{C}}HCH_2\underset{\displaystyle \underset{\displaystyle CH_3}{|}}{C}HCH_3$ 2,4-dimethylpentane

2-Ethylpentane is pictured on page 450.

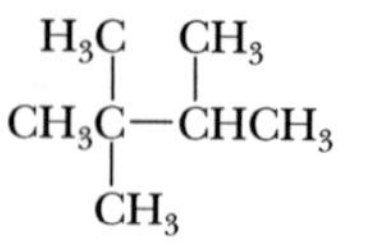

$CH_3\underset{\displaystyle \underset{\displaystyle CH_3}{|}}{\overset{\displaystyle \overset{\displaystyle H_3C}{|}}{C}}-\overset{\displaystyle \overset{\displaystyle CH_3}{|}}{C}HCH_3$ 2,2,3-trimethylbutane

(b) Two isomers, 3-methylhexane, and 2,3-dimethyl-pentane, are chiral.

10.2 The names accompany the structures in the answer to Exercise 10.1.

10.3 Isomers of C_6H_{12} in which the longest chain has six C atoms:

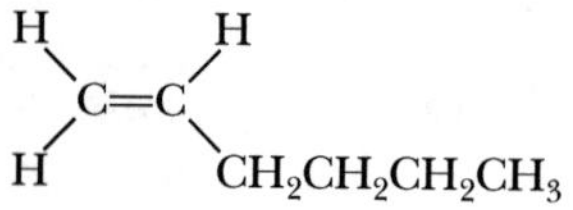

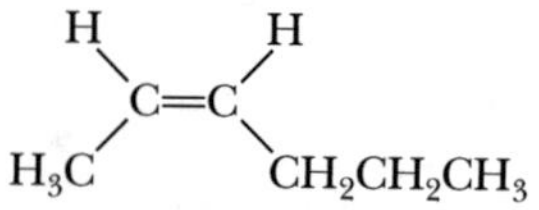

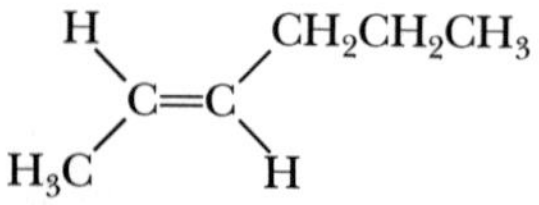

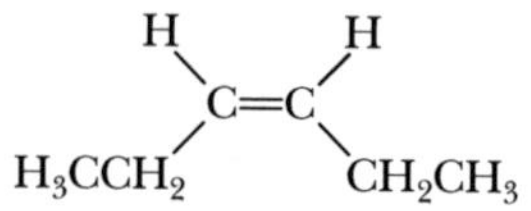

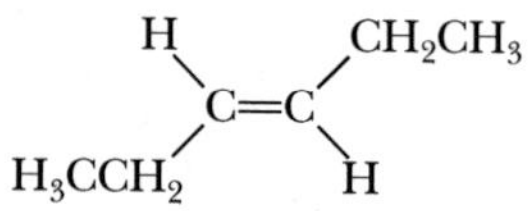

Names (in order, top to bottom): 1-hexene, *cis*-2-hexene, *trans*-2-hexene, *cis*-3-hexene, *trans*-3-hexene. None of these isomers is chiral.

10.4 (a)

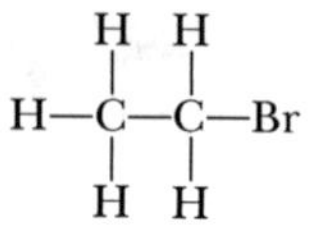

bromoethane

(b)

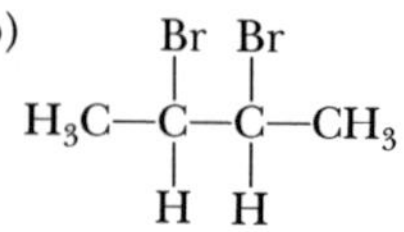

2,3-dibromobutane

10.5 1,4-diaminobenzene

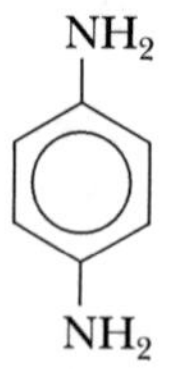

10.6 $CH_3CH_2CH_2CH_2OH$ 1-butanol

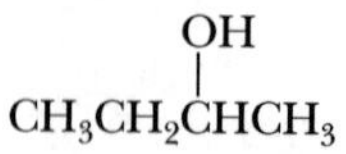

$CH_3CH_2\overset{\displaystyle OH}{\underset{\displaystyle |}{C}}HCH_3$ 2-butanol

$CH_3\underset{\displaystyle \underset{\displaystyle CH_3}{|}}{C}HCH_2OH$ 2-methyl-1-propanol

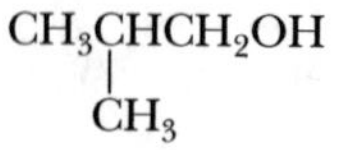

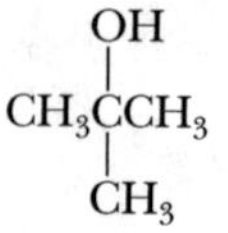

$CH_3\underset{\displaystyle \underset{\displaystyle CH_3}{|}}{\overset{\displaystyle \overset{\displaystyle OH}{|}}{C}}CH_3$ 2-methyl-2-propanol

0.7 (a)

$CH_3CH_2CH_2\overset{\overset{\displaystyle O}{\|}}{C}CH_3$ 2-pentanone

$CH_3CH_2\overset{\overset{\displaystyle O}{\|}}{C}CH_2CH_3$ 3-pentanone

$CH_3CH_2CH_2CH_2\overset{\overset{\displaystyle O}{\|}}{C}H$ pentanal

$CH_3\underset{\underset{\displaystyle CH_3}{|}}{C}HCH_2\overset{\overset{\displaystyle O}{\|}}{C}H$ 3-methylbutanal

(b) $CH_3\underset{\underset{\displaystyle OH}{|}}{C}HCH_2CH_2CH_3$, 2-pentanol

0.8 (a) 1-butanol gives butanal $CH_3CH_2CH_2\overset{\overset{\displaystyle O}{\|}}{C}H$

(b) 2-butanol gives butanone $CH_3CH_2\overset{\overset{\displaystyle O}{\|}}{C}CH_3$

(c) 2-methyl-1-propanol gives 2-methylpropanal

$CH_3\underset{\underset{\displaystyle CH_3}{|}}{\overset{\overset{\displaystyle H}{|}}{C}}\!-\!\overset{\overset{\displaystyle O}{\|}}{C}H$

The oxidation products from these three reactions are structural isomers.

0.9 (a) $CH_3CH_2\overset{\overset{\displaystyle O}{\|}}{C}OCH_3$ methyl propanoate

(b) $CH_3CH_2CH_2\overset{\overset{\displaystyle O}{\|}}{C}OCH_2CH_2CH_2CH_3$

                          butyl butanoate

(c) $CH_3CH_2CH_2CH_2CH_2\overset{\overset{\displaystyle O}{\|}}{C}OCH_2CH_3$

                          ethyl hexanoate

0.10 (a) Propyl acetate is formed from acetic acid and propanol:

$CH_3\overset{\overset{\displaystyle O}{\|}}{C}OH + CH_3CH_2CH_2OH$

(b) 3-Methylpentyl benzoate is formed from benzoic acid and 3-methylpentanol:

(c) Ethyl salicylate is formed from salicylic acid and ethanol:

10.11 (a) $CH_3CH_2CH_2OH$: 1-propanol, has an alcohol (—OH) group

CH_3CO_2H: ethanoic acid (acetic acid), has a carboxylic acid (—CO$_2$H) group

$CH_3CH_2NH_2$: ethylamine, has an amino (—NH$_2$) group

(b) 1-propyl ethanoate (propyl acetate)

(c) Oxidation of this primary alcohol first gives propanal, CH_3CH_2CHO. Further oxidation gives propanoic acid, $CH_3CH_2CO_2H$.

(d) *N*-ethylacetamide, $CH_3CONHCH_2CH_3$

(e) The amine is protonated by hydrochloric acid, forming ethylammonium chloride, $[CH_3CH_2NH_3]Cl$.

10.12 Kevlar is a polyamide polymer, prepared by the reaction of terephthalic acid and 1,4-diaminobenzene.

$n\,H_2NC_6H_4NH_2 + n\,HO_2CC_6H_4CO_2H \longrightarrow$
$\text{-(-HNC}_6\text{H}_4\text{NHCOC}_6\text{H}_4\text{CO-)}_n\text{- + } 2n\,H_2O$

Chapter 11

11.1 0.83 bar (0.82 atm) > 75 kPa (0.74 atm) > 0.63 atm > 250 mm Hg (0.33 atm)

11.2 $P_1 = 55$ mm Hg and $V_1 = 125$ mL; $P_2 = 78$ mm Hg and $V_2 = ?$

$V_2 = V_1(P_1/P_2) = (125\ \text{mL})(55\ \text{mm Hg}/78\ \text{mm Hg})$
$= 88$ mL

11.3 $V_1 = 45$ L and $T_1 = 298$ K; $V_2 = ?$ and $T_2 = 263$ K

$V_2 = V_1(T_2/T_1) = (45\ \text{L})(263\ \text{K}/298\ \text{K}) = 40.$ L

11.4 $V_2 = V_1(P_1/P_2)(T_2/T_1)$

$= (22\ \text{L})(150\ \text{atm}/0.993\ \text{atm})(295\ \text{K}/304\ \text{K})$

$= 3200$ L

At 5.0 L per balloon, there is sufficient He to fill 640 balloons.

11.5 44.8 L of O_2 is required; 44.8 L of $H_2O(g)$ and 22.4 L $CO_2(g)$ are produced.

11.6 $PV = nRT$

$(750/760\ \text{atm})(V) =$
$(1300\ \text{mol})(0.08206\ \text{L} \cdot \text{atm/mol} \cdot \text{K})(296\ \text{K})$

$V = 3.2 \times 10^4$ L

11.7 $d = PM/RT$; $M = dRT/P$

$M = (5.02 \text{ g/L})(0.082057 \text{ L} \cdot \text{atm/mol} \cdot \text{K})$
$(288.2 \text{ K})/(745/760 \text{ atm}) = 121 \text{ g/mol}$

11.8 $PV = (m/M)RT$; $M = mRT/PV$

$M = (0.105 \text{ g})(0.082057 \text{ L} \cdot \text{atm/mol} \cdot \text{K})$
$(296.2 \text{ K})/[(561/760) \text{ atm } 0.125 \text{ L})] = 27.7 \text{ g/mol}$

11.9 $n(H_2) = PV/RT$

$= (542/760 \text{ atm})(355 \text{ L})/(0.08206 \text{ L} \cdot \text{atm/mol} \cdot \text{K})$
(298.2 K)

$n(H_2) = 10.3 \text{ mol}$

$n(NH_3) = (10.3 \text{ mol } H_2)(2 \text{ mol } NH_3/3 \text{ mol } H_2)$
$= 6.87 \text{ mol } NH_3$

$P (125 \text{ L}) = (6.87 \text{ mol})(0.082057 \text{ L} \cdot \text{atm/mol} \cdot \text{K})$
(298.2 K)

$P(NH_3) = 1.35 \text{ atm}$

11.10 $P_{\text{halothane}} (5.00 \text{ L})$
$= (0.0760 \text{ mol})(0.08206 \text{ L} \cdot \text{atm/mol} \cdot \text{K})(298.2 \text{ K})$

$P_{\text{halothane}} = 0.372 \text{ atm (or 283 mm Hg)}$

$P_{\text{oxygen}} (5.00 \text{ L})$
$= (0.734 \text{ mol})(0.08206 \text{ L} \cdot \text{atm/mol} \cdot \text{K})(298.2 \text{ K})$

$P_{\text{oxygen}} = 3.59 \text{ atm (or 2730 mm Hg)}$

$P_{\text{total}} = P_{\text{halothane}} + P_{\text{oxygen}}$
$= 283 \text{ mm Hg} + 2730 \text{ mm Hg} = 3010 \text{ mm Hg}$

11.11 For He: Use Equation 11.9, with $M = 4.00 \times 10^{-3}$ kg/mol, $T = 298$ K, and $R = 8.314$ J/mol · K to calculate the rms speed of 1360 m/s. A similar calculation for N_2, with $M = 28.01 \times 10^{-3}$ kg/mol, gives an rms speed of 515 m/s.

11.12 The molar mass of CH_4 is 16.0 g/mol.

$$\frac{\text{Rate for } CH_4}{\text{Rate for unknown}} = \frac{n \text{ molecules/1.50 min}}{n \text{ molecules/4.73 min}} = \sqrt{\frac{M_{\text{unknown}}}{16.0}}$$

$M_{\text{unknown}} = 159 \text{ g/mol}$

11.13 $P(1.00 \text{ L})$
$= (10.0 \text{ mol})(0.082057 \text{ L} \cdot \text{atm/mol} \cdot \text{K})(298 \text{ K})$

$P = 245 \text{ atm (calculated by PV} = \text{nRT)}$

$P = 320 \text{ atm (calculated by van der Waals equation)}$

Chapter 12

12.1 Because F^- is the smaller ion, water molecules can approach most closely and interact more strongly. Thus, F^- should have the more negative enthalpy of hydration.

12.2

$$H_3C-O \overset{\displaystyle /}{\underset{\displaystyle \underset{\displaystyle CH_3}{\overset{\displaystyle H-O}{\cdot\cdot\cdot}}}{}} {}^{H}$$

Hydrogen bonding in methanol entails the attract of the hydrogen atom bearing a partial positive charge (δ^+) on one molecule to the oxygen atom bearing a partial negative charge (δ^-) on a second molecule. The strong attractive force of hydrogen bonding will cause the boiling point and the entha of vaporization of methanol to be quite high.

12.3 Water is a polar solvent, while hexane and CCl_4 are nonpolar. London dispersion forces are the prima forces of attraction between all pairs of dissimilar vents. For mixtures of water with the other solvent dipole–induced dipole forces will also be importar

12.4 (a) O_2: induced dipole–induced dipole forces only
(b) CH_3OH: strong hydrogen bonding (dipole–dipole forces) as well as induced dipole–induc dipole forces.
(c) Forces between water molecules: strong hydrog bonding and induced dipole–induced dipole forces. Between N_2 and H_2O: dipole–induced d pole forces and induced dipole–induced dipol forces.

Relative strengths: a < forces between N_2 and H in c < b < forces between water molecules in c

12.5 $(1.00 \times 10^3 \text{ g})(1 \text{ mol}/32.04 \text{ g})(35.2 \text{ kJ/mol})$
$= 1.10 \times 10^3 \text{ kJ}$

12.6 (a) At 40 °C, the vapor pressure of ethanol is abou 120 mm Hg.
(b) The equilibrium vapor pressure of ethanol at 60 °C is about 320 mm Hg. At 60 °C and 600 m Hg, ethanol is a liquid. If vapor is present, it w condense to a liquid.

12.7 $PV = nRT$

$P = 0.50 \text{ g} (1 \text{ mol}/18.02 \text{ g})(0.0821 \text{ L} \cdot \text{atm/mol} \cdot$
$(333 \text{ K})/5.0 \text{ L}$

$P = 0.15 \text{ atm.}$

Convert to mm Hg: $P = (0.15 \text{ atm})(760 \text{ mm Hg}/$ 1 atm) = 120 mm Hg. The vapor pressure of water 60 °C is 149.4 mm Hg (Appendix G). The calculat pressure is lower than this, so all the water (0.50 g evaporates. If 2.0 g of water is used, the calculated pressure, 460 mm Hg, exceeds the vapor pressure. this case, only part of the water will evaporate.

12.8 Use the Clausius–Clapeyron equation, with $P_1 = 57.0$ mm Hg, $T_1 = 250.4$ K, $P_2 = 534$ mm Hg, and $T_2 = 298.2$ K.

$\ln [P_2/P_1] = \Delta_{\text{vap}}H/R [1/T_1 - 1/T_2]$
$= [\Delta_{\text{vap}}H/R][(T_2 - T_1)/T_1T_2]$

$\ln [534/57.0] = \Delta_{\text{vap}}H/(0.0083145 \text{ kJ/K} \cdot \text{mol})$
$[47.8/(250.4)(298.2)]$

$\Delta_{\text{vap}}H = 29.1 \text{ kJ/mol}$

2.9 Glycerol is predicted to have a higher viscosity than ethanol. It is a larger molecule than ethanol, and there are higher forces of attraction between molecules because each molecule has three OH groups that hydrogen-bond to other molecules.

Chapter 13

3.1 The strategy to solve this problem is given in Example 13.1.

Step 1. Mass of the unit cell

= (197.0 g/mol)(1 mol/6.022 × 10^{23} atom/mol)(4 atoms/unit cell)

= 1.309 × 10^{-21} g/unit cell

Step 2. Volume of unit cell

= (1.309 × 10^{-21} g/unit cell)(1 cm^3/19.32 g)

= 6.773 × 10^{-23} cm^3/unit cell

Step 3. Length of side of unit cell

= [6.773 × 10^{-23} cm^3/unit cell]$^{1/3}$ = 4.076 × 10^{-8} cm

Step 4. Calculate the radius from the edge dimension.

Diagonal distance = 4.076 × 10^{-8} cm (2$^{1/2}$) = 4 (r_{Au})

r_{Au} = 1.441 × 10^{-8} cm (= 144.1 pm)

3.2 To verify a body centered cubic structure, calculate the mass contained in the unit cell. If the structure is bcc, then the mass will be the mass of 2 Fe atoms. (Other possibilities: fcc − mass of 4 Fe; primitive cubic − mass of 1 Fe atom). This calculation uses the four steps from the previous exercise in reverse order.

Step 1. Use radius of Fe to calculate cell dimensions. In a body-centered cube, atoms touch across the diagonal of the cube.

Diagonal distance = side dimension ($\sqrt{3}$) = 4 r_{Fe}

Side dimension of cube = 4 (1.26 × 10^{-8} cm)/($\sqrt{3}$) = 2.910 × 10^{-8} cm

Step 2. Calculate unit cell volume

Unit cell volume = (2.910 × 10^{-8} cm)^3 = 2.464 × 10^{-23} cm^3

Step 3. Combine unit cell volume and density to find the mass of the unit cell.

Mass of unit cell = 2.464 × 10^{-23} cm^3 (7.8740 g/cm^3) = 1.940 × 10^{-22} g

Step 4. Calculate the mass of 2 Fe atoms, and compare this to the answer from step 3.

Mass of 2 Fe atoms

= 55.85 g/mol (1 mol/6.022 × 10^{23} atoms)(2 atoms)

= 1.85 × 10^{-22} g).

This is a fairly good match, and clearly much better than the two other possibilities, primitive and fcc.

13.3 M$_2$X; In a face-centered cubic unit cell, there are four anions and eight tetrahedral holes in which to place metal ions. All of the tetrahedral holes are inside the unit cell, so the ratio of atoms in the unit cell is 2 : 1.

13.4 We need to calculate the mass and volume of the unit cell from the information given. The density of KCl will then be mass/volume. Select units so the density is calculated as g/cm^3

Step 1. Mass: the unit cell contains 4 K$^+$ ions and 4 Cl$^-$ ions

Unit cell mass = (39.10 g/mol)(1 mol/6.022 × 10^{23} K$^+$ ions)(4 K$^+$ ions) + (35.45 g/mol)(1 mol/6.022 × 10^{23} Cl$^-$ ions)(4 Cl$^-$ ions)

= 2.355 × 10^{-22} g + 2.597 × 10^{-22} g = 4.952 × 10^{-22} g

Step 2. Volume: assuming K$^+$ and Cl$^-$ ions touch along one edge of the cube, the side dimension = 2 r_{K^+} + 2 r_{Cl^-}. The volume of the cube is the cube of this value. (Convert the ionic radius from pm to cm.)

V = [2(1.33 × 10^{-8} cm) + 2(1.81 × 10^{-8} cm)]^3 = 2.477 × 10^{-22} cm^3

Step 3: density = mass/volume = 4.952 × 10^{-22} g/2.477 × 10^{-22} cm^3) = 2.00 g/cm^3

13.5 Use the Born–Haber cycle equation shown on pages 600–602. The unknown in this problem is the enthalpy of formation of NaI(s).

$\Delta_f H°$ [NaI(s)] = $\Delta H_{Step\ 1a}$ + $\Delta H_{Step\ 1b}$ + $\Delta H_{Step\ 2a}$ + $\Delta H_{Step\ 2b}$ + $\Delta_{lattice} H$

Step 1a. Enthalpy of formation of I(g)
= +106.8 kJ/mol (Appendix L)

Step 1b. ΔH for I(g) + e$^-$ → I$^-$(g) = −295 kJ/mol (Appendix F)

Step 2a. Enthalpy of formation of Na(g)
= +107.3 kJ/mol (Appendix L)

Step 2b. ΔH for Na(g) → Na$^+$(g) + e$^-$
= +496 kJ/mol (Appendix F)

Step 3 = $\Delta_{lattice} H$ = −702 kJ/mol (Table 13.2)

$\Delta_f H°$ [NaI(s)] = −287 kJ/mol

Chapter 14

14.1 (a) 10.0 g sucrose = 0.0292 mol;
250 g H$_2$O = 13.9 mol

$X_{sucrose}$ = (0.0292 mol)/(0.0292 mol + 13.9 mol) = 0.00210

$c_{sucrose}$ = (0.0292 mol sucrose)/(0.250 kg solvent) = 0.117 m

Weight % sucrose = (10.0 g sucrose/260 g soln)(100%) = 3.85%

(b) 1.08×10^4 ppm = 1.08×10^4 mg NaCl per 1000 g soln

$\quad$ = $(1.08 \times 10^4$ mg Na/1000 g soln$)$

$\qquad\qquad\qquad\qquad$ (1050 g soln/1 L)

$\quad$ = 1.13×10^4 mg Na/L

$\quad$ = 11.3 g Na/L

$\quad$ (11.3 g Na/L)(58.44 g NaCl/23.0 g Na) = 28.7 g NaCl/L

14.2 $\Delta_{soln}H° = \Delta_f H°$ [NaOH(aq)] $- \Delta_f H°$ [NaOH(s)]

$\quad$ = -469.2 kJ/mol $- (-425.9$ kJ/mol$)$

$\quad$ = -43.3 kJ/mol

14.3 Solubility of $CO_2 = k_H P_g = 0.034$ mol/kg $\cdot$ bar $\times$ 0.33 bar = 1.1×10^{-2} M

14.4 The solution contains sucrose [(10.0 g)(1 mol/342.3 g) = 0.0292 mol] in water [(225 g)(1 mol/18.02 g) = 12.5 mol].

$\quad X_{water} = (12.5$ mol $H_2O)/(12.5$ mol $+ 0.0292$ mol$)$

$\quad$ = 0.998

$\quad P_{water} = x_{water} P°_{water} = 0.998(149.4$ mm Hg$)$

$\quad$ = 149 mm Hg

14.5 $c_{glycol} = \Delta T_{bp}/K_{bp} = 1.0$ °C/(0.512 °C/m) = 1.95 m = 1.95 mol/kg

$\quad$ mass$_{glycol}$ = (1.95 mol/kg)(0.125 kg)(62.02 g/mol)

$\quad$ = 15 g

14.6 c_{glycol} = (525 g)(1 mol/62.07 g)/(3.00 kg) = 2.82 m

$\quad \Delta T_{fp} = K_{fp} \times m = (-1.86$ °C/m)(2.82 m) = -5.24 °C

$\quad$ You will be protected only to about -5 °C and not to -25 °C.

14.7 c (mol/L) = Π/RT = [(1.86 mm Hg)(1 atm/760 mm Hg)]/[(0.08206 L $\cdot$ atm/mol $\cdot$ K)(298 K)]

$\quad$ = 1.00×10^{-4} M

$\quad$ (1.00×10^{-4} mol/L)(0.100 L) = 1.0×10^{-5} mol

$\quad$ Molar mass = 1.40 g/1.00×10^{-5} mol

$\quad$ = 1.4×10^5 g/mol

$\quad$ (Assuming the polymer is composed of CH_2 units, the polymer is about 10,000 units long.)

14.8 c_{NaCl} = (25.0 g NaCl)(1 mol/58.44 g)/(0.525 kg)

$\quad$ = 0.815 m

$\quad \Delta T_{fp} = K_{fp} \times m \times i = (-1.86$ °C/m)(0.815 m)(1.85)

$\quad$ = -2.80 °C

Chapter 15

15.1 $-\frac{1}{2} (\Delta[NOCl]/\Delta t) = \frac{1}{2}(\Delta[NO]/\Delta t) = \Delta[Cl_2]/\Delta t$

15.2 For the first two hours:

$\quad -\Delta[\text{sucrose}]/\Delta t$ = [(0.033 $-$ 0.050) mol/L]/(2.0 h

$\qquad\qquad$ = 0.0080 mol/L $\cdot$ h

$\quad$ For the last two hours:

$\quad \Delta[\text{sucrose}]/\Delta t$ = $-[(0.010 - 0.015)$ mol/L]/(2.0 h

$\qquad\qquad$ = 0.0025 mol/L $\cdot$ h

$\quad$ Instantaneous rate at 4 h = 0.0045 mol/L $\cdot$ h. (Calculated from the slope of a line tangent to the curve at the defined concentration.)

15.3 Compare experiments 1 and 2: Doubling $[O_2]$ cause the rate to double, so the rate is first order in $[O_2]$. Compare experiments 2 and 4: Doubling [NO] causes the rate to increase by a factor of 4, so the rate is second order in [NO]. Thus, the rate law is

$\quad$ Rate = $k[NO]^2[O_2]$

$\quad$ Using the data in experiment 1 to determine k:

$\quad$ 0.028 mol/L $\cdot$ s = $k[0.020$ mol/L$]^2[0.010$ mol/L$]$

$\quad k = 7.0 \times 10^3$ L^2/mol^2 $\cdot$ s

15.4 Rate = $k[Pt(NH_3)_2Cl_2]$ = (0.27 h^{-1})(0.020 mol/L)

$\qquad$ = 0.0054 mol/L $\cdot$ h

15.5 ln ([sucrose]/[sucrose]$_o$) = $-kt$

$\quad$ ln ([sucrose]/[0.010]) = $-(0.21$ h^{-1})(5.0 h)

$\quad$ [sucrose] = 0.0035 mol/L

15.6 (a) The fraction remaining is $[CH_3N_2CH_3]/[CH_3N_2CH_3]_o$.

$\quad$ ln ($[CH_3N_2CH_3]/[CH_3N_2CH_3]_o$)

$\qquad\qquad$ = $-(3.6 \times 10^{-4}$ s^{-1})(150

$\quad [CH_3N_2CH_3]/[CH_3N_2CH_3]_o$= 0.95

$\quad$ (b) After the reaction is 99% complete $[CH_3N_2CH_3]/[CH_3N_2CH_3]_o$ = 0.010.

$\quad$ ln (0.010) = $-(3.6 \times 10^{-4}$ s^{-1})(t)

$\quad t = 1.3 \times 10^4$ s (220 min)

15.7 $1/[HI] - 1/[HI]_o = kt$

$\quad 1/[HI] - 1/[0.010$ M] = (30. L/mol $\cdot$ min)(12 min

$\quad$ [HI] = 0.0022 M

Concentration versus time

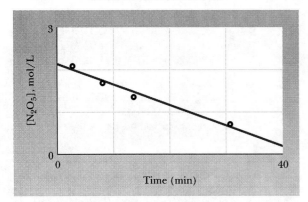

ln [N₂O₅] versus time

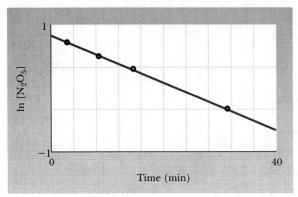

1/[N₂O₅] versus time

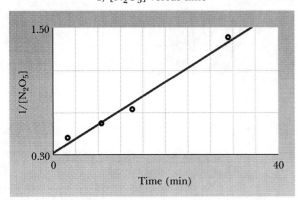

The plot of ln [N₂O₅] versus time has the best linear fit, indicating that this is a first-order reaction. The rate constant is determined from the slope:
$k = -\text{slope} = 0.038 \text{ min}^{-1}$.

.9 (a) For ^{241}Am, $t_{1/2} = 0.693/k = 0.693/(0.0016 \text{ y}^{-1})$
$= 430 \text{ y}$

For ^{125}I, $t_{1/2} = 0.693/(0.011 \text{ d}^{-1}) = 63 \text{ d}$

(b) ^{125}I decays much faster.

(c) $\ln [(n)/(1.6 \times 10^{15} \text{ atoms})] = -(0.011 \text{ d}^{-1})(2.0 \text{ d})$

$n/1.6 \times 10^{15} \text{ atoms} = 0.978; \ n = 1.57 \times 10^{15} \text{ atoms}$

Since the answer should have two significant figures, we should round this off to 1.6×10^{15} atoms. The approximately 2% that has decayed is not discernable within the limits of accuracy of the data presented.

15.10 $\ln (k_2/k_1) = (-E_a/R)(1/T_2 - 1/T_1)$

$\ln [(1.00 \times 10^4)/(4.5 \times 10^3)] = -(E_a/8.315 \times 10^{-3} \text{ kJ/mol} \cdot \text{K})(1/283 \text{ K} - 1/274 \text{ K})$

$E_a = 57 \text{ kJ/mol}$

15.11 All three steps are bimolecular.

For step 3: Rate $= k[\text{N}_2\text{O}][\text{H}_2]$.

There are two intermediates, $\text{N}_2\text{O}_2(g)$ and $\text{N}_2\text{O}(g)$.

When the three equations are added, N_2O_2 (a product in the first step and a reactant in the second step) and N_2O (a product in the second step and a reactant in the third step) cancel, leaving the net equation: $2 \text{ NO}(g) + 2 \text{ H}_2(g) \longrightarrow \text{N}_2(g) + 2 \text{ H}_2\text{O}(g)$.

15.12 (a) $2 \text{ NH}_3(aq) + \text{OCl}^-(aq) \longrightarrow \text{N}_2\text{H}_4(aq) + \text{Cl}^-(aq) + \text{H}_2\text{O}(\ell)$

(b) The second step is the rate-determining step.

(c) Rate $= k[\text{NH}_2\text{Cl}][\text{NH}_3]$

(d) NH_2Cl, N_2H_5^+, and OH^- are intermediates.

15.13 Overall reaction: $2 \text{ NO}_2\text{Cl}(g) \longrightarrow 2 \text{ NO}_2(g) + \text{Cl}_2(g)$

Rate $= k'[\text{NO}_2\text{Cl}]^2/[\text{NO}_2]$ (where $k' = k_1 k_2/k_1$)

Increasing $[\text{NO}_2]$ causes the reaction rate to decrease.

Chapter 16

16.1 (a) $K = [\text{CO}]^2/[\text{CO}_2]$
(b) $K = [\text{Cu}^{2+}][\text{NH}_3]^4/[\text{Cu}(\text{NH}_3)_4^{2+}]$
(c) $K = [\text{H}_3\text{O}^+][\text{CH}_3\text{CO}_2^-]/[\text{CH}_3\text{CO}_2\text{H}]$

16.2 (a) Both reactions are reactant-favored ($K < 1$).
(b) $[\text{NH}_3]$ in the second solution is greater. K for this reaction is larger, so the reactant, $\text{Cd}(\text{NH}_3)_4^{2+}$, dissociates to a greater extent.

16.3 (a) $Q = [2.18]/[0.97] = 2.3$. The system is not at equilibrium; $Q < K$. To reach equilibrium, [isobutane] will increase and [butane] will decrease.
(b) $Q = [2.60]/[0.75] = 3.5$. The system is not at equilibrium; $Q > K$. To reach equilibrium, [butane] will increase and [isobutane] will decrease.

16.4 $Q = [NO]^2/[N_2][O_2] = [4.2 \times 10^{-3}]^2/[0.50][0.25]$
$= 1.4 \times 10^{-4}$

$Q < K$, so the reaction is not at equilibrium. To reach equilibrium, [NO] will increase and [N_2] and [O_2] will decrease.

16.5 (a)

Equation	$C_6H_{10}I_2 \rightleftharpoons$	C_6H_{10} +	I_2
Initial (M)	0.050	0	0
Change (M)	−0.035	+0.035	+0.035
Equilibrium (M)	0.015	0.035	0.035

(b) $K = (0.035)(0.035)/(0.015) = 0.082$

16.6

Equation	H_2 +	I_2	$\rightleftharpoons$	2 HI
Initial (M)	6.00×10^{-3}	6.00×10^{-3}		0
Change (M)	$-x$	$-x$		$+2x$
Equilibrium (M)	$0.00600 - x$	$0.00600 - x$		$+2x$

$$K_c = 33 = \frac{(2x)^2}{(0.00600 - x)^2}$$

$x = 0.0045$ M, so [H_2] = [I_2] = 0.0015 M and [HI] = 0.0090 M.

16.7

Equation	$C(s) + CO_2\ (g)$	$\rightleftharpoons$	2 CO(g)
Initial (M)	0.012		0
Change (M)	$-x$		$+2x$
Equilibrium (M)	$0.012 - x$		$2x$

$$K_c = 0.021 = \frac{(2x)^2}{(0.012 - x)}$$

$x = [CO_2] = 0.0057$ M and $2x = [CO] = 0.011$ M

16.8 (a) $K' = K^2 = (2.5 \times 10^{-29})^2 = 6.3 \times 10^{-58}$
(b) $K'' = 1/K^2 = 1/(6.3 \times 10^{-58}) = 1.6 \times 10^{57}$

16.9 Manipulate the equations and equilibrium constants as follows:

$\frac{1}{2} H_2(g) + \frac{1}{2} Br_2(g) \rightleftharpoons HBr(g)$
$\qquad\qquad K_1' = (K_1)^{1/2} = 8.9 \times 10^5$

$H(g) \rightleftharpoons \frac{1}{2} H_2(g) \quad K_2' = 1/(K_2)^{1/2} = 1.4 \times 10^{20}$

$Br(g) \rightleftharpoons \frac{1}{2} Br_2(g) \quad K_3' = 1/(K_3)^{1/2} = 2.1 \times 10^7$

Net: $H(g) + Br(g) \rightleftharpoons HBr(g$
$\qquad\qquad K_{net} = K_1' K_2' K_3' = 2.6 \times 10^{33}$

16.10

Equation	butane	$\rightleftharpoons$	isobutane
Initial (M)	0.20		0.50
After adding 2.0 M more isobutene	0.20		2.0 + 0.50
Change (M)	$+x$		$-x$
Equilibrium (M)	$0.20 + x$		$2.50 - x$

$$K = \frac{[isobutane]}{[butane]} = \frac{(2.50 - x)}{(0.20 + x)} = 2.50$$

Solving for x gives $x = 0.57$ M. Therefore, [isobutene] = 2.50 − 0.55 = 1.93 M and [butane] = 0.20 + 0.57 = 0.77 M.

16.11 (a) Adding H_2 shifts the equilibrium to the right, increasing [NH_3]. Adding NH_3 shifts the equilibrium to the left, increasing [N_2] and [H_2].
(b) An increase in volume shifts the equilibrium to the left.

16.12 With an increase in temperature, the value of K will become larger. To adjust and attain equilibrium, [NOCl] will decrease.

Chapter 17

17.1 (a) $H_3PO_4(aq) + H_2O(\ell) \rightleftharpoons$
$\qquad\qquad H_3O^+(aq) + H_2PO_4^-(a$

$H_2PO_4^-$ can either donate or accept a proton; therefore, it is amphiprotic.

(b) $CN^-(aq) + H_2O(\ell) \rightleftharpoons HCN(aq) + OH^-(a$

CN^- is a Brønsted base; it is capable of accepting a proton.

17.2 NO_3^- is the conjugate base of the acid HNO_3; NH_4 is the conjugate acid of the base NH_3.

17.3 $[H_3O^+] = 4.0 \times 10^{-3}$ M; $[OH^-] = K_w/[H_3O^+]$
$= 2.5 \times 10^{-12}$ M

17.4 (a) $pOH = -\log [0.0012] = 2.92$; $pH = 14.00 - pO$
$= 11.08$
(b) $[H_3O^+] = 4.8 \times 10^{-5}$ mol/L; $[OH^-] = 2.1 \times 10^{-10}$ mol/L
(c) $pOH = 14.00 - 10.46 = 3.54$; $[OH^-] = 2.9 \times 10^{-4}$ mol/L. The solubility of $Sr(OH)_2$ is half of this value (because 1 mol $Sr(OH)_2$ gives two mo OH$^-$ when dissolved), or 1.4×10^{-4} mol/L.

17.5 Answer this question by comparing values of K_a and K_b from Table 17.3.
(a) H_2SO_4 is stronger than H_2SO_3.
(b) $C_6H_5CO_2H$ is a stronger acid than CH_3CO_2H.
(c) The conjugate base of boric acid, $B(OH)_4^-$, is a stronger base than the conjugate base of acetic acid, $CH_3CO_2^-$.
(d) Ammonia is a stronger base than acetate ion.
(e) The conjugate acid of acetate ion, CH_3CO_2H, is stronger acid than the conjugate acid of ammonia, NH_4^+.

17.6 (a) $pH = 7$
(b) $pH < 7$ (NH_4^+ is an acid)
(c) $pH < 7$ [$Al(H_2O)_6$]$^{3+}$ is an acid
(d) $pH > 7$ (HPO_4^{2-} is a stronger base than it is an acid)

7.7 (a) $pK_a = -\log [6.3 \times 10^{-5}] = 4.20$
(b) $ClCH_2CO_2H$ is stronger (the pK_a of 2.87 is less than a pK_a of 4.20)
(c) pK_a for NH_4^+, the conjugate acid of NH_3, is $-\log [5.6 \times 10^{-10}] = 9.26$. It is a weaker acid than acetic acid, for which $K_a = 1.8 \times 10^{-5}$.

7.8 K_b for the lactate ion $= K_w/K_a = 7.1 \times 10^{-11}$. It is a slightly stronger base than the formate, nitrite, and fluoride ions, and a weaker base than the benzoate ion.

7.9 (a) NH_4^+ is a stronger acid than HCO_3^-. CO_3^{2-}, the conjugate base of HCO_3^-, is a stronger base than NH_3, the conjugate base of NH_4^+.
(b) Reactant-favored; the reactants are the weaker acid and base.
(c) Reactant-favored; the reactants are the weaker acid and base.

7.10 (a) The two compounds react and form a solution containing HCN and NaCl. The solution is acidic (HCN is an acid).
(b) $CH_3CO_2H(aq) + SO_3^{2-}(aq) \rightleftharpoons$
$\qquad\qquad HSO_3^-(aq) + CH_3CO_2^-(aq)$
The solution is acidic, because HSO_3^- is a stronger acid than $CH_3CO_2^-$ is a base.

7.11 From the pH, we can calculate $[H_3O^+] = 1.9 \times 10^{-3}$ M. Also, $[butanoate^-] = [H_3O^+] = 1.9 \times 10^{-3}$ M. Use these values along with [butanoic acid] to calculate K_a.
$K_a = [1.9 \times 10^{-3}] [1.9 \times 10^{-3}]/(0.055 - 1.9 \times 10^{-3})$
$= 6.8 \times 10^{-5}$

7.12 $K_a = 1.8 \times 10^{-5} = [x][x]/(0.10 - x)$
$x = [H_3O^+] = [CH_3CO_2^-] = 1.3 \times 10^{-3}$ M;
$[CH_3CO_2H] = 0.099$ M; $pH = 2.89$

7.13 $K_a = 7.2 \times 10^{-4} = [x][x]/(0.015 - x)$
The x in the denominator cannot be dropped. This equation must be solved with the quadratic formula or by successive approximations.
$x = [H_3O^+] = [F^-] = 2.9 \times 10^{-3}$ M
$[HF] = 0.015 - 2.9 \times 10^{-3} = 0.012$ M
$pH = 2.54$

7.14 $OCl^-(aq) + H_2O(\ell) \rightleftharpoons HOCl(aq) + OH^-(aq)$
$K_b = 2.9 \times 10^{-7} = [x][x]/(0.015 - x)$
$x = [OH^-] = [HOCl] = 6.6 \times 10^{-5}$ M
$pOH = 4.18$; $pH = 9.82$

7.15 Equivalent amounts of acid and base react to form water, $CH_3CO_2^-$ and Na^+. Acetate ion hydrolyzes to a small extent, giving CH_3CO_2H and OH^-. We need to determine $[CH_3CO_2^-]$ and then solve a weak base equilibrium problem to determine $[OH^-]$.
Amount $CH_3CO_2^-$ = mol base = 0.12 mol/L × 0.015 L

$= 1.8 \times 10^{-3}$ mol
Total volume = 0.030 L, so $[CH_3CO_2^-] =$
$(1.8 \times 10^{-3}$ mol$)/0.030$ L $= 0.060$ M
$CH_3CO_2^-(aq) + H_2O(\ell) \rightleftharpoons$
$\qquad\qquad CH_3CO_2H(aq) + OH^-(aq)$
$K_b = 5.6 \times 10^{-10} = [x][x]/(0.060 - x)$
$x = [OH^-] = [CH_3CO_2H] = 5.8 \times 10^{-6}$ M
$pOH = 5.24$; $pH = 8.76$

17.16 $H_2C_2O_4(aq) + H_2O(\ell) \rightleftharpoons$
$\qquad\qquad H_3O^+(aq) + HC_2O_4^-(aq)$
$K_{a1} = 5.9 \times 10^{-2} = [x][x]/(0.10 - x)$
The x in the denominator cannot be dropped. This equation must be solved with the quadratic formula or by successive approximations.
$x = [H_3O^+] = [HC_2O_4^-] = 5.3 \times 10^{-2}$ M
$pH = 1.28$
$K_{b2} = [H_3O^+][C_2O_4^{2-}]/[HC_2O_4^-]$; because
$[H_3O^+] = [HC_2O_4^-]$
$[C_2O_4^{2-}] = K_{a2} = 6.4 \times 10^{-5}$ M

17.17 (a) Lewis base (electron-pair donor)
(b) Lewis acid (electron-pair acceptor)
(c) Lewis base (electron-pair donor)
(d) Lewis base (electron-pair donor)

17.18 (a) H_2SeO_4
(b) $Fe(H_2O)_6^{3+}$
(c) HOCl
(d) Amphetamine is a primary amine and a (weak) base. It is both a Brønsted base and a Lewis base.

Chapter 18

18.1 pH of 0.30 M HCO_2H:
$K_a = [H_3O^+][HCO_2^-]/[HCO_2H]$
$1.8 \times 10^{-4} = [x][x]/[0.30 - x]$
$x = 7.3 \times 10^{-3}$ M; $pH = 2.14$
pH of 0.30 M formic acid + 0.10 M $NaHCO_2$
$K_a = [H_3O^+][HCO_2^-]/[HCO_2H]$
$1.8 \times 10^{-4} = [x][0.10 + x]/(0.30 - x)$
$x = 5.4 \times 10^{-4}$ M; $pH = 3.27$

18.2 NaOH: (0.100 mol/L)(0.0300 L) $= 3.00 \times 10^{-3}$ mol
CH_3CO_2H: (0.100 mol/L)(0.0450 L) $=$
4.50×10^{-3} mol
3.00×10^{-3} mol NaOH reacts with 3.00×10^{-3} mol CH_3CO_2H, forming 3.00×10^{-3} mol $CH_3CO_2^-$; 1.50×10^{-3} mol unreacted CH_3CO_2H remains in solution. The total volume is 75.0 mL. Use these values to calculate $[CH_3CO_2H]$ and $[CH_3CO_2^-]$, and use these concentrations in a weak acid equilibrium calculation to obtain $[H_3O^+]$ and pH.

$[CH_3CO_2H] = 1.5 \times 10^{-3}$ mol/0.075 L = 0.0200 M
$[CH_3CO_2^-] = 3.0 \times 10^{-3}$ mol/0.075 L = 0.0400 M
$K_a = [H_3O^+][CH_3CO_2^-]/[CH_3CO_2H]$
$1.8 \times 10^{-5} = [x][0.0400 + x]/(0.0200 - x)$
$x = [H_3O^+] = 9.0 \times 10^{-6}$ M; pH = 5.05

18.3 pH = pK_a + log {[base]/[acid]}
pH = $-\log (1.8 \times 10^{-4})$ + log {[0.70]/[0.50]}
pH = 3.74 + 0.15 = 3.89

18.4 (15.0 g $NaHCO_3$)(1 mol/84.01 g) = 0.179 mol
$NaHCO_3$, and (18.0 g Na_2CO_3)(1 mol/106.0 g)
= 0.170 mol Na_2CO_3
pH = pK_a + log {[base]/[acid]}
pH = $-\log (4.8 \times 10^{-11})$ + log {[0.170]/[0.179]}
pH = 10.32 − 0.02 = 10.30

18.5 pH = pK_a + log {[base]/[acid]}
5.00 = $-\log (1.8 \times 10^{-5})$ + log {[base]/[acid]}
5.00 = 4.74 + log {[base]/[acid]}
[base]/[acid] = 1.8

To prepare this buffer solution, the ratio [base]/[acid] must equal 1.8. For example, you can dissolve 1.8 mol (148 g) of $NaCH_3CO_2$ and 1.0 mol (60.05 g) of CH_3CO_2H in enough water to make 1.0 L of solution.

18.6 Initial pH (before adding acid):
pH = pK_a + log {[base]/[acid]}
   = $-\log (1.8 \times 10^{-4})$ + log {[0.70]/[0.50]}
   = 3.74 + 0.15 = 3.89

After adding acid, the added HCl will react with the weak base (formate ion) and form more formic acid. The net effect is to change the ratio of [base]/[acid] in the buffer solution.

Initial amount HCO_2H = 0.50 mol/L × 0.500 L = 0.250 mol

Initial amount HCO_2^- = 0.70 mol/L × 0.50 L = 0.350 mol

Amount HCl added = 1.0 mol/L × 0.010 L = 0.010 mol

Amount HCO_2H after HCl addition = 0.250 mol + 0.010 mol = 0.26 mol

Initial amount HCO_2^- after HCl addition = 0.350 mol − 0.010 mol = 0.34 mol

pH = pK_a + log {[base]/[acid]}
pH = $-\log (1.8 \times 10^{-4})$ + log {[0.340]/[0.260]}
pH = 3.74 + 0.12 = 3.86

18.7 After addition of 25.0 mL base, half of the acid has been neutralized.

Initial amount HCl = 0.100 mol/L × 0.0500 L = 0.00500 mol

Amount NaOH added = 0.100 mol/L × 0.0250 L = 0.00250 mol

Amount HCl after reaction: 0.00500 − 0.00250 = 0.00250 mol HCl

[HCl] after reaction = 0.00250 mol/0.0750 L = 0.0333 M

This is a strong acid and completely ionized, so $[H_3O^+]$ = 0.0333 M and pH = 1.48.

After 50.50 mL base is added, a small excess of base is present in the 100.5 mL (0.1005 L) of solution. (Volume of excess base added is 0.50 mL = 5.0 × 10^{-4} L.)

Amount excess base = 0.100 mol/L × 5.0 × 10^{-4} L 5.0 × 10^{-5} mol

$[OH^-]$ = 5.0 × 10^{-5} mol/0.1005 L = 4.9 × 10^{-4} M
pOH = $-\log (4.9 \times 10^{-4})$ = 3.31; pH = 14.00 − pOH = 10.69

18.8 35.0 mL base will partially neutralize the acid.
Initial amount CH_3CO_2H = (0.100 mol/L)(0.1000 L) = 0.0100 mol

Amount NaOH added = (0.10 mol/L)(0.035 L) = 0.0035 mol

Amount CH_3CO_2H after reaction = 0.0100 − 0.0035 = 0.0065 mol

Amount $CH_3CO_2^-$ after reaction = 0.0035 mol
$[CH_3CO_2H]$ after reaction = 0.0065 mol/0.135 L = 0.0481 M
$[CH_3CO_2^-]$ after reaction = 0.00350 mol/0.135 L = 0.0259 M
$K_a = [H_3O^+][CH_3CO_2^-]/[CH_3CO_2H]$
$1.8 \times 10^{-5} = [x][0.0259 + x]/[0.0481 - x]$
$x = [H_3O^+] = 3.34 \times 10^{-5}$ M; pH = 4.48

18.9 75.0 mL acid will partially neutralize the base.
Initial amount NH_3 = (0.100 mol/L)(0.1000 L) = 0.0100 mol

Amount HCl added = (0.100 mol/L)(0.0750 L) = 0.00750 mol

Amount NH_3 after reaction = 0.0100 − 0.00750 = 0.0025 mol

Amount NH_4^+ after reaction = 0.00750 mol

Solve using the Henderson–Hasselbach equation; use K_a for the weak acid NH_4^+:
pH = pK_a + log {[base]/[acid]}
pH = $-\log (5.6 \times 10^{-10})$ + log {[0.0025]/[0.00750]}
pH = 9.25 − 0.48 = 8.77

18.10 An indicator that changes color near the pH at the equivalence point is required. Possible indicators include methyl red, bromcresol green, and Eriochrom black T; all change color in the pH range of 5–6.

18.11 (a) $AgI(s) \rightleftharpoons Ag^+(aq) + I^-(aq)$

$K_{sp} = [Ag^+][I^-]$; $K_{sp} = 8.5 \times 10^{-17}$

(b) $BaF_2(s) \rightleftharpoons Ba^{2+}(aq) + 2 F^-(aq)$

$K_{sp} = [Ba^{2+}][F^-]^2$; $K_{sp} = 1.8 \times 10^{-7}$

(c) $Ag_2CO_3(s) \rightleftharpoons 2 Ag^+(aq) + CO_3^{2-}(aq)$

$K_{sp} = [Ag^+]^2[CO_3^{2-}]$; $K_{sp} = 8.5 \times 10^{-12}$

18.12 $[Ba^{2+}] = 3.6 \times 10^{-3}$ M; $[F^-] = 7.2 \times 10^{-3}$ M

$K_{sp} = [Ba^{2+}][F^-]^2$

$K_{sp} = [3.6 \times 10^{-3}][7.2 \times 10^{-3}]^2 = 1.9 \times 10^{-7}$

18.13 $Ca(OH)_2(s) \rightleftharpoons Ca^{2+}(aq) + 2 OH^-(aq)$

$K_{sp} = [Ca^{2+}][OH^-]^2$; $K_{sp} = 5.5 \times 10^{-5}$

$5.5 \times 10^{-5} = [x][2x]^2$ (where x = solubility in mol/L)

$x = 2.4 \times 10^{-2}$ mol/L

Solubility in g/L = $(2.4 \times 10^{-2}$ mol/L)

$(74.1$ g/mol$) = 1.8$ g/L

18.14 (a) AgCl

(b) $Ca(OH)_2$

(c) Because these compounds have different stoichiometries, the most soluble cannot be identified without doing a calculation. The solubility of $Ca(OH)_2$ is 2.4×10^{-2} M (from Exercise 18.13); $Ca(OH)_2$ is more soluble than $CaSO_4$, whose solubility is 7.0×10^{-3} M $\{K_{sp} = [Ca^{2+}][SO_4^{2-}]; 4.9 \times 10^{-5} = [x][x]; x = 7.0 \times 10^{-3}$ M$\}$.

18.15 (a) In pure water:

$K_{sp} = [Ba^{2+}][SO_4^{2-}]$; $1.1 \times 10^{-10} = [x][x]$;

$x = 1.0 \times 10^{-5}$ mol/L

(b) In 0.010 M $Ba(NO_3)_2$, which furnishes 0.010 M Ba^{2+} in solution:

$K_{sp} = [Ba^{2+}][SO_4^{2-}]$; $1.1 \times 10^{-10} =$
$[0.010 + x][x]$; $x = 1.1 \times 10^{-8}$ mol/L

18.16 (a) In pure water:

$K_{sp} = [Zn^{2+}][CN^-]^2$; $8.0 \times 10^{-12} = [x][2x]^2 = 4x^3$

Solubility = $x = 1.3 \times 10^{-4}$ mol/L

(b) In 0.10 M $Zn(NO_3)_2$, which furnishes 0.10 M Zn^{2+} in solution:

$K_{sp} = [Zn^{2+}][CN^-]^2$; $8.0 \times 10^{-12} = [0.10 + x][2x]^2$

Solubility = $x = 4.5 \times 10^{-6}$ mol/L

18.17 When $[Pb^{2+}] = 1.1 \times 10^{-3}$ M, $[I^-] = 2.2 \times 10^{-3}$ M.

$Q = [Pb^{2+}][I^-]^2 = [1.1 \times 10^{-3}][2.2 \times 10^{-3}]^2 =$
5.3×10^{-9}

This value is less than K_{sp}, which means that the system has not yet reached equilibrium and more PbI_2 will dissolve.

18.18 $Q = [Sr^{2+}][SO_4^{2-}] = [2.5 \times 10^{-4}][2.5 \times 10^{-4}] =$
6.3×10^{-8}

This value is less than K_{sp}, which means that the system has not yet reached equilibrium. Precipitation will not occur.

18.19 $K_{sp} = [Pb^{2+}][I^-]^2$. Let x be the concentration of I^- required at equilibrium.

$9.8 \times 10^{-9} = [0.050][x]^2$

$x = [I^-] = 4.4 \times 10^{-5}$ mol/L. A concentration greater than this value will result in precipitation of PbI_2.

Let x be the concentration of Pb^{2+} in solution, in equilibrium with 0.0015 M I^-.

$9.8 \times 10^{-9} = [x][1.5 \times 10^{-3}]^2$

$x = [Pb^{2+}] = 4.4 \times 10^{-3}$ M

18.20 First, determine the concentrations of Ag^+ and Cl^-; then calculate Q, and see whether it is greater than or less than K_{sp}. Concentrations are calculated using the final volume, 105 mL, in the equation $C_{dil} \times V_{dil} = C_{conc} \times V_{conc}$.

$[Ag^+](0.105$ L$) = (0.0010$ mol/L$)(0.100$ L$)$

$[Ag^+] = 9.5 \times 10^{-4}$ M

$[Cl^-](0.105$ L$) = (0.025$ M$)(0.005$ L$)$

$[Cl^-] = 1.2 \times 10^{-3}$ M

$Q = [Ag^+][Cl^-] = [9.5 \times 10^{-4}][1.2 \times 10^{-3}] = 1.1 \times 10^{-6}$

Because $Q > K_{sp}$, precipitation occurs.

18.21 The logic for the solution of this exercise is outlined in Example 8.16.

Equation	$Ag(NH_3)_2^+ \rightleftharpoons$	$Ag^+ +$	$2 NH_3$
Initial (M)	0.005		$1.0 - 2(0.005)$
Change	$-x$	$+x$	$+2x$
Equilibrium (M)	$0.005 - x$	x	0.99

$K = 1/K_f = 1/1.1 \times 10^7 = [x][0.99]^2/0.005$

$x = [Ag^+] = 4.6 \times 10^{-10}$ mol/L

18.22 $Cu(OH)_2(s) \rightleftharpoons Cu^{2+}(aq) + 2 OH^-(aq)$

$K_{sp} = [Cu^{2+}][OH^-]^2$

$Cu^{2+}(aq) + 4 NH_3(aq) \rightleftharpoons Cu(NH_3)_4^{2+}(aq)$

$K_{form} = [Cu(NH_3)_4^{2+}]/[Cu^{2+}][NH_3]^4$

Net: $Cu(OH)_2(s) + 4 NH_3(aq) \rightleftharpoons$
$Cu(NH_3)_4^{2+}(aq) + 2 OH^-(aq)$

$K_{net} = K_{sp} \times K_{form} = (2.2 \times 10^{-20})(6.8 \times 10^{12}) = 1.5 \times 10^{-7}$

Chapter 19

19.1 (a) O_3; larger molecules generally have higher entropies than smaller molecules.

(b) $SnCl_4(g)$; gases have higher entropies than liquids.

19.2 (a) $\Delta_r S° = \Sigma S°(\text{products}) - \Sigma S°(\text{reactants})$

$\Delta_r S° = S°[NH_4Cl(aq)]) - S°[NH_4Cl(s)]$

$\Delta_rS° = (1 \text{ mol/mol-rxn})(169.9 \text{ J/mol} \cdot \text{K})$
$- (1 \text{ mol/mol-rxn})(94.85 \text{ J/mol} \cdot \text{K})$
$= 75.1 \text{ J/K} \cdot \text{mol-rxn}$

A gain in entropy for the formation of a mixture (solution) is expected.

(b) $\Delta_rS° = 2 \, S°(CO_2) + 3 \, S°(H_2O) -$
$[S°(C_2H_5OH) + 3 \, S°(O_2)]$

$\Delta_rS° = (2 \text{ mol/mol-rxn})(213.74 \text{ J/mol} \cdot \text{K})$
$+ (3 \text{ mol/mol-rxn})(188.84 \text{ J/mol} \cdot \text{K})$
$- [(1 \text{ mol/mol-rxn})(282.70 \text{ J/mol} \cdot \text{K})$
$+ (3 \text{ mol/mol-rxn})(205.07 \text{ J/mol} \cdot \text{K})]$

$\Delta_rS° = +96.09 \text{ J/K} \cdot \text{mol-rxn}$

An increase in entropy is expected because there is a increase in the number of moles of gases.

19.3 (a) Type 2
(b) Type 3
(c) Type 1
(d) Type 2

19.4 $\Delta S°(\text{system}) = 2 \, S°(HCl) - [S°(H_2) + S°(Cl_2)]$

$\Delta S°(\text{system}) = (2 \text{ mol/mol-rxn})(186.2 \text{ J/mol} \cdot \text{K})$
$- [(1 \text{ mol/mol-rxn})(130.7 \text{ J/mol} \cdot \text{K})$
$+ (1 \text{ mol/mol-rxn})(223.08 \text{ J/mol} \cdot \text{K})]$
$= 18.6 \text{ J/K} \cdot \text{mol-rxn}$

$\Delta S°(\text{surroundings}) = -\Delta H°(\text{system}) / T =$
$-(-184,620 \text{ J/mol-rxn}/298 \text{ K}) = 619.5 \text{ J/K} \cdot \text{mol-rxn}$

$\Delta S°(\text{universe}) = \Delta S°(\text{system}) + \Delta S°(\text{surroundings})$
$= 18.6 \text{ J/K} \cdot \text{mol-rxn} + 619.5 \text{ J/K} \cdot \text{mol-rxn} =$
$638.1 \text{ J/K} \cdot \text{mol-rxn}$

19.5 $\Delta S°(\text{system}) = \Delta_rS° = 560.7 \text{ J/K} \cdot \text{mol-rxn}$

At 298 K, $\Delta S°(\text{surroundings}) =$
$-(467,900 \text{ J/mol-rxn})/298 \text{ K}$
$= -1570 \text{ J/K} \cdot \text{mol-rxn}$

$\Delta S°_{\text{univ}} = \Delta S°(\text{system}) + \Delta S°(\text{surroundings})$
$= 560.7 \text{ J/K} \cdot \text{mol-rxn} - 1570 \text{ J/K} \cdot \text{mol-rxn}$
$= -1010 \text{ J/K} \cdot \text{mol-rxn}$

The negative sign indicates that the process is not spontaneous. At higher temperature, the value of $-\Delta H°(\text{system})/T$ will be less negative. At a high enough temperature, $\Delta S°(\text{surroundings})$ will outweigh $\Delta S°(\text{system})$ and the reaction will be spontaneous.

19.6 For the reaction $N_2(g) + 3 \, H_2(g) \longrightarrow 2 \, NH_3(g)$:

$\Delta_rH° = 2 \, \Delta_fH°$ for $NH_3(g) = (2 \text{ mol/mol-rxn})$
$(-45.90 \text{ kJ/mol}) = -91.80 \text{ kJ/mol-rxn}$

$\Delta_rS° = 2 \, S°(NH_3) - [S°(N_2) + 3 \, S°(H_2)]$

$\Delta_rS° = (2 \text{ mol/mol-rxn})(192.77 \text{ J/ mol} \cdot \text{K}) - [(1 \text{ mol/mol-rxn})(191.56 \text{ J/mol} \cdot \text{K}) + (3 \text{ mol/mol-rxn})(130.7 \text{ J/mol} \cdot \text{K})]$

$\Delta_rS° = -198.1 \text{ J/K} \cdot \text{mol-rxn} \, (= 0.198 \text{ kJ/K} \cdot \text{mol-rxn})$

$\Delta_rG° = \Delta_rH° - T\Delta_rS° =$
$-91.80 \text{ kJ/mol-rxn} - (298 \text{ K})(-0.198 \text{ kJ/K} \cdot \text{mol-rxn})$
$\Delta_rG° = -32.8 \text{ kJ/mol-rxn}$

19.7 $SO_2(g) + \frac{1}{2} \, O_2(g) \longrightarrow SO_3(g)$

$\Delta_rG° = \Sigma \, \Delta_fG°(\text{products}) - \Sigma \, \Delta_fG°(\text{reactants})$

$\Delta_rG° = (1 \text{ mol/mol-rxn})\Delta G°[SO_3(g)] - \{(1 \text{ mol/mol-rxn})\Delta G°[SO_2(g)] + 0.5 \text{ mol/mol-rxn}) \Delta G°[O_2(g)]\}$

$\Delta_rG° = -371.04 \text{ kJ/mol-rxn} - (-300.13 \text{ kJ/mol-rxn} + 0)$
$= -70.91 \text{ kJ/mol-rxn}$

19.8 $HgO(s) \longrightarrow Hg(\ell) + \frac{1}{2} \, O_2(g)$; determine the temperature at which $\Delta_rG° = \Delta_rH° - T\Delta_rS° = 0$. T the unknown in this problem.

$\Delta_rH° = [-\Delta_fH°$ for $HgO(s)] = 90.83 \text{ kJ/mol-rxn}$

$\Delta_rS° = S°[Hg(\ell)] + \frac{1}{2} \, S°(O_2) - S°[HgO(s)]$

$\Delta_rS° = (1 \text{ mol/mol-rxn})(76.02 \text{ J/mol} \cdot \text{K})$
$+ [(0.5 \text{ mol/mol-rxn})(205.07 \text{ J/mol} \cdot \text{K})$
$- (1 \text{ mol/mol-rxn})(70.29 \text{ J/mol} \cdot \text{K})]$
$= 108.26 \text{ J/K} \cdot \text{mol-rxn}$

$\Delta_rH° - T(\Delta_rS°) = 90,830 \text{ J/mol-rxn} -$
$T(108.27 \text{ J/mol-rxn})/\text{K}) = 0$

$T = 839 \text{ K} \, (566 \text{ °C})$

19.9 $C(s) + CO_2(g) \rightleftharpoons 2 \, CO(g)$

$\Delta_rG° = \Sigma \, \Delta_fG°(\text{products}) - \Sigma \, \Delta_fG°(\text{reactants})$
$\Delta_rG° = 2 \, \Delta_fG°(CO) - \Delta_fG°(CO_2)$
$\Delta_rG° = (2 \text{ mol/mol-rxn})(-137.17 \text{ kJ/mol}) -$
$(1 \text{ mol/mol-rxn})(-394.36 \text{ kJ/mol})$
$\Delta_rG° = 120.02 \text{ kJ/mol-rxn}$

$\Delta_rG° = -RT \ln K$

$120,020 \text{ J/mol-rxn}$
$= -(8.3145 \text{ J/mol-rxn} \cdot \text{K})(298 \text{ K})(\ln K)$

$K = 8.94 \times 10^{-22}$

Chapter 20

20.1 Oxidation half-reaction: $Al(s) \longrightarrow Al^{3+}(aq) + 3 \text{ e}$
Reduction half-reaction: $2 \, H^+(aq) + 2 \text{ e}^- \longrightarrow H_2(g)$

Overall reaction: $2 \, Al(s) + 6 \, H^+(aq) \longrightarrow 2 \, Al^{3+}(aq) + 3 \, H_2(g)$

Al is the reducing agent and is oxidized; $H^+(aq)$ is the oxidizing agent and is reduced.

20.2 $2 \, VO^{2+}(aq) + Zn(s) + 4 \, H^+(aq) \longrightarrow Zn^{2+}(aq) + 2 \, V^{3+}(aq) + 2 \, H_2O(\ell)$

$2 \, V^{3+}(aq) + Zn(s) \longrightarrow 2 \, V^{2+}(aq) + Zn^{2+}(aq)$

20.3 Oxidation (Fe^{2+}, the reducing agent, is oxidized): $Fe^{2+}(aq) \longrightarrow Fe^{3+}(aq) + e^-$

Reduction (MnO_4^-, the oxidizing agent, is reduced)

$$MnO_4^-(aq) + 8 H^+(aq) + 5 e^- \longrightarrow$$
$$Mn^{2+}(aq) + 4 H_2O(\ell)$$

Overall reaction:

$$MnO_4^-(aq) + 8 H^+(aq) + 5 Fe^{2+}(aq) \longrightarrow$$
$$Mn^{2+}(aq) + 5 Fe^{3+}(aq) + 4 H_2O(\ell)$$

20.4 (a) Oxidation half-reaction:

$$Al(s) + 3 OH^-(aq) \longrightarrow Al(OH)_3(s) + 3 e^-$$

Reduction half-reaction:

$$S(s) + H_2O(\ell) + 2 e^- \longrightarrow HS^-(aq) + OH^-(aq)$$

Overall reaction:

$$2 Al(s) + 3 S(s) + 3 H_2O(\ell) + 3 OH^-(aq) \longrightarrow$$
$$2 Al(OH)_3(s) + 3 HS^-(aq)$$

(b) Aluminum is the reducing agent and is oxidized; sulfur is the oxidizing agent and is reduced.

20.5 Construct two half-cells, the first with a silver electrode and a solution containing $Ag^+(aq)$, and the second with a nickel electrode and a solution containing $Ni^{2+}(aq)$. Connect the two half-cells with a salt bridge. When the electrodes are connected through an external circuit, electrons will flow from the anode (the nickel electrode) to the cathode (the silver electrode). The overall cell reaction is $Ni(s) + 2 Ag^+(aq) \longrightarrow Ni^{2+}(aq) + 2 Ag(s)$. To maintain electrical neutrality in the two half-cells, negative ions will flow from the $Ag \mid Ag^+$ half-cell to the $Ni \mid Ni^{2+}$ half-cell, and positive ions will flow in the opposite direction.

20.6 Anode reaction: $Zn(s) \longrightarrow Zn^{2+}(aq) + 2 e^-$

Cathode reaction: $2 Ag^+(aq) + 2 e^- \longrightarrow 2 Ag(s)$

$E°_{cell} = E°_{cathode} - E°_{anode} = 0.80 V - (-0.76 V)$
$= 1.56 V$

20.7 Mg is easiest to oxidize, and Au is the most difficult. (See Table 20.1.)

20.8 Use the "northwest–southeast rule" or calculate the cell voltage to determine whether a reaction is product-favored. Reactions (a) and (c) are reactant-favored; reactions (b) and (d) are product-favored.

20.9 Overall reaction: $2 Al(s) + 3 Fe^{2+}(aq) \longrightarrow$
$$2 Al^{3+}(aq) + 3 Fe(s)$$

($E°_{cell} = 1.22 V$, $n = 6$)

$E_{cell} = E°_{cell} - (0.0257/n) \ln \{[Al^{3+}]^2/[Fe^{2+}]^3\}$
$= 1.22 - (0.0257/6) \ln \{[0.025]^2/[0.50]^3\}$
$= 1.22 V - (-0.023) V = 1.24 V$

20.10 Overall reaction: $Fe(s) + 2 H^+(aq) \longrightarrow$
$$Fe^{2+}(aq) + H_2(g)$$

($E°_{cell} = 0.44 V$, $n = 2$)

$E_{cell} = E°_{cell} - (0.0257/n) \ln \{[Fe^{2+}]P_{H_2}/[H^+]^2\}$

$= 0.44 - (0.0257/2) \ln \{[0.024]1.0/[0.056]^2\}$
$= 0.44 V - 0.026 V = 0.41 V$

20.11 $\Delta_r G° = -nFE° = -(2 \text{ mol } e^-)(96,500 \text{ C/mol } e^-)$
$(-0.76 V)(1 J/1 C \cdot V)$
$= 146,680 J (= 150 \text{ kJ})$

The negative value of $E°$ and the positive value of $\Delta G°$ both indicate a reactant-favored reaction.

20.12 $E°_{cell} = E°_{cathode} - E°_{anode} = 0.80 V - 0.855 V$
$= -0.055 V$; $n = 2$

$E° = (0.0257/n) \ln K$

$-0.055 = (0.0257/2) \ln K$

$K = 0.014$

20.13 Cathode: $Zn^{2+}(aq) + 2 e^- \longrightarrow$
$$Zn(s) \quad E°_{cathode} = -0.76 V$$

Anode: $Zn(s) + 4 CN^-(aq) \longrightarrow$
$$[Zn(CN)_4^{2-}] + 2 e^- \quad E°_{anode} = -1.26 V$$

Overall: $Zn^{2+}(aq) + 4 CN^-(aq) \longrightarrow$
$$[Zn(CN)_4^{2-}] \quad E°_{cell} = 0.50 V$$

$E° = (0.0257/n) \ln K$

$0.50 = (0.0257/2) \ln K$

$K = 7.9 \times 10^{16}$

20.14 Cathode: $2 H_2O(\ell) + 2 e^- \longrightarrow$
$$2 OH^-(aq) + H_2(g)$$

$E°_{cathode} = -0.83 V$

Anode: $4 OH^-(aq) \longrightarrow O_2(g) + 2 H_2O(\ell) + 4 e^-$

$E°_{anode} = 0.40 V$

Overall: $2 H_2O(\ell) \longrightarrow 2 H_2(g) + O_2(g)$

$E°_{cell} = E°_{cathode} - E°_{anode} = -0.83 V - 0.40 V$
$= -1.23 V$

This is the minimum voltage needed to cause this reaction to occur.

20.15 O_2 is formed at the anode, by the reaction

$$2 H_2O(\ell) \longrightarrow 4 H^+(aq) + O_2(g) + 4 e^-.$$

$(0.445 A)(45 \text{ min})(60 \text{ s/min})(1 C/1 A \cdot s)(1 \text{ mol } e^-/96,500 C)(1 \text{ mol } O_2/4 \text{ mol } e^-)(32 \text{ g } O_2/1 \text{ mol } O_2) = 0.10 \text{ g } O_2$

20.16 The cathode reaction (electrolysis of molten NaCl) is

$$Na^+(melt) + e^- \longrightarrow Na(\ell).$$

$(25 \times 10^3 A)(60 \text{ min})(60 \text{ s/min})(1 C/1 A \cdot s)$
$(1 \text{ mol } e^-/96,500 C)(1 \text{ mol Na/mol } e^-)$
$(23 \text{ g Na/1 mol Na})$
$= 21,450 \text{ g Na} = 21 \text{ kg}$

Chapter 21

21.1 (a) $2 Na(s) + Br_2(\ell) \longrightarrow 2 NaBr(s)$
(b) $Ca(s) + Se(s) \longrightarrow CaSe(s)$
(c) $2 Pb(s) + O_2(g) \longrightarrow 2 PbO(s)$

Lead(II) oxide, a red compound commonly called litharge, is the most widely used inorganic lead compound. Maroon-colored lead(IV) oxide is the product of lead oxidation in lead-acid storage batteries (Chapter 21). Other oxides such as Pb_3O_4 also exist.

(d) $2\ Al(s) + 3\ Cl_2(g) \longrightarrow 2\ AlCl_3(s)$

21.2 (a) H_2Te
(b) Na_3AsO_4
(c) $SeCl_6$
(d) $HBrO_4$

21.3 (a) NH_4^+ (ammonium ion)
(b) O_2^{2-} (peroxide ion)
(c) N_2H_4 (hydrazine)
(d) NF_3 (nitrogen trifluoride)

21.4 (a) ClO is an odd-electron molecule, and Cl has the unlikely oxidation number of +2.
(b) In Na_2Cl, chlorine would have the unlikely charge of 2− (to balance the two positive charges of the two Na^+ ions).
(c) This compound would require either the calcium ion to have the formula Ca^+ or the acetate ion to have the formula $CH_3CO_2^{2-}$. In all of its compounds, calcium occurs as the Ca^{2+} ion. The acetate ion, formed from acetic acid by loss of H^+, has a 1− charge.
(d) No octet structure for C_3H_7 can be drawn. This species has an odd number of electrons.

21.5 $CH_4(g) + H_2O(g) \longrightarrow 3\ H_2(g) + CO(g)$
Bonds broken: 4 C—H and 2 O—H (sum = 2578 kJ)
$4\ \Delta H(C—H) = 4(413\ kJ) = 1652\ kJ$
$2\ \Delta H(O—H) = 4(463\ kJ) = 926\ kJ$
Bonds formed: 3 H—H and 1 C≡O (sum = 2354 kJ)
$3\ \Delta H(H—H) = 3(436\ kJ) = 1308\ kJ$
$\Delta H(CO) = 1046\ kJ$
Estimated energy of reaction = 2578 kJ − 2354 kJ
$= +224\ kJ$

21.6 Cathode reaction: $Na^+ + e^- \longrightarrow Na(\ell)$; 1 F, or 96,500 C, is required to form 1 mol of Na. There are (24 h) (60 min/h)(60 s/min) = 86,400 s in 1 day. 1000 kg = 1.000×10^6 g, so
$(1.000 \times 10^6$ g Na) (1 mol Na/23.00 g Na) (96,500 C/mol Na) (1 A · s/1 C) (1/86,400 s) = 4.855×10^4 A

21.7 Some interesting topics: gemstones of the mineral beryl; uses of Be in the aerospace industry and in nuclear reactors; beryllium–copper alloys; severe health hazards when beryllium or its compounds get into the lungs.

21.8 (a) $Ga(OH)_3(s) + 3\ H^+(aq) \longrightarrow Ga^{3+}(aq) + 3\ H_2O(\ell)$

$Ga(OH)_3(s) + OH^-(aq) \longrightarrow Ga(OH)_4^-(aq)$

(b) $Ga^{3+}(aq)$ $(K_a = 1.2 \times 10^{-3})$ is stronger acid than $Al^{3+}(aq)$ $(K_a = 7.9 \times 10^{-6})$

21.9

21.10 (a) :N≡N—Ö: ⟷ N̈=N=Ö ⟷ :N̈—N≡O:

    A   B   C

Resonance structure A has formal charges of N = 0, N = +1, O = −1 (from left to right) and is the most favorable structure. For B, N = −1, N = +1, O = 0, and for C, N = −2, N = +1, O = +1. Structure C is clearly unfavorable. B is not as favorable as A because the more electronegative atom (O) has a 0 charge whereas N is −1.

(b) $NH_4NO_3(s) \longrightarrow N_2O(g) + 2\ H_2O(g)$

$\Delta_rH° = \Sigma\Delta_fH°(products) - \Sigma\Delta_fH°(reactants)$

$\Delta_rH° = \Delta_fH°(N_2O) + 2\ \Delta_fH°(H_2O) - \Delta_fH°(NH_4NO_3)$

$= 82.05\ kJ + 2(-241.83\ kJ) - (-365.56\ kJ) = -36.05$

The reaction is exothermic.

21.11 First, calculate $\Delta_rG°$, $\Delta_rH°$, and $\Delta_rS°$ for this reaction using data from Appendix L.

$\Delta_rG° = \Sigma\Delta_fG°(products) - \Sigma\Delta_fG°(reactants)$

$\Delta_rG° = 2\ \Delta_fG°(ZnO) + 2\ \Delta_fG°(SO_2) - 2\ \Delta_fG°(ZnS) - 3\ \Delta_fG°(O_2)$

$= 2(-318.30\ kJ) + 2(-300.13\ kJ) - 2(-201.29\ kJ) - 0$

$= -834.28\ kJ$. The reaction is product-favored at 298 K.

$\Delta_rH° = 2\ \Delta_fH°(ZnO) + 2\ \Delta_fH°(SO_2) - 2\ \Delta_fH°(ZnS) - 3\ \Delta_fH°(O_2)$

$= 2(-348.28\ kJ) + 2(-296.84\ kJ) - [2(-205.98\ kJ) + 0] = -878.28\ kJ$

$\Delta_rS° = 2\ S°(ZnO) + 2\ S°(SO_2) - 2\ S°(ZnS) - 3\ S°(O_2)$

$= 2(43.64\ J/K) + 2(248.21\ J/K) - [2(57.7\ J/K) + 3(205.07\ J/K)]$

$= -146.9\ J/K$

This reaction is enthalpy favored and entropy disfavored. The reaction will become less favored at higher temperatures. See Table 19.2.

21.12 For the reaction $HX + Ag \longrightarrow AgX + \frac{1}{2}\ H_2$:

$\Delta_rG° = \Sigma\Delta_fG°(products) - \Sigma\Delta_fG°(reactants)$

$\Delta_rG° = \Delta_fG°(AgX) - \Delta_fG°(HX)$

For HF: $\Delta_rG° = +79.4\ kJ$; reactant favored

For HCl: $\Delta_rG° = -14.67\ kJ$; product favored

For HBr: $\Delta G° = -43.45\ kJ$; product favored

For HI: $\Delta_rG° = -67.75\ kJ$; product favored

.1 (a) $Co(NH_3)_3Cl_3$

(b) (i) $K_3[Co(NO_2)_6]$: a complex of cobalt(III) with a coordination number of 6

(ii) $Mn(NH_3)_4Cl_2$: a complex of manganese(II) with a coordination number of 6

.2 (a) hexaaquanickel(II) sulfate

(b) dicyanobis(ethylenediamine)chromium(III) chloride

(c) potassium amminetrichloroplatinate(II)

(d) potassium dichlorocuprate(I)

.3 (a) Geometric isomers are possible (with the NH_3 ligands in *cis* and *trans* positions).

(b) Only a single structure is possible.

(c) Only a single structure is possible.

(d) This compound is chiral; there are two optical isomers.

(e) Only a single structure is possible.

(f) Two structural isomers are possible based on coordination of the NO_2^- ligand through oxygen or nitrogen.

.4 (a) $[Ru(H_2O)_6]^{2+}$: An octahedral complex of ruthenium(II) (d^6). A low-spin complex has no unpaired electrons and is diamagnetic. A high-spin complex has four unpaired electrons and is paramagnetic.

(b) $[Ni(NH_3)_6]^{2+}$: An octahedral complex of nickel(II) (d^8). Only one electron configuration is possible; it has two unpaired electrons and is paramagnetic.

.5 (a) The $C_5H_5^-$ ligand is an anion (6 electrons), C_6H_6 is a neutral ligand (6 electrons), so Mn must be +1 (6 valence electrons). There is a total of 18 valence electrons.

(b) The ligands in this complex are all neutral, so the Mo atom must have no charge. The C_6H_6 ligand contributes six electrons, each Co contributes two electrons for a total of six, and Mo has six valence electrons. The total is 18 electrons.

hapter 23

.1 (a) $^{222}_{86}Rn \longrightarrow\ ^{218}_{84}Po +\ ^{4}_{2}\alpha$

(b) $^{218}_{84}Po \longrightarrow\ ^{218}_{85}At +\ ^{0}_{-1}\beta$

23.2 (a) E (per photon) $= h\upsilon = hc/\lambda$

$E = [(6.626 \times 10^{-34}\,J \cdot s/\text{photon})$
$(3.00 \times 10^8\,m/s)]/(2.0 \times 10^{-12})$

$E = 9.94 \times 10^{-14}\,J/\text{photon}$

E (per mole) $= (9.94 \times 10^{-14}\,J/\text{photon})$
$(6.022 \times 10^{23}\,\text{photons/mol})$

E (per mole) $= 5.99 \times 10^{10}\,J/\text{mol}$

23.3 (a) Emission of six α particles leads to a decrease of 24 in the mass number and a decrease of 12 in the atomic number. Emission of four β particles increases the atomic number by 4, but doesn't affect the mass. The final product of this process has a mass number of $232 - 24 = 208$ and an atomic number of $90 - 12 + 4 = 82$, identifying it as $^{208}_{82}Pb$.

(b) Step 1: $^{232}_{90}Th \longrightarrow\ ^{228}_{88}Ra +\ ^{4}_{2}\alpha$

Step 2: $^{228}_{88}Ra \longrightarrow\ ^{228}_{89}Ac +\ ^{0}_{-1}\beta$

Step 3: $^{228}_{89}Ac \longrightarrow\ ^{228}_{90}Th +\ ^{0}_{-1}\beta$

23.4 (a) $^{0}_{+1}\beta$ (b) $^{41}_{19}K$ (c) $^{0}_{-1}\beta$ (d) $^{22}_{12}Mg$

23.5 (a) $^{32}_{14}Si \longrightarrow\ ^{32}_{15}P +\ ^{0}_{-1}\beta$

(b) $^{45}_{22}Ti \longrightarrow\ ^{45}_{21}Sc +\ ^{0}_{+1}\beta$ or $^{45}_{22}Ti +\ ^{0}_{-1}e \longrightarrow$
$^{45}_{21}Sc$

(c) $^{239}_{94}Pu \longrightarrow \alpha +\ ^{45}_{22}U$

(d) $^{42}_{19}K \longrightarrow\ ^{42}_{20}Ca +\ ^{0}_{-1}\beta$

23.6 $\Delta m = 0.03438\,g/mol$

$\Delta E = (3.438 \times 10^{-5}\,kg/mol)(2.998 \times 10^8)^2$

$= 3.090 \times 10^{12}\,J/mol\ (= 3.090 \times 10^9\,kJ/mol)$

$E_b = 5.150 \times 10^8\,kJ/mol\ \text{nucleons}$

23.7 (a) 49.2 years is exactly 4 half-lives; quantity remaining $= 1.5\,mg(1/2)^4 = 0.094\,mg$

(b) 3 half-lives, 36.9 years

(c) 1% is between 6 half-lives, 73.8 years (1/64 remains), and 7 half-lives, 86.1 years (1/128 remains)

23.8 $\ln ([A]/[A_o]) = -kt$

$\ln ([3.18 \times 10^3]/[3.35 \times 10^3]) = -k(2.00\,d)$

$k = 0.0260\,d^{-1}$

$t_{1/2} = 0.693/k = 0.693/(0.0260\,d^{-1}) = 26.7\,d$

23.9 $k = 0.693/t_{1/2} = 0.693/200\,y = 3.47 \times 10^{-3}\,y^{-1}$

$\ln ([A]/[A_o]) = -kt$

$\ln ([3.00 \times 10^3]/[6.50 \times 10^{12}]) = -(3.47 \times 10^{-3}\,y^{-1})t$

$\ln (4.62 \times 10^{-10}) = -(3.47 \times 10^{-3}\,y^{-1})t$

$t = 6190\,y$

23.10 $\ln ([A]/[A_o]) = -kt$

$\ln ([9.32]/[13.4]) = -(1.21 \times 10^{-4}\,y^{-1})t$

$t = 3.00 \times 10^3\,y$

23.11 $3000\,dpm/x = 1200\,dpm/\ 60.0\,mg$

$x = 150\,mg$

Answers to Selected Study Questions

o

CHAPTER 1

1.1 (a) C, carbon
(b) K, potassium
(c) Cl, chlorine
(d) P, phosphorus
(e) Mg, magnesium
(f) Ni, nickel

1.3 (a) Ba, barium
(b) Ti, titanium
(c) Cr, chromium
(d) Pb, lead
(e) As, arsenic
(f) Zn, zinc

1.5 (a) Na (element) and NaCl (compound)
(b) Sugar (compound) and carbon (element)
(c) Gold (element) and gold chloride (compound)

1.7 (a) Physical property
(b) Chemical property
(c) Chemical property
(d) Physical property
(e) Physical property
(f) Physical property

1.9 (a) Physical (colorless liquid) and chemical (burns in air)
(b) Physical (shiny metal, orange liquid) and chemical (reacts with bromine)

1.11 (a) Qualitative: blue-green color, solid physical state
Quantitative: density = 2.65 g/cm³ and mass = 2.5 g
(b) Density, physical state, and color are intensive properties, whereas mass is an extensive property.
(c) Volume = 0.94 cm³

1.13 Observations c, e, and f are chemical properties

1.15 calcium, Ca; fluorine, F

The crystals are cubic in shape because the atoms a⟩ arranged in cubic structures.

1.17 The macroscopic view is the photograph of NaCl, a⟩ the particulate view is the drawing of the ions in a c⟩ bic arrangement. The structure of the compound at⟩ the particulate level determines the properties that⟩ are observed at the macroscopic level.

1.19 The density of the plastic is less than that of CCl₄, s⟩ the plastic will float on the liquid CCl₄. Aluminum i⟩ more dense than CCl₄, so aluminum will sink when⟩ placed in CCl₄.

1.21 The three liquids will form three separate layers wit⟩ hexane on the top, water in the middle, and perfluo⟩ rohexane on the bottom. The HDPE will float at the⟩ interface of the hexane and water layers. The PVC v⟩ float at the interface of the water and perfluorohex-⟩ ane layers. The Teflon will sink to the bottom of the⟩ cylinder.

1.23 HDPE will float in ethylene glycol, water, acetic acid⟩ and glycerol.

1.25 (a) (b) 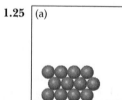 (c)

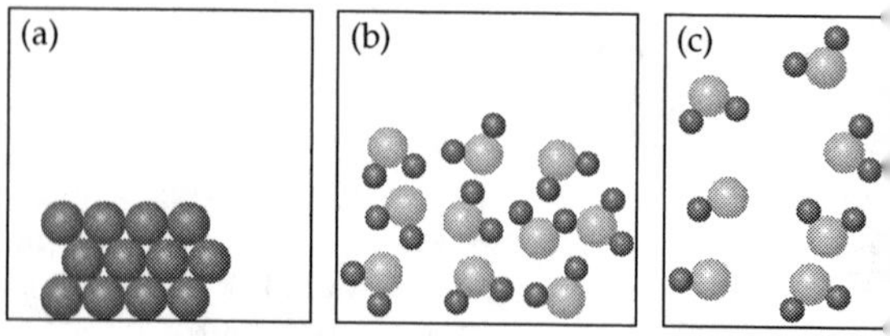

1.27 The sample's density and melting point could be co⟩ pared to those of pure silver.

1.29 If too much sugar is excreted, the density of the uri⟩ would be higher than normal. If too much water is ⟩ creted, the density would be lower than normal.

31 (a) Solid potassium metal reacts with liquid water to produce gaseous hydrogen and a homogeneous mixture (solution) of potassium hydroxide in liquid water.

(b) The reaction is a chemical change.

(c) The reactants are potassium and water. The products are hydrogen gas and a water (aqueous) solution of potassium hydroxide. Heat and light are also evolved.

(d) Among the qualitative observations are (i) the reaction is violent, and (ii) heat and light (a purple flame) are produced.

33 (a) The water could be evaporated by heating the solution, leaving the salt behind.

(b) Use a magnet to attract the iron away from lead, which is not magnetic.

(c) Mixing the solids with water will dissolve only the sugar. Filtration would separate the solid sulfur from the sugar solution. Finally, the sugar could be separated from the water by evaporating the water.

35 Separate the iron from a weighed sample of cereal by passing a magnet through a mixture of the cereal and water after the flakes have become a gooey paste. Remove the iron flakes from the magnet and weigh them to determine the mass of iron in this mass of cereal.

37 Physical change

ET'S REVIEW: THE TOOLS OF
QUANTITATIVE CHEMISTRY

298 K

(a) 289 K
(b) 97 °C
(c) 310 K (3.1 × 10² K)

42,195 m; 26.219 miles

5.3 cm²; 5.3 × 10⁻⁴ m²

250. cm³; 0.250 L, 2.50 × 10⁻⁴ m³; 0.250 dm³

1 2.52 × 10³ g

3 555 g

5 Choice (c), zinc

7 (a) Method A with all data included:
average = 2.4 g/cm³

Method B with all data included:
average = 3.480 g/cm³

For B, the 5.811 g/cm³ data point can be excluded because it is more than twice as large as all other points for case Method B. Using only the first three points, average = 2.703 g/cm³

(b) Method A: error = 0.3 g/cm³ or about 10%

Method B: error = 0.001 g/cm³ or about 0.04%

(c) Method A: standard deviation = 0.2 g/cm³

Method B (including all data points):
st. dev. = 1.554 g/cm³

Method B (excluding the 5.811 g/cm³ data point):
st. dev. = 0.002 g/cm³

(d) Method B's average value is both more precise and more accurate so long as the 5.811 g/cm³ data point is excluded.

19 (a) 5.4 × 10⁻² g, two significant figures
(b) 5.462 × 10³ g, four significant figures
(c) 7.92 × 10⁻⁴ g, three significant figures
(d) 1.6 × 10³ mL, two significant figures

21 (a) 9.44 × 10⁻³
(b) 5694
(c) 11.9
(d) 0.122

23

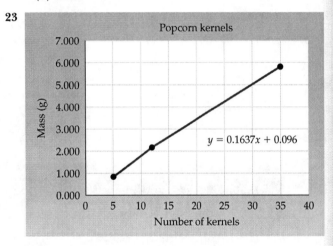

Slope: 0.1637 g/kernel

The slope represents the average mass of a popcorn kernel.

Mass of 20 popcorn kernels = 3.370 g

There are 127 kernels in a sample with a mass of 20.88 g.

25 (a) $y = -4.00x + 20.00$
(b) $y = -4.00$

27 $C = 0.0823$

29 $T = 295$

31 0.197 nm; 197 pm

33 (a) 7.5 × 10⁻⁶ m; (b) 7.5 × 10³ nm; (c) 7.5 × 10⁶ pm

35 50. mg procaine hydrochloride

37 The volume of the marbles is 99 mL − 61 mL = 38 mL. This yields a density of 2.5 g/cm³.

39 (a) 0.178 nm^3; $1.78 \times 10^{-22} \text{ cm}^3$
(b) $3.86 \times 10^{-22} \text{ g}$
(c) $9.68 \times 10^{-23} \text{ g}$

41 Your normal body temperature (about 98.6 °F) is 37 °C. As this is higher than gallium's melting point, the metal will melt in your hand.

43 (a) 15%
(b) 3.63×10^3 kernels

45 $8.0 \times 10^4 \text{ kg}$ of sodium fluoride per year

47 245 g sulfuric acid

49 (a) 272 mL ice
(b) The ice cannot be contained in the can.

51 7.99 g/cm^3

53 (a) 8.7 g/cm^3
(b) The metal is probably cadmium, but the calculated density is close to that of cobalt, nickel, and copper. Further testing should be done on the metal.

55 0.0927 cm

57 (a) 1.143×10^{21} atoms; 54.9% of the lattic is filled with atoms; 24% of the lattice is open space.

Atoms are spheres. When spheres are packed together, they touch only at certain points, therefore leaving spaces in the structure.

(b) Four atoms

59 Al, aluminum

61

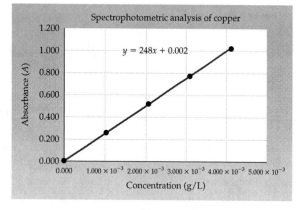

When absorbance = 0.635, concentration = $2.55 \times 10^{-3} \text{ g/L} = 2.55 \times 10^{-3} \text{ mg/mL}$

63

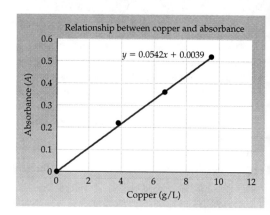

Slope = 0.054; y-intercept = 0.004; the absorbance for 5.00 g/L of copper is 0.27

CHAPTER 2

2.1 Atoms contain the following fundamental particles: protons (+1 charge), neutrons (zero charge), and electrons (−1 charge). Protons and neutrons are in the nucleus of an atom. Electrons are the least massive of the three particles.

2.3 (a) $^{27}_{12}\text{Mg}$
(b) $^{48}_{22}\text{Ti}$
(c) $^{62}_{30}\text{Zn}$

2.5

Element	Electrons	Protons	Neutrons
^{24}Mg	12	12	12
^{119}Sn	50	50	69
^{232}Th	90	90	142
^{13}C	6	6	7
^{63}Cu	29	29	34
^{205}Bi	83	83	122

2.7 $^{57}_{27}\text{Co}$, $^{58}_{27}\text{Co}$, $^{60}_{27}\text{Co}$

2.9 ^{205}Tl is more abundant than ^{203}Tl. The atomic mass thallium is closer to 205 than to 203.

2.11 $(0.0750)(6.015121) + (0.9250)(7.016003) = 6.94$

2.13 (c), About 50%. Actual percent $^{107}\text{Ag} = 51.839\%$

2.15 ^{69}Ga, 60.12%; ^{71}Ga, 39.88%

2.17

	Symbol	Atomic No.	Atomic Mass	Group	Period	
Titanium	Ti	22	47.867	4B(IUPAC 4)	4	Met
Thallium	Tl	81	204.3833	3A(IUPAC 13)	6	Met

2.19 Eight elements: periods 2 and 3. 18 elements: period 4 and 5. 32 elements: period 6.

.21 (a) Nonmetals: C, Cl
   (b) Main group elements: C, Ca, Cl, Cs
   (c) Lanthanides: Ce
   (d) Transition elements: Cr, Co, Cd, Ce, Cm, Cu, Cf
   (e) Actinides: Cm, Cf
   (f) Gases: Cl

.23 Metals: Na, Ni, Np
   Metalloids: None in this list
   Nonmetals: N, Ne

.25 Molecular Formula: H_2SO_4.
   Structural Formula:

$$O-\overset{\overset{\displaystyle O}{|}}{\underset{\underset{\displaystyle O-H}{|}}{S}}-O-H$$

The structure is not flat. The O atoms are arranged around the sulfur at the corners of a tetrahedron. The hydrogen atoms are connected to two of the oxygen atoms.

.27 (a) Mg^{2+}
   (b) Zn^{2+}
   (c) Ni^{2+}
   (d) Ga^{3+}

.29 (a) Ba^{2+}
   (b) Ti^{4+}
   (c) PO_4^{3-}
   (d) HCO_3^-
   (e) S^{2-}
   (f) ClO_4^-
   (g) Co^{2+}
   (h) SO_4^{2-}

.31 K loses one electron per atom to form a K^+ ion. It has the same number of electrons as an Ar atom.

.33 Ba^{2+} and Br^- ions. The compound's formula is $BaBr_2$.

.35 (a) Two K^+ ions and one S^{2-} ion
   (b) One Co^{2+} ion and one SO_4^{2-} ion
   (c) One K^+ ion and one MnO_4^- ion
   (d) Three NH_4^+ ions and one PO_4^{3-} ion
   (e) One Ca^{2+} ion and two ClO^- ions
   (f) One Na^+ ion and one $CH_3CO_2^-$ ion

.37 Co^{2+} gives CoO and Co^{3+} gives Co_2O_3

.39 (a) $AlCl_2$ should be $AlCl_3$ (based on an Al^{3+} ion and three Cl^- ions).
   (b) KF_2 should be KF (based on a K^+ ion and an F^- ion).
   (c) Ga_2O_3 is correct.
   (d) MgS is correct.

.41 (a) potassium sulfide
   (b) cobalt(II) sulfate
   (c) ammonium phosphate
   (d) calcium hypochlorite

2.43 (a) $(NH_4)_2CO_3$
   (b) CaI_2
   (c) $CuBr_2$
   (d) $AlPO_4$
   (e) $AgCH_3CO_2$

2.45 Compounds with Na^+: Na_2CO_3 (sodium carbonate) and NaI (sodium iodide). Compounds with Ba^{2+}: $BaCO_3$ (barium carbonate) and BaI_2 (barium iodide).

2.47 The force of attraction is stronger in NaF than in NaI because the distance between ion centers is smaller in NaF (235 pm) than in NaI (322 pm).

2.49 (a) nitrogen trifluoride
   (b) hydrogen iodide
   (c) boron triiodide
   (d) phosphorus pentafluoride

2.51 (a) SCl_2
   (b) N_2O_5
   (c) $SiCl_4$
   (d) B_2O_3

2.53 (a) 67 g Al
   (b) 0.0698 g Fe
   (c) 0.60 g Ca
   (d) 1.32×10^4 g Ne

2.55 (a) 1.9998 mol Cu
   (b) 0.0017 mol Li
   (c) 2.1×10^{-5} mol Am
   (d) 0.250 mol Al

2.57 Of these elements, He has the smallest molar mass, and Fe has the largest molar mass. Therefore, 1.0 g of He has the largest number of atoms in these samples, and 1.0 g of Fe has the smallest number of atoms.

2.59 (a) 159.7 g/mol
   (b) 117.2 g/mol
   (c) 176.1 g/mol

2.61 (a) 290.8 g/mol
   (b) 249.7 g/mol

2.63 (a) 1.53 g
   (b) 4.60 g
   (c) 4.60 g
   (d) 1.48 g

2.65 Amount of SO_3 = 12.5 mol
   Number of molecules = 7.52×10^{24} molecules
   Number of S atoms = 7.52×10^{24} atoms
   Number of O atoms = 2.26×10^{25} atoms

2.67 (a) 86.60% Pb and 13.40% S
   (b) 81.71% C and 18.29% H
   (c) 79.96% C, 9.394% H, and 10.65% O

2.69 66.46% copper in CuS. 15.0 g of CuS is needed to obtain 10.0 g of Cu.

2.71 $C_4H_6O_4$

2.73 (a) CH, 26.0 g/mol; C_2H_2
(b) CHO, 116.1 g/mol; $C_4H_4O_4$
(c) CH_2, 112.2 g/mol, C_8H_{16}

2.75 Empirical formula, CH; molecular formula, C_2H_2

2.77 Empirical formula, C_3H_4; molecular formula, C_9H_{12}

2.79 Empirical and molecular formulas are both $C_8H_8O_3$

2.81 XeF_2

2.83 ZnI_2

2.85

Symbol	^{58}Ni	^{33}S	^{20}Ne	^{55}Mn
Protons	28	16	10	25
Neutrons	30	17	10	30
Electrons	28	16	10	25
Name	nickel	sulfur	neon	manganese

2.87

S	N
B	I

2.89 (a) 1.0552×10^{-22} g for 1 Cu atom
(b) 6.286×10^{-22} dollars for 1 Cu atom

2.91 (a) strontium
(b) zirconium
(c) carbon
(d) arsenic
(e) iodine
(f) magnesium
(g) krypton
(h) sulfur
(i) germanium or arsenic

2.93 (a) 0.25 mol U
(b) 0.50 mol Na
(c) 10 atoms of Fe

2.95 40.2 g H_2 (b) < 103 g C   (c) < 182 g Al
(f) < 210 g Si   (d) < 212 g Na   (e) < 351 g Fe
(a) < 650 g $Cl_2(g)$

2.97 (a) Atomic mass of O = 15.873 u; Avogadro's
     number = 5.9802×10^{23} particles per mole
(b) Atomic mass of H = 1.00798 u; Avogadro's num-
     ber = 6.0279×10^{23} particles per mole

2.99 $(NH_4)_2CO_3$, $(NH_4)_2SO_4$, $NiCO_3$, $NiSO_4$

2.101 All of these compounds have one atom of some
element plus three Cl atoms. The highest mass percent of chlorine will occur in the compound having
the lightest central element. Here, that element is B,
so BCl_3 should have the highest mass percent of Cl
(90.77%).

2.103 The molar mass of adenine ($C_5H_5N_5$) is 135.13 g/mol
3.0×10^{23} molecules represents 67 g. Thus,
3.0×10^{23} molecules of adenine has a larger
mass than 40.0 g of the compound.

2.105 1.7×10^{21} molecules of water

2.107 245.75 g/mol. Mass percent: 25.86% Cu, 22.80%
N, 5.742% H, 13.05% S, and 32.55% O. In 10.5 g of
compound there are 2.72 g Cu and 0.770 g H_2O.

2.109 Empirical formula of malic acid: $C_4H_6O_5$

2.111 $Fe_2(CO)_9$

2.113 (a) $C_7H_5NO_3S$

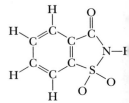

(b) 6.82×10^{-4} mol saccarin
(c) 21.9 mg S

2.115 (a) NaClO, ionic
(b) BI_3
(c) $Al(ClO_4)_3$, ionic
(d) $Ca(CH_3CO_2)_2$, ionic
(e) $KMnO_4$, ionic
(f) $(NH_4)_2SO_3$, ionic
(g) KH_2PO_4, ionic
(h) S_2Cl_2
(i) ClF_3
(j) PF_3

2.117 (a) Empirical formula = molecular formula =
     CF_2O_2
(b) Empirical formula = C_5H_4; molecular formula =
     $C_{10}H_8$

2.119 Empirical formula and molecular formula = $C_5H_{14}N$

2.121 $C_9H_7MnO_3$

2.123 68.42% Cr; 1.2×10^3 kg Cr_2O_3

2.125 Empirical formula = ICl_3; molecular formula = I_2C

2.127 7.35 kg of iron

2.129 (d) Na_2MoO_4

2.131 5.52×10^{-4} mol $C_{21}H_{15}Bi_3O_{12}$; 0.346 g Bi

2.133 The molar mass of the compound is 154 g/mol.
The unknown element is carbon.

2.135 n = 19.

2.137 (a) 2.3×10^{14} g/cm^3
(b) 3.34×10^{-3} g/cm^3
(c) The nucleus is much more dense than the space
     occupied by the electrons.

139 (a) 0.0130 mol Ni
(b) NiF_2
(c) nickel(II) fluoride

141 Formula is $MgSO_4 \cdot 7 H_2O$

143 Volume = 3.0 cm³; length of side = 1.4 cm

145 1.0028×10^{23} atoms C. If the accuracy is ± 0.0001 g, the maximum mass could be 2.0001 g, which also represents 1.0028×10^{23} atoms C.

147 Choice c. The calculated mole ratio is 0.78 mol H_2O per mol $CaCl_2$. The student should heat the crucible again and then reweigh it. More water might be driven off.

149 Required data: density of iron, molar mass of iron, Avogadro's number.

$$1.00 \ cm^3 \left(\frac{7.87 \ g}{1 \ cm^3}\right)\left(\frac{1 \ mol}{55.85 \ g}\right)\left(\frac{6.02 \times 10^{23} \ atoms}{1 \ mol}\right) = 8.49 \times 10^{22} \ atoms \ Fe$$

151 Barium would be more reactive than calcium, so a more vigorous evolution of hydrogen should occur. Reactivity increases on descending the periodic table, at least for Groups 1A and 2A.

153 When words are written with the pink, hydrated compound, the words are not visible. However, when heated, the hydrated salt loses water to form anhydrous $CoCl_2$, which is deep blue. The words are then visible.

CHAPTER 3

3.1 $C_5H_{12}(\ell) + 8 O_2(g) \rightarrow 5 CO_2(g) + 6 H_2O(g)$

3.3 (a) $4 Cr(s) + 3 O_2(g) \rightarrow 2 Cr_2O_3(s)$
(b) $Cu_2S(s) + O_2(g) \rightarrow 2 Cu(s) + SO_2(g)$
(c) $C_6H_5CH_3(\ell) + 9 O_2(g) \rightarrow 4 H_2O(\ell) + 7 CO_2(g)$

3.5 (a) $Fe_2O_3(s) + 3 Mg(s) \rightarrow 3 MgO(s) + 2 Fe(s)$
Reactants = iron(III) oxide, magnesium
Products = magnesium oxide, iron
(b) $AlCl_3(s) + 3 NaOH(aq) \rightarrow$
$Al(OH)_3(s) + 3 NaCl(aq)$
Reactants = aluminum chloride, sodium hydroxide
Products = aluminum hydroxide, sodium chloride
(c) $2 NaNO_3(s) + H_2SO_4(\ell) \rightarrow$
$Na_2SO_4(s) + 2 HNO_3(\ell)$
Reactants = sodium nitrate, sulfuric acid
Products = sodium sulfate, nitric acid
(d) $NiCO_3(s) + 2 HNO_3(aq) \rightarrow$
$Ni(NO_3)_2(aq) + CO_2(g) + H_2O(\ell)$
Reactants = nickel(II) carbonate, nitric acid
Products = nickel(II) nitrate, carbon dioxide, water

3.7 The reaction involving HCl is more product-favored at equilibrium.

3.9 Electrolytes are compounds whose aqueous solutions conduct electricity. Given an aqueous solution containing a strong electrolyte and another aqueous solution containing a weak electrolyte at the same concentration, the solution containing the strong electrolyte (such as NaCl) will conduct electricity much better than will be the one containing the weak electrolyte (such as acetic acid).

3.11 (a) $CuCl_2$
(b) $AgNO_3$
(c) All are water-soluble

3.13 (a) K^+ and OH^- ions
(b) K^+ and SO_4^{2-} ions
(c) Li^+ and NO_3^- ions
(d) NH_4^+ and SO_4^{2-} ions

3.15 (a) Soluble, Na^+ and CO_3^{2-} ions
(b) Soluble, Cu^{2+} and SO_4^{2-} ions
(c) Insoluble
(d) Soluble, Ba^{2+} and Br^- ions

3.17 $CdCl_2(aq) + 2 NaOH(aq) \rightarrow$
$Cd(OH)_2(s) + 2 NaCl(aq)$
$Cd^{2+}(aq) + 2 OH^-(aq) \rightarrow Cd(OH)_2(s)$

3.19 (a) $NiCl_2(aq) + (NH_4)_2S(aq) \rightarrow NiS(s) + 2 NH_4Cl(aq)$
$Ni^{2+}(aq) + S^{2-}(aq) \rightarrow NiS(s)$
(b) $3 Mn(NO_3)_2(aq) + 2 Na_3PO_4(aq) \rightarrow$
$Mn_3(PO_4)_2(s) + 6 NaNO_3(aq)$
$3 Mn^{2+}(aq) + 2 PO_4^{3-}(aq) \rightarrow Mn_3(PO_4)_2(s)$

3.21 $HNO_3(aq) + H_2O(\ell) \rightarrow H_3O^+(aq) + NO_3^-(aq)$

3.23 $H_2C_2O_4(aq) + H_2O(\ell) \rightarrow H_3O^+(aq) + HC_2O_4^-(aq)$
$HC_2O_4^-(aq) + H_2O(\ell) \rightarrow H_3O^+(aq) + C_2O_4^{2-}(aq)$

3.25 $MgO(s) + H_2O(\ell) \rightarrow Mg(OH)_2(s)$

3.27 (a) Acetic acid reacts with magnesium hydroxide to give magnesium acetate and water.
$2 CH_3CO_2H(aq) + Mg(OH)_2(s) \rightarrow$
$Mg(CH_3CO_2)_2(aq) + 2 H_2O(\ell)$
Brønsted acid: acetic acid; Brønsted base: magnesium hydroxide
(b) Perchloric acid reacts with ammonia to give ammonium perchlorate
$HClO_4(aq) + NH_3(aq) \rightarrow NH_4ClO_4(aq)$
Brønsted acid: perchloric acid; Brønsted base: ammonia

3.29 $Ba(OH)_2(aq) + 2 HNO_3(aq) \rightarrow$
$Ba(NO_3)_2(aq) + 2 H_2O(\ell)$

3.31 Strong Brønsted acid examples: hydrochloric acid, nitric acid

Strong Brønsted base example: sodium hydroxide

3.33 (a) $(NH_4)_2CO_3(aq) + Cu(NO_3)_2(aq) \rightarrow$
$$CuCO_3(s) + 2\ NH_4NO_3(aq)$$

$$CO_3^{2-}(aq) + Cu^{2+}(aq) \rightarrow CuCO_3(s)$$

(b) $Pb(OH)_2(s) + 2\ HCl(aq) \rightarrow PbCl_2(s) + 2\ H_2O(\ell)$

$$Pb(OH)_2(s) + 2\ H_3O^+(aq) + 2\ Cl^-(aq) \rightarrow$$
$$PbCl_2(s) + 4\ H_2O(\ell)$$

(c) $BaCO_3(s) + 2\ HCl(aq) \rightarrow$
$$BaCl_2(aq) + H_2O(\ell) + CO_2(g)$$

$$BaCO_3(s) + 2\ H_3O^+(aq) \rightarrow$$
$$Ba^{2+}(aq) + 3\ H_2O(\ell) + CO_2(g)$$

(d) $2\ CH_3CO_2H(aq) + Ni(OH)_2(s) \rightarrow$
$$Ni(CH_3CO_2)_2(aq) + 2\ H_2O(\ell)$$

$$2\ CH_3CO_2H(aq) + Ni(OH)_2(s) \rightarrow$$
$$Ni^{2+}(aq) + 2\ CH_3CO_2^-(aq) + 2\ H_2O(\ell)$$

3.35 (a) $AgNO_3(aq) + KI(aq) \rightarrow AgI(s) + KNO_3(aq)$

$$Ag^+(aq) + I^-(aq) \rightarrow AgI(s)$$

(b) $Ba(OH)_2(aq) + 2\ HNO_3(aq) \rightarrow$
$$Ba(NO_3)_2(aq) + 2\ H_2O(\ell)$$

$$OH^-(aq) + H_3O^+(aq) \rightarrow 2\ H_2O(\ell)$$

(c) $2\ Na_3PO_4(aq) + 3\ Ni(NO_3)_2(aq) \rightarrow$
$$Ni_3(PO_4)_2(s) + 6\ NaNO_3(aq)$$

$$2\ PO_4^{3-}(aq) + 3\ Ni^{2+}(aq) \rightarrow Ni_3(PO_4)_2(s)$$

3.37 $FeCO_3(s) + 2\ HNO_3(aq) \rightarrow$
$$Fe(NO_3)_2(aq) + CO_2(g) + H_2O(\ell)$$

Iron(II) carbonate reacts with nitric acid to give iron(II) nitrate, carbon dioxide, and water.

3.39 $(NH_4)_2S(aq) + 2\ HBr(aq) \rightarrow 2\ NH_4Br(aq) + H_2S(g)$

Ammonium sulfide reacts with hydrobromic acid to give ammonium bromide and hydrogen sulfide.

3.41 (a) $Br = +5$ and $O = -2$
(b) $C = +3$ each and $O = -2$
(c) $F = -1$
(d) $Ca = +2$ and $H = -1$
(e) $H = +1$, $Si = +4$, and $O = -2$
(f) $H = +1$, $S = +6$, and $O = -2$

3.43 (a) Oxidation–reduction
Zn is oxidized from 0 to +2, and N in NO_3^- is reduced from +5 to +4 in NO_2.
(b) Acid–base reaction
(c) Oxidation–reduction

Calcium is oxidized from 0 to +2 in $Ca(OH)_2$, and H is reduced from +1 in H_2O to 0 in H_2.

3.45 (a) O_2 is the oxidizing agent (as it always is) and so C_2H_4 is the reducing agent. In this process, C_2H_4 is oxidized, and O_2 is reduced.

(b) Si is oxidized from 0 in Si to +4 in $SiCl_4$. Cl_2 is reduced from 0 in Cl_2 to −1 in Cl^-. Si is the reducing agent, and Cl_2 is the oxidizing agent.

3.47 (a) Acid–base

$$Ba(OH)_2(aq) + 2\ HCl(aq) \rightarrow$$
$$BaCl_2(aq) + 2\ H_2O($$

(b) Gas-forming

$$2\ HNO_3(aq) + CoCO_3(s) \rightarrow$$
$$Co(NO_3)_2(aq) + H_2O(\ell) + CO_2($$

(c) Precipitation

$$2\ Na_3PO_4(aq) + 3\ Cu(NO_3)_2(aq) \rightarrow$$
$$Cu_3(PO_4)_2(s) + 6\ NaNO_3(a$$

3.49 a) Precipitation

$$MnCl_2(aq) + Na_2S(aq) \rightarrow MnS(s) + 2\ NaCl(aq)$$

$$Mn^{2+}(aq) + S^{2-}(aq) \rightarrow MnS(s)$$

(b) Precipitation

$$K_2CO_3(aq) + ZnCl_2(aq) \rightarrow ZnCO_3(s) + 2\ KCl(a$$

$$CO_3^{2-}(aq) + Zn^{2+}(aq) \rightarrow ZnCO_3(s)$$

3.51 (a) $CuCl_2(aq) + H_2S(aq) \rightarrow CuS(s) + 2\ HCl(aq)$
precipitation

(b) $H_3PO_4(aq) + 3\ KOH(aq) \rightarrow$
$$3\ H_2O(\ell) + K_3PO_4(a$$

acid–base

(c) $Ca(s) + 2\ HBr(aq) \rightarrow H_2(g) + CaBr_2(aq)$

oxidation–reduction and gas-forming

(d) $MgCl_2(aq) + 2\ H_2O(\ell) \rightarrow$
$$Mg(OH)_2(s) + 2\ HCl(a$$

precipitation

3.53 (a) $CO_2(g) + 2\ NH_3(g) \rightarrow NH_2CONH_2(s) + H_2O(\ell$
(b) $UO_2(s) + 4\ HF(aq) \rightarrow UF_4(s) + 2\ H_2O(\ell)$

$$UF_4(s) + F_2(g) \rightarrow UF_6(s)$$

(c) $TiO_2(s) + 2\ Cl_2(g) + 2\ C(s) \rightarrow$
$$TiCl_4(\ell) + 2\ CO(g$$

$$TiCl_4(\ell) + 2\ Mg(s) \rightarrow Ti(s) + 2\ MgCl_2(s)$$

3.55 (a) NaBr, KBr, or other alkali metal bromides; Group 2A bromides; other metal bromides except AgBr, Hg_2Br_2, and $PbBr_2$
(b) $Al(OH)_3$ and transition metal hydroxides
(c) Alkaline earth carbonates ($CaCO_3$) or transition metal carbonates ($NiCO_3$)
(d) Metal nitrates are generally water-soluble [e.g., $NaNO_3$, $Ni(NO_3)_2$].
(e) CH_3CO_2H, other acids containing the $-CO_2H$ group

3.57 Water soluble: $Cu(NO_3)_2$, $CuCl_2$. Water-insoluble: $CuCO_3$, $Cu_3(PO_4)_2$

.59 Spectator ion, NO_3^-. Acid–base reaction.

$$2\ H_3O^+(aq)\ +\ Mg(OH)_2(s) \rightarrow 4\ H_2O(\ell)\ +\ Mg^{2+}(aq)$$

.61 (a) Cl_2 is reduced (to Cl^-) and Br^- is oxidized (to Br_2).

(b) Cl_2 is the oxidizing agent and Br^- is the reducing agent.

.63 (a) $MgCO_3(s)\ +\ 2\ H_3O^+(aq) \rightarrow$
$$CO_2(g)\ +\ Mg^{2+}(aq)\ +\ 3\ H_2O(\ell)$$

Chloride ion (Cl^-) is the spectator ion.

(b) Gas-forming reaction

.65 (a) H_2O, NH_3, NH_4^+, and OH^- (and a trace of H_3O^+)

weak Brønsted base

(b) H_2O, CH_3CO_2H, $CH_3CO_2^-$, and H_3O^+ (and a trace of OH^-)

weak Brønsted acid

(c) H_2O, Na^+, and OH^- (and a trace of H_3O^+)

strong Brønsted base

(d) H_2O, H_3O^+, and Br^- (and a trace of OH^-)

strong Brønsted acid

.67 (a) $K_2CO_3(aq)\ +\ 2\ HClO_4(aq) \rightarrow$
$$2\ KClO_4(aq)\ +\ CO_2(g)\ +\ H_2O(\ell)$$
gas-forming

Potassium carbonate and perchloric acid react to form potassium perchlorate, carbon dioxide, and water

$$CO_3^{2-}(aq)\ +\ 2\ H_3O^+(aq) \rightarrow CO_2(g)\ +\ 3\ H_2O(\ell)$$

(b) $FeCl_2(aq)\ +\ (NH_4)_2S(aq) \rightarrow$
$$FeS(s)\ +\ 2\ NH_4Cl(aq)$$
precipitation

Iron(II) chloride and ammonium sulfide react to form iron(II) sulfide and ammonium chloride

$$Fe^{2+}(aq)\ +\ S^{2-}(aq) \rightarrow FeS(s)$$

(c) $Fe(NO_3)_2(aq)\ +\ Na_2CO_3(aq) \rightarrow$
$$FeCO_3(s)\ +\ 2\ NaNO_3(aq)$$
precipitation

Iron(II) nitrate and sodium carbonate react to form iron(II) carbonate and sodium nitrate

$$Fe^{2+}(aq)\ +\ CO_3^{2-}(aq) \rightarrow FeCO_3(s)$$

(d) $3\ NaOH(aq)\ +\ FeCl_3(aq) \rightarrow$
$$3\ NaCl(aq)\ +\ Fe(OH)_3(s)$$
precipitation

Sodium hydroxide and iron(III) chloride react to form sodium chloride and iron(III) hydroxide

$$3\ OH^-(aq)\ +\ Fe^{3+}(aq) \rightarrow Fe(OH)_3(s)$$

3.69 (a) Reactants: $Na(+1)$, $I(-1)$, $H(+1)$, $S(+6)$, $O(-2)$, $Mn(+4)$

Products: $Na(+1)$, $S(+6)$, $O(-2)$, $Mn(+2)$, $I(0)$, $H(+1)$

(b) The oxidizing agent is MnO_2, and NaI is oxidized. The reducing agent is NaI, and MnO_2 is reduced.

(c) Based on the picture, the reaction is product-favored.

(d) Sodium iodide, sulfuric acid, and manganese(IV) oxide react to form sodium sulfate, manganese(II) sulfate, and water.

3.71 Among the reactions that could be used are the following:

$$MgCO_3(s)\ +\ 2\ HCl(aq) \rightarrow$$
$$MgCl_2(aq)\ +\ CO_2(g)\ +\ H_2O(\ell)$$

$$MgS(s)\ +\ 2\ HCl(aq) \rightarrow MgCl_2(aq)\ +\ H_2S(g)$$

$$MgSO_3(s)\ +\ 2\ HCl(aq) \rightarrow$$
$$MgCl_2(aq)\ +\ SO_2(g)\ +\ H_2O(\ell)$$

In each case, the resulting solution could be evaporated to obtain the desired magnesium chloride.

3.73 The Ag^+ was reduced (to silver metal), and the glucose was oxidized (to $C_6H_{12}O_7$). The Ag^+ is the oxidizing agent, and the glucose is the reducing agent.

3.75 Weak electrolyte test: Compare the conductivity of a solution of lactic acid and that of an equal concentration of a strong acid. The conductivity of the lactic acid solution should be significantly less.

Reversible reaction: The fact that lactic acid is an electrolyte indicates that the reaction proceeds in the forward direction. To test whether the ionization is reversible, one could prepare a solution containing as much lactic acid as it will hold and then add a strong acid (to provide H_3O^+). If the reaction proceeds in the reverse direction, this will cause some lactic acid to precipitate.

3.77 (a) Several precipitation reactions are possible:

i. $BaCl_2(aq)\ +\ H_2SO_4(aq) \rightarrow$
$$BaSO_4(s)\ +\ 2\ HCl(aq)$$

ii. $BaCl_2(aq)\ +\ Na_2SO_4(aq) \rightarrow$
$$BaSO_4(s)\ +\ 2\ NaCl(aq)$$

iii. $Ba(OH)_2(aq)\ +\ H_2SO_4(aq) \rightarrow$
$$BaSO_4(s)\ +\ 2\ H_2O(\ell)$$

(b) Gas-forming reaction:

$$BaCO_3(s)\ +\ H_2SO_4(aq) \rightarrow$$
$$BaSO_4(s)\ +\ CO_2(g)\ +\ H_2O(\ell)$$

CHAPTER 4

4.1 4.5 mol O_2; 310 g Al_2O_3

4.3 22.7 g Br_2; 25.3 g Al_2Br_6

4.5 (a) CO_2, carbon dioxide, and H_2O, water
(b) $CH_4(g) + 2\ O_2(g) \rightarrow CO_2(g) + 2\ H_2O(\ell)$
(c) 102 g O_2
(d) 128 g products

4.7

Equation	2 PbS(s)	+ 3 O₂(g) →	2 PbO(s)	+ 2 SO₂(g)
Initial (mol)	2.5	3.8	0	0
Change (mol)	−2.5	−³⁄₂(2.5) = −3.8	+²⁄₂(2.5) = +2.5	+²⁄₂(2.5) = +2.5
Final (mol)	0	0	2.5	2.5

The amounts table shows that 2.5 mol of PbS requires $\frac{3}{2}(2.5) = 3.8$ mol of O_2 and produces 2.5 mol of PbO and 2.5 mol of SO_2.

4.9 (a) Balanced equation: $4\ Cr(s) + 3\ O_2(g) \rightarrow 2\ Cr_2O_3(s)$
(b) 0.175 g of Cr is equivalent to 0.00337 mol

Equation	4 Cr(s)	+ 3 O₂(g)	→	2 Cr₂O₃(s)
Initial (mol)	0.00337	0.00252 mol		0
Change (mol)	−0.00337	−³⁄₄(0.00337) = −0.00252		²⁄₄(0.00337) = +0.00168
Final (mol)	0	0		0.00168

The 0.00168 mol Cr_2O_3 produced corresponds to 0.256 g Cr_2O_3.
(c) 0.081 g O_2

4.11 0.11 mol of Na_2SO_4 and 0.62 mol of C are mixed. Sodium sulfate is the limiting reactant. Therefore, 0.11 mol of Na_2S is formed, or 8.2 g.

4.13 F_2 is the limiting reactant.

4.15 (a) CH_4 is the limiting reactant.
(b) 375 g H_2
(c) Excess H_2O = 1390 g

4.17 (a) $2\ C_6H_{14}(\ell) + 19\ O_2(g) \rightarrow 12\ CO_2(g) + 14\ H_2O(g)$
(b) O_2 is the limiting reactant. Products are 187 g of CO_2 and 89.2 g of H_2O.
(c) 154 g of hexane remains
(d)

Equation	2 C₆H₁₄(ℓ)	+ 19 O₂(g) →	12 CO₂(g)	+ 14 H₂O(g)
Initial (mol)	2.49	6.72	0	0
Change (mol)	−0.707	−6.72	+4.24	+4.95
Final (mol)	1.78	0	4.24	4.95

4.19 $(332\ g/407\ g)\,100\% = 81.6\%$

4.21 (a) 14.3 g $Cu(NH_3)_4SO_4$
(b) 88.3% yield

4.23 91.9% hydrate

4.25 84.3% $CaCO_3$

4.27 1.467% Tl_2SO_4

4.29 Empirical formula = CH

4.31 Empirical formula = CH_2; molecular formula = C_5H

4.33 Empirical formula = CH_3O; molecular formula = $C_2H_6O_2$

4.35 $Ni(CO)_4$

4.37 $[Na_2CO_3] = 0.254$ M; $[Na^+] = 0.508$ M; $[CO_3{}^{2-}] = 0.254$ M

4.39 0.494 g $KMnO_4$

4.41 5.08×10^3 mL

4.43 (a) 0.50 M $NH_4{}^+$ and 0.25 M $SO_4{}^{2-}$
(b) 0.246 M Na^+ and 0.123 M $CO_3{}^{2-}$
(c) 0.056 M H^+ and 0.056 M $NO_3{}^-$

4.45 A mass of 1.06 g of Na_2CO_3 is required. After weighing out this quantity of Na_2CO_3, transfer it to a 500.-mL volumetric flask. Rinse any solid from the neck of the flask while filling the flask with distilled water. Dissolve the solute in water. Add water until the bottom of the meniscus of the water is at the top of the scribed mark on the neck of the flask. Thoroughly mix the solution.

4.47 0.0750 M

4.49 Method (a) is correct. Method (b) gives an acid concentration of 0.15 M.

4.51 0.00340 M

4.53 $[H_3O^+] = 10^{-pH} = 4.0 \times 10^{-4}$ M; the solution is acidic.

4.55 HNO_3 is a strong acid, so $[H_3O^+] = 0.0013$ M. pH = 2.89.

4.57

	pH	$[H_3O^+]$	Acidic/Basic
(a)	1.00	0.10 M	Acidic
(b)	10.50	3.2×10^{-11} M	Basic
(c)	4.89	1.3×10^{-5} M	Acidic
(d)	7.64	2.3×10^{-8} M	Basic

4.59 268 mL

4.61 210 g NaOH and 190 g Cl_2

4.63 174 mL of $Na_2S_2O_3$

4.65 1.50×10^3 mL of $Pb(NO_3)_2$

4.67 44.6 mL

4.69 1.052 M HCl

4.71 104 g/mol

4.73 12.8% Fe

4.75

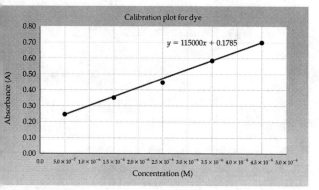

(a) slope = 1.2×10^5 M^{-1}; y-intercept = 0.18 M
(b) 3.0×10^{-6} M

4.77 (a) Products = $CO_2(g)$ and $H_2O(g)$
(b) $2\ C_6H_6(\ell) + 15\ O_2(g) \rightarrow 12\ CO_2(g) + 6\ H_2O(g)$
(c) 49.28 g O_2
(d) 65.32 g products (= sum of C_6H_6 mass and O_2 mass)

4.79 0.28 g arginine, 0.21 g ornithine

4.81 (a) titanium(IV) chloride, water, titanium(IV) oxide, hydrogen chloride
(b) 4.60 g H_2O
(c) 10.2 TiO_2, 18.6 g HCl

4.83 8.33 g NaN_3

4.85 Mass percent saccharin = 75.92%

4.87 SiH_4

4.89 C_3H_2O

4.91 1.85 kg H_2SO_4

4.93 The calculated molar mass of the metal is 1.2×10^2 g/mol. The metal is probably tin (118.67 g/mol).

4.95 479 kg Cl_2

4.97 66.5 kg CaO

4.99 1.29 g C_4H_8 (45.1%) and 1.57 g C_4H_{10} (54.9%)

4.101 62.2% Cu_2S and 26.8% CuS

4.103 (a) $MgCO_3(s) + 2\ H_3O^+(aq) \rightarrow$
$CO_2(g) + Mg^{2+}(aq) + 2\ H_2O(\ell)$
(b) Gas-forming reaction
(c) 0.15 g

4.105 15.0 g of $NaHCO_3$ require 1190 mL of 0.15 M acetic acid. Therefore, acetic acid is the limiting reactant. (Conversely, 125 mL of 0.15 M acetic acid requires only 1.58 g of $NaHCO_3$.) 1.54 g of $NaCH_3CO_2$ produced.

4.107 3.13 g $Na_2S_2O_3$, 96.8%

4.109 (a) pH = 0.979
(b) $[H_3O^+]$ = 0.0028 M; the solution is acidic.
(c) $[H_3O^+]$ = 2.1×10^{-10} M; the solution is basic.
(d) The new solution's concentration is 0.102 M HCl; the pH = 0.990

4.111 The concentration of hydrochloric acid is 2.92 M; the pH is -0.465

4.113 1.56 g of $CaCO_3$ required; 1.00 g $CaCO_3$ remain; 1.73 g $CaCl_2$ produced.

4.115 Volume of water in the pool = 7.6×10^4 L

4.117 (a) Au, gold, has been oxidized and is the reducing agent.

O_2, oxygen, has been reduced and is the oxidizing agent.

(b) 26 L NaCN solution

4.119 The concentration of Na_2CO_3 in the first solution prepared is 0.0275 M, in the second solution prepared the concentration of Na_2CO_3 is 0.00110 M.

4.121 (a) First reaction: oxidizing agent = Cu^{2+} and reducing agent = I^-

Second reaction: oxidizing agent = I_3^- and reducing agent = $S_2O_3^{2-}$

(b) 67.3% copper

4.123 x = 6; $Co(NH_3)_6Cl_3$.

4.125 11.48% 2,4-D

4.127 3.3 mol H_2O/mol $CaCl_2$

4.129 (a) Slope = 2.06×10^5; 0.024
(b) 1.20×10^{-4} g/L
(c) 0.413 mg PO_4^{3-}

4.131 The total mass of the beakers and products after reaction is equal to the total mass before the reaction (161.170 g) because no gases were produced in the reaction and there is conservation of mass in chemical reactions.

4.133 The balanced chemical equation indicates that the stoichiometric ratio of HCl to Zn is 2 mol HCl/1 mol Zn. In each reaction, there is 0.100 mol of HCl present. In reaction 1, there is 0.107 mol of Zn present. This gives a 0.93 mole HCl/mol Zn ratio, indicating that HCl is the limiting reactant. In reaction 2, there is 0.050 mol of Zn, giving a 2.0 mol HCl/mol Zn ratio. This indicates that the two reactants are present in exactly the correct stoichiometric ratio. In reaction 3, there is 0.020 mol of Zn, giving a 5.0 mol HCl/mol Zn ratio. This indicates that the HCl is present in excess and that the zinc is the limiting reactant.

4.135 If both students base their calculations on the amount of HCl solution pipeted into the flask (20 mL), then the second student's result will be (e), the same as the first student's. However, if the HCl concentration is calculated using the diluted solution volume, student 1 will use a volume of 40 mL, and student 2 will use a volume of 80 mL in the calculation. The second student's result will be (c), half that of the first student's.

4.137 150 mg/dL. Person is intoxicated.

CHAPTER 5

5.1 Mechanical energy is used to move the lever, which in turn moves gears. The device produces electrical energy and radiant energy.

5.3 5.0×10^6 J

5.5 170 kcal is equivalent to 710 kJ, considerably greater than 280 kJ.

5.7 0.140 J/g · K

5.9 2.44 kJ

5.11 32.8 °C

5.13 20.7 °C

5.15 47.8 °C

5.17 0.40 J/g · K

5.19 330 kJ

5.21 49.3 kJ

5.23 273 J

5.25 9.97×10^5 J

5.27 Reaction is exothermic because $\Delta_r H°$ is negative. The heat evolved is 2.38 kJ.

5.29 3.3×10^4 kJ

5.31 $\Delta H = -56$ kJ/mol CsOH

5.33 0.52 J/g · K

5.35 $\Delta_r H = +23$ kJ/mol-rxn

5.37 297 kJ/mol SO_2

5.39 3.09×10^3 kJ/mol $C_6H_5CO_2H$

5.41 0.236 J/g · K

5.43 (a) $\Delta_r H° = -126$ kJ/mol-rxn
(b)

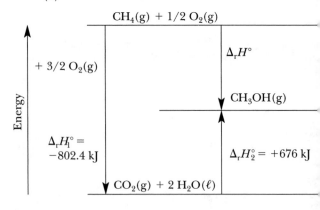

5.45 $\Delta_r H° = +90.3$ kJ/mol-rxn

5.47 $C(s) + 2 H_2(g) + 1/2 O_2(g) \rightarrow CH_3OH(\ell)$

$\Delta_f H° = -238.4$ kJ/mol

5.49 (a) $2 Cr(s) + 3/2 O_2(g) \rightarrow Cr_2O_3(s)$

$\Delta_f H° = -1134.7$ kJ/mol

(b) 2.4 g is equivalent to 0.046 mol of Cr. This will produce 26 kJ of energy transferred as heat.

5.51 (a) $\Delta H° = -24$ kJ for 1.0 g of phosphorus
(b) $\Delta H° = -18$ kJ for 0.2 mol NO
(c) $\Delta H° = -16.9$ kJ for the formation of 2.40 g of NaCl(s)
(d) $\Delta H° = -1.8 \times 10^3$ kJ for the oxidation of 250 g of iron

5.53 (a) $\Delta_r H° = -906.2$ kJ
(b) The heat evolved is 133 kJ for the oxidation of 10.0 g of NH_3

5.55 (a) $\Delta_r H° = +161.6$ kJ/mol-rxn; the reaction is endothermic.
(b)

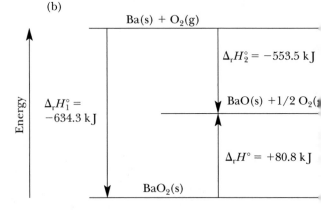

5.57 $\Delta_f H° = +77.7$ kJ/mol for naphthalene

5.59 (a) Exothermic: a process in which energy is transferred as heat from a system to its surroundings. (The combustion of methane is exothermic.)

Endothermic: a process in which energy is transferred as heat from the surroundings to the system. (Ice melting is endothermic.)

(b) System: the object or collection of objects being studied. (A chemical reaction—the system—taking place inside a calorimeter—the surroundings.)

Surroundings: everything outside the system that can exchange mass or energy with the system. (The calorimeter and everything outside the calorimeter comprise the surroundings.)

(c) Specific heat capacity: the quantity of energy that must be transferred as heat to raise the temperature of 1 gram of a substance 1 kelvin. (The specific heat capacity of water is 4.184 J/g · K.)

(d) State function: a quantity that is characterized by changes that do not depend on the path chosen to go from the initial state to the final state. (Enthalpy and internal energy are state functions.)

(e) Standard state: the most stable form of a substance in the physical state that exists at a pressure of 1 bar and at a specified temperature. (The standard state of carbon at 25 °C is graphite.)

(f) Enthalpy change, ΔH: the energy transferred as heat at constant pressure. (The enthalpy change for melting ice at 0 °C is 6.00 kJ/mol.)

(g) Standard enthalpy of formation: the enthalpy change for the formation of 1 mol of a compound in its standard state directly from the component elements in their standard states. ($\Delta_f H°$ for liquid water is -285.83 kJ/mol)

5.61 (a) System: reaction between methane and oxygen

Surroundings: the furnace and the rest of the universe. Energy is transferred as heat from the system to the surroundings.

(b) System: water drops

Surroundings: skin and the rest of the universe

Energy is transferred as heat from the surroundings to the system

(c) System: water

Surroundings: freezer and the rest of the universe

Energy is transferred as heat from the system to the surroundings

(d) System: reaction of aluminum and iron(III) oxide

Surroundings: flask, laboratory bench, and rest of the universe

Energy is transferred as heat from the system to the surroundings.

5.63 Standard state of oxygen is gas, $O_2(g)$.

$$O_2(g) \rightarrow 2\ O(g),\ \Delta_r H° = +498.34\ \text{kJ, endothermic}$$
$$3/2\ O_2(g) \rightarrow O_3(g),\ \Delta_r H° = +142.67\ \text{kJ}$$

5.65

$SnBr_2(s) + TiCl_2(s) \rightarrow SnCl_2(s) + TiBr_2(s)$		$\Delta_r H° = -4.2$ kJ
$SnCl_2(s) + Cl_2(g) \rightarrow SnCl_4(\ell)$		$\Delta_r H° = -195$ kJ
$TiCl_4(\ell) \rightarrow TiCl_2(s) + Cl_2(g)$		$\Delta_r H° = +273$ kJ
$SnBr_2(s) + TiCl_4(\ell) \rightarrow SnCl_4(\ell) + TiBr_2(s)$		$\Delta_r H° = +74$ kJ

5.67 $C_{Ag} = 0.24$ J/g · K

5.69 Mass of ice melted = 75.4 g

5.71 Final temperature = 278 K (4.8 °C)

5.73 (a) When summed, the following equations give the balanced equation for the formation of $B_2H_6(g)$ from the elements.

$2\ B(s) + 3/2\ O_2(g) \rightarrow B_2O_3(s)$	$\Delta_r H° = -1271.9$ kJ
$3\ H_2(g) + 3/2\ O_2(g) \rightarrow 3\ H_2O(g)$	$\Delta_r H° = -725.4$ kJ
$B_2O_3(s) + 3\ H_2O(g) \rightarrow B_2H_6(g) + 3\ O_2(g)$	$\Delta_r H° = +2032.9$ kJ
$2\ B(s) + 3\ H_2(g) \rightarrow B_2H_6(g)$	$\Delta_r H° = +35.6$ kJ

(b) The enthalpy of formation of $B_2H_6(g)$ is +35.6 kJ/mol

(c)

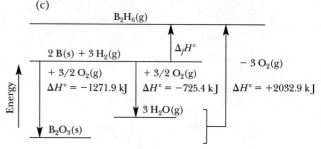

(d) The formation of $B_2H_6(g)$ is reactant-favored.

5.75 (a) $\Delta_r H° = +131.31$ kJ
(b) Reactant-favored
(c) 1.0932×10^7 kJ

5.77 Assuming $CO_2(g)$ and $H_2O(\ell)$ are the products of combustion:

$\Delta_r H°$ for isooctane is -5461.3 kJ/mol or -47.81 kJ per gram

$\Delta_r H°$ for liquid methanol is -726.77 kJ/mol or -22.682 kJ per gram

5.79 (a) Adding the equations as they are given in the question results in the desired equation for the formation of $SrCO_3(s)$. The calculated $\Delta_r H° = -1220.$ kJ/mol.

(b)

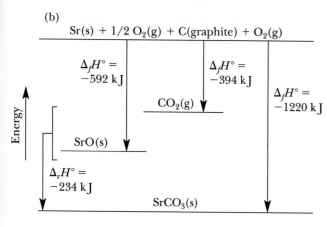

Sr(s) + 1/2 O₂(g) + C(graphite) + O₂(g)

$\Delta_f H° = -592\ kJ$

$\Delta_f H° = -394\ kJ$

$\Delta_f H° = -1220\ kJ$

$CO_2(g)$

$SrO(s)$

$\Delta_r H° = -234\ kJ$

$SrCO_3(s)$

5.81 $\Delta_r H° = -305.3\ kJ$

5.83 $C_{Pb} = 0.121\ J/g \cdot K$

5.85 $\Delta_r H = -69\ kJ/mol\ AgCl$

5.87 36.0 kJ evolved per mol of NH_4NO_3

5.89 The standard enthalpy change, $\Delta_r H°$, is $-352.88\ kJ$. The quantity of magnesium needed is 0.43 g.

5.91 (a) product-favored
(b) reactant-favored

5.93 The enthalpy change for each of the three reactions below is known or can be measured by calorimetry. The three equations sum to give the enthalpy of formation of $CaSO_4(s)$.

$Ca(s)\quad + 1/2\ O_2(g)$	$\rightarrow$	$CaO(s)$	$\Delta_r H° = \Delta_f H° = -635.09\ kJ$
$1/8\ S_8(s) + 3/2\ O_2(g)$	$\rightarrow$	$SO_3(g)$	$\Delta_r H° = \Delta_f H° = -395.77\ kJ$
$CaO(s)\quad + SO_3(g)$	$\rightarrow$	$CaSO_4(s)$	$\Delta_r H° = -402.7\ kJ$
$Ca(s) + 1/8\ S_8(s) + 2\ O_2(g)$	$\rightarrow$	$CaSO_4(s)$	$\Delta_r H° = \Delta_f H° = -1433.6\ kJ$

5.95

Metal	Molar Heat Capacity (J/mol · K)
Al	24.2
Fe	25.1
Cu	24.5
Au	25.4

All the metals have a molar heat capacity of 24.8 J/mol · K plus or minus 0.6 J/mol · K. Therefore, assuming the molar heat capacity of Ag is 24.8 J/mol · K, its specific heat capacity is 0.230 J/g · K. This is very close to the experimental value of 0.236 J/g · K.

5.97 120 g of CH_4 required (assuming $H_2O(g)$ as product)

5.99 1.6×10^{11} kJ released to the surroundings. This is equivalent to 3.8×10^4 tons of dynamite.

5.101 (a)

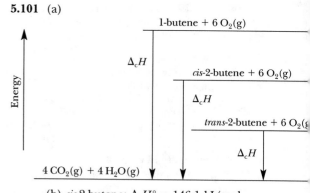

1-butene + 6 O₂(g)

$\Delta_c H$

cis-2-butene + 6 O₂(g)

$\Delta_c H$

trans-2-butene + 6 O₂(g)

$\Delta_c H$

4 CO₂(g) + 4 H₂O(g)

(b) cis-2-butene: $\Delta_f H° = 146.1\ kJ/mol$

trans-2-butene: $\Delta_f H° = 142.8\ kJ/mol$

1-butene: $\Delta_f H° = 155.3\ kJ/mol$

(c)

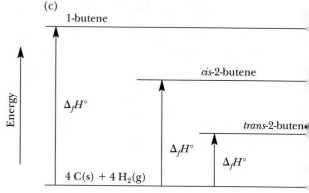

1-butene

cis-2-butene

trans-2-butene

$\Delta_f H°$

$\Delta_f H°$

$\Delta_f H°$

4 C(s) + 4 H₂(g)

(d) $-3.3\ kJ/mol$-rxn

5.103 (a) $-726\ kJ/mol\ Mg$
(b) 25.0 °C

5.105 (a) Methane
(b) Methane
(c) $-279\ kJ$
(d) $CH_4(g) + 2\ O_2(g) \rightarrow CH_3OH(\ell)$

5.107 (a) Metal Heated = 100.0 g of Al; Metal Cooled = 50.0 g of Au; Final Temperature = 26 °C
(b) Metal Heated = 50.0 g of Zn; Metal Cooled = 50.0 g of Al; Final Temperature = 21 °C

CHAPTER 6

6.1 (a) microwaves
(b) red light
(c) infrared

6.3 (a) Green light has a higher frequency than amber light
(b) $5.04 \times 10^{14}\ s^{-1}$

6.5 Frequency = $6.0 \times 10^{14}\ s^{-1}$; energy per photon = $4.0 \times 10^{-19}\ J$; energy per mol of photons = 2.4×10^5

7 Frequency = 7.5676×10^{14} s^{-1}; energy per photon = 5.0144×10^{-19} J; 302 kJ/mol of photons

9 In order of increasing energy: FM station < microwaves < yellow light < x-rays

11 Light with a wavelength as long as 600 nm would be sufficient. This is in the visible region.

13 (a) The light of shortest wavelength has a wavelength of 253.652 nm.
(b) Frequency = 1.18190×10^{15} s^{-1}. Energy per photon = 7.83139×10^{-19} J/photon.
(c) The lines at 404 (violet) and 436 nm (blue) are in the visible region of the spectrum.

15 The color is violet. $n_{initial} = 6$ and $n_{final} = 2$

17 (a) 10 lines possible
(b) Highest frequency (highest energy), $n = 5$ to $n = 1$
(c) Longest wavelength (lowest energy), $n = 5$ to $n = 4$

19 (a) $n = 3$ to $n = 2$
(b) $n = 4$ to $n = 1$; The energy levels are progressively closer at higher levels, so the energy difference from $n = 4$ to $n = 1$ is greater than from $n = 5$ to $n = 2$.

21 Wavelength = 102.6 nm and frequency = 2.923×10^{15} s^{-1}. Light with these properties is in the ultraviolet region.

23 Wavelength = 0.29 nm

25 The wavelength is 2.2×10^{-25} nm. (Calculated from $\lambda = h/m \cdot v$, where m is the ball's mass in kg and v is the velocity.) To have a wavelength of 5.6×10^{-3} nm, the ball would have to travel at 1.2×10^{-21} m/s.

27 (a) $n = 4$, $\ell = 0, 1, 2, 3$
(b) When $\ell = 2$, $m_\ell = -2, -1, 0, 1, 2$
(c) For a 4s orbital, $n = 4$, $\ell = 0$, and $m_\ell = 0$
(d) For a 4f orbital, $n = 4$, $\ell = 3$, and $m_\ell = -3, -2, -1, 0, 1, 2, 3$

29 Set 1: $n = 4$, $\ell = 1$, and $m_\ell = -1$
Set 2: $n = 4$, $\ell = 1$, and $m_\ell = 0$
Set 3: $n = 4$, $\ell = 1$, and $m_\ell = +1$

31 Four subshells. (The number of subshells in a shell is always equal to n.)

33 (a) ℓ must have a value no greater than $n - 1$.
(b) When $\ell = 0$, m_ℓ can only equal 0.
(c) When $\ell = 0$, m_ℓ can only equal 0.

35 (a) None. The quantum number set is not possible. When $\ell = 0$, m_ℓ can only equal 0.
(b) 3 orbitals
(c) 11 orbitals
(d) 1 orbital

6.37 (a) $m_s = 0$ is not possible. m_s may only have values of $\pm 1/2$.
One possible set of quantum numbers: $n = 4$, $\ell = 2$, $m_\ell = 0$, $m_s = +1/2$
(b) m_ℓ cannot equal -3 in this case. If $\ell = 1$, m_ℓ can only be $-1, 0,$ or 1.
One possible set of quantum numbers: $n = 3$, $\ell = 1$, $m_\ell = -1$, $m_s = -1/2$
(c) $\ell = 3$ is not possible in this case. The maximum value of ℓ is $n - 1$.
One possible set of quantum numbers: $n = 3$, $\ell = 2$, $m_\ell = -1$, $m_s = +1/2$

6.39 2d and 3f orbitals cannot exist. The $n = 2$ shell consists only of s and p subshells. The $n = 3$ shell consists only of s, p, and d subshells.

6.41 (a) For 2p: $n = 2$, $\ell = 1$, and $m_\ell = -1, 0,$ or $+1$
(b) For 3d: $n = 3$, $\ell = 2$, and $m_\ell = -2, -1, 0, +1,$ or $+2$
(c) For 4f: $n = 4$, $\ell = 3$, and $m_\ell = -3, -2, -1, 0, +1, +2,$ or $+3$

6.43 4d

6.45 (a) 2s has 0 nodal surfaces that pass through the nucleus ($\ell = 0$).
(b) 5d has 2 nodal surfaces that pass through the nucleus ($\ell = 2$).
(c) 5f has three nodal surfaces that pass through the nucleus ($\ell = 3$).

6.47 (a) Correct
(b) Incorrect. The intensity of a light beam is independent of frequency and is related to the number of photons of light with a certain energy.
(c) Correct

6.49 Considering only angular nodes (nodal surfaces that pass through the nucleus):

s orbital	0 nodal surfaces
p orbitals	1 nodal surface or plane passing through the nucleus
d orbitals	2 nodal surfaces or planes passing through the nucleus
f orbitals	3 nodal surfaces or planes passing through the nucleus

6.51

ℓ value	Orbital Type
3	f
0	s
1	p
2	d

6.53 Considering only angular nodes (nodal surfaces that pass through the nucleus):

Orbital Type	Number of Orbitals in a Given Subshell	Number of Nodal Surfaces
s	1	0
p	3	1
d	5	2
f	7	3

6.55 (a) Green light
(b) Red light has a wavelength of 680 nm, and green light has a wavelength of 500 nm.
(c) Green light has a higher frequency than red light.

6.57 (a) Wavelength = 0.35 m
(b) Energy = 0.34 J/mol
(c) Blue light (with λ = 420 nm) has an energy of 280 kJ/mol of photons.
(d) Blue light has an energy (per mol of photons) that is 840,000 times greater than a mole of photons from a cell phone.

6.59 The ionization energy for He^+ is 5248 kJ/mol. This is four times the ionization energy for the H atom.

6.61 $1s < 2s = 2p < 3s = 3p = 3d < 4s$

In the H atom orbitals in the same shell (e.g., $2s$ and $2p$) have the same energy.

6.63 Frequency = 2.836×10^{20} s^{-1} and wavelength = 1.057×10^{-12} m

6.65 260 s or 4.3 min

6.67 (a) size and energy
(b) ℓ
(c) more
(d) 7 (when ℓ = 3 these are f orbitals)
(e) one orbital
(f) (left to right) d, s, and p
(g) ℓ = 0, 1, 2, 3, 4
(h) 16 orbitals ($1s$, $3p$, $5d$, and $7f$) (= n^2)
(i) paramagnetic

6.69 (a) Drawing (a) is a ferromagnetic solid, (b) is a diamagnetic solid, and (c) is a paramagnetic solid.
(b) Substance (a) would be most strongly attracted to a magnet, whereas (b) would be least strongly attracted.

6.71 The pickle glows because it was made by soaking a cucumber in brine, a concentrated solution of NaCl. The sodium atoms in the pickle are excited by the electric current and release energy as yellow light as they return to the ground state. Excited sodium atoms are the source of the yellow light you see in fireworks and in certain kinds of street lighting.

6.73 (a) λ = 0.0005 cm = 5 μm
(b) The left side is the higher energy side, and the right side is the lower energy side.
(c) The interaction with O—H requires more energy

6.75 (c)

6.77 An experiment can be done that shows that the electron can behave as a particle, and another experiment can be done to show that it has wave properties. (However, no single experiment shows both properties of the electron.) The modern view of atomic structure is based on the wave properties of the electron.

6.79 (a) and (b)

6.81 Radiation with a wavelength of 93.8 nm is sufficient to raise the electron to the n = 6 quantum level (see Figure 6.10). There should be 15 emission lines involving transitions from n = 6 to lower energy levels. (There are five lines for transitions from n = 6 to lower levels, four lines for n = 5 to lower levels, three for n = 4 to lower levels, two lines for n = 3 to lower levels, and one line for n = 2 to n = 1.) Wavelengths for many of the lines are given in Figure 6.10. For example, there will be an emission involving an electron moving from n = 6 to n = 2 with a wavelength of 410.2 nm.

6.83 (a) Group 7B (IUPAC Group 7); Period 5
(b) n = 5, ℓ = 0, m_ℓ = 0, m_s = +1/2
(c) λ = 8.79×10^{-12} m; ν = 3.41×10^{19} s^{-1}
(d) (i) $HTcO_4(aq) + NaOH(aq) \rightarrow$
$H_2O(\ell) + NaTcO_4(aq)$
(ii) 8.5×10^{-3} g $NaTcO_4$ produced;
1.8×10^{-3} g NaOH needed
(e) 0.28 mg $NaTcO_4$; 0.00015 M

6.85 Six emission lines are observed. More than one line is observed because the following changes in energy levels are possible: from n = 4 to n = 3, n = 2, and n = 1 (three lines), from n = 3 to n = 2 and n = 1 (2 lines), and from n = 2 to n = 1 (one line).

CHAPTER 7

7.1 (a) Phosphorus: $1s^2 2s^2 2p^6 3s^2 3p^3$

[↑↓] [↑↓] [↑↓][↑↓][↑↓] [↑↓] [↑][↑][↑]
1s   2s   2p   3s   3p

The element is in the third period in Group 5A. Therefore, it has five electrons in the third shell.
(b) Chlorine: $1s^2 2s^2 2p^6 3s^2 3p^5$

[↑↓] [↑↓] [↑↓][↑↓][↑↓] [↑↓] [↑↓][↑↓][↑]
1s   2s   2p   3s   3p

The element is in the third period and in Group 7A. Therefore, it has seven electrons in the third shell.

(a) Chromium: $1s^2 2s^2 2p^6 3s^2 3p^6 3d^5 4s^1$
(b) Iron: $1s^2 2s^2 2p^6 3s^2 3p^6 3d^6 4s^2$

(a) Arsenic: $1s^2 2s^2 2p^6 3s^2 3p^6 3d^{10} 4s^2 4p^3$;
   $[Ar]3d^{10}4s^2 4p^3$
(b) Krypton: $1s^2 2s^2 2p^6 3s^2 3p^6 3d^{10} 4s^2 4p^6$;
   $[Ar]3d^{10}4s^2 4p^6 = [Kr]$

(a) Tantalum: This is the third element in the transition series in the sixth period. Therefore, it has a
   core equivalent to Xe plus two 6s electrons, 14 4f
   electrons, and three electrons in 5d:
   $[Xe]4f^{14}5d^3 6s^2$
(b) Platinum: This is the eighth element in the transition series in the sixth period. Therefore, it is predicted to have a core equivalent to Xe plus two
   6s electrons, 14 4f electrons, and eight electrons
   in 5d: $[Xe]4f^{14}5d^8 6s^2$. In reality, its actual configuration (Table 7.3) is $[Xe]4f^{14}5d^9 6s^1$.

Americium: $[Rn]5f^7 7s^2$ (see Table 7.3)

11 (a) 2
(b) 1
(c) none (because ℓ cannot equal n)

13 Magnesium: $1s^2 2s^2 2p^6 3s^2$

$$[Ne] \boxed{\uparrow\downarrow}$$
$$3s$$

Quantum numbers for the two electrons in the
3s orbital:

$n = 3$, $\ell = 0$, $m_\ell = 0$, and $m_s = +1/2$

$n = 3$, $\ell = 0$, $m_\ell = 0$, and $m_s = -1/2$

15 Gallium: $1s^2 2s^2 2p^6 3s^2 3p^6 3d^{10} 4s^2 4p^1$

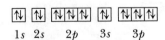
$$3d \qquad 4s \qquad 4p$$

Quantum numbers for the 4p electron:

$n = 4$, $\ell = 1$, $m_\ell = -1, 0,$ or $+1$, and $m_s = +\frac{1}{2}$ or $-\frac{1}{2}$

17 (a) Mg^{2+} ion

$$\boxed{\uparrow\downarrow}\ \boxed{\uparrow\downarrow}\ \boxed{\uparrow\downarrow}\boxed{\uparrow\downarrow}\boxed{\uparrow\downarrow}$$
$$1s \quad 2s \qquad 2p$$

(b) K^+ ion

$$\boxed{\uparrow\downarrow}\ \boxed{\uparrow\downarrow}\ \boxed{\uparrow\downarrow}\boxed{\uparrow\downarrow}\boxed{\uparrow\downarrow}\ \boxed{\uparrow\downarrow}\ \boxed{\uparrow\downarrow}\boxed{\uparrow\downarrow}\boxed{\uparrow\downarrow}$$
$$1s \quad 2s \qquad 2p \qquad 3s \qquad 3p$$

(c) Cl^- ion (Note that both Cl^- and K^+ have the same
   configuration; both are equivalent to Ar.)

$$\boxed{\uparrow\downarrow}\ \boxed{\uparrow\downarrow}\ \boxed{\uparrow\downarrow}\boxed{\uparrow\downarrow}\boxed{\uparrow\downarrow}\ \boxed{\uparrow\downarrow}\ \boxed{\uparrow\downarrow}\boxed{\uparrow\downarrow}\boxed{\uparrow\downarrow}$$
$$1s \quad 2s \qquad 2p \qquad 3s \qquad 3p$$

(d) O^{2-} ion

$$\boxed{\uparrow\downarrow}\ \boxed{\uparrow\downarrow}\ \boxed{\uparrow\downarrow}\boxed{\uparrow\downarrow}\boxed{\uparrow\downarrow}$$
$$1s \quad 2s \qquad 2p$$

7.19 (a) V (paramagnetic; three unpaired electrons)

$$[Ar] \boxed{\uparrow}\boxed{\uparrow}\boxed{\uparrow}\boxed{\ }\boxed{\ }\ \boxed{\uparrow\downarrow}$$
$$3d \qquad\qquad 4s$$

(b) V^{2+} ion (paramagnetic, three unpaired electrons)

$$[Ar] \boxed{\uparrow}\boxed{\uparrow}\boxed{\uparrow}\boxed{\ }\boxed{\ }\ \boxed{\ }$$
$$3d \qquad\qquad 4s$$

(c) V^{5+} ion. This ion has an electron configuration
   equivalent to argon, [Ar]. It is diamagnetic with
   no unpaired electrons.

7.21 (a) Manganese

$$[Ar] \boxed{\uparrow}\boxed{\uparrow}\boxed{\uparrow}\boxed{\uparrow}\boxed{\uparrow}\ \boxed{\uparrow\downarrow}$$
$$3d \qquad\qquad 4s$$

(b) Mn^{4+}

$$[Ar] \boxed{\uparrow}\boxed{\uparrow}\boxed{\uparrow}\boxed{\ }\boxed{\ }\ \boxed{\ }$$
$$3d \qquad\qquad 4s$$

(c) The 4^+ ion is paramagnetic to the extent of three
   unpaired electrons.
(d) 3

7.23 Increasing size: C < B < Al < Na < K

7.25 (a) Cl^-
(b) Al
(c) In

7.27 (c)

7.29 (a) Largest radius, Na
(b) Most negative electron affinity: O
(c) Ionization energy: Na < Mg < P < O

7.31 (a) Increasing ionization energy: S < O < F. S is less
   than O because the IE decreases down a group. F
   is greater than O because IE generally increases
   across a period.
(b) Largest IE: O. IE decreases down a group.
(c) Most negative electron affinity: Cl. Electron affinity becomes more negative across the periodic table and on ascending a group.
(d) Largest Size: O^{2-}. Negative ions are larger than
   their corresponding neutral atoms. F^- is thus
   larger than F. O^{2-} and F^- are isoelectronic, but
   the O^{2-} ion has only eight protons in its nucleus
   to attract the 10 electrons, whereas the F^- has
   nine protons, making the O^{2-} ion larger.

7.33 Uranium configuration: $[Rn]5f^36d^17s^2$

$$[Rn] \quad 5f \qquad 6d \qquad 7s$$

Uranium(IV) ion, U^{4+}: $[Rn]5f^2$

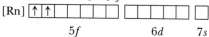

$$[Rn] \quad 5f \qquad 6d \qquad 7s$$

Both U and U^{4+} are paramagnetic.

7.35 (a) Atomic number = 20
(b) Total number of s electrons = 8
(c) Total number of p electrons = 12
(d) Total number of d electrons = 0
(e) The element is Ca, calcium, a metal.

7.37 (a) Valid. Possible elements are Li and Be.
(b) Not valid. The maximum value of ℓ is $(n - 1)$.
(c) Valid. Possible elements are B through Ne.
(d) Valid. Possible elements are Y through Cd.

7.39 (a) Neodymium, Nd: $[Xe]4f^46s^2$ (Table 7.3)

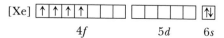

$$[Xe] \quad 4f \qquad 5d \qquad 6s$$

Iron, Fe: $[Ar]3d^64s^2$

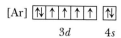

$$[Ar] \quad 3d \qquad 4s$$

Boron, B: $[He]2s^22p^1$

$$[He] \quad 2s \qquad 2p$$

(b) All three elements have unpaired electrons and so should be paramagnetic.
(c) Neodymium(III) ion, Nd^{3+}: $[Xe]4f^3$

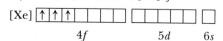

$$[Xe] \quad 4f \qquad 5d \qquad 6s$$

Iron(III) ion, Fe^{3+}: $[Ar]3d^5$

$$[Ar] \quad 3d \qquad 4s$$

Both neodymium(III) and iron(III) have unpaired electrons and are paramagnetic.

7.41 K < Ca < Si < P

7.43 (a) metal
(b) B
(c) A
(d) A
(e) Rb_2Se

7.45 In^{4+}: Indium has three outer shell electrons and so unlikely to form a 4+ ion.

Fe^{6+}: Although iron has eight electrons in its $3d$ and $4s$ orbitals, ions with a 6+ charge are highly unlikel The ionization energy is too large.

Sn^{5+}: Tin has four outer shell electrons and so is u likely to form a 5+ ion.

7.47 (a) Se
(b) Br^-
(c) Na
(d) N
(e) N^{3-}

7.49 (a) Na
(b) C
(c) Na < Al < B < C

7.51 (a) Cobalt
(b) Paramagnetic
(c) Four unpaired electrons

7.53 (a) 0.421 g
(b) paramagnetic; 2 unpaired electrons
(c) 99.8 mg; the nickel powder will stick to a magne

7.55 Li has three electrons ($1s^22s^1$) and Li^+ has only two electrons ($1s^2$). The ion is smaller than the atom be cause there are only two electrons to be held by thr protons in the ion. Also, an electron in a larger orbital has been removed. Fluorine atoms have nine electrons and nine protons ($1s^22s^22p^5$). The anion, F^-, has one additional electron, which means that 10 electrons must be held by only nine protons, and the ion is larger than the atom.

7.57 Element 1 comes from Group 4A (IUPAC Group 14 The first two IEs correspond to removing electrons from a p subshell. With the third IE, there is a fairly large jump in IE corresponding to removing an elec tron from an s subshell. The fourth electron remove comes from the same s subshell and therefore does not increase the IE by as much. None of the IEs are large enough to correspond to removing an electron from a lower energy level.

Element 2 comes from Group 3A (IUPAC Group 13 There is a large change in IE between the third and fourth IEs. The first three IEs correspond to removi electrons from the same energy level. The large jum at the fourth IE corresponds to having to remove th electron from a lower energy level.

7.59 Most stable: (d) The two electrons are in separate o bitals, following Hund's rule, and are of the same spin.

Least stable: (a) In this case the electrons violate bo Hund's rule and the Pauli exclusion principle.

61 K $(1s^22s^22p^63s^23p^64s^1) \rightarrow$ K$^+$ $(1s^22s^22p^63s^23p^6)$

K$^+$ $(1s^22s^22p^63s^23p^6) \rightarrow$ K^{2+} $(1s^22s^22p^63s^23p^5)$

The first ionization is for the removal of an electron from the valence shell of electrons. The second electron, however, is removed from the $3p$ subshell. This subshell is significantly lower in energy than the $4s$ subshell, and considerably more energy is required to remove this second electron.

.63 (a) In going from one element to the next across the period, the effective nuclear charge increases slightly and the attraction between the nucleus and the electrons increases.
(b) The size of fourth period transition elements, for example, is a reflection of the size of the $4s$ orbital. As d electrons are added across the series, protons are added to the nucleus. Adding protons should lead to a decreased atom size, but the effect of the protons is balanced by repulsions of the $3d$ electrons and $4s$ electrons, and the atom size is changed little.

.65 Among the arguments for a compound composed of Mg^{2+} and O^{2-} are:
(a) Chemical experience suggests that all Group 2A elements form 2^+ cations, and that oxygen is typically the O^{2-} ion in its compounds.
(b) Other alkaline earth elements form oxides such as BeO, CaO, and BaO.

A possible experiment is to measure the melting point of the compound. An ionic compound such as NaF (with ions having 1^+ and 1^- charges) melts at 990 °C, whereas a compound analogous to MgO, CaO, melts at a much higher temperature (2580 °C).

.67 (a) The effective nuclear charge increases, causing the valence orbital energies to become more negative on moving across the period.
(b) As the valence orbital energies become more negative, it is increasingly difficult to remove an electron from the atom, and the IE increases. Toward the end of the period, the orbital energies have become so negative that removing an electron requires significant energy. Instead, the effective nuclear charge has reached the point that it is energetically more favorable for the atom to gain an electron, corresponding to a more negative electron affinity.
(c) The valence orbital energies are in the order:

Li (-520.7 kJ) < Be (-899.3 kJ) > B (-800.8 kJ) < C (-1029 kJ)

This means it is more difficult to remove an electron from Be than from either Li or B. The energy is more negative for C than for B, so it is more difficult to remove an electron from C than from B.

7.69 The size declines across this series of elements while their mass increases. Thus, the mass per volume, the density, increases.

7.71 (a) Element 113: $[\text{Rn}]5f^{14}6d^{10}7s^27p^1$
Element 115: $[\text{Rn}]5f^{14}6d^{10}7s^27p^3$
(b) Element 113 is in Group 3A (with elements such as boron and aluminum), and element 115 is in Group 5A (with elements such as nitrogen and phosphorus).
(c) Americium ($Z = 95$) + argon ($Z = 18$) = element 113

7.73 (a) Sulfur electron configuration

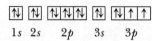
$1s$ $2s$ $2p$ $3s$ $3p$

(b) $n = 3$, $\ell = 1$, $m_\ell = 1$, and $m_s = +1/2$
(c) S has the smallest ionization energy and O has the smallest radius.
(d) S is smaller than S^{2-} ion
(e) 584 g SCl$_2$
(f) 10.0 g of SCl$_2$ is the limiting reactant, and 11.6 g of SOCl$_2$ can be produced.
(g) $\Delta_f H°[\text{SCl}_2(g)] = -17.6$ kJ/mol

7.75 (a) Z^* for F is 5.2; Z^* for Ne is 5.85. The effective nuclear charge increases from O to F to Ne. As the effective nuclear charge increases, the atomic radius decreases, and the first ionization energy increases.
(b) Z^* for a $3d$ electron in Mn is 13.7; for a $4s$ electron it is only 3.1. The effective nuclear charge experienced by a $4s$ electron is much smaller than that experienced by a $3d$ electron. A $4s$ electron in Mn is thus more easily removed.

CHAPTER 8

8.1. (a) Group 6A, six valence electrons
(b) Group 3A, three valence electrons
(c) Group 1A, one valence electron
(d) Group 2A, two valence electrons
(e) Group 7A, seven valence electrons
(f) Group 6A, six valence electrons

8.3 Group 3A, three bonds
Group 4A, four bonds
Group 5A, three bonds (for a neutral compound)
Group 6A, two bonds (for a neutral compound)
Group 7A, one (for a neutral compound)

8.5 (a) NF$_3$, 26 valence electrons

(b) ClO_3^-, 26 valence electrons

$$\left[\ddot{\text{O}}-\overset{..}{\underset{|}{\text{Cl}}}-\ddot{\text{O}}\text{:} \atop \ddot{\text{O}}\text{:}\right]^-$$

(c) HOBr, 14 valence electrons

$$\text{H}-\ddot{\text{O}}-\ddot{\text{Br}}\text{:}$$

(d) SO_3^{2-}, 26 valence electrons

$$\left[\ddot{\text{O}}-\overset{..}{\underset{|}{\text{S}}}-\ddot{\text{O}}\text{:} \atop \ddot{\text{O}}\text{:}\right]^{2-}$$

8.7 (a) $CHClF_2$, 26 valence electrons

$$\text{:}\ddot{\text{Cl}}-\overset{\text{H}}{\underset{\underset{:\ddot{\text{F}}:}{|}}{\text{C}}}-\ddot{\text{F}}\text{:}$$

(b) CH_3CO_2H, 24 valence electrons

$$\text{H}-\overset{\text{H}}{\underset{\text{H}}{\text{C}}}-\overset{:\text{O}:}{\underset{\|}{\text{C}}}-\ddot{\text{O}}-\text{H}$$

(c) CH_3CN, 16 valence electrons

$$\text{H}-\overset{\text{H}}{\underset{\text{H}}{\text{C}}}-\text{C}\equiv\text{N}\text{:}$$

(d) H_2CCCH_2, 16 valence electrons

$$\text{H}-\overset{\text{H}}{\text{C}}=\text{C}=\overset{\text{H}}{\text{C}}-\text{H}$$

8.9 (a) SO_2, 18 valence electrons

$$\text{:}\ddot{\text{O}}-\ddot{\text{S}}=\ddot{\text{O}} \longleftrightarrow \ddot{\text{O}}=\ddot{\text{S}}-\ddot{\text{O}}\text{:}$$

(b) HNO_2, 18 valence electrons

$$\text{H}-\ddot{\text{O}}-\ddot{\text{N}}=\ddot{\text{O}}$$

(c) SCN^-, 16 valence electrons

$$\left[\ddot{\text{S}}=\text{C}=\ddot{\text{N}}\right]^- \longleftrightarrow \left[\text{:}\text{S}\equiv\text{C}-\ddot{\text{N}}\text{:}\right]^- \longleftrightarrow \left[\text{:}\ddot{\text{S}}-\text{C}\equiv\text{N}\text{:}\right]^-$$

8.11 (a) BrF_3, 28 valence electrons

$$\text{:}\ddot{\text{F}}\text{:} \atop \ddot{\text{Br}}-\ddot{\text{F}}\text{:} \atop \text{:}\ddot{\text{F}}\text{:}$$

(b) I_3^-, 22 valence electrons

$$\left[\text{:}\ddot{\text{I}}\text{:} \atop \ddot{\text{I}}\text{:} \atop \text{:}\ddot{\text{I}}\text{:}\right]^-$$

(c) XeO_2F_2, 34 valence electrons

$$\text{:}\ddot{\text{O}}-\overset{:\ddot{\text{F}}:}{\underset{:\ddot{\text{F}}:}{\text{Xe}}}-\ddot{\text{O}}\text{:}$$

(d) XeF_3^+, 28 valence electrons

$$\text{:}\ddot{\text{F}}\text{:} \atop \text{:}\ddot{\text{Xe}}-\ddot{\text{F}}\text{:} \atop \text{:}\ddot{\text{F}}\text{:}$$

8.13 (a) N = 0; H = 0
(b) P = +1; O = −1
(c) B = −1; H = 0
(d) All are zero.

8.15 (a) N = +1; O = 0
(b) The central N is 0. The singly bonded O atom is −1, and the doubly bonded O atom is 0.

$$\left[\text{:}\ddot{\text{O}}-\ddot{\text{N}}=\ddot{\text{O}}\right]^- \longleftrightarrow \left[\ddot{\text{O}}=\ddot{\text{N}}-\ddot{\text{O}}\text{:}\right]^-$$

(c) N and F are both 0.
(d) The central N atom is +1, one of the O atoms is −1, and the other two O atoms are both 0.

$$\overset{0}{\text{H}}-\overset{}{\ddot{\text{O}}}-\overset{+1}{\text{N}}=\overset{0}{\ddot{\text{O}}} \atop \underset{-1}{\underset{:\ddot{\text{O}}:}{|}}$$

8.17 (a) Electron-pair geometry around N is tetrahedral. Molecular geometry is trigonal pyramidal.

$$\text{:}\ddot{\text{Cl}}-\overset{}{\underset{\underset{\text{H}}{|}}{\text{N}}}-\text{H}$$

(b) Electron-pair geometry around O is tetrahedral. Molecular geometry is bent.

$$\text{:}\ddot{\text{Cl}}-\ddot{\text{O}}-\ddot{\text{Cl}}\text{:}$$

(c) Electron-pair geometry around C is linear. Molecular geometry is linear.

$$\left[\ddot{\text{S}}=\text{C}=\ddot{\text{N}}\right]^-$$

(d) Electron-pair geometry around O is tetrahedral. The molecular geometry is bent.

$$\text{H}-\ddot{\text{O}}-\ddot{\text{F}}\text{:}$$

.19 (a) Electron-pair geometry around C is linear. Molecular geometry is linear.

$$\ddot{O}{=}C{=}\ddot{O}$$

(b) Electron-pair geometry around N is trigonal planar. Molecular geometry is bent.

$$\left[:\ddot{O}{-}\ddot{N}{=}\ddot{O}\right]^{-}$$

(c) Electron-pair geometry around O is trigonal planar. Molecular geometry is bent.

$$\ddot{O}{=}\ddot{O}{-}\ddot{O}:$$

(d) Electron-pair geometry around Cl atom is tetrahedral. Molecular geometry is bent.

$$\left[:\ddot{O}{-}\ddot{C}l{-}\ddot{O}:\right]^{-}$$

All have two atoms attached to the central atom. As the bond and lone pairs vary, the electron-pair geometries vary from linear to tetrahedral, and the molecular geometries vary from linear to bent.

.21 (a) Electron-pair geometry around Cl is trigonal bipyramidal. Molecular geometry is linear.

$$\left[:\ddot{F}{-}\ddot{C}l{-}\ddot{F}:\right]^{-}$$

(b) Electron-pair geometry around Cl is trigonal bipyramidal. Molecular geometry is T-shaped.

$$:\ddot{F}{-}\ddot{C}l{-}\ddot{F}:$$
$$|$$
$$:\ddot{F}:$$

(c) Electron-pair geometry around Cl is octahedral. Molecular geometry is square planar.

$$\left[\begin{array}{c}:\ddot{F}:\\ | \\ :\ddot{F}{-}\ddot{C}l{-}\ddot{F}:\\ | \\ :\ddot{F}:\end{array}\right]^{-}$$

(d) Electron-pair geometry around Cl is octahedral. Molecular geometry is a square pyramid.

$$\begin{array}{c}:\ddot{F}:\\ :\ddot{F}_{\!\!\!\!\diagdown}\ |\ _{\diagup}\ddot{F}:\\ Cl\\ :\ddot{F}\ \ \ \ddot{F}:\end{array}$$

.23 (a) Ideal O—S—O angle = 120°
(b) 120°
(c) 120°
(d) H—C—H = 109° and C—C—N angle = 180°

.25 1 = 120°; 2 = 109°; 3 = 120°; 4 = 109°; 5 = 109°

The chain cannot be linear because the first two carbon atoms in the chain have bond angles of 109° and the final one has a bond angle of 120°. These bond angles do not lead to a linear chain.

8.27

$\overrightarrow{\text{C}{-}\text{O}}$	$\overrightarrow{\text{C}{-}\text{N}}$
$+\delta\ \ -\delta$	$+\delta\ \ -\delta$

CO is more polar

$\overrightarrow{\text{P}{-}\text{Cl}}$	$\overrightarrow{\text{P}{-}\text{Br}}$
$+\delta\ \ -\delta$	$+\delta\ \ -\delta$

PCl is more polar

$\overrightarrow{\text{B}{-}\text{O}}$	$\overrightarrow{\text{B}{-}\text{S}}$
$+\delta\ \ -\delta$	$+\delta\ \ -\delta$

BO is more polar

$\overrightarrow{\text{B}{-}\text{F}}$	$\overrightarrow{\text{B}{-}\text{I}}$
$+\delta\ \ -\delta$	$+\delta\ \ -\delta$

BF is more polar

8.29 (a) CH and CO bonds are polar.
(b) The CO bond is most polar, and O is the most negative atom.

8.31 (a) OH⁻: The formal charge on O is −1 and on H it is 0.
(b) BH₄⁻: Even though the formal charge on B is −1 and on H is 0, H is slightly more electronegative than B. The four H atoms are therefore more likely to bear the −1 charge of the ion. The BH bonds are polar with the H atom the negative end.
(c) The CH and CO bonds are all polar (but the C—C bond is not). The negative charge in the CO bonds lies on the O atoms.

8.33 Structure C is most reasonable. The charges are as small as possible and the negative charge resides on the more electronegative atom.

$$\overset{-2\ \ \ \ +1\ \ \ +1}{:\ddot{N}{-}N{\equiv}O:}\longleftrightarrow\overset{-1\ \ \ +1\ \ \ \ 0}{\ddot{N}{=}N{=}\ddot{O}}\longleftrightarrow\overset{0\ \ \ +1\ \ \ -1}{:N{\equiv}N{-}\ddot{O}:}$$

A B C

8.35 (a)

$$\left[\overset{-1\ \ \ 0\ \ \ \ 0}{:\ddot{O}{-}\ddot{N}{=}\ddot{O}}\right]^{-}\longleftrightarrow\left[\overset{0\ \ \ \ 0\ \ \ -1}{\ddot{O}{=}\ddot{N}{-}\ddot{O}:}\right]^{-}$$

(b) If an H⁺ ion were to attack NO₂⁻, it would attach to an O atom because the O atoms bear the negative charge in this ion.

(c)

$$\text{H}{-}\ddot{O}{-}\ddot{N}{=}\ddot{O}:\longleftrightarrow:\ddot{O}{-}\ddot{N}{=}\ddot{O}{-}\text{H}$$

The structure on the left is strongly favored because all of the atoms have zero formal charge, whereas the structure on the right has a −1 formal charge on one oxygen and a +1 formal charge on the other.

8.37 (i) The most polar bonds are in H_2O (because O and H have the largest difference in electronegativity).
(ii) Not polar: CO_2 and CCl_4
(iii) The F atom is more negatively charged.

8.39 (a) $BeCl_2$, nonpolar linear molecule
(b) HBF_2, polar trigonal planar molecule with F atoms the negative end of the dipole and the H atom the positive end.
(c) CH_3Cl, polar tetrahedral molecule. The Cl atom is the negative end of the dipole and the three H atoms are on the positive side of the molecule.
(d) SO_3, a nonpolar trigonal planar molecule

8.41 (a) Two C—H bonds, bond order is 1; 1 C=O bond, bond order is 2.
(b) Three S—O single bonds, bond order is 1.
(c) Two nitrogen–oxygen double bonds, bond order is 2.
(d) One N=O double bond, bond order is 2; one N—Cl bond, bond order is 1.

8.43 (a) B—Cl
(b) C—O
(c) P—O
(d) C=O

8.45 NO bond orders: 2 in NO_2^+, 1.5 in NO_2^-; 1.33 in NO_3^-. The NO bond is longest in NO_3^- and shortest in NO_2^+.

8.47 The CO bond in carbon monoxide is a triple bond, so it is both shorter and stronger than the CO double bond in H_2CO.

8.49 $\Delta_r H = -126$ kJ

8.51 O—F bond dissociation energy = 192 kJ/mol

8.53

Element	Valence Electrons
Li	1
Ti	4
Zn	2
Si	4
Cl	7

8.55 SeF_4, BrF_4^-, XeF_4

8.57

Bond order = 3/2

8.59 To estimate the enthalpy change, we need energies for the following bonds: O=O, H—H, and H—O.

Energy to break bonds = 498 kJ (for O=O) + 2 × 436 kJ (for H—H) = +1370 kJ.

Energy evolved when bonds are made = 4 × 463 kJ (for O—H) = -1852 kJ

Total energy = -482 kJ

8.61 All the species in the series have 16 valence electrons and all are linear.
(a) $\ddot{O}=C=\ddot{O} \longleftrightarrow :\ddot{O}-C\equiv O: \longleftrightarrow :O\equiv C-\ddot{O}:$
(b)
$[\ddot{N}=N=\ddot{N}]^- \longleftrightarrow [:\ddot{N}-N\equiv N:]^- \longleftrightarrow [:N\equiv N-\ddot{N}:]^-$
(c)
$[\ddot{O}=C=\ddot{N}]^- \longleftrightarrow [:\ddot{O}-C\equiv N:]^- \longleftrightarrow [:O\equiv C-\ddot{N}:]^-$

8.63 The N—O bonds in NO_2^- have a bond order of 1.5, whereas in NO_2^+ the bond order is 2. The shorter bonds (110 pm) are the NO bonds with the higher bond order (in NO_2^+), whereas the longer bonds (124 pm) in NO_2^- have a lower bond order.

8.65 The F—Cl—F bond angle in ClF_2^+, which has a tetrahedral electron-pair geometry, is approximately 109°

$[:\ddot{F}-\ddot{C}l-\ddot{F}:]^+$

The ClF_2^- ion has a trigonal-bipyramidal electron-pair geometry with F atoms in the axial positions and the lone pairs in the equatorial positions. Therefore, the F—C—F angle is 180°.

$[:\ddot{F}-\ddot{C}l-\ddot{F}:]^-$

8.67 An H^+ ion will attach to an O atom of SO_3^{2-} and not to the S atom. The O atoms each have a formal charge of -1, whereas the S atom formal charge is +1.

$[:\ddot{O}-\overset{}{S}-\ddot{O}:]^{2-}$ with $:\ddot{O}:$ below

8.69 (a) Calculation from bond energies: $\Delta_r H° = -1070$ kJ/mol-rxn; $\Delta H° = -535$ kJ/mol CH_3OH
(b) Calculation from thermochemical data: $\Delta_r H° = -1352.3$ kJ/mol-rxn; $\Delta H° = -676$ kJ/mol CH_3O

8.71 (a)
$[:C\equiv N-\ddot{O}:]^- \longleftrightarrow [\ddot{C}=N=\ddot{O}]^- \longleftrightarrow [:\ddot{C}-N\equiv O:]^-$
$\quad -1 \quad +1 \quad -1 \qquad -2 \quad +1 \quad 0 \qquad -3 \quad +1 \quad +1$

(b) The first resonance structure is the most reasonable because oxygen, the most electronegative atom, has a negative formal charge, and the unfavorable negative charge on the least electronegative atom, carbon, is smallest.

(c) This species is so unstable because carbon, the least electronegative element in the ion, has a negative formal charge. In addition, all three resonance structures have an unfavorable charge distribution.

73

:—Xe—)120°   F—Cl—)120°

(a) XeF_2 has three lone pairs around the Xe atom. The electron-pair geometry is trigonal bipyramidal. Because lone pairs require more space than bond pairs, it is better to place the lone pairs in the equator of the bipyramid where the angles between them are 120°.

(b) Like XeF_2, ClF_3 has a trigonal bipyramidal electron-pair geometry, but with only two lone pairs around the Cl. These are again placed in the equatorial plane where the angle between them is 120°.

75 (a) Angle 1 = 109°; angle 2 = 120°; angle 3 = 109°; angle 4 = 109°; and angle 5 = 109°.

(b) The O—H bond is the most polar bond.

77 $\Delta_r H = +146$ kJ $= 2 (\Delta H_{C-N}) + \Delta H_{C=O} - [\Delta H_{N-N} + \Delta H_{C\equiv O}]$

79 (a) Two C—H bonds and one O=O are broken and two O—C bonds and two H—O bonds are made in the reaction. $\Delta_r H = -318$ kJ. The reaction is exothermic.

(b) Acetone is polar.

(c) The O—H hydrogen atoms are the most positive in dihydroxyacetone.

81 (a) The C=C bond is stronger than the C—C bond.

(b) The C—C single bond is longer than the C=C double bond.

(c) Ethylene is nonpolar, whereas acrolein is polar.

(d) The reaction is exothermic ($\Delta_r H = -45$ kJ).

83 $\Delta_r H = -211$ kJ

85 Methanol is a polar solvent. Methanol contains two bonds of significant polarity, the C—O bond and the O—H bond. The C—O—H atoms are in a bent configuration, leading to a polar molecule. Toluene contains only carbon and hydrogen atoms, which have similar electronegativites and which are arranged in tetrahedral or trigonal planar geometries, leading to a molecule that is largely nonpolar.

87 (a)

H   H
| |
H—C—S—C—H
| |
H   H

The bond angles are all approximately 109°.

(b) The sulfur atom should have a slight partial negative charge, and the carbons should have slight partial positive charges. The molecule has a bent shape and is polar.

(c) 1.6×10^{18} molecules

8.89 (a) Odd electron molecules: BrO (13 electrons)

(b) $Br_2(g) \rightarrow 2 Br(g)$ $\Delta_r H = +193$ kJ
$2 Br(g) + O_2(g) \rightarrow 2 BrO(g)$ $\Delta_r H = +96$ kJ
$BrO(g) + H_2O(g) \rightarrow HOBr(g) + OH(g)$
$\Delta_r H = 0$ kJ

(c) ΔH of formation $[HOBr(g)] = -101$ kJ/mol

(d) The reactions in part (b) are endothermic (or thermal-neutral for the third reaction), and the enthalpy of formation in part (c) is exothermic.

8.91 (a) BF_3 is a nonpolar molecule, but replacing one or two F atoms with an H atom (HBF_2 and H_2BF) gives polar molecules.

(b) $BeCl_2$ is not polar, whereas replacing a Cl atom with a Br atom gives a polar molecule ($BeClBr$).

CHAPTER 9

9.1 The electron-pair and molecular geometry of $CHCl_3$ are both tetrahedral. Each C—Cl bond is formed by the overlap of an sp^3 hybrid orbital on the C atom with a $3p$ orbital on a Cl atom to form a sigma bond. A C—H sigma bond is formed by the overlap of an sp^3 hybrid orbital on the C atom with an H atom $1s$ orbital.

:Cl:
|
H—C—Cl:
|
:Cl:

9.3

	Electron-Pair Geometry	Molecular Geometry	Hybrid Orbital Set
(a)	trigonal planar	trigonal planar	sp^2
(b)	linear	linear	sp
(c)	tetrahedral	tetrahedral	sp^3
(d)	trigonal planar	trigonal planar	sp^2

9.5 (a) C, sp^3; O, sp^3

(b) CH_3, sp^3; middle C, sp^2; CH_2, sp^2

(c) CH_2, sp^3; CO_2H, sp^2; N, sp^3

9.7 (a) Electron-pair geometry is octahedral. Molecular geometry is octahedral. S: sp^3d^2

[
  :F:
:F   F:
Si
:F   F:
  :F:
]$^{2-}$

(b) Electron-pair geometry is trigonal-bipyramidal. Molecular geometry is seesaw. Se: sp^3d

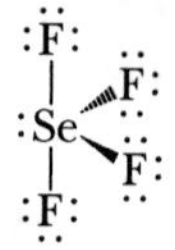

(c) Electron-pair geometry is trigonal-bipyramidal. Molecular geometry is linear. I: sp^3d

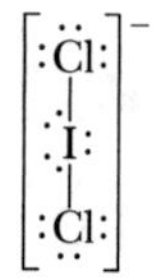

(d) Electron-pair geometry is octahedral. Molecular geometry is square-planar. Xe: sp^3d^2

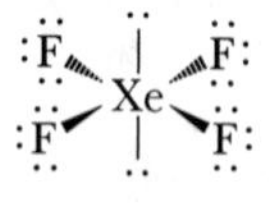

9.9 There are 32 valence electrons in both HPO_2F_2 and its anion. Both have a tetrahedral molecular geometry, and so the P atom in both is sp^3 hybridized.

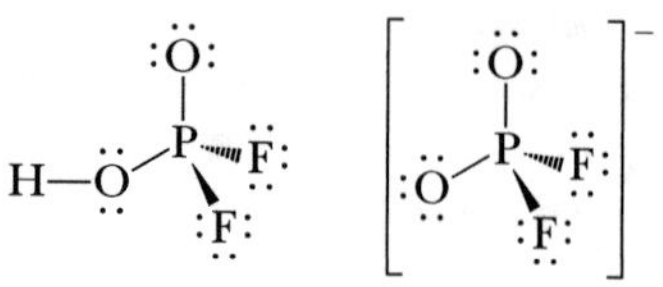

9.11 The C atom is sp^2-hybridized. Two of the sp^2 hybrid orbitals are used to form C—Cl sigma bonds, and the third is used to form the C—O sigma bond. The p orbital not used in the C atom hybrid orbitals is used to form the CO pi bond.

9.13

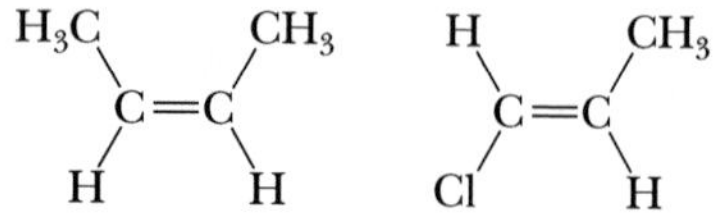

cis isomer   *trans* isomer

9.15 H_2^+ ion: $(\sigma_{1s})^1$. Bond order is 0.5. The bond in H_2^+ is weaker than in H_2 (bond order =1).

9.17 MO diagram for C_2^{2-} ion

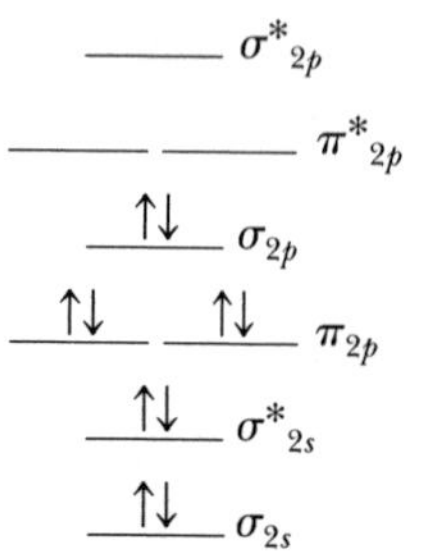

The ion has 10 valence electrons (isoelectronic with N_2). There are one net sigma bond and two net pi bonds, for a bond order of 3. The bond order increases by 1 on going from C_2 to C_2^{2-}. The ion is n paramagnetic.

9.19 (a) CO has 10 valence electrons

$$[core](\sigma_{2s})^2(\sigma^*_{2s})^2(\pi_{2p})^4(\sigma_{2p})^2$$

(b) σ_{2p}

(c) Diamagnetic

(d) There are net 1 σ bond and 2 π bonds; bond or der is 3.

9.21

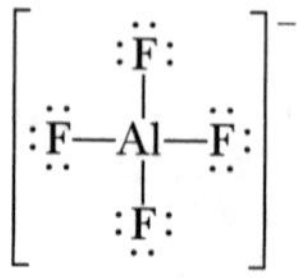

The electron pair and molecular geometries are bot tetrahedral. The Al atom is sp^3 hybridized, and so th Al—F bonds are formed by overlap of an Al sp^3 orbi with a p orbital on each F atom. The formal charge on each of the fluorines is zero, and that on the Al is -1. This is not a reasonable charge distribution b cause the less electronegative atom, aluminum, has the negative charge.

9.23

Molecule/Ion	O—S—O Angle	Hybrid Orbitals
SO_2	120°	sp^2
SO_3	120°	sp^2
SO_3^{2-}	109°	sp^3
SO_4^{2-}	109°	sp^3

9.25

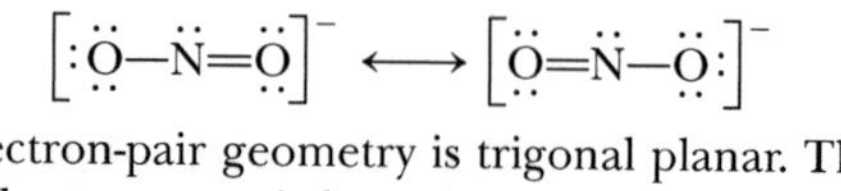

The electron-pair geometry is trigonal planar. The molecular geometry is bent (or angular). The O—N—O angle will be about 120°, the average N— bond order is 3/2, and the N atom is sp^2 hybridized.

9.27 The resonance structures of N_2O, with formal charg are shown here.

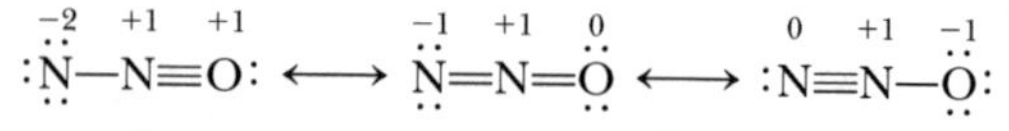

The central N atom is sp hybridized in all structures. The two sp hybrid orbitals on the central N atom are used to form N—N and N—O σ bonds. The two p o bitals not used in the N atom hybridization are used to form the required π bonds.

9.29 (a) All three have the formula C_2H_4O. They are usu- ally referred to as structural isomers.

(b) *Ethylene oxide:* Both C atoms are sp^3 hybridized. *Acetaldehyde:* The CH_3 carbon atom has sp^3 hybrid ization, and the other C atom is sp^2 hybridized. *Vinyl alcohol:* Both C atoms are sp^2 hybridized.

(c) *Ethylene oxide:* 109°.
   Acetaldehyde: 109°
   Vinyl alcohol: 120°.
(d) All are polar.
(e) Acetaldehyde has the strongest CO bond, and vinyl alcohol has the strongest C—C bond.

31 (a) CH_3 carbon atom: sp^3
      C=N carbon atom: sp^2
      N atom: sp^2
   (b) C—N—O bond angle = 120°

33 (a) C(1) = sp^2; O(2) = sp^3; N(3) = sp^3; C(4) = sp^3;
      P(5) = sp^3
   (b) Angle A = 120°; angle B = 109°; angle C = 109°;
      angle D = 109°
   (c) The P—O and O—H bonds are most polar
      ($\Delta\chi$ = 1.3).

35 (a) C=O bond is most polar.
   (b) 18 sigma bonds and five pi bonds
   (c)

   trans isomer   *cis* isomer

   (d) All C atoms are sp^2 hybridized.
   (e) All bond angles are 120°.

37 (a) The Sb in SbF_5 is sp^3d hybridized; whereas it is
      sp^3d^2 hybridized in SbF_6^-.
   (b) The molecular geometry of the H_2F^+ ion is bent
      or angular, and the F atom is sp^3 hybridized.

39 (a) The peroxide ion has a bond order of 1.

   (b) [core electrons]$(\sigma_{2s})^2(\sigma^*_{2s})^2(\sigma_{2p})^2(\pi_{2p})^4(\pi^*_{2p})^4$

      This configuration also leads to a bond order of 1.

   (c) Both theories lead to a diamagnetic ion with a
      bond order of 1.

41 Paramagnetic diatomic molecules: B_2 and O_2

   Bond order of 1: Li_2, B_2, F_2; Bond order of 2: C_2 and
   O_2; Highest bond order: N_2

43 CN has nine valence electrons
   [core electrons]$(\sigma_{2s})^2(\sigma^*_{2s})^2(\pi_{2p})^4(\sigma_{2p})^1$
   (a) HOMO, σ_{2p}
   (b, c) Bond order = 2.5 (0.5 σ bond and 2 π bonds)
   (d) Paramagnetic

9.45 (a) All C atoms are sp^3 hybridized
     (b) About 109°
     (c) Polar
     (d) The six-membered ring cannot be planar, owing
        to the tetrahedral C atoms of the ring. The bond
        angles are all 109°.

9.47 (a) The geometry about the boron atom is trigonal
        planar in BF_3, but tetrahedral in $H_3N—BF_3$.
     (b) Boron is sp^2 hybridized in BF_3 but sp^3 hybridized
        in $H_3N—BF_3$.
     (c) Yes
     (d) The ammonia molecule is polar with the N atom
        partially negative. While the BF_3 molecule is nonpolar overall, each of the B—F bonds is polarized
        such that the B has a partial positive charge. The
        partially negative N in NH_3 is attracted to the partially positive B in BF_3.
     (e) One of the lone pairs on the oxygen of H_2O can
        form a coordinate covalent bond with the B in
        BF_3. The resulting compound would be (the lone
        pairs on the F's not shown):

9.49 (a) NH_2^-: electron-pair geometry = tetrahedral, molecular geometry = bent, hybridization of N = sp^3

        SO_3: electron-pair geometry = molecular geometry = trigonal planar, hybridization of S = sp^2

     (b)

        The bond angles around the N and the S are all
        approximately 109°.
     (c) The N does not undergo any change in its hybridication; the S changes from sp^2 to sp^3.
     (d) The SO_3 is the acceptor of an electron pair in this
        reaction. The electrostatic potential map confirms
        this to be reasonable because the sulfur has a partial positive charge.

9.51 A C atom may form, at most, four hybrid orbitals
     (sp^3). The minimum number is two, for example, the
     sp hybrid orbitals used by carbon in CO. Carbon has
     only four valence orbitals, so it cannot form more
     than four hybrid orbitals.

9.53 (a) C, sp^2; N, sp^3

(b) The amide or peptide link has two resonance structures (shown here with formal charges on the O and N atoms). Structure B is less favorable, owing to the separation of charge.

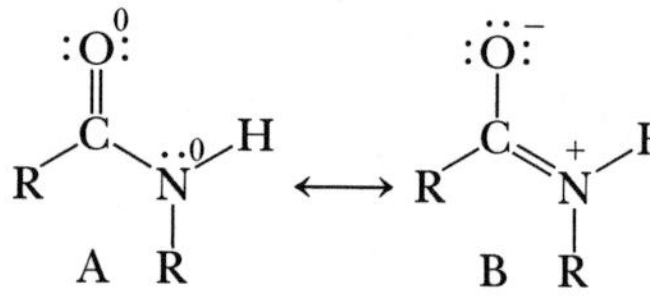

(c) The fact that the amide link is planar indicates that structure B has some importance.

The principal sites of positive charge are the nitrogen in the amide linkage, and the hydrogen of the —O—H group. The principal regions of negative charge are oxygen atoms and the nitrogen of the free —NH$_2$ group.

9.55 MO theory is better to use when explaining or understanding the effect of adding energy to molecules. A molecule can absorb energy and an electron can thus be promoted to a higher level. Using MO theory, one can see how this can occur. Additionally, MO theory is a better model to use to predict whether a molecule is paramagnetic.

9.57 Lowest Energy = Orbital C < Orbital B < Orbital A = Highest Energy

9.59 (a) The attractive forces must be greater than the repulsive forces if a covalent bond is to form.

(b) As the atoms approach each other, the energy drops as the electron clouds overlap and electron density increases between the two nuclei. If the atoms approach still more closely, electrostatic repulsion of the nuclei for each other and of the electrons for each other increases dramatically.

(c) In neon, all of the orbitals in the 2s and 2p sublevels are filled with paired electrons; there is no orbital available that can overlap with another orbital on another atom. In the case of fluorine, there is an orbital on each atom that is not completely filled that can overlap with another orbital to form a bond.

9.61 (a) The molecule with the double bond requires a great deal more energy because the π bond must be broken in order for the ends of the molecules to rotate relative to each other.

(b) No. The carbon–carbon double bonds in the molecule prevent the CH$_2$ fragments from rotating.

CHAPTER 10

10.1 Heptane

10.3 C$_{14}$H$_{30}$ is an alkane and C$_5$H$_{10}$ could be a cycloalkane

10.5 2,3-dimethylbutane

10.7 (a) 2,3-Dimethylhexane

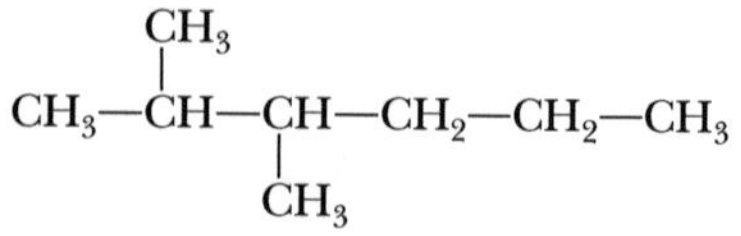

(b) 2,3-Dimethyloctane

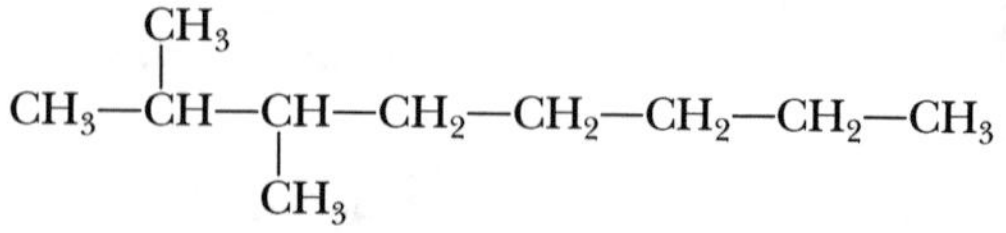

(c) 3-Ethylheptane

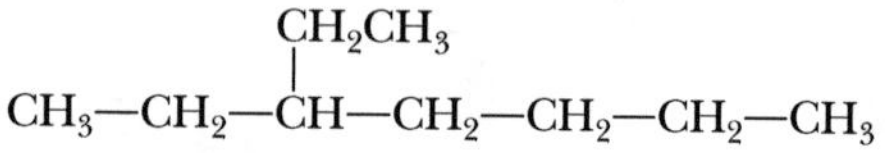

(d) 3-Ethyl-2-methylhexane

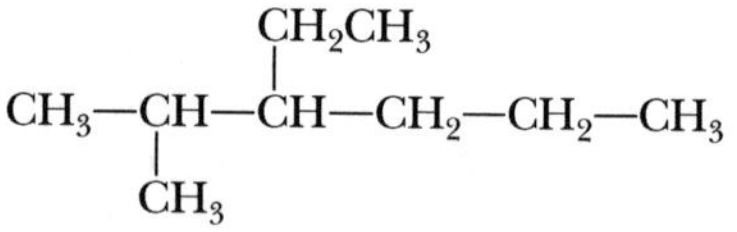

10.9

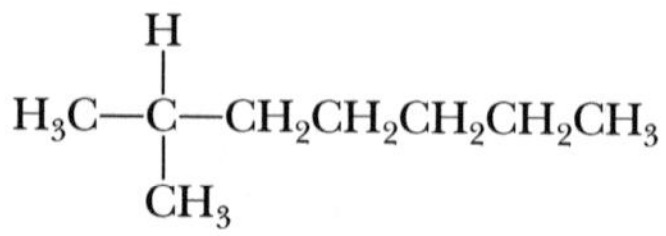

2-methylheptane

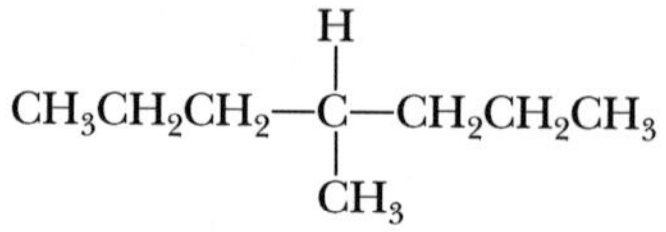

4-methylheptane

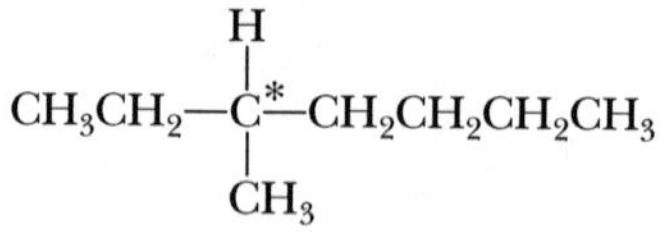

3-methylheptane. The atom with an asterisk is chiral.

10.11

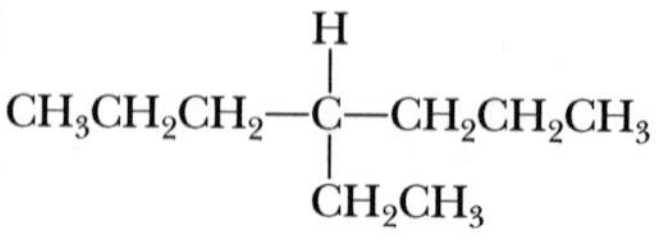

4-ethylheptane. The compound is not chiral.

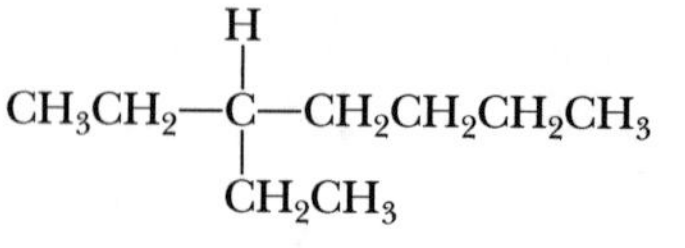

3-ethylheptane. Not chiral.

10.13 C$_4$H$_{10}$, butane: a low-molecular–weight fuel gas at room temperature and pressure. Slightly soluble in water.

C$_{12}$H$_{26}$, dodecane: a colorless liquid at room temperature. Expected to be insoluble in water but quite soluble in nonpolar solvents.

10.15

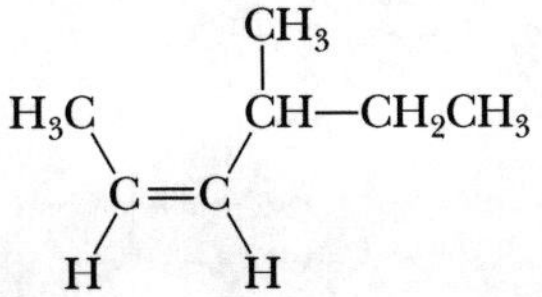

cis-4-methyl-2-hexene

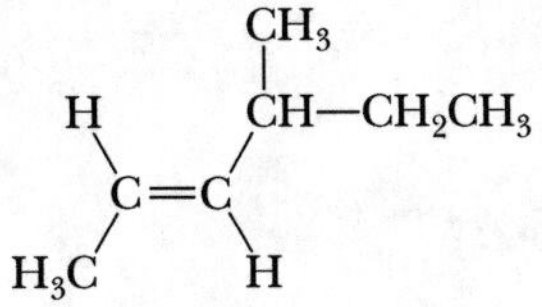

trans-4-methyl-2-hexene

10.17 (a)

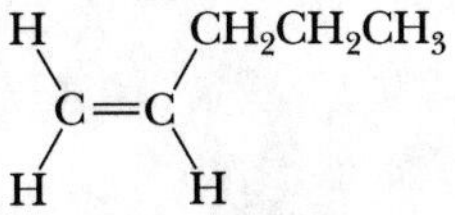

1-pentene

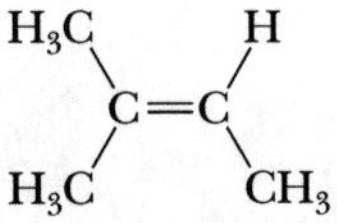

2-methyl-2-butene

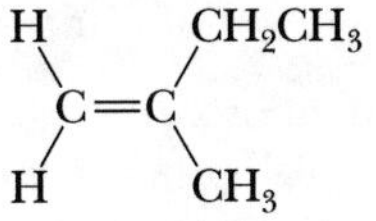

2-methyl-1-butene

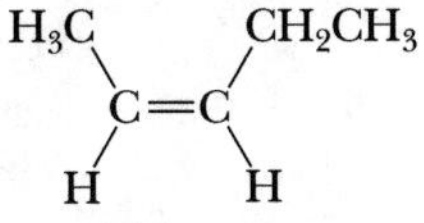

cis-2-pentene

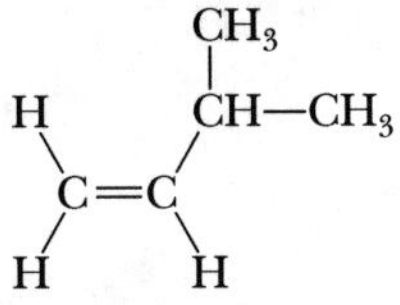

3-methyl-1-butene

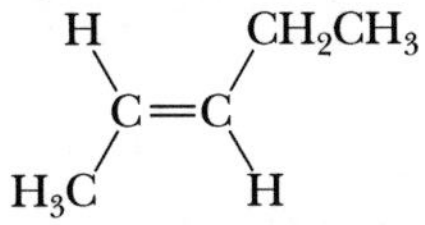

trans-2-pentene

(b)

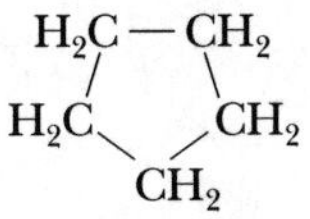

cyclopentane

10.19 (a) 1,2-Dibromopropane, $CH_3CHBrCH_2Br$
(b) Pentane, C_5H_{12}

10.21 1-Butene, $CH_3CH_2CH=CH_2$, or 1-butene

10.23 Four isomers are possible.

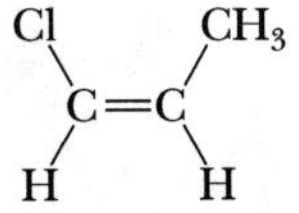

cis-1-chloropropene

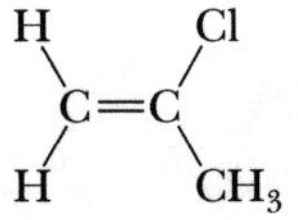

2-chloropropene

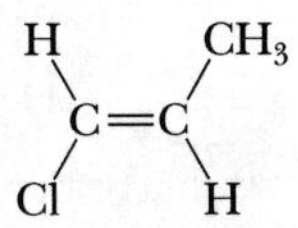

trans-1-chloropropene

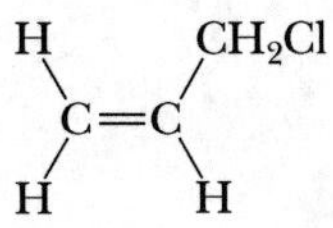

3-chloro-1-propene

10.25

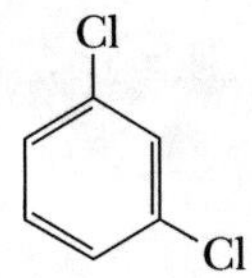

m-dichlorobenzene

o-bromotoluene

10.27

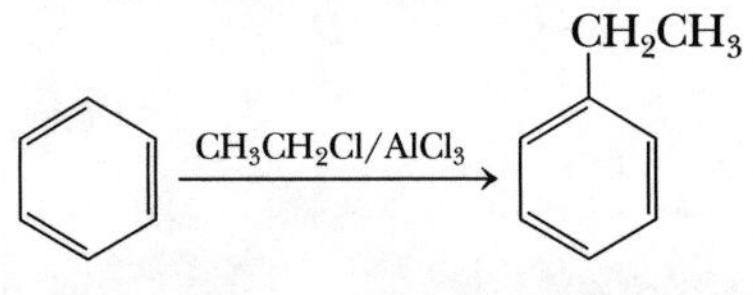

ethylbenzene

10.29

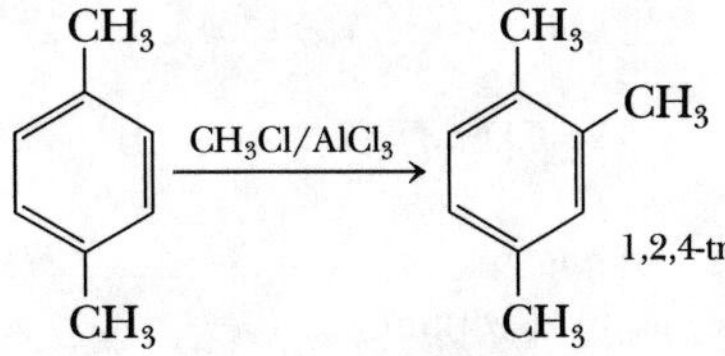

1,2,4-trimethylbenzene

10.31 (a) 1-Propanol, primary
(b) 1-Butanol, primary
(c) 2-Methyl-2-propanol, tertiary
(d) 2-Methyl-2-butanol, tertiary

10.33 (a) Ethylamine, $CH_3CH_2NH_2$
(b) Dipropylamine, $(CH_3CH_2CH_2)_2NH$

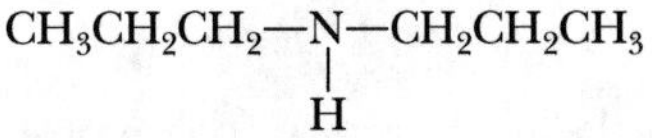

(c) Butyldimethylamine

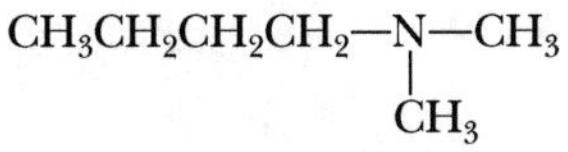

(d) triethylamine

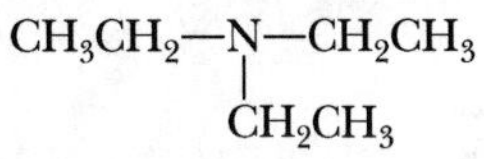

10.33 (a) 1-butanol, $CH_3CH_2CH_2CH_2OH$
(b) 2-butanol

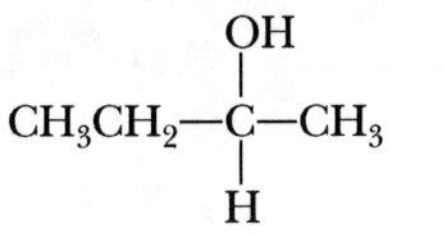

(c) 2-methyl-1-propanol

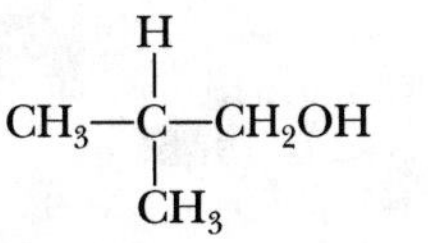

(d) 2-methyl-2-propanol

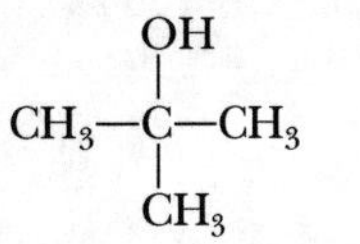

10.37 (a) $C_6H_5NH_2(aq) + HCl(aq) \rightarrow (C_6H_5NH_3)Cl(aq)$
(b) $(CH_3)_3N(aq) + H_2SO_4(aq) \rightarrow$
$$[(CH_3)_3NH]HSO_4(aq)$$

10.39

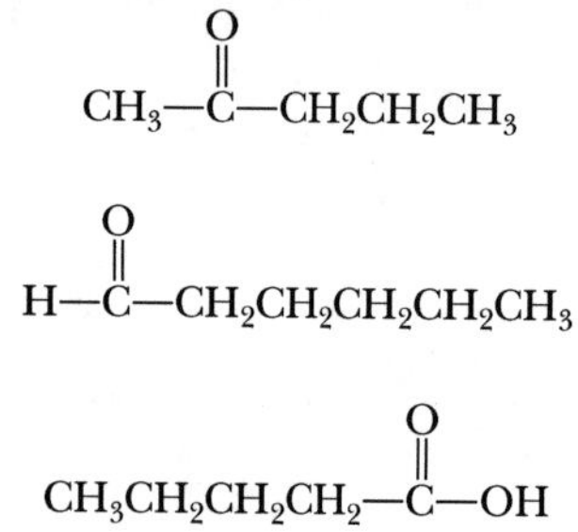

$$CH_3-\overset{\displaystyle O}{\overset{\|}{C}}-CH_2CH_2CH_3$$

$$H-\overset{\displaystyle O}{\overset{\|}{C}}-CH_2CH_2CH_2CH_2CH_3$$

$$CH_3CH_2CH_2CH_2-\overset{\displaystyle O}{\overset{\|}{C}}-OH$$

10.41 (a) Acid, 3-methylpentanoic acid
(b) Ester, methyl propanoate
(c) Ester, butyl acetate (or butyl ethanoate)
(d) Acid, p-bromobenzoic acid

10.43 (a) Pentanoic acid (see Question 39c)
(b) 1-Pentanol, $CH_3CH_2CH_2CH_2CH_2OH$

$$H_3C-\overset{\displaystyle OH}{\underset{\displaystyle H}{\overset{\|}{C}}}-CH_2CH_2CH_2CH_2CH_2CH_3$$

(c) 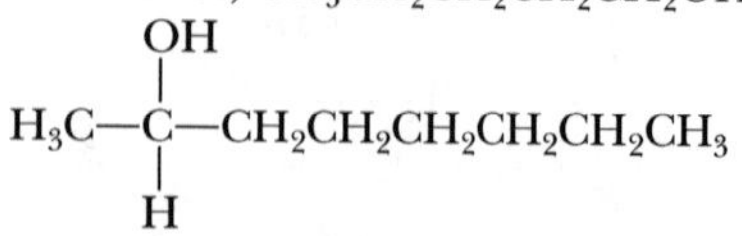
(d) No reaction. A ketone is not oxidized by $KMnO_4$.

10.45 Step 1: Oxidize 1-propanol to propanoic acid.

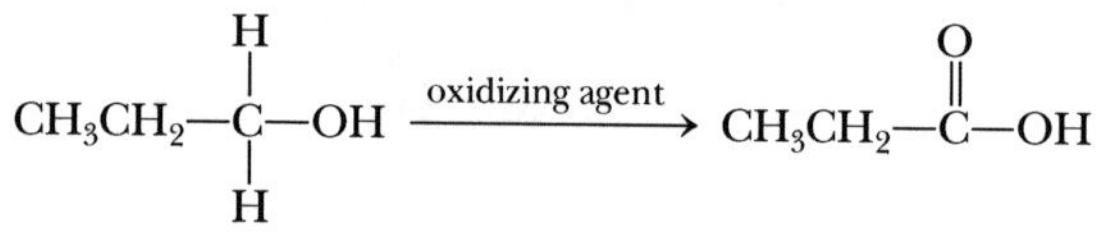

$$CH_3CH_2-\overset{\displaystyle H}{\underset{\displaystyle H}{\overset{\|}{C}}}-OH \xrightarrow{\text{oxidizing agent}} CH_3CH_2-\overset{\displaystyle O}{\overset{\|}{C}}-OH$$

Step 2: Combine propanoic acid and 1-propanol.

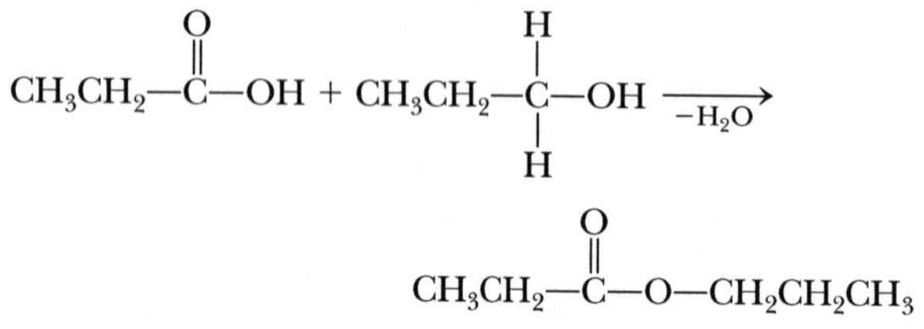

$$CH_3CH_2-\overset{\displaystyle O}{\overset{\|}{C}}-OH + CH_3CH_2-\overset{\displaystyle H}{\underset{\displaystyle H}{\overset{\|}{C}}}-OH \xrightarrow{-H_2O}$$

$$CH_3CH_2-\overset{\displaystyle O}{\overset{\|}{C}}-O-CH_2CH_2CH_3$$

10.47 Sodium acetate, $NaCH_3CO_2$, and 1-butanol, $CH_3CH_2CH_2CH_2OH$

10.49 (a) Trigonal planar
(b) 120°
(c) The molecule is chiral. There are four different groups around the carbon atom marked 2.
(d) The acidic H atom is the H attached to the CO_2H (carboxyl) group.

10.51 (a) Alcohol   (c) Acid
(b) Amide   (d) Ester

10.53 (a) Prepare polyvinyl acetate (PVA) from vinylaceta[te]

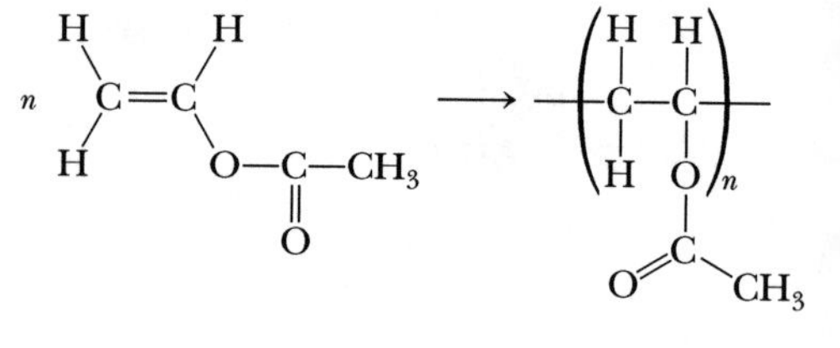

(b) The three units of PVA:

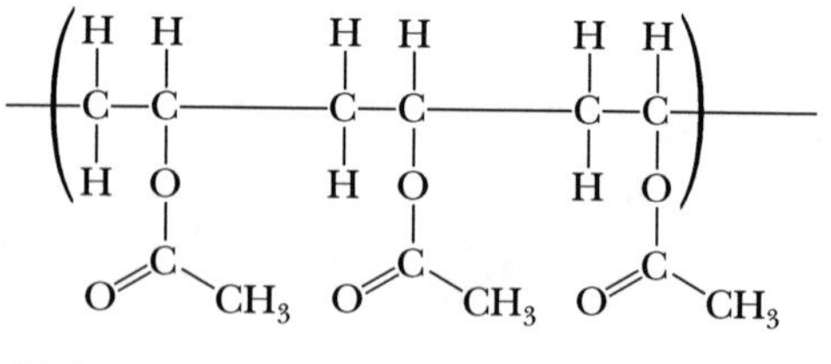

(c) Hydrolysis of polyvinyl alcohol

10.55 Illustrated here is a segment of a copolymer composed of two units of 1,1–dichloroethylene and two units of chloroethylene.

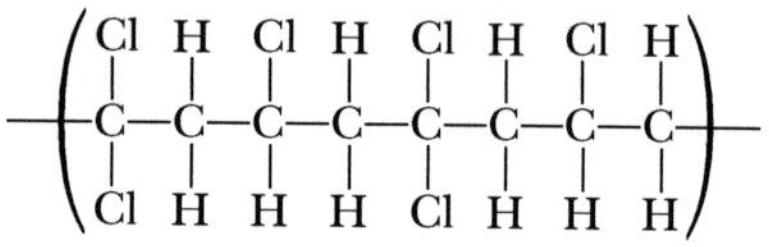

10.57 (a)   cis isomer   trans isomer   (b)

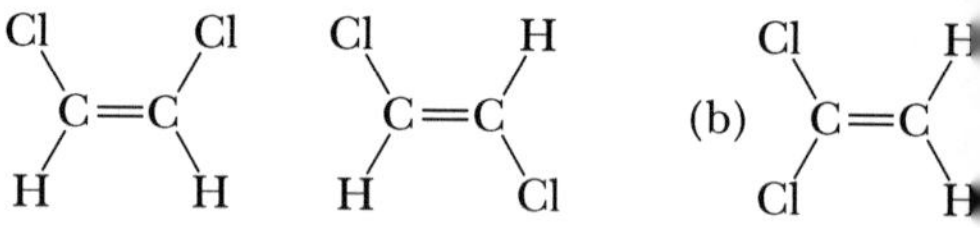

10.59

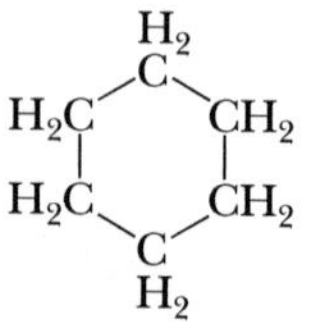

cyclohexane 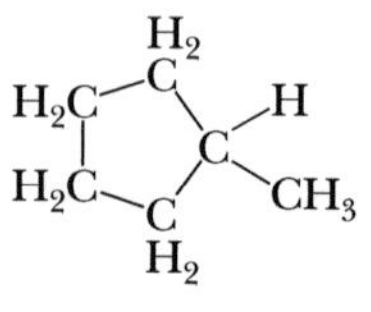   methylcyclopentane

$CH_3CH=CHCH$
2-hexene
Other isomers are po[...]
moving the double b[...]
with a branched chai[...]

10.61

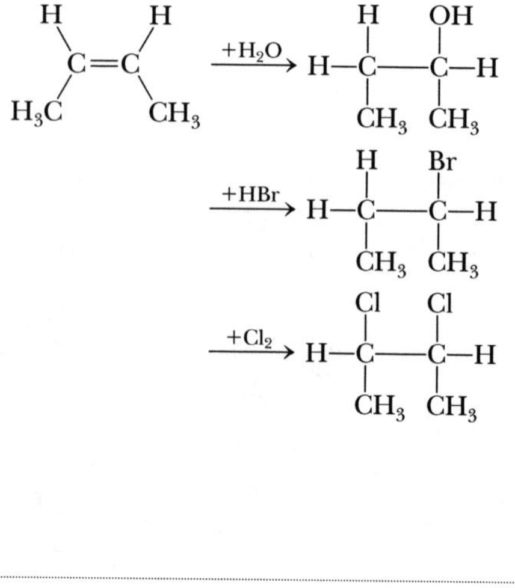

$$+H_2O \rightarrow H-\overset{\displaystyle H}{\underset{\displaystyle CH_3}{\overset{\|}{C}}}-\overset{\displaystyle OH}{\underset{\displaystyle CH_3}{\overset{\|}{C}}}-H$$

$$+HBr \rightarrow H-\overset{\displaystyle H}{\underset{\displaystyle CH_3}{\overset{\|}{C}}}-\overset{\displaystyle Br}{\underset{\displaystyle CH_3}{\overset{\|}{C}}}-H$$

$$+Cl_2 \rightarrow H-\overset{\displaystyle Cl}{\underset{\displaystyle CH_3}{\overset{\|}{C}}}-\overset{\displaystyle Cl}{\underset{\displaystyle CH_3}{\overset{\|}{C}}}-H$$

10.63 (a)

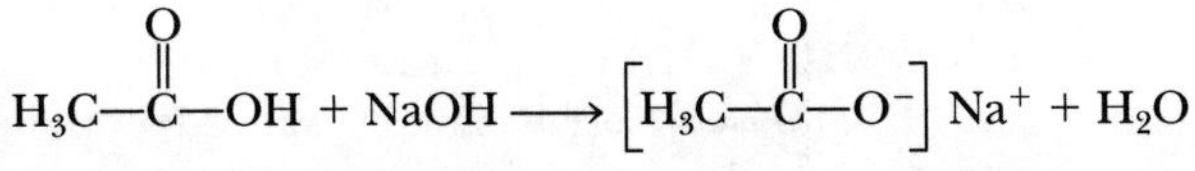

$$H_3C-\overset{\displaystyle O}{\overset{\displaystyle \|}{C}}-OH + NaOH \longrightarrow \left[H_3C-\overset{\displaystyle O}{\overset{\displaystyle \|}{C}}-O^- \right] Na^+ + H_2O$$

(b)

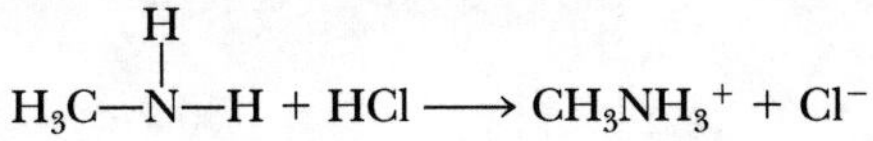

$$H_3C-\overset{\displaystyle H}{\overset{\displaystyle |}{N}}-H + HCl \longrightarrow CH_3NH_3{}^+ + Cl^-$$

10.65

$$n\, HOCH_2CH_2OH + n\, HO-\overset{\displaystyle O}{\overset{\displaystyle \|}{C}}-\underset{\text{(ring)}}{}-\overset{\displaystyle O}{\overset{\displaystyle \|}{C}}-OH \longrightarrow$$

$+\, n\, H_2O$

10.67 (a) 2, 3-Dimethylpentane

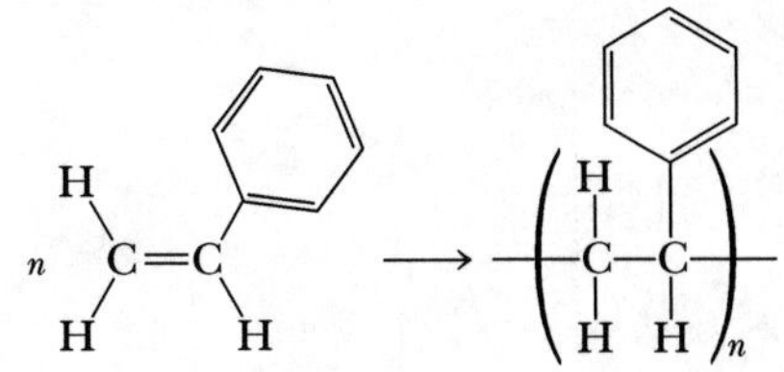

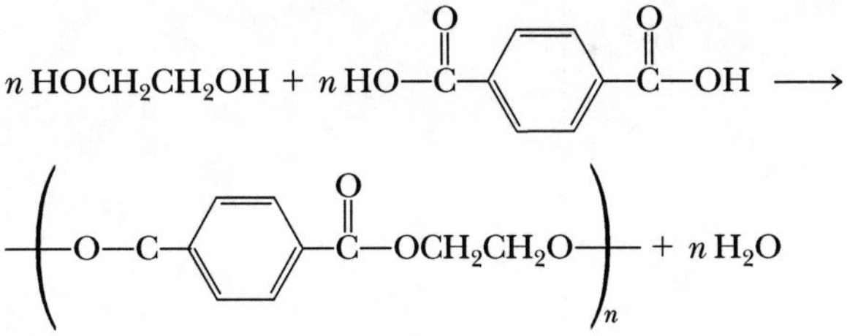

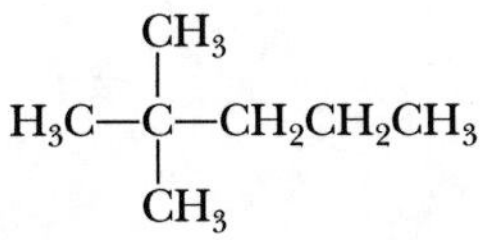

$$H_3C-\overset{\displaystyle CH_3}{\underset{\displaystyle CH_3}{\overset{\displaystyle |}{\underset{\displaystyle |}{C}}}}-CH_2CH_2CH_3$$

(b) 3, 3-Dimethylpentane

$$CH_3CH_2-\overset{\displaystyle CH_2CH_3}{\underset{\displaystyle CH_2CH_3}{\overset{\displaystyle |}{\underset{\displaystyle |}{C}}}}-CH_2CH_3$$

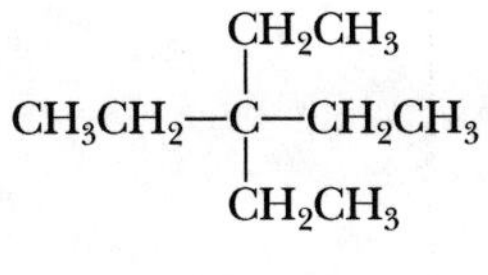

(c) 3-Ethyl-2-methylpentane

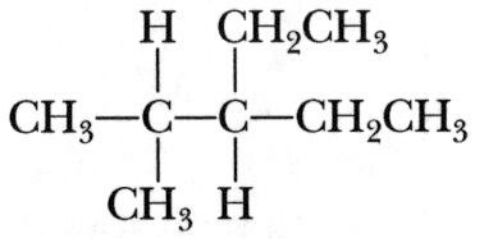

$$CH_3-\overset{\displaystyle H}{\underset{\displaystyle CH_3}{\overset{\displaystyle |}{\underset{\displaystyle |}{C}}}}-\overset{\displaystyle CH_2CH_3}{\underset{\displaystyle H}{\overset{\displaystyle |}{\underset{\displaystyle |}{C}}}}-CH_2CH_3$$

(d) 3-Ethylhexane

$$CH_3CH_2-\overset{\displaystyle CH_2CH_3}{\underset{\displaystyle H}{\overset{\displaystyle |}{\underset{\displaystyle |}{C}}}}-CH_2CH_2CH_3$$

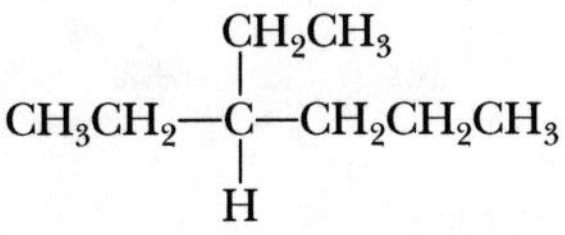

10.69

1,1-Dichloropropane $\quad H-\overset{\displaystyle Cl}{\underset{\displaystyle Cl}{\overset{\displaystyle |}{\underset{\displaystyle |}{C}}}}-CH_2CH_3$

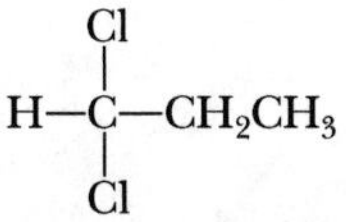

1,2-Dichloropropane $\quad H-\overset{\displaystyle Cl}{\underset{\displaystyle H}{\overset{\displaystyle |}{\underset{\displaystyle |}{C}}}}-\overset{\displaystyle Cl}{\underset{\displaystyle H}{\overset{\displaystyle |}{\underset{\displaystyle |}{C}}}}-CH_3$

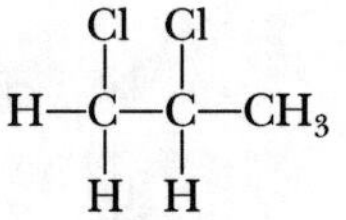

1,3-Dichloropropane $\quad H-\overset{\displaystyle Cl}{\underset{\displaystyle H}{\overset{\displaystyle |}{\underset{\displaystyle |}{C}}}}-\overset{\displaystyle H}{\underset{\displaystyle H}{\overset{\displaystyle |}{\underset{\displaystyle |}{C}}}}-\overset{\displaystyle Cl}{\underset{\displaystyle H}{\overset{\displaystyle |}{\underset{\displaystyle |}{C}}}}-H$

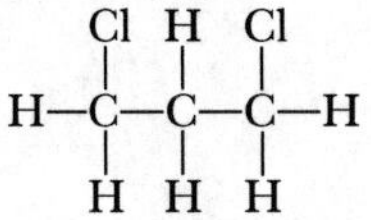

2,2-Dichloropropane $\quad H-\overset{\displaystyle H}{\underset{\displaystyle H}{\overset{\displaystyle |}{\underset{\displaystyle |}{C}}}}-\overset{\displaystyle Cl}{\underset{\displaystyle Cl}{\overset{\displaystyle |}{\underset{\displaystyle |}{C}}}}-\overset{\displaystyle H}{\underset{\displaystyle H}{\overset{\displaystyle |}{\underset{\displaystyle |}{C}}}}-H$

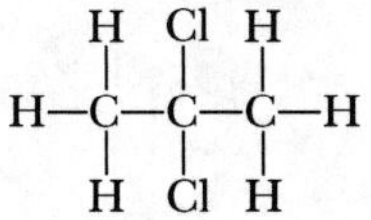

10.71

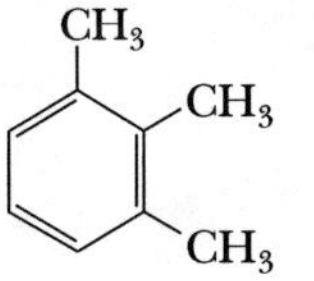

1,2,3-trimethylbenzene 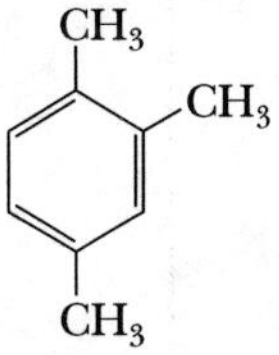 1,2,4-trimethylbenzene 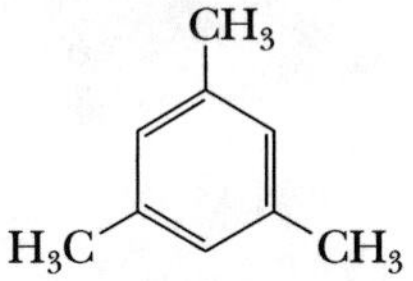 1,3,5-trimethylbenzene

10.73 Replace the carboxylic acid group with an H atom.

10.75

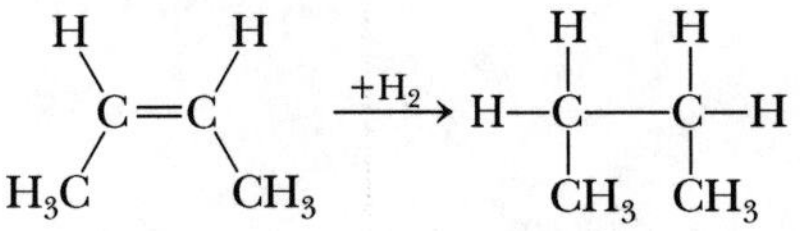

butane (not chiral)

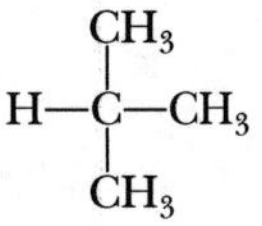

$$H-\overset{\displaystyle CH_3}{\underset{\displaystyle CH_3}{\overset{\displaystyle |}{\underset{\displaystyle |}{C}}}}-CH_3$$

10.77

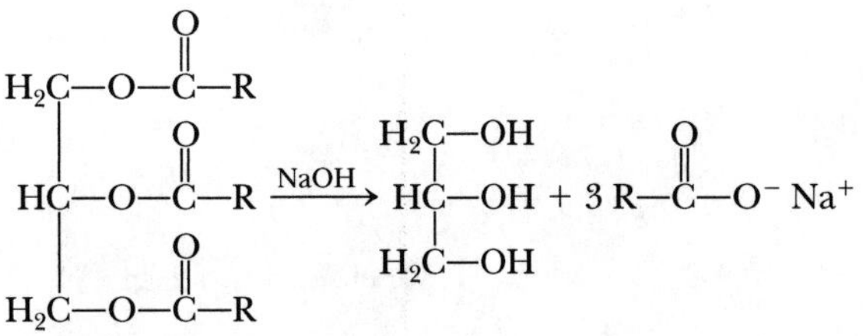

glyceryl trilaurate $\quad$ glycerol $\quad$ sodium laurate

10.79

add H₂ →
$H{-}C{-}C{-}H$ (H, CH₂OH top; H, H bottom)

$$\text{add H}_2 \rightarrow \begin{matrix} H & CH_2OH \\ H{-}C{-}C{-}H \\ H & H \end{matrix}$$

oxidize →
$$\begin{matrix} H & & CO_2H \\ & C{=}C & \\ H & & H \end{matrix}$$

(starting material)
$$\begin{matrix} H & & CH_2OH \\ & C{=}C & \\ H & & H \end{matrix}$$

polymerize →
$$\left(\begin{matrix} H & CH_2OH & H & CH_2OH \\ C{-}C & & C{-}C \\ H & H & H & H \end{matrix} \right)_n$$

CH_3CO_2H →
$$H_3C{-}\overset{O}{\overset{\|}{C}}{-}O{-}CH_2CH{=}CH_2$$

10.81 (a)

$$\begin{matrix} H & H \\ H{-}C{-}C{=}C{-}H \\ H & H \end{matrix} \xrightarrow{+HBr} \begin{matrix} H & Br & H \\ H{-}C{-}C{-}C{-}H \\ H & H & H \end{matrix}$$

2-bromopropane

(b)

$$\begin{matrix} H & CH_3 & H \\ H_3C{-}C{-}C{=}C{-}H \\ H \end{matrix} \xrightarrow{+H_2O} \begin{matrix} H & CH_3 & H \\ H_3C{-}C{-}C{-}C{-}H \\ H & OH & H \end{matrix}$$

2-methyl-2-butanol

(c)

$$\begin{matrix} H & CH_3 & H \\ H_3C{-}C{=}C{-}C{-}H \\ & & H \end{matrix} \xrightarrow{+H_2O} \begin{matrix} H & CH_3 & H \\ H_3C{-}C{-}C{-}C{-}H \\ H & OH & H \end{matrix}$$

10.83
Compound (b), acetaldehyde, and (c), ethanol, produce acetic acid when oxidized.

10.85
Cyclohexene, a cyclic alkene, will add Br_2 readily (to give $C_6H_{12}Br_2$). Benzene, however, needs much more stringent conditions to react with bromine; then Br_2 will substitute for H atoms on benzene and not add to the ring.

10.87
(a) The compound is either propanone, a ketone, or propanal, an aldehyde.

$$\begin{matrix} H & O & H \\ H{-}C{-}C{-}C{-}H \\ H & & H \end{matrix} \qquad \begin{matrix} H & H & O \\ H{-}C{-}C{-}C{-}H \\ H & H \end{matrix}$$

propanone (a ketone)   propanal (an aldehyde)

(b) The ketone will not undergo oxidation, but the aldehyde will be oxidized to the acid, $CH_3CH_2CO_2H$. Thus, the unknown is likely propanal.

(c) Propanoic acid

10.89
2-Propanol will react with an oxidizing agent such KMnO₄ (to give the ketone), whereas methyl ethyl ether ($CH_3OC_2H_5$) will not react. In addition, the cohol should be more soluble in water than the ether.

10.91

$$\begin{matrix} & CH_3 & H \\ H_2C{=}C{-}C{-}C{-}CH_3 \\ H & CH_3 & H \end{matrix}$$

X = 3,3-dimethyl-1-pentene

↓ +H₂O

$$\begin{matrix} OH & CH_3 & H \\ H_3C{-}C{-}C{-}C{-}CH_3 \\ H & CH_3 & H \end{matrix}$$

Y = 3,3-dimethyl-2-pentanol

oxidizing agent →

$$\begin{matrix} O & CH_3 & H \\ H_3C{-}C{-}C{-}C{-} \\ & CH_3 & H \end{matrix}$$

3,3-dimethyl-2-pentan

10.93

$$\begin{matrix} H \\ H{-}C{-}H \\ H \end{matrix}$$ methane   four single bonds

$$\begin{matrix} O \\ \| \\ C \\ H \quad H \end{matrix}$$ formaldehyde   one double bond and two single bonds

$$\begin{matrix} H & & H \\ C{=}C{=}C \\ H & & H \end{matrix}$$ allene   two double bonds

$H{-}C{\equiv}C{-}H$ acetylene   one single bond and o triple bond

10.95
(a) Cross-linking makes the material very rigid and inflexible.
(b) The OH groups give the polymer a high affinit for water.
(c) Hydrogen bonding allows the chains to form coils and sheets with high tensile strength.

10.97
(a) Ethane heat of combustion = −47.51 kJ/g
Ethanol heat of combustion = −26.82 kJ/g
(b) The heat obtained from the combustion of eth nol is less negative than for ethane, so partially oxidizing ethane to form ethanol decreases the amount of energy per mole available from the combustion of the substance.

10.99
(a) Empirical formula, CHO
(b) Molecular formula, $C_4H_4O_4$
(c)

$$\begin{matrix} O & & & O \\ \| & & & \| \\ HO{-}C{-}C{=}C{-}C{-}OH \\ & H & H \end{matrix}$$

(d) All four C atoms are sp^2 hybridized.
(e) 120°

CHAPTER 11

11.1 (a) 0.58 atm
(b) 0.59 bar
(c) 59 kPa

11.3 (a) 0.754 bar
(b) 650 kPa
(c) 934 kPa

11.5 2.70×10^2 mm Hg

11.7 3.7 L

11.9 250 mm Hg

11.11 3.2×10^2 mm Hg

11.13 9.72 atm

11.15 (a) 75 mL O_2
(b) 150 mL NO_2

11.17 0.919 atm

11.19 $V = 2.9$ L

11.21 1.9×10^6 g He

11.23 3.7×10^{-4} g/L

11.25 34.0 g/mol

11.27 57.5 g/mol

11.29 Molar mass = 74.9 g/mol; B_6H_{10}

11.31 0.039 mol H_2; 0.096 atm; 73 mm Hg

11.33 170 g NaN_3

11.35 1.7 atm O_2

11.37 4.1 atm H_2; 1.6 atm Ar; total pressure = 5.7 atm

11.39 (a) 0.30 mol halothane/1 mol O_2
(b) 3.0×10^2 g halothane

11.41 (a) CO_2 has the higher kinetic energy.
(b) The average speed of the H_2 molecules is greater than the average speed of the CO_2 molecules.
(c) The number of CO_2 molecules is greater than the number of H_2 molecules [$n(CO_2) = 1.8n(H_2)$].
(d) The mass of CO_2 is greater than the mass of H_2.

11.43 Average speed of CO_2 molecule = 3.65×10^4 cm/s

11.45 Average speed increases (and molar mass decreases) in the order $CH_2F_2 < Ar < N_2 < CH_4$.

11.47 (a) F_2 (38 g/mol) effuses faster than CO_2 (44 g/mol).
(b) N_2 (28 g/mol) effuses faster than O_2 (32 g/mol).
(c) C_2H_4 (28.1 g/mol) effuses faster than C_2H_6 (30.1 g/mol).
(d) $CFCl_3$ (137 g/mol) effuses faster than $C_2Cl_2F_4$ (171 g/mol).

11.49 36 g/mol

11.51 P from the van der Waals equation = 26.0 atm

P from the ideal gas law = 30.6 atm

11.53 (a) Standard atmosphere: 1 atm; 760 mm Hg; 101.325 kPa; 1.013 bar.
(b) N_2 partial pressure: 0.780 atm; 593 mm Hg; 79.1 kPa; 0.791 bar
(c) H_2 pressure: 131 atm; 9.98×10^4 mm Hg; 1.33×10^4 kPa; 133 bar
(d) Air: 0.333 atm; 253 mm Hg; 33.7 kPa; 0.337 bar

11.55 $T = 290.$ K or 17 °C

11.57 $2\ C_4H_9SH(g) + 15\ O_2(g) \rightarrow$
$8\ CO_2(g) + 10\ H_2O(g) + 2\ SO_2(g)$

Total pressure = 37.3 mm Hg. Partial pressures: CO_2 = 14.9 mm Hg, H_2O = 18.6 mm Hg, and SO_2 = 3.73 mm Hg.

11.59 4 mol

11.61 Ni is the limiting reactant; 1.31 g $Ni(CO)_4$

11.63 (a, b) Sample 4 (He) has the largest number of molecules and sample 3 (H_2 at 27 °C and 760 mm Hg) has the fewest number of molecules.
(c) Sample 2 (Ar)

11.65 8.54 g $Fe(CO)_5$

11.67 S_2F_{10}

11.69 (a) 28.7 g/mol $\simeq$ 29 g/mol
(b) X of O_2 = 0.17 and X of N_2 = 0.83

11.71 Molar mass = 86.4 g/mol. The gas is probably ClO_2F.

11.73 n(He) = 0.0128 mol

11.75 Weight percent $KClO_3$ = 69.1%

11.77 (a) $NO_2 < O_2 < NO$
(b) $P(O_2) = 75$ mm Hg
(c) $P(NO_2) = 150$ mm Hg

11.79 $P(NH_3) = 69$ mm Hg and $P(F_2) = 51$ mm Hg

Pressure after reaction = 17 mm Hg

11.81 At 20 °C, there is 7.8×10^{-3} g H_2O/L. At 0 °C, there is 4.6×10^{-3} g H_2O/L.

11.83 The mixture contains 0.22 g CO_2 and 0.77 g CO.

$P(CO_2) = 0.22$ atm; $P(O_2) = 0.12$ atm; $P(CO) = 1.22$ atm

11.85 The formula of the iron compound is $Fe(CO)_5$.

11.87 (a) $P(B_2H_6) = 0.0160$ atm
(b) $P(H_2) = 0.0320$ atm, so $P_{total} = 0.0480$ atm

11.89 Amount of $Na_2CO_3 = 0.00424$ mol
Amount of $NaHCO_3 = 0.00951$ mol
Amount of CO_2 produced = 0.0138 mol
Volume of CO_2 produced = 0.343 L

11.91 Decomposition of 1 mol of $Cu(NO_3)_2$ should give 2 mol NO_2 and ½ mol of O_2. Total actual amount = 4.72×10^{-3} mol of gas.
(a) Average molar mass = 41.3 g/mol.
(b) Mole fractions: $X(NO_2) = 0.666$ and $X(O_2) = 0.334$
(c) Amount of each gas: 3.13×10^{-3} mol NO_2 and 1.57×10^{-3} mol O_2
(d) If some NO_2 molecules combine to form N_2O_4, the apparent mole fraction of NO_2 would be smaller than expected (= 0.8). As this is the case, it is apparent that some N_2O_4 has been formed (as is observed in the experiment).

11.93 (a) 10.0 g of O_2 represents more molecules than 10.0 g of CO_2. Therefore, O_2 has the greater partial pressure.
(b) The average speed of the O_2 molecules is greater than the average speed of the CO_2 molecules.
(c) The gases are at the same temperature and so have the same average kinetic energy.

11.95 (a) $P(C_2H_2) > P(CO)$
(b) There are more molecules in the C_2H_2 container than in the CO container.

11.97 (a) Not a gas. A gas would expand to an infinite volume.
(b) Not a gas. A density of 8.2 g/mL is typical of a solid.
(c) Insufficient information
(d) Gas

11.99 (a) There are more molecules of H_2 than atoms of He.
(b) The mass of He is greater than the mass of H_2.

11.101 The speed of gas molecules is related to the square root of the absolute temperature, so a doubling of the temperature will lead to an increase of about $(2)^{1/2}$ or 1.4.

CHAPTER 12

12.1 (a) Dipole–dipole interactions (and hydrogen bonds)
(b) Induced dipole–induced dipole forces
(c) Dipole–dipole interactions (and hydrogen bonds)

12.3 (a) Induced dipole–induced dipole forces
(b) Induced dipole–induced dipole forces
(c) Dipole–dipole forces
(d) Dipole–dipole forces (and hydrogen bonding)

12.5 The predicted order of increasing strength is $Ne < CH_4 < CO < CCl_4$. In this case, prediction does not quite agree with reality. The boiling points are Ne (-246 °C) < CO (-192 °C) < CH_4 (-162 °C) < CCl_4 (77 °C).

12.7 (c) HF; (d) acetic acid; (f) CH_3OH

12.9 (a) LiCl. The Li^+ ion is smaller than Cs^+ (Figure 7.12) which makes the ion–ion forces of attraction stronger in LiCl.
(b) $Mg(NO_3)_2$. The Mg^{2+} ion is smaller than the Na^+ ion (Figure 7.12), and the magnesium ion has a 2+ charge (as opposed to 1+ for sodium). Both of these effects lead to stronger ion–ion forces of attraction in magnesium nitrate.
(c) $NiCl_2$. The nickel(II) ion has a larger charge than Rb^+ and is considerably smaller. Both effects mean that there are stronger ion–ion forces of attraction in nickel(II) chloride.

12.11 $q = +90.1$ kJ

12.13 (a) Water vapor pressure is about 150 mm Hg at 60 °C. (Appendix G gives a value of 149.4 mm Hg at 60 °C.)
(b) 600 mm Hg at about 93 °C
(c) At 70 °C, ethanol has a vapor pressure of about 520 mm Hg, whereas that of water is about 225 mm Hg.

12.15 At 30 °C, the vapor pressure of ether is about 590 mm Hg. (This pressure requires 0.23 g of ether in the vapor phase at the given conditions, so there is sufficient ether in the flask.) At 0 °C, the vapor pressure is about 160 mm Hg, so some ether condenses when the temperature declines.

12.17 (a) O_2 (-183 °C) (bp of $N_2 = -196$ °C)
(b) SO_2 (-10 °C) (CO_2 sublimes at -78 °C)
(c) HF ($+19.7$ °C) (HI, -35.6 °C)
(d) GeH_4 (-90.0 °C) (SiH_4, -111.8 °C)

12.19 (a) CS_2, about 620 mm Hg; CH_3NO_2, about 80 mm Hg

(b) CS_2, induced dipole–induced dipole forces; CH_3NO_2, dipole–dipole forces

(c) CS_2, about 46 °C; CH_3NO_2, about 100 °C

(d) About 39 °C

(e) About 34 °C

12.21 (a) 80.1 °C

(b) At about 48 °C, the liquid has a vapor pressure of 250 mm Hg.

The vapor pressure is 650 mm Hg at 75 °C.

(c) 33.5 kJ/mol (from slope of plot)

12.23 No, CO cannot be liquefied at room temperature because the critical temperature is lower than room temperature.

12.25 $Ar < CO_2 < CH_3OH$

12.27 Li^+ ions are smaller than Cs^+ ions (78 pm and 165 pm, respectively; see Figure 7.12). Thus, there will be a stronger attractive force between Li^+ ion and water molecules than between Cs^+ ions and water molecules.

12.29 (a) 350 mm Hg

(b) Ethanol (lower vapor pressure at every temperature)

(c) 84 °C

(d) CS_2, 46 °C; C_2H_5OH, 78 °C; C_7H_{16}, 99 °C

(e) CS_2, gas; C_2H_5OH, gas; C_7H_{16}, liquid

12.31 Molar enthalpy of vaporization increases with increasing intermolecular forces: C_2H_6 (14.69 kJ/mol; induced dipole) < HCl (16.15 kJ/mol; dipole) < CH_3OH (35.21 kJ/mol, hydrogen bonds). (The molar enthalpies of vaporization here are given at the boiling point of the liquid.)

12.33 5.49×10^{19} atoms/m^3

12.35 (a) 70.3 °C

(b)

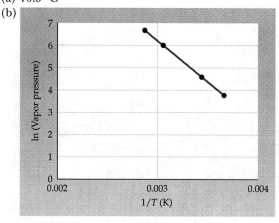

Using the equation for the straight line in the plot

$$\ln P = -3885 \, (1/T) + 17.949$$

we calculate that $T = 312.6$ K (39.5 °C) when $P = 250$ mm Hg. When $P = 650$ mm Hg, $T = 338.7$ K (65.5 °C).

(c) Calculated $\Delta_{vap}H = 32.3$ kJ/mol

12.37 When the can is inverted in cold water, the water vapor pressure in the can, which was approximately 760 mm Hg, drops rapidly—say, to 9 mm Hg at 10 °C. This creates a partial vacuum in the can, and the can is crushed because of the difference in pressure inside the can and the pressure of the atmosphere pressing down on the outside of the can.

12.39 Acetone and water can interact by hydrogen bonding.

12.41 Glycol's viscosity will be greater than ethanol's, owing to the greater hydrogen-bonding capacity of glycol.

12.43 (a) Water has two OH bonds and two lone pairs, whereas the O atom of ethanol has only one OH bond (and two lone pairs). More extensive hydrogen bonding is likely for water.

(b) Water and ethanol interact extensively through hydrogen bonding, so the volume is expected to be slightly smaller than the sum of the two volumes.

12.45 Two pieces of evidence for $H_2O(\ell)$ having considerable intermolecular attractive forces:

(a) Based on the boiling points of the Group 6A hydrides (Figure 12.6), the boiling point of water should be approximately −80 °C. The actual boiling point of 100 °C reflects the significant hydrogen bonding that occurs.

(b) Liquid water has a specific heat capacity that is higher than almost any other liquid. This reflects the fact that a relatively larger amount of energy is necessary to overcome intermolecular forces and raise the temperature of the liquid.

12.47 (a) HI, hydrogen iodide

(b) The large iodine atom in HI leads to a significant polarizability for the molecule and thus to a large dispersion force.

(c) The dipole moment of HCl (1.07 D, Table 9.8) is larger than for HI (0.38 D).

(d) HI. See part (b).

12.49 A gas can be liquefied at or below its critical temperature. The critical temperature for CF_4 (-45.7 °C) is below room temperature (25 °C), so it cannot be liquefied at room temperature.

12.51 Hydrogen bonding is most likely at the O—H group at the "right" end of the molecule, and at the C=O and N—H groups in the amide group (—NH—CO—).

CHAPTER 13

13.1 Two possible unit cells are illustrated here. The simplest formula is AB_8.

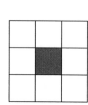 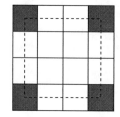

13.3 Ca^{2+} ions at eight corners = 1 net Ca^{2+} ion

O^{2-} ions in six faces = 3 net O^{2-} ions

Ti^{4+} ion in center of unit cell = 1 net Ti^{4+} ion

Formula = $CaTiO_3$

13.5 (a) There are eight O^{2-} ions at the corners and one in the center for a net of two O^{2-} ions per unit cell. There are four Cu ions in the interior in tetrahedral holes. The ratio of ions is Cu_2O.
(b) The oxidation number of copper must be +1.

13.7 Calcium atom radius = 197 pm

13.9 There are three ways the edge dimensions can be calculated:
(a) Calculate mass of unit cell ($= 1.103 \times 10^{-21}$ g/uc)

Calculate volume of unit cell from mass ($= 3.53 \times 10^{-22}$ cm³/uc)

Calculate edge length from volume ($= 707$ pm)

(b) Assume I^- ions touch along the cell diagonal (see Exercise 13.2) and use I^- radius to find the edge length. Radius $I^- = 220$ pm

Edge $= 4(220 \text{ pm})/2^{1/2} = 622$ pm

(c) Assume the I^- and K^+ ions touch along the cell edge (page 599)

Edge $= 2 \times I^-$ radius $+ 2 \times K^+$ radius $= 706$ pm

Methods (a) and (c) agree. It is apparent that the sizes of the ions are such that the I^- ions cannot touch along the cell diagonal.

13.11 Increasing lattice energy: RbI < LiI < LiF < CaO

13.13 As the ion–ion distance decreases, the force of attraction between ions increases. This should make the lattice more stable, and more energy should be required to melt the compound.

13.15 $\Delta_f H° = -607$ kJ/mol

13.17 (a) Eight C atoms per unit cell. There are eight corners (= 1 net C atom), six faces (= 3 net C atoms), and four internal C atoms.
(b) Face-centered cubic (fcc) with C atoms in the tetrahedral holes.

13.19 q (for fusion) $= -1.97$ kJ; q (for melting) $= +1.97$

13.21 (a) The density of liquid CO_2 is less than that of solid CO_2.
(b) CO_2 is a gas at 5 atm and 0 °C.
(c) Critical temperature = 31 °C, so CO_2 cannot be liquefied at 45 °C.

13.23 q (to heat the liquid) $= 9.4 \times 10^2$ kJ

q (to vaporize NH_3) $= 1.6 \times 10^4$ kJ

q (to heat the vapor) $= 8.8 \times 10^2$ kJ

$q_{total} = 1.83 \times 10^4$ kJ

13.25 O_2 phase diagram. (i) Note the slight positive slope the solid–liquid equilibrium line. It indicates that the density of solid O_2 is greater than that of liquid O_2. (ii) Using the diagram here, the vapor pressure of C at 77 K is between 150 mm Hg and 200 mm Hg.

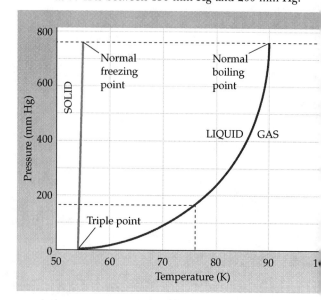

13.27 Radius of silver = 145 pm

13.29 1.356×10^{-8} cm (literature value is 1.357×10^{-8} cm

31 Mass of 1 CaF_2 unit calculated from crystal data = 1.2963×10^{-22} g. Divide molar mass of CaF_2 (78.077 g/mol) by mass of 1 CaF_2 to obtain Avogadro's number. Calculated value = 6.0230×10^{23} CaF_2/mol.

33 Diagram A leads to a surface coverage of 78.5%. Diagram B leads to 90.7% coverage.

35 (a) The lattice can be described as an fcc lattice of Si atoms with Si atoms in one half of the tetrahedral holes.
(b) There are eight Si atoms in the unit cell.

Mass of unit cell = 3.731×10^{-22} g

Volume of unit cell = 1.602×10^{-22} cm³

Density = 2.329 g/cm³ (which is the same as the literature value)

In the Si unit cell we cannot assume the atoms touch along the edge or along the face diagonal. Instead, we know that the Si atoms in the tetahedral holes are bonded to the Si atoms at the corner.

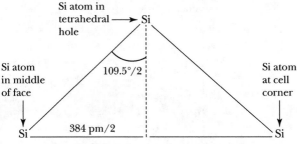

Distance = 1/2 (cell diagonal) = 384 pm

Distance across cell face diagonal = 768 pm

Sin $(109.5°/2)$ = 0.817 = (768 pm/2)/(Si–Si distance)

Distance from Si in tetrahedral hole to face or corner Si = 235 pm

Si radius = 118 pm

Table 7.8 gives Si radius as 117 pm

37 (a) Mg^{2+} ions are in ⅛ of the eight possible tetrahedral holes, and Al^{3+} ions are in ½ of the four available octahedral holes.
(b) Fe^{2+} ions are in ⅛ of the eight possible tetrahedral holes, and Cr^{3+} ions are in ½ of the four available octahedral holes.

39 Lead sulfide has the same structure as sodium chloride, not the same structure as ZnS. There are four Pb^{2+} ions and four S^{2-} ions per unit cell, a 1:1 ratio that matches the compound formula.

41 (a) $BBr_3(g) + PBr_3(g) + 3 H_2(g) \rightarrow$
$$BP(s) + 6 HBr(g)$$

(b) If B atoms are in an fcc lattice, then the P atoms must be in ½ of the tetrahedral holes. (In this way it resembles Si in Question 13.35.)
(c) Unit cell volume = 1.092×10^{-22} cm³
Unit cell mass = 2.775×10^{-22} g
Density = 2.54 g/cm³
(d) The solution to this problem is identical to Question 13.35. In the BP lattice, the cell face diagonal is 676 pm. Therefore, the calculated BP distance is 207 pm.

13.43 Assuming the spheres are packed in an identical way, the water levels are the same. A face-centered cubic lattice, for example, uses 74% of the available space, regardless of the sphere size.

CHAPTER 14

14.1 (a) Concentration (m) = 0.0434 m
(b) Mole fraction of acid = 0.000781
(c) Weight percent of acid = 0.509%

14.3 NaI: 0.15 m; 2.2%; $X = 2.7 \times 10^{-3}$

CH_3CH_2OH: 1.1 m; 5.0%; $X = 0.020$

$C_{12}H_{22}O_{11}$: 0.15 m; 4.9%; $X = 2.7 \times 10^{-3}$

14.5 2.65 g Na_2CO_3; $X(Na_2CO_3) = 3.59 \times 10^{-3}$

14.7 220 g glycerol; 5.7 m

14.9 16.2 m; 37.1%

14.11 Molality = 2.6×10^{-5} m (assuming that 1 kg of seawater is equivalent to 1 kg of solvent)

14.13 (b) and (c)

14.15 $\Delta_{soln}H°$ for LiCl = -36.9 kJ/mol. This is an exothermic enthalpy of solution, as compared with the very slightly endothermic value for NaCl.

14.17 Above about 40 °C the solubility increases with temperature; therefore, add more NaCl and raise the temperature.

14.19 2×10^{-3} g O_2

14.21 1130 mm Hg or 1.49 bar

14.23 35.0 mm Hg

14.25 $X(H_2O) = 0.869$; 16.7 mol glycol; 1040 g glycol

14.27 Calculated boiling point = 84.2 °C

14.29 $\Delta T_{bp} = 0.808$ °C; solution boiling point = 62.51 °C

14.31 Molality = 8.60 m; 28.4%

14.33 Molality = 0.195 m; $\Delta T_{fp} = -0.362$ °C

14.35 Molar mass = 360 g/mol; $C_{20}H_{16}Fe_2$

14.37 Molar mass = 150 g/mol

14.39 Molar mass = 170 g/mol

14.41 Freezing point = −24.6 °C

14.43 0.080 m $CaCl_2$ < 0.10 m NaCl < 0.040 m Na_2SO_4 < 0.10 sugar

14.45 (a) ΔT_{fp} = −0.348 °C; fp = −0.348 °C
(b) ΔT_{bp} = +0.0959 °C; bp = 100.0959 °C
(c) Π = 4.58 atm

The osmotic pressure is large and can be measured with a small experimental error.

14.47 Molar mass = 6.0 × 10³ g/mol

14.49 (a) $BaCl_2(aq)$ + $Na_2SO_4(aq)$ →
$$BaSO_4(s) + 2\ NaCl(aq)$$
(b) Initially, the $BaSO_4$ particles form a colloidal suspension.
(c) Over time, the particles of $BaSO_4(s)$ grow and precipitate.

14.51 Molar mass = 110 g/mol

14.53 (a) Increase in vapor pressure of water

0.20 m Na_2SO_4 < 0.50 m sugar < 0.20 m KBr < 0.35 m ethylene glycol

(b) Increase in boiling point

0.35 m ethylene glycol < 0.20 m KBr < 0.50 m sugar < 0.20 m Na_2SO_4

14.55 (a) 0.456 mol DMG and 11.4 mol ethanol; X(DMG) = 0.0385
(b) 0.869 m
(c) VP ethanol over the solution at 78.4 °C = 730.7 mm Hg
(d) bp = 79.5 °C

14.57 For ammonia: 23 m; 28%; $X(NH_3)$ = 0.29

14.59 0.592 g Na_2SO_4

14.61 (a) 0.20 m KBr; (b) 0.10 m Na_2CO_3

14.63 Freezing point = −11 °C

14.65 4.0 × 10² g/mol

14.67 4.7 × 10⁻⁴ mol/kg

14.69 (a) Molar mass = 4.9 × 10⁴ g/mol
(b) ΔT_{fp} = −3.8 × 10⁻⁴ °C

14.71 $\Delta_{soln}H°$ [Li_2SO_4] = −28.0 kJ/mol

$\Delta_{soln}H°$ [LiCl] = −36.9 kJ/mol

$\Delta_{soln}H°$ [K_2SO_4] = +23.7 kJ/mol

$\Delta_{soln}H°$ [KCl] = +17.2 kJ/mol

Both lithium compounds have exothermic enthalpies of solution, whereas both potassium compounds have endothermic values. Consistent with this is the fact that lithium salts (LiCl) are often more water-soluble than potassium salts (KCl) (see Figure 14.11).

14.73 X(benzene in solution) = 0.67 and X(toluene in solution) = 0.33

P_{total} = $P_{toluene}$ + $P_{benzene}$ = 7.3 mm Hg + 50. mm = 57 mm Hg

$$X\text{(toluene in vapor)} = \frac{7.3\ \text{mm Hg}}{57\ \text{mm Hg}} = 0.13$$

$$X\text{(benzene in vapor)} = \frac{50.\ \text{mm Hg}}{57\ \text{mm Hg}} = 0.87$$

14.75 i = 1.7. That is, there is 1.7 mol of ions in solution per mole of compound.

14.77 (a) Calculate the number of moles of ions in 10⁶ H_2O: 550. mol Cl^-; 470. mol Na^+; 53.1 mol Mg^{2+}; 9.42 mol SO_4^{2-}; 10.3 mol Ca^{2+}; 9.72 mol K^+; 0.84 mol Br^-. Total moles of ions = 1.103 × 10³ per 10⁶ g water. This gives ΔT_{fp} of −2.05 °C.
(b) Π = 27.0 atm. This means that a minimum pressure of 27 atm would have to be used in a reverse osmosis device.

14.79 (a) i = 2.06
(b) There are approximately two particles in solution, so H^+ + HSO_4^- best represents H_2SO_4 in aqueous solution.

14.81 The calculated molality at the freezing point of benzene is 0.47 m, whereas it is 0.99 m at the boiling point. A higher molality at the higher temperature indicates more molecules are dissolved. Therefore, assuming benzoic acid forms dimers like acetic acid (Figure 12.7), dimer formation is more prevalent at the lower temperature. In this process two molecules become one entity, lowering the number of separate species in solution and lowering the molality.

14.83 Molar mass in benzene = 1.20 × 10² g/mol; molar mass in water = 62.4 g/mol. The actual molar mass of acetic acid is 60.1 g/mol. In benzene, the molecules of acetic acid form "dimers." That is, two molecules form a single unit through hydrogen bonding. See Figure 12.7 on page 562.

14.85 (a) Molar mass = 97.6 g/mol; empirical formula, BF_2, and molecular formula, B_2F_4
(b)

14.87 See the discussion and data on page 558.
(a) The enthalpy of hydration of LiF is more negative than that for RbF because the Li^+ ion is much smaller than the Rb^+ ion.

(b) The enthalpy of hydration for $Ca(NO_3)_2$ is larger than that for KNO_3 owing to the $+2$ charge on the Ca^{2+} ion (and its smaller size).

(c) The enthalpy of hydration is greater for $CuBr_2$ than for $CsBr$ because Cu^{2+} has a larger charge than Cs^+, and the Cu^{2+} ion is smaller than the Cs^+ ion.

4.89 Li_2SO_4 should have a more negative enthalpy of hydration than Cs_2SO_4 because the Li^+ ion is smaller than the Cs^+ ion.

4.91 Colligative properties depend on the number of ions or molecules in solution. Each mole of $CaCl_2$ provides 1.5 times as many ions as each mole of NaCl.

4.93 Benzene is a nonpolar solvent. Thus, ionic substances such as $NaNO_3$ and NH_4Cl will certainly not dissolve. However, naphthalene is also nonpolar and resembles benzene in its structure; it should dissolve very well. (A chemical handbook gives a solubility of 33 g naphthalene per 100 g benzene.) Diethyl ether is weakly polar and will also be miscible to some extent with benzene.

4.95 The C—C and C—H bonds in hydrocarbons are nonpolar or weakly polar and tend to make such dispersions hydrophobic (water-hating). The C—O and O—H bonds in starch present opportunities for hydrogen bonding with water. Hence, starch is expected to be more hydrophilic.

4.97 $[NaCl] = 1.0$ M and $[KNO_3] = 0.88$ M. The KNO_3 solution has a higher solvent concentration, so solvent will flow from the KNO_3 solution to the NaCl solution.

CHAPTER 15

15.1 (a) $-\dfrac{1}{2}\dfrac{\Delta[O_3]}{\Delta t} = \dfrac{1}{3}\dfrac{\Delta[O_2]}{\Delta t}$

(b) $-\dfrac{1}{2}\dfrac{\Delta[HOF]}{\Delta t} = \dfrac{1}{2}\dfrac{\Delta[HF]}{\Delta t} = \dfrac{\Delta[O_2]}{\Delta t}$

15.3 $\dfrac{1}{3}\dfrac{\Delta[O_2]}{\Delta t} = -\dfrac{1}{2}\dfrac{\Delta[O_3]}{\Delta t}$ or $\dfrac{\Delta[O_2]}{\Delta t} = -\dfrac{2}{3}\dfrac{\Delta[O_2]}{\Delta t}$

so $\Delta[O_3]/\Delta t = -1.0 \times 10^{-3}$ mol/L $\cdot$ s.

15.5 (a) The graph of [B] (product concentration) versus time shows [B] increasing from zero. The line is curved, indicating the rate changes with time; thus the rate depends on concentration. Rates for the four 10-s intervals are as follows: 0–10 s, 0.0326 mol/L $\cdot$ s; from 10–20 s,

0.0246 mol/L $\cdot$ s; 20–30 s, 0.0178 mol/L $\cdot$ s; 30–40 s, 0.0140 mol/L $\cdot$ s.

(b) $-\dfrac{\Delta[A]}{\Delta t} = \dfrac{1}{2}\dfrac{\Delta[B]}{\Delta t}$ throughout the reaction

In the interval 10–20 s, $\dfrac{\Delta[A]}{\Delta t} = -0.0123 \dfrac{mol}{L \cdot s}$

(c) Instantaneous rate when $[B] = 0.750$ mol/L

$= \dfrac{\Delta[B]}{\Delta t} = 0.0163 \dfrac{mol}{L \cdot s}$

15.7 The reaction is second order in A, first order in B, and third order overall.

15.9 (a) Rate $= k[NO_2][O_3]$
(b) If $[NO_2]$ is tripled, the rate triples.
(c) If $[O_3]$ is halved, the rate is halved.

15.11 (a) The reaction is second order in [NO] and first order in $[O_2]$.

(b) $\dfrac{-\Delta[NO]}{\Delta t} = k[NO]^2[O_2]$

(c) $k = 13$ $L^2/mol^2 \cdot s$

(d) $\dfrac{-\Delta[NO]}{\Delta t} = -1.4 \times 10^{-5}$ mol/L $\cdot$ s

(e) When $-\Delta[NO]/\Delta t = 1.0 \times 10^{-4}$ mol/L $\cdot$ s, $\Delta[O_2]/\Delta t = 5.0 \times 10^{-5}$ mol/L $\cdot$ s and $\Delta[NO_2]/\Delta t = 1.0 \times 10^{-4}$ mol/L $\cdot$ s.

15.13 (a) Rate $= k[NO]^2[O_2]$
(b) $k = 50.$ $L^2/mol^2 \cdot h$
(c) Rate $= 8.5 \times 10^{-9}$ mol/L $\cdot$ h

15.15 $k = 3.73 \times 10^{-3}$ min^{-1}

15.17 5.0×10^2 min

15.19 (a) 153 min
(b) 1790 min

15.21 (a) $t_{1/2} = 10,000$ s (b) 34,000 s

15.23 0.1.87 g azomethane remains; 0.063 g N_2 formed

15.25 Fraction of ^{64}Cu remaining $= 0.030$

15.27 The straight line obtained in a graph of $\ln[N_2O]$ versus time indicates a first-order reaction.

$k = (-slope) = 0.0127$ min^{-1}

The rate when $[N_2O] = 0.035$ mol/L is 4.4×10^{-4} mol/L $\cdot$ min.

15.29 The graph of $1/[NO_2]$ versus time gives a straight line, indicating the reaction is second order with respect to $[NO_2]$ (see Table 15.1 on page 689). The slope of the line is k, so $k = 1.1$ L/mol $\cdot$ s.

15.31 $-\Delta[C_2F_4]/\Delta t = k[C_2F_4]^2 = (0.04$ L/mol $\cdot$ s$)[C_2F_4]^2$

15.33 Activation energy $= 102$ kJ/mol

15.35 $k = 0.3 \text{ s}^{-1}$

15.37

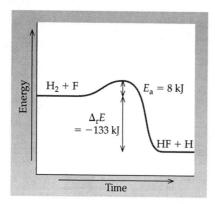

15.39 (a) Rate $= k[NO_3][NO]$
(b) Rate $= k[Cl][H_2]$
(c) Rate $= k[(CH_3)_3CBr]$

15.41 (a) The Second step   (b) Rate $= k[O_3][O]$

15.43 (a) NO_2 is a reactant in the first step and a product in the second step. CO is a reactant in the second step. NO_3 is an intermediate, and CO_2 is a product. NO is a product.
(b) Reaction coordinate diagram

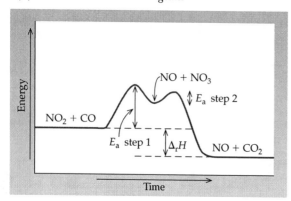

15.45 Doubling the concentration of A will increase the rate by a factor of 4 because the concentration of A appears in the rate law as $[A]^2$. Halving the concentration of B will halve the rate The net result is that the rate of the reaction will double.

15.47 After measuring pH as a function of time, one could then calculate pOH and then $[OH^-]$. Finally, a plot of $1/[OH^-]$ versus time would give a straight line with a slope equal to k.

15.49 72 s represents two half-lives, so $t_{1/2} = 36$ s.

15.51 (a) A plot of $1/[C_2F_4]$ versus time indicates the reaction is second order with respect to $[C_2F_4]$. The rate law is Rate $= k[C_2F_4]^2$.
(b) The rate constant (= slope of the line) is about 0.045 L/mol · s. (The graph does not allow a very accurate calculation.)

(c) Using $k = 0.045$ L/mol · s, the concentration ter 600 s is 0.03 M (to 1 significant figure).
(d) Time $= 2000$ s (using k from part a).

15.53 (a) A plot of $1/[NH_4NCO]$ versus time is linear, so the reaction is second order with respect to NH_4NCO.
(b) Slope $= k = 0.0109$ L/mol · min.
(c) $t_{1/2} = 200.$ min
(d) $[NH_4NCO] = 0.0997$ mol/L

15.55 Mechanism 2

15.57 $k = 0.018 \text{ h}^{-1}$ and $t_{1/2} = 39$ h

15.59 (a) After 125 min, 0.251 g remains. After 145, 0.144 g remains.
(b) Time $= 43.9$ min
(c) Fraction remaining $= 0.016$

15.61 The rate equation for the slow step is Rate $= k[O_3][O]$. The equilibrium constant, K, for step 1 is $K = [O_2][O]/[O_3]$. Solving this for $[O]$, we have $[O] = K[O_3]/[O_2]$. Substituting the expression for $[O]$ into the rate equation we find

$$\text{Rate} = k[O_3]\{K[O_3]/[O_2]\} = kK[O_3]^2/[O_2]$$

15.63 The slope of the ln k versus $1/T$ plot is -6370. From slope $= -E_a/R$, we derive $E_a = 53.0$ kJ/mol.

15.65 Estimated time at 90 °C $= 4.76$ min

15.67 After 30 min (one half-life), $P_{HOF} = 50.0$ mm Hg and $P_{total} = 125.0$ mm Hg. After 45 min, $P_{HOF} = 35.4$ mm Hg and $P_{total} = 132$ mm Hg.

15.69 (a) Reaction is first-order in NO_2NH_2 and -1 for H_3O^+.

(b, c) Mechanism 3.

In step 1, $K = k_4/k_4'$
$= [NO_2NH^-][H_3O^+]/[NO_2NH_2]$

Rearrange this and substitute into the rate law for the slow step.

Rate $= k_5[NO_2NH^-] = k_5K[NO_2NH_2]/[H_3O^+]$

This is the same as the experimental rate law, where the overall rate constant $k = k_5K$.

(d) Addition of OH^- ions will shift the equilibrium in step 1 to produce a larger concentration of NO_2NH^-, the reactant in the rate-determining step.

15.71 (a) Average rate for $t = 0$ to $t = 15$ is about 4.7×10^{-5} M/s. For $t = 100$ s to 125 s, the average rate is about 1.6×10^{-5} M/s. The rate slows because the rate of the reaction is dependent on the concentration of reactant and this concentration is declining with time.
(b) Instantaneous rate at 50 s is about 2.7×10^{-5} M/

(c) A plot of ln (concentration) versus time is a straight line with an equation of $y = -0.010\ x - 5.2984$. The slope, which is equal to $-k$, is -0.010, so $k = 0.010\ s^{-1}$.

(d) From the data the half-life is 69.3 s, and the same value comes from the relation $t_{1/2} = \ln 2/k$.

5.73 A plot of 1/Rate versus 1/[S] gives the equation

$$1/Rate = 94\ (1/[S]) + 7.5 \times 10^4$$

and so $Rate_{max} = 1/(7.5 \times 10^4) = 1.3 \times 10^{-5}\ M\ min^{-1}$.

5.75 The finely divided rhodium metal will have a significantly greater surface area than the small block of metal. This leads to a large increase in the number of reaction sites and vastly increases the reaction rate.

5.77 (a) False. The reaction may occur in a single step but this does not have to be true.
(b) True
(c) False. Raising the temperature increases the value of k.
(d) False. Temperature has no effect on the value of E_a.
(e) False. If the concentrations of both reactants are doubled, the rate will increase by a factor of 4.
(f) True

5.79 (a) True
(b) True
(c) False. As a reaction proceeds, the reactant concentration decreases and the rate decreases.
(d) False. It is possible to have a one-step mechanism for a third-order reaction if the slow, rate-determining step is termolecular.

5.81 (a) Decrease   (d) No change
(b) Increase   (e) No change
(c) No change   (f) No change

5.83 (a) There are three mechanistic steps.
(b) The overall reaction is exothermic.

5.85 (a) The average rate is calculated over a period of time, whereas the instantaneous rate is the rate of reaction at some instant in time.
(b) The reaction rate decreases with time as the dye concentration decreases.
(c) See part (b).

5.87 (a) Molecules must collide with enough energy to overcome the activation energy, and they must be in the correct orientation.
(b) In animation 2 the molecules are moving faster, so they are at a higher temperature.
(c) Less sensitive. The O_3 must collide with NO in the correct orientation for a reaction to occur. The O_3 and N_2 collisions do not depend to the same extent on orientation because N_2 is a symmetrical, diatomic molecule.

15.89 (a) I^- is regenerated during the second step in the mechanism.
(b) The activation energy is smaller for the catalyzed reaction.

CHAPTER 16

16.1 (a) $K = \dfrac{[H_2O]^2[O_2]}{[H_2O_2]^2}$

(b) $K = \dfrac{[CO_2]}{[CO][O_2]^{1/2}}$

(c) $K = \dfrac{[CO]}{[CO_2]}$

(d) $K = \dfrac{[CO_2]}{[CO]}$

16.3 $Q = (2.0 \times 10^{-8})^2/(0.020) = 2.0 \times 10^{-14}$
$Q < K$ so the reaction proceeds to the right.

16.5 $Q = 1.0 \times 10^3$, so $Q > K$ and the reaction is not at equilibrium. It proceeds to the left to convert products to reactants.

16.7 $K = 1.2$

16.9 (a) $K = 0.025$
(b) $K = 0.025$
(c) The amount of solid does not affect the equilibrium.

16.11 (a) $[COCl_2] = 0.00308\ M$; $[CO] = 0.00712\ M$
(b) $K = 144$

16.13 [isobutane] $= 0.024\ M$; [butane] $= 0.010\ M$

16.15 $[I_2] = 6.14 \times 10^{-3}\ M$; $[I] = 4.79 \times 10^{-3}\ M$

16.17 $[COBr_2] = 0.107\ M$; $[CO] = [Br_2] = 0.143\ M$
57.1% of the $COBr_2$ has decomposed.

16.19 (b)

16.21 (e) $K_2 = 1/(K_1)^2$

16.23 $K = 13.7$

16.25 (a) Equilibrium shifts to the right
(b) Equilibrium shifts to the left
(c) Equilibrium shifts to the right
(d) Equilibrium shifts to the left

16.27 Equilibrium concentrations are the same under both circumstances: [butane] $= 1.1\ M$ and [isobutane] $= 2.9\ M$.

16.29 $K = 3.9 \times 10^{-4}$

16.31 For decomposition of $COCl_2$, $K = 1/(K$ for $COCl_2$ formation) $= 1/(6.5 \times 10^{11}) = 1.5 \times 10^{-12}$

16.33 $K = 4$

16.35 Q is less than K, so the system shifts to form more isobutane.

At equilibrium, [butane] = 0.86 M and [isobutane] = 2.14 M.

16.37 The second equation has been reversed and multiplied by 2.
(c) $K_2 = 1/K_1^2$

16.39 (a) No change (d) Shifts right
(b) Shifts left (e) Shifts right
(c) No change

16.41 (a) The equilibrium will shift to the left on adding more Cl_2.
(b) K is calculated (from the quantities of reactants and products at equilibrium) to be 0.0470. After Cl_2 is added, the concentrations are: $[PCl_5]$ = 0.0199 M, $[PCl_3]$ = 0.0231 M, and $[Cl_2]$ = 0.0403 M.

16.43 $K_p = 0.215$

16.45 (a) Fraction dissociated = 0.15
(b) Fraction dissociated = 0.189. If the pressure decreases, the equilibrium shifts to the right, increasing the fraction of N_2O_4 dissociated.

16.47 $[NH_3]$ = 0.67 M; $[N_2]$ = 0.57 M; $[H_2]$ = 1.7 M; P_{total} = 180 atm

16.49 (a) $[NH_3]$ = $[H_2S]$ = 0.013 M
(b) $[NH_3]$ = 0.027 M and $[H_2S]$ = 0.0067 M

16.51 $P(NO_2)$ = 0.379 atm and $P(N_2O_4)$ = 0.960 atm; $P(total)$ = 1.339 atm

16.53 (a) $K_p = K_c$ = 56. Because 2 mol of reactants gives 2 mol of product, Δn does not change and $K_p = K_c$ (see page 730).

(b, c) Initial $P(H_2)$ = $P(I_2)$ = 2.6 atm and P_{total} = 5.2 atm

At equilibrium, $P(H_2)$ = $P(I_2)$ = 0.54 atm and $P(HI)$ = 4.1 atm. Therefore, P_{total} = 5.2 atm. The initial total pressure and the equilibrium total pressure are the same owing to the reaction stoichiometry. Percent dissociation = 69%

16.55 $P(CO)$ = 0.0010 atm

16.57 1.7×10^{18} O atoms

16.59 Glycerin concentration should be 1.7 M

16.61 (a) $K_p = 0.20$
(b) When initial $[N_2O_4]$ = 1.00 atm, the equilibrium pressures are $[N_2O_4]$ = 0.80 atm and $[NO_2]$ = 0.40 atm. When initial $[N_2O_4]$ = 0.10 atm, the equilibrium pressures are $[N_2O_4]$ = 0.050 atm and $[NO_2]$ = 0.10 atm. The percent dissociation is now 50.%. This is in accord with Le Chatelier's principle: If the initial pressure of the reactant

decreases, the equilibrium shifts to the right, increasing the fraction of the reactant dissociated See also Question 16.45.

16.63 (a) The flask containing $(H_3N)B(CH_3)_3$ will have t largest partial pressure of $B(CH_3)_3$.
(b) $P[B(CH_3)_3]$ = $P(NH_3)$ = 2.1 and $P[(H_3N)B(CH_3)_3]$ = 1.0 atm

P_{total} = 5.2 atm

Percent dissociation = 69%

16.65 (a) As more KSCN is added, Le Chatelier's princip predicts more of the red complex ion $[Fe(H_2O)_5(SCN)]^+$ will form.
(b) Adding Ag^+ ions leads to a precipitate of AgSC thus removing SCN^- ions from solution. The equilibrium shifts left, dropping the concentration of the red complex ion.

16.67 (a) False. The magnitude of K is always dependent on temperature.
(b) True
(c) False. The equilibrium constant for a reaction i the reciprocal of the value of K for its reverse.
(d) True
(e) False. Δn = 1 so $K_p = K_c(RT)$

16.69 (a) Product-favored, $K \gg 1$
(b) Reactant-favored, $K \ll 1$
(c) Product-favored, $K \gg 1$

16.71 The system is not at equilibrium because it continu to gain energy from the surroundings. The tempera ture of the water/ice mixture will remain at 0 °C u til all the ice is melted, then the temperature will rise as more energy is gained. Only if the beaker o water/ice were moved to a perfectly insulated com partment, also at 0 °C, would it attain equilibrium 0 °C. In this case, it would be a dynamic equilibriu with water molecules moving from the solid to the liquid phase and from the liquid to the solid phase The quantity of ice would not change. If a D_2O ice cube was added to some $H_2O(\ell)$, an equilibrium would be obtained. The amount of D_2O in the liqu phase would increase due to the continuing molecu lar exchange. The water could then be sampled for the presence of D_2O.

CHAPTER 17

17.1 (a) CN^-, cyanide ion
(b) SO_4^{2-}, sulfate ion
(c) F^-, fluoride ion

(a) $H_3O^+(aq) + NO_3^-(aq)$; $H_3O^+(aq)$ is the conjugate acid of H_2O, and $NO_3^-(aq)$ is the conjugate base of HNO_3.
(b) $H_3O^+(aq) + SO_4^{2-}(aq)$; $H_3O^+(aq)$ is the conjugate acid of H_2O, and $SO_4^{2-}(aq)$ is the conjugate base of HSO_4^-.
(c) H_2O + HF; H_2O is the conjugate base of H_3O^+, and HF is the conjugate acid of F^-.

.5 Brønsted acid: $HC_2O_4^-(aq) + H_2O(\ell) \rightleftharpoons$
$$H_3O^+(aq) + C_2O_4^{2-}(aq)$$

Brønsted base: $HC_2O_4^-(aq) + H_2O(\ell) \rightleftharpoons$
$$H_2C_2O_4(aq) + OH^-(aq)$$

.7

Acid (A)	Base (B)	Conjugate Base of A	Conjugate Acid of B
(a) HCO_2H	H_2O	HCO_2^-	H_3O^+
(b) H_2S	NH_3	HS^-	NH_4^+
(c) HSO_4^-	OH^-	SO_4^{2-}	H_2O

.9 $[H_3O^+] = 1.8 \times 10^{-4}$ M; acidic

.11 HCl is a strong acid, so $[H_3O^+]$ = concentration of the acid. $[H_3O^+] = 0.0075$ M and $[OH^-] = 1.3 \times 10^{-12}$ M. pH = 2.12.

.13 $Ba(OH)_2$ is a strong base, so $[OH^-] = 2 \times$ concentration of the base.

$[OH^-] = 3.0 \times 10^{-3}$ M; pOH = 2.52; and pH = 11.48

.15 (a) The strongest acid is HCO_2H (largest K_a) and the weakest acid is C_6H_5OH (smallest K_a).
(b) The strongest acid (HCO_2H) has the weakest conjugate base.
(c) The weakest acid (C_6H_5OH) has the strongest conjugate base.

.17 (c) HClO, the weakest acid in this list (Table 17.3), has the strongest conjugate base.

.19 $CO_3^{2-}(aq) + H_2O(\ell) \rightarrow HCO_3^-(aq) + OH^-(aq)$

.21 Highest pH, Na_2S; lowest pH, $AlCl_3$ (which gives the weak acid $[Al(H_2O)_6]^{3+}$ in solution)

.23 $pK_a = 4.19$

.25 $K_a = 3.0 \times 10^{-10}$

.27 2-Chlorobenzoic acid has the smaller pK_a value.

.29 $K_b = 7.09 \times 10^{-12}$

.31 $K_b = 6.3 \times 10^{-5}$

.33 $CH_3CO_2H(aq) + HCO_3^-(aq) \rightleftharpoons$
$$CH_3CO_2^-(aq) + H_2CO_3(aq)$$

Equilibrium lies predominantly to the right because CH_3CO_2H is a stronger acid than H_2CO_3.

17.35 (a) Left; NH_3 and HBr are the stronger base and acid, respectively.
(b) Left; PO_4^{3-} and CH_3CO_2H are the stronger base and acid, respectively.
(c) Right; $[Fe(H_2O)_6]^{3+}$ and HCO_3^- are the stronger acid and base, respectively.

17.37 (a) $OH^-(aq) + HPO_4^{2-}(aq) \rightleftharpoons$
$$H_2O(\ell) + PO_4^{3-}(aq)$$
(b) OH^- is a stronger base than PO_4^{3-}, so the equilibrium will lie to the right. (The predominant species in solution is PO_4^{3-}, so the solution is likely to be basic because PO_4^{3-} is the conjugate base of a weak acid.)

17.39 (a) $CH_3CO_2H(aq) + HPO_4^{2-}(aq) \rightleftharpoons$
$$CH_3CO_2^-(aq) + H_2PO_4^-(aq)$$
(b) CH_3CO_2H is a stronger acid than $H_2PO_4^-$, so the equilibrium will lie to the right.

17.41 (a) 2.1×10^{-3} M; (b) $K_a = 3.5 \times 10^{-4}$

17.43 $K_b = 6.6 \times 10^{-9}$

17.45 (a) $[H_3O^+] = 1.6 \times 10^{-4}$ M
(b) Moderately weak; $K_a = 1.1 \times 10^{-5}$

17.47 $[CH_3CO_2^-] = [H_3O^+] = 1.9 \times 10^{-3}$ M and $[CH_3CO_2H] = 0.20$ M

17.49 $[H_3O^+] = [CN^-] = 3.2 \times 10^{-6}$ M; $[HCN] = 0.025$ M; pH = 5.50

17.51 $[NH_4^+] = [OH^-] = 1.64 \times 10^{-3}$ M; $[NH_3] = 0.15$ M; pH = 11.22

17.53 $[OH^-] = 0.0102$ M; pH = 12.01; pOH = 1.99

17.55 pH = 3.25

17.57 $[H_3O^+] = 1.1 \times 10^{-5}$ M; pH = 4.98

17.59 $[HCN] = [OH^-] = 3.3 \times 10^{-3}$ M; $[H_3O^+] = 3.0 \times 10^{-12}$ M; $[Na^+] = 0.441$ M

17.61 $[H_3O^+] = 1.5 \times 10^{-9}$ M; pH = 8.81

17.63 (a) The reaction produces acetate ion, the conjugate base of acetic acid. The solution is weakly basic. pH is greater than 7.
(b) The reaction produces NH_4^+, the conjugate acid of NH_3. The solution is weakly acidic. pH is less than 7.
(c) The reaction mixes equal molar amounts of strong base and strong acid. The solution will be neutral. pH will be 7.

17.65 (a) pH = 1.17; (b) $[SO_3^{2-}] = 6.2 \times 10^{-8}$ M

17.67 (a) $[OH^-] = [N_2H_5^+] = 9.2 \times 10^{-5}$ M; $[N_2H_6^{2+}] = 8.9 \times 10^{-16}$ M
(b) pH = 9.96

17.69 (a) Lewis base
(b) Lewis acid

(c) Lewis base (owing to lone pair of electrons on the N atom)

17.71 CO is a Lewis base in its reactions with transition metal atoms. It donates a lone pair of electrons on the C atom.

17.73 HOCN should be a stronger acid than HCN because the H atom in HOCN is attached to a highly electronegative O atom. This induces a positive charge on the H atom, making it more readily removed by an interaction with water.

17.75 The S atom is surrounded by four highly electronegative O atoms. The inductive effect of these atoms induces a positive charge on the H atom, making it susceptible to removal by water.

17.77 pH = 2.671

17.79 Both $Ba(OH)_2$ and $Sr(OH)_2$ dissolve completely in water to provide M^{2+} and OH^- ions. 2.50 g $Sr(OH)_2$ in 1.00 L of water gives $[Sr^{2+}] = 0.021$ M and $[OH^-] = 0.041$ M. The concentration of OH^- is reflected in a pH of 12.61.

17.81 $H_2S(aq) + CH_3CO_2^-(aq) \rightleftarrows$
$$CH_3CO_2H(aq) + HS^-(aq)$$

The equilibrium lies to the left and favors the reactants.

17.83 $[X^-] = [H_3O^+] = 3.0 \times 10^{-3}$ M; $[HX] = 0.007$ M; pH = 2.52

17.85 $K_a = 1.4 \times 10^{-5}$; $pK_a = 4.86$

17.87 pH = 5.84

17.89 (a) Ethylamine is a stronger base than ethanolamine.
(b) For ethylamine, the pH of the solution is 11.82.

17.91 pH = 7.66

17.93 Acidic: $NaHSO_4$, NH_4Br, $FeCl_3$
Neutral: $KClO_4$, $NaNO_3$, LiBr
Basic: Na_2CO_3, $(NH_4)_2S$, Na_2HPO_4
$(NH_4)_2S$, highest pH. $NaHSO_4$, lowest pH.

17.95 $K_{net} = K_{a1} \times K_{a2} = 3.8 \times 10^{-6}$

17.97 For the reaction $HCO_2H(aq) + OH^-(aq) \rightarrow$ $H_2O(\ell) + HCO_2^-(aq)$, $K_{net} = K_a$ (for HCO_2H) $\times [1/K_w] = 1.8 \times 10^{10}$

17.99 To double the percent ionization, you must dilute 100 mL of solution to 400 mL.

17.101 $H_2O > H_2C_2O_4 > HC_2O_4^- = H_3O^+ > C_2O_4^{2-}$ $> OH^-$

17.103 Measure the pH of the 0.1 M solutions of the three bases. The solution containing the strongest base will have the highest pH. The solution having the weakest base will have the lowest pH.

17.105 The possible cation–anion combinations are NaC (neutral), NaOH (basic), NH_4Cl (acidic), NH_4OI (basic), HCl (acidic), and H_2O (neutral).

A = H^+ solution; B = NH_4^+ solution; C = Na^+ sol tion; Y = Cl^- solution; Z = OH^- solution

17.107 $K_a = 3.0 \times 10^{-5}$

17.109 (a) Aniline is both a Brønsted and a Lewis base. a proton acceptor it gives $C_6H_5NH_3^+$. The N atom can also donate an electron pair to give Lewis acid–base adduct, $F_3B \leftarrow NH_2C_6H_5$.
(b) pH = 7.97

17.111 Water can both accept a proton (a Brønsted base and donate a lone pair (a Lewis base). Water can also donate a proton (Brønsted acid), but it cann accept a pair of electrons (and act as a Lewis acid

17.113 (a) HOCl is the strongest acid (smallest pK_a and largest K_a), and HOI is the weakest acid.
(b) Cl is more electronegative than I, so the OCl anion is more stable than the OI⁻ anion.

17.115 (a) $HClO_4 + H_2SO_4 \rightleftarrows ClO_4^- + H_3SO_4^+$
(b) The O atoms on sulfuric acid have lone pairs of electrons that can be used to bind to an H ion.

$$H-\ddot{O}-\overset{\overset{\displaystyle :\ddot{O}:}{|}}{\underset{\underset{\displaystyle :\ddot{O}:}{|}}{S}}-\ddot{O}-H$$

17.117 (a) $\left[:\ddot{I}-\ddot{I}-\ddot{I}:\right]^-$
(b) $I^-(aq)$ [Lewis base] + $I_2(aq)$ [Lewis acid] $\rightarrow$ $I_3^-(aq)$

17.119 (a) For the weak acid HA, the concentrations at equilibrium are $[HA] = C_0 - \alpha C_0$, $[H_3O^+] =$ $[A^-] = \alpha C_0$. Putting these into the usual expression for K_a we have $K_a = \alpha^2 C_0/(1-\alpha)$.
(b) For 0.10 M NH_4^+, $\alpha = 7.5 \times 10^{-5}$ (reflecting the fact that NH_4^+ is a much weaker acid than acetic acid).

17.121 (a) Add the three equations.

$$NH_4^+(aq) + H_2O(\ell) \rightleftarrows NH_3(aq) + H_3O^+(aq$$
$$K_1 = K_w/K_b$$
$$CN^-(aq) + H_2O(\ell) \rightleftarrows HCN(aq) + OH^-(aq$$
$$K_2 = K_w/K_a$$
$$H_3O^+(aq) + OH^-(aq) \rightleftarrows 2 H_2O(\ell) \quad K_3 = 1/$$
$$\overline{NH_4^+(aq) + CN^-(aq) \rightleftarrows NH_3(aq) + HCN(a}$$
$$K_{net} = K_1 K_2 K_3 = K_w/K_a K_b$$

(b) The salts NH_4CN, $NH_4CH_3CO_2$, and NH_4F have K_{net} values of 1.4, 3.1×10^{-5}, and 7.7×10^{-7}, respectively. Only in the case of NH_4CN is the base (the cyanide ion) strong enough to remove a proton from the ammonium ion and produce a significant concentration of products.

(c) The pH of a solution will depend on the relative strengths of the anionic base and the cationic acid. In part (d) the anion and cation were equal in strength, so the solution was neutral. For NH_4CN, the CN^- ion is a stronger base ($K_b = 2.5 \times 10^{-5}$) than NH_4^+ is an acid ($K_a = 5.6 \times 10^{-10}$), so the solution is predicted to be basic.

CHAPTER 18

18.1 (a) Decrease pH; (b) increase pH; (c) no change in pH

18.3 pH = 9.25

18.5 pH = 4.38

18.7 pH = 9.12; pH of buffer is lower than the pH of the original solution of NH_3(pH = 11.17).

18.9 4.7 g

18.11 pH = 4.92

18.13 (a) pH = 3.59; (b) $[HCO_2H]/[HCO_2^-] = 0.45$

18.15 (b) $NH_3 + NH_4Cl$

18.17 The buffer must have a ratio of 0.51 mol NaH_2PO_4 to 1 mol Na_2HPO_4. For example, dissolve 0.51 mol NaH_2PO_4 (61 g) and 1.0 mol Na_2HPO_4 (140 g) in some amount of water.

18.19 (a) pH = 4.95; (b) pH = 5.05

18.21 (a) pH = 9.55; (b) pH = 9.50

18.23 (a) Original pH = 5.62
(b) $[Na^+] = 0.0323$ M, $[OH^-] = 1.5 \times 10^{-3}$ M, $[H_3O^+] = 6.5 \times 10^{-12}$ M, and $[C_6H_5O^-] = 0.0308$ M
(c) pH = 11.19

18.25 (a) Original NH_3 concentration = 0.0154 M
(b) At the equivalence point $[H_3O^+] = 1.9 \times 10^{-6}$ M, $[OH^-] = 5.3 \times 10^{-9}$ M, $[NH_4^+] = 6.25 \times 10^{-3}$ M.
(c) pH at equivalence point = 5.73

18.27 The titration curve begins at pH = 13.00 and drops slowly as HCl is added. Just before the equivalence point (when 30.0 mL of acid has been added), the curve falls steeply. The pH at the equivalence point is exactly 7. Just after the equivalence point, the curve flattens again and begins to approach the final pH of just over 1.0. The total volume at the equivalence point is 60.0 mL.

18.29 (a) Starting pH = 11.12
(b) pH at equivalence point = 5.28
(c) pH at midpoint (half-neutralization point) = 9.25
(d) Methyl red, bromcresol green
(e)

Acid (mL)	Added pH
5.00	9.85
15.0	9.08
20.0	8.65
22.0	8.39
30.0	2.04

18.31 See Figure 18.10 on page 832.
(a) Thymol blue or bromphenol blue
(b) Phenolphthalein
(c) Methyl red; thymol blue

18.33 (a) Silver chloride, AgCl; lead chloride, $PbCl_2$
(b) Zinc carbonate, $ZnCO_3$; zinc sulfide, ZnS
(c) Iron(II) carbonate, $FeCO_3$; iron(II) oxalate, FeC_2O_4

18.35 (a) and (b) are soluble, (c) and (d) are insoluble.

18.37 (a) $AgCN(s) \rightarrow Ag^+(aq) + CN^-(aq)$, $K_{sp} = [Ag^+][CN^-]$
(b) $NiCO_3(s) \rightarrow Ni^{2+}(aq) + CO_3^{2-}(aq)$, $K_{sp} = [Ni^{2+}][CO_3^{2-}]$
(c) $AuBr_3(s) \rightarrow Au^{3+}(aq) + 3 Br^-(aq)$, $K_{sp} = [Au^{3+}][Br^-]^3$

18.39 $K_{sp} = (1.9 \times 10^{-3})^2 = 3.6 \times 10^{-6}$

18.41 $K_{sp} = 4.37 \times 10^{-9}$

18.43 $K_{sp} = 1.4 \times 10^{-15}$

18.45 (a) 9.2×10^{-9} M; (b) 2.2×10^{-6} g/L

18.47 (a) 2.4×10^{-4} M; (b) 0.018 g/L

18.49 Only 2.1×10^{-4} g dissolves.

18.51 (a) $PbCl_2$; (b) FeS; (c) $Fe(OH)_2$

18.53 Solubility in pure water = 1.0×10^{-6} mol/L; solubility in 0.010 M SCN^- = 1.0×10^{-10} mol/L

18.55 (a) Solubility in pure water = 2.2×10^{-6} mg/mL
(b) Solubility in 0.020 M $AgNO_3$ = 1.0×10^{-12} mg/mL

18.57 (a) PbS
(b) Ag_2CO_3
(c) $Al(OH)_3$

18.59 $Q < K_{sp}$, so no precipitate forms.

18.61 $Q > K_{sp}$; $Zn(OH)_2$ will precipitate.

18.63 $[OH^-]$ must exceed 1.0×10^{-5} M.

18.65 Using K_{sp} for $Zn(OH)_2$ and K_{form} for $Zn(OH)_4{}^{2-}$, K_{net} for

$$Zn(OH)_2(s) + 2\ OH^-(aq) \rightleftharpoons Zn(OH)_4{}^{2-}(aq)$$

is 13.8. This indicates that the reaction is definitely product-favored.

18.67 K_{net} for $AgCl(s) + 2\ NH_3(aq) \rightleftharpoons Ag(NH_3)_2{}^+(aq) + Cl^-(aq)$ is 2.0×10^{-3}. When all the AgCl dissolves, $[Ag(NH_3)_2{}^+] = [Cl^-] = 0.050$ M. To achieve these concentrations, $[NH_3]$ must be 1.12 M. Therefore, the amount of NH_3 added must be 2×0.050 mol/L (to react with the AgCl) plus 1.25 mol/L (to achieve the proper equilibrium concentration). The total is 1.22 mol/L NH_3.

18.69 (a) Solubility in pure water $= 1.3 \times 10^{-5}$ mol/L or 0.0019 g/L.
(b) K_{net} for $AgCl(s) + 2\ NH_3(aq) \rightleftharpoons Ag(NH_3)_2{}^+(aq) + Cl^-(aq)$ is 2.0×10^{-3}. When using 1.0 M NH_3, the concentrations of species in solution are $[Ag(NH_3)_2{}^+] = [Cl^-] = 0.041$ M and so $[NH_3] = 1.0 - 2(0.041)$ M or about 0.9 M. The amount of AgCl dissolved is 0.041 mol/L or 5.88 g/L.

18.71 (a) $NaBr(aq) + AgNO_3(aq) \rightarrow$
$$NaNO_3(aq) + AgBr(s)$$
(b) $2\ KCl(aq) + Pb(NO_3)_2(aq) \rightarrow$
$$2\ KNO_3(aq) + PbCl_2(s)$$

18.73 $Q > K_{sp}$, so $BaSO_4$ precipitates.

18.75 $[H_3O^+] = 1.9 \times 10^{-10}$ M; pH $= 9.73$

18.77 $BaCO_3 < Ag_2CO_3 < Na_2CO_3$

18.79 Original pH $= 8.62$; dilution will not affect the pH.

18.81 (a) 0.100 M acetic acid has a pH of 2.87. Adding sodium acetate slowly raises the pH.
(b) Adding $NaNO_3$ to 0.100 M HNO_3 has no effect on the pH.
(c) In part (a), adding the conjugate base of a weak acid creates a buffer solution. In part (b), HNO_3 is a strong acid, and its conjugate base (NO_3^-) is so weak that the base has no effect on the complete ionization of the acid.

18.83 (a) pH $= 4.13$
(b) 0.6 g of $C_6H_5CO_2H$
(c) 8.2 mL of 2.0 M HCl should be added

18.85 $K = 2.1 \times 10^6$; yes, AgI forms

18.87 (a) $[F^-] = 1.3 \times 10^{-3}$ M; (b) $[Ca^{2+}] = 2.9 \times 10^{-5}$ M

18.89 (a) $PbSO_4$ will precipitate first.
(b) $[Pb^{2+}] = 5.1 \times 10^{-6}$ M

18.91 When $[CO_3{}^{2-}] = 0.050$ M, $[Ca^{2+}] = 6.8 \times 10^{-8}$ M This means only $6.8 \times 10^{-4}\ \%$ of the ions remain, or that essentially all of the calcium ions have been removed.

18.93 (a) Add H_2SO_4, precipitating $BaSO_4$ and leaving $Na^+(aq)$ in solution.
(b) Add HCl or another source of chloride ion. $PbCl_2$ will precipitate, but $NiCl_2$ is water-soluble.

18.95 (a) $BaSO_4$ will precipitate first.
(b) $[Ba^{2+}] = 1.8 \times 10^{-7}$ M

18.97 (a) pH $= 2.81$
(b) pH at equivalence point $= 8.72$
(c) pH at the midpoint $= pK_a = 4.62$
(d) Phenolphthalein
(e) After 10.0 mL, pH $= 4.39$.
After 20.0 mL, pH $= 5.07$.
After 30.0 mL, pH $= 11.84$.
(f) A plot of pH versus volume of NaOH added would begin at a pH of 2.81, rise slightly to the midpoint at pH $= 4.62$, and then begin to rise more steeply as the equivalence point is approached (when the volume of NaOH added is 27.0 mL). The pH rises vertically through the equivalence point, and then begins to level off above a pH of about 11.0.

18.99 The K_b value for ethylamine (4.27×10^{-4}) is found in Appendix I.
(a) pH $= 11.89$
(b) Midpoint pH $= 10.63$
(c) pH $= 10.15$
(d) pH $= 5.93$ at the equivalence point
(e) pH $= 2.13$
(f) Titration curve

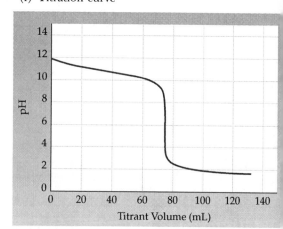

(g) Alizarin or bromcresol purple (see Figure 18.10)

18.101 110 mL NaOH

3.103 Add dilute HCl, say 1 M HCl, to a solution of the salts. Both AgCl and $PbCl_2$ will precipitate, but Cu^{2+} ions will stay in solution (as $CuCl_2$ is water-soluble). Decant off the copper-containing solution to leave a precipitate of white AgCl and $PbCl_2$. Lead(II) chloride ($K_{sp} = 1.7 \times 10^{-5}$) is much more soluble than AgCl ($K_{sp} = 1.8 \times 10^{-10}$). Warming the precipitates in water will dissolve the $PbCl_2$ and leave the AgCl as a white solid.

3.105 $Cu(OH)_2$ will dissolve in a nonoxidizing acid such as HCl, whereas CuS will not.

3.107 When Ag_3PO_4 dissolves slightly, it produces a small concentration of the phosphate ion, PO_4^{3-}. This ion is a strong base and hydrolyzes to HPO_4^{2-}. As this reaction removes the PO_4^{3-} ion from equilibrium with Ag_3PO_4, the equilibrium shifts to the right, producing more PO_4^{3-} and Ag^+ ions. Thus, Ag_3PO_4 dissolves to a greater extent than might be calculated from a K_{sp} value (unless the K_{sp} value was actually determined experimentally).

3.109 (a) Base is added to increase the pH. The added base reacts with acetic acid to form more acetate ions in the mixture. Thus, the fraction of acid declines and the fraction of conjugate base rises (i.e., the ratio $[CH_3CO_2H]/[CH_3CO_2^-]$ decreases) as the pH rises.

   (b) At pH = 4, acid predominates (85% acid and 15% acetate ions). At pH = 6, acetate ions predominate (95% acetate ions and 5% acid).

   (c) At the point the lines cross, $[CH_3CO_2H] = [CH_3CO_2^-]$. At this point pH = pK_a, so pK_a for acetic acid is 4.75.

3.111 (a) C—C—C angle, 120°; O—C=O, 120°; C—O—H, 109°; C—C—H, 120°

   (b) Both the ring C atoms and the C in CO_2H are sp^2 hybridized.

   (c) $K_a = 1 \times 10^{-3}$

   (d) 10%

   (e) pH at half-way point = pK_a = 3.0; pH at equivalence point = 7.3

CHAPTER 19

9.1 (a) For a given substance at a given temperature, a gas always has a greater entropy than the liquid. Matter and energy are more dispersed.

   (b) Liquid water at 50 °C

   (c) Ruby

   (d) One mole of N_2 at 1 bar

9.3 (a) $\Delta_r S° = +12.7$ J/K · mol-rxn. Entropy increases.

   (b) $\Delta_r S° = -102.55$ J/K · mol-rxn. Significant decrease in entropy.

(c) $\Delta_r S° = +93.2$ J/K · mol-rxn. Entropy increases.

   (d) $\Delta_r S° = -129.7$ J/K · mol-rxn. The solution has a smaller entropy (with H^+ forming H_3O^+ and hydrogen bonding occurring) than HCl in the gaseous state.

19.5 (a) $\Delta_r S° = +9.3$ J/K · mol-rxn; (b) $\Delta_r S° = -293.97$ J/K · mol-rxn

19.7 (a) $\Delta_r S° = -507.3$ J/K · mol-rxn; entropy declines as a gaseous reactant is incorporated in a solid compound.

   (b) $\Delta_r S° = +313.25$ J/K · mol-rxn; entropy increases as five molecules (two of them in the gas phase) form six molecules of products (all gases).

19.9 $\Delta_{sys} S° = -134.18$ J/K · mol-rxn; $\Delta_{sys} H° = -662.75$ kJ/mol-rxn; $\Delta_{surr} S° = +2222.9$ J/K · mol-rxn; $\Delta_{univ} S° = +2088.7$ J/K · mol-rxn

19.11 $\Delta_{sys} S° = +163.3$ J/K · mol-rxn; $\Delta_{sys} H° = +285.83$ kJ/mol-rxn; $\Delta_{surr} S° = -958.68$ J/K · mol-rxn; $\Delta_{univ} S° = -795.4$ J/K

The reaction is not spontaneous, because the overall entropy change in the universe is negative. The reaction is disfavored by energy dispersal.

19.13 (a) Type 2. The reaction is enthalpy-favored but entropy-disfavored. It is more favorable at low temperatures.

   (b) Type 4. This endothermic reaction is not favored by the enthalpy change nor is it favored by the entropy change. It is not spontaneous under any conditions.

19.15 (a) $\Delta_r H° = -438$ kJ/mol-rxn; $\Delta_r S° = -201.7$ J/K · mol-rxn; $\Delta_r G° = -378$ kJ/mol-rxn. The reaction is product-favored and is enthalpy-driven.

   (b) $\Delta_r H° = -86.61$ kJ/mol-rxn; $\Delta_r S° = -79.4$ J/K · mol-rxn; $\Delta_r G° = -62.9$ kJ/mol-rxn

The reaction is product-favored. The enthalpy change favors the reaction.

19.17 (a) $\Delta_r H° = +116.7$ kJ/mol-rxn; $\Delta_r S° = +168.0$ J/K mol-rxn; $\Delta_f G° = +66.6$ kJ/mol

   (b) $\Delta_r H° = -425.93$ kJ/mol-rxn; $\Delta_r S° = -154.6$ J/K · mol-rxn; $\Delta_f G° = -379.82$ kJ/mol

   (c) $\Delta_r H° = +17.51$ kJ/mol-rxn; $\Delta_r S° = +77.95$ J/K mol-rxn; $\Delta_f G° = -5.73$ kJ/mol

19.19 (a) $\Delta_r G° = -817.54$ kJ/mol-rxn; spontaneous

   (b) $\Delta_r G° = +256.6$ kJ/mol-rxn; not spontaneous

   (c) $\Delta_r G° = -1101.14$ kJ/mol-rxn; spontaneous

19.21 $\Delta_f G°$ [$BaCO_3(s)$] = -1134.4 kJ/mol

19.23 (a) $\Delta_r H° = +66.2$ kJ/mol-rxn; $\Delta_r S° = -121.62$ J/K · mol-rxn; $\Delta_r G° = +102.5$ kJ/mol-rxn

Both the enthalpy and the entropy changes indicate the reaction is not spontaneous. There is no temperature to which it will become spontaneous. This is a case like that in the right panel in Figure 19.12 and is a Type 4 reaction (Table 19.2).

(b) $\Delta_rH° = -221.05$ kJ/mol-rxn; $\Delta_rS° = +179.1$ J/K · mol-rxn; $\Delta_rG° = -283.99$ kJ/mol-rxn

The reaction is favored by both enthalpy and entropy and is product-favored at all temperatures. This is a case like that in the left panel in Figure 19.12 and is a Type 1 reaction.

(c) $\Delta_rH° = -179.0$ kJ/mol-rxn; $\Delta_rS° = -160.2$ J/K · mol-rxn; $\Delta_rG° = -131.4$ kJ/mol-rxn

The reaction is favored by the enthalpy change but disfavored by the entropy change. The reaction becomes less product-favored as the temperature increases; it is a case like the upper line in the middle panel of Figure 19.12.

(d) $\Delta_rH° = +822.2$ kJ/mol-rxn; $\Delta_rS° = +181.28$ J/K · mol-rxn; $\Delta_rG° = +768.08$ kJ/mol-rxn

The reaction is not favored by the enthalpy change but favored by the entropy change. The reaction becomes more product-favored as the temperature increases; it is a case like the lower line in the middle panel of Figure 19.12.

19.25 (a) $\Delta_rS° = +174.75$ J/K · mol-rxn; $\Delta_rH° = +116.94$ kJ/mol-rxn

(b) $\Delta_rG° = +64.87$ kJ/mol-rxn. The reaction is not spontaneous at 298 K.

(c) As the temperature increases, $\Delta_rS°$ becomes more important, so $\Delta_rG°$ can become negative at a sufficiently high temperature.

19.27 $K = 6.8 \times 10^{-16}$. Note that K is very small and that $\Delta G°$ is positive. Both indicate a reactant-favored process.

19.29 $\Delta_rG° = -100.24$ kJ/mol-rxn and $K_p = 3.64 \times 10^{17}$. Both the free energy change and K indicate a product-favored process.

19.31 (a) HBr
(b) $NH_4Cl(aq)$
(c) $C_2H_4(g)$
(d) NaCl(g)

19.33 $\Delta_rG° = -98.9$ kJ/mol-rxn. The reaction is spontaneous under standard conditions and is enthalpy-driven.

19.35 $\Delta_rH° = -1428.66$ kJ/mol-rxn; $\Delta_rS° = +47.1$ J/K · mol-rxn; $\Delta_{univ}S° = +4840$ J/K · mol-rxn. Combustion reactions are spontaneous, and this is confirmed by the sign of $\Delta_{univ}S°$.

19.37 (a) The reaction occurs spontaneously and is product-favored. Therefore, $\Delta_{univ}S°$ is positive and $\Delta_rG°$ is negative. The reaction is likely to be exothermic, so $\Delta_rH°$ is negative, and $\Delta_{surr}S°$ is positive. $\Delta_{sys}S°$ is

expected to be negative because two moles of g. form one mole of solid. The calculated values a as follows:

$\Delta_{sys}S° = -284.2$ J/K · mol-rxn

$\Delta_rH° = -176.34$ kJ/mol-rxn

$\Delta_{surr}S° = +591.45$ J/K · mol-rxn

$\Delta_{univ}S° = +307.3$ J/K · mol-rxn

$\Delta_rG° = -91.64$ kJ/mol-rxn

(b) $K_p = 1.13 \times 10^{16}$

19.39 $K_p = 1.3 \times 10^{29}$ at 298 K ($\Delta G° = -166.1$ kJ/mol-rxn). The reaction is already extremely product-favored at 298 K. A higher temperature, however, would make the reaction less product-favored because $\Delta_rS°$ has a negative value (-242.3 J/K · mol-rxn).

19.41 At the boiling point, $\Delta G° = 0 = \Delta H° - T\Delta S°$.

Here $\Delta S° = \Delta H°/T = 112$ J/K · mol-rxn at 351.15 K

19.43 $\Delta_rS°$ is $+137.2$ J/K · mol-rxn. A positive entropy change means that raising the temperature will increase the product favorability of the reaction (because $T\Delta S°$ will become more negative).

19.45 The reaction is exothermic, so $\Delta_rH°$ should be nega tive. Also, a gas and an aqueous solution are forme so $\Delta_rS°$ should be positive. The calculated values ar $\Delta_rH° = -183.32$ kJ/mol-rxn (with a negative sign a expected) and $\Delta_rS° = -7.7$ J/K · mol-rxn

The entropy change is slightly negative, not positive as predicted. The reason for this is the negative entropy change upon dissolving NaOH. Apparently th OH^- ions in water hydrogen-bond with water molecules, an effect that also leads to a small, negative entropy change.

19.47 $\Delta_rH° = +126.03$ kJ/mol-rxn; $\Delta_rS° = +78.2$ J/K · mol-rxn; and $\Delta_rG° = +103$ kJ/mol-rxn. The reactio is not predicted to be spontaneous under standard conditions.

19.49 $\Delta_rG°$ from K value $= 4.87$ kJ/mol-rxn

$\Delta_rG°$ from free energies of formation $= 4.73$ kJ/mol-rxn

19.51 $\Delta_rG° = -2.27$ kJ/mol-rxn

19.53 (a) $\Delta_rG° = +141.82$ kJ/mol-rxn, so the reaction is not spontaneous.

(b) $\Delta_rH° = +197.86$ kJ/mol-rxn; $\Delta_rS° = +187.95$ J/K · mol-rxn

$T = \Delta_rH°/ \Delta_rS° = 1052.7$ K or 779.6 °C

(c) $\Delta_rG°$ at 1500 °C (1773 K) $= -135.4$ kJ/mol-rxn

K_p at 1500 °C $= 1 \times 10^4$

9.55 $\Delta_r S° = -459.0$ J/K · mol-rxn; $\Delta_r H° = -793$ kJ/mol-rxn;

$\Delta_r G° = -657$ kJ/mol-rxn

The reaction is spontaneous and enthalpy-driven.

9.57 (a) $\Delta_r G°$ at 80.0 °C = +0.14 kJ/mol-rxn

$\Delta_r G°$ at 110.0 °C = -0.12 kJ/mol-rxn

Rhombic sulfur is more stable than monoclinic sulfur at 80 °C, but the reverse is true at 110 °C.

(b) $T = 370$ K or about 96 °C

9.59 $\Delta_r G°$ at 298 K = 22.64 kJ/mol; reaction is not product-favored.

It does become product-favored above 469 K (196 °C).

9.61 $\Delta_f G°$ [HI(g)] = -10.9 kJ/mol

9.63 (a) $\Delta_r G° = +194.8$ kJ/mol-rxn and $K = 6.68 \times 10^{-11}$

(b) The reaction is not spontaneous at 727 °C.

(c) Keep the pressure of CO as low as possible (by removing it during the course of the reciton).

9.65 $K_p = P_{Hg(g)}$ at any temperature.

$K_p = 1$ at 620.3 K or 347.2 °C when $P_{Hg(g)} = 1.000$ bar.

T when $P_{Hg(g)} = (1/760)$ bar is 393.3 K or 125.2 °C.

9.67 (a) True

(b) False. Whether an exothermic system is spontaneous also depends on the entropy change for the system.

(c) False. Reactions with $+ \Delta_r H°$ and $+ \Delta_r S°$ are spontaneous at higher temperatures.

(d) True

9.69 Dissolving a solid such as NaCl in water is a spontaneous process. Thus, $\Delta G° < 0$. If $\Delta H° = 0$, then the only way the free energy change can be negative is if $\Delta S°$ is positive. Generally the entropy change is the important factor in forming a solution.

9.71 $2 C_2H_6(g) + 7 O_2(g) \rightarrow 4 CO_2(g) + 6 H_2O(g)$

(a) Not only is this an exothermic combustion reaction, but there is also an increase in the number of molecules from reactants to products. Therefore, we would predict an increase in $\Delta S°$ for both the system and the surroundings and thus for the universe as well.

(b) The exothermic reaction has $\Delta_r H° < 0$. Combined with a positive $\Delta_{sys} S°$, the value of $\Delta_r G°$ is negative.

(c) The value of K_p is likely to be much greater than 1. Further, because $\Delta_{sys} S°$ is positive, the value of K_p will be even larger at a higher temperature. (See the left panel of Figure 19.12.)

19.73 Reaction 1: $\Delta_r S_1° = -80.7$ J/K · mol-rxn

Reaction 2: $\Delta_r S_2° = -161.60$ J/K · mol-rxn

Reaction 3: $\Delta_r S_3° = -242.3$ J/K · mol-rxn

$\Delta_r S_1° + \Delta_r S_2° = \Delta_r S_3°$

19.75 (a) $\Delta_r H° = -352.88$ kJ/mol-rxn and $\Delta_r S° = +21.31$ J/K · mol-rxn. Therefore, at 298 K, $\Delta_r G° = -359.23$ kJ/mol-rxn.

(b) 4.84 g of Mg is required.

19.77 (a) $N_2H_4(\ell) + O_2(g) \rightarrow 2 H_2O(\ell) + N_2(g)$

O_2 is the oxidizing agent and N_2H_4 is the reducing agent.

(b) $\Delta_r H° = -622.29$ kJ/mol-rxn and $\Delta_r S° = +4.87$ J/K · mol-rxn. Therefore, at 298 K, $\Delta_r G° = -623.77$ kJ/mol-rxn.

(c) 0.0027 K

(d) 7.5 mol O_2

(e) 4.8×10^3 g solution

(f) 7.5 mol $N_2(g)$ occupies 170 L at 273 K and 1.0 atm of pressure.

19.79 Iodine dissolves readily, so the process is spontaneous and $\Delta G°$ must be less than zero. Because $\Delta H° = 0$, the process is entropy-driven.

19.81 (a) The spontaneity decreases as temperature increases.

(b) There is no temperature between 400 K and 1000 K at which the decomposition is spontaneous.

19.83 (a, b)

Temperature (K)	$\Delta_r G°$ (kJ)	kJ/mol
298 K	-32.74 K	5.48×10^5
800 K	+72.92 K	1.73×10^{-5}
1300 K	+184.0 K	4.05×10^{-8}

(c) The largest mole fraction of NH_3 in an equilibrium mixture will be at 298 K.

CHAPTER 20

20.1 (a) $Cr(s) \rightarrow Cr^{3+}(aq) + 3 e^-$

Cr is a reducing agent; this is an oxidation reaction.

(b) $AsH_3(g) \rightarrow As(s) + 3 H^+(aq) + 3 e^-$

AsH_3 is a reducing agent; this is an oxidation reaction.

(c) $VO_3^-(aq) + 6 H^+(aq) + 3 e^- \rightarrow$
$$V^{2+}(aq) + 3 H_2O(\ell)$$

$VO_3^-(aq)$ is an oxidizing agent; this is a reduction reaction.

(d) $2 Ag(s) + 2 OH^-(aq) \rightarrow$
$$Ag_2O(s) + H_2O(\ell) + 2e^-$$

Silver is a reducing agent; this is an oxidation reaction.

20.3 (a) $Ag(s) \rightarrow Ag^+(aq) + e^-$

$e^- + NO_3^-(aq) + 2 H^+(aq) \rightarrow NO_2(g) + H_2O(\ell)$
———————————————————
$Ag(s) + NO_3^-(aq) + 2 H^+(aq) \rightarrow$
$$Ag^+(aq) + NO_2(g) + H_2O(\ell)$$

(b) $2[MnO_4^-(aq) + 8 H^+(aq) + 5 e^- \rightarrow$
$$Mn^{2+}(aq) + 4 H_2O(\ell)]$$

$5[HSO_3^-(aq) + H_2O(\ell) \rightarrow$
$$SO_4^{2-}(aq) + 3 H^+(aq) + 2 e^-]$$
———————————————————
$2 MnO_4^-(aq) + H^+(aq) + 5 HSO_3^-(aq) \rightarrow$
$$2 Mn^{2+}(aq) + 3 H_2O(\ell) + 5 SO_4^{2-}(aq)$$

(c) $4[Zn(s) \rightarrow Zn^{2+}(aq) + 2 e^-]$

$2 NO_3^-(aq) + 10 H^+(aq) + 8 e^- \rightarrow$
$$N_2O(g) + 5 H_2O(\ell)$$
———————————————————
$4 Zn(s) + 2 NO_3^-(aq) + 10 H^+(aq) \rightarrow$
$$4 Zn^{2+}(aq) + N_2O(g) + 5 H_2O(\ell)$$

(d) $Cr(s) \rightarrow Cr^{3+}(aq) + 3 e^-$

$3 e^- + NO_3^-(aq) + 4 H^+(aq) \rightarrow$
$$NO(g) + 2 H_2O(\ell)$$
———————————————————
$Cr(s) + NO_3^-(aq) + 4 H^+(aq) \rightarrow$
$$Cr^{3+}(aq) + NO(g) + 2 H_2O(\ell)$$

20.5 (a) $2[Al(s) + 4 OH^-(aq) \rightarrow$
$$Al(OH)_4^-(aq) + 3 e^-]$$

$3[2 H_2O(\ell) + 2 e^- \rightarrow H_2(g) + 2 OH^-(aq)]$
———————————————————
$2 Al(s) + 2 OH^-(aq) + 6 H_2O(\ell) \rightarrow$
$$2 Al(OH)_4^-(aq) + 3 H_2(g)$$

(b) $2[CrO_4^{2-}(aq) + 4 H_2O(\ell) + 3 e^- \rightarrow$
$$Cr(OH)_3(s) + 5 OH^-(aq)]$$

$3[SO_3^{2-}(aq) + 2 OH^-(aq) \rightarrow$
$$SO_4^{2-}(aq) + H_2O(\ell) + 2 e^-]$$
———————————————————
$2 CrO_4^{2-}(aq) + 3 SO_3^{2-}(aq) + 5 H_2O(\ell) \rightarrow$
$$2 Cr(OH)_3(s) + 3 SO_4^{2-}(aq) + 4 OH^-(aq)$$

(c) $Zn(s) + 4 OH^-(aq) \rightarrow Zn(OH)_4^{2-}(aq) + 2 e^-$

$Cu(OH)_2(s) + 2 e^- \rightarrow Cu(s) + 2 OH^-(aq)$
———————————————————
$Zn(s) + 2 OH^-(aq) + Cu(OH)_2(s) \rightarrow$
$$Zn(OH)_4^{2-}(aq) + Cu(s)$$

(d) $3[HS^-(aq) + OH^-(aq) \rightarrow$
$$S(s) + H_2O(\ell) + 2 e^-]$$

$ClO_3^-(aq) + 3 H_2O(\ell) + 6 e^- \rightarrow$
$$Cl^-(aq) + 6 OH^-(aq)$$
———————————————————
$3 HS^-(aq) + ClO_3^-(aq) \rightarrow$
$$3 S(s) + Cl^-(aq) + 3 OH^-(aq)$$

20.7 Electrons flow from the Cr electrode to the Fe electrode. Negative ions move via the salt bridge from the Fe/Fe^{2+} half-cell to the Cr/Cr^{3+} half-cell (and positive ions move in the opposite direction).

Anode (oxidation): $Cr(s) \rightarrow Cr^{3+}(aq) + 3 e^-$

Cathode (reduction): $Fe^{2+}(aq) + 2 e^- \rightarrow Fe(s)$

20.9 (a) Oxidation: $Fe(s) \rightarrow Fe^{2+}(aq) + 2 e^-$
Reduction: $O_2(g) + 4 H^+(aq) + 4 e^- \rightarrow 2 H_2O$
Overall: $2 Fe(s) + O_2(g) + 4 H^+(aq) \rightarrow$
$$2 Fe^{2+}(aq) + 2 H_2O$$

(b) Anode, oxidation: $Fe(s) \rightarrow Fe^{2+}(aq) + 2 e^-$
Cathode, reduction: $O_2(g) + 4 H^+(aq) + 4 e^- \rightarrow$
$$2 H_2O$$

(c) Electrons flow from the negative anode (Fe) to the positive cathode (site of the O_2 half-reaction). Negative ions move through the salt bridge from the cathode compartment in which the O_2 reduction occurs to the anode compartment in which Fe oxidation occurs (and positive ions move in the opposite direction).

20.11 (a) All are primary batteries, not rechargeable.
(b) Dry cells and alkaline batteries have Zn anodes. Ni-Cd batteries have a cadmium anode.
(c) Dry cells have an acidic environment, whereas the environment is alkaline for alkaline and Ni-Cd cells.

20.13 (a) $E°_{cell} = -1.298$ V; not product-favored
(b) $E°_{cell} = -0.51$ V; not product-favored
(c) $E°_{cell} = -1.023$ V; not product-favored
(d) $E°_{cell} = +0.029$ V; product-favored

20.15 (a) $Sn^{2+}(aq) + 2 Ag(s) \rightarrow Sn(s) + 2 Ag^+(aq)$

$E°_{cell} = -0.94$ V; not product-favored

(b) $3 Sn^{4+}(aq) + 2 Al(s) \rightarrow 3 Sn^{2+}(aq) + 2 Al^{3+}(aq)$

$E°_{cell} = +1.81$ V; product-favored

(c) $2 ClO_3^-(aq) + 10 Ce^{3+}(aq) + 12 H^+(aq) \rightarrow$
$$Cl_2(aq) + 10 Ce^{4+}(aq) + 6 H_2O$$

$E°_{cell} = -0.14$ V; not product-favored

(d) $3 Cu(s) + 2 NO_3^-(aq) + 8 H^+(aq) \rightarrow$
$$3 Cu^{2+}(aq) + 2 NO(g) + 4 H_2O$$

$E°_{cell} = +0.62$ V; product-favored

20.17 (a) Al

(b) Zn and Al

(c) $Fe^{2+}(aq) + Sn(s) \rightarrow Fe(s) + Sn^{2+}(aq)$; reactant-favored

(d) $Zn^{2+}(aq) + Sn(s) \rightarrow Zn(s) + Sn^{2+}(aq)$; reactant-favored

20.19 Best reducing agent, Cr(s). (Use Appendix M)

20.21 Ag^+

20.23 See Example 20.5

(a) F_2, most readily reduced

(b) F_2 and Cl_2

20.25 $E°_{cell} = +0.3923$ V. When $[Zn(OH)_4{}^{2-}] = [OH^-] = 0.025$ M and $P(H_2) = 1.0$ bar, $E_{cell} = 0.345$ V.

20.27 $E°_{cell} = +1.563$ V and $E_{cell} = +1.58$ V.

20.29 When $E°_{cell} = +1.563$ V, $E_{cell} = 1.48$ V, $n = 2$, and $[Zn^{2+}] = 1.0$ M, the concentration of $Ag^+ = 0.040$ M.

20.31 (a) $\Delta_rG° = -29.0$ kJ; $K = 1 \times 10^5$

(b) $\Delta_rG° = +88.6$ kJ; $K = 3 \times 10^{-16}$

20.33 $E°_{cell}$ for $AgBr(s) \rightarrow Ag^+(aq) + Br^-(aq)$ is -0.7281.

$K_{sp} = 4.9 \times 10^{-13}$

20.35 $K_{formation} = 2 \times 10^{25}$

20.37 See Figure 20.18. Electrons from the battery or other source enter the cathode where they are transferred to Na^+ ions, reducing the ions to Na metal. Chloride ions move toward the positively charged anode where an electron is transferred from each Cl^- ion, and Cl_2 gas is formed.

20.39 O_2 from the oxidation of water is more likely than F_2. See Example 20.10.

20.41 See Example 20.10.

(a) Cathode: $2 H_2O(\ell) + 2 e^- \rightarrow$
$$H_2(g) + 2 OH^-(aq)$$

(b) Anode: $2 Br^-(aq) \rightarrow Br_2(\ell) + 2 e^-$

20.43 Mass of Ni $= 0.0334$ g

20.45 Time $= 2300$ s or 38 min

20.47 Time $= 250$ h

20.49 (a) $UO_2{}^+(aq) + 4 H^+(aq) + e^- \rightarrow$
$$U^{4+}(aq) + 2 H_2O(\ell)$$

(b) $ClO_3{}^-(aq) + 6 H^+(aq) + 6 e^- \rightarrow$
$$Cl^-(aq) + 3 H_2O(\ell)$$

(c) $N_2H_4(aq) + 4 OH^-(aq) \rightarrow$
$$N_2(g) + 4 H_2O(\ell) + 4 e^-$$

(d) $ClO^-(aq) + H_2O(\ell) + 2 e^- \rightarrow$
$$Cl^-(aq) + 2 OH^-(aq)$$

20.51 (a,c) The electrode at the right is a magnesium anode. (Magnesium metal supplies electrons and is oxidized to Mg^{2+} ions.) Electrons pass through the wire to the silver cathode, where Ag^+ ions are reduced to silver metal. Nitrate ions move via the salt bridge from the $AgNO_3$ solution to the $Mg(NO_3)_2$ solution (and Na^+ ions move in the opposite direction).

(b) Anode: $Mg(s) \rightarrow Mg^{2+}(aq) + 2 e^-$

Cathode: $Ag^+(aq) + e^- \rightarrow Ag(s)$

Net reaction: $Mg(s) + 2 Ag^+(aq) \rightarrow$
$$Mg^{2+}(aq) + 2 Ag(s)$$

20.53 (a) For 1.7 V:

Use chromium as the anode to reduce $Ag^+(aq)$ to $Ag(s)$ at the cathode. The cell potential is $+1.71$ V.

(b) For 0.5 V:

(i) Use copper as the anode to reduce silver ions to silver metal at the cathode. The cell potential is $+0.46$ V.

(ii) Use silver as the anode to reduce chlorine to chloride ions. The cell potential would be $+0.56$ V. (In practice, this setup is not likely to work well because the product would be insoluble silver chloride.)

20.55 (a) $Zn^{2+}(aq)$ (c) $Zn(s)$

(b) $Au^+(aq)$ (d) $Au(s)$

(e) Yes, Sn(s) will reduce Cu^{2+} (as well as Ag^+ and Au^+).

(f) No, Ag(s) can only reduce $Au^+(aq)$.

(g) See part (e).

(h) $Ag^+(aq)$ can oxidize Cu, Sn, Co, and Zn.

20.57 (a) The cathode is the site of reduction, so the half-reaction must be $2 H^+(aq) + 2 e^- \rightarrow H_2(g)$. This is the case with the following half-reactions: $Cr^{3+}(aq)|Cr(s)$, $Fe^{2+}(aq)|Fe(s)$, and $Mg^{2+}(aq)|Mg(s)$.

(b) Choosing from the half-cells in part (a), the reaction of Mg(s) and $H^+(aq)$ would produce the most positive potential (2.37 V), and the reaction of H_2 with Cu^{2+} would produce the least positive potential ($+0.337$ V).

20.59 8.1×10^5 g Al

20.61 (a) $E°_{anode} = -0.268$ V

(b) $K_{sp} = 2 \times 10^{-5}$

20.63 $\Delta_rG° = -409$ kJ

20.65 6700 kWh; 820 kg Na; 1300 kg Cl_2

20.67 Ru^{2+}, $Ru(NO_3)_2$

20.69 9.5×10^6 g Cl_2 per day

20.71 (a) $2[Ag^+(aq) + e^+ \rightarrow Ag(s)]$

$$C_6H_5CHO(aq) + H_2O(\ell) \rightarrow$$
$$C_6H_5CO_2H(aq) + 2\ H^+(aq) + 2\ e^-$$

———————————————

$$2Ag^+(aq) + C_6H_5CHO(aq) + H_2O(\ell) \rightarrow$$
$$C_6H_5CO_2H(aq) + 2\ H^+(aq) + 2\ Ag(s)$$

(b) $3[CH_3CH_2OH(aq) + H_2O(\ell) \rightarrow$
$$CH_3CO_2H(aq) + 4\ H^+(aq) + 4\ e^-]$$

$2[Cr_2O_7{}^{2-}(aq) + 14\ H^+(aq) + 6\ e^- \rightarrow$
$$2\ Cr^{3+}(aq) + 7\ H_2O(\ell)]$$

———————————————

$3\ CH_3CH_2OH(aq) +$
$2\ Cr_2O_7{}^{2-}(aq) + 16\ H^+(aq) \rightarrow$
$3\ CH_3CO_2H(aq) + 4\ Cr^{3+}(aq) + 11\ H_2O(\ell)$

20.73 (a) 0.974 kJ/g
(b) 0.60 kJ/g
(c) The silver-zinc battery produces more energy per gram of reactants.

20.75 (a) $2\ NO_3{}^-(aq) + 3\ Mn^{2+}(aq) + 2\ H_2O(\ell) \rightarrow$
$$2\ NO(g) + 3\ MnO_2(s) + 4\ H^+(aq)$$

$3\ MnO_2(s) + 4\ H^+(aq) + 2\ NH_4{}^+(aq) \rightarrow$
$$N_2(g) + 3\ Mn^{2+}(aq) + 6\ H_2O(\ell)$$

(b) $E°$ for the reduction of $NO_3{}^-$ to NO is −0.27 V. $E°$ for the oxidation of $NH_4{}^+$ to N_2 is +1.50 V.

20.77 (a) $Fe^{2+}(aq) + 2\ e^- \rightarrow Fe(s)$
$2[Fe^{2+}(aq) \rightarrow Fe^{3+}(aq) + e^-]$
$3\ Fe^{2+}(aq) \rightarrow Fe(s) + 2\ Fe^{3+}(aq)$
(b) $E°_{cell} = -1.21$ V; not product-favored
(c) $K = 1 \times 10^{-41}$

20.79 (a)

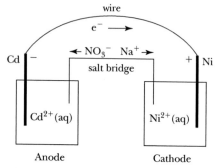

Anode   Cathode

(b) Anode: $Cd(s) \rightarrow Cd^{2+}(aq) + 2\ e^-$
Cathode: $Ni^{2+}(aq) + 2\ e^- \rightarrow Ni(s)$
Net: $Cd(s) + Ni^{2+}(aq) \rightarrow Cd^{2+}(aq) + Ni(s)$
(c) The anode is negative and the cathode is positive.
(d) $E°_{cell} = E°_{cathode} - E°_{anode} =$
$(-0.25\ V) - (-0.40\ V) = +0.15\ V$
(e) Electrons flow from anode (Cd) to cathode (Ni).
(f) Na^+ ions move from the anode compartment to the cathode compartment. Anions move in the opposite direction.
(g) $K = 1 \times 10^5$
(h) $E_{cell} = 0.21$ V
(i) 480 h

20.81 0.054 g Au

20.83 I^- is the strongest reducing agent of the three hal[i] ions. Iodide ion reduces Cu^{2+} to Cu^+, forming ins[o]uble CuI(s).

$$2\ Cu^{2+}(aq) + 4\ I^-(aq) \rightarrow 2\ CuI(s) + I_2(aq)$$

20.85 (a) 92 g HF required; 230 g CF_3SO_2F and 9.3 g H_2 isolated
(b) H_2 is produced at the cathode.
(c) 48 kWh

20.87 290 h

20.89 (a) 3.6 mol glucose and 22 mol O_2
(b) 86 mole electrons
(c) 96 amps
(d) 96 watts

CHAPTER 21

21.1 $4\ Li(s) + O_2(g) \rightarrow 2\ Li_2O(s)$

$Li_2O(s) + H_2O(\ell) \rightarrow 2\ LiOH(aq)$

$2\ Ca(s) + O_2(g) \rightarrow 2\ CaO(s)$

$CaO(s) + H_2O(\ell) \rightarrow Ca(OH)_2(s)$

21.3 These are the elements of Group 3A: boron, B; alum[i]num, Al; gallium, Ga; indium, In; and thallium, Tl.

21.5 $2\ Na(s) + Cl_2(g) \rightarrow 2\ NaCl(s)$

The reaction is exothermic and the product is ioni[c]. See Figure 1.4.

21.7 The product, NaCl, is a colorless solid and is solubl[e] in water. Other alkali metal chlorides have similar properties.

21.9 Calcium will not exist in the earth's crust because the metal reacts with water.

21.11 Increasing basicity: $CO_2 < SiO_2 < SnO_2$

21.13 (a) $2\ Na(s) + Br_2(\ell) \rightarrow 2\ NaBr(s)$
(b) $2\ Mg(s) + O_2(g) \rightarrow 2\ MgO(s)$
(c) $2\ Al(s) + 3\ F_2(g) \rightarrow 2\ AlF_3(s)$
(d) $C(s) + O_2(g) \rightarrow CO_2(g)$

21.15 $2\ H_2(g) + O_2(g) \rightarrow 2\ H_2O(g)$
$H_2(g) + Cl_2(g) \rightarrow 2\ HCl(g)$
$3\ H_2(g) + N_2(g) \rightarrow 2\ NH_3(g)$

21.17 $CH_4(g) + H_2O(g) \rightarrow CO(g) + 3\ H_2(g)$

$\Delta_r H° = +206.2$ kJ; $\Delta_r S° = +214.7$ J/K; $\Delta_r G° = +142.2$ kJ (at 298.15 K).

21.19 Step 1: $2\ SO_2(g) + 4\ H_2O(\ell) + 2\ I_2(s) \rightarrow$
$$2\ H_2SO_4(\ell) + 4\ HI(g)$$

Step 2: $2\ H_2SO_4(\ell) \rightarrow$
$$2\ H_2O(\ell) + 2\ SO_2(g) + O_2(g)$$

Step 3: $4 HI(g) \rightarrow 2 H_2(g) + 2 I_2(g)$

Net: $2 H_2O(\ell) \rightarrow 2 H_2(g) + O_2(g)$

.21 $2 Na(s) + F_2(g) \rightarrow 2 NaF(s)$

$2 Na(s) + Cl_2(g) \rightarrow 2 NaCl(s)$

$2 Na(s) + Br_2(\ell) \rightarrow 2 NaBr(s)$

$2 Na(s) + I_2(s) \rightarrow 2 NaI(s)$

The alkali metal halides are white, crystalline solids. They have high melting and boiling points, and are soluble in water.

.23 (a) $2 Cl^-(aq) + 2 H_2O(\ell) \rightarrow$
$Cl_2(g) + H_2(g) + 2 OH^-(aq)$
(b) If this were the only process used to produce chlorine, the mass of Cl_2 reported for industrial production would be 0.88 times the mass of NaOH produced (2 mol NaCl, 117 g, would yield 2 mol NaOH, 80 g, and 1 mol Cl_2, 70 g). The amounts quoted indicate a Cl_2-to-NaOH mass ratio 0.96. Chlorine is presumably also prepared by other routes than this one.

.25 $2 Mg(s) + O_2(g) \rightarrow 2 MgO(s)$

$3 Mg(s) + N_2(g) \rightarrow Mg_3N_2(s)$

.27 $CaCO_3$ is used in agriculture to neutralize acidic soil, to prepare CaO for use in mortar, and in steel production.

$CaCO_3(s) + H_2O(\ell) + CO_2(g) \rightarrow$
$Ca^{2+}(aq) + 2 HCO_3^-(aq)$

.29 1.4×10^6 g SO_2

.31

$B_3O_6{}^{3-}$

$B_2O_5{}^{4-}$

1.33 (a) $2 B_5H_9(g) + 12 O_2(g) \rightarrow 5 B_2O_3(s) + 9 H_2O(g)$
(b) Enthalpy of combustion of B_5H_9 = -4341.2 kJ/mol. This is more than double the enthalpy of combustion of B_2H_6.
(c) Enthalpy of combustion of $C_2H_6(g)$ [to give $CO_2(g)$ and $H_2O(g)$] = -1428.7 kJ/mol. C_2H_6 produces 47.5 kJ/g, whereas diborane produces much more (73.7 kJ/g).

1.35 $2 Al(s) + 6 HCl(aq) \rightarrow$
$2 Al^{3+}(aq) + 6 Cl^-(aq) + 3 H_2(g)$

$2 Al(s) + 3 Cl_2(g) \rightarrow 2 AlCl_3(s)$

$4 Al(s) + 3 O_2(g) \rightarrow 2 Al_2O_3(s)$

21.37 $2 Al(s) + 2 OH^-(aq) + 6 H_2O(\ell) \rightarrow$
$2 Al(OH)_4{}^-(aq) + 3 H_2(g)$

Volume of H_2 obtained from 13.2 g Al = 18.4 L

21.39 $Al_2O_3(s) + 3 H_2SO_4(aq) \rightarrow Al_2(SO_4)_3(s) + 3 H_2O(\ell)$

Mass of H_2SO_4 required = 860 g and mass of Al_2O_3 required = 298 g.

21.41 Pyroxenes have as their basic structural unit an extended chain of linked SiO_4 tetrahedra. The ratio of Si to O is 1 to 3.

21.43 This structure has a six-member ring of Si atoms with O atom bridges. Each Si also has two O atoms attached. The basic unit is $SiO_3{}^{2-}$, and the overall charge is -12 in $[(SiO_3)_6]^{-12}$. (Electron lone pairs are omitted in the following structure.)

21.45 Consider the general decomposition reaction:

$$N_xO_y \rightarrow {}^x/_2\, N_2 + {}^y/_2\, O_2$$

The value of $\Delta G°$ can be obtained for all N_xO_y molecules because $\Delta_r G° = -\Delta_f G°$. These data show that the decomposition reaction is spontaneous for all of the nitrogen oxides. All are unstable with respect to decomposition to the elements.

Compound	$-\Delta_f G°$ (kJ/mol)
NO(g)	-86.58
NO_2	-51.23
N_2O	-104.20
N_2O_4	-97.73

21.47 $\Delta_r H° = -114.4$ kJ; exothermic $\Delta_r G° = -70.7$ kJ, product-favored at equilibrium

21.49 (a) $N_2H_4(aq) + O_2(g) \rightarrow N_2(g) + 2 H_2O(\ell)$
(b) 1.32×10^3 g

21.51 (a) Oxidation number = $+3$
(b) Diphosphonic acid ($H_4P_2O_5$) should be a diprotic acid (losing the two H atoms attached to O atoms).

21.53 (a) 3.5×10^3 kg SO_2
(b) 4.1×10^3 kg $Ca(OH)_2$

21.55

$$\left[\ddot{S}\!-\!\ddot{S} \right]^{2-}$$

disulfide ion

21.57 $E°_{cell} = E°_{cathode} - E°_{anode} = +1.44$ V $- (+1.51$ V$) = -0.07$ V

The reaction is not product-favored under standard conditions.

21.59 $Cl_2(aq) + 2\ Br^-(aq) \rightarrow 2\ Cl^-(aq) + Br_2(aq)$

Cl_2 is the oxidizing agent, Br^- is the reducing agent; $E°_{cell} = 0.28$ V.

21.61 The reaction consumes 4.32×10^8 C to produce 8.51×10^4 g F_2.

21.63

Element	Appearance	State
Na, Mg, Al	Silvery metal	Solids
Si	black, shiny metalloid	Solid
P	White, red, and black allotropes; nonmetal	Solid
S	Yellow nonmetal	Solid
Cl	Pale green nonmetal	Gas
Ar	Colorless nonmetal	Gas

21.65 (a) $2\ K(s) + Cl_2(g) \rightarrow 2\ KCl(s)$

$Ca(s) + Cl_2(g) \rightarrow CaCl_2(s)$

$2\ Ga(s) + 3\ Cl_2(g) \rightarrow 2\ GaCl_3(s)$

$Ge(s) + 2\ Cl_2(g) \rightarrow GeCl_4(\ell)$

$2\ As(s) + 3\ Cl_2(g) \rightarrow 2\ AsCl_3(\ell)$

($AsCl_5$ has been prepared but is not stable.)

(b) KCl and $CaCl_2$ are ionic; the other products are covalent.
(c) $GaCl_3$ is planar trigonal; $AsCl_3$ is pyramidal.

21.67 (a) $2\ KClO_3(s) \rightarrow 2\ KCl(s) + 3\ O_2(g)$
(b) $2\ H_2S(g) + 3\ O_2(g) \rightarrow 2\ H_2O(g) + 2\ SO_2(g)$
(c) $2\ Na(s) + O_2(g) \rightarrow Na_2O_2(s)$
(d) $P_4(s) + 3\ KOH(aq) + 3\ H_2O(\ell) \rightarrow$
$\qquad PH_3(g) + 3\ KH_2PO_4(aq)$
(e) $NH_4NO_3(s) \rightarrow N_2O(g) + 2\ H_2O(g)$
(f) $2\ In(s) + 3\ Br_2(\ell) \rightarrow 2\ InBr_3(s)$
(g) $SnCl_4(\ell) + 2\ H_2O(\ell) \rightarrow SnO_2(s) + 4\ HCl(aq)$

21.69 1.4×10^5 metric tons

21.71 Mg: $\Delta_r G° = +64.9$ kJ

Ca: $\Delta_r G° = +131.40$ kJ

Ba: $\Delta_r G° = +219.4$ kJ

Relative tendency to decompose:
$MgCO_3 > CaCO_3 > BaCO_3$

21.73 (a) $\Delta_f G°$ should be more negative than $(-95.1$ kJ$) \times n$.
(b) Ba, Pb, Ti

21.75 O—F bond energy = 190 kJ/mol

21.77 (a) N_2O_4 is the oxidizing agent (N is reduced from +4 to 0 in N_2), and $H_2NN(CH_3)_2$ is the reduci agent.
(b) 1.3×10^4 kg N_2O_4 is required. Product masses 5.7×10^3 kg N_2; 4.9×10^3 kg H_2O; 6.0×10^3 CO_2.

21.79 $\Delta_r H° = -257.78$ kJ. This reaction is entropy-disfavored, however, with $\Delta_r S° = -963$ J/K becaus of the decrease in the number of moles of gases. Combining these values gives $\Delta_r G° = +29.19$ kJ, indicating that under standard conditions at 298 K the reaction is not spontaneous. (The reaction has favorable $\Delta_r G°$ at temperatures less than 268 K, ind cating that further research on this system might b worthwhile. Note that at that temperature water is solid.)

21.81 A = B_2H_6; B = B_4H_{10}; C = B_5H_{11}; D = B_5H_9; E = $B_{10}H_{14}$

21.83 (a) $2\ CH_3Cl(g) + Si(s) \rightarrow (CH_3)_2SiCl_2(\ell)$
(b) 0.823 atm
(c) 12.2 g

21.85 $5\ N_2H_5^+(aq) + 4\ IO_3^-(aq) \rightarrow$
$\qquad 5\ N_2(g) + 2\ I_2(aq) + H^+(aq) + 12\ H_2O$

$E°_{net} = 1.43$ V

21.87 (a) Br_2O_3
(b) The structure of Br_2O is reasonably well known Several possible structures for Br_2O_3 can be imagined, but experiment confirms the structu below.

21.89 (a) The NO bond with a length of 114.2 pm is a double bond. The other two NO bonds (with a length of 121 pm) have a bond order of 1.5 (a there are two resonance structures involving these bonds).

114.2 pm 121 pm (resonance structure of N–N oxide)

(b) $K = 1.90$; $\Delta_r S° = 141$ J/K · mol-rxn

(c) $\Delta_f H° = 82.9$ kJ/mol

1.91 The flask contains a fixed number of moles of gas at the given pressure and temperature. One could burn the mixture because only the H_2 will combust; the argon is untouched. Cooling the gases from combustion would remove water (the combustion product of H_2) and leave only Ar in the gas phase. Measuring its pressure in a calibrated volume at a known temperature would allow one to calculate the amount of Ar that was in the original mixture.

1.93 Generally, a sodium fire can be extinguished by smothering it with sand. The worst choice is to use water (which reacts violently with sodium to give H_2 gas and NaOH).

1.95 Nitrogen is a relatively unreactive gas, so it will not participate in any reaction typical of hydrogen or oxygen. The most obvious property of H_2 is that it burns, so attempting to burn a small sample of the gas would immediately confirm or deny the presence of H_2. If O_2 is present, it can be detected by allowing it to react as an oxidizing agent. There are many reactions known with low-valent metals, especially transition metal ions in solution, that can be detected by color changes.

1.97 3.5 kWh

1.99 The reducing ability of the Group 3A metals declines considerably on descending the group, with the largest drop occurring on going from Al to Ga. The reducing ability of gallium and indium are similar, but another large change is observed on going to thallium. In fact, thallium is most stable in the +1 oxidation state. This same tendency for elements to be more stable with lower oxidation numbers is seen in Groups 4A (Ge and Pb) and 5A (Bi).

CHAPTER 22

22.1 (a) Cr^{3+}: $[Ar]3d^3$, paramagnetic
(b) V^{2+}: $[Ar]3d^3$, paramagnetic
(c) Ni^{2+}: $[Ar]3d^8$, paramagnetic
(d) Cu^+: $[Ar]3d^{10}$, diamagnetic

22.3 (a) Fe^{3+}: $[Ar]3d^5$, isoelectronic with Mn^{2+}
(b) Zn^{2+}: $[Ar]3d^{10}$, isoelectronic with Cu^+
(c) Fe^{2+}: $[Ar]3d^6$, isoelectronic with Co^{3+}
(d) Cr^{3+}: $[Ar]3d^3$, isoelectronic with V^{2+}

22.5 (a) $Cr_2O_3(s) + 2\,Al(s) \rightarrow Al_2O_3(s) + 2\,Cr(s)$
(b) $TiCl_4(\ell) + 2\,Mg(s) \rightarrow Ti(s) + 2\,MgCl_2(s)$
(c) $2\,[Ag(CN)_2]^-(aq) + Zn(s) \rightarrow$
$$2\,Ag(s) + [Zn(CN)_4]^{2-}(aq)$$
(d) $3\,Mn_3O_4(s) + 8\,Al(s) \rightarrow 9\,Mn(s) + 4\,Al_2O_3(s)$

22.7 Monodentate: CH_3NH_2, CH_3CN, N_3^-, Br^-

Bidentate: en, phen (see Figure 22.14)

22.9 (a) Mn^{2+} (c) Co^{3+}
(b) Co^{3+} (d) Cr^{2+}

22.11 $[Ni(en)(NH_3)_3(H_2O)]^{2+}$

22.13 (a) $Ni(en)_2Cl_2$ (en = $H_2NCH_2CH_2NH_2$)
(b) $K_2[PtCl_4]$
(c) $K[Cu(CN)_2]$
(d) $[Fe(NH_3)_4(H_2O)_2]^{2+}$

22.15 (a) Diaquabis(oxalato)nickelate(II) ion
(b) Dibromobis(ethylenediamine)cobalt(III) ion
(c) Amminechlorobis(ethylenediamine)cobalt(III) ion
(d) Diammineoxalatoplatinum(II)

22.17 (a) $[Fe(H_2O)_5OH]^{2+}$
(b) Potassium tetracyanonickelate(II)
(c) Potassium diaquabis(oxalato)chromate(III)
(d) $(NH_4)_2[PtCl_4]$

22.19

cis   *trans*

cis   *trans*

fac   *mer*

Only one structure possible. (N—N is the bidentate ethylenediamine ligand.)

22.21 For a discussion of chirality, see Chapter 10, page 446).
(a) Fe^{2+} is a chiral center.
(b) Co^{3+} is not a chiral center.
(c) Neither of the two possible isomers is chiral.
(d) No. Square-planar complexes are never chiral.

22.23 (a) $[Mn(CN)_6]^{4-}$: d^5, low-spin Mn^{2+} complex is paramagnetic.

$$\underline{\uparrow\downarrow}\quad\underline{\uparrow\downarrow}\quad\underline{\uparrow}$$

(b) $[Co(NH_3)_6]^{3+}$: d^6, low-spin Co^{3+} complex is diamagnetic.

$$\underline{\uparrow\downarrow}\quad\underline{\uparrow\downarrow}\quad\underline{\uparrow\downarrow}$$

(c) $[Fe(H_2O)_6]^{3+}$: d^5, low-spin Fe^{3+} complex is paramagnetic (1 unpaired electron; same as part a).

(d) $[Cr(en)_3]^{2+}$: d^4, Cr^{3+} complex is paramagnetic (2 unpaired electrons).

$$\underline{\uparrow\downarrow}\quad\underline{\uparrow}\quad\underline{\uparrow}$$

22.25 (a) Fe^{2+}, d^6, paramagnetic, four unpaired electrons
(b) Co^{2+}, d^7, paramagnetic, three unpaired electrons
(c) Mn^{2+}, d^5, paramagnetic, five unpaired electrons
(d) Zn^{2+}, d^{10}, diamagnetic, zero unpaired electrons

22.27 (a) 6
(b) octahedral
(c) +2
(d) four unpaired electrons (high spin)
(e) paramagnetic

22.29 With four ligands, complexes of the d^8 Ni^{2+} ion can be either tetrahedral or square planar. The CN^- ligand is at one end of the spectrochemical series and leads to a large ligand field splitting, whereas Cl^- is at the opposite end and often leads to complexes with small orbital splitting. With ligands such as CN^- the complex will be square planar (and for a d^8 ion it will be diamagnetic). With a weak field ligand (Cl^-) the complex will be tetrahedral and, for the d^8 ion, two electrons will be unpaired, giving a paramagnetic complex.

22.31 The light absorbed is in the blue region of the spectrum (page 271). Therefore, the light transmitted—which is the color of the solution—is yellow.

22.33 (a) The Mn^+ ion in this complex has six d electrons. Each CO contributes two electrons, giving a total of 18 for the complex ion.
(b) The $C_5H_5^-$ ligand contributes six electrons, CO and PR_3 each contribute two electrons, for a total of 10 electrons for the ligands. The cobalt is effectively a Co^+ ion and contributes eight d electrons. The total is 18 electrons.
(c) The $C_5H_5^-$ ligand contributes six electrons, each CO contributes two electrons, for a total of 12 electrons for the ligands. The manganese is effectively a Mn^+ ion and contributes six d electrons. The total is 18 electrons.

22.35 Determine the magnetic properties of the complex. Square-planar Ni^{2+} (d^8) complexes are diamagnetic whereas tetrahedral complexes are paramagnetic.

22.37 Fe^{2+} has a d^6 configuration. Low-spin octahedral complexes are diamagnetic, whereas high-spin octahedral complexes of this ion have four unpaired electrons and are paramagnetic.

22.39 Square-planar complexes most often arise from d^8 transition metal ions. Therefore, it is likely that $[Ni(CN)_4]^{2-}$ (Ni^{2+}) and $[Pt(CN)_4]^{2-}$ (Pt^{2+}) are square planar. (See also Study Questions 22.29 and 22.65.)

22.41 Two geometric isomers are possible.

22.43 Absorbing at 425 nm means the complex is absorbing light in the blue-violet end of the spectrum. Therefore, red and green light are transmitted, and the complex appears yellow (see Figure 22.27).

22.45 (a) Mn^{2+}; (b) 6; (c) octahedral; (d) 5; (e) paramagnetic; (f) *cis* and *trans* isomers exist.

22.47 Name: tetraamminedichlorocobalt(III) ion

cis   trans

22.49 $[Co(en)_2(H_2O)Cl]^{2+}$

22.51

mer   fac

trans chlorides   cis chlorides

.53

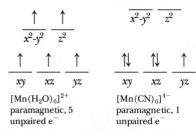

$[Co(NH_3)...]^{3+}$ complexes:

H_2O and NH_3
cis, chiral

H_2O *cis* and
NH_3 *trans*,
not chiral

H_2O *trans* and
NH_3 *cis*, not
chiral

.55 In $[Mn(H_2O)_6]^{2+}$ and $[Mn(CN)_6]^{4-}$, Mn has an oxidation number of $+2$ (Mn is a d^5 ion).

$[Mn(H_2O)_6]^{2+}$
paramagnetic, 5
unpaired e^-

$[Mn(CN)_6]^{4-}$
paramagnetic, 1
unpaired e^-

This shows that Δ_o for CN^- is greater than for H_2O.

.57 (a) ammonium tetrachlorocuprate(II)

(b) hexacarbonylmolybdenum(0)

(c) $[Cr(H_2O)_4Cl_2]Cl$

(d) $[Co(H_2O)(NH_2CH_2CH_2NH_2)_2(SCN)](NO_3)_2$

.59 (a) The light absorbed is in the orange region of the spectrum (page 1043). Therefore, the light transmitted (the color of the solution) is blue or cyan.

(b) Using the cobalt(III) complexes in Table 22.3 as a guide, we might place CO_3^{2-} between F^- and the oxalato ion, $C_2O_4^{2-}$.

(c) Δ_o is small, so the complex should be high spin and paramagnetic.

22.61

$N \frown O = H_2N-CH_2-CO_2^-$

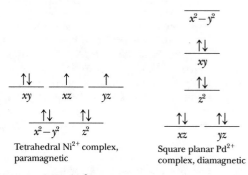

enantiometric pair

enantiometric pair

enantiometric pair

22.63 (a) In complexes such as $M(PR_3)Cl_2$ the metal is Ni^{2+} or Pd^{2+}, both of which are d^8 metal ions. If an Ni^{2+} complex is paramagnetic it must be tetrahedral, whereas the Pd^{2+} must be square planar. (A d^8 metal complex cannot be diamagnetic if it has a tetrahedral structure.)

Tetrahedral Ni^{2+} complex,
paramagnetic

Square planar Pd^{2+}
complex, diamagnetic

(b) A tetrahedral Ni^{2+} complex cannot have isomers, whereas a square planar complex of the type $M(PR_3)_2Cl_2$ can have *cis* and *trans* isomers. See page 1036.

22.65 A, dark violet isomer: $[Co(NH_3)_5Br]SO_4$

B, violet-red isomer: $[Co(NH_3)_5(SO_4)]Br$

$[Co(NH_3)_5Br]SO_4(aq) + BaCl_2(aq) \rightarrow$
$[Co(NH_3)_5Br]Cl_2(aq) + BaSO_4(s)$

22.67 (a) There is 5.41×10^{-4} mol of $UO_2(NO_3)_2$, and this provides 5.41×10^{-4} mol of U^{n+} ions on reduction by Zn. The 5.41×10^{-4} mol U^{n+} requires 2.16×10^{-4} mol MnO_4^- to reach the equivalence point. This is a ratio of 5 mol of U^{n+} ions to 2 mol MnO_4^- ions. The 2 mol MnO_4^- ions require 10 mol of e^- (to go to Mn^{2+} ions), so 5 mol of U^{n+} ions provide 10 mol e^- (on going to UO_2^{2+} ions, with a uranium oxidation number of +6). This means the U^{n+} ion must be U^{4+}.

(b) $Zn(s) \rightarrow Zn^{2+}(aq) + 2\,e^-$

$$UO_2^{2+}(aq) + 4\,H^+(aq) + 2\,e^- \rightarrow$$
$$U^{4+}(aq) + 2\,H_2O(\ell)$$
___
$$UO_2^{2+}(aq) + 4\,H^+(aq) + Zn(s) \rightarrow$$
$$U^{4+}(aq) + 2\,H_2O(\ell) + Zn^{2+}(aq)$$

(c) $5[U^{4+}(aq) + 2\,H_2O(\ell) \rightarrow$
$$UO_2^{2+}(aq) + 4\,H^+(aq) + 2\,e^-]$$

$2[MnO_4^-(aq) + 8\,H^+(aq) + 5\,e^- \rightarrow$
$$Mn^{2+}(aq) + 4\,H_2O(\ell)]$$
___
$5\,U^{4+}(aq) + 2\,MnO_4^-(aq) + 2\,H_2O(\ell) \rightarrow$
$$5\,UO_2^{2+}(aq) + 4\,H^+(aq) + 2\,Mn^{2+}(aq)$$

22.69

Ion	$K_{formation}$ (ammine complexes)
Co^{2+}	1.3×10^5
Ni^{2+}	5.5×10^8
Cu^{2+}	2.1×10^{13}
Zn^{2+}	2.9×10^9

The data for these hexammine complexes do indeed, verify the Irving-Williams series. In the book *Chemistry of the Elements* (N. N. Greenwood and A. Earnshaw: 2nd edition, p. 908, Oxford, England, Butterworth-Heinemann, 1997), it is stated: "the stabilities of corresponding complexes of the bivalent ions of the first transition series, irrespective of the particular ligand involved, usually vary in the Irving-Williams order, . . . , which is the reverse of the order for the cation radii. These observations are consistent with the view that, at least for metals in oxidation states +2 and +3, the coordinate bond is largely electrostatic. This was a major factor in the acceptance of the crystal field theory."

22.71 Wilkinson's catalyst and the EAN rule.

Step 1: Rhodium-containing reactant: Each PR_3 ligand donates two electrons as does the Cl^- ligand. The Rh^+ ion has 8 d electrons. Total electrons = 16.

Step 1: Rhodium-containing product. Assuming that the H ligand is H^-, each donates two electrons, as do Cl^- and the two PR_3 ligands. The metal center is Rh^{3+}, a d^6 metal ion. Total electrons = 18.

Step 2: The product has 16 electrons because one PR_3 ligand has been dissociated.

Step 3: The product has 18 electrons. The two-electron donor ligand CH_2CH_2 has replaced the dissociated PR_3 ligand.

Step 4: The product has 16 electrons. There are three anionic, two-electron donor ligands (Cl^-, H and $CH_3CH_2^-$), two two-electron donor PR_3 ligan and an Rh^{3+} ion (d^6).

Step 5: The product has 14 electrons. It is an Rh^+ complex (d^8) with two PR_3 ligands (two electrons each) and one Cl^- (two electrons). (It is likely a s vent molecule fills the vacant site here to give a tr sient, 16-electron complex.)

Step 6: The product is once again the active, 16-electron catalyst.

CHAPTER 23

23.11 (a) $^{56}_{28}Ni$; (b) $^{1}_{0}n$; (c) $^{32}_{15}P$; (d) $^{97}_{43}Tc$; (e) $_{-1}^{0}\beta$; (f) $^{0}_{1}e$ (positron)

23.13 (a) $_{-1}^{0}\beta$; (b) $^{87}_{37}Rb$; (c) $^{4}_{2}\alpha$; (d) $^{226}_{88}Ra$; (e) $_{-1}^{0}\beta$; (f) $^{24}_{11}N$

23.15 $^{235}_{92}U \rightarrow ^{231}_{90}Th + ^{4}_{2}\alpha$

$^{231}_{90}Th \rightarrow ^{231}_{91}Pa + {}_{-1}^{0}\beta$

$^{231}_{91}Pa \rightarrow ^{227}_{89}Ac + ^{4}_{2}\alpha$

$^{227}_{89}Ac \rightarrow ^{227}_{90}Th + {}_{-1}^{0}\beta$

$^{227}_{90}Th \rightarrow ^{223}_{88}Ra + ^{4}_{2}\alpha$

$^{223}_{88}Ra \rightarrow ^{219}_{86}Rn + ^{4}_{2}\alpha$

$^{219}_{86}Rn \rightarrow ^{215}_{84}Po + ^{4}_{2}\alpha$

$^{215}_{84}Po \rightarrow ^{211}_{82}Pb + ^{4}_{2}\alpha$

$^{211}_{82}Pb \rightarrow ^{211}_{83}Bi + {}_{-1}^{0}\beta$

$^{211}_{83}Bi \rightarrow ^{211}_{84}Po + {}_{-1}^{0}\beta$

$^{211}_{84}Po \rightarrow ^{207}_{82}Pb + ^{4}_{2}\alpha$

23.17 (a) $^{198}_{79}Au \rightarrow ^{198}_{80}Hg + {}_{-1}^{0}\beta$
(b) $^{222}_{86}Rn \rightarrow ^{218}_{84}Po + ^{4}_{2}\alpha$
(c) $^{137}_{55}Cs \rightarrow ^{137}_{56}Ba + {}_{-1}^{0}\beta$
(d) $^{110}_{49}In \rightarrow ^{110}_{48}Cd + ^{0}_{1}e$

23.19 (a) $^{80}_{35}Br$ has a high neutron/proton ratio of 45/35 Beta decay will allow the ratio to decrease: $^{80}_{35}Br \rightarrow ^{80}_{36}Kr + {}_{-1}^{0}\beta$. Some ^{80m}Br decays by gam emission.
(b) Alpha decay is likely: $^{240}_{98}Cf \rightarrow ^{236}_{96}Cm + ^{4}_{2}\alpha$
(c) Cobalt-61 has a high n/p ratio so beta decay is likely:

$^{61}_{27}Co \rightarrow ^{61}_{28}Kr + {}_{-1}^{0}\beta$

(d) Carbon-11 has only 5 neutrons so K-capture or positron emission may occur:

$$^{11}_{6}C + ^{0}_{-1}e \rightarrow ^{11}_{5}B$$

$$^{11}_{6}C \rightarrow ^{11}_{5}B + ^{0}_{1}e$$

23.21 Generally beta decay will occur when the n/p ratio is high, whereas positron emission will occur when the n/p ratio is low.
(a) Beta decay: $^{20}_{9}F \rightarrow ^{20}_{10}Ne + ^{0}_{-1}\beta$

$$^{3}_{1}H \rightarrow ^{3}_{2}He + ^{0}_{-1}\beta$$

(b) Positron emission

$$^{22}_{11}Na \rightarrow ^{22}_{10}Ne + ^{0}_{1}\beta$$

23.23 Binding energy per nucleon for $^{11}B = 6.70 \times 10^8$ kJ

Binding energy per nucleon for $^{10}B = 6.26 \times 10^8$ kJ

23.25 8.256×10^8 kJ/nucleon

23.27 7.700×10^8 kJ/nucleon

23.29 0.781 micrograms

23.31 (a) $^{131}_{53}I \rightarrow ^{131}_{54}Xe + ^{0}_{-1}\beta$
(b) 0.075 micrograms

23.33 9.5×10^{-4} mg

23.35 (a) $^{222}_{86}Rn \rightarrow ^{218}_{84}Po + ^{4}_{2}\alpha$
(b) Time = 8.87 d

23.37 (a) 15.8 y; (b) 88%

23.39 $^{239}_{94}Pu + + ^{4}_{2}\alpha \rightarrow ^{240}_{95}Am + ^{1}_{1}H + 2\,^{1}_{0}n$

23.41 $^{48}_{20}Ca + ^{242}_{94}Pu \rightarrow ^{287}_{114}Uuq + 3\,^{1}_{0}n$

23.43 (a) $^{115}_{48}Cd$ (b) $^{7}_{4}Be$ (c) $^{4}_{2}\alpha$ (d) $^{63}_{29}Cu$

23.45 $^{10}_{5}B + ^{1}_{0}n \rightarrow ^{7}_{3}Li + ^{4}_{2}\alpha$

23.47 Time $= 4.4 \times 10^{10}$ y

23.49 If $t_{1/2} = 14.28$ d, then $k = 4.854 \times 10^{-2}$ d^{-1}. If the original disintegration rate is 3.2×10^6 dpm, then (from the integrated first order rate equation), the rate after 365 d is 0.065 dpm. The plot will resemble Figure 23.5.

23.51 (a) $^{238}_{92}U + ^{1}_{0}n \rightarrow ^{239}_{92}U$
(b) $^{239}_{92}U \rightarrow ^{239}_{93}Np + ^{0}_{-1}\beta$
(c) $^{239}_{93}Np \rightarrow ^{239}_{94}Pu + ^{0}_{-1}\beta$
(d) $^{239}_{94}Pu + ^{1}_{0}n \rightarrow 2\,^{1}_{0}n + $ energy + other nuclei

23.53 About 2700 years old

23.55 Plot ln(activity) versus time. The slope of the plot is $-k$, the rate constant for decay. Here, $k = 0.0050$ d^{-1}, so $t_{1/2} = 140$ d.

23.57 Time $= 1.9 \times 10^9$ y

23.59 130 mL

23.61 Energy obtained from 1.000 lb (452.6 g) of $^{235}U = 4.05 \times 10^{-10}$ kJ

Mass of coal required $= 1.6 \times 10^3$ ton (or about 3 million pounds of coal)

23.63 27 fish tagged fish out of 5250 fish caught represents 0.51% of the fish in the lake. Therefore, 1000 fish put into the lake represent 0.51% of the fish in the lake, or 0.51% of 190,000 fish.

23.65 (a) The mass decreases by 4 units (with an $^{4}_{2}a$ emission) or is unchanged (with a $^{0}_{-1}\beta$ emission) so the only masses possible are 4 units apart.
(b) ^{232}Th series, $m = 4n$; ^{235}U series $m = 4n + 3$
(c) ^{226}Ra and ^{210}Bi, $4n + 2$ series; ^{215}At, $4n + 3$ series; ^{228}Th, $4n$ series)
(d) Each series is headed by a long-lived isotope (in the order of 10^9 years, the age of the Earth.) The $4n + 1$ series is missing because there is no long-lived isotope in this series. Over geologic time, all the members of this series have decayed completely.

23.67 (a) ^{231}Pa isotope belongs to the ^{235}U decay series (see Question 23.65b).
(b) $^{235}_{92}U \rightarrow ^{231}_{90}Th + ^{4}_{2}\alpha$

$$^{231}_{90}Th \rightarrow ^{231}_{91}Pa + ^{0}_{-1}\beta$$

(c) Pa-231 is present to the extent of 1 part per million. Therefore, 1 million grams of pitchblende need to be used to obtain 1 g of Pa-231.
(d) $^{231}_{91}Pa \rightarrow ^{227}_{89}Ac + ^{4}_{2}\alpha$

23.69 Pitchblende contains $^{238}_{92}U$ and $^{235}_{92}U$. Thus, both radium and polonium isotopes must belong to either the $4n + 2$ or $4n + 3$ decay series. Furthermore, the isotopes must have sufficiently long half-lives in order to survive the separation and isolation process. These criteria are satisfied by ^{226}Ra and ^{210}Po.

P | Answers to Selected Interchapter Study Questions

THE CHEMISTRY OF FUELS AND ENERGY SOURCES

1. (a) From methane: $H_2O(g) + CH_4(g) \rightarrow 3 H_2(g) + CO(g)$

100. g CH_4(1 mol CH_4/16.043 g)
(3 mol H_2/mol CH_4)(2.016 g H_2/1 mol H_2)
= 37.7 g of H_2 produced

(b) From petroleum: $H_2O(g) + CH_2(\ell) \rightarrow 2 H_2(g) + CO\ (g)$

100. g CH_2(1 mol CH_2/14.026 g CH_2)
(2 mol H_2/1 mol CH_2)(2.016 g H_2/1 mol H_2) = 28.7 g H_2 produced

(c) From coal: $H_2O(g) + C(s) \rightarrow H_2(g) + CO(g)$

100. g C(1 mol C/12.011 g C)
(1 mol H_2/mole C)(2.016 g H_2/1 mol H_2) = 16.8 g H_2 produced.

3. 70. lb(453.6 g/lb)(33 kJ/g) = 1.0×10^6 kJ

5. Assume burning oil produces 43 kJ/g (the value for crude petroleum in Table 2)

7.0 gal(3.785 L/gal)(1000 cm^3/L)(0.8 g/cm^3)(43 kJ/g) = 0.9×10^6 kJ. Uncertainty in the numbers is one significant figure. This value is close to the value for the energy obtained by burning from 70 kg of coal (calculated in Q.3.)

7. Per gram: (5.45×10^3 kJ/mol)(1 mol/114.26 g) = 47.7 kJ/g

Per liter: (47.7 kJ/g)(688 g/L) = 3.28×10^4 kJ/L

9. The factor for converting kW-h to kJ is 1 kW-h = 3600 kJ

(940 kW-h/yr)(3600 kJ/kW-h) = 3.4×10^6 kJ/yr

11. First, calculate $\Delta_r H°$ for the reaction $CH_3OH(\ell) + 1.5\ O_2(g) \rightarrow CO_2(g) + 2\ H_2O(\ell$ using enthalpies of formation ($\Delta_r H° = 726.7$ kJ/mol-rxn). Use molar mass and density to calculate energy per L [−726.7 kJ/mol-rxn (1 mol-rxn/32.04 g)(787 g/ L) = 17.9×10^3 kJ/L]. Then use the kW-h to kJ conversion fa tor from Q. 9 to obtain the answer [(17.9 × 10^3 kJ/L)(1 kW-h/3600 kJ) = 4.96 kW-h/L].

13. Area of parking lot = 325 m × 50.0 m = 1.63×10^4 m^2

2.6×10^7 J/m^2(1.63×10^4 m^2) = 4.3×10^{11} J

15. Amount of Pd = 1.0 cm^3(12.0 g/cm^3)(1 mol/106.4 g) = 0.113 mol

amount of H = 0.084 g(1 mol/1.008 g) = 0.0833 mol

mol H per mol Pd = 0.083/0.113 = 0.74: Simplest formula for this compound is PdH$_{0.7}$ (Because the compound is nonstoichiometric we will not write a formula with a whole number ratio. For these compounds, it is common practice to set the amount of metal [Pd] to be an integer and H as a non-integer.)

17. Energy per gal. of gas = (48.0 kJ/g)
$(0.737 \text{ g/cm}^3)(1000 \text{ cm}^3/\text{L})(3.785 \text{ L/gal})$ =
1.34×10^5 kJ/gal

Energy to travel 1 mile = (1.00 mile/
55.0 gal/mile)$(1.34 \times 10^5$ kJ/gal) = 2440 kJ

MILESTONES IN THE DEVELOPMENT OF CHEMISTRY AND THE MODERN VIEW OF ATOMS AND MOLECULES

1. Atoms are not solid, hard, or impenetrable. They have mass (an important aspect of Dalton's hypothesis), and we now know that atoms are in rapid motion at all temperatures above absolute zero (the kinetic-molecular theory).

3. mass e/mass p = 9.109383×10^{-28} g/1.672622×10^{-24} g = 5.446170×10^{-4}. (Mass of p and e obtained from Table 2.1, page 52.) The proton is 1,834 times more massive than an electron. Dalton's estimate was off by a factor of about 2.

THE CHEMISTRY OF LIFE: BIOCHEMISTRY

1. (a)

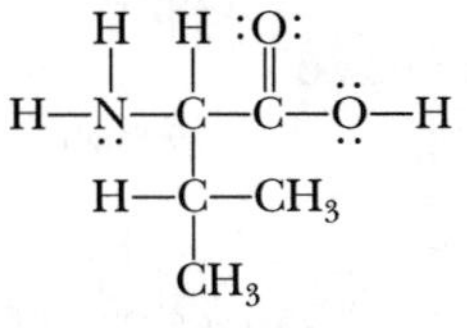

H—N—C—C—Ö—H
(with H, H, :O:, CH₃, H—C—CH₃, CH₃ substituents as drawn)

(b)

H—N⁺—C—C—Ö:⁻
(zwitterionic form as drawn)

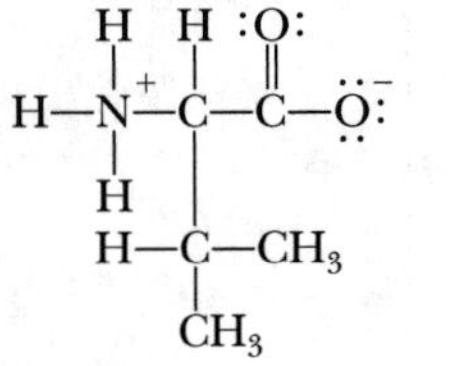

(c) The zwitterionic form is the predominant form at physiological pH.

3.

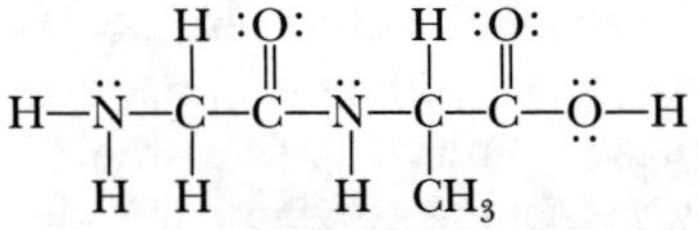

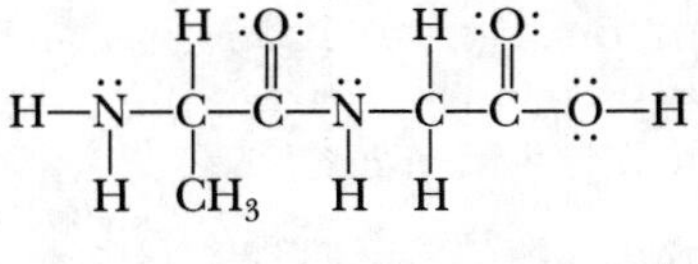

(dipeptide structures as drawn)

5.

(peptide structures with resonance as drawn)

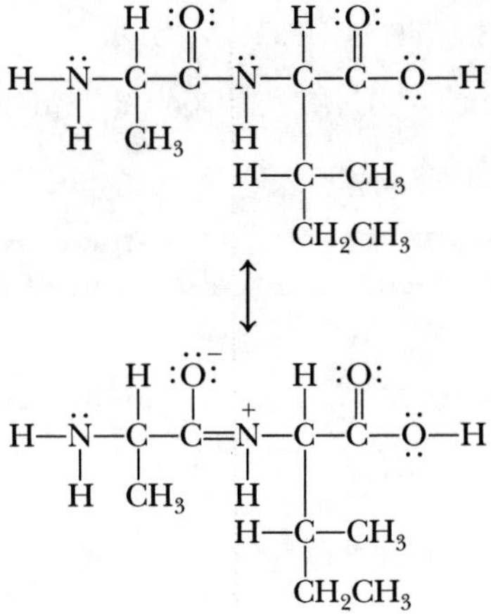

7. (a) The structure of ribose is given in Figure 13.

(b) Adenosine

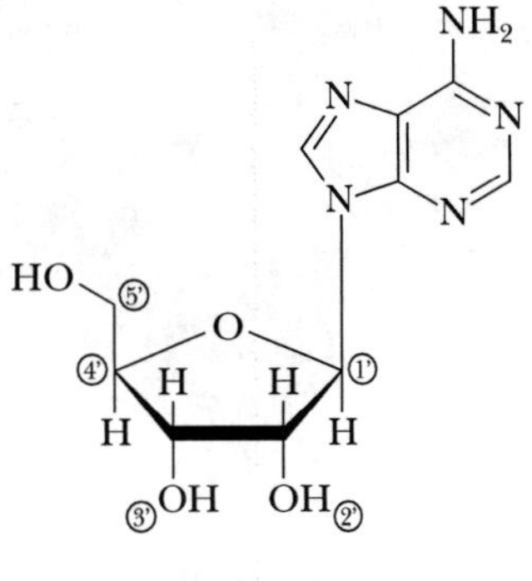

(structure of adenosine as drawn)

(c) Adenosine-5'-monophosphate

(structure of adenosine-5'-monophosphate as drawn)

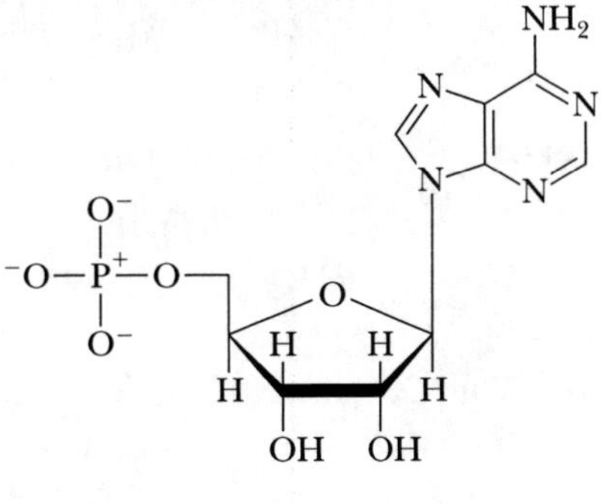

9. The sequences differ in the positions of attachments of the phosphate to deoxyribose on adjacent units. Consider the A-T attachments. In ATGC, the attachment is from the 5′ position on A to the 3′ position on T. In CGTA, the attachment is from the 3′ position on A to the 5′ position on T.

11. (a) 5′-GAATCGCGT-3′

    (b) 5′-GAAUCGCGU-3′

    (c) 5′-UUC-3′, 5′-CGA-3′, and 5′-ACG-3′

    (d) glutamic acid, serine, and arginine

13. (a) In transcription, a strand of RNA complementary to the segment of DNA is constructed.

    (b) In translation, an amino acid sequence is constructed based on the information in a mRNA sequence.

15. The 4-ring structure present in all steroids is given in Figure 18a.

17. (a) False (b) True (c) True (d) True

19. (a) $6\ CO_2(g) + 6\ H_2O(\ell) \rightarrow$
    $$C_6H_{12}O_6(s) + 6\ O_2(g)$$

    $\Delta_r H° = \Delta_f H°(\text{products}) - \Delta_f H°(\text{reactants})$

    $\Delta_r H° = (1\ \text{mol}\ C_6H_{12}O_6/\text{mol-rxn})$
    $[\Delta_f H°(C_6H_{12}O_6)] - (6\ \text{mol}\ H_2O/\text{mol-rxn})$
    $[\Delta_f H°(H_2O)] - (6\ \text{mol}\ CO_2/\text{mol-rxn})$
    $[\Delta_f H°(CO_2)]$

    $\Delta_r H° = (1\ \text{mol}\ C_6H_{12}O_6/\text{mol-rxn})$
    $(-1273.3\ \text{kJ/mol}\ C_6H_{12}O_6) - (6\ \text{mol}$
    $H_2O/\text{mol-rxn})(-285.8\ \text{kJ/mol}\ H_2O) -$
    $(6\ \text{mol}\ CO_2/\text{mol-rxn})(-393.5\ \text{kJ/mol}\ CO_2)$

    $\Delta_r H° = +2{,}803\ \text{kJ/mol-rxn}$

    (b) $(2803\ \text{kJ/mol})(1\ \text{mol}/6.022 \times 10^{23}$
    $\text{molecules})(1000\ \text{J/1 kJ}) = 4.655 \times$
    $10^{-18}\ \text{J/molecule}$

    (c) $\lambda = 650\ \text{nm}(1\ \text{m}/10^9\ \text{nm}) = 6.50 \times 10^{-7}\ \text{m}$

    $E = hc/\lambda = (6.626 \times 10^{-34}\ \text{J} \cdot \text{s})$
    $(3.00 \times 10^8\ \text{m} \cdot \text{s}^{-1})/(6.50 \times 10^{-7}\ \text{m}) =$
    $3.06 \times 10^{-19}\ \text{J}$

    (d) The amount of energy per photon is less than the amount of required per molecule of glucose, therefore multiple photons must be absorbed.

THE CHEMISTRY OF MODERN MATERIALS

1. The GaAs band gap is 140 kJ/mol. Use the equations $E = h\nu$ and $\lambda \times \nu = c$ to calculate wavelength of 854 nm corresponding to this energy. Radiation of this wavelength is in the infrared portion of the spectrum.

3. The amount of light falling on a single solar cell = 925 W/m² [(1 m²/10⁴ cm²) (1.0 cm²/cell) = 0.0925 W/cell.] Using the conversion factor 1 W = 1 J/s, the energy incident on the cell is (0.0925 W/cell) (1J/W · s)(60 sec/min) = 5.55 J/(min · cell) At 25% efficiency, the energy absorbed for each cell is 1.39 J/min.

5. The density of dry air at 25 °C and 1.0 atm. i 1.2 g/L (see page 526), so the mass of air in aerogel is 0.99(1.2 × 10⁻³ g) = 1.2 × 10⁻³ g. Add to this 0.023 g, the mass of 0.010 cm³ of SiO₂ (density of SiO₂, from web, is 2.3 g/cm³ mass of 0.010 cm³ is 0.023 g). Thus, the total mass is 0.0012 g + 0.023 g = 0.024 g, and th density of aerogel is 0.024 g/cm³.

ENVIRONMENTAL CHEMISTRY

1. $[Na^+] = 0.460$ mol/L, $[Cl^-] = 0.550$ mol/L; larger amount of chloride than sodium ion is present in a sample of seawater.

3. The amount of NaCl is limited by the amoun of sodium present. From 1.0 L sample of seawater, a maximum of 0.460 mol NaCl could b obtained. The mass of this amount of NaCl is 26.9 g [(0.460 mol/L)(1.00 L)(58.43 g NaCl/ 1 mol NaCl) = 26.9 g].

5. For gases, ppm refers to numbers of particle and hence to mole fractions (see footnote to Table 1). Gas pressure exerted is directly proportional to mole fraction. Thus, 40,000 ppm water vapor would exert a pressure of 40,000/1,000,000ᵗʰ of one atmosphere, or 30.4 mm Hg (0.040 × 760 mm Hg). This would be the case at a little over 29 °C, at 100% humidity.

7. The concentration of Mg^{2+} in seawater is 52 mmol/L (Table 2). Assuming that all this is converted to Mg metal, one would expect to obtain 1.26 g from 1.0 L of seawater [0.052 mol(24.31 g/mol) = 1.26 g]. To obtain 100 kg of Mg, 79,000 L of seawater [100. kg(1000 g/kg)(1 L/1.26 g) = 7.9×10^4 L] would be needed.

9. (a) The volume occupied by 25 g of ice is 33 cm^3 [25 g(1 cm^3/0.92 g) = 33 cm^3]. However, only 92% of the ice is submerged and the water displaced by ice (the volume of ice under the surface of water) is 25 cm^3 (0.92 × 33 cm^3 = 25 cm^3). Thus, the liquid level in the graduated cylinder will be 125 mL.

(b) Melting 25 g of ice will produce 25 mL of liquid water. The water level will be 125 mL (the same as in (a), that is the water level won't rise as the ice melts).

Index/Glossary

air bags, 515, 522, *523*
alanine, 498
 zwitterionic form, 808
albite, dissolved by rain
  water, 186
albumin, precipitation of, 719
alchemy, 339, 1061
alcohol(s) Any of a class of
  organic compounds characterized by the presence of a
  hydroxyl group bonded to a
  saturated carbon atom,
  461–465
 energy content of, 215
 naming of, A-19
 oxidation to carbonyl compounds, 468
 solubility in water, 465
aldehyde(s) Any of a class of
  organic compounds characterized by the presence of a
  carbonyl group, in which the
  carbon atom is bonded to at
  least one hydrogen atom,
  468–470
aldehydes, naming of, A-19
alkali metal(s) The metals in
  Group 1A of the periodic
  table, 62
 electron configuration of,
  311
 ions, enthalpy of hydra-
  tion, 557, 558t
 reaction with oxygen, 973
 reaction with water, 62, *63*,
  971, 973
 reduction potentials of,
  973
alkaline battery, 912
alkaline earth metal(s) The
  elements in Group 2A of the
  periodic table, 62, 975–979
 biological uses of, 977
 electron configuration of,
  311
alkalosis, 822
alkane(s) Any of a class of
  hydrocarbons in which each
  carbon atom is bonded to
  four other atoms, 448–452
 derivatives of, 462t
 general formula of, 447t
 naming of, A-17
 properties of, 452
 reaction with chlorine, 452
 reaction with oxygen, 452
 standard enthalpies of
  vaporization of, 572t
AlkA-Seltzer®, *149*, 760
 composition of, 104

alkene(s) Any of a class of
  hydrocarbons in which there
  is at least one carbon–carbon double bond, 453–457
 general formula of, 447t
 hydrogenation of, 457
 naming of, A-18
alkyl groups Hydrocarbon substituents, 451
alkylation, of benzene, 461
alkyne(s) Any of a class of
  hydrocarbons in which there
  is at least one carbon–carbon triple bond, 456
 general formula of, 447t
 naming of, A-19
allene, structure of, 440, 444
allergy, to nickel, 896
allicin, 541
allotrope(s) Different forms of
  the same element that exist
  in the same physical state
  under the same conditions of
  temperature and pressure, 63
 boron, 981
 carbon, 63
 oxygen, 1001. *See also* ozone.
 phosphorus, 65, 992
 sulfur, 65, 1001
alloy(s),
 iron, 1027
 magnesium in, 976
 memory metal, 1018
alnico V, 1028
 ferromagnetism of, 292
alpha particle(s), 1061
 bombardment with, 1077
 predicting emission of,
  1068
alpha plot(s), 857
alpha radiation Radiation that
  is readily absorbed, 343
alpha-hydroxy acid(s), *787*
altitude sickness, 514
alum, formula of, 110
alumina, amphoterism of,
  1012
aluminosilicates, 989
 separation of, 982
aluminum, abundance of,
  63
 chemistry of, 985
 density of, 44
 production of, 981–982
 reaction with bromine, 67,
  207
 reaction with copper ions,
  900
 reaction with iron(III)
  oxide, 147

reaction with potassium
  hydroxide, 199
reaction with sodium
  hydroxide, 970
reaction with water, 904
reduction by sodium, 972
aluminum bromide, dimer-
  ization of, 985
aluminum carbide, reaction
  with water, 169
aluminum chloride, prepa-
  ration of, 197
aluminum hydroxide,
  amphoterism of, 790,
  792
aluminum oxide, 982
 amphoterism of, 982
aluminum sulfate, 1012
amalgam, 925
americium, 1079
amide link, 486
amide(s) Any of a class of
  organic compounds characterized by the presence of an
  amino group, 468, 475–478
amine(s) A derivative of
  ammonia in which one or
  more of the hydrogen atoms
  are replaced by organic
  groups, 466
 as acids and bases, 798
α-amino acid(s) An amino acid
  in which the amine group
  and the carboxyl group are
  both attached to the same
  carbon atom.
 chirality of, 498
 zwitterionic form, 808
amino group A functional
  group related to ammonia,
  in which some or all of the
  hydrogen atoms are replaced
  by organic groups, 468,
  475
2-aminobenzoic acid, 494
ammonia, aqueous, equilibrium constant expres-
  sion for, 728
 bond angles in, 370, *371*
 combustion of, balanced
  equation for, 118
 decomposition of, 679,
  689, 715
 as Lewis base, 793
 as ligand, 1031
 molecular polarity of, 383
 orbital hybridization in,
  411
 oxidation of, 163, *164*
 percent composition of, 89

pH of, 179
production of, as equili[brium]
  rium process, 119
 by Haber process, 749
 equilibrium constant f[or]
  743
 spontaneity of, 875
 stoichiometry of, 527
reaction with acetic acid[,]
  780
reaction with boron tri[flu]
  oride, 364, 438
reaction with copper su[l]
  fate, 197
reaction with hydrochlo[ric]
  acid, 779
reaction with hydrogen
  chloride, 138, 533, 8[ ]
reaction with nickel(II)
  nitrate and ethylene[di]
  amine, 758
reaction with sodium hy[po]
  chlorite, 993
reaction with water, 136
relation to amines, 466
synthesis of, equilibrium
  constant, 885
titration with hydrogen
  chloride, 828–830
waste product of fish
  metabolism, 994
as weak base, 771
ammonium carbamate, di[s]
  sociation of, 756
ammonium chloride,
  decomposition of, 87[ ]
 in dry cell battery, 911
 reaction with calcium
  oxide, 196
ammonium cyanate, conv[er]
  sion to urea, 718
ammonium dichromate,
  decomposition of, 15[0,]
  550
ammonium formate, solu[bil]
  ity of, 652
ammonium hydrogen sul[ ]
  fide, decomposition o[f,]
  754, 755
ammonium iodide, dissoc[ia]
  tion of, 756
ammonium ion, 73
 in Lewis adduct, 790
ammonium nitrate, decor[m]
  position of, 250
 dissolution of, 862
 enthalpy of solution, 62[ ]
 in cold pack, 245
ammonium perchlorate, i[n]
  rocket fuel, 1009, 101[ ]

azomethane, decomposition of, 688, 690, 714

azurite, *21, 1025*

background radiation, 1083

back-titration, 204

bacteria, copper production by, 1028

thermophilic, 16

bain-Marie, 339

baking powder, *780,* 1000

baking soda, 140, 974

reaction with vinegar, 777

balance, laboratory, precision of, *35*

balanced chemical equation A chemical equation showing the relative amounts of reactants and products, 116–118

enthalpy and, 227

equilibrium constant and, 741–744

ball-and-stick model(s) A diagram in which spheres represent atoms, and sticks represent the bonds holding them together, 70, 445

balloon, hot air, 208, *525*

hydrogen and helium, 968

models of electron pair geometries, 368

weather, *521*

Balmer, Johann, 276

Balmer series A series of spectral lines that have energies in the visible region, 276, 279

band of stability, nuclear, 1067

bar A unit of pressure; 1 bar = 100 kPa, 516, A-8

barium carbonate, decomposition of, 755

barium chloride, as strong electrolyte, 124

precipitation of, 845

reaction with sodium sulfate, 130

barium nitrate, in fireworks, 281

barium sulfate, as x-ray contrast agent, 977

precipitation of, 845

solubility of, 835

barometer An apparatus used to measure atmospheric pressure, 516

base(s) A substance that, when dissolved in pure water, increases the concentration of hydroxide ions,

131–139. *See also* Brønsted base(s), Lewis base(s).

acids and, 760–809. *See also* acid–base reaction(s).

Arrhenius definition of, 132

Brønsted definition, 761

Brønsted-Lowry definition, 133–136

common, 132t

Lewis definition of, 789–793

of logarithms, A-2

reaction with acids, 136–138

strengths of, 769. *See also* strong base, weak base.

direction of reaction and, 776

base ionization constant (K_b) The equilibrium constant for the ionization of a base in aqueous solution, 769, 770t

relation to conjugate acid ionization constant, 775

base units, SI, 25t, A-11

basic oxide(s) An oxide of a metal that acts as a base, 139

basic oxygen furnace, 1027

basic solution A solution in which the concentration of hydronium ions is less than the concentration of hydroxide ion, 766

battery A device consisting of two or more electrochemical cells, 911

energy per kilogram, 914t

bauxite, 982

Bayer process, 982

becquerel The SI unit of radioactivity, 1 decomposition per second, 1082

Becquerel, Henri, 342

Beer-Lambert law The absorbance of a sample is proportional to the path length and the concentration, 191

Beethoven, Ludwig van, 991

bends, 626

benzaldehyde, structure of, 469

benzene, boiling point elevation and freezing point depression constants for, 633t

bonding in, resonance structures in, 361, 421

derivatives of, 459, A-19

liquid and solid volumes, *556*

molecular orbital configuration of, 432

in organometallic compounds, 1051

reactions of, 461

structure of, 342, 459

vapor pressure of, 583, 632

benzenesulfonic acid, structure of, 805

benzoic acid, 471t

buffer solution of, 817

structure of, 245, 459, 653

benzonitrile, structure of, 444

benzyl acetate, 475

benzyl butanoate, 474t

beryllium dichloride, orbital hybridization in, 414

beta particle(s) An electron ejected at high speed from certain radioactive substances, 1061

predicting emission of, 1068

beta radiation Radiation of a penetrative character, 343

bicarbonate ion. *See also* hydrogen carbonate ion.

in biological buffer system, 822

bidentate ligands, 1031

bimolecular process A process that involves two molecules, 703

binary compound(s) A compound formed from two elements, 81

binding energy The energy required to separate a nucleus into individual protons and neutrons, 1069–1072

per nucleon, 1070

biochemistry, thermodynamics and, 884

biodiesel, 479

birefringence, *976*

bismuth subsalicylate, formula of, 109

in Pepto-Bismol, *128*

black powder, 281

black smokers, metal sulfides from, 112

black tongue, Pepto-Bismol and, *128*

blackbody radiation, 272

blast furnace, 1026

entropy and, 876

bleach, detection in food tampering, 188

hypochlorite ion in, 10

sodium hypochlorite in, 619

blood, buffers in, 814, 82

oxygen saturation of, 5

pH of, 179, 822

blood alcohol level (BAI 207

blue vitriol, 97

boat form, 453

body-centered cubic (bc unit cell, 591

Bohanan, Art, 579

Bohr, Christian, 1033

Bohr, Niels, 276, 346

Bohr effect, in hemoglot 1033

boiling point The temperat at which the vapor press of a liquid is equal to the external pressure on the uid, 576

of common compound 572t

hydrogen bonding and 561

intermolecular forces a 560t

boiling point elevation, 6

boiling point elevation cc stant (K_{bp}), 633

Boltzmann, Ludwig, 536, 866

Boltzmann distribution curves. *See* Maxwell-Boltzmann distributi curves.

bomb calorimeter, 231, 2

bombardier beetle, *677*

bond(s) An interaction between two or more ato that holds them together reducing the potential energy of their electrons, 349. *See also* bonding.

coordinate covalent, 36 789, 1031

covalent, 349

formation of, 349

ionic, 349

multiple, 354

molecular geometry a 373

polar, 375–379

properties of, 386–391

nitrosyl bromide, decomposition of, 754
formation of, 701, 713
nitrosyl ion, 435
nitrous acid, 996
strength of, 794
nitrous oxide. *See* dinitrogen oxide.
nitryl chloride, decomposition of, 710
electrostatic potential map of, 400
nitryl fluoride, 718
Nobel, Alfred, *464*
noble gas electron configuration, in ions, 330
noble gas(es) The elements in Group 8A of the periodic table, 66
compounds of, 365, 404
electron affinity of, 325
electron configuration of, 73, 313, 351, 964
noble gas notation An abbreviated form of spdf notation that replaces the completed electron shells with the symbol of the corresponding noble gas in brackets, 311
noble metals, 996
nodal surface A surface on which there is zero probability of finding an electron, 290, 291
node(s) A point of zero amplitude of a wave, 270, 284
nonbonding electrons. *See* lone pair(s).
nonelectrolyte A substance that dissolves in water to form an electrically nonconducting solution, 124
nonequilibrium conditions, reaction quotient at, 732, 925
nonideal gases, 542
nonideal solutions, 629
nonmetal(s) An element characterized by a lack of metallic properties, 60
anions formed by, 72
binary compounds of, 81
electron affinity of, 324
electronegativity of, 376
nonpolar covalent bond A covalent bond in which there is equal sharing of the bonding electron pair, 375
nonpolar molecules, 383
interactions of, 565–568

nonspontaneous reaction, 861. *See also* reactant-favored reaction(s).
normal boiling point The boiling point when the external pressure is 1 atm, 576
for common compounds, 572t
northern lights, 268
northwest–southeast rule A product-favored reaction involves a reducing agent below and to the right of the oxidizing agent in the table of standard reduction potentials, 921
novocaine, 805
nuclear binding energy The energy required to separate the nucleus of an atom into protons and neutrons, 1069–1072
nuclear charge, effective, 308, 309t
nuclear chemistry, 1060–1097
nuclear energy, 1081
nuclear fission A reaction in which a large nucleus splits into two or more smaller nuclei, 1080
nuclear fusion A reaction in which several small nuclei react to form a larger nucleus, 1081
nuclear magnetic resonance (NMR) spectrometer, *169*, 294
nuclear medicine, 1085
nuclear reaction(s) A reaction involving one or more atomic nuclei, resulting in a change in the identities of the isotopes, 1062–1067
artificial, 1077–1080
predicting types of, 1068
rates of, 1072–1077
nuclear reactor A container in which a controlled nuclear reaction occurs, 1080
breeder, 1094
natural, 1060, 1093
nuclear spin, quantization of, 294
nucleation, of gas bubbles, 641
nucleon A nuclear particle, either a neutron or a proton, 1070

nucleus The core of an atom, made up of protons and neutrons, 51
demonstration of, 344, *345*
stability of, 1067–1072
nutrition label, energy content on, 215
Nyholm, Ronald S., 368
nylon, 486

octahedral electron-pair geometry, orbital hybridization and, *410*, 414
octahedral holes, 596
octahedral molecular geometry, 369, 1036
octane, combustion of, 116
heat of combustion, 232
reaction with oxygen, 547
vapor pressure of, 583
octet A stable configuration of eight electrons surrounding an atomic nucleus, 351
octet rule When forming bonds, atoms of main group elements gain, lose, or share electrons to achieve a stable configuration having eight valence electrons, 352
exceptions to, 353, 364–367
odd-electron compounds, 366, 429, 995
odors, 541
oil(s) A liquid triester of a long-chain fatty acid with glycerol, 476
soaps and, 645
Oklo, natural nuclear rector at, 1060
oleic acid, 471t
olivine, 988
Olympic Analytical Laboratory, 1
optical isomers Isomers that are nonsuperimposable mirror images of each other, 445, 1038
orbital(s) The matter wave for an allowed energy state of an electron in an atom or molecule, 285
atomic. *See* atomic orbital(s).
molecular. *See* molecular orbital(s).
orbital box diagram A notation for the electron configuration of an atom in which each orbital is shown as a box and the number and

spin direction of the electrons are shown by arrows, 305, 309
orbital hybridization The combination of atomic orbitals to form a set of equivalent hybrid orbitals that minimize electron-pair repulsions, 408–416
orbital overlap Partial occupation of the same region of space by orbitals from two atoms, 406
order, bond. *See* bond order.
reaction. *See* reaction order.
ore(s) A sample of matter containing a desired mineral element, usually with large quantities of impurities, 1025
insoluble salts in, 842
organic compounds, bonding in, 443–495
naming of, 448t, 450, A-17
organometallic chemistry, 1048–1053
orientation of reactants, effect on reaction rate, 695
Orlon, 481t
ornithine, 201
orpiment, 810
ortho position, 459
orthophosphoric acid, 999
orthorhombic sulfur, 1001
orthosilicates, 988
osmium, density of, 1020
osmosis The movement of solvent molecules through a semipermeable membrane from a region of lower solute concentration to a region of higher solute concentration, 635
osmotic pressure (II) The pressure exerted by osmosis in a solution system at equilibrium, 636
Ostwald, Friedrich Wilhelm, 83
Ostwald process, 996
overlap, orbital, 406
overvoltage, 935
oxalate ion, as ligand, 1031
oxalic acid, 471t
as polyprotic acid, 763t
molar mass of, 87
titration of, 183, 827

Project Stardust, 607
promethium, 1079
propane, as fuel, 249
   combustion of, balanced
      equation for, 117
   enthalpy of combustion,
      228
   percent composition of, 89
   structure of, 444
   use in hot air balloons, 208
1,2,3-propanetriol, 463t
propanoic acid, as weak
      acid, 771
propanol, 463t
propene, 453, 685
   hydrogenation of, 390
   reaction with bromine,
      457
propionic acid, 472t
proportionality constant,
      518, 535
proportionality symbol, 678
propyl alcohol, 463t
propyl propanoate, 478
propylene, 453
propylene glycol, 616
   as antifreeze, 465
protein(s),
   as hydrophilic colloids, 644
   energy content of, 215
proton exchange membrane
      (PEM), 914
proton(s) A positively charged
      subatomic particle found in
      the nucleus, 51
   bombardment with, 1078
   demonstration of, 345
   donation by Brønsted acid,
      134, 761
   name of, 341
   nuclear stability and, 1067
Prout, William, 341
Prussian blue, 1020
purification, of mixtures, 11
Purkinji, John, 579
putrescine, 466
pyridine, resonance struc-
      tures of, 494
   structure of, 798
   substitutions on, 807
pyrite, iron, 13, 14
pyrometallurgy Recovery of
      metals from their ores by
      high-temperature processes,
      1026
pyroxenes, structure of,
      988
pyruvate, production of
      lactate from, 895

quadratic equations, A-5
quadratic formula, use in
      concentration prob-
      lems, 738
qualitative information Non-
      numerical experimental
      observations, such as
      descriptive or comparative
      data, 5, 25
quantitative analysis, 169
quantitative information
      Numerical experimental
      data, such as measurements
      of changes in mass or vol-
      ume, 5, 25
quantity, of pure substance,
      82
quantization A situation in
      which only certain energies
      are allowed, 346
   of electron potential
      energy, 276, 284
   of electron spin, 293
   of nuclear spin, 294
   Planck's assumption of,
      272
quantum mechanics A general
      theoretical approach to
      atomic behavior that
      describes the electron in
      an atom as a matter wave,
      283–287
quantum number(s) A set of
      numbers with integer values
      that define the properties of
      an atomic orbital, 284–287,
      291
   allowed values of, 285
   angular momentum, 285
   in macroscopic system,
      867
   magnetic, 286
   Pauli exclusion principle
      and, 305
   principal, 277, 285
quartz, 987
   structure of, 603
quinine, 103, 467

rad A unit of radiation dosage,
      1082
radial distribution plot,
      288
radiation, background,
      1083
   cancer treatment with,
      1086
   cosmic, 1083
   electromagnetic, 269–271

health effects of, 1082–
      1084
   safe exposure, 1084
   treatment of food with,
      1088
   units of, 1082
radiation absorbed dose
      (rad), 1082
radioactive decay series A
      series of nuclear reactions
      by which a radioactive iso-
      tope decays to form a stable
      isotope, 1063–1066
radioactivity, discovery of,
      342, 343
radiochemical dating,
      1075
radium, 342
   from decay of uranium,
      1064
radon, as environmental
      hazard, 1065
   from decay of uranium,
      1064
   radioactive half-life of, 691
Raoult, François M., 629
Raoult's law The vapor pressure
      of the solvent is propor-
      tional to the mole fraction of
      the solvent in a solution,
      629
rare gas(es). See noble
      gas(es).
Raschig reaction, 707, 993
rate. See reaction rate(s).
rate constant (k) The propor-
      tionality constant in the rate
      equation, 678–680
   Arrhenius equation for,
      696
   half-life and, 690
   units of, 680
rate constant, for radioactiv-
      ity, 1074
rate equation(s) The mathe-
      matical relationship between
      reactant concentration and
      reaction rate, 678
   determining, 680
   first-order, nuclear, 1074
   for elementary step, 704
   graphical determination
      of, 687–689
   integrated, 683–692
   integrated, for nuclear
      decay, 1074
   reaction mechanisms and,
      705–710
   reaction order and, 679

rate law. See rate
      equation(s).
rate-determining step The
      slowest elementary step
      reaction mechanism, 70∎
reactant(s) A starting sub-
      stance in a chemical rea∎
      tion, 18, 114
   effect of adding or rem∎
      ing, 745
   in equilibrium constan∎
      expression, 728
   heat as, 748
   rate of concentration
      change, 673
   reaction rate and,
      677–683
reactant-favored reaction(∎
      A system in which, when
      reaction appears to stop∎
      reactants predominate o∎
      products, 121
   equilibrium constant fc∎
      730
   predicting, 874, 878
reaction(s) A process in wh∎
      substances are changed ∎
      other substances by rear∎
      rangement, combination∎
      separation of atoms, 18.∎
      also under element, com-
      pound, or chemical grou∎
      interest.
   (n, γ), 1078
   acid–base, 136–138, 149
   addition, 456
   aquation, 720
   in aqueous solution, 12∎
      stoichiometry of,
         182–189
      types of, 149
   autoionization, 765
   chain, 1080
   condensation, 484
   coupling of, 884
   direction of, acid–base
      strength and, 776
      reaction quotient and,
         732
   disproportionation, 100∎
   electron transfer, 896–9∎
      See also oxidation–
      reduction reaction(s)∎
   enthalpy change for,
      227–229
   esterification, 472
   exchange, 121, 149
   free energy change for,
      877

Friedel–Crafts, 791–792
gas laws and, 527–530
gas-forming, 139–141, 150
hydrogenation, 390
hydrolysis, 473
moles of, 167, 227
neutralization, 137, 779
neutron capture, 1078
nuclear, 1062–1067
  artificial, 1077–1080
  rates of, 1072–1077
order of. *See* reaction
  order.
oxidation–reduction,
  141–148, 150, 896–947.
  See also oxidation–
  reduction reaction(s).
precipitation, 127–131,
  149, 832–842
  solubility product con-
  stant and, 842–845
product-favored vs. reac-
  tant-favored, 121, 239,
  730, 861
  predicting, 874, 878
rate of. *See* reaction rate(s).
reductive carbonylation,
  1050
reverse, equilibrium con-
  stant expression for, 742
reversibility of, 118, 726
standard enthalpy of, 227
standard reduction poten-
  tials of, 917, 920t
substitution, 461
trans-esterification, 479
water gas, 263, 969
reaction coordinate dia-
  gram, 694, 697
reaction intermediate A species that is produced in one
  step of a reaction mechanism and completely consumed in a later step,
  700
  in rate law, 708
reaction mechanism(s) The
  sequence of events at the
  molecular level that control
  the speed and outcome of a
  reaction, 671, 701–710
  effect of catalyst on, 700
  rate equation and,
  705–710
reaction order The exponent of
  a concentration term in the
  reaction's rate equation, 679
  determining, 681
  molecularity and, 704

reaction quotient (Q) The
  product of concentrations of
  products divided by the
  product of concentrations of
  reactants, each raised to the
  power of its stoichiometric
  coefficient in the chemical
  equation, 732–734. *See also*
  equilibrium constant.
  Gibbs free energy change
  and, 878–879
  relation to cell potential,
  925
  solubility product constant
  and, 843
reaction rate(s) The change in
  concentration of a reagent
  per unit time, 671–675
  Arrhenius equation and,
  696
  average vs. instantaneous,
  674
  catalysts and, 699–701
  collision theory of, 692
  conditions affecting, 676
  effect of temperature,
  693
  expression for. *See* rate
  equation(s).
  initial, 680
  radioactive disintegration,
  1072–1077
  redox reactions, 935
  stoichiometry and, 673,
  674
receptor proteins, 509
rechargeable battery, 911
redox reaction(s). *See* oxidation–reduction
  reaction(s).
reducing agent(s) The substance that donates electrons and is oxidized in an
  oxidation–reduction reaction, 141, 898
  relative strengths of, 917,
  923
reduction The gain of electrons
  by an atom, ion, or molecule, 141
  of transition metals, 1021
reduction potential(s), standard, 917, 920t
reduction reaction(s), of
  aldehydes and ketones,
  469
reductive carbonylation
  reaction, 1050
reference dose (RfD), 96

reformation, in petroleum
  refining, 461
refrigerator, pot-in-pot, 222
rem A unit of radiation dosage
  to biological tissue, 1082
replication, of DNA, 504
resin, in ion exchanger, 980
resonance, in amides, 477
  molecular orbital theory
  and, 431
resonance stabilization, 460
resonance structure(s) The possible structures of a molecule
  for which more than one
  Lewis structure can be written, differing by the number
  of bond pairs between a
  given pair of atoms, 361–363
  benzene, 361, 421
  carbonate ion, 362
  effect on acid strength, 796
  nitrate ion, 362
  nitrite ion, 363
  ozone, 361
respiration, 511
  production of ATP by, 884
reverse osmosis, 957
reversibility, equilibrium
  and, 725
  of chemical reactions, 118
reversible process A process for
  which it is possible to return
  to the starting conditions
  along the same path without
  altering the surroundings,
  864
Rhazes (Abu Bakr Moham-
  mad ibn Zakariyya al-
  Razi), 339
rhodochrosite, 154, 810
ring structure, in benzene,
  421
RNA. *See* ribonucleic acid.
Roberts, Ainé, *533*
rock salt structure, 598
roentgen A unit of radiation
  dosage, 1082
root-mean-square (rms)
  speed The square root of the
  average of the squares of the
  speeds of the molecules in a
  sample, 536
roots, calculating with logarithms, A-4
  on calculator, 34
Rosenberg, Barnett, 1049
rotation, A-7
  around bonds in alkanes,
  449

around sigma and pi
  bonds, 420
  of polarized light, 445
rounding off, 37
ROY G BIV, 1045
rubber, isoprene in, 483
  natural and synthetic,
  483
  styrene-butadiene, 484
  vulcanized, 483
rubidium, radiochemical
  dating with, 1093
ruby, ion charges in, 75
  synthetic, 985
Rush, Benjamin, 442
rust, 1023. *See also* iron(III)
  oxide.
Rutherford, Ernest, 51, 341,
  343, 1061, 1077
rutile, unit cell of, 611
Rydberg, Johannes, 276
Rydberg constant, 276
Rydberg equation, 276

s-block elements Elements
  with the valence electron
  configuration of ns1 or ns2,
  312
s orbital(s). *See* atomic
  orbital(s).
saccharin, 202
  structure of, 108, 458, 806
safety match, 998
salad dressing, as emulsion,
  644
salicylic acid, 168, 474, 760
  structure of, 858
salt(s) An ionic compound
  whose cation comes from a
  base and whose anion comes
  from an acid, 136–138
  acid–base properties of,
  773
  calculating pH of aqueous
  solution, 785
  concentration in sea water,
  186
  electrolysis of, 932
  hydrated, 559
  insoluble, precipitation of,
  842–845
  solubility of, 832–842
  solubility product con-
  stants of, 834t
salt bridge A device for maintaining the balance of ion
  charges in the compartments
  of an electrochemical cell,
  905

saltpeter, 971, 975
sandwich compounds, 1052
saponification The hydrolysis of an ester, 476
sapphire, 985
saturated compound(s) A hydrocarbon containing only single bonds, 448. *See also* alkanes.
saturated solution(s) A stable solution in which the maximum amount of solute has been dissolved, 620
reaction quotient in, 844
saturation, of fatty acids, 476
scanning electron microscopy (SEM), 27
Scheele, Carl Wilhelm, 114, 1005, 1016
Schrödinger, Erwin, 283, 346
science, goals of, 6
methods of, 3–7
scientific notation A way of presenting very large or very small numbers in a compact and consistent form that simplifies calculations, 32–35, A-3
operations in, 34
Scott Couper, Archibald, 342
screening, of nuclear charge, 308
SCUBA diving, gas laws and, 542
Henry's law and 626
sea slug, sulfuric acid excreted by, 772
sea water, density of, 39
ion concentrations in, 122t, 653t
magnesium in, 976
pH of, 181
salt concentration in, 186
sodium and potassium ions in, 971
Seaborg, Glenn T., 1078
sebum, 579
second, definition of, A-11
second law of thermodynamics The entropy of the universe increases in a spontaneous process, 863
secondary alcohols, 468
secondary battery A battery in which the reactions can be reversed, so the battery can be recharged, 911

second-order reaction, 679
half-life of, 690
integrated rate equation, 686
seesaw molecular geometry, 372
selenium, uses of, 1002
semimetals. *See* metalloid(s).
semipermeable membrane A thin sheet of material through which only certain types of molecules can pass, 635
shielding constant, effective nuclear charge and, 337
SI Abbreviation for Système International d'Unités, a uniform system of measurement units in which a single base unit is used for each measured physical quantity, 25, A-11
siderite, 154
sievert The SI unit of radiation dosage to biological tissue, 1082
sigma (s) bond(s) A bond formed by the overlap of orbitals head to head, and with bonding electron density concentrated along the axis of the bond, 407
sign conventions, for electron affinity, 325
for energy calculations, *217*, 224t, 226
for voltaic cells, 906
significant figure(s) The digits in a measured quantity that are known exactly, plus one digit that is inexact to the extent of ±1, 35–38
in atomic masses, 84
logarithms and, A-3
silicate ion, in minerals, 810
silane, comparison to methane, 962
reaction with oxygen, 547
silica, 987
silica aerogel, 607
silica gel, 988
silicates, minerals containing, 988
structure of, 603
silicon,
bond energy compared to carbon, 446
chemistry of, 986–990

purification of, 986
reaction with methyl chloride, 549
similarity to boron, 979
similarity to carbon, 962
unit cell of, 613
silicon carbide, 1014
unit cell of, 614
silicon dioxide, 987
comparison to carbon dioxide, 962
in gemstones, 810, 985
reaction with hydrogen fluoride, 1008
silicon tetrachloride, 986
molecular geometry, 369
silicone polymers, 990
Silly Putty, 990
silt, formation of, 644
silver, as bacteriocide, 148
density of, 44
isotopes of, 101
silver acetate, solubility of, 838
silver bromide, reaction with sodium thiosulfate, 198
solubility of, 832–833
silver chloride, free energy change of dissolution, 885
reaction with potassium nitrate, 122, 127, 129
solubility of, 837
in aqueous ammonia, 742, 847
silver chromate, 186
formation by precipitation, 129
solubility of, 837, 839
silver coulometer, 946
silver nitrate, reaction with potassium chloride, 122, 127, 129
silver(I) oxide, decomposition of, 892
silver oxide battery, 912
silver sulfide, reaction with aluminum, 156
silver-zinc battery, 945
simple cubic (sc) unit cell, 591
single bond A bond formed by sharing one pair of electrons; a sigma bond, 407
slag, in blast furnace, 1027
Slater's rules, 337
slime, 483
slope, of straight-line graph, 40, 687

Smalley, Richard, 255
smog, photochemical, 26
snot-tites, 1004
soap A salt produced by the hydrolysis of a fat or oil [by] strong base, 476, 645
hard water and, 980
soapstone, 976
soda ash. *See* sodium carbonate.
soda-lime process, 974
Soddy, Frederick, 344, 1062
sodium, in fireworks, 281
preparation of, 971
reaction with chlorine, 146, 349, *350*
reaction with water, 5
sodium acetate, calculati[ng] pH of aqueous soluti[on] 785
in heat pack, 620
sodium azide, in air bags, *515*, 522, 528, 547
preparation of, 202, 553
sodium bicarbonate, 974. *also* sodium hydrogen carbonate.
reaction with acetic acid 777
sodium borohydride, 984 1016
as reducing catalyst, 470
sodium carbonate, 177
calculating pH of aqueo[us] solution, 787
industrial uses, 974
primary standard for aci[d] base titration, 187
sodium chloride, as stron[g] electrolyte, 123
composition of, *4*, 13
crystal lattice of, 79
electrolysis of, 527, 932, *933*, 972
entropy of solution process, 873
ion charges in, 74
lattice enthalpy calculati[on] for, 601
melting ice and, 639
standard enthalpy of formation of, 236
structure of, 596, *597*
sodium fluoride, 47
sodium hydrogen carbonate, reaction with citr[ic] acid, 149
reaction with tartaric aci[d] 140

dium hydrosulfite, preparation of, 202

dium hydroxide, commercial preparation of, 974

enthalpy of solution, 623

eaction with acetic acid, 137

eaction with aluminum, 970

eaction with formic acid, 779

eaction with hydrogen chloride, 136

eaction with methyl acetate, 680

itration of acetic acid, 824, 826

itration with hydrogen chloride, 823

dium hypochlorite, 188

n bleach, 619

eaction with ammonia, 993

dium iodide, aqueous, electrolysis of, 934

eaction with thallium(I) sulfate, 197

dium ions, in ion exchanger, 980

dium laurylbenzenesulfonate, structure of, 645

dium monohydrogen phosphate, 1000

dium nitrite, reaction with sulfamic acid, 551

dium peroxide, 973

dium pertechnetate, 303

dium phosphate, 1000

dium polyacrylate, in disposable diapers, 487

dium silicate, 988

dium stearate, as soap, 645

dium sulfate, quantitative analysis of, 169, *170*

eaction with barium chloride, 130

dium sulfide, preparation of, 196

dium sulfite, 1013

dium thiosulfate, reaction with iodine, 188

eaction with silver bromide, 198

itration with iodine, 203

A colloidal dispersion of a solid substance in a fluid medium, 642t, 643

lar panel, *243*

solid(s) The phase of matter in which a substance has both definite shape and definite volume, 7
- amorphous, 603
- chemistry of, 588–615
- compressibility of, 556
- concentration of, in equilibrium constant expression, 728
- dissolution in liquids, 622
- ionic, 596–599
- molecular, 602
- network, 602
- types of, 589t

solubility The concentration of solute in equilibrium with undissolved solute in a saturated solution, 621
- common ion effect and, 838
- of complex ions, 846–848
- estimating from solubility product constant, 834–838
- factors affecting, 626–628
- of gases in water, 566t
- intermolecular forces and, 560
- of ionic compounds in water, 125
- of minerals and gems, 810
- of salts, 832–842

solubility product constant (K_{sp}) An equilibrium constant relating the concentrations of the ionization products of a dissolved substance, 833
- reaction quotient and, 843
- standard potential and, 930
- values of, A-26t

solute The substance dissolved in a solvent to form a solution, 121, 617

solution(s) A homogeneous mixture in a single phase, 10–11, 616–655
- acidic and basic, redox reactions in, 901–905
- aqueous, 121
  - balancing redox equations, 901–905
  - pH and pOH of, 179–182, 767
  - reactions in, 121
- boiling process in, 632
- buffer. See buffer solution(s).

concentrations in, 174–179
- enthalpy of, 623–626
- Henry's law, 626
- ideal, 629
- osmosis in, 635
- process of forming, 620–626
- Raoult's law, 629
- saturated, 620

solvation, effect on acid strength, 795
- enthalpy of, 557

Solvay process, 974, 1049

solvent The medium in which a solute is dissolved to form a solution, 121, 617

sound energy, 210

space-filling models, 70, 445

spdf **notation** A notation for the electron configuration of an atom in which the number of electrons assigned to a subshell is shown as a superscript after the subshell's symbol, 309

specific heat capacity (C) The quantity of heat required to raise the temperature of 1.00 g of a substance by 1.00 °C, 215
- determining, 217
- units of, 218

spectator ion(s) An ion that is present in a solution in which a reaction takes place, but that is not involved in the net process, 129

spectrochemical series An ordering of ligands by the magnitudes of the splitting energies that they cause, 1046–1048

spectrophotometer, 49, 1047

spectrophotometry The quantitative measurement of light absorption and its relation to the concentration of the dissolved solute, 189–192

spectroscope, 341

spectrum, absorption, 1047
- electromagnetic, *271*, 1045
- continuous, 275
- of heated body, 271, *272*
- line, 275, *276*
- light absorption, 190
- mass, 54, 95
  - isotope ratio, 58
- nuclear magnetic resonance, 294

speed(s), of gas molecules, 533
- distribution of, 535
- of wave, 270

spinel(s), 335
- structure of, 614

sponge, skeletal structure of, *27, 28*

spontaneous reaction, 861. *See also* product-favored reaction(s).
- effect of temperature on, 875
- Gibbs free energy change and, 877–879

square planar molecular geometry, 372, 1036

square-pyramidal molecular geometry, 372

stability, band of, 1067
- standard enthalpy of formation and, 237

stainless steel, 1028

stalactites and stalagmites, 119, *833*

standard atmosphere (atm) A unit of pressure; 1 atm = 760 mm Hg, 516, A-8

standard conditions In an electrochemical cell, all reactants and products are pure liquids or solids, or 1.0 M aqueous solutions, or gases at a pressure of 1 bar, 916

standard deviation A measure of precision, calculated as the square root of the sum of the squares of the deviations for each measurement from the average divided by one less than the number of measurements, 31

standard free energy change of reaction ($\Delta_r G°$) The free energy change for a reaction in which all reactants and products are in their standard states, 877

standard hydrogen electrode (SHE), 916, 918

standard molar enthalpy of formation ($\Delta_f H°$) The enthalpy change of a reaction for the formation of one mole of a compound directly from its elements, all in their standard states, 236, 862

thyroid gland, imaging of, 1087
treatment of hyperthyroidism, 1089
thyroxine, 1006, 1089
tin, density of, 44
tin(II) chloride, aqueous, electrolysis of, 935
tin iodide, formula of, 93
tin(IV) oxide, 1017
titanium, density of, 44
in memory metal, 1018
titanium(IV) chloride, reaction with water, 201
synthesis of, 155
titanium(IV) oxide, 1004
as pigment, 1020
quantitative analysis of, 171
reaction with carbon, 892
titrant The substance being added during a titration, 823
titration A procedure for quantitative analysis of a substance by an essentially complete reaction in solution with a measured quantity of a reagent of known concentration, 183–185
acid–base, 183, 821–832
curves for, 823, 825
oxidation–reduction, 188-189
Tollen's test, 157
toluene, structure of, 458
tonicity, 639
torr A unit of pressure equivalent to one millimeter of mercury, 516, A-8
Torricelli, Evangelista, 516
tracer, radioactive, 1086
trans-esterification reaction, 479
trans-fats, 476
transition, *d*-to-*d*, 1046
transition elements Some elements that lie in rows 4 to 7 of the periodic table, comprising scandium through zinc, yttrium through cadmium, and lanthanum through mercury, 66, 1018–1059
atomic radii, 320, *321*
cations formed by, 72
commercial production of, 1025–1028
electron configuration of, 315, 317, 1021

naming in ionic compounds, 77
oxidation numbers of, 1021
properties of, 1019–1025
transition state The arrangement of reacting molecules and atoms at the point of maximum potential energy, 694
translation, A-7
of RNA, 506
transmittance (T) The ratio of the amount of light passing through the sample to the amount of light that initially fell on the sample, 190
transmutation, 1077. *See also* nuclear reaction(s).
transport proteins, 509
transuranium elements Elements with atomic numbers greater than 92, 1078
travertine, 16
trenbolone, 3
trichlorobenzene, isomers of, 460
trigonal-bipyramidal electron-pair geometry, orbital hybridization and, *410*, 414
trigonal-bipyramidal molecular geometry, 369
axial and equatorial positions in, 372
trigonal-planar electron-pair geometry, orbital hybridization and, *410*, 413
trigonal-planar molecular geometry, 369
in carbon compounds, 443
trigonal-pyramidal molecular geometry, 370
triiodide ion, orbital hybridization in, 416
trimethylamine, 789
structure of, 798
trimethylborane, dissociation of, 757
triple bond A bond formed by sharing three pairs of electrons, one pair in a sigma bond and the other two in pi bonds, 354
valence bond theory of, 419
triple point The temperature and pressure at which the

solid, liquid, and vapor phases of a substance are in equilibrium, 607
tritium, 54, 968, 1093
fusion of, 1082
trona, 974
T-shaped molecular geometry, 372
tungsten, enthalpy of fusion of, 604
melting point of, 1020
unit cell of, 613
tungsten(IV) oxide, reaction with hydrogen, 155
turquoise, 810
density of, 21
Tyndall effect The scattering of visible light caused by particles of a colloid that are relatively large and dispersed in a solvent, 643

U.S. Anti-Doping Agency (USADA), 1, 58
U.S. Environmental Protection Agency (EPA), 96
U.S. Food and Drug Administration (FDA), 188, 215
ultraviolet catastrophe, 272
ultraviolet radiation, 270
skin damage and, *275*
uncertainty principle. *See* Heisenberg's uncertainty principle.
unimolecular process A process that involves one molecule, 703
unit cell(s) The smallest repeating unit in a crystal lattice, 590
number of atoms in, 592
shapes of, *591*
unit(s), of measurement, 25–29, 516
SI, 25, A-11
universe, entropy change for, 872
total energy of, 211
unpaired electrons, paramagnetism of, 292
unsaturated compound(s) A hydrocarbon containing double or triple carbon-carbon bonds, 456
unsaturated solution(s), reaction quotient in, 844
uracil, structure of, 402, 809

uranium(VI) fluoride, synthesis of, 155
uranium, fission reaction 1080
isotopes of, 1060
isotopic enrichment, 1080
isotopic separation of, 5 1008
radioactive series from, 1064
uranium-235, fission of, 1080
uranium-238, radioactive half-life, 1072
uranium hexafluoride, 54 1008, 1024
uranium(IV) oxide, 110
uranyl(IV) nitrate, 1059
urea, 789
conversion to ammoniu cyanate, 718
production of, 201
structure of, 397
synthesis of, 155
uric acid, 789
urine, phosphorus distille from, 997

valence bond (VB) theory A model of bonding in whic bond arises from the over of atomic orbitals on two atoms to give a bonding orbital with electrons loca ized between the atoms, 405–422
valence electron(s) The oute most and most reactive el trons of an atom, 311, 34 351
Lewis symbols and, 351
of main group elements, 964
valence shell electron pair repulsion (VSEPR) model model for predicting the shapes of molecules in wh structural electron pairs a arranged around each ato to maximize the angles between them, 368
valency, 341
valeric acid, 472t
van der Waals, Johannes, 543
van der Waals equation A mathematical expression that describes the behavio of nonideal gases, 543

yield, of product in a chemical reaction, 168

Zeise's salt, 430, 1051
zeolite(s), 989
  in ion exchanger, 980
zeroes, as significant figures, 36

zero-order reaction, 679
  half-life of, 690
  integrated rate equation, 687
zinc, density of, 44
  reaction with dioxovanadium(V) ion, 901–902

reaction with hydrochloric acid, *132*, 206
zinc blende, structure of, 597
zinc chloride, in dry cell battery, 911
zinc sulfide, 596, *597*
zinc-oxygen battery, 912

zone refining, 987
Zosimos, 339
zwitterion An amino acid in which both the amine gr⬤ and the carboxyl group a⬤ ionized, 808

PHYSICAL AND CHEMICAL CONSTANTS

Avogadro's number	$N = 6.0221415 \times 10^{23}/\text{mol}$
Electronic charge	$e = 1.60217653 \times 10^{-19}$ C
Faraday's constant	$F = 9.6485338 \times 10^{4}$ C/mol electrons
Gas constant	$R = 8.314472$ J/K · mol
	$= 0.082057$ L · atm/K · mol

π	$\pi = 3.1415926536$
Planck's constant	$h = 6.6260693 \times 10^{-34}$ J · sec
Speed of light (in a vacuum)	$c = 2.99792458 \times 10^{8}$ m/sec

USEFUL CONVERSION FACTORS AND RELATIONSHIPS

Length
SI unit: Meter (m)

1 kilometer = 1000 meters
          = 0.62137 mile
1 meter = 100 centimeters
1 centimeter = 10 millimeters
1 nanometer = 1.00×10^{-9} meter
1 picometer = 1.00×10^{-12} meter
    1 inch = 2.54 centimeter (exactly)
1 Ångstrom = 1.00×10^{-10} meter

Mass
SI unit: Kilogram (kg)

1 kilogram = 1000 grams
  1 gram = 1000 milligrams
  1 pound = 453.59237 grams = 16 ounces
   1 ton = 2000 pounds

Volume
SI unit: Cubic meter (m^3)

1 liter (L) = 1.00×10^{-3} m^3
        = 1000 cm^3
        = 1.056710 quarts
1 gallon = 4.00 quarts

Energy
SI unit: Joule (J)

1 joule = 1 kg · m^2/s^2
      = 0.23901 calorie
      = 1 C × 1 V
1 calorie = 4.184 joules

Pressure
SI unit: Pascal (Pa)

1 pascal = 1 N/m^2
       = 1 kg/m · s^2
1 atmosphere = 101.325 kilopascals
       = 760 mm Hg = 760 torr
       = 14.70 lb/in^2
       = 1.01325 bar
  1 bar = 10^5 Pa (exactly)

Temperature
SI unit: kelvin (K)

0 K = -273.15 °C
K = °C + 273.15°C
? °C = (5 °C/9 °F)(°F $-$ 32 °F)
? °F = (9 °F/5 °C)(°C) + 32 °F

LOCATION OF USEFUL TABLES AND FIGURES

Atomic and Molecular Properties

Atomic electron configurations	Table 7.3
Atomic radii	Figures 7.8, 7.9
Bond dissociation enthalpies	Table 8.9
Bond lengths	Table 8.8
Electron affinity	Figure 7.11, Appendix F
Electronegativity	Figure 8.11
Elements and their unit cells	Figure 13.5
Hybrid orbitals	Figure 9.5
Ionic radii	Figure 7.12
Ionization energies	Figure 7.10, Table 7.5

Thermodynamic Properties

Enthalpy, free energy, entropy	Appendix L
Lattice energies	Table 13.2
Specific heat capacities	Appendix D

Acids, Bases and Salts

Common acids and bases	Table 3.2
Formation constants	Appendix K
Ionization constants for weak acids and bases	Table 17.3, Appendix H, I
Names and composition of polyatomic ions	Table 2.4
Solubility guidelines	Figure 3.10
Solubility constants	Appendix J

Miscellaneous

Charges on common monatomic cations and anions	Figure 2.18
Common polymers	Table 10.12
Oxidizing and reducing agents	Table 3.4
Selected alkanes	Table 10.2
Standard reduction potentials	Table 20.1, Appendix M